Volkswagen New Beetle

1998, 1999

Service Manual

2.0L gasoline, 1.9L TDI diesel

RB

Bentley, Publishers
Cambridge, Massachusetts

RB ROBERT BENTLEY, INC. | AUTOMOTIVE PUBLISHERS

Information that makes the difference.®

1734 Massachusetts Avenue
Cambridge, MA 02138 USA
800-423-4595 / 617-547-4170
http://www.rb.com
e-mail: sales@rb.com
tech@rb.com

WARNING—Important Safety Notice

Do not use this manual unless you are familiar with basic automotive repair procedures and safe workshop practices. This manual illustrates the workshop procedures required for most service work; it is not a substitute for full and up-to-date information from the vehicle manufacturer or for proper training as an automotive technician. Note that it is not possible for us to anticipate all of the ways or conditions under which vehicles may be serviced or to provide cautions as to all of the possible hazards that may result.

The vehicle manufacturer will continue to issue service information updates and parts retrofits after the editorial closing of this manual. Some of these updates and retrofits will apply to procedures and specifications in this manual. We regret that we cannot supply updates to purchasers of this manual.

We have endeavored to ensure the accuracy of the information in this manual. Please note, however, that considering the vast quantity and the complexity of the service information involved, we cannot warrant the accuracy or completeness of the information contained in this manual.

FOR THESE REASONS, NEITHER THE PUBLISHER NOR THE AUTHOR MAKES ANY WARRANTIES, EXPRESS OR IMPLIED, THAT THE INFORMATION IN THIS BOOK IS FREE OF ERRORS OR OMISSIONS AND WE EXPRESSLY DISCLAIM THE IMPLIED WARRANTIES OF MERCHANTABILITY AND OF FITNESS FOR A PARTICULAR PURPOSE, EVEN IF THE PUBLISHER OR AUTHOR HAVE BEEN ADVISED OF A PARTICULAR PURPOSE, AND EVEN IF A PARTICULAR PURPOSE IS INDICATED IN THE MANUAL. THE PUBLISHER AND AUTHOR ALSO DISCLAIM ALL LIABILITY FOR DIRECT, INDIRECT, INCIDENTAL OR CONSEQUENTIAL DAMAGES THAT RESULT FROM ANY USE OF THE EXAMPLES, INSTRUCTIONS OR OTHER INFORMATION IN THIS BOOK. IN NO EVENT SHALL OUR LIABILITY WHETHER IN TORT, CONTRACT OR OTHERWISE EXCEED THE COST OF THIS MANUAL.

Your common sense and good judgment are crucial to safe and successful service work. Read procedures through before starting them. Think about whether the condition of your car, your level of mechanical skill, or your level of reading comprehension might result in or contribute in some way to an occurrence which might cause you injury, damage your car, or result in an unsafe repair. If you have doubts for these or other reasons about your ability to perform safe repair work on your car, have the work done at an authorized Volkswagen dealer or other qualified shop.

Part numbers listed in this manual are for identification purposes only, not for ordering. Always check with your authorized Volkswagen dealer to verify part numbers and availability before beginning service work that may require new parts.

Before attempting any work on your Volkswagen, read the warnings and cautions on page vii, and any warning or caution that accompanies a procedure in the service manual. Review the warnings and cautions on page vii each time you prepare to work on your Volkswagen.

Special tools required to perform certain service operations are identified in the manual and are recommended for use. Use of tools other than those recommended in this service manual may be detrimental to the car's safe operation as well as the safety of the person servicing the car.

Copies of this manual may be purchased from authorized Volkswagen dealers, from selected booksellers and automotive accessories and parts dealers, or directly from the publisher by mail.

The publisher encourages comments from the reader of this manual. These communications have been and will be considered in the preparation of this and other manuals. Please write to Robert Bentley, Inc., Publishers at the address listed below.

This manual was prepared, published and distributed by Robert Bentley, Inc., 1734 Massachusetts Avenue, Cambridge, MA 02138. All information in this Manual is based on the latest product information available from Volkswagen at the time of the editorial closing date. Volkswagen has not reviewed and does not vouch for the accuracy or completeness of the technical specifications and work procedures described and given.

Library of Congress Cataloging-in-Publication Data

Volkswagen New Beetle 1998, 1999 : service manual, 2.0L gasoline, 1.9L TDI diesel
p. cm.
Includes index.
ISBN 0-8376-0385-4
1. Volkswagen Beetle automobile--Maintenance and repair--Handbooks, manuals, etc. I. Robert Bentley, inc. II. Title: Volkswagen New Beetle.
TL215.V6V6145 1999
629.28'722--dc21 99-22856
CIP

VWoA Inc. Part No. LPV 800 401
Bentley Stock No. VB99

Editorial closing 01/29/99

03 02 01 00 99 5 4 3 2 1

The paper used in this publication is acid free and meets the requirements of the National Standard for Information Sciences-Permanence of Paper for Printed Library Materials. ∞

Manufactured in the United States of America

Volkswagen Service Manuals from Robert Bentley

New Beetle Service Manual: 1998-1999
2.0L gasoline, 1.9L TDI diesel
Robert Bentley. ISBN 0-8376-0385-4
Volkswagen Part No. LPV 800 401

Jetta, Golf, GTI, Cabrio Service Manual: 1993-early 1999
including, Jetta$_{III}$, Golf$_{III}$, VR6, and TDI
Robert Bentley. ISBN 0-8376-0366-8
Volkswagen Part No. LPV 800 116

EuroVan Official Factory Repair Manual: 1992-1999
Gasoline, Diesel, TDI, 5-cylinder and VR6, including MultiVan and CV Camper. Volkswagen of America.
ISBN 0-8376-0335-8. *Volkswagen Part No. LPV 800 149*

Volkswagen Inspection/Maintenance (I/M) Emission Test Handbook: 1980-1997 Overview and Troubleshooting for Volkswagen Cars, Vans, and Pickups. Volkswagen of America and Robert Bentley. ISBN 0-8376-0394-3
Volkswagen Part No. LPV 800 901

Passat Official Factory Repair Manual: 1995-1997
Gasoline, Turbo Diesel, and TDI, including wagon
Volkswagen United States. ISBN 0-8376-0380-3
Volkswagen Part No. LPV 800 207

GTI, Golf, Jetta Service Manual: 1985-1992
Gasoline, Diesel, and Turbo Diesel, including 16V.
Robert Bentley. ISBN 0-8376-0342-0
Volkswagen Part No. LPV 800 112

Corrado Official Factory Repair Manual: 1990-1994
Volkswagen United States. ISBN 0-8376-0387-0
Volkswagen Part No. LPV 800 300

Passat Service Manual: 1990-1993 including Wagon.
Robert Bentley. ISBN 0-8376-0378-1
Volkswagen Part No. LPV 800 205

Cabriolet, Scirocco Service Manual: 1985-1993
including Scirocco 16V. Robert Bentley.
ISBN 0-8376-0362-5
Volkswagen Part No. LPV 800 113

Volkswagen Fox Service Manual: 1987-1993
including GL, GL Sport and Wagon.
Robert Bentley ISBN 0-8376-0363-3
Volkswagen Part No. LPV 800 504

Quantum Official Factory Repair Manual: 1982-1988
Gasoline and Turbo Diesel, including Wagon and Syncro.
Volkswagen United States. ISBN 0-8376-0341-2
Volkswagen Part No. LPV 800 202

Vanagon Official Factory Repair Manual: 1980-1991 Including Diesel, Syncro and Camper.
Volkswagen United States. ISBN 0-8376-0336-6
Volkswagen Part No. LPV 800 148

Rabbit, Scirocco, Jetta Service Manual: 1980-1984 Gasoline Models, including Pickup Truck, Convertible, and GTI.
Robert Bentley. ISBN 0-8376-0183-5
Volkswagen Part No. LPV 800 104

Rabbit, Jetta Service Manual: 1977-1984 Diesel Models, including Pickup Truck and Turbo Diesel.
Robert Bentley. ISBN 0-8376-0184-3
Volkswagen Part No. LPV 800 122

Rabbit, Scirocco Service Manual: 1975-1979 Gasoline Models. Robert Bentley. ISBN 0-8376-0107-X
Volkswagen Part No. LPV 997 174

Dasher Service Manual: 1974-1981 including Diesel.
Robert Bentley. ISBN 0-8376-0083-9
Volkswagen Part No. LPV 997 335

Super Beetle, Beetle and Karmann Ghia Official Service Manual Type 1: 1970-1979
Volkswagen United States. ISBN 0-8376-0096-0
Volkswagen Part No. LPV 997 109

Beetle and Karmann Ghia Official Service Manual Type 1: 1966-1969
Volkswagen United States. ISBN 0-8376-0416-8
Volkswagen Part No. LPV 997 169

Station Wagon/Bus Official Service Manual Type 2: 1968-1979 Volkswagen United States.
ISBN 0-8376-0094-4
Volkswagen Part No. LPV 997 288

Fastback and Squareback Official Service Manual Type 3: 1968-1973 Volkswagen United States.
ISBN 0-8376-0057-X
Volkswagen Part No. LPV 997 383

Volkswagen 1200 Workshop Manual: 1961-1965, Type 11, 14 and 15 Beetle, Beetle Convertible, Karmann Ghia Coupe and Karmann Ghia Convertible
Robert Bentley. ISBN 0-8376-0390-0
Volkswagen Part No. LPV 800 121

Volkswagen Transporter Workshop Manual: 1963-1967, Type 2 including Kombi, Micro Bus, Micro Bus De Luxe, Pick-up, Delivery Van and Ambulance.
Robert Bentley. ISBN 0-8376-0391-9
Volkswagen Part No. LPV 800 135

Volkswagen Workshop Manual: 1952-1957, Type 11, 14 and 15 (Beetle, Beetle Convertible, Karmann Ghia Coupe)
Robert Bentley. ISBN 0-8376-0389-7
Volkswagen Part No. LPV 800 136

Audi Service Manuals from Robert Bentley

Audi 100, A6 Official Factory Repair Manual: 1992-1997, including S4, S6, quattro and Wagon models. Audi of America. ISBN 0-8376-0374-9
Audi Part No. LPV 800 702

Audi 80, 90, Coupe Quattro Official Factory Repair Manual: 1988-1992 including 80 Quattro, 90 Quattro and 20-valve models. Includes Electrical Troubleshooting Manual.
Audi of America. ISBN 0-8376-0367-6
Audi Part No. LPV 800 604

Audi 100, 200 Official Factory Repair Manual: 1989-1991, including 100 Quattro, 200 Quattro, Wagon, Turbo and 20V Turbo. Audi of America. ISBN 0-8376-0372-2
Audi Part No. LPV 800 701

Audi 5000S, 5000CS Official Factory Repair Manual: 1984-1988 Gasoline, Turbo, and Turbo Diesel, including Wagon and Quattro. Audi of America. ISBN 0-8376-0370-6
Audi Part No. LPV 800 445

Audi 5000, 5000S Official Factory Repair Manual: 1977-1983
Gasoline and Turbo Gasoline, Diesel and Turbo Diesel.
Audi of America. ISBN 0-8376-0352-8
Audi Part No. LPV 800 443

Audi 4000S, 4000CS, and Coupe GT Official Factory Repair Manual: 1984-1987 including Quattro and Quattro Turbo.
Audi of America. ISBN 0-8376-0373-0
Audi Part No. LPV 800 424

Audi 4000, Coupe Official Factory Repair Manual: 1980-1983
Gasoline, Diesel, and Turbo Diesel.
Audi of America. ISBN 0-8376-0349-8
Audi Part No. LPV 800 422

Foreword

Service to Volkswagen owners is a top priority of the Volkswagen organization and has always included the continuing development and introduction of new and expanded services. In line with this purpose, Robert Bentley, Inc., in cooperation with Volkswagen of America, Inc., has introduced this Volkswagen New Beetle Service Manual.

This manual covers Volkswagen New Beetles for the model years 1998 through 1999. This manual was created specifically to cover only those models built for sale in the United States and Canada.

For the Volkswagen owner with basic mechanical skills and for independent auto service professionals, this manual includes the specifications and procedures that were available in an authorized Volkswagen dealer service department as this manual went to press. The Volkswagen owner with no intention of working on his or her car will find that owning and referring to this manual will make it possible to be better informed and to more knowledgeably discuss repairs with a professional automotive technician. The aim throughout has been clarity and completeness, with step-by-step procedures and accurate specifications.

The Volkswagen owner intending to do maintenance and repair should have screwdrivers, a set of metric wrenches and sockets, and metric hex wrenches, since these basic hand tools are needed for most of the work described in this manual. Most procedures will also require a torque wrench to ensure that fasteners are tightened properly and in accordance with specifications. In some cases, the text refers to special tools that are recommended or required to accomplish adjustments or repairs. These tools are identified by their Volkswagen special tool number and illustrated. A thorough pre-reading of each procedure is recommended to determine in advance the need for particular tools and for essential replacement parts such as gaskets.

Some of the information in this manual applies only to cars of a particular model year or range of years. For example, "1998 m.y." refers to the 1998 model year. The model year does not necessarily match the calendar year in which the car was manufactured or sold. To be sure of the model year of a particular car, check the vehicle identification number (VIN) on the car. Technical changes made in production within a model year are identified in this manual by listing the VIN for the first car produced with this change.

The VIN is a unique sequence of 17 characters assigned by Volkswagen to identify each individual car. 3VWBB61C1WM031159 is an example. Each of the 17 letters and numbers indicates certain facts about the car and its manufacture. VINs used to distinguish information in this manual may refer only to the last eleven digits—the characters 1C1WM031159 in the example above.

Your Volkswagen's VIN can be found on a plate mounted on the top of the instrument panel, on the driver's side where the number can be seen through the windshield. The 10th character is the model year code. The letters "I", "O", "Q" and "U" are not used for model year designation, for example, "W" for 1998 m.y., "X" for 1999 m.y., etc. This manual covers Volkswagen New Beetles for the model years 1998 through 1999. The table below explains some of the various codes in the VIN numbers of models covered by this manual.

3 V W	B	B	6	1 C	1	W	M	1 2 3 4 5 6
Manufactuer Information	Body	Engine Type	Restraint Type	Body Type	Check Digit	Model Year	Factory	Sequential Chassis No.
3VW-Mexican Passenger car WVW-German passenger car	Depends on model year		6-Airbag front & side driver/pass. 8-Airbag front only driver/pass	1C-New Beetle		W-1998 X-1999	M- Puebla, Mexico	000001-Begin production 999999-End production

We have endeavored to insure the accuracy of the information in this manual. When the vast array of data presented in the manual is taken into account, however, no claim to infallibility can be made. We therefore cannot be responsible for the result of any errors that may have crept into the text. The publisher encourages comments from the readers of this manual with regard to errors, and also, suggestions for improvement in the presentation of the technical material. These communications have been and will be carefully considered in the preparation of this and other manuals. Please write or e-mail to Robert Bentley, Inc., at the address at the beginning of this manual.

Volkswagen offers extensive warranties, especially on components of the fuel delivery and emission control systems. Therefore, before deciding to repair a Volkswagen that may be covered wholly or in part by any warranties issued by Volkswagen of America, Inc., consult your authorized Volkswagen dealer. You may find that the dealer can make the repair either free or at minimum cost. Regardless of its age, or whether it is under warranty, your Volkswagen is both an easy car to service and an easy car to get serviced. So if at any time a repair is needed that you feel is too difficult to do yourself, a trained Volkswagen technician is ready to do the job for you.

Please read these warnings and cautions before proceeding with maintenance and repair work.

WARNING—

- Some repairs may be beyond your capability. If you lack the skills, tools and equipment, or a suitable workplace for any procedure described in this manual, we suggest you leave such repairs to an authorized Volkswagen dealer service department, or other qualified shop.

- Volkswagen is constantly improving its cars. Sometimes these changes, both in parts and specifications, are made applicable to earlier models. Therefore, before starting any major jobs or repairs to components on which passenger safety may depend, consult your authorized Volkswagen dealer about Technical Bulletins that may have been issued since the editorial closing of this manual.

- Do not re-use any fasteners that are worn or deformed in normal use. Many fasteners are designed to be used only once and become unreliable and may fail when used a second time. This includes, but is not limited to, nuts, bolts, washers, self-locking nuts or bolts, circlips and cotter pins. Always replace these fasteners with new parts.

- Never work under a lifted car unless it is solidly supported on stands designed for the purpose. Do not support a car on cinder blocks, hollow tiles or other props that may crumble under continuous load. Never work under a car that is supported solely by a jack. Never work under the car while the engine is running.

- If you are going to work under a car on the ground, make sure that the ground is level. Block the wheels to keep the car from rolling. Disconnect the battery negative (–) terminal (Ground strap) to prevent others from starting the car while you are under it.

- Never run the engine unless the work area is well ventilated. Carbon monoxide kills.

- Finger rings, bracelets and other jewelry should be removed so that they cannot cause electrical shorts, get caught in running machinery, or be crushed by heavy parts.

- Tie long hair behind your head. Do not wear a necktie, a scarf, loose clothing, or a necklace when you work near machine tools or running engines. If your hair, clothing, or jewelry were to get caught in the machinery, severe injury could result.

- Do not attempt to work on your car if you do not feel well. You increase the danger of injury to yourself and others if you are tired, upset or have taken medication or any other substance that may keep you from being fully alert.

- Illuminate your work area adequately but safely. Use a portable safety light for working inside or under the car. Make sure the bulb is enclosed by a wire cage. The hot filament of an accidentally broken bulb can ignite spilled fuel or oil.

- Catch draining fuel, oil, or brake fluid in suitable containers. Do not use food or beverage containers that might mislead someone into drinking from them. Store flammable fluids away from fire hazards. Wipe up spills at once, but do not store the oily rags, which can ignite and burn spontaneously.

- Always observe good workshop practices. Wear goggles when you operate machine tools or work with battery acid. Gloves or other protective clothing should be worn whenever the job requires working with harmful substances.

- Friction materials such as brake or clutch discs may contain asbestos fibers. Do not create dust by grinding, sanding, or by cleaning with compressed air. Avoid breathing asbestos fibers and asbestos dust. Breathing asbestos can cause serious diseases such as asbestosis or cancer, and may result in death.

- Disconnect the battery negative (–) terminal (ground strap) whenever you work on the fuel system or the electrical system. Do not smoke or work near heaters or other fire hazards. Keep an approved fire extinguisher handy.

- Batteries give off explosive hydrogen gas during charging. Keep sparks, lighted matches and open flame away from the top of the battery. If hydrogen gas escaping from the cap vents is ignited, it will ignite gas trapped in the cells and cause the battery to explode.

- Connect and disconnect battery cables, jumper cables or a battery charger only with the ignition switched off, to prevent sparks. Do not disconnect the battery while the engine is running.

- Do not quick-charge the battery (for boost starting) for longer than one minute. Wait at least one minute before boosting the battery a second time.

- Do not allow battery charging voltage to exceed 16.5 volts. If the battery begins producing gas or boiling violently, reduce the charging rate. Boosting a sulfated battery at a high charging rate can cause an explosion.

- The air-conditioning system is filled with chemical refrigerant, which is hazardous. The A/C system should be serviced only by trained technicians using approved refrigerant recovery/recycling equipment, trained in related safety precautions, and familiar with regulations governing the discharging and disposal of automotive chemical refrigerants.

- Do not expose any part of the A/C system to high temperatures such as open flame. Excessive heat will increase system pressure and may cause the system to burst.

- Some aerosol tire inflators are highly flammable. Be extremely cautious when repairing a tire that may have been inflated using an aerosol tire inflator. Keep sparks, open flame or other sources of ignition away from the tire repair area. Inflate and deflate the tire at least four times before breaking the bead from the rim. Completely remove the tire from the rim before attempting any repair.

- Most cars covered by this manual are equipped with a supplemental restraint system (SRS), that automatically deploys an airbag in the event of a frontal impact. The airbag is inflated by an explosive device. Handled improperly or without adequate safeguards, it can be accidently activated and cause serious injury.

- To prevent personal injury or airbag system failure, **only factory trained Volkswagen service technicians** should test, disassemble or service the airbag system.

- Disconnect the power supply before working on the airbag system, or when doing repairs that require removing airbag system components. Disconnect the battery negative (–) terminal and cover the battery.

continued on next page

Please read these warnings and cautions before proceeding with maintenance and repair work.

WARNING (continued) —

- On airbag-equipped cars, never apply stickers or any other type of covering on the steering wheel. Do not let chemical cleaners, oil or grease come into contact with vinyl covering of the airbag unit.

- Never open or otherwise attempt to repair airbag system parts. Always use new parts. Never leave airbag parts or the partially disassembled airbag system unattended.

- Never use a test light to conduct electrical tests on the airbag system. The system must only be tested by trained Volkswagen Service technicians using the Volkswagen VAG 1551/1552 Scan Tool (ST) or an approved equivalent. The airbag unit must never be electrically tested while it is not installed in the car.

- Do not expose the airbag unit to temperatures above 194°F (90°C), even for brief periods. Keep clear of heat sources such as hot plates, soldering irons, heat lamps and welding equipment.

- When driving or riding in an airbag-equipped vehicle, never hold test equipment in your hands or lap while the vehicle is in motion. Objects between you and the airbag can increase the risk of injury in an accident.

- Greases, lubricants and other automotive chemicals contain toxic substances, many of which are absorbed directly through the skin. Read manufacturer's instructions and warnings carefully. Use hand and eye protection. Avoid direct skin contact.

CAUTION—

- If you lack the skills, tools and equipment, or a suitable workshop for any procedure described in this manual, we suggest you leave such repairs to an authorized Volkswagen dealer or other qualified shop. We especially urge you to consult an authorized Volkswagen dealer before beginning repairs on any car that may still be covered wholly or in part by any of the extensive warranties issued by Volkswagen of America.

- Volkswagen offers extensive warranties, especially on components of fuel delivery and emission control systems. Therefore, before deciding to repair a Volkswagen that may still be covered wholly or in part by any warranties issued by Volkswagen United States, Inc., consult your authorized Volkswagen dealer. You may find that he can make the repair for free, or at minimal cost.

- Volkswagen part numbers listed in this manual are for identification purposes only, not for ordering. Always check with your authorized Volkswagen dealer to verify part numbers and availability before beginning service work that may require new parts.

- Before starting a job, make certain that you have all the necessary tools and parts on hand. Read all the instructions thoroughly, do not attempt shortcuts. Use tools appropriate to the work and use only replacement parts meeting Volkswagen specifications. Makeshift tools, parts and procedures will not make good repairs.

- Use pneumatic and electric tools only to loosen threaded parts and fasteners. Never use these tools to tighten fasteners, especially on light alloy parts. Always use a torque wrench to tighten fasteners to the tightening torque specification listed.

- Be mindful of the environment and ecology. Before you drain the crankcase, find out the proper way to dispose of the oil. Do not pour oil onto the ground, down a drain, or into a stream, pond or lake. Consult local ordinances that govern the disposal of wastes.

- On cars equipped with anti-theft radios, make sure you know the correct radio activation code before disconnecting the battery or removing the radio. If the wrong code is entered into the radio when power is restored, that radio may lock up and be rendered inoperable, even if the correct code is then entered.

- Connect and disconnect a battery charger only with the battery charger switched off.

- Do not quick-charge the battery (for boost starting) for longer than one minute. Wait at least one minute before boosting the battery a second time.

- Sealed or "maintenance free" batteries should be slow-charged only, at an amperage rate that is approximately 10% of the battery's ampere-hour (Ah) rating.

- Do not allow battery charging voltage to exceed 16.5 volts. If the battery begins producing gas or boiling violently, reduce the charging rate. Boosting a sulfated battery at a high charging rate can cause an explosion.

0 Maintenance

TABLES

GENERAL

All of the maintenance work described in this repair group is important and should be carried out at the specified time or mileage interval. The Owner's Manual, the Maintenance Record, and the Warranty Booklet originally supplied with the car contain the maintenance schedules that apply to your Volkswagen. Following these schedules will ensure safe and dependable operation. In addition, many of the maintenance procedures are necessary to maintain warranty protection.

NOTE —
Volkswagen is constantly updating their recommended maintenance procedures and requirements. The information contained here may not include updates or revisions made by Volkswagen since publication of the Owner's Manual, the Maintenance Record, and the Warranty Booklet supplied with the car. If there is any doubt about what procedures apply to a specific model or model year, or what intervals should be followed, remember that an authorized Volkswagen dealer has the latest maintenance information.

CAUTION —
Disconnecting the negative (–) battery cable may erase fault codes and basic settings in the engine management and automatic transmission control modules. Some driveability problems may be noticed until the system re-adapts to operating conditions. OBD II readiness codes, which may be required for emissions testing, may also be erased. Convenience electronics (alarm system, interior light control, power locks, mirrors, and windows) may need to be re-set using a VAG 1551/1552 or equivalent scan tool.

HOW TO USE THIS MANUAL

The manual is divided into 10 main sections, or partitions:

0 Maintenance
1 Engine
2 Engine Management, Exhaust, and Engine Electrical
3 Clutch, Transmission, and Final Drive
4 Suspension, Brakes, and Steering
5 Body–Assembly
6 Body–Components and Accessories
7 Body–Interior Trim
8 Heating and Air Conditioning
9 Electrical System

0 Maintenance covers the recommended schedules and service procedures needed to do the Volkswagen-specified scheduled maintenance work.

The remaining nine partitions (1 through 9) are repair oriented and are broken down into individual repair groups. Some main partitions begin with a general information group, e.g. **1 General Information.** These general groups are mostly descriptive in nature, covering topics such as theory of operation and troubleshooting. The remainder of the repair groups contain the more involved and more detailed system repair information.

A master listing of the 10 partitions and the corresponding individual repair groups can be found on the inside book cover.

Thumb tabs are used on the first page of each repair group page to help locate the groups quickly. Page numbers throughout the manual are organized according to the repair group system. For example, you can expect to find information on engine removal and installation (Repair Group 10) beginning on page 10-1. A comprehensive index can be found on the last pages of the manual.

Warnings, Cautions and Notes

Throughout this manual are many passages with the headings **WARNING**, **CAUTION**, or **NOTE**. These very important headings have different meanings.

WARNING —
The text under this heading warns of unsafe practices that are very likely to cause injury, either by direct threat to the person(s) doing the work or by increased risk of accident or mechanical failure while driving. Warnings are always contained in a box.

CAUTION —
A caution calls attention to important precautions to be observed during the repair work that will help prevent accidentally damaging the car or its parts. Cautions are always contained in a box.

NOTE —
A note contains helpful information, tips that will help in doing a better job and completing it more easily.

Please read every **WARNING**, **CAUTION**, and **NOTE** at the front of the manual and as they appear in repair procedures. They are very important. Read them before you begin any maintenance or repair job.

Some **WARNING**s and **CAUTION**s are repeated wherever they apply. Read them all. Do not skip any. These messages are important, even to the owner who never intends to work on the car.

Work Safety

Although an automobile presents many hazards, common sense and good equipment can help ensure safety. Many accidents happen because of carelessness. Pay attention and stick to these few important safety rules.

> ***WARNING —***
>
> *• Never run the engine in the work area unless it is well-ventilated. The exhaust should be vented to the outside. Carbon Monoxide (CO) is an odorless and colorless gas. Carbon Monoxide (CO) in the exhaust kills.*
>
> *• Remove all neckties, scarfs, loose clothing, and jewelry when working near running engines or power tools. Tuck in shirts. Tie long hair and secure it under a cap. Severe injury can result from these things being caught in rotating parts.*
>
> *• Remove rings, watches, and bracelets. Aside from the dangers of moving parts, metallic jewelry conducts electricity and may cause shorts, sparks, burns, or damage to the electrical system when accidentally contacting the battery or other electrical terminals.*
>
> *• Disconnect the battery negative (–) (GND) cable whenever working on or near the fuel system, airbag system or anything that is electrically powered. Accidental electrical contact may damage the electrical system, cause fire, or result in serious personal injury.*
>
> *• Never work under a lifted car unless it is solidly supported on jack stands that are intended for that purpose. Do not support a car on cinder blocks, bricks, or other objects that may shift or crumble under continuous load. Never work under a car that is supported only by a jack.*
>
> *• The fuel system retains pressure even when the ignition is off. Loosen the fuel lines very slowly to allow the residual pressure to dissipate gradually. Cover fittings with a suitable shop cloth to avoid spraying fuel.*
>
> *• Fuel is highly flammable. When working around fuel, do not smoke or work near fire hazards. Keep an approved fire extinguisher handy. Be aware that water and building heaters may have standing pilot lights.*
>
> *• Illuminate the work area adequately and safely. Use a portable safety light for working inside or under the car. A fluorescent type light is best because it gives off less heat. If using a light with a normal incandescent bulb, use rough service bulbs to avoid breakage. The hot filament of an accidentally broken bulb can ignite spilled fuel or oil.*
>
> *• Keep sparks, lighted matches, and open flame away from the top of the battery. Hydrogen gas emitted by the battery is highly flammable. Any nearby source of ignition may cause the battery to explode.*
>
> *• Never lay tools or parts in the engine compartment or on top of the battery. They may fall and be difficult to retrieve, become caught in belts or other rotating parts, or cause electrical shorts and damage to the electrical system.*

IDENTIFICATION PLATES AND LABELS

Vehicle Identification Number (VIN)

The vehicle year and model can be determined from the VIN or the identification plate. Because stickers can fall off, be painted over, or be moved, it is best to rely on numbers stamped into the chassis.

The VIN (Chassis number) is stamped into the rear floor pan under the rear seat. See Fig. 1.

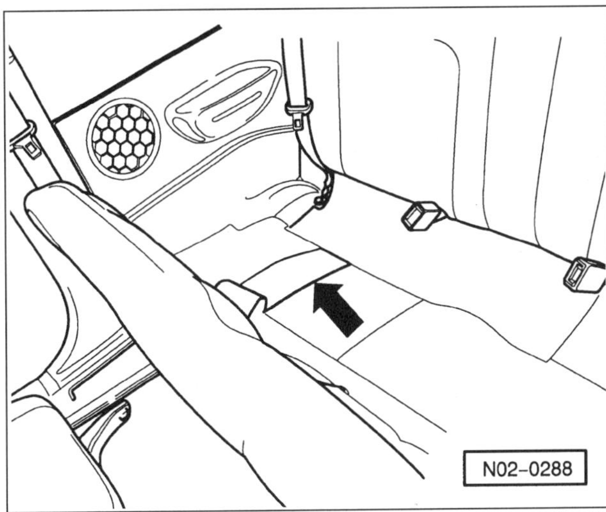

N02-0288

Fig. 1. Partial vehicle identification number (**arrow**) stamped into rear floor pan under rear seat. Pull up rear seat cushion and fold up. Lift carpet on right side for access.

The identification plate is located on the driver's side of the padded dash panel. See Fig. 2. Additional vehicle identification information is also found on stickers attached to the driver's side door post and in the trunk.

> ***NOTE —***
>
> *Additional information on the 17 digit VIN is given in the Foreword on page vi, at the front of the manual.*

0024319

Fig. 2. Full 17 digit VIN plate (**arrow**) on driver's side of padded dash. Trim covers have been removed for other repairs.

Engine identification

The engines used in New Beetles covered by this manual are identified by a three letter code followed by a six digit number such as: AEG 029 452. The engine code and the engine number are located on the engine block.

Engine Codes

- AEG .... 2.0L 4-cylinder gasoline
- ALH .... 1.9L 4-cylinder turbo diesel

- **AEG** and **ALH** engine code letters and numbers are located at the rear of the cylinder block. This information is stamped into the cylinder block casting near the oil filter flange close to the joint between the engine and transmission. See Fig. 3. Additionally, the engine codes can often be found on a sticker on the upper section of the toothed belt guard. See Fig. 4.

0024320

Fig. 3. Engine code letters and numbers (**arrow**) shown on AEG engine. ALH engine letters and numbers are in the same location.

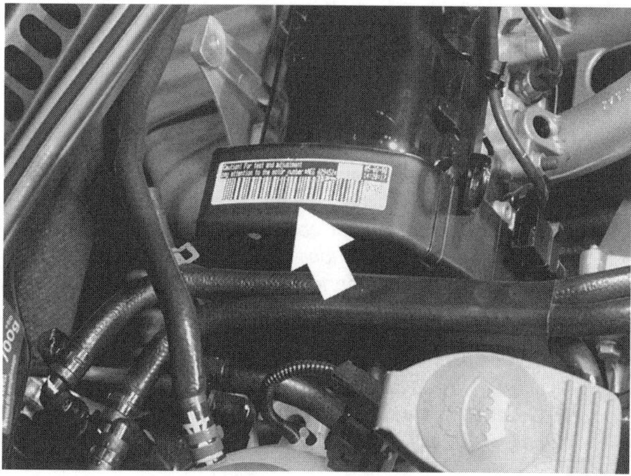

0024321

Fig. 4. Sticker with engine codes (**arrow**) is often attached to upper section of toothed belt guard.

Transmission identification

The transmissions used in New Beetles covered by this manual are identified by a three letter code followed by a five digit number such as: DQY 17078. The digits indicate the transmission build date and all transmissions built on any given day will have the same number. Two transmissions types are available; a five speed manual and a four speed automatic. Each transmission type comes in two versions, depending on engine type.

02J 5-speed manual transmission: code DZQ is used with AEG gas engines and code DQY is used with ALH TDI diesel engines. See Fig. 5.

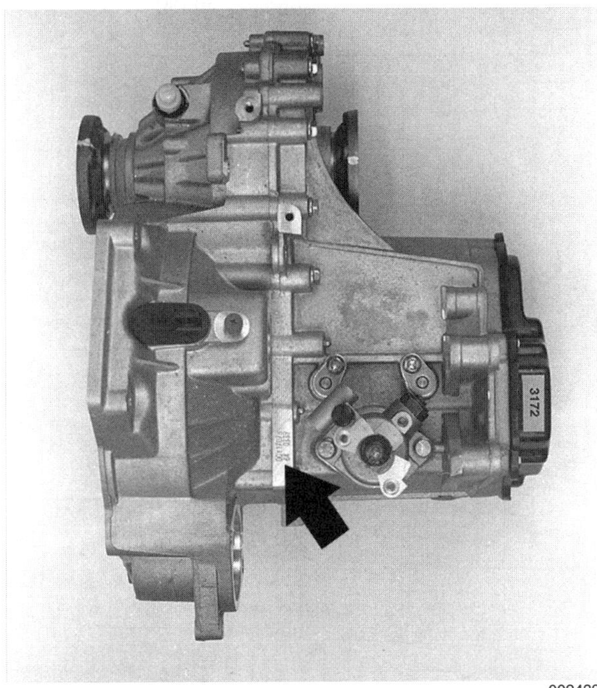

0024322

Fig. 5. Transmission code (**arrow**) stamped into machined area of case for manual transmissions. Other numbers may be stamped into this area of the case but are not relevant to the code.

01M 4-speed automatic transmission: code DYQ is used with AEG gas engines and code DMP is used with ALH TDI diesel engines. See Fig. 6.

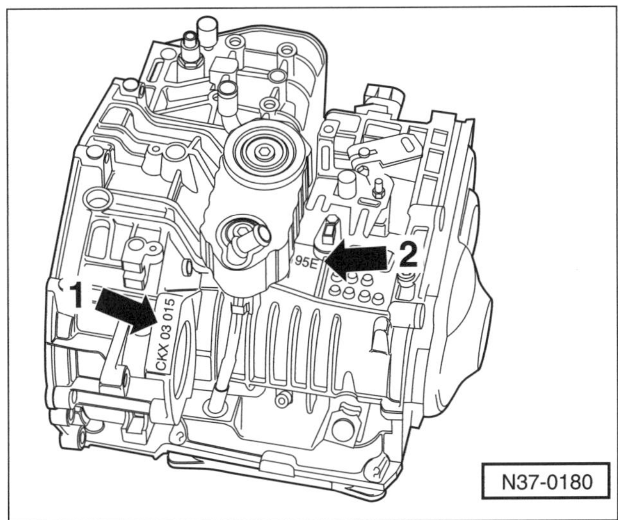

N37-0180

Fig. 6. Transmission code (**arrow 1**) stamped into machined area of case for automatic transmissions. Other numbers (**arrow 2**) may be cast into the case but are not relevant to the code.

TOWING

Emergency towing with commercial equipment

The following information is to be used by commercial tow truck operators who know how to operate their equipment safely. To prevent damage to the vehicle, read and understand all of the following information before proceeding.

CAUTION —
- *The New Beetle cannot be towed with conventional sling-type equipment or non-self-loading wheel dollies. Towing with this type of equipment will cause bumper and body panel damage.*
- *If an automatic transmission vehicle cannot be towed with wheel lift equipment in combination with self-loading wheel dollies, it must be transported with a car carrier (flatbed) to avoid damage to the transmission due to lack of lubrication.*

WARNING —
Never allow passengers to ride in a towed vehicle for any reason.

NOTE —
- *Always follow the manufacturer's recommendations for commercial towing equipment.*
- *Always be thoroughly familiar with specific towing equipment being used.*
- *Always observe all State, Provincial and Local laws regarding such items as warning signals, night illumination, speed, licensing, etc.*

- Whenever possible, tow with the front wheels off the ground.
- The vehicle may be lifted at the rear and moved a short distance to a better position for front wheel lifting.
- If a vehicle with a manual transmission must be towed with the front wheels on the ground, make sure that the transmission oil has not leaked out or been drained.
- If a vehicle is to be towed on its drive wheels, the transmission and differential MUST be operable. Place the transmission in NEUTRAL.
- If any doubt exists about the condition of the transmission or differential, tow the vehicle with the drive wheels lifted, use self-loading wheel dollies or wheel lift equipment.
- Excessive towing speeds and distances may damage both manual and automatic transmissions.
- Move the vehicle only within the recommended speeds and distances.
- During any tow, the raised wheels can contact the road or other ground surfaces, so they need to rotate freely.

(continued on following page)

- The anti-theft steering column lock is not strong enough to withstand shocks transmitted from the wheels while towing. Before towing, always unlock the steering wheel with the ignition key and secure the steering wheel with a steering wheel clamp which has been specifically designed for towing service.
- To reduce the risk of serious personal injury and vehicle damage, never attempt to rock or pivot the vehicle on jack stands to allow positioning on the dolly.
- Always release the parking brake.
- When the ignition key is not available, DO NOT tow from the rear or serious damage to vehicle systems will result.
- The front of the vehicle must be lifted to prevent damage to the steering column anti-theft lock.

> ***CAUTION —***
> *To reduce the risk of accident and serious personal injury, always stay within manufacturer's rated equipment capacities. Exceeding manufacturer's design specifications is dangerous.*

- To reduce the risk of accident and serious injury, never tow any vehicle at a speed in excess of 50 mph for any reason whenever towing with a conventional tow truck, with or without the use of a self-loading wheel dolly.
- Safe operating speeds always depend on weather, road, traffic, visibility, conditions; as well as the condition of the towed vehicle.
- A tow truck is an emergency vehicle to be used to move disabled vehicles to a suitable place of repair. It must not be used for transporting vehicles long distances.
- Towed vehicles should be raised until lifted wheels are a minimum of 6 inches from the ground and there is adequate clearance at opposite end of lifted vehicle.
- Always inspect points of attachment to the disabled vehicle. If they appear to be damaged or deteriorated, select other attachment points at a substantial structural member of the frame.
- Never allow the fuel tank to support any of the vehicle's weight during towing. Before moving the vehicle, carefully secure or remove any loose or protruding parts of damaged vehicles; such as hoods, fenders, trim, etc.
- To avoid serious vehicle damage, never lift or tow any vehicle by attaching towing chains or hooks to shock absorbers, stabilizer bars, or front strut rods.
- Never go under the vehicle while it is lifted by the towing equipment, unless the vehicle is adequately supported by safety stands.
- The safety of the operator and all others in the vicinity of the wrecker or the towed vehicle must be the first consideration at all times during a towing operation.

Vehicle hook-up, front

1. Attach wheel lift equipment to wheels.
2. Attach safety straps to wheels. See Fig. 7.

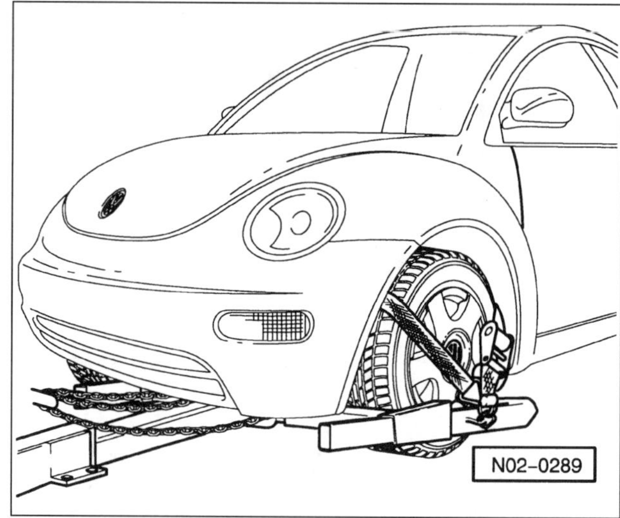

N02-0289

Fig. 7. New Beetle shown attached to appropriate towing equipment for front-first towing.

3. Attach safety chains to lower control arms.

> ***NOTE —***
> - *Always use a safety chain system which is completely independent of the primary lifting and towing attachments.*
> - *During installation of safety chains, be careful not to damage lights, bumpers, or painted surfaces.*
> - *To prevent damage to brake lines and front driveshaft boots, always position hooks and chains cautiously to prevent damage to these components.*
> - *Prior to towing the vehicle, ensure that all attachment points are firmly secured.*
> - *Towing clearance: 6-12 inches between tires and ground.*

Vehicle hook-up, rear

> ***CAUTION—***
> - *Do not tow cars with automatic transmission from the rear.*
> - *Do not tow cars with manual transmission from the rear unless transmission is in nuetral and ignition is unlocked. Secure steering wheel with a steering wheel clamp which has been specificially desinged for towing service.*

1. Attach wheel lift equipment to wheels.
2. Attach safety straps to wheels. See Fig. 8.

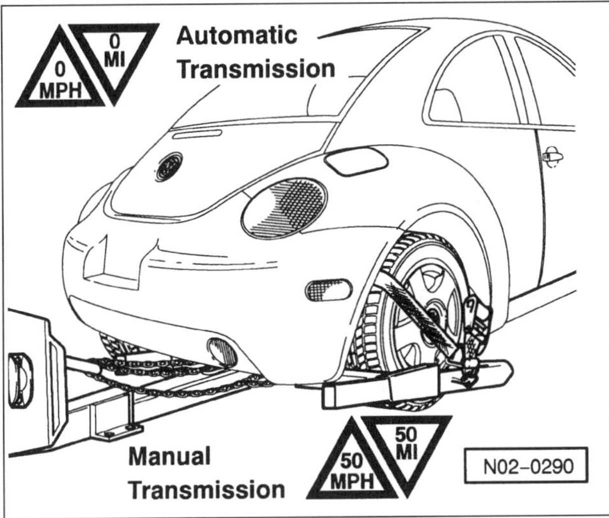

N02-0290

Fig. 8. New Beetle shown attached to appropriate towing equipment for rear-first towing on a manual transmission vehicle.

3. Attach safety chains to axle beam.

> ***NOTE—***
> *Observe all notes associated with front vehicle hook-up.*

Towing eyes

To be able to pull or be pulled, a towing eye must be threaded into the mount at right front of vehicle. The detachable towing eye is in the vehicle tool kit.

1. Pry cover off forward with flat blade screwdriver. See Fig. 9.
2. Thread towing eye fully into mount and tighten with wheel lug wrench. See Fig. 10.
3. After use, unscrew towing eye and return to vehicle tool kit.
4. Reinstall cover.

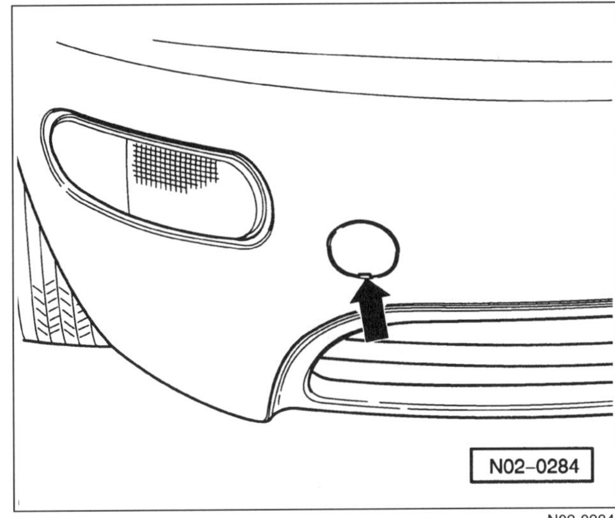

N02-0284

Fig. 9. Towing eye cover (**arrow**) in right front section of bumper.

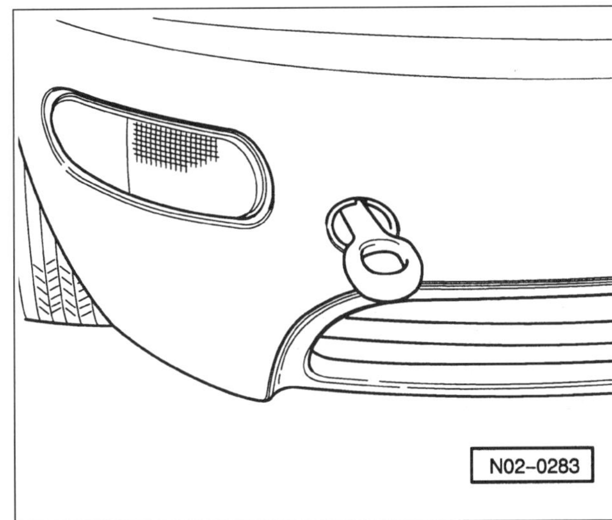

N02-0283

Fig. 10. Installed front towing eye.

> ***NOTE—***
> *The rear towing eye is welded to the vehicle and is located under rear bumper on right side.*

LIFTING VEHICLE

Lifting with hoist or floor jack

New Beetles may be raised for service and repairs by floor jacks and/or hoists. For repairs that require raising the vehicle, proper jacking points must be used. There are four jack points, two on each side of the car, marked by indentations in the lower panel sheet metal just behind the front fender or just in front of rear fender. If using a hoist, similar lift points are just inboard of the aforementioned indentations.

Lifting points

To lift the front of vehicle, place floor jack or hoist at appropriate front lifting point. See Fig. 11.

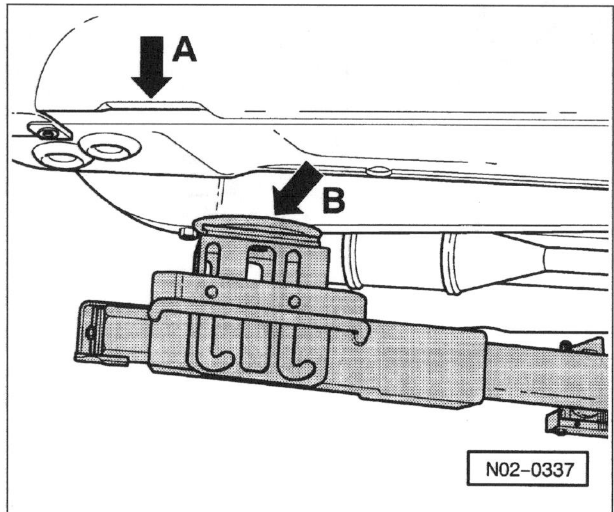

Fig. 11. Front lifting points; when using a floor jack, lift at indentation (**arrow A**). When using a hoist, place pad under long member (**arrow B**) on flat surface behind curve.

To lift the rear of vehicle, use appropriate rear lifting points. See Fig. 12. Always use a suitable rubber or wooden block between the jack and the vehicle.

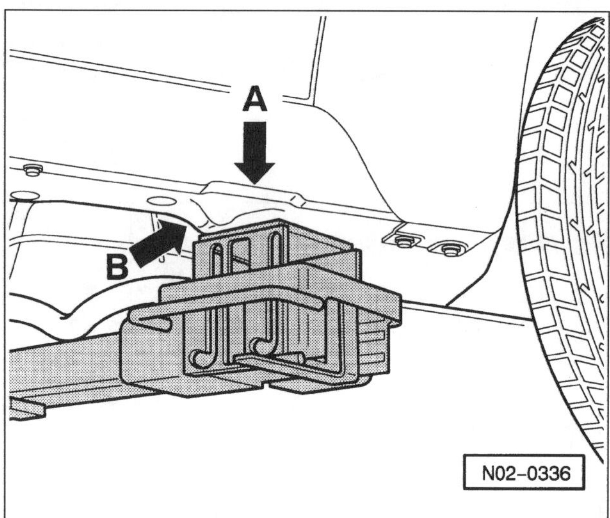

Fig. 12. Rear lifting points; when using a floor jack, lift at indentation (**arrow A**). When using a hoist, place pad under rear cross-member (**arrow B**).

> ***CAUTION —***
> *Do not lift vehicle at engine oil pan, transmission, or on front or rear axle as serious damage may result.*

1. Place car on a flat level area with a surface capable of supporting jacks and jackstands, e.g. concrete.
2. Block the wheels to prevent the car from rolling.
3. Place the jack proper lifting points as shown previously.
4. Operate the jack or hoist and raise the car slowly. If working under the car, support the weight of the car using jack stands.

> ***WARNING —***
> *If work is to be performed under vehicle it must be supported by suitable jack stands.*

> ***CAUTION —***
> - *Vehicle may only be lifted at points indicated in order to avoid damaging vehicle floor pan and to prevent the vehicle from tipping.*
> - *Never start engine and engage a gear with vehicle lifted if any drive wheel has contact with the floor! (There is danger of an accident if this is not observed).*
> - *Before driving on to a vehicle hoist, ensure there is sufficient clearance between low lying vehicle components and the hoist platform.*

Working under the vehicle

When working under any vehicle, the following points should be observed:

1. Disconnect the negative (GND) battery cable so that no one else can start the car. Let others know that you will be under the vehicle.
2. Place at least two jack stands under the car. A jack is a temporary lifting device and should not be used alone to support the car while you are under it. Use positively locking jack stands that are designed for the purpose of supporting a car.
3. If you are using a hoist, be sure that the safety locks are engaged and that the weight of the vehicle is resting on the locks, not the hydraulic system.
4. Lower the car slowly until its weight is fully supported by the jack stands or hoist. Watch to make sure that jack stands do not tip or lean as the car settles on them, and that jack stands and hoist arms are placed solidly and will not move.

> ***WARNING —***
> *Check to make sure vehicle is stable before working under car.*

5. Observe all jacking precautions again when raising the car to remove the jack stands.

MAINTENANCE SCHEDULES

The maintenance schedules list all of the routine maintenance specified by Volkswagen, as well as the mileage intervals at which they should be performed. In any instance where the publisher has recommended maintenance or a maintenance interval that differs from that specified by Volkswagen, such recommendations are more conservative, and still meet Volkswagen's maintenance requirements.

In addition to the specified mileage intervals, Volkswagen also recommends that services be carried out on the basis of time. For 1998 and 1999 model years, the time interval is generally 6 months after delivery, 12 months after delivery, and every 12 months thereafter.

NOTE—

- *Aside from keeping your Volkswagen in the best possible condition, scheduled maintenance plays a role in maintaining full coverage under Volkswagen's extensive warranties. If in doubt about the terms and conditions of your car's warranty, consult an authorized Volkswagen dealer.*
- *Volkswagen continually updates maintenance schedules to suit changing conditions through the issuance of Maintenance Schedule Service Circulars. If in doubt about any of the requirements for your vehicle, consult an authorized Volkswagen dealer.*

Table a. First 5,000 mile (8000 kilometer), service

Maintenance item	Tools required	New parts/fluids required	Warm engine required	Dealer service recommended
Engine compartment maintenance				
Change oil and oil filter	*	*	*	
Water separator: drain water (TDI Diesel)	*			
Timing belt: check condition (TDI Diesel)	*			

Table b. Every 10,000 miles (16,000 kilometers), service

Maintenance item	Tools required	New parts/fluids required	Warm engine required	Dealer service recommended
Engine compartment maintenance				
Change oil and oil filter	*	*	*	
Water separator: drain water (TDI Diesel)	*			
Timing belt: check condition (TDI Diesel)	*			
Windshield washer: check fluid level, add as necessary		*		
Dust/pollen filter: replace[1)]		*		
Under car maintenance				
Tires and spare: check condition and pressures	*			
Rotate tires front to rear	*			
Brake system: check for damage and/or leaks; check pad thickness and brake fluid level	*	*		
Road Test				
Automatic shift lock (where applicable): check operation including park/neutral position switch				

1)Dust and pollen filter: 1999 models replace every 20,000 miles; 1998 models, replace every 10,000 miles.

Table c. Every 20,000 miles (30,000 kilometers), service

Maintenance item	Tools required	New parts/fluids required	Warm engine required	Dealer service recommended
Engine compartment maintenance				
Change oil and oil filter	*	*	*	
Water separator: drain water (TDI Diesel)	*			
Timing belt: check condition (TDI Diesel)	*			
Windshield washer: check fluid, add as necessary		*		
Dust/pollen filter: replace[1)]		*		
Battery: check electrolyte level and add if necessary. DO NOT attempt to check or add fluid to a maintenance free battery.	*	*		
Check engine coolant level, add if necessary		*		
Fuel filter: replace (TDI Diesel)[2)]	*	*		
Brake fluid: check level, add if necessary; replace every 2 years regardless of mileage	*	*		
Under car maintenance				
Brake system: check for damage and/or leaks; check pad thickness	*			
Rotate tires front to rear	*			
Tires and spare: check condition and pressures	*			
Automatic transmission final drive: check oil level, add if necessary, check for leaks	*	*		
Manual transmission: check oil level, add if necessary, check for leaks	*	*		
Drive axle shafts: check boots for tears, cracks or damage				
Body and interior maintenance				
Door check straps and hinge mechanism: lubricate		*		
On Board Diagnostic system: check Diagnostic Trouble Code (DTC) Memory with VAG 1551/1552 Scan tool (ST) and erase if necessary.	*	*		*
Road Test				
Automatic shift lock (where applicable): check operation including park/neutral position switch				
Check A/T transmission kickdown, braking, steering, heating, ventilation, air conditioning, power accessories and electrical systems				
After Road Test				
Engine: check for leaks				
Power steering: check fluid level		*		
Exhaust system: check for damage and leaks				
On Board Diagnostic system: check Diagnostic Trouble Code (DTC) Memory with VAG 1551/1552 Scan tool (ST) and erase if necessary.	*		*	*

1)Dust and pollen filter: 1999 models replace every 20,000 miles; 1998 models, replace every 10,000 miles.

2)Fuel filter: Gasoline engine fuel filter replacement is not part of Volkswagen's scheduled maintenance.

Table d. Every 40,000 miles (60,000 kilometers), service

Maintenance item	Tools required	New parts/fluids required	Warm engine required	Dealer service recommended
Engine compartment maintenance				
Change oil and oil filter	*	*	*	
Water separator: drain water (TDI Diesel)	*			
Timing belt: check tension and condition, adjust if necessary [1)] Replace (TDI Diesel)	*	*		*
Timing belt tensioner: replace (TDI Diesel)	*	*		*
Ribbed belt: check condition	*			
Windshield washer: check fluid, add as necessary		*		
Dust/pollen filter: replace[2)]		*		
Spark plugs: replace	*	*		
Battery: check electrolyte level and add if necessary. DO NOT attempt to check or add fluid to a maintenance free battery.	*	*		
Check engine coolant level, add if necessary		*		
Fuel filter: replace (TDI Diesel)	*	*		
Air filter: replace filter element (required every 40,000 miles and every 4 years)	*	*		
Brake fluid: check level, add if necessary; replace every 2 years regardless of mileage	*	*		
Under car maintenance				
Brake system: check for damage and/or leaks; check pad thickness	*			
Rotate tires front to rear	*			
Tires and spare: check condition and pressures	*			
Automatic transmission final drive: check oil level, add if necessary, check for leaks	*	*		
Automatic transmission: check ATF level [3)]				
Manual transmission: check oil level, add if necessary, check for leaks	*	*		
Drive axle shafts: check boots for tears, cracks or damage				
Front axle: check dust seals on ball joints and tie rod ends, check tie rods for play/wear	*			

[1)]Volkswagen does not specify a replacement interval for the camshaft drive belt on 4-cylinder gasoline engines. The publisher recommends periodic inspection of the belt and replacement at least every 90k miles or 5 years.

[2)]Dust and pollen filter: 1999 models replace every 20,000 miles; 1999 models, replace every 10,000 miles.

[3)]Volkswagen does not specify a change interval due in part to the synthetic ATF used. The publisher recommends that in the case of severe conditions, such as extremely high temperatures, continuous mountain driving, trailer towing or predominantly stop-and-go traffic conditions, the ATF should be changed every 30,000 miles. During this time the ATF sump should be removed and cleaned and the ATF strainer and sump gasket replaced.

Table d. Every 40,000 miles (60,000 kilometers), service

Maintenance item	Tools required	New parts/fluids required	Warm engine required	Dealer service recommended
Body and interior maintenance				
Door check straps and hinge mechanism: lubricate		*		
On Board Diagnostic system: check Diagnostic Trouble Code (DTC) Memory with VAG 1551/1552 Scan tool (ST) and erase if necessary.	*	*		*
Road Test				
Automatic shift lock (where applicable): check operation including park/neutral position switch				
Check A/T transmission kickdown, braking, steering, heating, ventilation, air conditioning, power accessories and electrical systems				
After Road Test				*
Engine: check for leaks				
Power steering: check fluid level		*		
Exhaust system: check for damage and leaks				
On Board Diagnostic system: check Diagnostic Trouble Code (DTC) Memory with VAG 1551/1552 Scan tool (ST) and erase if necessary.	*		*	*

Table e. Every 2 years, service

Maintenance item	Tools required	New parts /fluids required	Warm engine required	Dealer service recommended
Engine compartment maintenance				
Brake fluid: replace regardless of mileage	*	*		

Table f. Every 4 years, service

Maintenance item	Tools required	New parts /fluids required	Warm engine required	Dealer service recommended
Engine compartment maintenance				
Air cleaner: replace regardless of mileage	*	*		

Table g. At 4 and 8 years, and every 2 years thereafter, inspection

Maintenance item	Tools required	New parts /fluids required	Warm engine required	Dealer service recommended
Passenger compartment maintenance				
Air bags: To assure continued reliability, the Air Bag System must be inspected by an authorized Volkswagen dealer at 4 and 8 years from the date of manufacture and every two years thereafter.	✻	✻		✻

ENGINE COMPARTMENT MAINTENANCE

The jobs listed under this heading are the engine compartment maintenance items from the maintenance tables. The jobs follow the same general sequence in which they appear in the tables.

Sound absorber panels, removing and installing

1. Removing lower center, AEG gasoline engines. See Fig. 13.
   - Remove 4 bolts on each side.
   - Pull sound absorber to the rear off of the bumper and remove.

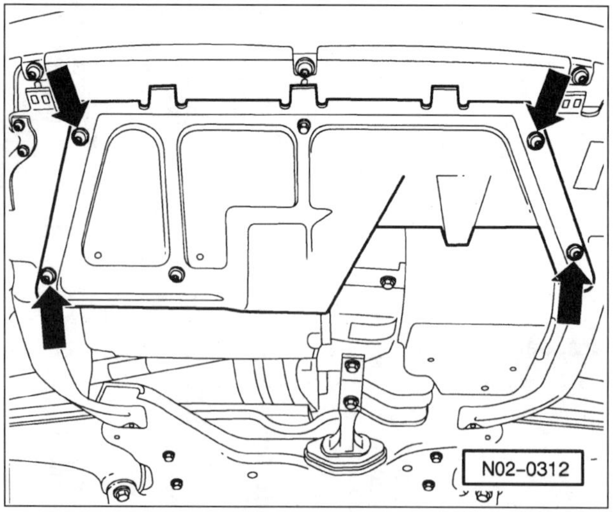

N02-0312

Fig. 13. Remove bolts (**arrows**) and pull sound absorber panel to rear.

2. Removing lower center, ALH TDI diesel engines. See Fig. 14.
   - Remove 4 bolts on each side.
   - Remove 2 bolts in the rear.
   - Pull sound absorber to the rear off of the bumper and remove.

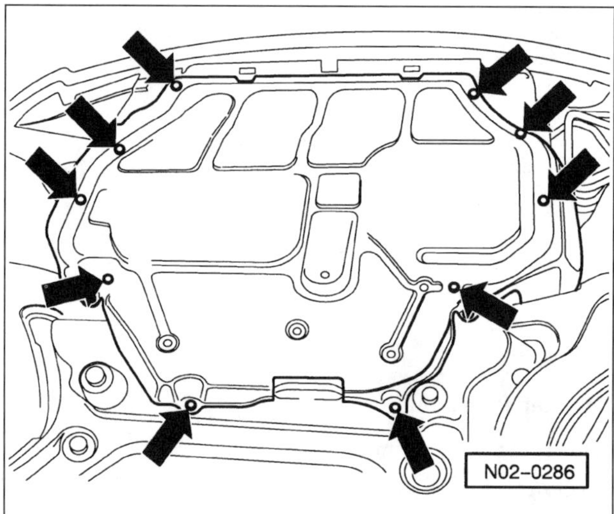

N02-0286

Fig. 14. Remove bolts (**arrows**) and pull sound absorber panel to rear.

3. Installing lower center, ALH and AEG engines.
   - Push sound absorber forward over bumper cover.
   - Install all bolts.

4. Removing and installing lower side panels. See Fig. 15. and Fig. 16.
   - Remove screws and speed clips.
   - Pull side panels down and out of retainers.

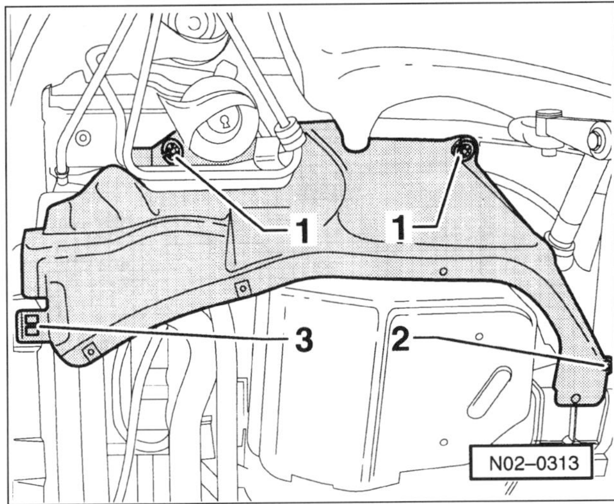

N02-0313

Fig. 15. Remove speed clips (**1**), screws (**2**) and driver's side panel from retainers (**3**).

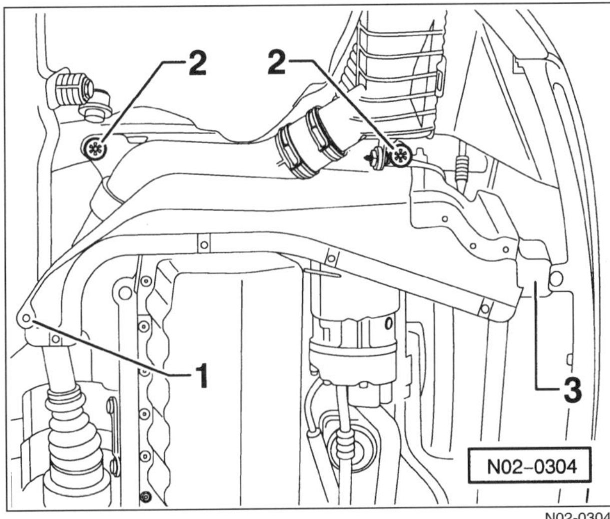

N02-0304

Fig. 16. Remove speed clips (**2**), screw (**1**) and passenger's side panel from retainer (**3**).

5. Removing and installing upper sound absorber panel. See Fig. 17.
   - Pry out plastic plugs and remove nuts underneath.
   - Loosen nut in rear slightly.
   - Remove dipstick,
   - Pull cover forward and up to remove.
   - Installation is the reverse.

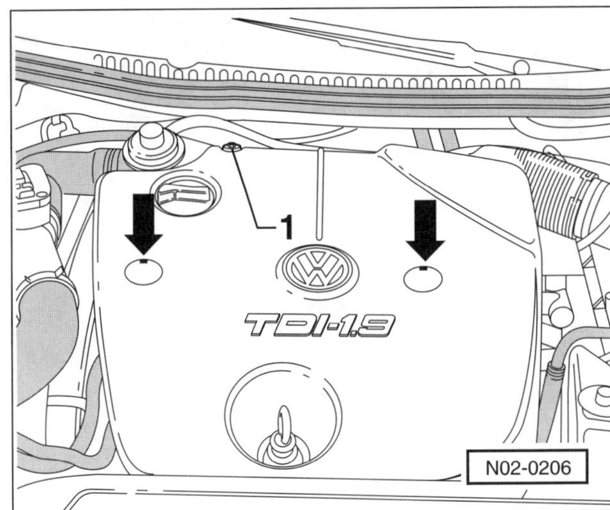

N02-0206

Fig. 17. Carefully pry off plastic plugs (**arrows**) and remove nuts. Loosen rear nut (**1**) slightly. ALH engine shown, AEG is similar.

Engine oil, level checking

It is normal for your engine to consume a small amount of oil. The rate of consumption will depend on the quality and viscosity of the oil and operating conditions. Make it a habit to check oil level at every fuel filling.

1. After switching ignition OFF, wait at least 3 minutes to allow the oil to flow back into the oil pan.
2. Remove dipstick located in front of intake manifold. Wipe dipstick with a clean cloth and fully re-insert into tube.
3. Remove dipstick again and read oil level. The oil level must be at the top edge of the shaded area but on no account above the maximum level mark. If oil level is below shaded area, fill to top mark. See Fig. 18.

> ***CAUTION —***
> *Risk of damage to the catalytic converter if oil level is too high.*

Select an oil that conforms to the standards of the American Petroleum Institute (API). A symbol can be found on the oil container with the API rating and viscosity grade. Gasoline engines can use either petroleum or synthetic oils. Volkswagen does, however, recommend that only 5W30 synthetic oil be used in all TDI diesel engines.

Recommended engine oils

- AEG engines . . . . .API service rating SG
- ALH engines (5W30 synthetic) . . . . API service rating CD

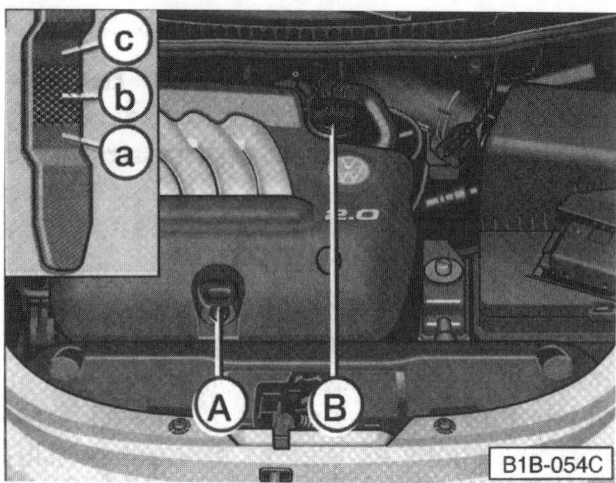

B1B-054C

Fig. 18. Oil dipstick shown at **A** and filler cap at **B**. The end of the dipstick is shown in the upper left inset. Oil level in shaded area (**b**) is normal and does not need to be topped up. Oil level must be no higher than **c**. Oil level at **a** or lower must be topped up and rechecked. AEG engine shown, ALH engine similar.

Engine oil, changing

1. Warm car to normal operating temperature.
2. Shut off engine and apply parking brake.
3. Raise car and support on jackstands designed for the purpose.

> ***WARNING —***
> *Jack stands should be placed on hard level surface (e.g. concrete).*

4. Remove lower sound absorber panel (belly pan) from beneath engine compartment. Remove drain plug from oil pan and allow oil to drain. See **17 Engine—Lubrication System** for drain plug location.

> ***WARNING —***
> *Hot oil can scald. Wear protective clothing, gloves and eye protection.*

> ***CAUTION —***
> - *Always replace oil-drain plug sealing ring anytime the drain plug is removed.*
> - *Dispose of oil properly at a facility equipped for recycling or storage.*

5. Replace oil filter. See **Engine Oil filter, replacing** for applicable engine.
6. Install oil drain plug with a new seal. Tighten drain plug to proper torque.

Tightening torque
- Oil drain plug to oil pan. . . . . 30 Nm (22 ft-lb)

7. Fill engine with proper quantity and type of oil.

Engine oil capacity, with filter change
- AEG engine . . . . 4.0 liters (4.2 qt.)
- ALH engine. 4.5 liters (4.7 qt.)

8. Run engine and check for leaks. Shut off engine and reinstall sound dampening pan. Check oil level after about 3 minutes.

> ***CAUTION —***
> *After changing the engine oil and the oil filter, observe the following at the first engine start:*
> - *The engine must only run at idling speed as long as the oil pressure warning light in the instrument cluster is on. Do not rev the engine! If the engine is revved with the warning light on, the turbocharger on TDI engines could be damaged or fail completely.*
> - *The full oil pressure is not attained until the warning light has gone out. Only then can the engine be revved.*

Engine oil filter, replacing (AEG engine)

1. Remove center of lower sound absorber panel.
2. Position drain pan under oil filter to catch spills.
3. Working from under engine, loosen and remove oil filter with oil filter strap or suitable wrench. See Fig. 19.
4. Clean sealing surface on oil filter flange.
5. Lightly lubricate rubber seal with clean oil.
6. Thread on new filter and tighten by hand.

> ***CAUTION —***
> *Observe all applicable regulations concerning disposal of used oil filters.*

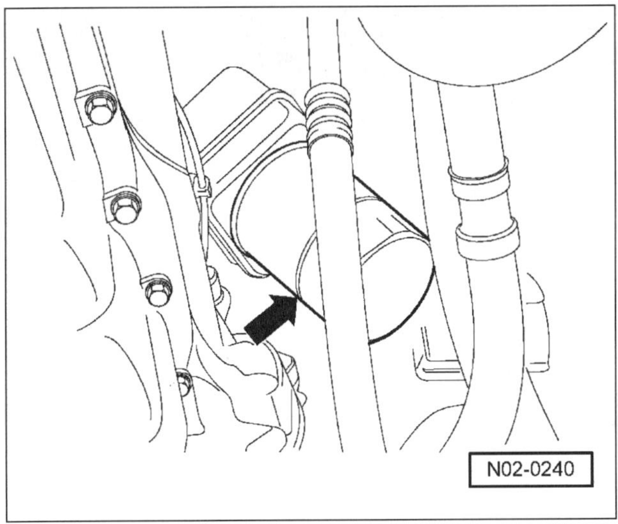

N02-0240

Fig. 19. AEG engine oil filter from underneath.

Engine oil filter, replacing (ALH engine)

1. Remove upper sound absorber panel.
2. Working from above the engine, loosen and remove oil filter sealing cap.
3. Pull filter up and out.
4. Install new filter and gaskets. See Fig. 20.

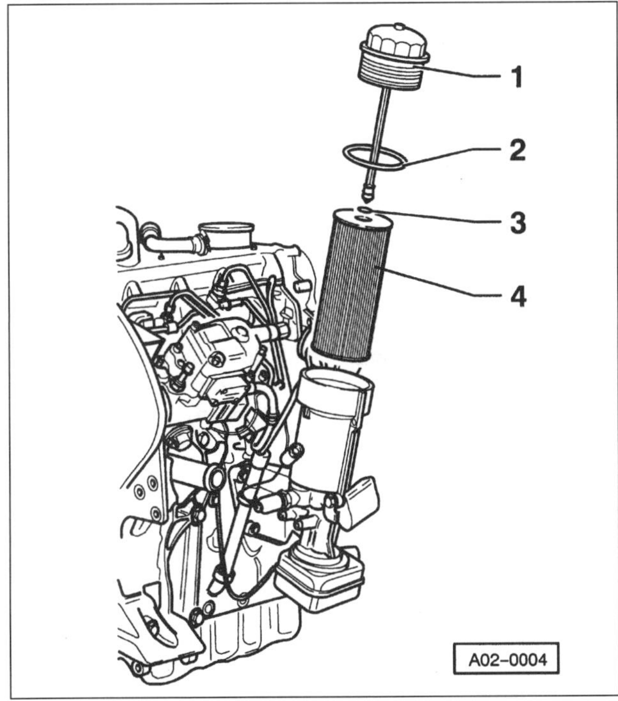

A02-0004

Fig. 20. Install new oil filter (**4**) with new gaskets (**2**) and (**3**). Install sealing cap and torque.

5. Install sealing cap.

Tightening torque
- Oil filter sealing cap . . . . 25 Nm (18 ft-lb)

---

6. Install upper sound absorber panel.

> ***CAUTION —***
> *Observe all applicable regulations concerning disposal of used oil filters.*

Coolant, checking

Cooling system maintenance consists of maintaining coolant level, checking coolant freezing point, and inspecting hoses. Coolant flushing is not part of Volkswagen's scheduled maintenance.

NOTE —
Volkswagen does not require replacing the coolant as part of routine maintenance. The cooling system has been filled at the factory with a permanent coolant. For coolant system draining and refilling procedures, see **19 Engine-Cooling System.**

> ***WARNING —***
> - *Hot coolant can scald. Do not work on the cooling system until it has fully cooled.*
> - *Use extreme care when draining and disposing of coolant. Coolant is poisonous and lethal. Children and pets are attracted to it because of its sweet smell and taste. See a doctor or veterinarian immediately if any amount is ingested.*

> ***CAUTION —***
> - *Use only Volkswagen original anti-freeze when filling the cooling system. Use of any other anti-freeze may be harmful to the cooling system. Do not use an anti-freeze containing phosphates.*
> - *Do not use tap water in cooling system. Use distilled water only to mix anti-freeze.*

Volkswagen uses only one type of coolant in New Beetles. It can be identified by its red color. This coolant/antifreeze is phosphate free and also silicate free. When supplied by Volkswagen, this coolant/antifreeze is known as G12.

The advantages of G12 over earlier types include improvements in corrosion protection, thermal stability, heat transfer/control, hard water tolerance and environmental protection.

A translucent expansion tank, or overflow reservoir, provides easy monitoring of coolant level without opening the system. See Fig. 21.

0024323

Fig. 21. Coolant expansion tank (**A**) on passenger's side of engine compartment is partially obscured by windshield washer reservoir (**B**).

> ***CAUTION —***
> - *G12 (Red Coolant) must NEVER be mixed with ANY other coolant. Engine damage will result!*
> - *Contamination of G12 with other colored coolants is identifiable by discoloration (brown, purple, etc.). This mixture causes a foamy deposit to appear in the expansion tank/radiator and MUST be drained immediately.*
> - *The cooling system must be completely free of this mixture before refilling with the correct type of coolant/antifreeze.*

The coolant level should always be checked when engine is cold. The coolant level should be between the maximum and minimum mark on the expansion tank. See Fig. 22.

Inspect hoses by first checking that all connections are tight and dry. Coolant seepage indicates that either the hose clamp is loose, that the hose is damaged, or that the connection is dirty or corroded. Dried coolant has a chalky appearance. Check hose condition by pinching them. Hoses should be firm and springy. Replace any hose that is cracked, that has become soft and limp, or has been contaminated by oil or diesel fuel. See Fig. 23.

To check freezing point of the coolant, (and also the boiling point), use a refractometer. With the engine cold, remove cap from expansion tank and draw up some coolant with refractometer siphon. Volkswagen recommends using a 50/50 mixture of anti-freeze and water, which has a freezing point of -35°F (-38°C). If the freezing point is too high, drain a small amount of coolant from the system and add new anti-freeze until proper protection level is obtained.

0024130

Fig. 22. Coolant level should be between **max** and **min** marks on expansion tank.

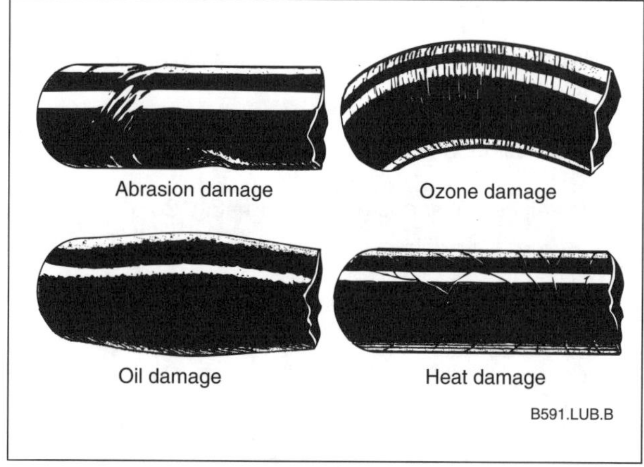

B9110

Fig. 23. Examples of damaged coolant hoses. Any of the conditions shown is cause for replacement. (Courtesy of Gates Rubber Inc.)

> ***NOTE —***
> *For protection to approx. -40°C (-40°F) the percentage of anti-freeze may be increased up to 60%. The percentage of anti-freeze must not exceed 60%, as higher amounts will decrease frost protection and cooling capacity.*

Brake fluid level, checking

Routine maintenance of the brake system includes maintaining an adequate level of brake fluid in the reservoir, replacing brake fluid every 2 years, checking brake pads for wear, checking hand brake function, and inspecting system for fluid leaks or other damage. See **Under Car Maintenance** for pad inspection and brake system inspection.

> ***WARNING —***
> - *Use only new, previously unopened brake fluid conforming to US Standard FMVSS 166 DOT 4.*
> - *Brake fluid is poisonous. DO NOT ingest brake fluid. Wash thoroughly with soap and water if brake fluid comes into contact with skin.*

> ***CAUTION —***
> - *DO NOT let brake fluid come in contact with paint. Wash immediately with soap and water.*
> - *Brake fluid absorbs moisture from the air and must be stored in an airtight container.*
> - *DO NOT allow brake fluid to exceed the maximum level in the fluid reservoir.*

The brake fluid level will drop slightly as the brakes wear. Check fluid level at brake fluid reservoir, located on driver's side of engine compartment, under air cleaner connecting hose.

Brake fluid
- Type . . . . FVMSS 116 SAE DOT 4

> ***WARNING —***
> *Do not mix DOT 5 (silicone) brake fluid with DOT 4 brake fluid as severe component corrosion will result. Such corrosion could lead to brake system failure.*

Brake fluid, replacing

Brake fluid readily absorbs moisture from the atmosphere. This moisture can cause brake system corrosion and adversely affect braking performance. Therefore, the old brake should be flushed out of the system and new, fresh fluid added at least every 2 years, regardless of mileage. See **47 Brakes–Hydraulic System** for brake system bleeding procedures and brake fluid replacement.

> ***NOTE —***
> *Vehicles equipped with ABS can be bled using conventional methods.*

Power steering fluid level, checking

There are two methods for checking the power steering fluid level.

COLD - When cold checking the power steering fluid level, the engine should not be running and the front wheels should be in the straight ahead position. Use a screwdriver to remove the cap. See Fig. 24. Use a clean shop cloth to wipe the dipstick end and screw the cap back on hand tight only. Remove the dipstick from the fluid reservoir again and check the level on the dipstick. The level should be within ± 2 mm of the **min** mark. See Fig. 25. Adjust the fluid level if required and screw the cap back on hand tight when done.

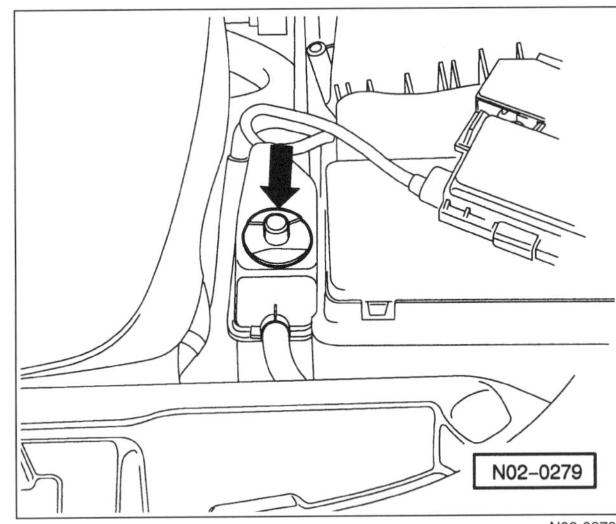

N02-0279

Fig. 24. Power steering fluid reservoir cap (**arrow**) with attached dipstick.

HOT - When hot checking the power steering fluid level, start the engine and let it run until the power steering fluid temperature is above 50°C (122°F). The front wheels should be in the straight ahead position. Use a screwdriver to remove the cap. See Fig. 24. Use a clean shop cloth to wipe the dipstick end and screw the cap back on hand tight only. Remove the dipstick from the fluid reservoir again and check the level on the dipstick. The level should be between the **min** and **max** marks. See Fig. 25. Adjust the fluid level if required and screw the cap back on hand tight when done.

Power steering fluid
- Type . . . . hydraulic oil (VW part no. G 002 000)

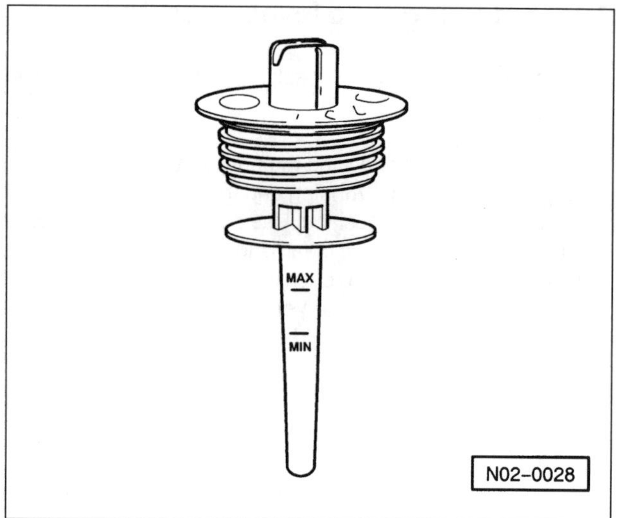

N02-0028

Fig. 25. Dipstick section of power steering reservoir cap. Note **min** and **max** marks.

> ***CAUTION—***
> - *Use only Volkswagen hydraulic oil G 002 000 in the power steering system. Do not use ATF or other non-approved types of power steering fluid. If the wrong fluid is used, power steering components may fail.*
> - *Volkswagen part numbers are given for reference only! Always consult your Volkswagen parts department or aftermarket parts specialist for the latest parts information.*

NOTE—
- *The power steering system uses a special hydraulic oil and not ATF.*
- *If fluid level is above (approx. 2 mm) the MIN mark, some fluid must be extracted.*
- *If fluid level is below (approx. 2 mm) the MIN mark, the hydraulic system must be checked for leaks. It is not sufficient to top-up with fluid.*

Fluid leaks

Check the engine compartment for signs of fluid leaks. Fluid leaks attract dust making them easier to spot. Many expensive repairs can be avoided by prompt repair of minor fluid leaks.

Inspect for leaks in engine, cooling, fuel, heating and air conditioning systems. Visually inspect hoses and hose connections for leaks, worn areas, porosity and brittleness.

Fuel filter, draining (ALH engines)

The diesel fuel filter functions to trap water. As water is heavier than diesel fuel, it settles to the bottom of filter and can be drained off.

> ***CAUTION—***
> *Do not allow diesel fuel to contact coolant hoses or other rubber parts. Wipe diesel fuel off hoses immediately and wash with soap and water.*

1. Remove control valve retaining clip. See Fig. 26.

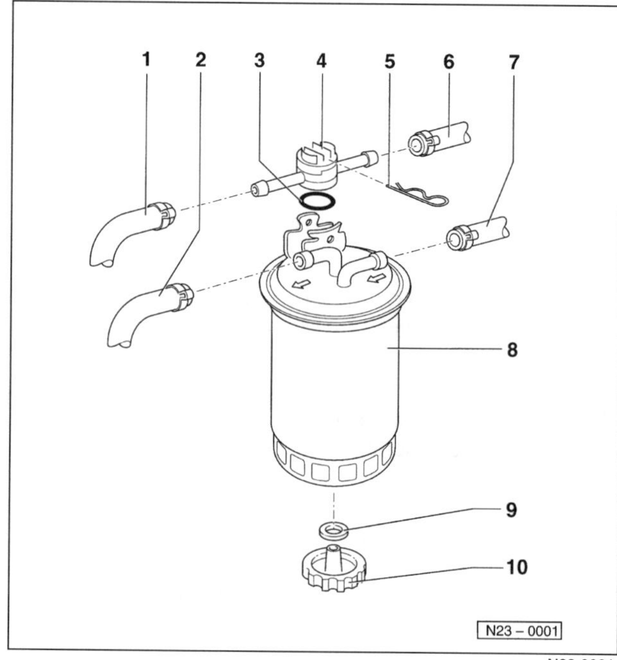

N23-0001

Fig. 26. Diesel fuel filter shown with related components.

The numbered list below applies to Fig. 26.

1. **Fuel return line**
   - From diesel injection pump
2. **Fuel supply line**
   - To diesel injection pump
3. **O-ring**
   - Always replace
4. **Fuel control valve**
   - Recirculates fuel to filter at temperatures below 15°C (59°F)
   - Returns fuel to tank at temperatures above 31°C (88°F)
   - Installed position: arrow points toward fuel tank
5. **Retaining clip**
6. **Fuel return line**
   - To fuel tank
7. **Fuel supply line**
   - From fuel tank
8. **Diesel fuel filter**
   - Fill with diesel fuel before installing
   - Observe fuel flow direction marked on top
9. **Gasket**
10. **Water drain plug**

2. Pull fuel control valve up with fuel lines connected.

3. Loosen water drain plug on bottom of filter and drain out approximately 100cc (1.7 oz.) of fuel/water.

4. Install fuel control valve with a new O-ring.

5. Attach retaining clip and tighten drain plug.

6. Check fuel system for leaks (visual inspection) with the engine running. Raise engine speed several times and let idle. Fuel flow through transparent pipe must be observed.

Fuel filter, replacing (ALH engines)

1. Remove control valve retaining clip. See Fig. 26.

2. Pull fuel control valve up with fuel lines connected.

3. Label and disconnect fuel filter inlet and outlet lines.

4. Unbolt filter bracket from body and remove with filter.

5. Loosen bracket and remove filter.

6. Install new filter.

7. Installation is the reverse of removal, noting the following:
   - Install fuel filter inlet and outlet lines.
   - Install fuel control valve with a new O-ring and attach retaining clip.

8. Check fuel system for leaks (visual inspection) with the engine running. Raise engine speed several times and let idle. Fuel flow through transparent pipe must be observed.

Fuel filter, replacing (AEG engines)

Volkswagen specifies that the fuel filter used on gasoline engines is designed to last the life of the car. Replacement is only necessary if the filter becomes clogged due to contaminated fuel or failure to keep the fuel tank sealed. If dirt in the fuel filter is suspected, also check the screen on the bottom of the fuel delivery unit for contamination. **See 20 Fuel Storage and Supply.**

Battery service

Under normal operating conditions, the battery is maintenance free. At high outside temperatures, however, it is advisable to check the electrolyte level through the translucent battery housing. The electrolyte level should be just above the battery plates and their separators. The battery plates can be seen once the filler caps are removed. If the electrolyte level is low, replenish it by adding distilled water only. When servicing the battery, observe the following points:

- All cell caps must be equipped with an O-ring seal.
- The electrolyte level on batteries with visible minimum and maximum markings on the outside of the (semi-transparent) battery case is checked by visual inspection.
- The electrolyte level must be above the minimum marking or just reach the maximum marking.
- On batteries where the exterior markings are difficult to recognize (due to installation location, battery case opaqueness or dirt), the cell caps must be removed and individual cell electrolyte levels checked from inside the battery.
- The electrolyte level must align with the internal electrolyte level indicator (lip). This equates to the external “maximum” marking on the battery case.
- Check that battery is securely located and clamping bolt is tight.
- When the electrolyte level is too low and the cell plates are exposed, a loss of battery capacity will result (loss of power). If the cell plates are not completely submerged by electrolyte, (sulfuric acid/water mixture) corrosion will occur on the plates, plate bridges and cell connector. Optimum battery function is not possible under these conditions!
- When electrolyte level is too high, electrolyte (sulfuricacid/water mixture) may leak out and damage the surrounding areas such as the battery tray and engine compartment.
- Only use distilled water to top-up batteries. This prevents electrolyte impurities which cause self-discharging.
- DO NOT overfill the battery.
- Overfilled batteries can boil over.
- Too little electrolyte reduces the service life of the battery.
- Excess electrolyte MUST be extracted using a hydrometer.
- Dispose of electrolyte (sulfuric acid) properly! Waste electrolyte must only be disposed of in appropriate waste disposal sites. Refer to local regulations pertaining to electrolyte disposal.
- Volkswagen recommends that only new generation batteries with central gas venting are to be installed.

For battery testing and service, see **27 Engine Electrical**.

Ribbed V-belt, checking

On AEG and ALH engines, the ribbed V-belt is self-adjusting and does not require any routine maintenance aside from periodic inspection for wear. When checking, observe the following points:

- Subsurface cracks, core ruptures and cross-sectional breaks
- Layer separation
- Fraying of cord strands
- Flank wear, material condition, fraying, brittleness, glassiness and cracks
- Traces of oil and grease

> ***NOTE —***
> *It is essential to replace the ribbed belt if it is found to be faulty.*

Ribbed V-belt, replacing (AEG engine)

1. Remove right side lower sound absorber panel as given earlier.

2. Mark direction of rotation on ribbed V-belt with chalk or crayon.

3. Swing tension roller off of belt with a wrench and hold. See Fig. 27.

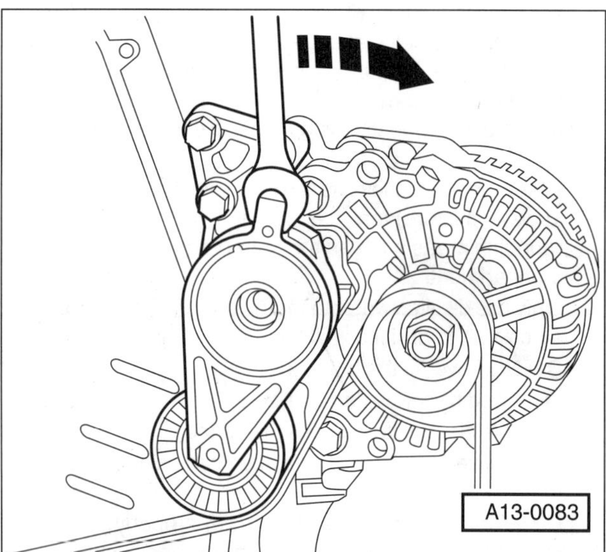

A13-0083

Fig. 27. Using a 15 mm wrench, swing tensioner out of way (**arrow**).

4. Lock tensioner in released position with suitable tool. See Fig. 28.

5. Remove belt.

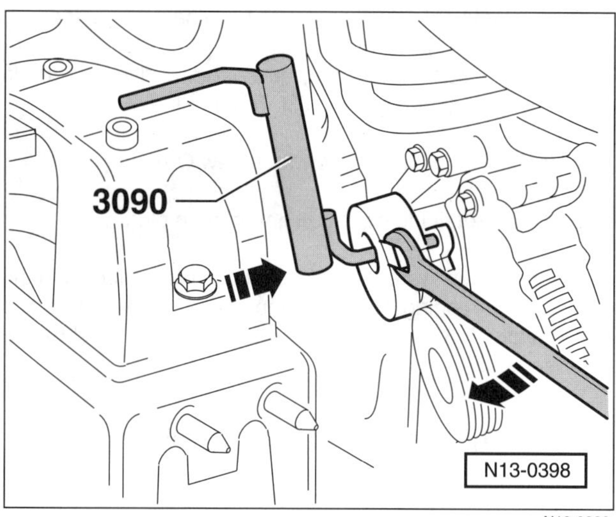

N13-0398

Fig. 28. While holding tensioner, insert special tool (VW 3090 connecting rod support shown) into tensioner to lock in position.

6. Installation is the reverse of removal. Observe belt routing. See Fig. 29. and Fig. 30.

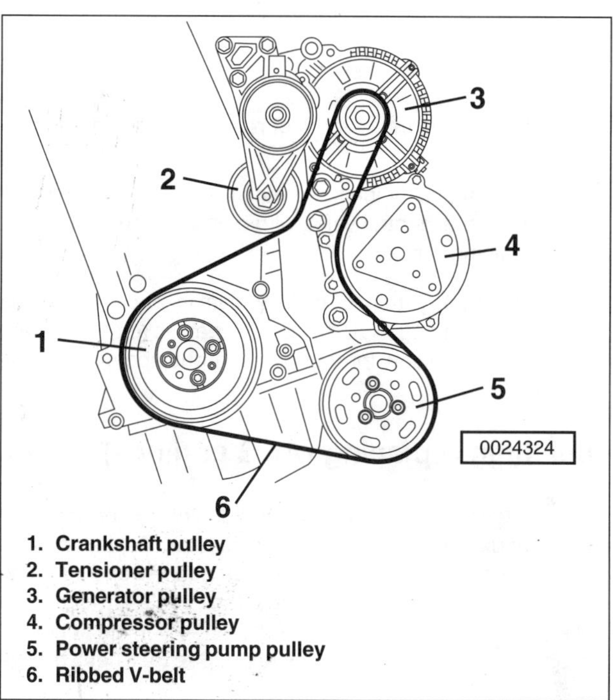

1. **Crankshaft pulley**
2. **Tensioner pulley**
3. **Generator pulley**
4. **Compressor pulley**
5. **Power steering pump pulley**
6. **Ribbed V-belt**

0024324

Fig. 29. Ribbed V-belt routing for AEG engines with air conditioning.

> ***CAUTION —***
> *Ensure correct seating of ribbed V-belt in pulleys. Failure to seat belt properly will severely damage ribbed V-belt.*

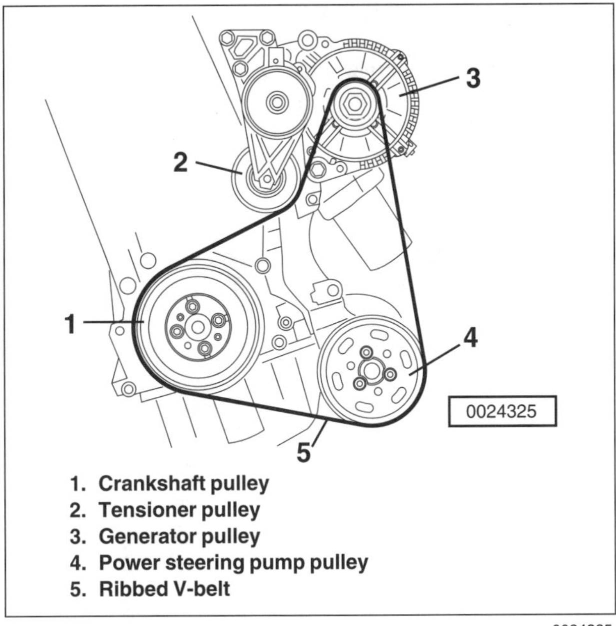

0024325

Fig. 30. Ribbed V-belt routing for AEG engines without air conditioning.

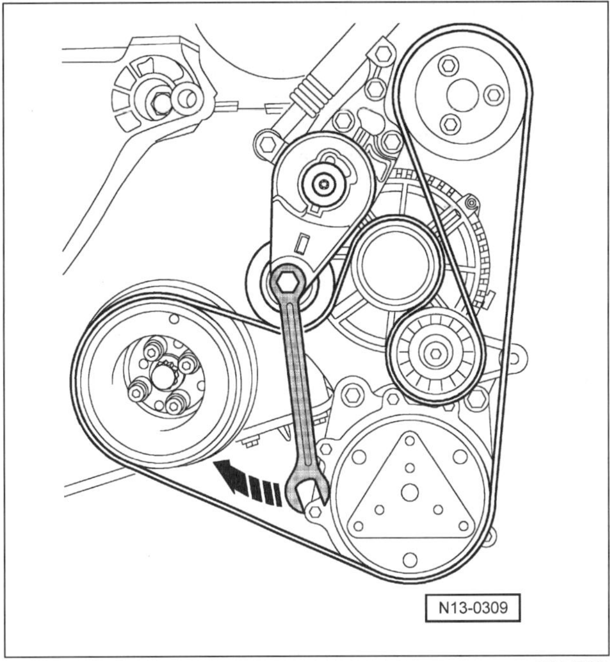

N13-0309

Fig. 31. Using a 15 mm wrench, swing tensioner out of the way (arrow) and hold while removing belt from pulleys.

Ribbed V-belt, replacing (ALH engine)

1. Remove right side lower sound absorber panel as given earlier.

2. Remove connecting pipe between intercooler and turbocharger.

3. Mark direction of rotation on ribbed V-belt with chalk or crayon.

4. Swing tension roller off of belt with a wrench and hold while removing belt. See Fig. 31.

5. Installation is the reverse of removal. Observe belt routing. See Fig. 32. and Fig. 33.

> ***CAUTION —***
> *Ensure correct seating of ribbed V-belt in pulleys. Failure to seat belt properly will severely damage ribbed V-belt very quickly.*

NOTE —
On engines with air conditioning, slip belt off of compressor pulley first and install to compressor pulley last.

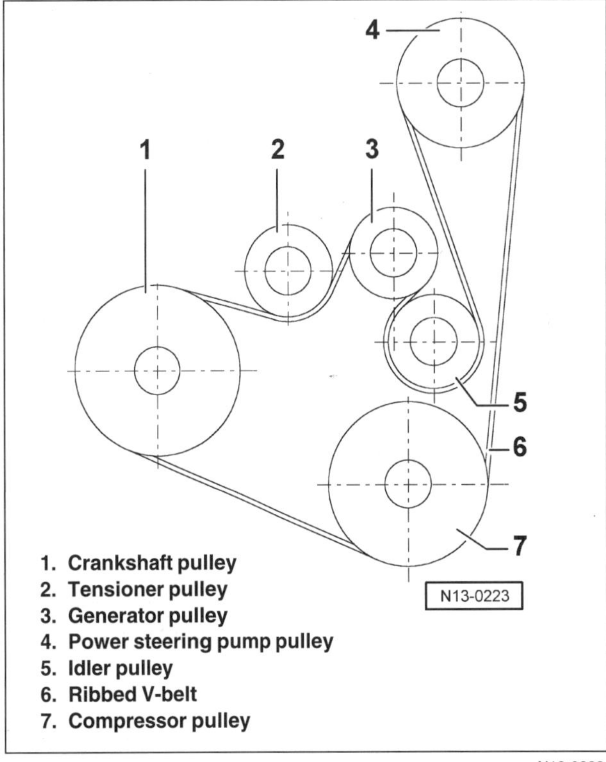

N13-0223

Fig. 32. Ribbed V-belt routing for ALH engines with air conditioning.

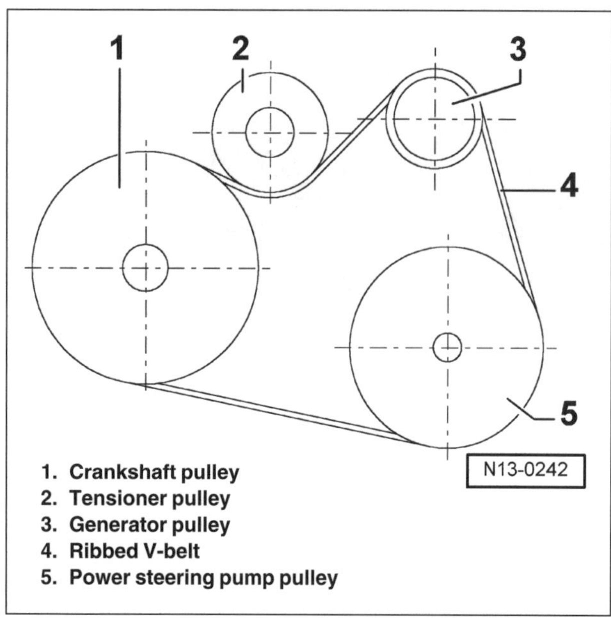

Fig. 33. Ribbed V-belt routing for ALH engines without air conditioning.

> ***NOTE —***
> *On engines without air conditioning, slip belt off of generator pulley first and install to generator pulley last.*

Toothed belt, checking

The toothed belt, also called the camshaft drive belt or the timing belt, is a reinforced rubberized belt that drives that camshaft. On diesel engines, the belt also drives the injection pump. The belt is subjected to high temperatures and should be inspected during scheduled maintenance intervals. On ALH TDI engines, Volkswagen specifies replacement of the belt and tensioner every 40,000 miles.

> ***NOTE —***
> *Volkswagen does not specify a replacement interval for the camshaft drive belt on gasoline engines. However, the publisher recommends the belt be inspected periodically and replaced at least every 90k miles or 5 years.*

To inspect the toothed belt, the upper section of the toothed belt guard belt must first be removed. Inspect belt for tears, separation of layers, fraying of belt cords, surface cracks, or traces of oil and grease. Replace belt if any faults are found.

Toothed belts found on both AEG and ALH engines use semi-automatic tensioners that do not generally require adjustments. See **15a Cylinder Head and Valvetrain (AEG Engine)** or **15b Cylinder Head and Valvetrain (ALH Engine)** for replacement procedures.

Spark plugs, replacing

Spark plugs are generally replaced during scheduled maintenance services. Due to the design of the combustion chambers and shape of the cylinder head, spark plug replacement can easily be accomplished without removal of intake manifold. See Fig. 34.

Fig. 34. Spark plug wires shown with upper section of intake manifold removed for clarity. Note that spark plugs for cylinders #1 and #2 are angled to the left and that spark plugs for cylinders #3 and #4 are angled to the right.

1. Remove the upper sound absorber panel.
2. Remove the spark plug wire from cylinder 1 with a suitable tool such as VW special tool 3277. Do not pull on the wire.

> ***NOTE —***
> *It may be necessary to unplug the injector wire and gently turn the injector in the mounts for access.*

3. Remove spark plug with a 5/8 in. (16 mm) spark plug socket and an extension.
4. Check gap on new spark plug and install, re-install injector wire and plug wire.
5. Repeat for each remaining cylinder.
6. Install upper sound absorber panel.

Specification

- Spark Plugs-Long Life
  Original equipment number. 101-000-033-AA
  Manufacturers number . . . . NGK BKUR 6 ET-10
- Gap. . . . . .0.9 to 1.1 mm (0.035 to 0.043 in)

NOTE —
Volkswagen part numbers are given for reference only. Always consult with your Volkswagen parts department or aftermarket parts specialist for the latest parts information.

Tightening torque
- Spark plugs .... 30 Nm (22 ft-lb)

Air filter element, replacing (AEG engine)

The air filter element should generally be replaced as specified in the maintenance tables. Under severe conditions, however, such as driving on dirt or desert roads, or in dusty areas, it is advisable to replace the element more frequently.

1. Disconnect harness connector for mass air flow sensor (MAF). See Fig. 35.

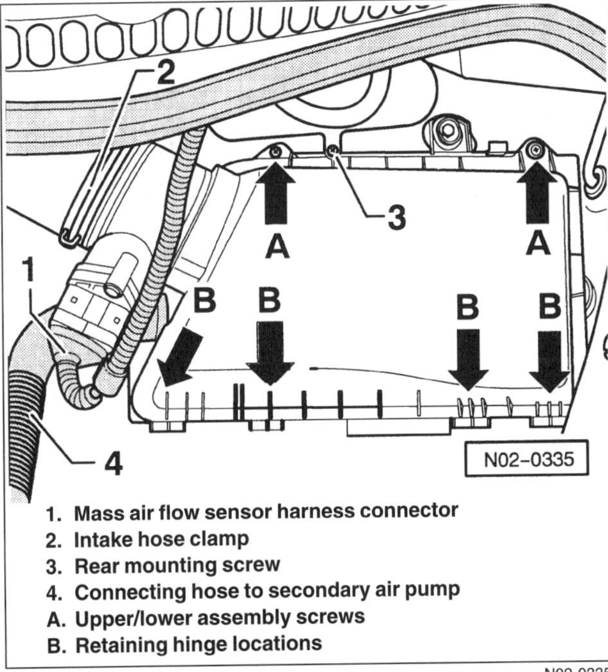

Fig. 35. AEG air cleaner assembly shown from above.

2. Loosen hose clamp on intake hose and take hose off of mass air flow sensor.
3. Loosen mounting screw at rear of air cleaner assembly.
4. Remove connecting hose to secondary air pump.
5. Remove two screws holding upper and lower sections together.
6. Lift upper filter housing and remove from lower filter housing.
7. Remove old filter element.
8. Clean filter housing.
9. Install new filter element.
10. Remainder of installation is the reverse of removal.

Air filter element, replacing (ALH engine)

The air filter element should generally be replaced as specified in the maintenance tables. Under severe conditions, however, such as driving on dirt or desert roads, or in dusty areas, it is advisable to replace the element more frequently.

1. Disconnect harness connector for mass air flow sensor (MAF). See Fig. 36.

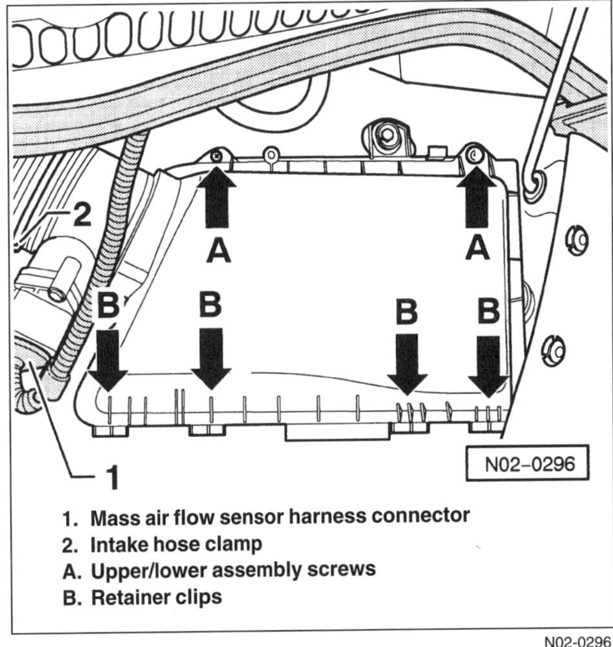

Fig. 36. ALH air cleaner assembly shown from above.

2. Loosen clamp on intake hose and take hose off of mass air flow sensor.
3. Remove 2 screws holding upper and lower sections together.
4. Lift upper filter housing and remove from retainer.
5. Remove old filter element.
6. Clean filter housing.
7. Install new filter element.
8. Remainder of installation is the reverse of removal.

UNDER CAR MAINTENANCE

Under car maintenance requires that the car be raised on a lift or properly supported on jackstands. Under car maintenance should not be carried out unless proper (safe) lifting equipment is available. See **Lifting Vehicle** for more information on lifting and working under the car.

> ***WARNING —***
> - *Do not work under a car supported solely by a jack. Jack stands must always be used when working under the car.*
> - *Jack stands must be placed on a hard, level surface (e.g. concrete).*

Tire service

Tire pressure should be checked on a regular basis. It is best to check pressures when the tires are cold. Refer to the data label on the fuel filler flap for proper inflation pressures. Be sure to also check the spare tire pressure. Check that all tires are the same type and tread pattern. Measure tread depth. If the tread wear has exceeded the minimum specification listed, the tire should be replaced.

Tire tread depth
- Minimum . . . . 1.6 mm (2/32 in.)

> ***CAUTION —***
> *Wheel alignment must be checked after replacing tires to ensure maximum tire life.*

The tires should also be checked for abnormal wear patterns.The tread wear pattern on the front tires is an indication of whether the toe and camber settings need to be checked. "Feathering" on the tread indicates incorrect toe. If the tread is worn on one side, this is usually caused by incorrect camber.

To extended tire life and minimize wear, Volkswagen recommends that the tires be rotated front to rear every 10,000 miles. For more information on tires, see **44 Wheels–Tires, Wheel Alignment**.

Brake system, visual inspection

Check the brake master cylinder, vacuum brake booster (also hydraulic unit if anti-lock brake system is fitted), brake pressure regulator, and brake calipers for leaks and damage.

- Brake hoses must not be twisted.
- Brake hoses must not touch any part of the vehicle when steering is at full lock.
- Check brake hoses for porosity and deterioration, brake hoses and brake lines for chafing points.
- Check brake connections and attachments for correct seating, leaks and corrosion.
- Any faults found must be repaired.

Brake pads (front and rear), checking

To accurately check the front brake pad thickness, the front wheels should be removed. With the wheel removed, measure the thickness of outer and inner pads. If pad thickness (including backing plate) is 7 mm (0.28 in.) or less, the brake pads should be replaced. See Fig. 37.

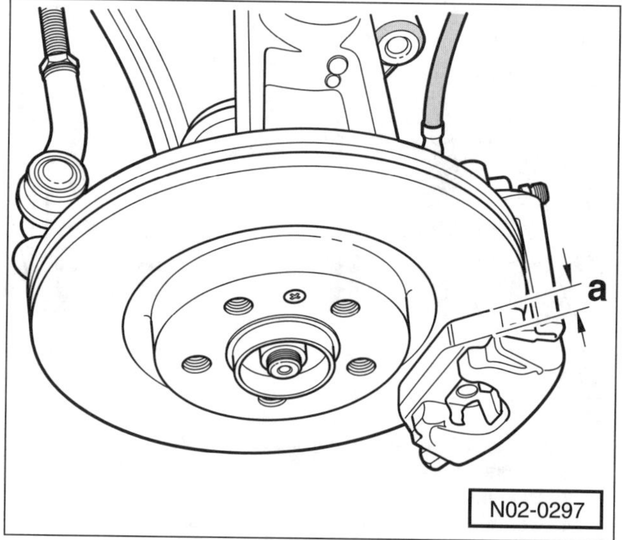

N02-0297

Fig. 37. Brake pad thickness must be at least 7 mm (0.028 in.) including backing plate as indicated by dimension (**a**). Front brake pad shown, rear pads are similar and have the same specification.

Brake pad wear limit
- Minimum width
  (including backing plate) 7 mm (0.28 in.)

NOTE —
- *Before removing the front wheels, mark their position in relation to the brake rotor so the wheel can be reinstalled in the same position.*
- *Brake pad wear may be minimally greater on the front passenger's side than on the driver's side. It is therefore recommended that inspection always be performed on passenger's side front wheel.*
- *When tightening wheel bolts, tighten the bolts in stages using a criss-cross pattern.*

Tightening torque
- Wheel bolt to wheel hub. . . . . 120 Nm (87 ft-lb)

Parking brake, adjusting

The parking brake acts on the rear brakes and is self-adjusting to compensate for wear. Adjustment of the parking brake is only necessary if brake components are replaced. See **46 Brakes–Mechanical Components** for parking brake adjustment and service procedures. The parking brake should begin to hold after approximately two clicks of the lever.

Drive axles, checking boots

There are inner and outer CV boots on each front axle shaft. The boots should be regularly inspected for tears, cracks, or deterioration. Once the boot is open to the weather, abrasive road debris can enter the joint and quickly destroy it. If boot replacement is carried out promptly, chances are good that the joint can be saved. See **40 Front Suspension and Drive Axles** for drive boot replacement procedures.

Front suspension components, checking

Check ball joint dust boots for damage and correct seating. Check for play in ball joints. Check inner and outer tie rod end boots for damage and correct seating. Check for play by moving tie rods and wheels. Check attachment of ball joints and tie rod ends. See **40 Front Suspension and Drive Axles** for suspension component replacement.

Transmission, checking for leaks

Inspect the transmission for signs of fluid leakage. Pay particular attention to the axle seals. Repair any leaks found, see **34 Manual Transmission.**

Final drive oil level, checking

On cars with manual transmission, the final drive lubricant shares a common supply with the transmission lubricant. For final drive and transmission fluid level checking, see **Transmission oil level, checking (manual transmission)**.

On cars with automatic transmission, the final drive oil level is checked by removing the speedometer drive gear from the transmission housing and using the drive gear as a dipstick. The car should be on a level surface when making the check.

1. Remove speedometer drive, wipe clean with a cloth and install again.

2. Remove drive and check oil level. See Fig. 38.

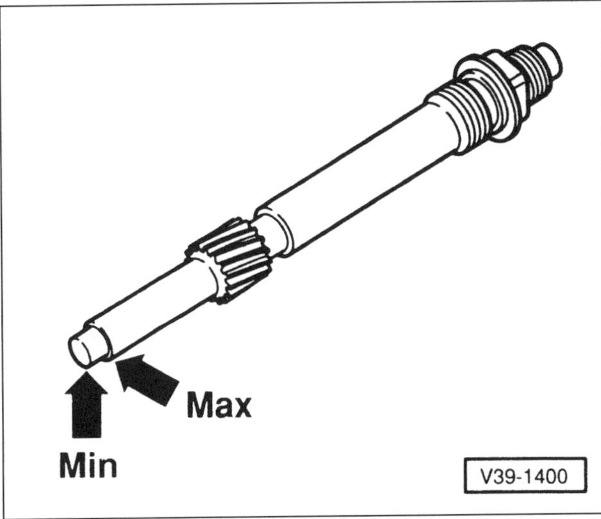

V39-1400

Fig. 38. Automatic transmission speedometer drive doubles as a dipstick. Fluid level should be between **min** and **max** marks.

NOTE —
- *The oil level must between the MIN and MAX markings.*
- *The amount of oil between the MIN and MAX markings is approximately 0.1 Liter (0.1 qt).*

3. If oil level is too low, add oil in small amounts until proper level is reached.

Specification
- Automatic transmission, final drive lubricant G 052 145 A2 . . . . SAE 75 W90 (Synthetic oil)

NOTE —
Volkswagen part numbers are given for reference only! Always consult with your Volkswagen Parts Department or aftermarket parts specialist for the latest parts information.

4. If oil level is too high, suction out excess.

5. When proper level is obtained, install speedometer drive.

Transmission oil level, checking (manual transmission)

1. Remove oil filler plug with 17 mm Allen wrench. See Fig. 39.

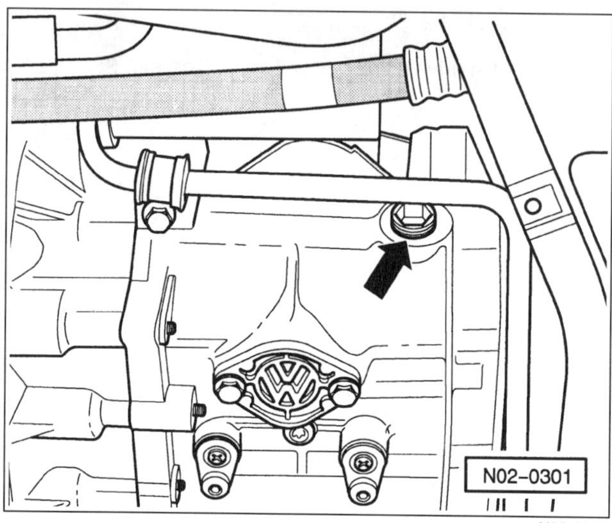

Fig. 39. Manual transmission fill plug (**arrow**).

2. Check oil level.

NOTE—
Oil level must be to lower edge of filler plug hole.

3. If oil level is too low, add oil in small amounts until proper level is reached.

4. Install oil filler plug.

Specification

- Manual transmission lubricant
G 052 145 A2. . . . . SAE 75 W90 (Synthetic oil)

NOTE—
Volkswagen part numbers are given for reference only! Always consult with your Volkswagen Parts Department or aftermarket parts specialist for the latest parts information.

Transmission fluid (ATF) level, checking and adjusting (automatic transmission)

The 01M automatic transmission does not have a dipstick and the procedure requires measuring and maintaining a specified ATF temperature (which is neither cold nor hot, but in between) during the ATF level checking. Special Volkswagen tools are required for this operation and it is therefore recommended that ATF level checking on 01M transmission be left to an authorized Volkswagen dealer.

Before starting, be sure that the following checking conditions are met:

- Transmission not in limp-home mode, ATF temperature not above approx. 30°C (86° F)
- Vehicle must be level
- Selector lever in "P"
- Center and left sound absorber panels removed

1. Attach container of ATF filler VAG 1924 to vehicle. See Fig. 40.

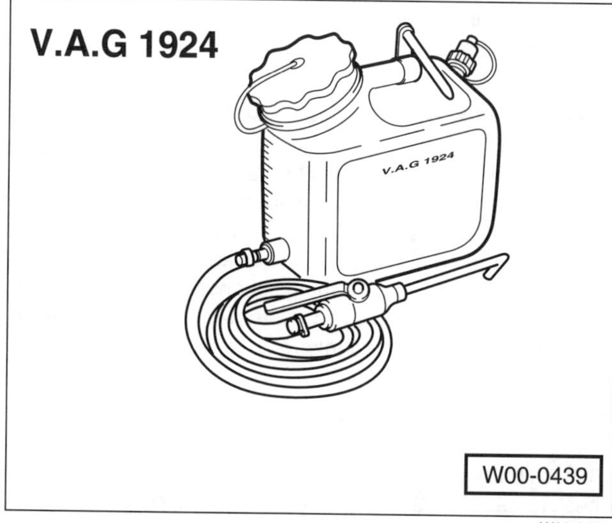

Fig. 40. Volkswagen special tool VAG 1924 used for filling automatic transmissions.

2. Start engine.

3. Connect suitable scan tool and access Transmission Control Module. If using a Volkswagen supplied VAG 1551/1552, observe the following sequence in the scan tool display window:
   - 1 - Rapid Data
   - Address word 02 - Transmission electronics
   - Advance to Read Measuring Value Blocks - 08
   - Select display group 05
   - Observe display field 1 for transmission temperature (must be below 30°C at start)

4. Lift vehicle.

5. Place container under transmission.

6. Bring ATF to test temperature.

ATF test temperature

- 35 to 45°C (95 to 113°F)

---

7. Remove ATF level plug from oil pan. See Fig. 41.

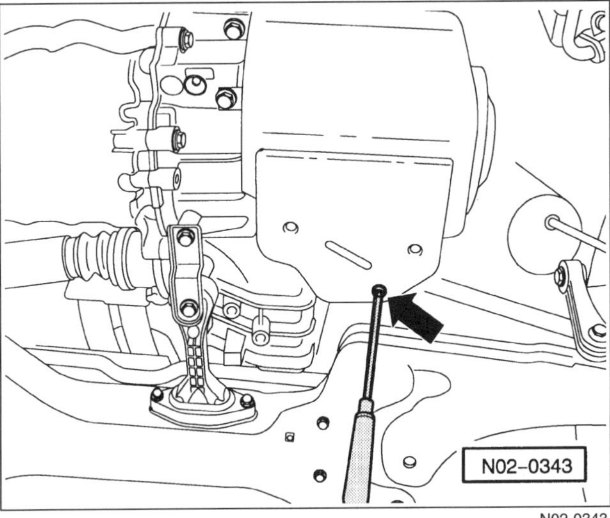

N02-0343

Fig. 41. Remove ATF level plug (**arrow**) in transmission oil pan.

8. If ATF drips out of hole when temperature is between 35°C to 45°C, ATF level is correct and no further action is required. Install new seal on level plug and torque. This completes the ATF check.

Tightening torque

- ATF level plug with new seal .... 15 Nm (11 ft-lb)

---

9. If no ATF drips out of hole by the time the temperature reaches 45°C (113°F), fill through the filler tube until fluid comes out of the level checking hole. See Fig. 42. and Fig. 43.

10. Install plug on filler tube and secure with new seal. Install new seal on level plug and torque. This completes the ATF check.

If ATF ran out immediately when plug was removed from level checking hole, transmission was overfilled. Allow fluid to run out until temperature on scan tool is between 35°C and 45°C. Install new seal on level plug and torque. This completes the ATF check.

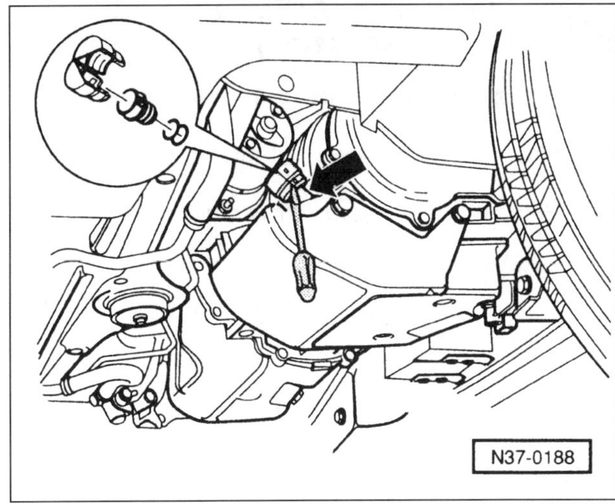

N37-0188

Fig. 42. Pry off plug and seal (**arrow**) with screwdriver. The seal will be destroyed, always replace.

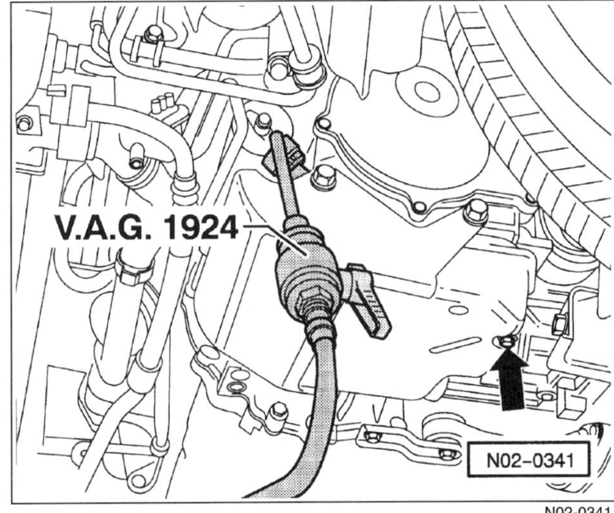

N02-0341

Fig. 43. Special tool VAG 1924 shown inserted into filler tube for automatic transmission filling.

Transmission fluid (ATF), changing (automatic transmission)

1. Remove center and left sound absorber panels.
2. Place suitable container under transmission.
3. Remove ATF level plug from oil pan. See Fig. 44.

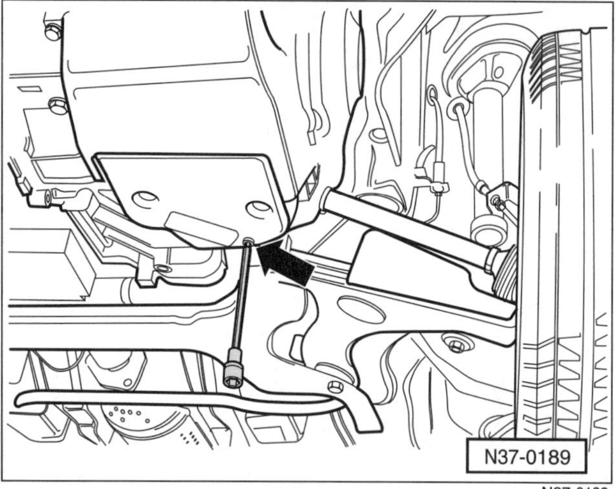

N37-0189

Fig. 44. Remove ATF level plug (**arrow**) and unscrew inner overflow pipe.

4. Remove overflow pipe from within level plug hole. ATF will flow out.
5. Drain ATF.
6. When fluid has drained, install overflow pipe.
7. Install level plug (with old seal) and tighten hand-tight.
8. Fill with 3 liters (3.2 qt) of ATF through filler line using VAG 1924. See Fig. 43.
9. Start engine and shift through all selector lever positions with the vehicle stationary.
10. Check and top up ATF level as given earlier.

Exhaust system, checking

> ***WARNING —***
> - *The exhaust system operates at extremely high temperatures. Do not touch the exhaust system while the engine is running.*
> - *Allow exhaust system to cool at least one hour before touching.*

Inspect exhaust system for leaks or damage. Inspect exhaust system mounts. Replace faulty, missing or deteriorated parts.

Underbody sealant, checking

When performing the visual inspection for damage to the underbody sealant, also check the underbody, wheel housings and sill panels. Any faults found should be promptly repaired.

BODY AND INTERIOR MAINTENANCE

Body exterior

Automobile finishes are subjected to abuse from industrial fumes, corrosive road salt, acid rain, and other damaging airborn elements. Regular and correct care will contribute to maintaining and preserving the exterior of your Volkswagen.

NOTE —
Proper care may be a condition for upholding the new car warranty, should corrosion damage or paint defects occur.

The best protection against environmental influences is frequent washing and waxing. How often this is required depends on the environment where the vehicle is used.

Under certain circumstances weekly washing may be necessary. Under other conditions, a monthly washing and waxing may be adequate. Even if a wax solution is used when washing your vehicle, it is advisable to protect the paint with a coat of hard wax at least twice a year. Check the paint for chips and scratches. Paint defects should be touched up soon after they occur to prevent corrosion.

After the winter, the underside of the vehicle should be thoroughly washed.

Exterior plastic and vinyl should be kept clean. Occasionally apply a colorless vinyl or leather preservative. DO NOT wax plastic or vinyl.

Exterior lights, checking

Check operation of headlights (high and low beam), marker lights, taillights, turn signal lights, brake lights, reverse lights and emergency flasher lights. Use a helper when checking lights. See **94 Lights, Accessories–Exterior**.

Interior lights, checking

Check operation of indicator and instrument cluster warning bulbs. Check operation of interior cabin illumination bulbs. See **96 Lights, Accessories-Interior**.

Dust and pollen filter, replacing

All New Beetles are equipped with a ventilation air dust and pollen filter. This filter prevents most dusts and pollens from entering the passenger compartment. Volkswagen specifies replacement of this filter at regular mileage intervals. **See 80 Heating and Ventilation.**

Airbag unit, visual inspection

All models are fitted with driver's side and passenger's side airbags. In addition, all models are fitted with side airbags built into the front seat backrest..

> ***WARNING —***
> - *The padded airbag covers on the steering wheel and instrument panel must not be covered over or have any objects affixed to them.*
> - *Do not apply any chemical treatment to airbag unit covers. Clean with a dry or water moistened cloth only.*

Inspect padded airbag unit covers on steering wheel and instrument panel and side airbag units for signs of external damage. Check with an authorized Volkswagen dealer if any faults are found.

Inspect seats for covers that may obstruct or hinder proper deploymentof side airbag.

> ***WARNING —***
> *Volkswagen of America has issued a directive specifically warning against the installation of aftermarket upholstery on any vehicle equipped with side airbags. The factory-installed upholstery is designed to separate in specific places at specific rates, and in specific directions. Installation of non-factory upholstery including, but not limited to, "beads" and "sheepskins", may cause seat mounted airbags to deploy when they are not supposed to; fail to deploy when they should; or to deploy in some manner other than designed. This is a safety hazard and could result in serious injury or death to occupants of the vehicle.*

Door check straps and hinges, lubrication

The door checks straps and door hinges should be lubricated periodically. Use a lithium grease for the job. Lubricate the hinge securing bolt with lock cylinder spray. It is a good idea to clean the old grease away before applying the new lubricant. See Fig. 45.

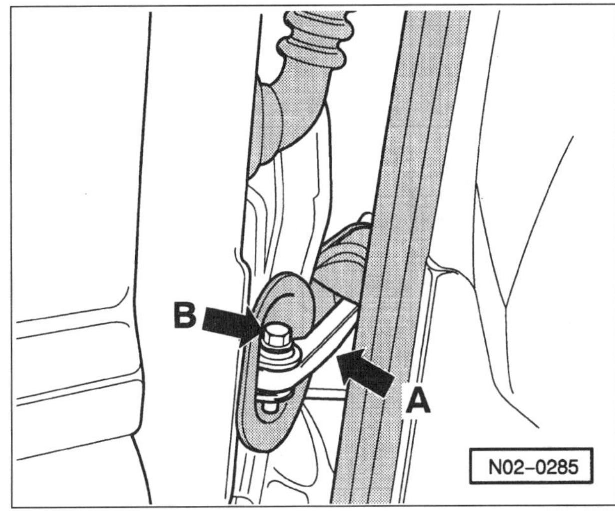

N02-0285

Fig. 45. Lubricate door check strap (**arrow A**) with Volkswagen special grease G 000 400 and securing bolt (**arrow B**) with special lock cylinder lubricant spray G 000 400 01.

Windshield wipers and washers, checking

Inspect windshield wiper blades, front and rear. Replace damaged or deteriorated parts. Check spray pattern of windshield washers, front and rear, adjust as necessary. Fill reservoir for windshield cleaning system. Always add a windshield cleaner to the water (windshield washer antifreeze in winter). See **92 Wipers and Washers**.

In cases where cleaning of the windshield and replacement of the wiper blades or inserts fails to eliminate streaking conditions, a more complete cleaning of the windshield may be needed. Thoroughly clean the outside of the windshield with a non-abrasive cleaner such as Bon Ami® or Soft Scrub® using a soft cloth and water. Rub until windshield is completely clean of all foreign material. Rinse windshield thoroughly.

On board diagnostics (OBD), checking

A final part of Volkswagen's maintenance program specifies checking the On-board Diagnostic (OBD) system memory. The ODB system is integrated into the engine management control module and monitors emissions-related and other electrical components on the car, including the adaptive automatic transmission, the ABS system, and the airbag system. Checking the OBD memory for faults requires special tools and training. Therefore, it is recommended that this job be carried out by an authorized Volkswagen dealer or qualified independent repair shop.

QUALITY REVIEW

When you have finished working under the hood and around other areas of the vehicle, it is advisable to take a moment to quality check or review your work. This helps to insure that the operation or repair has been completed properly with all affected systems functioning within normal parameters. These may include the following:

Road test

Upon completion of the maintenance work, the vehicle should be road tested. Check the following systems during the road test:

Automatic transmission shift lock

1. Turn ignition on, but do not start engine. Apply parking brake.
2. With gearshift selector in park attempt to shift into a drive or reverse. The selector lever should not move.
3. Press brake pedal. The selector lever should move into gear.
4. Place gear selector lever in neutral and release brake pedal.
5. Attempt to shift into gear. The selector lever should not move.
6. Press the brake pedal. The selector lever should move into gear.
7. If shift lock does not operate as described, see **37 Automatic Transmission**.

Automatic park/neutral position switch

Apply the parking brake and step on the brake pedal. Place the gear shift selector in park and attempt to start car. Repeat for all gears. The engine should only start in park or neutral. See **37 Automatic Transmission**.

Brake pedal and parking brake

Check pedal and handbrake travel (free play) and operation.

- Travel of brake pedal: max. 1/3 of overall pedal travel
- Travel of parking brake lever: 2 notches (clicks)

Manual gearshift

Check for smooth operation of the transmission and its gearshift.

Steering

Check steering play with vehicle weight on the wheels by turning steering wheel back and forth (wheels in straight ahead position).

- Steering play: zero play with engine running

Kickdown operation

Depress accelerator pedal fully to floor. Depending on vehicle speed and engine speed, upshift is either delayed or the transmission shifts down into the next lower gear.

Air conditioner and heater

Check the full range of the heater and the air conditioner for proper function. Cold or warm air must flow out of the vents.

Additional checks

Perform the following checks in accordance with the vehicle equipment and the road conditions available during the road test:

- Engine performance, idle speed, acceleration, cold and hot starting.
- Clutch operation, smoothness and pedal pressure.
- Brake operation, noise and function of ABS if equipped.
- Cruise control system operation.
- Radio operation, and reception.
- General vehicle handling and dynamics such as pulling to the side, cornering, vibrations in steering wheel and unusual noises.

1 Engine–General

GENERAL

This general information group gives engine application information and general technical data for the engines used in the Volkswagen New Beetle. Engines are the same for both the United States and Canada.

Much of the engine repair information in **1 Engine** is organized according to engine code. It is therefore important to know the code of the engine installed in your New Beetle. For engine code location see **0 Maintenance**.

Engine Codes

- AEG . . . . 2.0L 4-cylinder gasoline, 115 HP
- ALH . . . . 1.9L 4-cylinder turbo diesel, 90 hp

AEG ENGINE

The AEG engine is a design evolution of the 4-cylinder gasoline engines used on previous models of the Volkswagen Golf and Jetta. And although this new engine looks familiar to the older versions, there has been significant development of the basic 4-cylinder engine for the New Beetle. See Fig. 1.

Technical Data - Engine Code AEG

- Type . . . . 4-cylinder inline, 2 valves/cylinder
- Displacement . . . . .2.0L, 1984 cc (121.1 cubic inches)
- Bore . . . . 82.5 mm
- Stroke. . . . . 92.8 mm
- Compression Ratio. 10.0:1
- Horsepower . . . . 85 kW (115 HP) @2600 RPM
- Fuel requirement . . . . . . Gasoline, Regular Unleaded
- Engine Management . . . . . . .Motronic M5.9.2, OBD II

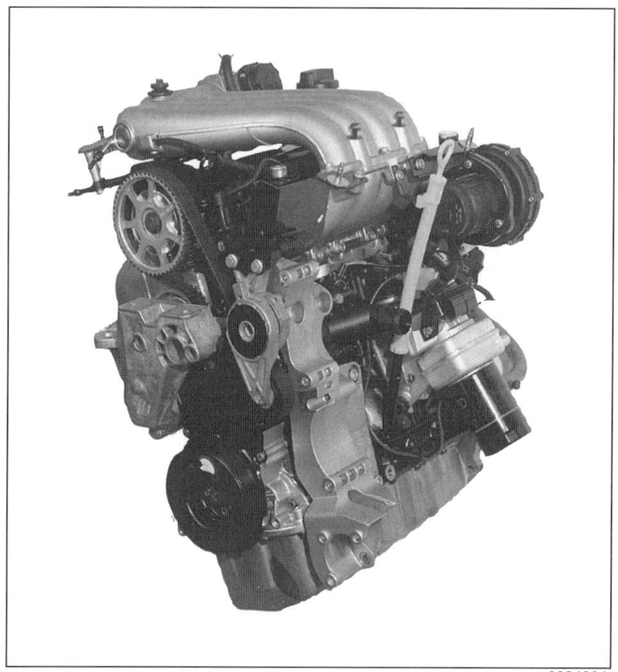

0024304

Fig. 1. 2.0 Liter gas engine used in New Beetles.

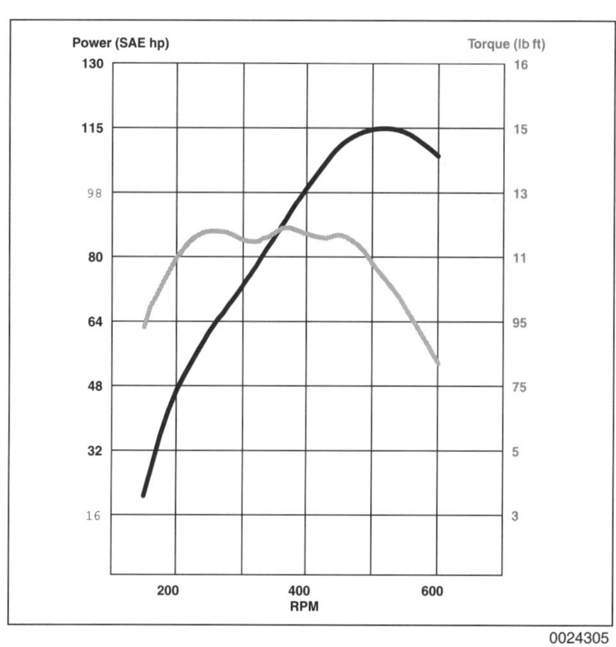

0024305

Fig. 2. Engine performance data of 2.0 Liter (AEG) engine.

AEG engine design features:

- Cast iron cylinder block, light alloy crossflow cylinder head and aluminum oil pan.
- Crankshaft with 5 main bearings.
- Single overhead camshaft driven by a toothed belt with semi-automatic belt tensioner.
- Lightweight valvetrain, 2 valves per cylinder.
- Transverse mounting with "Pendulum" type engine mounts.
- Chain-drive internal gear oil pump driven from the front of the crankshaft.
- Coolant pump built into the cylinder block and driven by the toothed camshaft belt.
- Thermostat integral with the cylinder block.
- Two-piece aluminum intake manifold.
- Tubular stainless steel exhaust manifold.
- Distributorless ignition.
- External engine accessories driven by a single poly-rib belt with tensioner.
- Bosch Motronic M5.9.2 Multi-point Sequential Fuel Injection (MFI) system.

ALH ENGINE

The ALH engine is a design evolution of the 4 cylinder diesel engines used on previous models of the Volkswagen Golf and Jetta. Just as in the gas versions, this new engine looks familiar to the older versions, but again there has been significant development. See Fig. 3.

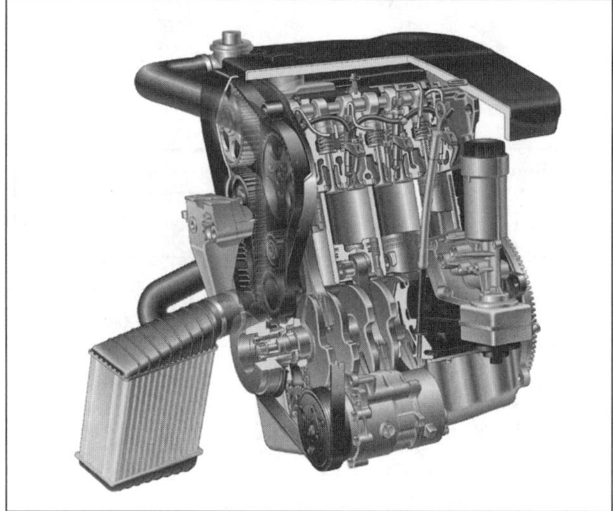

0024307

Fig. 3. 1.9 Liter TDI diesel engine used in New Beetles.

ALH engine design features:

- Cast iron cylinder block, light alloy cylinder head and aluminum oil pan and cylinder head cover.
- Piston oil spray nozzles.
- Crankshaft with 5 main bearings.
- Single overhead camshaft driven by a toothed belt with semi-automatic belt tensioner and two guide pulleys.
- Lightweight valvetrain, 2 valves per cylinder.
- Transverse mounting with "Pendulum" type engine mounts.
- Chain-drive internal gear oil pump driven from the front of the crankshaft.
- Camshaft-driven vacuum pump.
- Coolant pump built into the cylinder block and driven by the toothed camshaft belt.
- Thermostat integral with the cylinder block.
- Cartridge-type oil filter.
- External engine accessories driven by a single poly-rib belt with tensioner.
- Turbo Direct Injection (TDI) Diesel Fuel Injection.

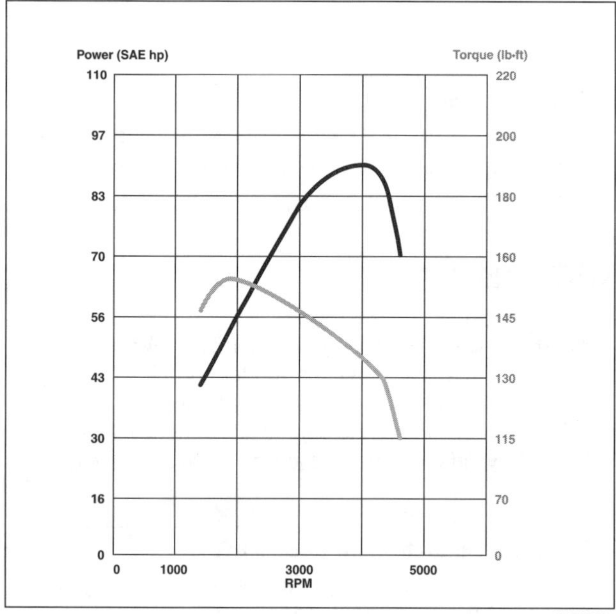

0024306

Fig. 4. Engine performance data of 1.9 Liter (ALH) engine.

Technical Data - Engine Code ALH

- Type . . . . 4-cylinder inline, 2 valves/cylinder
- Displacement . . . . 1.9L, 1896 cc (115.7 cubic inches)
- Bore . . . . 79.9 mm
- Stroke . . . . 95.5 mm
- Compression Ratio. 19.5:1
- Horsepower . . . . 66 kW (90 HP) @4000 RPM
- Fuel requirement . . . . Diesel 45 Cetane
- Engine Management . . . . Turbo Direct Injection (TDI) Diesel OBD II

10 Engine–Removing and Installing

GENERAL

The engine and transmission are removed as a unit from below and separated from each other once removed from the vehicle.

The operations needed to remove the engine and transmission assembly are generally grouped into two main areas: jobs under the hood and jobs under the vehicle. The steps below follow this general sequence. Most of the operations are simple and straight forward. References to additional repair groups are provided in bold type where additional information may be helpful to complete a step.

Engine Codes

- AEG . . . . 2.0L 4-cylinder gasoline
- ALH . . . . 1.9L 4-cylinder turbo diesel

CAUTION —
Disconnecting the negative (–) battery cable may erase fault codes and basic settings in the engine management and automatic transmission control modules. Some driveability problems may be noticed until the system re-adapts to operating conditions. OBD II readiness codes, which may be required for emissions testing, may also be erased. Convenience electronics (alarm system, interior light control, power locks, mirrors, and windows) may need to be re-set using a VAG 1551/1552 or equivalent scan tool.

NOTE —
- *It will be necessary to cut many wire tie wraps when removing the engine. The tie wraps are installed to prevent the wiring harnesses from chaffing or contacting engine parts. Be sure to make note of all tie wraps removed and install new ones during engine installation.*
- *Most of the hardware used in the vehicles covered by this repair manual is specially coated to prevent corrosion. This coating is known as "dacromet" or "delta tone" and is identified by a green tinted finish. Always use replacement hardware with the same specification.*

ENGINE, REMOVING AND INSTALLING

Engine/transmission assembly, removing

1. Ensure ignition is switched off. Disconnect battery negative (–) terminal and then positive (+) terminal.

   NOTE —
   Be sure to have the anti-theft radio code on hand before disconnecting the battery.

2. Remove upper sound absorber panel.
3. Remove power steering reservoir from battery support, but do not loosen the hoses. Temporarily tie reservoir to hood lock carrier.
4. Remove the fuse holder on the top of the battery, the battery and the mounting bracket, see **27 Engine Electrical**.
5. Remove air cleaner assembly and connecting hoses and ducts.
6. On ALH engines, remove connecting pipe between turbocharger and intercooler and intercooler and intake manifold complete with the EGR vacuum regulator solenoid valve.
7. Disconnect and label fuel lines.
   - Gas engine: Disconnect fuel supply and return lines at fuel rail. See Fig. 1. Disconnect accelerator cable.
   - Diesel engine: Disconnect fuel supply and return lines at injection pump. See Fig. 2.

WARNING —
Fuel will be expelled when disconnecting fuel hoses. Wrap a cloth around the fuel line fittings before disconnecting them. Do not smoke or work near heaters or other fire hazards. Have a fire extinguisher handy.

Fig. 1. Fuel line connections at fuel rail on gas engine. Disconnect pressure line from tank (**1**) and return line (**2**). Seal off all hoses and fittings.

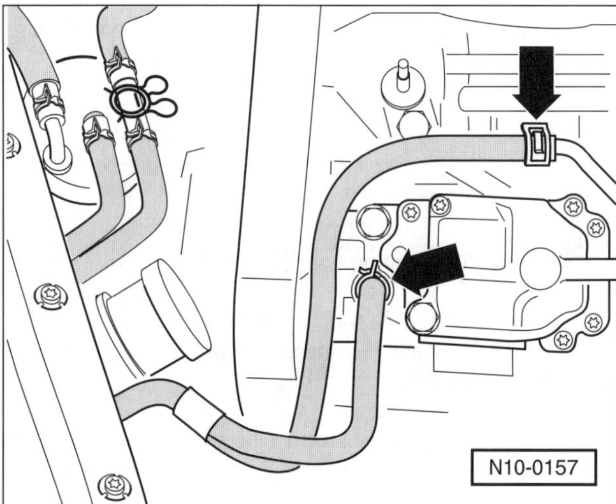

Fig. 2. Fuel line connections at diesel injection pump. Disconnect supply line from tank (**bottom arrow**) and return line (**top arrow**). Seal off all hoses and fittings.

8. Plug fuel line fittings and open fuel lines to prevent contamination and fuel spillage.

9. Disconnect shift linkage.
   - Manual transmission vehicles: Disconnect cables from selector mechanism and unbolt support bracket, see **34 Manual Transmission**. Unbolt hydraulic clutch slave cylinder and secure to the side with a tie wrap. Do not disconnect the hydraulic line.
   - Automatic transmission vehicles: Disconnect selector cable at selector lever, see **37 Automatic Transmission**.

> ***CAUTION—***
> *Do not depress the clutch pedal with the slave cylinder removed, damage will result.*

10. Remove lower sound absorber panel (belly pan).

11. Drain coolant, see **19 Cooling System**.

> ***WARNING—***
> *Hot coolant can scald. Drain the coolant only with engine cold.*

12. Mark running direction and remove ribbed V-belt, see **0 Maintenance**.

13. Remove auxiliary cooling fan on right side of vehicle, if equipped.

14. Disconnect coolant hoses to radiator and heater.

15. Remove power steering lines from mounting clamps on cylinder block.

16. Remove power steering pump with its mounting bracket and carefully lay aside with hoses remaining connected, see **48 Steering**.

17. Remove retaining clamp(s) from A/C refrigerant lines. Remove A/C compressor with refrigerant lines still attached, see **87 Air Conditioning**.

18. Attach A/C compressor to lower section of body with a suitable support so that refrigerant lines are not stressed. See Fig. 3.

NOTE—
To prevent damage to the condenser and to the refrigerant lines/hoses, ensure that the lines and hoses are not stretched, kinked or bent.

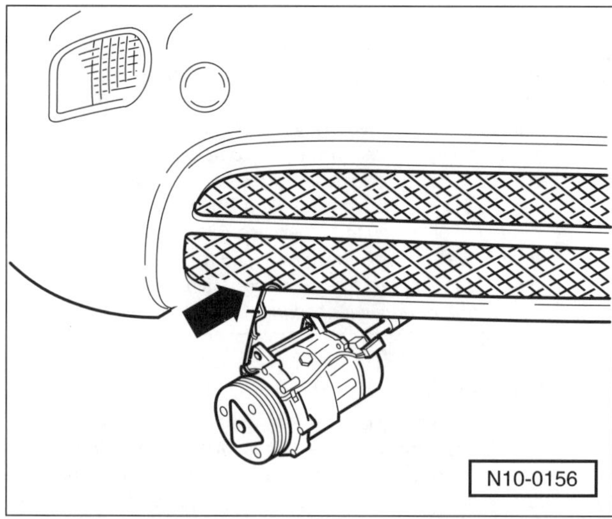

Fig. 3. A/C compressor shown hanging from front of vehicle with a suitable support (**arrow**). Refrigerant lines are still attached.

19. Label and remove all electrical connections on engine, transmission, generator (alternator) and starter.

20. Label and remove all vacuum and breather hoses.

21. On AEG engines, unbolt secondary air injection pump and remove from bracket, see **26 Exhaust System and Emission Controls**.

22. Raise car and support with jack stands or lift. See **0 Manintence** for proper lifting procedure.

> ***WARNING —***
> *Observe all warnings and cautions associated with lifting vehicle in* **0 Maintenance**.

23. Remove starter motor, see **27 Engine Electrical**.

24. Unbolt and remove pendulum support. See Fig. 4.

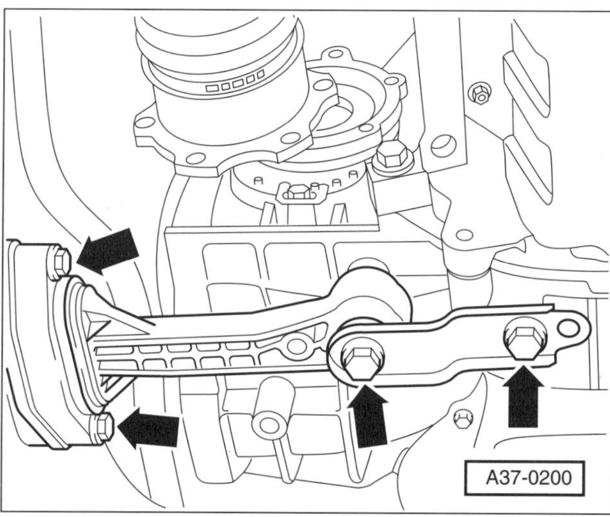

A37-0200

Fig. 4. Pendulum support view from under vehicle. Unbolt at arrows.

25. Remove right side inner CV joint protective cover from engine if equipped.

26. Remove axle nuts from right side outer CV joint and unbolt both inner CV or triple-rotor joints from the transmission. Remove the right side drive axle, see **40 Front Suspension and Drive Axles**. Tie wrap left side axle up and out of way as far as possible taking care not to damage the coating on the axle.

27. Unbolt front exhaust pipe with catalytic converter from exhaust manifold or turbocharger. Loosen clamp at connection to center muffler and remove front pipe, see **26 Exhaust System/Emission Controls**.

28. Install a suitable engine supporting device from below, using supporting points. See Fig. 5.

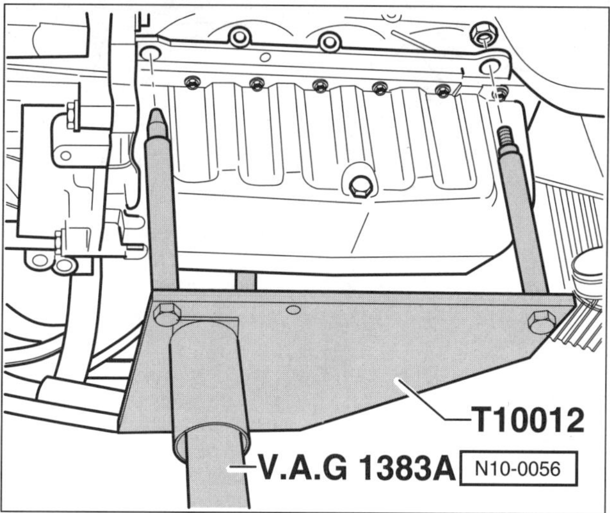

N10-0056

Fig. 5. Engine support tools supplied by Volkswagen shown being installed under vehicle. Use of support as shown is necessary for proper weight distribution and safe support and removal.

29. Remove supporting bracket for coolant hose under engine block.

30. Lift supporting device slightly, so that weight of engine and transmission is on supporting device.

31. Unbolt right side engine mount from support on engine. See Fig. 6.

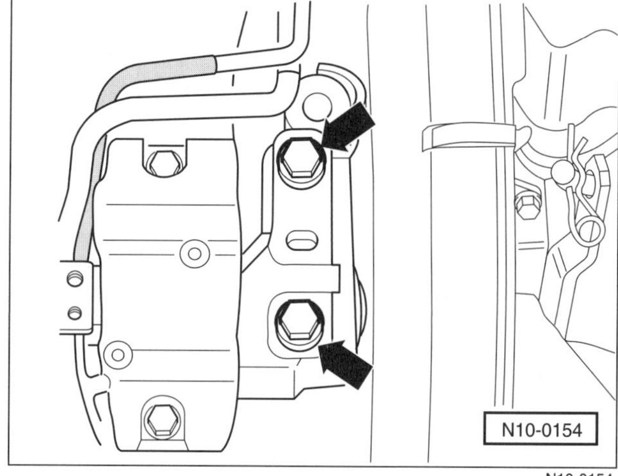

N10-0154

Fig. 6. Top view of right side engine mount. Remove bolts (**arrows**) to disconnect mount from engine.

32. Unbolt left side transmission mount from support on transmission. See Fig. 7.

33. Carefully lower engine and transmission assembly out of vehicle using caution to guide assembly past power steering and refrigerant lines.

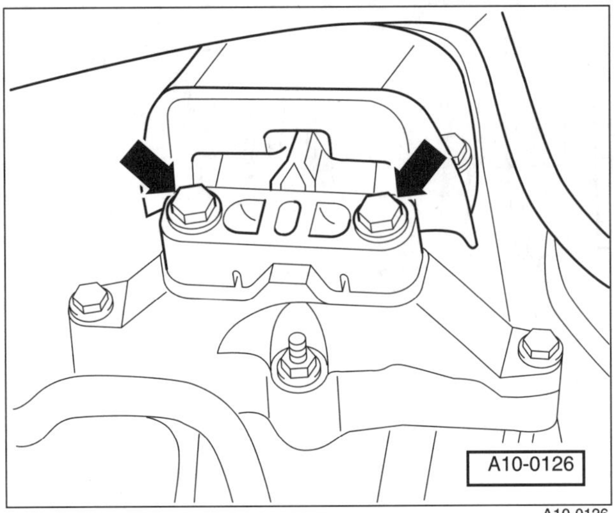

Fig. 7. Pendulum mount on left side supporting the transmission. Remove bolts (**arrows**) to disconnect mount from transmission.

> ***CAUTION —***
> *Before removing the engine and transmission assembly, be sure that the vehicle is properly supported in the rear. Removal of such a large amount of weight from the front can cause an improperly supported vehicle to pivot on the lift and fall to the rear.*

NOTE —
Carefully guide the engine/transmission assembly during the lowering process to prevent damage to it and to the bodywork.

Engine/transmission assembly, installing

1. With engine/transmission assembly on same device as was used for removal, carefully raise assembly up and into position.

2. Guide power steering fluid lines around transmission and the A/C lines around the engine to avoid damage.

3. While raising engine into position, ensure sufficient clearance for drive axle on left side.

4. When engine/transmission assembly is in position, adjust mounts so that there is a distance of approximately 10mm between engine mount and engine support on the body. See Fig. 8.

NOTE —
Do not stress the engine and transmission mounts during installation. Make sure they are aligned parallel to each other.

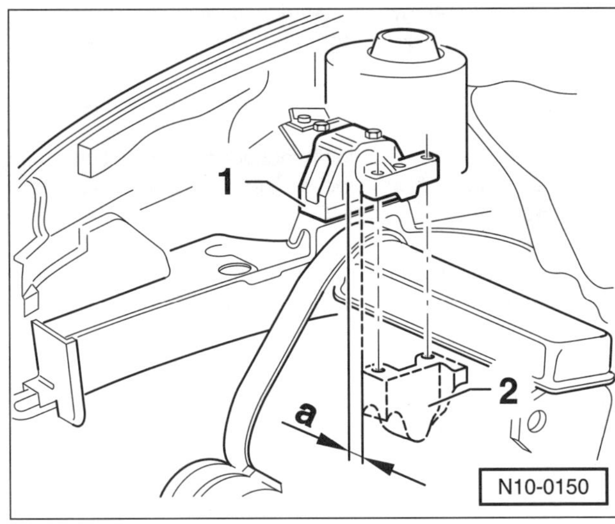

Fig. 8. Engine is properly positioned in mounts when gap between bracket on engine (**2**) and support on body (**1**) is 10 mm (**dimension a**).

5. Install engine, transmission and pendulum mounts with new bolts where indicated and torque to specification, see **Engine and Transmission Mounts**.

6. Install front exhaust pipe with catalytic converter, see **26 Exhaust System/Emission Controls**.

7. Attach left side drive shaft to transmission and install right side drive axle and protective cover, see **40 Front Suspension and Drive Axles**.

8. Install A/C compressor and secure A/C lines, see **87 Air Conditioning**.

9. Install power steering pump and lines, see **48 Steering**.

10. Connect shift linkage.
    - Manual transmission vehicles: Connect cables from selector mechanism and attach support bracket. Adjust shift linkage, see **34 Manual Transmission**. Install hydraulic clutch slave cylinder.
    - Automatic transmission vehicles: Connect selector cable and adjust, see **37 Automatic Transmission**.

11. Install starter motor and connect wiring.

12. Install secondary air injection pump, and auxiliary fan where equipped.

13. Note running direction and install ribbed V-belt, see **13 Crankshaft/Cylinder Block**.

14. Reinstall fuel supply and return lines.
    - On AEG engines, attach accelerator cable and adjust for full throttle. Have an assistant depress throttle pedal to floor while adjusting throttle cable at manifold to insure that throttle plate is wide open.

15. Install vacuum and breather hoses.

16. Install heater and coolant hoses.

17. Install auxiliary coolant fan, as applicable.

18. Refill cooling system with appropriate ratio of distilled water and G12 coolant and check for leaks, see **19 Engine – Cooling System**.

19. Install all remaining electrical connectors and check for proper routing of wires.

20. Install air cleaner assembly, connecting hoses and ducts.
    - On ALH engines, install connecting pipe between turbocharger and intercooler and intercooler and intake manifold complete with EGR vacuum regulator solenoid valve.

NOTE —

Install bottom portion of air cleaner housing first, then air filter and top half of housing.

21. Install battery mounting bracket, battery and battery fuse holder.

22. Mount power steering reservoir to battery mounting bracket.

23. Ensure that all removed tie wraps are replaced, and that all electrical wiring and hoses are properly routed and secured.

24. Connect battery cables.

25. Start engine and let it idle. Inspect for oil and coolant leaks. Check for smooth operation of shifter and clutch as required. Road test as required.

26. Shut off engine and install lower sound absorber panel (belly pan) and upper engine cover.

Tightening torques

- Engine to transmission bolts,
  - M10 bolts . . . . 60 Nm (33 ft-lb)
  - M12 bolts . . . . 80 Nm (59 ft-lb)
- Triple rotor/CV joint to transmission . . 40 Nm (30 ft-lb)
- Torque converter to drive plate. . . . . . 60 Nm (44 ft-lb)
- Bolts & nuts, not specifically listed
  - M6. . . . . 10 Nm (7 ft-lb)
  - M7. . . . . 15 Nm (10 ft-lb)
  - M8. . . . . 25 Nm (18 ft-lb)
  - M10. . . . . 40 Nm (30 ft-lb)
  - M12. . . . . 60 Nm (44 ft-lb)

ENGINE AND TRANSMISSION, MOUNTS

The engine and transmission assembly is suspended on its rotational axis by the engine mount on the right side and the transmission mount on the left side. Engine movement known as torque reaction is limited by the pendulum support mounted in the center underneath. Engine mounts differ slightly depending on transmission type (manual vs. automatic); and engine type (gasoline vs. diesel), but are all visually similar, see Fig. 9 through 11.

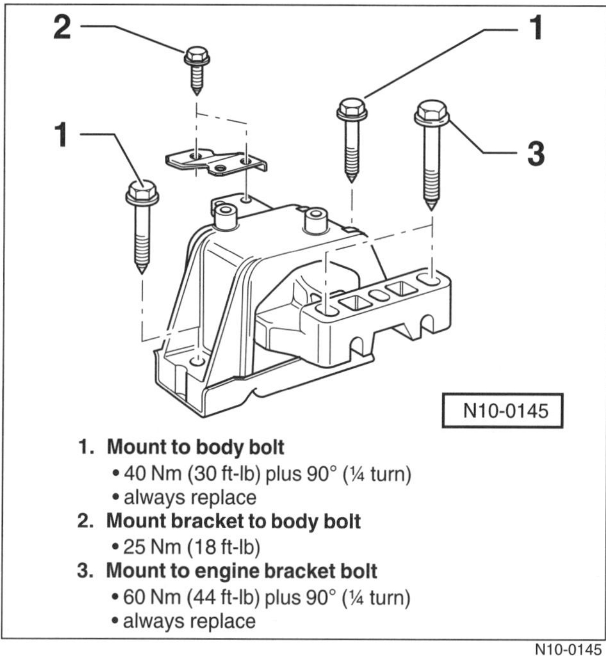

Fig. 9. Right side engine mount.

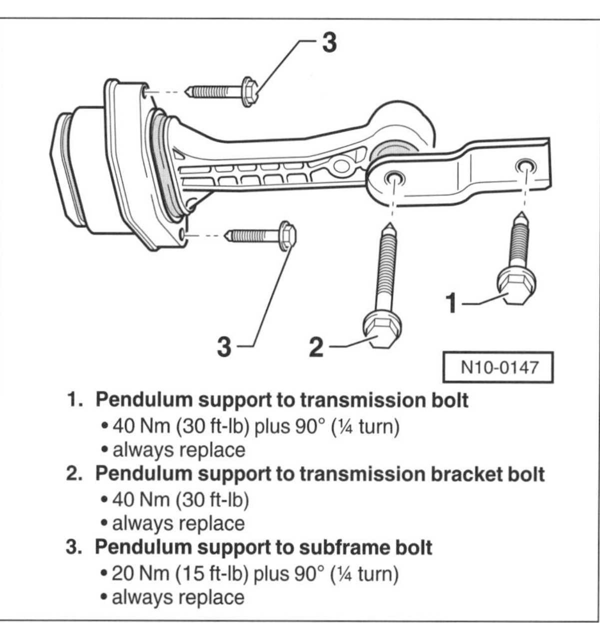

3
1
3
2
N10-0147
1. Pendulum support to transmission bolt
• 40 Nm (30 ft-lb) plus 90° (¼ turn)
• always replace
2. Pendulum support to transmission bracket bolt
• 40 Nm (30 ft-lb)
• always replace
3. Pendulum support to subframe bolt
• 20 Nm (15 ft-lb) plus 90° (¼ turn)
• always replace
N10-0147

Fig. 10. Pendulum support, lower center.

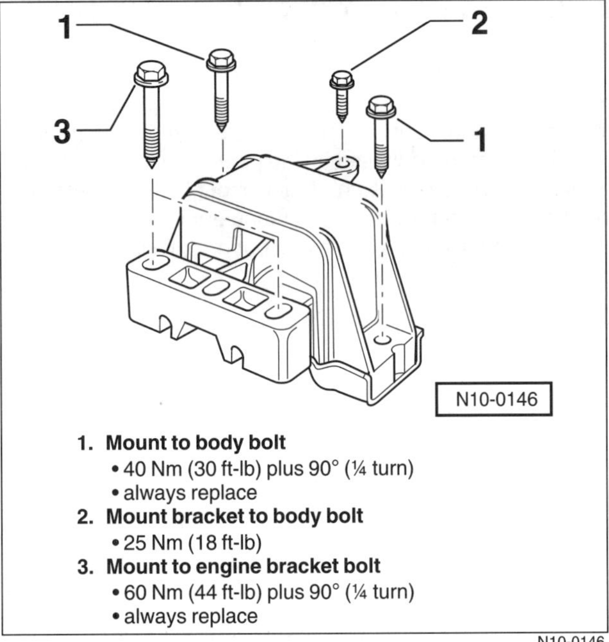

Fig. 11. Transmission mount, left side.

ENGINE/TRANSMISSION, SEPARATING

1. Support engine with device used to remove engine/transmission and rest transmission on work bench.

2. Remove small cover plate from behind right side axle flange if equipped. See Fig. 12.

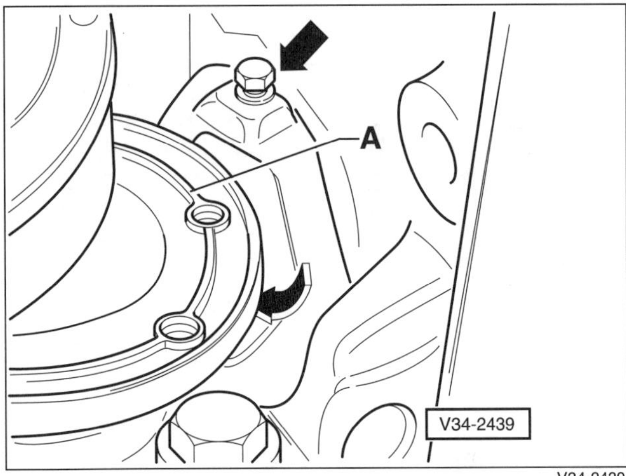

Fig. 12. Remove small cover plate (**A**) near right side drive flange if equipped.

3. Remove engine oil pan bolts from transmission.

4. Remove nuts from torque converter from engine side of the transmission, if equipped.

5. Remove bolts holding engine and transmission together.

6. Slide transmission off of engine.

NOTE —
On automatic transmissions, the torque converter should come off with transmission. Secure the torque converter to the transmission to prevent damage.

CAUTION —
- *On cars with automatic transmissions, be sure the drive plate separates cleanly from the torque converter without pulling the torque converter off of its support. Once the engine and transmission are separated, install a suitable bar across the open bell bellhousing to keep the torque converter from falling out.*
- *On cars with manual transmissions, be sure that the weight of the transmission or the engine is never supported on the transmission mainshaft. Clutch or transmission damage could result.*
- *When reattaching the transmission to the engine, check that the guide sleeves are installed into the engine block. Replace them if they are missing.*
- *Clutch or drive plate damage may result if guide sleeves are not installed.*

7. Attaching engine to transmission is the reverse of separating. Observe the following points:
   - Lightly lubricate manual transmission mainshaft with molybdenum disulfide (MoS2) grease.
   - Inspect clutch components, see **30 Clutch**.
   - Install torque converter to stator support on automatic transmission before attaching.

QUALITY REVIEW

When you have finished working under the hood and around other areas of the vehicle it is advisable to take a moment to quality check or review your work. This helps to ensure that the operation or repair has been completed properly with all affected systems functioning within normal parameters. This may include the following:

- Make sure that the radiator fan cycles properly and that the coolant level and concentration are correct.
- Ensure that all cable ties and hose clamps that were removed as part of the repair are replaced.
- Check and adjust all other applicable fluid levels.
- Make sure that there are no fluid leaks.
- Make sure there are no air, vacuum or exhaust leaks.
- Make sure that all components involved in the repair are positioned correctly and function properly.
- Male sure all tools, shop cloths, fender covers, and protective tape are removed.
- Clean grease from painted surfaces and steering wheel.

In addition to the above noted points, the ECM and TCM may need to be checked using the Volkswagen supplied VAG 1551 or 1552 scan tool as mentioned at the start of this repair.

13 Crankshaft/Cylinder Block

TABLES

GENERAL

This repair group provides the special reconditioning information necessary to repair the Volkswagen short block. The information contained here is intended to be used as a reconditioning guide for the professional or experienced automotive technician. Many of the operations and specifications listed require precision measuring equipment.

Engine Codes
- AEG . . . . 2.0L 4-cylinder gasoline
- ALH . . . . 1.9L 4-cylinder turbo diesel

CYLINDER BLOCK OIL SEALS

The front crankshaft oil seal can be replaced with the engine installed. Replacement of the rear crankshaft oil seal requires that the engine be separated from the transmission. See Fig. 1.

NOTE —
In some instances, individual seals may not be available separately. See an authorized Volkswagen parts dealer, or an aftermarket parts specialist, for the latest in parts information.

Cylinder block oil seals, assembly

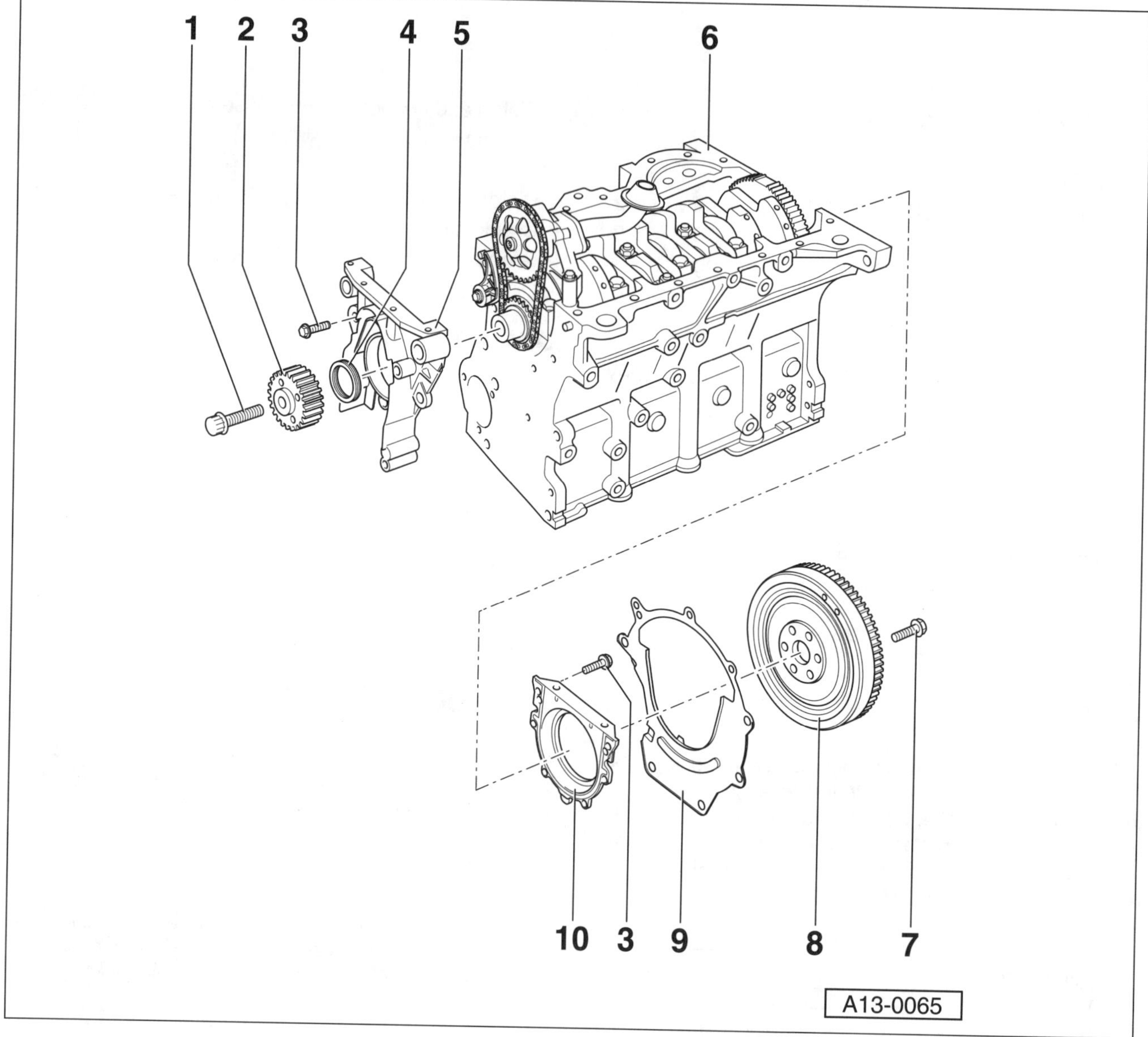

A13-0065

Fig. 1. Exploded view of crankshaft seals in cylinder block. AEG engine shown, ALH block is similar.

1. **Bolt**
   - Tighten to:
     AEG: 90 Nm (66 ft-lb) + ¼ turn (90°)
     ALH: 120 Nm (88 ft-lb)
   - Always replace
2. **Crankshaft toothed belt sprocket**
3. **Bolt**
   - Tighten to 15 Nm (11 ft-lb)
4. **Front crankshaft oil seal**
5. **Front oil seal flange**
6. **Engine block**
7. **Bolt**
   - Tighten to 60 Nm (44 ft-lb) + ¼ turn (90°)
   - Always replace
8. **Flywheel/driveplate**
   - Flywheel: remove and install with 3067 counterholder
9. **Intermediate plate**
   - Must be located on dowel sleeves
   - Do not damage or bend when assembling
10. **Rear oil seal flange**
    - May need to replace as complete unit (w/integral oil seal)
    - Lightly oil lip on seal
    - Install new sealing flange with guide sleeve
    - Guide sleeve protects seal during installation

Front crankshaft oil seal, replacing

1. Remove camshaft drive belt, see **15a Cylinder Head and Valvetrain (Engine Code AEG)**, or **23 Fuel Injection (Engine Code ALH)**.

2. Hold the crankshaft stationary with a suitable counterholder and loosen the crankshaft sprocket (hub) center bolt. Remove the bolt and sprocket. See Fig. 2.

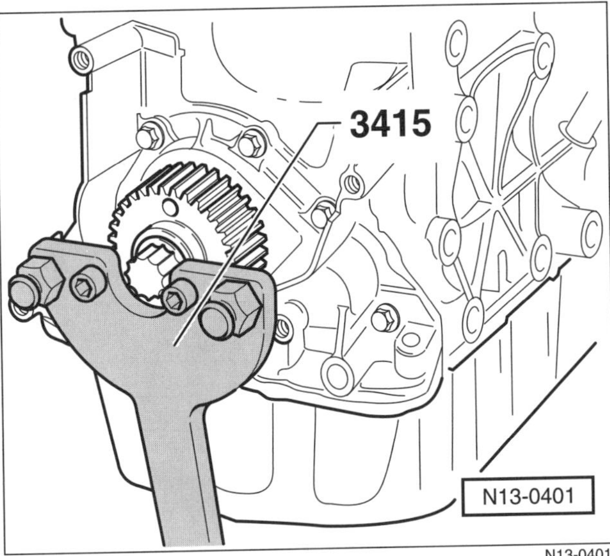

N13-0401

Fig. 2. Counterholder threaded into sprocket to allow removal of center bolt.

3. Reinstall the removed bolt into the crankshaft to prevent damage to the end of the crankshaft when using the seal extractor. Remove the oil seal from the flange using an appropriate seal extractor or by carefully prying it out. See Fig. 3.

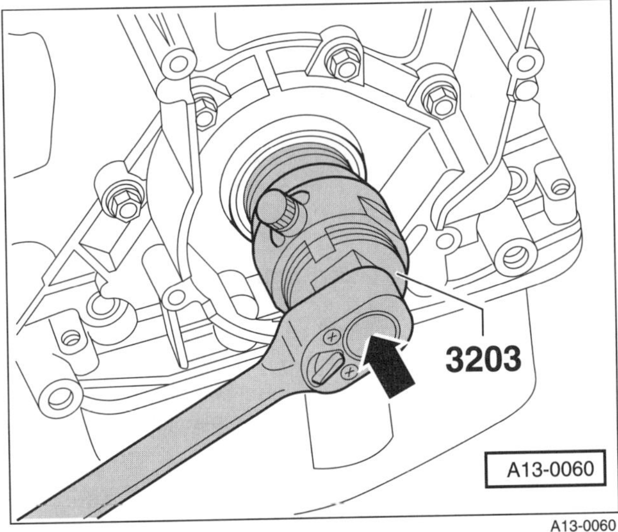

A13-0060

Fig. 3. Seal removal tool threaded into seal. Wrench (**arrow**) is being used to remove crankshaft oil seal.

4. Install new seal, lubricated with clean engine oil, with closed side facing out. Use a guide sleeve to protect seal from sharp edges of the crankshaft as necessary. Carefully press seal into place until it is fully seated. See Fig. 4.

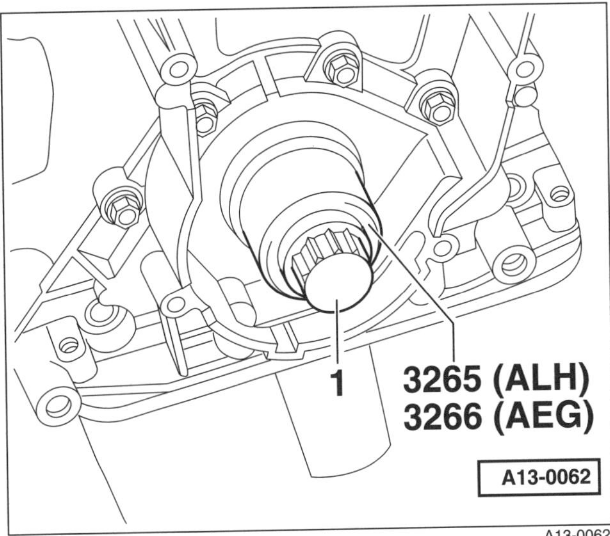

A13-0062

Fig. 4. Front crankshaft oil seal being pressed in using Volkswagen special tools and old crankshaft sprocket bolt (**1**).

5. Align locating key on sprocket with cutout on the end of crankshaft and install sprocket onto the crankshaft with a new bolt. Hold the crankshaft with the counterholder and torque to specification.

6. Install remaining removed components.

> ***CAUTION —***
> *Always replace the crankshaft sprocket bolt. It is a stretch bolt designed to be used only once.*

Tightening torques

- Crankshaft sprocket bolt, engine code AEG (stretch bolt - always replace)
  - stage I . . . . 90 Nm (66 ft-lb)
  - stage II . . . . additional ¼ turn (90°)
- Crankshaft sprocket bolt, engine code ALH (stretch bolt - always replace)
  - stage I . . . . 120 Nm (88 ft-lb)
  - stage II . . . . additional ¼ turn (90°)

Front oil seal flange, removing and installing

1. Remove crankshaft drive sprocket as described earlier.
2. Drain engine oil and remove oil pan. See **17 Engine–Lubrication System**.
3. Unbolt front oil seal flange from cylinder block and remove. It may be necessary to lightly tap flange with a soft faced mallet to remove it.
4. Thoroughly remove all the old sealant residue from the flange. See Fig. 5.

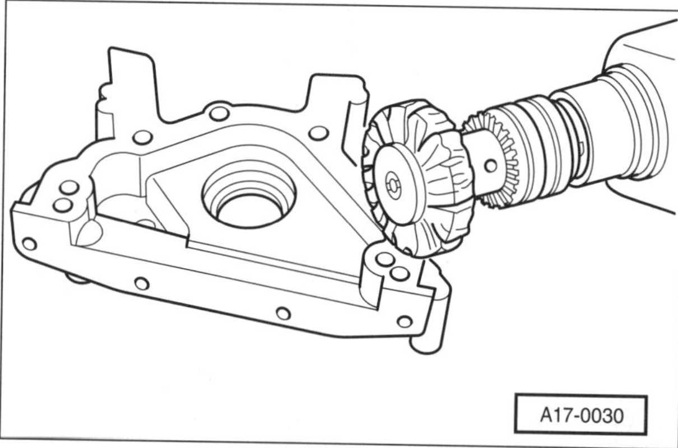

A17-0030

Fig. 5. Old sealant residue being removed with a cleaning pad attached to a drill motor. Use care not to scratch or gouge the aluminum housing.

NOTE —
The front oil seal flange does not use a paper gasket. Special silicone sealant is used instead. Surface must be clean and free from oil and grease before sealant is applied.

5. Apply a 2 to 3 mm (slightly less than 1/8 inch) bead of new sealant to flange as shown in Fig. 6.

NOTE —
Flange must be installed within 5 minutes of applying sealant.

> ***CAUTION —***
> *The sealing compound bead thickness must not be wider than 3 mm (slightly less than 1/8 inch). If this width is exceeded, excess sealing compound will enter the oil pan and could block the oil pump pick-up tube strainer.*

6. Use a guide sleeve as necessary to protect the oil seal and install the flange on the guide pins of the cylinder block. Torque the bolts in a staggered pattern.
7. Install the oil pan.

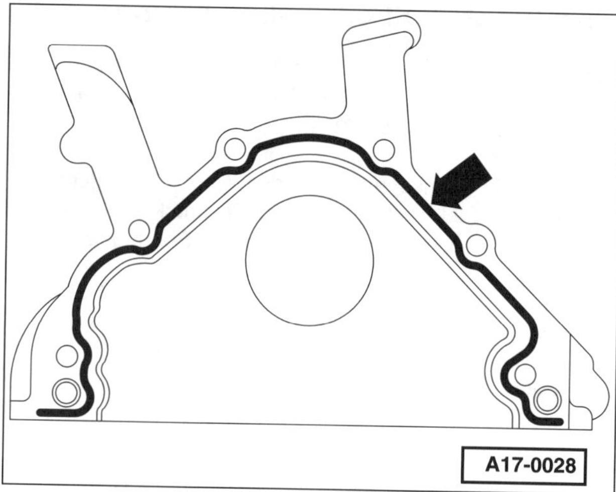

A17-0028

Fig. 6. Apply sealant bead 2 to 3 mm (slightly less than 1/8 inch) wide (**arrow**). Front flange is shown; sealant is applied to the rear seal flange in a similar manner.

8. Install remaining removed components.

Tightening torques
- Front or rear flange to cylinder block (M7) . . . . 15 Nm (11 ft-lb)
- Oil pan to cylinder block (M7) . . . . 15 Nm (11 ft-lb)
- Oil pan to transmission (M10) . . . . . . 45 Nm (33 ft-lb)

Rear crankshaft oil seal, replacing

NOTE —
The rear crankshaft oil seal may not be available separately from the rear crankshaft oil seal flange. See an authorized Volkswagen parts dealer, or an aftermarket parts specialist for the latest in parts information.

1. If engine is still in car, remove transmission as described in **34 Manual Transmission** or **37 Automatic Transmission**, as applicable.
2. If engine and transmission are out of car, separate engine from transmission as described in **10 Engine–Removing and Installing**.
3. Remove flywheel or driveplate as described later.
4. Remove seal from flange by carefully prying it out.
5. Install the new seal, lubricated with clean engine oil, with closed side facing out using a suitable seal installation tool.
6. Install remaining removed components.

Rear oil seal flange, removing and installing

1. If engine is still in car, remove transmission as described in **34 Manual Transmission** or **37 Automatic Transmission**, as applicable.

2. If engine and transmission are out of car, separate engine from transmission as described in **10 Engine– Removing and Installing**.

3. Remove flywheel or drive plate as described later.

4. Drain engine oil and remove oil pan, see **17 Engine–Lubrication System**.

5. Unbolt rear oil seal flange from cylinder block and remove. It may be necessary to lightly tap the flange with a soft faced mallet to remove it.

6. The rear oil seal flange does not use a paper gasket. Special silicone sealant is used instead.

7. Apply a 2 to 3 mm (slightly less than 1/8 inch) bead of new sealant to the flange as shown in Fig. 6.

   NOTE —
   Flange must be installed within 5 minutes of applying sealant.

> ***CAUTION —***
> *The sealing compound bead thickness must not be wider than 3 mm (slightly less than 1/8 inch). If this width is exceeded, excess sealing compound will enter the oil pan and could block the oil pump pick-up tube strainer.*

8. Use a guide sleeve as necessary to protect the oil seal and install the flange on the guide pins of the cylinder block. Torque the bolts in a staggered pattern.

9. Install the oil pan, see **17 Engine–Lubrication System**.

10. Install remaining removed components.

FLYWHEEL OR DRIVEPLATE

Removal of the flywheel or driveplate requires that the engine be separated from the transmission. Remove the clutch on manual transmission vehicles, see **30 Clutch**.

> ***CAUTION —***
> - *On vehicles with automatic transmissions, special mounting and measuring procedures are required when installing the driveplate.*
> - *The flywheel on manual transmission vehicles and the driveplate on automatic transmission vehicles are mounted to the crankshaft using stretch bolts that are designed to be used only once. Always replace.*

Flywheel or driveplate, removing and installing

1. Attach a suitable holder to the engine and flywheel on manual transmission vehicles or the engine and driveplate on automatic transmission vehicles. See Fig. 7.

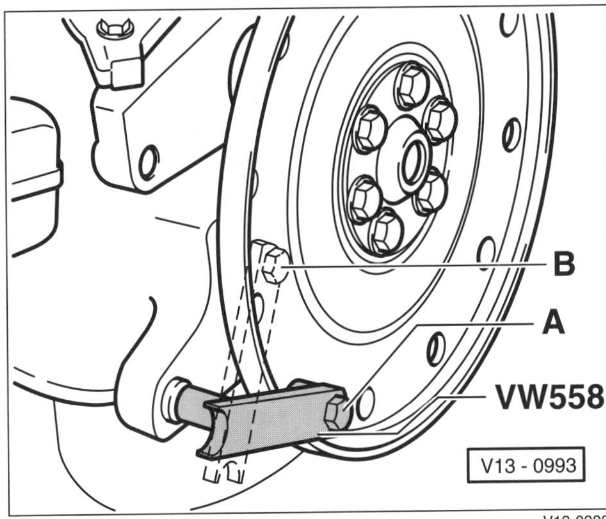

V13-0993

Fig. 7. Driveplate secured with holding fixture VW558. Position **A** is used to loosen and position **B** for tightening. Flywheel is similar.

2. Loosen securing bolts diagonally and remove flywheel or drive plate and any shims.

3. Installation is the reverse of removal observing the following points:
   - Install any removed shims and mount the flywheel or drive plate with new bolts.
   - Check driveplate clearance (as applicable) as described later.
   - Attach the holder and torque diagonally to specifications.

Tightening torques
- Flywheel or driveplate to crankshaft (stretch bolt, always replace)
  - stage I . . . . 30 Nm (22 ft-lb)
  - stage II . . . . 60 Nm (44 ft-lb)
  - stage III . . . . additional ¼ turn (90°)

Driveplate clearance, adjusting (cars with automatic transmission)

Component replacement or other circumstances may necessitate adjustment of the driveplate clearance. Incorrect clearance may result in premature starter wear.

1. Install drive plate with new bolts and backing plate, but without shim(s). See Fig. 8.

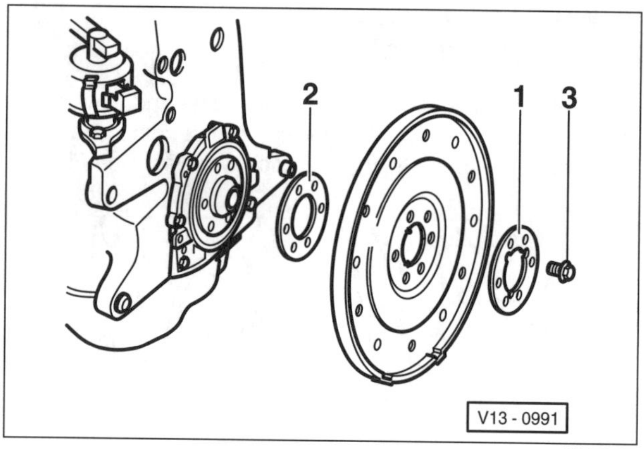

V13-0991

Fig. 8. Automatic transmission driveplate assembly. Shim (**2**) may or may not be present. Backing plate (**1**) is used only with automatic transmission driveplate.

Tightening Torque

- Driveplate checking torque. . . . . 30 Nm (22 ft-lb)

---

2. Measure distance from machined surface on cylinder block to outer edge of driveplate with a suitable measuring tool at three points. Measuring tool must fit through hole in driveplate. See Fig. 9.

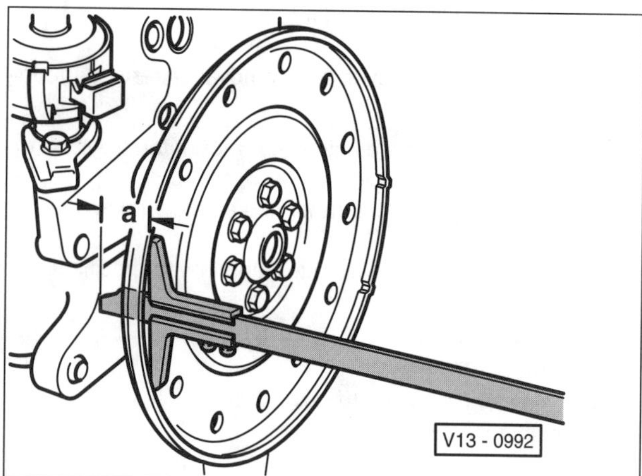

V13-0992

Fig. 9. Measuring tool inserted into hole in drive plate to obtain distance from machined surface of block to outer edge of driveplate, dimension (**a**).

3. Average the three readings to get **dimension a**.

Specification

- Cylinder block to outer edge of driveplate (automatic transmission only), **dimension a**. . . 19.5 mm – 21.1mm (0.77 – 0.83 in.)

---

4. If specification is not obtained, remove driveplate add shim(s) and recheck.

5. When specification is obtained, attach holding fixture and torque to final specification.

Tightening torques

- Flywheel or driveplate to crankshaft (stretch bolt, always replace)
  - stage I . . . . 30 Nm (22 ft-lb)
  - stage II . . . . 60 Nm (44 ft-lb)
- stage III. additional ¼ turn (90°)

CYLINDER BLOCK INTERNAL COMPONENTS

During engine block disassembly, be sure to mark the position and orientation of all parts as they are removed. This includes connecting rods, rod bearings and caps, piston pins, pistons, main bearings and caps. This ensures that re-used parts are put back in to service in the location where they have been "run-in". Certain cylinder block components such as connecting rod caps and main bearing caps are matched to another part during manufacture and will not fit properly to any other part. Knowing which components came from which location can also be a used to diagnose internal engine problems.

To minimize wear during initial engine start-up, clean engine oil should be used to lubricate all friction surfaces during assembly.

Pistons and Connecting Rods

Pistons, piston pins, piston rings, connecting rods, and bearings should never be interchanged if they are to be reused. Mark cylinder number and installation orientation on pistons, connecting rods and connecting rod bearing caps before removal.

Components of one piston and connecting rod assembly are shown in Fig. 10. Pistons for ALH engines are not all the same. Valve relief pockets machined into the piston crown for cylinders 1 and 2 are the same. Pockets in cylinders 3 and 4 are also the same, but are different from cylinders 1 and 2.

The piston pin should require only a slight push to remove or install. If difficult, heat the piston to approximately 60°C (160°F). Replace the piston and the pin if the fit is excessively loose.

Inspect the connecting rod for any bending, distortion, heat damage or other visual damage. Connecting rod specifications are listed in **Table a**. Connecting rods should always be replaced in complete sets due to weight and dimensional considerations.

NOTE —

- *When checking radial clearance, reuse the old bolt or nut, and lubricate the contact surface of the nut or bolt before tightening. Tighten the nut or bolt only to the 30 Nm (22 ft-lb) specification and not the additional ¼ turn.*
- *If connecting rod radial clearance is excessive, the crankshaft connecting rod journals should be checked. If crankshaft journal diameters are within specifications, recheck radial clearance using new bearing shells.*

Piston and connecting rod, assembly

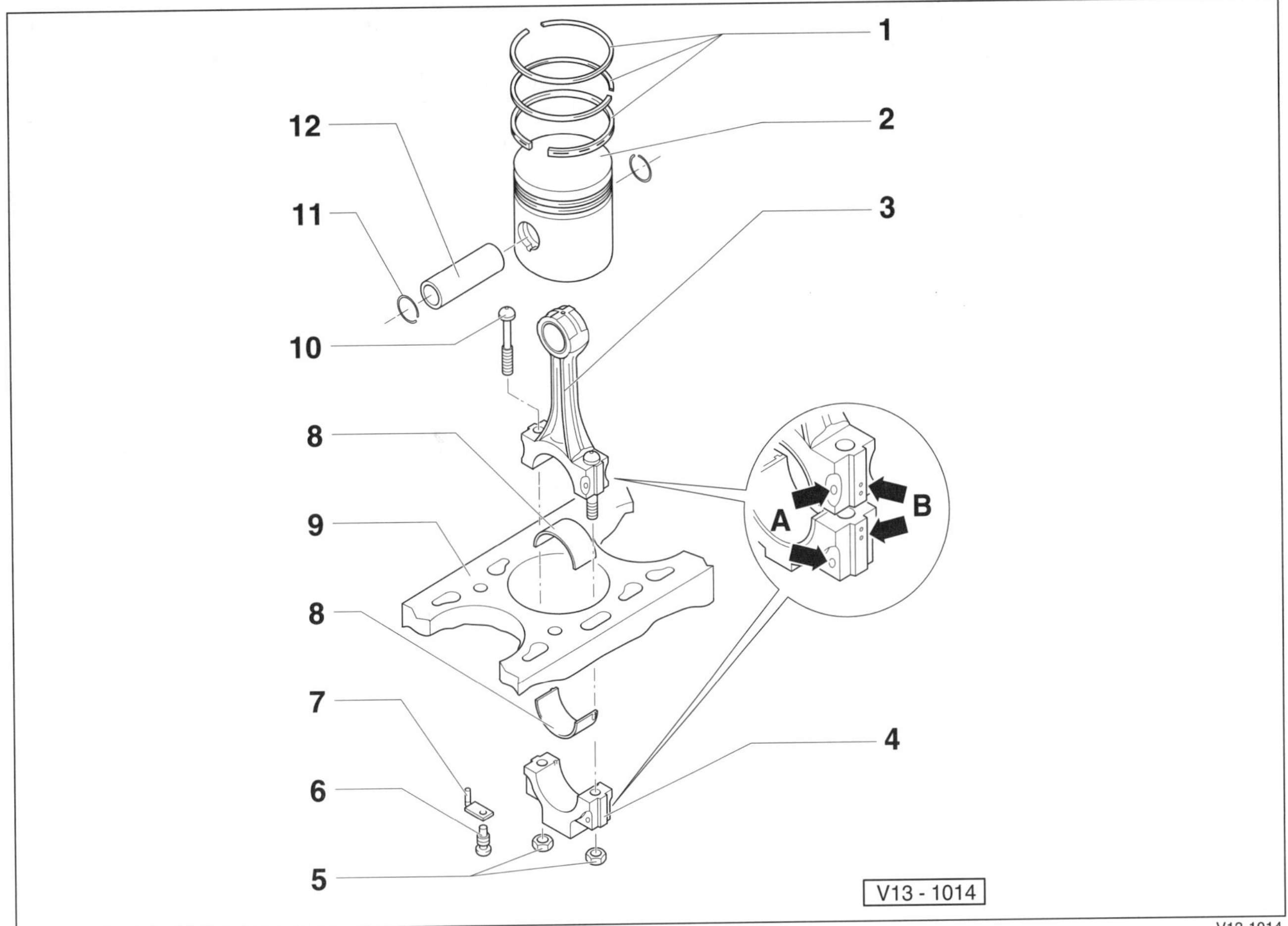

Fig. 10. Exploded view of piston and connecting rod assembly.

1. **Piston ring**
   - Offset gaps by 120°
   - Remove and install using piston ring pliers
   - "TOP" faces piston crown

2. **Piston**
   - Mark installation position and cylinder number
   - Arrow on piston crown points to pulley end
   - Install using piston ring clamp **see** Ⓐ

3. **Connecting rod**
   - Only replace as a set
   - Mark cylinder number (**B**)
   - Installation position: mark (**A**) faces toward pulley end

4. **Connecting rod bearing cap**
   - Note installation position

5. **Nuts**
   - Tighten to 30 Nm (22 ft-lb) + ¼ turn (90°)
   - Always replace
   - Oil threads and contact surfaces
   - To measure radial clearance tighten to 30 Nm (22 ft-lb), but no further

6. **Pressure relief valve**
   - Not on AEG engine
   - Tighten to 27 Nm (20 ft-lb)
   - Opening pressure: 2.5 to 3.2 bar (36 to 46 psi)

7. **Oil spray jet**
   - Not on AEG engine
   - For piston cooling

8. **Bearing shell**
   - Note installation position
   - Do not interchange used bearing shells
   - Ensure retaining lugs fit tightly in recesses
   - Do not rotate crankshaft when checking radial clearance
   - With oil hole for piston bolt lubrication

9. **Engine block**

10. **Connecting rod bolt**

11. **Circlip**

12. **Piston pin**
    - If difficult to remove, heat piston to 60°C (140°F)
    - Remove and install with VW 222a

A Piston orientation (ALH engine)

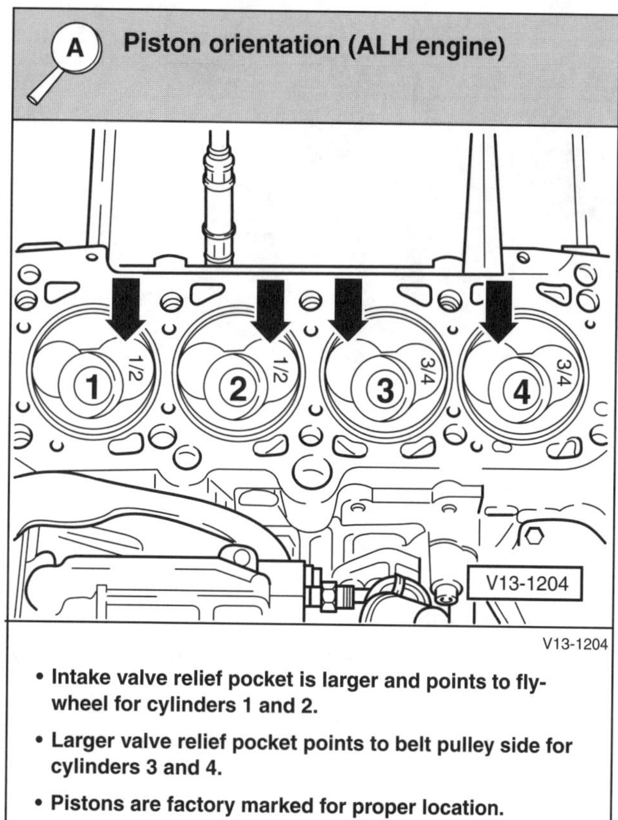

V13-1204

- **Intake valve relief pocket is larger and points to flywheel for cylinders 1 and 2.**
- **Larger valve relief pocket points to belt pulley side for cylinders 3 and 4.**
- **Pistons are factory marked for proper location.**

Table a. Connecting Rod Specifications

Radial clearance (Plastigage®)	
new (AEG, ALH)	0.01–0.06 mm (0.0004–0.0024 in.)
wear limit	
AEG engine	0.12 mm (0.0047 in.)
ALH engine	0.08 mm (0.0031 in.)
Axial (side) clearance	
new (AEG, ALH)	0.05–0.31 mm (0.0020–0.0122 in.)
wear limit	
AEG, ALH engines	0.37 mm (0.0145 in.)
Checking torque	30 Nm (22 ft-lb)
Assembly torque	30 Nm (22 ft-lb) plus ¼ turn (90°)

Piston Rings

Piston ring end gaps are checked with the piston rings inserted evenly approximately 15 mm (5/8 in.) from the bottom of the cylinder. This is because wear in this area of the cylinder is negligible. See Fig. 11. **Table b** lists piston ring end gap specifications.

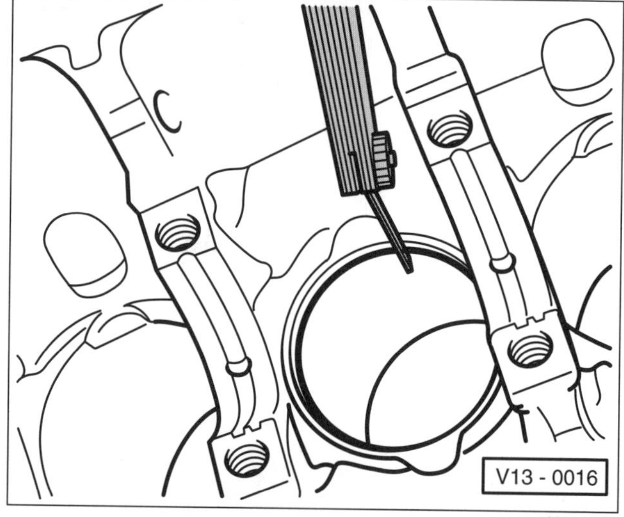

V13-0016

Fig. 11. Piston ring shown inserted into the bottom of the cylinder. Measure gap with a feeler gauge.

Table b. Piston Ring End Gaps

	New	**Wear limit**
Top compression ring		
AEG engine	0.20–0.40 mm (.0079–.0157 in.)	0.8 mm (.0315 in.)
ALH engine	0.20–0.40 mm (.0079–.0157 in.)	1.0 mm (.0394 in.)
Bottom compression ring		
AEG engine	0.20–0.40 mm (.0079–.0157 in.)	0.8 mm (.0315 in.)
ALH engine	0.20–0.40 mm (.0079–.0157 in.)	1.0 mm (.0394 in.)
Oil scraper ring		
AEG engine	0.25–0.50 mm (.0098–.0197 in.)	0.8 mm (.0315 in.)
ALH engine	0.25–0.50 mm (.0098–.0197 in.)	1.0 mm (.0394 in.)

Piston ring side clearance (ring to groove clearance) is checked using feeler gauges. Measure each ring in its original groove. See Fig. 12. Piston ring side clearance specifications are listed in **Table c**.

NOTE —
Piston ring groove should be thoroughly cleaned before checking ring side clearance.

Table c. Piston Ring Side Clearances

	New	Wear limit
Top compression ring		
AEG engine	0.06–0.09 mm (.0024–.0035 in.)	0.20 mm (.0079 in.)
ALH engine	0.06–0.09 mm (.0024–.0035 in.)	0.25 mm (.0098 in.)
Bottom compression ring		
AEG engine	0.06–0.09 mm (.0024–.0035 in.)	0.20 mm (.0079 in.)
ALH engine	0.05–0.08 mm (.0020–.0031 in.)	0.25 mm (.0098 in.)
Oil scraper ring		
AEG engine	0.03–0.06 mm (.0012–.0024 in.)	0.15 mm (.0059 in.)
ALH engine	0.03–0.06 mm (.0012–.0024 in.)	0.15 mm (.0059 in.)

Specification

- Piston wear–maximum allowable deviation from nominal piston diameter
  - AEG engine . . . . 0.04 mm (.0016 in.)
  - ALH engine . . . . .no factory specification

Specification

- Cylinder wear–maximum allowable deviation from nominal cylinder bore
  - AEG engine . . . . 0.08 mm (.0031 in.)
  - ALH engine . . . . 0.10 mm (.0039 in.)

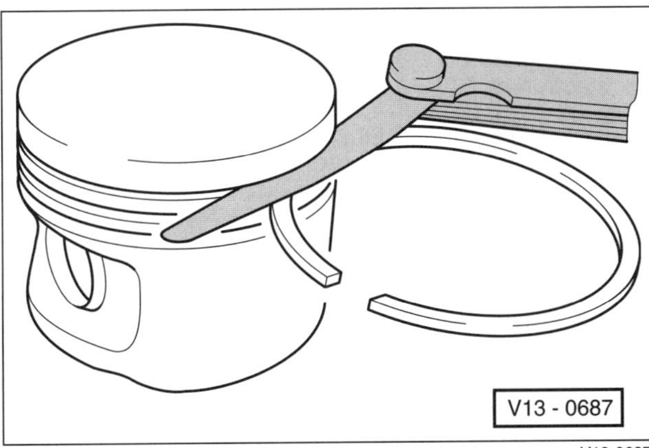

V13-0687

Fig. 12. Piston ring side clearance (ring to groove clearance) being measured with a feeler gauge.

Cylinder Block

Measure cylinder bores at three places; approximately the top, the middle and the bottom of the piston travel. Make measurements parallel to the crankshaft and at right angles (90°). See Fig. 13.

The top and bottom measurements should be made approximately 10 mm (3/8 in.) from the ends of the cylinder. Measure pistons from the bottom of the piston skirt and at right angles (90°) to the piston pin. See Fig. 14. Nominal piston and cylinder bore diameter specifications are given in **Table d**. Nominal piston diameters are also marked on the piston crowns.

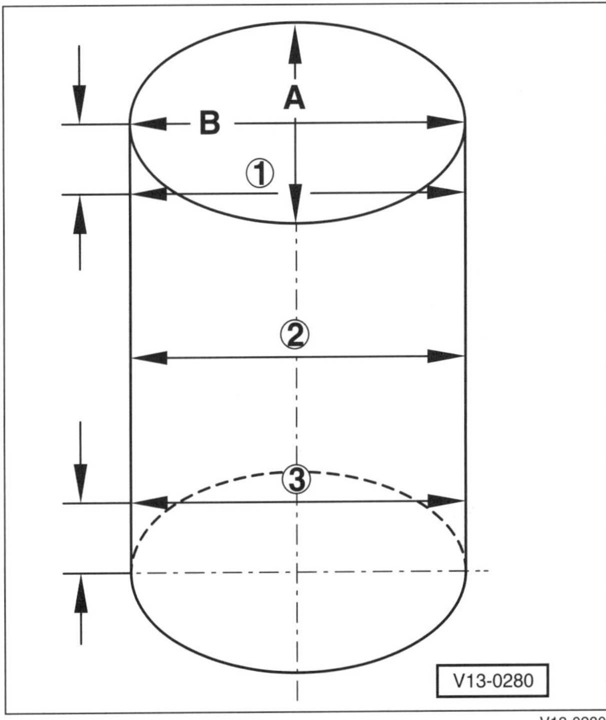

V13-0280

Fig. 13. Measure cylinder bore in directions both perpendicular to the crankshaft (**A**) and parallel to crankshaft (**B**). Make measurements at 3 locations in each cylinder.

CAUTION —
Mounting the bare cylinder block to an engine stand can distort its shape and cause inaccurate cylinder bore measurement. Always check cylinder bores with the block resting unstressed and without mounting brackets on a flat surface.

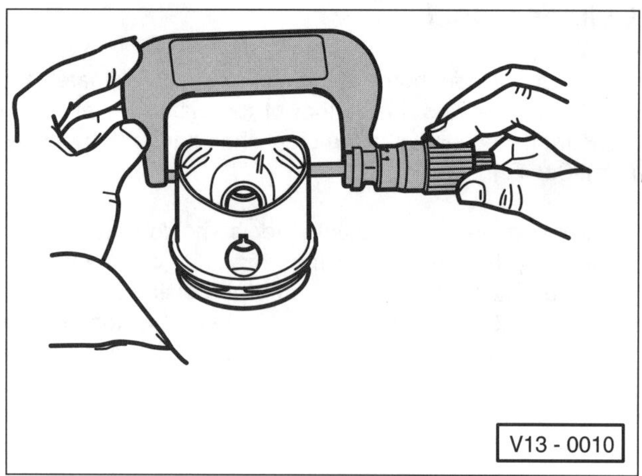

V13-0010

Fig. 14. Check piston diameter approximately 6–10 mm (0.236–0.394 in.) from bottom of skirt at right angle to piston pin. If piston is graphite coated, (dark gray color) allow up to 0.02 mm (0.0008 in.) additional, as the graphite coating will wear

Table d. Piston and Cylinder Diameters

Engine code	Piston diameter in mm (in.)	Cylinder bores in mm (in.)
AEG		
standard	82.465* (3.2466)	82.51 (3.2484)
1st oversize	82.965* (3.2663)	83.01 (3.2681)
ALH		
standard	79.47 (3.1287)	79.51 (3.1303)
1st oversize	79.72 (3.1386)	79.76 (3.1401)
2nd oversize	79.97 (3.1484)	80.01 (3.1500)

* Dimension without graphite coating (thickness 0.02 mm (.0008 in.). The graphite coating wears away.

Piston Projection at TDC (ALH engine)

Diesel engine pistons protrude slightly out of the block at TDC due to design considerations. The amount of protrusion varies slightly between engines as a result of production tolerance. In order to achieve proper compression ratios, one of three different thickness head gaskets are used to adjust compression height. Piston projection must be measured and adjusted any time components that affect it are replaced. These components include: crankshaft, piston, connecting rod and block. Measure piston height on all 4 cylinders. See Fig. 15.

Select a suitable head gasket based on the highest reading obtained from the available head gaskets listed in **Table e**. The different gaskets are identified by the number of holes punched in an identification tab on the front of the gasket. See Fig. 16.

NOTE—

Cylinder measurements that differ substantially from each other could be an indication of internal engine damage.

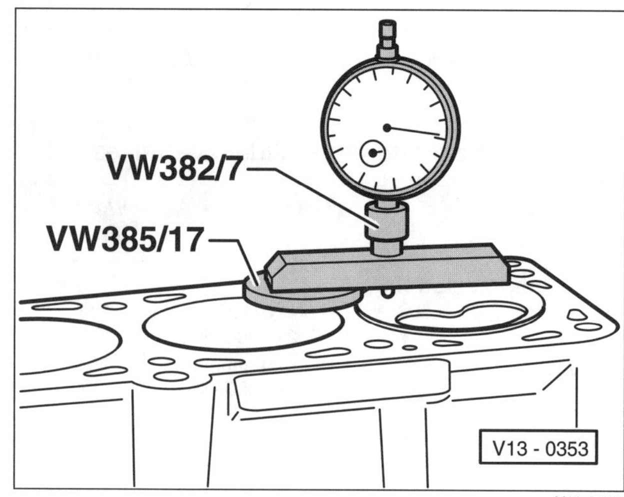

V13-0353

Fig. 15. Piston projection being measured with a dial gauge and suitable adapters.

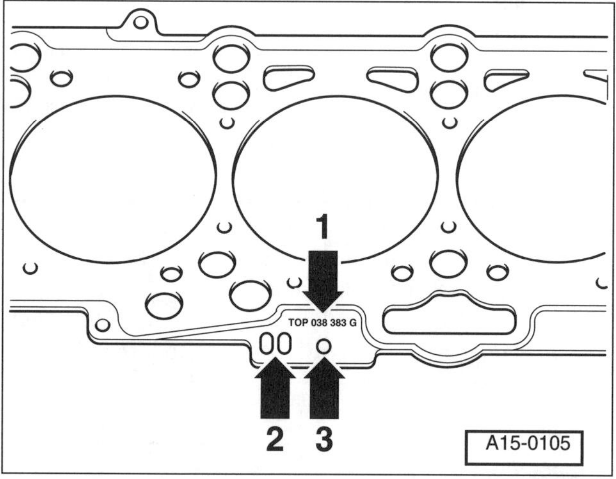

A15-0105

Fig. 16. ALH cylinder head gasket identification markings: **arrow 1** = part number, **arrow 2** = production information (disregard), **arrow 3** = identification holes.

Table e. ALH Diesel Cylinder Head Gasket Selection

Measured piston projection at TDC	Gasket identification	Thickness
0.91 – 1.00 mm (.0358 – .0394 in.)	1 hole	1.45 mm (.0571 in.)
1.01 – 1.10 mm (.0398 – .0433 in.)	2 holes	1.53 mm (.0602 in.)
1.11 – 1.20 mm (.0437 – .0472 in.)	3 holes	1.61 mm (.0634 in.)

Crankshaft

The crankshaft assemblies and related components for AEG and ALH engines are shown in Fig. 17 and Fig. 18, respectively. Observe the installation notes for any components that are to be reused. The crankshaft mounts a sensor wheel for the engine management system that will only fit on the crankshaft in one position. The sensor wheel on ALH engines uses a dowel pin.

Crankshaft bearing specifications are listed in **Table f** and journal diameters are listed in **Table g**. If a crankshaft must be replaced, a Volkswagen remanufactured crankshaft is available from an authorized Volkswagen Dealer.

> ***CAUTION —***
> *Many of the fasteners used in the cylinder block are stretch bolts that must be replaced once loosened. Review the repair information to identify all bolts and nuts that must be replaced during cylinder block repairs or reconditioning.*

NOTE —

- *On cars with an automatic transmission, see* **Flywheel or Driveplate** *given earlier when reinstalling the driveplate. Special installation procedures apply.*
- *Attach engine to suitable engine stand when disassembling and assembling.*

Table f. Crankshaft Bearing Specifications

Main bearing radial clearance (Plastigage®)	
new parts	
AEG engine	0.01–0.04 mm (.0004–.0016 in.)
ALH engine	0.03–0.08 mm (.0012–.0031 in.)
wear limit	
AEG engine	0.15 mm (.0059 in.)
ALH engine	0.17 mm (.0067 in.)
Crankshaft axial play (side clearance)	
new parts	
AEG engine	0.07–0.23 mm (.0028–.0091 in.)
ALH engines	0.07–0.17 mm (.0028–.0067 in.)
wear limit	
AEG engine	0.30 mm (.0118 in.)
ALH engine	0.37 mm (.0146 in.)

Table g. Crankshaft Journal Diameters

Journal diameters (nominal)	mm (in.)
Basic dimension	
AEG engine	
main	54.00 (2.1260) $^{-0.017\ (0.00067)}_{-0.037\ (0.00146)}$
connecting rod	47.80 (1.8819) $^{-0.022\ (0.00087)}_{-0.042\ (0.00165)}$
ALH engine	
main	54.00 (2.1260) $^{-0.022\ (0.00087)}_{-0.042\ (0.00165)}$
connecting rod	47.80 (1.8819) $^{-0.022\ (0.00087)}_{-0.042\ (0.00165)}$
1st undersize (0.25 mm)	
AEG engine	
main	53.75 (2.1161) $^{-0.017\ (0.00067)}_{-0.037\ (0.00146)}$
connecting rod	47.55 (1.8720) $^{-0.022\ (0.00087)}_{-0.042\ (0.00165)}$
ALH engine	
main	53.75 (2.1161) $^{-0.022\ (0.00087)}_{-0.042\ (0.00165)}$
connecting rod	47.55 (1.8720) $^{-0.022\ (0.00087)}_{-0.042\ (0.00165)}$
2nd undersize (0.50 mm)	
AEG engine	
main	53.50 (2.1063) $^{-0.017\ (0.00067)}_{-0.037\ (0.00146)}$
connecting rod	47.30 (1.8622) $^{-0.022\ (0.00087)}_{-0.042\ (0.00165)}$
ALH engine	
main	53.50 (2.1063) $^{-0.022\ (0.00087)}_{-0.042\ (0.00165)}$
connecting rod	47.30 (1.8622) $^{-0.022\ (0.00087)}_{-0.042\ (0.00165)}$
3rd undersize (0.75 mm)	
AEG engine	
main	53.25 (2.0965) $^{-0.017\ (0.00067)}_{-0.037\ (0.00146)}$
connecting rod	47.05 (1.8524) $^{-0.022\ (0.00087)}_{-0.042\ (0.00165)}$
ALH engine	
main	53.25 (2.0965) $^{-0.022\ (0.00087)}_{-0.042\ (0.00165)}$
connecting rod	47.05 (1.8524) $^{-0.022\ (0.00087)}_{-0.042\ (0.00165)}$

Crankshaft assembly (AEG engine)

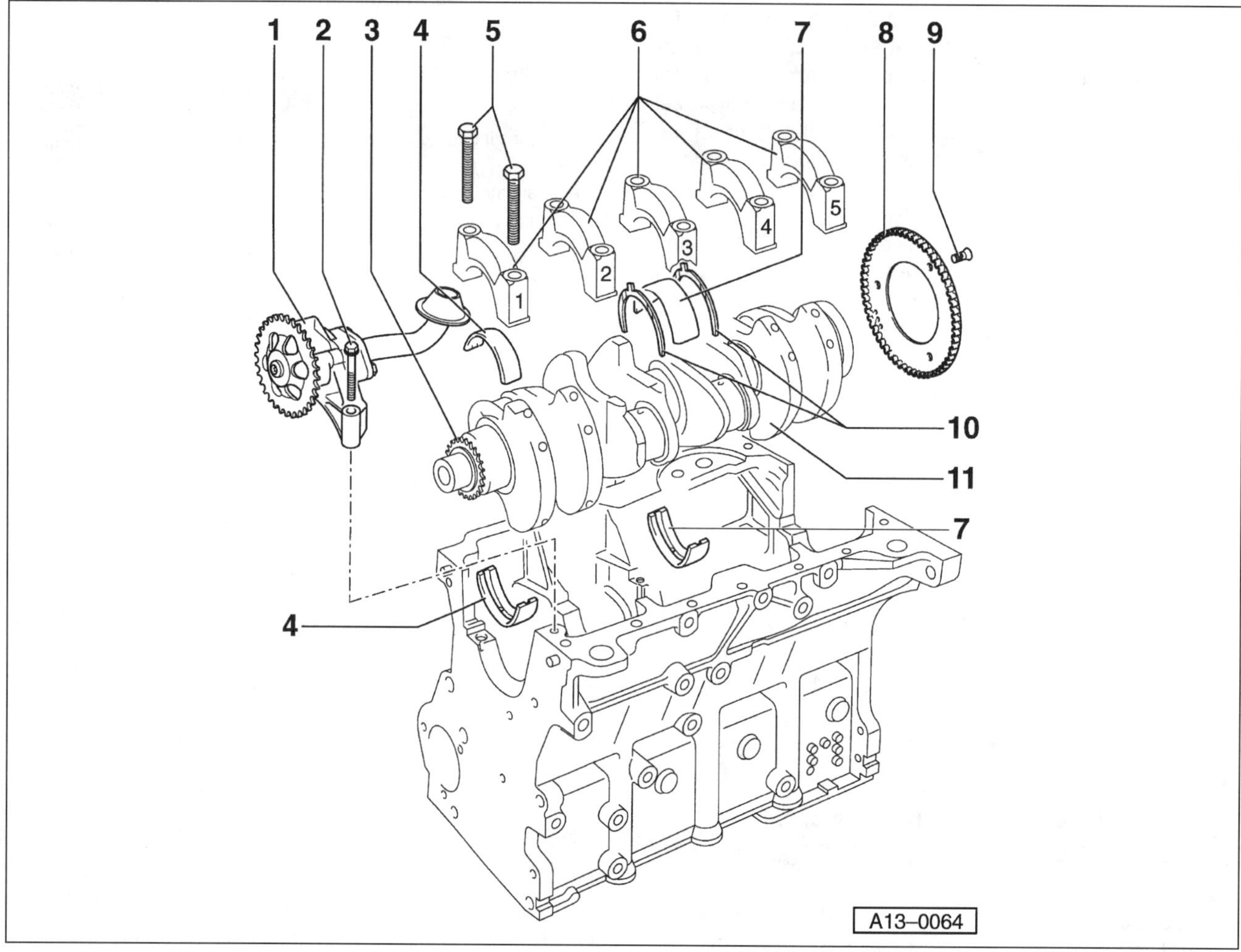

A13-0064

Fig. 17. Exploded view of crankshaft and related components of AEG engine.

1. **Oil pump**
2. **Bolt**
   - Tighten to 15 Nm (11 ft-lb)
3. **Chain sprocket**
   - For oil pump drive
4. **Bearing caps 1, 2, 4 and 5**
   - For bearing cap without oil groove
   - For cylinder block with oil groove
   - Do not interchange used bearing shells (mark)
5. **Bolts**
   - Tighten to 65 Nm (48 ft-lb) + ¼ turn (90°)
   - Always replace
   - Threaded along complete length
   - Tighten to 65 Nm (48 ft-lb) to measure radial clearance
6. **Bearing cap**
   - Bearing cap 1: pulley end
   - Bearing cap 3 with recesses for thrust washers
   - Bearing shell retaining lugs engine block/bearing cap must be on the same side
7. **Bearing shell 3**
   - For bearing cap without oil groove
   - For cylinder block with oil groove
   - Do not interchange used bearing shells (mark)
8. **Sensor wheel**
   - For engine speed sensor (G28)
   - Can only be installed in one position, holes are offset
9. **Bolt**
   - Tighten to 10 Nm (7 ft-lb) + ¼ turn (90°)
   - Always replace
10. **Thrust washer**
    - For bearing 3 bearing cap
    - Note installation position
11. **Crankshaft**
    - Check radial clearance with Plastigage
    - Do not rotate crankshaft when checking radial clearance

Crankshaft assembly (ALH engine)

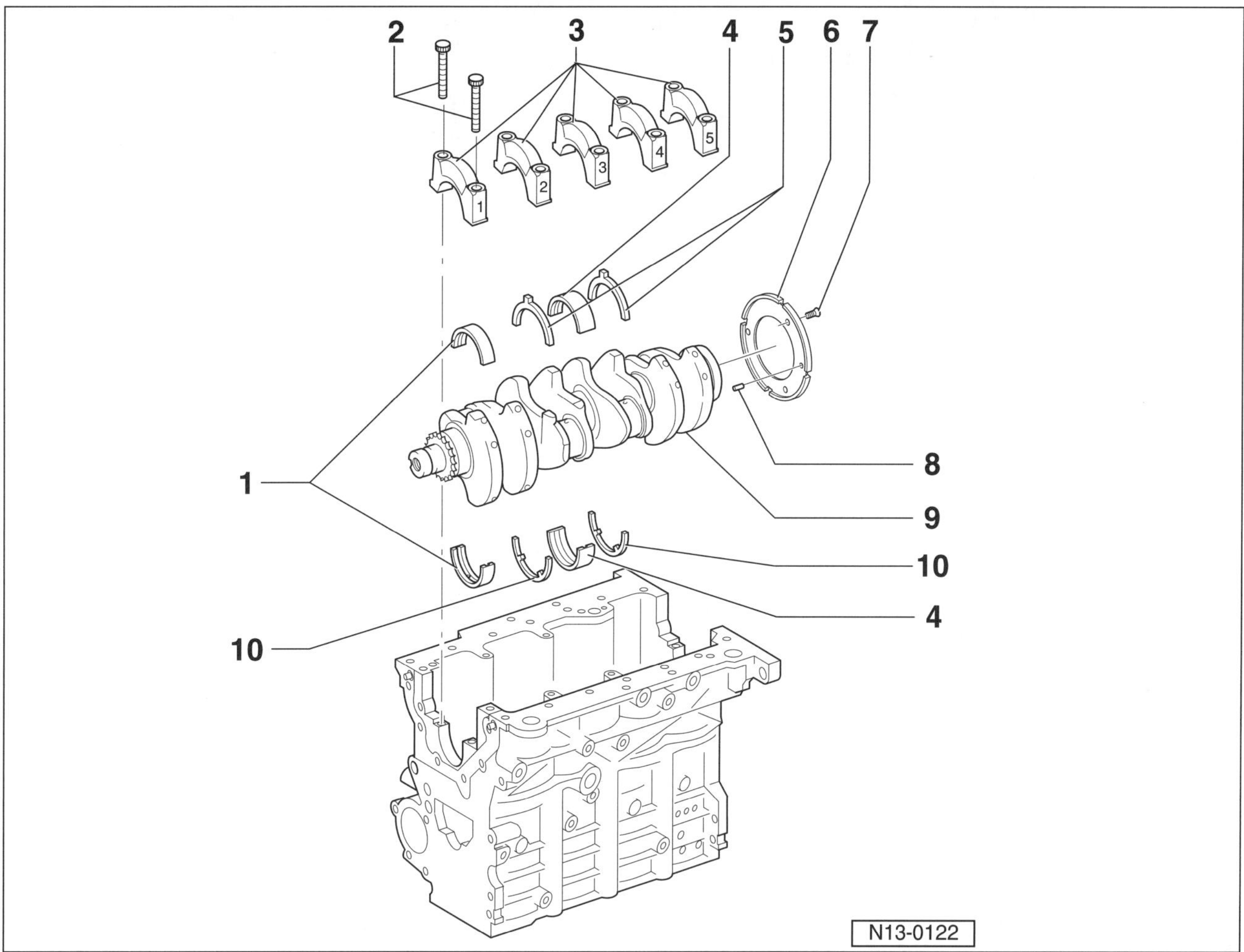

N13-0122

Fig. 18. Exploded view of crankshaft and related components on ALH engine.

1. **Bearing shells 1, 2, 4 and 5**
   - For bearing caps without oil groove
   - For engine block with oil groove
   - Do not interchange used bearing shells (mark)
2. **Bolt**
   - Tighten to 65 Nm (48 ft-lb) + ¼ turn (90°)
   - Always replace
   - Threaded along complete length
   - Tighten to 65 Nm (48 ft-lb) to measure radial clearance
3. **Bearing cap**
   - Bearing cap 1: pulley end
   - Bearing cap 3 with recesses for thrust washers
   - Bearing shell retaining lugs engine block/bearing cap must be on the same side
4. **Bearing shell 3**
   - Bearing cap without oil groove
   - For engine block with oil groove
5. **Thrust washer**
   - For bearing cap 3
   - Note installation position
6. **Sensor wheel**
   - For engine speed sensor
7. **Bolt**
   - Tighten to 10 Nm (7 ft-lb) + ¼ turn (90°)
   - Always replace
8. **Dowel pin**
   - For installation position, **see** Ⓐ
9. **Crankshaft**
   - Check radial clearance with Plastigage
   - Do not rotate crankshaft when checking radial clearance
10. **Thrust washer**
    - For engine block, bearing 3
    - Note installation position

A Dowel pin and sensor wheel (ALH engine)

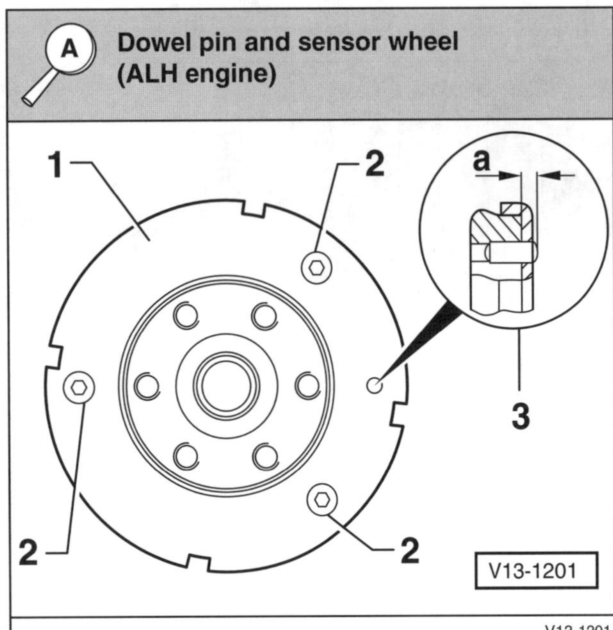

V13-1201

- **ALH engine only.**
- **Sensor wheel (1) mounted on crankshaft with screws (2).**
- **A single dowel pin (3) extends 2.5 – 3.0 mm (.098 – .118 in.) from the flange end, dimension (a).**

QUALITY REVIEW

When you have finished working under the hood and around other areas of the vehicle it is advisable to take a moment to quality check or review your work. This helps to ensure that the operation or repair has been completed properly with all affected systems functioning within normal parameters. This may include the following:

- Make sure that the radiator fan cycles properly and that the coolant level and concentration are correct.
- Ensure that all cable ties and hose clamps that were removed as part of the repair are replaced.
- Check and adjust all other applicable fluid levels.
- Make sure that there are no fluid leaks.
- Make sure that there are no air, vacuum or exhaust leaks.
- Make sure that all components involved in the repair are positioned correctly and function properly.
- Male sure all tools, shop cloths, fender covers, and protective tape are removed.
- Clean grease from painted surfaces and steering wheel.
- Unlock the anti-theft radio and reset the clock.

In addition to the above noted points, the ECM and TCM may need to be checked using the Volkswagen supplied VAG 1551 or 1552 scan tool as mentioned at the start of this repair.

15a Cylinder Head and Valvetrain (AEG Engine)

TABLES

GENERAL

This section covers cylinder head and valvetrain service and repair work for the AEG 4-cylinder, 2 valve per cylinder, gasoline engine. For information on short block engine rebuilding and internal engine specifications, see **13 Crankshaft/Cylinder Block**.

Most of the operations described in this repair group require special equipment and experience. If you lack the skills, tools, or a suitable workplace for servicing or repairing the cylinder head, we suggest that you leave these repairs to an authorized Volkswagen dealer or other qualified shop.

Engine Codes
- AEG . . . . . 2.0L 4-cylinder gasoline
- ALH . . . . . 1.9L 4-cylinder turbo diesel

DIAGNOSTIC TESTING

The tests that follow can be used to help isolate engine problems, to better understand a problem before starting expensive and extensive repairs, or to just periodically check engine condition.

Compression Test

A compression test will tell a lot about the overall condition of the engine without the need for taking it apart. Testing is relatively simple and straightforward.

1. Remove two plastic caps and retaining nuts on upper sound absorber panel. Loosen the rear retaining nut slightly. Remove dipstick and lift cover up slightly and pull forward. See Fig. 1.

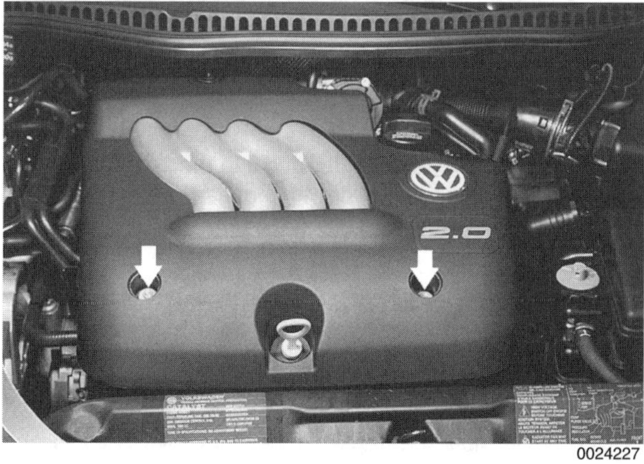

Fig. 1. Remove dipstick and nuts (**arrows**) to remove engine cover.

2. Replace dipstick and warm-up the engine until it is a minimum of 30°C (86°F).

3. Disconnect spark plug wires from the spark plugs by gently pulling on the boot, do not pull on the wire. Label all wires to avoid confusion during reinstallation.

4. Use compressed air to clear the area around the spark plugs. Remove all spark plugs and lay aside in proper order.

5. Disable ignition system by unplugging 4-pin harness connector from ignition coil power output stage. See Fig. 2.

Fig. 2. Disconnect 4-pin harness connector (**arrow**) for ignition coil power output stage. Secondary air pump removed for clarity.

> ***CAUTION —***
> *Failure to disable the ignition system during testing can result in damage to the Motronic ECM or the ignition power output stage due to the high voltage developed in the ignition coil.*

6. Remove fuse 28 for the fuel pump.

7. Fit the compression tester into the spark plug hole.

8. Have a helper:
   - depress clutch pedal fully
   - put the transmission in neutral or park
   - depress the accelerator pedal to the floor
   - crank the engine over with the starter motor

> ***NOTE —***
> *Cranking the engine with the ignition system disabled and components disconnected may cause Diagnostic trouble codes (DTCs) to be stored in engine management system memory.*

9. Engine should be cranked a minimum of 4 to 5 revolutions.

10. Record readings, release pressure in the gauge and repeat procedure for each cylinder.

11. Compare readings to specification.

Specification
- Compression pressures (AEG engine)
  new . . . . 10 to 13 bar (147 - 191 psi)
  wear limit. . . . . .7.5 bar (110 psi)
  maximum difference
  between cylinders . . . . 3 bar (44 psi)

12. When all cylinders have been checked, reinstall spark plugs and wires, connect harness connector for ignition coil power output stage and install the upper engine cover.

Tightening torque
- Spark plug to cylinder head . . . . 30 Nm (22 ft-lb)

Cylinder Leakdown Test

The most conclusive diagnosis of low compression symptoms requires a cylinder leak-down test. Using a special tester and a supply of compressed air, each cylinder is pressurized. The rate at which the air leaks out of the cylinder, as well as the sound and location of the escaping air can more accurately pinpoint the magnitude and source of the leakage. Any engine compression diagnosis that will require major disassembly should first be confirmed by a cylinder leak-down test. Because this test requires special equipment and experience, it may be desirable to have it performed by a Volkswagen dealer or other qualified repair shop.

CYLINDER HEAD SERVICE

Many cylinder head repairs can be accomplished without removing the cylinder head from the engine. The cylinder head cover (valve cover) gasket, the camshaft, the camshaft oil seal, the valve guide oil seals, the valve springs, and the camshaft followers are all accessible with the cylinder head installed. This heading describes those repairs that can be done with the cylinder head installed.

Fig. 3 shows an exploded view of the internal cylinder head components and Fig. 4 shows the external cylinder head components.

Internal cylinder head assembly

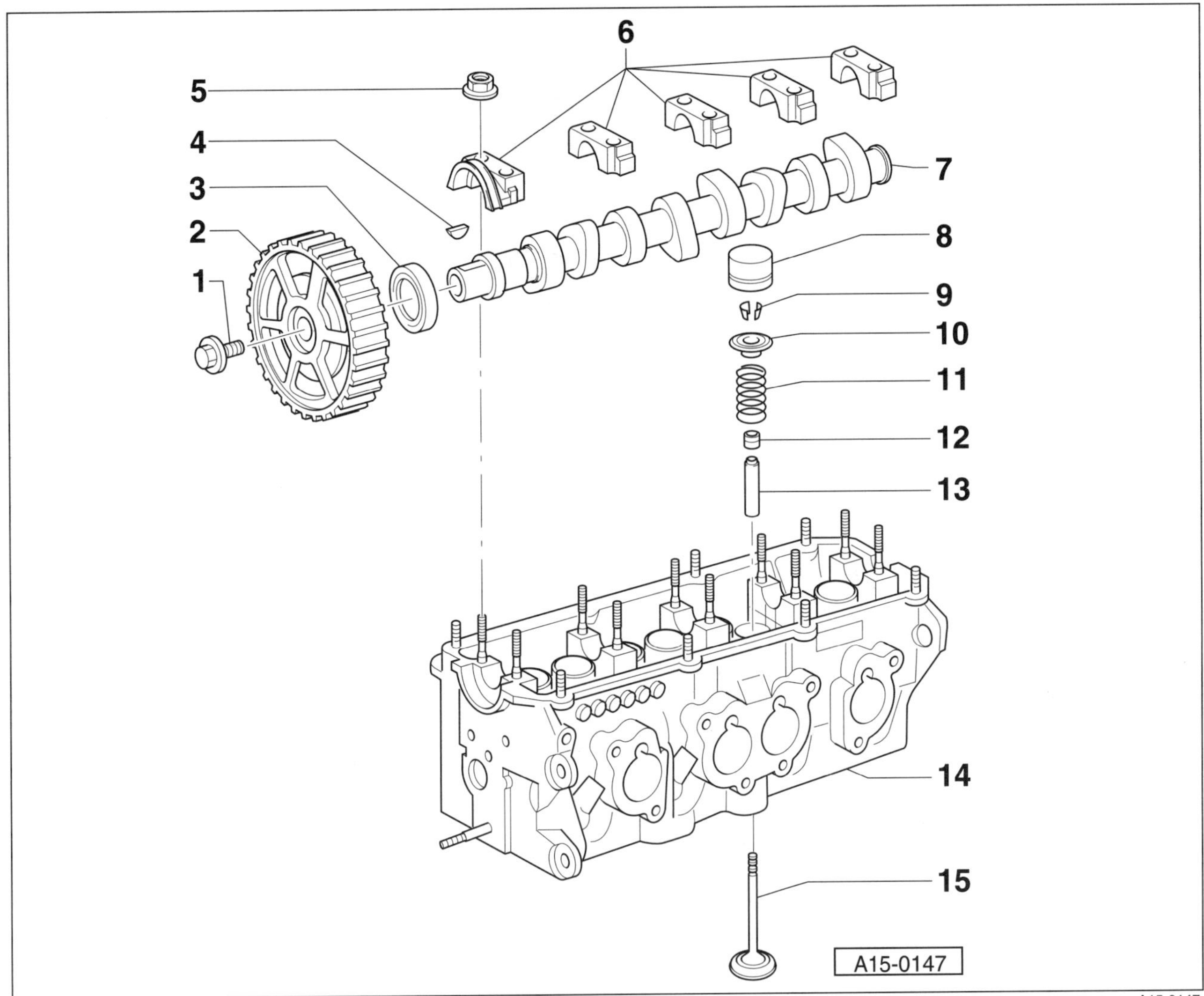

A15-0147

Fig. 3. Exploded view of internal cylinder head components.

1. **Camshaft sprocket bolt**
   - Tighten to 100 Nm (74 ft-lb)
   - Use 3036 counterholder to loosen and tighten
2. **Camshaft sprocket**
3. **Oil seal**
4. **Woodruff key**
   - Ensure tight fit
5. **Bearing cap nut**
   - Tighten to 20 Nm (15 ft-lb)
6. **Bearing cap**
   - Lightly coat bearing cap 1 cylinder head mating surface with sealant
7. **Camshaft**
   - Radial clearance, checking with plastigage
     Wear limit: 0.1 mm (.004 in.)
   - Run-out: max. 0.01mm (.0004 in.)
8. **Hydraulic lifter**
   - Do not interchange
   - Equipped with hydraulic clearance compensation
   - Store with cam contact surface facing downwards
   - Oil contact surfaces
9. **Keepers**
10. **Valve spring retainer, upper**
11. **Valve spring**
12. **Valve stem seal**
13. **Valve guide**
    - Service version with collar
14. **Cylinder head**
15. **Intake and exhaust valves**
    - Do not rework! Only lapping is permitted

External cylinder head assembly

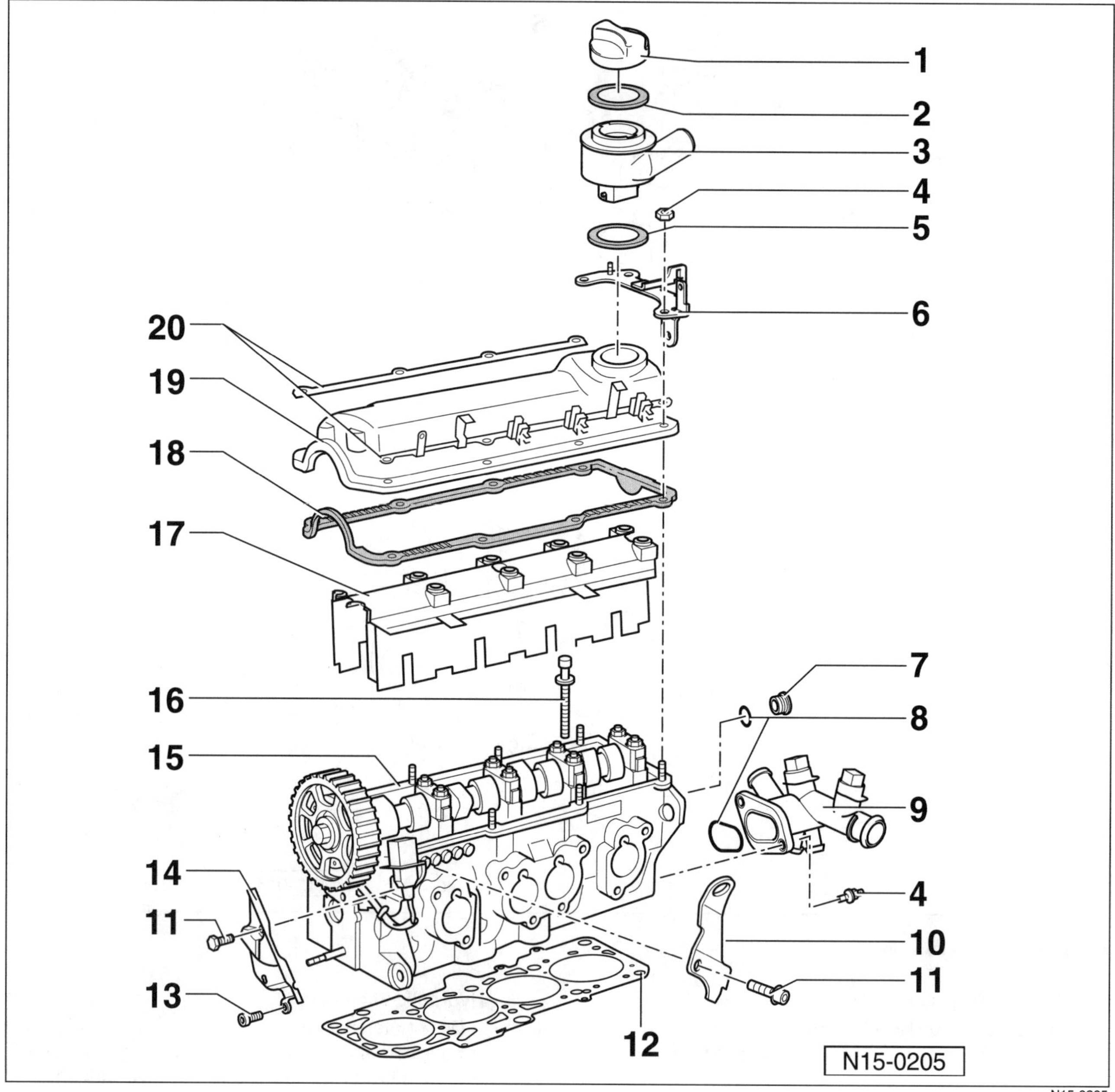

N15-0205

Fig. 4. Exploded view of external cylinder head components.

1. **Cap**
2. **Gasket**
3. **Vent housing**
   - Turn clockwise to remove
4. **Nut**
   - Tighten to 10 Nm (7 ft-lb)
5. **Gasket**
   - Replace if damaged
6. **Bracket**
7. **Sealing plug**
   - Tighten to 15 Nm (11 ft-lb)
   - Always replace
8. **Oil seal**
   - Always replace
9. **Coolant connection flange**
10. **Lifting eye**

11. Bolt
- Tighten to 20 Nm (15 ft-lb)

12. Cylinder head gasket
- Always replace
- Replace engine coolant if replacing gasket

13. Bolt
- Tighten to 15 Nm (11 ft-lb)

14. Toothed belt guard, rear

15. Cylinder head
- Replace engine coolant if removing head

16. Cylinder head bolt
- Always replace

17. Oil deflector

18. Valve cover gasket
- Replace if damaged
- Before installing gasket coat bearing cap 1 cylinder head mating surface with sealant

19. Valve cover

20. Reinforcing strip

Cylinder head (valve) cover, removing and installing

1. Remove upper sound absorber panel and disconnect intake boot from throttle housing.

2. Disconnect accelerator cable from throttle body.

3. Disconnect all hoses and electrical connectors from upper intake manifold.

4. Remove bolts from warm air deflector plate on the back side of upper intake manifold. See Fig. 5.

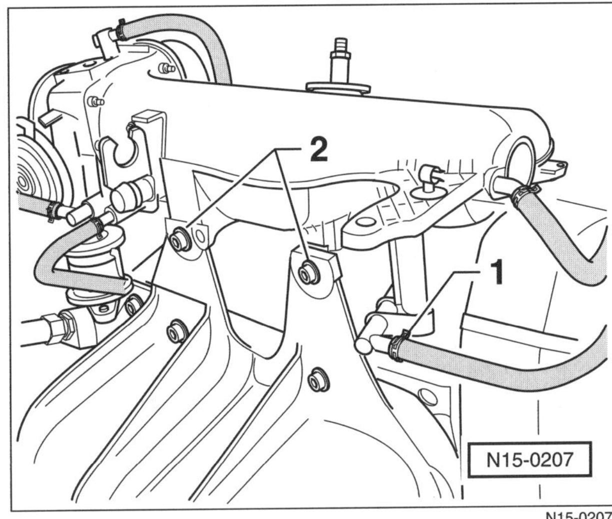

N15-0207

Fig. 5. Rear view of intake manifold showing vent line (**1**) and warm air deflector bolts (**2**).

5. Remove upper intake manifold bolts. Carefully separate upper manifold from lower manifold. Cover open intake runner openings in lower manifold with clean shop rags. See Fig. 6.

0024228

Fig. 6. Remove bolts (**arrows**) that hold upper manifold to lower manifold

6. Disconnect crankcase breather valve from cylinder head cover.

7. Remove nuts from cylinder head cover.

8. Unclip and remove upper camshaft drive belt cover. Remove small protection cover from back of camshaft drive sprocket.

9. Remove both reinforcing strips from cylinder head cover.

10. Lift off cylinder head cover and gasket.

11. Installation is reverse of removal noting the following additional points:
    - Be sure to remove the shop rags from the lower intake manifold runner openings.
    - Use new gaskets where appropriate.
    - Apply a small amount of sealer to the area where the cylinder head cover gasket and the number one camshaft bearing cap meet.

Tightening Torques
- Cylinder head cover to cylinder head (M6) . . . . 10 Nm (89 in-lb)
- Upper intake manifold to lower manifold (M8) . . . . 20 Nm (15 ft-lb)
- Warm air deflector to upper intake manifold (M8) . . . . 25 Nm (18 ft-lb)

Camshaft oil seal, replacing

1. Remove upper engine cover and unclip and remove toothed belt guard, upper section. See **Toothed belt – Camshaft drive**, given later.

2. Set engine to TDC for cylinder 1 by turning crankshaft until timing mark on camshaft sprocket aligns with mark on toothed belt upper rear guard. See Fig. 7.

3. Release tensioning roller and slide toothed belt off of camshaft sprocket.

4. Turn crankshaft back off of TDC slightly.

5. Using a suitable spanner, remove camshaft sprocket bolt. See Fig. 8.

6. Remove camshaft drive sprocket and woodruff key.

7. Remove seal using a suitable seal extractor. See Fig. 9.

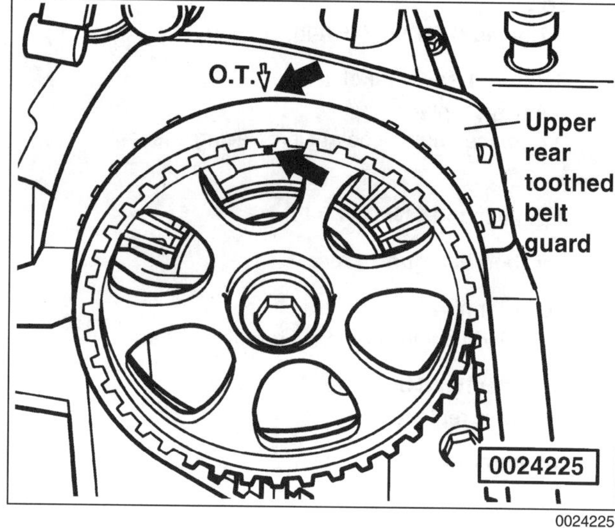

0024225

Fig. 7. Line up camshaft timing marks (**arrows**) as shown.

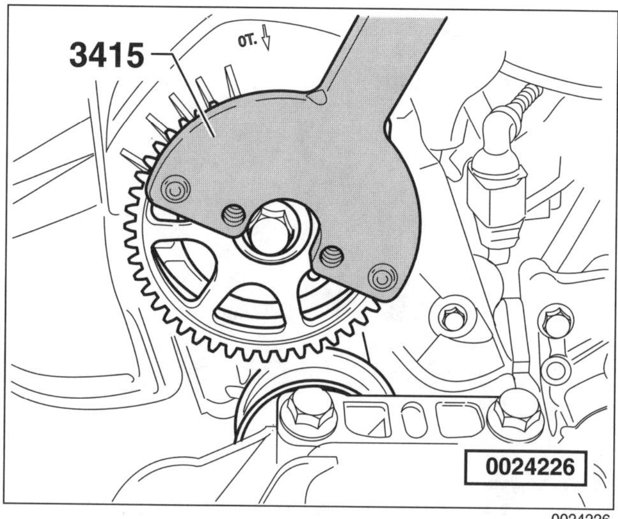

0024226

Fig. 8. Spanner or counterholder tool shown holding camshaft sprocket to facilitate removal of securing bolt.

8. Install the new oil seal noting the following points:
    - Lubricate new seal with clean engine oil.
    - Install with closed end facing out.
    - Use a suitable guide sleeve and installation tool.
    - Press seal into the bottom of recess.

9. Install woodruff key and camshaft sprocket, hold sprocket with a spanner and torque bolt.

Tightening torque
- Camshaft sprocket to camshaft . . . . 100 Nm (74 ft-lb)

10. Turn crankshaft back to TDC.

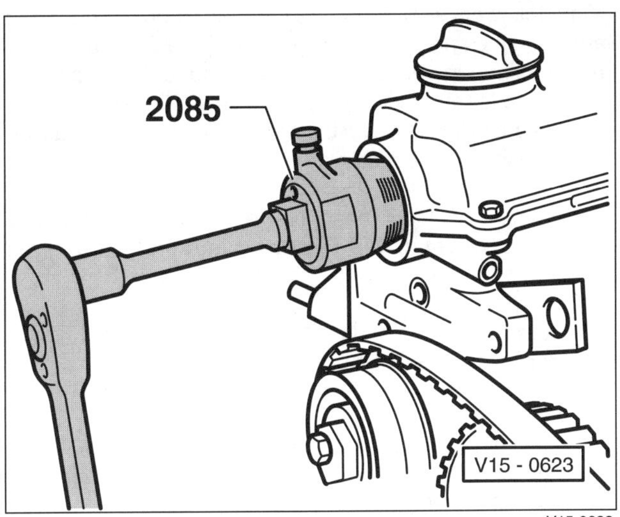

Fig. 9. Volkswagen seal removal tool being used to remove camshaft seal.

11. Install toothed belt and adjust tension, see **Toothed Belt–Camshaft Drive**, given later.

12. Install upper camshaft drive belt cover, upper engine cover and any other removed components.

13. Be sure to quality check your work, see **Quality Review** at the end of this repair group.

Camshaft, removing and installing

The camshaft can be removed and installed with the cylinder head installed. Removing the camshaft allows access to the hydraulic cam followers, the valve springs and the valve stem oil seals.

1. Remove upper engine cover and unclip and remove upper camshaft drive belt cover.

2. Turn engine by hand until timing mark on camshaft sprocket aligns with mark on toothed belt upper rear guard. See Fig. 7.

3. Release tensioning roller and slide toothed belt off of camshaft sprocket.

4. Turn crankshaft back off of TDC slightly.

   NOTE —
   Turning the crankshaft away from TDC slightly minimizes the chances of contact between pistons and valves upon re-assembly.

5. Using a suitable spanner, remove the camshaft sprocket bolt. See Fig. 8.

6. Remove camshaft drive sprocket and woodruff key.

7. Remove cylinder head (valve) cover and gasket as described previously.

8. Lift off plastic oil deflector to expose camshaft.

9. Loosen and remove the bearing caps from positions 5, 1 and 3 in that order. Position 1 is closest to the belt end of the camshaft.

   NOTE —
   Mark each bearing cap before removing. Each cap is machined to each journal and must be reinstalled to that exact location to prevent damage.

10. Loosen nuts on bearing cap 2 slightly and then loosen nuts on bearing cap 4 slightly. Loosen nuts alternately and evenly a little at a time on each of the two bearing caps. Remove nuts (and washers, if equipped), and remove bearing caps.

11. Lift out camshaft and lay aside.

    NOTE —
    Once removed, the camshaft should be checked for wear and other visible damage as described later under **Cylinder Head Components**.

12. Oil bearing surfaces of cylinder head and camshaft and install camshaft into cylinder head with lobes for cylinder number 1 pointing up.

13. Install bearing caps 2 and 4. Install nuts (and washers, if camshaft is drawn down fully and evenly into bearing saddles. Torque to specification.

Tightening torque
- Camshaft bearing cap to cylinder head . . . . 20 Nm (15 ft-lb)

CAUTION —
Be sure to install bearing caps correctly. The caps are bored off-center and only fit properly one way. Caps are matched to the cylinder head by the machining process and are not available separately. Broken caps will require the replacement of the cylinder head. See Fig. 10.

14. Install bearing cap number 1 with a small amount of sealer on the cylinder head mating surface. Install all remaining bearing caps and torque to specification.

15. Install the plastic oil deflector.

16. Install the camshaft drive sprocket and woodruff key using a suitable spanner as shown earlier. See Fig. 8.

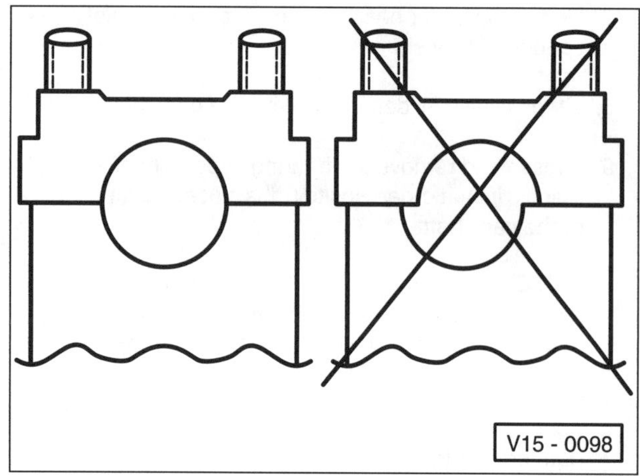

V15-0098

Fig. 10. Bearing caps are bored off-center. If necessary, test install caps without camshaft to confirm installation direction.

NOTE —

Ensure that camshaft lobes for cylinder #1 are still pointing up.

Tightening torque

- Camshaft sprocket to camshaft . . . . 100 Nm (74 ft-lb)

---

17. Install cylinder head (valve) cover and rear upper toothed belt guard.

18. Install toothed camshaft drive belt and adjust tension, see **Toothed Belt - Camshaft Drive** given later.

19. Install upper camshaft drive belt cover, upper engine cover and any other removed components.

20. Be sure to quality check your work, see **Quality Review** at the end of this repair group.

Hydraulic cam followers, checking

The 2.0 liter AEG engine installed in the New Beetle is equipped with hydraulic cam followers which are also known as lifters.The cam followers are pumped up by engine oil pressure, expanding as necessary to fill the gap between the valve stem and the camshaft lobe. This occurs continuously and automatically to keep the valve in proper adjustment at all times.

Some valve noise at start-up and during the warm-up period is normal at times due to hydraulic cam followers that have bled down while the engine was not running. Before checking noisy cam followers, check that the engine oil is new and fresh, of the correct weight, and that the level is correct. Allow 2 minutes with a warm engine running at a fast idle for the lubrication system to properly pump up the cam followers.

Cam followers should only be checked when the engine is warm. Run the engine until the radiator fan has switched on at least one time. Increase the engine speed to 2,500 rpm and hold it there for approximately 2 minutes. If the hydraulic cam followers are still noisy, shut the engine off and proceed as follows while the engine is still warm.

1. Remove cylinder head (valve) cover. See **Cylinder head (valve) cover, removing and installing**, given earlier.

2. Turn engine by hand until both camshaft lobes of cylinder #1 are pointing approximately up.

NOTE —

Hydraulic cam follower clearance can be checked on any cam follower (lifter) that is not being depressed by the camshaft lobe.

3. Check clearance between cam follower and cam lobe on cylinder #1 by lightly depressing cam follower with a wooden or plastic wedge and inserting a feeler gauge into the gap. See Fig. 11. If clearance exceeds specified limit, the lifter is faulty and should be replaced.

Specification

- Hydraulic cam follower maximum clearance (AEG engine) . . . . 0.2 mm (0.008 in.)

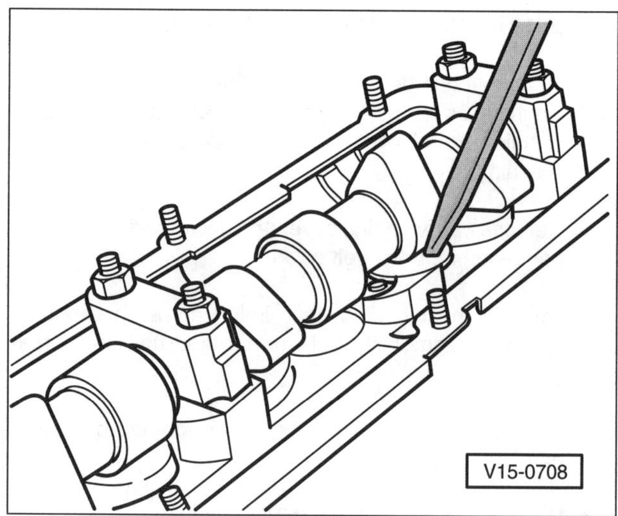

V15-0708

Fig. 11. Hydraulic cam follower shown being pushed down lightly with a plastic wedge.

4. Turn engine by hand and repeat procedure until all cam followers have been checked.

5. Replace a faulty cam follower by removing camshaft as previously described and pulling the follower from the cylinder head. Faulty hydraulic cam followers can be replaced individually but only as a complete assembly.

CAUTION—
After installing new cam followers, the engine should not be started for at least 30 minutes. New cam followers are usually at full extended height and must be allowed to bleed down to their proper height once installed. Failure to do so may cause the valves to strike the pistons resulting in serious damage.

NOTE—
Store removed hydraulic cam followers in order on a clean surface with the camshaft contact surface facing down to minimize bleed down. Cover with a clean lint-free shop cloth.

Valve stem oil seals, replacing

The sign of faulty valve stem seals is excessive oil consumption and oil smoke from the exhaust. This is usually most noticeable during periods of high manifold vacuum such as deceleration. If compression and leak-down testing confirm the integrity of the piston rings, but the engine consumes oil, it is likely that faulty valve stem seals are present. It should also be noted that worn valve stem seals could be due to worn valve guides and that the worn valve guides are the major cause of the oil consumption. See **Cylinder Head Components** for more information on checking valve guides.

Replacing the valve stem oil seals requires removal of the camshaft, cam followers, and the valve springs. This can be done with the cylinder head installed or removed. In either case, several Volkswagen special tools are required to compress the valve springs and remove and install the seals.

Working with the cylinder head installed:

1. Remove cylinder head cover, camshaft, and hydraulic cam followers as described earlier.

2. Remove spark plugs and apply a continuous supply of compressed air with a minimum of 6 bar (87 psi) into the first spark plug hole with an adapter. This must be done to hold the valves in place while the springs are removed. Continue with step 5.

CAUTION—
Compressed air supply must be able to maintain at least 6 bar (87 psi) during this repair. If air supply is interrupted while valve spring is removed, valve will fall into the cylinder and may require cylinder head removal to retrieve.

Working with the cylinder head removed:

3. Secure cylinder head to the workbench. Use care to avoid damage to the head gasket surfaces.

4. Remove camshaft and hydraulic cam followers as described earlier. Continue with step 5.

Working with cylinder head removed or installed:

5. Install appropriate valve spring compressor tools. See Fig. 12. Compress the spring for the first cylinder and remove the spring retainer, both keepers, and the valve spring. If spring will not compress, lightly tap the tool to release the stuck keepers. Use a small magnet to retrieve the keepers.

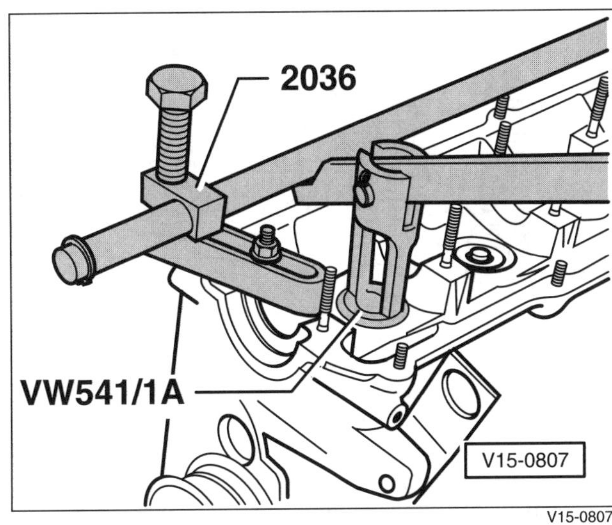

V15-0807

Fig. 12. Valve spring compressor tools being used to compress valve spring for removal of keepers. Numbers identify Volkswagen special tools.

6. Remove valve stem seals with special slide hammer tool. See Fig. 13.

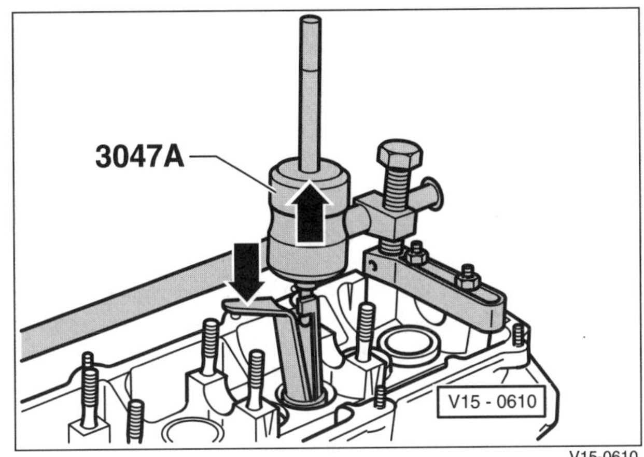

V15-0610

Fig. 13. Valve stem seal removal tool shown in position to remove valve stem seal. Push down on tool (**left arrow**) while sliding hammer up (**right arrow**)

7. Begin installation of new seal by temporarily fitting a protective plastic fitting sleeve over the valve stem. This sleeve is usually included with the new seal set and will prevent damage to the seal due to the sharp edges of the keeper grooves. Lubricate new seal with clean engine oil and fit it to the installation tool. See Fig. 14.

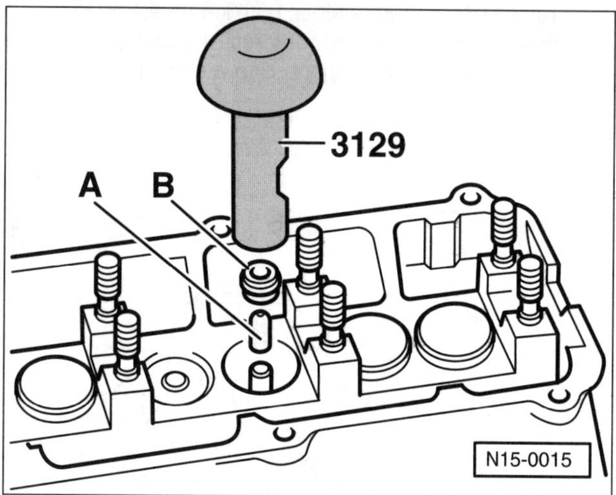

N15-0015

Fig. 14. Plastic fitting sleeve (**A**), shown with valve stem seal (**B**) and plastic installation tool 3129 available from Volkswagen.

8. Push the tool (with seal) down over the valve stem until the seal is fully seated on the guide. Remove the tool and the protective fitting sleeve.

9. Reinstall the valve spring, retainer and keepers.

10. Repeat for the second valve on the cylinder.

11. When both valve seals have been replaced on the first cylinder, transfer the compressed air adapter (if working with cylinder head installed) to the next cylinder and repeat the process until all valve seals have been replaced.

12. Remaining installation is the reverse of removal.

> ***CAUTION —***
> *To prevent cylinder head or camshaft damage, be sure to follow the camshaft installation procedure when tightening the camshaft bearing caps. See* **Camshaft, removing and installing**.

Tightening torque

- Spark plug to cylinder head . . . . 30 Nm (22 ft-lb)

13. Be sure to quality check your work, see **Quality Review** at the end of this repair group.

TOOTHED BELT - CAMSHAFT DRIVE

The camshaft drive belt and its related parts are shown in Fig. 15. Although no maintenance interval is specified, the publisher recommends periodic inspection of the belt, and replacement at 60,000 miles or every 4 years. This will help prevent damage to the engine due to belt stretch and the long term effects of heat. The camshaft drive belt is also known as a toothed belt and both terms are used interchangeably.

The following component list applies to Fig. 15

1. **Bolt**
   - Tighten to 45 Nm (33 ft-lb)
2. **Engine support**
3. **Bolt**
   - Tighten to 25 Nm (18 ft-lb)
4. **Bracket**
5. **Toothed belt guard, upper section**
6. **Toothed belt guard, center section**
7. **Nut**
   - Tighten to 20 Nm (15 ft-lb)
8. **Washer**
9. **Tensioner**
   - Semi-automatic toothed belt tensioning roller
10. **Toothed belt**
    - Mark engine direction of rotation before removing
    - Check for wear
    - Do not kink
11. **Toothed belt guard, rear**
12. **O-ring**
    - Always replace
13. **Coolant pump**
14. **Bolt**
    - Tighten to 15 Nm (11 ft-lb)

Drive belts, assembly

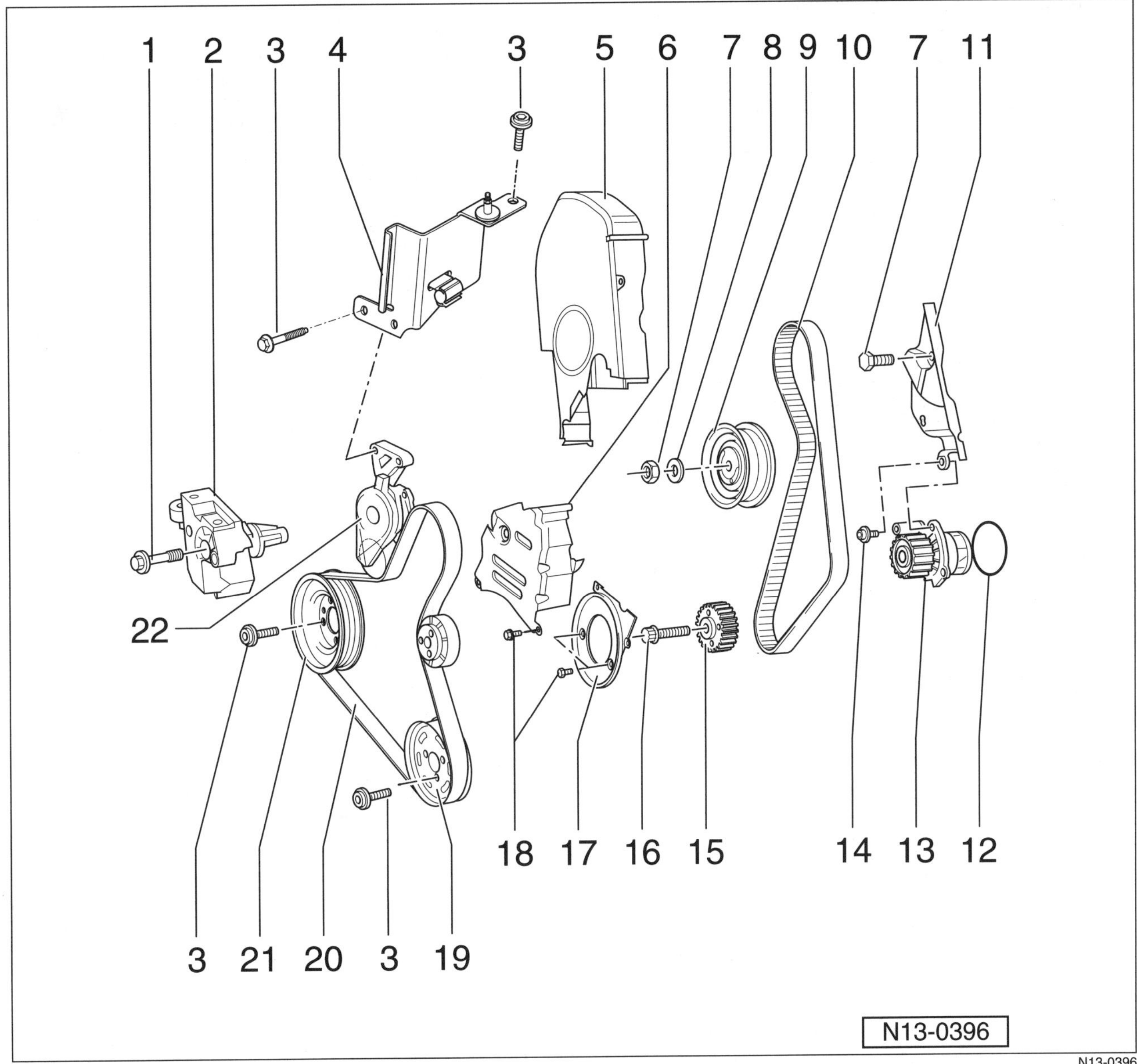

Fig. 15. Exploded view of the ribbed V-belt, the toothed belt and their related components.

15. Toothed belt sprocket (crankshaft)

16. Bolt
- Tighten to 90 Nm (66 ft-lb) + ¼ turn (90°)
- Always replace
- Threads and shoulder must be free of grease

17. Toothed belt guard, lower section

18. Bolt
- Tighten to 10 Nm (7 ft-lb)

19. Pulley
- For power steering pump

20. Ribbed belt
- Mark direction of rotation before removing

21. Belt pulley/vibration damper
- Can only be installed in one position, holes are offset
- Note position when installing toothed belt

22. Ribbed belt, tensioning device
- Loosen ribbed belt by turning with open-ended wrench

Toothed belt for camshaft drive, removing

1. Remove the lower sound absorber panel (belly pan).
2. Remove the upper engine cover.
3. Remove the ribbed V-belt and tensioner.
4. Turn the engine to top dead center, TDC, for cylinder number 1. See Fig. 16.

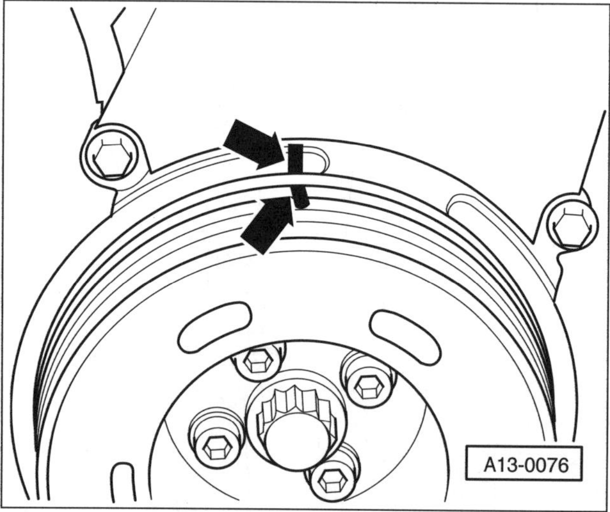

A13-0076

Fig. 16. Mark on belt pulley (**lower arrow**) shown aligned with mark on toothed belt guard, center section (**upper arrow**).

5. Remove the upper toothed belt cover.
6. Support the engine with a suitable fixture that is designed to support the weight of the engine and transmission without damaging the body. See Fig. 17.

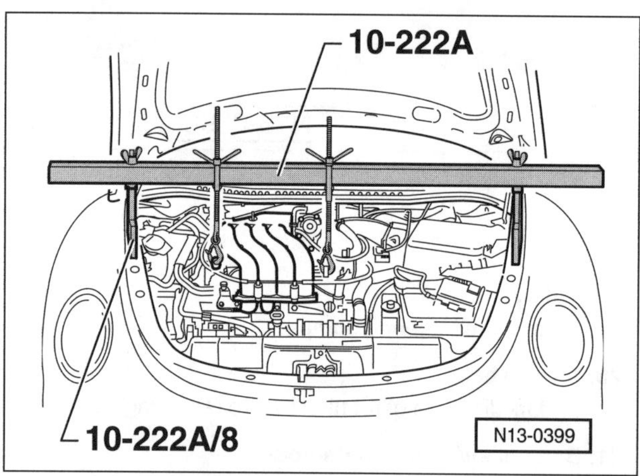

N13-0399

Fig. 17. Volkswagen supplied engine support tools shown attached to the engine.

7. Lift the supporting device slightly, so that the weight of the engine and transmission is on the supporting device.
8. Remove right side engine mount from body and carrier on engine. See Fig. 18.

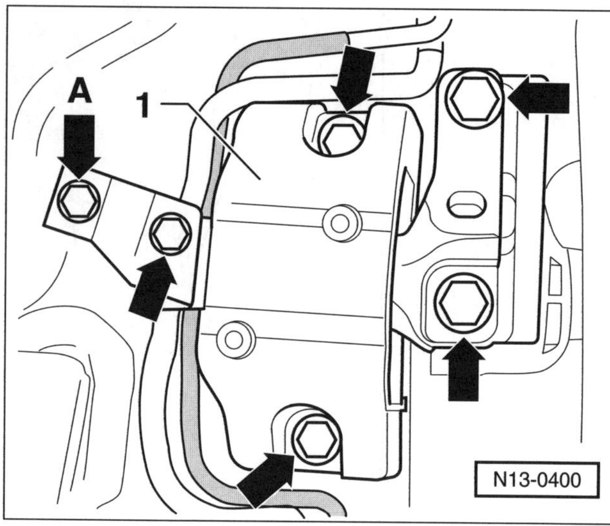

N13-0400

Fig. 18. Right side engine mount (**1**) as viewed from above. Remove the 5 bolts (**arrows**), and loosen body bolt (**arrow A**).

9. Remove the 4 bolts holding the belt pulley to the toothed belt sprocket and remove the belt pulley.
10. Remove the center and lower sections of the toothed belt guard.
11. Remove the right side engine mount bracket from the block. There will not be sufficient room to withdraw the bolts, so the mount and the bolts are all removed at the same time. See Fig. 19.

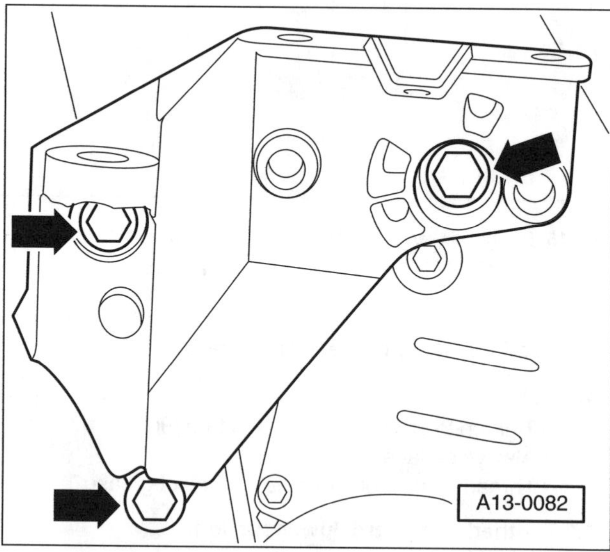

A13-0082

Fig. 19. Completely loosen the 3 long bolts (**arrows**) that secure right side engine mount bracket to cylinder block.

12. Mark running direction of the belt.

13. Loosen the securing nut on the tensioner to release it and remove the belt.

Toothed belt for camshaft drive, installing

1. Align the mark on the camshaft with the mark on the toothed belt guard. This brings the camshaft to TDC for cylinder number 1. See Fig. 20.

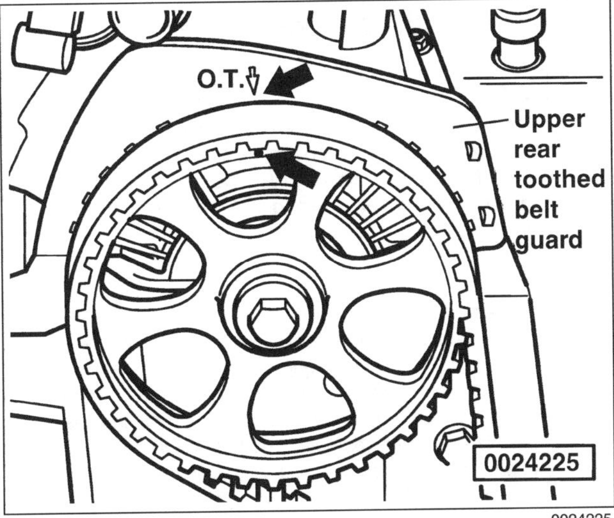

0024225

Fig. 20. Line up camshaft timing marks (**arrows**) as shown.

> ***CAUTION —***
>
> *• Due to engine design, care must be used when turning the camshaft with the toothed belt removed. If valves are allowed to open with the piston at TDC, serious internal damage will result.*
>
> *• Belt tension must not be adjusted on a hot engine. Allow to cool sufficiently before proceeding. Engine temperature must be no hotter than warm to the touch.*

2. Install toothed belt onto the crankshaft drive sprocket, coolant pump and camshaft drive sprocket.

> ***NOTE —***
>
> *If re-using an old belt, be sure to note running direction marks placed on it before removal.*

3. Install bolts into the right side engine mount bracket and install to the cylinder block. See Fig. 19 given earlier.

Tightening torques

• Right side engine mount bracket to cylinder block (M10) . . . . 45 Nm (33 ft-lb)

---

4. Install the center and lower sections of the toothed belt guard.

5. Install the vibration dampener/ribbed belt pulley to the toothed belt drive sprocket.

Tightening torques

• Vibration dampener/ribbed belt pulley to toothed belt drive sprocket (M8). . . . . 25 Nm (18 ft-lb)

---

6. Ensure that crankshaft is at TDC for cylinder 1 by aligning mark on belt pulley with the mark on the toothed belt guard, center section. See Fig. 16.

7. Ensure that camshaft is still at TDC for cylinder number 1.

8. Install right side engine mount using new stretch bolts. See Fig. 21.

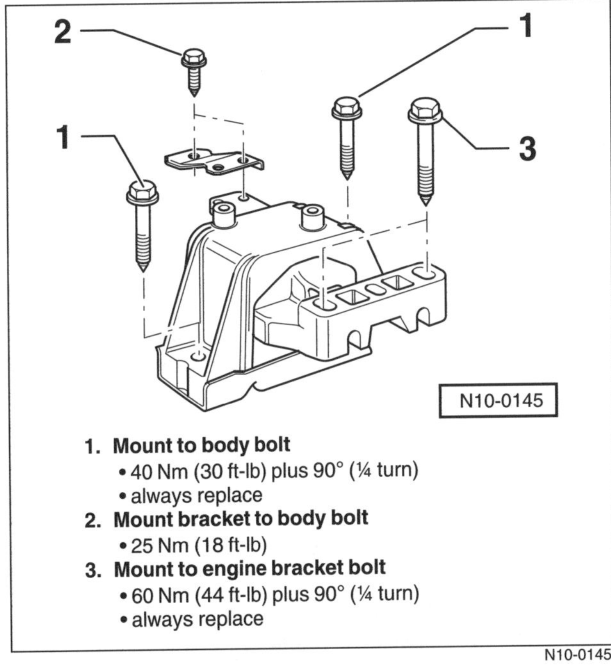

2
1
1
3
N10-0145
1. Mount to body bolt
• 40 Nm (30 ft-lb) plus 90° (¼ turn)
• always replace
2. Mount bracket to body bolt
• 25 Nm (18 ft-lb)
3. Mount to engine bracket bolt
• 60 Nm (44 ft-lb) plus 90° (¼ turn)
• always replace

N10-0145

Fig. 21. Right side engine mount.

9. Remove engine support fixture.

10. Install the toothed belt onto the tensioner and check for correct placement of belt on all sprockets. Securing nut should be just tight enough to allow movement of the center section.

11. Ensure that camshaft and crankshaft are still at TDC.

12. Tension the toothed belt by turning the center section eccentric of the tensioner with a 2 pin spanner wrench until the notch and the indictor pointer line up. When marks line up, tighten the securing nut. See Fig. 22.

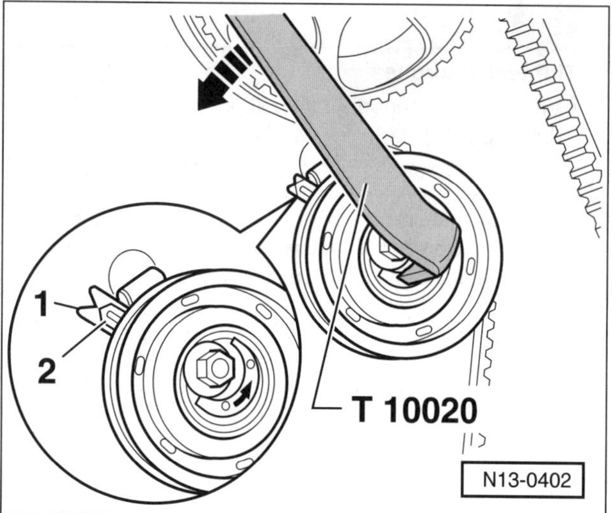

N13-0402

Fig. 22. Move spanner (VW special tool T10020 shown) in direction of **arrow** to align notch (**1**) with pointer (**2**).

Tightening torques

- Toothed belt tensioner (M8) . . . . 20 Nm (15 ft-lb)

13. Ensure that marks on camshaft sprocket and dampener/pulley still align with their respective TDC marks. If they do not align, repeat until they do.

NOTE —

Some movement of the sprockets and their marks is to be expected as belt tension is adjusted. Keep in mind that the smallest possible increment of adjustment is one whole tooth of the belt or sprocket.

14. With all marks in proper alignment, rotate the crankshaft two revolutions in the running direction and recheck the belt tension marks on the tensioner.

15. Install toothed belt guard, upper section.

16. Install ribbed belt tensioner and belt.

Tightening torque

- Ribbed belt tensioner to bracket (M8) 25 Nm (18 ft-lb)

17. Install the lower sound absorber panel (belly pan) and the upper engine cover.

18. Install any remaining parts and quality check your work, see **Quality Review** at the end of this repair group.

CYLINDER HEAD, REMOVING AND INSTALLING

The cylinder head can be removed and installed with the engine in the vehicle. Fig. 2, given earlier, shows a view of the AEG cylinder head and related components. Note that the cylinder head bolts are stretch type fasteners and should never be reused. In addition, whenever the cylinder head or the cylinder head gasket is replaced, the coolant must also be replaced, see **19 Engine–Cooling System**.

Cylinder head, removing

WARNING —

Do not start work on a hot engine. Allow to cool sufficiently before proceeding. Engine temperature must be no hotter than warm to the touch. Cylinder head warpage can result due to uneven cooling rates.

NOTE —

- *Disconnecting the battery cables will erase fault codes and basic settings in the engine management and automatic transmission control unit memories. Some driveability problems may be noticeable until the system re-adapts to operating conditions. OBD II readiness codes, which may be required for emissions testing, may also be erased. See* ***24 Fuel Injection – Motronic (AEG engine)*** *for additional information. In some instances proper diagnosis will require the use of a scan tool such as the Volkswagen supplied VAG 1551 or 1552. Use and operation of this tool is outside the scope of this repair manual.*
- *Cylinder head will be removed with the exhaust manifold and the lower section of the intake manifold still attached.*

1. With ignition switched off, disconnect the battery negative terminal from the battery.

NOTE —

Be sure to have the anti-theft radio code on hand before disconnecting the battery.

2. Position the crankshaft so that pistons are NOT at TDC.
3. Remove the upper engine cover.
4. Remove the lower sound absorber panel (belly pan).
5. Drain engine coolant, see **19 Engine–Cooling System**.
6. Disconnect fuel supply line, fuel return line and vacuum connection for the leak detection pump (LDP). See Fig. 23.

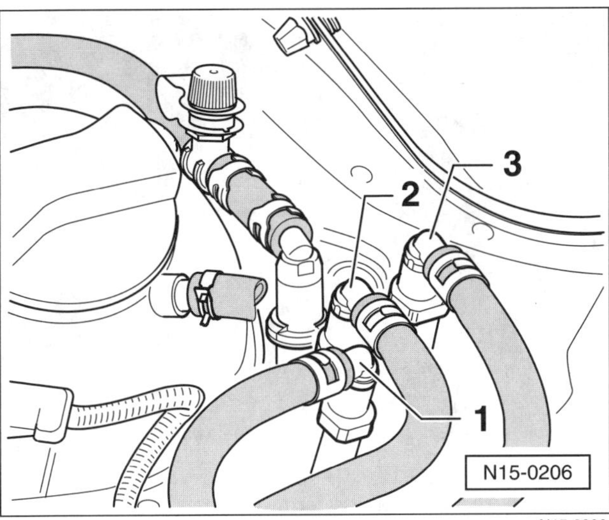

N15-0206

Fig. 23. Separate fuel supply line (**3**), fuel return line (**2**), and vacuum connection (**1**) for leak detection pump (LDP) as shown.

> ***WARNING —***
> *Fuel will be expelled when disconnecting fuel hoses. Wrap a cloth around the fuel line fittings before disconnecting them. Do not smoke or work near heaters or other fire hazards. Have a fire extinguisher handy.*

7. Seal off disconnected fuel and vacuum lines to prevent contamination.

8. Remove air cleaner assembly and connecting hose to throttle housing.

9. Disconnect accelerator cable from the throttle control module linkage and the cable retainers.

10. Unplug the wiring harness connector from the throttle control module.

11. Remove the 2 coolant hoses from throttle control module that connect to the reservoir and cylinder head.

12. Disconnect vacuum hose connection for the power brake booster on the back of intake manifold and any remaining connections on the intake manifold.

13. Loosen and remove the bolts holding the upper and lower sections of the intake manifold together. See Fig. 24.

0024228

Fig. 24. Remove bolts (**arrows**) that hold upper manifold to lower manifold.

14. On the rear upper section of the intake manifold, remove vent line and t bolts for warm air deflector plate. See Fig. 25.

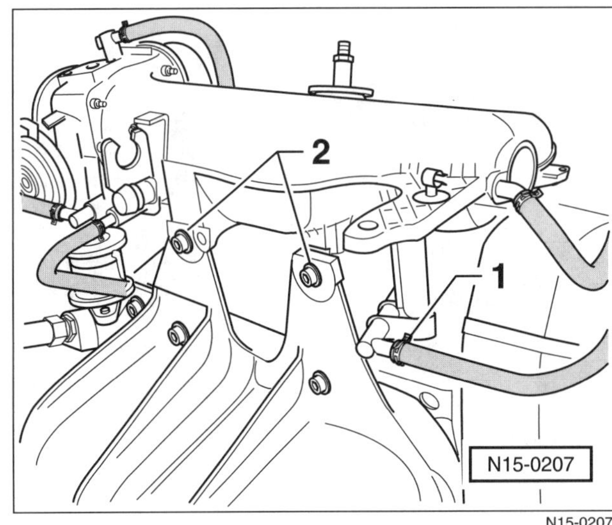

N15-0207

Fig. 25. Rear view of intake manifold showing vent line (**1**) and warm air deflector bolts (**2**).

15. Lift off the upper section of the intake manifold and lay aside. Block off the exposed open ports on the lower section with wide tape or other suitable material. See Fig. 26.

Fig. 26. Cover intake manifold (**arrow**) holes after removing upper section.

16. Unbolt the coolant connection flange from the end of the cylinder head and carefully move aside. The coolant hoses stay connected. See Fig. 27.

Fig. 27. Coolant connection flange mounting bolts (**arrows**).

17. Disconnect the intake and pressure hoses from the Secondary Air Injection pump. Unbolt nuts holding pump to bracket and disconnect harness connector. Remove pump. See Fig. 28.

18. Disconnect the following electrical components/connections:

- Fuel Injectors (and unclip the wiring from the holders)
- Camshaft Position Sensor
- Spark Plug Wires

19. Remove the ribbed V-belt from the tensioner and remove the tensioner.

Fig. 28. Disconnect air intake (**A**), pressure hose (**B**), harness connector (**C**) and unbolt nuts (**arrows**) to remove secondary air injection pump from its mounting bracket.

20. Remove the upper toothed belt cover.

21. Release the toothed belt tensioning roller and take the toothed belt off the camshaft sprocket.

22. Remove the upper bolt from the rear toothed belt guard where it is attached to the cylinder head, see Fig. 15 given earlier.

23. Unbolt the front exhaust pipe from the exhaust manifold, see **26 Exhaust System and Emission Controls**.

24. Remove cylinder head (valve) cover as described earlier.

25. Loosen the socket head bolts slightly in sequence. See Fig. 29. Do not remove the bolts until all 10 have been loosened. Discard the head bolts.

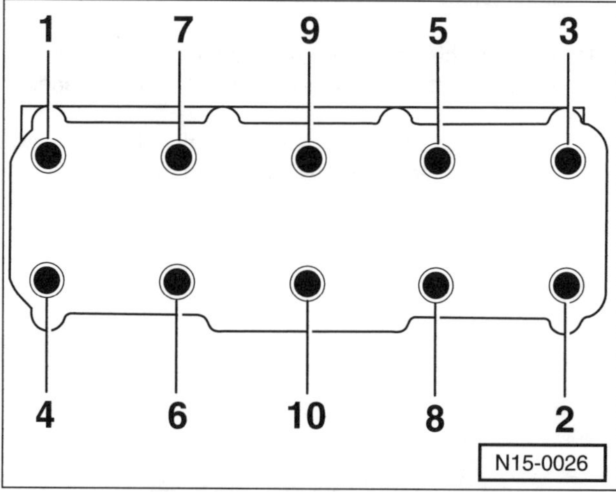

Fig. 29. Loosen the cylinder head bolts in the order shown. Loosen all bolts slightly the first time around, repeat the order, finish loosening and then remove.

26. Carefully lift off cylinder head and place in a clean area. If the head is stuck, use a soft-faced mallet or pry gently with a wooden stick.

> ***CAUTION —***
> *Some of the valves will be open. Use extra care when removing and handling to avoid damage. Place the cylinder head on the bench or table so that the weight of the cylinder head will not rest on the valves.*

Cylinder head, installing

Before proceeding with the installation of the cylinder head, whether an original or a new unit, observe the following important points:

- Check the cylinder head and block for distortion and warpage, see **Cylinder Head Components**, given later in this section.
- Carefully clean the cylinder block and cylinder head sealing surfaces being sure to avoid scratching them during the cleaning process. Do not use metal scrapers or wire brushes.
- When using abrasive paper do not use any grades coarser than 100 grit (such as 80 grit). Lower numbers are coarser.
- If cylinder head will not be reinstalled immediately, take precautions to prevent rust from forming on the cylinder block walls and gasket sealing surfaces.
- When cleaning the old gasket material off of the cylinder block, take precautions to keep the old gasket material and the abrasive particles and dirt out of the cooling and oiling system passages. Place a clean shop cloth over the cylinders to prevent contamination from getting between the cylinder wall and the piston.
- Do not take the new cylinder head gasket out of the packaging until ready to use. Handle the new gasket with extreme care as any damage will lead to leaks.
- There MUST NOT BE any oil or coolant in the head bolt holes in the cylinder block. Any fluids in the holes creates the danger of hydrolock while torquing which could lead to structural damage of the cylinder block. Use thread chasers to remove foreign material as required. Be sure that all 10 bolt holes are clean and dry.
- When all traces of the old gasket material have been removed from the cylinder block and head, carefully remove all traces of metal particles, abrasives and lint. All gasket sealing surfaces and bolt holes must be clean and dry to ensure a proper seal.
- Always use new cylinder head bolts and a new cylinder head gasket.
- Do not use any gasket sealer on the new cylinder head gasket.
- If installing a Volkswagen supplied replacement cylinder head, be sure to inspect for and remove any plastic packaging materials used to protect the head and the open valves.

1. Position the crankshaft so that pistons are NOT at TDC.

2. Install alignment pins into bolt holes of cylinder block. Use of this tool allows for proper alignment of the head on the block. preventing slippage and damage to the head gasket. See Fig. 30.

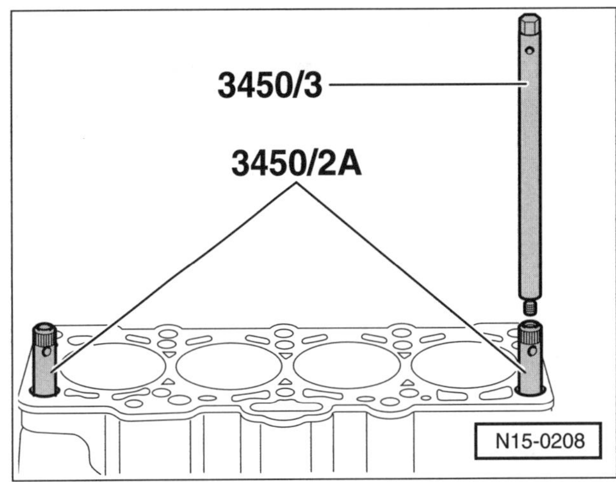

N15-0208

Fig. 30. Volkswagen supplied installation tool for assembly of cylinder head onto the block.

3. Install the new cylinder head gasket onto the block with the numbers and letters facing up. Be sure that none of the wiring or any vacuum hoses are caught between the cylinder head and the block.

4. Carefully install the cylinder head onto the block over the alignment pins and screw in 8 of the new head bolts. Tighten the bolts hand-tight only.

5. Remove the alignment pins from the bolt holes with the tool and install the remaining 2 new head bolts. Tighten these bolts hand-tight.

6. Tighten the 10 cylinder head bolts in three stages following the tightening order. See Fig. 31.

Tightening torque

- Cylinder head to cylinder block, engine code AEG (stretch bolt – always replace)
  stage I . . . . 40 Nm (30 ft-lb)
  stage II . . . . additional ¼ turn (90°)
  stage III . . . . additional ¼ turn (90°)

---

7. Lubricate the camshaft and followers and install the cylinder head (valve) cover.

8. Install the toothed belt, adjust the tension and the belt timing.

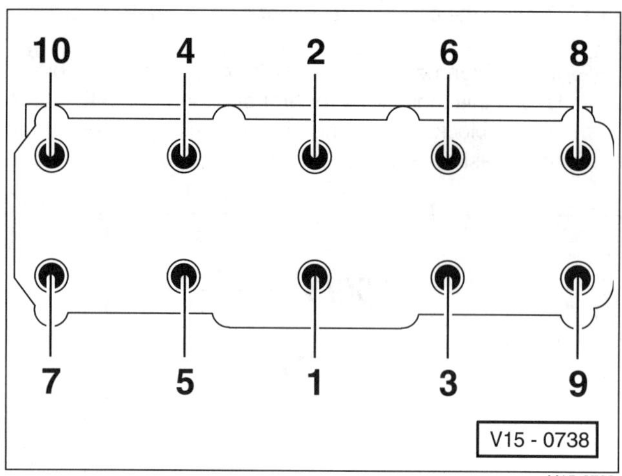

Fig. 31. Tighten the cylinder head bolts in the order shown.

9. Install the upper bolt for the rear toothed belt guard where it is attached to the cylinder head.
10. Install the upper toothed belt cover.
11. Install the ribbed V-belt tensioner and the belt.
12. Remove whatever material was used to seal the exposed lower section of the intake manifold and install the upper section of the intake manifold. Re-attach the vacuum fitting and warm air deflector plate.
13. Reconnect all coolant flanges and lines.
14. Reconnect all vacuum hoses connections.
15. Reconnect fuel supply and return hoses and vacuum hose to leak detection pump.
16. Reconnect accelerator cable and check for smooth operation and full throttle.
17. Reconnect all disconnected electrical components and connections including spark plug wires.
18. Refill cooling system with fresh coolant in the appropriate ratio. See **19 Engine–Cooling System.**

> ***CAUTION —***
> - *Use only Volkswagen original anti-freeze when filling the cooling system. Use of any other anti-freeze may be harmful to the cooling system. Do not use an anti-freeze containing phosphates.*
> - *Do not use tap water in cooling system. Use distilled water only to mix anti-freeze.*

19. Install air cleaner assembly and connecting hoses.
20. Attach the front exhaust pipe to the exhaust manifold with new nuts. See **26 Exhaust System and Emission Controls**.
21. Install the lower sound absorber panel (belly pan).
22. Install the upper engine cover.
23. Reconnect the battery only after all parts/electrical connections have been reinstalled and reconnected.
24. Be sure to quality check your work, see **Quality Review** at the end of this repair group.

Tightening torques

- Cylinder head cover to cylinder head (M6) . . . . 10 Nm (89 in-lb)
- Upper intake manifold bolts to lower manifold (M8) . . . . 20 Nm (15 ft-lb)
- Warm air deflector to upper intake manifold (M8). . . . . 25 Nm (18 ft-lb)
- Cylinder head to cylinder block, engine code AEG (stretch bolt - always replace)
  - stage I . . . . 40 Nm (30 ft-lb)
  - stage II . . . . additional ¼ turn (90°)
  - stage III . . . . additional ¼ turn (90°)
- Front exhaust pipe to exhaust manifold (special nuts - always replace)(M10) . 40 Nm (30 ft-lb)
- Coolant outlet flange to cylinder head (M6) . . . . 10 Nm (89 in-lb)
- Rear toothed belt guard to cylinder head (M8) . . . . 20 Nm (15 ft-lb)
- Ribbed belt tensioner to bracket (M8) 25 Nm (18 ft-lb)
- Toothed belt tensioner (M8) . . . . 20 Nm (15 ft-lb)
- Secondary air pump to support bracket nut (M6) . . . . 10 Nm (89 in-lb)

CYLINDER HEAD COMPONENTS

This section provides the specifications and special information necessary to repair the cylinder head that has been removed from the Volkswagen AEG engine. Special service tools and machine shop services are required for most cylinder head repair.

> ***NOTE —***
> - *The information given under this heading assumes that the cylinder head is removed. For cylinder head removal procedures, see **Cylinder head, removing** given earlier.*
> - *Fig. 3 and Fig. 4, given earlier, show exploded views of the cylinder head and valve train assemblies.*

Cylinder Head and Camshaft

Check the cylinder head for warpage and distortion with an accurate straight edge and a feeler gauge. See Fig. 32. The cylinder head can be resurfaced provided that the distance from the valve cover gasket surface to the head gasket surface is never less than specified. See Fig. 33. Resurfacing the cylinder head will require that the valves be set deeper into the seat by the same amount as was removed by the surfacing operation. This can be done by reworking the valve seats. Machining too much material off of this surface will change the compression ratio and will affect engine emissions.

Specification

- Maximum cylinder head distortion/warpage . . . . 0.1 mm (0.004 in.)
- Minimum cylinder dimension (valve cover gasket surface to the head gasket surface) . . . . 132.6 mm (5.22 in.)

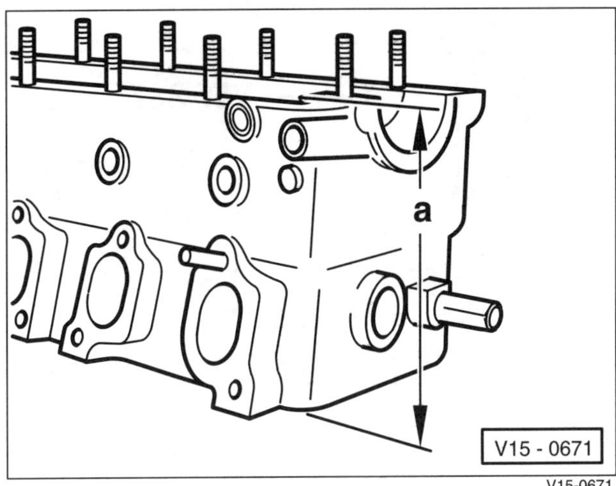

V15-0671

Fig. 33. Dimension (**a**) must not be less than 132.6 mm (5.22 in.) after reworking cylinder head sealing surface.

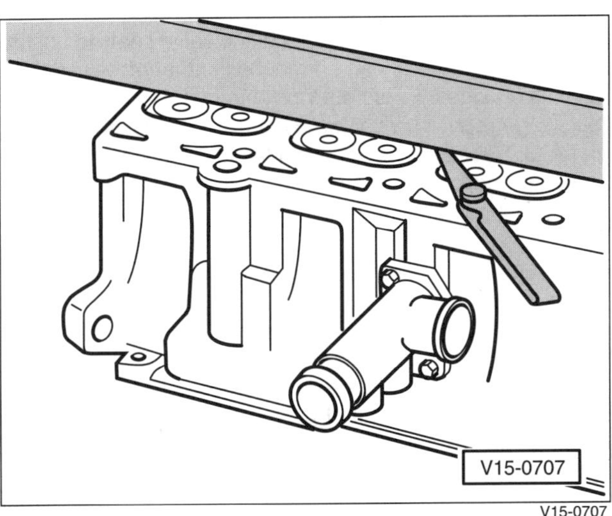

V15-0707

Fig. 32. Cylinder head being checked for distortion with a feeler gauge.

The camshaft for the AEG engine is easily identified by markings cast into it during manufacture. See Fig. 34.

Specification

- Valve timing at 1 mm valve lift, engine code AEG
  - Intake opens ATDC . . . . 4.6°
  - Intake closes ABDC . . . . 40.85°
  - Exhaust opens BBDC . . . . 37.4°
  - Exhaust closes BTDC . . . . 1.15°

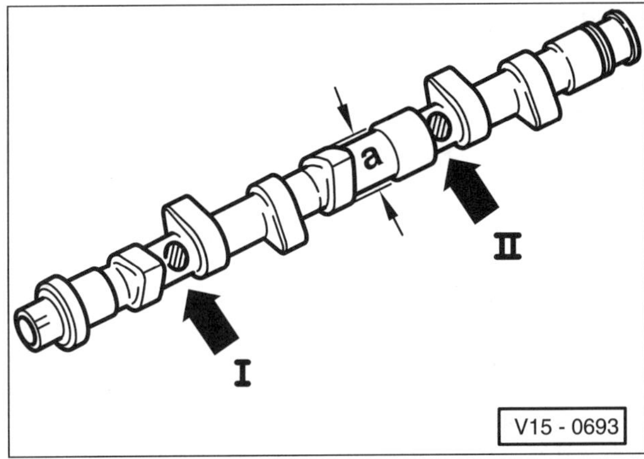

V15-0693

Fig. 34. Camshaft identification marks for AEG engines; **a** is the base diameter of 34 mm, **arrow I** should show the letter -B-, and **arrow II** should show the number -050-.

The in and out movement of the camshaft is known as axial play and is measured with the cam followers removed and only the first and last bearing caps installed.

A dial gauge is set up on the sprocket end of the camshaft and the camshaft clearance is checked by moving the camshaft as far as it can go in each direction. See Fig. 35.

Specification

- Camshaft axial clearance . . . . 0.15 mm (0.006 in.)

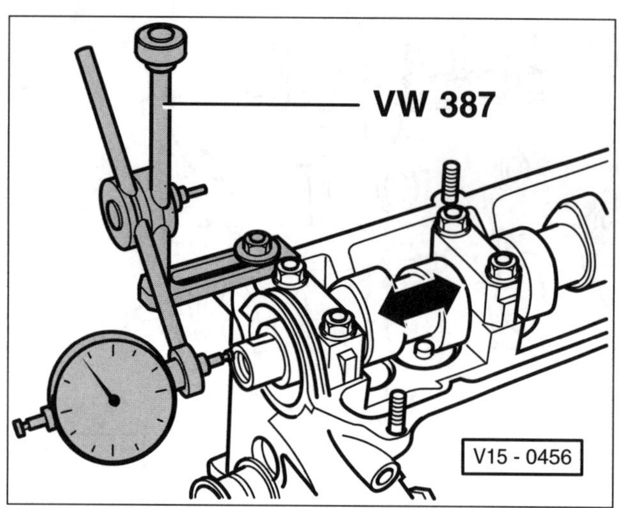

V15-0456

Fig. 35. Dial gauge set up on camshaft to measure axial play (**arrow**).

Valves

Valves should not be re-worked on a machine. Only lapping by hand with valve compound is permitted. Valve dimensions listed in **Table a** apply to the valve shown in Fig. 36.

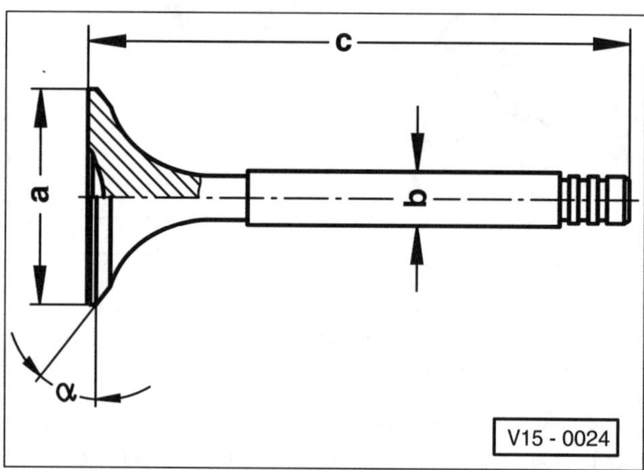

V15-0024

Fig. 36. Valve dimensions are referenced in **Table a**.

Table a. Valve Dimensions

Engine Code	AEG
Valve head diameter (**a**)	
intake	39.5 mm ± 0.15 mm (1.555 in. ± 0.006 in)
exhaust	32.9 mm ± 0.15 mm (1.295 in. ± 0.0008 in.)

Table a. Valve Dimensions

Engine Code	AEG
Valve stem diameter (**b**)	
intake	6.92 mm ± 0.02 mm (0.272 in. ± 0.0008 in.)
exhaust	6.92 mm ± 0.02 mm (0.272 in. ± 0.0008 in.)
Valve length (**c**)	
intake	91.85 mm (3.616 in.)
exhaust	91.15 mm (3.588 in.)
Valve face angle (α)	
intake	45°
exhaust	45°

Valve guides

Special tools and a press are required to replace the valve guides. Check valve guide wear with a new valve. Always use an intake valve in an intake guide and an exhaust valve in an exhaust guide. See Fig. 37. Inspect the valve seats to ensure that the cylinder head can be reconditioned before installing new valve guides. Press out worn original valve guides with Volkswagen special driver tool 3121 from the camshaft side of the head. Replacement valve guides have a shoulder on the camshaft side to limit the installed depth and must be pressed out from the combustion chamber side.

When installing new valve guides, lubricate with clean engine oil and press in from the camshaft side down to the shoulder. The cylinder head should be cold for this operation. Once the shoulder of the valve guide contacts the cylinder head, do not allow the pressure on the guide to exceed 2000 psi (1 ton) otherwise the cylinder head or the guide will be damaged. When the guide has been replaced, ream it to the proper size and continue with the reworking of the valve seats.

Specification

- Valve guide (wear limits-maximum play) with new valve
  - intake valve guide . . . . 1.0 mm (0.039 in.)
  - exhaust valve guide. . . . . 1.3 mm (0.051 in.)

NOTE —

Due to the close tolerances found in the valve guides, it is recommended that Volkswagen special tool 3121 be used for removal and installation and special tool 3120 be used to ream the valve guide to size.

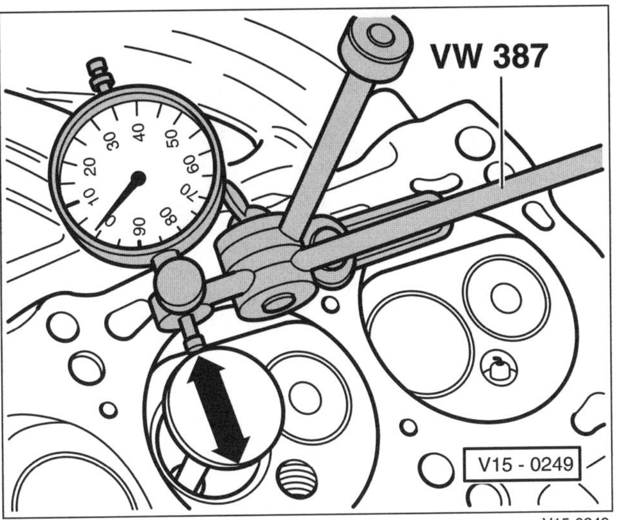

V15-0249

Fig. 37. Valve guide wear being checked with new valve. Insert valve until stem end is flush with end of guide. Rock valve back and forth (**arrow**) to check total travel.

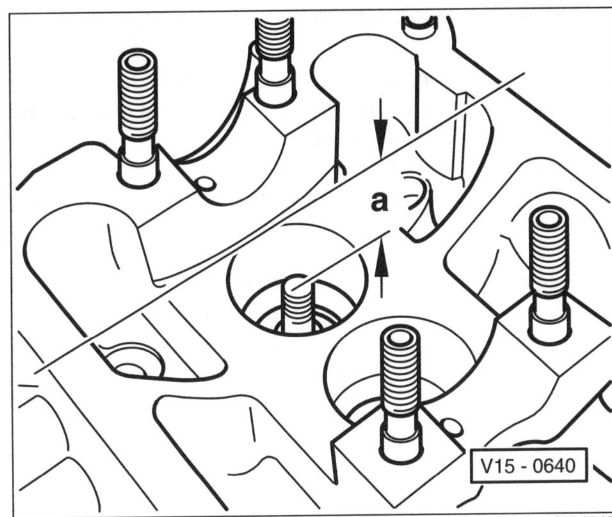

V15-0640

Fig. 38. Dimension (**a**), distance between top of valve stem and gasket surface of cylinder head, is used to calculate maximum valve seat refacing dimensions.

Valve seats

When resurfacing valve seats, there is a limit to the amount of material that can be removed to bring the seat back into specification. If too much material is removed, the final assembly will leave too little space for the hydraulic cam follower to function properly. The maximum refacing dimension, that is, the maximum amount of material that can be removed from the valve seat, is calculated from the measurement shown in Fig. 38.

Measure dimension **a** in Fig. 38, and subtract the minimum dimension, as given in **Table b**. The difference is the maximum amount of material that can be removed from the valve seat.

Table b. Minimum Dimensions for Calculating Valve Seat Refacing Dimensions

Engine Code	Intake	Exhaust
AEG	33.8 mm (1.331 in.)	34.1 mm (1.343 in.)

NOTE—
Use care when reworking the exhaust valve seats to avoid changing the shape of the port. This can upset the flow characteristics of the valve.

Table c. Valve Seat Dimensions

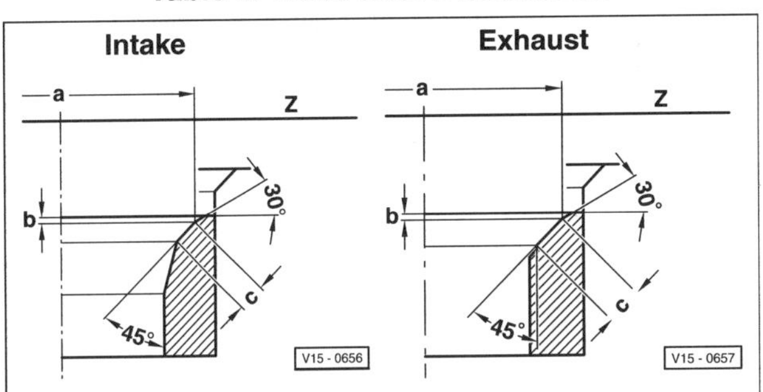

Engine Code: AEG	Intake	Exhaust
Seat diameter (**a**)	39.2 mm (1.543 in.)	32.4 mm (1.276 in.)
Maximum refacing dimension (**b**)	Calculated See Fig. 38.	Calculated See Fig. 38.
Seat width (**c**)	approx. 2.0 mm (0.079 in.)	approx. 2.4 mm (0.094 in.)
Valve seat angle	45°	45°
Correction angle, upper	30°	30°

NOTE—
Z shows cylinder head surface reference.

QUALITY REVIEW

When you have finished working under the hood and around other areas of the vehicle it is advisable to take a moment to quality check or review your work. This helps to ensure that the operation or repair has been completed properly with all affected systems functioning within normal parameters. This may include the following:

- Make sure that the radiator fan cycles properly and that the coolant level and concentration are correct.
- Ensure that all cable ties and hose clamps that were removed as part of the repair are replaced.
- Check and adjust all other applicable fluid levels.
- Make sure that there are no fluid leaks.
- Make sure that there are no air, vacuum or exhaust leaks.
- Make sure that all components involved in the repair are positioned correctly and function properly.
- Male sure all tools, shop cloths, fender covers, and protective tape are removed.
- Clean grease from painted surfaces and steering wheel.
- Unlock the anti-theft radio and reset the clock.

In addition to the above noted points, the ECM and TCM may need to be checked using the Volkswagen supplied VAG 1551 or 1552 scan tool as mentioned at the start of this repair.

15b Cylinder Head and Valvetrain (ALH Engine)

GENERAL

This section covers most cylinder head and valvetrain service and repair work for the ALH 4-cylinder, 2 valve per cylinder, diesel engine. For information on short block engine rebuilding and internal engine specifications, see **13 Crankshaft/Cylinder Block**.

Most of the operations described in this repair group require special equipment and experience. If you lack the skills, tools, or a suitable workplace for servicing or repairing the cylinder head, we suggest that you leave these repairs to an authorized Volkswagen dealer or other qualified shop.

Engine Codes
- AEG . . . . 2.0L 4-cylinder gasoline
- ALH . . . . 1.9L 4-cylinder turbo diesel

DIAGNOSTIC TESTING

The tests that follow can be used to help isolate engine problems, to better understand a problem before starting expensive and extensive repairs, or to just periodically check engine condition.

Compression Test

A compression test will tell a lot about the overall condition of the engine without the need for taking it apart. Testing is relatively simple and straightforward.

1. Remove two plastic caps and retaining nuts on upper sound absorber panel. Loosen the rear retaining nut slightly. Remove dipstick, lift cover up slightly and pull forward.

2. Warm-up the engine until it is a minimum of 30°C (86°F).

3. Disconnect harness connectors for fuel cut-off valve and quantity adjuster from diesel injection pump. See Fig. 1. and Fig. 2.

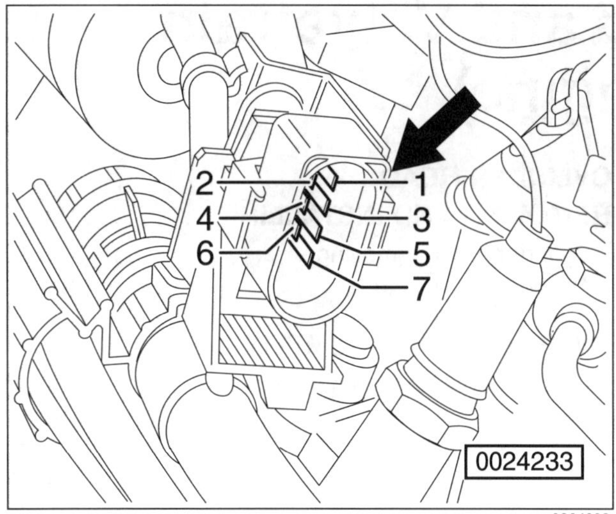

0024233

Fig. 1. Harness connector for quantity adjuster (**arrow**) on diesel injection pump. Numbers indicate pin numbers of connector.

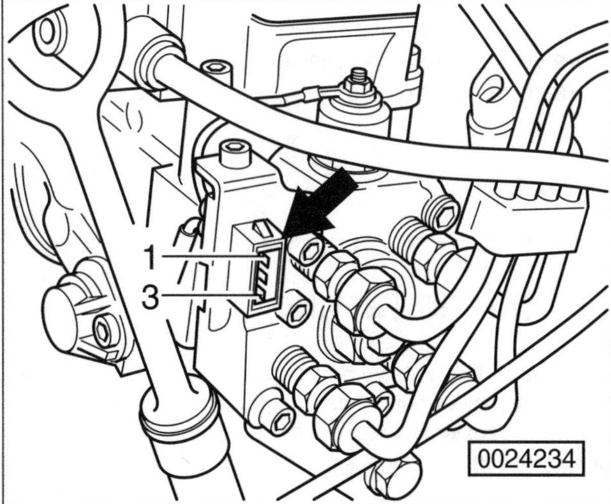

0024234

Fig. 2. Harness connector (**arrow**) for fuel cut off valve on diesel injection pump. Numbers indicate pin numbers of connector.

4. Disconnect bus connector from each glow plug by gently pulling up on it. Lay the complete bus connector aside.

5. Use compressed air to clear area around the glow plugs.

6. Using a 10 mm deep socket and swivel or Volkswagen special tool 3220, remove all glow plugs and lay aside in proper order.

7. Install compression tester into glow plug hole.

8. Have a helper:
   - depress clutch pedal fully
   - put the transmission in neutral or park
   - crank the engine over with the starter motor

> ***NOTE —***
> *Cranking the engine over with the diesel injection system components disconnected may Diagnostic Trouble Codes (DTCs) to be stored in engine management system memory.*

9. Engine should be cranked a minimum of 4 to 5 revolutions.

10. Record readings, release pressure in the gauge and repeat procedure for each cylinder.

11. Compare readings to specification.

Specification

- Compression pressures (ALH engine)
  - new . . . . 25 to 31 bar (368 - 456 psi)
  - wear limit . . . . 19 bar (279 psi)
  - maximum difference between cylinders . . . . 5 bar (74 psi)

12. When all cylinders have been checked, reinstall glow plugs and bus connector, connect harness connector for quantity adjuster and fuel cut-off valve. Install the upper engine cover.

Tightening torque

- Glow plug to cylinder head . . . . 15 Nm (11 ft-lb)

Cylinder leakdown test

The most conclusive diagnosis of low compression symptoms requires a cylinder leak-down test. Using a special tester and a supply of compressed air, each cylinder is pressurized. The rate at which the air leaks out of the cylinder, as well as the sound and location of the escaping air can more accurately pinpoint the magnitude and source of the leakage. Any engine compression diagnosis that will require major disassembly should first be confirmed by a cylinder leak-down test. Because this test requires special equipment and experience, it may be desirable to have it performed by a Volkswagen dealer or other qualified repair shop.

CYLINDER HEAD SERVICE

Many cylinder head repairs can be accomplished without removing the cylinder head from the engine. The cylinder head cover (valve cover) gasket, the camshaft, the camshaft oil seal, the valve guide oil seals, the valve springs, and the camshaft followers are all accessible with the cylinder head installed. This heading describes those repairs that can be done with the cylinder head installed.

Fig. 3 shows an exploded view of the internal cylinder head components and Fig. 4 shows the external cylinder head components.

Internal cylinder head assembly

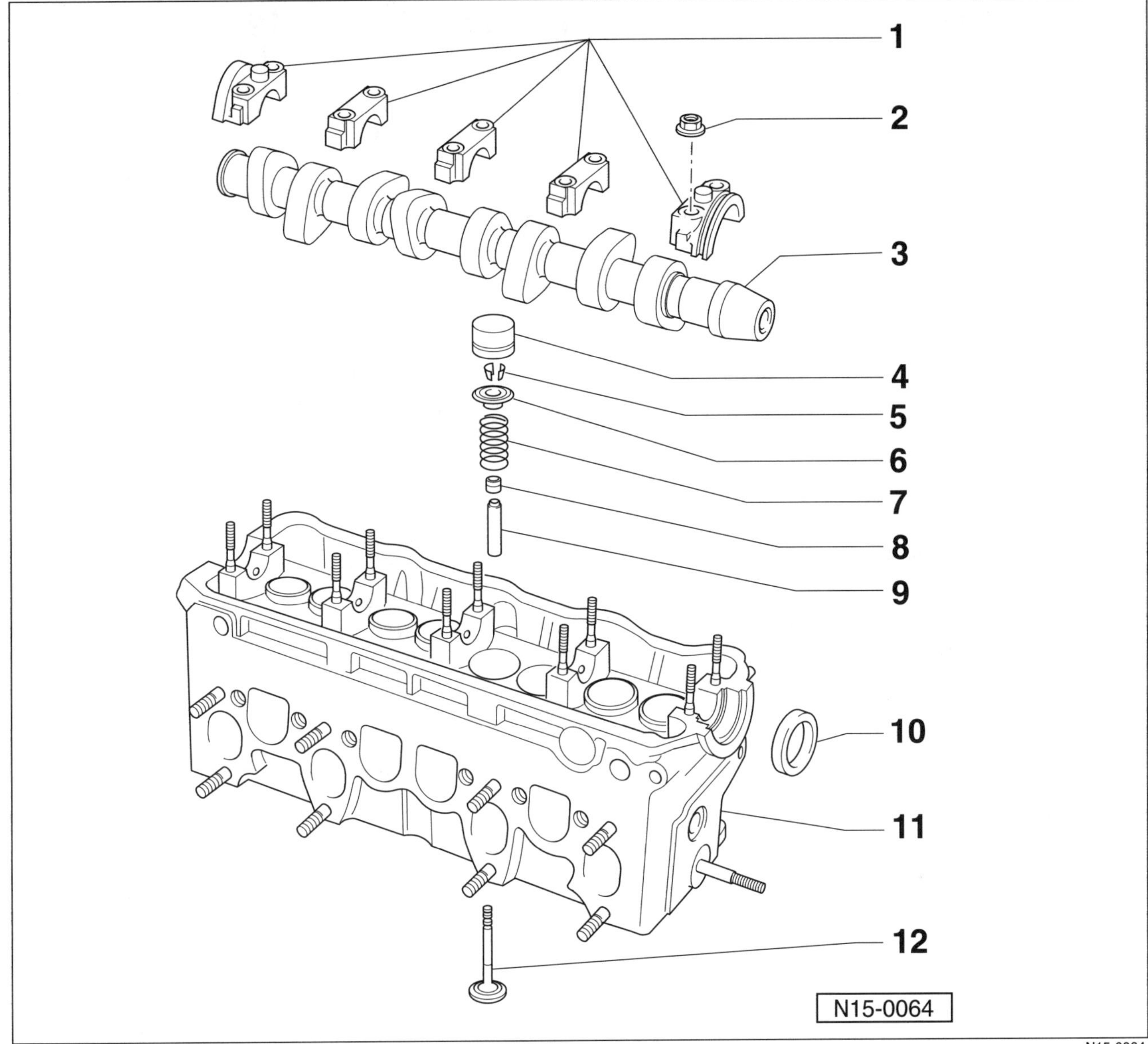

N15-0064

Fig. 3. Exploded view of internal cylinder head components.

1. **Bearing cap**
2. **Nut**
   - Tighten to 20 Nm (15 ft-lb)
3. **Camshaft**
   - Checking radial clearance with plastigage wear limit: 0.11 mm (.0043 in.)
   - Run-out: max. 0.01 mm (.0004 in.)
4. **Hydraulic lifter**
   - Do not interchange
   - Store with cam contact surface facing downwards
   - Before installing, check camshaft axial clearance, see **Cylinder Head Components**
   - Oil contact surfaces
5. **Keepers**
6. **Upper valve spring plate**
7. **Valve spring**
8. **Valve stem seal**
9. **Valve guide**
10. **Oil seal**
    - To remove and install, remove bearing cap
11. **Cylinder head**
12. **Valves**

External cylinder head assembly

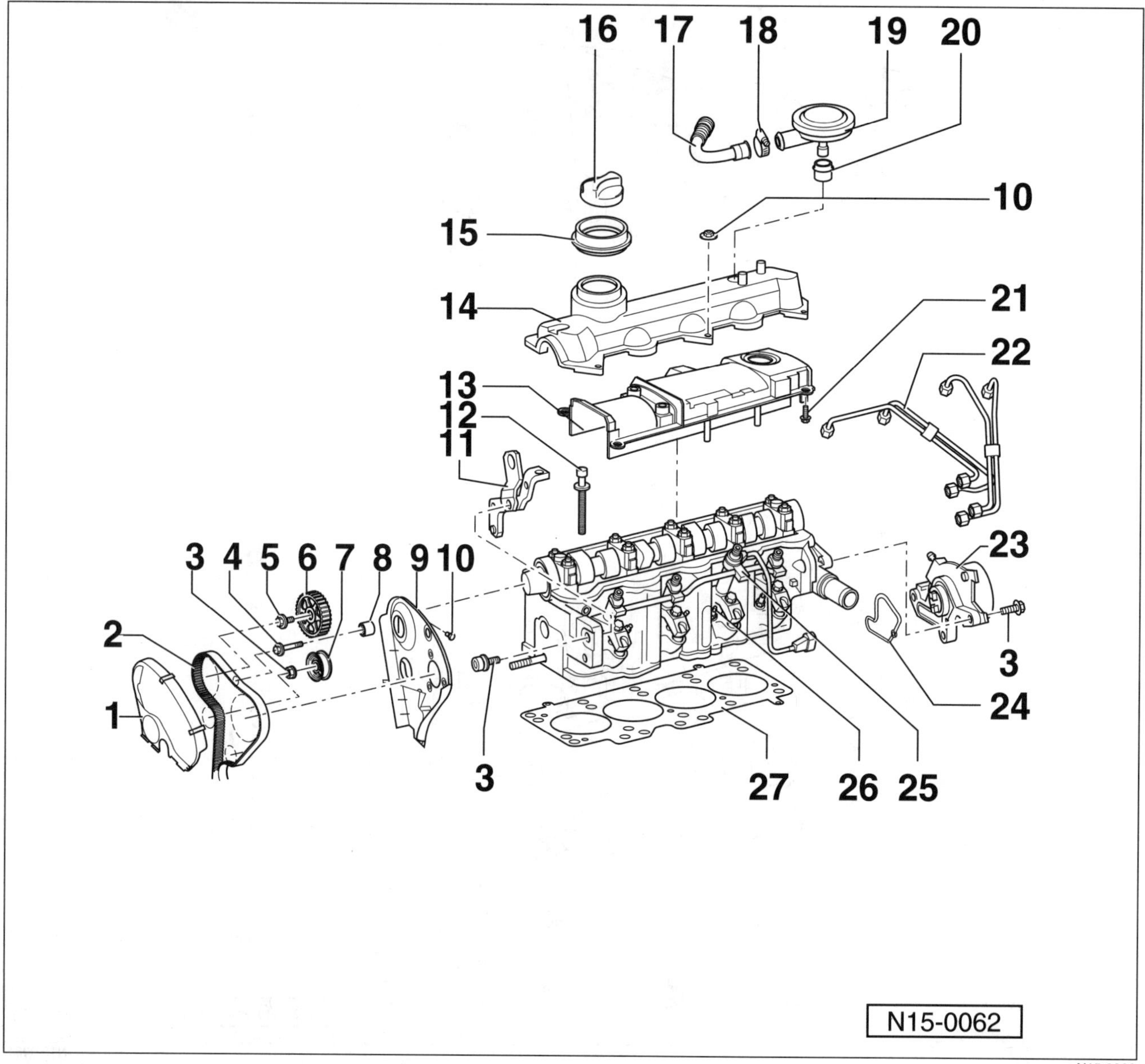

N15-0062

Fig. 4. Exploded view of external cylinder head components.

1. **Toothed belt guard, upper section**
2. **Toothed belt**
   - Mark direction of engine rotation before removing
   - Check for wear
   - Do not kink
3. **Nut**
   - Tighten to 20 Nm (15 ft-lb)
4. **Bolt**
   - Tighten to 20 Nm (15 ft-lb)
5. **Bolt**
   - Tighten to 45 Nm (33 ft-lb)
6. **Camshaft sprocket**
   - Drive off of camshaft taper using hammer and drift through toothed belt guard openings
7. **Tensioning roller (semi-automatic, toothed belt)**
8. **Idler roller**
9. **Toothed belt guard, rear**
10. **Nut**
    - Tighten to 10 Nm (7 ft-lb)
11. **Lifting eye**

12. Cylinder head bolt
- Always replace
- Note sequence when loosening and tightening, see **Cylinder head, removing and installing**

13. Oil deflector

14. Valve cover

15. Seal
- Replace if damaged

16. Cap
- Replace seal if damaged

17. Breather pipe

18. Retaining clip

19. Pressure regulating valve
- For positive crankcase ventilation valve

20. Gasket
- Replace if damaged

21. Bolt
- Tighten to 5 Nm (44 in-lb)

22. Fuel injector lines
- Tighten to 25 Nm (18 ft-lb)
- Remove using 3035 offset tubing wrench
- Always remove fuel line cluster as an assembly
- Do not bend, kink or alter shape

23. Exhauster
- For brake booster

24. Gasket
- Always replace

25. Fuel injector
- Removing and installing, see **23 Diesel Fuel Injection**

26. Glow plug
- Tighten to 15 Nm (11 ft-lb)
- Checking, see **28 Ignition/Glow Plug System**

27. Cylinder head gasket
- Always replace
- If replaced; also replace entire engine coolant

Cylinder head (valve) cover, removing and installing

NOTE —

The valve cover gasket is vulcanized into the rigid aluminum cover and is not available as a separate part.

1. Remove the upper engine cover.
2. Remove connecting pipe between the intercooler and the intake hose.
3. Disconnect the breather hose from the breather valve.
4. Remove 4 cylinder head cover securing bolts from the rear and 3 from the front.
5. Lift off cover with attached oil separator and gasket.
6. Installation is the reverse of removal.

Tightening torque
- Cylinder head cover to cylinder head . 10 Nm (89 in-lb)

Camshaft oil seal, replacing

1. Remove the upper engine cover.
2. Remove connecting pipe between the intercooler and the intake hose.
3. Remove the upper toothed belt guard.
4. Remove cylinder head (valve) cover.
5. Remove brake booster vacuum pump from the end of the cylinder head.
6. Set the engine to TDC for cylinder 1 by turning the crankshaft until the timing mark on the flywheel or torque converter aligns with mark on the transmission case. See Fig. 5. See Fig. 6.

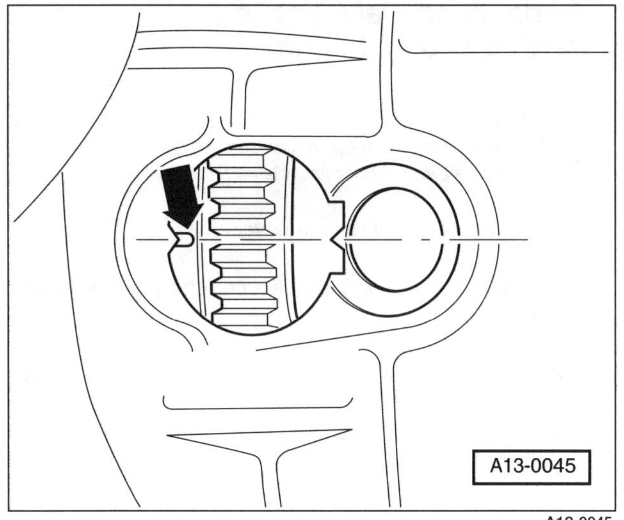

Fig. 5. TDC for manual transmissions: align mark on flywheel (**arrow**) with pointer on transmission case.

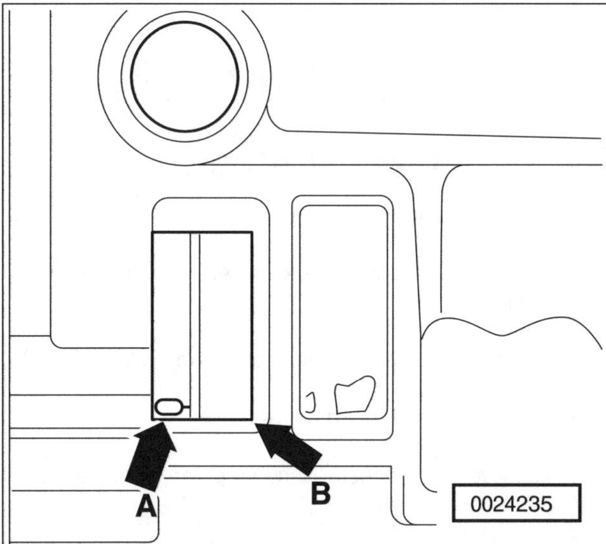

Fig. 6. TDC for automatic transmissions: align mark on torque converter (**A**) with lower edge of opening in transmission case (**B**).

7. Lock the camshaft at TDC with the setting bar. See Fig. 7.

8. Loosen camshaft sprocket mounting bolt about ½ turn. Release camshaft sprocket from camshaft taper by tapping with a hammer on a soft drift inserted through the hole in rear of toothed belt guard. See Fig. 8.

9. Release the tensioning roller and slip toothed belt off the camshaft sprocket.

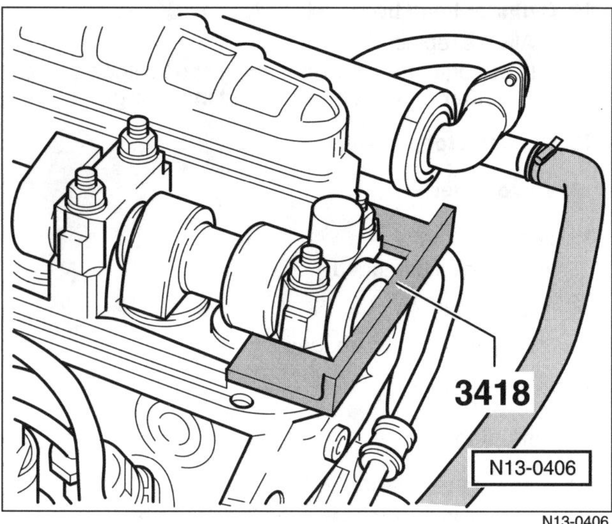

Fig. 7. Volkswagen special tool 3418 shown in position on the vacuum pump end of the camshaft to lock camshaft at TDC.

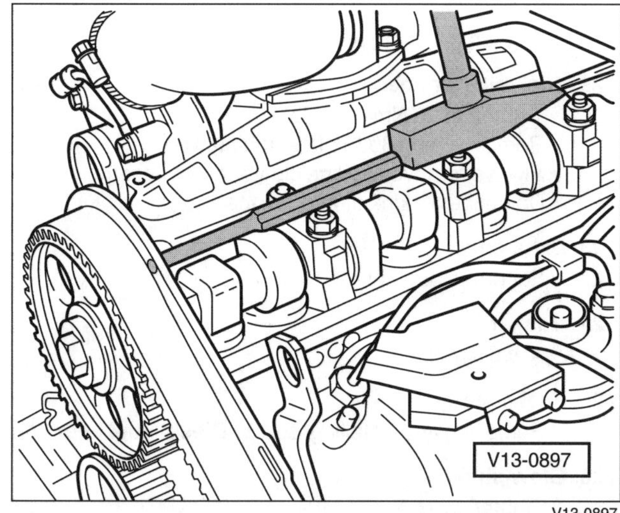

Fig. 8. Drift shown inserted through hole in rear toothed belt guard to loosen camshaft sprocket.

NOTE —

The camshaft end is tapered. Loosening the sprocket will allow the camshaft sprocket to rotate independently of the camshaft. There may be a keyway cut into the end of the camshaft. However, there is no matching keyway cut into the sprocket nor is there a Woodruff key.

10. Remove the camshaft sprocket mounting bolt and sprocket.

11. Loosen and remove camshaft bearing cap 1.

    NOTE —
    Position 1 is closest to the belt end of the camshaft.

12. Slide the seal through the rear toothed belt guard and off the end of the camshaft.

13. Install new seal noting the following points:
    - Lubricate the new seal with clean engine oil.
    - Install with the closed end facing out.
    - Use a suitable installation tool.
    - Press seal into the bottom of the recess.

14. Install bearing cap 1.

Tightening torque
- Camshaft bearing cap to cylinder head . . . . 20 Nm (15 ft-lb)
- Camshaft sprocket to camshaft . . . . . 45 Nm (33 ft-lb)

15. Install camshaft drive belt sprocket.

16. Install toothed belt and adjust tension, see **Toothed Belt–Camshaft Drive**, given later.

17. Install brake booster vacuum pump, cylinder head (valve) cover, and upper toothed belt guard.

18. Install connecting pipe between the intercooler and the intake hose.

19. Check that all components are installed, properly secured, and install upper engine cover.

20. Be sure to quality check your work, see **Quality Review** at the end of this repair group.

Camshaft, removing and installing

The camshaft can be removed and installed with the cylinder head installed. Removing the camshaft allows access to the hydraulic cam followers, the valve springs and the valve stem oil seals.

1. Remove upper sound absorber panel.

2. Remove connecting pipe between intercooler and intake hose.

3. Remove upper toothed belt guard.

4. Remove cylinder head (valve) cover.

5. Remove brake booster vacuum pump from end of the cylinder head.

6. Turn crankshaft to top dead center, TDC, for cylinder 1, see Fig. 5 or Fig. 6, given earlier.

7. Lock camshaft with setting bar as shown earlier. See Fig. 7.

8. Loosen camshaft sprocket mounting bolt about ½ turn. Release camshaft sprocket from camshaft taper by tapping with a hammer on a soft drift inserted through the hole in rear of toothed belt guard. See Fig. 8.

9. Release tensioning roller and slide toothed belt off the camshaft sprocket.

10. Remove camshaft sprocket mounting bolt and sprocket.

    NOTE —
    Mark each bearing cap before removing. Each cap is machined to each journal and must be reinstalled to that exact location to prevent damage.

11. Loosen and remove bearing caps from positions 5, 1 and 3 in that order.

    NOTE —
    Position 1 is closest to the belt end of the camshaft.

12. Loosen the nuts on bearing cap 2 slightly and then loosen the nuts on bearing cap 4 slightly. Loosen the nuts alternately and evenly a little at a time on each of the two bearing caps. Remove the nuts (and washers, if equipped), and remove the bearing caps.

13. Lift out camshaft and lay aside.

    NOTE —
    Once removed, the camshaft should be checked for wear and other visible damage as described later under **Cylinder Head Components**.

14. Oil the bearing surfaces of the cylinder head and camshaft and install the camshaft into the cylinder head with the lobes for cylinder number 1 pointing up.

15. Install bearing caps 2 and 4. Install nuts (and washers, if equipped) and tighten nuts alternately and evenly so that camshaft is drawn down fully and evenly into bearing saddles. Torque to specification. See Fig. 9.

Tightening torque
- Camshaft bearing cap to cylinder head 20 Nm (15 ft-lb)

CAUTION —
Be sure to install bearing caps correctly. The caps are bored off-center and only fit properly one way. Caps are matched to the cylinder head by the machining process and are not available separately. Broken caps will require the replacement of the cylinder head. See Fig. 9.

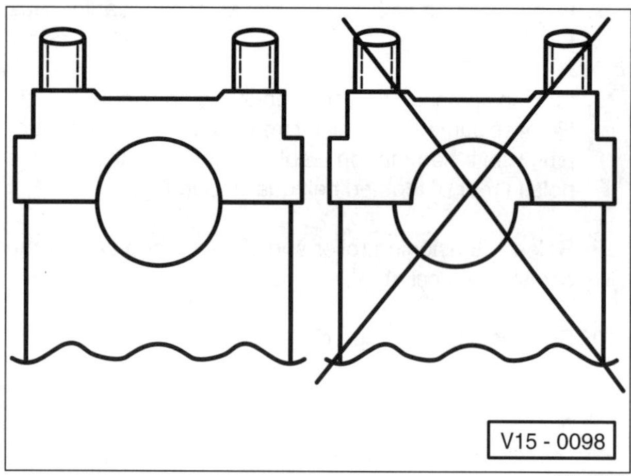

V15-0098

Fig. 9. Bearing caps are bored off-center. If necessary, test install caps without camshaft to confirm installation direction.

16. Install all remaining bearing caps and torque to specification.

17. Install the camshaft drive belt sprocket.

    NOTE —
    Ensure that camshaft lobes for cylinder #1 are still pointing up.

Tightening torque

- Camshaft sprocket to camshaft . . . . . 45 Nm (33 ft-lb)

18. Install the toothed belt and adjust tension, see **Toothed Belt – Camshaft Drive** given later.

19. Install brake booster vacuum pump, cylinder head (valve) cover, and upper toothed belt guard.

20. Install the connecting pipe between the intercooler and the intake hose.

21. Install upper engine cover.

22. Be sure to quality check your work, see **Quality Review** at the end of this repair group.

Hydraulic cam followers, checking

The 1.9 liter ALH engine is equipped with hydraulic cam followers which are also known as lifters.The cam followers are pumped up by engine oil pressure, expanding as necessary to fill the gap between the valve stem and the camshaft lobe. This occurs continuously and automatically to keep the valve in proper adjustment at all times.

Some valve noise at start-up and during the warm-up period is normal at times due to hydraulic cam followers that have bled down while the engine was not running. Before checking noisy cam followers, check that the engine oil is new and fresh, of the correct weight, and that the level is correct. Allow 2 minutes with a warm engine running at a fast idle for the lubrication system to properly pump up the cam followers.

Cam followers should only be checked when the engine is fully up to operating temperature. Run the engine until the radiator fan has switched on at least one time. Increase the engine speed to 2,500 rpm and hold it there for approximately 2 minutes. If the hydraulic cam followers are still noisy, shut the engine off and proceed as follows while the engine is still warm.

1. Remove the cylinder head (valve) cover. See **Cylinder head (valve) cover, removing and installing**, given earlier.

2. Turn the engine by hand until both camshaft lobes of cylinder #1 are pointing approximately up.

    NOTE —
    Hydraulic cam follower clearance can be checked on any cam follower (lifter) that is not being depressed by the camshaft lobe.

3. Check the clearance between the cam follower and the cam lobe on cylinder #1 by lightly depressing the cam follower with a wooden or plastic wedge and inserting a feeler gauge into the gap. See Fig. 10. If the clearance exceeds the specified limit, the lifter is faulty and should be replaced.

Specification

- Hydraulic cam follower maximum clearance (ALH engine) . . . . 0.1 mm (0.004 in.)

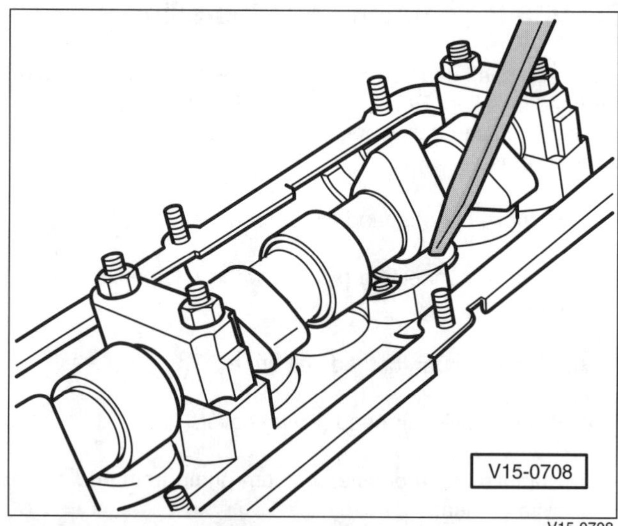

V15-0708

Fig. 10. Hydraulic cam follower shown being pushed down lightly with plastic wedge.

4. Turn engine by hand and repeat procedure until all cam followers have been checked.

5. Replace a faulty cam follower by removing camshaft as previously described and pulling the follower from the cylinder head. Faulty hydraulic cam followers can be replaced individually but only as a complete assembly.

> ***CAUTION —***
> *After installing new cam followers, the engine should not be started for at least 30 minutes. New cam followers are usually at full extended height and must be allowed to bleed down to their proper height once installed. Failure to do so may cause the valves to strike the pistons resulting in serious damage.*

NOTE —
Store removed hydraulic cam followers in order on a clean surface with the camshaft contact surface facing down to minimize bleed down. Cover with a clean lint-free shop cloth.

Valve stem oil seals, replacing

The sign of faulty valve stem seals is excessive oil consumption and oil smoke from the exhaust. This is usually most noticeable during periods of high manifold vacuum such as deceleration. If compression and leak-down testing confirm the integrity of the piston rings, but the engine consumes oil, it is likely that faulty valve stem seals are present. It should also be noted that worn valve stem seals could be due to worn valve guides and that the worn valve guides are the major cause of the oil consumption. See **Cylinder Head Components** for more information on checking valve guides.

Replacing the valve stem oil seals requires removal of the camshaft, cam followers, and the valve springs. This can be done with the cylinder head installed or removed. In either case, several Volkswagen special tools are required to compress the valve springs and remove and install the seals.

Working with the cylinder head installed:

1. Remove the cylinder head cover, camshaft, and hydraulic cam followers as described earlier.

2. Turn the crankshaft so that cylinder #1 is at TDC. Continue with step 5.

NOTE —
Compressed air is not used as on other engines. When the spring is removed, the valve is properly supported by the piston crown at TDC.

Working with the cylinder head removed:

3. Secure the cylinder head to the workbench. Use care to avoid damage to the head gasket surfaces.

4. Remove the camshaft and hydraulic cam followers as described earlier. Continue with step 5.

Working with cylinder head removed or installed:

5. Install the appropriate valve spring compressor tools. See Fig. 11. Compress the spring for the first cylinder and remove the spring retainer, both keepers, and the valve spring. If spring will not compress, lightly tap the tool to release the stuck keepers. Use a small magnet to retrieve the keepers. See Fig. 11.

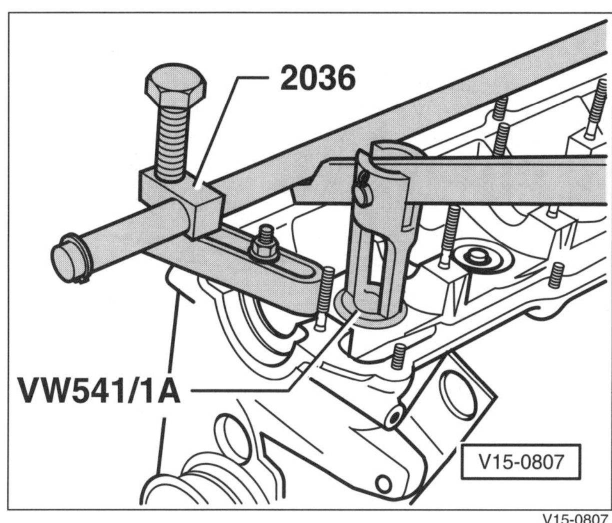

V15-0807

Fig. 11. Valve spring compressor tools being used to compress valve spring for removal of keepers. Numbers identify Volkswagen special tools.

6. Remove the valve stem seals with the special slide hammer tool. See Fig. 12.

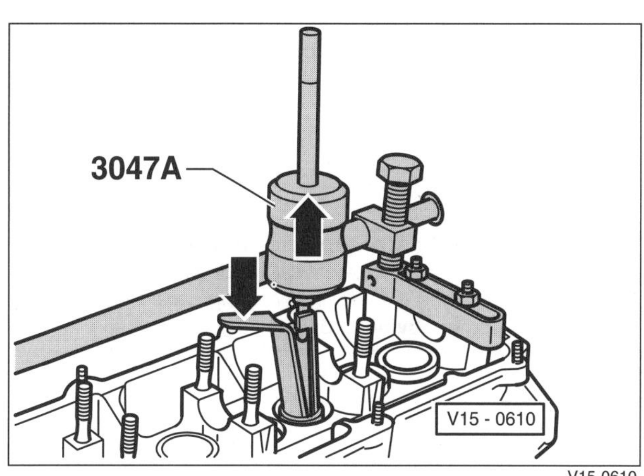

V15-0610

Fig. 12. Valve stem seal removal tool shown in position to remove valve stem seal. Push down on tool (**left arrow**) while sliding hammer up (**right arrow**).

7. Begin installation of new seal by temporarily fitting a protective plastic fitting sleeve over the valve stem. This sleeve is usually included with the new seal set and will prevent damage to the seal due to the sharp edges of the keeper grooves. Lubricate the new seal with clean engine oil and fit it to the installation tool. See Fig. 13.

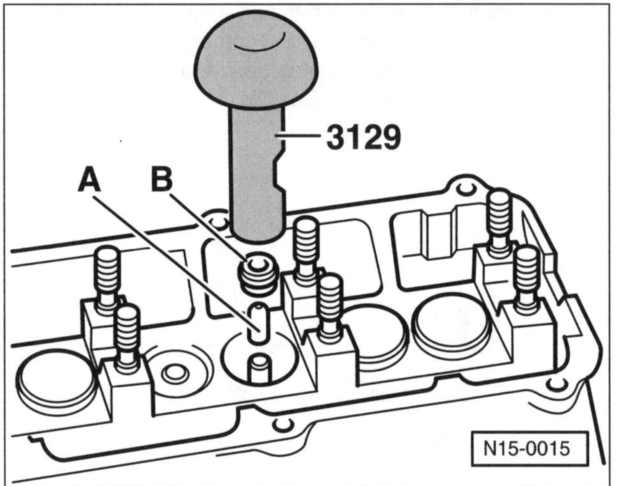

N15-0015

Fig. 13. Plastic fitting sleeve (**A**), shown with valve stem seal (**B**) and plastic installation tool 3129 available from Volkswagen.

8. Push the tool (with seal) down over the valve stem until the seal is fully seated on the guide. Remove the tool and the protective fitting sleeve.

9. Reinstall valve spring, retainer and keepers.

10. Repeat for the second valve on the cylinder.

11. When both valve seals have been replaced on the first cylinder, turn the crankshaft to TDC for the next cylinder (if working with cylinder head installed) and repeat the process until all valve seals have been replaced.

12. Remaining installation is the reverse of removal.

> ***CAUTION —***
> *To prevent cylinder head or camshaft damage, be sure to follow the camshaft installation procedure when tightening the camshaft bearing caps. See* **Camshaft, removing and installing**.

Tightening torque

- Spark plug to cylinder head . . . . 30 Nm (22 ft-lb)

13. Be sure to quality check your work, see **Quality Review** at the end of this repair group.

Toothed Belt - Camshaft Drive

The camshaft drive belt and its related parts are shown in Fig. 14. Required maintenance involves inspection at 5,000, 10,000, 20,000, 30,000, and 50,000 miles. Belt tension is to be adjusted at 40,000 miles and the belt and the tensioner are to be replaced at 60,000 miles. The factory does not specify a time interval on the above noted maintenances, however the publisher also recommends replacing the belt and tensioner at 4 years or 60,000 miles, whichever occurs first. The cycle should then be repeated. This will help prevent damage to the engine due to belt stretch and the long term effects of heat. The camshaft drive belt is known also as a toothed belt and both terms are used interchangeably.

The following component list applies to Fig. 14

1. **Bolt**
   - Always replace
   - Tighten to 120 Nm (88 ft-lb) + ¼ turn (90°)
   - To loosen and tighten, counter-hold with 3099
   - Threads and shoulder must be free of oil and grease
   - The additional quarter turn can be obtained in several stages
2. **Bolt**
   - Always replace
   - Tighten to 40 Nm (30 ft-lb) + ¼ turn (90°)
3. **Bolt**
   - Tighten to 15 Nm (11 ft-lb)
4. **Bolt**
   - Tighten to 22 Nm (16 ft-lb)
5. **Toothed belt guard, lower section**
6. **Bolt**
   - Tighten to 10 Nm (7 ft-lb)
7. **Toothed belt guard, lower section**
8. **Bolt**
   - Tighten to 45 Nm (33 ft-lb)
9. **Right engine bracket**
10. **Toothed belt guard, upper section**
11. **Toothed belt**
    - Mark engine direction of rotation before removing
    - Check for wear
    - Do not kink
12. **Idler wheel**
13. **Bolt**
    - Always replace
    - Tighten to 20 Nm (15 ft-lb) + ¼ turn (90°)
14. **Bolt**
    - Tighten to 20 Nm (15 ft-lb)
15. **Bolt**
    - Tighten to 20 Nm (15 ft-lb)
    - To loosen and tighten bolt, counter-hold using 3036

Drive belts, assembly

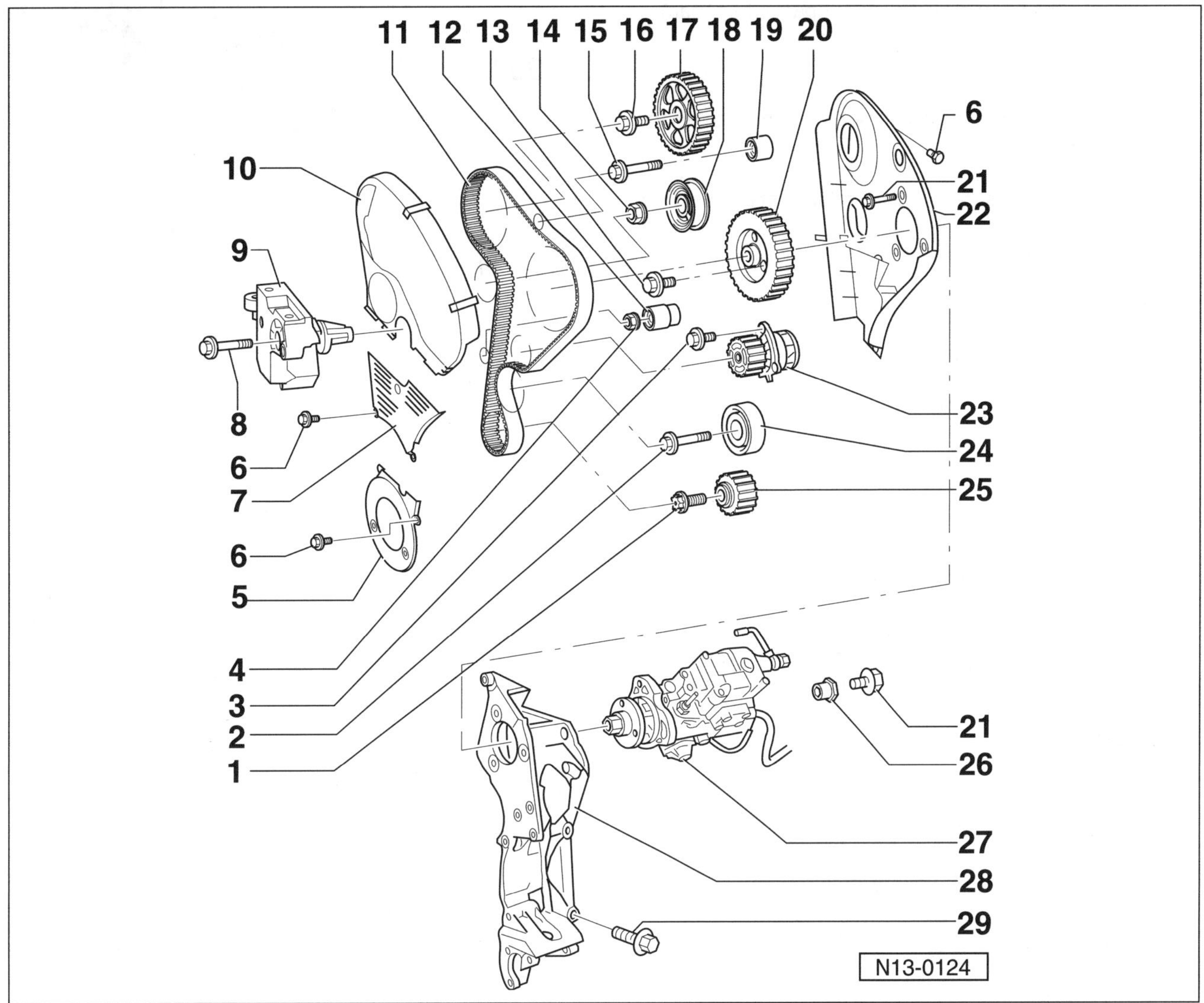

N13-0124

Fig. 14. Exploded view of the toothed belt for the camshaft drive and related components.

16. Bolt
- Tighten to 45 Nm (33 ft-lb)
- To loosen and tighten bolt, counter-hold using 3036

17. Camshaft sprocket
- Drive camshaft off of taper using hammer and drift through toothed belt guard openings

18. Tensioning roller
- Semi-automatic toothed belt tensioning roller

19. Idler wheel

20. Injection pump sprocket
- Two piece construction

21. Bolt
- Tighten to 30 Nm (22 ft-lb)

22. Toothed belt guard, rear

23. Coolant pump

24. Idler wheel
- First remove, to remove coolant pump

25. Crankshaft toothed belt sprocket

26. Bushing

27. Diesel injection pump

28. Assembly bracket
- For diesel injection pump, generator and power steering pump
- For vehicles with A/C

29. Bolt
- Tighten to 45 Nm (33 ft-lb)

Toothed belt for camshaft drive, removing

1. Remove the lower sound absorber panel (belly pan).
2. Remove the upper engine cover.
3. Remove connecting pipe between the intercooler and the intake hose.
4. Disconnect fuel supply and return lines at the fuel filter.
5. Remove fuel filter from the mounting bracket.
6. Remove upper toothed belt guard.
7. Remove cylinder head (valve) cover.
8. Remove brake booster vacuum pump from the end of the cylinder head.
9. Remove connecting pipe between the intercooler and the turbocharger.
10. Remove ribbed V-belt and tensioner.
11. Turn the engine to top dead center (TDC) for cylinder #1, as shown earlier. If engine and transmission are separated use alternate procedures shown below. See Fig. 15. See Fig. 16.

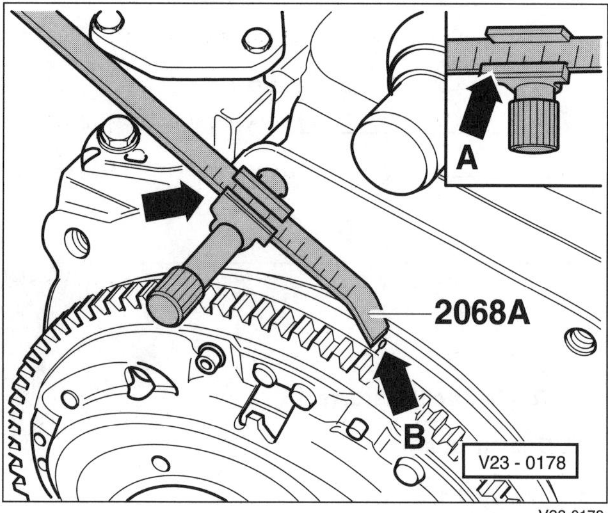

V23-0178

Fig. 15. Alternate procedure for setting TDC for manual transmissions. Install Volkswagen special tool 2068A as shown. Set adjustment to 96 mm (**arrow A**) and align with TDC mark on flywheel (**arrow B**).

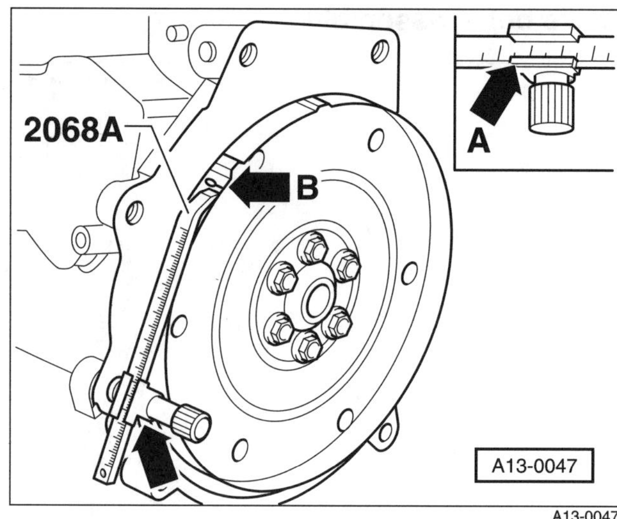

A13-0047

Fig. 16. Alternate procedure for setting TDC for automatic transmissions. Install Volkswagen special tool 2068A as shown. Set adjustment to 96 mm (**arrow A**) and align with TDC mark on driveplate (**arrow B**).

12. Lock camshaft with the setting bar and shim between the gasket surface and both sides of Volkswagen special tool 3418 with equal thickness of feeler gauges. This will insure that the camshaft is at actual TDC. See Fig. 17.

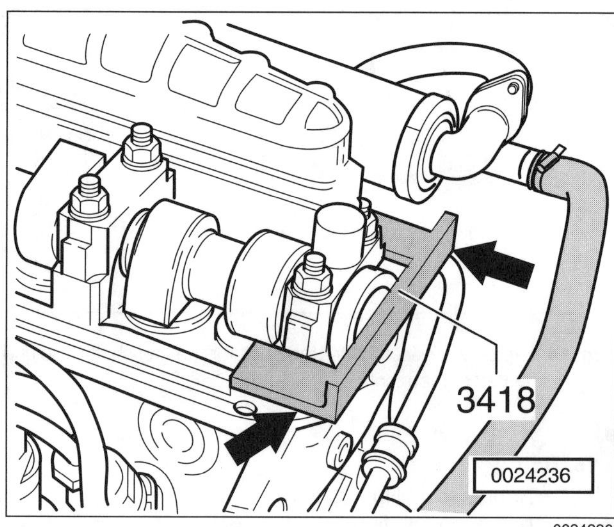

0024236

Fig. 17. Right side engine mount (**1**) as viewed from above. Remove the 5 bolts (**arrows**), and loosen body bolt (**arrow A**).

13. Lock the injection pump sprocket with an appropriate locking tool and loosen injection pump sprocket mounting bolts. See Fig. 18.

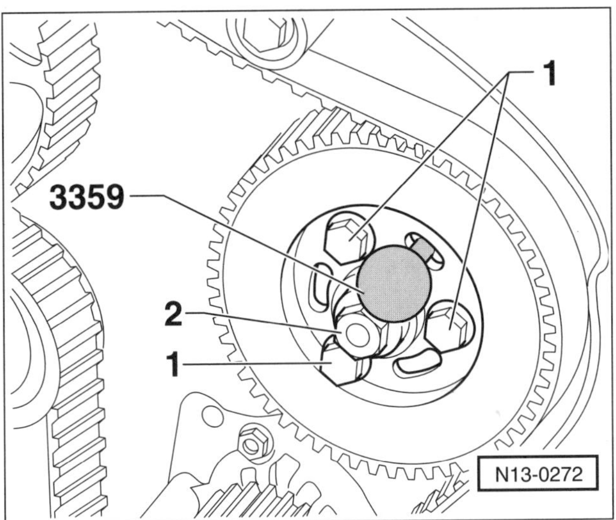

N13-0272

Fig. 18. Volkswagen special tool 3359 installed in injection pump sprocket locking it. Loosen bolts (**1**) only. Do not loosen hub bolt (**2**).

> ***CAUTION —***
> *Do not loosen or remove the hub from the Diesel injection pump. The hub is pressed onto the tapered end of the camshaft and NOT keyed to the pump drive shaft! If removed, it will no longer be correctly indexed to the pump. Correct indexing requires special equipment and training available only at specialized Bosch service centers and is beyond the scope of this manual.*

14. Loosen tensioner for toothed belt.

15. Support the engine with a suitable fixture that is designed to support the weight of the engine and transmission without damaging the body. See Fig. 19.

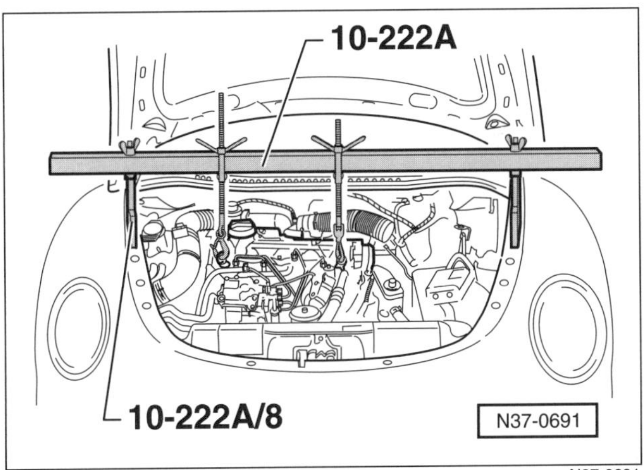

N37-0691

Fig. 19. Volkswagen supplied engine support tools shown attached to the engine.

16. Lift the supporting device slightly, so that the weight of the engine and transmission is on the supporting device.

17. Unbolt the right side engine mount from the body and the engine support bracket and remove the mount. See Fig. 20.

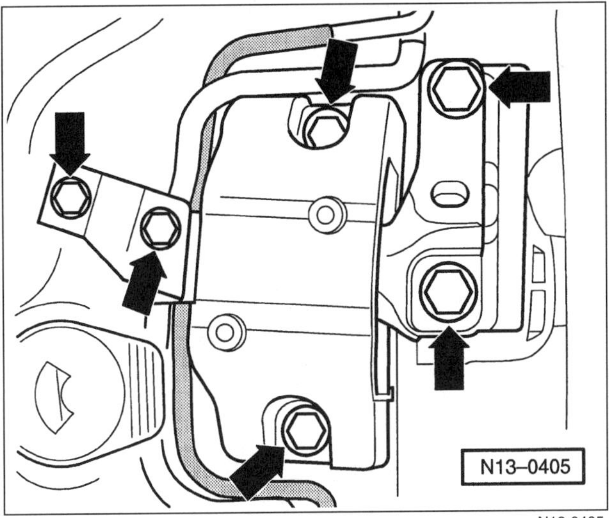

N13-0405

Fig. 20. Remove the bolts (**arrows**) securing the right side engine mount to the body and the engine support bracket.

18. Remove the right side engine support bracket.

19. Remove the vibration dampener/belt pulley from the crankshaft.

20. Remove the center and lower toothed belt guards.

21. Mark the running direction of the toothed belt and remove.

Toothed belt for camshaft drive, installing

1. Ensure that the engine is at Top Dead Center (TDC) for cylinder #1. See Fig. 5. and Fig. 6.
   If engine and transmission are separated use alternate procedure to set TDC. See Fig. 15. and Fig. 16.

2. Loosen camshaft sprocket mounting bolt about ½ turn. Release camshaft sprocket from camshaft tapered end. See Fig. 8. Locking bar and feeler gauges remain in place.

3. Install new mounting bolts into injection pump sprocket, but do not torque at this time.

4. Install toothed belt (noting directional mark if re-using old belt) on crankshaft toothed belt sprocket, idler wheels, injection pump sprocket and coolant pump.

5. When the belt is properly positioned, slip the camshaft sprocket into the toothed belt and slide onto the camshaft. Install the securing bolt only enough to hold the sprocket in place.

6. Ensure that tab on rear of tensioning roller is positioned into oil galley hole. See Fig. 21.

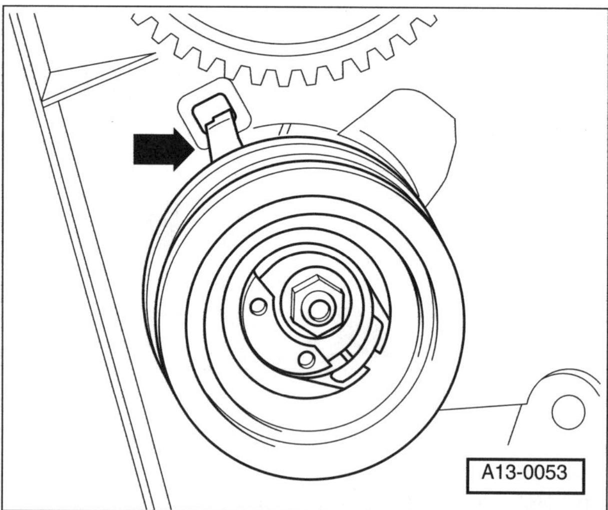

A13-0053

Fig. 21. Positioning tab shown in proper location in oil galley plug (**arrow**).

7. Tension the toothed belt using a two pin spanner in the holes in the eccentric center section. Belt is tensioned properly when notch and the raised mark are aligned. See Fig. 22.

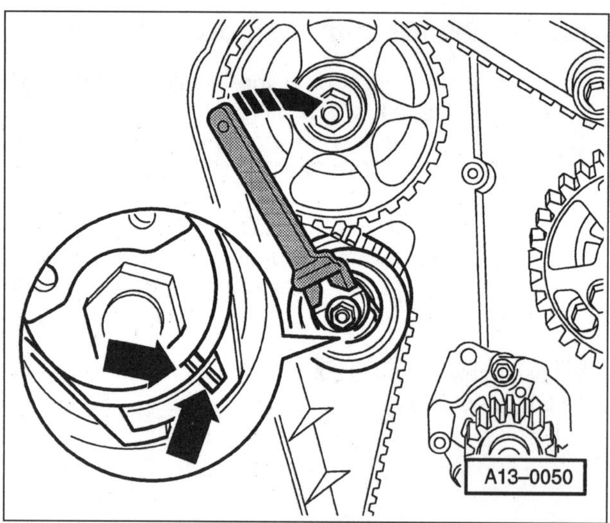

A13-0050

Fig. 22. Two pin spanner wrench shown in position to tension toothed belt. Adjustment is correct when notch and raised mark align (**inset arrows**).

8. Tighten the lock nut on the tensioner.

Tightening torque
- Toothed belt tensioner (M8) . . . . 20 Nm (15 ft-lb)

9. Ensure that crankshaft is still at TDC.

10. Tighten camshaft sprocket mounting bolt and remove setting bar and feeler gauges.

Tightening torques
- Camshaft sprocket . . . . 45 Nm (33 ft-lb)

> ***NOTE —***
> *Tighten the new injection pump sprocket mounting bolts to stage I only and remove the locking pin.*

11. The injection pump sprocket mounting bolts should only be used one time, since by design they have a reduced shank and are stretch bolts.

12. Turn crankshaft two rotations in the running direction and recheck toothed belt tension.

13. Dynamically check diesel injection pump timing, see **23 Diesel Fuel Injection (Engine Code ALH)**. If engine is removed, diesel pump injection timing must be checked and adjusted after engine has been installed.

14. Return engine to TDC for cylinder #1. Install locking pin tool 3359 and tighten injection pump sprocket mounting bolts to final torque (stage II).

Tightening torque
- Injection pump sprocket - always replace
  stage I . . . . 20 Nm (15 ft-lb)
- stage II . . . . additional ¼ turn (90°)

15. Install the center and lower toothed belt guards.

16. Install the vibration dampener/ribbed belt pulley onto the crankshaft.

Tightening torque
- Vibration dampener/ribbed belt pulley to toothed belt drive sprocket (M8). . . . . 25 Nm (18 ft-lb)

17. Insert bolts into right side engine mount bracket and attach bracket to block.

Tightening torque
- Right side engine mount bracket to cylinder block (M10) . . . . 45 Nm (33 ft-lb)

18. Install right side engine mount with new stretch bolts. See Fig. 23.

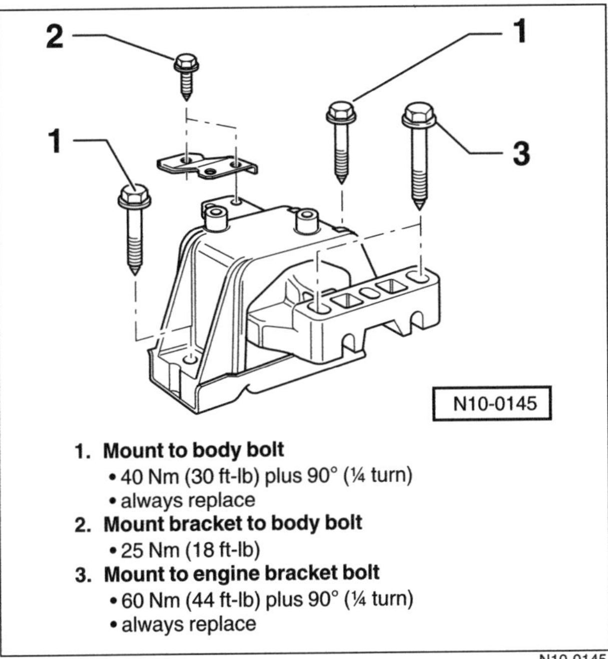

Fig. 23. Right side engine mount.

19. Remove the engine support device.

20. Install ribbed V-belt and tensioner.

Tightening torque

• Ribbed V-belt tensioner (M8) . . . . 25 Nm (18 ft-lb)

---

21. Install the brake booster vacuum pump.

22. Install the cylinder head (valve) cover.

23. Install the connecting pipe between the intercooler and the turbocharger and between the intercooler and the intake hose.

24. Install upper toothed belt guard.

25. Install the fuel filter back into the mounting bracket and connect the fuel lines.

26. Start engine and re-check diesel injection pump timing, see **23 Diesel Fuel Injection (Engine Code ALH)**.

27. Install lower sound absorber panel (belly pan).

28. Install upper engine cover.

29. Be sure to quality check your work, see **Quality Review** at the end of this repair group.

CYLINDER HEAD, REMOVING AND INSTALLING

The cylinder head can be removed and installed with the engine in the vehicle. Fig. 4, given earlier shows a view of the ALH cylinder head and related components. Note that the cylinder head bolts are stretch type fasteners and should never be reused. In addition, whenever the cylinder head or the cylinder head gasket is replaced, the coolant must also be replaced, see **19 Engine–Cooling System**.

Cylinder head, removing

The cylinder head will be removed with the exhaust manifold, turbo-charger and the intake manifold still attached. The plenum close-out panel at the base of the windshield will be removed to allow easier access to the cylinder head and provide space needed for an engine support.

> ***WARNING —***
> *Do not start work on a hot engine. Allow to cool sufficiently before proceeding. Engine temperature must be no hotter than warm to the touch. Cylinder head warpage can result due to uneven cooling rates.*

NOTE —
Disconnecting the battery cables will erase fault codes and basic settings in the engine management and automatic transmission control unit memories. Some driveability problems may be noticeable until the system re-adapts to operating conditions. OBD II readiness codes, which may be required for emissions testing, may also be erased. See **23 Fuel Injection – Diesel (ALH)** *for additional information. In some instances proper diagnosis will require the use of a scan tool such as the Volkswagen supplied VAG 1551 or 1552. Use and operation of this tool is outside the scope of this repair manual.*

1. With ignition switched off, disconnect the battery negative terminal from the battery.

NOTE —
Be sure to have the anti-theft radio code on hand before disconnecting the battery.

2. Position crankshaft so that pistons are NOT at TDC.

3. Remove upper engine cover.

4. Remove air cleaner assembly and connecting pipe.

5. Remove connecting pipe and hose between the intercooler and intake manifold/EGR solenoid.

6. Remove connecting pipe and hoses between turbo-charger and intercooler.

7. Remove lower sound absorber panel (belly pan).

8. Drain engine coolant, see **19 Engine–Cooling System**.

9. Disconnect and label fuel supply and return lines at the fuel filter. See Fig. 24.

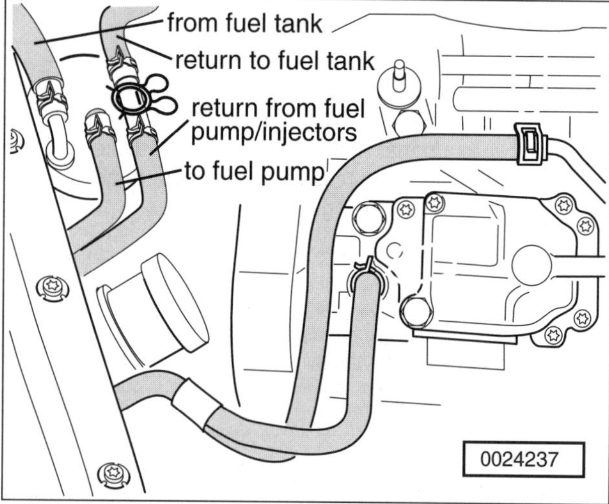

0024237

Fig. 24. Disconnect and label fuel lines at the fuel filter.

> ***WARNING —***
> *Fuel will be expelled when disconnecting fuel hoses. Wrap a cloth around the fuel line fittings before disconnecting them. Do not smoke or work near heaters or other fire hazards. Have a fire extinguisher handy.*

10. Seal off disconnected fuel and vacuum lines to prevent contamination.

11. Remove the fuel filter and bracket.

12. Unbolt front exhaust pipe from the turbo-charger, see **26 Exhaust System/Emission Controls**.

13. Remove the ribbed V-belt and tensioner.

14. Remove both wiper arms and plenum close-out panel at base of windshield, see **92 Wipers and Washers**.

15. Remove the coolant flange from the end of the cylinder head and disconnect the coolant hoses from the EGR cooler.

16. Disconnect breather and vacuum hoses from cylinder head.

17. Disconnect all electrical connectors from cylinder head including the glow plug bus connector.

18. Remove coolant reservoir from the bracket with the hoses still attached and place to the side.

19. Remove upper toothed belt guard.

20. Remove cylinder head (valve) cover.

21. Remove brake booster vacuum pump.

22. Disconnect oil return line at turbo-charger, see **21 Turbocharger and Intercooler**.

23. Disconnect turbo-charger oil supply line and support bracket.

24. Remove metal fuel injector lines.
    - Remove all four lines together as a set.
    - Use an offset flare nut wrench such as Volkswagen special tool 3035 to loosen the fittings of the injector lines.
    - Take care not to bend the lines or change the shape.

25. Remove the small injector fuel return hoses.

26. Install a suitable engine support fixture tool onto the body with both hooks moved to the belt side of the engine.

27. Attach center hook to the lifting eye on the cylinder head and tighten sufficiently to relieve tension from engine mount.

> ***NOTE —***
> *The lifting eye on the cylinder head will only be used temporarily to support the engine while the engine mount bracket is removed. A lifting eye adapter must be attached to the block after the engine mount bracket is removed. The engine support must then be transferred to the adapter because the lifting eye on the head will remain attached to the cylinder head when the head is removed.*

28. Remove right side engine mount and the support bracket on the cylinder block and lift the engine slightly with the engine fixture support hook.

29. Install a lifting eye adapter tool into the block and attach the remaining hook from the engine support fixture to adapter. See Fig. 25.

30. Lift engine slightly using the engine support hook attached to the adapter and remove hook from lifting eye on cylinder head.

31. Loosen camshaft sprocket as shown earlier and slip the toothed belt off of the camshaft sprocket. See Fig. 7. See Fig. 8.

32. Position engine to TDC for cylinder #1 and remove toothed belt tensioning roller and camshaft sprocket.

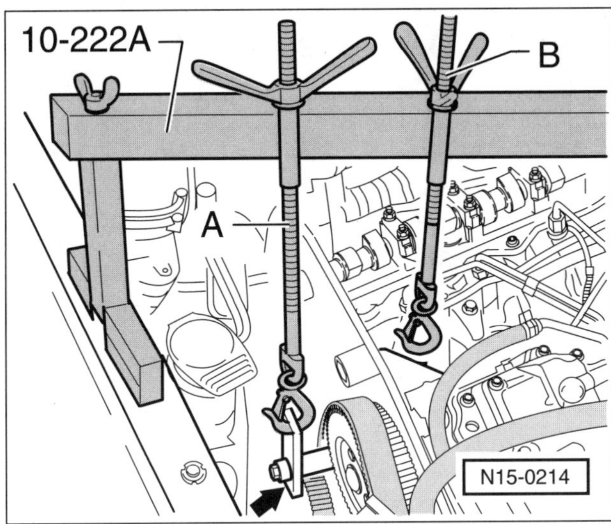

Fig. 25. Engine support tool shown installed in final position. Hook **A** is shown attached to the temporary lifting eye adapter (**arrow**) threaded into the cylinder block. Hook **B** has been released from the lifting eye on the cylinder head.

33. Remove upper bolt from rear toothed belt guard.

34. Loosen the socket head bolts slightly in sequence but do not remove until all 10 bolts have been loosened. Discard the head bolts. See Fig. 26.

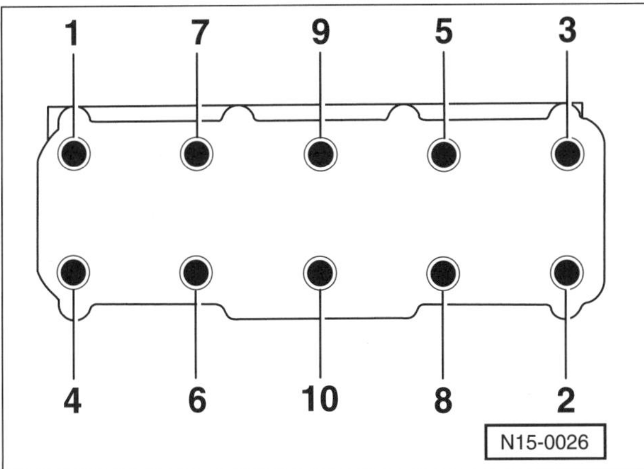

Fig. 26. Loosen the cylinder head bolts in the order shown. Loosen all bolts slightly the first time around, repeat the order, finish loosening and then remove.

35. Carefully lift off cylinder head and place in a clean area. If the head is stuck, use a soft-faced mallet or pry gently with a wooden stick.

> ***CAUTION —***
> *Some of the valves will be open. Use extra care when removing and handling to avoid damage. Place the cylinder head on the bench or table so that the weight of the cylinder head will not rest on the valves.*

Cylinder head, installing

Before proceeding with the installation of the cylinder head, whether an original or a new unit, observe the following important points:

- Check the cylinder head and block for distortion and warpage, see **Cylinder Head Components**, given later in this section.
- Carefully clean the cylinder block and cylinder head sealing surfaces being sure to avoid scratching them during the cleaning process. Do not use metal scrapers or wire brushes.
- When using abrasive paper do not use any grades coarser than 100 grit (such as 80 grit). Lower numbers are coarser.
- If the cylinder head will not be reinstalled immediately, take precautions to prevent rust from forming on the cylinder block walls and gasket sealing surfaces.
- When cleaning the old gasket material off of the cylinder block, take precautions to keep the old gasket material and the used abrasive particles and dirt out of the cooling and oiling system passages. Place a clean shop cloth over the cylinders to prevent contamination from getting between the cylinder wall and the piston.
- Do not take the new cylinder head gasket out of the packaging until ready to use. Handle the new gasket with extreme care as any damage will lead to leaks.
- There MUST NOT BE any oil or coolant in the head bolt holes in the cylinder block. Any fluids in the holes creates the danger of hydrolock while torquing which could lead to structural damage of the cylinder block. Use thread chasers to remove foreign material as required. Be sure that all 10 bolt holes are clean and dry.
- When all traces of the old gasket material have been removed from the cylinder block and head, carefully remove all traces of metal particles, abrasives and lint. All gasket sealing surfaces and bolt holes must be clean and dry to ensure a proper seal.
- Always use a new cylinder head gasket.
- Do not use any gasket sealer on the new cylinder head gasket.
- If installing a Volkswagen supplied replacement cylinder head, be sure to inspect for and remove any plastic packaging materials used to protect the head and the open valves.

1. Position the crankshaft to TDC for cylinder #1 and then turn backwards until all pistons are equally spaced below TDC.

2. Install pins from installation tool into bolt holes of cylinder block. Use of this tool allows for quick and easy alignment of the head on the block. This keeps the head from sliding off of the block and prevents damage to the head gasket. See Fig. 27.

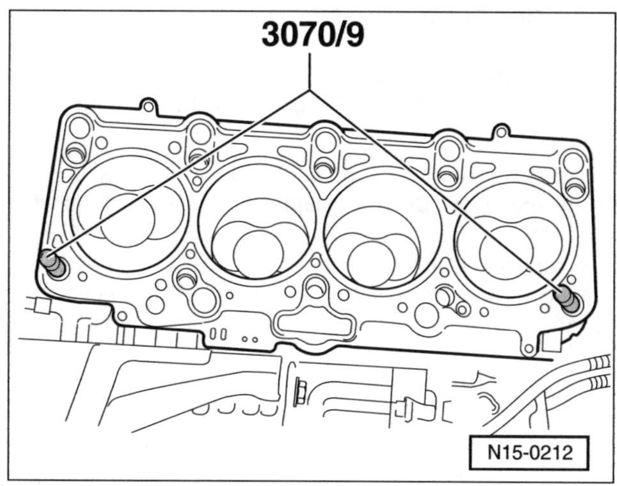

N15-0212

Fig. 27. Volkswagen supplied installation tool for assembly of cylinder head onto the block.

3. Install the new cylinder head gasket onto the block with the numbers and letters facing up. Be sure that none of the wiring or any vacuum hoses are caught between the cylinder head and the block.

4. Carefully install the cylinder head onto the block over the alignment pins and screw in 8 of the new head bolts. Tighten the bolts hand-tight only.

5. Remove the alignment pins from the bolt holes with the tool and install the remaining 2 new head bolts. Tighten these bolts hand-tight.

6. Tighten the 10 cylinder head bolts in three stages following the tightening order. See Fig. 28.

Tightening torque

- Cylinder head to cylinder block, engine code AEG (stretch bolt - always replace)
  - stage I . . . . 40 Nm (30 ft-lb)
  - stage II . . . . 60 Nm (44 ft-lb)
  - stage III . . . . additional ¼ turn (90°)
  - stage IV . . . . additional ¼ turn (90°)

---

7. Ensure that setting bar remains in place on the end of the camshaft as shown earlier. See Fig. 7.

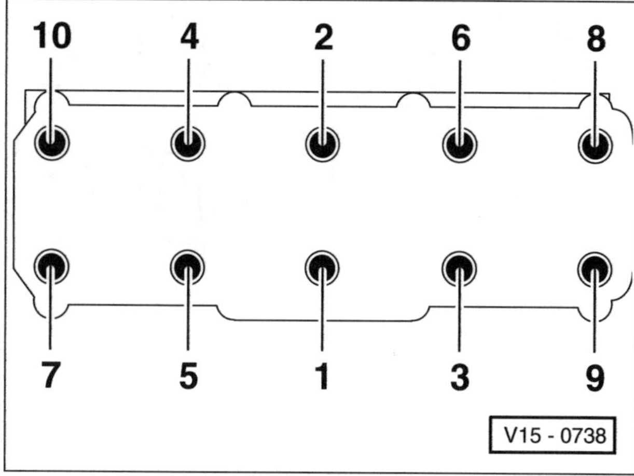

V15-0738

Fig. 28. Tighten the cylinder head bolts in the order shown. The same pattern is used for all four stages of the sequence

8. Attach the available support hook from the engine support fixture tool to the lifting eye on the cylinder head. Slightly lift this support hook to relieve the tension on the other support hook and remove it along with the adapter.

9. Install upper bolt for the rear toothed belt guard where it is attached to the cylinder head.

10. Position crankshaft at TDC for cylinder #1 by carefully turning in the normal running direction.

11. Install toothed belt, sprocket and tensioner, see **Toothed belt for camshaft drive, installing**, given earlier.

12. Install brake booster vacuum pump.

13. Install cylinder head (valve) cover.

14. Install bolts into right side engine support bracket and attach bracket to block.

15. Install engine mount with new stretch bolts, see **10 Engine–Removing and Installing**.

16. Relieve tension on the engine support bracket hook and remove the fixture.

17. Install metal fuel injector lines and small fuel return hoses.

18. Connect turbo-charger oil lines.

19. Attach front exhaust pipe to the turbo-charger with new nuts.

20. Install lower sound absorber panel (belly pan).
21. Install upper toothed belt guard.
22. Install ribbed V-belt and tensioner.
23. Install plenum close-out panel and the wiper arms.
24. Install coolant flange and hoses to the cylinder head.
25. Install coolant reservoir and refill the cooling system with fresh coolant of the appropriate ratio. See **19 Engine–Cooling System**.

> ***CAUTION —***
> - *Use only Volkswagen original anti-freeze when filling the cooling system. Use of any other anti-freeze may be harmful to the cooling system. Do not use an anti-freeze containing phosphates.*
> - *Do not use tap water in cooling system. Use distilled water only to mix anti-freeze.*

26. Install fuel filter, bracket and fuel hoses.
27. Install breather and vacuum hoses.
28. Install all electrical connectors including glow plug bus.
29. Install connecting pipes between the intercooler, turbocharger and intake manifold.
30. Install air cleaner assembly and connecting pipe.
31. Install upper sound absorber panel.
32. Reconnect the battery only after all parts have been reinstalled and reconnected.
33. Start engine and re-check diesel injection pump timing, see **23 Diesel Fuel Injection (Engine Code ALH)**.
34. Be sure to quality check your work, see **Quality Review** at the end of this repair group.

Tightening torques

- Cylinder head cover to cylinder head (M6) . . . . 10 Nm (89 in-lb)
- Cylinder head to cylinder block, engine code ALH (stretch bolt - always replace)
  - stage I . . . . 40 Nm (30 ft-lb)
  - stage II . . . . 60 Nm (44 ft-lb)
  - stage III . . . . additional ¼ turn (90°)
  - stage IV . . . . additional ¼ turn (90°)
- Front exhaust pipe to exhaust manifold (special nuts - always replace)(M8) . . 25 Nm (18 ft-lb)
- Coolant outlet flange to cylinder head (M6) . . . . 10 Nm (7 ft-lb)
- Rear toothed belt guard to cylinder head (M6) . . . . 10 Nm (7 ft-lb)
- Ribbed belt tensioner to bracket (M8) 25 Nm (18 ft-lb)
- Toothed belt tensioner (M8) . . . . 20 Nm (15 ft-lb)
- Fuel injector line flare nut . . . . 25 Nm (18 ft-lb)
- Vacuum pump to cylinder head . . . . . 20 Nm (15 ft-lb)
- Camshaft sprocket to camshaft . . . . . 45 Nm (33 ft-lb)
- Right side engine mount bracket to cylinder block (M10) . . . . 45 Nm (33 ft-lb)

CYLINDER HEAD COMPONENTS

This section provides the specifications and special information necessary to repair the cylinder head that has been removed from the Volkswagen ALH engine. Special service tools and machine shop services are required for most cylinder head repair.

> ***NOTE —***
> - *The information given under this heading assumes that the cylinder head is removed. For cylinder head removal procedures, see* ***Cylinder head, removing*** *given earlier.*
> - *Fig. 3 and Fig. 4 show exploded views of the cylinder head and valvetrain assemblies.*

Cylinder Head and Camshaft

Check the cylinder head for warpage and distortion with an accurate straight edge and a feeler gauge. See Fig. 29. Resurfacing of the cylinder head is specifically not recommended by Volkswagen. Excessively warped or distorted cylinder heads must be replaced.

Specification

- Maximum cylinder head distortion/warpage . . . . 0.1 mm (0.004 in.)

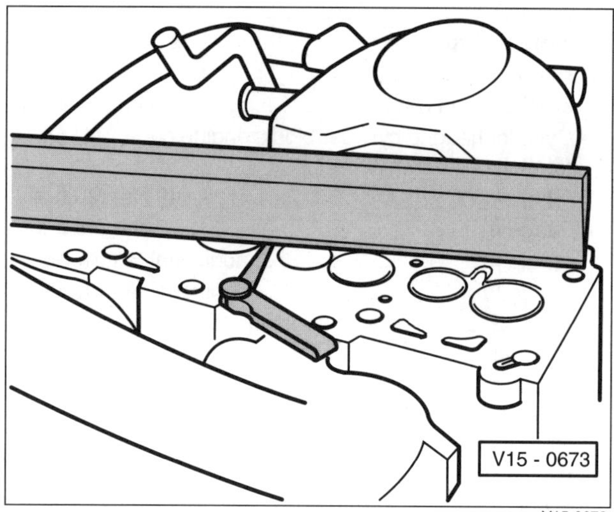

V15-0673

Fig. 29. Cylinder head being checked for distortion with a feeler gauge.

The camshaft for the ALH engines is easily identified by markings cast into it during manufacture. See Fig. 30.

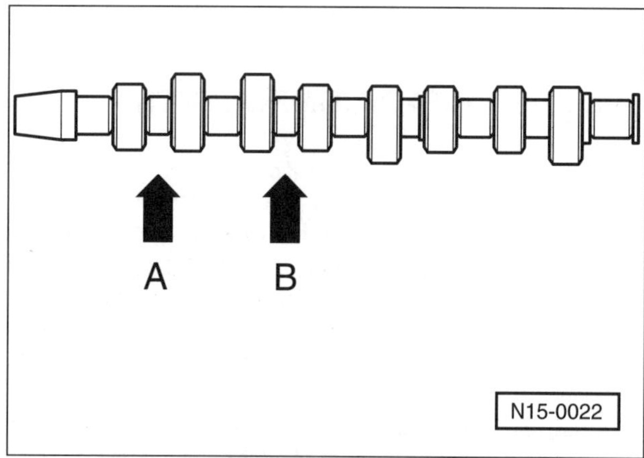

N15-0022

Fig. 30. Camshaft identification marks for ALH engines: **arrow a** identifier is -38K-, and **arrow B** identifier is -DE-.

Specification

- Valve timing at 1 mm valve lift, engine code ALH
  - Intake opens ATDC . . . . 16°
  - Intake closes ABDC . . . . 25°
  - Exhaust opens BBDC . . . . 28°
  - Exhaust closes BTDC . . . . 19°

The in and out movement of the camshaft is known as axial play and is measured with the cam followers removed and only the first and last bearing caps installed.

A dial gauge is set up on the sprocket end of the camshaft and the camshaft clearance is checked by moving the camshaft as far as it can go in each direction. See Fig. 31.

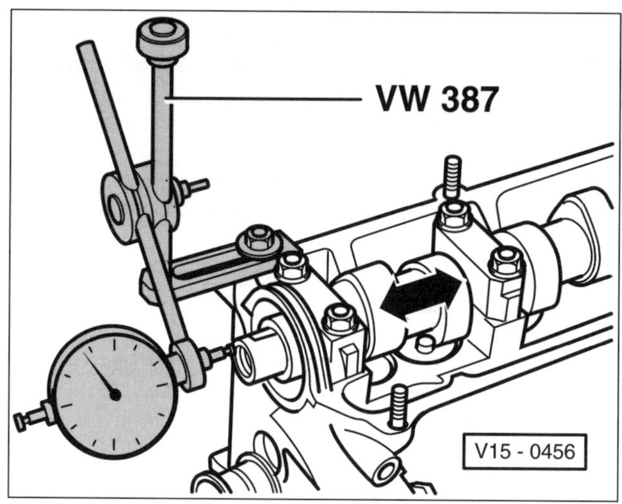

V15-0456

Fig. 31. Dial gauge set up on a camshaft to measure the axial play (**arrow**). AEG cylinder head shown, ALH is similar.

Specification

- Camshaft axial clearance . . . . 0.15 mm (0.006 in.)

Valves

Valves should not be re-worked on a machine. Only lapping by hand with valve compound is permitted. Valve dimensions listed in **Table a** apply to the valve shown in Fig. 32 which is representative of both intake and exhaust valves.

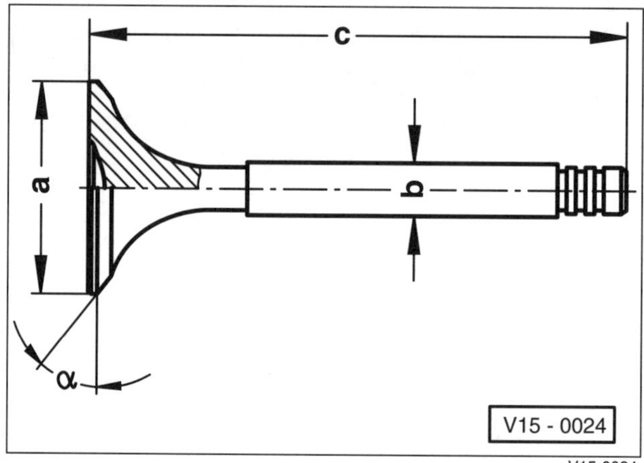

V15-0024

Fig. 32. Valve dimensions are referenced in **Table a**.

Table a. Valve Dimensions

Engine Code	ALH
Valve head diameter (**a**) intake exhaust	 35.95 mm (1.415 in.) 31.45 mm (1.238 in.)
Valve stem diameter (**b**) intake exhaust	 6.963 mm (0.274 in.) 6.943 mm (0.273 in.)
Valve length (**c**) intake exhaust	 96.85 mm (3.813 in.) 96.85 mm (3.813 in.)
Valve face angle (α) intake exhaust	 45° 45°

Valve guides

Special tools and a press are required to replace the valve guides. Check valve guide wear with a new valve. Always use an intake valve in an intake guide and an exhaust valve in an exhaust guide. See Fig. 33. Inspect the valve seats to ensure that the cylinder head can be reconditioned before installing new valve guides. Press out worn original valve guides with Volkswagen special driver tool 3121 from the camshaft side of the head. Replacement valve guides have a shoulder on the camshaft side to limit the installed depth and must be pressed out from the combustion chamber side.

When installing new valve guides, lubricate with clean engine oil and press in from the camshaft side down to the shoulder. The cylinder head must be cold for this operation. Once the shoulder of the valve guide contacts the cylinder head, do not allow the pressure on the guide to exceed 2000 psi (1 ton) otherwise the cylinder head or the guide will be damaged. When the guide has been replaced, ream it to the proper size and continue with the reworking of the valve seats.

Specification

- Valve guide (wear limits-maximum play) with new valve
  intake and exhaust valve guide. . . 1.3 mm (0.051 in.)

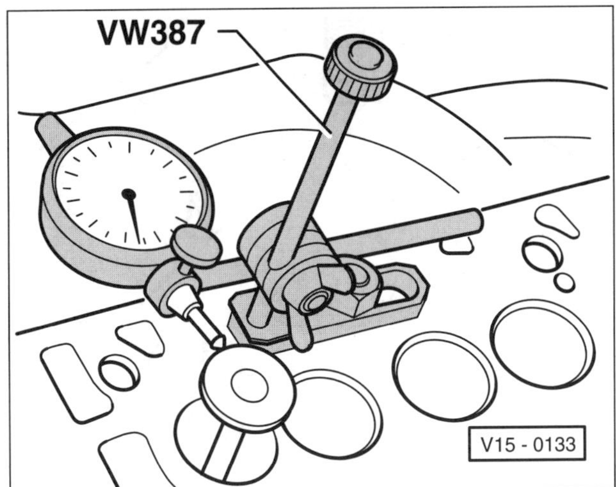

V15-0133

Fig. 33. Valve guide wear being checked with new valve. Insert valve until stem end is flush with end of guide. Rock valve back and forth to check total travel.

NOTE —
Due to the close tolerances found in the valve guides, it is recommended that Volkswagen special tool 3121 be used for removal and installation and special tool 3120 be used to ream the valve guide to size. Be sure to use the appropriate cutting fluid during the reaming operation.

Valve seats

When resurfacing valve seats, there is a limit to the amount of material that can be removed to bring the seat back into specification. If too much material is removed, the final assembly will leave too little space for the hydraulic cam follower to function properly. The maximum refacing dimension, that is, the maximum amount of material that can be removed from the valve seat, is calculated from the measurement shown in Fig. 34.

Measure dimension **a** in Fig. 34, and subtract the minimum dimension, as given in **Table b**. The difference is the maximum amount of material that can be removed from the valve seat.

Table b. Minimum Dimensions for Calculating Valve Seat Refacing Dimensions

Engine Code	Intake	Exhaust
ALH	35.8 mm (1.409 in.)	35.8 mm (1.409 in.)

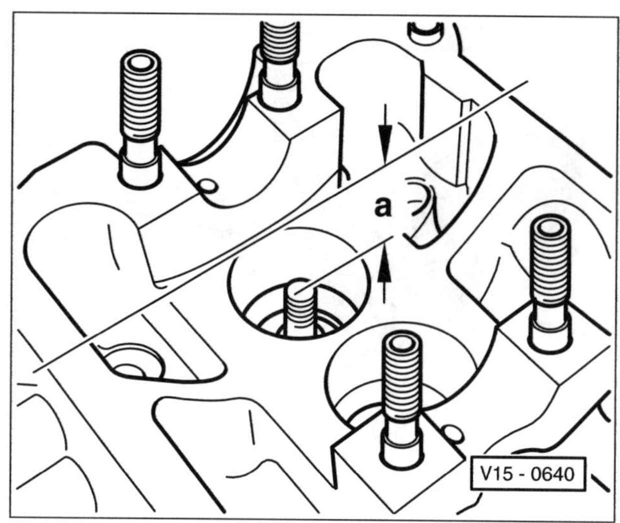

V15-0640

Fig. 34. Dimension (**a**), distance between top of valve stem and gasket surface of cylinder head, is used to calculate maximum valve seat refacing dimensions.

NOTE —

Use care when reworking the exhaust valve seats to avoid changing the shape of the port. The 30° lower valve seat chamfer is necessary to ensure that the intake channel flow characteristics are maintained.

Table c. Valve Seat Dimensions

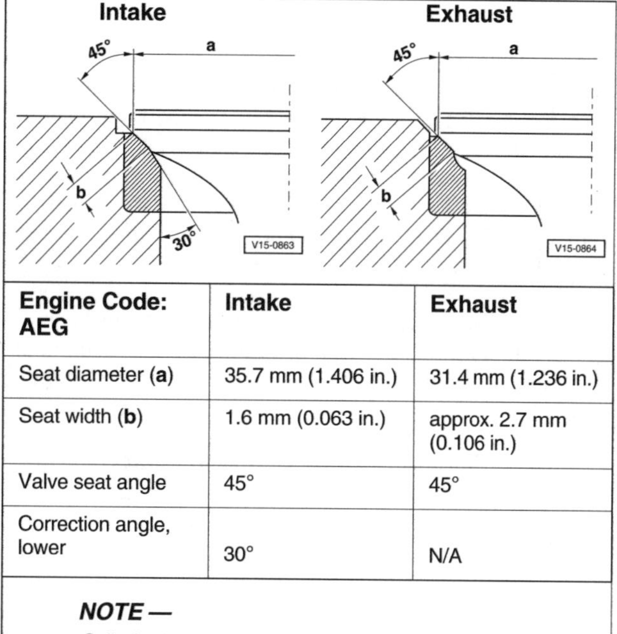

Engine Code: AEG	**Intake**	**Exhaust**
Seat diameter (**a**)	35.7 mm (1.406 in.)	31.4 mm (1.236 in.)
Seat width (**b**)	1.6 mm (0.063 in.)	approx. 2.7 mm (0.106 in.)
Valve seat angle	45°	45°
Correction angle, lower	30°	N/A

NOTE —

*Cylinder head surface reference line is (**Z**).*

QUALITY REVIEW

When you have finished working under the hood and around other areas of the vehicle it is advisable to take a moment to quality check or review your work. This helps to ensure that the operation or repair has been completed properly with all affected systems functioning within normal parameters. This may include the following:

- Make sure that the radiator fan cycles properly and that the coolant level and concentration are correct.
- Ensure that all cable ties and hose clamps that were removed as part of the repair are replaced.
- Clean off any diesel fuel that may have spilled onto rubber hoses and belts. It will cause deterioration.
- Check and adjust all other applicable fluid levels.
- Make sure that there are no fluid leaks.
- Make sure that there are no air, vacuum or exhaust leaks.
- Make sure that all components involved in the repair are positioned correctly and function properly.
- Male sure all tools, shop cloths, fender covers, and protective tape are removed.
- Clean grease from painted surfaces and steering wheel.
- Unlock the anti-theft radio and reset the clock.

In addition to the above noted points, the ECM and TCM may need to be checked using the Volkswagen supplied VAG 1551 or 1552 scan tool as mentioned at the start of this repair.

17 Engine–Lubrication System

GENERAL

Proper engine lubrication relies on a constant supply of oil, fed to the moving parts under pressure. Pressure is supplied by a gear-type oil pump located inside the engine oil pan. Engine oil returns to the oil pan by way of internal passages in the cylinder block and head. The returned oil collects in the oil pan where it is stored for eventual pickup by the oil pump. Additionally, engines with turbo-chargers have external oil supply and return lines. Fig. 1 shows an exploded view of the lubrication system.

Engine Codes

- AEG . . . . .2.0L 4-cylinder gasoline
- ALH . . . . 1.9L 4-cylinder turbo diesel

NOTE —
Oil and oil filter information is covered in **0 Maintenance Program**.

Lubrication system, assembly

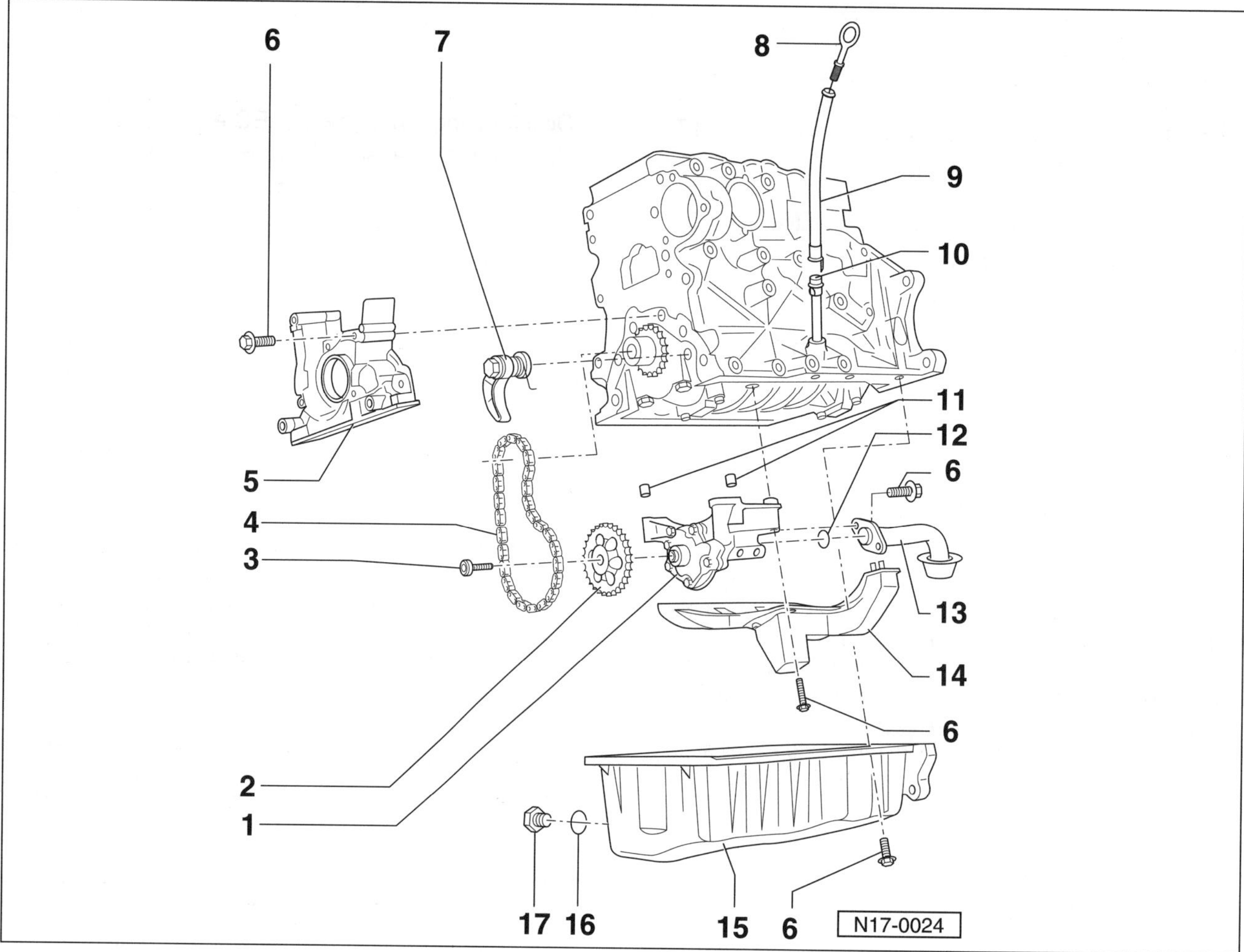

N17-0024

Fig. 1. Exploded view of lubrication system on AEG and ALH engines.

1. **Oil pump**
   - 12 bar (174 psi) pressure relief valve
   - Before installing, ensure that both centering dowels are installed
   - Replace if any running surfaces or gears are scored
2. **Chain sprocket**
3. **Bolt**
   - Tighten to 25 Nm (18 ft-lb)
4. **Chain**
5. **Sealing flange**
   - Insert with silicone sealer D176 404 A2
6. **Bolt**
   - Tighten to 15 Nm (11 ft-lb)
7. **Chain tensioner (with tensioning rail)**
   - Tighten to 15 Nm (11 ft-lb)
   - To install, first pretension spring
8. **Dipstick**
   - Oil level must NOT be above MAX mark!
9. **Guide**
10. **Guide tube**
11. **Centering dowels**
12. **O-ring**
    - Always replace
13. **Suction pipe**
    - Clean strainer if soiled
14. **Baffle plate**
15. **Oil pan**
    - Clean oiling surfaces before installing
    - Install with silicone sealant D 176 404 A2
16. **Seal**
    - Always replace
17. **Oil drain plug**
    - Tighten to 30 Nm (22 ft-lb)

OIL PRESSURE WARNING SYSTEM

To prevent serious engine damage, a dynamic oil pressure warning system warns the driver of insufficient oil pressure. The dynamic oil pressure system includes a single oil pressure switch, an electric control unit, a warning light and a buzzer. The electronic control unit with buzzer and warning light is integrated into the instrument cluster.

Oil pressure warning system, checking

With the ignition off, the single oil pressure switch is open (no continuity between the terminal connection and the switch body). When the ignition is switched on, but the engine is not started, the oil pressure warning light should come on for approximately 3 seconds and then go out.

When the engine is started and the oil pressure rises, the oil pressure switch should close at the specified pressure completing a circuit to ground. When the engine reaches approximately 1,500 rpm, the electronic control unit checks to see if the ground is complete and if so, the system is functioning normally. If the ground is not complete, the warning light and buzzer are activated. Several small time delays are programmed into the system to prevent accidental warnings due to normal minor fluctuations in pressure.

> ***CAUTION—***
> *If the warning indicators stay on after the engine is started, or while driving, always assume that there is insufficient oil pressure. Check oil level and test oil pressure before proceeding.*

A quick-check of the system can be accomplished as follows:

1. Check instrument cluster warning light.
   - Turn key on, but do not start engine.
   - Warning light should come on for about 3 seconds and then go out.
2. Turn key off.
3. Disconnect and ground the wire at oil pressure switch.
4. Turn key on, but do not start engine.
5. Warning light should flash and the buzzer should beep 3 times.
6. Turn key off.
7. Remove oil pressure switch wire from ground but do not re-connect to oil pressure switch.
8. Start engine and let idle.
   - Warning light and buzzer should not come on.
9. Increase engine speed above approximately 1,500-2,000 rpm.
   - Warning light and buzzer should come on after a 2-3 second delay.

If the above tests give results as noted, the oil pressure warning system is functioning within normal parameters.

If the above test results deviate from specification, continue by testing the oil pressure and the oil pressure switch, given later.

> ***NOTE—***
> *Since oil temperature can have a considerable influence on oil pressure, it may be advisable to conduct the above noted tests on both a cold and a warmed-up engine.*

Oil pressure and oil pressure switch, testing

It is possible for the oil pressure warning system to be functioning properly and still give an occasional indication of a malfunction. In this case, it is advisable to check the oil pressure switch. This switch is located on the oil filter flange for both gas and diesel engines, see **Oil filter flange, assembly**, given later.

The oil pressure switch can be accurately tested by removing it from the oil filter flange and temporarily installing it into an oil pressure tester such as the Volkswagen supplied VAG 1342. See Fig. 2.

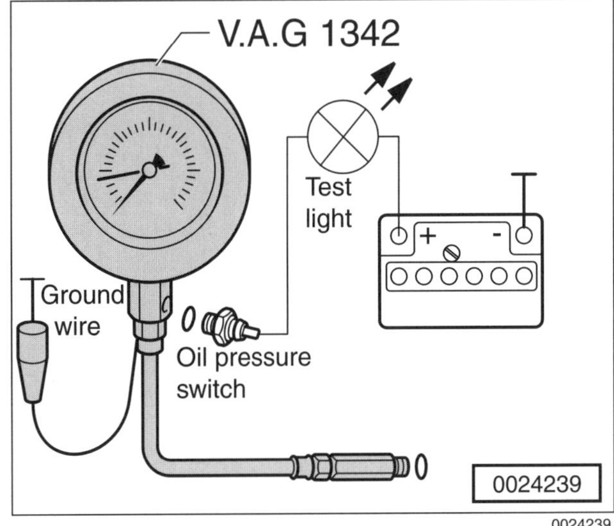

0024239

Fig. 2. Pressure gauge and test light setup for testing oil pressure and oil pressure switch. Oil pressure switch is installed in tester and test light is connected between the switch terminal and battery positive.

1. Disconnect wire from oil pressure switch and leave it unplugged for this test.

2. Remove oil pressure switch and thread it into tester.
3. Thread oil pressure tester hose into hole previously occupied by switch.
4. Connect ground wire from tester to a good ground.
5. Connect a test light from battery positive to switch terminal.
6. Start engine and let it warm up.
7. When radiator fan has cycled at least once, accelerate engine until test light comes on and observe pressure gauge. The light must come on at the specified value. If light does not illuminate at specified value, switch is defective and should be replaced.
8. Continue system test by checking oil pressure. With tester still attached, run engine at specified speeds and compare readings on gauge to specification. If specification is not reached, oil pump deficiencies are indicated.

Specification

- Oil pressure switch closing pressure
  - AEG engine
    - black switch, (1.4 bar). . . . . . 1.2-1.6 bar (18-24 psi)
  - ALH engine
    - gray switch, (0.9 bar) . . . . . . 0.7-1.1 bar (10-16 psi)

> ***NOTE—***
> *Incorrect engine oil viscosity can influence engine oil pressures. Before performing repairs, ensure that the engine has a sufficient quantity of fresh oil of the correct viscosity.*

Specification

- Oil pressure at 80°C (176°F)
  - AEG engine
    - at idle . . . . minimum 2.0 bar (29 psi)
    - at 2,000 rpm . . . . 3.0 to 4.5 bar (44 to 66 psi)
    - maximum . . . . no factory specification available
  - ALH engine
    - at idle . . . . no factory specification available
    - at 2,000 rpm . . . . minimum 2.0 bar (29 psi)
    - maximum . . . . 7.0 bar (103 psi)

---

9. When testing is completed, remove the test light and tester. Install the oil pressure switch and the wiring.

> ***NOTE—***
> *If an oil pressure switch seal is leaking, a new sealing washer should be installed. The sealing washer is held captive on the switch and must be cut off. New sealing rings are available from authorized Volkswagen parts dealers or aftermarket parts specialists.*

LUBRICATION SYSTEM COMPONENTS

Oil filter flange

The oil filter flange mounts the oil cooler and the oil filter. The AEG engine uses a spin-on oil filter mounted from below. See Fig. 3. The ALH engine uses a cartridge-type filter accessed from above. See Fig. 4. Both flanges have valves that bypass the filter if it should be unable to flow correctly.

Oil filter flange, assembly (AEG engine)

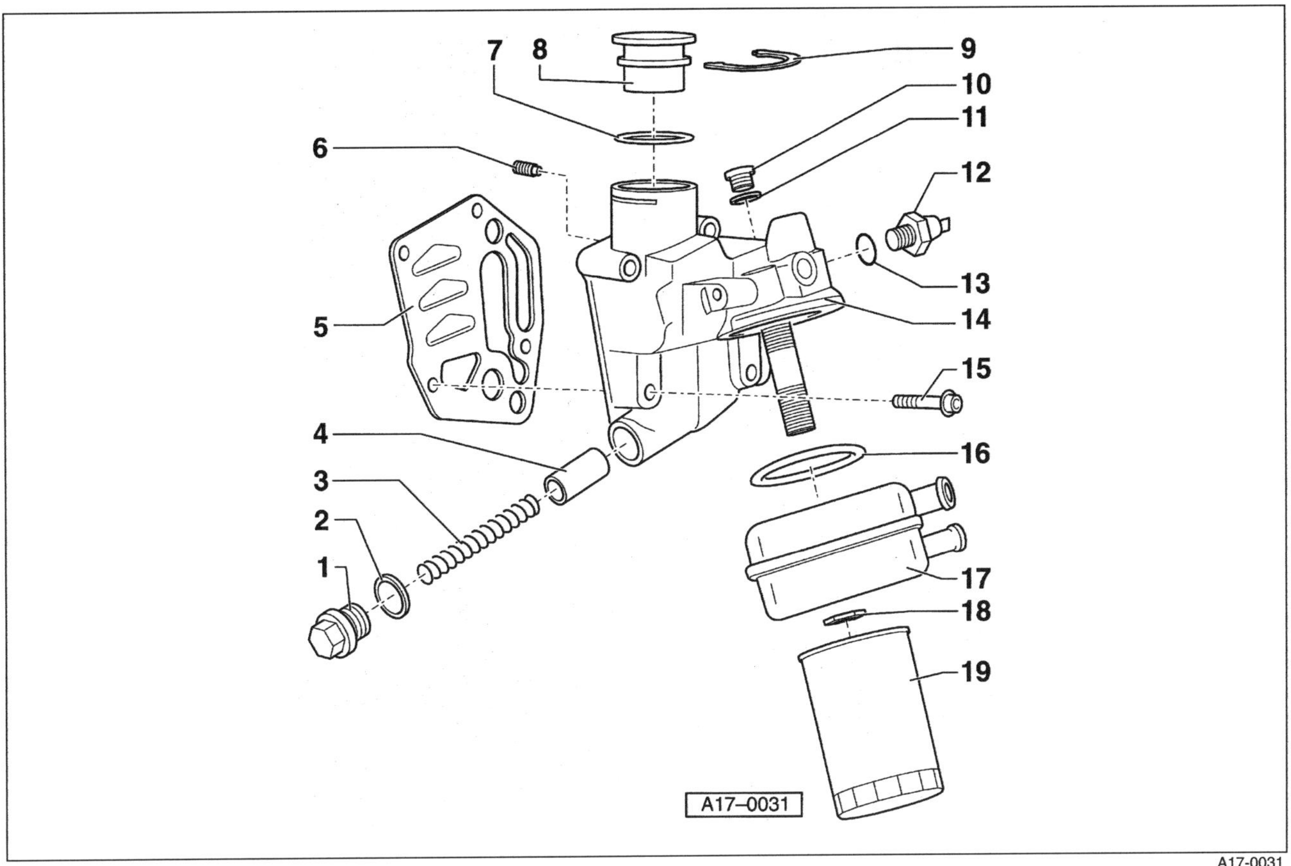

Fig. 3. Oil filter flange with related components for AEG engine.

1. **Sealing plug**
   - Tighten to 40 Nm (30 ft-lb)
2. **Seal**
3. **Spring**
   - For pressure relief valve, approx. 4 bar (58 psi)
4. **Piston**
   - For pressure relief valve
5. **Gasket**
   - Always replace
6. **Check valve**
   - Tighten to 8 Nm (71 in-lb)
7. **Seal**
   - Install onto sealing cap and shoulder (item 8)
8. **Sealing cap**
9. **Retaining clip**
10. **Sealing plug**
    - Tighten to 15 Nm (11 ft-lb)
11. **Seal**
    - If sealing ring is leaking, cut open and replace
12. **Oil pressure switch (1.4 bar)**
    - Tighten to 25 Nm (18 ft-lb)
    - Black
13. **Seal**
    - If sealing ring is leaking, cut open and replace
14. **Oil filter flange**
15. **Nut**
    - Tighten to 15 Nm (11 ft-lb) + ¼ turn (90°) further
    - Always replace
16. **Gasket**
    - Always replace
    - Fit into groove on oil cooler
17. **Oil cooler**
    - Installed position: must be turned fully clockwise (viewed from below) until touching its own bracket
18. **Nut**
    - Tighten to 25 Nm (18 ft-lb)
19. **Oil filter**
    - Loosen with strap wrench
    - Hand tighten
    - Observe installation instructions on oil filter

Oil filter flange, assembly (ALH engine)

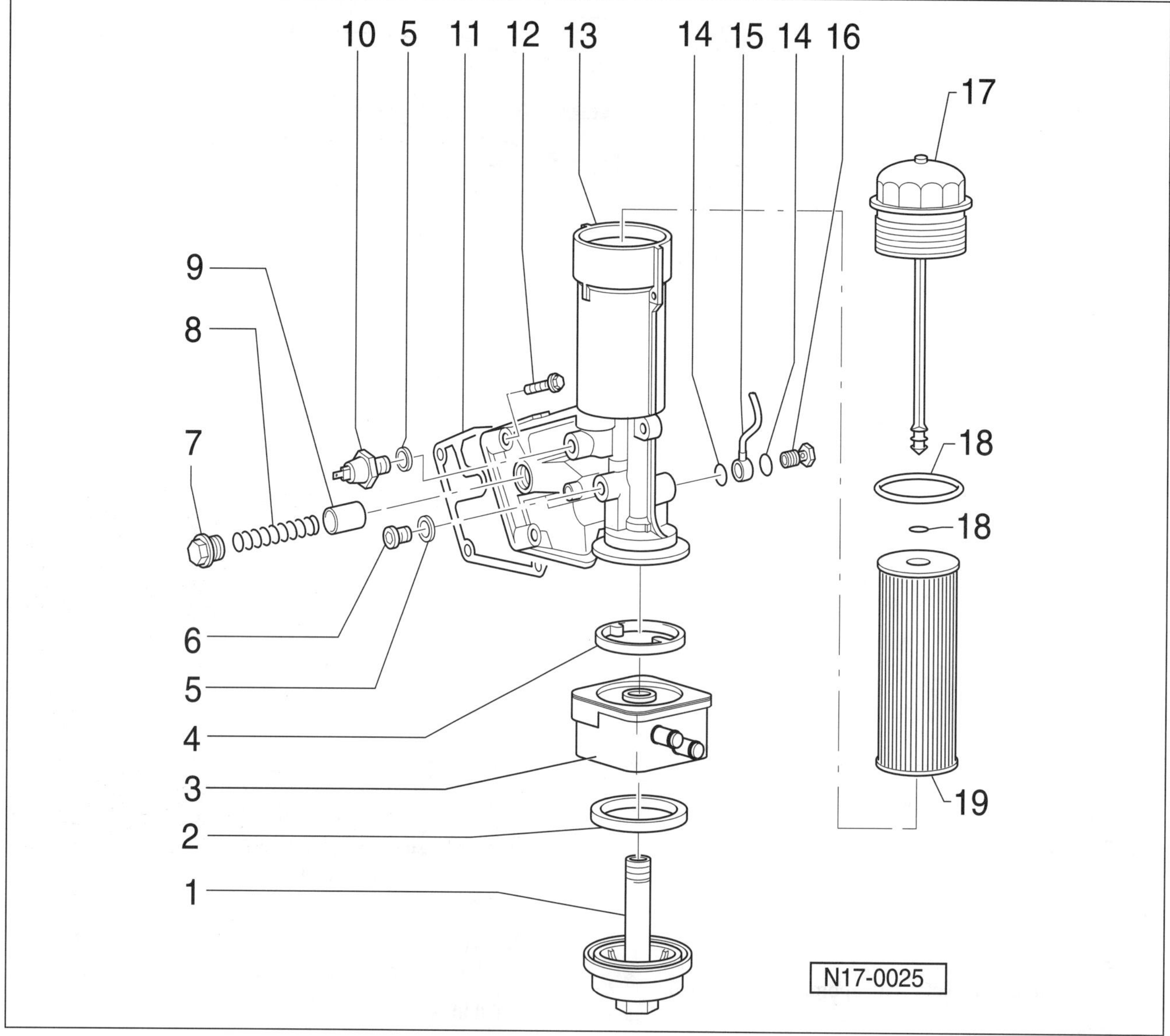

N17-0025

Fig. 4. Oil filter flange with related components for ALH engine.

1. **Sealing plug**
   - Tighten to 25 Nm (18 ft-lb)
2. **Gasket**
   - Always replace
3. **Oil cooler**
   - Installed position: must be turned fully clockwise (viewed from below) until touching its own bracket
4. **Gasket**
   - Always replace
   - Install into oil cooler groove
5. **Seal**
   - If seal leaks, cut open and replace
6. **Plug**
   - Tighten to 10 Nm (7 ft-lb)
7. **Sealing plug**
   - Do NOT open
8. **Spring**
   - For pressure relief valve, approx. 5 bar (72.5 psi)
9. **Piston**
   - For pressure relief valve, approx. 5 bar (72.5 psi)
10. **Oil pressure switch (0.9 bar)**
    - Tighten to 25 Nm (18 ft-lb)
    - Gray

11. **Gasket**
    - Always replace
12. **Bolt**
    - Tighten to 15 Nm (11 ft-lb) + ¼ turn (90°) further
    - Always replace
    - Place bolts first top left and right, then tighten all four bolts diagonally
13. **Oil filter bracket**
14. **Seal**
    - Always replace
15. **Oil supply pipe**
    - To turbocharger
16. **Banjo bolt**
    - Tighten to 20 Nm (15 ft-lb)
17. **Sealing cap**
    - Tighten to 25 Nm (18 ft-lb)
    - Loosen and tighten using 3417 oil filter wrench
18. **O-ring**
    - Always replace
19. **Oil filter element**

Oil pan, removing

The engine oil pan is a cast aluminum design bolted to both the cylinder block and the transmission. This new design uses silicone sealant instead of a conventional gasket at the joint to the cylinder block.

Oil pan removal is a straight-forward operation.

1. Remove lower sound absorber panel (belly pan).
2. Remove oil drain plug and drain oil into a suitable container.
3. Remove M10 bolts (quantity 3) holding the oil pan to the transmission.
4. Remove the M7 bolts (quantity 20) holding the oil pan to the cylinder block. See Fig. 5.

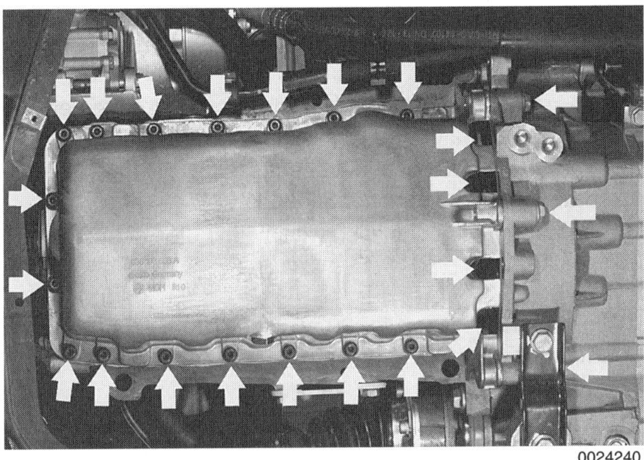

Fig. 5. Engine oil pan as viewed from below. Remove bolts at **arrows** to separate oil pan from engine and transmission.

5. Remove oil pan. It may be necessary to free oil pan by tapping it lightly with a rubber hammer.
6. Remove old sealant residue from cylinder block with a flat scraper.
7. Remove old sealant residue from oil pan with a suitable rotating brush/pad. See Fig. 6.

> ***WARNING —***
> *Always wear suitable eye protection when using a rotating brush/pad.*

8. Clean sealing surfaces on oil pan and cylinder block so that there are no traces of oil or grease.

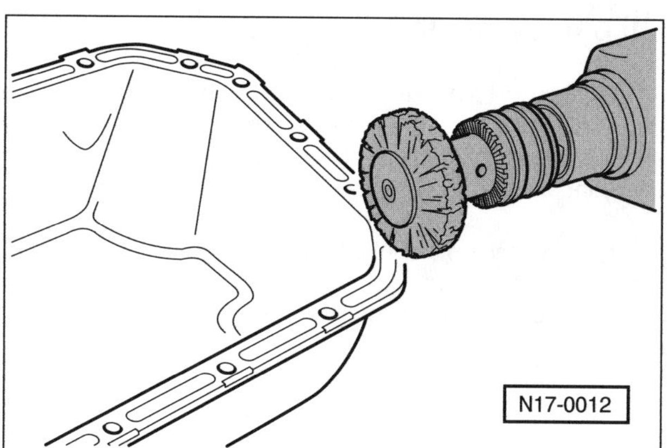

Fig. 6. Old sealant residue being removed with a cleaning pad attached to a drill motor. Use care to avoid scratching aluminum oil pan.

Oil pan, installing

Before installing the oil pan, observe the following points:

- Volkswagen recommends using special silicone sealant D 176 404 A2 on the oil pan and cylinder block.
- The above sealant is date coded. Observe the "Use by date" on the sealant container.
- Oil pan must be installed within 5 minutes of applying sealant.

Allow sealant to cure for 30 minutes before adding engine oil to the pan.

> ***NOTE —***
> *Volkswagen part numbers are given for reference only! Always consult with your Volkswagen Parts Department or aftermarket parts specialist for the latest parts information.*

1. Be sure that the sealing surfaces on the oil pan and cylinder block are clean with no traces of oil or grease.

2. Cut sealant tube nozzle at first mark and apply a 2 to 3 mm (slightly less than 1/8 inch) bead of new sealant to cylinder block sealing surface. Be sure to run bead on inside of bolt holes. See Fig. 7.

> ***CAUTION —***
> *The sealing compound bead thickness must not be wider than 3 mm (slightly less than 1/8 inch). If this width is exceeded, excess sealing compound will enter the oil pan and could block the oil pump pickup tube strainer.*

3. Apply a 2 to 3 mm (slightly less than 1/8 inch) bead of new sealant to oil pan sealing surface. Be sure to run bead on the inside of the bolt holes. See Fig. 8.

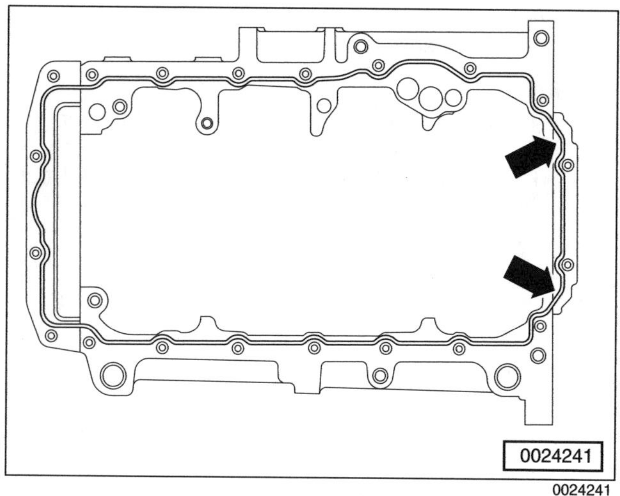

Fig. 7. Sealant bead (**arrows**) applied to cylinder block. Note how sealant is applied inside of bolt holes.

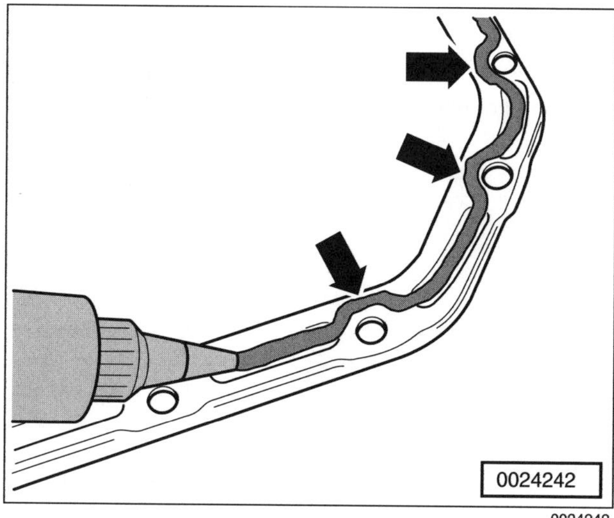

Fig. 8. Sealant bead (**arrows**) applied to cylinder block. Note how sealant is applied inside of bolt holes.

4. Immediately install oil pan to cylinder block and loosely install M7 bolts (quantity 20) diagonally.

> ***NOTE —***
> *If the engine and transmission are separated for this operation, install the oil pan flush with the flywheel edge of the cylinder block.*

5. Install and lightly tighten M10 bolts (quantity 3) securing oil pan to transmission.

6. Diagonally tighten M7 oil pan bolts further, but not to final torque.

7. Torque M10 bolts securing oil pan to transmission.

8. Diagonally torque M7 bolts securing oil pan to cylinder block.

Tightening torques
- Oil pan to transmission (M10) . . . . . . 45 Nm (33 ft-lb)
- Oil pan to cylinder block (M7). . . . . . . 15 Nm (11 ft-lb)
- Oil drain plug (M14) . . . . 30 Nm (22 ft-lb)

9. Install drain plug.

10. Install lower sound absorber panel (belly pan).

11. Wait 30 minutes as prescribed and refill with proper viscosity and quantity of engine oil.

12. Be sure to quality check your work, see **Quality Review** at the end of this repair group.

Oil pump

The oil pump is located inside the engine oil pan and is bolted to the cylinder block below the front of the crankshaft. The oil pump is driven by a short chain connected directly to the crankshaft rather than by an intermediate shaft as on previous 4-cylinder Volkswagen engines. A spring loaded tensioner takes up any slack in the chain.

There is normally no need to remove and inspect the oil pump unless oil pressure is inadequate. Check the oil pressure as described earlier in **Oil pressure and oil pressure switch, testing**.

There are no serviceable parts inside the oil pump, however the pump can be disassembled and visually inspected for scoring and wear on the gears and running surfaces. If abnormal scoring is found, the pump must be replaced.

Tightening torques
- Oil pump to cylinder block (M7) . . . . . 15 Nm (11 ft-lb)
- Sprocket to oil pump (M8) . . . . 25 Nm (18 ft-lb)
- Oil pump cover to body (M6) . . . . 10 Nm (7 ft-lb)
- Suction pipe to body (M7) . . . . 15 Nm (11 ft-lb)

Oil spray nozzles (AHU engine)

ALH TDI engines are equipped with oil spray nozzles attached to the cylinder block at the base of the cylinder bore. See Fig. 9. The oil spray nozzles atomize a fine mist of engine oil and direct it against the bottom of the piston for additional cooling and lubrication. The oil spray nozzle is regulated by the valve that secures it to the cylinder block. The valve only opens to allow flow when oil pressure is greater than 2.5 to 3.2 bar (37 to 47 psi). To access the oil spray nozzles, the oil pan must first be removed.

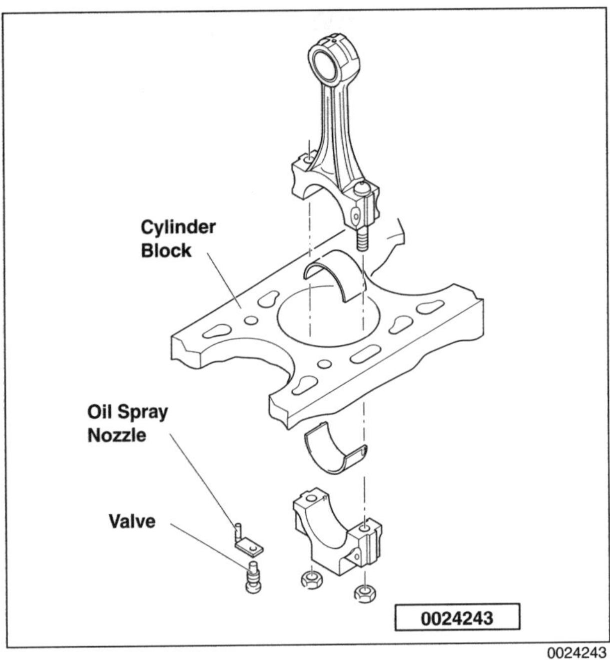

0024243

Fig. 9. Oil spray nozzle is secured to the base of the cylinder block by the valve.

Oil cooler

The oil cooler is an oil-to-coolant heat exchanger. Engine oil flows through one part of the cooler and gives up heat to the engine coolant flowing through the other part of the cooler. During warm-up, the process is reversed and engine coolant gives up heat to the engine oil because the engine coolant gets warm first. This speeds the warm-up process and gets the engine to operating temperature more quickly. See Fig. 3 or Fig. 4 given earlier for oil cooler location.

NOTE —
- *The oil cooler should be replaced if metal particles or metal shavings are found in the engine oil. The cooler cannot be cleaned.*
- *The cooler is a potential source of leakage between the lubrication system and the cooling system and should be considered whenever such leakage is suspected.*

Remove the cooler only if it needs to be inspected or replaced. Check to see that there is adequate space for the coolant hose connections and that the cooler is properly positioned.

Tightening torque
- Oil cooler sealing cap or nut to filter flange . . . . 25 Nm (18 ft-lb)

QUALITY REVIEW

When you have finished working under the hood and around other areas of the vehicle, it is advisable to take a moment to quality check or review your work. This helps to insure that the operation or repair has been completed properly with all affected systems functioning within normal parameters. These may include the following:

- Ensure that all cable ties and hose clamps that were removed as part of the repair are replaced.
- Check and adjust engine oil and all other applicable fluid levels.
- Make sure that there are no oil leaks.
- Make sure that all components involved in the repair are positioned correctly and function properly.
- Make sure that all tools, shop cloths, fender covers and protective tapes are removed before closing the hood.
- Clean grease and fingerprints from painted surfaces and steering wheel.

19 Engine–Cooling System

GENERAL

This section covers repairs and troubleshooting for the engine cooling system. For heater core and related heating and air conditioning components, see **80 Heating and Air Conditioning**. For information on the engine oil cooler, see **17 Engine-Lubrication**. For information on the ATF cooler used on vehicles with automatic transmissions, see **37 Automatic Transmission**.

Engine Codes

- AEG . . . . 2.0L 4-cylinder gasoline
- ALH . . . . 1.9L 4-cylinder turbo diesel

Warnings and cautions

The following warnings and cautions should be observed when working on the cooling system.

WARNING —

- *Hot coolant can scald and result in serious personal injury. Do not work on the cooling system until it has fully cooled.*
- *At normal operating temperature the cooling system is pressurized. Allow the system to cool as long as possible before opening, a minimum of an hour, then release the cap slowly to allow safe release of the pressure.*

WARNING —

- *Releasing the cooling system pressure lowers the coolant's boiling point, and the coolant may boil suddenly. Use heavy gloves and wear eye and face protection to guard against scalding.*
- *Use extreme care when working at or near the radiator cooling fans when the engine is hot. The fan can come on at any time, even if the ignition key is switched off.*
- *Use extreme care when draining and disposing of engine coolant. Coolant is poisonous and lethal. Children and pets are attracted to coolant because of its sweet smell and taste. See a doctor or veterinarian immediately if any amount of coolant is ingested.*
- *Disposal of used coolant must be done in conformance with all applicable local, state and federal laws. Do not pour into the ground or down drains or sewers. Contamination of ground water will result.*

CAUTION —

Avoid adding cold water to the cooling system while the engine is hot or overheated. If it is necessary to add coolant to a hot system, do so only with the engine running and the coolant pump operating.

Coolant, pump and thermostat

Volkswagen uses only one type of antifreeze/coolant in the New Beetle, regardless of engine type. This antifreeze/coolant is phosphate and silicate free and is identified by its red color. When supplied by Volkswagen, this coolant is known as G12. Due to its special characteristics it should never be mixed with any other type of coolant. See **0 Maintenance** for additional information and cautions.

For best overall performance, the coolant additive proportion must be at least 40%, but not more than 60% to maintain the antifreeze protection and cooling efficiency. Distilled water should always be used due to the various chemicals and minerals usually associated with tap water. Under no circumstances should 100% coolant/antifreeze be used. This will generally result in overheating and poor heater operation due to the poor heat transfer characteristics of pure anti/freeze. For accurate testing of antifreeze/coolant protection, a refractometer such as VW tool CEN5021 should be used, see **Coolant/antifreeze protection, testing**. A 50/50 mixture is generally preferred and will provide freeze protection to -34°F (-37°C).

An impeller-type coolant pump is mounted into cylinder block. The pump is crankshaft-driven by the same toothed belt that drives the camshaft and circulates coolant through the system whenever the engine is running.

The thermostat controls coolant flow through the radiator. When the engine is cold, the thermostat restricts flow through the radiator to allow the engine to reach operating temperature quicker. As the engine heats up, the thermostat opens and coolant circulates through the whole system, including the radiator.

Radiator and cooling fan

A radiator cooling fan assembly provides auxiliary air flow through the radiator. The fan assembly is electrically operated and thermostatically controlled so that it runs only when extra air flow is required to maintain proper coolant temperature.

The radiator is a cross-flow design constructed of an aluminum core and plastic side tanks. A translucent expansion tank, or overflow reservoir, provides for the expansion of the coolant at higher temperatures, easy monitoring of the coolant level and a convenient location for adding coolant.

An electric radiator cooling fan assembly is controlled by a thermoswitch located in the side of the radiator. At higher coolant temperatures, the switch closes to start the cooling fans. Any time the coolant temperature rises to higher than normal levels, the fan will start and continue to run until coolant temperature returns to a normal range. On vehicles with air conditioning, rising refrigerant pressures will also activate the cooling fans.

> ***WARNING —***
> *The electric cooling fans can come on at any time, even if the key is out of the ignition. To avoid personal injury, use extreme caution when working at or near the cooling fan if the engine is hot. As a safety precaution, always disconnect the harness connector from the fan when working around the radiator, fans and associated components.*

Coolant temperature/level warning lights

The New Beetle is not equipped with a conventional coolant temperature gauge. In place of the gauge is a symbol on the instrument cluster that changes color to provide information about cooling system operation. See Fig. 1.

0024244

Fig. 1. Engine coolant temperature and level warning light symbol in instrument cluster (**arrow**).

The coolant temperature and level symbol will change color to indicate the following cooling system functions:

- Steady BLUE
  May come on when the engine is first started to indicate a cold engine.
- Flashing BLUE
  Comes on to indicate a malfunction within the electrical section of the cooling system.
- Steady RED
  Comes on when the ignition is first switched on as a functional check and self-test, flashes several times and goes out.
- Flashing RED
  Comes on when driving to indicate a low coolant level condition or an overheat situation. A warning buzzer may also sound.
- Not Illuminated (no light)
  If self test is OK, no light indicates normal cooling system operation.

The coolant temperature and level warning lights have Onboard Diagnostic (OBD) capabilities included with the diagnostic capabilities of the instrument cluster. In order to access these capabilities, a scan tool such as the Volkswagen VAG 1551 or 1552 is required. Due to the specialized nature of this particular tool, its use and operation are outside the scope of this manual.

TROUBLESHOOTING

When investigating the cause of overheating or coolant loss, begin with a visual inspection of the system. Check the coolant level and inspect for evidence of coolant leaks.

The system becomes pressurized at normal operating temperatures. Leaks may prevent the system from becoming pressurized and allow the coolant to boil at a lower temperature. If visual evidence is inconclusive, a cooling system pressure test will determine whether the system leaks and may help to indicate the source.

If the cooling system holds pressure, the most probable causes of overheating are an electrical fault with the cooling fans, a faulty thermostat, or poor coolant circulation due to restrictions in the system.

Table a lists overheating and underheating symptoms, their probable causes, and suggested corrective actions. The bold type refers to areas outside of this repair group for suggested repairs.

NOTE —
- *Coolant also circulates through the heater core in the passenger compartment. For problems associated with the heater core and the heating system, see* **8 Heating and Air Conditioning**.
- *Overheating problems may also be caused by an engine fault that leaks hot combustion gases into the cooling system. See* **1 Engine** *for additional information concerning the cylinder block and head.*

Table a. Cooling system troubleshooting

Symptom	Probable cause	Corrective action
1. Engine overheats, red overheat warning light flashes	**a.** Low coolant level	**a.** Fill expansion tank to the MAX mark on a cold engine. Check cooling system for leaks with pressure tester.
	b. Incorrect coolant concentration	**b.** Adjust coolant concentration to a mix of 50% coolant additive and 50% distilled water.
	c. Poor air flow through radiator	**c.** Check for debris (leaves, bugs, etc.) buildup on front of radiator. Clean radiator exterior using compressed air.
	d. Radiator fan not switching on	**d.** Test thermoswitch and fan. Replace faulty parts.
	e. Faulty radiator cap	**e.** Pressure test radiator cap. Replace faulty cap.
	f. Faulty thermostat	**f.** Remove and test thermostat. Replace faulty thermostat.
	g. Coolant pump faulty	**g.** Remove and inspect for spun impeller or pulley hub.
	h. Radiator hose restricted (lower hose may collapse at high engine or highway speeds)	**h.** Check hoses for soft, spongy areas. Replace faulty hoses.
	i. Clogged radiator	**i.** Clean or replace faulty radiator.
	j. Internal engine mechanical fault	**j.** Check internal engine condition, see **15a or 15b Cylinder Head and Valvetrain**.
2. Blue low temperature warning light on, poor heater output	**a.** Incorrect coolant concentration	**a.** Adjust coolant concentration to a mix of 50% coolant additive and 50% distilled water.
	b. Faulty thermostat	**b.** Remove and test thermostat. Replace faulty thermostat.
	c. Radiator fan not switching off	**c.** Test thermoswitch. Replace faulty parts.
3. Blue low temperature warning light on, heater output normal	**a.** Faulty instrument cluster or coolant temperature sensor	**a.** Test instrument cluster and sensor. Replace parts as required.
4. Blue and red warning lights operate normally, poor heater output	**a.** Installed position of heater hoses reversed	**a.** Inspect routing of heater hoses, see **80 Heating and Ventilation**.
	b. Heater hose restriction	**b.** Inspect heater hoses for ply separation and clogging. Replace hoses as required.
	c. Heat core restricted or clogged	**c.** Clean or replace faulty heater core.
	d. Heater or A/C ventilation controls or flaps not operating correctly	**d.** Check operation and adjustment of controls, see **80 Heating and Ventilation**
5. Blue warning light flashes	**a.** Malfunction with guage, Engine Coolant Temperature sensor (ECT), or wiring	**a.** Visually inspect ECT wiring in engine compartment. See **Cooling System, Components** for ECT location. **b.** Troubleshoot with suitable scan tool.

Diagnostic checks

The following checks and tests should generally be performed prior to any major tear down or repair work. This will help insure that the full extent or nature of the problem is known beforehand and may prevent unneeded repair work.

Coolant/antifreeze concentration, testing

1. Using a refractometer (VW tool CEN5021), take a small amount of coolant and place it onto measuring prism. See Fig. 2.

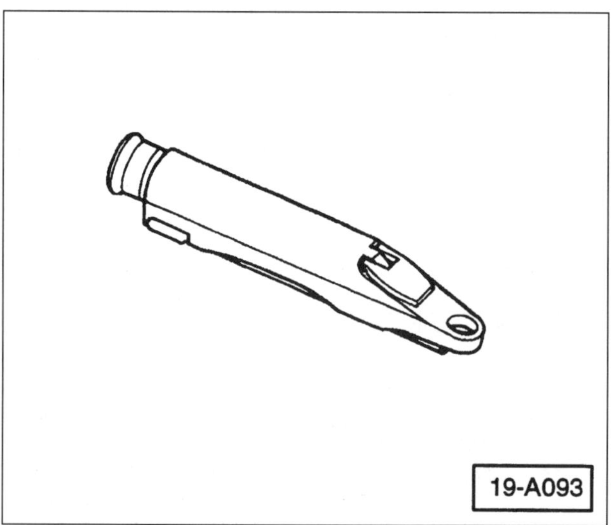

19-A093

Fig. 2. Anti-freeze tester (refractometer), VW special tool CEN5021.

2. Close the cover and hold tester up to a light source.

3. Look into the eyepiece and read the scale for ethylene glycol. The measure point is where the black and white come together. A 50/50 mixture is generally preferred and will provide freeze protection to -34°F (-37°C). See **Coolant, pump and thermostat** given earlier.

4. Rinse the tester clean.

5. Periodically check calibration by placing distilled water onto the prism and closing the cover. The measure point should be at 32°F (0°C) which is the freezing point for pure water. If this reading is not obtained, follow the instructions that came with tester for calibration and adjustment.

Cooling system, pressure testing

A pressure test uses a special tester in place of the cap on the expansion tank to pressurize the system and simulate normal operating conditions. If the system is unable to hold pressure, the engine will overheat more easily and fluid will be lost.

NOTE—
A pressure test also checks for internal leakage. Some of the common sources of internal leakage include a faulty cylinder head gasket, a cracked cylinder head, and a cracked cylinder block.

1. With engine at normal operating temperature, pressure test the system using a cooling system pressure tester with suitable adapters.

2. Observe the gauge reading. If the pressure drops, there is a leak in the system. A rapid drop may indicate a faulty cylinder head gasket if no external leaks can be found. Remove the spark plugs or glow plugs to inspect for coolant in the cylinders.

3. Using the correct tester adapter, test coolant expansion tank cap opening pressure. Compare opening pressure to specification and replace the cap if opening pressure is outside of specification.

NOTE—
It is not unusual for opening pressure to be slightly above specification when pressure is first applied due to slight sticking of the internal valve. Subsequent pressure applications should open the valve within specification, otherwise, replace the cap.

Specification

- Cooling system test pressures (AEG and ALH engines)
  testing pressure (max) . . . . .1.25 bar (18 psi)
  cap opening pressure . . . . . 1.4 - 1.6 bar (20 - 23 psi)

---

4. Inspect gasket in expansion tank cap for cuts and damage.

Cooling fans and thermoswitch, testing

New Beetles use a pair of 2 speed electric cooling fans to pull air across the radiator (and A/C condenser where equipped). A thermo-switch and a fan control module are used to control fan operation. See Fig. 3. The engine will overheat if the electric cooling fans are not operating properly, especially in traffic where speeds are low and there is insufficient natural air flow across the radiator. A/C operation will also be affected and damage to the system could result. In normal operation, the fans will switch on and off according to engine coolant temperature at the radiator thermo-switch or whenever the A/C is on.

Fig. 3. Radiator fan thermo-switch (**A**) and fan control module (**B**) shown from under the left front section of the vehicle. The lower sound absorber panel (belly pan) has been removed. Radiator drain (**C**) is also visible.

> ***WARNING —***
> *Use extreme care when working at or near the radiator cooling fans when the engine is hot. The fan can come on at any time, even if the ignition key is switched off.*

NOTE —
If the cooling fans fail to operate normally use the following procedure to help determine where the problem lies.

1. Check fuses #3 and #8 in the holder on battery cover and fuse #16 in the dash fuse box. Replace as necessary. See wiring diagrams for circuitinformation. **See 97 Wiring Diagrams, Fuses and Relays**.

2. Disconnect harness connector from radiator fan thermo-switch on lower left side of radiator.

3. Using a fused jumper wire, bridge the red wire and red/white wire. Both fans should run on the first speed.

4. Remove jumper wire from the red/white wire and move it to the red/yellow wire so that the red wire and red/yellow wire are jumped. Both fans should run on the second speed.

5. If the fans run with the jumpers installed, This indicates the fans are functionng properly and the radiator thermo-switch may be faulty. Switch opening and closing specifications are given below for more accurate testing of the thermo-switch. Drain coolant before replacing a faulty switch.

Tightening torque
- Thermo-switch to radiator. . . . . 35 Nm (26 ft-lb)

6. If the fans do not run, check for battery voltage at the red wire in the harness connector. No voltage at harness connector indicates a blown fuse or a break in wiring from the fuse. See **97 Wiring Diagrams, Fuses and Relays**.

7. If the fans do not run and voltage is present at the thermo-switch harness connector, reconnect jumper to the red wire and red/white wire.

8. Unplug left side fan motor and plug a suitable test light into terminals 1 and 2 of harness connector. The light should light.

9. Repeat step 8 for right side fan motor. The light should light.

10. If the light does not come on for steps 8 and 9 check for broken or shorted wiring between the fan control module and the thermo-switch or between the fan control module and the fans. See **97 Wiring Diagrams, Fuses and Relays**. If the wiring is in order, then the fan control module is faulty. If the test light comes on, this indicates that the radiator fan is faulty and should be replaced.

The above tests check first speed fan operation. The second speed can be checked by connecting the jumper to the red wire and red/yellow wire at the thermo-switch harness and a test light to terminals 1 and 3 of the fan harness connectors. As with the first speed, if the light does not come on for steps 8 and 9, check for broken or shorted wiring between the fan control module and the thermo-switch or between the fan control module and the fans. See **97 Wiring Diagrams, Fuses and Relays**. If the wiring is in order, than the fan control module is faulty. If the test light comes on, this indicates that the radiator fan is faulty and should be replaced.

Specification
- Radiator fan thermo-switch operating temperatures
  Stage I
  switch on. . . . . .197° - 206°F (92° - 97°C)
  switch off. . . . . .183° - 195°F (84° - 91°C)
  Stage II
  switch on. . . . . .210° - 221°F (99° - 105°C)
  switch off. . . . . .195° - 208°F (91° - 98°C)

Thermostat, testing

A thermostat that is stuck open will cause the engine to warm up slowly and generally run below normal operating temperature at highway speed. A thermostat that is stuck closed will restrict coolant flow to the radiator and cause overheating.

Accurate testing of the thermostat requires removal and observation while being warmed in a container of hot water. An accurate thermometer is used to note the temperatures at which it begins to open and at which it is fully open.

Specification

- Coolant thermostat operating parameters
  - Opening starts at approx. . . . . 85°C (185°F)
  - Fully open by approx. . . . . 105°C (221°F)
  - Valve travel, min.. . . . . 7mm (0.28 in.)

To quickly check if the thermostat is opening and if coolant is circulating through the radiator, allow a cold engine to run at idle and warm up. As the temperature of the coolant rises, carefully feel the heater and expansion tank hoses. They will get hot. Feel the radiator hoses, particularly the lower hose. They will stay relatively cool to the touch. When the thermostat opens, the radiator hoses will quickly get hot and the radiator fan should cycle on shortly thereafter.

> ***CAUTION —***
> *If the engine runs long enough for the warning light in the instrument cluster to indicate an overheat condition, shut down the engine immediately.*

Check the radiator hoses. If they are not hot, then the thermostat has not opened or the radiator is clogged. If the hoses are hot, but the radiator fan did not come on, troubleshoot the radiator fans as per instructions given earlier in this section.

COOLING SYSTEM, DRAINING AND FILLING

> ***CAUTION —***
> *Always use a mixture of genuine Volkswagen coolant/anti-freeze and distilled water to avoid the formation of harmful deposits in the cooling system. Use of coolant/anti-freeze with phosphate compounds or tap water can be harmful to the cooling system.*

When refilling the engine coolant, keep in mind the following points:

- Use only Volkswagen G12 or equivalent phosphate and silicate free coolant/anti-freeze identified by the red color.
- Under no circumstances should G12 be mixed with any other type of coolant/anti-freeze. If the fluid in the expansion tank is brown, mixing with other types has occurred and the system must be flushed and the coolant/anti-freeze changed.
- Under no circumstances should straight coolant/anti-freeze or straight water be used. A 50/50 mix of coolant/anti-freeze to water provides freeze protection to -34°F (-35°C) and boiling protection to 226°F (108°C). The coolant/anti-freeze percentage should always be a minimum of 40% and a maximum of 60%.
- Hoses are secured with spring clamps. If replacement is needed, always replace with spring clamps due to their ability to expand with engine heat and remain tight.
- Most hoses have alignment marks to ensure correct positioning on the appropriate fitting; always line up the marks to ensure stress free installation.

1. Remove lower sound absorber panel (belly pan).
2. With engine fully cold, remove cap from the coolant expansion tank.
3. Position a drain pan under left front part of the radiator.
4. Unscrew drain plug at lower radiator hose fitting and allow coolant to drain. See Fig. 4.

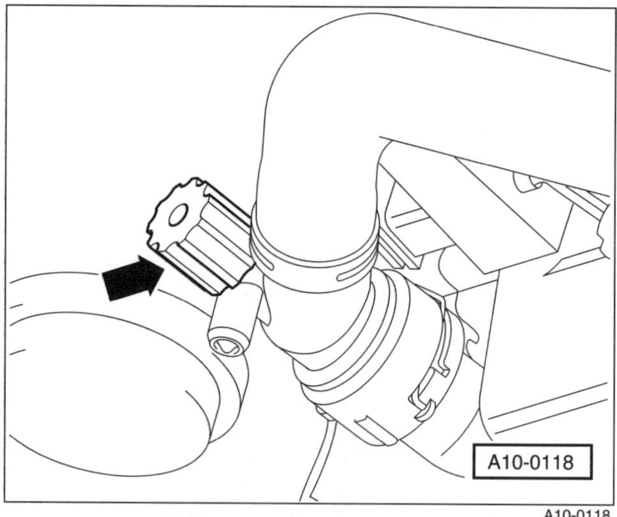

A10-0118

Fig. 4. Drain plug (**arrow**) at lower radiator hose fitting.

5. Remove lower hose from oil cooler to drain cylinder block and allow coolant to drain. See Fig. 5.

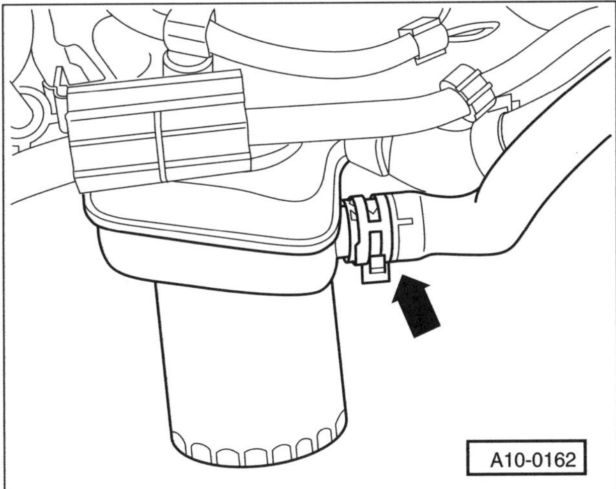

A10-0162

Fig. 5. Remove lower oil cooler hose (**arrow**) to drain coolant from cylinder block. AEG engine shown, ALH TDI engine similar.

> ***NOTE—***
> *Dispose of used coolant properly.*

6. Close drain plug on lower radiator hose fitting.

7. Reconnect the lower oil cooler hose.

8. Slowly fill expansion tank with the appropriate mixture of coolant/anti-freeze while allowing the air to escape.

Specification

- Cooling system capacity
  Engine code AEG . . . . 5.3 quarts (5.0 liters)
  Engine code ALH . . . . 6.3 quarts (6.0 liters)

> ***NOTE—***
> *If a cooling system pressure tester is available, connect it to the expansion tank and pressurize the system. This will force the coolant/anti-freeze past the thermostat and into many of the hoses that drained and will speed up the entire process.*

9. Install expansion tank cap, start engine and allow to run until the radiator fans cycle at least once.

> ***NOTE—***
> *If the expansion tank empties completely during warm-up, shut off the engine, carefully remove the expansion tank cap and refill to the **max** marks on the side. Restart the engine and continue until the fans cycle.*

10. Recheck the level in the expansion tank when the engine has cooled. See Fig. 6.

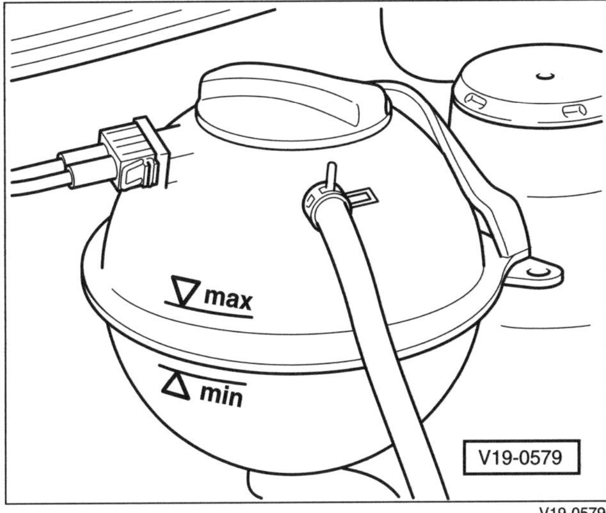

V19-0579

Fig. 6. Coolant/anti-freeze expansion tank showing **min** and **max** marks.

> ***NOTE—***
> *The coolant/anti-freeze level should be at the **max** mark with the engine at operating temperature and between the **min** and **max** marks when cold. The final level is best checked when the cooling system is fully cold.*

COOLING SYSTEM, COMPONENTS

A schematic view of the cooling systems for the AEG and ALH engines is shown in Fig. 7 and Fig. 8, respectively. Fig. 9 and Fig. 10 are exploded views of the various cooling system components on the AEG and ALH engines.

Cooling system, schematic (AEG engine)

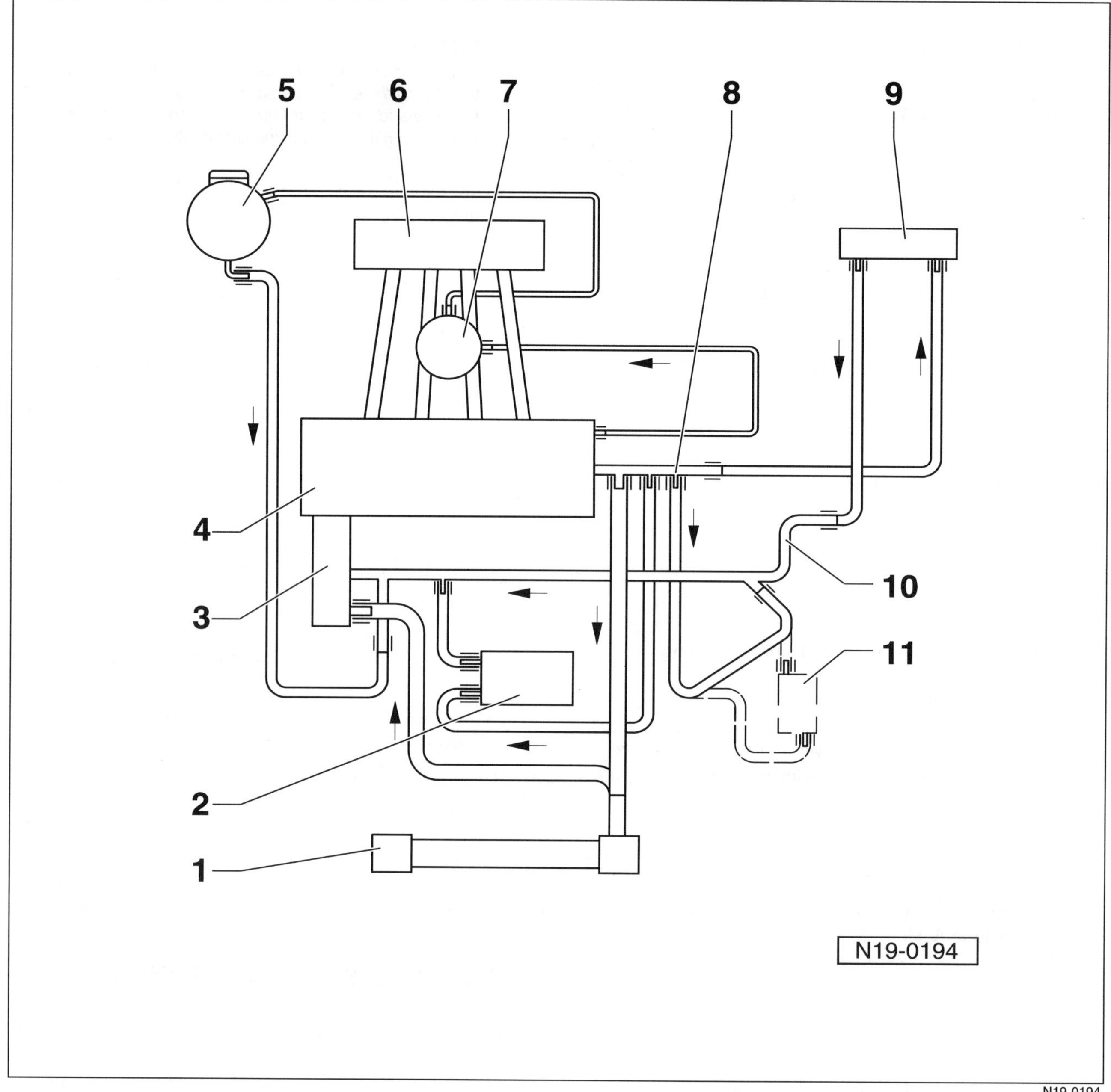

N19-0194

Fig. 7. AEG engine coolant flow and general component layout.

1. **Radiator**
2. **Oil cooler**
3. **Coolant pump/coolant thermostat**
4. **Cylinder head/engine block**
5. **Expansion tank**
6. **Intake manifold**
7. **Throttle control module**
8. **Connection**
9. **Heat exchanger**
10. **Coolant pipe**
11. **Transmission cooler**
    - Vehicles with automatic transmission

Cooling system, schematic (ALH engine)

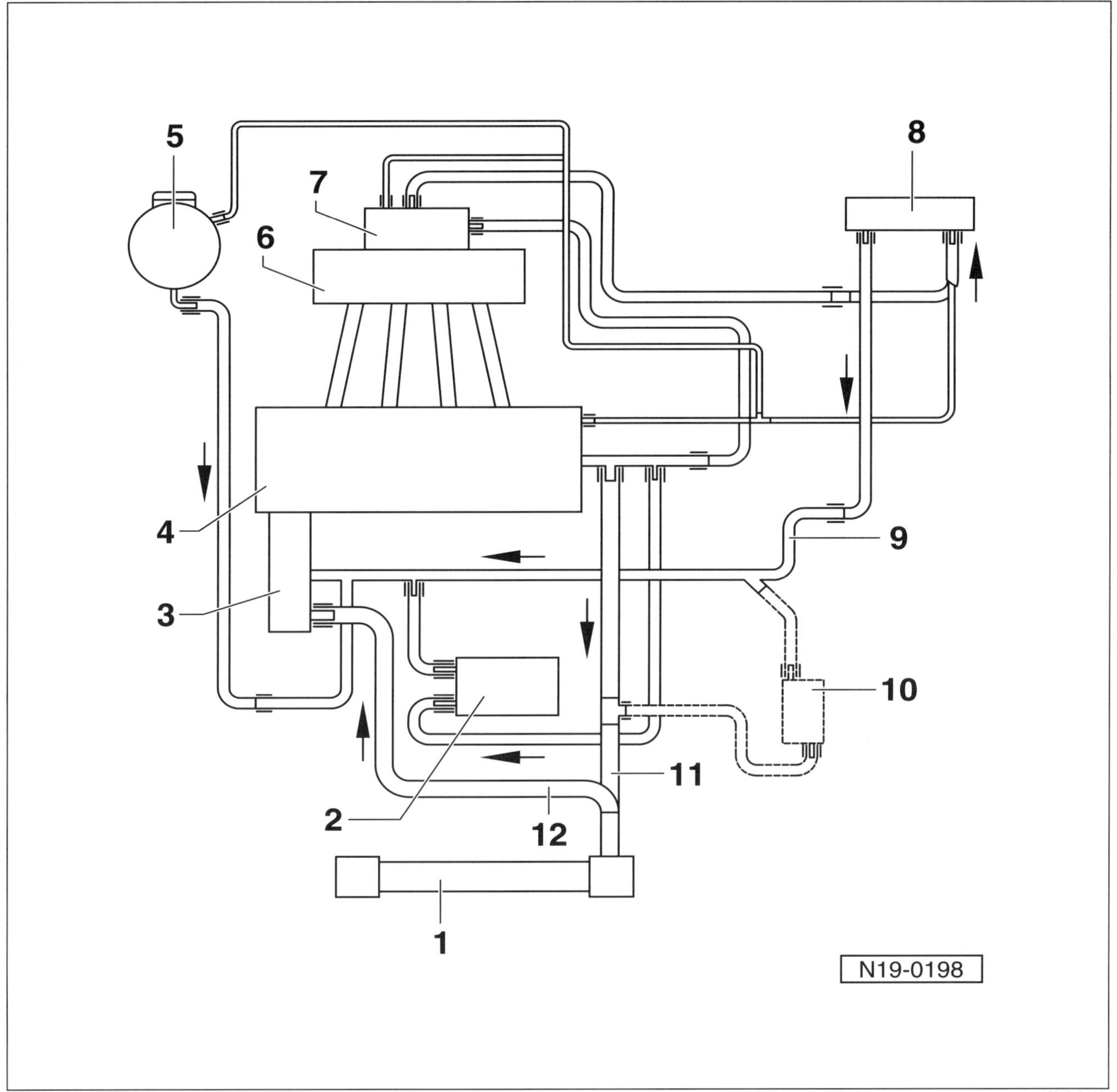

Fig. 8. ALH diesel engine coolant flow and general component layout.

1. **Radiator**
2. **Oil cooler**
3. **Coolant pump**
4. **Engine block**
5. **Expansion tank**
6. **Intake manifold**
7. **EGR cooler**
8. **Heating system heat exchanger**
9. **Coolant pipe**
10. **Transmission cooler**
    - Vehicles with automatic transmission
11. **Coolant hose, upper**
12. **Coolant hose, lower**

Cooling system, components (AEG engine)

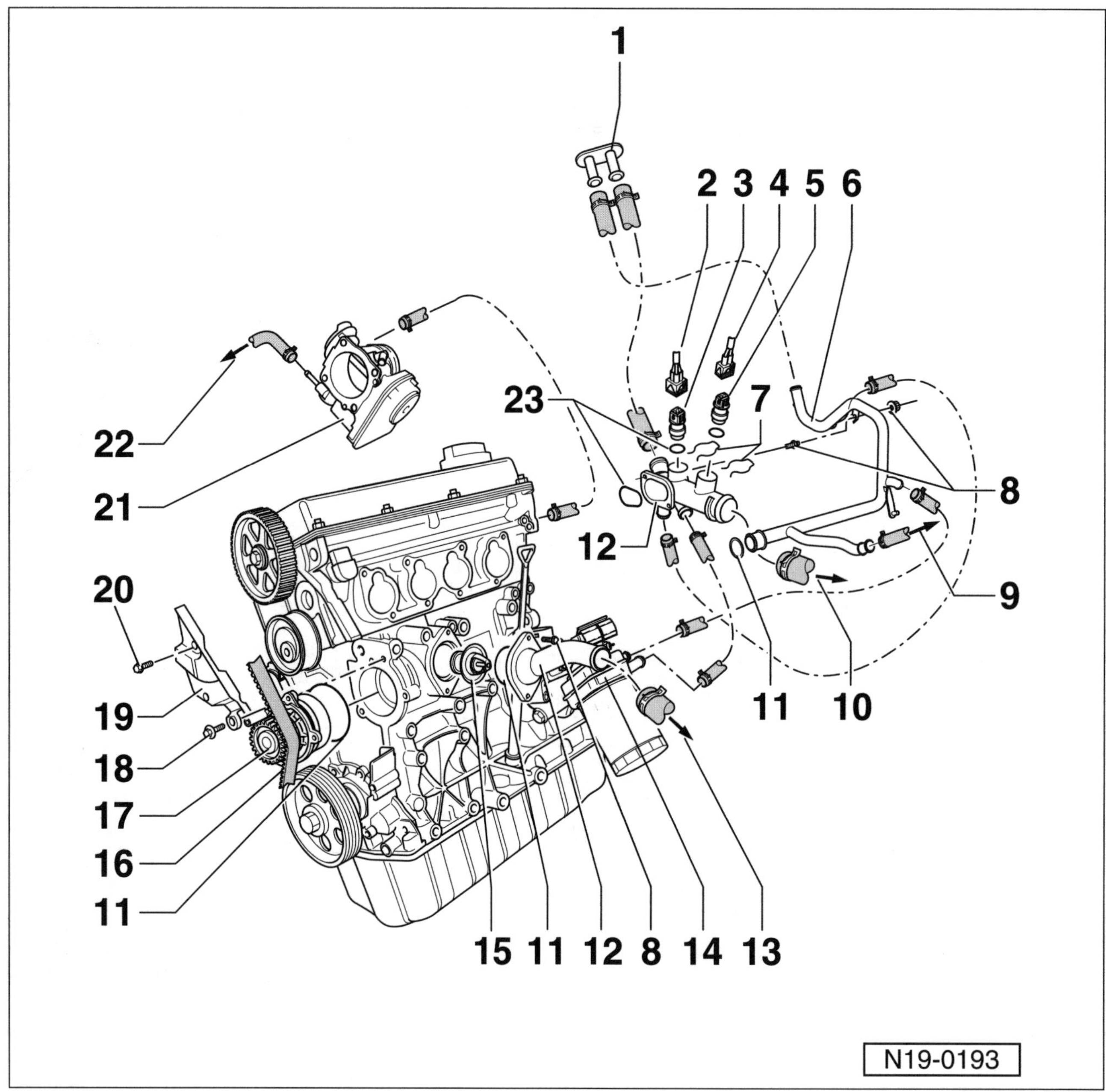

N19-0193

Fig. 9. Coolant pump and related cooling system components on AEG engine.

1. **Heater core**
   - For passenger compartment heat
2. **4-pin harness connector**
   - Wiring cavities 1 and 3 for engine coolant temperature sensor
   - Terminals 1 and 3: gold plated
3. **Engine coolant temperature sensor (G62)**
   - For engine control module
   - With engine coolant temperature warning light sensor (G2)
   - If necessary, release cooling system pressure before removing
4. **2-pin harness connector**
   - For vehicles with A/C only

(continued from previous page)

5. **A/C cut-out thermal switch (F163)**
   - For vehicles with A/C only
6. **Coolant pipe**
7. **Retaining clip**
   - Ensure clip is securely seated
8. **Stepped stud and nut**
   - Tighten to 10 Nm (7 ft-lb)
9. **To expansion tank**
10. **To top of radiator**
11. **O-ring**
    - Replace
12. **Flange**
13. **To bottom of radiator**
14. **Oil cooler**
15. **Engine coolant thermostat**
    - Checking: heat-up thermostat in water
    - Opening starts at approx. 187°F (86°C)
    - Opening lift: 7 mm minimum
16. **Toothed belt**
    - Mark engine direction of rotation before removing
    - Check for wear
    - Do not kink
17. **Coolant pump**
    - Check pulley for ease of movement
    - If damaged and leaking replace complete assembly
    - Note installation position, **see (A)**
18. **Bolt**
    - Tighten to 15 Nm (11 ft-lb)
19. **Toothed belt guard, rear**
20. **Bolt**
    - 20 Nm (15 ft-lb)
21. **Throttle control module**
    - Heated by engine coolant
22. **To expansion tank, upper**
23. **O-ring**
    - Replace if damaged

Coolant pump, replacing (AEG engine)

1. Drain coolant as previously described.
2. Remove ribbed V-belt and tensioner, see **0 Maintenance**.
3. Remove upper and center toothed belt guards.

(A) Coolant pump (AEG engine)

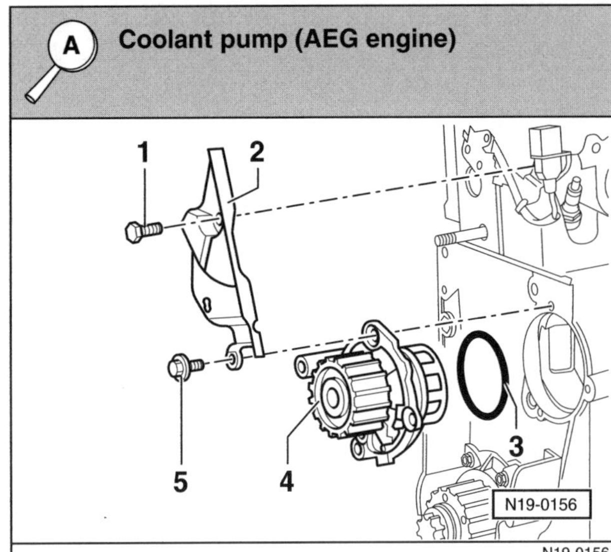

N19-0156

1. **Bolt**
   - Tighten to 20 Nm (15 ft-lb)
2. **Rear toothed belt guard**
3. **O-ring seal**
4. **Coolant pump**
   - Installed position: plug in housing points downward
5. **Bolt**
   - Tighten to 15 Nm (11 ft-lb)

4. Turn the crankshaft to TDC for cylinder 1 and release the toothed belt tensioning roller, see **15a Cylinder Head and Valvetrain**. The toothed belt should be left in position on the crankshaft sprocket.
5. Take toothed belt off coolant pump drive sprocket.
6. Remove mounting bolts from rear toothed belt guard.
7. Remove coolant pump mounting bolts and remove coolant pump.
8. Installation is reverse of removal, noting the following:
   - Clean pump mating surface on cylinder block.
   - Always use new O-rings and hardware as indicated.
   - Lubricate O-rings with coolant before installing.

Tightening torque
- Coolant pump to cylinder block ..... 15 Nm (11 ft-lb)
- Rear toothed belt guard to cylinder block .... 20 Nm (15 ft-lb)

9. Fill cooling system as described previously.
10. Start engine and check for leaks. Be sure to quality check your work, see **Quality Review** at the end of this repair group.

Cooling system, components (ALH engine)

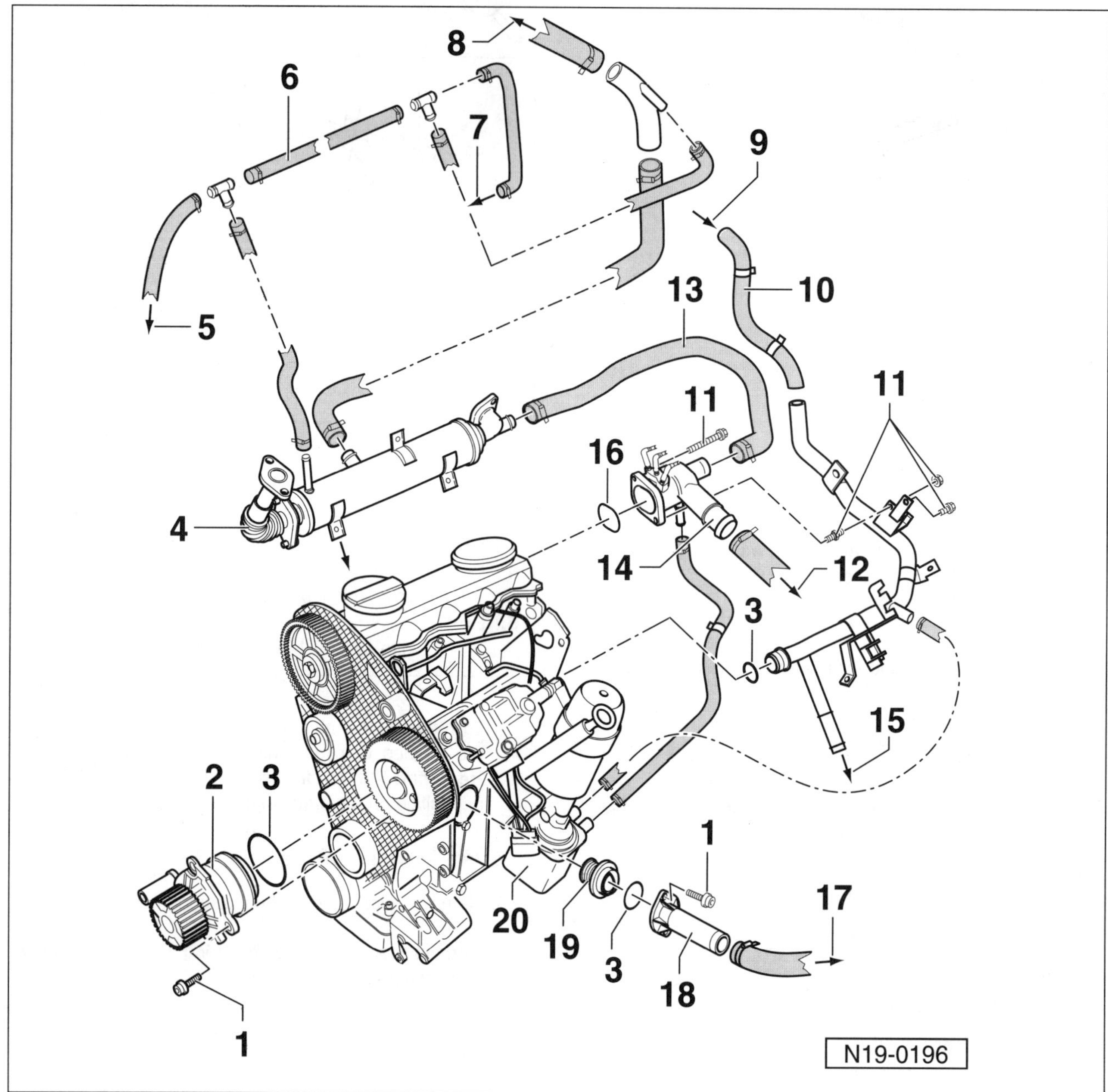

N19-0196

Fig. 10. Coolant pump and related cooling system components on ALH engine.

1. **Bolt**
   - Tighten to 25 Nm (18 ft-lb)
2. **Coolant pump**
   - Check pulley for ease of movement
   - If damaged and leaking replace complete assembly
   - Note installation position, **see** Ⓐ
3. **O-ring**
   - Always replace
4. **EGR cooler**
5. **To expansion tank**
6. **Coolant hose, upper**
7. **To cylinder head**
8. **To heater core**
9. **From heater core**

(continued from previous page)

10. Coolant pipe

11. Bolt
- Tighten to 10 Nm (7 ft-lb)

12. To expansion tank, lower

13. EGR cooler supply

14. Flange
- With glow plugs for auxiliary heater

15. To top of radiator
- Clipped to the firewall

16. O-ring
- Ensure it is seated securely
- Always replace

17. To bottom of radiator

18. Connection
- For thermostat

19. Coolant thermostat
- Checking: heat-up thermostat in water
- Opening starts at approx. 185°F (85°C)
- Ends approx. 221°F (105°C)
- Opening lift: 7 mm minimum

20. Oil cooler

A Coolant pump (ALH engine)

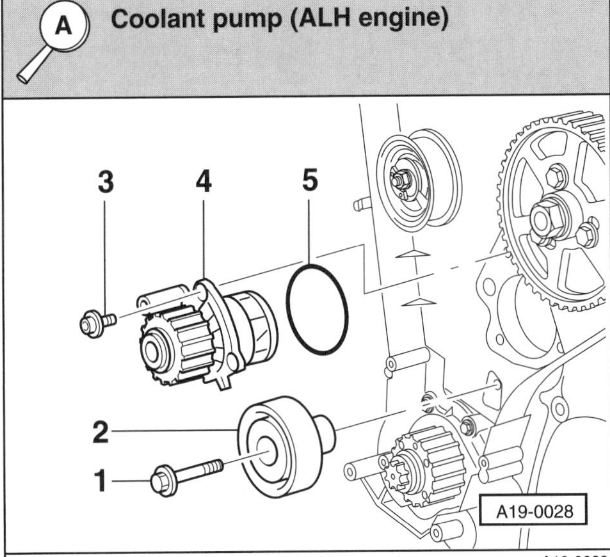

A19-0028

1. **Bolt**
   - Tighten to 40 Nm (30 ft-lb) plus ¼ turn (90°)
   - Always replace
2. **Idler pulley**
3. **Bolt**
   - Tighten to 15 Nm (11 ft-lb)
4. **Coolant pump**
   - Installation position: plug in housing points downward
5. **O-ring seal**

Coolant pump, replacing (ALH engine)

1. Drain coolant as previously described.
2. Remove ribbed V-belt and tensioner, see **0 Maintenance**.
3. Disconnect fuel supply and return lines at fuel filter.
4. Remove connecting pipe between intercooler and intake manifold.
5. Remove fuel filter and mounting bracket.
6. Remove upper and center toothed belt guards.
7. Turn crankshaft to TDC for cylinder 1 and release toothed belt tensioning roller, see **15b Cylinder Head and Valvetrain**. Remove toothed belt from camshaft, injection pump and coolant pump sprockets, but leave it in position on crankshaft sprocket.
8. Remove bolt from idler pulley and work the pulley free from cylinder block. Discard bolt.
9. Remove coolant pump mounting bolts and carefully lift coolant pump from cylinder block between engine mount support and rear toothed belt guard.
10. Installation is reverse of removal, noting the following:
    - Clean pump mating surface on cylinder block.
    - Always use new O-rings and hardware as indicated.
    - Lubricate O-rings with coolant before installing.
11. Fill cooling system as described previously.
12. Start engine and check for leaks Be sure to quality check your work, see **Quality Review** at the end of this repair group.

Tightening torques

- Coolant pump to cylinder block (M7) . . . . 15 Nm (11 ft-lb)
- Idler pulley bolt, engine code ALH (M10) (always replace)
  - stage I . . . . 40 Nm (30 ft-lb)
  - stage I . . . . additional ¼ turn (90°)
- Rear toothed belt guard to cylinder block (M8) . . . . 20 Nm (15 ft-lb)

Radiator and cooling fans, assembly

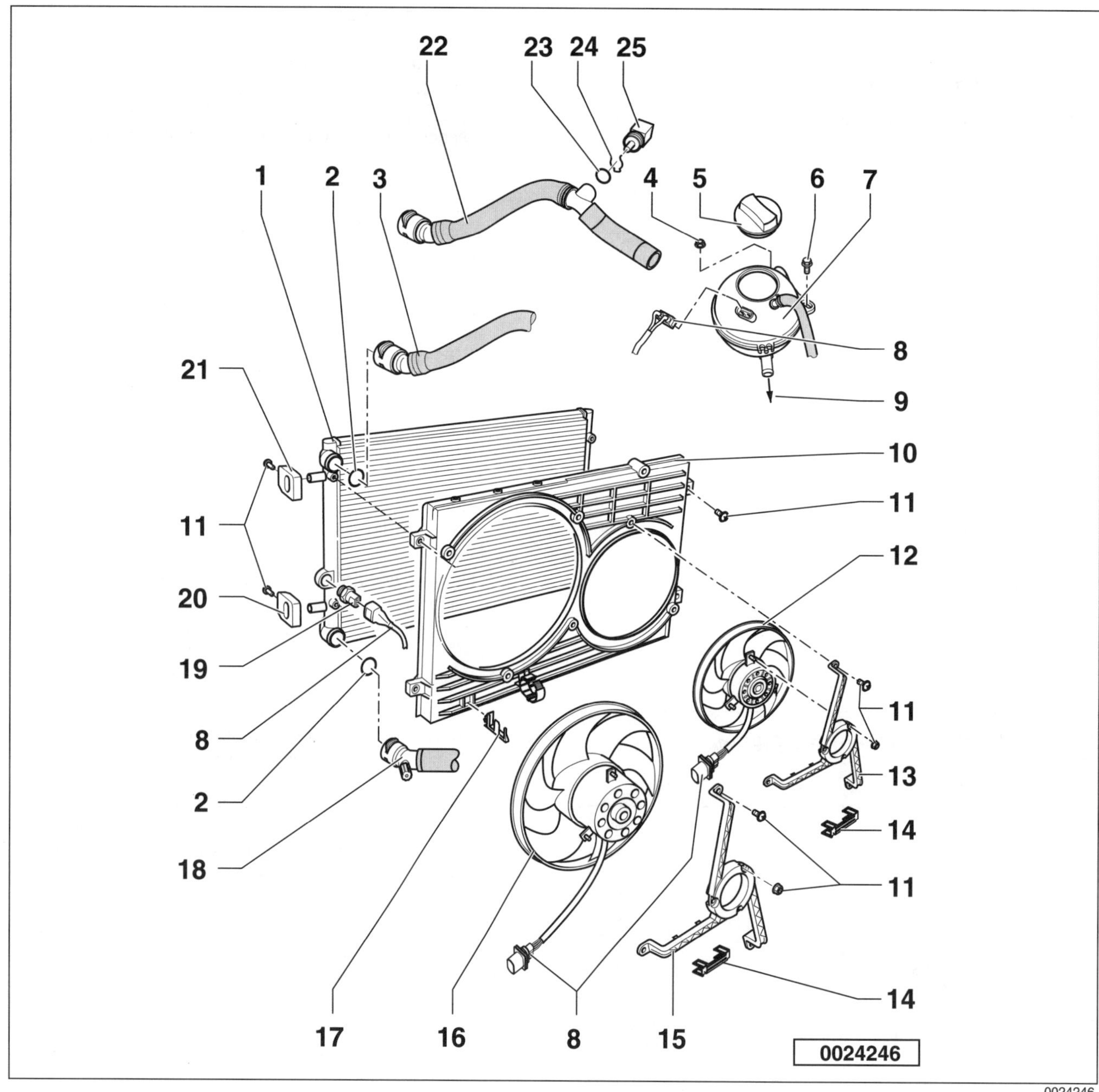

0024246

Fig. 11. Radiator and cooling fans for AEG and ALH engines.

1. **Radiator**
   - If replaced, flush cooling system and use new coolant
2. **O-ring**
   - Always replace
3. **Coolant hose, upper**
   - Attached to radiator with retaining clip
   - AEG engine only
4. **Nut**
   - Tighten to 4 Nm (35 in-lb)
5. **Cap**
6. **Bolt**
   - Tighten to 2 Nm (18 in-lb)
7. **Expansion tank**
8. **Connector**
9. **To coolant hose**
10. **Air ducting**

(continued from previous page)

11. Bolt
- Tighten to 10 Nm (7 ft-lb)

12. Additional fan

13. Fan ring

14. Retaining clip
- Ensure it is seated securely

15. Fan ring

16. Radiator fan

17. Bracket
- For radiator fan connector

18. Coolant hose, lower
- Attached to radiator with retaining clip

19. Thermoswitch (F18)
- Tighten to 35 Nm (26 ft-lb)
- For electric fan
- Stage 1 switching temperatures:
  ON: 198 to 207°F (92 to 97°C)
  OFF: 183 to 196°F (84 to 91°C)
- Stage 2 switching temperatures:
  ON: 210 to 221°F (99 to 105°C)
  OFF: 196 to 208°F (91 to 98°C)

20. Bracket
- For radiator, lower

21. Bracket
- For radiator, upper
- Note installation position

22. Coolant hose, upper
- Attached to radiator with retaining clip
- ALH engine only

23. O-ring
- Always replace
- ALH engine only

24. Retaining clip
- Ensure it is seated securely
- ALH engine only

25. Engine coolant temperature sensor (G62)
- ALH engine only

Radiator and cooling fans, removing and installing

The cooling fans provide additional air flow through the radiator. A faulty cooling fan motor or thermoswitch may be the cause of insufficient air flow and overheating.

The Volkswagen New Beetle models covered by this manual are equipped with dual two-speed radiator fans.

> ***WARNING —***
> *The electric cooling fans can come on at any time, even if the key is out of the ignition. To avoid personal injury, use extreme caution when working at or near the cooling fan if the engine is hot. As a safety precaution, always disconnect the harness connector from the fan when working around the radiator, fans and associated components.*

1. Drain coolant as previously described.
2. Remove front body section and move lock carrier to service position, see **50 Body-Front**.
3. Disconnect coolant hoses from radiator.
4. Disconnect thermo-switch harness connector.
5. Remove ribbed V-belt and tensioner, see **0 Maintenance**.
6. Remove radiator fans from the ducting.
7. Remove retaining clamps from A/C hoses near condenser.
8. Remove radiator mounting bolts from both sides and slide radiator slightly to rear. See Fig. 12.
9. Unbolt A/C condenser from radiator, support condenser and remove radiator.

NOTE —
Do not discharge the A/C refrigerant. Support the A/C condenser with wire and avoid stretching or kinking the hoses.

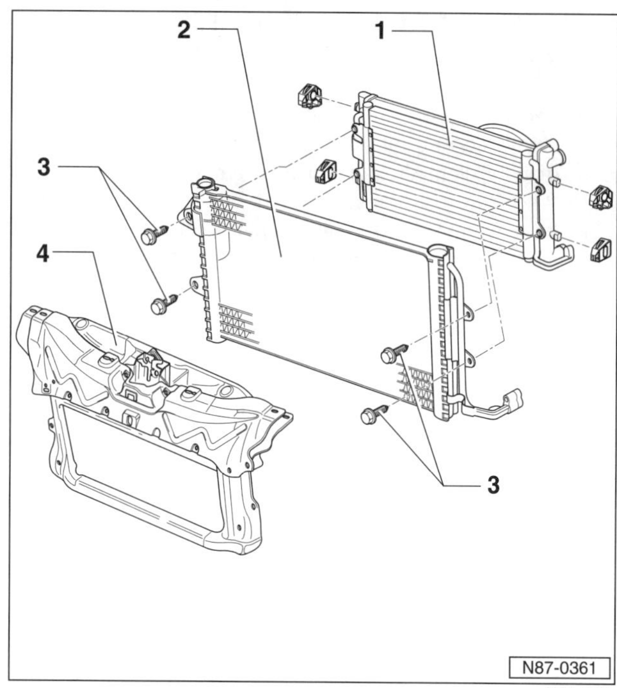

N87-0361

Fig. 12. Radiator (**1**), condenser (**2**), mounting bolts (**3**) and lock carrier (**4**) for AEG and ALH engines.

10. Installation is the reverse of removal.

Tightening torque
- A/C condenser to radiator . . . . 8 Nm (71 in-lb)

11. Fill the cooling system as described previously. Start engine and check for leaks. Be sure to quality check your work, see **Quality Review** below.

Thermostat, replacing

A thermostat mounted in the cylinder block provides primary control of coolant temperature by regulating the flow of coolant to the radiator. The thermostat remains closed when coolant is below the specified temperature allowing the engine to reach operating temperature quickly and providing immediate heat to the passenger compartment. Thermostats for the AEG engine and the ALH engine operate within the same temperature ranges, but are not interchangeable, see Fig. 11 and Fig. 12.

1. Drain coolant as previously given.

2. Disconnect lower radiator hose from flange on cylinder block.

3. Remove the outlet flange mounting bolts and remove the flange and O-ring seal.

4. Remove the thermostat:
   - AEG engines, carefully pull the thermostat out.
   - ALH engines, rotate the thermostat ¼ turn, (90°), counterclockwise and pull out.

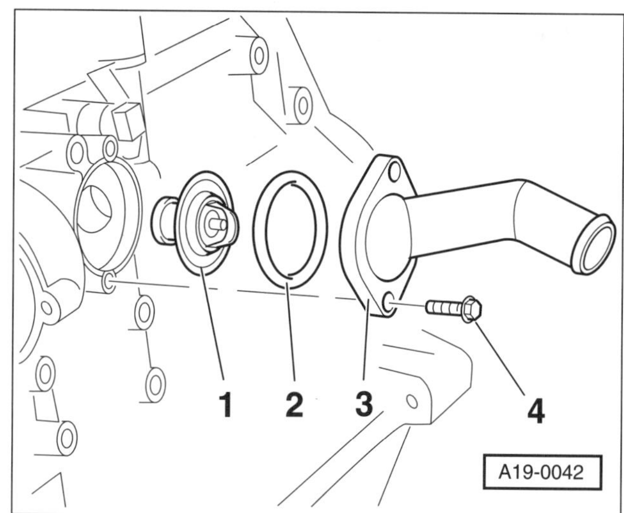

A19-0042

Fig. 13. Thermostat (**1**), O-ring (**2**), flange (**3**) and mounting bolt (**4**) on AEG engine.

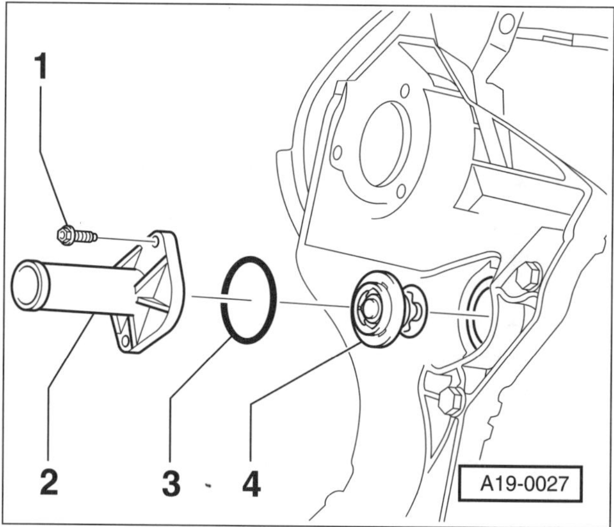

A19-0027

Fig. 14. Mounting bolt (**1**), flange (**2**), O-ring (**3**), and thermostat (**4**) on ALH engine.

5. Install thermostat into cylinder block:
   - AEG engines, fit thermostat into cylinder block.
   - ALH engines, fit thermostat into cylinder block and rotate ¼ turn (90°) clockwise.

NOTE —
On AEG engines the support brace on the thermostat must be almost vertical when installed.

6. Remaining installation is the reverse of removal noting the following:
   - Clean mating surface on cylinder block before installing outlet flange.
   - Always use new O-rings with coolant before installing.
   - Fill cooling system as described previously.

Tightening torque

- Thermostat flange (AEG and ALH engines) . . . . 15 Nm (11 ft-lb)

---

7. Start engine and check for leaks. Be sure to quality check your work, see **Quality Review** at the end of this repair group.

QUALITY REVIEW

When you have finished working under the hood and around other areas of the vehicle, it is advisable to take a moment to quality check or review your work. This helps to insure that the operation or repair has been completed properly with all affected systems functioning within normal parameters. These may include the following:

- Ensure that all cable ties and hose clamps that were removed as part of the repair are replaced.
- Check and adjust coolant level and all other applicable fluid levels.
- Make sure that there are no coolant leaks.
- Make sure that the radiator fans cycle properly.
- Make sure that all other components involved in the repair are positioned correctly and function properly.
- Make sure that all tools, shop cloths, fender covers and protective tapes are removed before closing the hood.
- Clean grease and fingerprints from painted surfaces and steering wheel.

2 Fuel, Ignition, and Exhaust Systems

GENERAL

This general information group covers application information and system descriptions for the repair groups listed under 2 Fuel, Ignition and Exhaust Systems.

> ***NOTE —***
> - *For general information on the battery, starter and alternator, see* **27 Engine Electrical Systems**.
> - *For emission control system application information, see* **26 Exhaust System and Emission Controls**.

FUEL SUPPLY

The plastic fuel tank is mounted beneath the rear of the vehicle. On gasoline engines, an electric fuel pump with integral level sensor is submersed in the tank. On diesel engines, only the fuel the level sensor is mounted in the tank, as the engine-mounted diesel injection pump handles fuel delivery to the engine.

This gasoline fuel pump/fuel level sensor assembly is called the fuel delivery unit. An inlet strainer provides course filtration and prevents dirt and debris from entering the fuel system. Built into the fuel delivery unit is a check valve and a relief valve. The check valve is on the outlet side of the pump and holds pressure in the system after the engine is shut off. The relief valve prevents high pressure from damaging the system. The check valve and relief valve are not replaceable.

The fuel tank is designed to prevent overfilling and allow for fuel expansion. The fuel cap contains a valve to prevent a vacuum from forming in the tank.

On all engines, fuel is supplied to the engine and excess fuel is returned to the tank through special plastic fuel lines. In addition, diesel engines with automatic transmissions use a fuel cooler on the supply line to the pump.

FUEL INJECTION

Two types of engine management are used on the engines covered in this manual, one gasoline and one diesel as noted below.

Engine Codes

- AEG .... 2.0L 4 cylinder gasoline Motronic 5.9.2
- ALH .... 1.9L 4 cylinder turbo diesel TDI Diesel Direct Fuel Injection

Motronic 5.9.2 engine management

The AEG (2.0 liter) engine is equipped with an enhanced version of the sophisticated Bosch Motronic engine management system. See Fig. 1. This version complies with the federal and state government mandated On-Board Diagnostic (OBD) II standards.

Basic fuel metering is determined by engine speed and engine load. The Engine Control Module (ECM) receives engine speed and crankshaft position information from the engine speed and reference sensor, and engine load information from the Mass Air Flow sensor (MAF). The ECM then meters fuel to the engine by sequentially triggering the fuel injectors at a rate proportional to engine speed and load. The length of time the injectors remain open determines fuel quantity.

The ECM uses the same information to determine the correct ignition firing point. A small output signal is generated and sent to the Power Output Stages built into the Ignition Coils. The Camshaft Position Sensor (CMP), identifies cylinder number 1 firing position for cylinder-selective injection and ignition knock control. The Engine Coolant Temperature sensor (ECT), supplies engine temperature information to the ECM.

Motronic 5.9.2, overview

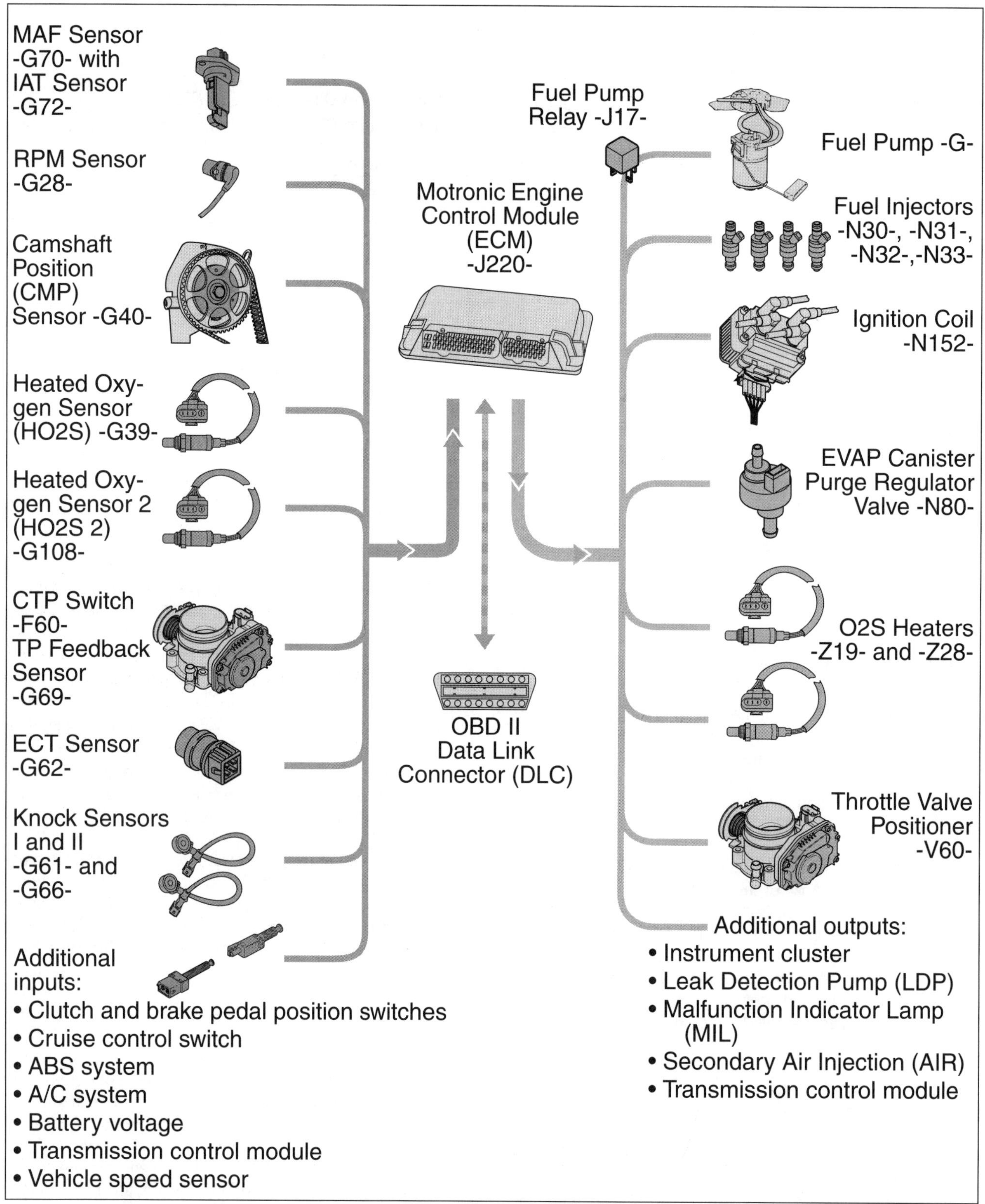

Fig. 1. Bosch Motronic 5.9.2 engine management system. Inputs (**left**) to the ECM are used to control and adapt output signals (**right**) to the individual components. Volkswagen component codes are indicated within dashes (–).

The Throttle Actuator Control Module (TACM), combines 4 functions. Three are used on the input side: the Throttle Position Sensor (TPS), which signals throttle angle; the Closed Throttle Position switch (CTP), which signals fully closed throttle plate; and the Throttle Position Feedback sensor, which signals position of the electric motor used for idle stabilization and cruise control function.

The Pre-Catalyst Heated Oxygen Sensor (HO2S), signals combustion efficiency, and the Post-Catalyst Heated Oxygen Sensor (HO2S), monitors efficiency of the Three-Way Catalytic Converter (TWC).

The Knock Sensors (KS1 and KS2), supply engine knock information for ignition timing regulation and the Intake Air Temperature sensor (IAT), is used for idle stabilization and as a correction factor for ignition timing.

Based on all of the input signals, the ECM precisely controls the following output components:

- Fuel Injectors
- Power Output Stage and Ignition Coil
- Throttle Position Actuator
- Evaporative Canister Purge Valve (EVAP)
- Fuel Pump and Relay

In addition, certain versions have additional outputs controlled by the ECM:

- Secondary Air Pump Relay (AIR); Air Injection Solenoid Control Valve and Secondary Air Injection Pump
- Leak Diagnosis Pump (LDP); and Control Relay

The ECM also controls cruise control functions.

A warning light known as a Malfunction Indicator Lamp (MIL), is located in the instrument cluster and signals the vehicle operator when certain systems have failed. In some instances, it will come on if relatively small malfunctions have been recorded, such as running very low on fuel or leaving off the gas cap. Most malfunctions that occur will cause the light to stay on steadily, but certain very serious situations such as an overheating catalytic converter may cause it to blink.

Because of the Motronic 5.9.2 system is quite complex, proper diagnosis and repair requires the use of a specialized scan tool such as Volkswagen special tool VAG 1551 or VAG 1552.

In addition to diagnostics, Motronic 5.9.2 systems include the ability to record proper operation of as many as 8 monitored functions. These functional checks are called readiness codes and are set when the proper operating parameters are reached at least one time. These codes are important because some areas with emissions testing check these codes first. If the readiness code is NOT set, the vehicle will not pass the specialized test. Readiness codes may be erased if the battery is disconnected or runs low, if the ECM is disconnected, or if faults or DTCs are erased with a scan tool. Generally speaking, the readiness codes in Volkswagen systems will reset themselves after the vehicle has been started and driven under varying conditions several times. They can also be reset using the scan tool.

Diesel Turbo Direct Injection (TDI)

The ALH (1.9 liter) engine is equipped with the Diesel Turbo Direct Injection System that features engine controls that closely resemble those of a gasoline engine. See Fig. 2. The TDI system combines sophisticated computer control of fuel management and emissions with system monitoring and diagnostics. An exhaust driven turbocharger and an intercooler work with a specially designed combustion chamber and cylinder head to produce more efficient combustion and lower fuel consumption. This also results in reduced engine noise and increased power.

In addition, the accelerator pedal is directly connected to the Engine Control Module (ECM) via a potentiometer. This eliminates the need for an accelerator cable and is known as "drive by wire". The ECM also controls all glow plug functions, auxiliary coolant glow plug functions and cruise control.

Basic fuel metering is determined by engine speed and engine load. When the key is switched on and the engine is started, the fuel cut-off valve opens and fuel flows into the injection pump. The ECM receives engine RPM from the engine speed sensor and engine load information from the Throttle Position Sensor (TPS). These signals are modified by the Engine Coolant Temperature sensor (ECT), the Mass Air Flow Sensor (MAF), and the Fuel Temperature Sensor. The ECM then signals the quantity adjuster which allows the proper quantity of fuel to be metered sequentially to the mechanical injectors. The ECM also uses the same information to determine the correct moment of injection which is the ignition firing point. An output signal is generated and sent to the cold start valve at the correct time.

The ECM monitors the operation of the quantity adjuster via a signal received from the modulating piston displacement sensor and makes corrections to the fuel quantity as required.

The ECM monitors the operation of the cold start valve via a signal received from the needle lift sensor attached to injector number 3 and again makes corrections as required.

Turbocharger boost pressure is regulated by the ECM based on a signal from the Intake Air Temperature sensor (IAT), the Mass Air Flow (MAF) sensor, and an ambient pressure signal from an internal Barometric Pressure Sensor (BARO). The wastegate bypass regulator valve receives output from the ECM and controls a vacuum signal sent to the turbocharger wastegate.

Diesel Turbo Direct Injection, overview

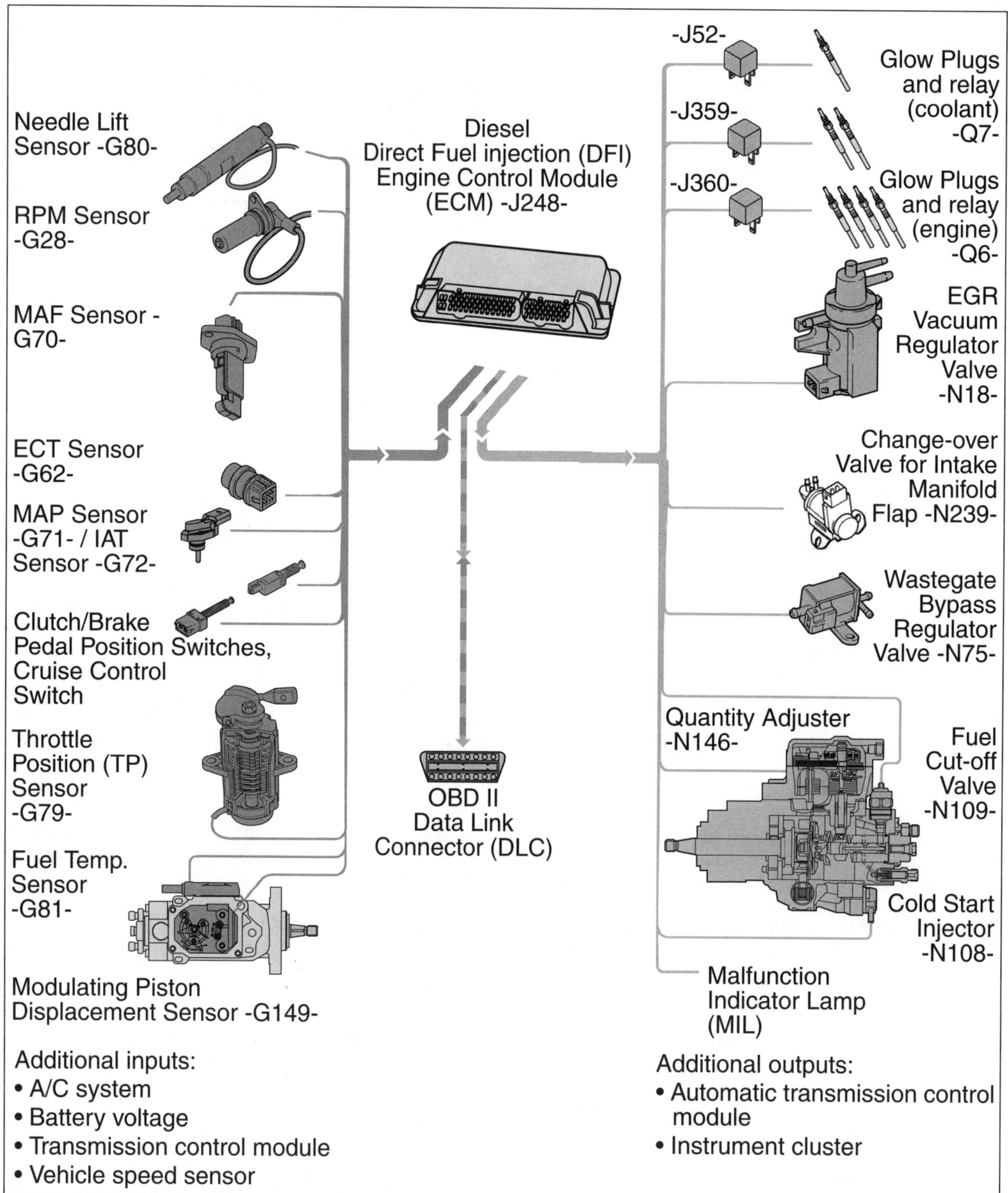

Fig. 2. Diesel Turbo Direct Injection engine management system. Inputs (**left**) to the ECM are used to control and adapt output signals (**right**) to the individual components. Volkswagen component codes are indicated within dashes (-).

In order to prevent possible damage from simultaneous application of the brake, clutch and accelerator pedals, the brake pedal switch, brake light switch, and clutch pedal switch signal their respective positions to the ECM. These signals are also used by the ECM during in cruise control mode.

Based on all of the input signals, the ECM precisely controls the following output components:

- Quantity Adjuster
- Cold Start Injector
- Fuel Cut-off Valve
- Wastegate Bypass Regulator Valve
- EGR Vacuum Regulator Valve
- Intake Manifold Change-over Valve

In addition, the ECM uses various sensors to control these additional outputs:

- Glow Plugs
- Glow Plug Relay
- Auxiliary Heater Coolant Glow Plugs
- Coolant Glow Plug Relay

When the ECM receives the signal to shut down, a signal is sent to a flap valve mounted in the intake tract. This valve, known as the intake manifold change-over valve, closes and blocks the flow of air to the still-turning engine. Blocking the flow of air during the shut-down cycle reduces the abruptness associated with stopping a diesel engine.

Tailpipe emissions are further reduced by a two-way oxidation-type catalytic converter.

TDI equipped New Beetles have two warning lights in the instrument cluster to advise of system status. The glow plug indicator light operates when the key is first turned on to indicate the need to wait for the glow plugs to pre-heat the combustion chambers. The Malfunction Indicator Lamp (MIL), lights if a failure of a monitored component occurs. In some serious failure modes, both warning indicators can be lit.

Owing to the complex nature, most diagnosis and repair of the TDI system requires the use of specialized scan tools such as Volkswagen special tool VAG 1551 or VAG 1552.

IGNITION SYSTEM

The ignition function is handled through the fuel injection/engine management system on all engines.

On gasoline engines, the Motronic ECM computes ignition timing based on inputs from the various sensors. Crankshaft position and speed are the main inputs to the ECM used for starting. The other sensors are used to adapt the basic timing map for varying operating conditions. Motronic engines incorporate adaptive knock control to adjust the ignition timing for individual cylinders. See **28a Ignition System (AEG engine)** for more information.

On diesel engines, the ECM uses the same information that was used to compute the fuel quantity to determine the correct moment of injection. When the fuel is injected into the combustion chamber, heat generated by the high compression ratio causes the fuel to spontaneously burn. This is the ignition firing point. There is no separate ignition system as such. In spite of this high compression ratio, cold engines do not have sufficient heat to burn the fuel. For this reason, glow plugs are used to provide supplementary heat. See **28b Ignition System (ALH engine)** for more information.

EMISSION CONTROLS

Gas and diesel engines use different emission controls. Most functions are integral with the engine management systems and are monitored by the On-Board Diagnostic (OBD) system. Most of these functions cannot be isolated. For additional information on those functions, see **26 Exhaust System and Emission Controls**.

20 Fuel Storage and Supply

20

GENERAL

This repair group covers the fuel supply portion of the fuel system. For AEG engines, this includes the components that store and supply fuel under pressure to the fuel injection section of the engine management system. For ALH engines, this includes the components that store and supply fuel to the diesel injection pump. For general system descriptions and overviews, see **2 General Information**.

> ***NOTE —***
> *Fuel filter replacement is covered in* **0 Maintenance**.

Safety Precautions

Please read and be familiar with the following warnings and cautions before working on the fuel pump, fuel tank or fuel lines.

> ***WARNING —***
> - *Always disconnect the negative (-) battery cable and cover the terminal with an insulated material whenever working on any fuel related component.*
> - *Gasoline and diesel fuel are dangerous to your health. Wear suitable hand and skin protection when working on the fuel system. Do not breath fuel vapors. Always work in a well-ventilated area.*
> - *Fuel and fuel vapors will be present during many of the operations described in this repair group. Do not smoke or create sparks. Be aware of pilot lights in gas operated equipment (heating systems, water heaters, etc.). Have an approved fire extinguisher handy.*

> ***WARNING —***
> - *Gasoline fuel supply systems are designed to maintain pressure in the system after the engine is turned off. Fuel will be expelled under pressure as fuel lines are disconnected. This can be a fire hazard, especially if the engine is warm. Always wrap a clean shop rag around any fuel line fitting before loosening or disconnecting it.*
> - *Exercise extreme caution when using spray-type cleaners on a warm engine. Observe all manufacturer recommendations.*

> ***CAUTION —***
> - *Cleanliness is essential when working on any part of the fuel system. Thoroughly clean fuel line unions and hose fittings before disconnecting them. Use only clean tools.*
> - *Use only spring-type clamps on fuel hoses. Do not use screw-type hose clamps, they do not expand and contract with engine heat and will leak.*
> - *Keep removed components clean. Seal or cover them with plastic or paper, especially if the repair cannot be completed immediately. Seal open fuel supply and return lines to prevent contamination.*
> - *When replacing parts, install only new, clean components. Seals and O-rings should always be replaced rather than reused.*

FUEL PUMP TROUBLESHOOTING (AEG ENGINE)

The fuel supply system is an integral part of the operation of the fuel injection system. Problems such as a no-start condition, hesitation, or stalling may be due to poor fuel delivery. The fuel pump itself is not directly monitored as part of the OBD II system, however, the fuel pump relay is monitored and several Diagnostic Trouble Codes (DTCs) are associated with it. In addition, the Motronic 5.9.2 fuel injection system will try to adjust for poor fuel delivery and the resultant lean running condition may exceed the system's ability to compensate. This will store DTCs in the system memory. Suspected fuel pump problems should first be investigated with an appropriate scan tool such as the Volkswagen supplied VAG 1551 or 1552. Use of these specialized tools must be in accordance with instructions with the tool by the manufacturer and are outside the scope of this service manual.

There are some preliminary tests that can be used to determine if the fuel pump or its electrical circuits are causing problems. Some of the tests described below require special test equipment such as a fuel pressure gauge and fittings.

The electrical current that operates the fuel pump is controlled by a relay and protected by a 15-amp fuse. This helps to handle the high current load of the pump and also ensures that the pump will not continue to run in the event of an accident or if the engine stalls. If, for any reason, electric power to run the pump is interrupted, the engine will not run.

Begin troubleshooting with a simple check of the fuel pump electrical circuit. The pump should run while cranking the engine with the starter. If necessary, remove the floor cover and access plate in the luggage compartment and listen or feel to verify that the fuel pump is running. If the pump does not run, see **Fuel pump, checking electrical circuit**.

> ***CAUTION—***
> *In cold weather, water in the fuel may freeze in the pump causing the circuit to overload and the fuse to fail. Be sure to check the fuel pump fuse in the dashboard fuse/relay panel. See* **97 Wiring Diagrams, Fuses and Relays** *for fuse locations.*

If the fuel pump runs, begin troubleshooting with a check of the fuel pump delivery rate as described later in this section. The test will indicate whether further tests are necessary. This is especially important on higher mileage cars, where normal pump wear may decrease delivery volume. Also check for correct pump installation and for a clogged or restricted pump inlet screen.

The electric fuel pump operates only when the car is running or being started. Because many of the fuel pump and fuel injection tests require that the pump be operated with the engine off, the fuel pump relay can be temporarily bypassed during testing.

All tests assume that there is sufficient fuel in the tank. If there is any doubt regarding fuel quantity, add more. The fuel gauge may not indicate true fuel level. Avoid running the fuel pump when the tank is empty.

Fuel pump, operating for testing

The procedure below uses a temporary wiring connection to bypass the fuel pump fuse and run the pump directly from the battery by way of the fuse panel connection. The preferred method is to use a remote switch such as Volkswagen special tools VAG 1348/3A and VAG 1348/3-2. See Fig. 1. You can also accomplish the same thing with a homemade fused jumper wire and an in-line switch. See Fig. 2.

> ***CAUTION—***
> - *A homemade jumper wire with a switch should be at least 1.5mm metric wire size (14 gauge AWG) and, for safety, include a 15-amp in-line fuse.*
> - *To avoid damaging the fuse panel sockets, the ends of the jumper wires should be flat-blade connectors that are the same size as the fuse blades.*
> - *Connect and disconnect the remote switch or jumper wire only with the switch in the off position.*

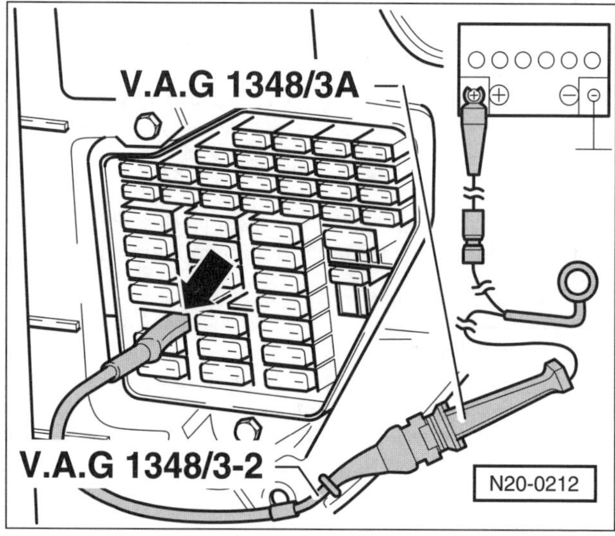

N20-0212

Fig. 1. Fuel pump fuse removed from position 28 of the dashboard fuse panel with one lead of the remote switch in place. Connect the remaining lead to the positive terminal of the battery.

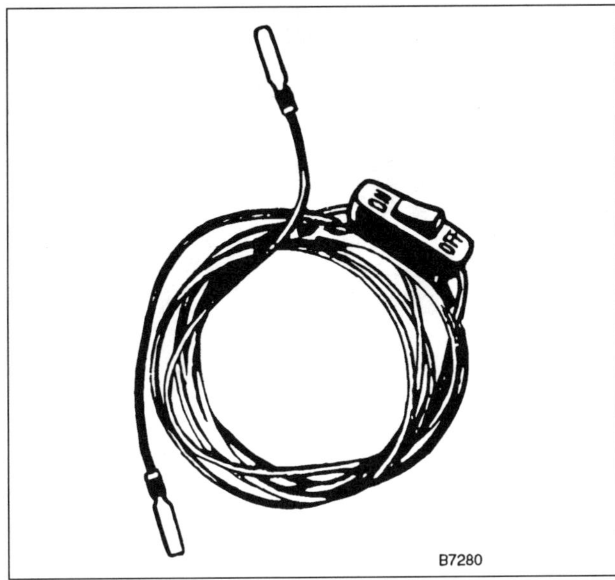

B7280

Fig. 2. Homemade jumper wire with flat blade terminals and switch/fuse for running fuel pump.

1. Remove fuse from position 28 of dashboard fuse panel. See Fig. 3.

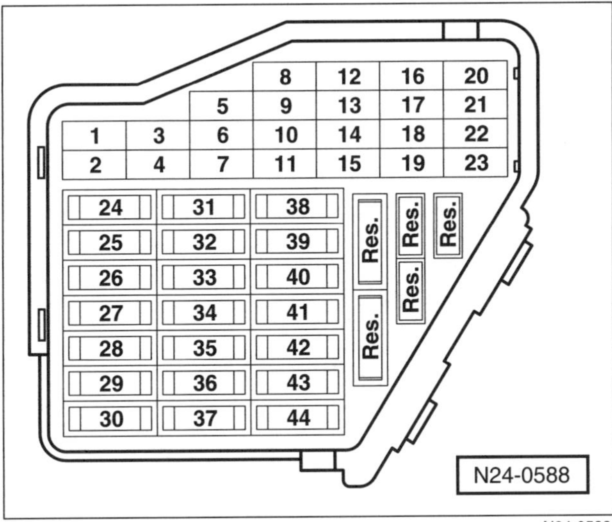

N24-0588

Fig. 3. Dashboard fuse panel showing fuse identification numbers. Be sure to inspect fuse 28.

2. With the ignition switched off, connect one lead of the fused jumper wire to the rear terminal of the fuse holder number 28.

3. Connect the other lead of the fused jumper to the positive terminal of the battery.

4. Turn the jumper wire switch on to run the pump.
   - If the pump does not run, remove the jumper lead from the rear terminal of fuse holder number 28 and put it in the front terminal.
   - If the pump still does not run, the problem is most likely in the wiring to the pump or the pump itself is faulty. See **Fuel pump, checking electrical circuit**.
   - If the pump runs only with the jumper connected, the relay, the engine control module (ECM), the circuit wiring or fuse 28 is faulty. See **97 Wiring Diagrams, Fuses and Relays**.

Fuel pump, checking electrical circuit

The fuel pump receives power from the fuel pump relay which is energized by the engine control module (ECM). The test given below checks for power at the fuel pump.

1. Check that the battery is fully charged and that fuse 28 is good.

2. Fold down rear seat, pull back floor cover and remove the access plate to the fuel delivery unit.

3. While a helper listens at the fuel pump, turn the ignition key on. The pump may run briefly. If not, turn the key to the start position and crank the engine. If the pump runs, the circuit is probably operating correctly. If the pump does not run, proceed to step 4.

   NOTE —
   Listen carefully for the pump to run, in operation it is barely audible.

4. Remove the fuel pump fuse and run the fuel pump as described in **Fuel pump, operating for testing**.
   - If the pump runs only with the jumper connected, the relay, the engine control module (ECM), the circuit wiring or fuse 28 is faulty. See **97 Wiring Diagrams, Fuses and Relays**.
   - If the pump does not run, leave the jumper connected and go to step 5.

5. Disconnect the 4 pin harness connector from the fuel delivery unit.

6. Check for voltage at the pump harness connector. See Fig. 4.

7. If voltage is not present at the connector, check the wiring between the dashboard fuse panel and the fuel pump harness connector. See **97 Wiring Diagrams, Fuses and Relays**.

8. If voltage is present, remove the pump and check for open circuits and internal grounds in the delivery unit. If no faults can be found, the fuel pump is probably faulty.

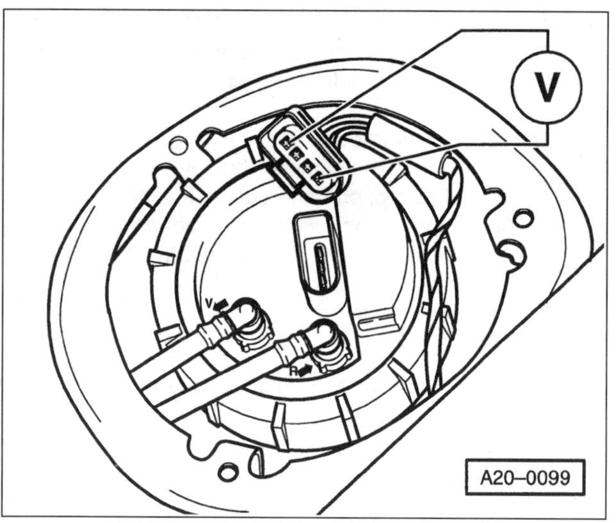

A20-0099

Fig. 4. Voltage supply to fuel pump being checked at outer terminals of connector (terminals 1 and 4).

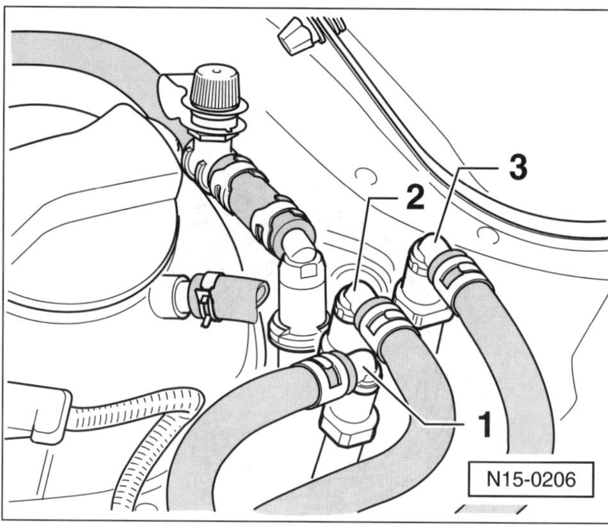

N15-0206

Fig. 5. Separate fuel supply line (**3**) from supply pipe. Fuel may be under pressure; cover connections with a clean shop cloth before disconnecting hoses. Connection (**2**) is fuel return and connection (**1**) is vacuum supply for leak detection pump.

Specification

- Voltage available at fuel pump . . . . battery voltage minus 2 volts maximum
- Fuel pump amperage (current) draw with engine at idle . . . . 8 amps maximum

Fuel pump, checking delivery rate

The tests given below require an accurate fuel pressure gauge with a shutoff valve and a range of 0-6 bar (approximately 0-100 psi). Volkswagen special tool VAG 1318 with appropriate adapters, or equivalent, can be used to check fuel delivery rate.

1. Connect jumper wire with switch to the fuel pump circuit as described in **Fuel pump, operating for testing**, given earlier.

2. Remove the fuel filler cap from the fuel tank.

3. Working in the engine compartment, disconnect the fuel supply hose from the supply pipe at the firewall and connect it to the fuel pressure gauge. See Fig. 5.

> ***WARNING —***
> *Fire Hazard! Fuel will be expelled under pressure when fuel lines are disconnected. Do not smoke or work near heaters or other fire hazards. Keep a fire extinguisher handy.*

4. Connect fuel pressure gauge to supply pipe with appropriate adapters. See Fig. 6.

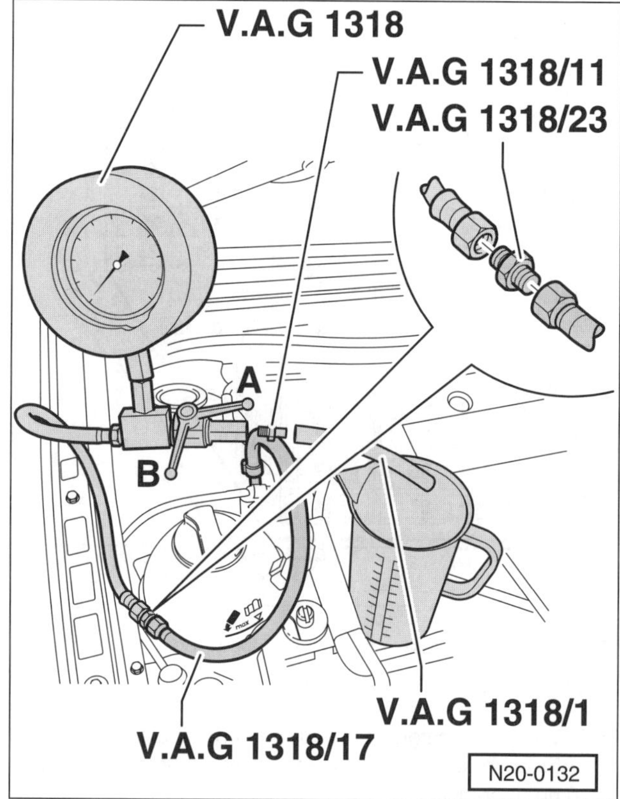

N20-0132

Fig. 6. Volkswagen fuel pressure gauge VAG 1318 and adapters shown connected to fuel supply pipe with valve positioned to regulate fuel flow.

5. Connect one end of a length of hose to the valve side of the gauge and place the other end into a clean, fuel resistant measurement container with at least 1 liter (1 quart) capacity.

6. Open the pressure gauge valve.

7. Operate the fuel pump with the jumper wire switch while slowly closing the valve on the gauge until the pressure reads 3 bar (44 psi).

8. Without moving the valve, shut off fuel pump and empty the measuring container back into the tank.

9. Connect a voltmeter to the battery and record reading.

> ***NOTE —***
> *Fuel pump delivery volume is dependent on the voltage available at the pump. For purposes of this test, the factory assumes a 2 volt drop between the battery and the pump.*

10. Operate the fuel pump with the jumper wire switch for 30 seconds and note the voltage reading on the meter.

11. Subtract 2 volts from the voltage reading at battery and compare the measured fuel quantity with the graph shown. See Fig. 7.

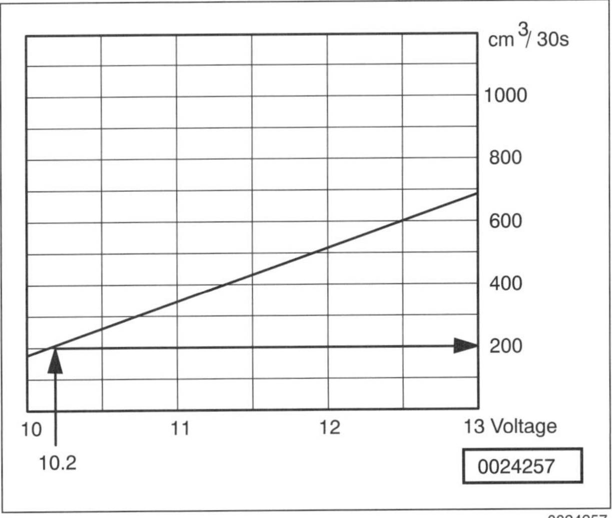

0024257

Fig. 7. Fuel delivery graph showing the minimum quantity of fuel to be delivered by the fuel pump in 30 seconds based on calculated voltage at the fuel pump. Fuel quantity must be above the diagonal line.

> ***NOTE —***
> *The line in the graph (Fig. 7.) represents the minimum quantity of fuel at a given voltage. For example, at battery voltage of 13 volts the measured volume was 500 cubic centimeters (cm^3) after 30 seconds. Subtract 2 volts to get 11 volts, locate 11 volts on the graph and note that the minimum volume for that voltage is approximately 350 cm^3. 500 cm^3 is greater than 350 cm^3 and is therefore within specification.*

12. If fuel delivery is below specification, check for kinks, blockage or other restrictions in the lines, a blocked or restricted fuel filter or tank strainer, or fuel leakage. If no faults are found, the fuel pump/fuel delivery unit is probably worn or otherwise faulty and should be replaced.

13. When testing is completed, empty the measuring container back into the tank. Remove the pressure gauge, jumper wire switch and volt meter, connect all fuel lines and check for leaks.

Fuel pump, checking system pressures

Checking fuel pressure is a fundamental part of troubleshooting and diagnosing the Motronic Engine Management System. Fuel pressure has a direct effect on fuel mixture and driveability. Low fuel pressure may set oxygen sensor-related Diagnostic Trouble Codes (DTC) in the Engine Control Module (ECM) as the system attempts to compensate for low pressure. This test will also check the fuel pressure regulator, the fuel pump check valve and the fuel injectors for internal leaks.

Before making the tests described below, make sure the fuel pump is operating correctly and that the fuel pump delivery rate is within specification as given earlier in this section. The tests given below require an accurate fuel pressure gauge with a range of 0-6 bar (approximately 0-100 psi). Volkswagen special tool VAG 1318 with appropriate adapters, or equivalent, can be used to measure fuel pressure.

> ***WARNING —***
> *Fire Hazard! Fuel will be expelled under pressure when fuel lines are disconnected. Do not smoke or work near heaters or other fire hazards. Keep a fire extinguisher handy.*

1. Working in the engine compartment, disconnect the fuel supply hose at the fuel rail. See Fig. 8.

2. Connect the fuel pressure gauge between the fuel line and the fuel rail. See Fig. 9. Make sure that if the gauge is equipped with a valve, it is in the open position.

3. Start the engine, let it run at idle speed and make sure that there are no leaks.

0024256

Fig. 8. Fuel supply hose (**arrow**) on fuel rail in engine compartment.

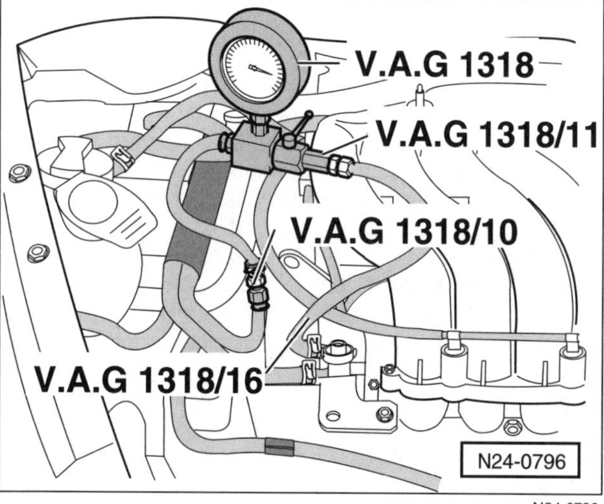

N24-0796

Fig. 9. Volkswagen fuel pressure gauge VAG 1318 with adapters shown installed to measure fuel pressure.

> ***NOTE —***
> *If engine does not start, operate the fuel pump with a jumper wire with switch as given earlier in* **Fuel pump, operating for testing**.

4. Observe fuel pressure on the gauge with the engine at idle:
   - If system pressure is too high, check for a blocked or restricted fuel line from the fuel pressure regulator. Check the vacuum line to the fuel pressure regulator. If the fuel line has no restrictions and the vacuum line is properly connected, the fuel pressure regulator is probably faulty and should be replaced.
   - If system pressure is too low, check for leaks in the fuel supply lines. Also check for restrictions in the fuel supply lines or a clogged fuel filter. If there are no leaks or restrictions, the fuel pressure regulator is probably faulty and should be replaced.

5. If fuel pressure is OK, disconnect and plug the small vacuum hose on the fuel pressure regulator and check that the fuel pressure increases as specified.
   - If fuel pressure does not increase, check the vacuum hose for kinks, restrictions and proper connections.

Specification

- Fuel pressure at idle. . . . . approx. 2.0 bar (36 psi)
- Fuel pressure (regulator hose disconnected). . . . . approx. 3.0 bar (44 psi)
- Residual pressure, after 10 minutes . . . . minimum 2.0 bar (29 psi)

---

6. Switch off engine.

7. Check for leaks and residual pressure by observing pressure drop on gauge after 10 minutes.

8. If pressure drops below specification, restart engine and let idle. While simultaneously closing valve on the pressure gauge, switch off engine.

9. Observe pressure gauge.
   - If pressure drops below specification, check for leaks in the fuel lines between the gauge and the fuel pump. If no leaks are found, the fuel pump check valve is probably faulty and should be replaced.
   - If pressure does not drop, clamp off the return fuel line just past the fuel pressure regulator with a suitable clamp and open the valve. If the pressure drops, check for leaks in the fuel injector rail. If no leaks are found, the fuel injectors are probably leaking. Remove the injector rail and inspect the injectors.
   - If the pressure does not drop when the valve is opened, remove the clamp from the return line and observe the pressure gauge. If it drops, the check valve in the fuel pressure regulator is faulty and the fuel pressure regulator must be replaced.

FUEL PUMP (FUEL DELIVERY UNIT)

The fuel delivery unit is mounted in the top of the tank and retained by a threaded retaining ring.

> ***NOTE —***
> *The procedure given below also applies to removing and installing the fuel level sensor on diesel engines.*

Fuel delivery unit, removing and installing

1. With the ignition switched off, disconnect the negative (-) battery cable.

> ***NOTE —***
> *Be sure to have the anti-theft radio code on hand before disconnecting the battery.*

2. Fold down rear seat, pull back floor cover and remove the access plate to the fuel delivery unit.

3. Disconnect the 4-pin harness connector from the fuel delivery unit.

4. Disconnect the fuel supply and return lines and wrap with a cloth to prevent fuel spillage. See Fig. 10.

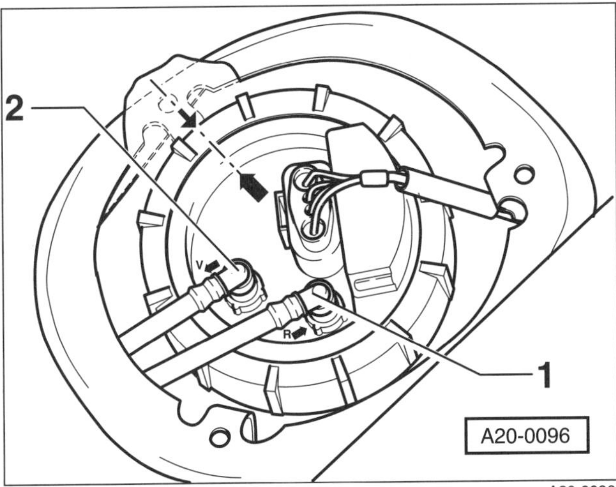

A20-0096

Fig. 10. Fuel pump return line (**1**) is identified with blue markings, fuel supply line (**2**) is identified with black markings. Alignment marks (**arrows**) must match during re-assembly.

> ***WARNING —***
> *Fuel will be discharged and dangerous fuel vapors will be present. Work in a well ventilated area. Do not disconnect wires that could cause sparks. Do not smoke or work near heaters or other fire hazards. Keep a fire extinguisher handy.*

5. Unscrew and remove the fuel pump retaining ring. See Fig. 11.

6. Carefully lift the delivery unit from the tank. Empty fuel delivery unit into a suitable container once it is removed.

7. Installation is the reverse of removal noting the following points:
   - Inspect and clean the intake screen as needed.
   - Do not bend the fuel gauge sending unit arm when installing.
   - Inspect the fuel tank seal and replace if damaged or distorted. Moisten the seal with fuel when installing.

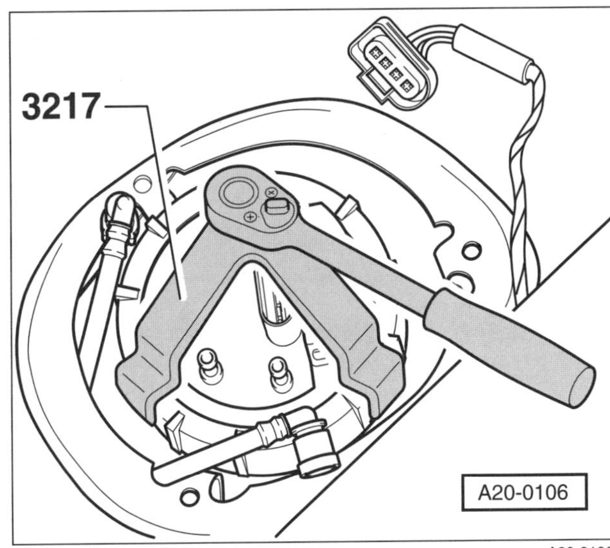

A20-0106

Fig. 11. Volkswagen special tool 3217 shown in position to remove the delivery unit retaining ring.

> ***NOTE —***
> - *Note the installed position of the fuel delivery unit; marks on the fuel delivery unit must align with marks on the tank as shown in Fig. 10.*
> - *Check for leaks before final installation of access plate.*

EVAPORATIVE EMISSIONS (AEG ENGINE)

All New Beetles with gasoline engines are equipped with evaporative emissions system monitoring. This system is referred to as the Leak Detection System or LDP after one of its major components. See Fig. 12.

The ECM determines when the appropriate conditions are met and activates the Leak Detection Pump (LDP) to pump a small amount of air pressure into the fuel tank and lines. The pump runs until a pre-determined pressure or time is reached. If the system does not hold the pressure, a fault or DTC is stored in the ECM memory.

Basic troubleshooting should begin with a visual inspection of the evaporative system hoses and components with particular attention paid to the fuel cap and seal. Further testing will require use of a scan tool such as Volkswagen special tool VAG 1551 or VAG 1552.

Leak detection system, assembly

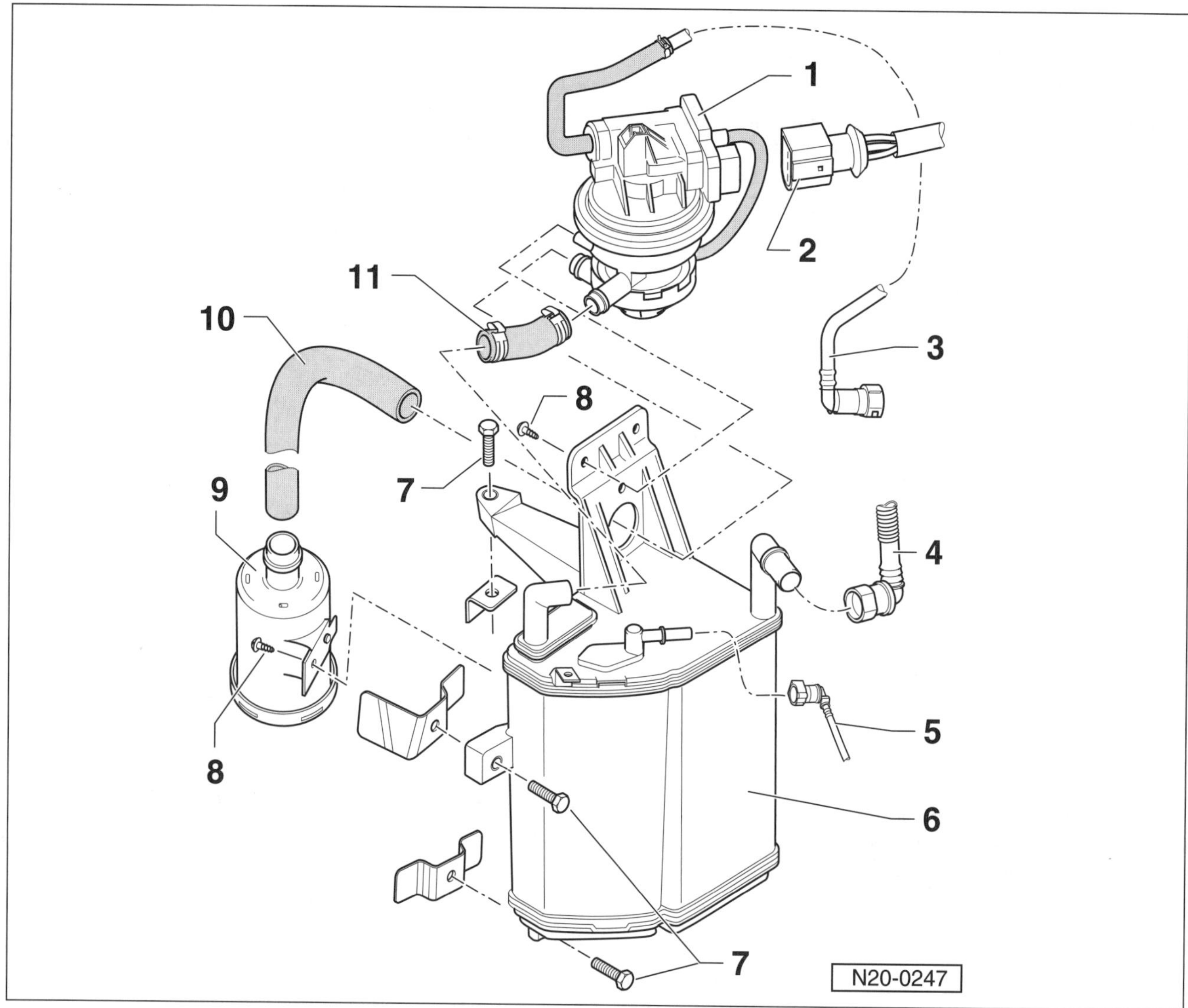

N20-0247

Fig. 12. Evaporative emissions leak detection system on New Beetles with gasoline engine.

1. **Leak detection pump (V144)**
   - On EVAP canister
2. **3-pin harness connector**
3. **Vacuum line**
   - To intake pipe upper section
   - Press together at front to release
4. **Vent line**
   - From fuel tank change-over valve
5. **To EVAP canister purge regulator valve (N80)**
   - In engine compartment on air cleaner
6. **Evaporative emissions (EVAP) canister**
   - In rear left wheel housing under wheel housing liner
   - To remove and install: remove the taillight
7. **Bolt**
   - Tighten to 10 Nm (7 ft-lb)
8. **Bolt**
   - Tighten to 2 Nm (17 in-lb)
9. **Air cleaner**
   - For leak detection pump
10. **Connecting hose**
    - Suction side
11. **Connecting hose**
    - Pressure side

FUEL TANK AND LINES

Fuel tank assembly (AEG engine)

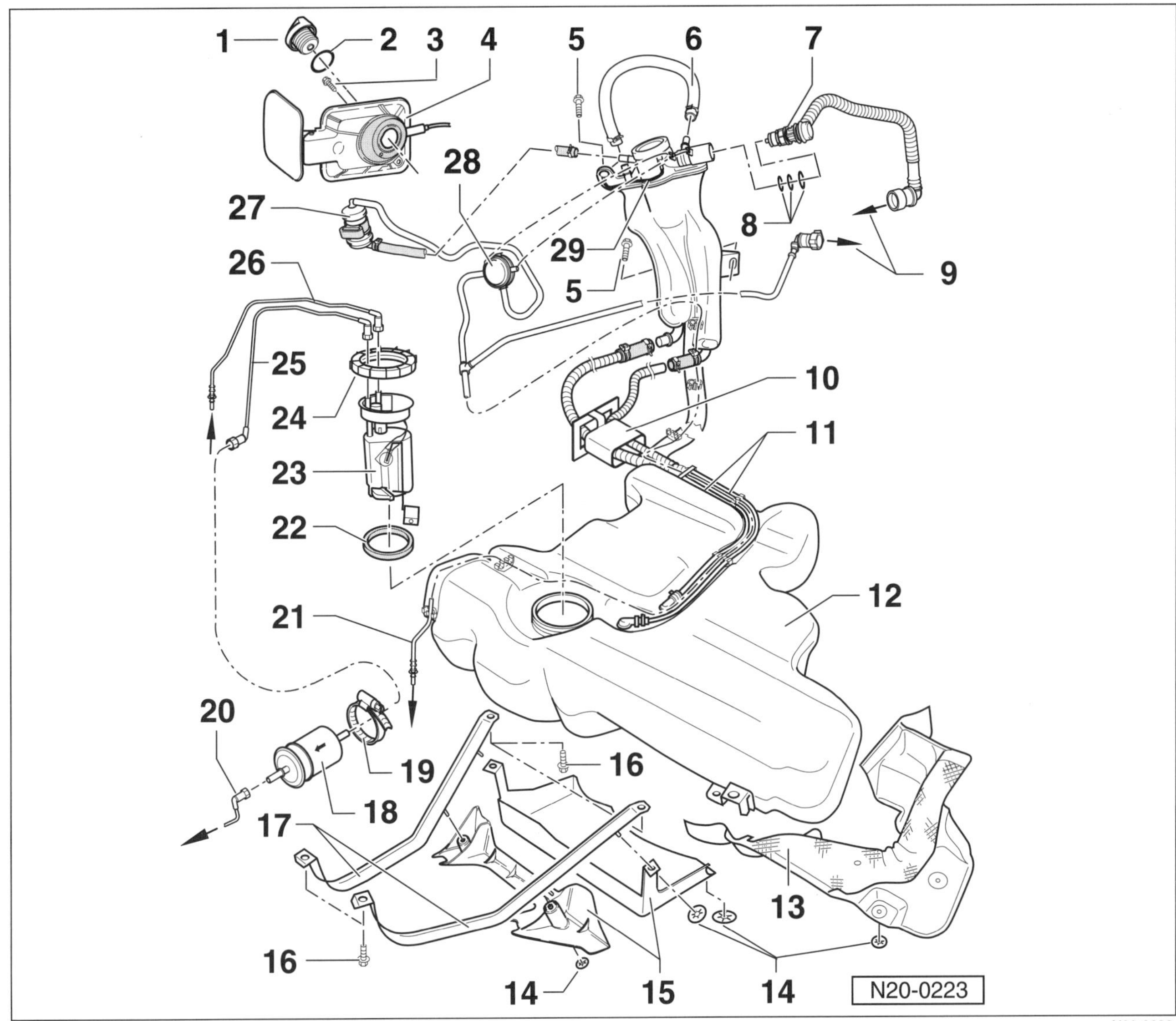

N20-0223

Fig. 13. Gasoline fuel tank assembly and related components

1. **Sealing cap**
2. **Seal**
   - Replace if damaged
3. **Bolt**
   - Tighten to 1 Nm (9 in-lb)
4. **Tank flap unit**
   - With rubber cup
5. **Bolt**
   - Tighten to 10 Nm (7 ft-lb)
6. **Vent pipe**
7. **Change-over valve**
   - Removing: unclip out of side support
   - Before installing, remove sealing cap (item 1)
8. **O-ring**
   - Replace if damaged
9. **EVAP canister**
10. **Wiring routing**
    - In floor pan long member
11. **Vent pipe**
    - Ensure it is securely seated
    - Secure using spring clips

(continued on following page)

(continued from previous page)

12. Fuel tank
- Support with VAG 1383A engine/transmission jack when removing

13. Heat shield
- For fuel tank

14. Clamping washer

15. Fuel tank cover

16. Bolt
- Tighten to 25 Nm (18 ft-lb)

17. Mounting straps
- Note differing lengths
- Installed position: attaching points (holes) point in direction of travel

18. Fuel filter
- Installed position: arrow points in direction of flow

19. Screw clip

20. Supply line
- Black
- To fuel rail
- Ensure it is securely seated

21. Vent line
- White
- Clipped onto top of fuel tank
- With EVAP canister purge regulator valve (N80)
- Ensure it securely seated

22. Sealing ring
- Replace if damaged
- Coat with fuel when installing

23. Fuel delivery unit
- Note installed position on fuel tank
- Clean strainer if soiled

24. Retaining ring
- Remove and install using 3217 wrench

25. Supply line
- Black
- Clipped to side of fuel tank
- Ensure it is securely seated

26. Return line
- Blue or blue markings
- Clipped to side of fuel tank
- Ensure it is securely seated
- From fuel rail

27. Gravity overflow valve
- Check valve for flow
  valve vertical: OPEN
  valve tilted 45°: CLOSED

28. Pressure retention valve
- For fuel reservoir ventilation

29. Ground connection
- Ensure it is securely seated

> ***WARNING —***
> *If working on a lift or hoist be sure to support the front of the vehicle before removing the fuel tank. The sudden removal of the fuel tank and associated components can unbalance the vehicle sufficiently to cause the vehicle to fall.*

> ***CAUTION —***
> *When removing or installing the fuel tank, the tank should be as empty as possible to facilitate easier handling.*

Fuel tank assembly (ALH engine)

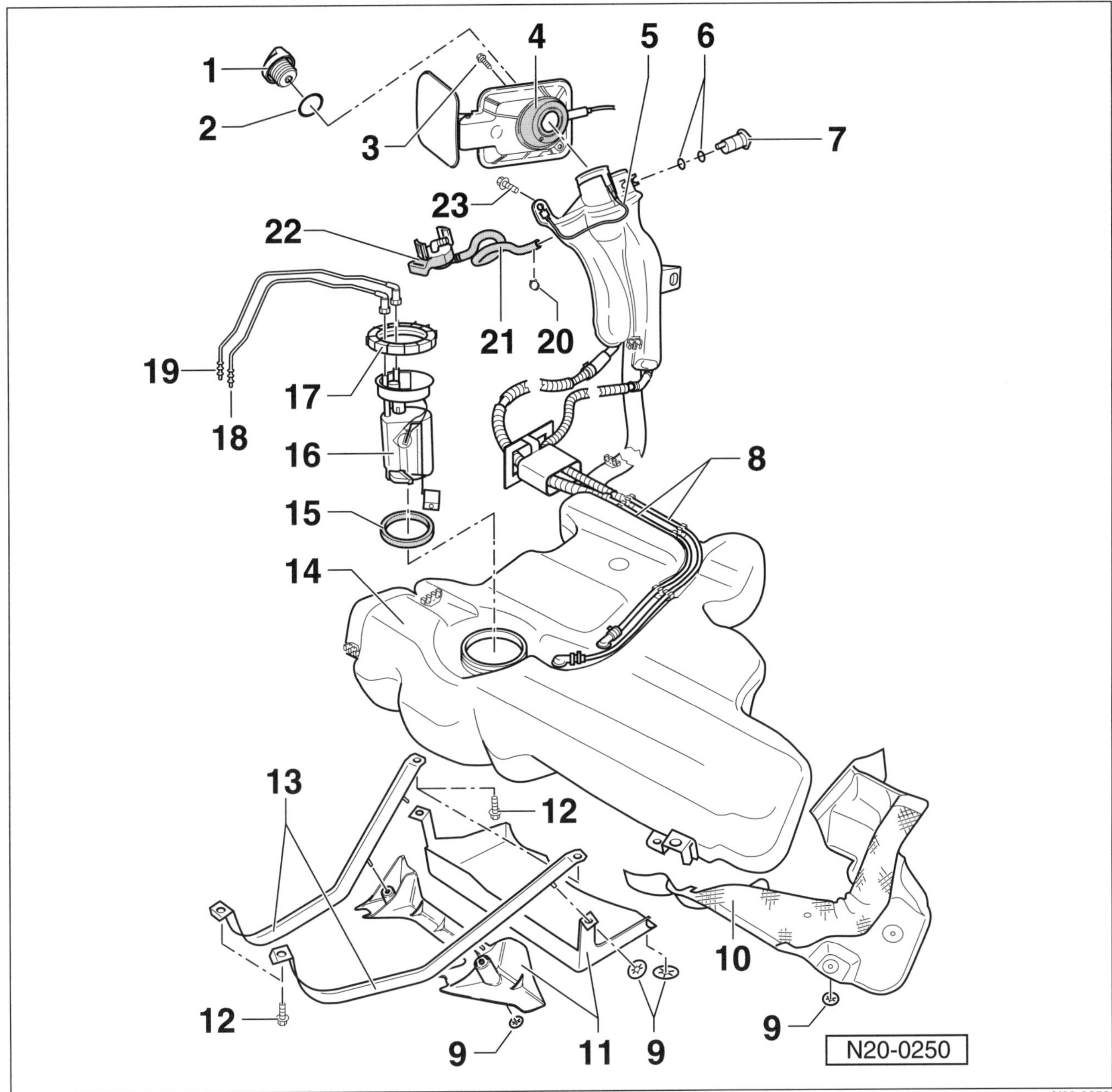

Fig. 14. Diesel fuel tank assembly and related components.

1. **Sealing cap**
2. **Seal**
   - Replace if damaged
3. **Bolt**
4. **Tank flap unit**
   - With rubber cup
5. **Ground connection**
6. **O-ring**
   - Always replace
7. **Vent valve**
   - To remove: unclip valve out of side support
   - Before installing, remove sealing cap (item 1)
8. **Vent line**
   - Ensure it is securely seated
9. **Clamping washer**

(continued on following page)

(continued from previous page)

10. Heat shield

11. Fuel tank cover

12. Bolt
- Tighten to 25 Nm (18 ft-lb)

13. Mounting straps
- Note differing lengths

14. Fuel tank
- Support with VAG 1383A engine/transmission jack when removing

15. Sealing ring
- Replace if damaged
- Moisten with fuel when installing

16. Fuel gauge sensor
- Note installed position on fuel tank

17. Retaining ring
- Remove and install using 3217 wrench

18. Supply line
- Black
- To fuel filter
- Clipped onto fuel tank
- Ensure it is securely seated
- To remove from flange, press down on tabs at connection

19. Return line
- Blue or blue markings
- From fuel filter
- At connection -R-
- Clipped onto fuel tank
- Ensure it is securely seated
- To remove from flange, press down on tabs at connection

20. Clamp
- Replace clamps

21. Hose

22. Gravity overflow valve
- To remove, unclip upwards out of support
- Check valve for flow
  valve vertical: OPEN
  valve tilted 45°: CLOSED

23. Bolt
- Tighten to 10 Nm (7 ft-lb)

> ***WARNING —***
> *If working on a lift or hoist be sure to support the front of the vehicle before removing the fuel tank. The sudden removal of the fuel tank and associated components can unbalance the vehicle sufficiently to cause the vehicle to fall.*

> ***CAUTION —***
> *When removing or installing the fuel tank, the tank should be as empty as possible to facilitate easier handling.*

21 Turbocharger and Intercooler

21

GENERAL

This section covers turbocharger and intercooler service and repair for the ALH diesel engine. Turbocharger boost pressure is not adjustable and separate parts for the turbocharger are not generally available from Volkswagen. The turbocharger and exhaust manifold are integral components. If the turbocharger is found to be faulty, the complete turbocharger/exhaust manifold assembly must be replaced.

Read the following warnings and cautions before servicing the turbocharger or exhaust system.

> ***WARNING —***
> *The turbocharger and related components operate at very high temperature. Always allow the system to cool or use proper protective clothing to prevent severe burns.*

> ***CAUTION —***
> - *Thoroughly clean all joints, pipe unions and connections, before disconnecting or reconnecting the turbocharger or any of its related components.*
> - *Take measures to prevent dust and dirt contamination. Cover all components with dust-free paper or seal them in plastic bags. Do not use cloth material. Avoid nearby use of compressed air. Do not move the car or work in dusty conditions while the turbocharger is open or removed. Install only clean components. Do not remove components from packaging until just before installation. Avoid use of components that have been stored loose.*

A cutaway view of the turbocharger is shown in Fig. 1. The exhaust-driven turbocharger vanes spin at very high speeds and are precisely balanced. The turbocharger is cooled and lubricated with engine oil. The boost pressure is limited by a mechanical wastegate. When the boost pressure exceeds a predetermined level, the wastegate opens to bypass some of the exhaust gases around the turbine. As the turbocharger compresses the incoming air, it also raises the air temperature. Output from the turbocharger is routed to an air-to-air radiator called an intercooler. The intercooler removes the excess heat allowing for greater boost pressure.

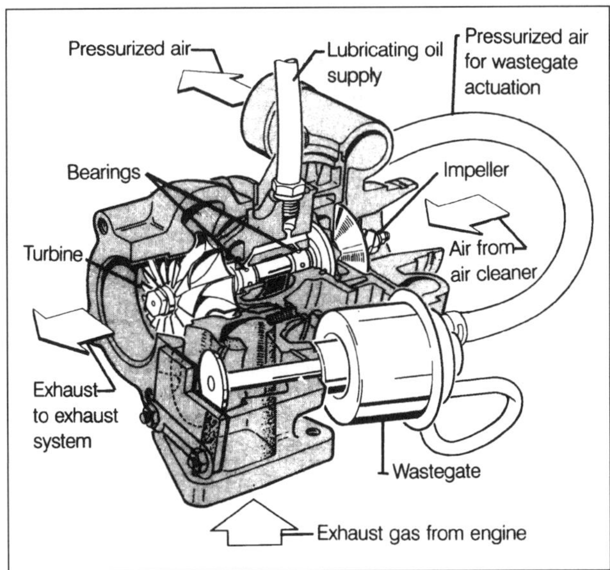

Fig. 1. Cutaway view of representative turbocharger used on ALH engines. The turbocharger unit is not adjustable and must be replaced as a complete assembly with the exhaust manifold if faulty.

TURBOCHARGER DIAGNOSTICS

Due to the extremely high speeds and temperatures, proper lubrication of the turbocharger is critical. Small oil passages are drilled into the turbocharger housing and bearings. Seals are placed around the shaft at each end to prevent oil from entering the compressor and turbine housing. When the turbocharger bearings and seals become worn, the lubricating oil can slip past the seals and into the combustion chamber or exhaust system. The result is blue-gray oil smoke from the tailpipe. When the bearings become severely worn, the turbocharger compressor and turbine impeller may contact the turbocharger housing, making loud screeching or thumping noises.

The major cause of turbocharger bearing and seal failure is "coking", or baking of the oil in the turbocharger's oil passages. During operation, the temperature of the turbocharger housing can exceed the boiling point of the oil running through it. Because the oil is constantly circulating, it stays cool enough to prevent coking. If the oil pipes are clogged or if the engine is turned off before the turbocharger has had time to cool down, the oil can quickly turn to coke. When these carbon deposits form, oil flow to the turbocharger is reduced. In addition, this substance is abrasive and can wear the seals, bearing and shafts prematurely.

If engine performance is low, and low boost pressure is suspected, first check for any loose or broken hoses or fittings. Make sure the control line to the wastegate is not blocked, loose, or leaking. Make sure there are no restrictions in the intake air system, such as a dirty air filter element or damage to the intercooler. Check the exhaust system for restrictions such as a damaged catalytic converter or clogged muffler. If no visible faults can be found, check the turbo boost pressure with a scan tool such as Volkswagen supplied VAG 1551 or 1552.

NOTE —

Suspected engine performance problems must first be investigated with an appropriate scan tool such as the Volkswagen supplied VAG 1551 or 1552. Diagnostic Trouble Codes (DTCs) stored in ECM memory must be repaired and the DTCs erased before proceeding. Use of these specialized tools must be in accordance with instructions with the tool by the manufacturer and are outside the scope of this service manual.

Turbo boost pressure, checking

Boost pressure measurements with a conventional pressure gauge are generally not possible due to the lack of an attachment fitting for a gauge. Volkswagen specifies testing with scan tool VAG 1551 or 1552. The use and operation of this scan tool requires extensive knowledge and training which are outside the scope of this manual.

Basic Requirements

- Intake and exhaust systems free of leaks and restrictions
- Engine temperature at 80°C minimum
- Engine compression OK. See **1 Engine**
- No DTCs in ECM memory

Specification

- Boost pressure measured with scan tool VAG 1551 or 1552 with basic requirements met (ALH engine) at 1500 rpm, wide open throttle........1700 to 2200 mbar

TURBOCHARGER, REMOVING AND INSTALLING

When replacing the turbocharger, the oil return and supply pipes/lines should be removed and thoroughly cleaned using a stiff brush and solvent. If the pipes cannot be completely cleaned, they should be replaced. The engine oil and oil filter should also be changed. If the impeller blades are damaged, inspect the intake connecting pipes and the intercooler for debris and clean or replace as needed. Be sure to check the boost pressure once installation is complete. An exploded view of the turbocharger system found on ALH engines is shown in Fig. 2.

NOTE —

If the turbocharger is being replaced because of excessive exhaust smoke, there will probably be some residual oil in the exhaust upon start-up. Be sure to test drive the car long enough to clear the left over oil from the exhaust system.

Turbocharger assembly

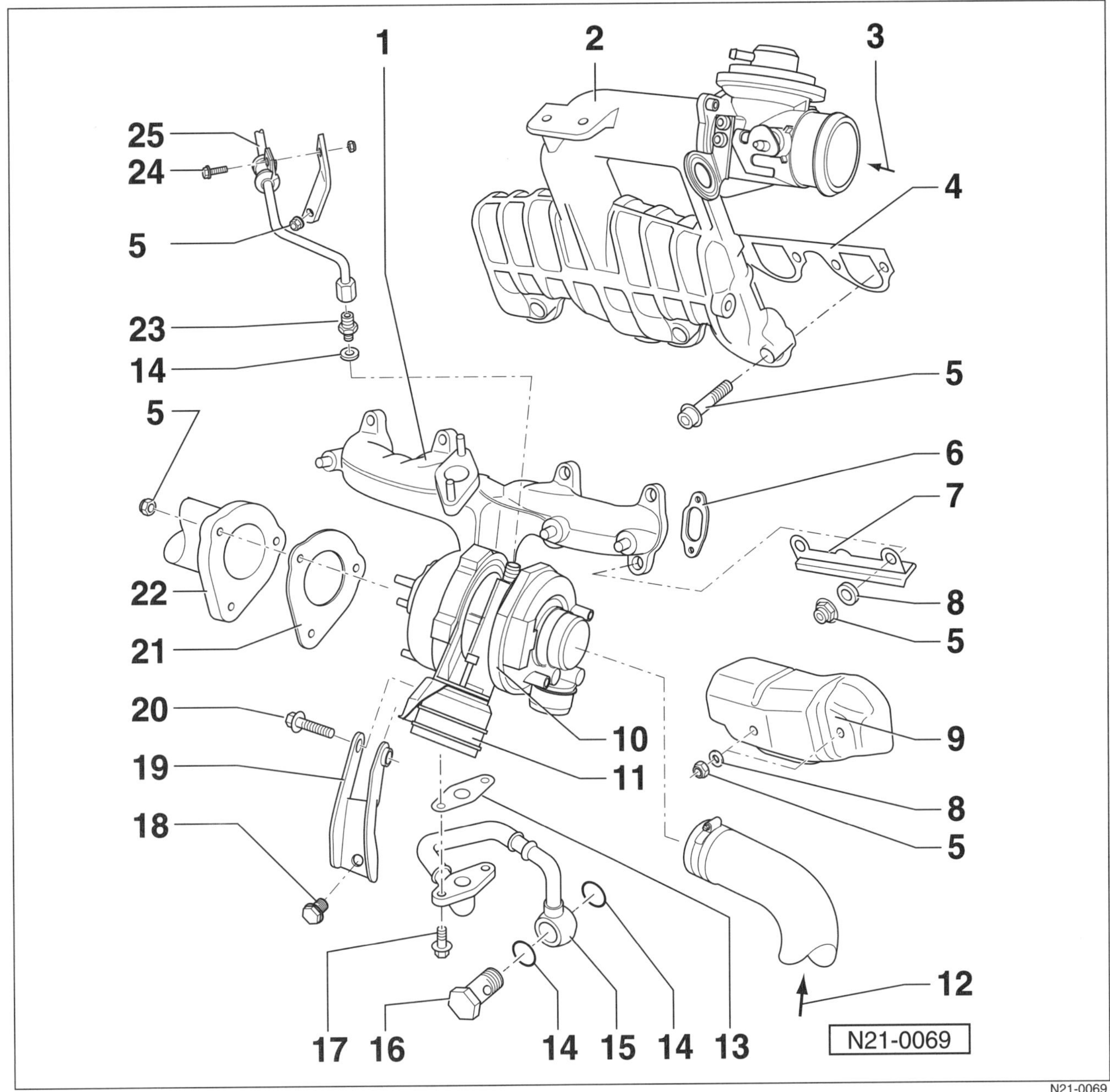

N21-0069

Fig. 2. Exploded view of turbocharger, exhaust manifold and related components on ALH engines.

1. **Exhaust manifold**
   - Integral with turbocharger
2. **Intake manifold**
   - Shown with EGR valve and manifold flap
3. **Air flow in from intercooler**
4. **Gasket**
   - Always replace
   - Coated (beaded) side faces intake manifold
5. **Bolt**
   - Tighten to 25 Nm (18 ft-lb)
6. **Gasket**
   - Always replace
   - Note installation position
7. **Bracket**
   - For heat shield

(continued on following page)

(continued from previous page)

8. **Washer**
9. **Heat shield**
10. **Turbocharger**
    - Integral with exhaust manifold
11. **Pressure unit (servo) for wastegate**
12. **Air flow in from air cleaner**
13. **Gasket**
    - Always replace
14. **Seal ring**
    - Always replace
15. **Oil return pipe**
    - To cylinder block
16. **Banjo bolt**
    - Tighten to 25 Nm (18 ft-lb)
17. **Bolt**
    - Tighten to 15 Nm (11 ft-lb)
18. **Bolt**
    - Tighten to 40 Nm (30 ft-lb)
19. **Bracket**
20. **Bolt**
    - Tighten to 25 Nm (18 ft-lb)
21. **Gasket**
    - Always replace
22. **Front exhaust pipe**
23. **Fitting**
24. **Bolt**
    - Tighten to 10 Nm (7 ft-lb)
25. **Oil supply pipe**
    - From oil filter flange

Turbocharger hose connections

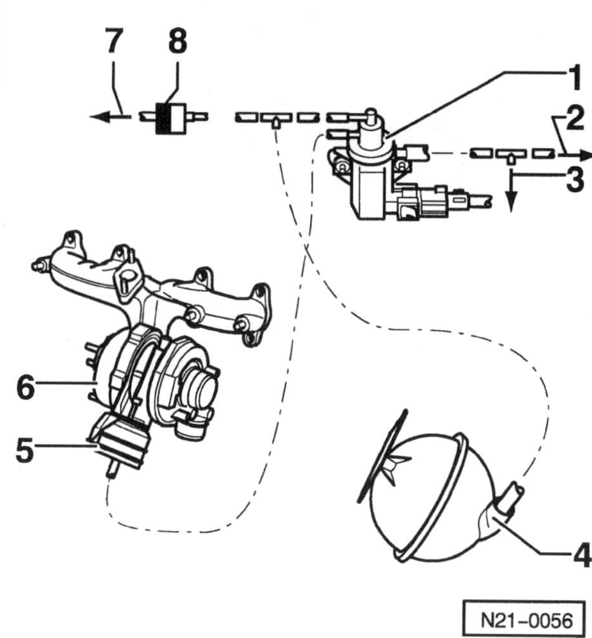

1. **Wastegate regulator valve**
2. **Connection to EGR regulator valve**
3. **Connection to air filter**
4. **Connection to vacuum reservoir/vacuum pump**
5. **Pressure unit (servo) for wastegate**
6. **Exhaust manifold with turbocharger**
7. **Connection to change-over valve for intake manifold**
8. **Check valve**

N21-0056

Fig. 3. Schematic view of hose connections to the turbocharger and wastegate regulator valve.

INTERCOOLER

Fig. 4 shows an exploded view of the intercooler on the ALH TDI engine. The intercooler is used to reduce the temperature associated with compressing the air by the turbocharger. This reduction in air temperature increases the density of the air which contributes to a reduction of Nitrous Oxide (NOS) gases and an improvement in performance.

Intercooler assembly

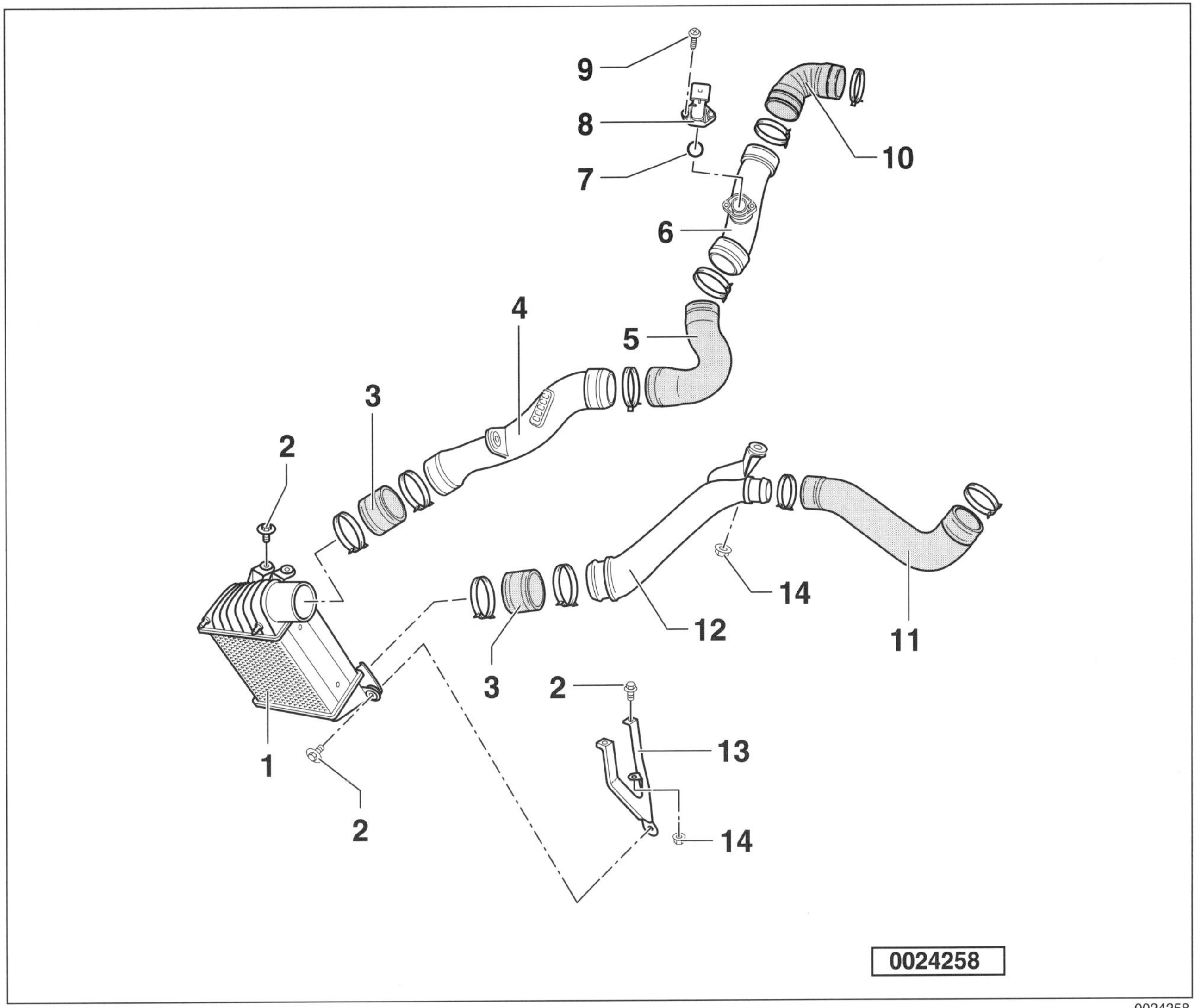

0024258

Fig. 4. Exploded view of intercooler system on ALH TDI engine.

1. **Intercooler**
2. **Bolt**
   - Tighten to 10 Nm (7 ft-lb)
3. **Connecting hose**
4. **Connecting pipe**
   - Between intercooler and intake manifold
   - Lower
5. **Connecting hose**
6. **Connecting pipe**
   - Between intercooler and intake manifold
   - Upper
7. **O-ring**
   - Replace if damaged
8. **Intake Air Temperature (IAT) sensor (G72)**
9. **Bolt**
   - Tighten to 5 Nm (44 in-lb)
10. **Connecting hose**
    - From intercooler to intake manifold
11. **Connecting hose**
12. **Connecting pipe**
    - Between turbocharger and intercooler
13. **Support bracket**
14. **Nut**
    - Tighten to 10 Nm (7 ft-lb)

23 Fuel Injection-Diesel (TDI)

TABLES

GENERAL

This repair group covers the diesel fuel injection system for the ALH 1.9 liter Turbo Direct Injection (TDI) diesel engine. Testing on the diesel glow plug system is covered in **28b Ignition System–Diesel (ALH engine)**.

Most major components of the diesel injection system are shown in Fig. 1.

Fig. 1 does not show the following components:

- Brake pedal switch (F47) and brake light switch (F); located in one housing on brake pedal.
- Throttle position sensor (G79); located in footwell on throttle pedal. In case of malfunction, the scan tool display is Throttle Position Sensor G69
- Clutch pedal switch (F36); located in footwell on clutch pedal.

NOTE—
Volkswagen identifies electrical components by a letter and/or a number in the electrical schematics. See **97 Wiring Diagrams, Fuses and Relays**. *These electrical identifiers are listed as an aid to electrical troubleshooting.*

CAUTION—

- *Repairs and adjustments to the injection pump require specialized equipment, and parts for rebuilding are not generally available. Faulty pumps must be serviced by the manufacturer. Internal problems usually require replacement of the pump.*
- *Adjustments and repairs to the fuel injection system should be made carefully. Cleanliness is especially important. Always clean fuel unions before removing lines*
- *Diesel fuel is damaging to rubber. Wipe off any fuel that spills on hoses, wiring, and rubber steering and suspension parts and wash with soap and water. If coolant hoses have been contaminated with diesel fuel, they must be replaced.*
- *Disconnecting the negative (–) battery cable may erase fault codes and basic settings in the engine management and automatic transmission control modules. Some driveability problems may be noticed until the system re-adapts to operating conditions. OBD II readiness codes, which may be required for emissions testing, may also be erased. Convenience electronics (alarm system, interior light control, power locks, mirrors, and windows) may need to be re-set using a VAG 1551/1552 or equivalent scan tool.*

Diesel injection system, component overview

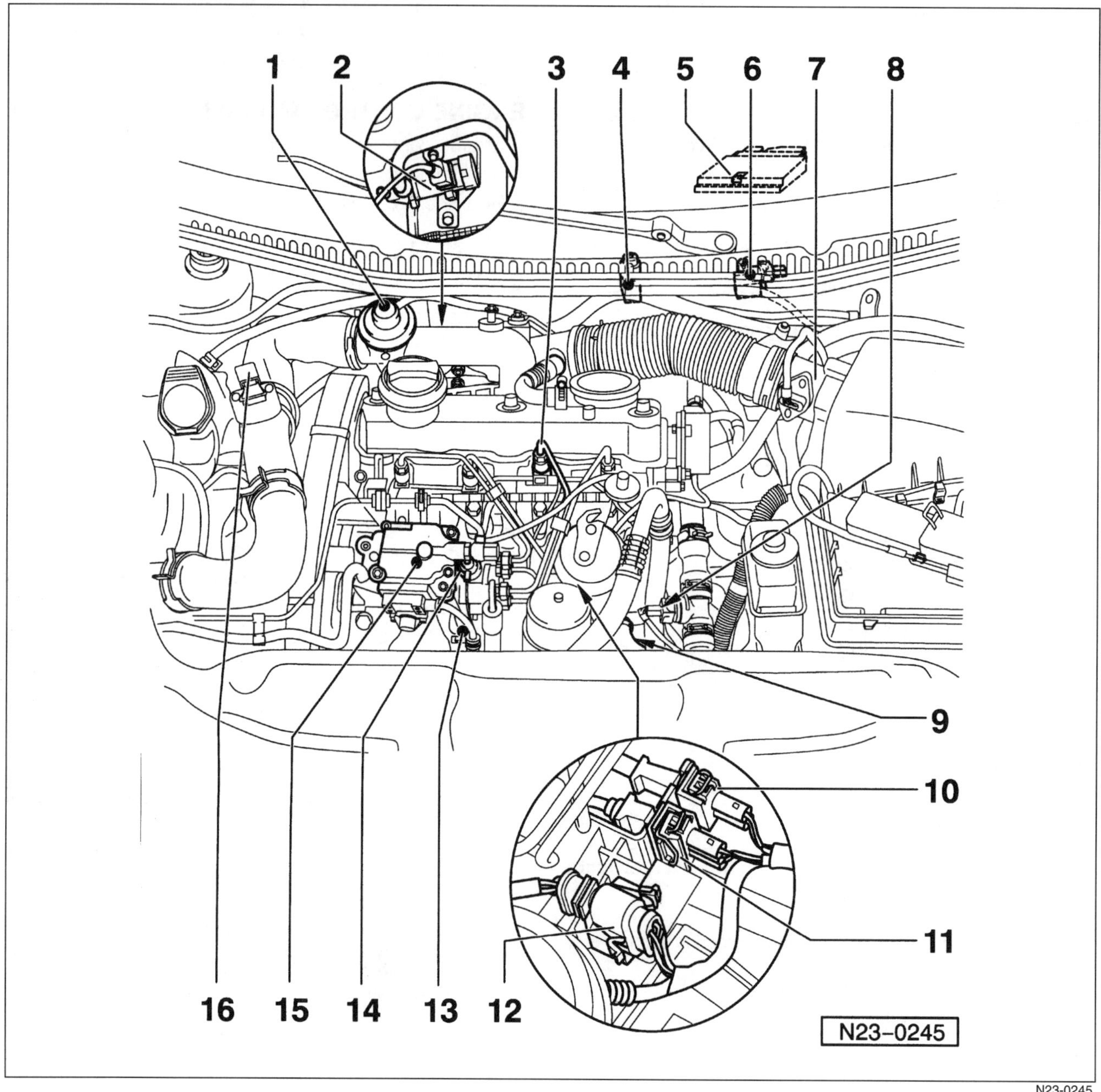

N23-0245

Fig. 1. Major components of diesel injection system.

1. **EGR valve**
2. **Intake manifold change-over valve (N239)**
3. **Injector with needle lift sensor (G80)**
4. **EGR vacuum regulator solenoid valve (N18)**
5. **Diesel direct injection system ECM (J248)**
   - With BARO sensor (F96)
6. **Wastegate bypass regulator valve (N75)**
7. **Mass air flow sensor (G70)**
8. **Engine coolant temperature sensor (G62)**
9. **Engine speed sensor (G28)**
10. **Harness connector**
    - For needle lift sensor (G80)
11. **Harness connector**
    - For engine speed sensor (G28)

(continued from previous page)

12. Harness connector
- For fuel temperature sensor (G81)
- For quantity adjuster (N146)
- For modulating piston displacement sensor (G149)
- For fuel shut-off valve (N109)
- For cold start injector

13. Cold start injector

14. Fuel shut-off valve (N109)

15. Injection pump quantity adjuster
- With fuel temperature sensor
- With quantity adjuster (N146)
- With modulating piston displacement sensor (G149)

16. Manifold absolute pressure sensor (G71) and intake air temperature sensor (G72)

NOTE—
Volkswagen identifies electrical components by a letter and/or a number in the electrical schematics. See **97 Wiring Diagrams, Fuses and Relays**. *These electrical identifiers are listed as an aid to electrical troubleshooting.*

TROUBLESHOOTING

Proper operation of the diesel engine requires a supply of clean fuel under pressure, an unrestricted supply of air, and properly timed fuel delivery. Fuel must be of the proper grade and properly winterized for cold-start and cold-running conditions. Dirt and water can interfere with combustion and will cause problems.

Good compression is especially necessary for the engine to run well. Engine mechanical faults leading to poor compression can cause problems that may seem to be injection related. Engine lubricating oil that leaks past worn piston rings, valve stem seals or turbocharger seals may produce exhaust smoke that also can be mistaken for fuel injection problems.

A faulty glow plug system may contribute to cold starting problems. See **28b Ignition System–Diesel (ALH engine)**. The battery must have the correct electrical capacity and the starter must be able to turn the engine fast enough (generally at least 150 rpm) to begin compression ignition. See **27 Engine Electrical System**. Insufficient engine power can also be the result of turbocharger or intercooler malfunctions. See **21 Turbocharger and Intercooler**.

Because the diesel engine speed is controlled by the amount of fuel injected and not by the amount of air admitted past a throttle plate, the air intake must be unrestricted. A clogged air filter, faulty turbocharger, or restricted intercooler can lower the air flow and reduce power output.

The injection pump, under the control of the Engine Control Module (ECM), produces the high pressure necessary to open the injectors and spray fuel. Fuel leaks or air in the fuel lines may reduce system pressure. Since power is controlled by the amount of fuel injected, low pressure may cause sluggish performance.

For cold starting, when the compression heat necessary for combustion is dissipated quickly by a cold engine, injection timing is automatically advanced by the ECM to give the fuel more time to burn. At higher rpm, there is less time for fuel to burn, so injection timing is advanced to start the fuel burning sooner. Since the injection pump is driven by the engine and externally mounted, its precise fuel metering and timing can be degraded by such things as a loose timing belt, worn sprocket, or loose mounting bolts. Correct Cetane rating as specified by the vehicle's Owner's Manual will profoundly influence starting and overall performance as well.

Most of the in-depth troubleshooting of this electronically controlled engine management system will require the use of a scan tool such as the Volkswagen supplied VAG 1551 or VAG 1552. However, there are several basic tests that should not be overlooked. **Table a** lists symptoms, their probable causes, and corrective actions. The boldface type refers to other sections in the manual where the repairs are described.

NOTE—
Engine performance problems should first be investigated with an appropriate scan tool such as the Volkswagen supplied VAG 1551 or 1552. Diagnostic Trouble Codes (DTCs) stored in ECM memory must be re-set and the DTCs erased before proceeding. Use of these specialized tools must be in accordance with instructions with the tool by the manufacturer and are outside the scope of this service manual.

Diagnostic quick checks

These tests are used to isolate and diagnose diesel fuel system problems. It is assumed that the glow plug system is functioning within normal parameters and that injection pump timing and valve timing are correct.

NOTE—
Testing and repair information on the diesel glow plug system is covered in **28b Ignition System–Diesel (ALH engine).**

Table a. TDI Diesel Fuel Injection Troubleshooting

Problem	Probable cause	Corrective action
1. Engine does not start	**a.** Cranking speed too low or will not crank	**a.** Repair starting system or charge/replace battery. See **27 Engine Electrical Systems.**
	b. No fuel or wrong fuel in fuel tank	**b.** Verify sufficient fuel of correct type in tank. Add as necessary.
	c. No voltage at fuel cut-off valve on injection pump. Fuel cut-off valve loose or faulty	**c.** Valve should click each time ignition is turned on and off. If not, check for voltage at connector. See **97 Wiring Diagrams, Fuses and Relays.** Replace a faulty solenoid.
	d. No voltage at glow plug bus or glow plug(s) faulty	**d.** The glow plug circuit is activated by the Engine Control Module. See **28b Ignition System–Diesel (ALH engine)** for glow plug testing and repair information.
	e. Excessive air in fuel system	**e.** Check fuel supply lines from fuel tank for cracks and connections for leaks, especially at and around fuel filter and injection pump inlet.
	f. Injection pump not delivering fuel	**f.** Check for basic fuel delivery to engine. Check for cracked or damaged lines, clogged fuel filter or other fuel supply problems.
	g. Injection timing incorrect	**g.** Adjust injection timing. Requires scan tool VAG 1551/1552.
	h. Faulty injectors	**h.** Test and, if necessary, replace injectors.
	i. Engine mechanical faults	**i.** Test compression. See **15b Cylinder Head and Valvetrain (ALH engine)**.
	j. Faulty injection pump	**j.** Replace pump.
	k. Fault in engine speed sensor (G28)	**k.** Test sensor at connector.
	l. Fault in ECM or other engine management system component	**l.** Interrogate permanent fault memory. Repair or replace components as required. Requires scan tool VAG 1551/1552.
2. Glow plug warning light not working	**a.** Bulb burned out or malfunction in glow plug relay circuit	**a.** Test and repair as described in **28b Ignition System–Diesel (ALH engine)**.
3. Idle speed incorrect, rough or irregular	**a.** Accelerator pedal or linkage binding	**a.** Remove driver's side trim panels under dash and inspect pedal and linkage for free movement. Repair as required.
	b. Excessive air in fuel system	**b.** Check fuel supply line from fuel tank for cracks, kinks, or leaks.
	c. Clogged fuel filter, or fuel return line and injector pipes leaking, dirty, kinked, or damaged at connectors	**c.** Inspect and, if necessary, replace lines and hoses, replace fuel filter. See **0 Maintenance**.
	d. Faulty injectors	**d.** Test and, if necessary, replace injector.
	e. Injection timing incorrect	**e.** Adjust injection timing. Requires scan tool VAG 1551/1552.
	f. Engine mechanical faults	**f.** Test compression. See **15b Cylinder Head and Valvetrain (ALH engine)**.
	g. Faulty injection pump	**g.** Replace pump.
4. Smoky exhaust (black, blue, or white)	**a.** Faulty injectors	**a.** Check and, if necessary, replace injectors.
	b. Injection timing incorrect	**b.** Adjust injection timing. Requires scan tool VAG 1551/1552.
	c. Turbocharger leaking internally	**c.** Inspect and repair, or replace turbocharger.
	d. Engine mechanical faults	**d.** Test compression. See **15b Cylinder Head and Valvetrain (ALH engine)**.
	e. Faulty injection pump	**e.** Replace pump.
	f. Fault in ECM or other engine management system component	**f.** Interrogate permanent fault memory. Repair or replace components as required. Requires scan tool VAG 1551/1552.

Table a. TDI Diesel Fuel Injection Troubleshooting

Problem	Probable cause	Corrective action
5. Poor power output, slow acceleration or top speed	a. Accelerator pedal or linkage binding	a. Remove driver's side trim panels under dash and inspect pedal and linkage for free movement. Repair as required.
	b. Air filter dirty or restricted	b. Clean or replace air filter. Inspect housing and ducting for debris. See **0 Maintenance**.
	c. Clogged fuel filter; or fuel return line and injection pipes leaking, dirty, kinked, or damaged at connections	c. Check for basic fuel delivery to engine. Inspect and, if necessary, replace lines and hoses, replace fuel filter. See **0 Maintenance**.
	d. Excessive air in fuel system	d. Check fuel supply line from fuel tank for cracks, kinks, or leaks, especially at and around fuel filter and injection pump inlet.
	e. Faulty injectors	e. Check and, if necessary, replace injectors.
	f. Injection timing incorrect	f. Adjust injection timing. Requires scan tool VAG 1551/1552.
	g. Engine mechanical faults	g. Test compression. See **15b Cylinder Head and Valvetrain (ALH engine)**.
	h. Faulty injection pump	h. Replace pump.
	i. Fault in ECM or other engine management system component	i. Interrogate permanent fault memory. Repair or replace components as required. Requires scan tool VAG 1551/1552.
6. Engine runs at a high constant idle and speed does not vary	a. Throttle position sensor (G79), malfunctioning	a. Interrogate permanent fault memory. Repair or replace components as required. Requires scan tool VAG 1551/1552.
7. Excessive fuel consumption	a. Air filter dirty or restricted	a. Clean or replace air filter element. Inspect housing and ducting for debris. See **0 Maintenance**.
	b. Fuel leaks	b. Check and, if necessary, replace or tighten all pipes, hoses and connections.
	c. Fuel return pipe blocked or restricted	c. Check return line for kinks and dents; replace faulty lines. If line is clogged, blow it out with compressed air, then bleed fuel system.
	d. Faulty injectors	d. Test and, if necessary, repair or replace injectors.
	e. Injection timing incorrect	e. Adjust injection timing. Requires scan tool VAG 1551/1552.
	f. Faulty injection pump	f. Replace pump.
	g. Fault in ECM or other engine management system component	g. Interrogate permanent fault memory. Repair or replace components as required. Requires scan tool VAG 1551/1552.

Fuel shut-off valve, checking

The diesel engine is stopped by cutting off its fuel supply. This is done by means of an electrical solenoid located on the diesel injection pump and that is closed with power off. An electrical signal from the Engine Control Module (key ON) opens the valve. If the valve is not working, the engine will not start. Conversely, a faulty valve could also allow the engine to continue running after the key is switched off.

1. Turn ignition key on and off without operating the starter. Listen for the valve to operate.
   - The fuel cut-off valve should click open when the key is turned on and click closed when the key is turned off. Do not confuse this sound with continuous sounds coming from other electronic components on the pump.
2. If valve does not operate, check for voltage at harness connector with key on.
   - If voltage is not present, check for wiring faults. See **97 Wiring Diagrams, Fuses and Relays.**
   - If voltage is present, disconnect battery ground (GND) strap from battery negative (–) terminal and proceed with step 3. See the **Caution** at the beginning of this repair group regarding battery disconnection.

> ***CAUTION—***
> *Before disconnecting battery cables, be sure to obtain radio anti-theft code.*

3. Clean the area around fuel shut-off valve and remove the valve, spring and plunger. See Fig. 2.

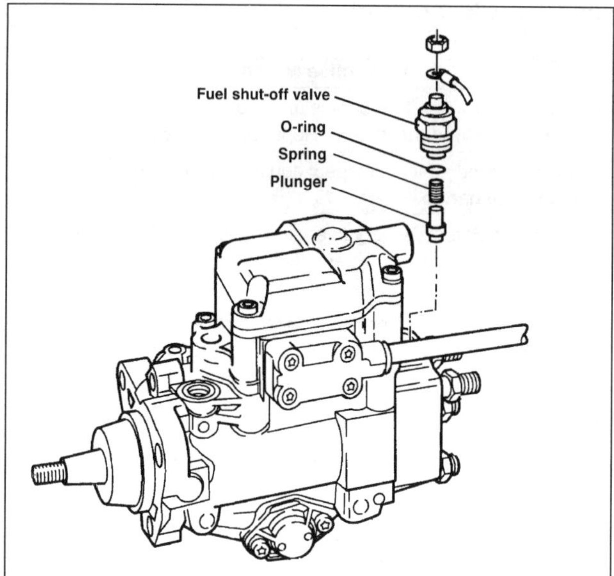

Fig. 2. Fuel shut-off valve removed from injection pump.

> ***WARNING —***
> *Fuel will be expelled. Do not smoke or work near heaters or other fire hazards. Have a fire extinguisher handy.*

4. Clean and inspect solenoid plunger and seat. Slide plunger into the valve without spring and check for free movement. If plunger does not move freely, replace valve assembly.

5. Carefully check for dirt and metal particles in valve bore of injection pump. The slightest amount of debris can cause malfunctions.

6. Install fuel cut-off valve using a new O-ring.

7. Reconnect battery negative (–) terminal.

Tightening Torque

- Fuel shut-off valve to injection pump . 40 Nm (30 ft-lb)

---

8. Be sure to quality check your work, see **Quality Review** at the end of this repair group.

Basic fuel delivery, checking

This test checks if fuel is being delivered to the pump and fuel injectors. Make this test when experiencing hard starting or no-start problems.

1. Check visually for fuel leaks on injector pump and especially around injector line unions.

2. If no leaks are found, clean the fuel union nut for cylinder No. 1 fuel injector pipe at the injector. Slightly loosen the fuel union nut. See Fig. 3.

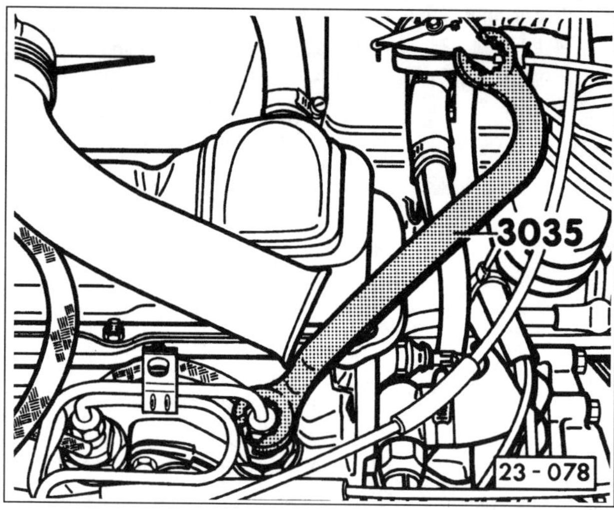

Fig. 3. Flare-nut wrench (Volkswagen special tool 3035) being used to loosen injector union nut for cylinder #4 on an earlier diesel engine version. The same tool is used on ALH diesel engines which are similar.

> ***WARNING —***
> - *Loosen the nut only about one-half turn to limit the amount of fuel leakage. The fuel injection system operates at very high pressure. Keep hands and eyes clear. Wear heavy gloves and eye protection. Wrap a cloth around the nut when loosening.*
> - *Fuel will be expelled. Do not smoke or work near heaters or other fire hazards. Have a fire extinguisher handy.*

3. Crank the engine and look for fuel to run out of the loosened union nut at the injector.

> ***CAUTION —***
> *Diesel fuel is damaging to rubber. Wipe off any fuel that spills on hoses, wiring, and rubber steering and suspension parts and wash with soap and water. If coolant hoses have been contaminated with diesel fuel, they must be replaced.*

4. If no fuel is observed, the most likely cause is a restriction or air leak in fuel lines between fuel tank and injection pump, or possibly a clogged fuel filter. It is also possible that vehicle has run out of fuel regardless of fuel gauge readings. If vehicle has a semi-transparent plastic fuel pipe on the supply side of diesel injection pump, check for movement of fuel in the line.

NOTE —
A stream of tiny air bubbles moving in the line is normal (unlike previous versions of the diesel engine).

5. If fuel is observed, but engine still fails to start, consult **Table a**, given earlier, for additional troubleshooting checks.

NOTE—
It is not necessary to test for basic fuel delivery on the remaining three cylinders due to the way the TDI system operates.

6. When finished testing, tighten the fuel union nuts and check for leaks. Clean up any spilled fuel.

Tightening torque
- Fuel injector union nut to injector or pump . . . . 25 Nm (18 ft-lb)

7. Be sure to quality check your work, see **Quality Review** at the end of this repair group.

THROTTLE POSITION SENSOR

Fuel quantity is controlled by the Engine Control Module (ECM) in TDI equipped vehicles. There is no accelerator cable connection between the pedal and the engine. This system is described as "drive by wire". A throttle position sensor is mounted on the inside of the bulkhead near the upper end of the pedal. See Fig. 4. A very short cable and cam connect the sensor and the pedal.

Testing and adjustment of the throttle position sensor requires the use of a scan tool such as VAG 1551 or VAG 1552. Faults related to the throttle position sensor will be stored as diagnostic trouble codes (DTCs) in the ECM. If the fault is severe enough, the ECM will ignore the throttle position sensor completely and run the engine at a constant high idle speed. This should enable the driver to reach the nearest workshop.

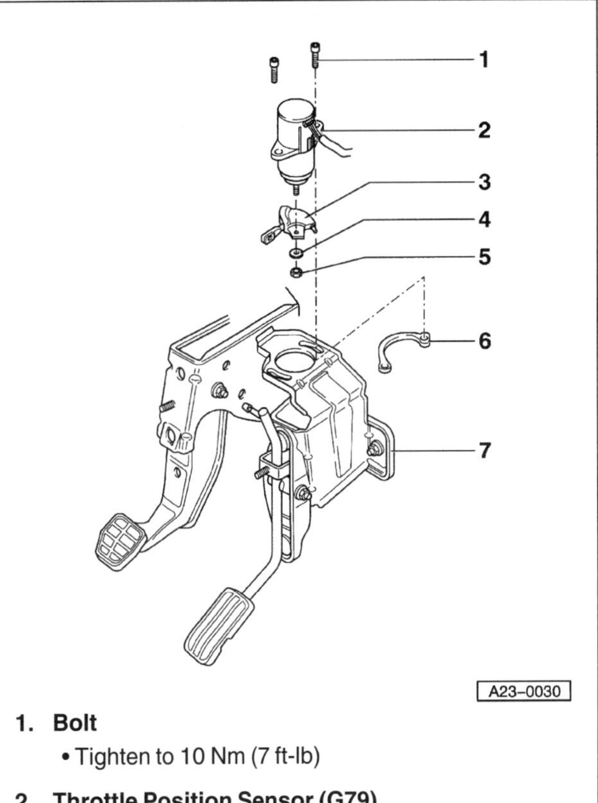

1. **Bolt**
   - Tighten to 10 Nm (7 ft-lb)
2. **Throttle Position Sensor (G79)**
3. **Cable cam**
4. **Spring washer**
5. **Nut**
   - Tighten to 10 Nm (7 ft-lb)
6. **Threaded retainer plate**
7. **Pedal mounting bracket**
   - Bracket supports accelerator and brake pedals

A23-0030

Fig. 4. Throttle position sensor, pedal assembly and mounting hardware.

TOOTHED BELT - CAMSHAFT/INJECTION PUMP DRIVE

Any time the camshaft drive belt is removed or installed, camshaft and injection pump timing must be checked and adjusted as required. Special tools are required for setting drive belt tension, camshaft TDC position, and injection pump timing. In addition, a scan tool such as the VAG 1551 or VAG 1552 is required to properly set injection pump timing on this electronically controlled diesel injection system. Fig. 5 shows an exploded view of the camshaft/injection pump drive belt assembly on the ALH Turbo Direct Injection diesel engine. See **15b Cylinder Head and Valvetrain (ALH Engine)** for toothed belt removal and installation.

Toothed belt - camshaft drive, assembly

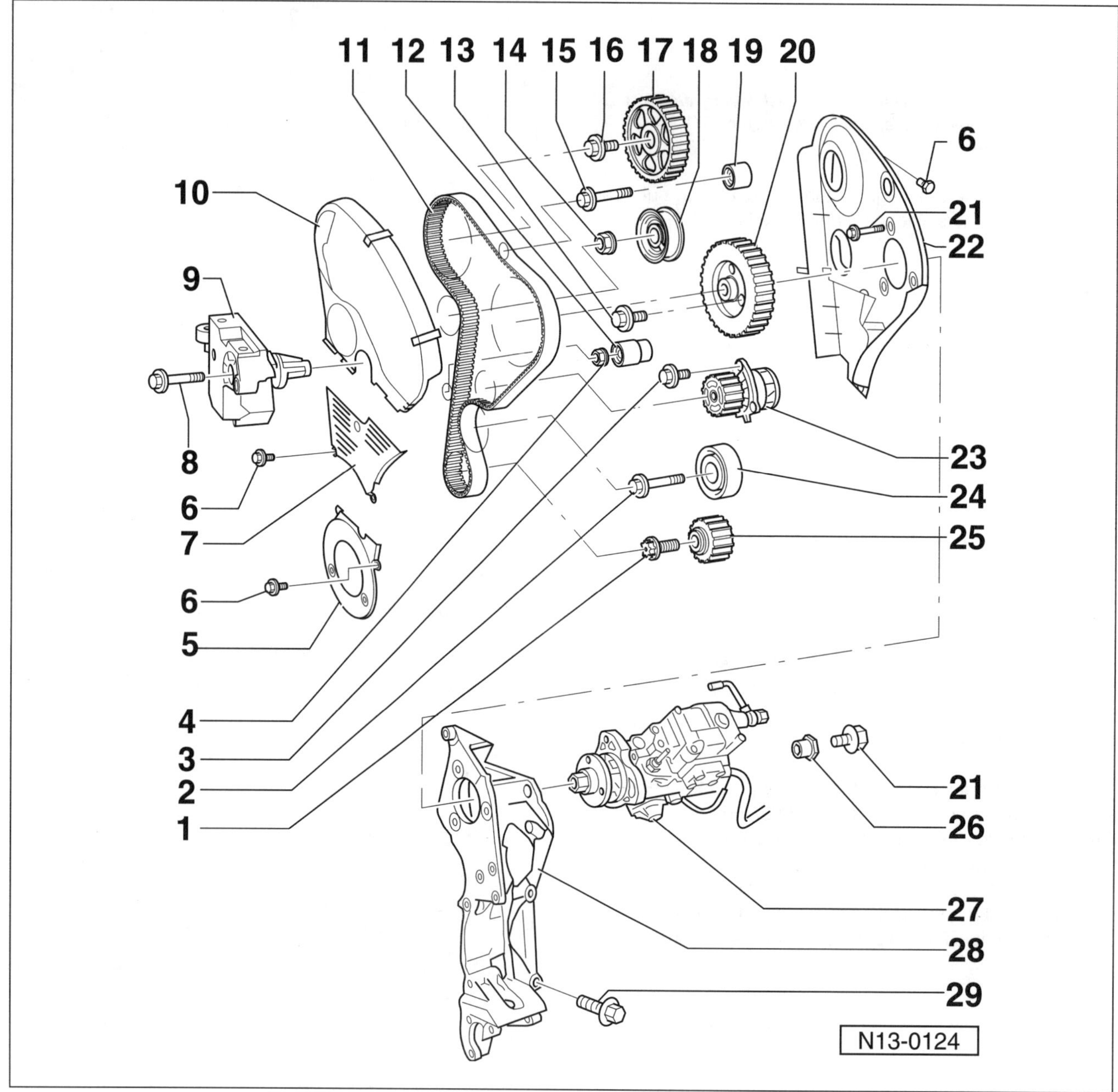

Fig. 5. Toothed belt for camshaft and injection pump drive and related components.

1. **Bolt**
   - Always replace
   - Tighten to 120 Nm (88 ft-lb) + ¼ turn (90°)
   - To loosen and tighten, counter hold with VW special tool 3099, or similar
   - Threads and shoulder must be free of oil and grease
2. **Bolt**
   - Always replace
   - Tighten to 40 Nm (30 ft-lb) + ¼ turn
3. **Bolt**
   - Tighten to 15 Nm (11 ft-lb)
4. **Bolt**
   - Tighten to 22 Nm (16 ft-lb)
5. **Toothed belt guard, lower section**
6. **Bolt**
   - Tighten to 10 Nm (7 ft-lb)

(continued from previous page)

7. **Toothed belt guard, center section**
8. **Bolt**
   - Tighten to 45 Nm (33 ft-lb)
9. **Right engine bracket**
10. **Toothed belt guard, upper section**
11. **Toothed belt**
    - Mark engine direction of rotation before removing
    - Check for wear
    - Do not kink
12. **Idler wheel**
13. **Bolt**
    - Always replace
    - Tighten to 20 Nm (15 ft-lb) + ¼ turn (90°)
14. **Nut**
    - Tighten to 20 Nm (15 ft-lb)
15. **Bolt**
    - Tighten to 20 Nm (15 ft-lb)
16. **Bolt**
    - Tighten to 45 Nm (33 ft-lb)
    - To loosen and tighten, counter hold with VW special tool 3036, or similar
17. **Camshaft sprocket**
    - Drive camshaft sprocket off camshaft taper using a hammer and drift through rear toothed belt guard opening
18. **Tensioning roller**
    - Semi-automatic toothed belt tensioning roller
19. **Idler roller**
20. **Injection pump sprocket**
    - Two piece construction
21. **Bolt**
    - Tighten to 30 Nm (22 ft-lb)
22. **Toothed belt guard, rear**
23. **Coolant pump**
24. **Idler wheel**
    - Must be removed before coolant pump
25. **Crankshaft toothed belt sprocket**
26. **Bushing**
27. **Diesel injection pump**
28. **Assembly bracket**
    - For diesel injection pump, generator and power steering pump
    - For A/C compressor if equipped
29. **Bolt**
    - Tighten to 45 Nm (33 ft-lb)

INJECTION PUMP

The diesel fuel injection pump is controlled by the ECM and performs three primary functions:

- It takes the fuel from the tank and pressurizes it to over 3000 psi.
- It precisely times the delivery of fuel to the injectors.
- It accurately meters the quantity of fuel delivered to the injectors.

The pump is driven by the same toothed drive belt that drives the camshaft at 1/2 crankshaft speed. Internal parts are lubricated and cooled by the diesel fuel. No routine maintenance is required or possible because no internal repair parts are available.

Because the Turbo Direct Injection system is fully electronic, the ECM can detect and store most faults associated with the injection pump. These faults are known as DTCs and are held in the ECM memory. Most DTCs will turn on the malfunction indicator light (MIL) and/or the glow plug light, alerting the driver to this condition. In addition, the ECM has diagnostic capabilities that allow an experienced technician with a scan tool to view certain operating parameters of the injection pump and other parts of the system. These must be investigated before a decision is made to replace an injection pump.

Fig. 6 shows the diesel injection pump with related components and mounting hardware.

> ***NOTE—***
> *Volkswagen identifies electrical components by a letter and/or a number in the electrical schematics. See* **97 Wiring Diagrams, Fuses and Relays**. *These electrical identifiers are listed as an aid to electrical troubleshooting.*

Injection pump assembly

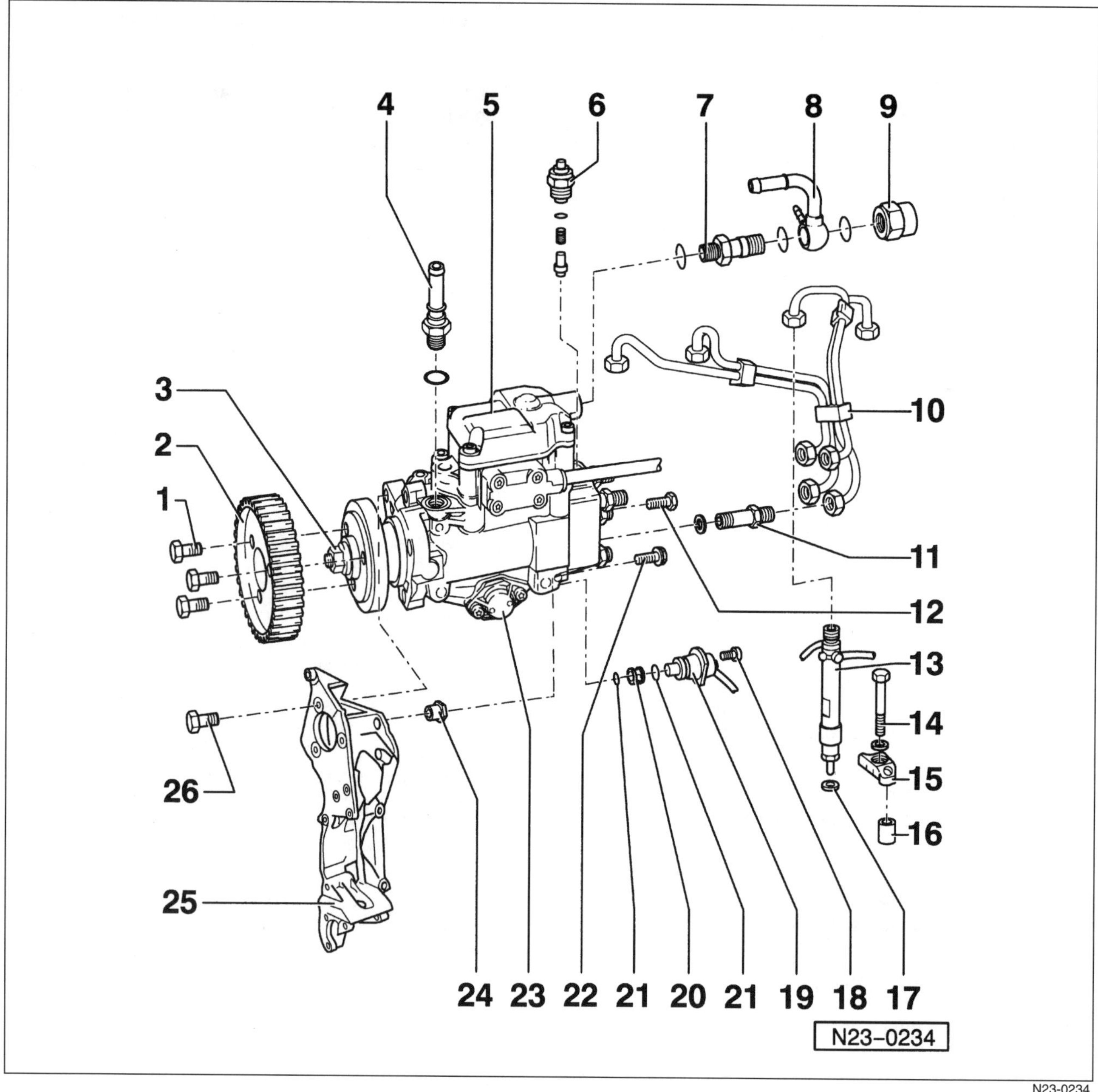

N23-0234

Fig. 6. Diesel injection pump with related fuel system components and mounting parts.

1. **Bolts**
   - Tighten to 20 Nm (15 ft-lb) plus ¼ turn (90°)
   - Always replace
2. **Injection pump sprocket**
3. **Injection pump sprocket nut**
   - Do not loosen for any reason!
4. **Union**
   - Supply line from fuel filter
   - Tighten to 25 Nm (18 ft-lb)
5. **Diesel injection pump**
   - With quantity adjuster (N146)
   - With modulating piston displacement sensor (G149)
   - With Fuel Temperature Sensor (G81)
6. **Fuel shut off valve (N109)**
   - Tighten to 40 Nm (30 ft-lb)
7. **Union**
   - Return line from diesel injection pump

(continued from previous page)

8. **Return line**
   - To control valve on fuel filter
9. **Cap nut**
   - Tighten to 25 Nm (18 ft-lb)
10. **Fuel injector lines**
    - Tighten to 25 Nm (18 ft-lb)
    - Always remove as a complete assembly
    - Do not bend, kink or alter shape
11. **Union**
    - To injector lines
    - With check valve
    - Tighten to 45 Nm (33 ft-lb)
12. **Bolt**
    - Tighten to 25 Nm (18 ft-lb)
13. **Fuel injector**
    - Cylinder # 3 with needle lift sensor (G80)
14. **Bolt**
    - Tighten to 20 Nm (15 ft-lb)
15. **Injector retainer**
    - Use special washer only
16. **Injector retainer mounting**
    - Fits into machined hole in cylinder head
17. **Sealing washer**
    - Always replace
18. **Bolt**
    - Bolt
    - Tighten to 10 Nm (7 ft-lb)
19. **Cold Start Injector (N108)**
    - Controls start of injection (timing)
20. **Strainer**
21. **O-ring**
    - Always replace
22. **Bolt**
    - Tighten to 25 Nm (18 ft-lb)
23. **Cover**
24. **Rear sleeve nut**
25. **Assembly bracket**
26. **Bolt**
    - Tighten to 25 Nm (18 ft-lb)

Injection pump, removing

Removal of the injection pump requires partial removal of the toothed belt driving the camshaft and the injection pump. Special Volkswagen tools including scan tool VAG 1551 or VAG 1552 are required to remove and install the diesel injection pump and properly set it up.

1. Remove upper engine cover.
2. Remove connecting pipes between intercooler and intake hose. Remove intercooler and turbocharger.
3. Remove fuel supply and return lines at injector pump.
4. Remove injector fuel lines as an assembly using a flair nut wrench as shown earlier. See Fig. 3.

> ***WARNING —***
> *Fuel will be expelled. Do not smoke or work near heaters or other fire hazards. Have a fire extinguisher handy.*

NOTE —
Cover all open fuel fittings with a clean cloth to prevent contamination.

5. Remove upper toothed belt guard.
6. Remove vacuum pump from end of cylinder head.
7. Remove cylinder head (valve) cover.
8. Set engine to top dead center (TDC), for cylinder #1 by turning crankshaft until timing mark on flywheel or torque converter aligns with mark on transmission case.
   - Manual transmission equipped vehicles: See Fig. 7.
   - Automatic transmission equipped vehicles: See Fig. 8.

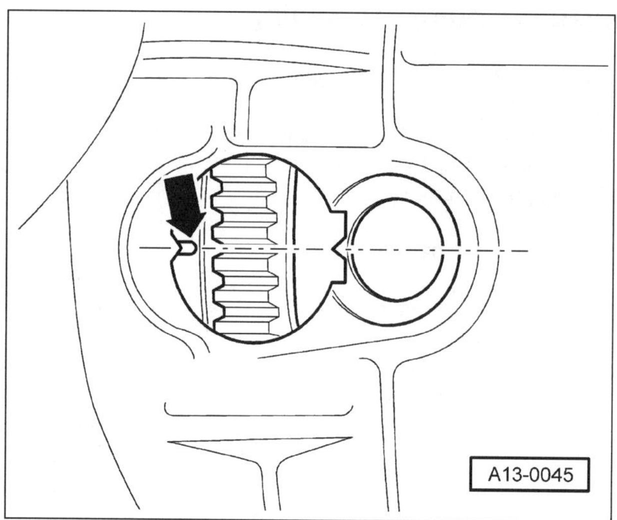

A23-0045

Fig. 7. TDC for manual transmissions: align mark on flywheel (**arrow**) with pointer on transmission case.

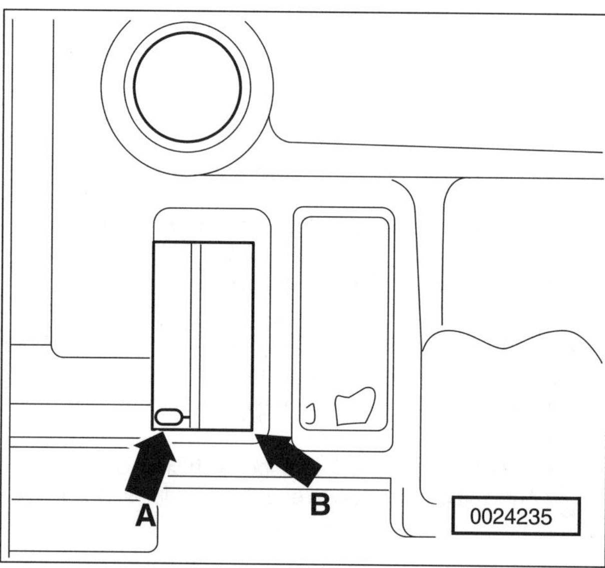

0024235

Fig. 8. TDC for automatic transmissions: align mark on torque converter (**A**) with lower edge of opening in transmission case (**B**).

9. Lock camshaft at TDC with a setting bar such as Volkswagen special tool 3418 and centralize using feeler gauges. See Fig. 9.

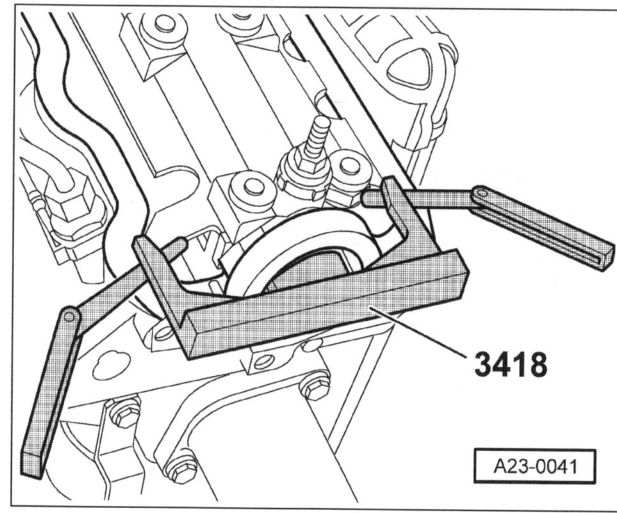

A23-0041

Fig. 9. Volkswagen special tool 3418 shown in position on the vacuum pump end of the camshaft locking it at TDC. Equal thicknesses of feeler gauges are placed under the ends of the tool to ensure exact camshaft TDC.

10. Remove injection pump sprocket mounting bolts and discard. See Fig. 10.

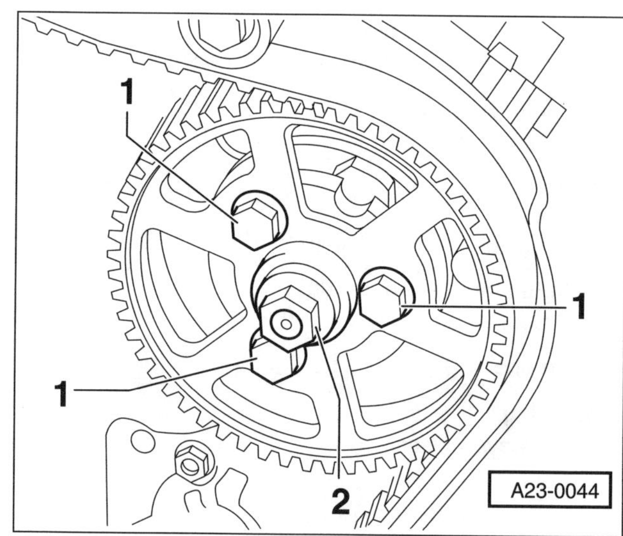

A23-0044

Fig. 10. Remove injection pump sprocket mounting bolts (**1**). Do not loosen center sprocket nut (**2**).

> ***CAUTION—***
> *Do not loosen the center sprocket nut for any reason. Loosening this nut will allow the sprocket to move on the shaft resulting in altered basic settings which CANNOT be reset with normal workshop equipment.*

11. Loosen toothed belt tension roller nut to relieve toothed belt tension.

12. Slip toothed belt off injection pump sprocket and remove sprocket from pump shaft hub.

13. Loosen camshaft sprocket mounting bolt about ½ turn. Release camshaft sprocket from camshaft taper by tapping with a hammer on a soft drift inserted through the hole in rear of toothed belt guard. See Fig. 11.

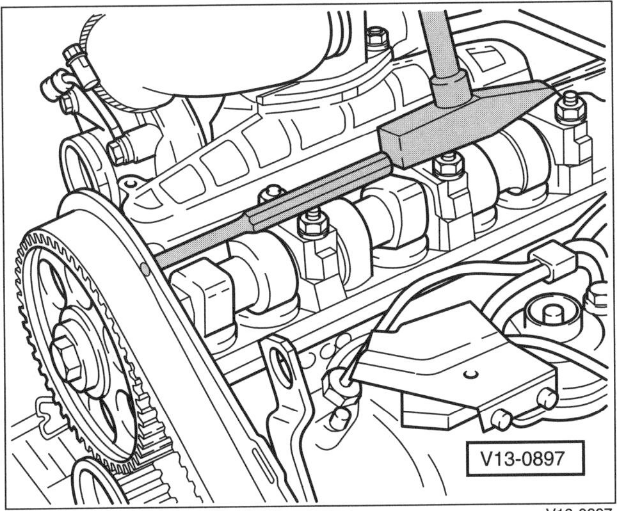

Fig. 11. Drift shown inserted through hole in rear toothed belt guard.

NOTE—
The camshaft end is tapered. Loosening the bolt and tapping the sprocket will allow the camshaft sprocket to rotate independently of the camshaft. There may be a keyway cut into the end of the camshaft. However, there is no matching keyway cut into the sprocket nor is there a woodruff key installed.

14. Remove camshaft sprocket mounting bolt and sprocket.

15. Disconnect the harness connector for the diesel pump electronics and unclip the connector from the retaining bracket. See Fig. 12.

16. Remove front injection pump mounting bolts from assembly bracket. See Fig. 13.

17. Remove rear injection pump mounting bolt from support bracket. See Fig. 14.

Fig. 12. Harness connector (**arrow**) for diesel pump electronics.

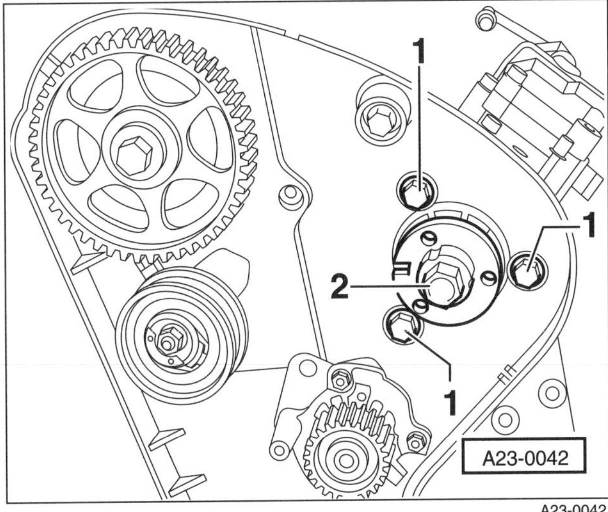

Fig. 13. Front injection pump mounting bolts (**1**). Do not loosen center sprocket nut (**2**).

18. Carefully slide pump shaft out of assembly bracket and lift pump out.

19. If pump will not be immediately reinstalled, take steps to insure that no dirt can get into any of pump openings or injector unions. Store pump so that diesel fuel in the pump will not drain out.

20. Be sure to quality check your work, see **Quality Review** at the end of this repair group.

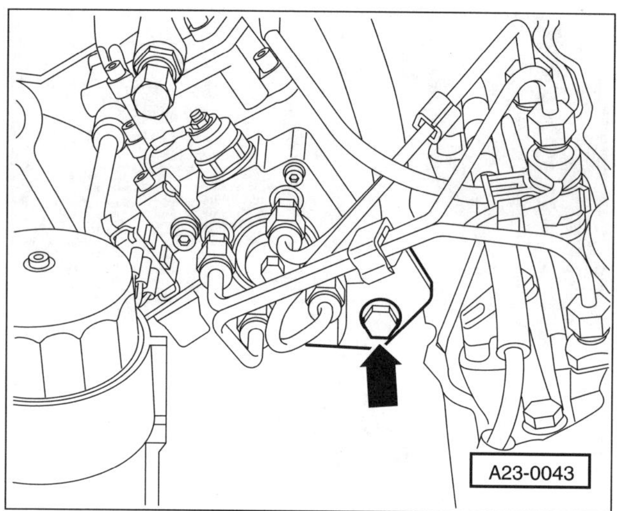

A23-0043

Fig. 14. Rear injection pump mounting bolt (**arrow**) threaded into rear sleeve nut (not visible).

Injection pump, installing

Before installing a new injection pump or if reusing the original, remove all packaging materials and plugs sealing port openings.

1. Install injection pump into assembly bracket and hand tighten rear injection pump mounting bolt. See Fig. 14.

2. Position pump in assembly bracket. Install and torque front injection pump mounting bolts and torque rear injection pump mounting bolt.

Tightening torque

- Injection pump bolts, front (M8) . . . . . 25 Nm (18 ft-lb)
- Injection pump bolt, rear (M8) . . . . . . 25 Nm (18 ft-lb)

3. Install new bolts into injection pump sprocket and mount sprocket to injection pump hub. Hand tighten only at this time.

4. Position pump sprocket so that bolts are in the middle of the elongated holes

5. Lock injection pump sprocket using Volkswagen special tool 3359. See Fig. 15.

6. Ensure that crankshaft is at TDC for cylinder #1 as shown earlier. See Fig. 7. See Fig. 8.

7. Ensure that camshaft is locked in position as shown earlier. See Fig. 9.

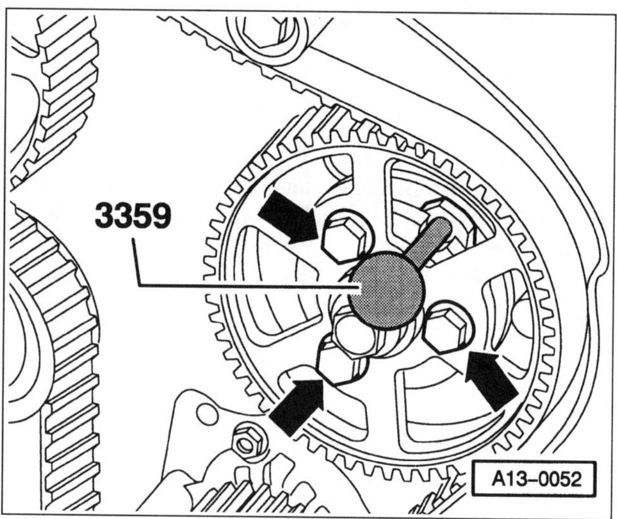

A13-0052

Fig. 15. Injection pump sprocket installed with new bolts (**arrows**) and secured with locking pin 3359.

8. Place toothed belt onto injection pump sprocket and tensioning roller and thread under idler roller. Be sure tensioning roller retaining hook is correctly seated in hole in toothed belt guard and cylinder head. See Fig. 16.

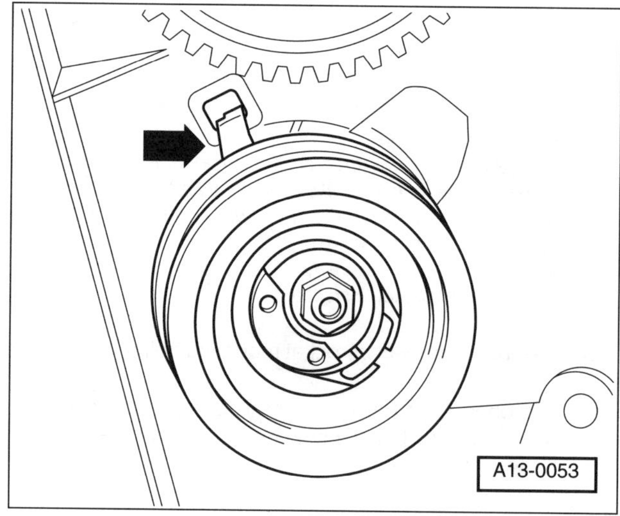

A13-0053

Fig. 16. Tensioning roller retaining lug (**arrow**) shown in proper position through toothed belt guard and into hole in cylinder head.

9. Place camshaft sprocket into toothed belt and slide sprocket onto camshaft. Thread sprocket mounting bolt loosely into camshaft but leave it sufficiently loose to allow sprocket to move.

10. Tension toothed belt using a two-pin spanner in the center holes of the eccentric belt tensioner. Belt is tensioned properly when notch and raised mark are aligned. See Fig. 17.

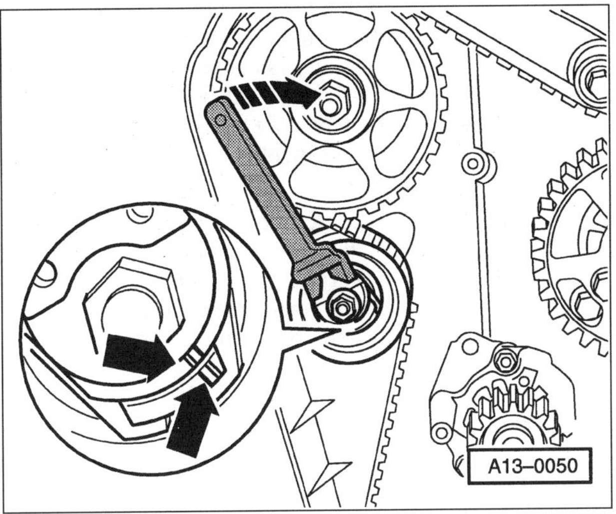

A13-0050

Fig. 17. Two-pin spanner wrench shown in position to tension toothed belt. Adjustment is correct when notch and raised mark align (**inset, arrow**).

11. Tighten lock nut on tensioner while maintaining belt tension.

Tightening torque
- Toothed belt tensioner (M8) . . . . 20 Nm (15 ft-lb)

12. Ensure that crankshaft is still at TDC.

13. Tighten new injection pump sprocket mounting bolts to **stage I** specification only.

NOTE—
- *Tighten the new injection pump sprocket mounting bolts to stage I only at this time. Final torque (stage II) will be done after timing has been dynamically checked/adjusted.*
- *Injection pump sprocket mounting bolts must only be used one time, since by design, they have a reduced shank and are stretch bolts.*

Tightening torque
- Injection pump sprocket bolt - always replace
  stage I . . . . 20 Nm (15 ft-lb)
  stage II . . . . additional ¼ turn (90°)
- Camshaft sprocket bolt . . . . 45 Nm (33 ft-lb)

14. Tighten camshaft sprocket mounting bolt and remove setting bar and feeler gauges.

15. Remove locking pin from injection pump sprocket.

16. Turn crankshaft two rotations in the running direction and recheck toothed belt tension.

17. Connect harness connector for diesel pump electronics and slip connector into retaining bracket.

18. Install cylinder head (valve) cover.

19. Install vacuum pump.

20. Install injector fuel line assembly.

21. Install fuel supply line and draw fuel into pump with a hand operated vacuum pump. See Fig. 18.

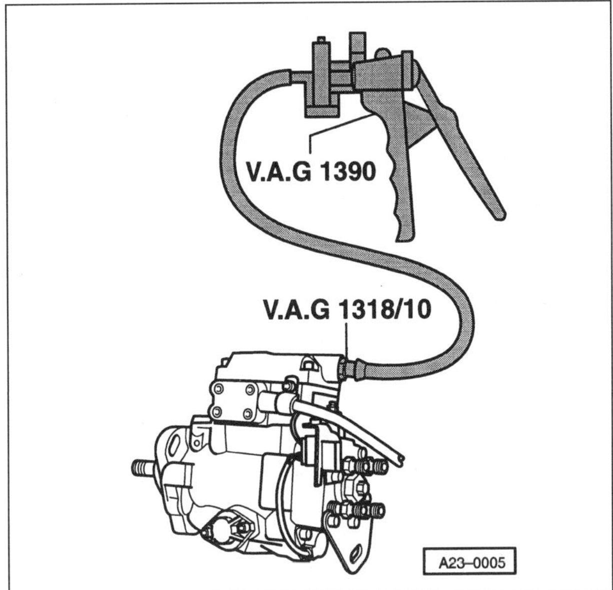

A23-0005

Fig. 18. Plastic hand operated vacuum pump shown connected to diesel injection pump with clear tubing at fuel return port.

CAUTION—
Do not attempt to start engine with a dry diesel injection pump, severe damage can result. Always ensure that pump is full of fuel before cranking engine.

NOTE—
Do not draw diesel fuel into hand operated vacuum pump made of plastic!

22. Install fuel return line.

23. Dynamically check diesel injection pump timing as given later in this section.

Injection pump timing, checking and adjusting

Diesel injection pump timing must be set using Volkswagen scan tool VAG 1551, VAG 1552, or equivalent in a mode known as Basic Setting. Injection pump timing is correlated to several factors, including fuel temperature. Failure to properly set injection pump timing will result in hard starting, poor performance, poor fuel economy, excessive noise, smoking and increased emissions. The vehicle may not be drivable.

If timing adjustment is necessary, special adjustment tools and new pump sprocket mounting bolts are required.

The following instructions assume that the individual technician already has a good working knowledge of the operation and use of the VAG 1551 or VAG 1552 scan tool.

1. Connect scan tool to vehicle Data Link Connector (DLC) located in lower left side of the dash panel. The scan tool will be powered up when plugged into the DLC.

2. Start the engine and let it idle.

3. Observe the following sequence in the scan tool display window:

   - 1 – Rapid Data
   - Address Word 01 – Engine Electronics
   - Function 04 – Basic Settings
   - Display Group – 000
   - The display will show 10 fields (groups) of information. See Fig. 19.

System in Basic Setting 000
XX 53 XX XX XX XX XX XX 90 XX

0024190

Fig. 19. Typical VAG 1551/1552 display shows 90 in field 9 and 53 in field 2.

NOTE—
Data is only available in the format shown in Fig. 19 through use of scan tool VAG 1551 or VAG 1552. Scan tools from other manufacturers may provide the same data, but in a different format.

4. Use the graph to find timing value. See Fig. 20. Observe the number in field 9 on the scan tool display. This is a fuel temperature value and is assigned **B** in the table. The timing value must fall within shaded area of the table and is assigned the value **A**. If value is within shaded area, no adjustment is needed. When value is obtained, shut off engine.

   - If this procedure was done for diagnosis purposes, and timing value is within specification, remove scan tool.
   - If this procedure was done as part of injection pump removal and installation, and timing value is not within specification, continue procedure steps.

Example:

- This example assumes the engine is running. Note that the fuel temperature value in the scan tool display window, field 9, is 90. This is value **B**. Look on the table along the B axis until you see 90. Follow the line from 90 up into the shaded area. The shaded area is the range of timing values. Find the center of the shaded area and look to the left for the value on the **A** axis. In this case it is 53. Adjust the pump until the value in the scan tool display field 2 reads 53.

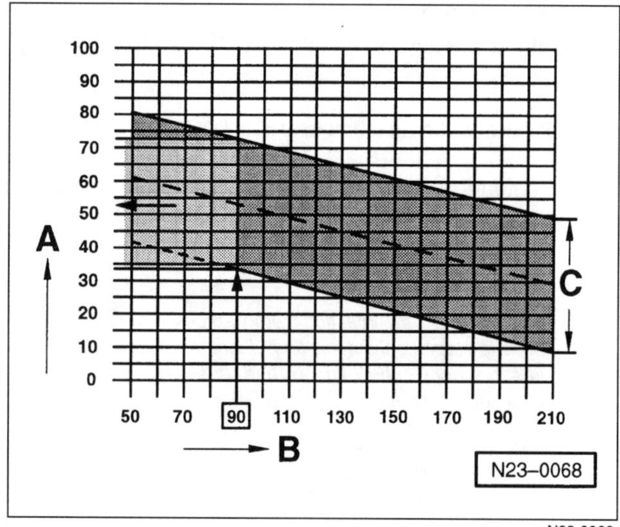

N23-0068

Fig. 20. Graph showing relationship between fuel temperature value **B** and start of injection timing **A**.

5. If timing adjustment is required, access injection pump sprocket. See **Injection pump, removing** given earlier for appropriate steps.

6. Loosen two of the injection pump sprocket mounting bolts. See Fig. 21.

NOTE—
It is permissible to counterhold the pump shaft during loosening using a 22 mm wrench on the center nut. Under no circumstances should the center nut be loosened or used as a counterholder during tightening sequences.

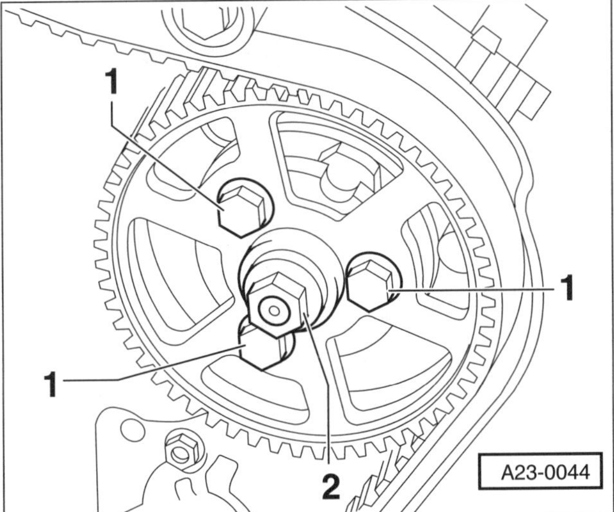

Fig. 21. Remove injection pump sprocket mounting bolts (**1**). Do not loosen center sprocket nut (**2**). Early version sprocket shown, later version is similar.

CAUTION—
Do not loosen the center sprocket nut for any reason. Loosening this nut will allow the sprocket to move on the shaft resulting altered basic settings which CANNOT be reset with normal workshop equipment.

7. Loosen the third injection pump sprocket mounting bolt only enough to allow movement of the sprocket on the hub. Move the hub/injection pump shaft to adjust timing. See Fig. 22.

Specification
- Advance timing (start of injection) . . . . Move hub to the left (counter-clockwise)
- Retard timing (start of injection) . . . . Move hub to the right (counter-clockwise)

Fig. 22. Injection pump sprocket shown with one mounting bolt removed (**arrow**). Elongated slot for bolt allows sprocket position to vary on the hub.

8. Tighten injection pump sprocket bolts to **stage I** specification only, start engine and recheck timing value as given earlier. Repeat procedure as necessary to obtain correct timing value.

Tightening torque
- Injection pump sprocket bolt - always replace
  stage I . . . . 20 Nm (15 ft-lb)
  stage II . . . . additional ¼ turn (90°)

9. When a satisfactory timing value is obtained, remove and replace 3 pump sprocket with new bolts one at a time. See Fig. 22.

NOTE—
If bolts were already replaced as part of injection pump installation and/or replacement, it is not necessary to install new bolts as described in the above step.

10. Lock injection pump sprocket. See Fig. 23. Tighten all injection pump sprocket mounting bolts to stage I value if not previously done. Tighten injection pump sprocket mounting bolts to **stage II** specification.

11. With scan tool still connected, check for any Diagnostic Trouble Codes (DTCs) that may have been set. Repair and erase as required.

12. Disconnect scan tool.

13. Install all remaining fasteners, fuel lines, electrical connectors and components that were removed.

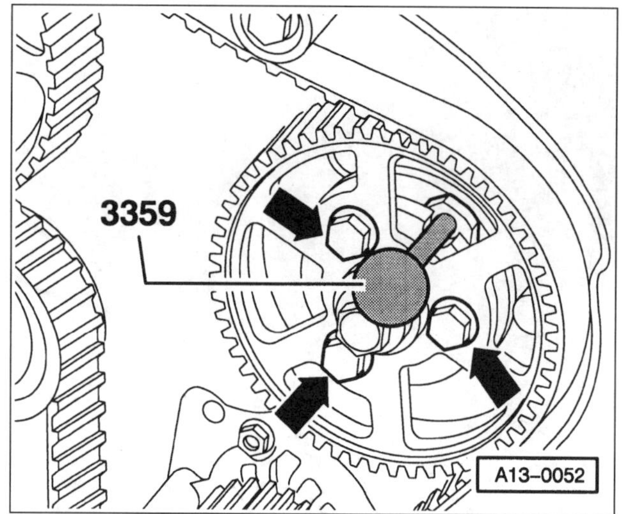

A13-0052

Fig. 23. Injection pump sprocket installed with new bolts (**arrows**) and secured with locking pin 3359.

14. Verify that all fuel lines are secure and that there are no leaks.

15. Install upper sound absorber panel.

16. Be sure to quality check your work, see **Quality Review** at the end of this repair group.

ENGINE CONTROL MODULE

Diesel engine management is controlled by an Electronic Control Module (ECM). The ECM is located at the very rear of the engine compartment in the air plenum on the driver's side. Due to the shape of the body in this area, the Engine Control Module is accessed through the interior. See Fig. 24.

Engine control module coding

The Engine Control Module must "know" what equipment is installed in the vehicle. This process is known as coding and must be performed whenever the ECM is replaced, as new ECMs areun-coded. If the ECM is moved between vehicles such as might be the case for diagnostic testing, the coding will need to be changed if equipment is different. Coding memory is, however, retained when the battery is disconnected. If a new ECM is installed without being coded, the engine will usually run poorly and the automatic transmission and anti-lock braking system (if equipped) will not function properly. The MIL will be illuminated.

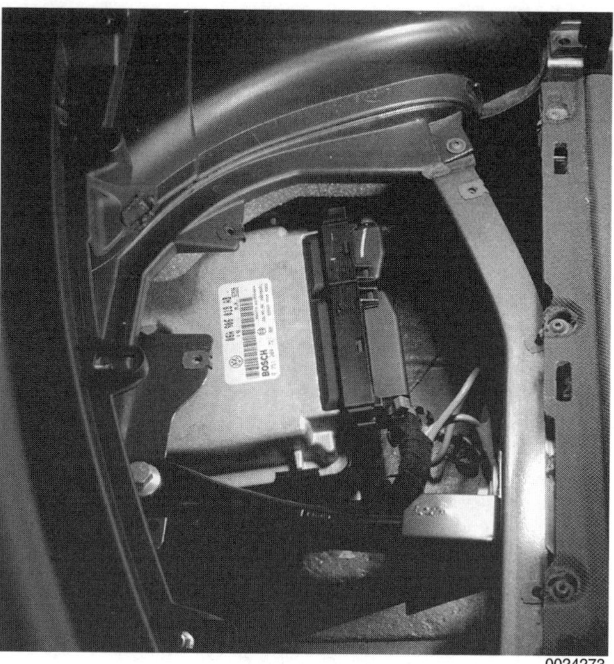

0024273

Fig. 24. Engine Control Module shown with the dashboard trim and covers removed. View is through the windshield on the driver's side. Motronic ECM shown, TDI ECM is similar.

This coding process can only be done with Volkswagen scan tool VAG 1551/1552 or equivalent. The appropriate code is electronically programmed into the ECM according to instructions provided by the scan tool manufacturer. See **Table b**.

Table b. ECM Coding

Coding	Vehicle and Equipment
00001	New Beetle with Automatic Transmission and ABS
00002	New Beetle with Manual Transmission and ABS
00004	New Beetle with Automatic Transmission without ABS
00002	**New Beetle with ECM 038-906-018BD ONLY** New Beetle with Manual Transmission without ABS

Readiness code, checking

Legislation requires that all auto manufacturers build into their engine management systems the ability to check for proper operation of up to 8 functions. These functions are known collectively as the readiness code. For the TDI system on the ALH engine, only the exhaust gas recirculation system code is relevant. Most of the time, the readiness code will set itself after the appropriate conditions have been met. These may include a cold or a hot start, operation at a certain load or speed for a certain period of time, or operation at different temperatures. After repairs, it may be advantageous to verify component operation. Setting the readiness code rather than waiting to see if it sets on it's own can confirm a proper repair. The setting procedure is simple and requires the scan tool VAG 1551/1552 to confirm the setting.

1. Connect the scan tool to the vehicle Data Link Connector (DLC) located in the lower left side of the dash panel. The scan tool will be powered up when plugged into the DLC. Start the engine and let it idle. Observe the following sequence in the scan tool display window:
   - 1 – Rapid Data
   - Address Word 01– Engine Electronics
   - Function 08–Measure Value Blocks
   - Display Group 017
   - The display will show four fields of information

> ***CAUTION—***
> *These instructions assume that the technician already has a good working knowledge of the operation and use of the VAG 1551 or VAG 1552 scan tool.*

2. Fig. 25 shows information as it appears on scan tool screen. Disregard information shown as the letter x. These x spaces will have either a 1 or a 0 and do not affect this procedure. The readiness code is the 8 digit number in fields 2 and 4. If scan tool screen displays ones in the indicated fields as shown here, readiness code is not set.

```
Read Measuring Value Block                17
xxxxxxxx  x111xxxx  xxxxxxxx  1xxxxxxx
```

0024262

Fig. 25. Display that shows that readiness code is not set.

3. If the scan tool screen displays zeros in the indicated fields, readiness code is set and no further action is required. See Fig. 26.

```
Read Measuring Value Block                17
xxxxxxxx  x000xxxx  xxxxxxxx  0xxxxxxx
```

0024263

Fig. 26. Display that shows that readiness code is set and no further action is required.

4. If the readiness code is set, disconnect the scan tool.

5. If readiness code is not set, unplug scan tool and proceed as follows.

Readiness code, setting

1. Start engine and allow to idle for at least 35 seconds.
   - Engine temperature must be over 10° C (50°F)
   - Engine must remain running during test sequence unless directed otherwise.
   - Adhere to test sequence and do not interrupt it.

2. Road test vehicle. When conditions allow, accelerate to 2,000 rpm as indicated on the tachometer.

> ***CAUTION—***
> *Observe all applicable traffic and safety laws while road testing to this procedure. Accelerate only where conditions are appropriate.*

3. At 2,000 rpm, accelerate to wide open throttle (WOT) in 3rd gear for 5 seconds, and allow engine speed to return to 2,200 rpm.

4. At 2,200 rpm, accelerate to WOT in 2nd or 3rd gear for 8 seconds and allow engine to return to idle.

5. When conditions permit, switch off engine, wait at least 10 seconds. Repeat steps 1 through 4.

6. Check readiness code as previously described.
   - If the scan tool screen displays zeros in the indicated fields, readiness code is set and no further action is required. See Fig. 26.
   - If the scan tool screen displays ones in the indicated fields, readiness code is not set. Unplug scan tool and repeat from step 1. If the code does not set after a second attempt, it is likely that there is a malfunction in the system. Consult scan tool directions for additional information on checking for DTCs.

INTAKE MANIFOLD CHANGE-OVER VALVE

The intake manifold change-over valve is a flap valve that closes for approximately 3 seconds when the engine stops, blocking the air to the engine. This reduces the suddenness of the diesel engine shut-down. The valve re-opens once the engine has stopped. See Fig. 27.

Intake manifold change-over valve, assembly

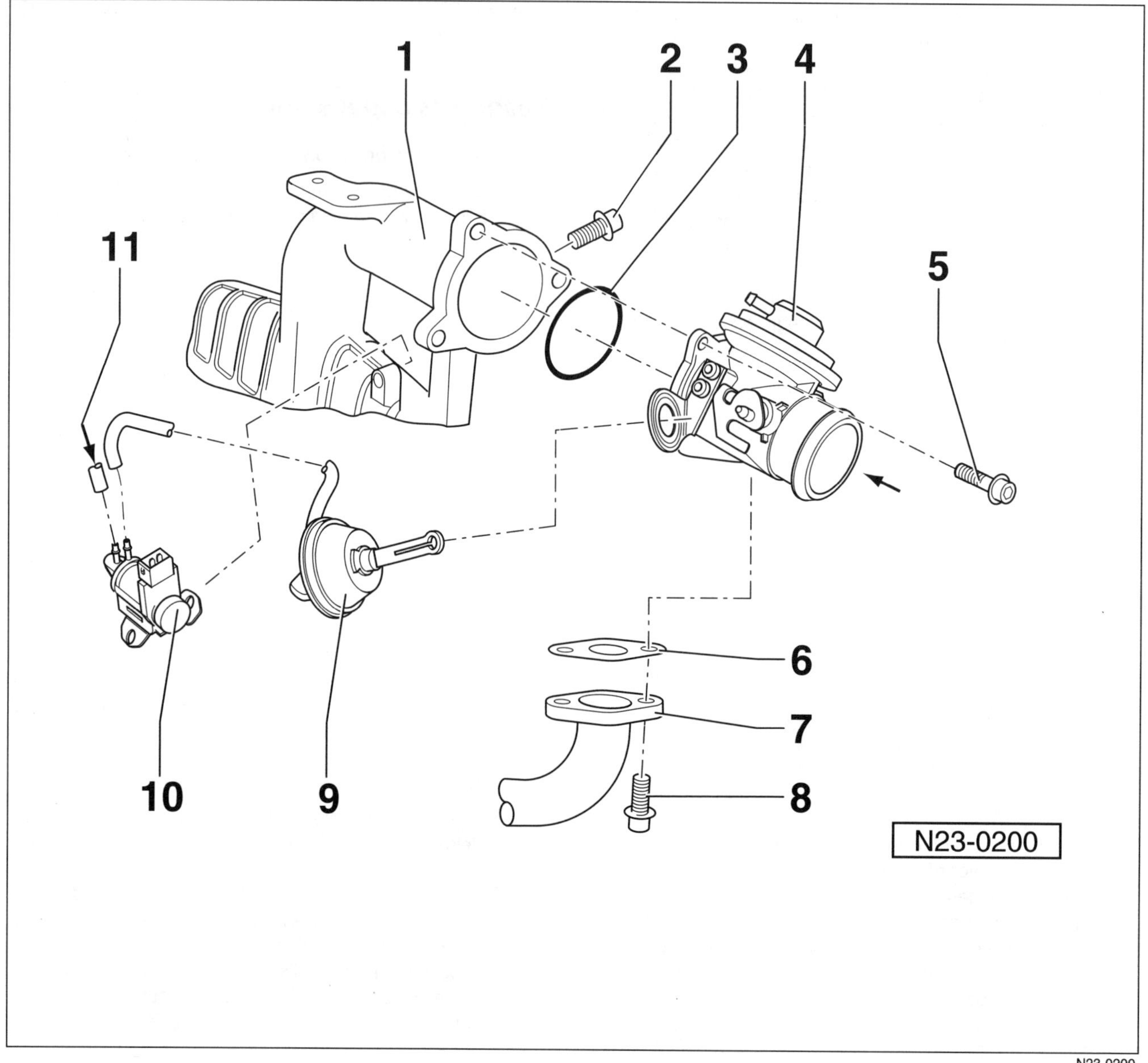

N23-0200

Fig. 27. Intake manifold change-over valve with EGR valve and related components.

1. **Intake manifold**
2. **Bolt**
   - Tighten to 10 Nm (7 ft-lb)
3. **O-ring**
   - Always replace
4. **Connecting flange**
   - With EGR valve
   - With intake manifold change-over valve
5. **Bolt**
   - Tighten to 10 Nm (7 ft-lb)
6. **Gasket**
   - Always replace
7. **Connecting pipe**
   - From EGR cooler
8. **Bolt**
   - Tighten to 25 Nm (18 ft-lb)
9. **Vacuum servo**
10. **Intake manifold change-over vacuum control valve**
11. **Vacuum supply**
    - From vacuum source

FUEL INJECTORS

The ALH TDI diesel engine uses a two-spring injector that enables the fuel to be injected in two stages for "softer" combustion. In addition, the injectors are a 5-hole design that spray fuel from 5 ports in a more lateral direction rather than in a single conical pattern. Injector opening pressures are approximately 220 to 230 bar (3190-3335 psi). All 4 injectors are functionally the same. However, injector for cylinder #3 carries the needle lift sensor (G80). This injector must always be installed in cylinder #3 to prevent erroneous DTCs or performance problems from occurring.

The signs of injector trouble usually appear as misfiring and knocking noises from one or more cylinders, engine overheating, loss of power, smoky black exhaust, and excessive blue smoke during cold starting.

> ***CAUTION—***
> *When working on the injectors, everything must be kept absolutely clean. Clean all pipe unions before disconnecting.*

Fuel injectors, checking

A defective injector (or a weak cylinder) can often be identified by simply "turning it off". This can be done by relieving the fuel pressure so that the injector can not open and inject fuel into the cylinder. Idle speed may not substantially change, however, because the ECM will often be able to compensate for the weak cylinder.

1. Clean area around fuel unions where the fuel pipes meet the injectors.

2. Start engine and let it run at idle.

3. Wrap a cloth around the union nut for cylinder #1 fuel injector at the injector. Slightly loosen the nut. Cylinder #1 is closest to the drive belt. See Fig. 28.
   - If a particular cylinder is defective, the noise or smoke will cease when union nut is loosened.
   - If the problem was roughness, the roughness will be affected very little or not at all because that cylinder was already malfunctioning. Tighten the union nut.

> ***WARNING—***
> - *Loosen the nut only about one half turn to limit the amount of fuel leakage. The fuel injection system operates at very high pressures. Keep hands and eyes clear. Wear heavy duty gloves and eye protection. Wrap a cloth around the nut when loosening. Fuel will be expelled.*
> - *Do not smoke or work near heaters or other fire hazards.*
> - *Have a fire extinguisher handy.*

4. Repeat procedure for other suspected cylinders.

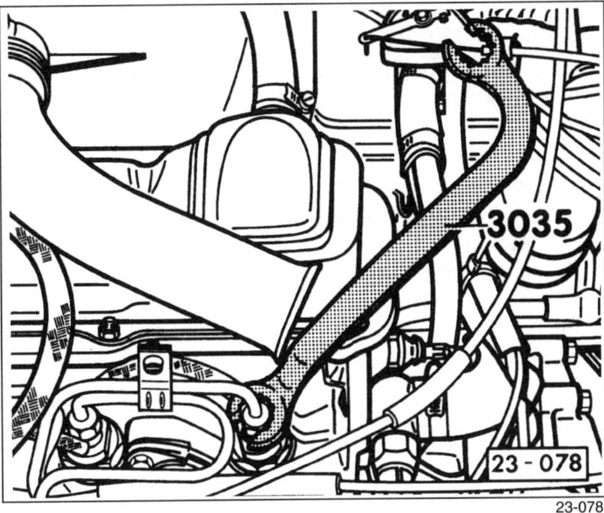

23-078

Fig. 28. Flare-nut wrench (Volkswagen special tool 3035) being used to loosen injector union nut for cylinder 4 on an earlier version diesel engine. The same tool is used on ALH diesel engines.

5. When finished, verify that all fuel lines are secure and that there are no fuel leaks. Thoroughly clean any spilled fuel.

> ***CAUTION—***
> *Diesel fuel is damaging to rubber. Wipe off any fuel that spills on hoses, wiring, and rubber steering and suspension parts and wash with soap and water. If coolant hoses are contaminated with diesel fuel, they must be replaced.*

Fuel injectors, replacing

1. Unscrew fuel pipe union nuts at injection pump and injectors. Remove injector fuel pipes as one assembly taking care not to bend them.

2. Remove fuel return hoses from between injectors.

3. Unplug harness connector for the needle lift sensor (G80) on the injector for cylinder #3.

4. Loosen and remove bolt, special washer and hold down clamp for each injector. Lift out injectors.

5. Remove small copper sealing washer from tip of injector or from injector port in head. Discard.

> ***NOTE—***
> *The crush-type sealing washers must always be replaced to prevent compression leaks.*

6. Install injector with a new copper sealing washer and torque the bolt to specification.

Tightening torque
- Injector line union . . . . 25 Nm (18 ft-lb)
- Injector clamp mounting bolt (M8) . . . 20 Nm (15 ft-lb)

7. Install metal fuel pipes and fuel return hoses. Due to the higher pressures involved, injectors will seldom need to have air bleed from them. Reconnect harness connector to needle lift sensor.

8. When finished, verify that all fuel lines are secure and that there are no fuel leaks.

Fuel injectors, pressure testing

1. Remove injector as described previously.

2. Install fuel injector on pressure tester according to manufacturer's directions. Place a suitable container under injector to catch the spray. See Fig. 29.

> ***WARNING—***
> *When testing fuel injectors, make sure that the high pressure discharge does not contact the hands or any other bare skin. The high pressure spray can be injected directly into the skin causing severe injuries or health complications. Always wear eye protection!*

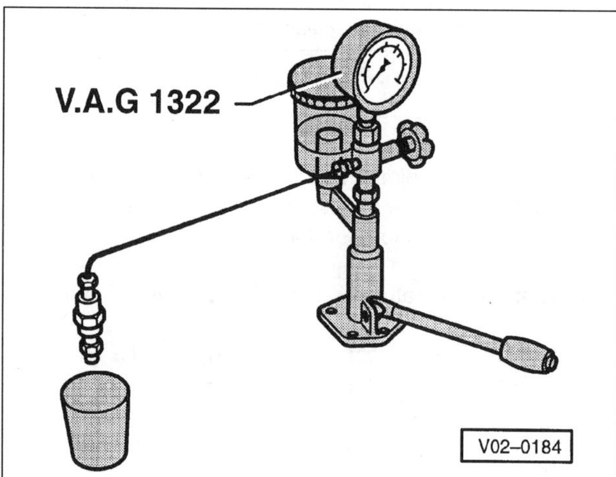

V02-0184

Fig. 29. Injector installed on hand pressure pump. Volkswagen special tool VAG 1322 shown. This tester is designed to work best with mineral spirits. Older version US1111 will also work with suitable fittings.

3. Pump lever to increase pressure. Read opening pressure when spray begins.

Injector Opening Pressure
- New . . . . 220–230 bar (3190–3335 psi)
- Wear limit . . . . 200 bar (2900 psi)

4. Spray should discharge evenly from all 5 ports. See Fig. 30.

> ***WARNING—***
> *Fire hazard! No smoking! Do not have anything in the area that can ignite the spray discharged by the injectors. This includes overhead heating units and hidden sources such as water heaters with standing pilot lights.*

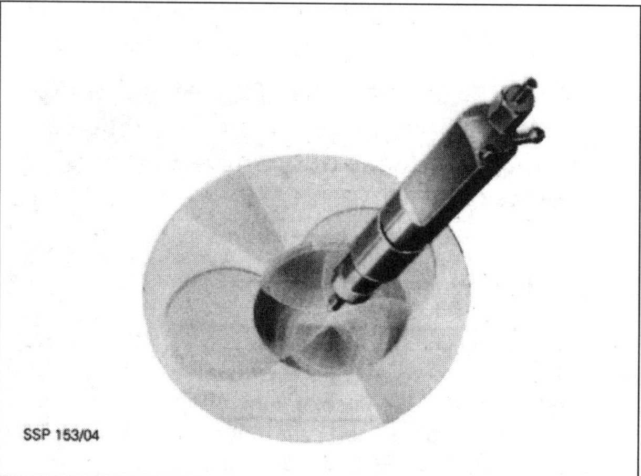

SSP153/04

Fig. 30. TDI fuel injector spray pattern discharging from all 5 ports.

5. Pump lever slowly to a pressure of approximately 150 bar (2175 psi) for 10 seconds. Check for leaks from injector tip. No fuel should leak.

6. If any injector fails to meet opening pressure or leak specifications, it should be replaced. No repairs are possible to the fuel injectors.

QUALITY REVIEW

When you have finished working under the hood and around other areas of the vehicle, it is advisable to take a moment to quality check or review your work. This helps to insure that the operation or repair has been completed properly with all affected systems functioning within normal parameters. These may include the following:

- Make sure that there are no air, fuel, or vacuum leaks.
- Be sure to wipe up any diesel fuel spills, using soap and water as necessary, especially on any rubber or painted surfaces.
- Make sure that all components involved in the repair are positioned correctly and function properly.
- Make sure all tools and shop cloths are removed.
- Road test vehicle to confirm proper engine operation.

24 Fuel Injection–Motronic (AEG engine)

TABLES

GENERAL

This repair group covers the fuel injection/engine management system for the AEG 2.0 liter gasoline engine. The operation of the Bosch Motronic 5.9.2 engine management system is described in **2 Fuel, Ignition and Exhaust Systems.**

Special testing equipment may be necessary for some of the tests and repair procedures given here.

NOTE —

- *AEG engines are equipped with the Bosch Motronic 5.9.2 engine management system which is OBD II compliant. It is recommended that fault diagnosis and troubleshooting be carried out using Volkswagen scan tools VAG 1551/VAG 1552 or equivalent.*
- *Fuel pump and fuel tank testing and repair along with EVAP information is covered in* **20 Fuel Storage and Supply**.
- *Ignition system testing and repair is covered in* **28a Ignition System.**
- *Related systems such as Exhaust Gas Recirculation (EGR) and catalytic converters are covered in* **26 Exhaust System and Emission Controls**.

The Motronic 5.9.2 system combines the ignition and fuel injection functions into one system managed by a single Engine Control Module (ECM). The system is fully adaptive and features built-in diagnostics that are capable of detecting and storing coded fault information. There are no basic adjustments or settings that can be made to the system without specialized equipment.

CAUTION —
Disconnecting the negative (–) battery cable may erase fault codes and basic settings in the engine management and automatic transmission control modules. Some driveability problems may be noticed until the system re-adapts to operating conditions. OBD II readiness codes, which may be required for emissions testing, may also be erased. Convenience electronics (alarm system, interior light control, power locks, mirrors, and windows) may need to be re-set using a VAG 1551/1552 or equivalent scan tool.

Safety precautions

The following warnings and cautions should be adhered to whenever working on the engine management system.

WARNING —

- *Fuel may be discharged during fuel system repairs. Do not smoke or work near heaters or other fire hazards. Have a fire extinguisher handy. Work only in a well-ventilated area.*
- *Wear suitable hand and eye protection when working with gasoline. Prolonged contact with fuel can cause illness and skin disorders.*
- *Fuel hoses in engine compartment must only be secured with spring-type clips. The use of clamp or screw-type clips will damage fuel lines and cause fuel leaks.*

CAUTION —

- *Connect and disconnect wires and test equipment only with the ignition switched off.*
- *Before making any electrical tests that require the engine to be cranked using the starter, disable the ignition system as described in* **28a Ignition System.**
- *Do not use sealants containing silicones. Particles of silicone drawn into the engine will not be burned in the engine and will damage the heated oxygen sensor. Use only sealants and engine chemicals marked as safe for oxygen sensors.*
- *During testing, it is possible for the Engine Control Module to recognize and store a diagnostic trouble code (DTC) that was due solely to the testing procedure. Therefore, after completing repairs, the DTC memory must be checked and erased as necessary with a scan tool such as VAG 1551/1552 or equivalent*
- *Cleanliness is essential when working on the fuel system. Thoroughly clean fuel line connections and surrounding areas before loosening. Avoid the use of compressed air. Avoid moving the vehicle. Only install clean components.*

ON BOARD DIAGNOSTICS (OBD)

On Board Diagnostics, found on the Bosch Motronic 5.9.2 Engine Management Systems monitor many aspects of engine operation. The current generation OBD II is integrated into all Volkswagen New Beetle gasoline engines. For a description of the system and an overview of operation, see **2 Fuel, Ignition, and Exhaust Systems.**

Because of the large number of operating parameters monitored and the vast quantity of data available, fault diagnosis can only be properly carried out using a suitable scan tool such as Volkswagen special tool VAG 1551 or VAG 1552 or equivalent. The engine control module or ECM also supports certain limited functions in a government-mandated generic scan tool mode. These functions are standardized for all OBD II compliant vehicles, but are not as comprehensive as those found by using the VAG 1551/1552 in the original mode of operation.

During repairs where the battery must be disconnected, consideration must be given to the effect that this will have on the vehicle in general and the engine management system in particular.

- Diagnostic Trouble Codes may be erased.
- Readiness codes may be erased.
- Fault counters that monitor certain functions will be reset to zero.
- Adaptive leaning values will be set to default.

Because the ignition, fuel injection, and emission control functions are even more inter-related than on previous Motronic versions, it is difficult, if not impossible to isolate general driveability problems by examining individual components of the system. For this reason, a suitable scan tool must be used for diagnosis if driveability problems occur or if the malfunction indicator light is illuminated. Access for the scan tool is through the Data Link Connector (DLC) under the lower left side of the instrument panel. See Fig. 1.

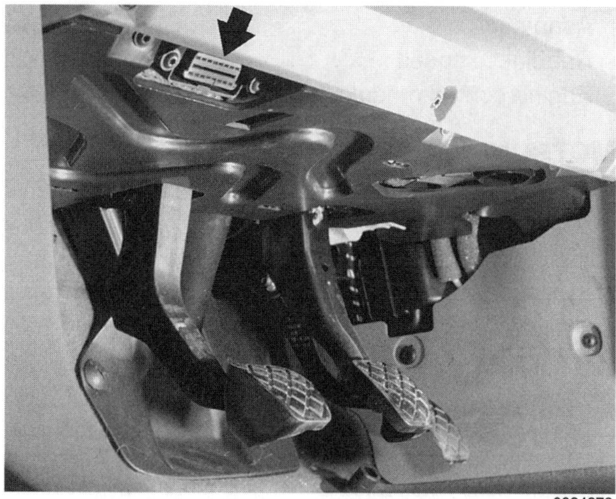

0024272

Fig. 1. Data Link Connector (DLC), (**arrow**) under left lower side of instrument panel.

Adaptation

The Motronic 5.9.2 engine management system is adaptive. Idle speed, ignition timing, injection timing and quantity automatically compensate and adapt to changes in the engine due to wear and operating conditions. Minor problems such as mixture changes due to small vacuum leaks can be eliminated. As a result, idle speed, fuel mixture (CO%) and ignition timing are non-adjustable.

NOTE —

Beginning in 1994 (1993 in California) automakers are required by law to apply uniform terminology, words and terms for certain components according to SAE standard J1930. These standardized terms are used throughout this section.

Readiness Codes

Federal and state legislation requires that all auto manufacturers build into their engine management systems the ability to check for proper operation of up to 8 functions. For the Motronic engine management system, the exact number depends on the equipment level of each particular vehicle. Most of the time, the readiness code will set itself after the appropriate conditions have been met. These may include a cold or a hot start, operation at a certain load or speed for a certain period of time, or operation at different temperatures. After repairs, it may be advantageous to confirm repairs rather than wait to see if they set on their own. Other than waiting, the only other method of setting the readiness codes on the Motronic 5.9.2 system is with a scan tool. This method requires Volkswagen scan tool VAG 1551, VAG 1552, or an equivalent aftermarket scan tool, and extensive knowledge of its operation and capabilities. Readiness codes are then generated according to instructions provided by the scan tool manufacturer. For the significance of the 8 digit readiness code, see **Table a**

Table a. Readiness code values

Digit position								Diagnostic Function
1	2	3	4	5	6	7	8	
							0	Three Way Catalyst
						0		Catalyst Heating (always 0)
					0			Evaporative Emissions System (Fuel tank vent system)
				0				Secondary Air Injection System (always 0)
			0					Air Conditioning (no current diagnostic function-always 0)
		0						Oxygen Sensor
	0							Oxygen Sensor Heater
0								Exhaust Gas Recirculation - EGR (always 0)

The readiness code can be displayed in any of several areas within the ECM's diagnostic memory depending on the individual scan tool. It will always have a format consisting of 8 digits. If the 8 digit code contains characters other than the number 0, such as 10100110, than the readiness code is NOT set. When the code displays all zeros, i.e. 00000000, the readiness code IS set and no further action is required. The specifics of **Table a** apply to the AEG engine only. While the format is required to be the same for all engines, certain equipment may not be used on each engine. For example, the AEG engine does not use EGR and as such, digit number 8 will always show 0. Other engines that use EGR, such as the ALH diesel, will show either a 1 or a 0 as appropriate.

Engine control module coding

The engine control module (ECM) must be supplied with appropriate power sources and grounds to function properly. Also, the engine control module must "know" what equipment is installed in the vehicle. This process is known as coding and must be performed whenever the ECM is replaced as new ECMs are un-coded. If an ECM is moved between vehicles such as might be the case for diagnostic testing, the coding will need to be changed if equipment is different. Coding memory is, however, retained when the battery is disconnected. If a new ECM is installed without being coded, the engine will usually run poorly and the automatic transmission and anti-lock braking system (if equipped) will not function properly. The MIL will be illuminated.

This coding process can only be done with Volkswagen scan tool VAG 1551/1552 or equivalent. The appropriate code is electronically programmed into the ECM according to instructions provided by the scan tool manufacturer. See **Table b**.

Table b. ECM Coding

Coding	Vehicle and Equipment
00000	New Beetle with Manual Transmission and ABS
00001	New Beetle with Automatic Transmission and ABS
00040	New Beetle with Manual Transmission without ABS
00041	New Beetle with Automatic Transmission without ABS

NOTE —
The appropriate code is electronically programmed into the ECM according to instructions provided by the scan tool manufacturer.

MOTRONIC ENGINE MANAGEMENT COMPONENTS

Fig. 2 through 5 show the various components of the Motronic engine management fuel injection system.

NOTE —
Volkswagen identifies electrical components by a letter and/or a number in the electrical schematics. See **97 Wiring Diagrams, Fuses and Relays**. *These electrical identifiers are listed in parenthesis as an aid to electrical troubleshooting.*

Fuel injection system component locations, overview

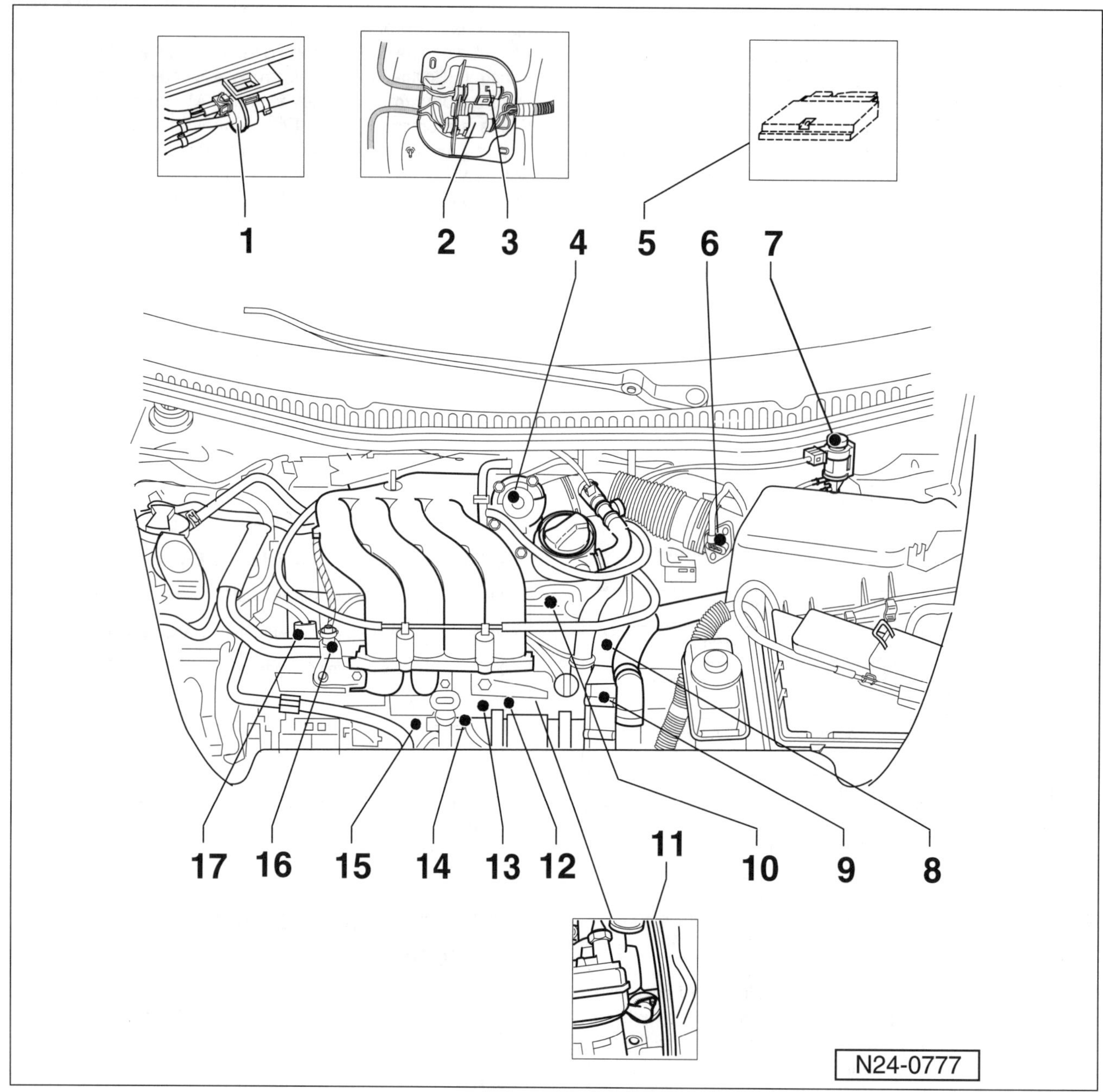

N24-0777

Fig. 2. Motronic component locations on AEG engine.

1. **Evaporative emissions (EVAP) canister purge regulator valve (N80)**
   - Location: right side of engine compartment over wheel housing
2. **4-pin harness connector**
   - Black
   - For pre-catalyst heated oxygen sensor (G39) and oxygen sensor heater (Z19)
   - Location: right underside of vehicle in plastic shield
3. **4-pin harness connector**
   - Brown
   - For post-catalyst heated oxygen sensor (G130) and oxygen sensor heater (Z29)
   - Location: right underside of vehicle in plastic shield
4. **Throttle control module (J338)**
5. **Motronic engine control module (J220)**
   - Location: in air plenum at forward part of instrument panel near base of windshield on driver's side.

(continued from previous page)

6. **Mass air flow sensor (G70), with intake air temperature sensor (G42)**
7. **Secondary air injection solenoid valve (N112)**
8. **Engine coolant temperature sensor (G62)**
   - Combined with sensor (G2) for instrument panel warning light
9. **Secondary air injection pump motor (V101)**
10. **Fuel injectors (N30 to N33)**
11. **Engine speed sensor (G28)**
    - Location: on cylinder block near oil filter
    - Inductive type sensor
12. **Ignition coils (N, N128)**
    - Combined with power output stage (N122)
13. **3-pin harness connector**
    - Grey
    - For engine speed sensor (G28)
14. **Knock sensor 2 (G66)**
    - Brown connector
15. **Knock sensor 1 (G61)**
    - Black connector
16. **Fuel pressure regulator**
    - Location: on fuel rail
17. **Camshaft position sensor (G40)**
    - Location: on cylinder head behind camshaft sprocket

Fuel injection system components, removing and installing

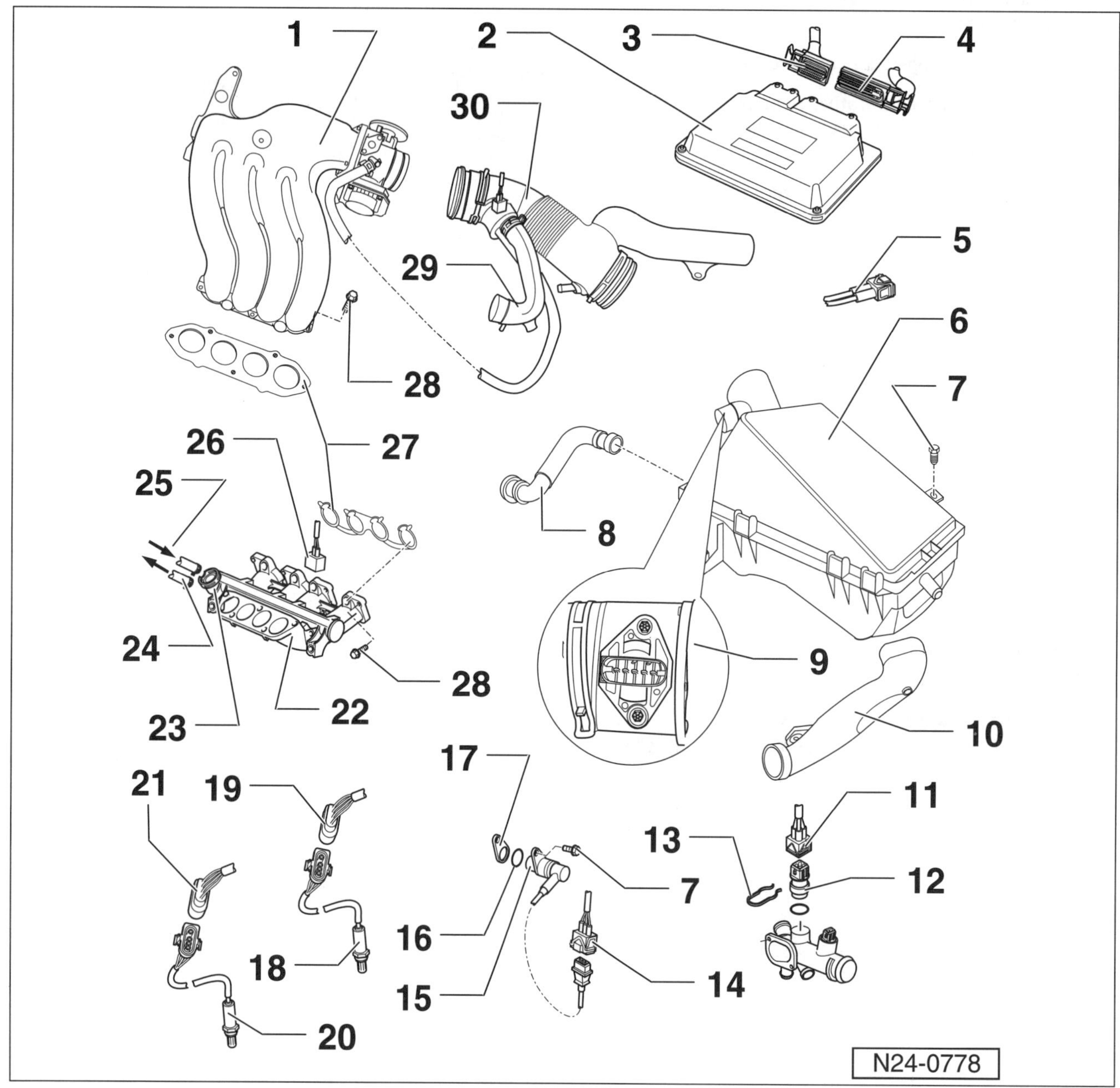

N24-0778

Fig. 3. Motronic system elements and related components.

1. **Intake manifold, upper section**
   - Shown with throttle control module (J338)
2. **Engine control module (J220)**
   - Location: in air plenum at forward part of instrument panel near base of the windshield on driver's side
3. **28-pin harness connector (T28)**
   - Only disconnect or connect with ignition switched OFF
4. **52-pin connector (T52)**
   - Only disconnect or connect with ignition switched OFF
5. **2-pin harness connector**
   - For secondary air injection solenoid valve (N112)
6. **Air filter assembly**
7. **Bolt**
   - Tighten to 10 Nm (7 ft-lb)

(continued from previous page)

8. **Connecting hose**
   - To secondary air injection pump (V101)

9. **Mass air flow sensor (G70)**

10. **Intake air duct**
    - Location: in left front wheel housing

11. **4-pin harness connector**
    - Blue
    - For engine coolant temperature sensor (G62 & G2)

12. **Engine coolant temperature sensor (G62)**
    - Blue
    - For engine control module
    - Combined with sensor (G2) for instrument panel warning light

13. **Retaining clip**
    - Ensure clip is securely seated

14. **3-pin harness connector**
    - Grey
    - For engine speed sensor

15. **Engine speed sensor (G28)**
    - Location: on cylinder block near oil filter
    - Inductive type sensor

16. **O-ring**
    - Replace if damaged

17. **Spacer**

18. **Oxygen sensor, post-catalyst (G130)**
    - Monitors catalytic converter efficiency
    - Location: threaded into rear of catalytic converter
    - Tighten to 50 Nm (37 ft-lb)
    - Lubricate threads only with high temperature anti-seize G5
    - Do not allow anti-seize compound into the slots on the sensor body

19. **4-pin harness connector**
    - Brown
    - For post-catalyst heated oxygen sensor (G130) and oxygen sensor heater (Z29)
    - Right underside of vehicle in plastic shield

20. **Oxygen sensor, pre-catalyst (G39)**
    - Monitors combustion efficiency
    - Location: Threaded into front exhaust pipe
    - Tighten to 50 Nm (37 ft-lb)
    - Lubricate threads only with high temperature anti-seize G5
    - Do not allow anti-seize compound into the slots on the sensor body

21. **4-pin harness connector**
    - Black
    - For pre-catalyst heated oxygen sensor (G39) and oxygen sensor heater (Z19)
    - Right underside of vehicle in plastic shield

22. **Intake manifold, lower section**

23. **Fuel rail, with fuel injectors (N30-N33) and fuel pressure regulator**

24. **Fuel return line/hose**
    - Identification color - blue
    - Secure with spring clips only
    - Ensure coupling is securely seated
    - To fuel delivery unit in fuel tank

25. **Fuel supply line/hose**
    - Identification color - black
    - Secure with spring clips only
    - Ensure coupling is securely seated
    - From fuel filter

26. **2-pin harness connector**
    - Black
    - For injectors N30 to N33

27. **Gasket**
    - Replace if damaged

28. **Bolt**
    - Tighten to 20 Nm (15 ft lb)

29. **Connecting hose**
    - To positive crankcase ventilation valve

30. **Intake hose**
    - Between air cleaner assembly and throttle control module/intake manifold

Air cleaner assembly

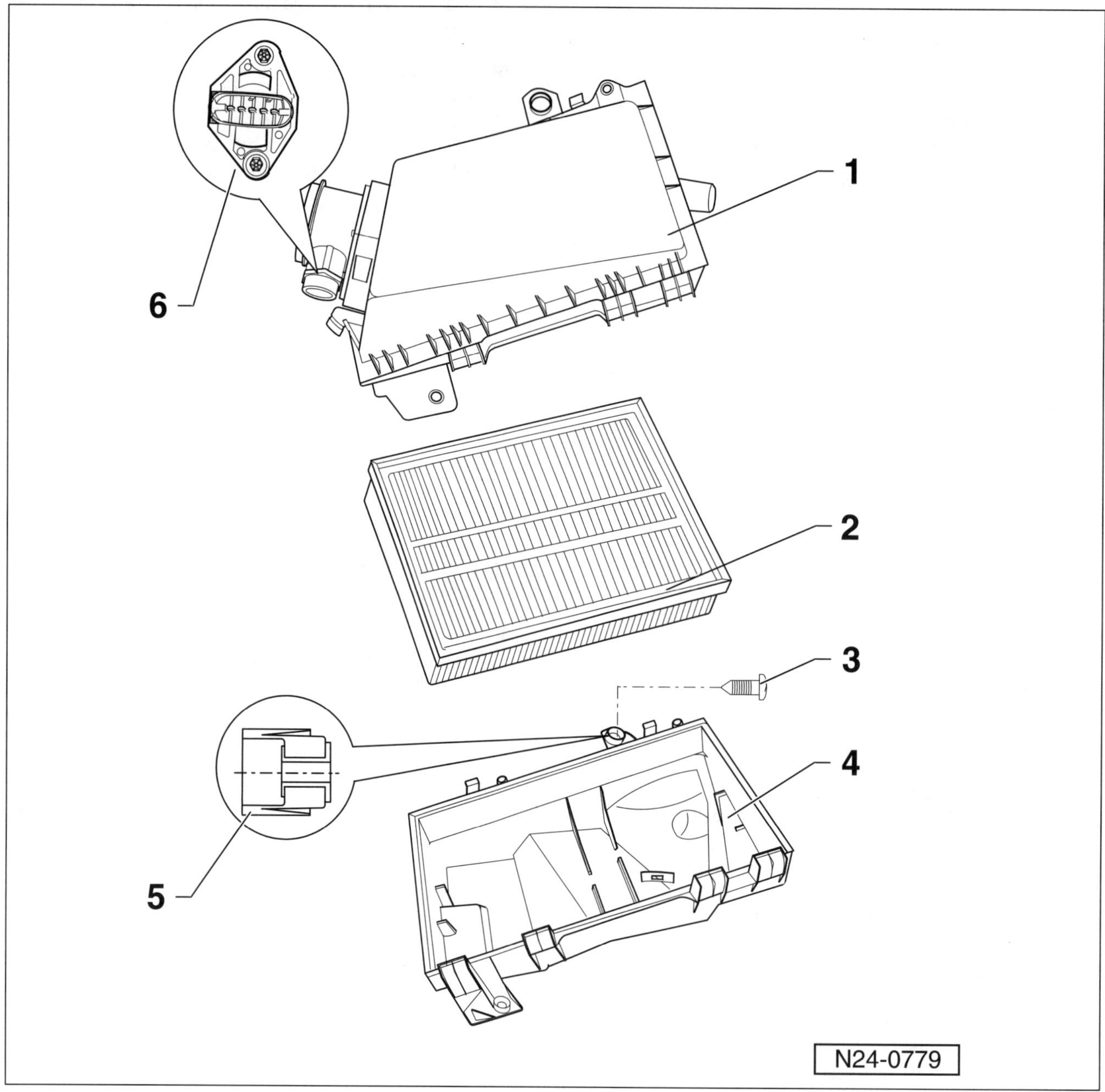

N24-0779

Fig. 4. Air filter assembly shown with element and related components.

1. **Air cleaner housing, upper section**
2. **Filter element**
3. **Bolt**
   - Tighten to 10 Nm (7 ft-lb)
4. **Air cleaner housing, lower section**
5. **Rubber mounting grommet**
   - Note installation position
6. **Mass air flow sensor (G70)**
   - 5-pin harness connector

Intake manifold, lower section assembly

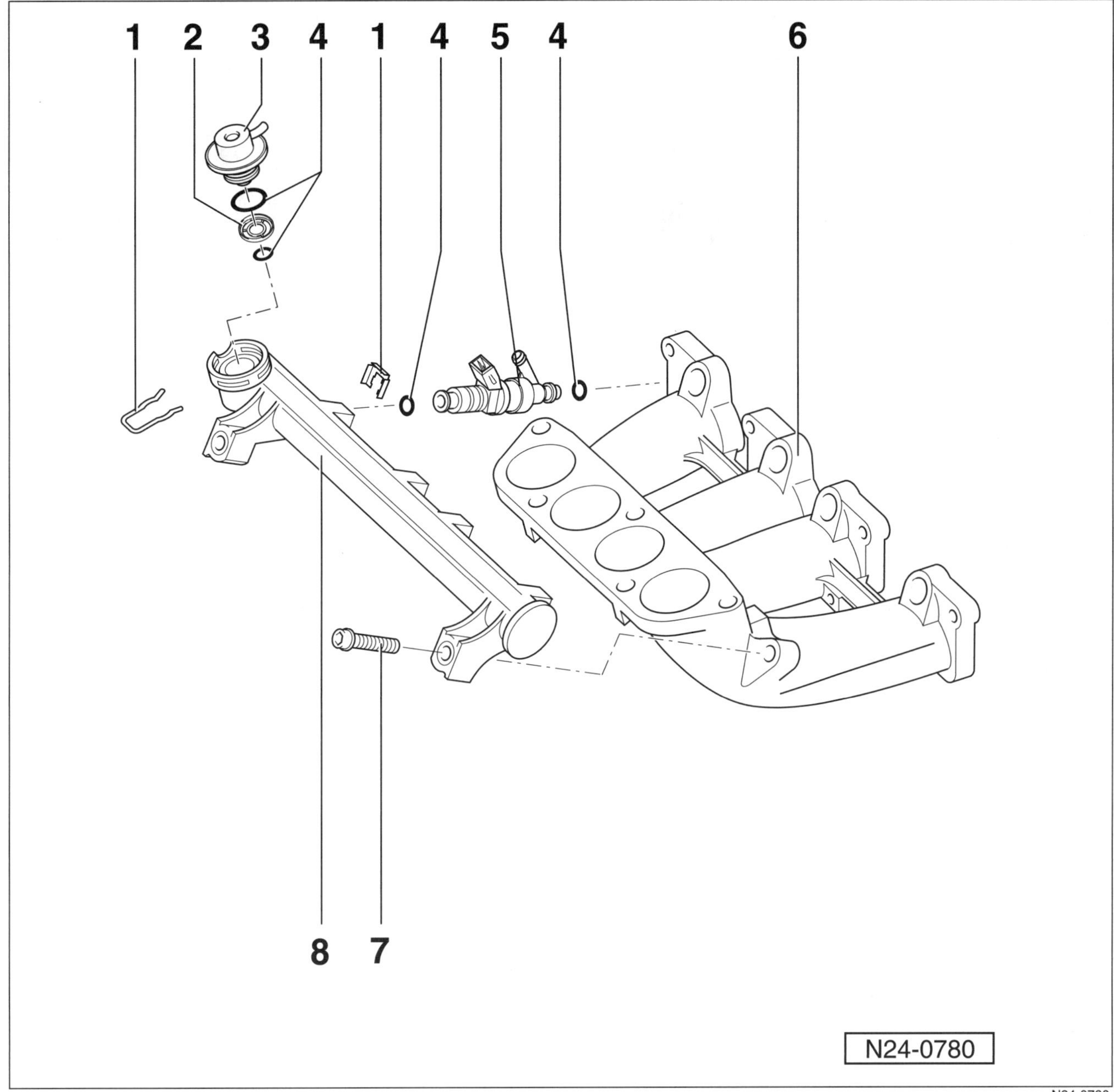

Fig. 5. Lower section of the two-piece Intake manifold showing fuel rail and injectors.

1. **Retaining clip**
   - Ensure it is securely seated
2. **Strainer**
3. **Fuel pressure regulator**
   - Fuel pressure regulator with residual check valve
4. **O-ring**
   - Replace if damaged
5. **Fuel injectors (N30, N31, N32, N33)**
6. **Intake manifold, lower section**
7. **Bolt**
   - Tighten to 10 Nm (7 ft-lb)
8. **Fuel rail**

Engine Control Module (ECM)

The Engine control module is located at the very rear of the engine compartment in the air plenum on the left side. Due to the shape of the body in this area, the ECM is accessed through the interior. See Fig. 6.

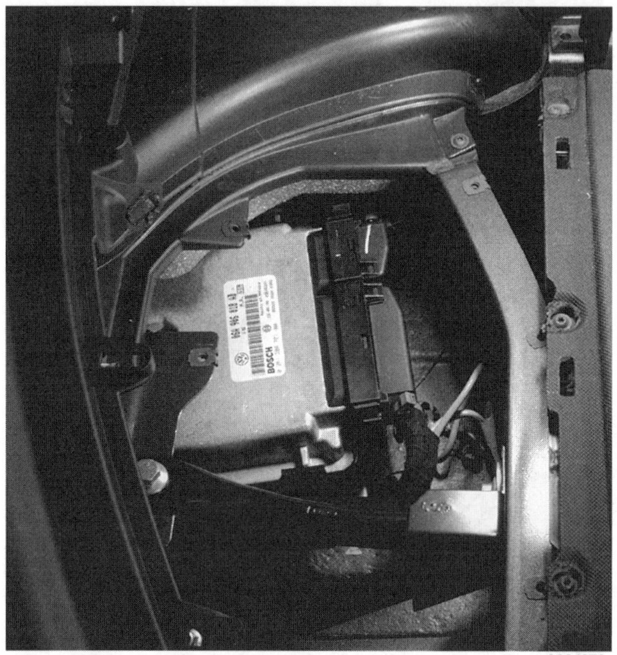

Fig. 6. ECM shown with the dashboard trim and covers removed. View is through the windshield on the driver's side.

Engine speed sensor

Operation of the engine management system depends on a wide variety of input sensors. Failure of most of these sensors will allow the engine to continue to run, albeit poorly. One major exception to this is the engine speed sensor (G28). Failure of this sensor will prevent the engine from starting and running and will set a diagnostic trouble code in the ECM.

Note that most diagnostic functions require the use of a scan tool such as the VAG 1552/1552 or equivalent, however a quick check can be accomplished as follows:

1. Disconnect the grey 3-pin harness connector from the engine speed sensor plug near the secondary air injection pump. See Fig. 7.

2. Connect an accurate ohmmeter between terminals 2 and 3 and measure resistance.

3. Measure resistance between terminals 1 and 3, and between terminals 1 and 2.

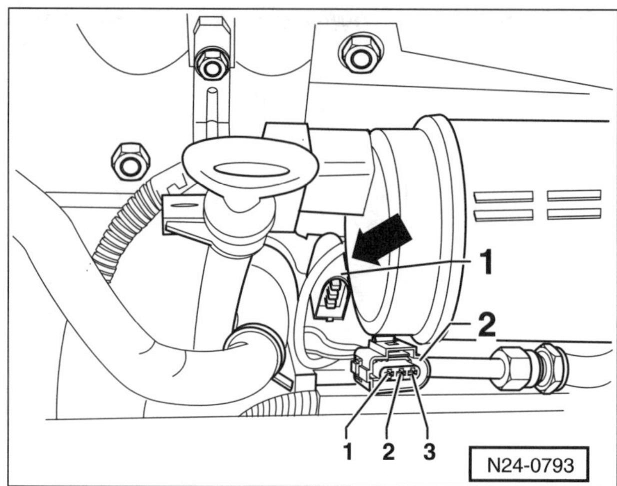

Fig. 7. Engine speed sensor (G28) harness connector (**1**) shown unplugged near secondary air injection pump.

Specification

- Engine speed sensor resistance values
  Between terminals 2 and 3 . . . . 480 to 1000 Ω
  Between terminals 1 and 2 . . . . infinity Ω
  Between terminals 1 and 3 . . . . infinity Ω

4. If specification is not obtained, replace engine speed sensor.

5. If specification is obtained, and engine will not start, additional testing with a suitable scan tool will be required.

QUALITY REVIEW

When you have finished working under the hood and around other areas of the vehicle, it is advisable to take a moment to quality check or review your work. This helps to insure that the operation or repair has been completed properly with all affected systems functioning within normal parameters. These may include the following:

- Make sure that there are no air, fuel, or vacuum leaks.
- Be sure to wipe up any fuel or oil spills.
- Make sure that all components involved in the repair are positioned correctly and function properly.
- Make sure all tools and shop cloths are removed.
- Road test vehicle to confirm proper engine operation.

26 Exhaust System and Emission Controls

GENERAL

This repair group covers repair and troubleshooting for the emission control systems and removal and installation of exhaust components.

Engine Codes

- AEG . . . . . 2.0L 4-cylinder gasoline
- ALH . . . . . 1.9L 4-cylinder turbo diesel

NOTE —

- *Oxygen sensor (Lambda) system repair and troubleshooting is covered in* **23 Fuel Injection–Diesel or 24 Fuel Injection–Gasoline**.
- *All cars have a self-diagnostic program to detect emissions-related problems and store coded fault information in electronic memory. When diagnosing an emissions-related faults, first check for stored fault codes using VAG 1551/1552 or suitable scan tool.*
- *The cars covered by this manual have a vacuum hose routing diagram (sticker) located in the engine compartment which can be helpful when working with vacuum hoses.*

Service Precautions

To help guard against personal injury or damage to car components, the following warnings and cautions apply when servicing the exhaust system.

WARNING —

- *Exhaust gases are colorless, odorless, and very toxic. Run the engine only in a well-ventilated area. Immediately repair any leaks in the exhaust system or structural damage to the car body that might allow exhaust gases to enter the passenger compartment.*
- *The exhaust system, catalytic converter and other emission control systems operate at very high temperatures. Allow these components to cool before servicing, or wear protective clothing to prevent burns. Do not use flammable chemicals near a hot catalytic converter.*
- *Old corroded exhaust system components crumble easily and often have exposed sharp edges. To avoid injury, wear eye protection and heavy gloves when working with such parts.*
- *Do not work under a lifted car unless it is solidly supported on jack stands designed for that purpose. Never work under a car that is supported solely by a jack.*

> ***CAUTION —***
> *Disconnecting the negative (–) battery cable may erase fault codes and basic settings in the engine management and automatic transmission control modules. Some driveability problems may be noticed until the system re-adapts to operating conditions. OBD II readiness codes, which may be required for emissions testing, may also be erased.*

EXHAUST SYSTEM

For safe and proper exhaust system operation, all components must be free of holes and all connections must be airtight. Check the system immediately if it becomes noisy or an exhaust odor is detected inside the car.

NOTE —
Excessive exhaust system back pressure can cause driveability problems such as a rough idle or stalling. Back pressure problems are caused by external damage such as crushed or collapsed parts, or internal damage such as a plugged catalytic converter.

Exhaust System Replacement

Fig.1 and Fig. 2 show the exhaust system used on the AEG engine. Fig. 3 and Fig. 4 shows the exhaust system used on the ALH diesel engine. Use these illustrations as a guide for removal and installation. Tightening torques and other relevant installation information are given in the component lists.

A liberal application of penetrating oil to cold exhaust system nuts, bolts and slip joints will make removal easier. New fasteners, clamps and rubber mounts are always recommended when replacing exhaust components. Gaskets should be replaced whenever flange joints are disconnected. Use high-temp anti-seize compound on threaded fasteners to extend their service life and make future replacement easier. Some slight smoking and/or odor is normal as new exhaust system parts become hot for the first time.

> ***WARNING —***
> *Inspect the exhaust system heat shields on the car underbody and repair or replace any damaged parts. Heat shields protect the car occupants, undercoating, and various other components from excessive heat. Damaged or missing shields, particularly those above the catalytic converter, will increase interior temperatures and create a fire hazard.*

NOTE —

- *After performing repairs on the exhaust system, ensure that the system is not under stress and that it has sufficient clearance from the body. If necessary, loosen the double clamps and align the muffler and exhaust pipe so sufficient clearance is maintained to the body while the support rings are evenly loaded.*
- *When performing repairs, always replace self-locking nuts.*

Exhaust manifold and front catalyst (AEG engine)

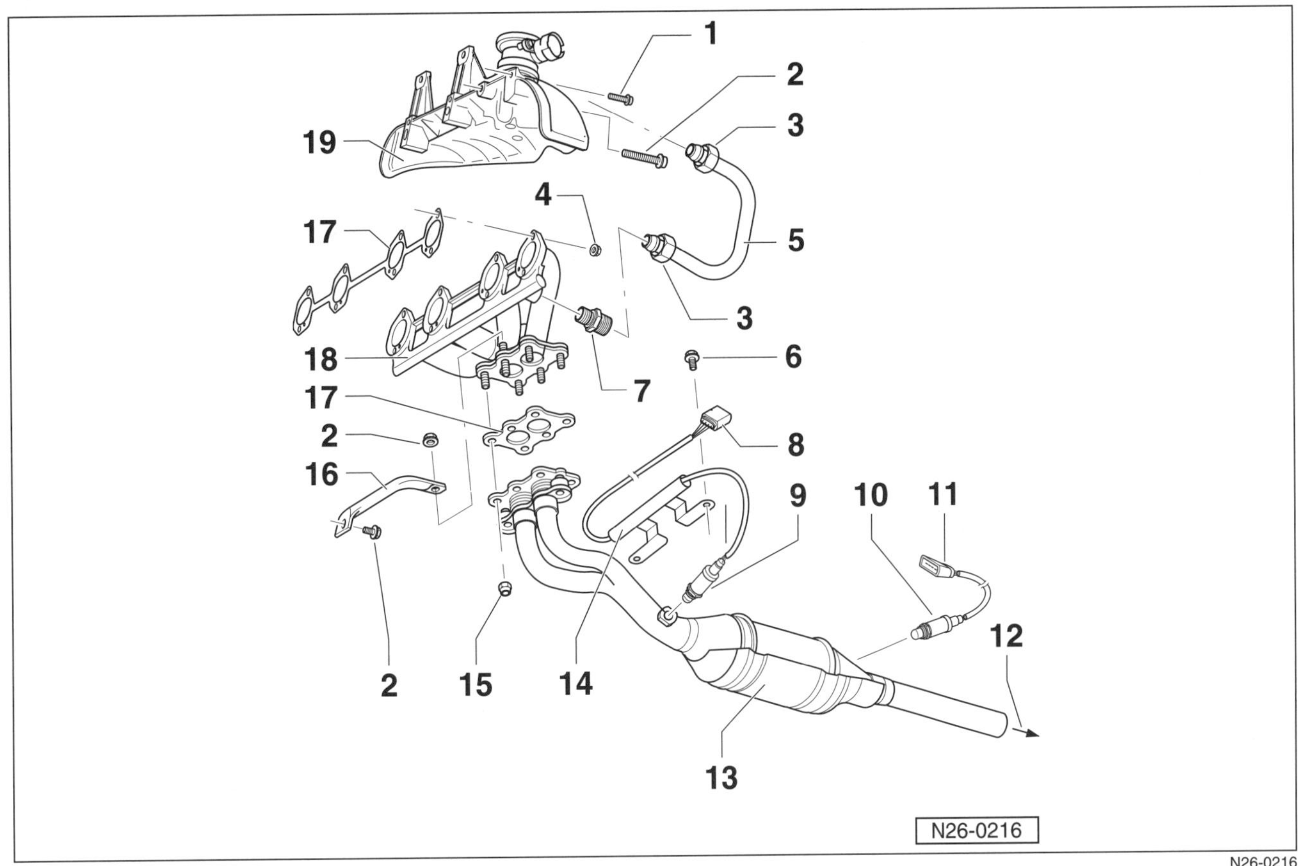

N26-0216

Fig. 1. Exhaust manifold, front exhaust pipe and catalyst for AEG engine.

1. **Bolt**
   - Tighten to 10 Nm (7 ft-lb)
2. **Bolt**
   - Tighten to 25 Nm (18 ft-lb)
3. **Flare nut**
   - Tighten to 30 Nm (22 ft-lb)
4. **Nut**
   - Tighten to 25 Nm (18 ft-lb)
   - Always replace
5. **Connecting pipe for secondary air combi-valve**
6. **Bolt**
   - Tighten to 15 Nm (11 ft-lb)
7. **Union**
   - Tighten to 35 Nm (26 ft-lb)
8. **4-pin harness connector**
   - For Oxygen sensor and Oxygen sensor heating
9. **Oxygen sensor 1 (G39)**
   - Tighten to 50 Nm (37 ft-lb)
   - Coat threads with high-temp anti-seize compound; do not allow compound to enter slots on sensor body
10. **Oxygen sensor 2 (G130)**
    - Tighten to 50 Nm (37 ft-lb)
    - Coat threads with high-temp anti-seize compound; do not allow compound to enter slots on sensor body
11. **4-pin harness connector**
    - For Oxygen sensor and Oxygen sensor heating
12. **To center muffler**
13. **Front exhaust pipe with catalyst**
14. **Guide tube**
15. **Nut**
    - Tighten to 40 Nm (30 ft-lb)
    - Always replace
16. **Exhaust manifold support brace**
17. **Gasket**
    - Always replace
18. **Exhaust manifold**
19. **Warm air collector plate**

Muffler system, overview (AEG engine)

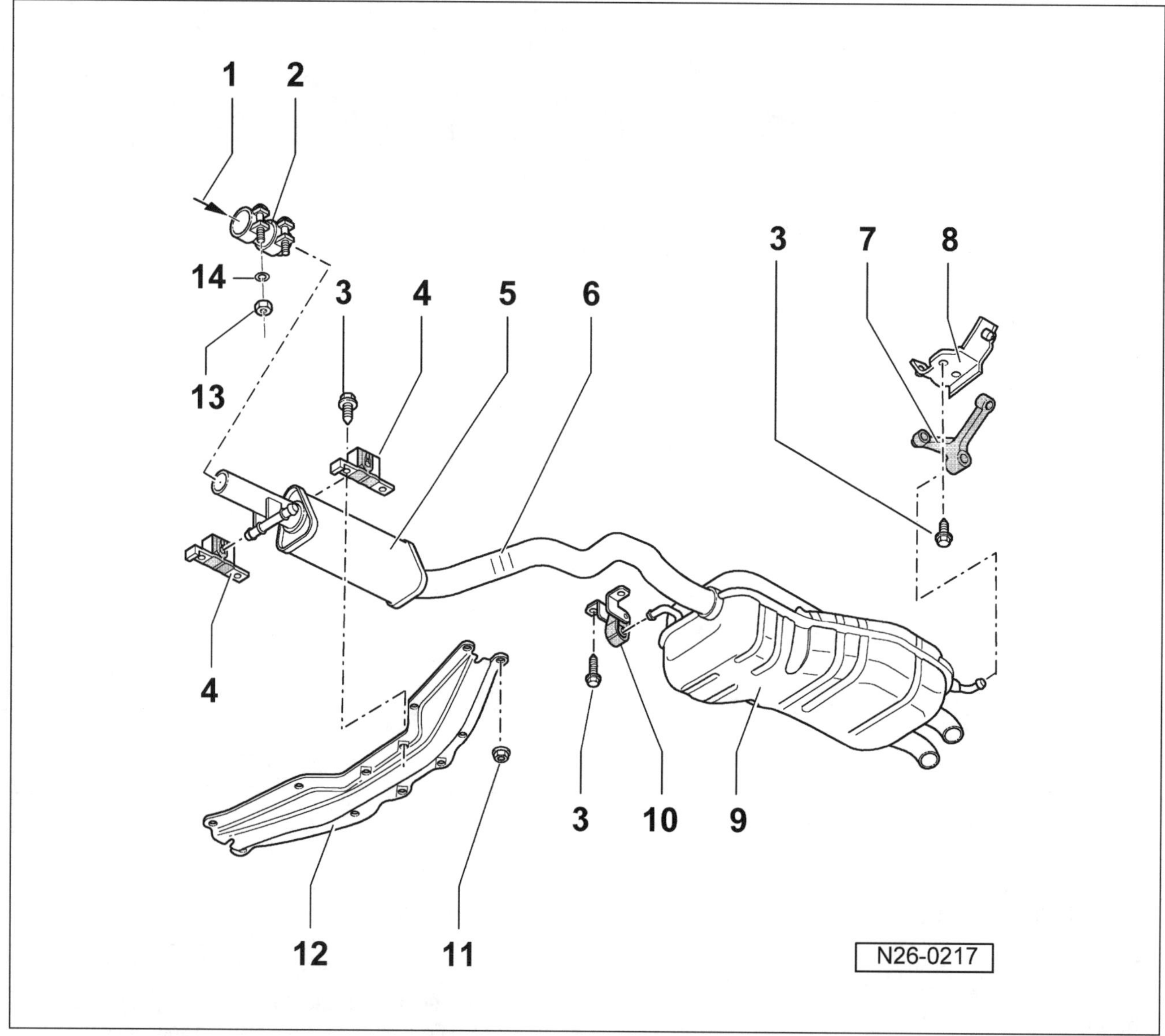

N26-0217

Fig. 2. Muffler system with related hardware for AEG engine.

1. **From front catalyst**
2. **Double clamp**
3. **Bolt**
   - Tighten to 25 Nm (18 ft-lb)
4. **Mount**
5. **Center muffler**
6. **Separation point**
   - Center and rear mufflers are installed as one unit but can be obtained individually when replacing
   - Saw through connecting pipe at separation point to replace mufflers individually
7. **Mount**
8. **Bracket**
9. **Rear muffler**
10. **Mount**
11. **Nut**
    - Tighten to 20 Nm (15 ft-lb)
12. **Tunnel bridge**
13. **Nut**
    - Tighten to 40 Nm (30 ft-lb)
14. **Washer**

Front exhaust pipe and catalyst (ALH engine)

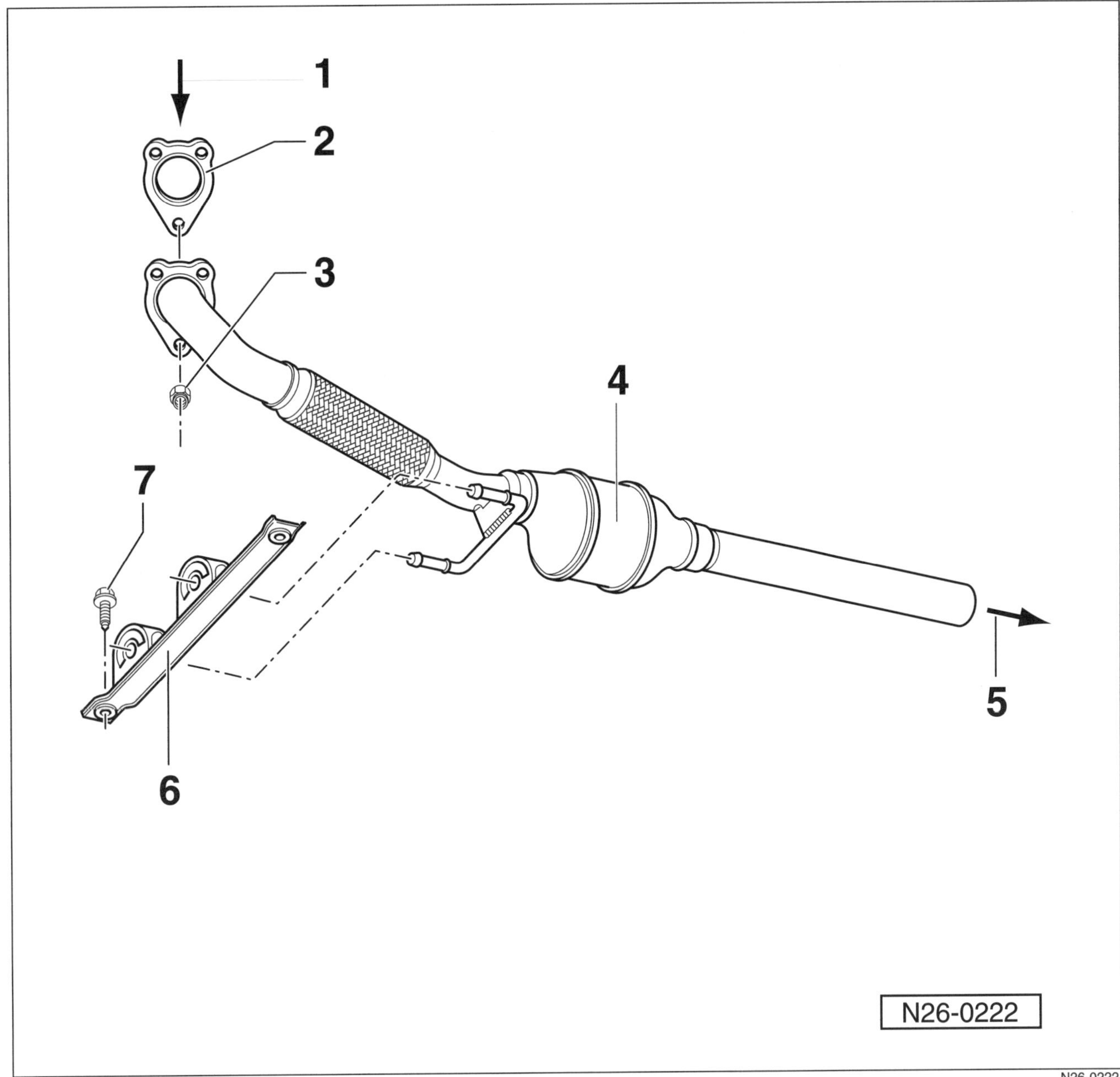

Fig. 3. Front exhaust pipe and catalyst for ALH engine.

1. **From turbocharger**
2. **Gasket**
   - Always replace
3. **Nut**
   - Tighten to 25 Nm (18 ft-lb)
4. **Catalyst**
5. **To center muffler**
6. **Front support**
7. **Bolt**
   - Tighten to 25 Nm (18 ft-lb)

Muffler system, overview (ALH engine)

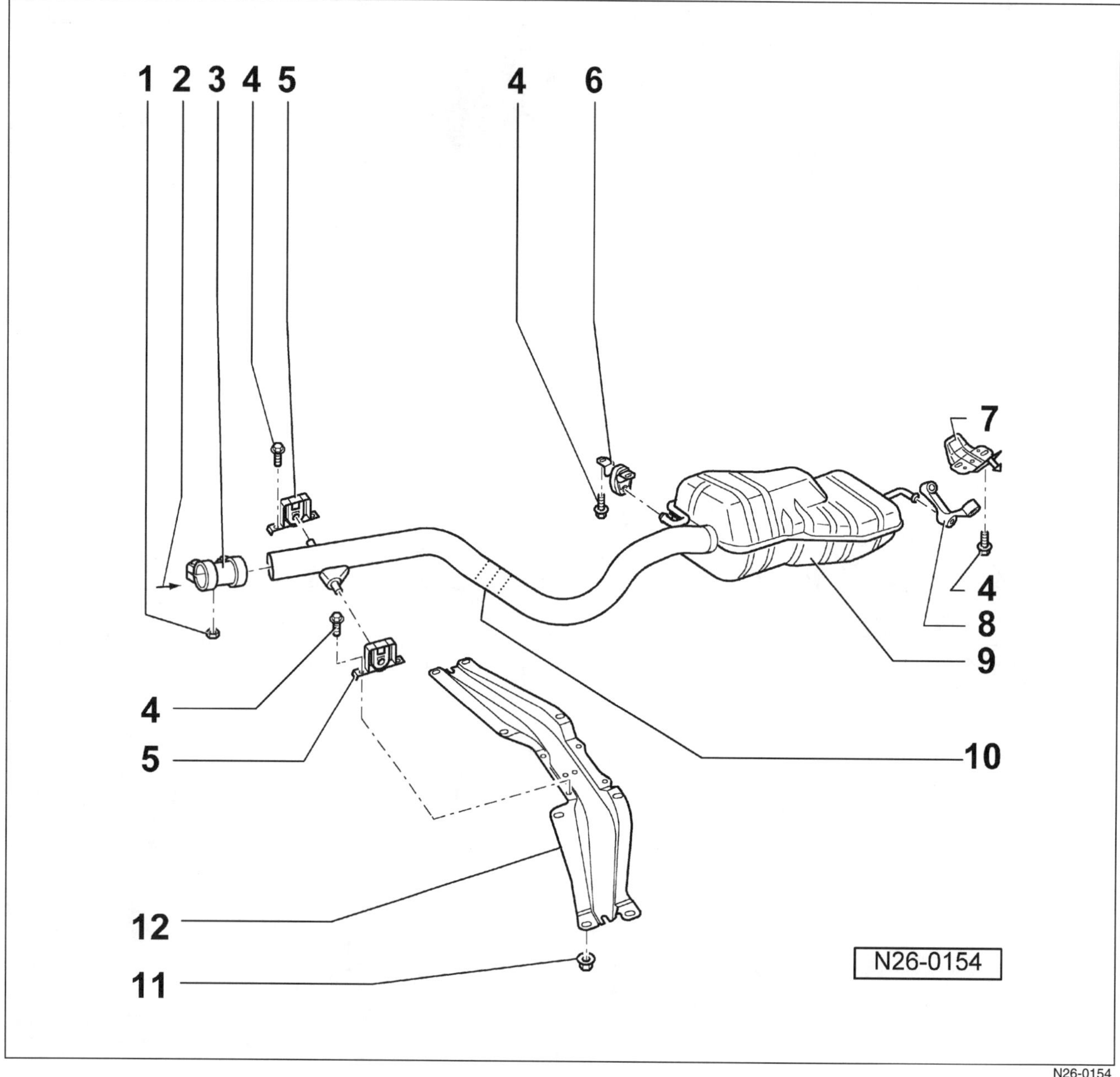

N26-0154

Fig. 4. Muffler and related hardware for ALH engine.

1. **Nut**
   - Tighten to 25 Nm (18 ft-lb)
2. **From catalyst**
3. **Double clamp**
4. **Bolt**
   - Tighten to 25 Nm (18 ft-lb)
5. **Mount**
6. **Mount**
7. **Bracket**
8. **Mount**
9. **Rear muffler**
10. **Separation point**
    - Center and rear mufflers are installed as one unit but can be obtained individually when replacing
    - Saw through connecting pipe at separation point to replace mufflers individually
11. **Nut**
    - Tighten to 25 Nm (18 ft-lb)
12. **Tunnel bridge**

Exhaust system, installation details

Figs. 5 through 8 show various details relevant to installing exhaust components on both the AEG and ALH engines.

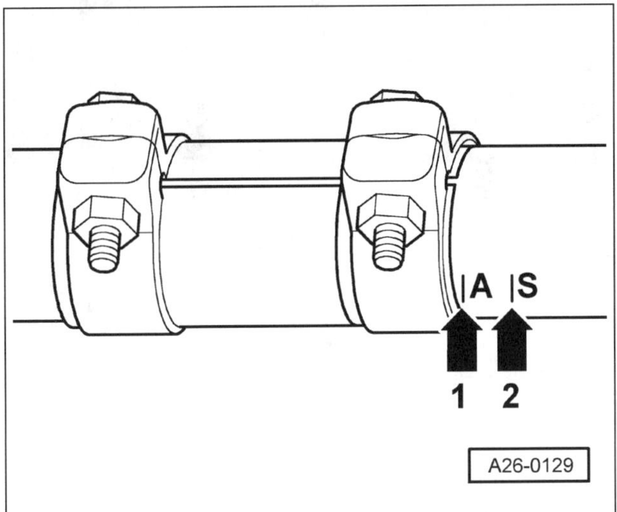

A26-0129

Fig. 5. Installation position of double clamp that attaches front and rear exhaust sections. Position clamp approx. 5 mm from **A** (**arrow 1**) for most vehicles. For vehicles with AEG engine and manual transmission position clamp 5 mm from **S** (**arrow 2**).

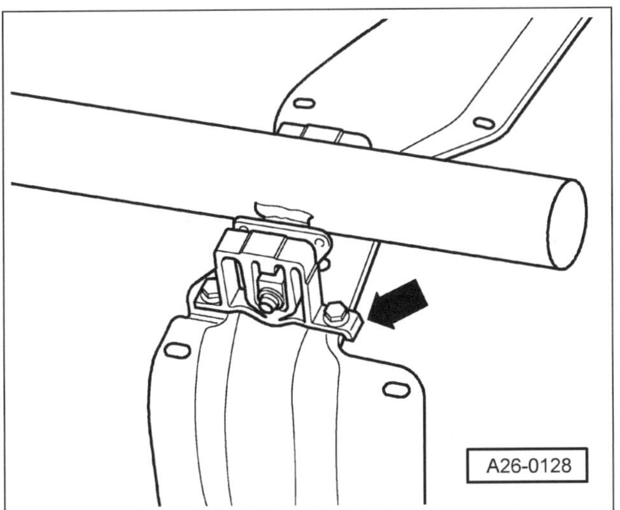

A26-0128

Fig. 6. Exhaust mount located behind double clamp. Ensure that tab (**arrow**) on foot of mount points forward.

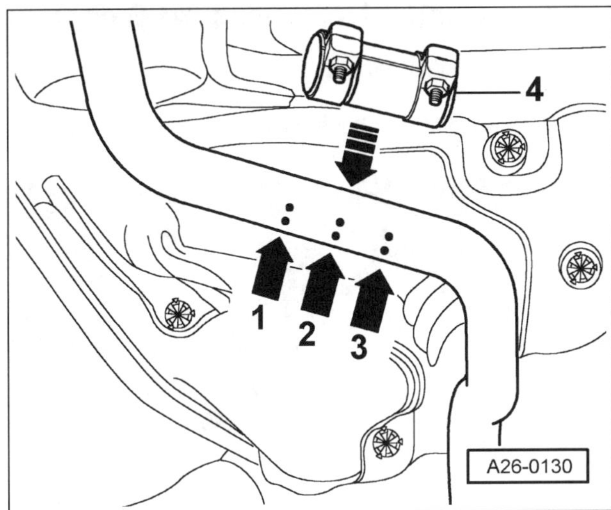

A26-0130

Fig. 7. Exhaust pipe separation point. Cut pipe at right angles at **arrow 2**. Repair clamp (**4**) is then positioned between **arrow 1** and **arrow 3**.

Tightening torque

- Exhaust pipe repair clamp bolts . . . . . 40 Nm (30 ft-lb)

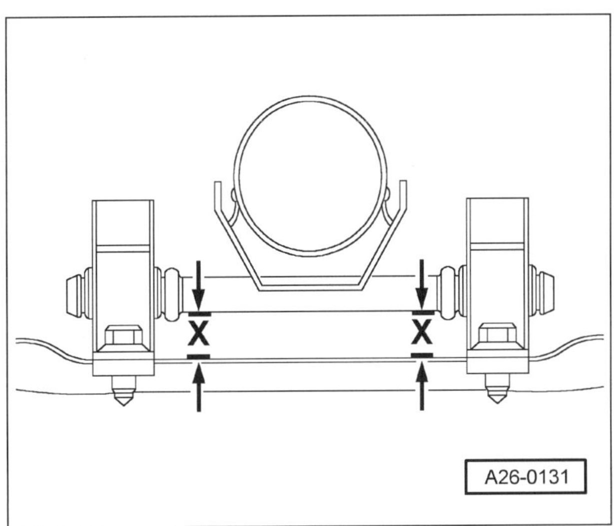

A26-0131

Fig. 8. Ensure that rear muffler is aligned stress free. Mounting pins on exhaust pipe must run parallel with tunnel bridge (dimension **X** should be equal on left and right sides).

Exhaust manifold, removing (AEG engine)

1. Remove engine cover.

2. Remove intake air hose. See Fig. 9.

Fig. 9. Remove intake air hose (**arrow**).

3. Remove pressure and vacuum hoses from secondary air injection valve (combi-valve). See **Secondary air injection system, components**, given later.

NOTE —
The combi-valve is located behind the upper intake manifold.

4. Remove connecting pipe between combi-valve and exhaust manifold. See **Exhaust manifold and front catalyst (AEG engine)**, given earlier.

5. Remove warm air collector plate. See **Exhaust manifold and front catalyst (AEG engine)**, given earlier.

6. Remove right side inner CV joint protective cover (if installed). See Fig. 10.

Fig. 10. Remove bolts (**arrows**) for CV joint protective cover.

7. Unbolt right side inner CV joint and secure drive axle with stiff wire.

8. Remove nuts (qty. 6) securing front exhaust pipe to exhaust manifold. See Fig. 1 given earlier.

9. Unbolt exhaust manifold support brace from engine block.

10. Remove exhaust manifold bolts (qty. 8) and manifold with support brace still attached.

11. Installation is the reverse of the removal noting the following:
    - Replace all gaskets and self-locking nuts/bolts.
    - See **Exhaust manifold and front catalyst (AEG engine)** given earlier, for tightening torques.
    - Use high-temp anti-seize compound on threaded fasteners to extend their service life and make future replacement easier.

12. Be sure to quality check your work, see **Quality Review** at the end of this repair group.

EMISSION CONTROLS

Evaporative emission (EVAP) controls, schematic diagram

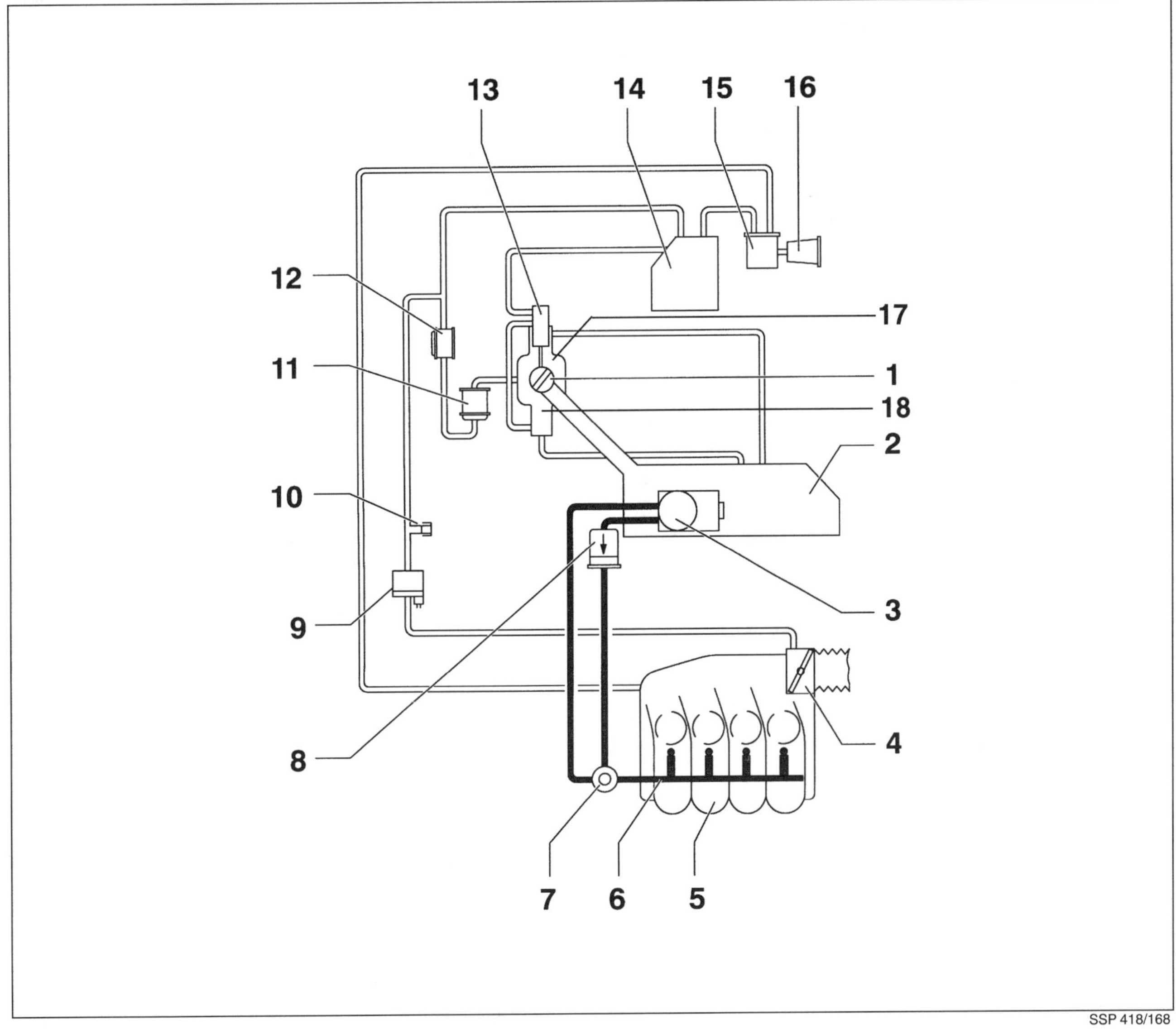

Fig. 11. Schematic diagram of EVAP controls.

1. **Filler flap**
   - Location: at top of fuel filler neck
2. **Fuel tank**
3. **Fuel pump**
   - Location: in fuel delivery unit
4. **Throttle valve**
5. **Intake manifold**
6. **Fuel rail with injectors**
7. **Fuel pressure regulator**
8. **Fuel filter**
9. **EVAP canister purge regulator valve (N80)**
10. **Pressure test port (IM 240)**
11. **Roll-over valve**
12. **Pressure holding valve**
13. **Breather valve**
14. **EVAP canister**
15. **Leak detection pump**
16. **LDP filter**
17. **Operating breather bottle**
18. **Filler breather bottle**

Positive Crankcase Ventilation (PCV)

The PCV system traps crankcase vapors and routes them back into the intake air stream to be burned.

The system consists simply of a breather hose between the valve cover and the intake air boot. The valve cover contains a flame trap to prevent ignition of the crankcase vapors in the event of a backfire. To prevent icing during cold weather, a heating element is integrated into the breather hose.

> ***CAUTION —***
> *Replace PCV hoses only with parts designed for PCV or fuel system service. Conventional vacuum and heater hoses deteriorate rapidly when exposed to oil vapors and combustion gasses.*

Fig. 12. PCV hose on AEG engine (**arrow**). ALH engine is similar.

Most crankcase ventilation problems result when the hoses or valves become clogged with oily residues. Restrictions create excessive crankcase pressure that can eventually cause driveability problems. PCV system service is limited to inspecting and cleaning the breather valves, hoses, and replacing faulty parts.

Exhaust Gas Recirculation (EGR) (ALH engine)

The EGR system installed on the ALH diesel engine reduces emissions by directing a small quantity of exhaust gases back into the intake manifold to dilute the air/fuel mixture effectively. An EGR cooler reduces the exhaust gas temperature by as much as 122°F. This reduces the amount of oxides of nitrogen (NO_x) pollutants in the exhaust.

The function of the EGR system is managed by the diesel direct injection system Engine Control Module (ECM) via the EGR vacuum regulator solenoid valve. The cone shaped plunger in the mechanical EGR valve ensures that various cross sectional openings are possible at different plunger heights. Every possible valve position is provided via pulsed control from the EGR vacuum regulator solenoid valve.

EGR valve, checking (ALH engine)

1. Remove engine cover.
2. Disconnect pipe between charge air cooler and intake manifold at intake manifold.
3. Disconnect vacuum hose from EGR valve.
4. Connect hand vacuum pump, such as VAG 1390 or equivalent, to EGR valve.
5. Operate pump and observe if membrane rod moves. See Fig. 13.

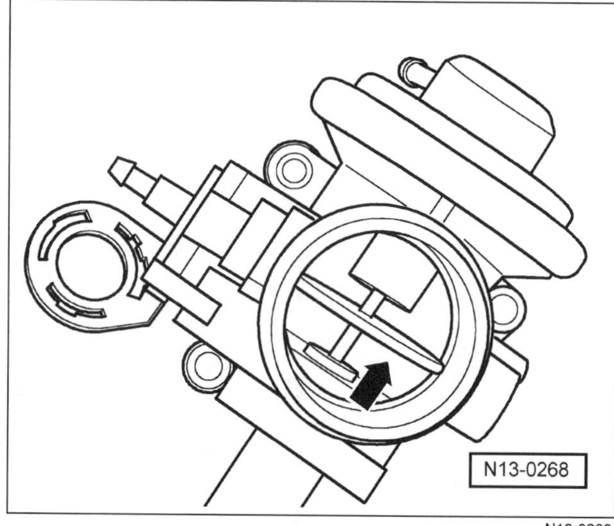

Fig. 13. Membrane rod must move in direction of **arrow** when vacuum is applied to the EGR valve.

6. Disconnect hand vacuum pump hose from EGR valve.
7. Membrane rod must move back to its original position.
8. If the membrane rod did not move then the EGR valve is faulty and should be replaced. If the rod does move correctly then the problem may be with the EGR vacuum regulator solenoid valve. Check the wiring to the solenoid valve and check for a duty cycle (on-off) signal at the valve. If no faults can be found, the signal from the ECM may be missing or the valve or ECM may be faulty.

The EGR system and its various components is shown in Fig. 14.

EGR system, assembly (ALH engine)

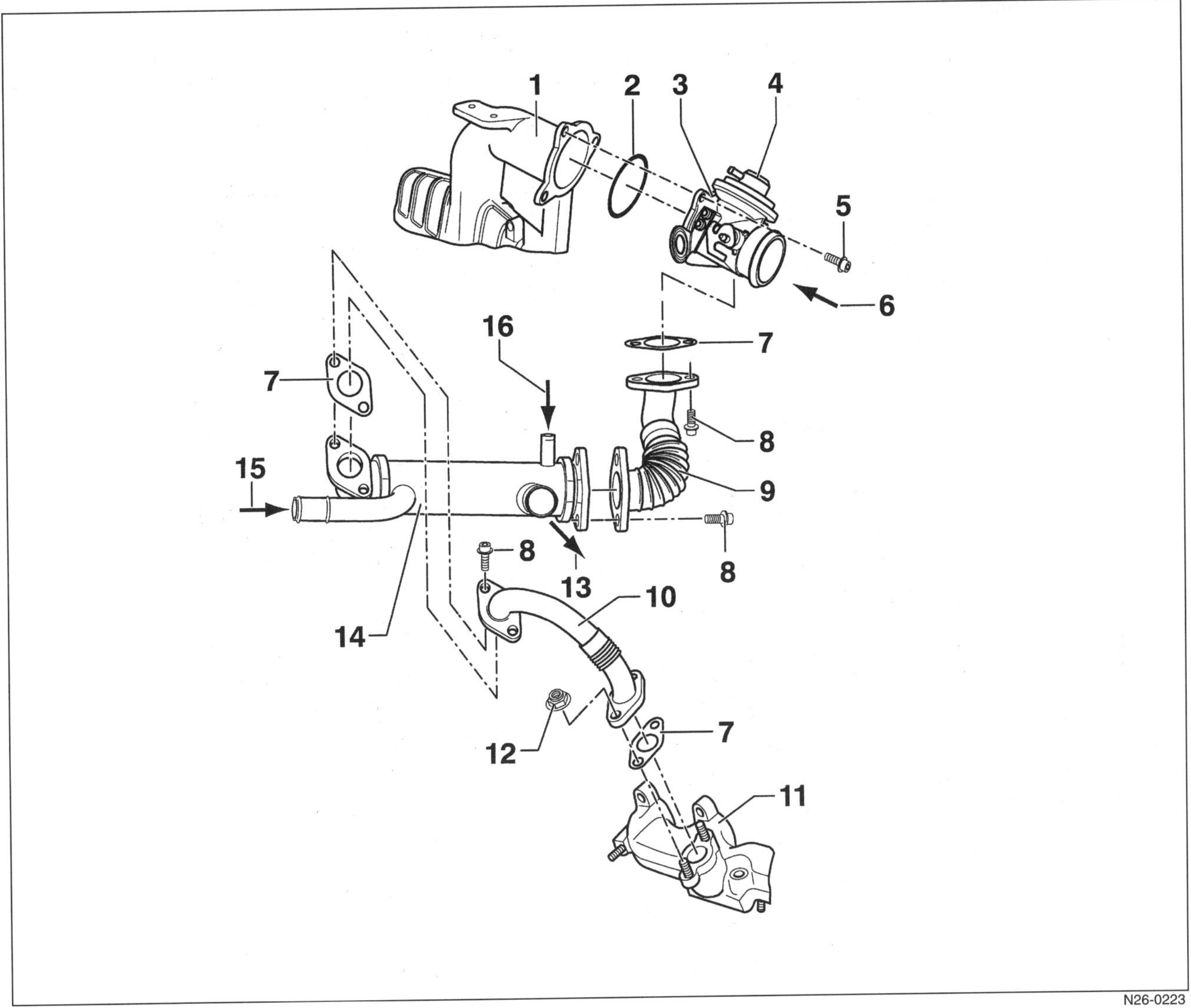

Fig. 14. EGR system on ALH diesel engine.

1. **Intake manifold**
2. **O-ring**
   - Always replace
3. **Throttle valve**
   - With EGR valve and control flap
4. **Exhaust Gas Recirculation (EGR) valve**
   - Can only replace with intake support assembly
   - Vacuum hose connection, **see** Ⓐ
5. **Bolt**
   - Tighten to 10 Nm (7 ft-lb)
6. **Intake air from air cleaner**
7. **Gasket**
   - Always replace
8. **Bolt**
   - Tighten to 25 Nm (18 ft-lb)
9. **Connecting pipe**
   - EGR cooler to intake support
10. **Connecting pipe**
    - EGR cooler to exhaust elbow
11. **Exhaust manifold**
12. **Nut**
    - Tighten to 25 Nm (18 ft-lb)
13. **To heat exchanger**
14. **EGR cooler**
15. **Connection**
    - From heater
16. **Connection**
    - From coolant expansion tank

Vacuum hose connections (ALH engine)

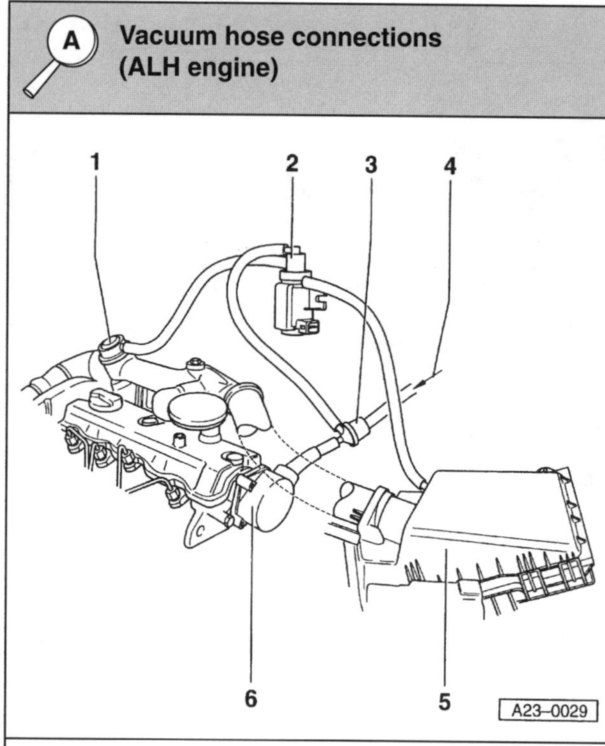

A23-0029

1. **EGR valve**
2. **EGR vacuum regulator solenoid valve (N18)**
3. **Check valve**
4. **from Brake servo**
5. **Air cleaner**
6. **Vacuum pump**

Secondary Air Injection System (AEG Engine)

The Secondary Air Injection (AIR) system on the AEG gasoline engine uses an air pump to inject fresh air behind the exhaust valves for approximately 65 seconds during cold starting.

Specification

- Engine coolant temperature for Secondary Air Injection on initial start-up. . . . . 15–35°C (59–95°F)

Also, after each subsequent engine start (up to an 85°C (185°F) max. engine coolant temperature), the secondary air injection system will, after a 20 second delay, switch in for 5 seconds during idle and is then monitored by the system.

The purpose of the AIR system is to reduce exhaust emissions during engine warm-up when the Motronic engine management system is in open loop. The AIR system produces an oxygen rich exhaust gas, causes afterburning and reduces the duration of the catalyst heat-up phase. Activation initiates from the Motronic ECM via the secondary air injection pump relay to the secondary air injection solenoid valve, then to the change-over valve and combi-valve.

The system consists of the electric air pump, the vacuum-operated shut-off valve (combi-valve), the inlet (solenoid) valve, and the related duct work. Fig. 15 shows an exploded view of the AIR system.

Secondary air injection system, components (AEG engine)

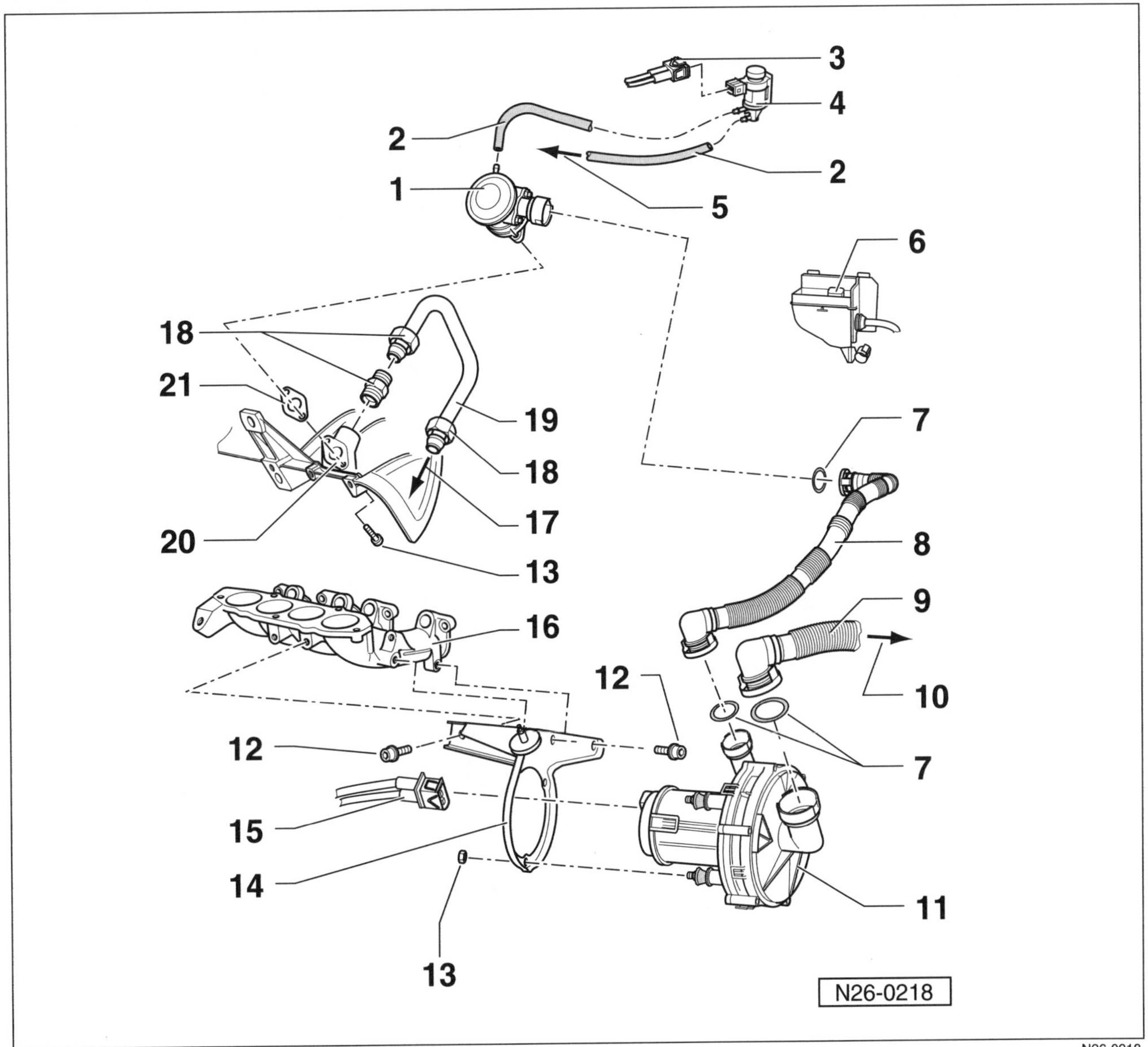

N26-0218

Fig. 15. Components of the secondary air injection system on AEG engines only.

1. **Combi-valve**
   - Checking **see** Ⓐ
2. **Vacuum hose**
3. **2-pin harness connector**
4. **Secondary air injection solenoid valve**
   - Fastened to close-out panel
5. **to Brake booster**
6. **Secondary air injection pump motor relay (J299)**
   - In fuse relay panel (slide in wire routing next to brake master cylinder)
7. **O-ring**
   - Always replace
8. **Pressure hose**
   - Ensure hose is tightly sealed
   - Press together at front to release
9. **Intake hose**
10. **to Air cleaner**
11. **Secondary air injection pump motor (V101)**

(continued on following page)

(continued from previous page)

12. Bolt
- Tighten to 25 Nm (18 ft-lb)

13. Nut
- Tighten to 10 Nm (7 ft-lb)

14. Bracket
- Attached to intake manifold

15. 2-pin harness connector

16. Fuel rail – lower section

17. To union on exhaust manifold

18. Flare nut
- Tighten to 30 Nm (22 ft-lb)

19. Connecting pipe for combi-valve

20. Warm air collector plate
- With mount for combi-valve

21. Gasket
- Always replace

A Combi-valve, checking

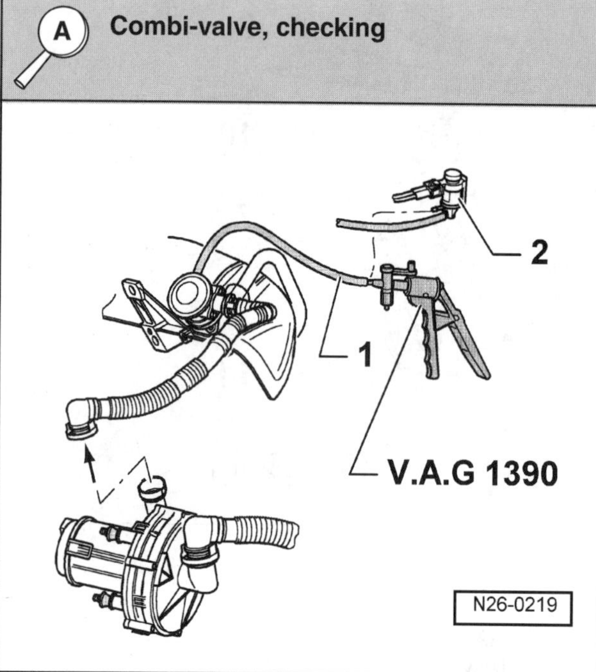

N26-0219

- **Disconnect vacuum hose (1) from AIR solenoid valve (2)**
- **Connect hand vacuum pump (i.e. VAG 1390)**
- **Remove pressure hose (arrow) from pump motor**
- **Blow into pressure hose with slight pressure**
  Do not use compressed air!
- **Both valves must be closed**
- **Operate hand vacuum pump**
- **Combi valve should open - replace if doesn't open**

Secondary air injection pump, testing

1. Disconnect the pressure hose from the outlet on the rear of the secondary air injection (AIR) pump. See Fig. 15.

2. With the engine fully warm, start and allow the engine to idle. Approximately 20 seconds after starting, the air pump should run for about five seconds and secondary air should be felt coming from the pump outlet.
   - If the air pump does not run, check the fuse on top of the battery.
   - If fuse is OK check the secondary air injection pump relay (J299).

NOTE —
*Wiring diagrams are given in **97 Wiring Diagrams, Fuses and Relays**. If no faults are found, continue testing.*

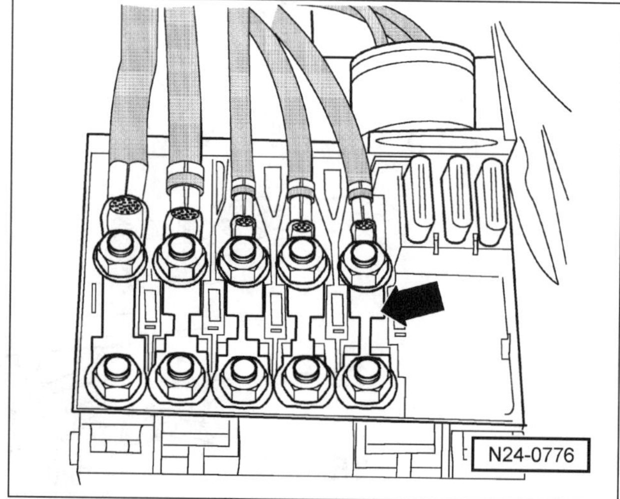

N24-0776

Fig. 16. Fuse (**arrow**) for secondary air pump, located on top of battery.

3. If the pump does not run and no wiring faults can be found, check the signal from the ECM to the pump. Disconnect the harness connector from the pump and connect a voltmeter to the connector. Start the engine while checking for voltage 20 seconds after starting.
   - If voltage is present, the pump is most likely faulty and should be replaced.
   - If voltage is not present, check the wiring at the AIR relay and between the ECM and the AIR relay. If no faults are found, the relay or ECM may be faulty.

Secondary air injection solenoid valve, checking

NOTE —
- *Engine oil temperature should be between 5–33°C (41–91°F).*
- *Ensure that secondary air injection pump motor is OK.*

1. Disconnect the vacuum hose at solenoid valve. See Fig. 17.

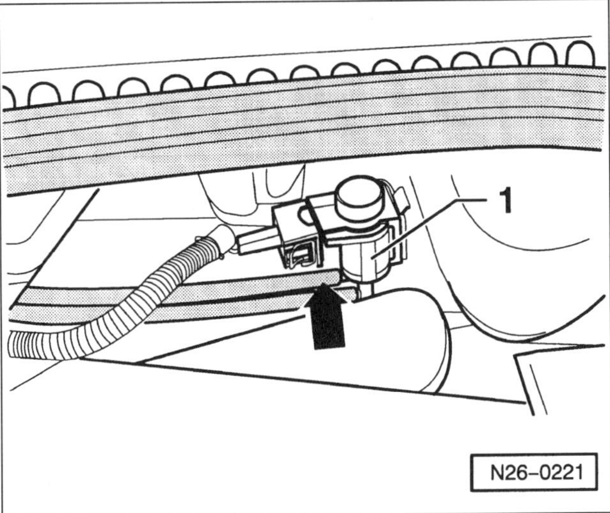

N26-0221

Fig. 17. Disconnect vacuum line (arrow) at AIR solenoid valve

2. Start the engine while checking for vacuum at the hose 20 seconds after starting. If vacuum is present, the valve is functioning correctly.
3. If vacuum is not present, shut off engine and disconnect the harness connector from the solenoid valve and connect a voltmeter to the harness connector. Start the engine while checking for voltage 20 seconds after starting.
   - If voltage is present, the solenoid valve is most likely faulty and should be replaced.
   - If voltage is not present, check the wire between solenoid valve and the ECM. If no faults are found, the ECM may be faulty.

Combi-valve, removing and installing

NOTE —
- *Always replace all seals and gaskets.*
- *Installation is best accomplished using a helper.*

1. Remove engine cover.
2. Remove intake hose between air cleaner and secondary air injection pump motor.
3. Remove pressure and vacuum hoses from combi-valve.
4. Unbolt connecting pipe from combi-valve.
5. Working underneath the car, remove protective cover from above right inner CV joint (if applicable) as shown earlier. See Fig. 10.
6. Unbolt connecting pipe from exhaust manifold.
7. Unscrew combi-valve from warm air collector plate using 4 mm ball-headed allen wrench.
8. To install, thread front bolts through the warm air collector plate from below.
9. Have helper hold fastener tight from above and position combi-valve during installation of second bolt.

Tightening torque
- Combi-valve to warm air collector plate 10 Nm (7 ft-lb)

Catalytic converter

The three-way catalytic converter chemically reduces pollutants in the engine exhaust. A properly operating converter provides a 90-95 percent reduction of the three major exhaust gas pollutants (nitrogen (NO_x), carbon monoxide (CO), and unburned hydrocarbons (HC).

The catalytic converter works correctly only when the air/fuel ratio is kept within a very narrow range. The oxygen sensor provides the feedback for control of the air/fuel mixture. For more information see **24 Fuel Injection–Gasoline (AEG engine)**.

The catalytic converter itself does not require any routine maintenance. However, any problem that increases converter temperature beyond its normal operating range (incorrect ignition timing or air/fuel mixture, engine misfire, prolonged idling or extended high engine loads) can damage the converter. Reduced power, stalling, exhaust system rattles and excessive emissions are symptoms that may be caused by a faulty catalytic converter.

Catalytic converters on New Beetles with AEG engine use a second heated oxygen sensor to monitor the operation of the catalyst. If the converter fails to properly oxidize the spent combustion gasses, the heated oxygen sensor will detect this malfunction and a fault code (DTC) will be stored in the ECM.

Exhaust leaks anywhere in the system, but especially between the cylinder head and the catalytic converter, can cause running problems, false DTCs or converter failure.

> ***WARNING —***
> *Do not operate the starter for long periods if the engine fails to start. Extended cranking may allow excess fuel to enter the catalytic converter, creating a fire hazard and possibly damaging the converter.*

Accurately testing the function of the catalytic converter requires an infrared exhaust gas analyzer to check the air/fuel mixture adjustment (% CO) at the exhaust system test port upstream of the catalytic converter, and then again at the tailpipe. If the converter is working properly, the tailpipe reading will be lower than the test port reading. If the reading is the same or only slightly less, the converter is probably faulty.

QUALITY REVIEW

When you have finished working under the hood and around other areas of the vehicle, it is advisable to take a moment to quality check or review your work. This helps to insure that the operation or repair has been completed properly with all affected systems functioning within normal parameters. These may include the following:

- Ensure that the exhaust system is not under stress, and that it has sufficient clearance from the body. If necessary, loosen the double clamps and align the muffler and exhaust pipe so sufficient clearance is maintained to the body while the support rings are evenly loaded.
- Confirm that all heat shields are in place.
- Make sure that there are no air, vacuum or exhaust leaks.
- Make sure that all components involved in the repair are positioned correctly and function properly.
- Make sure all tools and shop cloths are removed.

27 Engine Electrical

TABLES

GENERAL

This repair group covers battery, starter, and generator troubleshooting and repair.

NOTE —

- *The alternator is identified as generator by the vehicle manufacturer. Car makers must by law use uniform words and terms (nomenclature) to describe certain components and or systems. The uniform word for alternator is generator. Therefore, the component labeled "Generator (GEN)" in the wiring diagrams is the alternator.*
- *Wiring diagrams for the battery, charging system and starter motor are given in* **97 Wiring Diagrams, Fuses and Relays**.

The six-cell, 12-volt lead-acid battery capacity is rated in Ampere/hours (Ah) and cold cranking amps (CCA). The Ah rating is determined by the average amount of current the battery can deliver over time without dropping below a specified voltage. The CCA rating is determined by the battery's ability to deliver starting current at 0°F (–18°C). The battery is installed in the engine compartment, behind the left headlight assembly.

The charging system consists of a belt-driven 14-volt generator and a voltage regulator. The voltage regulator, which is mounted in the generator, also serves as the generator brush holder. The charging system provides the current necessary to keep the battery charged and to operate the vehicle's electrical accessories.

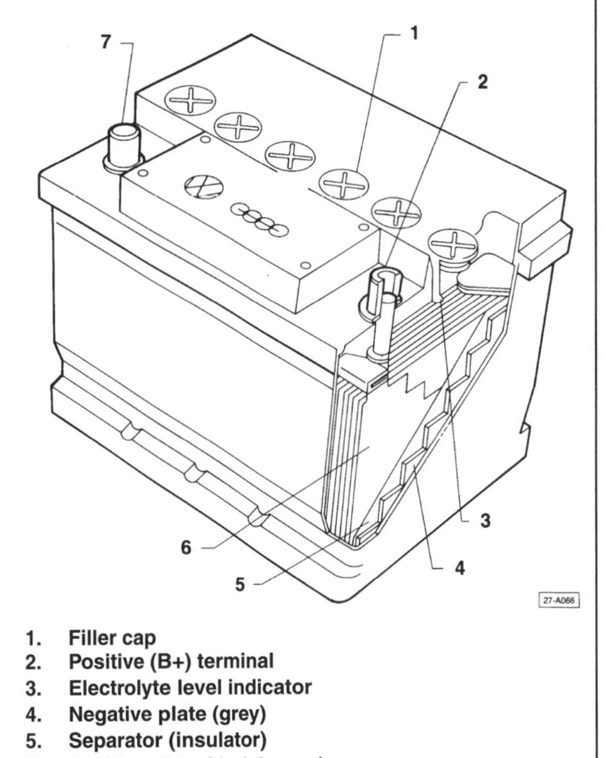

1. **Filler cap**
2. **Positive (B+) terminal**
3. **Electrolyte level indicator**
4. **Negative plate (grey)**
5. **Separator (insulator)**
6. **Positive plate (dark brown)**
7. **Negative (–) terminal**

27-A066

Fig. 1. Battery.

Please read the following warnings and cautions before doing any work on any parts of the engine electrical system.

WARNING —

- *Wear goggles, rubber gloves, and a rubber apron when working around batteries and battery acid (electrolyte). Battery acid contains sulfuric acid and can cause skin irritation and burning. If acid is spilled on your skin or clothing, flush the area at once with large quantities of water. If electrolyte gets into your eyes, bathe them with large quantities of clean water for several minutes and call a physician.*
- *Batteries that are being charged or are fully charged give off explosive hydrogen gas. Keep sparks and open flames away. Do not smoke.*

CAUTION —

- *Disconnecting the negative (–) battery cable may erase fault codes and basic settings in the engine management and automatic transmission control modules. Some driveability problems may be noticed until the system re-adapts to operating conditions. OBD II readiness codes, which may be required for emissions testing, may also be erased.Convenience electronics (alarm system, interior light control, power locks, mirrors, and windows) may need to be re-set using a VAG 1551/1552 or equivalent scan tool.*
- *Do not disconnect the battery cables while the engine is running. The generator will be damaged.*
- *Never operate the generator with its output terminal (B+ or 30) disconnected and the other terminals connected. Never short, bridge, or ground any terminals of the charging system.*
- *Always disconnect the negative (–) battery cable when working at or near the generator. Battery voltage is always present at the rear of the generator, even with the ignition key off.*
- *Always allow a frozen battery to thaw before attempting to recharge it.*
- *Always disconnect the battery cables during battery charging. This will prevent damage to the generator and any solid-state components. Do not exceed 16.5 volts at the battery.*
- *Never reverse the battery terminals. Even a momentary wrong connection can damage the generator or electrical components.*
- *Replace the battery if the case is cracked or leaking. Electrolyte can damage the car. If electrolyte is spilled, clean the area with a solution of baking soda and water.*

BATTERY SERVICE

If the battery discharges when the vehicle is not driven, there may be a constant drain or current draw causing it to discharge when the ignition is off. Depending on the draw and the condition of the battery, a full discharge can happen overnight or it may take a few weeks. Although a small static drain on the battery is normal (for example to operate the clock or radio memory), a large drain such as a relay sticking on or a faulty switch will cause the battery to quickly discharge. Make a static current draw test as the first step when experiencing battery discharge.

If the current draw on the battery is not excessive and the battery still discharges, the condition of the battery should be tested. Battery testing determines the state of battery charge. The most common methods are open-circuit and load voltage testing. Batteries with filler caps can also be tested by checking the specific gravity of the electrolyte. Inexpensive specific gravity testers are available at most auto supply stores.

Some New Beetles are equipped with batteries with a central gas venting system with anti-flash protection. The anti-flash protection consists of a small round fiberglass mat with a diameter of approximately 15 mm and a thickness of 2 mm. Its purpose is to vent gasses that form in the battery. The gasses that form while charging can vent centrally through an opening on the upper side of the battery cover. The anti-flash protection is also installed to prevent ignition of the flammable gasses in the battery.

CAUTION —

- *Use new generation batteries with central gas venting when replacing the battery.*
- *Always use genuine VW battery cell caps. Caps must be fitted with an O-ring seal.*
- *Before diagnosing electrical problems visually inspect the battery for clean and tight connections at all terminals.*

Static current draw, checking

1. Make sure the ignition and all electrical accessories are switched off.
2. Disconnect the negative (–) cable from the battery. See the Cautions at the beginning of this repair group regarding battery disconnection.

NOTE —

Be sure to have the anti-theft radio code on hand before disconnecting the battery.

3. Connect a digital ammeter between the battery negative post and the negative battery cable and measure the current draw. See Fig. 2.

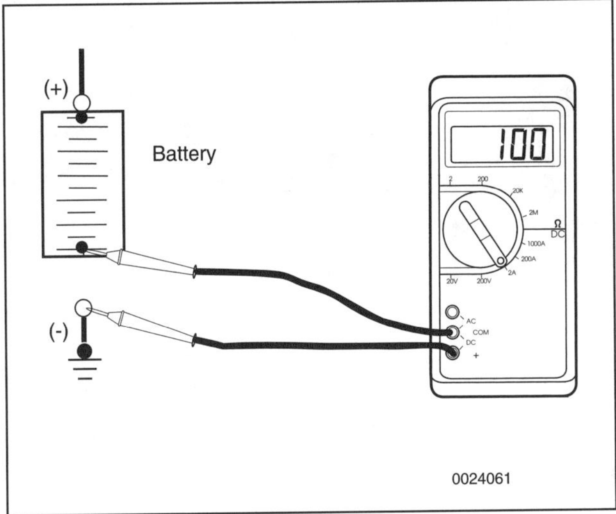

0024061

Fig. 2. Electrical system static current draw being measured.

A range of about 0 to 100 milliamps is normal, depending on the number of accessories that need constant power. A current of 500 milliamps (0.5 amp) or more indicates a problem. To determine the circuit or component causing the problem, remove one fuse at a time until the current drops to a normal range. Use the wiring diagrams shown in **97 Wiring Diagrams, Fuses and Relays** to locate wiring or component faults.

Open-circuit voltage test

An open-circuit voltage test checks battery voltage by connecting an accurate digital voltmeter to the battery posts after disconnecting the battery ground cable. Before making an open-circuit voltage test on a battery, first load the battery with 15 amps for one minute, for example by turning on the headlights without the engine running. See **Table a** for open-circuit voltage levels and their corresponding percentages of charge.

Table a. Open-Circuit Voltage and Battery Charge

Open-circuit voltage	State of charge
12.6 V or more	Fully charged
12.4 V	75% charged
12.2 V	50% charged
12.0 V	25% charged
11.7 V or less	Fully discharged

The battery is in satisfactory condition if the open-circuit voltage is at least 12.4 volts. If the open-circuit voltage is at this level or above, but the battery still lacks power for starting, make a load voltage test to determine the battery's service condition. If the open-circuit voltage is below 12.4 volts, recharge the battery. If the battery cannot be recharged to at least 75%, it should be replaced.

Load voltage testing

A load voltage battery test is made by connecting a specific resistive load to the battery terminals and then measuring the battery's voltage. The test requires a special tester and can generally be performed quickly and inexpensively by an authorized VW dealer or other qualified repair facility.

The battery should be fully charged and at room temperature for the most accurate results. If the equipment is available, disconnect the negative (–) battery cable. Then apply the specified load for 15 seconds and measure the battery's voltage. If the voltage is below that listed, the battery should be replaced. **Table b** lists load current and minimum voltages for original-equipment VW batteries.

> ***WARNING —***
> *Always wear protective goggles and clothing when performing a load test.*

Battery charging

Discharged batteries can be recharged using a battery charger. Prolonged charging causes gassing that will evaporate the electrolyte to a level that can damage the battery.

Table b. Battery Load Current and Minimum Voltage

Battery Capacity	Cold Cranking Amps (CCA)	Load Current	Minimum voltage
70 Amp-hour	340	200	9.5

Always read and follow the instructions provided by the battery charger's manufacturer. A slow-charging rate (10% of battery capacity) is best to prevent battery damage caused by overheating.

> ***WARNING —***
> - *The gasses given off by the battery during charging are explosive. Do not smoke. Keep open flames away from the top of the battery, and prevent electrical sparks by turning off the battery charger before connecting or disconnecting it.*
> - *Battery cell caps must not be removed while charging.*
> - *Batteries are damaged by quick charging. It should only be used as a last alternative when slow charging is not possible.*
> - *Never quick charge a totally discharged battery.*
> - *Do not allow the battery charging rate to exceed 16.5 volts.*
> - *If the battery begins gassing (boiling) violently when charging, reduce the charging rate immediately.*
> - *Ensure that the battery is charged in a well ventilated area.*
> - *Precision tools must not be kept in the same room where batteries are being charged. Tools may corrode due to chemical reaction.*

Battery, removing and installing

1. Switch ignition off.
2. Press locking tabs together to open hinged battery cover. See Fig. 3. Fold the top part of the battery blanket up.

Fig. 3. Press locking tabs (**arrows**) to open hinged battery cover.

3. Disconnect battery ground (GND) strap from battery negative (-) terminal.

> ***CAUTION —***
> *Be sure to have the anti-theft radio code on hand before disconnecting the battery.*

4. Open fuse cover on top of battery and remove carefully.
5. Remove rear wiring cover by pulling upward.
6. Remove hex nut for positive (+) battery terminal lead. See Fig. 4. Position battery cover out of the way.

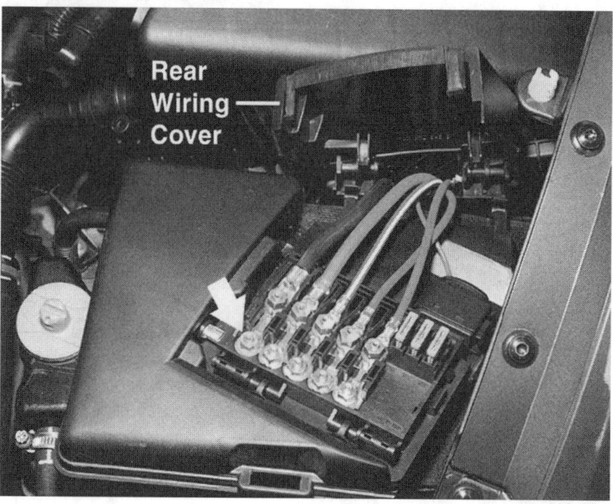

Fig. 4. Remove hex nut for positive battery terminal lead (**arrow**) and remove rear wiring cover by pulling upward.

7. Remove positive (+) battery clamp from battery and position cable out of the way.
8. Remove bolt securing power steering reservoir to battery tray. Position reservoir out of the way without disconnecting power steering lines.
9. Remove nut securing plastic battery shroud, pull shroud off of front and left side locating tabs. Remove shroud. See Fig. 5.

Fig. 5. Remove power steering reservoir bolt (**A**), battery shroud nut (**B**), and pull shroud off locating tabs (**arrows**).

10. Remove battery clamping bracket. See Fig. 6.

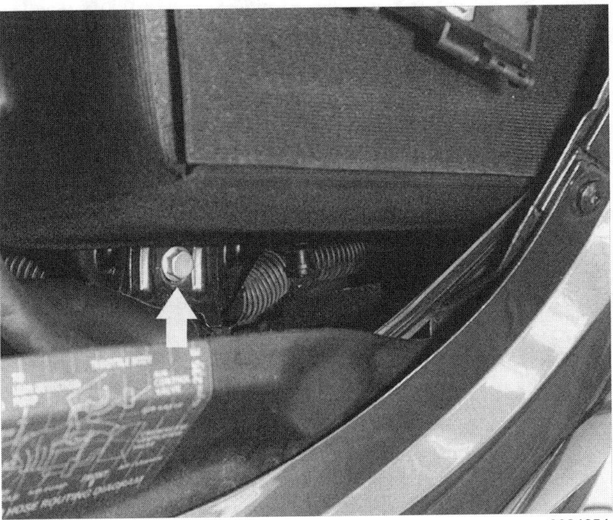
0024254

Fig. 6. Remove bolt and battery clamping bracket (**arrow**).

11. Remove battery with insulating blanket (if applicable).

12. Install battery so lug of battery tray engages in battery groove. The battery is correctly installed when the center groove in the battery foot strip aligns with threaded hole in the battery carrier. See Fig. 7.

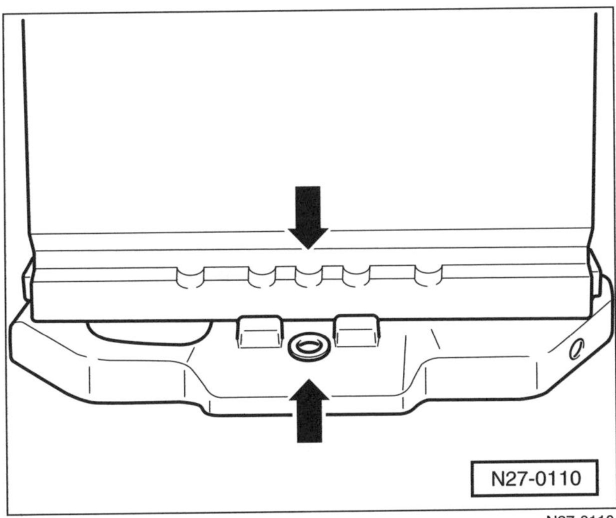

N27-0110

Fig. 7. Correct installation position of battery.

> ***CAUTION —***
> - *To be sure the battery seats securely, only install batteries with a 10.5 mm battery foot strip.*
> - *It must not be possible to move the battery to the left or to the right.*

13. Install battery clamping bracket and tighten securing bolt.

> ***CAUTION —***
> - *On batteries with hose for central venting make sure venting hose is not kinked. Only then can battery vent freely.*
> - *On batteries without hose for central venting make sure opening on upper side of battery cover is not blocked.*

Tightening torque
- Battery clamping bracket bolt . . . . 22 Nm (16 ft-lb)

14. Remaining installation is the reverse of removal, noting the following points:
    - Be sure to properly position plastic battery shroud on locating tabs.
    - Connect all battery positive (+) connections before installing negative (-) battery clamp.

Tightening torque
- Battery terminal clamps . . . . 6 Nm (53 in-lb)

> ***CAUTION —***
> *After installing, check if the battery is seated securely. If the battery is not secured properly, the following will result:*
> - *Shortened battery life due to vibration damage*
> - *Battery cell and plate damage*
> - *Electrolyte leakage due to battery case damage*
> - *Poor collision safety*

15. Be sure to quality check your work, see **Quality Review** at the end of this repair group.

CHARGING SYSTEM SERVICE

Charging system trouble is indicated by an illuminated generator warning light on the instrument panel, or by an under or overcharged battery.

The generator generates electrical current by electrical induction. When the engine is running, part of the current it produces energizes its electromagnetic field. When starting, some other current must be provided to initially energize the field and begin the current generating process. This current is provided by the battery through the generator warning light in the instrument cluster. If the lamp burns out, the generator will not charge the battery properly.

> ***CAUTION —***
> - *Always disconnect the negative (–) battery cable before servicing the charging system. The large red wire at the rear of the generator comes directly from the battery and is not fuse protected.*
> - *Disconnecting the negative (–) battery cable may erase fault codes and basic settings in the engine management and automatic transmission control modules. Some driveability problems may be noticed until the system re-adapts to operating conditions. OBD II readiness codes, which may be required for emissions testing, may also be erased.*

As a quick-check, measure the voltage across the battery terminal with the key off and then again with the engine running. The battery voltage should be about 12.6 volts with key off and approximately 14.0 volts with the engine running. If the voltage does not increase when the engine is running, there is a fault in the charging system.

NOTE —
The regulated voltage (engine running) should be roughly between 13.8 and 14.5 volts, depending on temperature and operating conditions. If the voltage is much higher than 14.5 volts, the voltage regulator is most likely faulty.

Charging system, testing

1. Inspect the poly-ribbed drive belt for cracking, glazing or wear. Replace the belt if any faults are found. Check that the belt is not slipping and that the belt tension is correct.

2. Make sure the battery is fully charged and capable of holding a charge. Make sure the battery terminals are clean and tight.

3. Check that the charge warning lamp comes on when the key is on. If the light comes on, proceed to step 4. If the light does not come on, repair any wiring or bulb faults before continuing to test.

NOTE —
The charge warning light must come on when the ignition is switched on or the system may not charge. If any faults are found, see **97 Wiring Diagrams, Fuses and Relays** *for electrical schematics.*

4. Check for battery voltage between ground and terminal **B+** (large red wire) at the back of the generator. Check that the wire is securely fastened.

5. Turn the ignition key on and check for battery voltage between terminal **D+** and ground. If voltage is not present, check the wiring from the warning light in the instrument cluster.

6. If no faults are found up to this point, have the generator tested with a load tester, such as the Sun VAT40.

NOTE —
If a load test is not possible, an imperfect output test can be done by running the engine at about 2000 rpm and turning on many of the electrical loads such as fans, lights and heated window, wipers, etc. When loaded, the battery should still be 12 volts or higher.

Generator, removing and installing

1. Disconnect the battery ground (GND) strap from battery negative (-) terminal. See the Cautions at the beginning of this repair group regarding battery disconnection.

NOTE —
Be sure to have the anti-theft radio on hand before disconnecting the battery cables.

2. Mark the running direction on the poly-ribbed drive belt and then remove the belt from the generator pulley. See **0 Maintenance Program**.

3. Disconnect the wiring from the rear of the generator.

4. Remove the upper and lower generator through-bolts and remove the generator from its bracket.

5. Installation is the reverse of removal. Tightening torques are given in the alternator overview. See Fig. 8.

6. Be sure to quality check your work, see **Quality Review** at the end of this repair group.

Generator overview

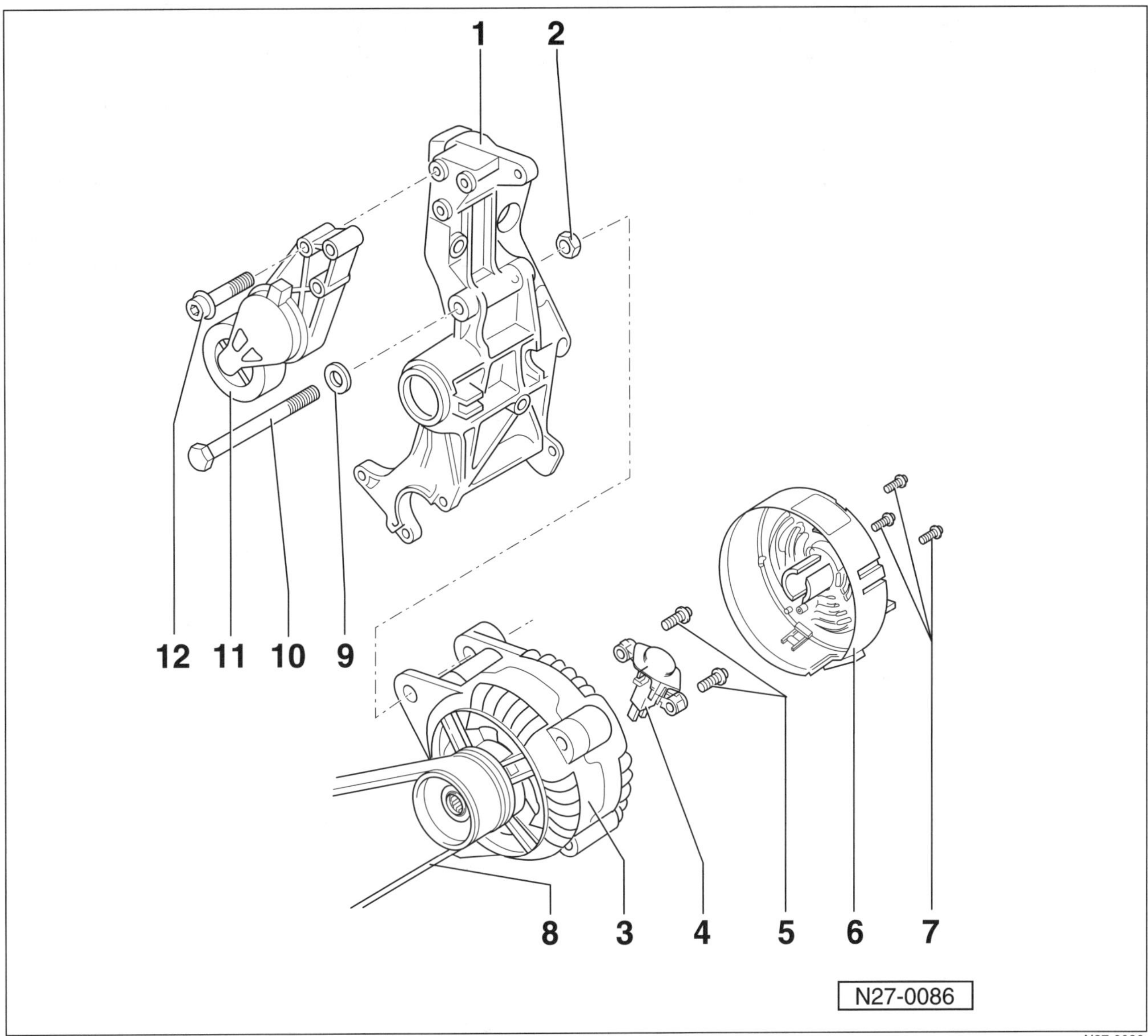

N27-0086

Fig. 8. Overview of alternator on ALH engine equipped with power steering and air-conditioning. Other applications are similar.

1. **Bracket**
2. **Hex nut**
    - Tighten to 30 Nm (22 ft lb)
3. **Generator**
    - Tighten nut of B+ wire to generator to 15 Nm (11 ft-lb)
4. **Voltage regulator**
    - To remove and install, remove items 7, 6, 5
    - Checking carbon brushes, **see** Ⓐ
5. **Phillips-head screw**
    - M4 x 25mm
6. **End cap**
7. **Hex bolts**
    - M3 x 18mm
8. **Ribbed belt**
    - Removing and installing, see **0 Maintenance**
9. **Washer**
10. **Hex bolt**
    - M8 x 85mm
    - Tighten to 25 Nm (18 ft-lb)
11. **Tensioning roller**
12. **Socket-head bolt**
    - M8 x 85mm
    - Tighten to 25 Nm (18 ft-lb)

A Alternator carbon brushes, checking

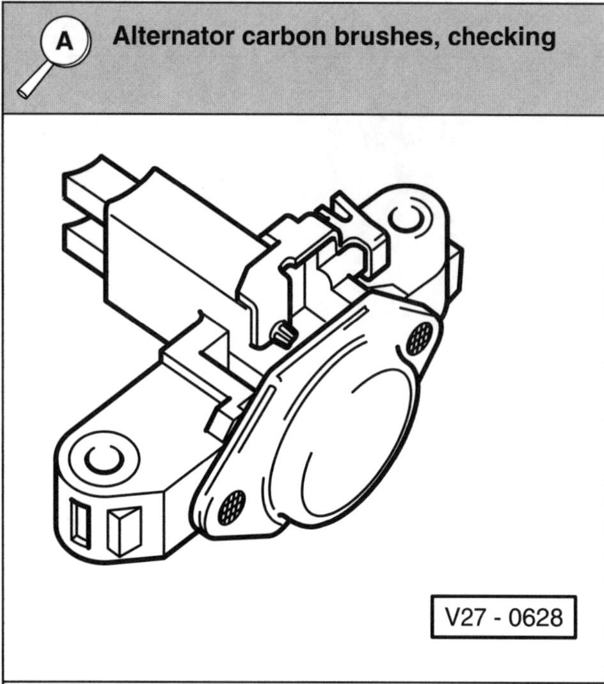

V27-0628

- **Length of new carbon brushes = 12 mm (0.5 in.)**
- **Wear limit = 5 mm (0.19 in.)**
- **Tolerance = +1 mm (0.03 in.)**

STARTER SERVICE

The starter is located below the engine on the left-hand (driver's) side, bolted to the forward part of the transmission. The starter and solenoid are removed together as an assembly. The solenoid can be separated from the starter motor once the starter has been removed. Although the starter is generally replaced as an exchange unit, the solenoid and other parts are available from an authorized Volkswagen dealer.

All vehicles have a lock-out relay for the starter which is controlled by the alarm system. For location of relays, see **97 Wiring Diagrams, Fuses and Relays**.

In addition, vehicles equipped with manual transmissions have a starter lock-out function requiring the clutch pedal to be depressed before the starter can be activated. This system consists of a pedal switch and a relay on the fuse-relay panel. See Fig. 9.

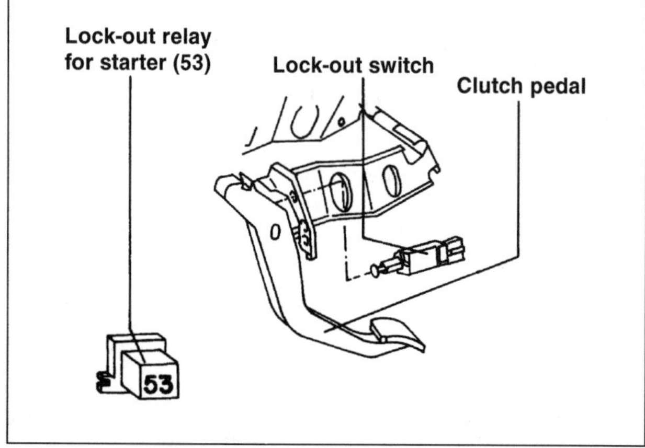

0024256

Fig. 9. Starter lock-out switch and relay for vehicles with manual transmission.

Vehicles equipped with automatic transmissions have a park/neutral position relay that prevents the vehicles from being started if the gear selector is not in the P (Park) or N (Neutral) position.

Before troubleshooting the starter, make sure the battery is fully charged and the battery cables and ground connections are free of corrosion and in good condition. Troubleshooting information for the starting system appears in **Table c**.

> ***NOTE —***
> *Starter cranking speed is affected by engine oil viscosity, especially in cold weather. Make sure the correct oil is in the engine. See* **0 Maintenance.**

Specification

- Starter rating
  - AEG engine . . . . 1.0 KW (1.34 hp)
  - ALH engine . . . . 1.8 KW (2.41 hp)

Table c. Starter System Troubleshooting

Symptom	Probable cause	Corrective action
1. Starter does not operate when ignition switch is turned to START	a. Ignition switch or wire leading from ignition switch to solenoid faulty (less than 8 volts to solenoid)	a. Test for voltage at terminal 50 of solenoid with ignition at START. If not at least 8 volts, test for voltage at terminal 50 of ignition switch with switch at START. Replace ignition switch or eliminate open circuit between ignition switch and solenoid.
	b. Automatic transmission Park/Neutral position (PNP) relay faulty	b. Test relay. See **97 Wiring Diagrams, Fuses and Relays** and **37 Automatic Transmission.**
	c. Starter lock-out switch or relay faulty (manual transmission only)	c. Test switch and relay. See **97 Wiring Diagrams, Fuses and Relays.**
2. Starter turns slowly or fails to turn engine	a. Dirty, loose, or corroded starter connections	a. Clean, and tighten connections. If necessary check voltage drop between the battery and the starter as described in **9 Electrical System—General.**
	b. Dirty, loose, or corroded ground strap between engine and body	b. Remove and clean or replace strap
	c. Starter worn or faulty	c. Repair or replace starter
3. Starter operates, but does not turn engine	a. Flywheel or driveplate teeth missing or damaged	a. Replace flywheel or driveplate. See **1 ENGINE.**
	b. Starter drive or armature shaft faulty	b. Repair or replace starter
	c. Solenoid mechanism faulty	c. Replace starter solenoid

Starter, removing and installing

1. Disconnect battery ground (GND) strap from battery negative (-) terminal. See the **Cautions** at the beginning of this repair group regarding battery disconnection.

   NOTE—
   Be sure to have the anti-theft radio code on hand before disconnecting the battery.

2. Remove lower sound absorber (belly pan).

3. Remove coolant hose bracket and starter mounting bolts. See Fig. 10.

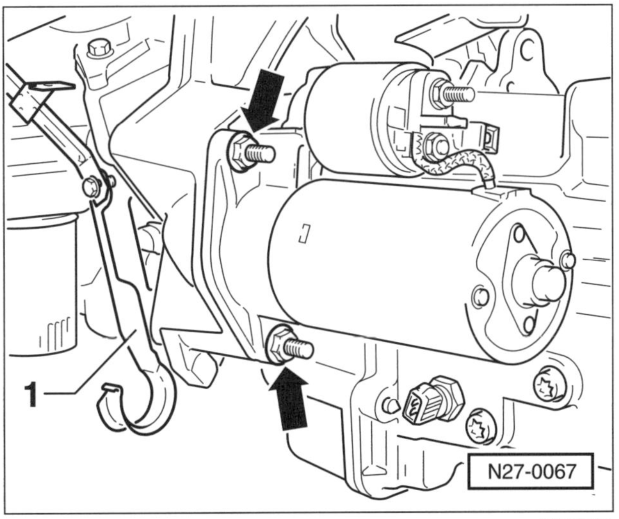

N27-0067

Fig. 10. Remove coolant hose bracket (**1**) and starter mounting bolts (**arrows**)

Tightening torque

- Starter to engine block . . . . 60 Nm (44 ft-lb)

4. Release and disconnect starter switch harness connector (terminal 50) and battery positive (+) cable (terminal 30) from starter. See Fig. 11.

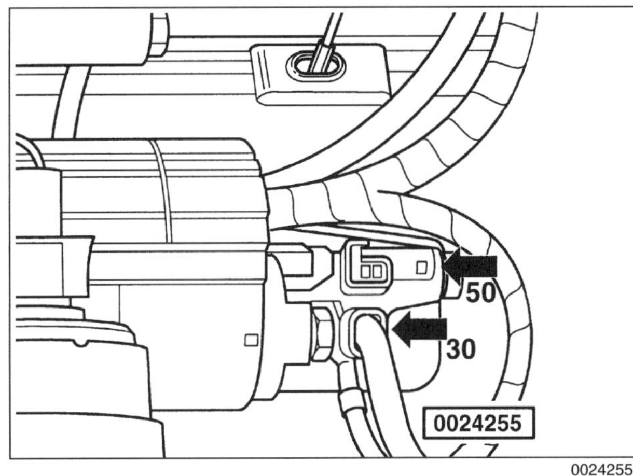

0024255

Fig. 11. Disconnect ignition switch and battery connection at starter (**arrows**, with terminal designations).

Starter terminal designation

- Switched battery positive (+) from ignition/starter switch . . . . terminal 50
- Battery positive (+), hot at all times . . . . . . terminal 30

5. Remove starter. Installation is the reverse of removal. Be sure to install a new starter bushing as described below.

Tightening torque
- Battery positive (+) cable to starter . . .13 Nm (10 ft lb)

Starter bushing, removing and installing

1. Remove starter as describe above.
2. Use Volkswagen special tool VW 228b, or similar to extract the starter bushing. See Fig. 12.

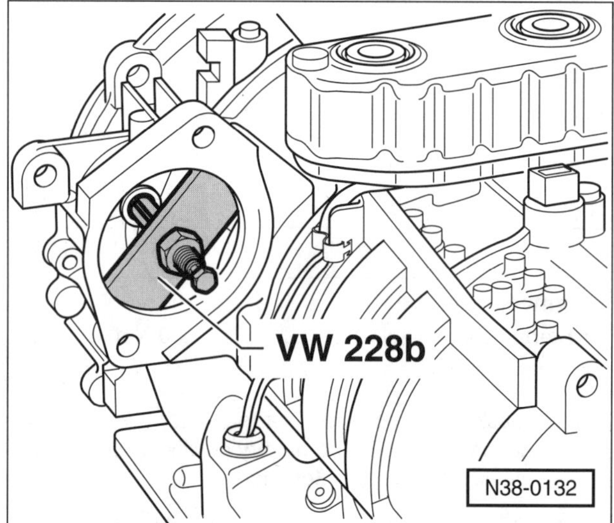

N38-0132
Fig. 12. Starter bushing being removed with special tool VW 228b.

3. Use Volkswagen special tool VW 222a or similar to install a new starter bushing. See Fig. 13.

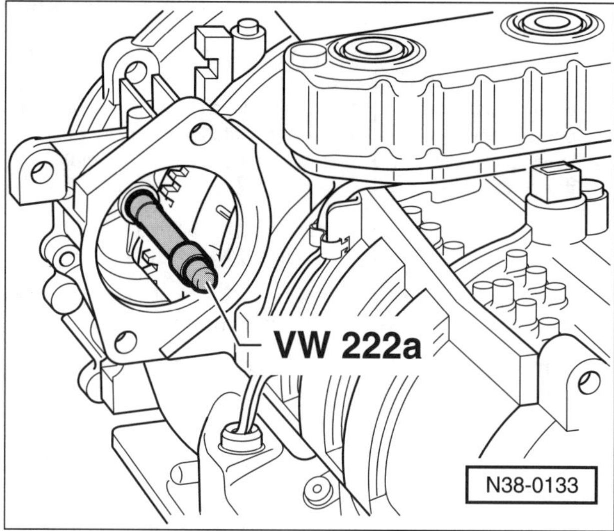

N38-0133
Fig. 13. Starter bushing being installed with special tool VW 222a.

QUALITY REVIEW

When you have finished working under the hood and around other areas of the vehicle, it is advisable to take a moment to quality check or review your work. This helps to insure that the operation or repair has been completed properly with all affected systems functioning within normal parameters. These may include the following:

- Ensure battery is securely mounted, cables connections are tight, and battery cover is in place.

If the battery has been disconnected:

- Re-code radio and set clock.
- Check the operation of power windows and reset as necessary, see **57 Doors**.
- Reset basic setting for automatic transmission (as applicable) using VAG 1551/1552 or a suitable scan tool, or see **37 Automatic Transmission**.
- Reset basic settings for engine and OBD II readiness codes as required using VAG 1551/1552 or a suitable scan tool. See **23 Fuel Injection–Diesel (ALH engine)** or **24 Fuel Injection–Gasoline (AEG engine)** as applicable.

28a Ignition System–Gasoline (AEG engine)

28a

GENERAL

The ignition functions on the AEG gasoline engine are handled by the Motronic engine management system. The Engine Control Module (ECM) computes ignition timing based on inputs from various sensors. Crankshaft speed from the crankshaft position sensor (G28) and engine load from the mass air flow sensor (G70) are the two main inputs used to calculate the basic ignition timing point. The other sensors, including the two knock sensors, are used by the ECM to modify and correct the ignition timing point to changing operating conditions. The distributor-less ignition system features a single double-ended ignition coil pack with power output stage, dual knock sensors, and a camshaft position sensor mounted to the cylinder head behind the camshaft sprocket

> ***WARNING —***
> *Disconnecting the negative (–) battery cable may erase fault codes and basic settings in the engine management and automatic transmission control modules. Some driveability problems may be noticed until the system re-adapts to operating conditions. OBD II readiness codes, which may be required for emissions testing, may also be erased. Convenience electronics (alarm system, interior light control, power locks, mirrors, and windows) will need to be re-set using a VAG 1551/1552 or equivalent scan tool.*

NOTE —
AEG engines are equipped with the Bosch Motronic 5.9.2 engine management system which is OBD II compliant. It is recommended that fault diagnosis and troubleshooting be carried out using Volkswagen scan tools VAG 1551 or VAG 1552 or equivalent.

Service precautions

Ignition system service and repair work must be carried out carefully. The ignition system contains sensitive electronic components. To guard against system damage, and for personal and general safety, the following warnings and cautions apply to any ignition system troubleshooting, maintenance or repair work.

> ***WARNING —***
> - *Ignition systems operate in a dangerous voltage range that could prove to be fatal if exposed terminals or live parts are contacted. Use extreme caution when working on a vehicle with the ignition on or the engine running.*
> - *Connect and disconnect ignition system wires, terminal connectors and test equipment leads only while the ignition is off unless specifically instructed otherwise. Do not touch or disconnect any of the high voltage wires from the coil pack or spark plugs while the engine is running or being cranked by the starter.*

Disabling ignition system

If the engine must be turned at starter speed without starting, the ignition system should be disabled to prevent the discharge of dangerously high voltage. This should be done any time repairs or maintenance are performed on the engine with the ignition key on or if the starter needs to be operated without running the engine. The ignition coils are mounted low on the front of the cylinder block behind the secondary air injection pump.

1. Disconnect 4-pin harness connector from ignition coil Power Output Stage. See Fig. 1.

Fig. 1. Ignition coil connector (**arrow**) must be disconnected before cranking engine to prevent dangerous high voltage discharge. Secondary air pump has been removed for clarity.

2. Remove fuse 28 (for fuel pump). See Fig. 2.

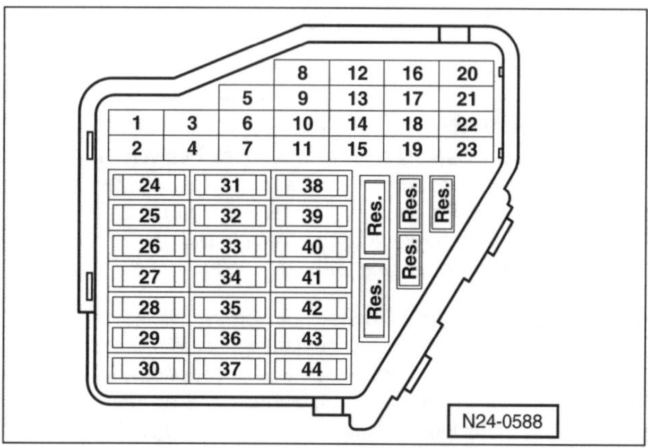

Fig. 2. Fuse 28 **(arrow)** protects fuel pump circuit.

IGNITION SYSTEM TROUBLESHOOTING

Poor driveability may have a variety of causes. The fault may lie with the ignition system, the fuel system, parts of the emission control system, or a combination of the three. Because of the interrelated functions of these systems, it is often difficult to know where to begin looking for problems. For this reason, when troubleshooting always consider these systems in unison, as one major system.

A complete failure of the ignition system to produce spark at the spark plugs is self-evident. For other problems such as rough idle, misfiring, or poor starting the cause may not be so clear. The engine management system has a built in diagnostic circuit that monitors the ignition system components and detects and stores system faults. Before troubleshooting the ignition system, always check for diagnostic trouble codes (DTCs) using a suitable scan tool such as VAG 1551/1552 or equivalent

> ***NOTE —***
> *Continued operation of the engine with a misfire will result in serious damage to the catalytic converter.*

Quick-check of ignition system

The first step in troubleshooting a no-start condition is to determine whether the problem is caused by the ignition system or some other system, such as a fuel delivery problem. This is done by checking that the spark plugs are firing. If no spark is present, a more detailed testing of the ignition system is necessary.

To make the check, turn the ignition off and remove a spark plug wire from a spark plug. Connect to the plug wire to a known good spark plug. Position the plug so that the outer electrode is grounded on the engine. For accurate test results, the battery should be fully charged.

> ***CAUTION —***
> *Never let the spark plug gap (between electrode and ground) exceed 5 mm (0.20 in.) when checking for a spark, as the power output stage may be damaged. Always ground the plug on the engine when checking for spark.*

While a helper actuates the starter, look and listen for a spark at the plug. A bright blue spark indicates a healthy ignition system. If there is no spark, visually ensure that the engine speed sensor plug is connected properly and that the speed sensor is secured into the mount in the cylinder block. If the above inspection reveals no obvious defects, then test the ignition coil output stage and the ignition coil as described later.

> ***WARNING —***
> - *Do not hold the spark plug or its connector during the test, even if using insulated pliers.*
> - *If ignition system failure is not the problem, the engine may start during this test. Be prepared to switch the ignition off immediately. Running the engine with a spark plug wire disconnected may damage the catalytic converter.*

Specification
- Ignition firing order, (AEG engine) 1-3-4-2

IGNITION SYSTEM COMPONENTS

The ignition system of the AEG engine requires little or no periodic maintenance due to the distributor-less nature of its design. Most of the components are monitored by the engine management system and a failure will cause a fault (DTC) to be stored in the engine control module. Engine misfiring can even result in a DTC being stored due to the potential for damage to the catalytic converter. Fig. 3 shows the various ignition system components.

Ignition system components, overview

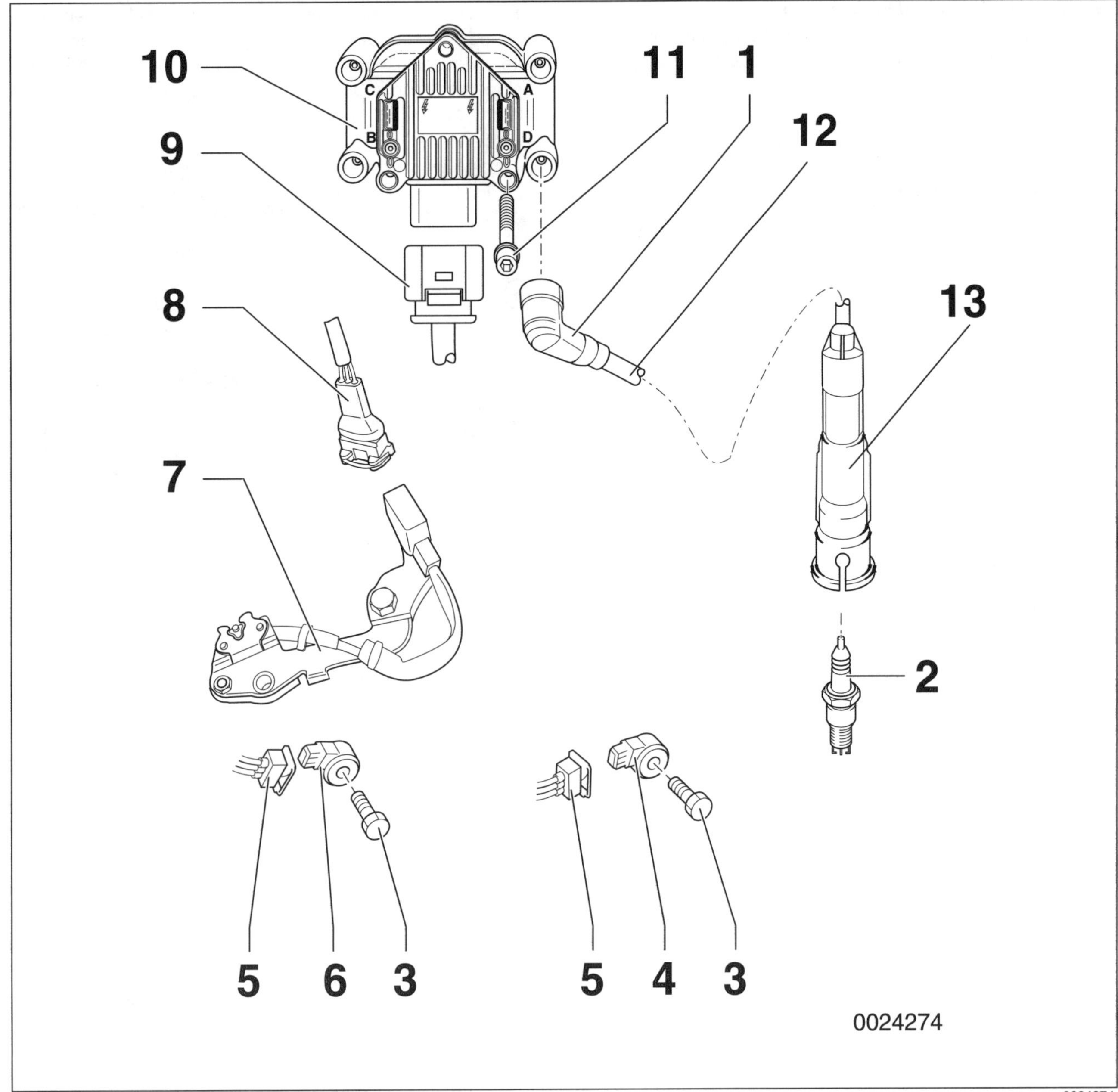

Fig. 3. Primary and secondary ignition system components of the AEG engine.

1. **Ignition coil connector**
   - RF suppressor
   - Resistance: 1000Ω
2. **Spark plug**
   - Tighten to 30 Nm (22 ft lb)
   - Remove and install with 5/8 spark plug socket
3. **Bolt**
   - Tighten to 20 Nm (15 ft-lb)
   - Tightening torque influences knock sensor function
4. **Knock sensor 1 (G61)**
   - Sensor and connector terminals are gold-plated
5. **3-pin harness connectors**
   - Terminals gold plated
   - Black for knock sensor 1 (G61)
   - Brown for knock sensor 2 (G66)
6. **Knock sensor 2 (G66)**
   - Sensor and connector terminals are gold-plated

(continued from previous page)

7. **Camshaft position sensor (G40)**
   - Mounted on cylinder head behind camshaft sprocket
   - Shutter wheel (rotor) mounted on camshaft sprocket
8. **3-pin harness connector**
   - Black
   - For camshaft position sensor (G40)
9. **5-pin harness connector**
   - Black
10. **Ignition coils N, N128**
    - With power output stage (N122)
    - Marked for ignition cables:
    - A = Cylinder 1
    - B = Cylinder 2
    - C = Cylinder 3
    - D = Cylinder 4
11. **Bolt**
    - Tighten to 10 Nm (7 ft lb)
12. **Spark plug wire**
    - Individual lengths for each cylinder
    - Remove with special tool 3277
    - Do not pull on wire
    - Ignition coil and spark plug connectors integral with wire
13. **Spark plug connector**
    - RF suppressor
    - Resistance 5000Ω

Spark plugs, removing and installing

Spark plugs are generally replaced during scheduled maintenance services. Due to the design of the combustion chambers and the shape of the cylinder head, spark plug replacement can easily be accomplished without removal of the intake manifold. See Fig. 4.

Fig. 4. Spark plug wires shown with upper section of intake manifold removed for clarity. Note that spark plugs for cylinders **1** and **2** are angled to the left and that spark plugs for cylinders **3** and **4** are angled to the right.

1. Remove the upper engine cover.
2. Remove the spark plug wire from cylinder no. 1 with a suitable tool such as VW special tool 3277. Do not pull on the wire.

   NOTE —
   It may be necessary to unplug the injector wire and gently turn the injector in the mounts for access.

3. Remove the spark plug with a 5/8 in. (16 mm) spark plug socket and an extension.
4. Check gap on new spark plug and install, re-install injector wire and plug wire.

Specifications

- Spark Plugs-Long Life
  Original equipment number. 101-000-033-AA
  Manufacturers number . . . . .NGK BKUR 6 ET-10
- Gap. . . . . .0.9 to 1.1 mm (.035 to .043 in)
- Tightening torque . . . . 30 Nm (22 ft-lb)

---

5. Repeat for each remaining cylinder.
6. Install upper engine cover.
7. Be sure to quality check your work, see **Quality Review** at the end of this repair group.

Ignition cables

Ignition cables suppress radio frequency (RF) interference through the use of resistors built in to the ends.

1. Disconnect 4-pin harness connector from ignition coil Power Output Stage. See Fig. 1.

2. Disconnect spark plug wire from spark plug.

3. Disconnect spark plug wire from ignition coil.

4. Measure resistance of spark plug wires.

Specification
- Spark plug wire with connectors . .4000 to 6000 ohms

Camshaft position sensor

A camshaft position sensor is mounted to the front of the cylinder head behind the camshaft drive sprocket. See Fig. 5.

Fig. 5. Camshaft position sensor **(arrow)** behind camshaft drive sprocket on cylinder head.

A shutter wheel or rotor is permanently mounted on the camshaft drive sprocket. See Fig. 6.

Fig. 6. Shutter wheel **(arrow)** on inside of camshaft drive sprocket.

Ignition coil and power output stage, testing

Two double-ended ignition coils are mounted in a common housing together with an power output stage. The power output stage takes the low power signal from the ECM and boosts it to a level usable by the ignition coils. The signal to fire a spark plug results in both spark plugs on that particular coil firing at the same time. One spark is "wasted" by the un-used cylinder because it occurs at a time when it is not needed. The other simultaneous spark is used to fire the mixture in the normal manner. The un-used spark causes no additional wear on the spark plug because it occurs at a time when there is minimal heat and pressure on the plug. The power output stage cannot be directly tested, but the signal from the ECM along with power and ground can be easily tested. The ignition coil can also be checked.

1. Remove 4-pin harness connector from ignition coil power output stage as shown earlier. See Fig. 1.

2. Connect a voltmeter to disconnected connector at terminals 2 and 4. See Fig. 7.

3. Switch on ignition and read voltage. If voltage is present, proceed to next step. If no voltage is present, check for breaks or open circuits in the wiring, **see 97 Wiring Diagrams, Fuses and Relays.**

Specification
- Voltage supply
  power output stage. . . . . 11.5 Volts minimum

4. Switch off ignition.

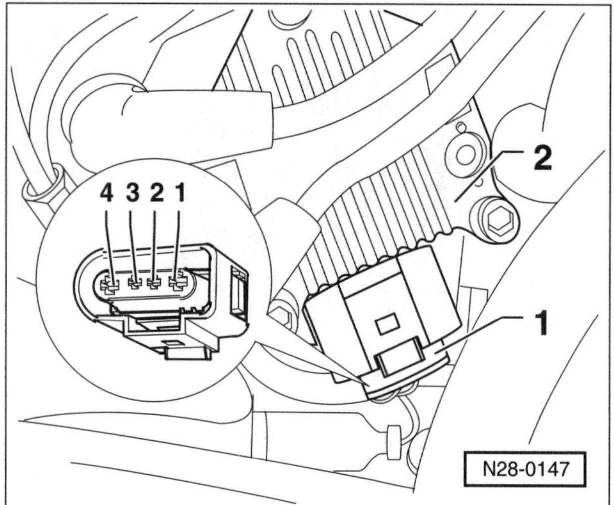

N28-0147

Fig. 7. Disconnected 4-pin harness connector to power output stage. Connect voltmeter between pins 2 and 4.

5. Remove fuse 32 (for fuel injectors) as shown earlier. See Fig. 2.

6. Connect an LED test light only (such as VAG 1527B) to the disconnected connector at terminals 2 and 4.

7. Operate starter and check for a signal from the ECM. LED test light must flicker.

8. Repeat steps 6 and 7 with the LED test light in terminals 3 and 4.
   - If LED test light flickers, signal from ECM is good and ignition coil with power output stage should be replaced.
   - If test light does not flicker, check for break in wiring, **see 97 Wiring Diagrams, Fuses and Relays.** If no faults are found, check ECM for DTCs with a suitable scan tool.

> ***CAUTION —***
> - *Use a high-quality digital automotive multimeter and an LED test light to make the tests. An analog (swing-needle) meter and conventional test light should not be used as they can permanently damage electronic components.*
> - *Always connect and disconnect the ECM connector and meter probes with the ignition off to avoid damage to electronic components.*

The secondary (high voltage) side of the ignition coil can also be checked with an ohmmeter.

1. Label and disconnect spark plug wires from coil terminals.

2. Connect an accurate ohmmeter between terminals 3 and 2 and again between 1 and 4. See Fig. 8.

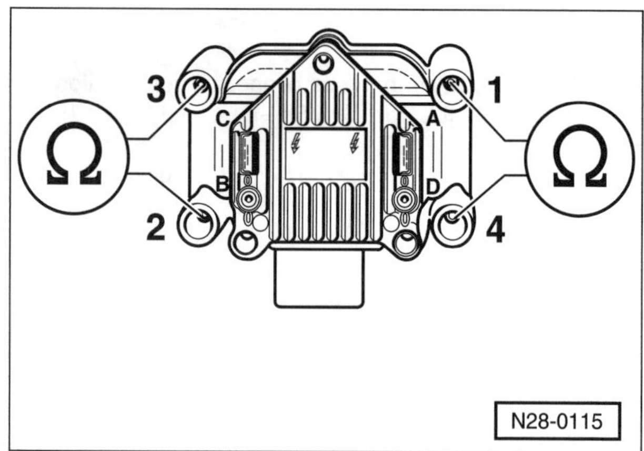

N28-0115

Fig. 8. Connect an ohmmeter to ignition coil terminals as shown. Resistance should be within specification. Open circuits and short circuits to ground are not acceptable.

Specification
- Ignition coil secondary resistance at 20°C (68°F) . . . . 4000 to 6000 ohms

3. Reconnect all terminals disconnected for testing and replace all parts removed. Install new components as needed. Be sure to quality check your work, see **Quality Review** at the end of this repair group

NOTE —
- *Ignition coils and Power output stages are a combined unit.*
- *Ignition coil primary resistance cannot be measured.*

QUALITY REVIEW

When you have finished working under the hood and around other areas of the vehicle, it is advisable to take a moment to quality check or review your work. This helps to insure that the operation or repair has been completed properly with all affected systems functioning within normal parameters. These may include the following:

- Ensure that all harness connectors that were removed are securely snapped into place and that all seals in the terminal housing are in place.
- Ensure that all cable ties and clips that were removed as part of the repair are replaced.
- Make sure that all other components involved in the repair are positioned correctly and function properly.
- Make sure that all tools, shop cloths, fender covers and protective tapes are removed before closing the hood.

28b Ignition System–Diesel (ALH engine)

GENERAL

The ignition system of a diesel engine is based on heat generated by the compression of air in the cylinder. Fuel is injected into this hot air at a precise time to obtain ignition and the exact time is varied by the injection pump to obtain ignition advance. Diesel engines are therefore said to be compression-ignition engines. As a result of this design, diesel engines do not require spark plugs and their associated components. A cold diesel engine can be difficult to start, however, because the compression heat generated is quickly dissipated into the surrounding structure leaving the combustion chamber too cold to support combustion. Extra heat is required to overcome this cold starting limitation. Volkswagen ALH diesel engines use glow plugs to provide the additional heat required during a cold start.

> ***CAUTION —***
> *Disconnecting the negative (–) battery cable may erase fault codes and basic settings in the engine management and automatic transmission control modules. Some driveability problems may be noticed until the system re-adapts to operating conditions. OBD II readiness codes, which may be required for emissions testing, may also be erased. Convenience electronics (alarm system, interior light control, power locks, mirrors, and windows) may need to be re-set using a VAG 1551/1552 or equivalent scan tool.*

NOTE —
The TDI engine management system found on ALH engines has a built in diagnostic circuit that detects and stores a limited number of system faults related to the glow plug system. These faults are known as Diagnostic Trouble Codes (DTCs). It is recommended that fault diagnosis and troubleshooting be carried out using the special Volkswagen scan tool VAG 1551/1552 or equivalent.

Service precautions

Ignition system service and repair work must be carried out carefully. The ignition system contains sensitive electronic components. To guard against system damage, and for general safety, the following warnings apply to any ignition system troubleshooting, maintenance or repair work.

> ***WARNING —***
> *Glow plug systems operate at high current levels. For this reason, always insure that electrical connections that have been disturbed during testing are properly secured when done.*

> ***CAUTION —***
> *Disconnecting engine management components with the key in the "on" position during some procedures will cause diagnostic trouble codes to be stored in the engine control module. Erasing these DTCs and resetting the readiness code will require Volkswagen scan tool VAG 1551/1552 or equivalent.*

Diesel Glow Plug System

The TDI diesel engine uses four glow plugs. Because of the TDI combustion chamber design, the glow plugs are installed in a vertical manner and are fitted with push-on electrical connectors similar to spark plug connectors. The glow plugs assist combustion during cold starts by providing additional heat for ignition. Due to the efficiency of the TDI engine design, the additional heat that the glow plugs provide is not needed until temperatures drop to approximately 48°F (9°C). This function is known as preglow. In addition to preglowing, the glow plugs will continue to operate after the engine is started. This is known as afterglowing and is used to reduce engine noise, improve idle quality and reduce hydrocarbon emissions. The afterglow function is enabled after every start, both hot and cold until the specified time has expired or the engine speed exceeds 2,500 rpm.

The glow plug system is controlled by the Engine Control Module (ECM) and the Engine Coolant Temperature (ECT) sensor. The period of preglow depends on the temperature of the engine coolant as determined by the ECT. A dash mounted indicator light signals the driver that preglowing is operating. See Fig. 1. Preglowing is not linked to operation of the driver's door as in some earlier Volkswagen diesel systems.

> ***WARNING —***
> *Disconnecting engine management components for this procedure will cause diagnostic trouble codes to be stored in the engine control module. Erasing these DTCs and resetting the readiness code will require Volkswagen scan tool VAG 1551/1552 or equivalent.*

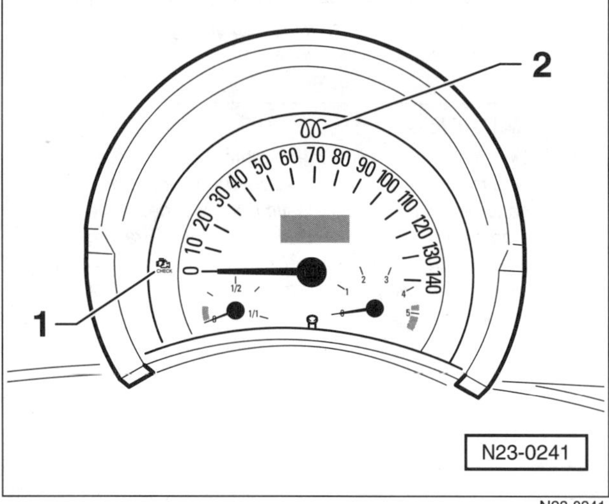

N23-0241

Fig. 1. Glow plug warning light (**2**) and Malfunction indicator light (**1**) on instrument cluster.

NOTE —

- *For more information on troubleshooting diesel cold starting problems, see* **23 Fuel Injection—Diesel (ALH engine)**.
- *See* **97 Wiring Diagrams, Fuses and Relays** *for a complete wiring diagram of the glow plug electrical circuits.*

Testing and replacing glow plugs

Basic checks of the glow plug system are similar to earlier diesel systems.

1. Remove upper engine cover.
2. Disconnect the harness connector from the Engine Coolant Temperature (ECT) sensor. See Fig. 2.

NOTE —
Disconnecting the ECT harness connector simulates a cold engine when the ignition key is switched on.

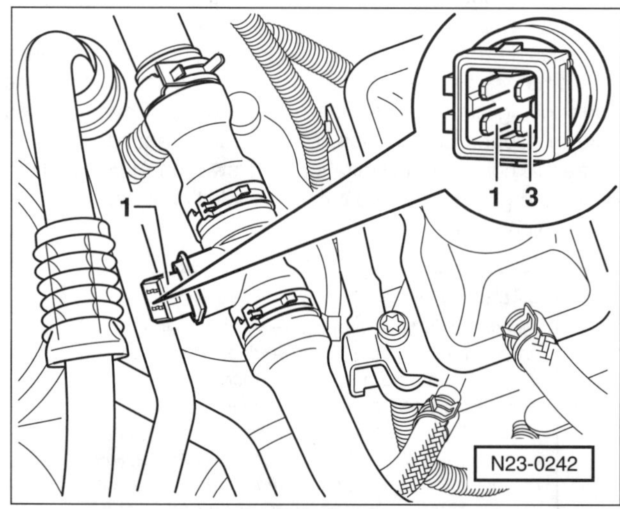

N23-0242

Fig. 2. Engine coolant temperature sensor (**1**) in the upper radiator hose. Disconnecting the harness connector simulates a cold engine and operates the glow plugs for the maximum length of time.

3. Disconnect the bus connector from the glow plugs by gently pulling it off. See Fig. 3.
4. Connect an accurate voltmeter between the bus connector for cylinder #1 and ground.
5. Turn on the key and observe battery voltage. Voltage should be present for approximately 20 seconds.
6. Repeat for remaining cylinders.
7. If no voltage is present, check glow plug fuses, see **97 Wiring Diagrams, Fuses and Relays.**

Fig. 3. Glow plug bus connector (**1**) shown attached to each glow plug (**arrows**).

> ***NOTE —***
> *Glow plug fuses are located in the fuse holder on the battery cover.*

8. If voltage is present, switch off ignition.

9. Connect a suitable test light to battery positive and touch the other end to the disconnected terminal on the glow plug. See Fig. 4. The low resistance of the glow plug will cause the test light to light up if the glow plug is good.

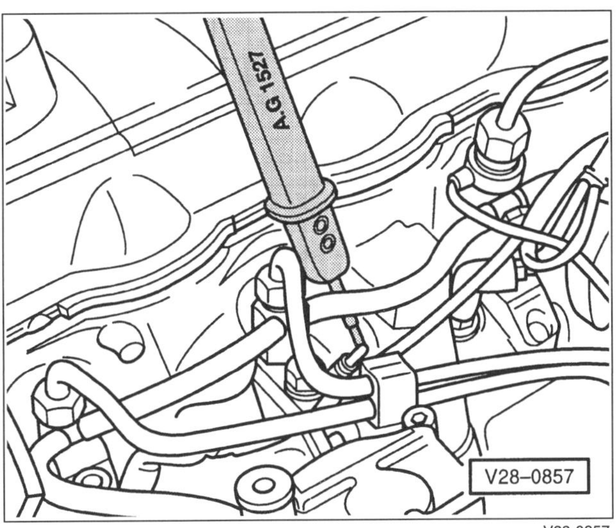

Fig. 4. A test light with one terminal connected to the battery and the other terminal touching glow plug #2. The test light will light if the glow plug is good.

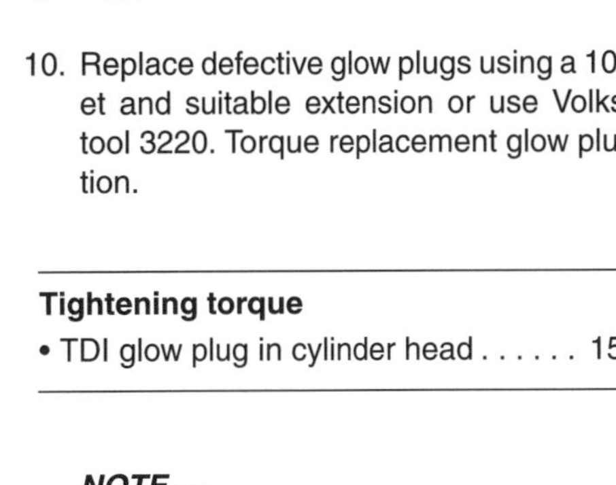

10. Replace defective glow plugs using a 10mm deep socket and suitable extension or use Volkswagen special tool 3220. Torque replacement glow plugs to specification.

Tightening torque
- TDI glow plug in cylinder head . . . . . . 15 Nm (11 ft-lb)

> ***NOTE —***
> *Advanced testing of the glow plug system requires the use of Volkswagen scan tool VAG 1551 or 1552 or equivalent.*

COOLANT GLOW PLUGS/AUXILIARY HEATER

Because of its outstanding efficiency, the ALH TDI engine develops very little waste heat. In certain circumstances, there may not be sufficient heat with manual transmission vehicles to warm the vehicle interior. An auxiliary heater consisting of three coolant glow plugs is installed to provide additional coolant heat when needed. See Fig. 5. The coolant glow plugs are operated by two coolant glow plug relays which are controlled by the engine control module. The coolant glow plug relays are located under the hood.

The coolant glow plugs can operate in one of three modes depending on the amount of heat required. Coolant glow plug #1 can operate separately, or #2 and #3 together, or all three at the same time.

Testing and replacing coolant glow plugs

Complete testing of the coolant glow plug system requires the use of Volkswagen scan tool VAG 1551/1552 or equivalent. The coolant glow plugs can, however, be checked in the same manner as the glow plugs used for starting.

1. Visually inspect the fuse for the coolant glow plugs in the fuse holder on battery cover. See **97 Wiring Diagrams, Fuses and Relays**. Replace as required.

2. Pull the electrical connectors off of the coolant glow plugs. See Fig. 5.

3. Connect a suitable test light to battery positive and touch the other end to the end of the coolant glow plug. The light will glow due to the low resistance of the glow plug if it is good. Faulty coolant glow plugs will not light the test light.

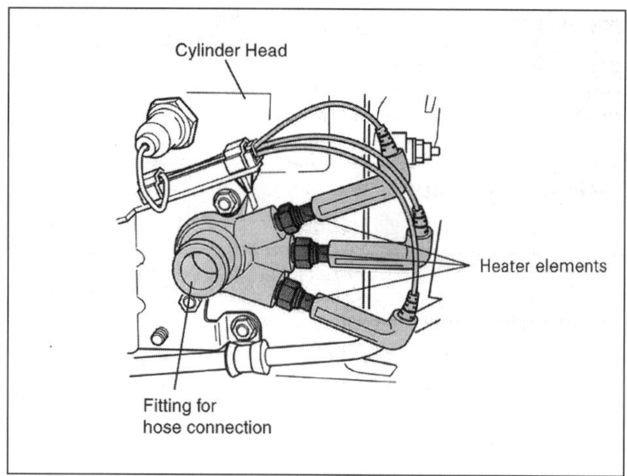

Fig. 5. Coolant glow plugs (**heater elements**) in the flange on the end of the cylinder head with the electrical connectors in place. Early version shown, ALH engine is similar.

4. If defective glow plugs are found, unscrew and replace as necessary. Coolant will leak out of the system when unscrewing glow plugs.

> ***WARNING —***
> - *Hot coolant can scald and result in serious personal injury. Do not work on the cooling system until it has fully cooled.*
> - *At normal operating temperature the cooling system is pressurized. Allow the system to cool as long as possible before opening—a minimum of an hour—then release the cap very slowly to allow safe release of pressure.*
> - *Releasing the cooling system pressure lowers the coolant's boiling point, and the coolant may boil suddenly. Use heavy gloves and wear eye and face protection to guard against scalding.*
> - *Use extreme care when working at or near the cooling fan when the engine is hot. The fan can come on at any time–even if the ignition key is off.*
> - *Use extreme care when draining and disposing of engine coolant. Coolant is poisonous and lethal. Children and pets are attracted to coolant because of its sweet smell and taste. See a doctor or veterinarian immediately if any amount of coolant is ingested.*

5. Re-attach electrical connectors and replace lost coolant.

QUALITY REVIEW

When you have finished working under the hood and around other areas of the vehicle, it is advisable to take a moment to quality check or review your work. This helps to insure that the operation or repair has been completed properly with all affected systems functioning within normal parameters. These may include the following:

- Make sure that there are no fuel or coolant leaks.
- Make sure that the coolant is at the proper concentration and level.
- Ensure that all cable ties and hose clamps that were removed as part of the repair are replaced.
- Be sure to wipe up any diesel fuel spills using soap and water as necessary, especially on any rubber or painted surfaces.
- Make sure that all components involved in the repair are positioned correctly and function properly.
- Make sure that the radiator fans cycles properly.
- Make sure all tools and shop cloths are removed.
- Clean grease and fingerprints from painted surfaces, steering wheel and shifter.
- Road test vehicle as required to confirm proper cooling system operation.

30 Clutch

GENERAL

Servicing of the clutch assembly requires that the transmission be removed from the engine. Special tools and equipment are required to remove the transmission and service the clutch. See **34 Manual Transmission** for transmission removal procedures. Read the procedures through to fully understand the scope and nature of the job.

> ***WARNING —***
> - *The cars covered by this manual use an airbag system that automatically deploys the airbags in the event of a frontal or side impact. The airbags are inflated by an explosive device. Handled improperly or without adequate safeguards, the system can be very dangerous. Special precautions must be observed prior to any work at or near the steering wheel or steering column, including the pedal assembly. See* **69 Seatbelts, Airbags**.
> - *To guard against personal injury or airbag system failure, only trained Volkswagen service technicians should test, disassemble or service the airbag system.*

> ***CAUTION —***
> *Disconnecting the negative (–) battery cable may erase fault codes and basic settings in the engine management and automatic transmission control modules. Some driveability problems may be noticed until the system re-adapts to operating conditions. OBD II readiness codes, which may be required for emissions testing, may also be erased. Convenience electronics (alarm system, interior light control, power locks, mirrors, and windows) may need to be re-set using a VAG 1551/1552 or equivalent scan tool.*

CLUTCH ACTUATING MECHANISM

Fig. 1 shows components of the pedal assembly. Be sure to lubricate all bearings and friction surfaces with poly-resin grease (VW Part No. G 052 142 A2). Always replace self-locking nuts and circlips during repairs.

> ***CAUTION —***
> *Before working on the pedal cluster, obtain anti-theft radio code and then disconnect battery ground (–) strap.*

Pedal Cluster, assembly

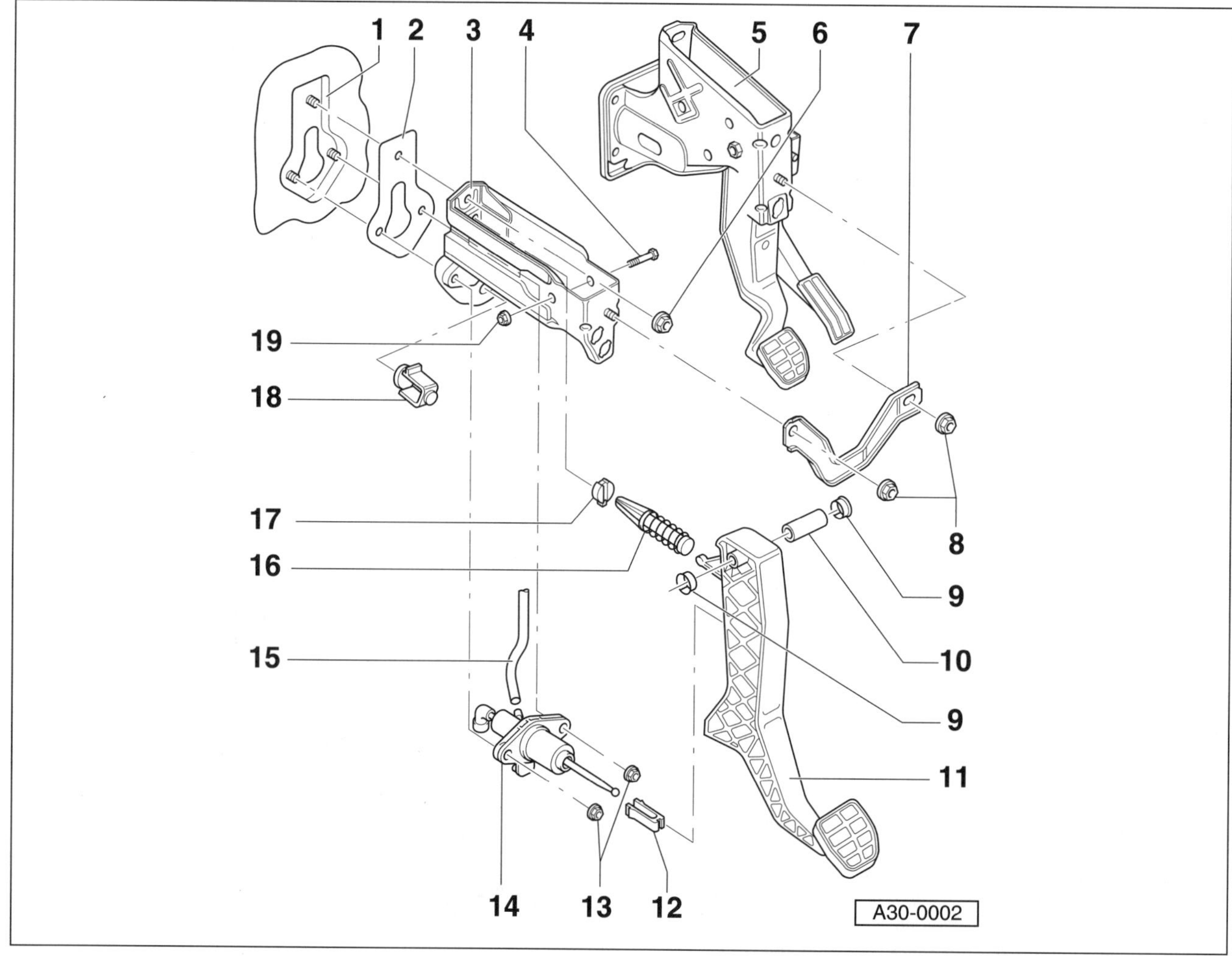

A30-0002

Fig. 1. Clutch actuating mechanism and related parts.

1. **Bulkhead**
2. **Seal**
    - Always replace
3. **Clutch pedal mounting bracket**
4. **Pivot bolt**
5. **Accelerator and brake pedal mounting bracket**
6. **Self-locking nut**
    - Tighten to 25 Nm (18 ft-lb)
    - Always replace
7. **Connecting plate**
8. **Self-locking nut**
    - Tighten to 25 Nm (18 ft-lb)
    - Always replace
9. **Bushing**
10. **Fulcrum pin**
11. **Clutch pedal**
12. **Retainer**
13. **Self-locking nut**
    - Tighten to 25 Nm (18 ft-lb)
    - Always replace
14. **Clutch master cylinder**
15. **Supply hose**
    - from brake fluid reservoir
16. **Over-center spring**
17. **Over-center spring mount**
    - See Clutch master cylinder, removing and installing
18. **Clutch pedal stop**
19. **Self-locking nut**
    - Tighten to 25 Nm (18 ft-lb)
    - Always replace

Over-center spring, removing and installing

1. Remove drivers side lower trim to access pedal assembly.

2. Compress clutch pedal over-center spring by pushing clutch pedal forward, then install retaining clamp. See Fig. 2.

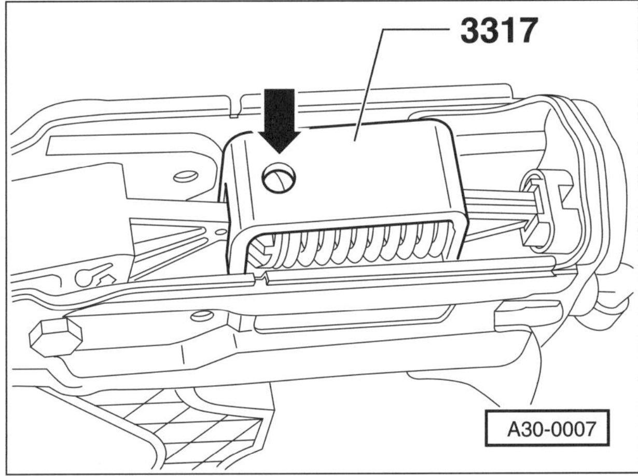

A30-0007

Fig. 2. Volkswagen special tool 3317 (retaining clamp) installed to compress clutch pedal over-center spring. Hole (**arrow**) should be positioned toward clutch pedal.

3. Move clutch pedal to rest position and remove over-center spring with retaining clamp still installed.

4. To install over-center spring, push clutch pedal forward and insert over-center spring (with retaining clamp) into rear mount. Operate clutch pedal until spring seats on mounting lug of clutch pedal. See Fig. 3.

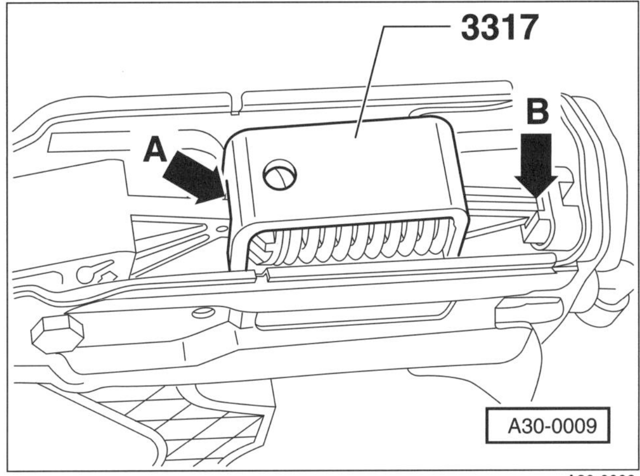

A30-0009

Fig. 3. Install over-center spring with retaining clamp into rear mount (**B**), then operate clutch pedal to seat mounting lug (**A**).

5. Remove retaining clamp while moving clutch pedal to rest position.

Clutch pedal, removing and installing

1. Remove clutch pedal over-center spring.

2. Separate clutch pedal from clutch master cylinder, see **Clutch master cylinder, removing and installing**.

3. Push master cylinder operating rod toward engine compartment onto stop.

4. Remove clutch pedal mounting bolt. See items 4 and 19 in Fig. 1, given earlier.

5. Install clutch pedal and mounting bolt.

6. Install clutch over-center spring as described earlier.

7. Ensure that retainer is correctly installed on master cylinder operating rod. Press clutch pedal down to engage retainer. See Fig. 4.

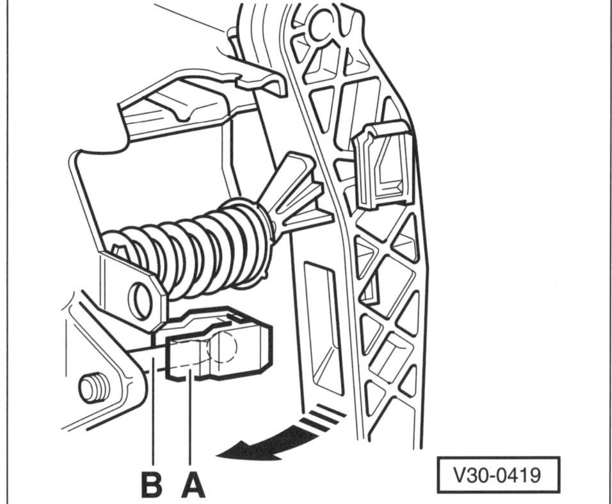

V30-0419

Fig. 4. Retainer (**A**) must be installed on the master cylinder operating rod (**B**). Press clutch in direction of **arrow** to engage retainer.

8. Remove over-center spring retaining clamp.

9. Bleed clutch system if hydraulic fluid level is below MIN marking on brake fluid reservoir. See **Clutch hydraulic system, bleeding**.

10. Fill brake fluid reservoir up to MAX marking.

Specification

- Hydraulic (brake) fluid. .DOT 4

---

11. Be sure to quality check your work, see **Quality Review** at the end of this repair group.

CLUTCH HYDRAULIC SYSTEM

Clutch hydraulic system, assembly

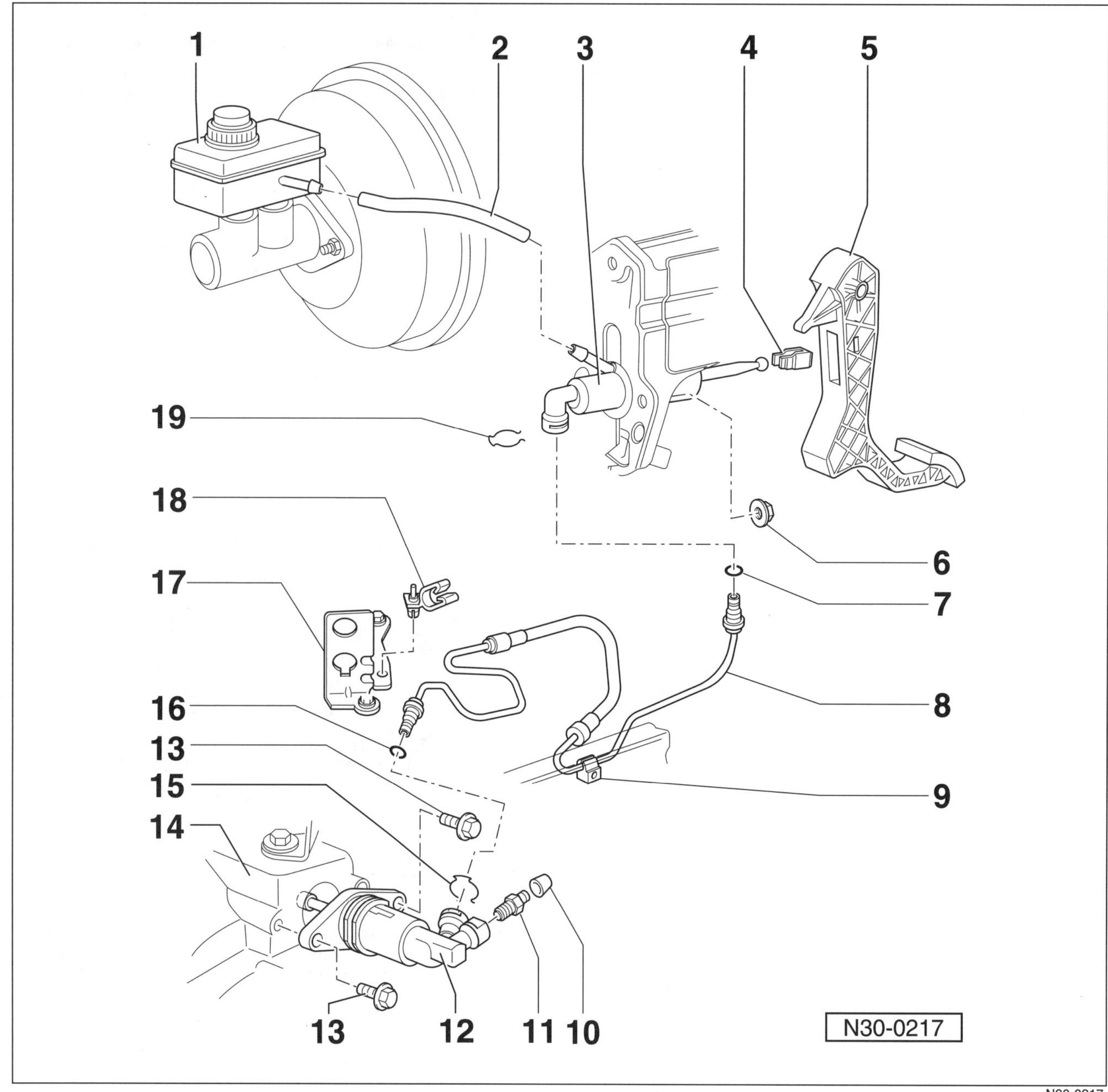

N30-0217

Fig. 5. Clutch hydraulic system and related components.

1. **Hydraulic (brake) fluid reservoir**
2. **Supply hose**
3. **Master cylinder**
4. **Retainer**
   - Replace only with master cylinder removed
   - Removing **see** Ⓐ, installing **see** Ⓑ
5. **Clutch pedal**
6. **Self-locking nut**
   - Tighten to 25 Nm (18 ft-lb)
   - Always replace
7. **O-ring**
   - Coat with hydraulic fluid
   - Pull into line/hose connection
8. **Hydraulic line/hose assembly**

(continued from previous page)

9. Bracket
- Attached to body

10. Dust cap

11. Bleeder valve

12. Slave cylinder
- Remove the following components before removing slave cylinder (see **34 Manual Transmission**):
  - gear selector cable from selector lever
  - relay lever and actuating arm for gate selector cable
- After installing adjust gear selector mechanism

13. Bolt
- Tighten to 25 Nm (18 ft-lb)
- With collar

14. Transmission

15. Clip

16. O-ring
- Coat with hydraulic fluid
- Pull onto/hose connection

17. Cable support bracket

18. Hose bracket
- Secure to cable support bracket

19. Clip

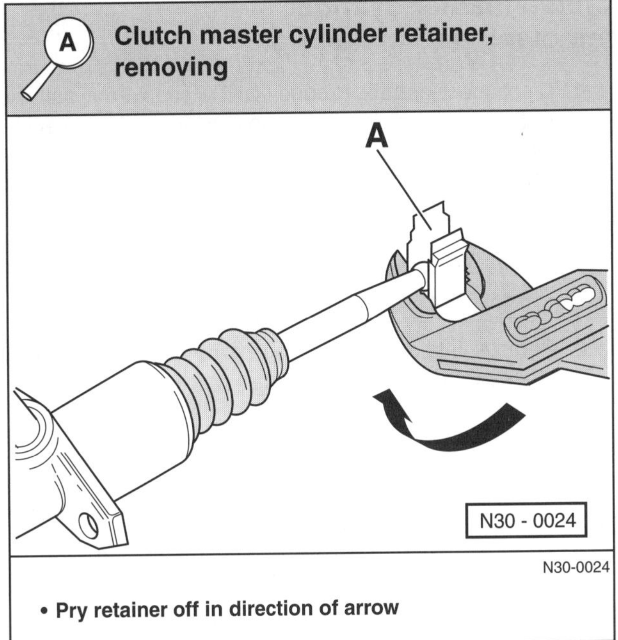

(A) Clutch master cylinder retainer, removing

- **Pry retainer off in direction of arrow**

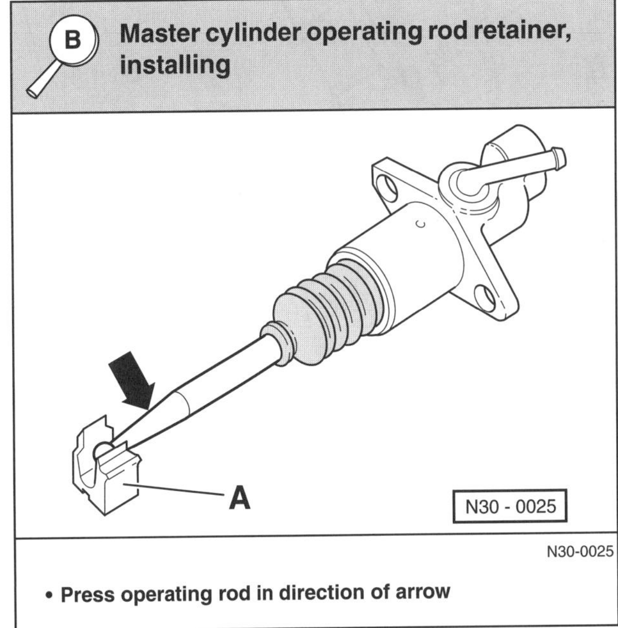

(B) Master cylinder operating rod retainer, installing

- **Press operating rod in direction of arrow**

Clutch master cylinder, removing and installing

1. Disconnect battery ground (GND) strap from battery negative (–) terminal. See the **Cautions** at the beginning of this repair group regarding battery disconnection.

   NOTE —

   Be sure to have the anti-theft radio code on hand before disconnecting the battery.

2. Remove intake air hose and harness connector from Mass Air Flow (MAF) sensor.

3. Remove mounting bolts for air cleaner and lift out air cleaner assembly. See Fig. 6.

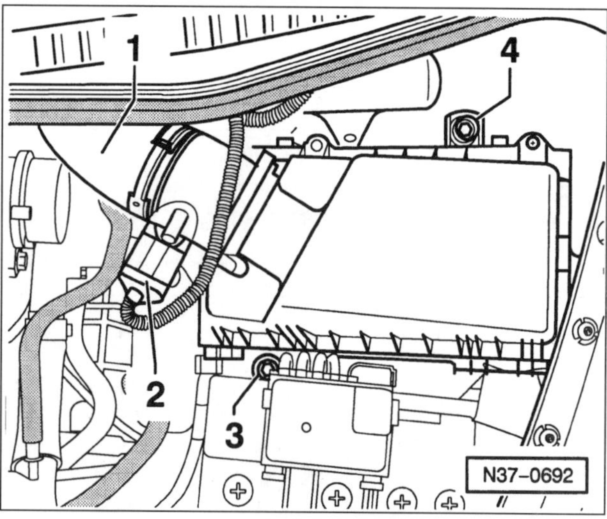

N37-0692

Fig. 6. Remove intake air hose (**1**), harness connector (**2**), and air cleaner mounting bolts (**3**, **4**).

4. Remove hydraulic fluid reservoir supply hose and seal end to prevent dirt or moisture from entering.

5. Pry out clip for brake line and hose assembly at master cylinder. See Fig. 7.

6. Disconnect hydraulic brake line/hose assembly from rear of master cylinder and seal end to prevent dirt or moisture from entering.

7. Remove drivers side lower trim to access pedal assembly.

8. Remove connecting plate for clutch and brake pedal assemblies, then remove self-locking nuts for clutch pedal mounting bracket. See Fig. 8.

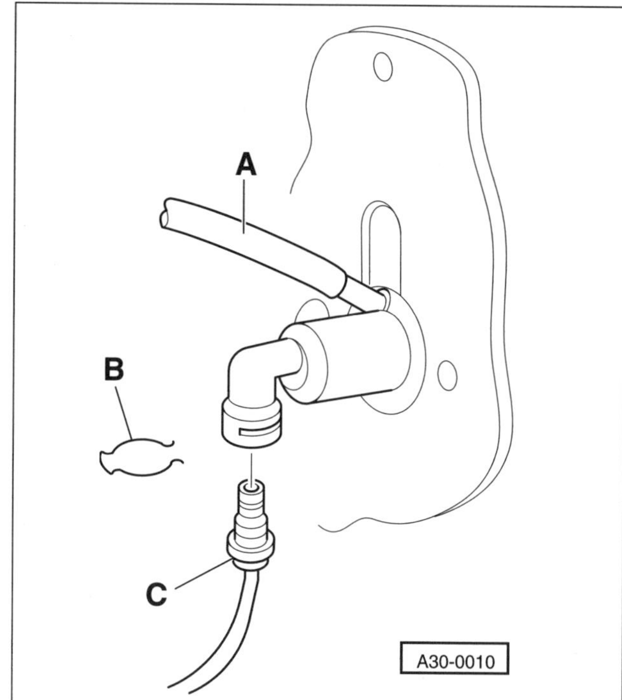

A30-0010

Fig. 7. Remove supply hose (**A**), pry out clip (**B**) and remove brake line/hose assembly (**C**).

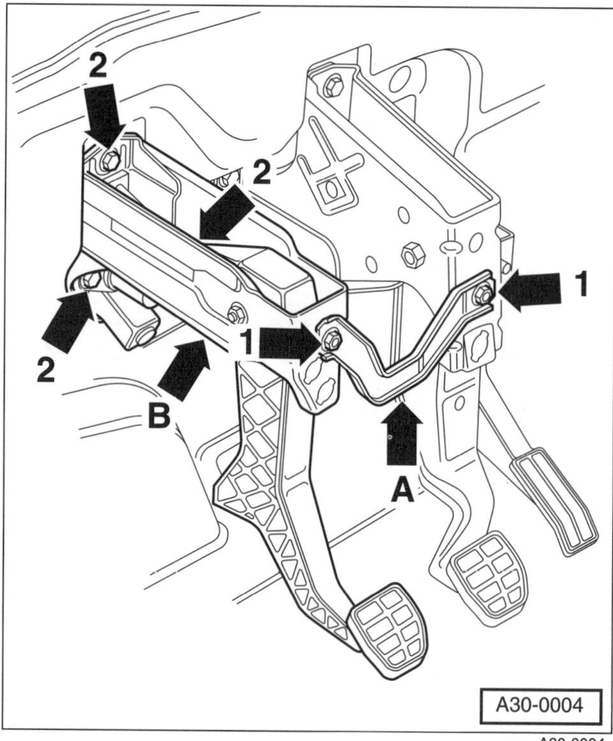

A30-0004

Fig. 8. Remove nuts (**1**) for connecting plate (**A**) and nuts (**2**) for mounting bracket (**B**). Lower two nuts (**2**) also secure clutch master cylinder to bulkhead.

9. Separate master cylinder operating rod from clutch pedal as follows:
   - Insert Volkswagen special tool 3309 (release tool) in clutch peal cutout with inscription "top/oben" pointing away from clutch pedal.
   - Position Volkswagen special tool 10-208A (valve shim pliers) or similar, in recess on sides of clamp and press clamp together. See Fig. 9.

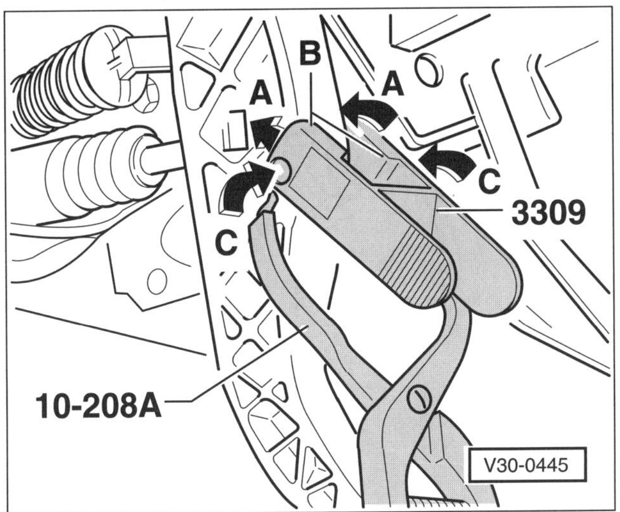

V30-0445

Fig. 9. Volkswagen special tool 3309 positioned in clutch pedal cutout (**A**) with "top/oben" (**B**) pointing away from pedal. Use special pliers 10-208A to press clamp together (**C**).

10. Turn clutch pedal stop counterclockwise and remove. See Fig. 10.

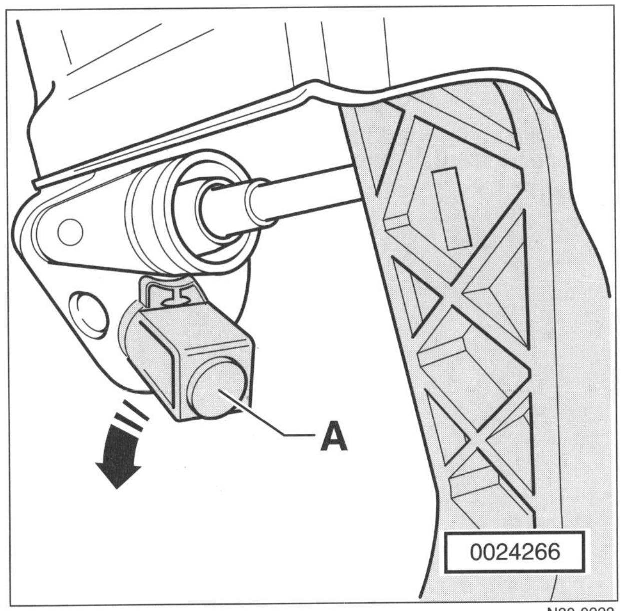

N30-0223

Fig. 10. Turn clutch pedal stop (**A**) in direction of **arrow** and remove.

11. Push master cylinder down onto stop and swing downward out of mounting bracket.

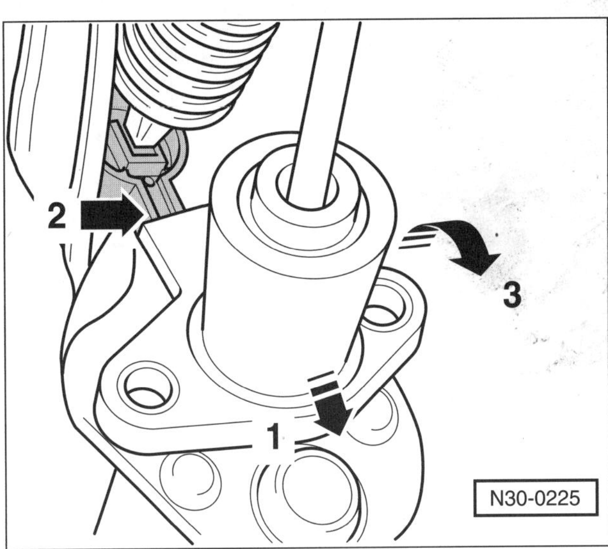

N30-0225

Fig. 11. Remove master cylinder by pushing down (**1**) and swinging downward (**3**).

NOTE —

*The master cylinder must not be blocked in the upper area by the over-center spring mount (**arrow 2** above).*

12. Installation is reverse of removal, noting the following:
    - When installing master cylinder be sure to position clutch pedal retainer properly as shown earlier. See Fig. 4.
    - Position master cylinder behind slave cylinder and install mounting nuts.
    - Install clutch pedal stop with arm pointing towards master cylinder. See Fig. 12.
    - Bleed clutch system after installing master cylinder, see **Clutch hydraulic system, bleeding**.
    - Be sure to quality check your work, see **Quality Review** at the end of this repair group.

Tightening torque

- Clutch master cylinder mounting nuts (always replace) . . . . 25 Nm (18 ft-lb)

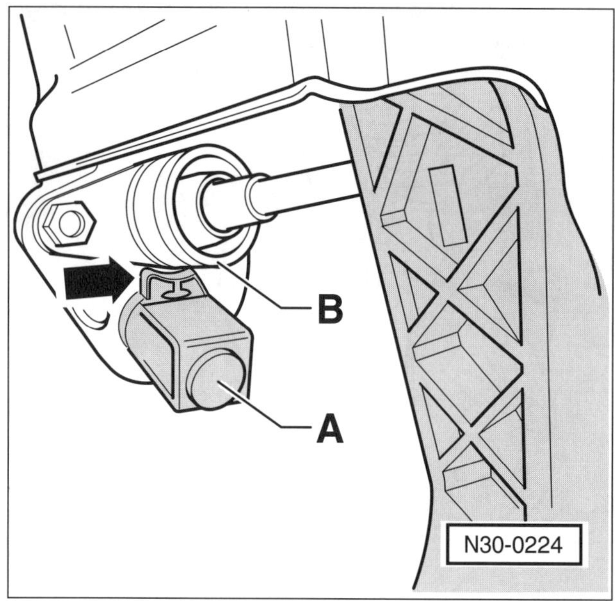

Fig. 12. Clutch pedal stop (**A**) installed with arm (**arrow**) positioned against slave cylinder (**B**).

Clutch hydraulic system, bleeding

Bleed clutch hydraulic system using VAG 1869 or US 1116 brake filling and bleeding unit or equivalent power bleeding equipment.

1. To bleed system, connect approximately 670 mm (26 in.) of bleeder hose to pressure hose fitting on collector bottle of power bleeder.

2. Connect bleeder hose to slave cylinder and open bleeder valve to bleed system. See Fig. 13.

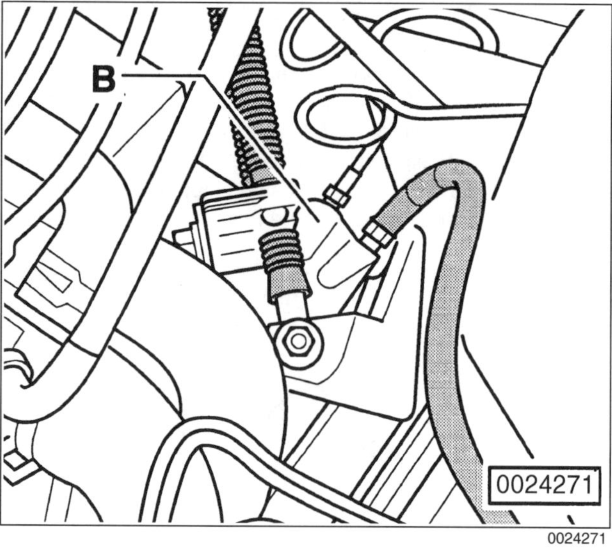

Fig. 13. Connect bleeder hose to slave cylinder (**B**) and open bleeder valve.

3. Depress clutch pedal several times after completing bleeding process.

4. Top off hydraulic fluid in reservoir.

Specification
- Hydraulic (brake) fluid. .DOT 4

CLUTCH RELEASE MECHANISM

Fig. 14 shows the clutch release mechanism components. The clutch slave cylinder can be replaced with the transmission installed in the car. Replacement of the other clutch release components require that the transmission be removed from the car. See **34 Manual Transmission** for transmission removal and replacement procedures.

Clutch release mechanism, assembly

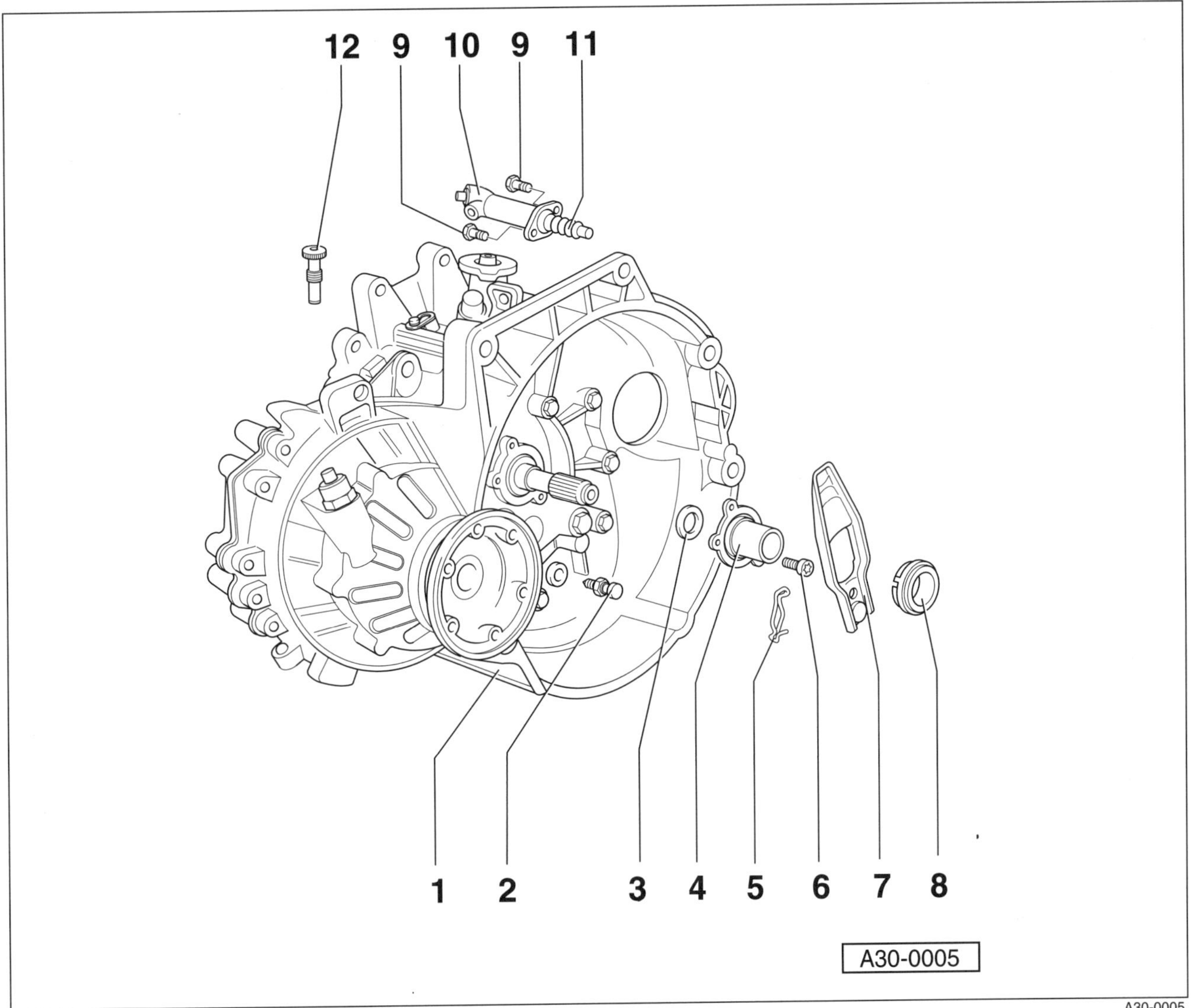

Fig. 14. Clutch release mechanism.

1. **Transmission**
2. **Ball stud**
   - Tighten to 25 Nm (18 ft lb)
   - Lubricate with MoS_2
3. **Input shaft oil seal**
4. **Guide sleeve**
   - With vulcanized O-ring
   - If damaged, replace guide sleeve and O-ring
   - Lubricate guide sleeve in area of release bearing with MoS_2 grease
5. **Retaining spring**
   - Secure to clutch release lever
6. **Bolt**
   - Tighten to 20 Nm (15 ft-lb)
7. **Clutch release lever**
8. **Release bearing**
   - Do not wash bearing out, only wipe
   - Replace noisy bearings
   - Lubricate surfaces which contact release lever with MoS_2 grease
9. **Bolt**
   - Tighten to 20 Nm (15 ft-lb)
10. **Slave cylinder**
11. **Plunger**
    - Grease end of plunger with MoS_2 grease
12. **Assembly bolt**
    - Secures clutch release lever when installing trans.
    - Remove after transmission has been installed
    - An M8 x 35 bolt can be used in place of assembly bolt

CLUTCH, SERVICING (TRANSMISSION REMOVED)

Clutch assembly

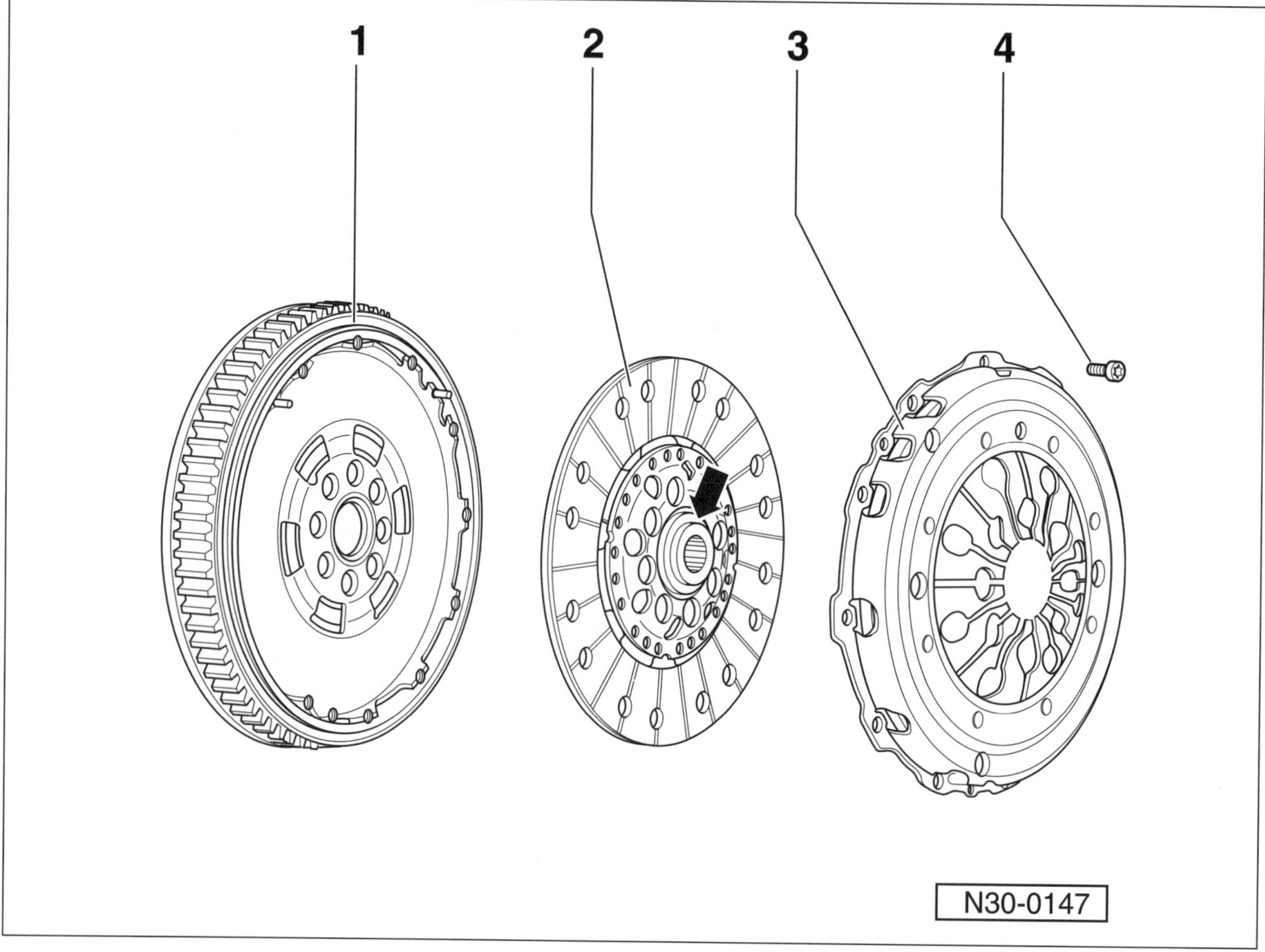

Fig. 15. Clutch assembly.

N30-0147

1. **Flywheel**
   - Make sure centering pins fit tightly
   - Contact surfaces for clutch disc must be free of grooves, oil and grease
   - Removing/installing, see **13 Crankshaft/Cylinder Block**
2. **Clutch disc**
   - Installation position with two-piece flywheel: shorter hub end (**arrow**) points toward pressure plate
   - Installation position with one-piece flywheel: spring cage faces pressure plate
   - Clean and lightly grease splines
   - After light greasing, move clutch plate back and forth on input shaft until hub moves freely on shaft
   - Centering, **see** Ⓐ
3. **Pressure plate**
   - Removing and installing, **see** Ⓐ
   - Clean contact surface only
   - Check ends of diaphragm spring, **see** Ⓑ
4. **Bolt**
   - Select correct flywheel bolt for two- or one-piece flywheel
   - Loosen and tighten gradually and diagonally
   - Two-piece flywheel:
     Tighten to 13 Nm (10 ft-lb)
   - One-piece flywheel:
     Tighten to 20 Nm (15 ft-lb)

NOTE —

- *Replace clutch plates and pressure plates that have damaged or loose rivets.*
- *Select the correct clutch plate and pressure plate according to engine code.*

A Clutch disc, centering
Pressure plate, removing/installing

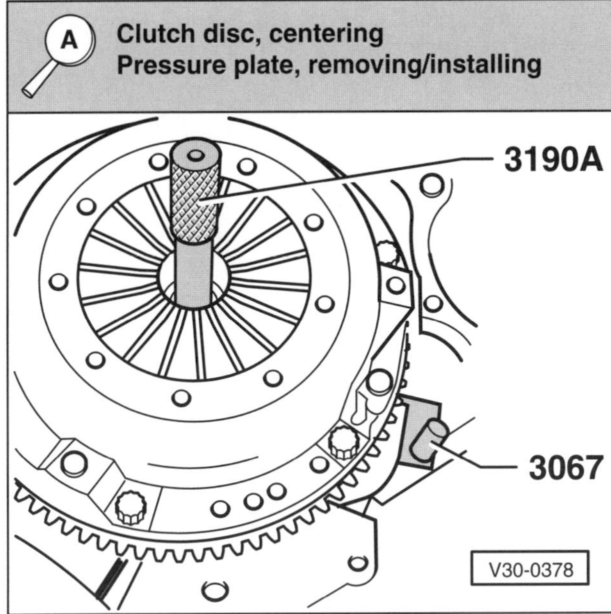

V30-0378

- VW special tool 3190A being used to center clutch disc
- Loosen and tighten bolts gradually and diagonally
- When removing, reverse position of flywheel locking tool (VW 3067 shown)
- Pressure plate contact surface and clutch disc must make full contact with flywheel.

B Diaphragm spring, checking ends

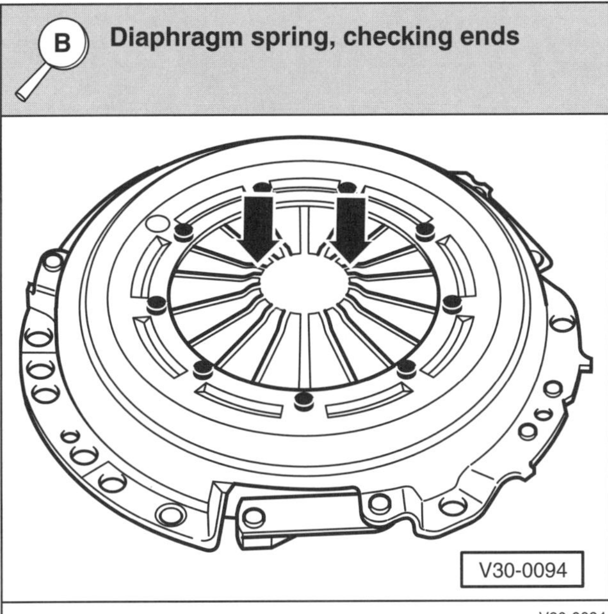

V30-0094

- Check pressure plate diaphragm spring for wear (arrows)
- Maximum wear: up to half of original diaphragm spring thickness

QUALITY REVIEW

When you have finished working under the hood and around other areas of the vehicle, it is advisable to take a moment to quality check or review your work. This helps to insure that the operation or repair has been completed properly with all affected systems functioning within normal parameters. These may include the following:

- Make sure that all components involved in the repair are positioned correctly and function properly.
- Make sure all tools and shop cloths are removed.
- Be sure to top off hydraulic (brake) fluid.
- Be careful not to spill hydraulic fluid as it can damage painted surfaces. Wipe up any spills immediately.
- Check for smooth operation of clutch pedal.
- Before road testing vehicle, confirm that clutch operates properly.
- Road test the vehicle to check operation of clutch and transmission.

34 Manual Transmission

TABLES

34

GENERAL

This repair group covers repair information for the cable-operated gear shift mechanism and the removal and installation of the 02J manual transmission. This repair group does not cover transaxle or transmission teardown and disassembly.

NOTE —
- *For information on drive axles, including drive flange oil seals, see* **39 Differential and Final Drive**.
- *To check manual transmission oil, see* **0 Maintenance**.

CAUTION —
- *Before working on the transmission or gear selector lever mechanism disconnect the negative (–) battery cable.*
- *Disconnecting the negative (–) battery cable may erase fault codes and basic settings in the engine management and automatic transmission control modules. Some driveability problems may be noticed until the system re-adapts to operating conditions. OBD II readiness codes, which may be required for emissions testing, may also be erased. Convenience electronics (alarm system, interior light control, power locks, mirrors, and windows) may need to be re-set using a VAG 1551/1552 or equivalent scan tool.*
- *Be sure to have the anti-theft radio code on hand before disconnecting the battery.*

The close ratio 02J transmission uses a hydraulic clutch release mechanism and a cable operated shift mechanism. **Table a** lists the engine applications, gear ratios, and other data for the various manual transmissions. The transmission code and production number can be found stamped on the transmission case near the shift linkage.

Table a. Manual transmission specifications

Designation		02J	
Code letters		DZQ	DQY
Engine application		2.0L, 115hp (AEG)	1.9L, 90hp (ALH)
Ratio: Z_2:Z_1	Final drive	72:17 = 4.235	61:18 = 3.389
	1st gear	34:9 = 3.778	34:9 = 3.788
	2nd gear	36:17 = 2.118	36:17 = 2.118
	3rd gear	34:25 = 1.360	34:25 = 1.360
	4th gear	35:34 = 1.029	34:35 = 0.971
	5th gear	36:43 = 0.837	34:45 = 0.756
	Reverse gear	18:9 x 36:20 = 3.600	18:9 x 36:20 = 3.600
Lubricant	Capacity	2.0 liters (2.1 qt.)	
	Specification	G50 synthetic oil, SAE 75W/90	
Clutch control		hydraulic	
Clutch disc diameter		215 mm	219 mm
Ratio, overall in top gear		3.545	2.562

GEAR SELECTOR MECHANISM

Fig. 1 shows the gear selector cables and related components. Access to the gear selector mechanism may be difficult without partially removing the exhaust system, see **26 Exhaust System and Emission Controls**.

NOTE —
During reassembly, lubricate all mounting and contact surfaces with Polyuric grease (VW part no. G 052 142 A2). As the final step, adjust the gear selector mechanism, see **Gear selector mechanism, adjusting**.

Gear selector cables, assembly

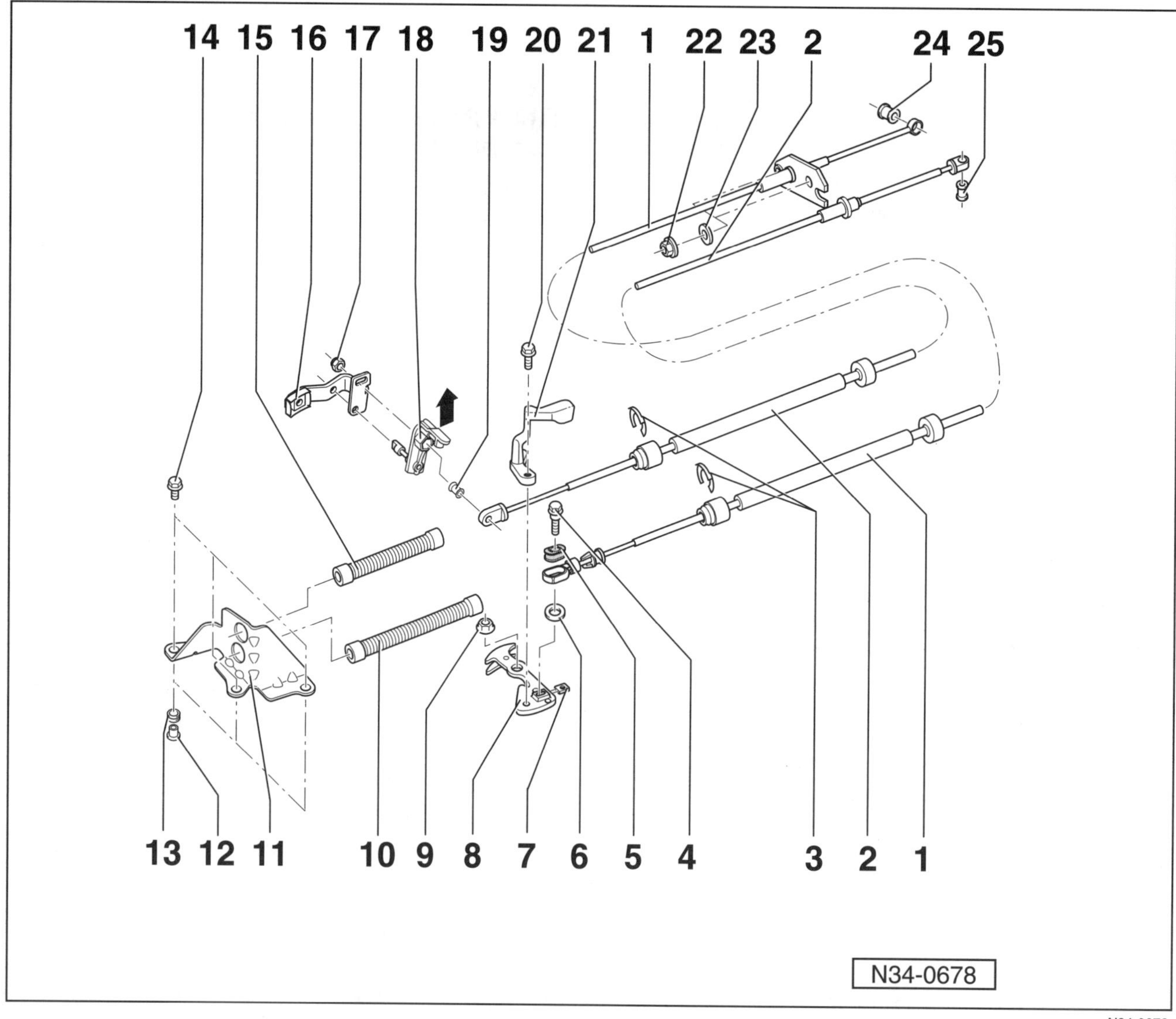

N34-0678

Fig. 1. Shift lever control cable and related parts.

1. **Gear change cable**
   - Installation position, **see** Ⓐ
2. **Gate selector cable**
   - Pull off actuating arm (item 18) by pulling tab in direction of **arrow**
   - Install before installing gear selector cable
   - Installation position, **see** Ⓐ
3. **Circlip**
   - When removing do not damage boot
4. **Bolt**
   - Tighten to 25 Nm (18 ft-lb)
   - With shoulder
   - Gear selector cable to gear change lever
5. **Rubber bushing**
   - For gear change cable to gear selector lever
   - To replace boot press out of end piece
6. **Washer**
   - Install between gear selector cable and selector lever
7. **Square nut**
   - Insert into gear selector lever
8. **Gear selector lever**
   - Only fits in one position
   - After installing adjust gear selector mechanism
   - Installation position **see** Ⓑ

(continued from previous page)

9. **Self-locking nut**
   - Tighten to 25 Nm (18 ft lb)
   - For gear selector lever
10. **Boot**
   - Carefully pull over gear selector cable end piece
   - Use MoS_2 grease
11. **Cable support bracket**
12. **Spacer**
13. **Bushing**
   - Cable support bracket mounting to transmission
14. **Bolt**
   - Tighten to 25 Nm (18 ft-lb)
   - For cable support bracket (item 11)
15. **Boot**
   - Carefully pull over gear selector cable end piece
   - Use MoS_2 grease
16. **Relay lever**
   - Remove before removing clutch controls
   - Installation position **see** (B)
17. **Self-locking nut**
   - Tighten to 15 Nm (11 ft-lb)
   - For relay lever to actuating arm
   - Only loosen to adjust selector mechanism
18. **Actuating arm**
   - With pivot pin to mount relay lever
   - Installation position **see** (B)
19. **Rubber bushing**
   - For gate selector cable to actuating arm
   - Press in and out with a drift
20. **Bolt**
   - Tighten to 25 Nm (18 ft-lb)
   - For balance weight
21. **Balance weight**
   - Remove to adjust selector mechanism
22. **Self-locking nut**
   - Tighten to 15 Nm (11 ft-lb)
   - For selector cable to selector housing
23. **Rubber washer**
24. **Rubber bushing**
   - For gear selector cable/gear change lever
   - Press in and out with a drift
25. **Rubber bushing**
   - For gate selector cable/selector bracket
   - Press in and out with a drift

(A) Gear selector mechanism, installation position

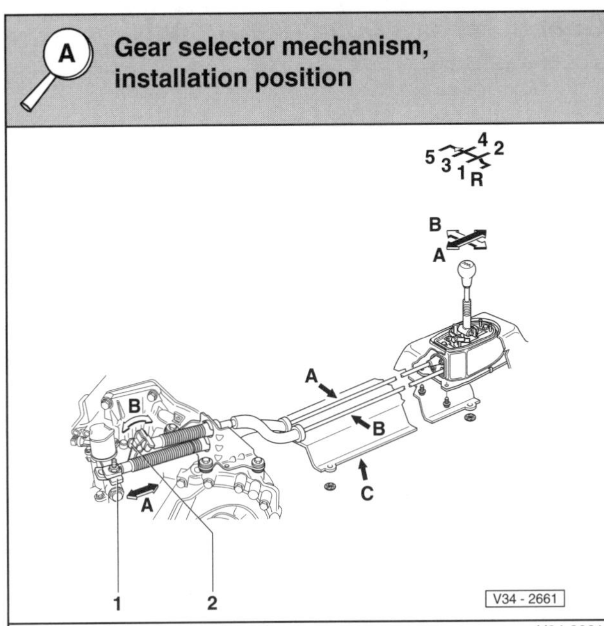

V34-2661

- **Gear change cable (A) controls forward/back travel.**
- **Gear selector cable (B) controls side-to-side travel.**
- **Heat shield (C) holds cables in position.**

(B) Gear selector lever and relay lever, installation position

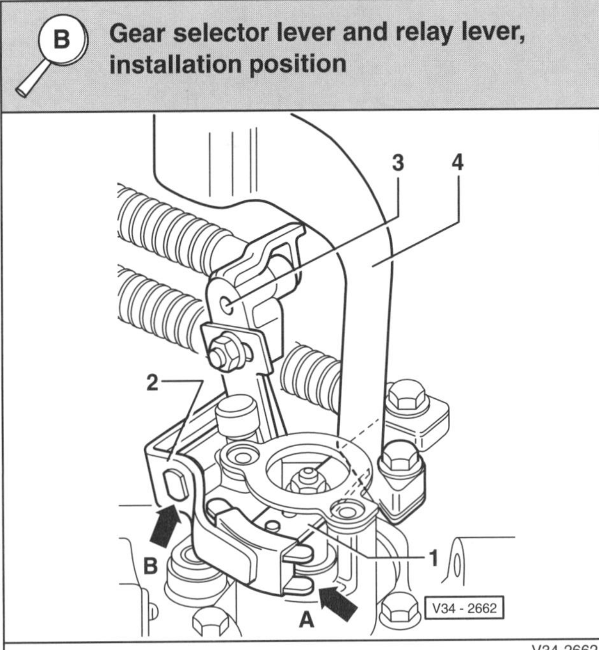

V34-2662

1. **Gear selector lever**
2. **Relay lever**
   - Locates in guide rail of gear shift lever (**arrow A**)
   - Lubricate with MoS_2 grease
3. **Actuating arm**
   - Relay lever only fits in one position (**arrow B**)
4. **Balance weight**
   - Bolt on to gear selector lever

Gear selector housing, assembly

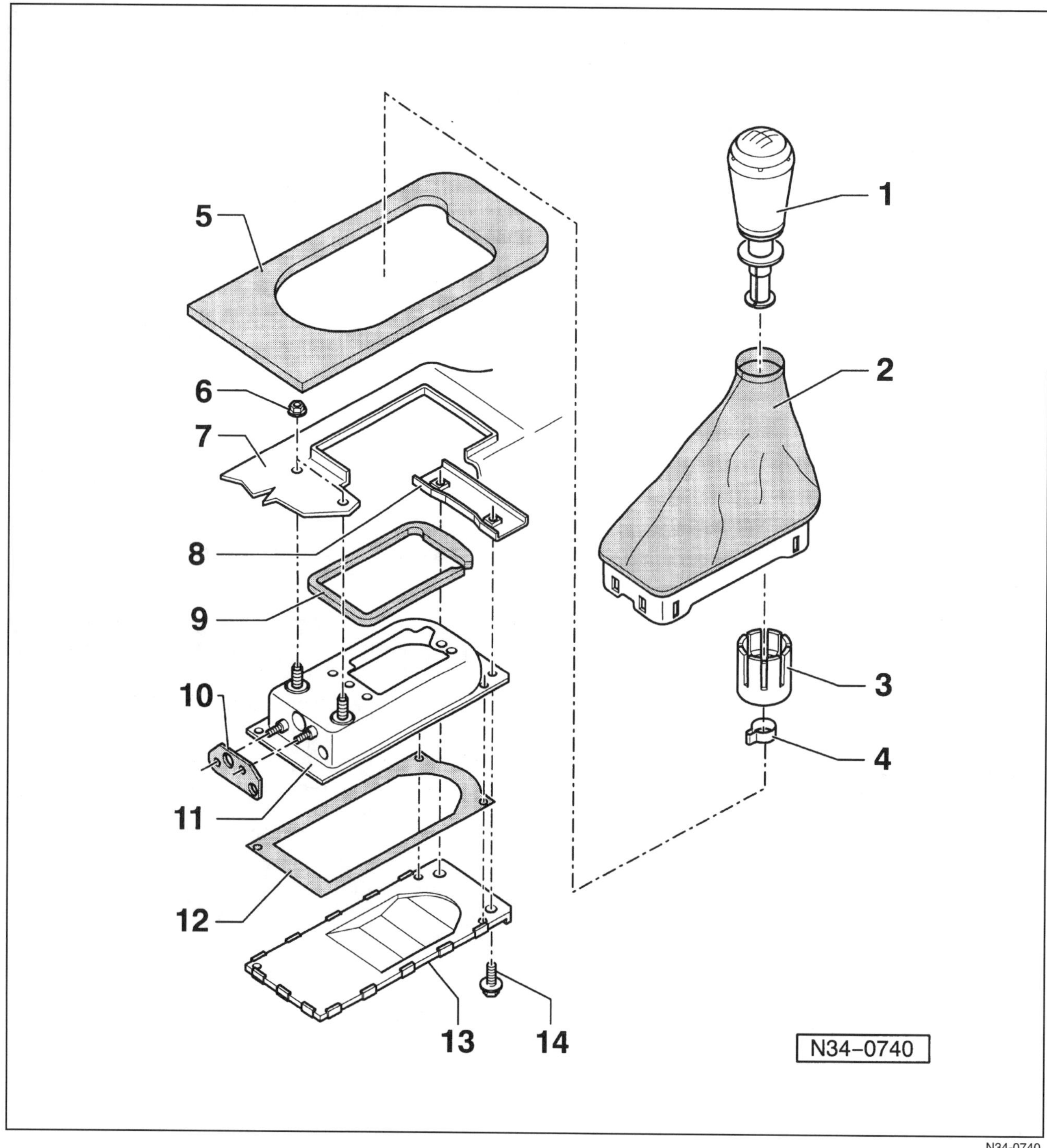

N34-0740

Fig. 2. Gear selector housing and related parts.

1. **Gear lever knob**
2. **Boot with frame**
   - Remove and install together with gear lever knob
   - Separating from gear lever knob, **see** Ⓐ
3. **Clamping sleeve**
4. **Retaining clip**
   - Cut clip to remove gear lever knob from gear lever
5. **Cover**

(continued from previous page)

6. **Nut**
   - Tighten to 25 Nm (18 ft-lb)
7. **Floor panel**
8. **Retainer**
   - For gear lever housing
9. **Gasket**
   - Between gear lever housing and floor
   - Self-adhesive
   - Bond to gear lever housing
10. **Gasket**
    - Between selector cables and gear lever housing
11. **Gear lever housing**
12. **Gasket**
    - Self-adhesive
    - Bond underneath gear lever housing
13. **Cover plate**
14. **Bolt**
    - Tighten to 25 Nm (18 ft-lb)

(A) Gearshift boot, removing and installing from gear lever knob

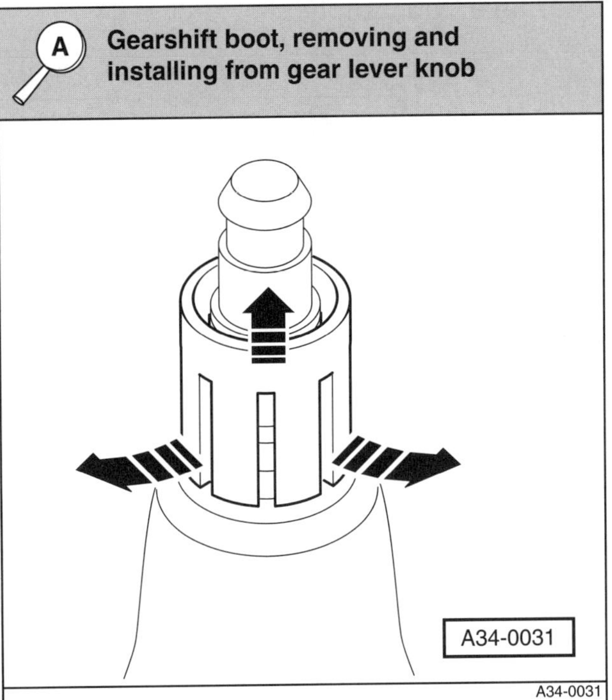

A34-0031

- **Cut retaining clip to remove gear lever knob from gear lever**
- **Turn boot inside out.**
- **Carefully pry clamping sleeve legs with small screw-driver in direction of lower arrows while simultaneously pulling gear lever knob out.**
- **When installing insert gear lever knob in boot.**
- **Push sleeve onto gear lever knob and engage.**
- **Install knob and boot together on gear lever.**

Gear lever, assembly

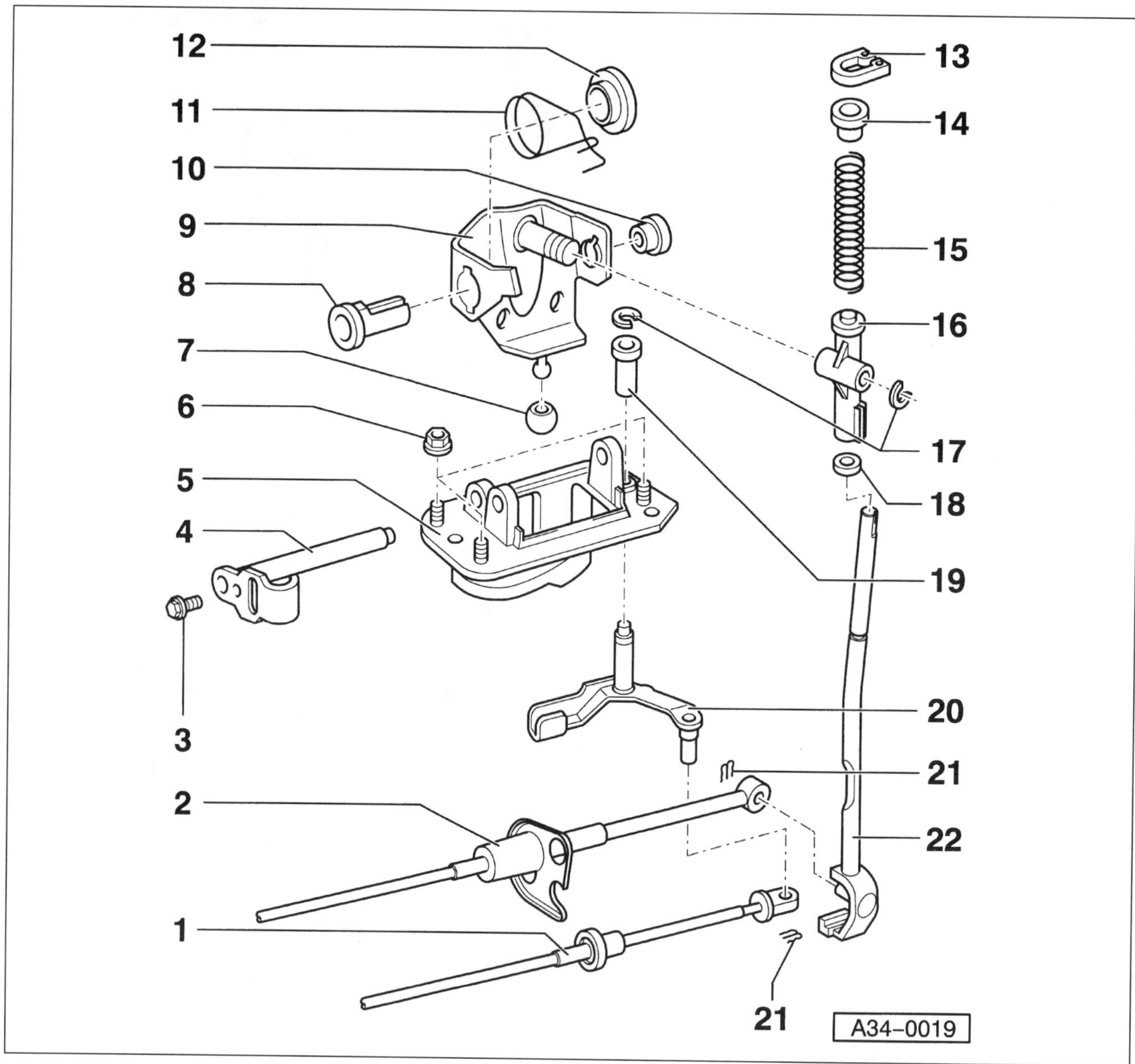

Fig. 3. Gear shift lever and related components.

A34-0019

NOTE —

Lubricate all mountings and sliding surfaces with Polyuric grease (VW part no. G 052 142 A2, or equivalent).

1. **Gate selector cable**
   - On gate selector bracket
2. **Gear selector cable**
   - On gear lever
3. **Bolt**
   - Tighten to 15 Nm (11 ft-lb)
   - For fulcrum pin to mounting plate
4. **Fulcrum pin**
5. **Mounting plate**
6. **Nut**
   - Tighten to 20 Nm (15 ft-lb)
   - For mounting plate to gear lever housing
   - Self-locking
   - Always replace
7. **Cap**
   - Installing, **see** Ⓐ
8. **Bushing**
   - Only fits in one position

(continued from previous page)

9. **Gate selector housing**
   - Install into mounting plate after installing complete gear lever
10. **Bushing**
11. **Spring**
12. **Guide bushing**
    - Position on bushing (item 8)
13. **Circlip**
    - Removing and installing, **see** Ⓒ
14. **Spacer sleeve**
15. **Spring**
16. **Gear lever guide**
17. **Lock plate**
    - Removing, **see** Ⓑ
18. **Damping washer**
19. **Bushing**
    - Only fits in one position
20. **Gate selector bracket**
21. **Spring clip**
22. **Gear lever**

A Gate selector housing cap, installing

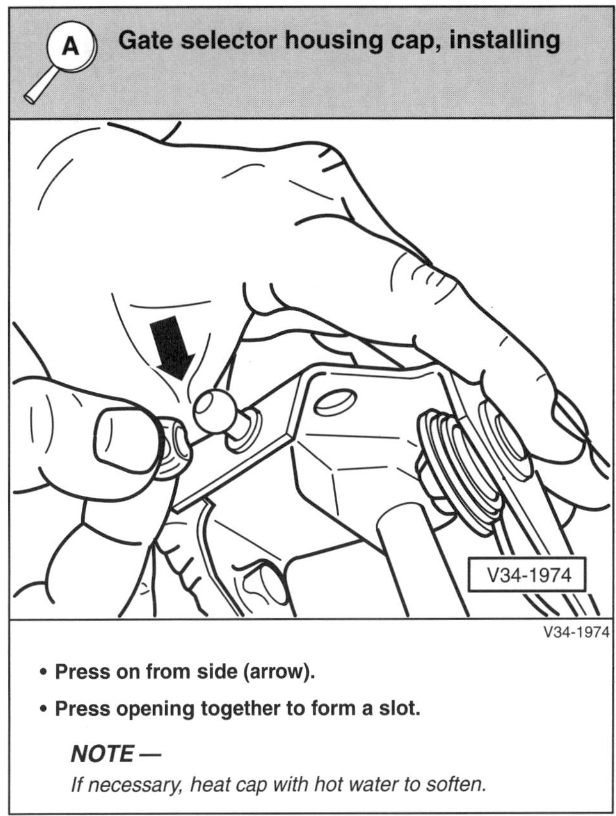

V34-1974

- **Press on from side (arrow).**
- **Press opening together to form a slot.**

NOTE —
If necessary, heat cap with hot water to soften.

B Lock plate for gate selector bracket and gate selector housing, removing

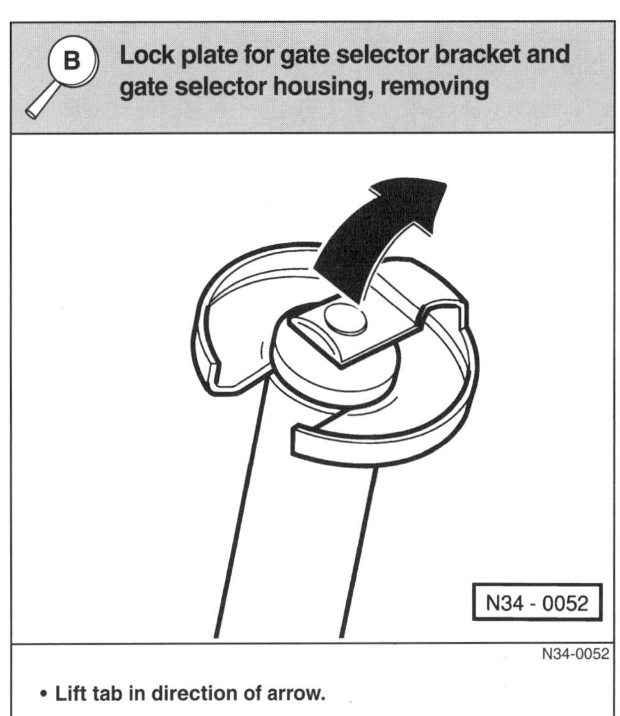

N34-0052

- **Lift tab in direction of arrow.**

C Circlip for gear lever guide, removing

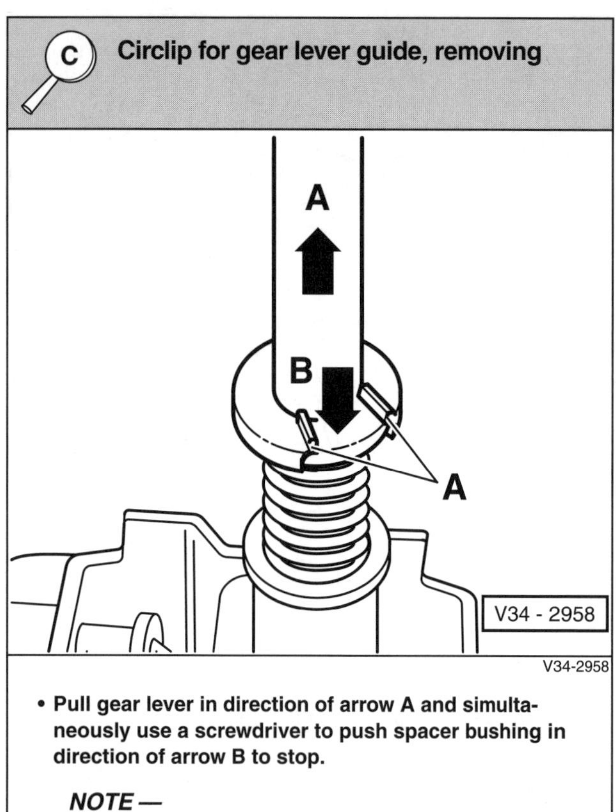

V34-2958

- **Pull gear lever in direction of arrow A and simultaneously use a screwdriver to push spacer bushing in direction of arrow B to stop.**

NOTE —

Do not tilt spacer bushing when pushing down. Carefully release pressure at groove in shift lever for circlip

Gear selector mechanism, adjusting

NOTE —

Special VW tools are required to accurately adjust the shift mechanism. Read the procedure through to determine what tools will be necessary.

1. Place transmission in neutral.
2. Carefully pry boot off center console. See Fig. 4.

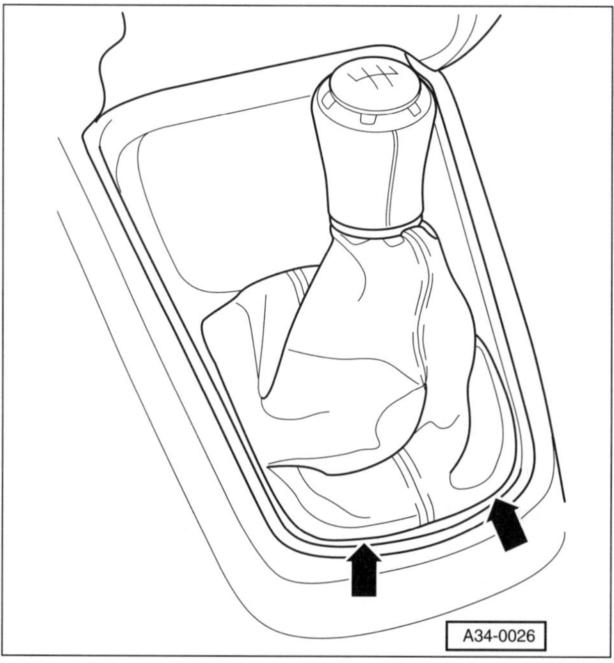

A34-0026

Fig. 4. Pry gear shift boot off at **arrows**.

3. Pull boot to rear off center console.
4. Cut off retaining clip under boot and pull gear lever knob off with boot. See Fig. 5.
5. Remove rubber cover, if installed.
6. Working at the transmission, remove balance weight from shift lever. See Fig. 1, given earlier.

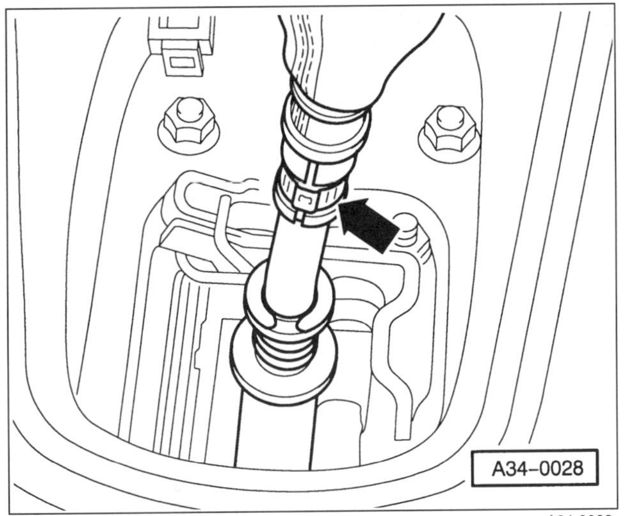

A34-0028

Fig. 5. Cut off retaining clip (**arrow**) for gear shift boot.

7. Loosen bolt and nut for gear selector cables. See Fig. 6. Gear selector cables and actuating arm/gate selector cable should now move freely in elongated holes.

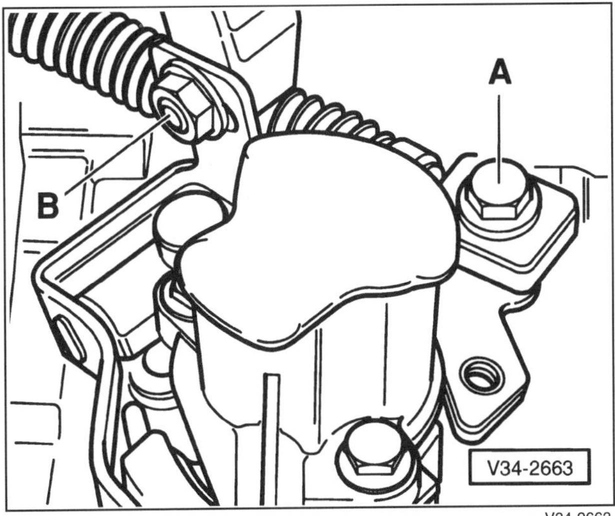

V34-2663

Fig. 6. Gear selector cables mounting bolt (**A**) and nut (**B**).

8. Working in shift lever housing, loosen adjustment bolt. See Fig. 7.

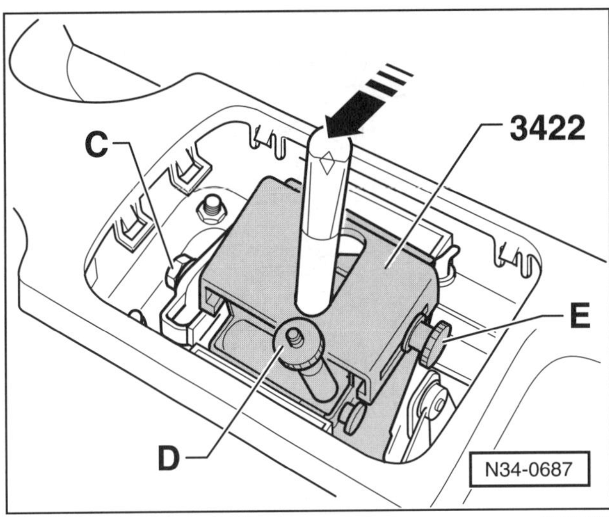

N34-0687

Fig. 7. Shift lever housing adjustment bolt to be loosened (**C**). Shift linkage alignment gauge (VW special tool no 3192) shown installed over shift lever.

NOTE —

Pull off foam seal in area of adjustment bolt if necessary.

9. Install shift linkage gauge (VW special tool 3422) over shift lever. Then pivot gauge mounting hook under mounting plate and tighten clamping nut (D in Fig. 7).

10. Press shift lever into left-hand detent of slide then press on shift lever and slide toward left stop (direction of arrow in Fig. 7). Tighten clamping bolt (bolt E in Fig. 7).

11. Press shift lever toward right-hand detent (opposite direction of arrow in Fig. 7) and then tighten shift lever housing bolt previously loosened (bolt C in Fig. 7).

12. Install special wedge (VW special tool 3192/1) and pin to shift mechanism. See Fig. 8. Slide wedge between gear selector lever and selector cover plate so that there is no play.

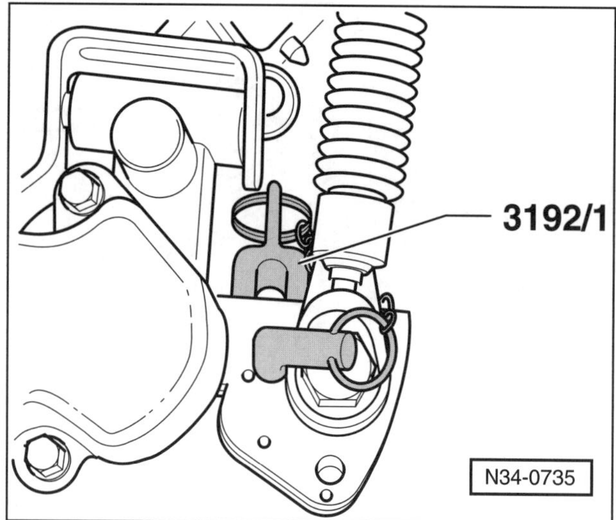

N34-0735

Fig. 8. Shift lever alignment wedge and pin (VW special tool 3192/1) shown installed on shift linkage at transmission.

> ***NOTE—***
> *When installing the wedge, use care so that the wedge does not cause the shift lever to lift.*

13. Secure gear selector cable and actuating arm/selector cable by tightening nut and bolt. Refer to Fig. 6. Check that the wedge is still correctly positioned.
14. Remove shift linkage alignment gauge, wedge, and pin.
15. Install balance weight, shift lever knob and boot.
16. Be sure to quality check your work, see **Quality Review** at the end of this repair group.

Gear selector mechanism, functional check

1. With transmission in neutral, make sure shift lever is in 3rd/4th gear gate
2. Depress clutch pedal and start engine.
3. Wait approximately 3-6 seconds to allow transmission input shaft to come to a standstill.
4. Select each gear several times, checking all gears. Pay particular attention to operation of reverse gear.

> ***NOTE—***
> *Should any gear fail to engage smoothly after being selected repeatedly, the selector shaft play (lift) should be checked as described below.*

5. Have a helper select 1st gear and then press shift lever to left stop, then release. At same time, observe selector shaft on transmission. The selector shaft must move approximately 1 mm (0.04 in.). See Fig. 9.

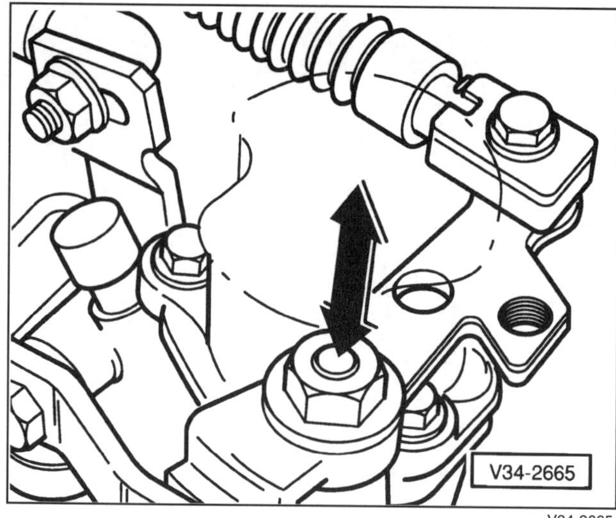

V34-2665

Fig. 9. When moving shift lever to 1st gear stop, transmission selector lever should move in direction of arrow approximately 1.0 mm (0.04 in.).

6. If any faults are found, disengage 1st gear, then loosen nut at actuating arm/gate selector cable mounting. See Fig. 10. Take up gate selector cable play by lightly pressing on actuating arm and retighten nut.

> ***NOTE—***
> *Gate selector cable has some play at mounting due to transfer elements, i.e. minimal play at mounting is normal.*

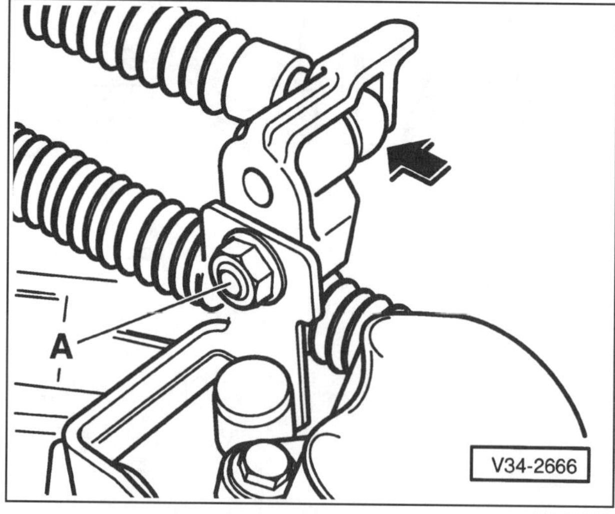

V34-2666

Fig. 10. Actuating arm/gate selector cable mounting nut (**A**). With nut loosened, press lightly on actuating arm (direction of **arrow**) and retighten nut.

TRANSMISSION, REMOVING AND INSTALLING

This procedure describes the removal and installation of the manual transmission. Special engine lifting and jacking equipment is needed to support and reposition the engine as the transmission is removed from below.

Volkswagen recommended special tools

- VW 457/1 support rails
- 10-222A transmission support kit
- 10-222A/8 adapter
- 3282 transmission support
- 3282/8 adjustment plate
- 3300A engine support
- 3336 transmission lifting beam
- VAG 1331 torque wrench
- VAG 1332 torque wrench
- VAG 1383A engine/transmission jack
- VAS 5024 mounting pliers

Special tools, modifying

Two of the Volkswagen recommended special tools will need to be modified as follows.

To secure support rail VW 457/1 to the subframe a new hole is required. See Fig. 11.

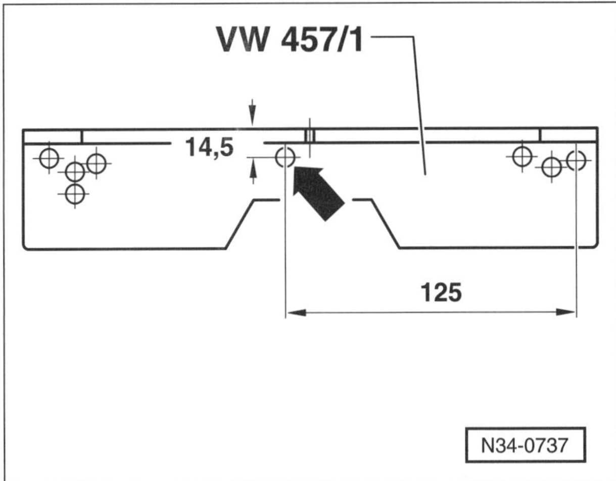

N34-0737

Fig. 11. Drill an 8.5 mm (0.335 in.) diameter hole (**arrow**) in VW 457/1 support rail. Dimensions are provided in mm.

The engine support bridge 10-222A is used to support the engine/transmission assembly. A new hole is required to mount the adapter 10-222A/8 to the guide 10-222A/21. See Fig. 12.

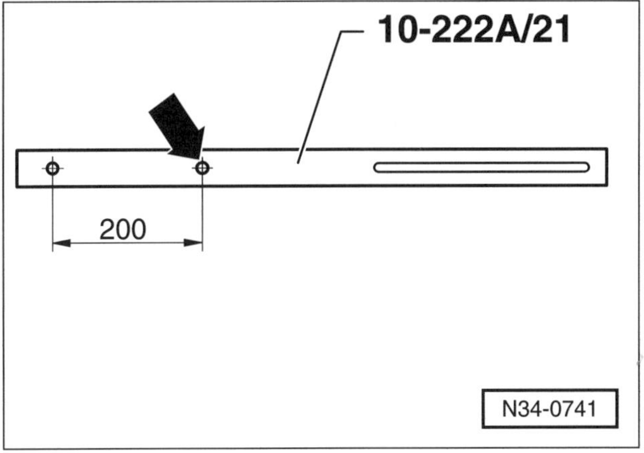

N34-0741

Fig. 12. Drill a 12.5 mm (0.50 in.) diameter hole (**arrow**) in the guide 10-222A/21. Dimensions are provided in mm.

Transmission, removing

1. Remove engine cover.
2. Disconnect battery ground (GND) strap from battery negative (–) terminal. See the **Cautions** at the beginning of this repair group regarding battery disconnection.

   NOTE —
   Be sure to have the anti-theft radio code on hand before disconnecting the battery.

3. Remove power steering reservoir from battery bracket but do not loosen hoses. Tie reservoir up to upper radiator support.
4. Disconnect battery positive (+) cable and remove battery and battery tray. See **27 Engine Electrical**.
5. Remove intake hose and harness connector from Mass Air Flow (MAF) sensor.
6. Remove air cleaner mounting bolts and pull out air cleaner. See Fig. 13.

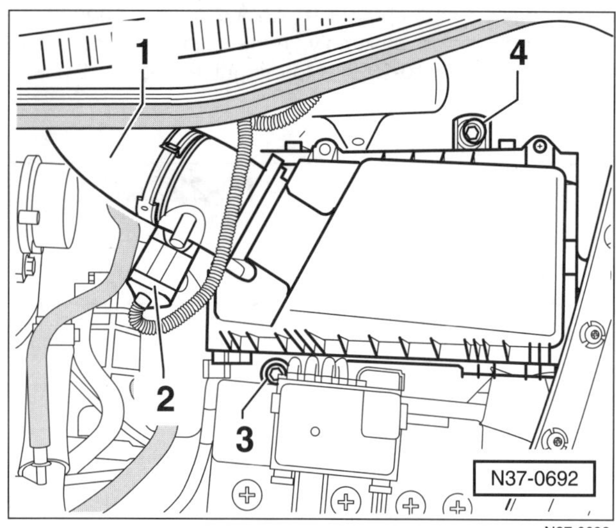

N37-0692

Fig. 13. Remove intake air hose (**1**), harness connector (**2**), and air cleaner mounting bolts (**3**, **4**).

7. Disconnect harness connector from vehicle speed sensor and back-up light switch. See Fig. 14.

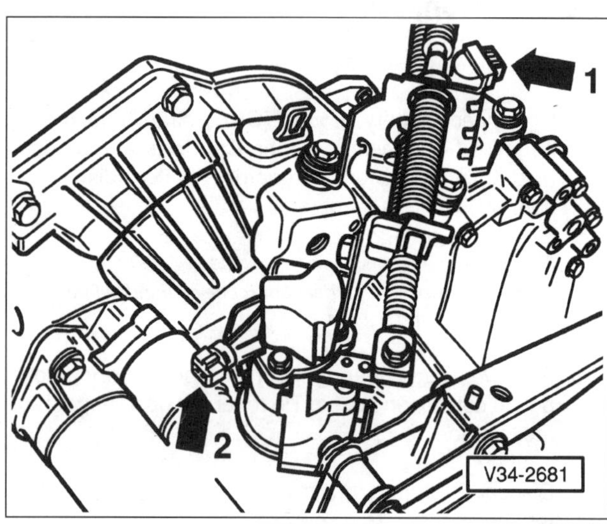

V34-2681

Fig. 14. Vehicle speed sensor (**1**) and backup light switch (**2**) harness connectors to be disconnected from transmission.

8. Remove balance weight and gear selector cable from gear selector lever. Take off gear selector cable with washer and square nut. Lift actuating arm/relay lever upward and remove gate selector cable. See Fig. 15.

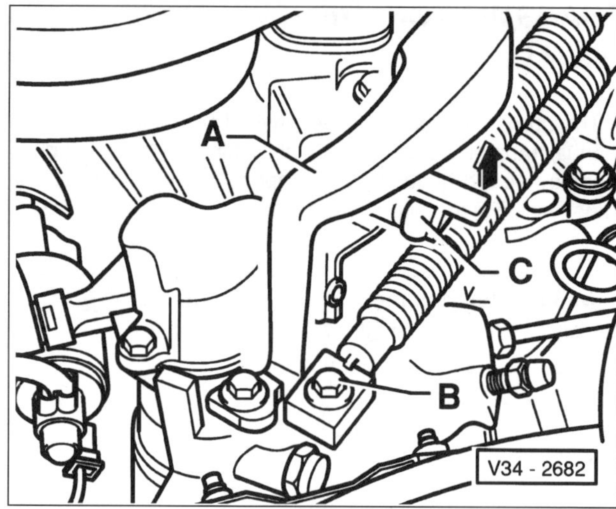

V34-2682

Fig. 15. Gear selector lever balance weight (**A**) on transmission shift lever. Disconnect gear selector cable by removing bolt at (**B**). Disconnect gate selector cable at actuating arm/relay lever (**C**) by pulling tab in direction of **arrow**.

9. Remove cable retaining bracket from transmission. See Fig. 16.

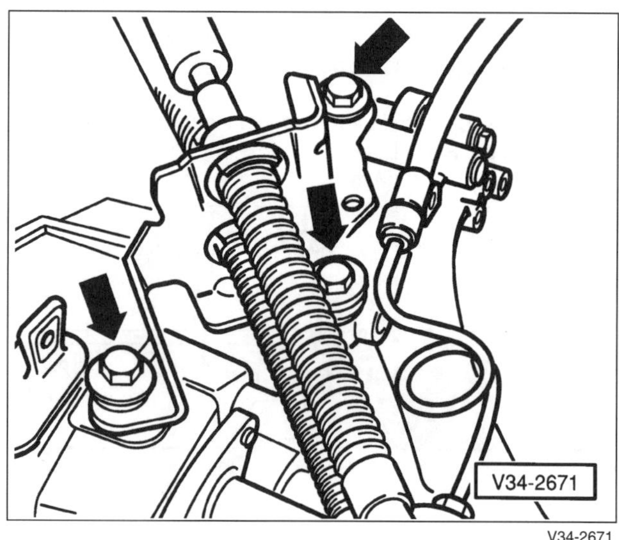

V34-2671

Fig. 16. Cable retaining bracket mounting bolts (**arrows**).

NOTE —

If necessary unclip hydraulic hose at cable support bracket before removing bracket.

10. Remove slave cylinder and secure to side with wire. Do not disconnect hydraulic lines. See Fig. 17.

CAUTION —

Do not depress clutch pedal with slave cylinder removed.

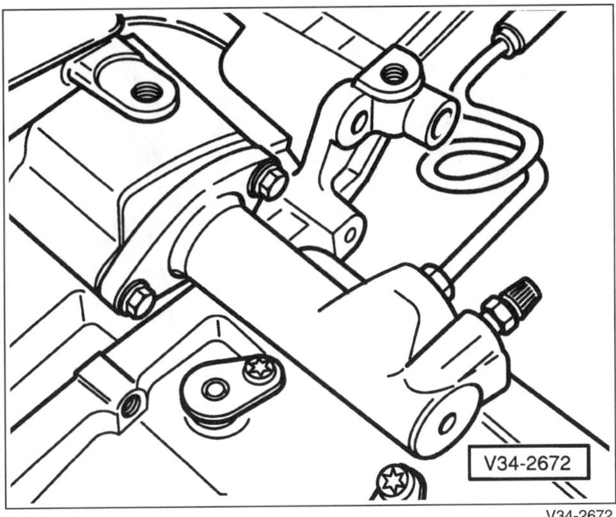

Fig. 17. Clutch slave cylinder on transmission.

11. Remove cable retainer and upper mounting bolt on starter. See Fig. 18.

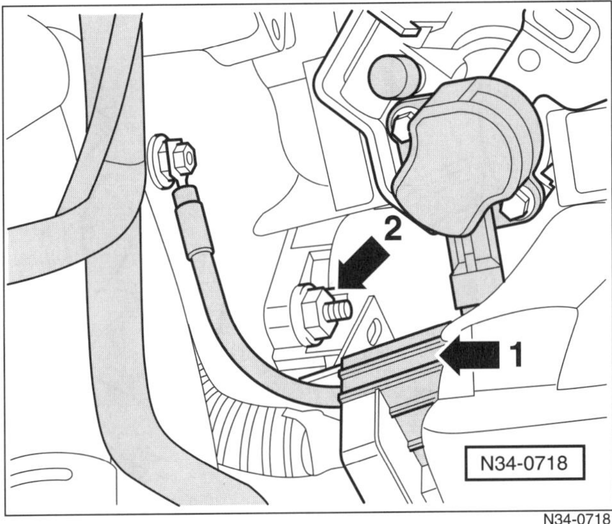

Fig. 18. Remove cable retainer (**arrow 1**) and upper mounting bolt (**arrow 2**) on starter.

12. Remove ground strap at engine-to-transmission upper securing bolt.

13. Remove upper engine-to-transmission mounting bolts.

14. On vehicles with 1.9L TDI (ALH engine), remove intake air duct between intake air cooler and turbocharger, see **21 Turbocharger and Intercooler**.

15. Attach engine lifting equipment (VW sling 10-222A and adjust 10-222A/8 adapters, or equivalent) to engine lifting eyes. Adjust the lifting sling until the weight of the engine is fully supported. See Fig. 19.

NOTE —
The engine support bridge guide (VW special tool 10-222 A/21) must modified to mount the adapter (VW special tool 10-222A/8) by drilling an additional hole as described earlier under **Special tools, modifying**.

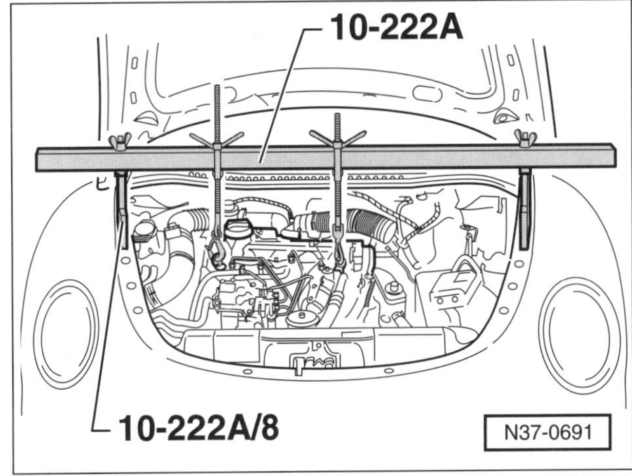

Fig. 19. Engine lifting equipment used to support weight of engine. Numbers shown are for VW special tools.

CAUTION —
- *Before installing the engine lifting hooks, disconnect all hoses and wiring in the vicinity of the engine lifting eyes, to prevent damage.*
- *Do not position adapters 10-222 A/8 on the fender mounting bolts.*

16. Raise car and support with jack stands or lift. See **0 Maintenance** for proper lifting procedure.

WARNING —
Observe all warnings and cautions associated with lifting vehicle in **0 Maintenance**.

17. Remove lower sound absorber panel (belly pan). See Fig. 20.

18. Remove drivers side lower sound insulator. See Fig. 21.

NOTE —
Sound insulator fasteners may best be removed and installed with needle nose pliers.

0024267

Fig. 20. Remove screws (**arrows**) for belly pan.

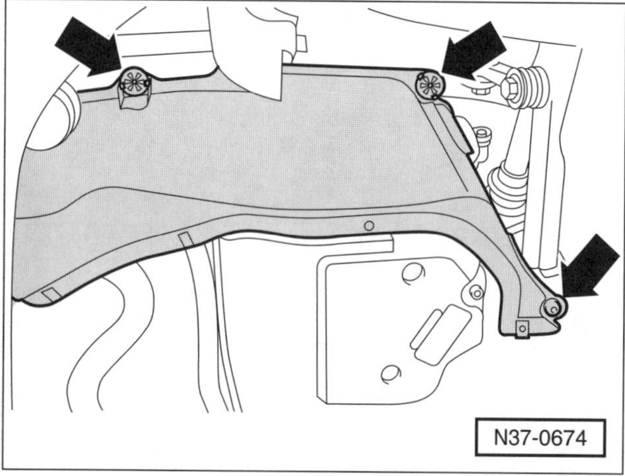

N37-0674

Fig. 21. Remove left sound insulator panel by unscrewing fasteners (**arrows**).

19. Remove power steering line from starter and transmission mounts.

NOTE —

Use care not to damage the power steering line.

20. Remove starter, see **27 Engine Electrical**.

21. Remove right inner constant velocity joint protective cover from engine if installed. See Fig. 22.

22. Turn wheels all the way to the left.

23. Disconnect axle shafts from axle flanges and tie up as high as possible.

NOTE —

When tying up axle shafts use care not to damage the paint on the body panels or the axle boots.

0024260

Fig. 22. Remove bolts (**arrows**) for CV joint protective cover.

24. Remove flywheel small cover plate behind right axle flange, if installed. See Fig. 23.

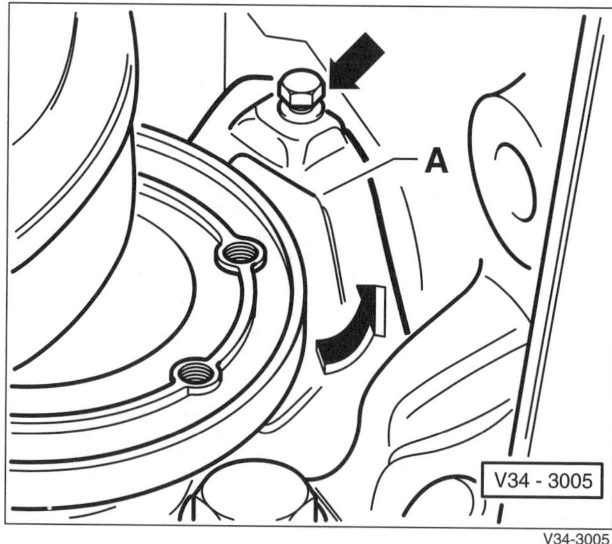

V34-3005

Fig. 23. Remove flywheel small cover plate (**A**) behind right axle flange (**arrows**), if installed.

25. If installed, remove lower flywheel cover plate.

26. Separate exhaust system at front exhaust pipe, see **26 Exhaust System/Emission Controls**.

27. Remove bolts for pendulum mount. See Fig. 24.

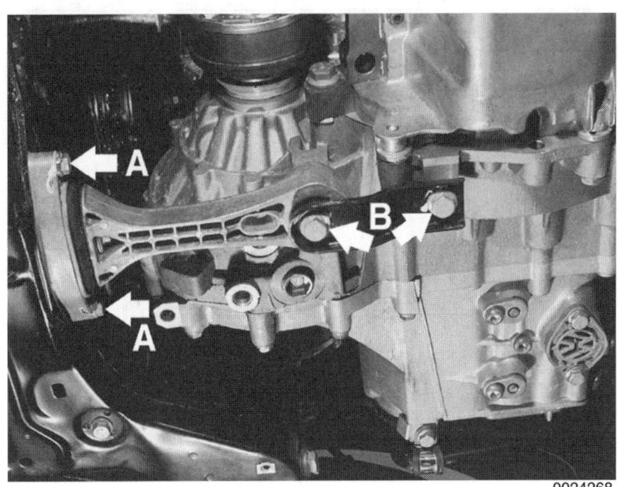

Fig. 24. Remove pendulum mounting bolts (**A** and **B**).

28. Remove transmission support from transmission and bolts from left assembly mount. See Fig. 25.

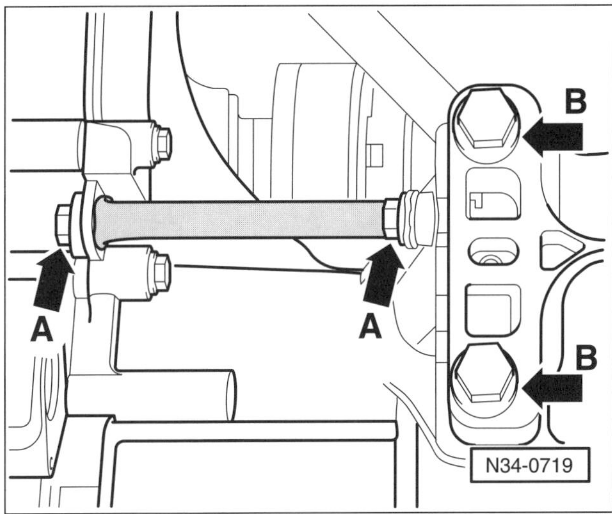

Fig. 25. Remove transmission support (**arrows A**) and left assembly mount bolts (**arrows B**).

29. Incline engine/transmission assembly by lowering it via left-side spindle of support bar (VW 10-222A, or equivalent).

30. Remove bolts for transmission mount. See Fig. 26.

31. Remove additional radiator cooling fan, if installed, on right side of vehicle, see **19 Engine–Cooling System**.

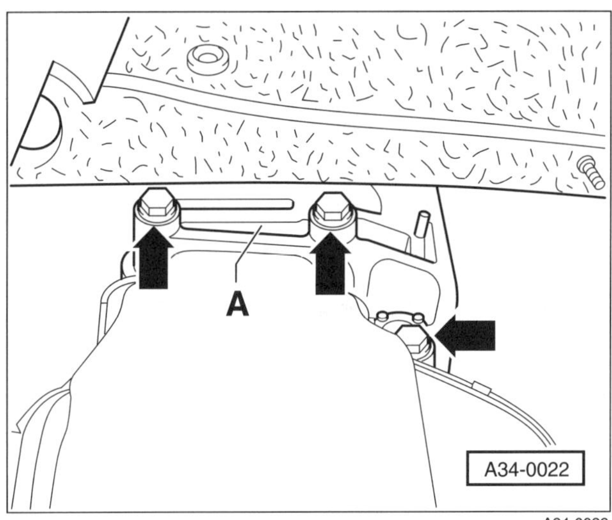

Fig. 26. Remove bolts (**arrows**) for transmission mount (**A**).

32. Bolt support rail (VW 457/1 or equivalent) to the pendulum support securing holes on subframe. See Fig. 27.

NOTE —

- *Volkswagen special tool 457/1 must be modified as described earlier under* **Special tools, modifying**.
- *Spacers totaling a thickness of 6 mm must be inserted between the subframe and the support rail VW 457/1.*

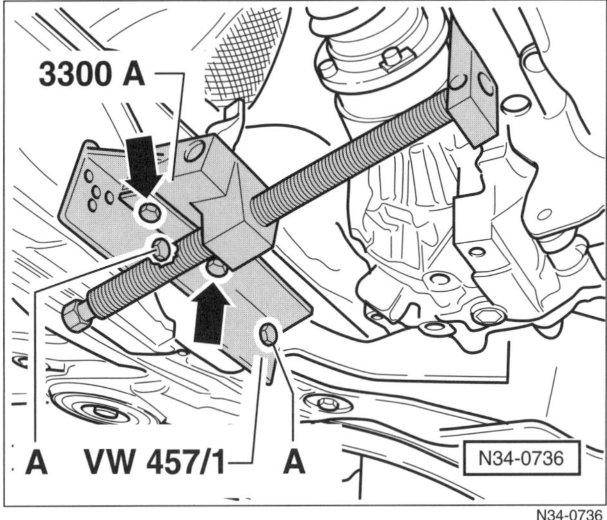

Fig. 27. Use two M8 x 25 bolts (**A**) to attach support rail to the pendulum mount securing holes on subframe. Install support 3300A to support rail (**arrows**). Numbers shown are for VW special tools.

33. Install support (VW 3300A) to support rail (VW 457/1) and secure. Refer to Fig. 27.

34. Press engine/transmission assembly forward carefully.

NOTE —
Do not damage power steering line when moving engine/transmission assembly.

35. Assemble transmission jack with support 3282, adjustment plate 3282/8 (same as for 02A transmission) and support elements. See Fig. 28.
    - Place adjustment plate 3282/8 on transmission support 3282. (Adjustment plate only fits in one position).
    - Position transmission support arms according to holes in adjustment plate.

NOTE —
Arrow on adjustment plate 3282/8 should point toward front of vehicle.

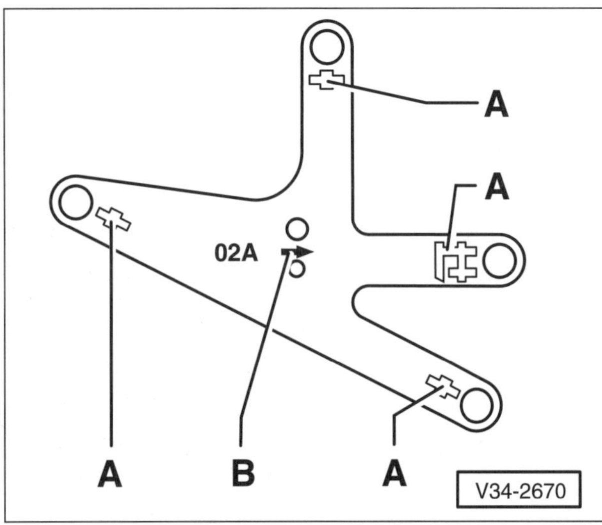

V34-2670

Fig. 28. Adjustment plate 3282/8 to be used with Volkswagen transmission jack 3282. Position transmission support arms at **A**. Arrow (**B**) should point toward front of vehicle.

36. Place transmission jack under vehicle. See Fig. 29.

37. Align adjustment plate parallel to transmission and lock safety supports on transmission jack.

38. Remove lower engine/transmission securing bolts.

> ***WARNING —***
> *Before unbolting lower engine-to-transmission mounting bolts be sure to support the weight of the vehicle at all four corners with jack stands designed for that purpose. Removal of the transmission can upset the weight balance of the vehicle and cause it to fall off the lift.*

39. Press transmission off alignment dowel sleeves and carefully swing toward subframe. See Fig. 30.

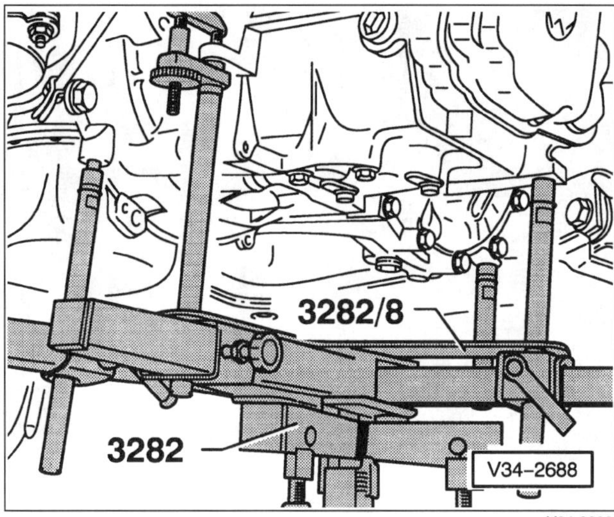

V34-2688

Fig. 29. Transmission jack correctly placed under transmission. Numbers shown are for VW transmission jack and adapters.

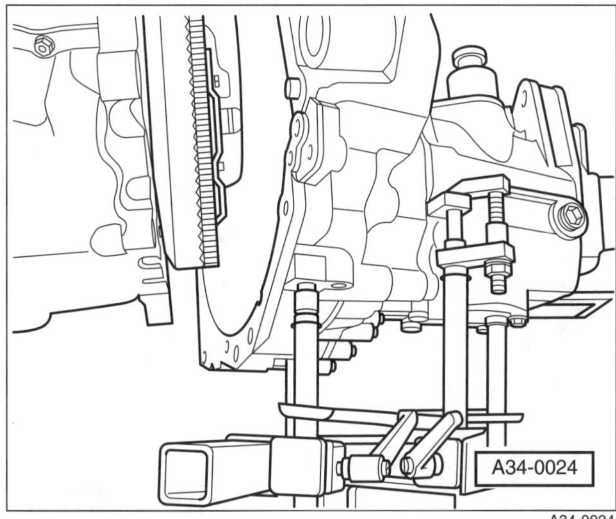

A34-0024

Fig. 30. Press transmission off dowel sleeves and carefully swing toward sub-frame.

40. Lower transmission carefully while guiding right flange shaft past flywheel. Guide left flange shaft past subframe. See Fig. 31.

NOTE —
- *When lowering the transmission change its position using the transmission support 3282 spindles.*
- *Do not damage the power steering line when lowering the transmission.*

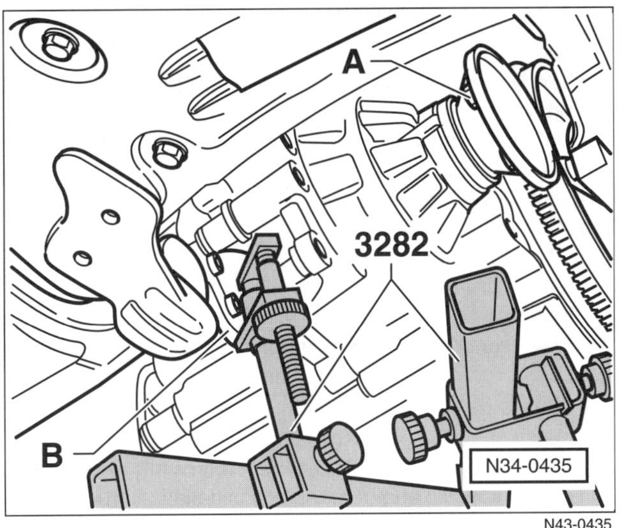

N43-0435

Fig. 31. Lower transmission carefully while guiding right flange shaft (**A**) past flywheel. Guide left flange shaft (**B**) past subframe.

Transmission, installing

Install the transmission in the reverse order of removal. Check that all engine-to-transmission dowel pins are installed in the engine block. Replace any that are missing. Clean the hub splines of the transmission input shaft and apply a light coat of G 000 100 grease before installing. If replacing the transmission assembly, transfer the vehicle speed sensor, the back-up light switch, and the transmission relay lever to the new transmission.

Before installing the transmission to the engine, press the clutch release lever toward the transmission case and secure the lever in position using a M8 x 35 bolt. See Fig. 32.

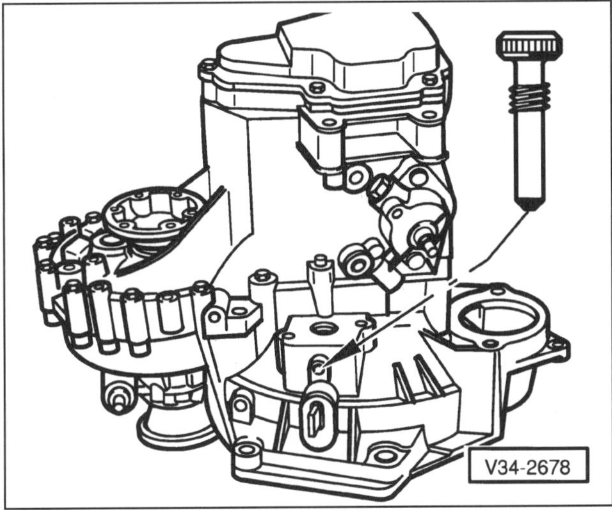

V34-2678

Fig. 32. Press clutch release lever into operating position and secure by inserting M8 x 35 bolt through bellhousing. Remove bolt once transmission is installed.

Transmission-to-engine bolt specifications and tightening torques are listed in **Table b**. See Fig. 33.

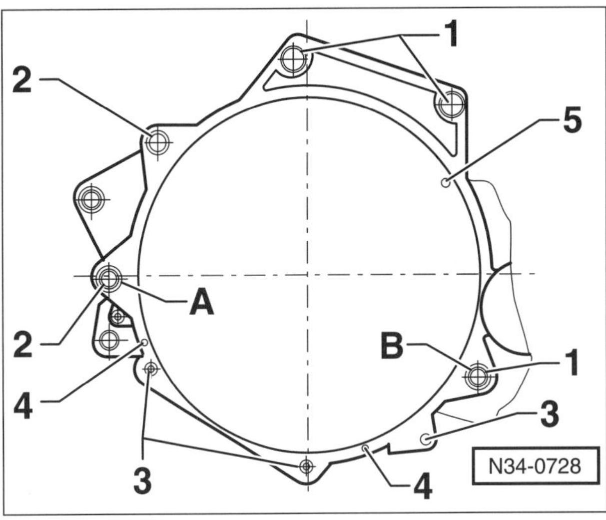

N34-0728

Fig. 33. Engine-to-transmission mounting bolt locations to be used in conjunction with **Table b**. Alignment dowel sleeves shown at **A** and **B**.

Table b. Transmission to engine fasteners

Fastener	Size	Qty.	Tightening torque
1	M12 X 55	3	80 Nm (59 ft-lb)
2*	M12 X 150	2	80 Nm (59 ft-lb)
3**	M10 X 50	3	45 Nm (33 ft-lb)
4***	M7 X 12	2	10 Nm (7 ft-lb)
5****	M7 X 12	1	10 Nm (7 ft-lb)

* Also starter to transmission
** Only on engines with an aluminum oil pan
*** Large cover plate for flywheel, only on engines with sheet steel oil pan (painted black)
**** Small cover plate for flywheel

Remaining transmission installation tightening torques are given below with corresponding Fig. # as necessary for clarification.

Tightening torques

Always replace all stretch bolts (stretch bolts have plus ¼ turn (90°) specification)

- Transmission mount to transmission (See Fig. 26.) . . . . 50 Nm (37 ft-lb) plus ¼ turn (90°)
- Transmission to body
  (**arrow A**, See Fig. 25.) . . . . 25 Nm (18 ft-lb)
  (**arrow B**, See Fig. 25.) . . . . 60 Nm (44 ft-lb) plus ¼ turn (90°)
- Pendulum mount to body (**arrow A**, See Fig. 24.) . . . . 20 Nm (15 ft-lb) plus ¼ turn (90°)
- Pendulum mount bracket (**arrow B**, See Fig. 24.) . . . . 40 Nm (30 ft-lb) plus ¼ turn (90°)
- Axle shaft to axle flange. . . . . 40 Nm (30 ft-lb)
- Balance weight to transmission selector lever . . . . 25 Nm (18 ft-lb)
- Clutch slave cylinder mounting bolts . 25 Nm (18 ft-lb)
- CV joint to drive flange on transmission . . . . 40 Nm (30 ft-lb)
- CV joint protective cover to engine. . . 35 Nm (26 ft-lb)
- Engine-to-transmission bolts, M10. . . 60 Nm (44 ft-lb)
- Engine-to-transmission bolts, M12. . . 80 Nm (59 ft-lb)
- Selector cable support bracket to transmission. . . . . 25 Nm (18 ft-lb)
- Selector cable bolt to transmission lever . . . . 25 Nm (18 ft-lb)
- Starter to transmission. . . . . 80 Nm (59 ft-lb)

QUALITY REVIEW

When you have finished working under the hood and around other areas of the vehicle, it is advisable to take a moment to quality check or review your work. This helps to insure that the operation or repair has been completed properly with all affected systems functioning within normal parameters. These may include the following:

- Make sure that there are no air, vacuum or exhaust leaks.
- Make sure that all components involved in the repair are positioned correctly and function properly.
- Make sure all tools and shop cloths are removed.
- Install the engine/transmission mounts so that they are free of tension. See **10 Engine–Removing and Installing** for specific engine/transaxle installation procedures.
- Check the transmission oil level. See **0 Maintenance**.
- Adjust gear selector mechanism, see **Gear selector mechanism, adjusting**.
- Check the operation of the clutch hydraulics. See **30 Clutch**.
- Top off transmission with appropriate gear oil, see **0 Maintenance**.
- Road test vehicle and check for proper gear selection and transmission operation.

37 Automatic Transmission

TABLES

GENERAL

Cars covered by this manual with automatic transmissions are equipped with the 01M 4-speed automatic transmission. The 01M automatic transmission is controlled electro-hydraulically and features adaptive programming and On-Board Diagnostic (OBD) capabilities. **Table a** lists the engine applications, gear ratios, and other data for the various automatic transmissions. The transmission code and production number can be found stamped on the transmission case near the Automatic Transmission Fluid (ATF) cooler, see **ATF Cooler**, given later. The transmission code letters can also be found on the vehicle data plate.

NOTE —
- *For information on drive axles, including drive flange oil seals, see* **39 Differential and Final Drive**.
- *ATF draining and filling procedures, including ATF screen (filter) replacement, is covered in* **0 Maintenance**.

CAUTION —
- *Before working on the transmission or gear selector mechanism, disconnect the negative (–) battery cable.*
- *Disconnecting the negative (–) battery cable may erase fault codes and basic settings in the engine management and automatic transmission control modules. Some driveability problems may be noticed until the system re-adapts to operating conditions. OBD II readiness codes, which may be required for emissions testing, may also be erased. Convenience electronics (alarm system, interior light control, power locks, mirrors, and windows) will need to be re-set using a VAG 1551/1552 or equivalent scan tool.*

Table a. Automatic transmission specifications

Designation		01M	
Code letters		DYQ	DMP
Engine application		2.0L, 115hp (AEG)	1.9L, 90hp (ALH)
Ratio:	Final drive	4.875	4.875
	Intermediate drive	1.033	0.978
	1st gear	2.714	2.714
	2nd gear	1.551	1.441
	3rd gear	1.000	1.000
	4th gear	0.679	0.742
	Reverse	2.111	2.884
Transmission Lubricant	Initial filling	5.3 Liters (5.6 qt.)	
	Oil change	approx. 3.0 Liters (3.2 qt.)	
	Specification	VW ATF	
Final drive lubricant	Initial filling	0.75 Liters (0.8 qt.)	
	Oil change	Filled for life, no change	
	Specification	Synthetic oil, SAE 75/90W	
Drive shaft		tripodic	
Torque converter code letter		QBDC	QCDC
Valve body code letter		QEB	QEB

BASIC SETTINGS

The automatic Transmission Control Module (TCM) and the Engine Control Module (ECM) share data concerning engine and transmission operation. One piece of data that the TCM may not always "know" is the full throttle position. This is known as a basic setting. The basic setting influences automatic transmission shifting and is set at the time that the vehicle is new. The basic setting will be lost if the battery is disconnected or runs down, or if the TCM is disconnected. It will change if the TCM or the throttle control module is replaced. In these circumstances, the basic settings must be restored to insure proper automatic transmission operation.

Basic settings, restoring

Basic settings can be restored using a suitable scan tool and following the manufacturer's instructions or by using the procedure outlined below. In either case, the kickdown switch on the accelerator cable must fuction properly.

1. Switch on the ignition but do not start the engine.
2. Push the accelerator pedal all the way to the floor and hold it there for a minimum of 5 seconds.

   NOTE —
   Be sure that floor mats do not prevent the accelerator pedal from being completely depressed.

3. Release the accelerator pedal and switch off the ignition.

Basic requirements

1. Check that the ATF level is correct. Check that the fluid is clean and of the correct type. See **0 Maintenance**.

   CAUTION —
   The 01M transmission uses a special VW-only ATF. If the fluid was changed, check to make sure that the correct fluid was installed. VW ATF is yellowish in color.

2. Make a visual check of the components shown in Fig. 1. Check the wiring and harness connectors for loose, damaged or corroded wiring. Check that all related grounds are firmly connected and in good condition. Consult the wiring diagrams shown in **97 Wiring Diagrams, Fuses and Relays**.
3. Check the shift mechanism for proper function. See **Shift Mechanism**.
4. Review the list given below.
   - Engine control module (ECM) replaced
   - New, reconditioned, or used engine installed
   - New or altered/adjusted throttle housing
   - New or altered/adjusted throttle position sensor
   - Transmission control module (TCM) replaced

If any of the above conditions are met, the TCM must be reset to its "basic settings" using the VAG 1551/1552 scan tool or the procedure described above. If the TCM basic settings are not re-established, driveability problems may be encountered.

5. If no faults are found up to this point, the next logical step is to have an authorized VW dealer check for faults using the special VW scan tool, VAG 1551 or 1552. If the transmission problem is electrical/electronic in nature, specific DTCs will most likely be stored in memory.

   NOTE —
   - *Volkswagen identifies electrical components by a letter/number code in the electrical schematics. These component codes are given in the numbered list below as an aid in using the wiring diagrams. See* ***97 Wiring Diagrams, Fuses, and Relays****.*
   - *If engine or transmission control modules are replaced, the system must be returned to basic setting.*

Automatic transmission electronic/electrical components

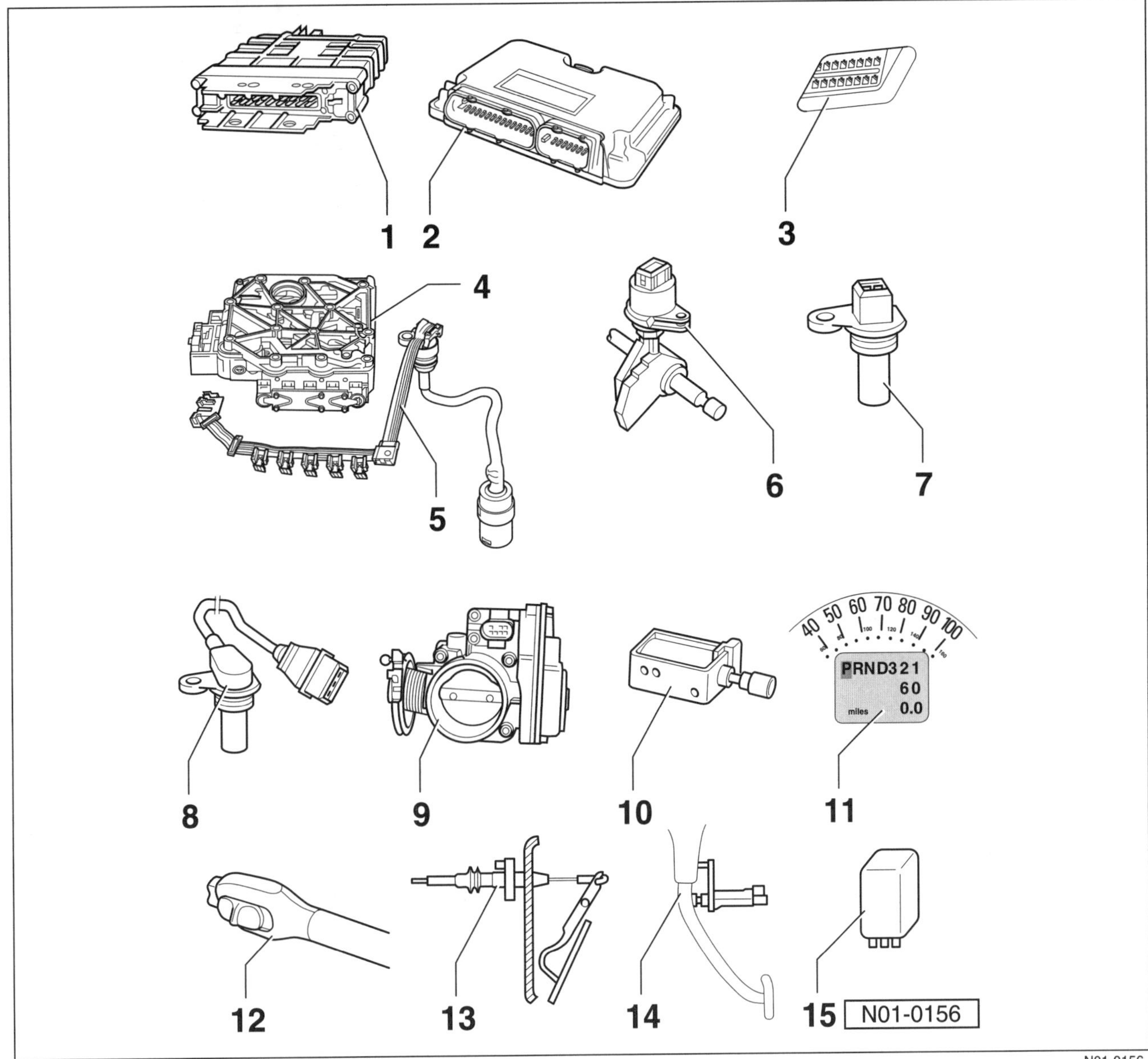

Fig. 1. Electrical/electronic components for automatic transmission.

1. **Transmission control module (J217)**
   - Located in center plenum
   - Factory coded, no user changes possible
2. **Engine control module**
   - Located in plenum, driver's side
   - Removing and installing, see **23 Fuel Injection–Diesel (ALH engine)** or **24 Fuel Injection–Motronic (AEG engine)**
3. **Data Link Connector (DLC)**
   - Located under dashboard on driver's side
4. **Valve body**
   - Located above oil pan
   - Solenoid valves (N88, N89, N90, N91, N92, N93, N94) are attached to the valve body
   - Valves are checked by On-Board Diagnostics (OBD)
5. **Conductor strip with integrated transmission fluid temperature sensor (G93)**
   - Located in oil pan, on valve body
   - Checked by OBD
   - Can be replaced without removing valve body or transmission

(continued on following page)

(continued from previous page)

6. **Multi-function transmission range switch (F125)**
   - Location and removing and installing, **see** Ⓐ
   - Checked by OBD
7. **Transmission vehicle speed sensor (G38)**
   - Located on top of transmission
   - Removing and installing, **see** Ⓑ
   - Checked by OBD
8. **Vehicle speed sensor (G68)**
   - Location and removing and installing **see** Ⓒ
   - Checked by OBD
9. **Throttle position sensor (G69)**
   - Checked by OBD
   - Gasoline engines:
     located on throttle valve housing,
     part of throttle valve control module (J338)
   - Diesel engines:
     throttle valve signal is generated in the throttle position sensor (G79) located near accelerator pedal
10. **Shift Lock Solenoid (N110)**
    - Location, see **Shift mechanism, assembly**
    - Checked by OBD
11. **Transmission range selector lever display (Y5)**
    - Located in instrument cluster
12. **Cruise control switch (E45)**
13. **Kick down switch (F8)**
    - Engines with accelerator cable (gasoline):
      kickdown switch is integrated into cable and located on bulkhead in engine compartment
    - Engines without accelerator cable (diesel):
      kickdown signal is generated in the throttle position sensor (G79) located near accelerator pedal
14. **Brake light switch (F)**
    - Located on pedal cluster
15. **Park/Neutral Position (PNP) Relay -J226-**
    - Located on additional relay panel under instrument panel, left side
    - Marked with number "175"

Ⓐ Multi-function transmission range switch (F125), replacing

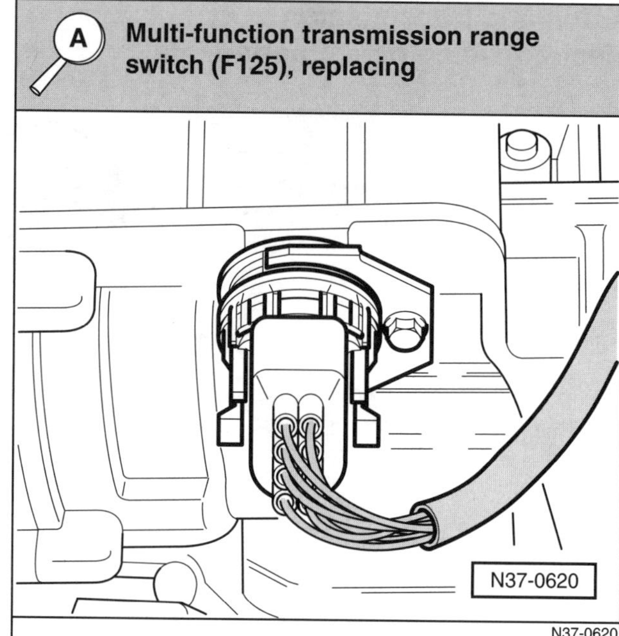

N37-0620

- **Switch off ignition, remove harness connector, bolt, and retaining bracket.**
- **When installing, replace seal.**
- **Tighten retaining clamp bolt to 10 Nm (7 ft-lb).**

Ⓑ Transmission vehicle speed sensor (G38), removing and installing

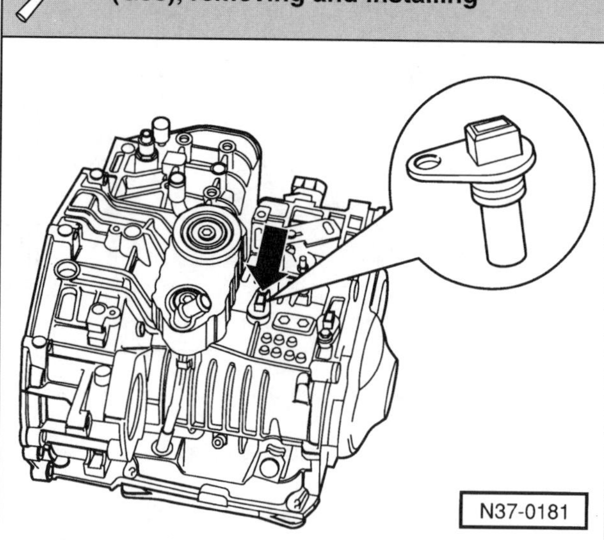

N37-0181

- **Switch off ignition, remove harness connector and retaining bolt.**
- **When installing, replace seal.**
- **Tighten retaining clamp bolt to 10 Nm (7 ft-lb).**

Vehicle speed sensor (G68), removing and installing

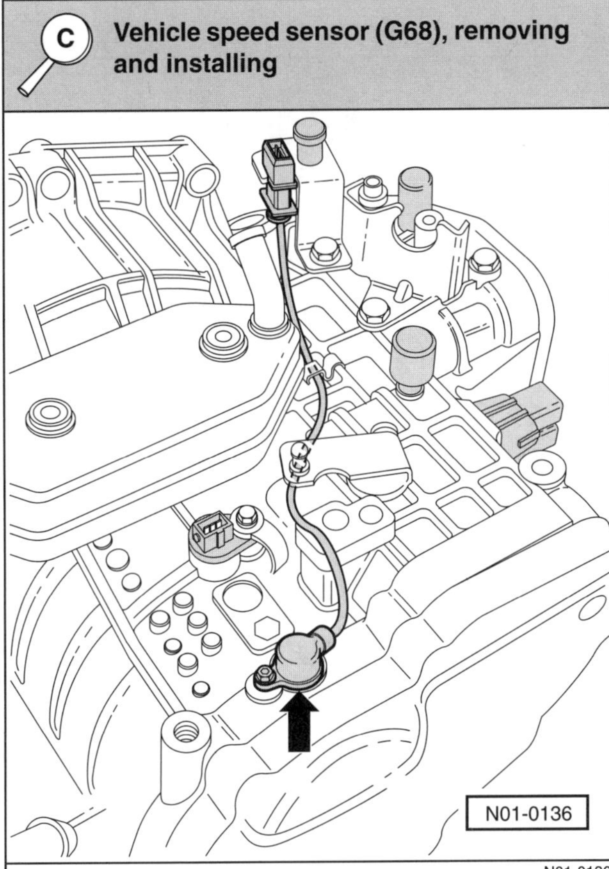

N01-0136

- **When transmission is installed the sensor is covered by left transmission mount.**
- **Transmission must be unbolted from mounts and lowered approximately 2.5 in. to access sensor, see Transmission, Removing and Installing, given later.**
- **Disconnect harness connector from sensor and remove sensor retaining bolt.**
- **When installing, replace seal.**
- **Tighten retaining bolt to 10 Nm (7 ft-lb).**

SHIFT MECHANISM

Selector lever cable, checking and adjusting

1. Switch ignition off and set parking brake.
2. Open hood and locate selector lever cable and selector shaft lever on transmission.
3. Use a screwdriver to pry selector lever cable off selector shaft lever and move cable aside so that the end is free to move. See Fig. 2.

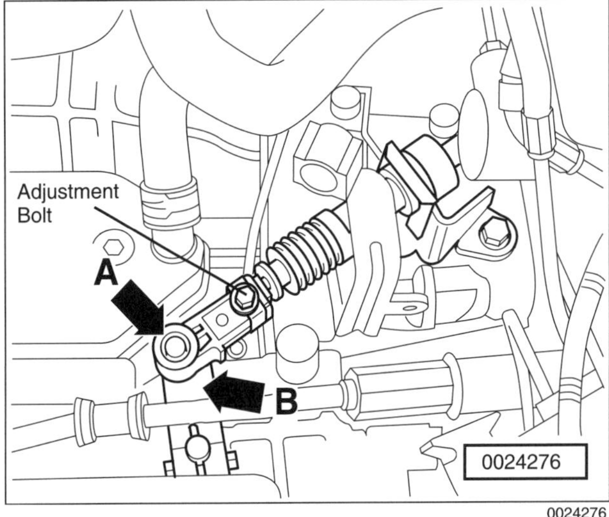

0024276

Fig. 2. Selector lever cable (**A**), selector shaft lever (**B**), and adjustment bolt for automatic transmission.

4. Move selector lever from "**P**" to "**1**" and check that shift mechanism and selector lever cable move freely. If necessary replace selector lever cable or service shift mechanism.
5. Check protective bellows at front of selector cable for damage. If protective bellow is damaged, replace selector cable.
6. To adjust cable, install selector lever cable on selector shaft lever and move selector lever to "**P**".
7. Loosen adjustment bolt. See Fig. 2.
8. Place selector shaft lever into position "**P**" on transmission then tighten adjustment bolt. Shift through all gear positions and check for smooth operation.

NOTE—
*With selector lever in "**P**" position, the transmission locking lever must engage, locking both front wheels.*

Tightening torque
- Selector lever adjustment bolt . . . . 5 Nm (44 in-lb)

Shift mechanism, assembly

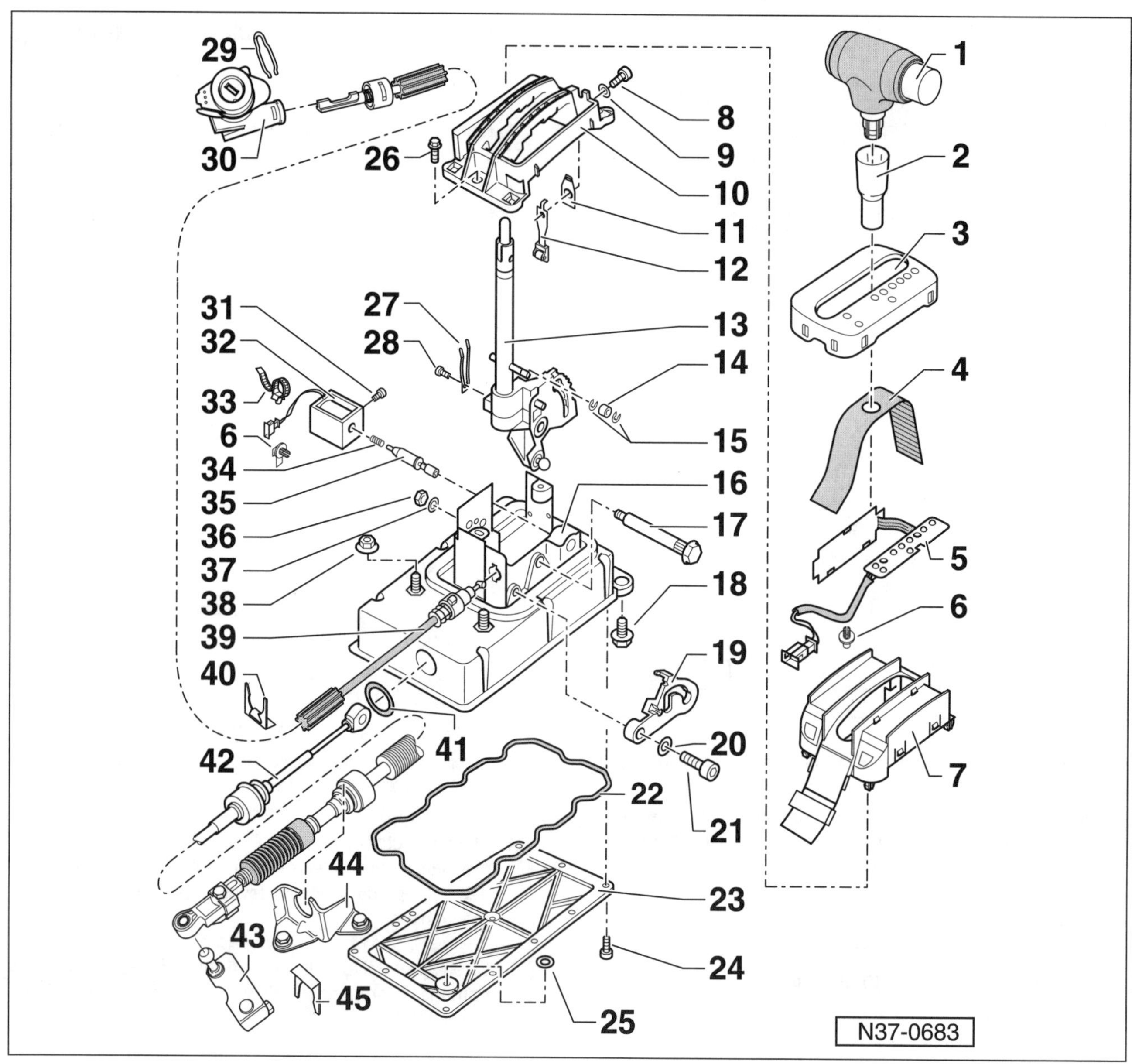

N37-0683

Fig. 3. Shift mechanism for automatic transmission.

NOTE —

Lubricate mounting points and contact surfaces with grease (VW part no. G 052 142 A2).

1. **Selector lever handle**
   - Removing: push sleeve (item 2) down and while depressing knob, remove handle upward
   - Installing: while depressing knob, install handle until lock engages. Push sleeve up to lock.
2. **Sleeve**
   - Locks selector lever handle
   - Prevents selector lever handle from being pulled off
3. **Cover**
   - With selector indicator
   - Snapped into bracket (item 7)
4. **Cover strip**
   - Insert in bracket (item 7)
5. **Selector lever position display**
   - Printed circuit for selector lever position illuminated display is held in position by clips
6. **Retainer**
   - To position connector in bracket (item 7)

(continued from previous page)

7. **Bracket**
    - Carefully pry off at corners
    - Push into cover strip (item 4)
    - Installation position: ribs must face down
    - Carefully position printed circuits and wiring (item 5)
    - When installing be careful not to damage contact springs (item 27) for selector lever position display

8. **Bolt**
    - Tighten to 7 Nm (62 in-lb)
    - Attaches locating spring (item 12) and plate (item 11) to bracket (item 7)

9. **Washer**

10. **Locking segment**
    - Place on centering elements of selector lever housing

11. **Plate**

12. **Locating spring with roller**
    - Engages in detent in selector lever

13. **Selector lever**
    - With pull rod, spring, detent, contact spring for selector lever position and locking cable release

14. **Roller**
    - For releasing locking cable

15. **Circlip**

16. **Selector lever housing**
    - Does not need not be removed to replace most individual parts, with the exception of selector lever and shift lock solenoid

17. **Fulcrum pin**
    - Apply grease to shank
    - Do not turn when installing selector lever

18. **Bolt**
    - Tighten to 25 Nm (18 ft-lb)

19. **Locking lever**
    - For locking cable
    - For locking selector lever in "**P**"

20. **Washer**

21. **Bolt**

22. **Gasket**
    - Always replace

23. **Cover**
    - For selector lever housing

24. **Bolt (qty. 14)**

25. **O-ring**
    - Always replace

26. **Bolt (qty. 2)**
    - Tighten to 8 Nm (71 in-lb)

27. **Contact spring**
    - For selector lever position display

28. **Bolt**
    - Tighten to 4 Nm (35 in-lb)
    - Place selector lever in "**P**" to loosen and tighten

29. **Clip**

30. **Steering lock**

31. **Bolt (qty. 2)**
    - Attaches solenoid to selector lever housing

32. **Shift lock solenoid (N110)**
    - Checked via OBD
    - Remove/install only with selector lever in position "**1**"
    - Look out for spring and locking pin when removing
    - Install together with locking pin and spring while moving selector lever slightly back and forth

33. **Cable tie**
    - Attaches wiring/solenoid to selector lever housing
    - Always replace

34. **Spring**

35. **Locking pin**

36. **Nut**
    - Tighten to 13 Nm (10 ft-lb)
    - Always replace

37. **Washer**

38. **Nut (qty. 2)**
    - Tighten to 25 Nm (18 ft-lb)
    - Always replace

39. **Shift-lock cable**
    - Do not kink
    - See **Automatic Shift Lock**, given later

40. **Clip**
    - Always replace
    - Mounts selector lever cable to selector lever housing
    - Install angled end toward inside of selector housing

41. **Gasket**
    - Always replace

42. **Selector lever cable**
    - Do not bend or kink
    - If outer cable sleeve is damaged, replace selector lever cable.
    - Lightly grease ball socket and cable ends before installing

43. **Lever**
    - For selector shaft

44. **Support bracket**
    - For mounting selector lever cable on transmission

45. **Clip**
    - Always replace

AUTOMATIC SHIFT LOCK

Automatic shift-lock is used on cars with automatic transmission. Turning the ignition key on and off operates a bowden cable to lock and unlock the selector lever. See Fig. 4.

When the key is turned to the off position (shift lever in **P**), the cable pushes the stop lever into the shift lever. This locks the lever button and also allows the ignition key to be withdrawn from the lock cylinder. The key can only be removed from the ignition with the lever in the "**P**" position. With the key out of the ignition, the selector lever cannot be shifted out of "**P**" position.

When the key is in the **ON** position, the cable pulls the stop lever away from the shift lever, allowing the shift lever to be moved out of park.

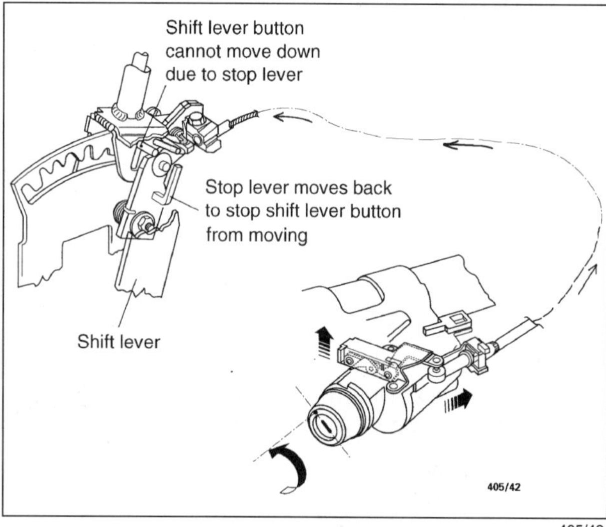

405/42

Fig. 4. Automatic shift lock shown in the "key-off" position.

Shift-lock cable, removing and installing

The shift-lock cable is routed through the dashboard and under the center console. Be sure to route the cable correctly when installing.

1. Disconnect battery ground (GND) strap from battery negative (–) terminal. See the **Cautions** at the beginning of this repair group regarding battery disconnection.

NOTE —
Be sure to have the anti-theft radio code on hand before disconnecting the battery.

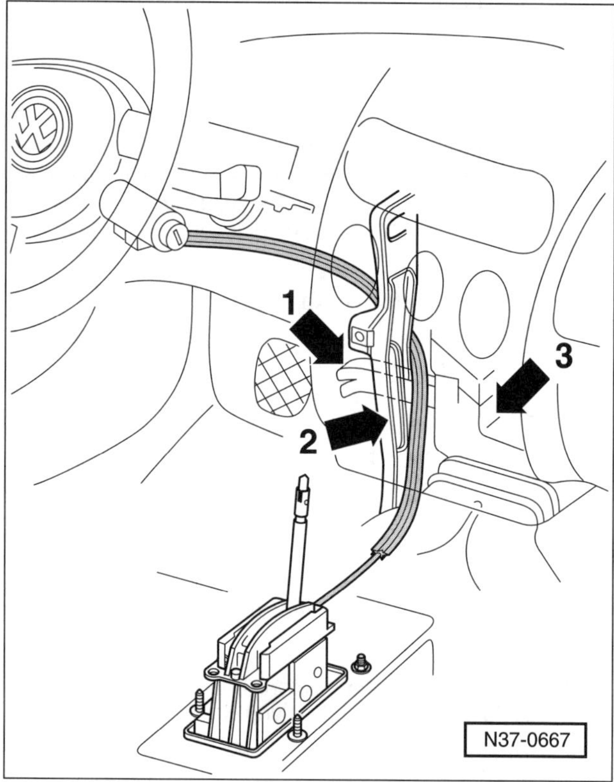

N37-0667

Fig. 5. Installation position of shift-lock cable showing footwell vents (**1**), instrument panel support (**2**), and heater unit (**3**).

2. Remove steering wheel, handle for steering height and reach adjustment and cover for ignition/starter lock, see **48 Steering**.

3. Turn ignition **ON** and move selector lever to "**P**".

4. Remove shift-lock cable clip and pull cable out of ignition/steering lock assembly. See Fig. 6.

5. Push down sleeve on selector lever handle.

6. While depressing knob, remove selector lever handle by pulling upward.

7. Remove center console, arm rest (if installed), and switch bracket, see **70 Trim–Interior**.

8. Disconnect shift-lock cable from locking lever at selector mechanism.

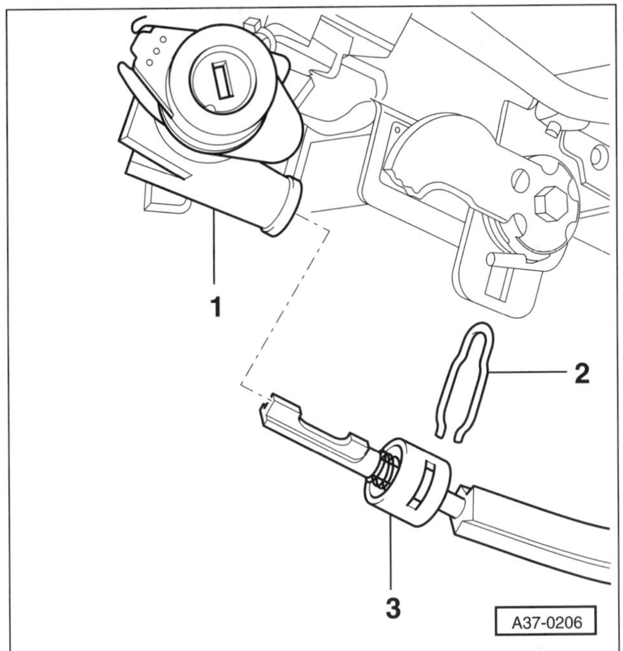

A37-0206

Fig. 6. Remove clip (**2**) for shift-lock cable (**3**) and pull out of steering lock (**1**).

9. Press tabs of shift lock cable retaining clip together and pull locking cable out of selector mechanism. See Fig. 7.

10. To install, move selector lever to "**P**".

> ***CAUTION—***
> *• Be sure to route cable correctly when installing.*
> *• Do not kink cable.*
> *• Be sure to adjust cable after installation.*

11. Press shift-lock cable into support bracket on selector lever housing until tabs on retaining clip spread.

12. Attach locking cable in locking lever.

13. Turn ignition **ON**.

14. Push locking cable into ignition/steering lock assembly.

15. Install clip onto cable.

NOTE—
Be sure that clip is properly located.

Shift-lock cable, adjusting

> ***CAUTION—***
> *Follow the adjustment procedure exactly as outlined.*

1. Remove ignition key.

2. Working at center console, slide cable sleeve forward and release clip by pushing up. See Fig. 7.

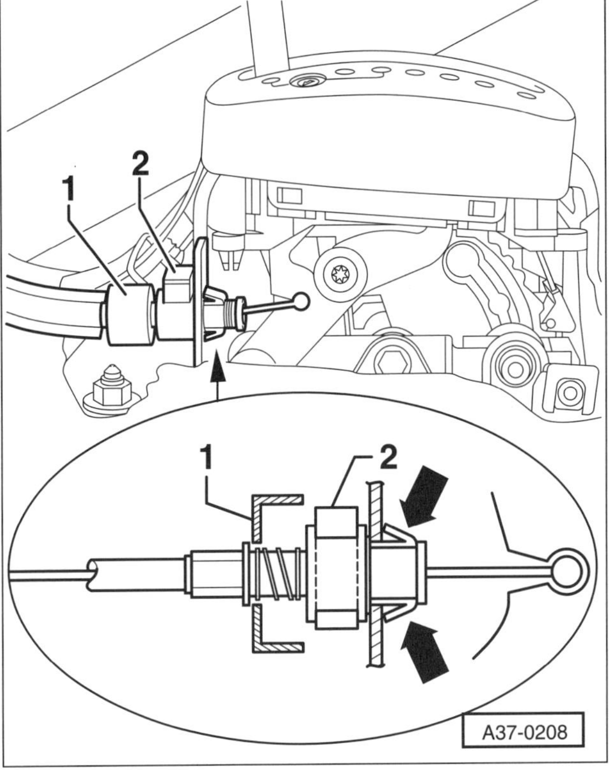

A37-0208

Fig. 7. Slide sleeve (**1**) forward and release clip (**2**) by pushing up. **Arrows** are for removal and installation of shift-lock cable clip.

3. Carefully pry up at four corners of shift lever bracket and remove.

NOTE—
Be careful not to damage the contact spring for shift lever position indicator.

4. Slide 0.8 mm feeler gauge between locking lever and selector lever roller.

5. Pull outer sleeve of shift-lock cable slightly forward in direction of travel and push red clip down until it engages. See Fig. 8.

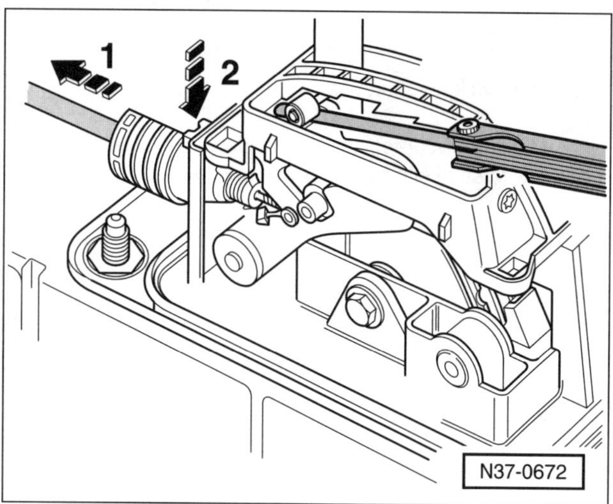

N37-0672

Fig. 8. Pull shift-lock cable outer sleeve forward slightly (**1**) and push clip down (**2**) until it engages.

6. Push sliding sleeve over clip.

7. Check for proper ignition key removal.

8. Replace center console, arm rest (if applicable), and switch bracket.

TRANSMISSION, REMOVING AND INSTALLING

This procedure describes the removal and installation of the automatic transmission. Special engine lifting and jacking equipment is needed to support and reposition the engine as the transmission is removed from below.

Volkswagen recommended special tools

- VW 457/1 support rails
- 10-222A transmission support kit
- 10-222A/8 adapter
- 3094 hose clamps
- 3282 transmission support
- 3282/2 adjustment plate
- 3300A engine support
- 3336 transmission lifting beam
- VAG 1331 torque wrench
- VAG 1332 torque wrench
- VAG 1383A engine/transmission jack
- V/175 socket

Special tools, modifying

Two of the Volkswagen recommended special tools will need to be modified as follows.

To secure support rail VW 457/1 to the subframe a new hole is required. See Fig. 9.

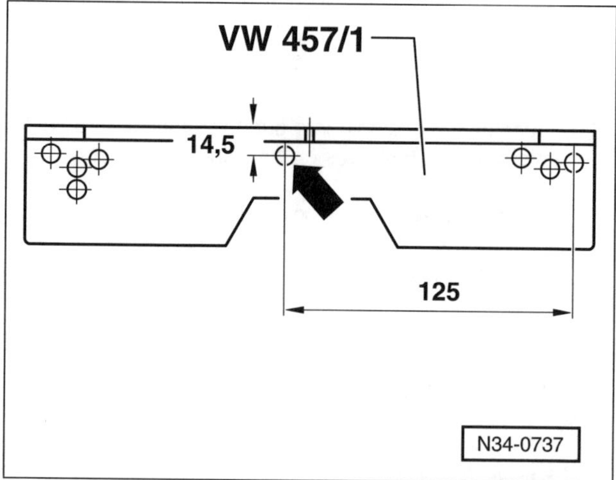

N34-0737

Fig. 9. Drill an 8.5 mm (0.335 in.) diameter hole (**arrow**) in VW 457/1 support rail. Dimensions are provided in mm.

The engine support bridge 10-222A is used to support the engine/transmission assembly. A new hole is required to mount the adapter 10-222A/8 to the guide 10-222A/21. See Fig. 10.

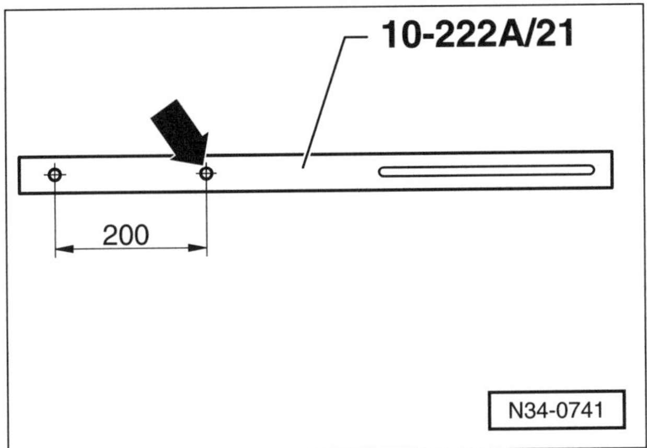

N34-0741

Fig. 10. Drill a 12.5 mm (0.50 in.) diameter hole (**arrow**) in the guide 10-222A/21. Dimensions are provided in mm.

Transmission, removing

1. Remove engine cover.

2. Disconnect battery ground (GND) strap from battery negative (–) terminal. See the **Cautions** at the beginning of this repair group regarding battery disconnection.

   NOTE —
   Be sure to have the anti-theft radio code on hand before disconnecting the battery.

3. Remove power steering reservoir from battery bracket but do not loosen hoses. Tie reservoir up to upper radiator support.

4. Disconnect battery positive (+) cable and remove battery and battery tray. See **27 Engine Electrical**.

5. Remove intake hose and harness connector from Mass Air Flow (MAF) sensor.

6. Remove air cleaner mounting bolts and pull out air cleaner. See Fig. 11.

7. Disconnect harness connector from solenoid valves, vehicle speed sensor, multi-function transmission range sensor, and transmission vehicle speed sensor. See Fig. 12.

8. Remove wiring harness from retainer on transmission and move aside.

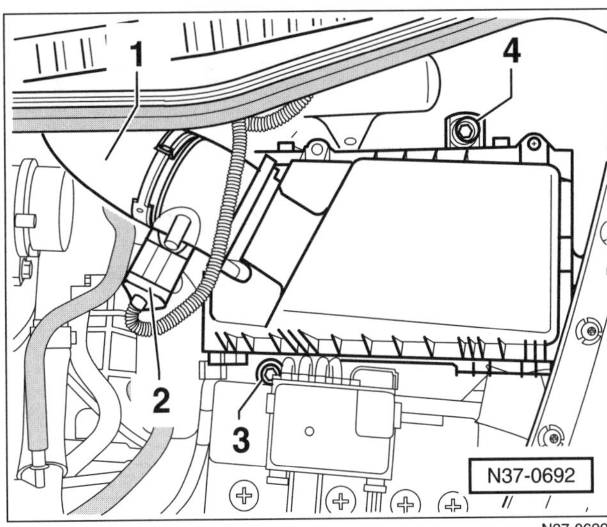

N37-0692

Fig. 11. Remove intake air hose (**1**), harness connector (**2**), and air cleaner mounting bolts (**3**, **4**).

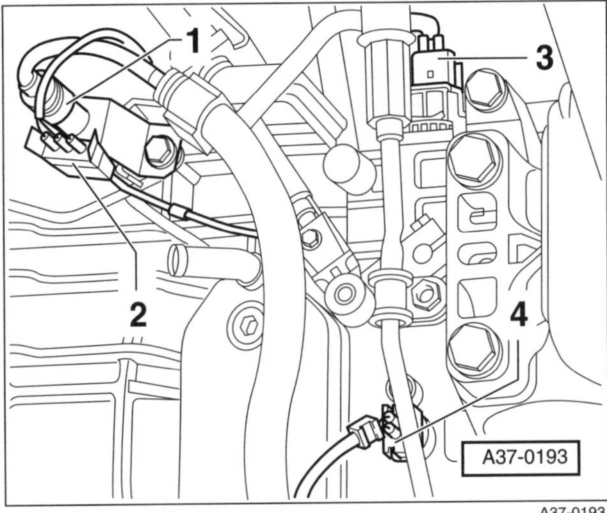

A37-0193

Fig. 12. Solenoid valves (**1**), vehicle speed sensor (**2**), multi-function transmission range switch (**3**), and transmission vehicle speed sensor (**4**) harness connectors to be disconnected from transmission.

9. Remove bracket for power steering hose with retainer for wiring harness from transmission.

10. Move selector lever to "**P**". Using a screwdriver, pry selector lever cable off selector shaft lever. See Fig. 13.

11. Remove clip at selector lever cable support bracket and remove selector lever cable. See Fig. 13.

    NOTE —
    Do not kink selector lever cable.

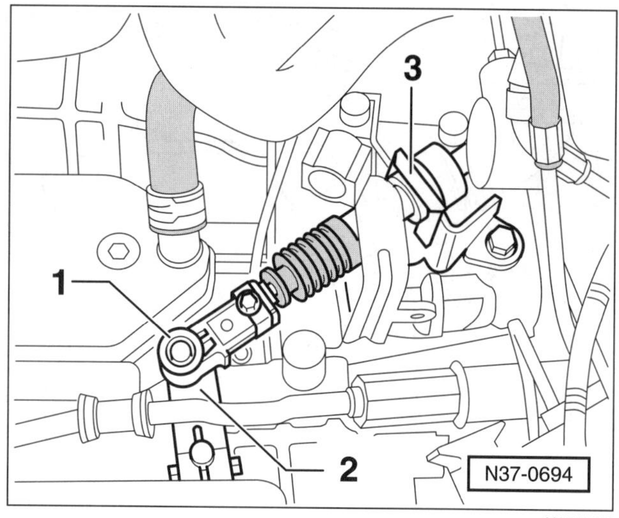

N37-0694

Fig. 13. Pry selector lever cable (**1**) off lever/selector shaft lever (**2**). Remove clip (**3**) and selector lever cable.

12. On vehicles with 2.0L engine, remove vehicle speed sensor and heat shield for exhaust manifold. See Fig. 14.

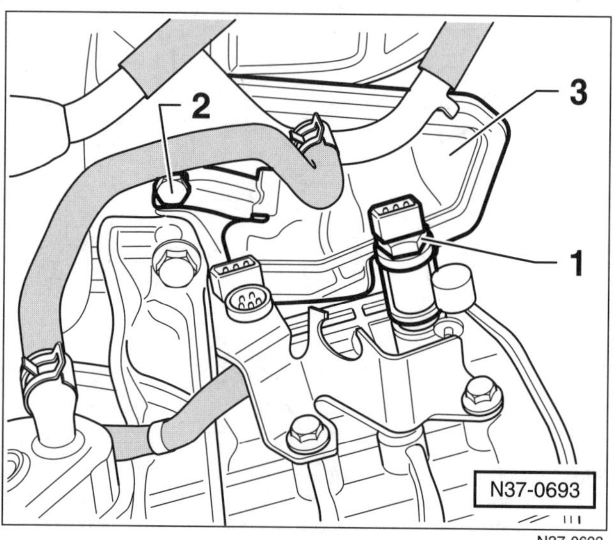

N37-0693

Fig. 14. On vehicles with 2.0L engine, remove vehicle speed sensor (**1**), bolt (**2**), and heat shield (**3**) for exhaust manifold.

13. For all vehicles, disconnect ground cable from upper engine/transmission bolt, electrical connections at starter motor and harness connector on top of starter motor. See Fig. 15.

14. Pull harness connector out of retainer on top of starter motor and remove retainer.

15. Remove upper starter mounting bolt.

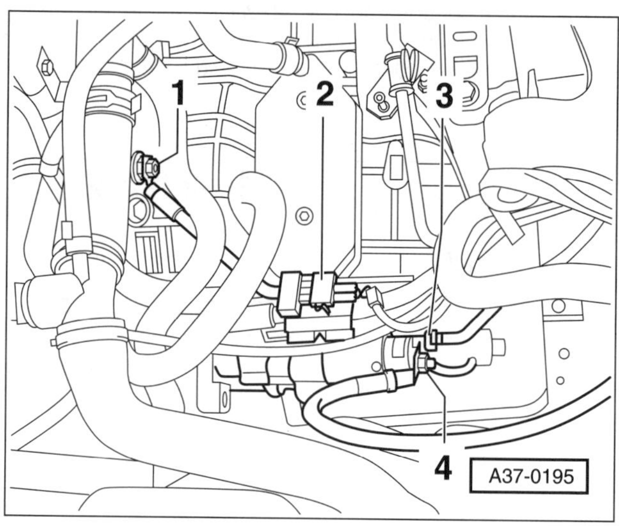

A37-0195

Fig. 15. Disconnect ground cable (**1**) from upper engine/transmission bolt, electrical connections at starter motor (**3** and **4**), and harness connector on top of starter motor (**2**).

16. Clamp-off ATF cooler hoses and detach at ATF cooler. Seal ATF cooler with clean plugs. See Fig. 16.

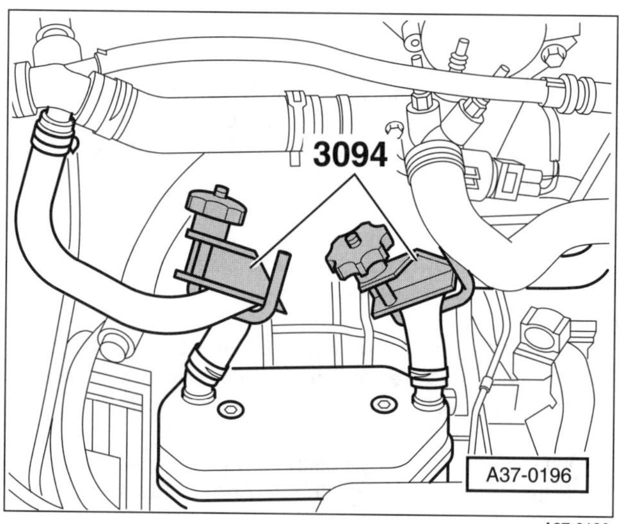

A37-0196

Fig. 16. Volkswagen special tool 3094 being used to clamp off ATF hoses.

17. Remove upper engine/transmission bolts.

18. Attach engine lifting equipment (VW sling 10-222A and adjust 10-222A/8 adapters, or equivalent) to engine lifting eyes. Adjust the lifting sling until the weight of the engine is fully supported. See Fig. 17.

NOTE —
The engine support bridge guide (VW special tool 10-222 A/21) must be modified to mount the adapter (VW special tool 10-222A/8) by drilling an additional hole as described earlier under **Special tools, modifying**.

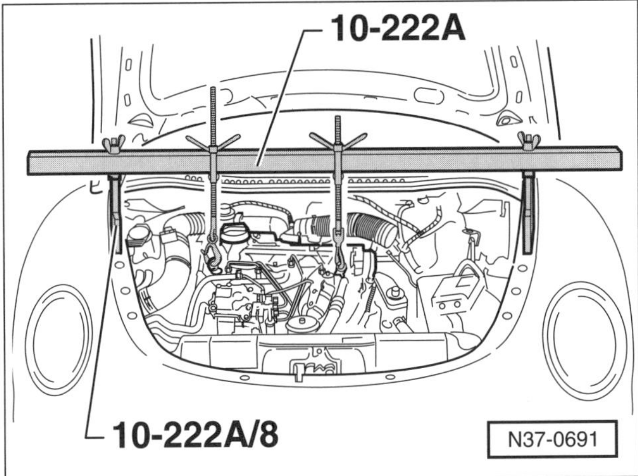

N37-0691

Fig. 17. Engine lifting equipment used to support weight of engine. Numbers shown are for VW special tools.

CAUTION —
- *Before installing the engine lifting hooks, disconnect all hoses and wiring in the vicinity of the engine lifting eyes, to prevent damage.*
- *Do not position adapters 10-222 A/8 on the fender mounting bolts.*

19. Loosen left front wheel bolts and lift vehicle.

20. Raise car and support with jack stands or lift. See **0 Maintenance** for proper lifting procedure.

WARNING —
Observe all warnings and cautions associated with lifting vehicle in **0 Maintenance**.

21. Remove left front wheel.

22. Remove lower sound absorber panel (belly pan). See Fig. 18.

23. Remove drivers side lower sound insulator. See Fig. 19.

NOTE —
Sound insulator fasteners may best be removed and installed with needle nose pliers.

0024267

Fig. 18. Remove screws (**arrows**) for belly pan.

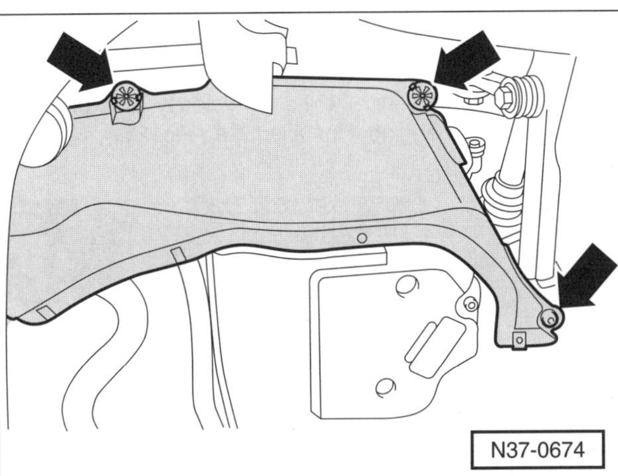

N37-0674

Fig. 19. Remove left sound insulator panel by unscrewing fasteners (**arrows**).

24. On vehicles with 1.9L TDI engine, remove intake air cooler and turbocharger, see **21 Turbocharger and Intercooler**.

25. Remove passenger side lower sound insulator.

26. Remove ATF pan protective cover. See Fig. 20.

27. Remove power steering line from starter and transmission mounts.

NOTE —
Use care not to damage the power steering line.

28. Remove starter, see **27 Engine Electrical**.

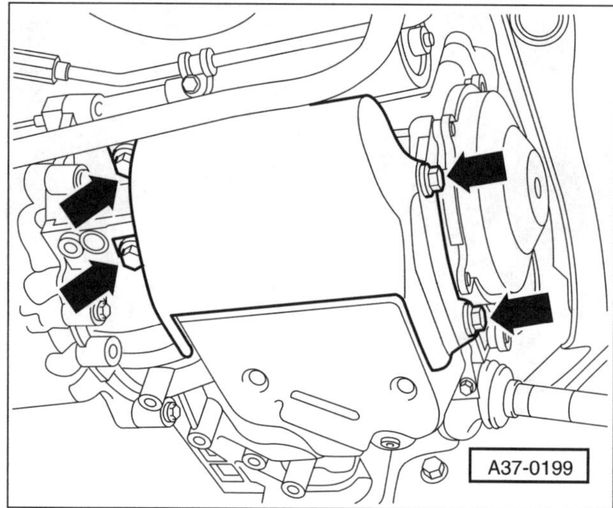

A37-0199

Fig. 20. Unbolt ATF pan protective cover (**arrows**).

29. Remove right inner constant velocity joint protective cover from engine if installed. See Fig. 21.

0024260

Fig. 21. Remove bolts (**arrows**) for CV joint protective cover.

30. Disconnect drive shafts from transmission flanges and tie up as high as possible.

NOTE —

When tying up axle shafts use care not to damage the paint on the body panels or the axle boots.

31. Remove bolts for pendulum mount. See Fig. 22.

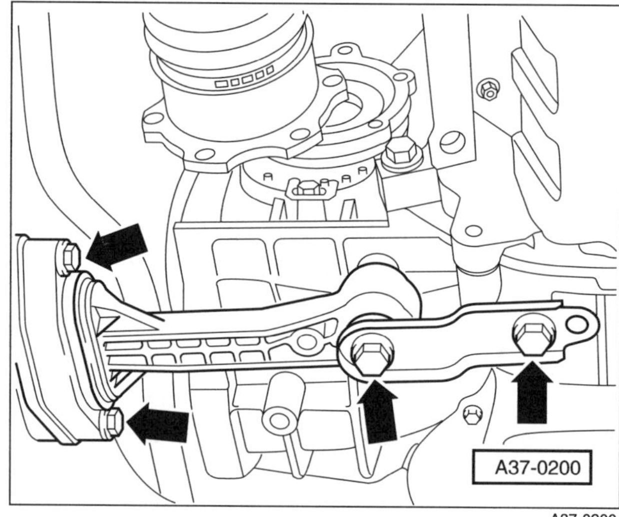

A37-0200

Fig. 22. Remove pendulum mounting bolts (**arrows**).

32. Remove additional radiator cooling fan, if installed, on right side of vehicle, see **19 Engine–Cooling System**.

33. Remove cap for torque converter nut cover.

34. Remove torque converter nuts (qty. 3) with special socket (V/175 or equivalent). See Fig. 23.

NOTE —

Turn crankshaft 120° to access each nut.

35. Turn steering fully to left.

36. Mark installation position of axle joint boots on left control arm.

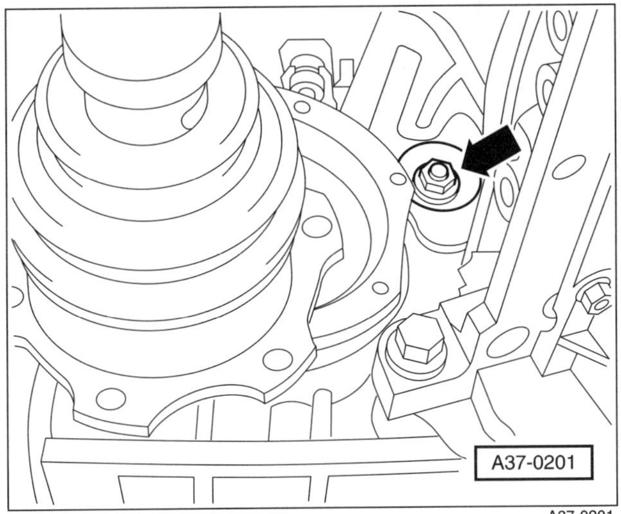

Fig. 23. Remove torque converter nuts (**arrow**).

37. Remove left control arm bolts. See Fig. 24.

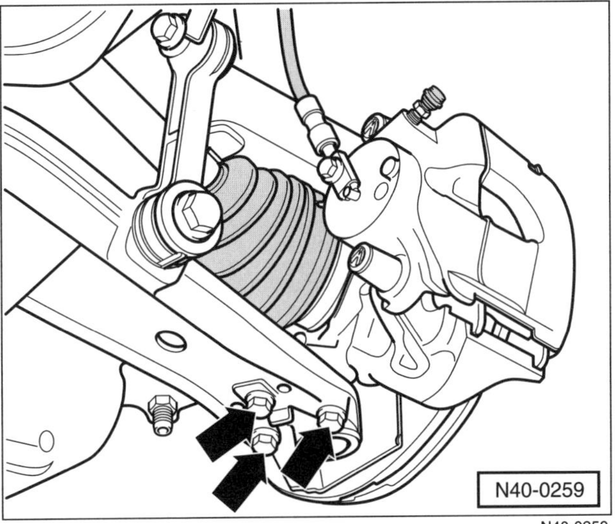

Fig. 24. Remove control arm bolts (**arrows**).

38. Unbolt left stabilizer coupling rod from control arm and turn coupling rod upward. Swing wheel bearing housing outward and guide left drive shaft out between subframe and transmission. Lift drive shaft and secure to suspension strut with wire. See Fig. 25.

39. Disconnect exhaust at front double clamp. Remove front exhaust support if necessary, see **26 Exhaust System/Emission Controls**.

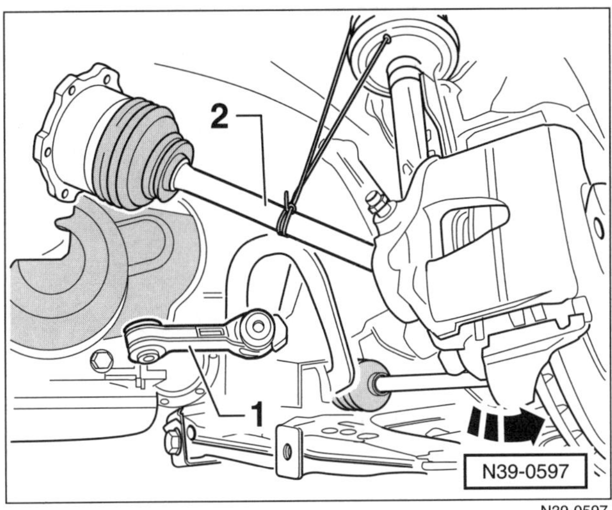

Fig. 25. Remove stabilizer coupling rod (**1**), swing wheel bearing housing outward (**arrow**), and move left drive shaft (**2**) away from transmission.

40. Remove mounting bolts for left engine/transmission mount. See Fig. 26.

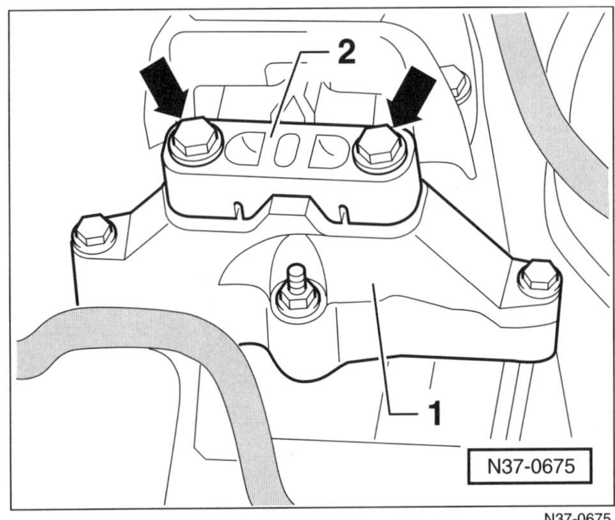

Fig. 26. Remove bolts (**arrows**) of left engine/transmission mount (**2**) from left support (**1**).

41. Carefully tilt engine/transmission assembly by lowering left-side spindle of support bar (VW 10-222A, or equivalent) by approximately 60 mm (2.3 in.).

42. Remove left support from transmission. See Fig. 27.

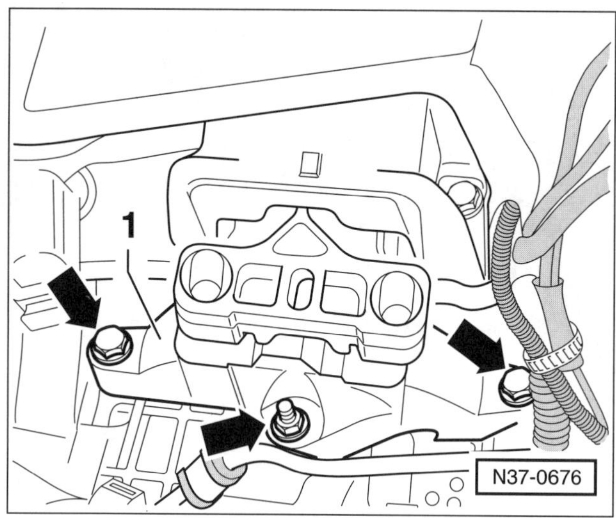

N37-0676

Fig. 27. Remove bolts and nut (**arrows**) for left support (**1**).

43. Bolt support rail (VW 457/1 or equivalent) to the pendulum support securing holes on subframe. See Fig. 28.

NOTE —

- *Volkswagen special tool 457/1 must be modified as described earlier under* **Special tools, modifying**.
- *Spacers totaling a thickness of 6 mm must be inserted between the subframe and the support rail VW 457/1.*

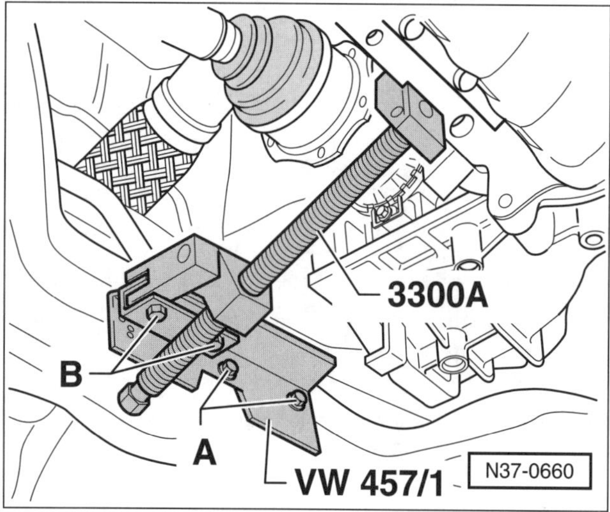

N37-0660

Fig. 28. Use two M8 x 25 bolts (**A**) to attach support rail to the pendulum mount securing holes on subframe. Install support 3300A to support rail and tighten with bolts (**B**). Numbers shown are for VW special tools.

44. Install support (VW 3300A) to support rail (VW 457/1) and secure. Refer to Fig. 28.

45. Press engine/transmission assembly forward carefully.

NOTE —

Do not damage power steering line when moving engine/transmission assembly.

46. Assemble transmission jack with support 3282, adjustment plate 3282/2 and support elements. See Fig. 29.

- Place adjustment plate 3282/2 on transmission support 3282. (Adjustment plate only fits in one position).
- Position transmission support arms according to holes in adjustment plate.

NOTE —

Arrow on adjustment plate 3282/2 should point toward front of vehicle.

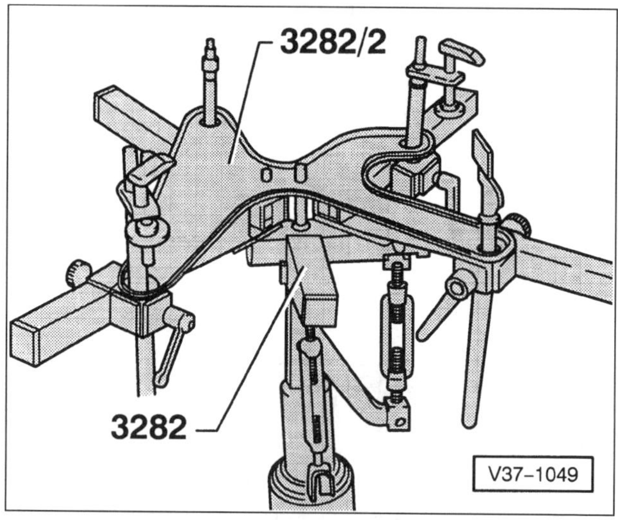

V37-1049

Fig. 29. Volkswagen transmission jack 3282 with adjustment plate 3282/2.

47. Place transmission jack under vehicle. See Fig. 30.

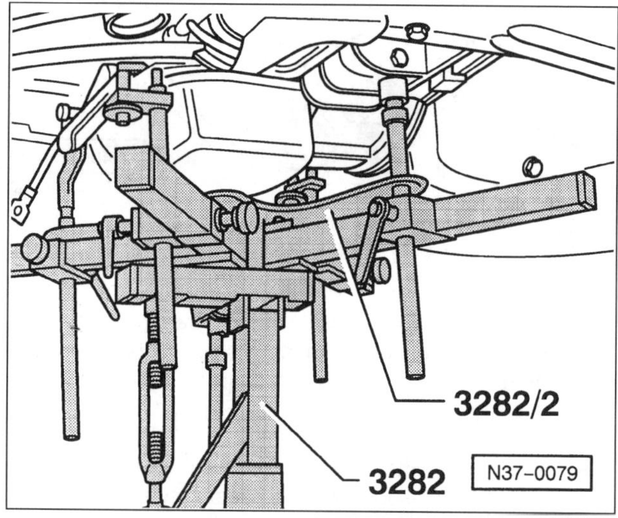

N37-0079

Fig. 30. Transmission jack correctly placed under transmission. Numbers shown are for VW transmission jack and adapters.

48. Align adjustment plate parallel to transmission and lock safety supports on transmission jack.

49. Place safety support pin on oil pan and secure it to transmission housing. See Fig. 31.

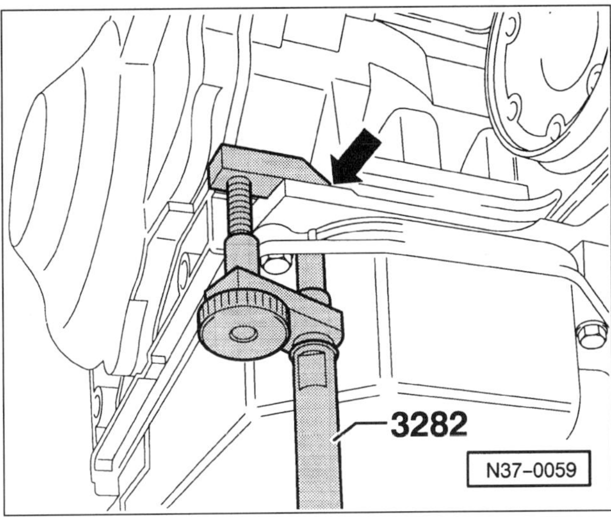

Fig. 31. Safety support pin placed on oil pan and secured to transmission housing (**arrow**).

50. Turn right transmission output flange to the right until flat section is vertical.

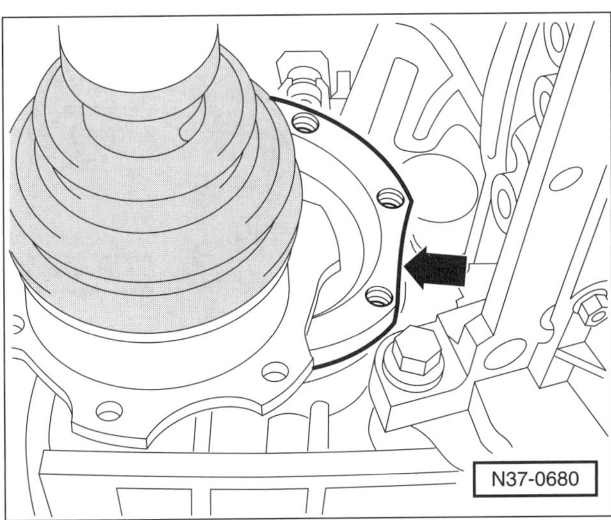

Fig. 32. Turn transmission flange to the right until flat section (**arrow**) is vertical.

51. Remove lower engine/transmission securing bolts.

> ***WARNING —***
> *Before unbolting lower engine-to-transmission mounting bolts be sure to support the weight of the vehicle at all four corners with jack stands designed for that purpose. Removal of the transmission can upset the weight balance of the vehicle and cause it to fall off the lift.*

52. Separate transmission from engine while pushing torque converter away from drive plate.

> ***NOTE —***
> *On automatic transmissions, the torque converter should come off with the transmission. Secure the torque converter to the transmission to prevent damage.*

53. Lower transmission slightly.

54. While lowering transmission, guide power steering pressure line past transmission.

55. Turn transmission and carefully lower.

56. While lowering transmission, guide right axle joint at engine past support 3300 A.

> ***NOTE —***
> *Be careful not to let multi-function switch contact engine/transmission mount.*

Transmission, installing

> ***NOTE —***
> *If torque converter has been removed, the torque converter seal will need to be replaced as described later.*

The transmission is installed in the reverse order of removal, noting the following:

1. When installing torque converter, be sure that both drive pins engage in the ATF pump inner wheel recesses.
2. Before installing transmission, be sure that the dowel sleeves are correctly located.
3. When installing transmission, check torque converter contact pattern on drive plate.
4. Replace selector cable locking circlip.
5. Adjust selector lever cable, see **Selector lever cable, adjusting**.
6. Check and top up ATF level.
7. Connect VAG 1551/1552, or equivalent, and check diagnostic trouble code memory.
8. Have the front wheels professionally aligned once installation is complete.

Use the following tightening torques when installing the automatic transmission.

Tightening torques

- Drive shaft to transmission drive flange . . . . 40 Nm (30 ft-lb)
- Torque converter to drive plate. . . . . . 60 Nm (44 ft-lb)
- Transmission to engine (M12) . . . . . . 80 Nm (59 ft-lb)
- Transmission to oil pan (M10) . . . . . . 45 Nm (33 ft-lb)
- Axle joint to control arm . . . . 20 Nm (15 ft-lb) plus ¼ turn (90°)
- Coupling rod to control arm . . . . 45 Nm (33 ft-lb)
- Left mount to transmission. . . . . 25 Nm (18 ft-lb)
- Wheel bolts to wheel hub. . . . . 120 Nm (89 ft-lb)
- Protective cap to drive shaft at engine 33 Nm (24 ft-lb)

Remaining transmission installation tightening torques are given below with corresponding Fig. # as necessary for clarification.

Tightening torques

Always replace all stretch bolts (with plus ¼ turn spec.)

- Transmission to body
  - (bolts **A**, See Fig. 33.). . . . . 60 Nm (44 ft-lb) plus ¼ turn (90°)
  - (bolts **B**, See Fig. 33.). . . . . 60 Nm (44 ft-lb) plus ¼ turn (90°)
- Pendulum mount to body (bolts **A**, See Fig. 34.) . . . . 20 Nm (15 ft-lb) plus ¼ turn (90°)
- Pendulum mount bracket (bolts **B**, See Fig. 34.) . . . . 40 Nm (30 ft-lb) plus ¼ turn (90°)

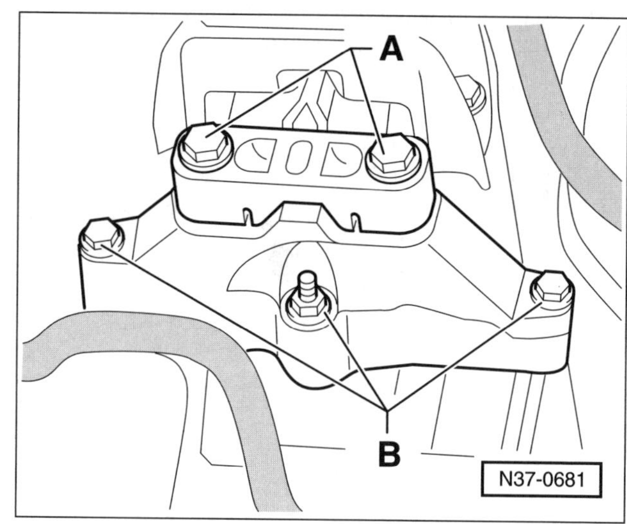

N37-0681

Fig. 33. Transmission to body mount.

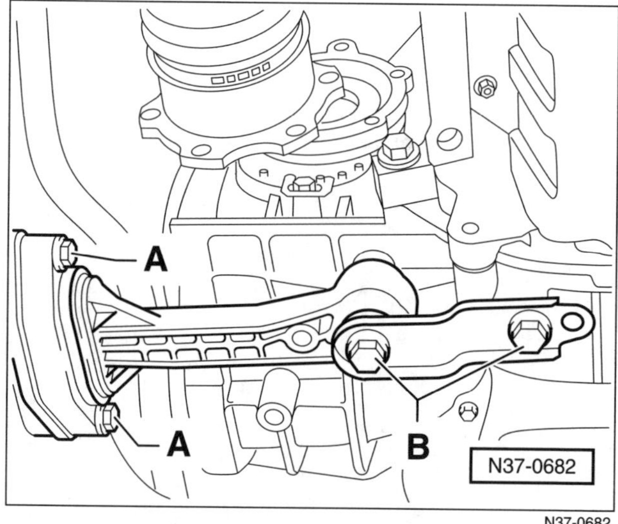

N37-0682

Fig. 34. Rear transmission pendulum mount.

TORQUE CONVERTER

When replacing the torque converter, always note the torque converter code number. The code number can be found in one of two places. See Fig. 35. and Fig. 36. The replacement torque converter must have the same code number, as it is matched to the transmission/engine application.

> ***CAUTION—***
> *When installing the torque converter, make sure that both drive pins engage in the recesses in the ATF pump inner wheel.*

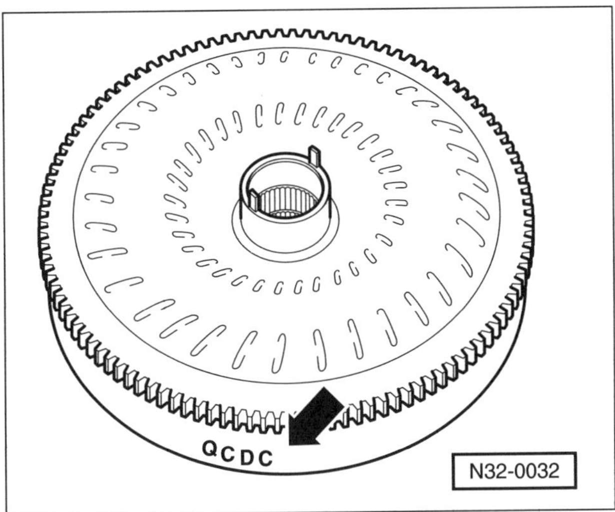

N32-0032

Fig. 35. Torque converter code letter location (**arrow**).

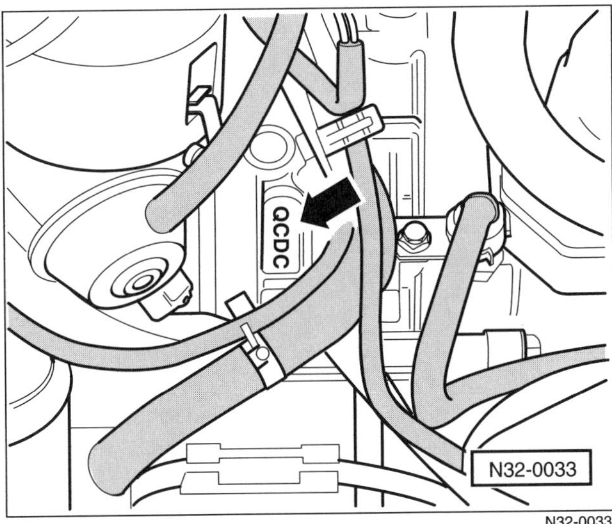

N32-0033

Fig. 36. Torque converter code letters visible through access hole with transmission installed (**arrow**).

If the torque converter has become contaminated by particles resulting from wear or abrasion, or in the course of a major overhaul of the transmission, always flush the torque converter with clean ATF. The torque converter can be flushed with commercially-available extraction equipment, such as EZ1 fluid evacuator, or Volkswagen special tools VAG 1358A and VAG 1358 A/1 probe.

Torque converter oil seal, replacing (transmission removed)

1. Remove the torque converter seal using a seal extractor. See Fig. 37.

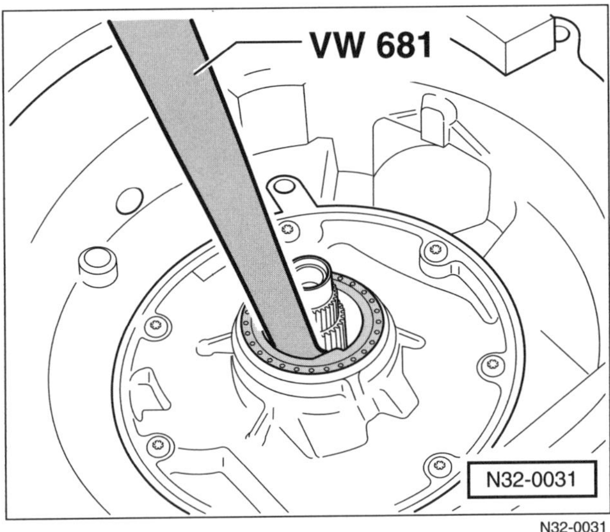

N32-0031

Fig. 37. Torque converter seal being removed from bell housing. Volkswagen special tool VW 681 shown.

2. Using a seal driver, drive seal in until flush. See Fig. 38.

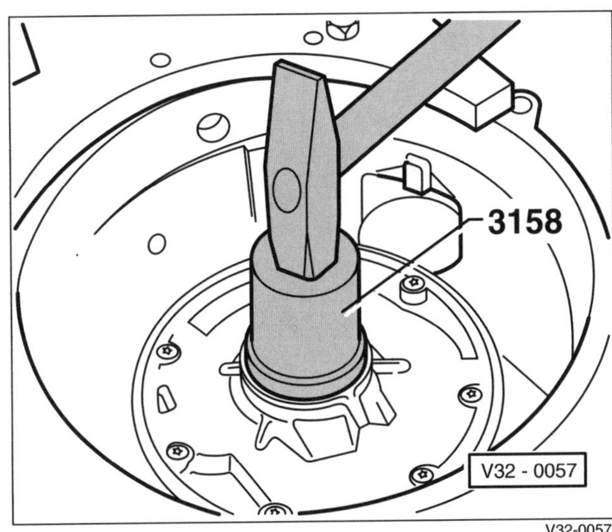

V32-0057

Fig. 38. Installing torque converter seal with seal driver. Volkswagen special tool 3158 shown.

ATF COOLER

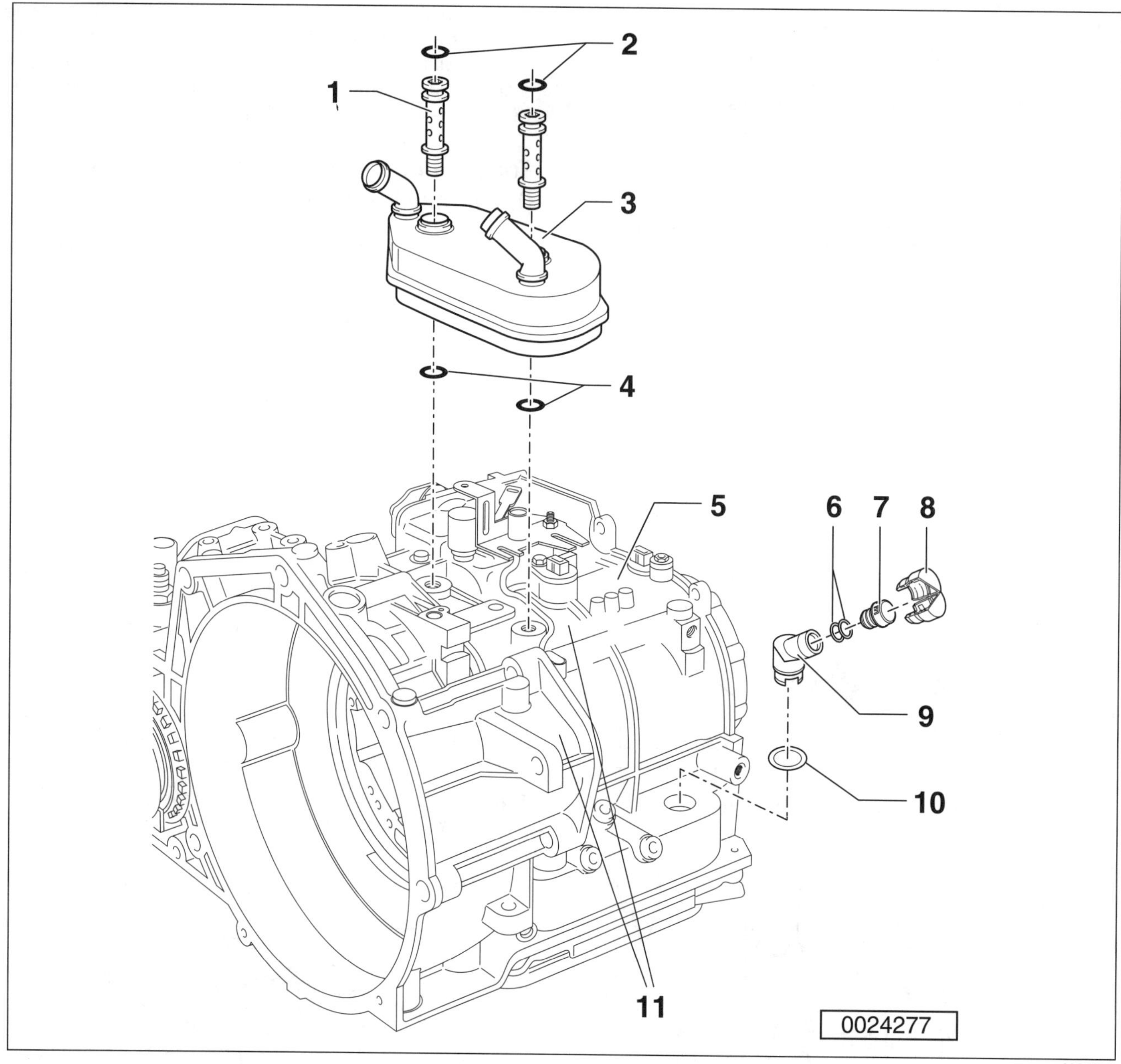

0024277

Fig. 39. ATF cooler for automatic transmission.

1. **Banjo bolt**
   - Tighten to 35 Nm (26 ft-lb)
2. **O-ring**
   - Always replace
3. **ATF cooler**
4. **O-ring**
   - Always replace
5. **Transmission housing**
6. **Seal**
   - Always replace
7. **Plug**
8. **Cap**
   - To secure ATF level plug after checking ATF level
   - Always replace
9. **ATF filler tube**
10. **O-ring**
    - Always replace
11. **Location of transmission code and production number**

40 Front Suspension and Drive Axles

GENERAL

Special tools, equipment and procedures are required for most front suspension repair and component replacement. In addition, front wheel alignment is almost always disturbed when suspension components are removed or replaced.

This section covers repairs to the front suspension and related components. For rear suspension servicing and repair information, see **42 Rear Suspension**. For wheel alignment specifications, see **44 Wheels, Tires, Wheel Alignment**.

Also covered are the drive axle assemblies with Constant Velocity (CV) joints as installed in vehicles with manual transmissions, as well as drive axles with triple roller joints installed in vehicles with automatic transmissions.

WARNING —
- *Do not re-use any fasteners that are worn or deformed in normal use. Most fasteners are designed to be used only once and become unreliable and may fail when used a second time. This includes, but is not limited to, nuts, bolts, washers, circlips cotter pins, self-locking nuts and bolts. For replacements, always use new parts.*
- *Do not reinstall bolts and nuts coated with undercoating wax, as correct tightening torque cannot be ensured. Always clean the threads of removed bolts and nuts that are to be re-used with a suitable solvent before installation. Ensure that new parts are clean.*

WARNING —
- *Do not use standard nuts and bolts in place of green colored parts. The green color denotes a special anti-corrosion process known as "dacromet" or "delta-tone". Torque specifications are given based on use of these parts only.*
- *Always replaced rusted or corroded bolts, nuts and washers even if not specifically indicated.*
- *DO NOT attempt to straighten or weld suspension struts, wheel bearing housings, control arms or any other wheel locating or load bearing components of the front suspension.*

CAUTION —
If a vehicle has to be moved (rolled) after removing the drive axle, install an outer constant velocity joint into the wheel bearing/housing and tighten the nut to 50 Nm (37 ft-lb). Otherwise the wheel bearing will be damaged.

SUBFRAME AND CONTROL ARMS

The control arms and the subframe are mounted in replaceable rubber bushings that are subject to wear. The subframe supports the steering gear and the lower engine/transmission pendulum mount. Always understand and observe the warnings and cautions listed above before working on the suspension components. Fig. 1 shows the subframe, stabilizer bar and control arm assembly.

40

Subframe/stabilizer bar/control arm assembly

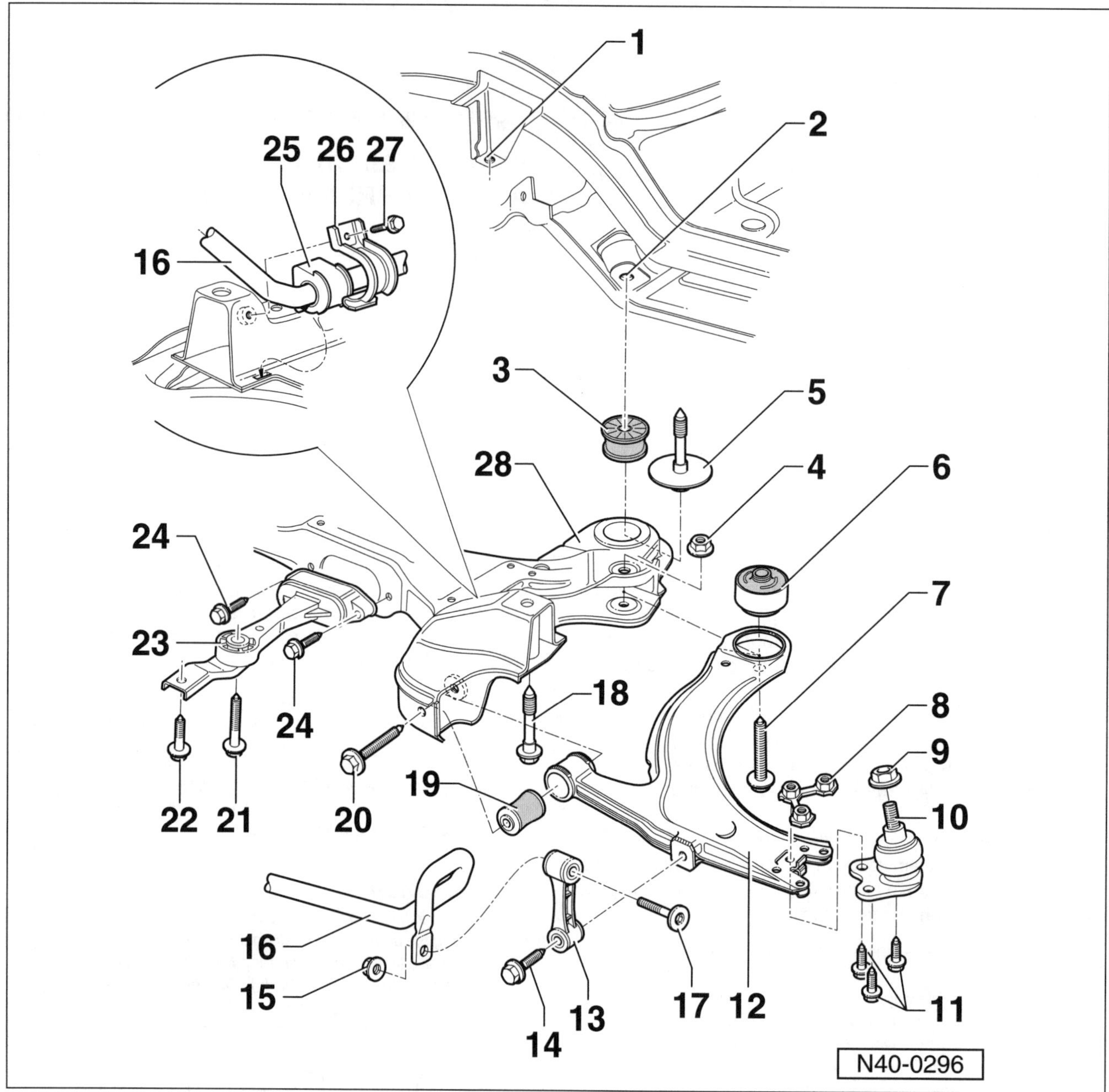

N40-0296

Fig. 1. Subframe with left control arm and related components.

1. **Subframe retaining bracket (on body)**
2. **Welded nut (in body)**
3. **Rear bonded rubber bushing for subframe**
4. **Nut, self-locking**
   - Always replace
5. **Bolt**
   - Always replace
   - Tighten to 100 Nm (74 ft-lb) + ¼-turn (90°)
6. **Rear bonded rubber bushing for control arm**
   - Installed position, **see** (A)
   - Pressing out/in, **see** (B)
7. **Bolt**
   - Always replace
   - Tighten to 70 Nm (52 ft-lb) + ¼-turn (90°)
8. **Nut plate**
9. **Nut, self-locking**
   - Always replace
   - Tighten to 45 Nm (33 ft-lb)

(continued from previous page)

10. Ball joint
- Checking, **see** (C)

11. Bolts
- Always replace
- Tighten to 20 Nm (15 ft-lb) + ¼-turn (90°)

12. Control arm

13. Stabilizer connecting link

14. Bolt
- Tighten to 45 Nm (33 ft-lb)

15. Nut, self-locking
- Always replace
- Tighten to 30 Nm (22 ft-lb)

16. Stabilizer bar
- Subframe must be lowered to remove and install

17. Bolt

18. Bolt
- Always replace
- Tighten to 100 Nm (74 ft-lb) + ¼-turn (90°)

19. Front bonded rubber bushing for control arm
- Pressing out, **see** (D)
- Pressing in, **see** (E)

20. Bolt
- Always replace
- Tighten to 70 Nm (52 ft-lb) + ¼-turn (90°)

21. Bolt
- Always replace
- Tighten to 40 Nm (30 ft-lb) + ¼-turn (90°)

22. Bolt
- Always replace
- Tighten to 40 Nm (30 ft-lb) + ¼-turn (90°)

23. Pendulum support

24. Bolts
- Always replace
- Tighten to 20 Nm (15 ft-lb) + 1/4-turn (90°)

25. Stabilizer bar bushing

26. Stabilizer bar mounting bracket

27. Bolt
- Tighten to 25 Nm (18 ft-lb)

28. Subframe

(A) Rear bushing for control arm, installed position

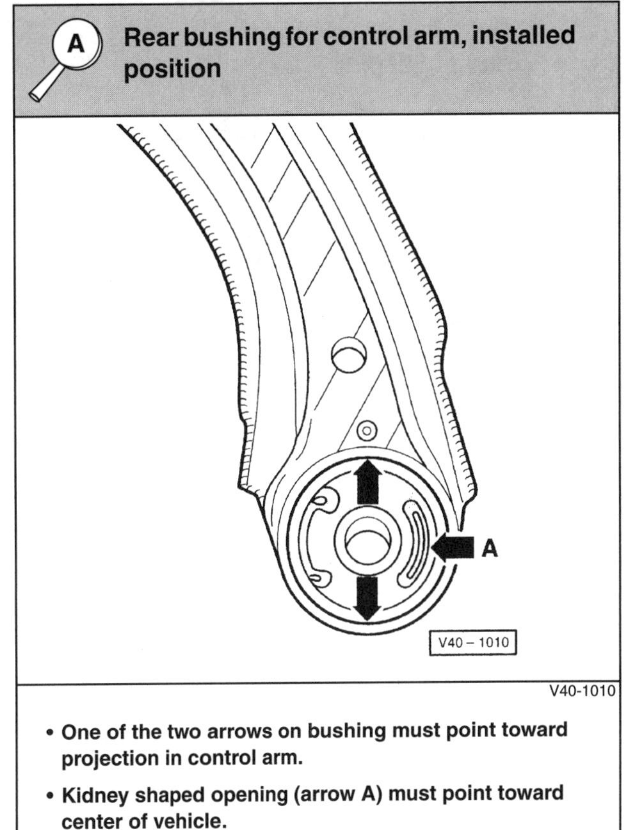

V40-1010

- **One of the two arrows on bushing must point toward projection in control arm.**
- **Kidney shaped opening (arrow A) must point toward center of vehicle.**

(B) Rear bushing for control arm, pressing out/in

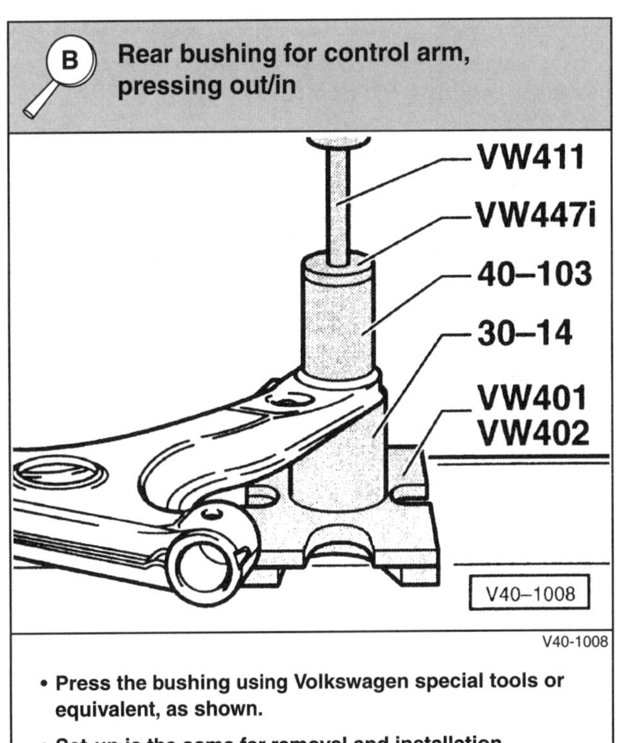

V40-1008

- **Press the bushing using Volkswagen special tools or equivalent, as shown.**
- **Set-up is the same for removal and installation.**

C Ball joint, checking axial and radial play

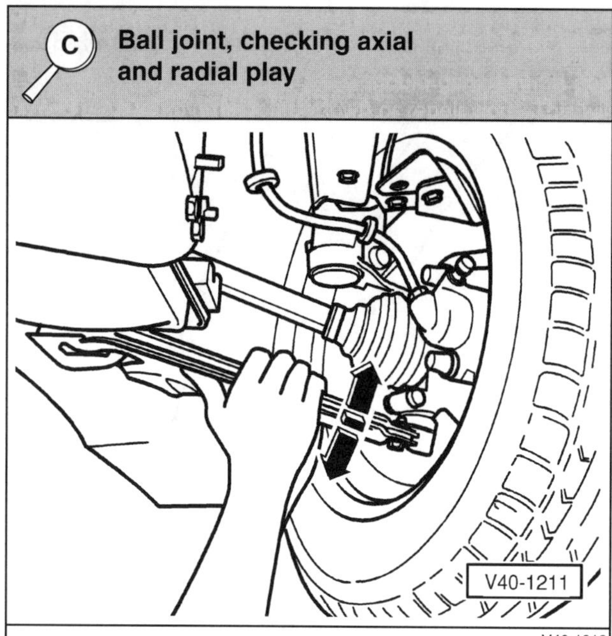

V40-1212

- Forcibly pull ball joint down and press up again (arrows).
- Forcibly push lower part of wheel in and out.
- There must not be any perceptible play as a result of either check. Do not confuse with upper suspension strut mount or wheel bearing play.
- Replace ball joint if dust boot is damaged.

D Pressing out front bonded rubber bushing for control arm

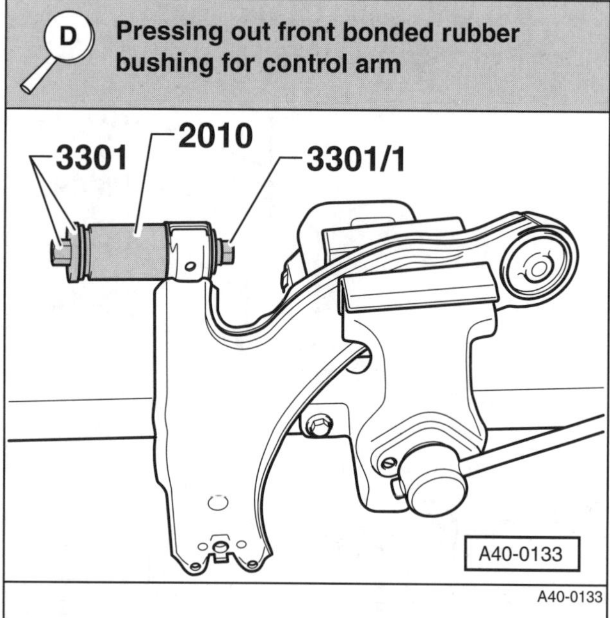

A40-0133

- Support control arm securely in vise as shown.

E Pressing in front bonded rubber bushing for control arm

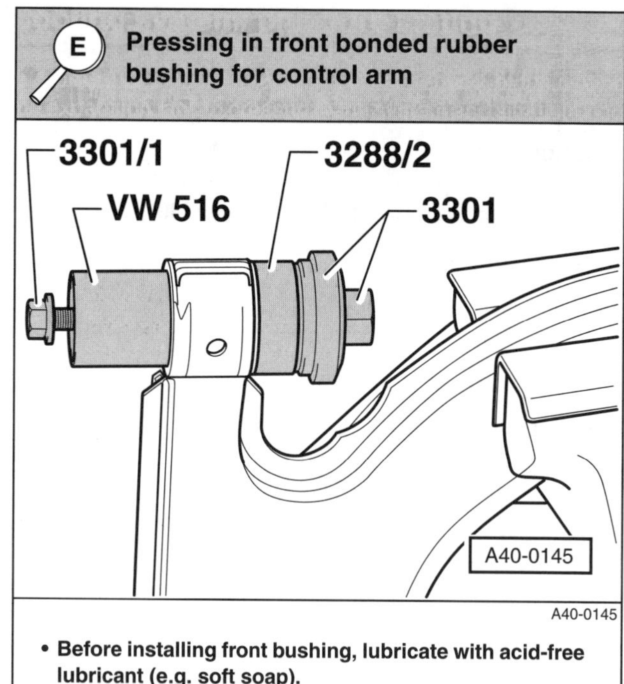

A40-0145

- Before installing front bushing, lubricate with acid-free lubricant (e.g. soft soap).
- Never use grease.

WHEEL BEARINGS

Removal and/or replacement of the front wheel bearings requires special tools and equipment. Note that the wheel bearing is destroyed any time it is removed. Always understand and observe the warnings and cautions listed at the beginning of this section. Fig. 2 shows the front wheel bearing housing with related suspension components.

Front wheel bearing housing assembly

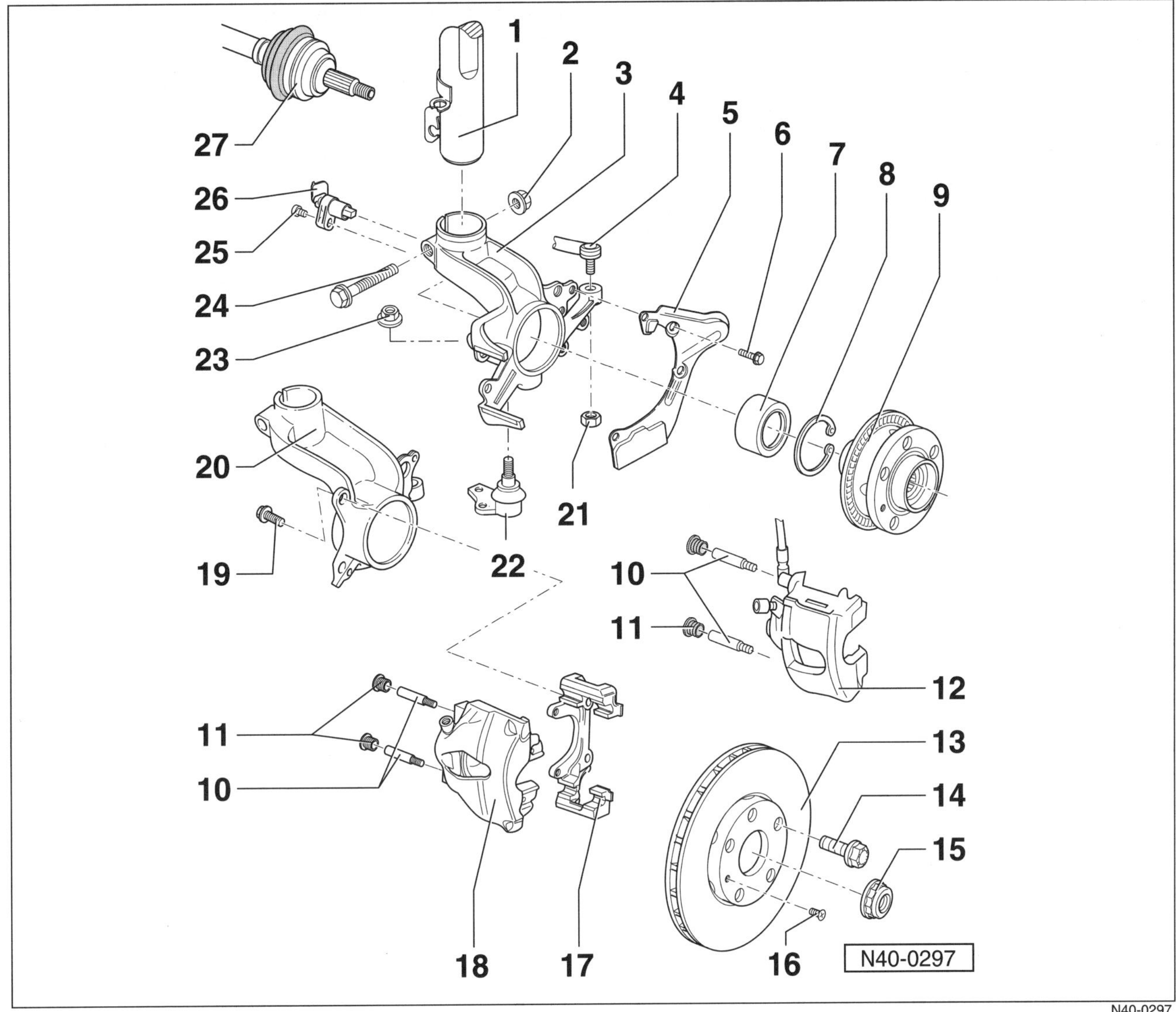

N40-0297

Fig. 2. Front wheel bearing with related components on the left side.

1. **Suspension strut**
2. **Nut, self-locking**
   - Always replace
   - Tighten to 50 Nm (37 ft-lb) + ¼-turn (90°)
   - Never less than 90°
   - Turning angle tolerance 90°–120°
3. **Wheel bearing housing**
   - Engine code ALH - 1.9 Liter TDI
   - Engine code AEG - 2.0 Liter Gasoline
4. **Tie rod end**
5. **Splash plate**
6. **Bolt**
   - Tighten to 10 Nm (7 ft-lb)
7. **Wheel bearing**
   - Always replace (bearing is destroyed when removed)
   - Pressing out, **see** (A)
   - Pressing in, **see** (B)
8. **Circlip**
   - Make sure clip is correctly seated
9. **Wheel hub with ABS wheel speed sensor rotor**
   - Rotor welded to wheel hub
   - Pressing out of wheel bearing housing, **see** (C)
   - Pressing into wheel bearing, **see** (D)
10. **Guide pins**
    - Tighten to 27.5 Nm (20 ft-lb)

(continued on following page)

(continued from previous page)

11. Protective caps

12. Brake caliper
- Engine code ALH - 1.9 Liter TDI
- Engine code AEG - 2.0 Liter Gasoline
- Do not loosen the brake hose when working on the front suspension
- Do not allow the caliper to hang by the brake hose. The unsupported weight can stretch and damage the hose. Suspend the brake caliper using a piece of wire or similar.

13. Ventilated brake disc (rotor)

14. Wheel (lug) bolts
- Tighten to 120 Nm (87 ft-lb)

15. Axle nut, self-locking
- Always replace
- Any paint residue and/or corrosion on threads of outer joint must be removed before nut is installed
- Recommended tightening procedure, **see** Ⓔ
- Alternate tightening procedure, **see** Ⓕ

16. Screw
- Tighten to 4 Nm (35 in-lb)

17. Brake carrier
- Engine code APH - 1.8 Liter

18. Brake caliper
- Engine code APH - 1.8 Liter
- Do not loosen the brake hose when working on the front suspension
- Do not allow the caliper to hang by brake hose. The unsupported weight can stretch and damage hose. Suspend brake caliper using a piece of wire or similar.

19. Bolt, self-locking
- Tighten to 125 Nm (92 ft-lb)
- Clean ribs on under side of bolt head

20. Wheel bearing housing
- Engine code APH - 1.8 Liter

21. Nut, self-locking
- Always replace
- Tighten to 45 Nm (33 ft-lb)

22. Ball joint

23. Nut, self-locking
- Always replace
- Tighten to 45 Nm (33 ft-lb)

24. Bolt
- Always replace

25. Bolt
- Tighten to 8 Nm (71 in-lb)

26. ABS wheel speed sensor

27. Drive axle
- Pressing drive axle out/in from wheel hub, **see** Ⓖ

Ⓐ Wheel bearing, pressing out

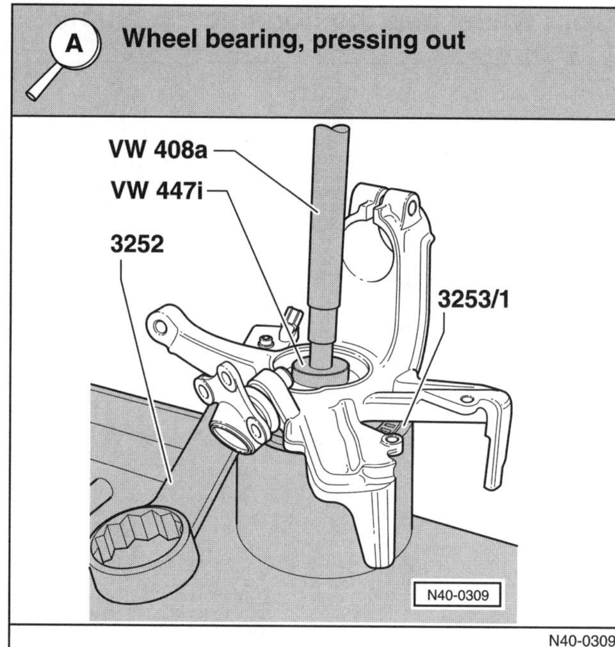

N40-0309

- **Press the bushing using Volkswagen special tools or equivalent, as shown.**

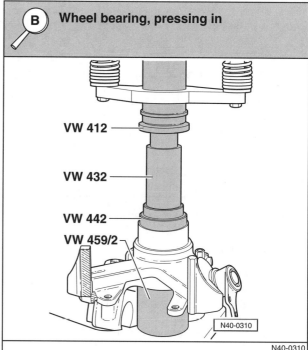

Ⓑ Wheel bearing, pressing in

N40-0310

- **Install circlip in housing with open end at the bottom of the wheel bearing housing.**
- **Be sure that circlip is properly seated.**
- **Press the bushing using Volkswagen special tools or equivalent, as shown.**

C Wheel hub, pressing out of housing

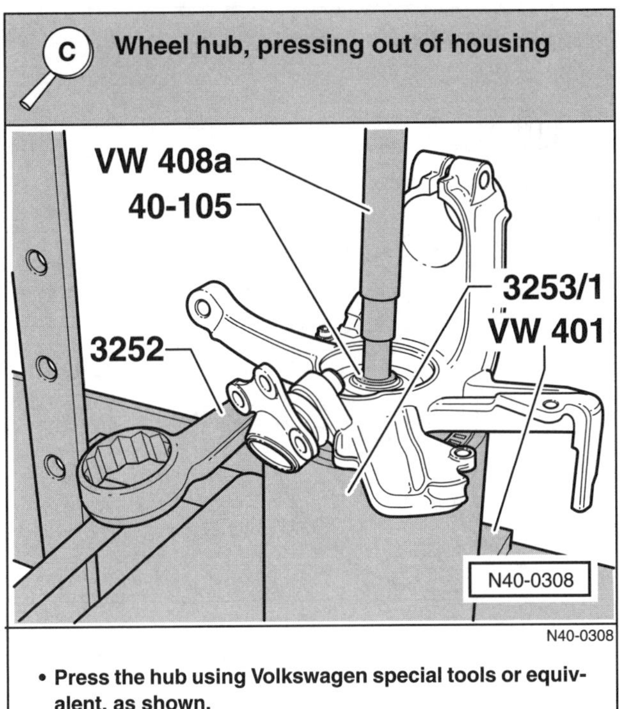

N40-0308

- Press the hub using Volkswagen special tools or equivalent, as shown.

D Wheel hub, pressing into wheel bearing

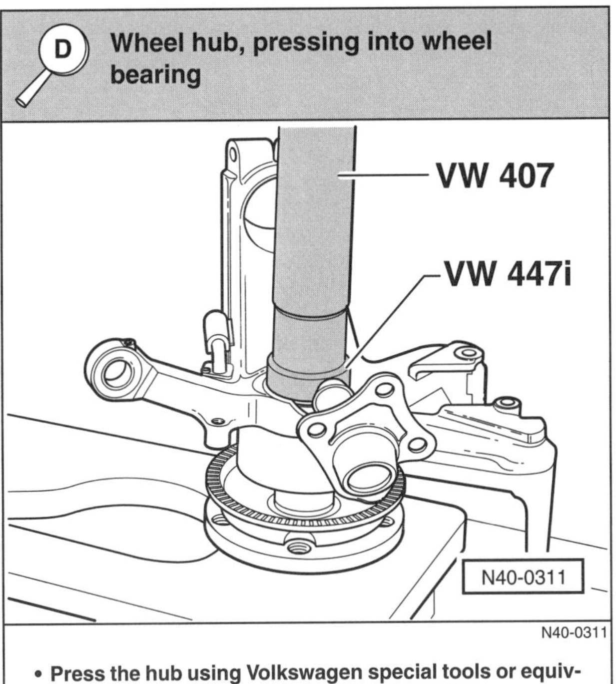

N40-0311

- Press the hub using Volkswagen special tools or equivalent, as shown.

E Axle nut, final tightening - recommended procedure

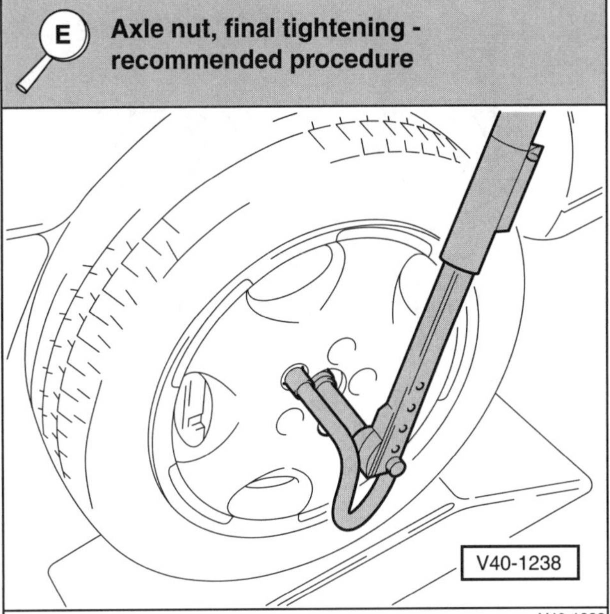

V40-1238

- Weight of vehicle MUST be on its wheels.
- Tighten 12-point nut to 300 Nm (221 ft-lb) and then loosen one full turn.
- Tighten to 50 Nm (37 ft-lb).
- Using a torque angle measuring wrench, tighten 1/12 of a turn (30°)

> *WARNING —*
> *Loosen and tighten axle nuts only when weight of vehicle is on the wheels. The leverage required for this operation is sufficient to topple the vehicle to the ground if supported on a lift or jack stands.*

F Axle nut, final tightening - alternate procedure

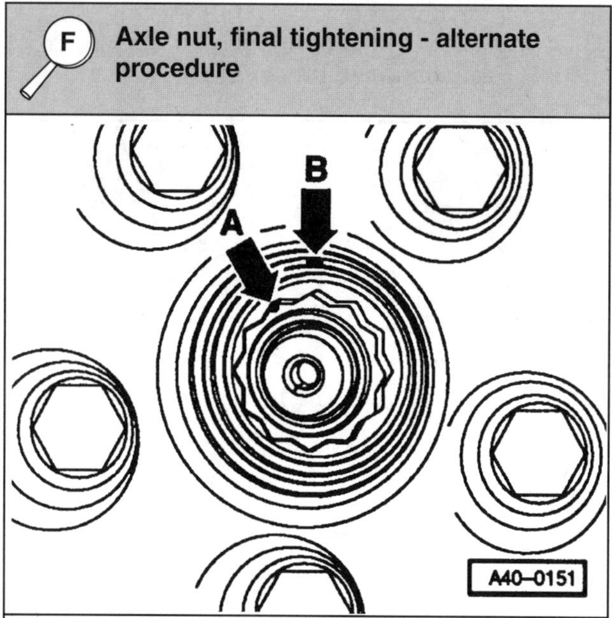

A40-0151

- Weight of vehicle MUST be on its wheels.
- Tighten 12-point nut to 300 Nm (221 ft-lb) and then loosen one full turn.
- Tighten to 50 Nm (37 ft-lb).
- Make a mark on nut point with line (arrow A).
- Make a second mark on the wheel hub (arrow B) one nut point away from the first. (The distance between each nut point on a 12-point nut is 30°)
- Tighten the axle nut until both marks line up.

G Drive axle/constant velocity joint, pressing out

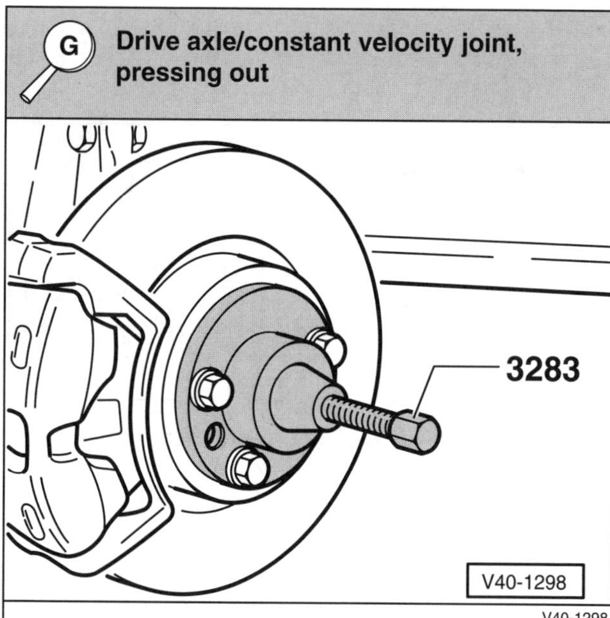

V40-1298

- Press end of axle out using Volkswagen special tools or equivalent, as shown.
- Be sure there is sufficient clearance before pressing.

> ***WARNING —***
> *Loosen and tighten axle nuts only when weight of vehicle is on the wheels. The leverage required for this operation is sufficient to topple the vehicle to the ground if supported on a lift or jack stands.*

SUSPENSION STRUTS

Removal and/or replacement of the front suspension struts requires special tools and equipment. Note that the strut is a sealed unit integral with the shock absorber. Always understand and observe the warnings and cautions listed at the beginning of this section. Fig. 3 shows the front strut with related components.

Front suspension strut assembly

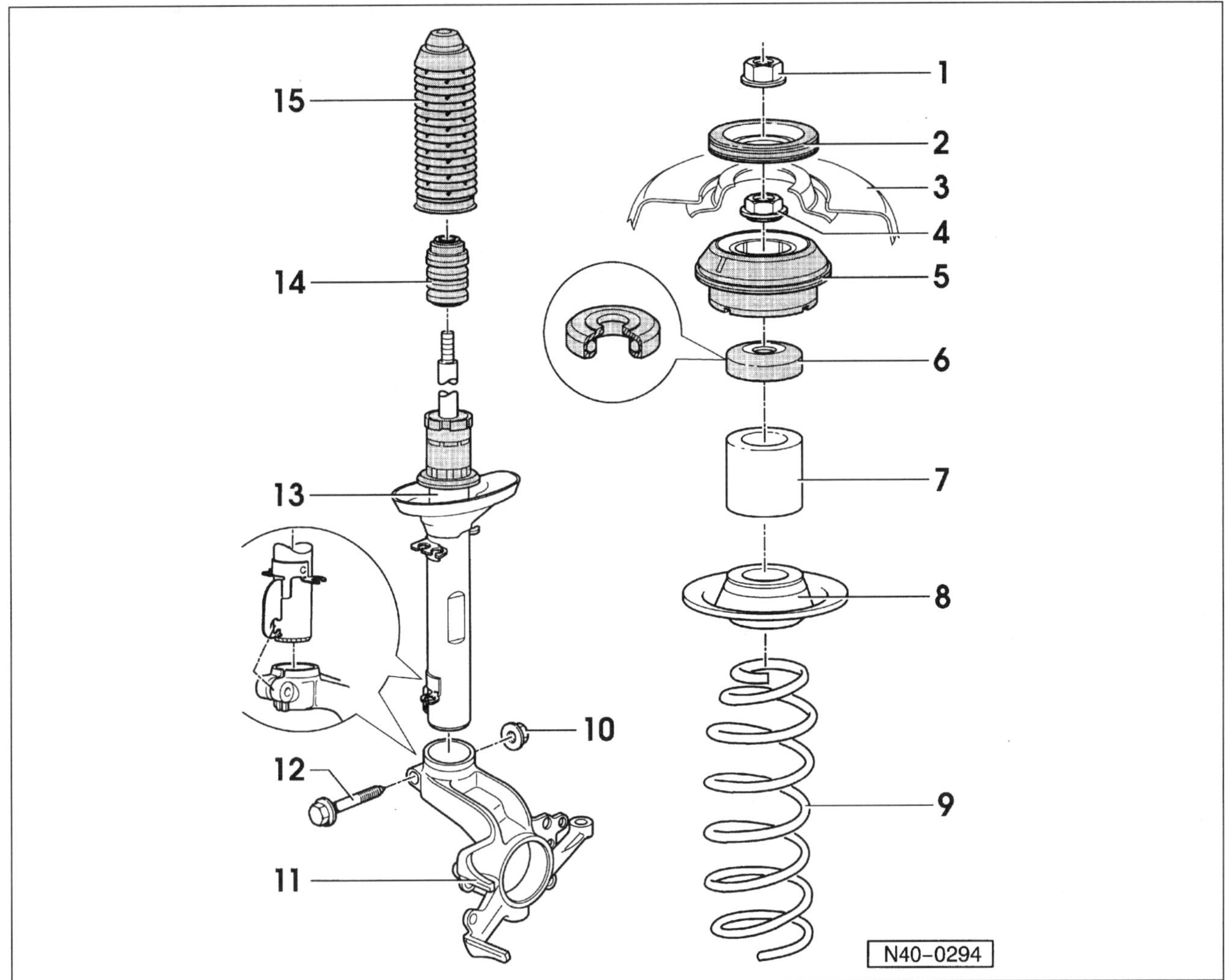

Fig. 3. Suspension strut with coil spring and related components.

1. **Outer nut, self-locking**
   - Always replace
   - Tighten to 60 Nm (44 ft-lb)
2. **Stop plate**
3. **Suspension strut turret**
   - Welded to inner wheel housing
4. **Inner nut**
   - Tighten to 60 Nm (44 ft-lb)
5. **Suspension strut mount, upper**
6. **Axial ball bearing**
7. **Bushing**
   - Not applicable for US/Canada
8. **Spring seat, upper**
9. **Coil spring**
   - Note color-code marking for identification
   - Outer surface of spring must not be damaged
10. **Nut, self-locking**
    - Always replace
    - Tighten to 50 Nm (37 ft-lb) + ¼-turn (90°)
    - Never less than 90°
    - Turning angle tolerance 90°–120°
11. **Wheel bearing housing**
12. **Bolt**
    - Always replace
13. **Shock absorber**
    - Can be replaced individually
    - Slight traces of oil do not necessitate replacement
14. **Bump stop**
15. **Protective sleeve**

Front suspension strut, removing and installing

WARNING —
- *Suspension strut springs are compressed and under pressure when installed on struts.*
- *DO NOT attempt to disassemble or repair suspension without proper tools and experience. Serious injury will result from using improper tools or procedures.*
- *Suspension strut is removed and installed as an assembly. DO NOT disassemble or attempt repair while assembly is still installed in vehicle.*
- *Front wheel alignment may be altered during suspension strut repairs. Wheel alignment should be checked and adjusted any time repairs are made to the suspension strut area.*

1. Raise vehicle and properly support.

WARNING —
- *Be sure to use jack stands designed for the purpose.*
- *Jack stands should be on a level hard surface.*
- *If a vehicle lift/hoist is used, be sure vehicle is lifted according to manufacturer's instructions.*

2. Remove wheel assembly.
3. Remove both guide pins from brake caliper. See Fig. 4.

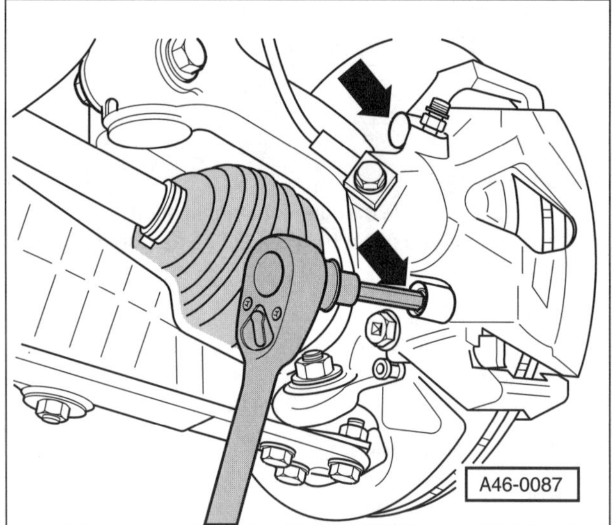

A46-0087

Fig. 4. Remove guide pins (**arrows**) from brake caliper and support caliper with a wire hanger.

4. Remove brake caliper and suspend using wire.

NOTE —
- *Suspend the brake caliper using a piece of wire or similar.*
- *Do not allow the caliper to hang by the brake hose. The unsupported weight can stretch and damage the hose.*

5. Remove connecting link from control arm.
6. Disconnect ABS wheel speed sensor wiring from suspension strut (where applicable).
7. When removing right side suspension strut the following additional work is required
   - Remove lower sound absorber panel (belly pan).
   - Vehicles with TDI engine, remove intake air duct between charge air cooler and turbocharger.
   - Remove right side noise insulation.
   - Disconnect drive axle from transmission drive flange.
8. For left and right sides, remove bolt and nut from wheel bearing housing and suspension strut connection. See Fig. 5.

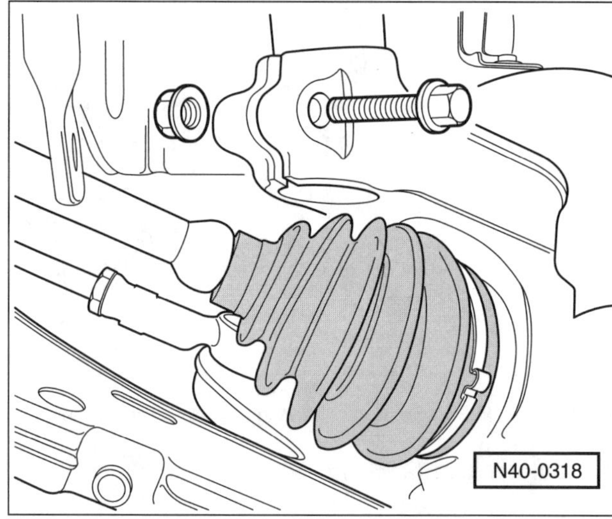

N40-0318

Fig. 5. Bolt and nut securing wheel bearing housing and suspension strut.

9. Insert Volkswagen special spreader tool 3424 into gap in wheel bearing housing and turn ¼-turn in either direction to spread apart. See Fig. 6.
10. Push brake disc in direction of suspension strut by hand to prevent shock absorber tube from canting in wheel bearing housing opening.
11. Pull wheel bearing housing down and clear of shock absorber.

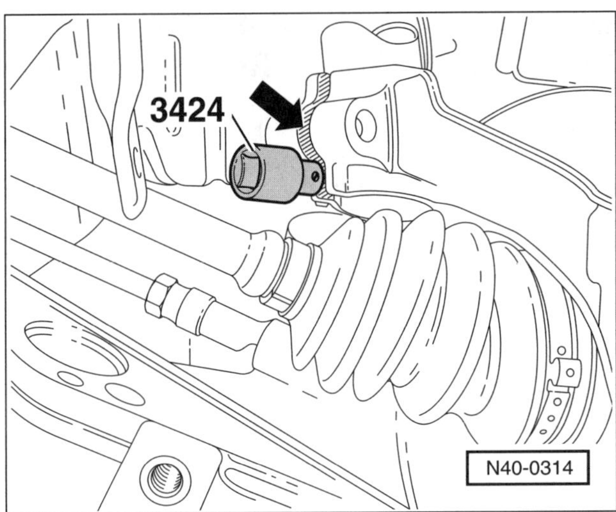

N40-0314

Fig. 6. Volkswagen special tool 3424 (**arrow**) shown inserted into gap in wheel bearing housing. Turn with a ½-inch ratchet.

12. Remove wiper arms and cowl panel, see **92 Wipers and Washers.**

13. Remove outer nut and stop plate for upper shock absorber mount using Volkswagen special tools or equivalent. See Fig. 7.

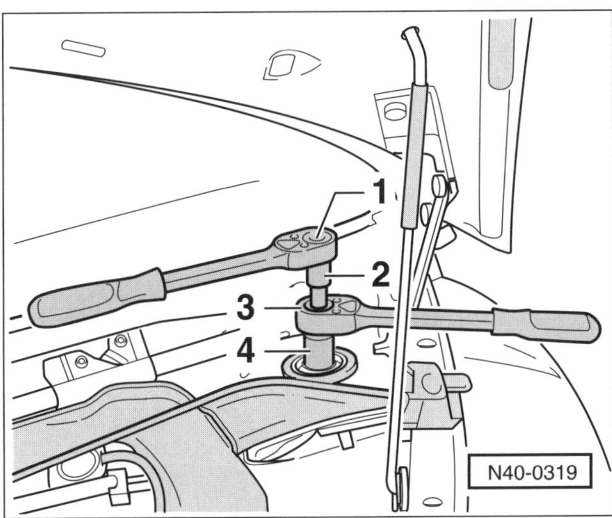

N40-0319

Fig. 7. Set-up for removing suspension strut from vehicle using tools from Volkswagen special tool kit T10001; (**1**) ½-inch ratchet, (**2**) T10001/8, (**3**) T10001/11, (**4**) T10001/5.

14. Carefully remove suspension strut from below.

Coil spring, removing and installing

1. Using VAG1752 spring compressor or equivalent, compress coil spring until upper spring seat is free. See Fig. 8.

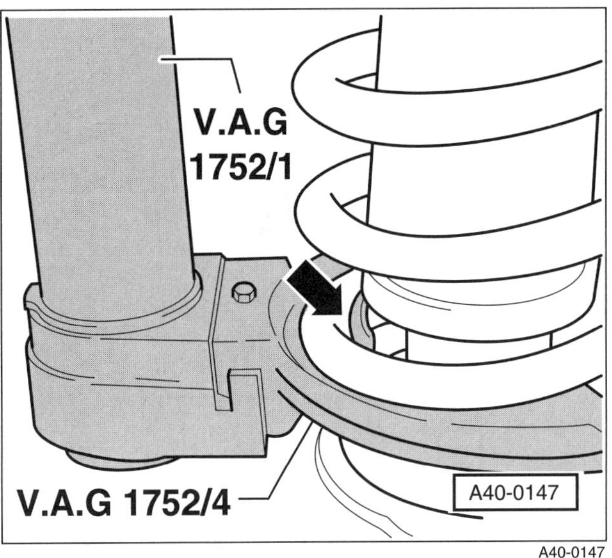

A40-0147

Fig. 8. Insure that coil spring is seated securely (**arrow**) into Volkswagen spring compressor VAG 1752/4.

2. With coil spring properly compressed, remove inner nut. See Fig. 9.

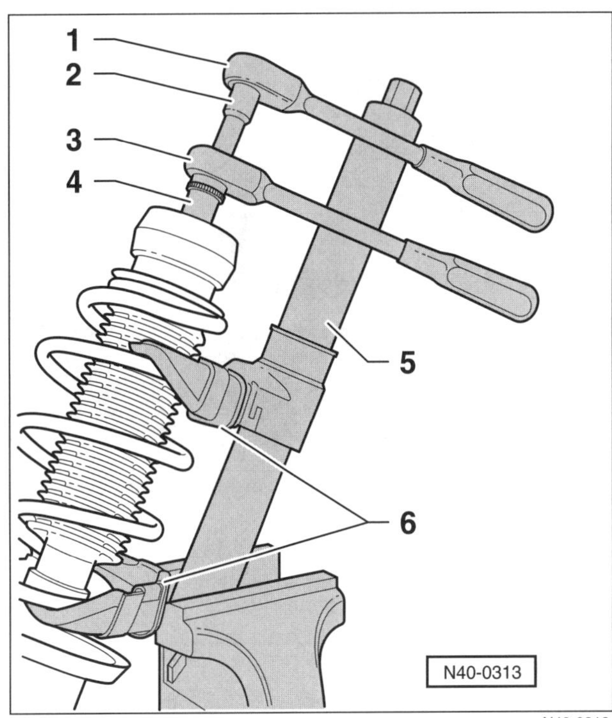

N40-0313

Fig. 9. Set-up for removing coil spring from suspension strut using Volkswagen special tools; (**1**) ½-inch ratchet, (**2**) T10001/8, (**3**) T10001/11, (**4**) T10001/5, (**5**) VAG 1752, (**6**) VAG 1752/4. Volkswagen special tool 3186 is also suitable.

3. Remove components of suspension strut.

4. When re-installing coil spring, fit end of coil against stop in lower spring seat on strut. Fig. 10.

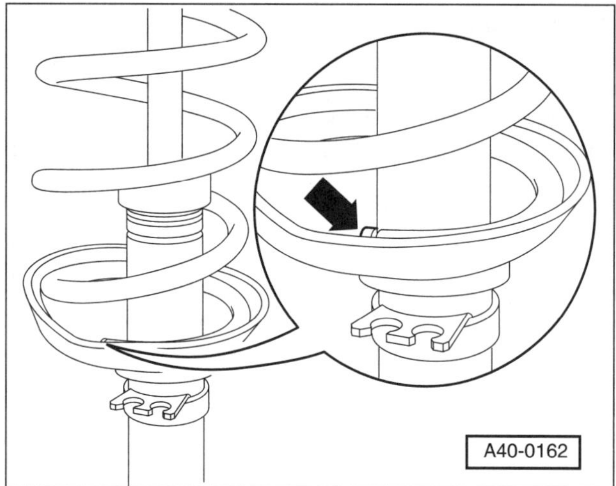

A40-0162

Fig. 10. Install end of coil spring against stop (**arrow**) in lower spring seat on strut.

5. If coil springs are to be replaced, note identifying paint marks on coils for proper matching. See Fig. 11.

0024281

Fig. 11. Colored paint marks (**arrows**) are used to identify coil springs with different spring rates.

6. Installation is the reverse of disassembly.

Tightening torque

- Inner suspension strut nut . . . . 60 Nm (44 ft-lb)
- Outer suspension strut nut, always replace . . . . 60 Nm (44 ft-lb)

DRIVE AXLES WITH CONSTANT VELOCITY AND TRIPLE ROTOR JOINTS

Removal and/or replacement of the front axle with constant velocity or triple rotor joints requires special tools and equipment. In some cases, constant velocity and triple rotor joints are supplied only with axles. Lubricate all axle joints with special high temperature molybdenum-disulfide "moly" grease. Always understand and observe the warnings and cautions listed at the beginning of this section.

Specification

- Molybdenum-disulfide constant velocity and triple rotor joint lubricant
  VW part # G 000 603 . . . . 90 G (3.2 oz)
  VW part # G 000 633 . . . . 120 G (4.2 oz)

NOTE —

Volkswagen part numbers are given for reference only! Always consult with your Volkswagen Parts Department or aftermarket parts specialist for the latest parts information.

Fig. 12 shows the drive axles with the Constant Velocity (CV) joints.

Drive axles with constant velocity joints, assembly

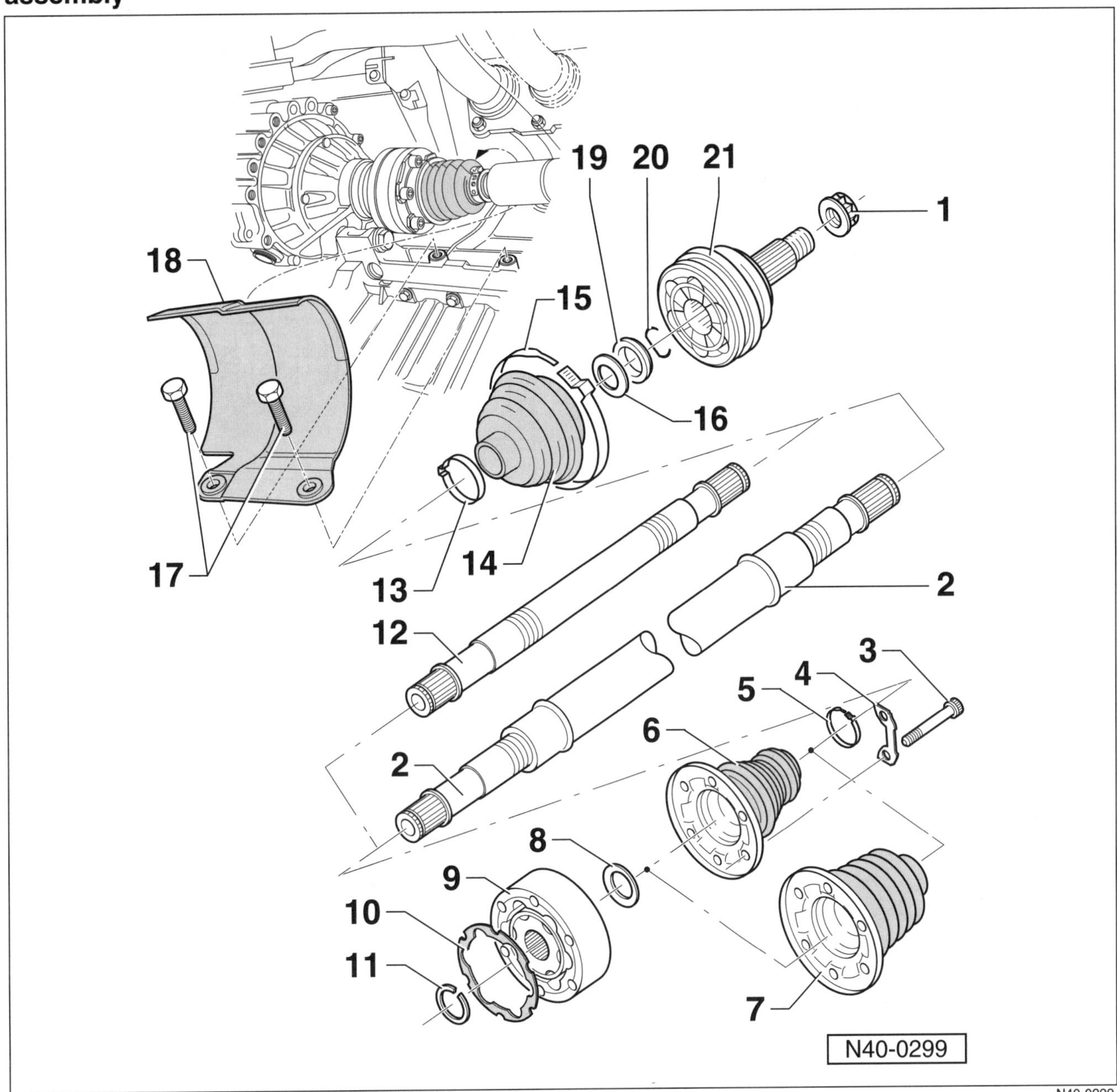

Fig. 12. Constant velocity (CV) joints with axles and related components.

1. **Axle nut, self-locking**
   - Always replace
   - Any paint residue and/or corrosion on threads of outer joint must be removed before nut is installed
   - For tightening procedure see **Front wheel bearing housing assembly** given earlier
2. **Axle shaft, right side (tube shaft)**
3. **Bolt**
   - Tighten to 40 Nm (30 ft-lb)
4. **Lock plate**
5. **Clamp**
   - Always replace
6. **CV joint boot, inner**
   - Material: Hytrel (Polyelastomer)
   - No vent hole
   - Check for tears and chafing
   - Drive off CV joint using drift

(continued on following page)

(continued from previous page)

7. **CV joint boot, inner**
   - Material: Rubber
   - With vent hole
   - Check for tears and chafing
   - Drive off CV joint using drift
   - Installation position for left drive axle, **see** (A)
   - Installation position for right drive axle, **see** (B)
8. **Spring washer**
   - Installation position, **see** (C)
9. **Inner CV joint**
   - Only replace complete unit
   - Support hub and press off of axle
   - Install with chamfer on inner diameter of hub facing stop on axle shaft
   - Press up to stop
   - Install new circlip
10. **Gasket**
    - Always replace
    - Adhesive surface on CV joint must be free of oil and grease
    - Remove protective foil and stick gasket onto CV joint.
11. **Circlip**
12. **Axle shaft, left side (solid shaft)**
13. **Clamp**
    - Always replace
14. **CV joint boot, outer**
    - Check for tears and chafing
    - Material: Hytrel (Polyelastomer)
15. **Clamp**
    - Always replace
16. **Spring washer**
    - Installation position, **see** (D)
17. **Bolts**
    - Tighten to 35 Nm (26 ft-lb)
18. **Heat shield**
19. **Thrust washer**
    - Installation position, **see** (D)
20. **Circlip**
    - Always replace
    - Install in shaft groove
21. **Outer CV joint**
    - Only replace complete unit
    - Drive off axle with plastic/brass/aluminum hammer
    - Drive onto shaft up to stop using plastic/brass/aluminum hammer

(A) Left (solid) axle CV joint boot, installed position

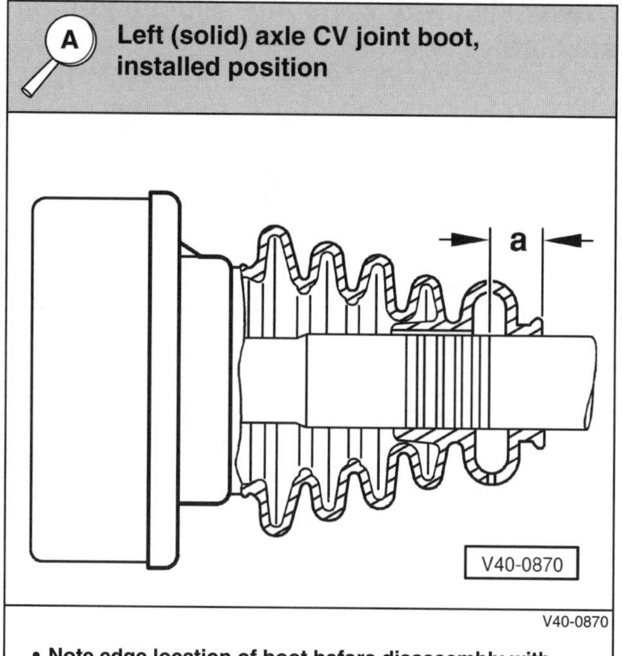

V40-0870

- **Note edge location of boot before disassembly with paint or tape mark. Do not mark by scratching axle.**
- **Install to dimension (a); 17 mm (0.669 in)**

(B) Right (hollow) axle CV joint boot, installed position

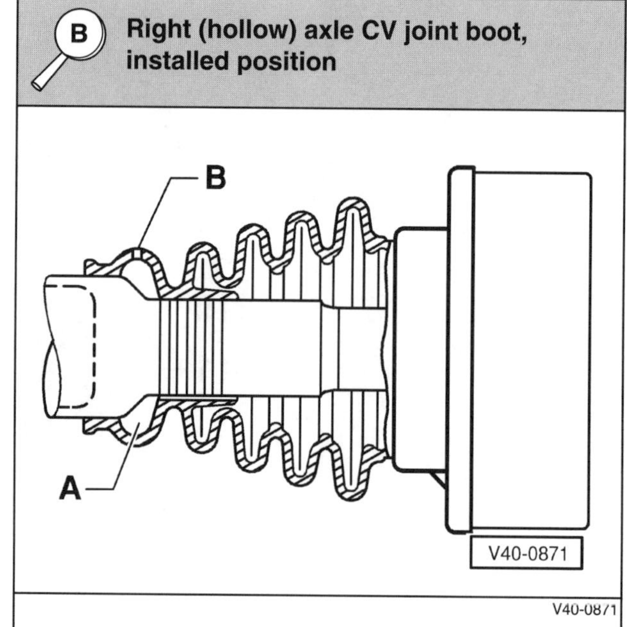

V40-0871

- **Position boot to allow for vent chamber (A).**
- **Vent hole (B) must open into vent chamber (A).**

C **Spring washer on inner CV joints, installed position**

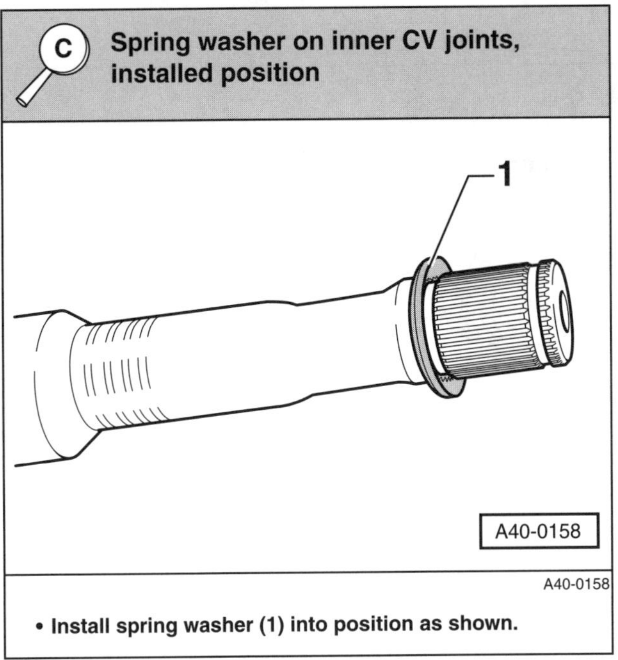

A40-0158

- **Install spring washer (1) into position as shown.**

D **Spring washer and thrust washer on outer CV joints, installed position**

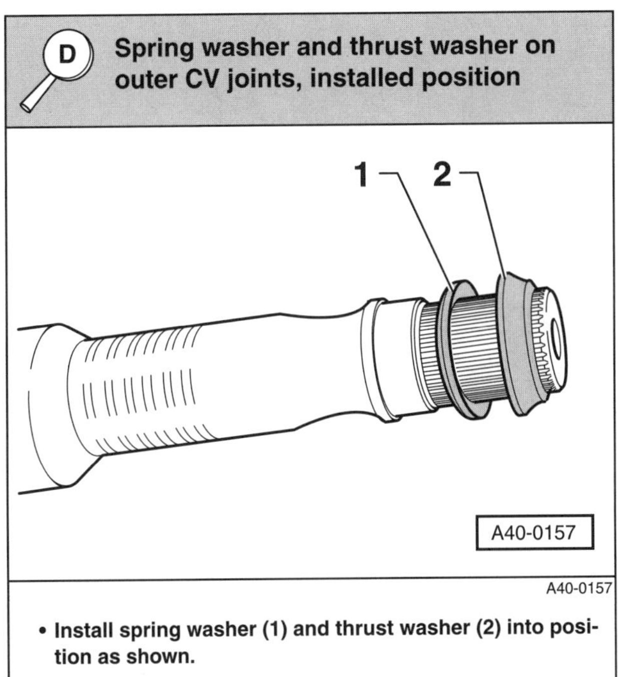

A40-0157

- **Install spring washer (1) and thrust washer (2) into position as shown.**

Drive axles with triple-rotor joint, assembly

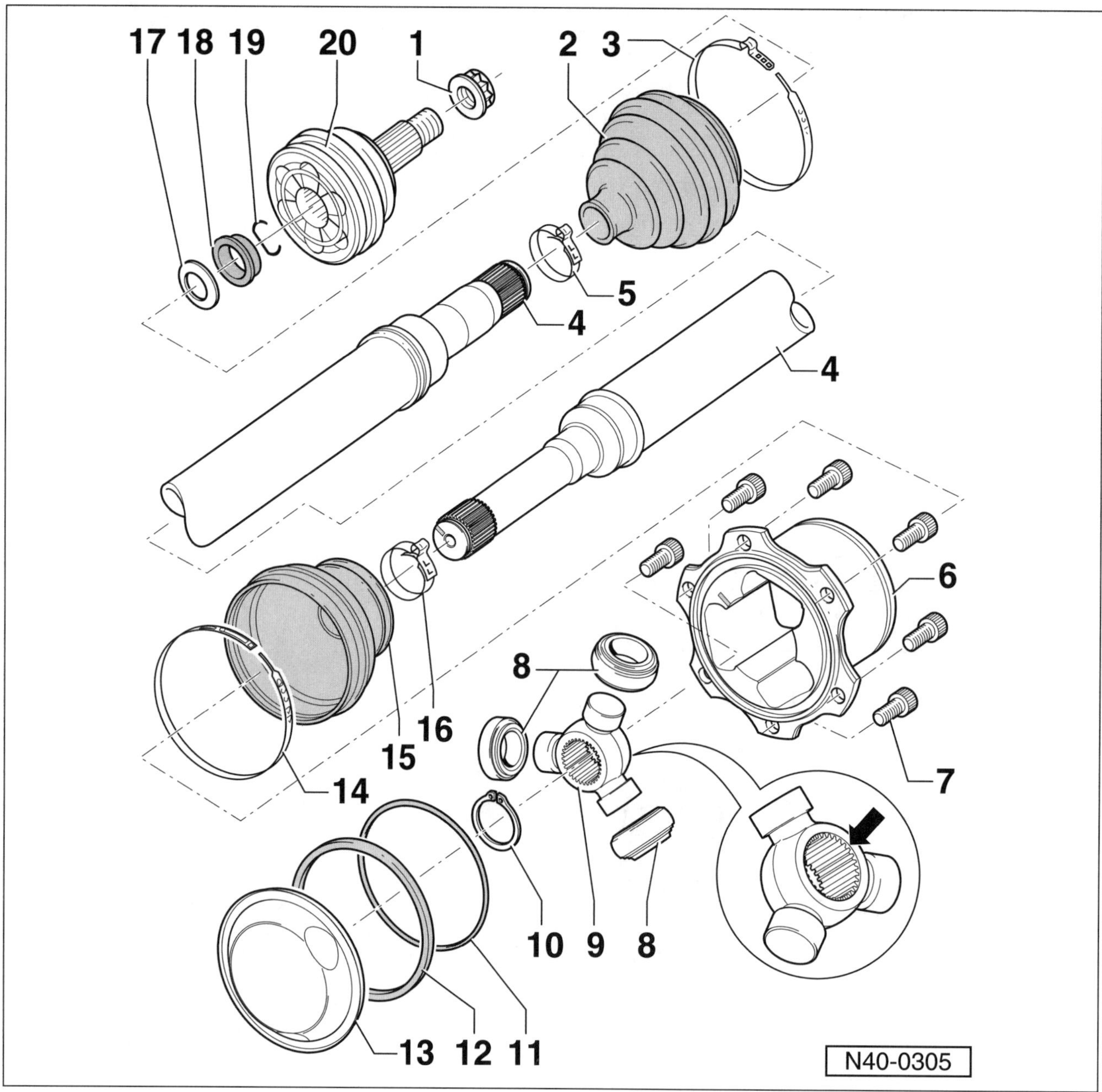

N40-0305

Fig. 13. Triple rotor joints with axle and related components.

1. **Axle nut, self-locking**
   - Always replace
   - Any paint residue and/or corrosion on threads of outer joint must be removed before nut is installed
   - For tightening procedure see **Front wheel bearing housing assembly** given earlier
2. **CV joint boot, outer**
   - Check for tears and chafing
3. **Clamp**
   - Always replace
4. **Axle shaft**
5. **Clamp**
   - Always replace
6. **Triple rotor joint housing**
   - Also called "tripot" and "tripod" joints
   - Only replace complete unit
   - Use caution on re-assembly to prevent axle from inadvertently falling apart, **see** Ⓐ

(continued from previous page)

7. **Bolt**
   - Tighten to 40 Nm (30 ft-lb)
8. **Rollers**
9. **Triple-rotor star (hub)**
   - Chamfer faces opposite end of drive axle
10. **Circlip**
    - Always replace
    - Install in shaft groove
11. **O-ring**
    - Not required for assembly
12. **Rectangular section seal**
    - Seal is part of repair kit; not installed in production
13. **Cover**
    - Destroyed when disassembling
    - Not required for assembling; not supplied as replacement part
14. **Clamp**
    - For triple-rotor joint
    - Only installed to left side on production vehicles
15. **Triple-rotor joint boot**
16. **Clamp**
17. **Spring washer**
    - Installation position, see **Drive axles with constant velocity joints, assembly** given earlier
18. **Thrust washer**
    - Installation position, see **Drive axles with constant velocity joints, assembly** given earlier
19. **Circlip**
    - Always replace
    - Install in shaft groove
20. **Outer constant velocity (CV) joint**
    - Only replace complete unit
    - Drive off of axle with plastic/brass/aluminum hammer
    - Drive onto shaft up to stop using plastic/brass/aluminum hammer

(A) Triple rotor joint, installation precautions

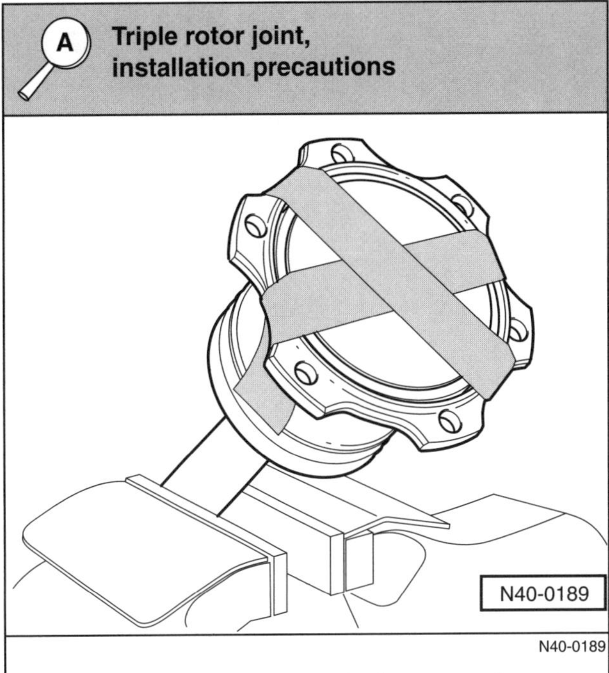

N40-0189

- **Secure triple rotor joint with adhesive tape as shown to prevent housing from accidently sliding down axle shaft.**
- **Remove tape just prior to bolting securely to drive flange.**

QUALITY REVIEW

When you have finished working under the hood and around other areas of the vehicle, it is advisable to take a moment to quality check or review your work. This helps to insure that the operation or repair has been completed properly with all affected systems functioning within normal parameters. These may include the following:

- Ensure that all cable ties and clamps that were removed as part of the repair are replaced.
- Ensure that all fasteners and hardware were replaced and torqued as specified.
- Make sure that all other components involved in the repair are positioned correctly, properly torqued and function properly.
- Make sure that all tools, shop cloths, fender covers and protective tapes are removed before closing the hood.
- Clean grease and fingerprints from painted surfaces, steering wheel and shifter.

42 Rear Suspension

GENERAL

Special tools, equipment and procedures are required for most front suspension repair and component replacement. In addition, wheel alignment is almost always disturbed when suspension components are removed or replaced.

This section covers repairs to the rear suspension and related components. For front suspension servicing and repair information, see **40 Front Suspension**. For wheel alignment specifications, see **44 Wheels, Tires, Wheel Alignment**.

WARNING —

- *Do not re-use any fasteners that are worn or deformed in normal use. Most fasteners are designed to be used only once and become unreliable and may fail when used a second time. This includes, but is not limited to, nuts, bolts, washers, circlips, cotter pins, self-locking nuts and bolts. For replacements, always use new parts.*
- *Do not reinstall bolts and nuts coated with undercoating wax, as correct tightening torque cannot be ensured. Always clean the threads of removed bolts and nuts that are to be re-used with a suitable solvent before installation. Ensure that new parts are clean.*

WARNING —

- *Do not use standard nuts and bolts in place of green colored parts. The green color denotes a special anti-corrosion process known as "dacromet" or "delta-tone". Torque specifications are given based on use of these parts only.*
- *Always replaced rusted or corroded bolts, nuts and washers even if not specifically indicated.*
- *DO NOT attempt to straighten or weld suspension struts, wheel bearing housings, control arms or any other wheel locating or load bearing components of the front suspension.*

REAR SUSPENSION

The beam-type rear axle is a one-piece welded assembly consisting of an axle beam, trailing arms, stabilizer bar, and coil spring seat. Rear wheel stub axles are bolted to the trailing arms. Coil springs are mounted low on the beam with the upper spring seats attached to the rear body structure. Gas-pressure telescopic rear shock absorbers are bolted to the outside of the wheel wells and are easily removed independent of the springs. Rear wheel bearings are sealed into the hub assembly and are not serviceable. Fig. 1 shows the rear suspension with related components.

42

Rear suspension overview

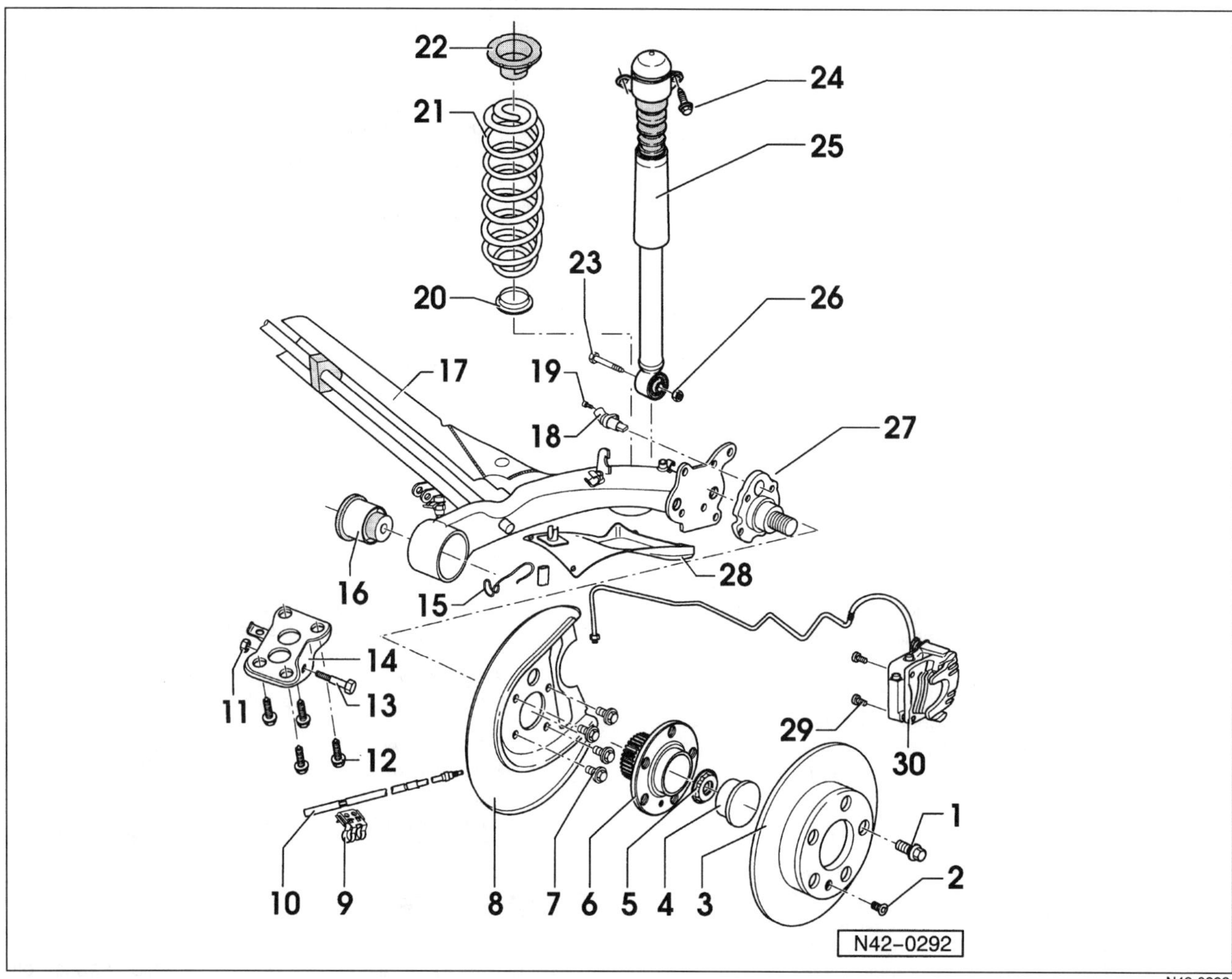

N42-0292

Fig. 1. Rear axle beam with left side suspension and brake components.

1. **Wheel lug bolts**
   - Tighten to 120 Nm (89 ft-lb)
2. **Screw**
   - Tighten to 4 Nm (35 in-lb)
3. **Brake disc (rotor)**
4. **Dust cap**
   - Always replace
   - Proper function and long service life can only be ensured by the perfect seal of a new dust cap
5. **Nut, self-locking**
   - Always replace
   - Tighten to 175 Nm (129 ft-lb)
6. **Wheel bearing/hub unit with ABS wheel speed sensor rotor**
   - Wheel bearing, wheel hub and wheel speed sensor rotor are installed together in housing
   - Wheel bearing/hub unit is maintenance and adjustment free
7. **Bolt**
   - Always replace
   - Tighten to 60 Nm (44 ft-lb)
8. **Splash shield**
9. **Parking brake cable bracket**
10. **Parking brake cable**
11. **Nut, self-locking**
    - Always replace
    - Tighten to 80 Nm (59 ft-lb)
12. **Bolt**
    - Always replace
    - Tighten to 75 Nm (55 ft-lb)
    - If threads in welded nut in longitudinal member (rear body structure) are damaged, repair using Heli-Coil
    - Do not repair more than one welded nut on each side with Heli-Coils

(continued from previous page)

13. Bolt
- Always replace
- Tighten to 80 Nm (59 ft-lb)

14. Rear axle mounting bracket
- Check and if necessary adjust rear axle total toe after installation
- If possible do not loosen when removing rear axle

15. Parking brake cable bracket

16. Bonded rubber bushing
- Installed position, **see** (A)

17. Axle beam
- Stub axle contact surfaces and threaded holes must be free of paint and dirt

18. ABS wheel speed sensor

19. Bolt
- Tighten to 8 Nm (71 in-lb)

20. Spacer bushing
- Material: zinc
- Check for damage

21. Coil spring
- Note color-code marking for identification
- Outer surface of spring must not be damaged

22. Spring seat, upper
- End of coil spring must lie against spring seat stop, **see** (B)

23. Lower shock bolt
- Always replace
- Tighten to 60 Nm (44 ft-lb)

24. Upper shock bolt
- Always replace
- Tighten to 30 Nm (22 ft-lb) + ¼-turn (90°)

25. Shock absorber
- Gas pressure
- Can be replaced individually

26. Nut
- Always replace
- Axle beam must be in middle position when tightening nut to insure proper shock bushing preload
- Load rear of vehicle with weight of one person when tightening

27. Stub axle
- Do not attempt to straighten stub axle
- Do not attempt to re-cut threads

28. Stone protection plate

29. Bolts
- Always replace
- Tighten to 65 Nm (48 ft-lb)

30. Rear brake caliper

(A) Bonded rubber axle beam bushing, installed position

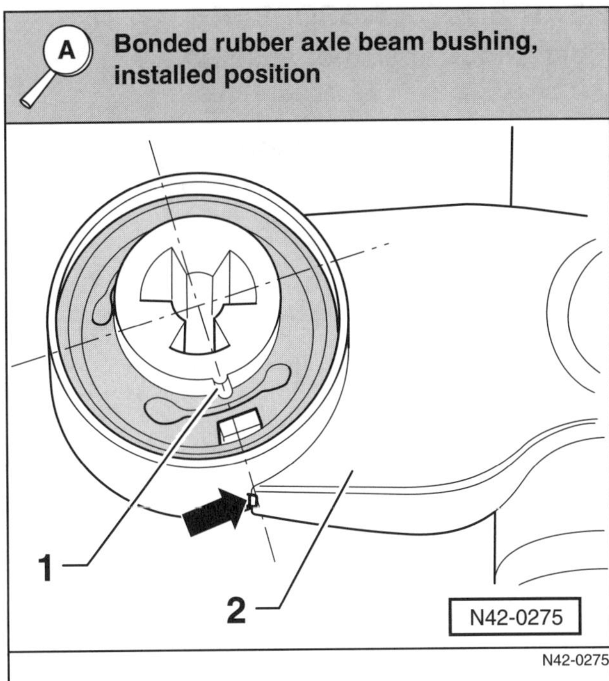

N42-0275

- **Identification mark (1) on face of bonded rubber bushing must align with edge of trailing arm (arrow) on axle beam (2).**

(B) Upper spring seat and coil spring, installed position

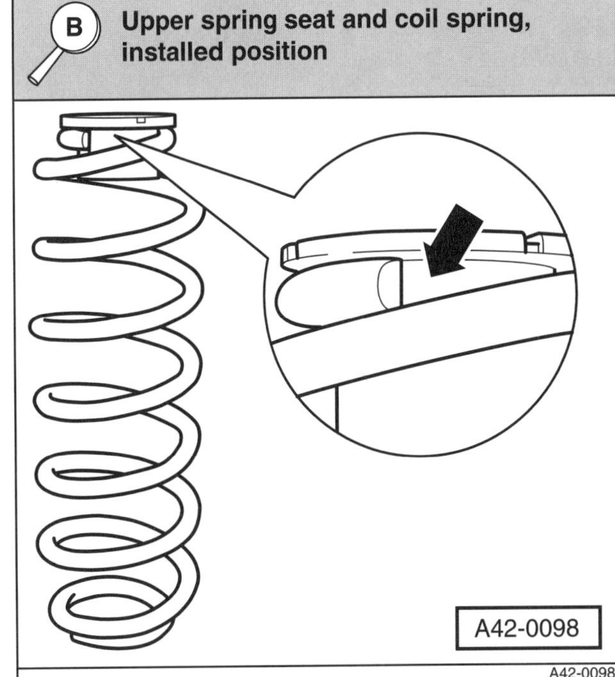

A42-0098

- **Make sure that zinc lower spacer bushing is not damaged; replace as required.**
- **Install coil spring and upper spring seat together.**
- **Install end of coil spring against stop (arrow) in upper spring seat.**

REAR SHOCK ABSORBERS

Rear shock absorber assembly

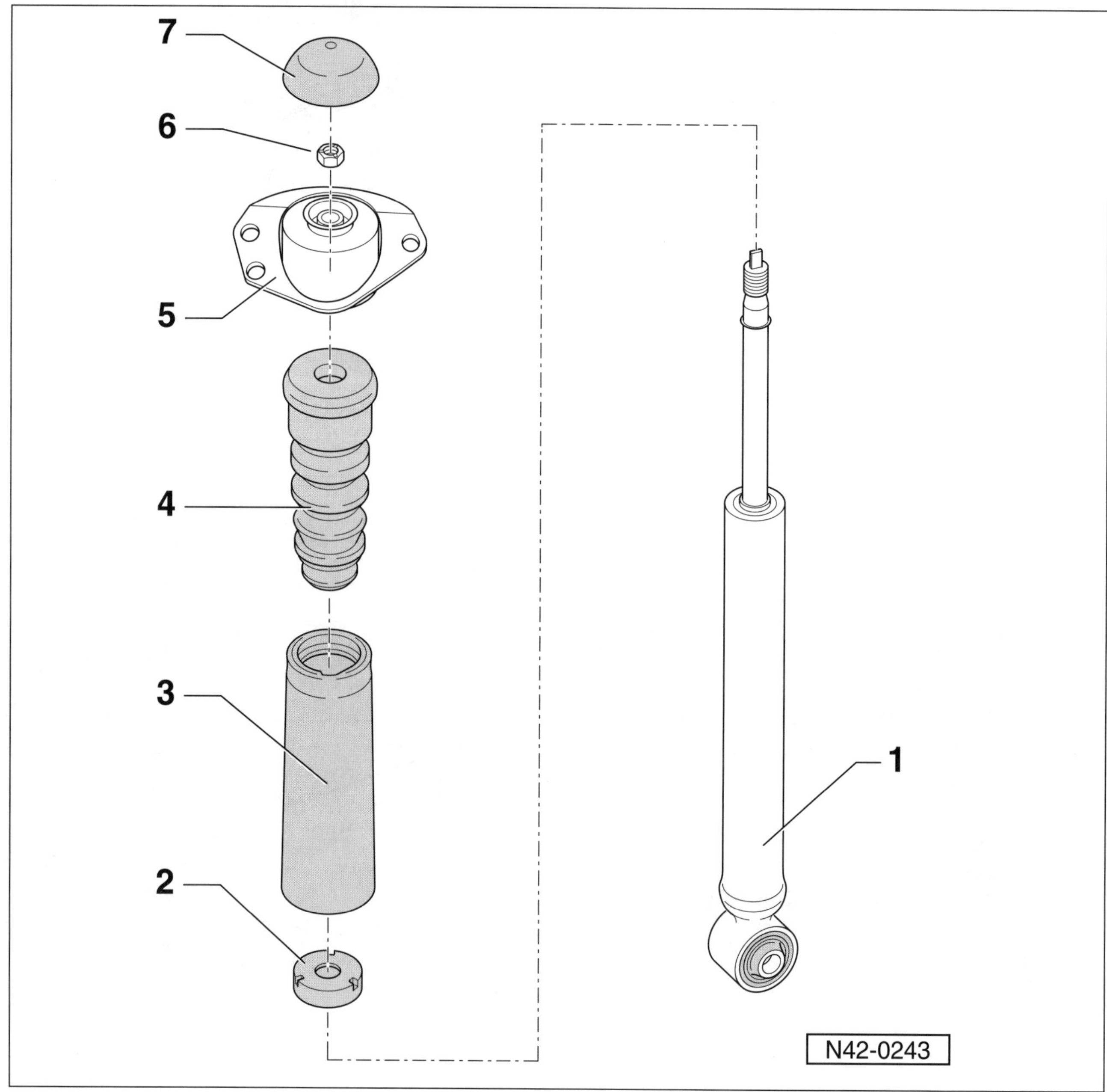

N42-0243

Fig. 2. Rear shock absorber and related components with upper mount.

1. **Gas-filled shock absorber**
   - Can be replaced individually
   - Slight traces of oil do not necessitate replacement
   - Note markings for identification
2. **Protective cap**
3. **Protective tube**
4. **Bump stop**
5. **Upper shock absorber mount**
6. **Nut, self-locking**
   - Always replace
   - Tighten to 25 Nm (18 ft-lb)
7. **Protective sleeve**

Rear shock absorber, checking

1. Remove shock absorber as described below.
2. Compress shock absorber by hand. Piston rod must move over its complete length smoothly and with even force.
3. If gas pressure is sufficient, piston rod will return to its fully extended position.
4. If piston rod does not return to its fully extended position and there is no loss of oil, then shock absorber is still OK.

Rear shock absorber, removing and installing

1. Raise vehicle slightly with a lift or floor jack, but leave weight of vehicle on the wheels.

   NOTE —

   Rear suspension must not be allowed to extend fully. Spring will fall out when shock absorber is unbolted if some vehicle weight is not supported by the rear wheel.

2. Remove upper shock mounting bolts. See Fig. 3.

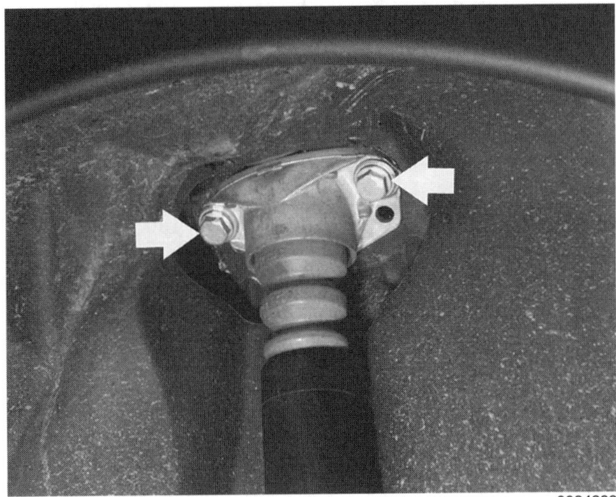

0024282

Fig. 3. Remove bolts (**arrows**) with the vehicle still resting on its wheels.

3. Raise vehicle slightly to relieve coil spring pressure.
4. Remove lower shock absorber bolt on rear axle. See Fig. 4.
5. Remove shock absorber.
6. Remove upper shock mount. See Fig. 5.
7. Installation is the reverse of removal.

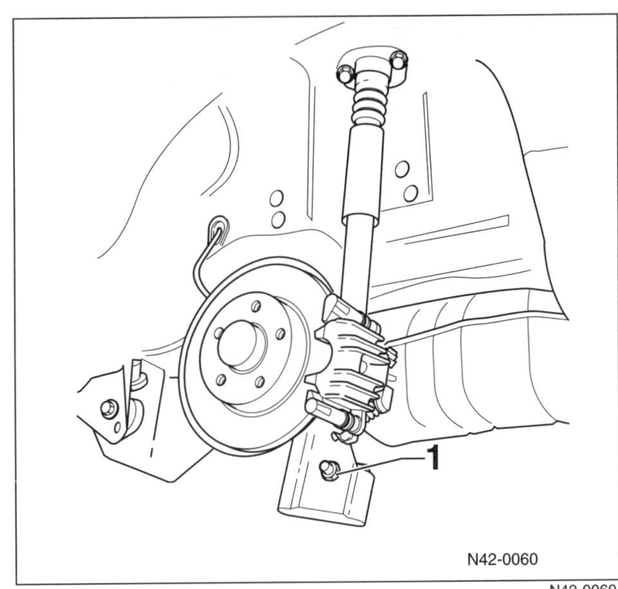

N42-0060

Fig. 4. Remove lower shock bolt (**1**) holding shock to axle beam. Wheel and tire shown removed for clarity, but should remain installed.

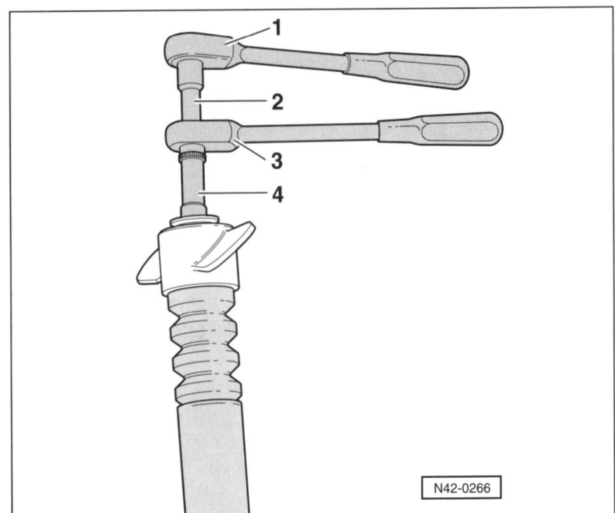

N42-0266

Fig. 5. Set-up for removing nut holding upper shock mount using Volkswagen special tools; (**1**) ½-inch ratchet, (**2**) T10001/9, (**3**) T10001/11, (**4**) T10001/1. Volkswagen special tool 3079 is also suitable.

Tightening torque

- Upper shock bolt (M10) always replace .... 75 Nm (55 ft-lb)
- Lower shock bolt and nut (M10) always replace .... 60 Nm (44 ft-lb)

Rear coil spring, removing and installing

1. Disconnect harness connector for ABS wheel speed sensor (where applicable).

2. Unclip wheel speed sensor wiring from retainer. See Fig. 6.

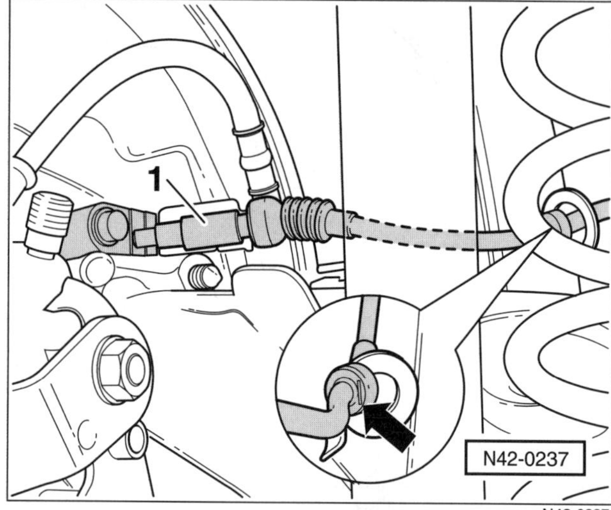

N42-0237

Fig. 6. Unplug ABS wheel speed sensor **(1)** as required and unclip sensor wiring from retainer **(arrow)**.

3. Raise vehicle slightly with a lift or floor jack, but leave vehicle resting on its wheels.

4. Remove upper shock mounting bolts as shown earlier. See Fig. 3.

5. Raise vehicle further to relieve coil spring pressure.

6. Remove coil spring.

7. Installation is the reverse of removal, noting the following:
   - Make sure spacer bushing (zinc) is not damaged, replace if necessary.
   - Install spring together with spring seat.
   - Observe spring installation position, given earlier.
   - Press rear axle upward using transmission jack.
   - Using new bolts, bolt shock absorber to body.

> ***WARNING —***
> *If vehicle is supported on a vehicle lift or hoist, ensure that transmission jack does not push up on the suspension sufficient to topple the vehicle off.*

Tightening torque
- Upper shock bolt (M10)
  always replace . . . . 75 Nm (55 ft-lb)

REAR WHEEL BEARINGS

Inner and outer rear wheel bearings along with the hub and ABS speed sensor rotor are combined into a single integrated assembly. This assembly must be replaced as a complete unit as there are no individually serviceable components. See Fig. 7.

Rear wheel bearing/hub unit, assembly

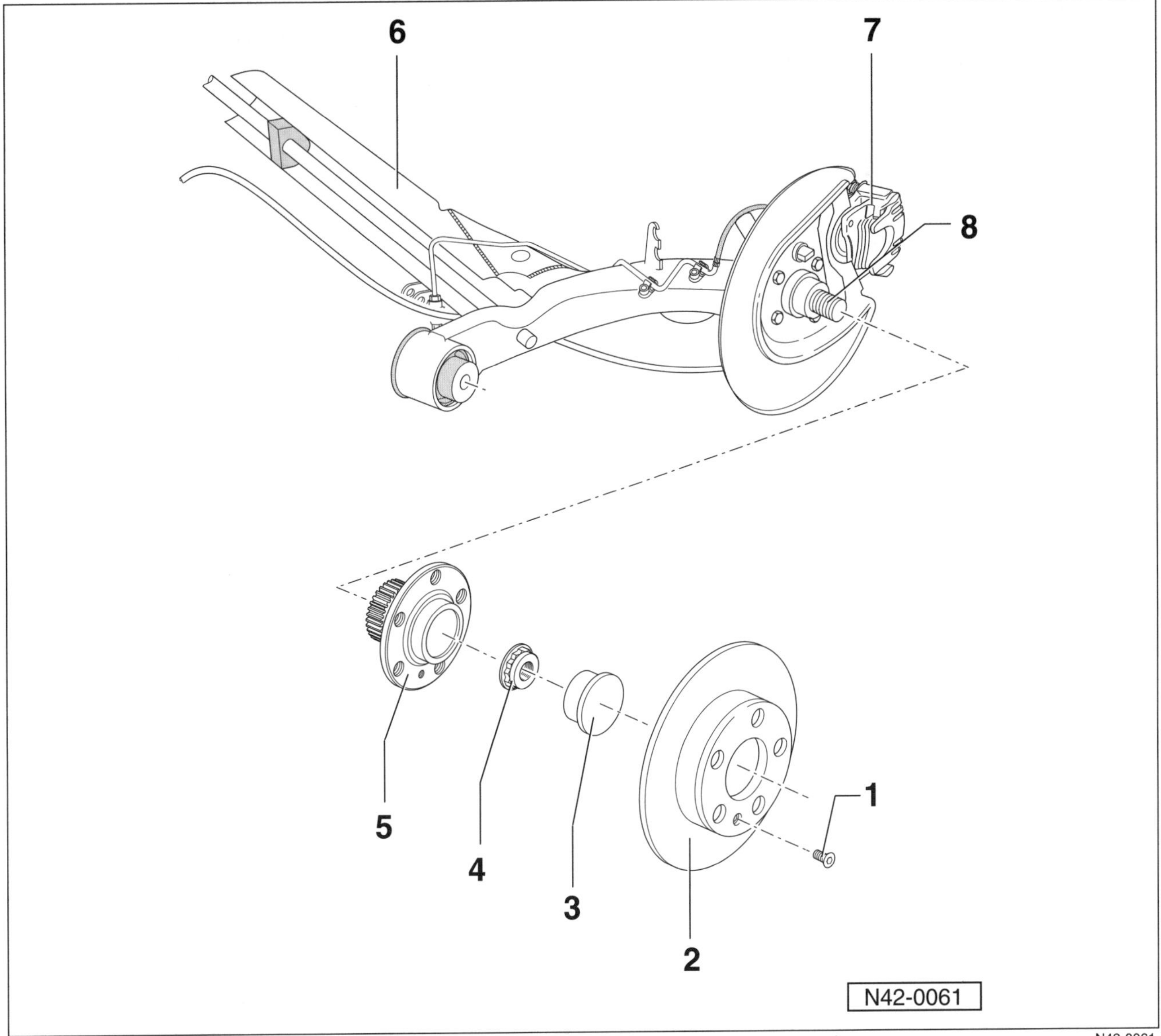

Fig. 7. Left rear wheel bearing/hub unit assembly and related components. Right side is similar.

1. **Screw**
   - Tighten to 4 Nm (35 in-lb)
2. **Brake disc (rotor)**
3. **Dust cap**
   - Always replace
   - Proper function and long service life can only be ensured by the perfect seal of a new dust cap
4. **Nut, self-locking**
   - Always replace
   - Tighten to 175 Nm (129 ft-lb)
5. **Wheel bearing/hub unit with ABS wheel speed sensor rotor**
   - Wheel bearing, wheel hub and wheel speed sensor rotor are installed together in housing
   - Wheel bearing/hub unit is maintenance and adjustment free
6. **Axle beam assembly**
7. **Rear brake caliper**
8. **Stub axle**
   - Do not attempt to straighten stub axle
   - Do not attempt to re-cut threads

Rear wheel bearing/hub unit, removing

1. Remove wheel assembly.

2. Remove rear hub dust cap from seat on rotor. See Fig. 8.

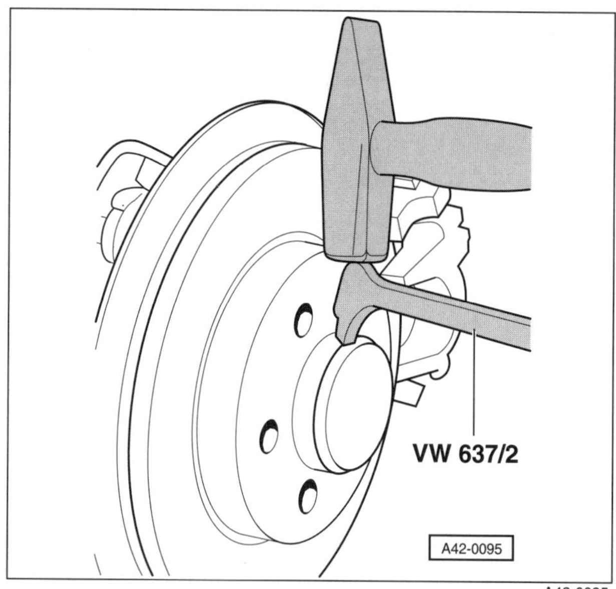

A42-0095

Fig. 8. Tap on dust cap with suitable tools to loosen, then pry off with suitable tools.

3. Remove brake caliper. See Fig. 9.

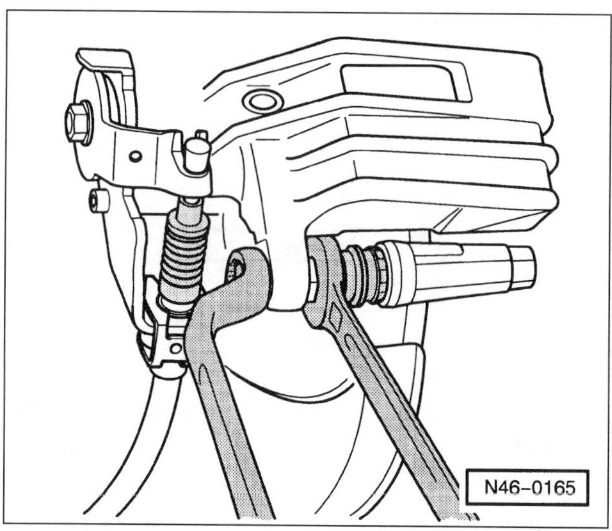

N46-0165

Fig. 9. Counterhold guide pins and remove mounting bolts from brake caliper.

> ***CAUTION—***
> *Do not allow the caliper to hang by the brake hose. The unsupported weight can stretch and damage the hose.*

4. Remove phillips head screw from brake disc (rotor) and remove brake disc.

5. Remove self-locking nut at center of hub assembly.

6. Using a suitable puller, remove bearing/hub unit. See Fig. 10.

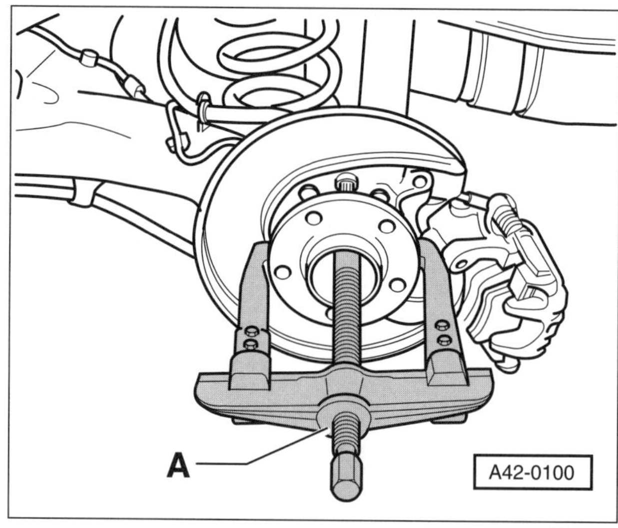

A42-0100

Fig. 10. Kukko 20/2 puller (**A**) shown pulling off bearing/hub unit.

7. Pulling the bearing/hub unit may leave the inner wheel bearing on the stub axle. Using a suitable puller, carefully remove the inner bearing. See Fig. 11.

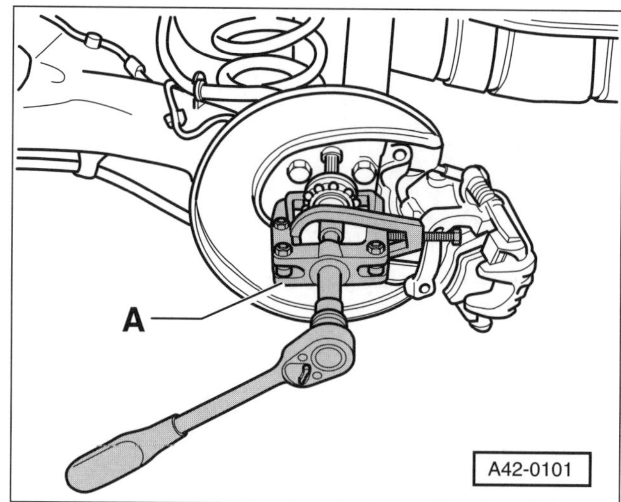

A42-0101

Fig. 11. Kukko 204-2 puller (**A**) shown pulling off inner wheel bearing. Use only a puller with leg clamps to prevent the jaws from spreading and damaging the bearing.

8. Remove stub axle.

Rear wheel bearing/hub unit, installing

1. Install stub axle to axle beam with new bolts.

Tightening torque
- Stub axle bolts to axle beam (M10) always replace . . . . 60 Nm (44 ft-lb)

---

2. Place inner wheel bearing into hub (if applicable) and install wheel bearing/hub unit as far as possible onto stub axle.

3. Attach Volkswagen assembly tool 3420 and pull wheel bearing/hub unit all the way onto stub axle. See Fig. 12.

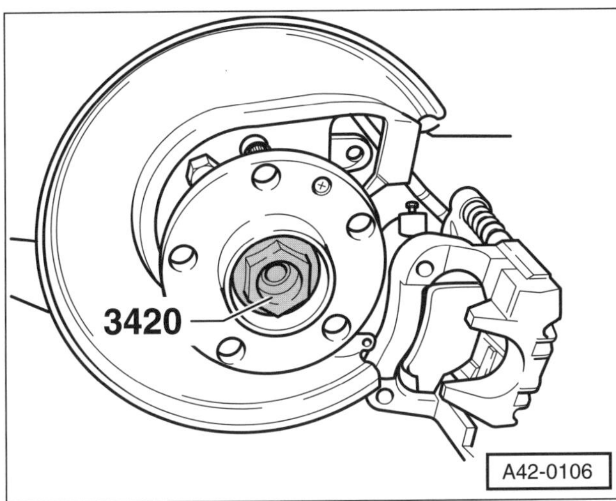

A42-0106

Fig. 12. Volkswagen special tool 3420 shown installed to pull wheel bearing/hub unit onto stub axle.

4. Remove Volkswagen assembly tool 3420 and install a new self-locking 12-point nut.

Tightening torque
- Stub axle nut, self-locking, shouldered (M20) always replace . . . . 175 Nm (129 ft-lb)
- Screw, brake rotor (M6) . . . . 4 Nm (35 in-lb)
- Bolt, brake caliper . . . . 65 Nm (48 ft-lb)
- Wheel bolt to wheel hub. . . . . 120 Nm (87 ft-lb)

---

5. Install brake disc (rotor) and caliper.

6. Install new dust cap. See Fig. 13.

NOTE —
Use care when installing new dust cap as dented and damaged dust caps allow moisture contamination that shortens bearing life.

7. Install and torque wheel assembly.

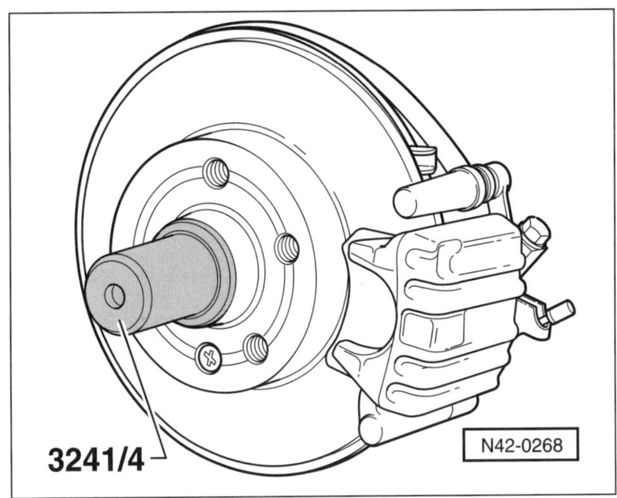

N42-0268

Fig. 13. Volkswagen special tool 3241/4 shown in place to drive new dust cap onto hub.

QUALITY REVIEW

When you have finished working under the vehicle and around other areas, it is advisable to take a moment to quality check or review your work. This helps to insure that the operation or repair has been completed properly with all affected systems functioning within normal parameters. These may include the following:

- Ensure that all cable ties and clamps that were removed as part of the repair are replaced.
- Ensure that all fasteners and hardware were replaced and torqued as specified.
- Make sure that all other components involved in the repair are positioned correctly, properly torqued and function properly.
- Make sure that all tools, shop cloths, fender covers and protective tapes are removed before closing the hood.
- Clean grease and fingerprints from painted surfaces, steering wheel and shifter.

44 Wheels–Tires, Wheel Alignment

TABLES

GENERAL

This repair group covers basic tire, wheel, and wheel alignment information. Also covered here is wheel alignment specifications to be used in conjunction with professional alignment tools and measuring equipment.

Wheels and tires

Wheels and tires approved by the manufacturer have been matched to the vehicle and contribute largely to road handling and driving characteristics. To retain the handling characteristics, it is recommended that the tires be replaced only with tires having the same specifications with regard to size, design, load carrying capacity, speed rating, tread pattern, tread depth, etc. This information can be found on the tire's sidewall. See Fig. 1. Various tire and wheel applications can be found in **Table a**.

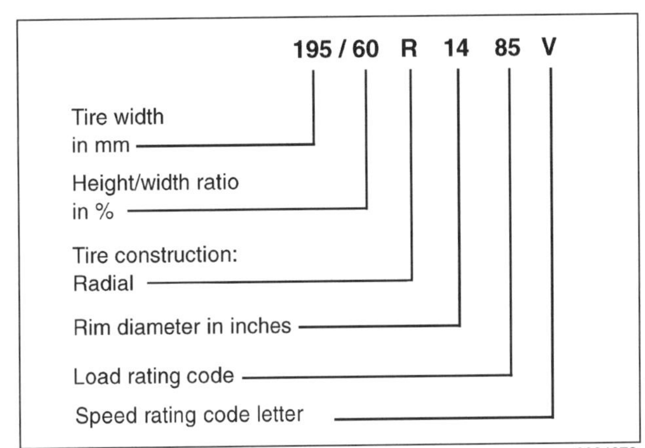

Fig. 1. Tire sidewalls are marked with important tire specifications.

Volkswagen recommends that the tires be rotated front to back, with the tires remaining on the same side of the vehicle. Only when tires show unusual wear should they be rotated diagonally. See **0 Maintenance** for maintenance schedules regarding tire rotation.

Tightening torque

- Wheel bolt to hub (diagonally and evenly). . . . . 120 Nm (87 ft-lb)

Table a. Wheel and Tire applications

Engine (code), output	Tire size	Wheel	Offset mm	Snow chains permissible
1.9L (ALH), 90 Hp Diesel	195/65 R 15 91 T	6 J x 15	38	Yes
2.0L (AEG), 115 Hp Gasoline	195/65 R 15 91 H	6 J x 15	38	Yes
1.8L (APH), 150 Hp Gasoline	195/65 R 15 91 V	6 J x 15	38	Yes
1.9L (ALH), 90 Hp Diesel 2.0L (AEG), 115 Hp Gasoline	205/60 R 15 91 H	6½ J x 15	43	No
1.8L (APH), 150 Hp Gasoline	205/60 R 15 91 V	6½ J x 15	43	No
1.9L (ALH), 90 Hp Diesel 2.0L (AEG), 115 Hp Gasoline	205/55 R 16 91 H	6½ J x 16	42	No
1.8L (APH), 150 Hp Gasoline	205/55 R 16 91 V	6½ J x 16	42	No
Temporary spare	T 125/70 R 18 98 M	3½ J x 18	38	–

WHEEL ALIGNMENT

Tire pressures, tire wear, and wheel alignment will all influence how the car feels and responds on the road. For stability and control, all four wheels and tires must be in good condition, balanced, and be properly aligned. Precise wheel alignment can only be accomplished when the tires, the suspension, and the steering are in good condition. Reputable wheel alignment technicians will always inspect the front and rear suspension and the steering for worn parts before an alignment, and will recommend that any necessary repairs be made before proceeding. The important front wheel alignment angles are camber, caster, and toe. In the rear, the important angles are camber, toe and thrust line. Although rear alignment angles are not generally adjustable, they should be checked because of the effect that they have on rear tire wear and straight-line stability of the vehicle.

Camber is the angle that the wheels tilt from vertical when viewed from front or rear. See Fig. 2. Wheels which tilt out at the top have positive (+) camber. Wheels that tilt in at the top have negative (–) camber. On the Volkswagens covered by this manual, camber is non-adjustable and corrections must be made by moving the front subframe slightly.

Camber influences cornering, directional stability, and tire wear. Different camber on the two front wheels may cause the car to pull to one side. Incorrectly adjusted camber will cause uneven tire wear.

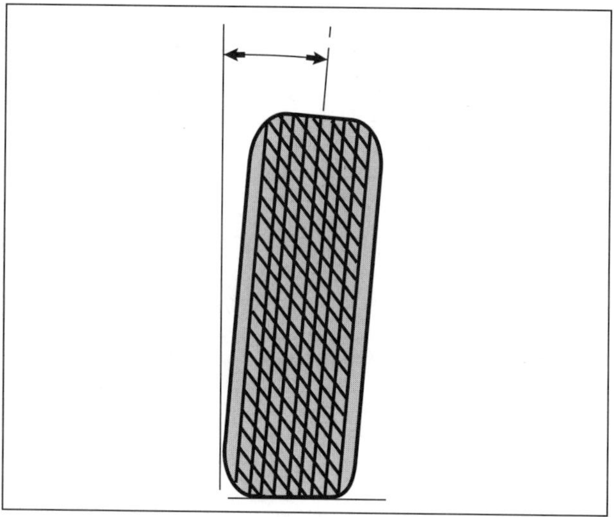

Fig. 2. Camber is the wheel/tire deviation from vertical as viewed from front or rear.

Caster is the angle at which the steering axis deviates from vertical. See Fig. 3. Most cars are designed with positive caster, which improves directional stability and tends to make the steering more self-centering. Caster angle should be checked as part of wheel alignment, but it is not adjustable on cars covered by this manual.

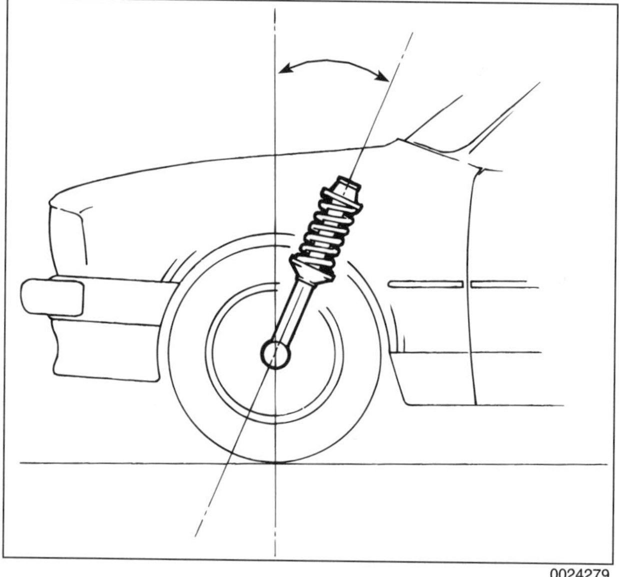

Fig. 3. Caster is the angle of steering axis inclination from vertical.

Toe is a measurement of the amount that two wheels on the same axle point toward each other (toe-in) or away from each other (toe-out). Toe affects directional stability and tire wear. Toe also affects response to steering input. Too much toe will cause tires to "scrub" and to wear unevenly and quickly. Too little toe may cause the car to be less stable and wander at highway speeds. See Fig. 4.

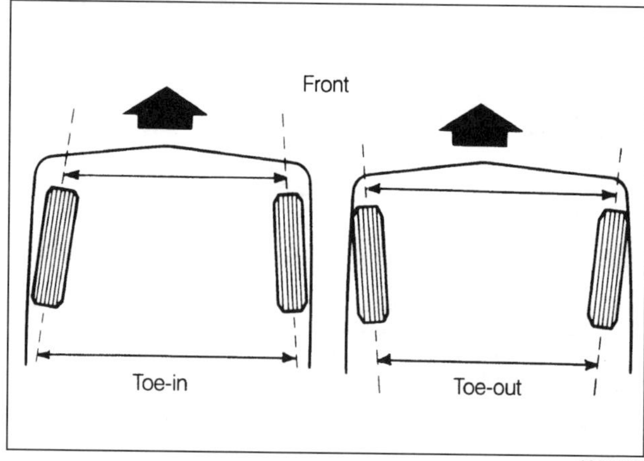

Fig. 4. Front wheel toe.

Wheel alignment, checking

Accurate wheel alignment will best be obtained by having your Volkswagen dealer or a certified alignment shop perform the procedure. Following are a list of required conditions and alignment specifications.

> ***CAUTION —***
> - *It is recommended that both the front and rear axles are measured (thrust angle) when carrying out alignment measurements.*
> - *If the installation position of the rear axle (which affects the direction of travel of the vehicle) is not taken into account the steering wheel may not be centered.*

Before evaluating alignment, be sure that steering wheel and steering column are aligned. See Fig. 5.

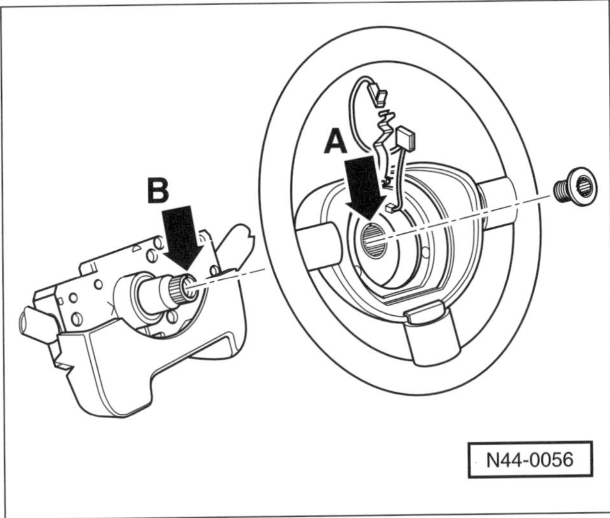

N44-0056

Fig. 5. Mark on steering wheel (**A**) and steering column (**B**) should always line up.

NOTE —
Steering columns supplied as a replacement parts do not have a center punch mark.

> ***WARNING —***
> - *Do not remove air bag without reviewing cautions and warnings in* **69 Seatbelts, Airbags**.
> - *To remove steering wheel and airbag, see* **48 Steering**.

Alignment requirements

- Vehicle at curb weight
- Fuel tank full
- Spare wheel and vehicle tools are stored at correct locations
- Fluid reservoir for windshield/headlight washer system full
- Equal tread depth for both tires on each axle, with difference between two not more than 2 mm (0.079 in.)
- Tires inflated to correct pressure
- Test equipment must be properly adjusted and attached to vehicle. Observe all instructions, cautions and warnings of the test equipment manual
- Vehicle accurately positioned, suspension bounced and rocked several times
- Suspension, steering and steering linkage in proper condition; without excessive play or damage

NOTE —
The vehicle alignment should not be checked before the vehicle has completed 1000-2000 km (600-1200 miles) so that the coil springs can have a chance to settle.

Wheel alignment specifications

Table b. Wheel Alignment Data—Front Suspension

Suspension (version)	**Base suspension (1GJ)**	**Sport suspension (1GD)**
Total toe 1) (wheels not pressed)	0° ± 10'	
Camber 1) (in straight-ahead position)	–30' ± 30'	–33' ± 30'
Maximum permissible difference between left and right	max. 30'	
Toe angle difference at 20° lock from left to right	+1° 30' ± 20'	+1° 31' ± 20'
Caster (not adjustable)	+7° 40' ± 30'	+7° 50' ± 30'
Maximum permissible difference between left and right	30'	30'

1)Camber adjustments are not possible. Corrections are possible by moving the subframe slightly. Adjustment approx. 10′ to 15′.

Table c. Wheel Alignment Data—Rear Suspension

Suspension (version)	**Base suspension (1JD, 1JN)**	**Sport suspension (1JC)**
Camber	–1°27' ± 10'	
Maximum permissible difference between left and right	30'	
Total toe (with specified camber)	+20' ± 10'	+25' ± 10'
Maximum permissible deviation from direction of travel (thrust angle)	20'	

Thrust angle, calculating

Thrust angle (deviation from direction of travel) can be calculated using one of the two following examples. The result is the deviation of the actual running direction from the longitudinal center line of the vehicle.

If alignment readings for rear toe are both positive or both negative (+/+ or -/-), subtract smaller figure from larger figure to determine total toe angle, then divide by 2.

Example:

- Left rear wheel track. . . . . + 15'
- Right rear wheel track . . . . + 5'

15' - 5' = 10'

10' ÷ 2 = 5'

- Thrust angle (deviation from direction of travel): 5′

If alignment readings for rear toe are different signs, one positive and one negative (+/-), add two figures to determine total toe angle, then divide by 2.

Example:

- Left rear wheel track. . . . . + 15'
- Right rear wheel track . . . . - 5'

15' + 5' = 20'

10' ÷ 2 = 10'

- Thrust angle (deviation from direction of travel): 10′

---

45 Anti-lock Brakes (ABS)

GENERAL

This repair group covers the optional ITT (Teves) Mark 20 IE anti-lock brake system (ABS) found on the Volkswagen New Beetle. This 3-channel system includes electronic brake-pressure distribution (EBD) which eliminates the need for an axle-mounted mechanical brake pressure regulator. Brake pedal pressure is boosted pneumatically by a vacuum brake booster in this dual-diagonal system.

NOTE —
- *The ABS system features built-in diagnostic circuitry that detects and stores Diagnostic Trouble Code (DTC) information. When the system detects a fault, a DTC is generated and stored in the ABS control module's permanent memory. These fault codes can be accessed through the data link connector using Volkswagen scan tool VAG 1551/1552*
- *If an ABS malfunction is stored, the ABS warning light comes on. ABS and EBD functions may be switched off depending on the nature of the fault. However, normal vacuum and hydraulic brake function is retained.*

CAUTION —
Disconnecting the negative (–) battery cable may erase fault codes and basic settings in the engine management and automatic transmission control modules. Some driveability problems may be noticed until the system re-adapts to operating conditions. OBD II readiness codes, which may be required for emissions testing, may also be erased. Convenience electronics (alarm system, interior light control, power locks, mirrors, and windows) may need to be re-set using a VAG 1551/1552 or equivalent scan tool.

WARNING —
- *ABS is a vehicle safety system; appropriate knowledge and special equipment are necessary to properly work on the system.*
- *The ABS system must be bled after repairs requiring opening of the brake hydraulic system.* *See* **47 Brakes-Hydraulic System.**
- *If you drive an ABS-equipped vehicle after a fault has been detected by the On-Board Diagnostics, keep in mind that the function of the brake system may be limited and there is a risk of accident. The brake pressure at the rear wheels is no longer controlled by the Electronic Brake Distribution (EBD) function. This can result in excessive braking at the rear, and the vehicle may skid unexpectedly under braking.*

Special precautions for ABS equipped vehicles

The ABS control module processes precise, low-level electronic signals and can be very sensitive to changes in the power supply and the environment. The following precautions apply to vehicles with ABS.

WARNING —
- *When driving or riding in an airbag-equipped vehicle, NEVER hold the scan tool or other test equipment in your hands or lap while in motion. Objects between you and the airbag increase the risk of injury in an accident.*
- *During a test drive in an air-bag equipped vehicle, test equipment must always be fastened to and operated from the rear seat by a helper.*
- *Brake fluid is poisonous!*

CAUTION—
- *When working on the electrical sections of the ABS, only disconnect harness connectors with the ignition switched off.*
- *If the ABS warning light illuminates, there is a fault in the system. Determine the cause of the malfunction using the On-Board Diagnostic (OBD) program. Check the fault memory with a suitable scan tool such as Volkswagen scan tool VAG 1551/1552 or equivalent before proceeding.*
- *Certain faults will only be detected and stored as DTCs at speeds greater than 20 kph (13 mph).*
- *The ABS and brake system warning lights are not capable of monitoring all brake system functions; visual inspections are still required for the system.*
- *Brake fluid must not contact any painted surfaces; it will remove paint.*
- *Brake fluid absorbs moisture from the surrounding air and must be replaced every two years. Use only new brake fluid that complies with Federal Motor Vehicle Safety Standards 116, DOT 4.*
- *Do not use silicone-based brake fluids (DOT 5). This fluid is incompatible with the brake system and even the smallest trace can cause severe corrosion.*
- *Absolute cleanliness is required when working on the ABS system. Do not use any products that contain mineral oil such as oil, grease, etc.*
- *Thoroughly clean all connections and the area immediately around them before loosening. Do not use aggressive cleaning agents such as brake cleaner, gasoline or thinners.*
- *Place removed parts on a clean surface and cover them. Only use clean plastic covering or paper. Do not use rags that may contain lint.*
- *Carefully seal or cover opened components if repairs cannot be completed immediately.*
- *After separating the control module from the hydraulic unit, use the transportation protection for the valve dome.*
- *Only install replacement parts from original packaging. Only remove the parts from the package immediately before installation.*
- *Do not work with compressed air nearby whenever the hydraulic system is open. Do not move the vehicle with the hydraulic system open.*
- *Be very careful not to let any brake fluid enter any wiring harness connectors.*
- *Do not re-use fasteners that are worn or deformed from normal use.*

ABS COMPONENTS

The ITT (Teves) Mark 20 IE Anti-Lock brake system (ABS) uses electronic, electrical, hydraulic and mechanical components. For an overview of the major electronic and electrical components, see Fig. 1. For an overview of the major hydraulic and mechanical components, see Fig. 2.

Electrical/electronic ABS components

The following numbered list applies to Fig. 1.

1. **ABS hydraulic unit**
   - Secured to mounting bracket on left side of engine compartment near the strut tower
   - Hydraulic pump
   - Valve block with inlet/outlet valves
   - Combined assembly does not separate
   - If exchanging, use plugs from new unit to seal openings
2. **ABS control module**
   - Mounted to underside of hydraulic unit
   - Hydraulic unit and control module form one unit that can only be separated when removed from vehicle
   - New control modules (replacement parts) are not coded and must be coded after installation
   - Disconnect harness connector only with ignition switched off
   - Check for Diagnostic Trouble Codes (DTCs) with scan tool before disconnecting harness connector
3. **Bolt**
   - Tighten to 8 Nm (71 in-lb)
4. **Bolt**
   - Tighten to 8 Nm (71 in-lb)
5. **Brake light switch**
   - Open circuit in rest position
   - Removing, adjusting see **96 Lights, Accessories–Interior**
6. **Data Link Connector**
   - Located in left lower area of dash panel
7. **Brake system warming light**
   - Operation, **see** (A)
8. **ABS warning light**
   - Operation, **see** (B)
9. **ABS wheel speed sensor, front**
   - Clean inner surface in wheel bearing housing before installing and lubricate with grease (VW part no. G 000 650 or equivalent)
   - Check to be sure wiring is not twisted in wheel well before connecting
10. **Wheel hub with ABS wheel speed sensor rotor**
    - Rotor welded to wheel hub

Electrical/electronic ABS components

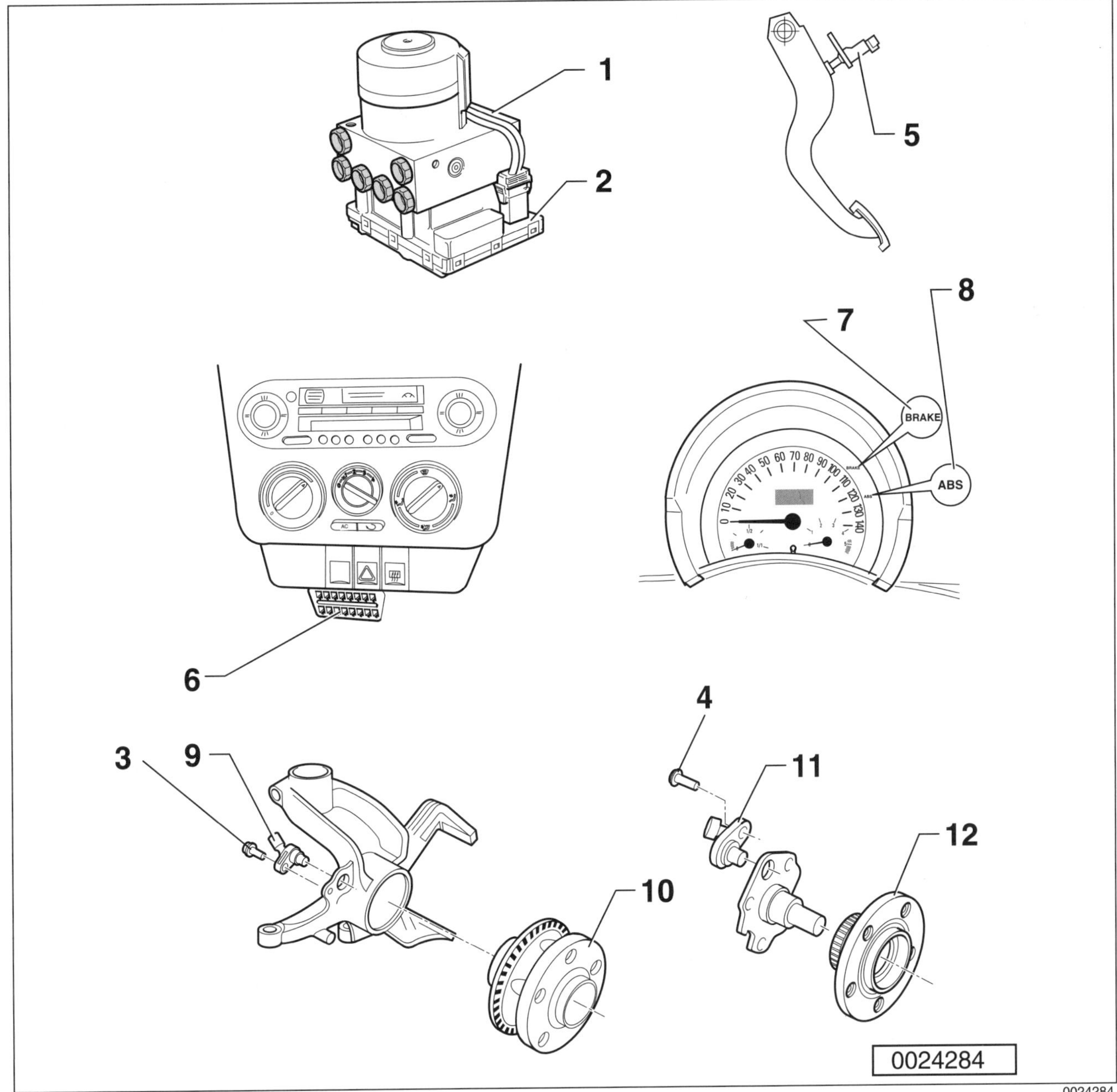

Fig. 1. Major electrical/electronic components of the ITT (Teves) Mark 20 IE ABS.

11. **ABS wheel speed sensor, rear**
    - Clean inner surface in wheel bearing housing before installing and lubricate with grease (VW part no. G 000 650 or equivalent)
    - Check to be sure wiring is not twisted in wheel well before connecting

12. **Wheel bearing/hub unit with ABS wheel speed sensor rotor**
    - Wheel bearing, wheel hub and wheel speed sensor rotor are installed together in housing

A Brake system warning light functions

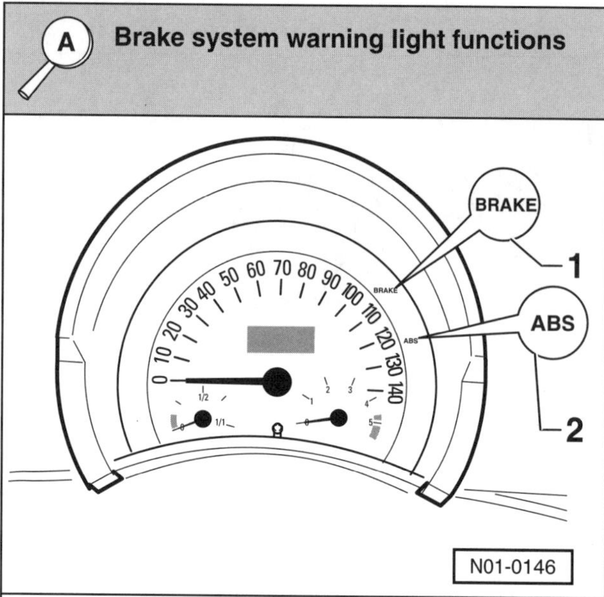

N01-0146

Brake warning light (1):

- Lights momentarily and goes out if key is switched on and parking brake is not applied (as a self test).
- Lights if key is switched on and parking brake is applied.
- Lights if key is switched on and parking brake is not applied if brake fluid level is low (may flicker).
- May light in conjunction with ABS warning light if certain Diagnostic Trouble Codes are present.

B ABS warning light functions

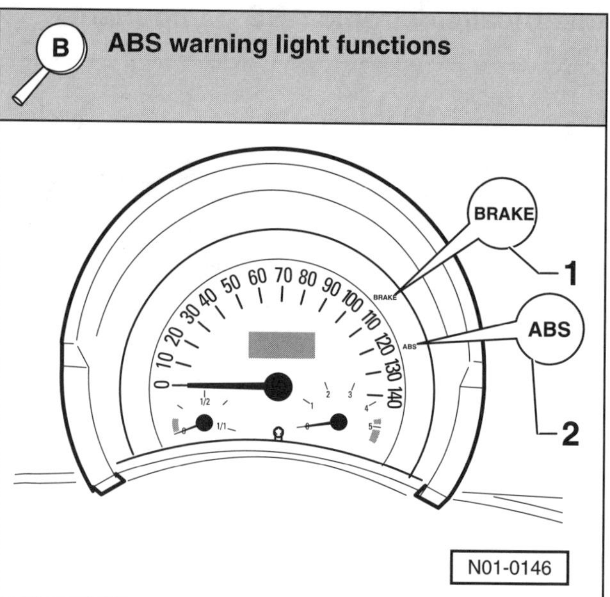

N01-0146

ABS warning light (2):

- Lights momentarily and goes out if key is switched on and ABS system is functioning within normal parameters (as a self test).
- Lights if supply voltage drops below 10.0 volts.
- Lights if ABS system has a malfunction (ABS system is automatically switched off if light is on).
- Lights after vehicle speed exceeds 20 km/h (13 mph) to indicate wheel speed sensor malfunction.
- May light if instrument cluster or wiring malfunction is present.

Hydraulic/mechanical ABS Components

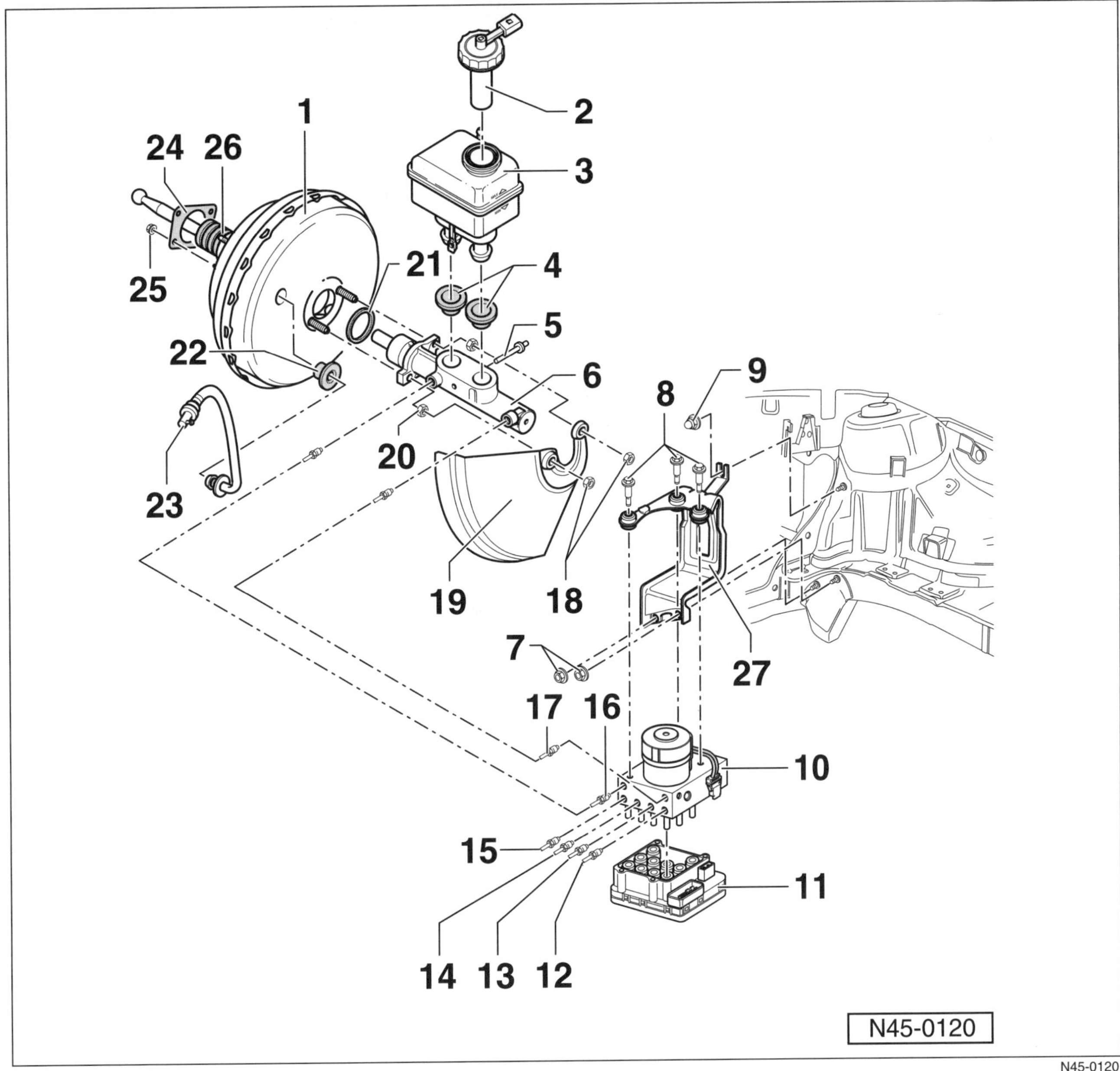

Fig. 2. Major hydraulic/mechanical components of the ITT (Teves) Mark 20 IE ABS.

1. **Brake booster**
   - On gasoline engines vacuum is taken from intake manifold
   - Diesel engines have a vacuum pump to create required vacuum
   - Complete master cylinders and brake boosters can be replaced separately
2. **Cap**
   - With fluid level sensor
3. **Brake fluid reservoir**
   - Also supplies brake fluid to hydraulic clutch for manual transmission
4. **Sealing plug**
   - Moisten with brake fluid and press into reservoir
5. **Retainer pin**
   - Insert through brake master cylinder
6. **Tandem brake master cylinder**
   - Cannot be repaired
   - If faulty, replace as complete unit
7. **Nut, self-locking**
   - Always replace
   - Tighten to 20 Nm (15 ft-lb)

(continued on following page)

(continued from previous page)

8. **Bolt**
   - Tighten to 9 Nm (80 in-lb)
9. **Nut**
   - Tighten to 9 Nm (80 in-lb)
10. **ABS hydraulic unit**
11. **ABS control module**
    - Separating from hydraulic unit, **see** 
12. **Brake line connection**
    - Hydraulic unit to left front brake caliper
13. **Brake line connection**
    - Hydraulic unit to right rear caliper
14. **Brake line connection**
    - Hydraulic unit to left rear caliper
15. **Brake line connection**
    - Hydraulic unit to right front brake caliper
16. **Brake line**
    - Brake master cylinder/primary piston circuit to hydraulic unit
17. **Brake line**
    - Master brake cylinder/secondary piston circuit to hydraulic unit
18. **Nut, self-locking**
    - Always replace
    - Tighten to 20 Nm (15 ft-lb)
19. **Heat shield**
    - Only for vehicles with AEG engine
20. **Nut, self-locking**
    - Always replace
    - Tighten to 20 Nm (15 ft-lb)
21. **Seal**
    - Always replace
22. **Seal**
23. **Vacuum hose**
    - Insert into brake booster
24. **Gasket**
    - For brake booster
25. **Nut, self-locking**
    - Always replace
    - Tighten to 20 Nm (15 ft-lb)
26. **Boot**
    - Ensure proper seating
27. **Bracket**

A — ABS control module, separating from hydraulic unit

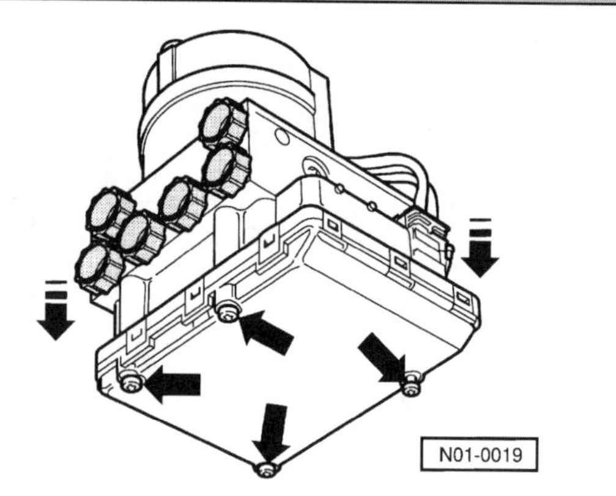

N01-0019

- **Assembly must be removed from vehicle.**
- **Unplug pump motor from control module.**
- **Remove bolts (solid arrows) from control module.**
- **Pull control module and hydraulic unit straight apart (dashed arrows) to separate.**
- **Always use new attaching bolts.**
- **Do not tilt hydraulic valve dome against solenoid valves.**

CAUTION —
- *Only remove sealing plugs on the new hydraulic unit just before installing the corresponding brake line.*
- *If the sealing plugs are removed too early, brake fluid can escape. It can then no longer be guaranteed that the unit is sufficiently filled or adequately bled.*
- *Cover the control module magnetic coils with a plastic covering. Do not use rags.*
- *After separating the control module and hydraulic unit, use transportation protection for the valve dome.*
- *When assembling the control module and hydraulic unit, be sure that the hydraulic unit valve dome is not tilted against the control module solenoid valves.*

Tightening torques
- Control module to hydraulic unit always replace (M4) . . . . 4 Nm (35 in-lb)
- Hydraulic unit bolt to bracket (M6) . . . . 8 Nm (71 in-lb)
- Master cylinder nut to booster (M8) . . 20 Nm (15 ft-lb)
- Brake lines to ABS unit (M10/M12) . . 15 Nm (11 ft-lb)
- Mounting bracket to body (M8). . . . . . 20 Nm (15 ft-lb)

ABS CONTROL MODULE

The ABS control module is attached to the bottom of the ABS hydraulic unit located in the engine compartment. Control unit replacement is only possible if the hydraulic unit has been removed.

Vehicles equipped with ABS link the ABS control module to the engine control module and the automatic transmission control module (where applicable). Linking the systems allows certain types of vehicle data to be shared for functional and diagnostic purposes. Linking systems to share data is generally known as multiplexing. Volkswagen uses a 2-wire system called a CAN-bus. See Fig. 3.

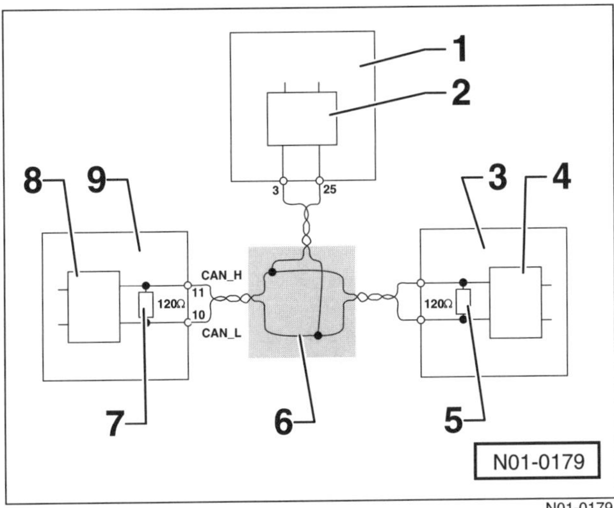

Fig. 3. Schematic view of linked control modules if all systems were installed in a given vehicle. Numbers identify various components.

1. **Automatic transmission control module (TCM)**
2. **Communications circuitry**
3. **Engine control module (ECM)**
4. **Communications circuitry**
5. **Terminating impedance**
6. **CAN-bus multiplexing**
7. **Terminating impedance**
8. **Communications circuitry**
9. **Anti -lock brakes control module (ABS)**

Most service and repair to the ITT (Teves) Mark 20 IE ABS system requires the use of a scan tool such as the Volkswagen VAG 1551/1552 or equivalent. Access is via the Data Link Connector (DLC). See Fig. 4. This includes coding of replacement control modules. Although all control modules carry the same code at this time, replacement parts are shipped uncoded and will not function properly when installed in an uncoded condition. Because of the specialized nature of these repairs, servicing should be referred to an authorized Volkswagen dealer or qualified independent repair shop. ABS control module coding numbers are shown in **Table a**.

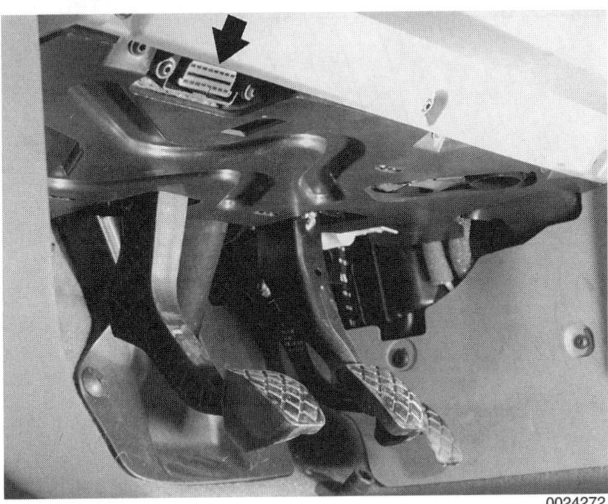

Fig. 4. Data Link Connector (DLC), (**arrow**) under left lower side of instrument panel.

Table a. ABS control module coding

Engine Code	System	ABS Control Module Code
AEG	ABS	03504
ALH	ABS	03504

WHEEL SPEED SENSORS

Each wheel has a separate speed sensor to supply data to the ABS control module. Each sensor is also monitored by the control module and malfunctions will cause a DTC to be stored. The system checks the sensors for proper resistance when the ignition is first switched on and again for proper signal when the vehicle is in motion.

Front wheel speed sensor, removing and installing

1. Raise car and support with jack stands or lift. See **0 Maintenance** for proper lifting procedure.

> ***WARNING —***
> *Observe all warnings and cautions associated with lifting vehicle in* **0 Maintenance**.

2. Disconnect harness connector from wheel speed sensor.

3. Remove bolt from wheel bearing housing. See Fig. 5.

4. Remove sensor from bearing housing.

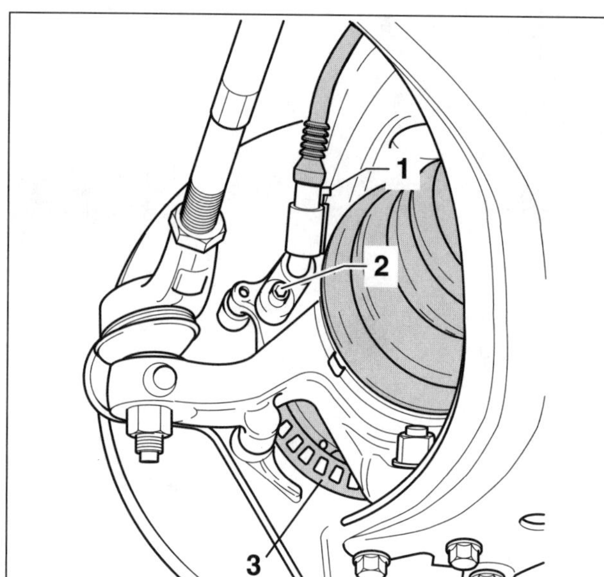

0024285

Fig. 5. Front ABS wheel speed sensor harness connector (**1**), securing bolt (**2**) and sensor rotor (**3**).

Specification

- ABS wheel speed sensor resistance, front and rear . . . . 1000-1300 ohms

Tightening torque

- Wheel speed sensor mounting bolt, front and rear, M6. . . . . 8 Nm (71 in-lb)

5. Before installing sensor into bearing housing, clean mounting hole and lubricate with grease (VW part no. G 000 650 or equivalent).

6. Install sensor and bolt, reconnect harness connector.

7. Turn wheels fully to left and then to right. Check sensor wiring for interference and clearance.

Rear wheel speed sensor, removing and installing

1. Raise car and support with jack stands or lift. See **0 Maintenance** for proper lifting procedure.

> ***WARNING —***
> *Observe all warnings and cautions associated with lifting vehicle in* **0 Maintenance**.

2. Disconnect harness connector from wheel speed sensor.

3. Remove ABS wheel sensor mounting bolt from stub axle. See Fig. 6.

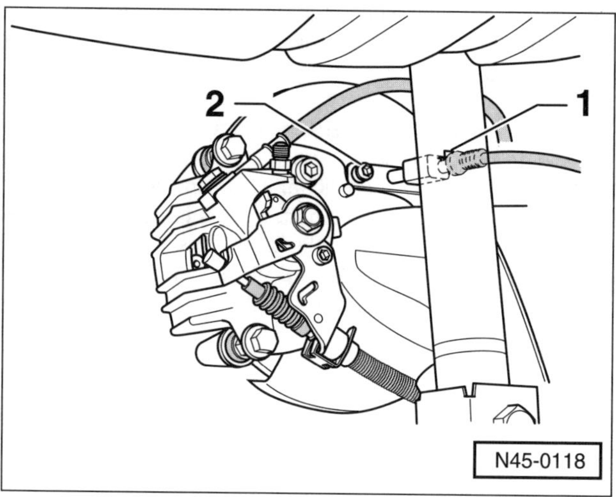

N45-0118

Fig. 6. Rear ABS wheel speed sensor harness connector (**1**) and securing bolt (**2**).

4. Pull ABS wheel speed sensor out of stub axle.

5. Before installing sensor into bearing housing, clean mounting hole and lubricate with grease (VW part no. G 000 650 or equivalent).

6. Install sensor and bolt, reconnect harness connector.

7. Check sensor wiring for interference and clearance around suspension components.

QUALITY REVIEW

When you have finished working under the hood and around other areas of the vehicle, it is advisable to take a moment to quality check or review your work. This helps to insure that the operation or repair has been completed properly with all affected systems functioning within normal parameters. These may include the following:

- During the final road test make at least one controlled brake test where the brake pedal is felt to pulsate (ABS operation).
- Ensure that all cable ties and clamps that were removed as part of the repair are replaced.
- Ensure that all fasteners and hardware were replaced and torqued as specified.
- Check and adjust brake fluid level.
- Make sure that all other components involved in the repair are positioned correctly, properly torqued and function properly.
- Make sure that all tools, shop cloths, fender covers and protective tapes are removed before closing the hood.
- Clean grease and fingerprints from painted surfaces, steering wheel and shifter.

46 Brakes–Mechanical Components

GENERAL

This repair groups covers service and repair to the brake friction components; brake pads and rotors. Also included here is parking brake service.

Cars covered by this manual are equipped with disc brakes on all four wheels. Some cars with four-wheel disc brakes are also equipped with anti-lock brakes (ABS).

> ***NOTE —***
> - *For brake caliper and rear brake wheel cylinder repair information, see* **47 Brakes–Hydraulic System**.
> - *For information on the ABS hydraulic unit and ABS service, see* **45 Anti-Lock Brakes (ABS)**.
> - *Brake fluid should be flushed from the system every two years. See* **47 Brakes–Hydraulic System**.

> ***WARNING —***
> - *A properly functioning brake system is essential to safe driving. If the red brake/parking warning light or ABS warning light illuminates while driving, it is imperative that the system be given a thorough check, even if braking action still seems satisfactory. The brakes should be inspected regularly.*
> - *Brake fluid is poisonous. Wear safety glasses when working with brake fluid, and wear rubber gloves to prevent brake fluid from entering the bloodstream through cuts or scratches. Do not siphon brake fluid by mouth.*
> - *New brake pads and shoes require some break-in. Allow for slightly longer stopping distances for the first 100 to 150 miles of city driving, and avoid hard stops.*

> ***CAUTION —***
> - *All brake work must be done with cleanliness, careful attention to specifications, and proper working procedures. If you lack the skills, the tools, or a clean workplace for servicing the brake system, we suggest you leave these repairs to an authorized VW dealer or other qualified shop.*
> - *After replacing brake components, depress the brake pedal firmly several times to seat the brakes in their normal operating position.The pedal should be firm and at its normal height, if not, further work is required before driving vehicle.*
> - *Brake fluid is very damaging to paint. Immediately wipe up any brake fluid that spills on the vehicle.*

FRONT BRAKES

Two types of front discs are used on the cars covered by this manual. Repair procedures vary depending on caliper/rotor application. See the appropriate (FS III or FN 3) assembly view.

Caliper application
- 2.0L (AEG engine) . . . . FS III
- 1.9L (ALH engine) . . . . FS III
- 1.8L (APH engine) . . . . FN 3

Rotors should be inspected for cracks, scoring, glazing and warpage. Rotors must be replaced (in pairs) if either disc is worn below the minimum thickness specification or if any of the above listed defects are found.

> ***NOTE —***
> *The minimum brake rotor thickness specification is stamped into the rotor's hub and also listed in the appropriate illustration.*

46

Front brake assembly (FS III caliper)

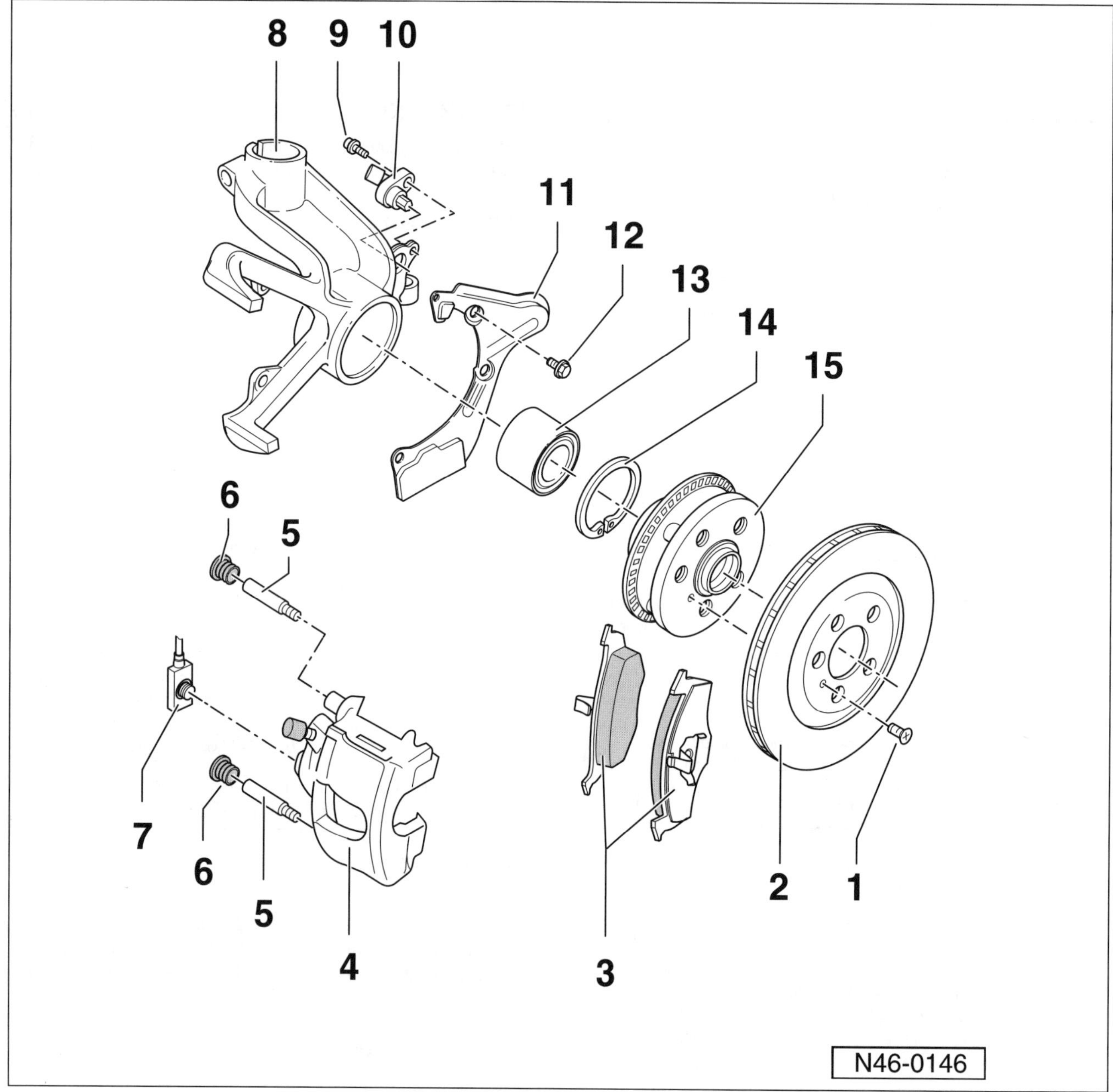

Fig. 1. Front brake assembly with FS III brake caliper.

1. **Screw**
   - Tighten to 4 Nm (35 in-lb)
2. **Brake disc**
   - Diameter: 280 mm (11.02 in.)
   - Thickness: 22 mm (0.866 in.)
   - Wear limit: 19 mm (0.748 in.)
   - When worn always replace on both sides
   - Remove brake caliper before removing disc
   - Never remove brake discs from hub by using force. If necessary use penetrating fluid, otherwise brake discs can be damaged.
3. **Brake pads**
   - Thickness 14 mm (0.551 in.)
   - Checking thickness, see **0 Maintenance**
   - Always replace all pads on one axle at same time
   - Wear limit: 7 mm (0.276 in.) including backing plate
4. **Brake caliper**
   - Do not loosen hydraulic line when replacing pads
5. **Guide pin**
   - Tighten to 28 Nm (21 ft-lb)

(continued from previous page)

6. **Protective cap**
7. **Brake hose with union and banjo bolt**
   - Tighten to 35 Nm (26 ft-lb)
8. **Wheel bearing housing**
9. **Socket-head bolt**
   - Tighten to 8 Nm (71 in-lb)
10. **ABS wheel speed sensor**
    - Before inserting sensor, clean hole inner surface and coat with grease (VW part no. G 000 650)
11. **Splash shield**
12. **Bolt**
    - Tighten to 10 Nm (7 ft-lb)
13. **Wheel bearing**
    - Replace each time after removing
    - Pressing out and in, see **40 Front Suspension and Drive Axles**
14. **Circlip**
15. **Wheel hub with rotor**
    - Removing and installing, see **40 Front Suspension and Drive Axles**

Front brake pads, removing and installing (FS III caliper)

1. Raise car and support with jack stands or lift. See **0 Maintenance** for proper lifting procedure.

> ***WARNING —***
> *Observe all warnings and cautions associated with lifting vehicle in* **0 Maintenance***.*

2. Remove front wheels.
3. Remove guide pin protective caps.
4. Remove both guide pins from brake caliper.

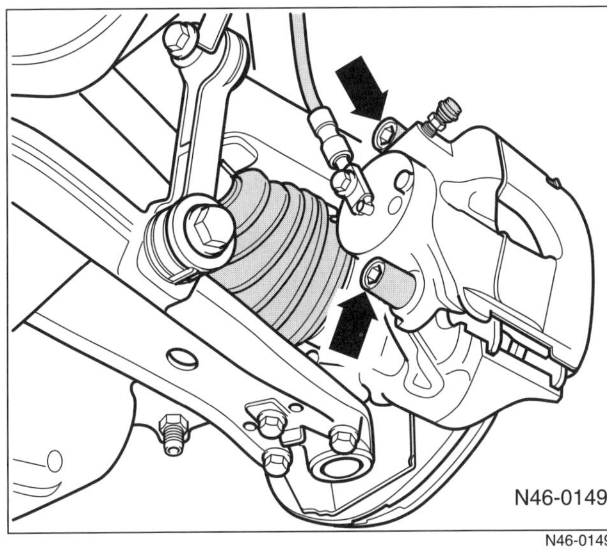

N46-0149

Fig. 2. Remove caliper guide pins (**arrows**)

5. Remove brake caliper housing and hang up with wire.

> ***CAUTION —***
> - *Do not allow caliper to hang by the brake hose. The unsupported weight can stretch and damage the hose.*
> - *Do not disconnect the brake hose from the caliper when removing brake pads.*

6. Remove brake pads from brake caliper housing.
7. Before installing new pads extract some of the brake fluid from the brake fluid reservoir.

> ***WARNING —***
> *Brake fluid is poisonous. Never siphon by mouth.*

> ***CAUTION —***
> *A full brake fluid reservoir may allow brake fluid to flow out and cause damage when pistons are pushed back.*

8. Press piston into caliper housing. See Fig. 3.

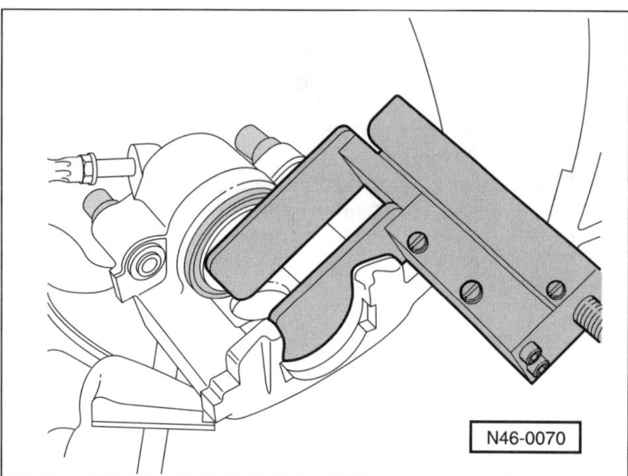

N46-0070

Fig. 3. Caliper piston being pressed into caliper using VW special tool.

9. Install brake pads with retaining spring in brake caliper housing.

10. Install brake caliper onto wheel bearing housing.
    - Position lower brake caliper housing on first.
    - The brake caliper housing tab must be behind the wheel bearing housing guide. See Fig. 4.

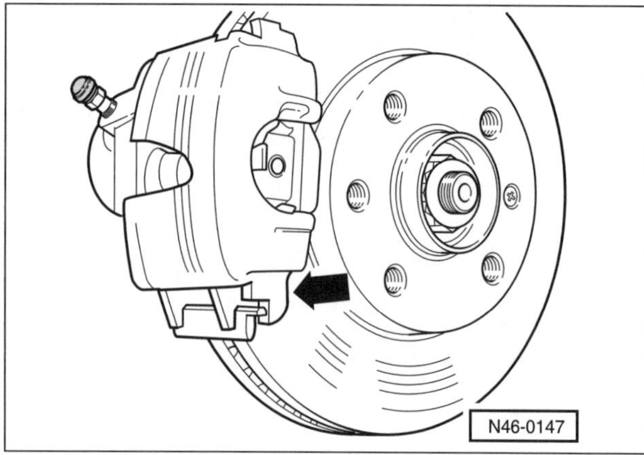

N46-0147

Fig. 4. Brake caliper housing tab (**arrow**) must be behind the wheel bearing housing guide.

11. Mount brake caliper housing to brake carrier with both guide pins and install guide pin protective caps.

12. Install wheels and lower vehicle.

Tightening torques
- Brake caliper to bearing housing . . . . 28 Nm (21 ft-lb)
- Wheel bolt to hub . . . . 120 Nm (87 ft-lb)

---

13. Depress brake pedal firmly several times to seat brake pads to brake disc. Check brake fluid level.

Front brake assembly (FN 3 caliper)

The followiong numbered list applies to Fig. 5.

1. **Screw**
    - Tighten to 4 Nm (35 in-lb)
2. **Brake disc**
    - Diameter: 288 mm (11.34 in.)
    - Thickness: 25 mm (0.984 in.)
    - Wear limit: 22 mm (0.866 in.)
    - When worn always replace brake disc pairs on both sides
3. **Brake pads**
    - Thickness: 14 mm (0.551 in.)
    - Checking thickness, see **0 Maintenance**
    - Always replace all pads on one axle at same time
    - Wear limit: 7 mm (0.276 in.) including backing plate
4. **Retaining spring**
    - Insert in both brake caliper housings
5. **Brake carrier**
    - Supplied as replacement part
    - If protective caps are damaged, use repair kit
    - Use grease packet supplied to lubricate guide pins
6. **Brake caliper housing**
    - Do not disconnect brake hose when changing brake pads
7. **Guide pins**
    - Tighten to 28 Nm (21 ft-lb)
8. **Protective cap**
9. **Brake hose with union and banjo bolt**
    - Tighten to 15 Nm (11 ft-lb)
10. **Ribbed bolt**
    - Tighten to 125 Nm (92 ft-lb)
11. **Wheel bearing housing**
12. **Socket-head bolt**
    - Tighten to 10 Nm (7 ft-lb)
13. **ABS wheel speed sensor**
    - Before inserting sensor, clean hole inner surface and coat with grease (VW part no. G 000 650)
14. **Splash shield**

(continued on following page)

Front brake assembly (FN 3 caliper)

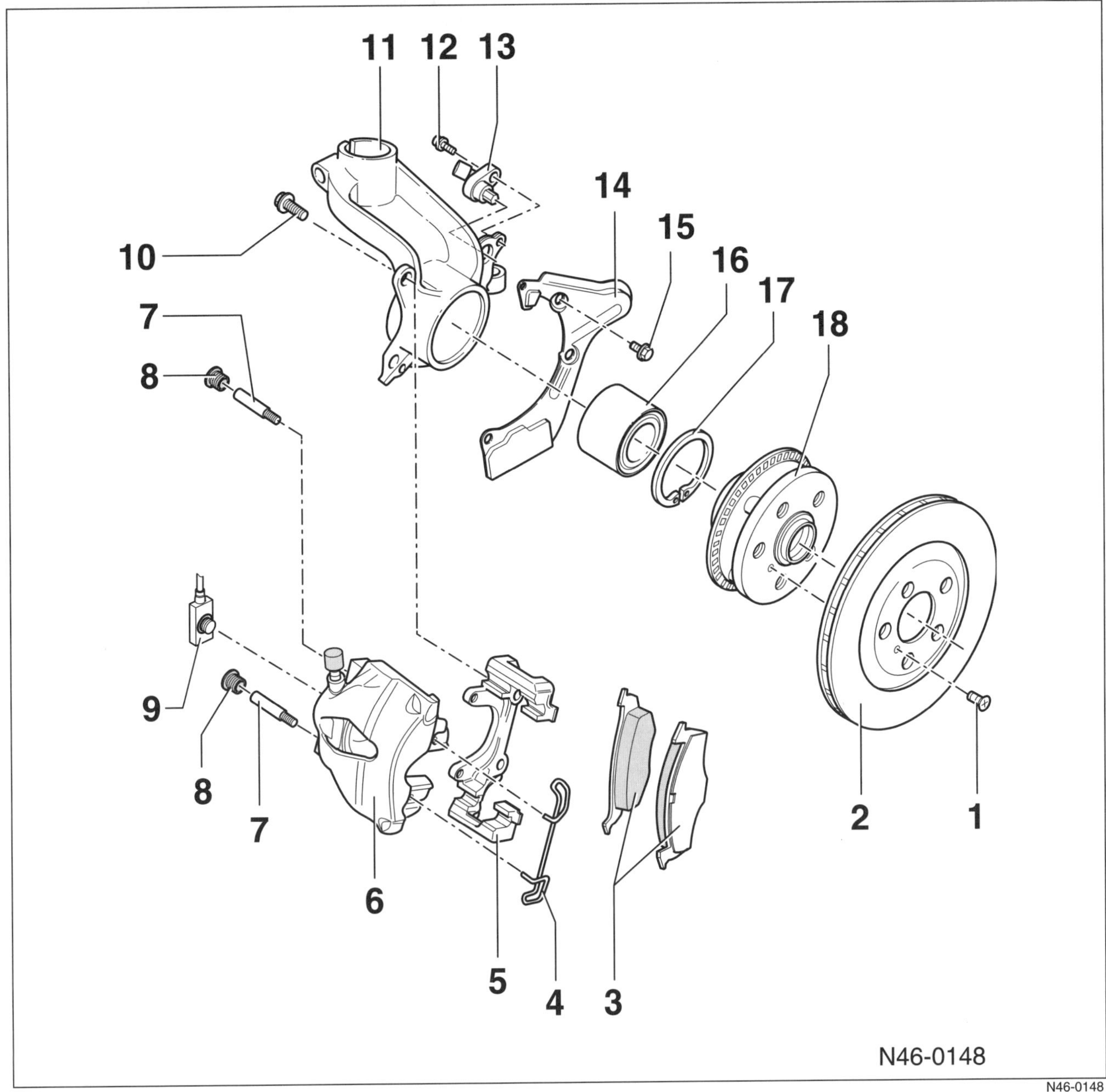

N46-0148

Fig. 5. Front brake assembly with FN 3 brake caliper.

15. Bolt
- Tighten to 10 Nm (7 ft-lb)

16. Wheel bearing
- Replace each time after removing
- Removing and installing, see **40 Front Suspension and Drive Axles**

17. Circlip

18. Wheel hub with rotor
- Removing and installing, see **40 Front Suspension and Drive Axles**

Front brake pads, removing and installing (FN 3 caliper)

1. Raise car and support with jack stands or lift. See **0 Maintenance** for proper lifting procedure.

> ***WARNING —***
> *Observe all warnings and cautions associated with lifting vehicle in* **0 Maintenance**.

2. Remove front wheels.
3. Remove guide pin protective caps.
4. Using a screwdriver, pry brake pad retaining spring out of brake caliper housing and remove.

> ***WARNING —***
> *Wear appropriate eye protection when removing retaining spring.*

5. Remove both guide pins from brake caliper. See Fig. 6.

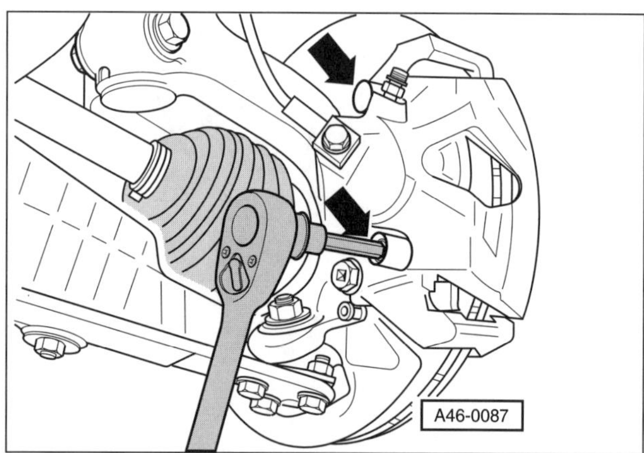

A46-0087

Fig. 6. Remove caliper guide pins (**arrows**).

6. Remove brake caliper housing and hang up with wire.

> ***CAUTION —***
> - *Do not allow caliper to hang by the brake hose. The unsupported weight can stretch and damage the hose.*
> - *Do not disconnect the brake hose from the caliper when removing brake pads.*

7. Remove brake pads.
8. Clean brake caliper housing, especially bonding surface for brake pad. Surfaces must be free of adhesive or grease residue.
9. Before installing new pads extract some of the brake fluid from the brake fluid reservoir.

> ***WARNING —***
> *Brake fluid is poisonous. Never siphon brake fluid by mouth.*

> ***CAUTION —***
> *A full brake fluid reservoir may allow brake fluid to flow out and cause damage when pistons are pushed back.*

10. Be sure to install correct brake pads into left and right caliper. See Fig. 7.

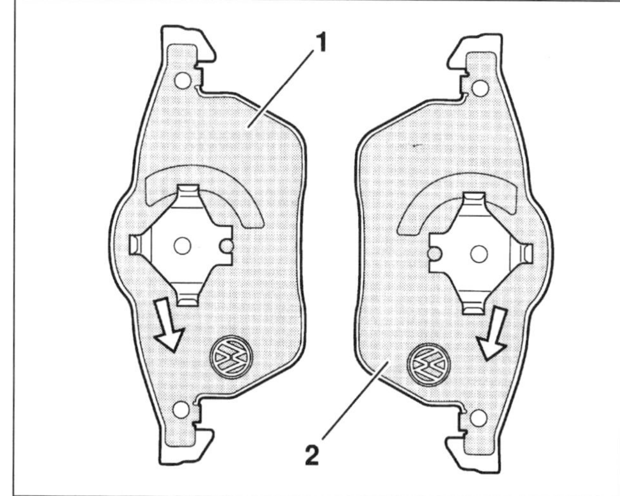

N46-0058

Fig. 7. Right-hand piston side brake pad (**1**) and left-hand piston side brake pad (**2**). **Arrow** on brake pad backing plate must point downward when installed in caliper.

11. Press piston into caliper housing and install brake pads.
12. Install outer brake pad in brake caliper.
13. Pull protective foil off outer brake pad backing plate.
14. Install brake caliper housing with both guide pins to brake carrier.
15. Install guide pin protective caps.
16. Insert retaining spring into brake caliper housing.
17. Install wheels and lower vehicle.

Tightening torques
- Brake caliper to bearing housing . . . . 28 Nm (21 ft-lb)
- Wheel bolt to hub . . . . 120 Nm (87 ft-lb)

18. Depress brake pedal firmly several times to seat brake pads to brake disc. Check brake fluid level and add as necessary.

REAR BRAKES

Rear disc brake assembly

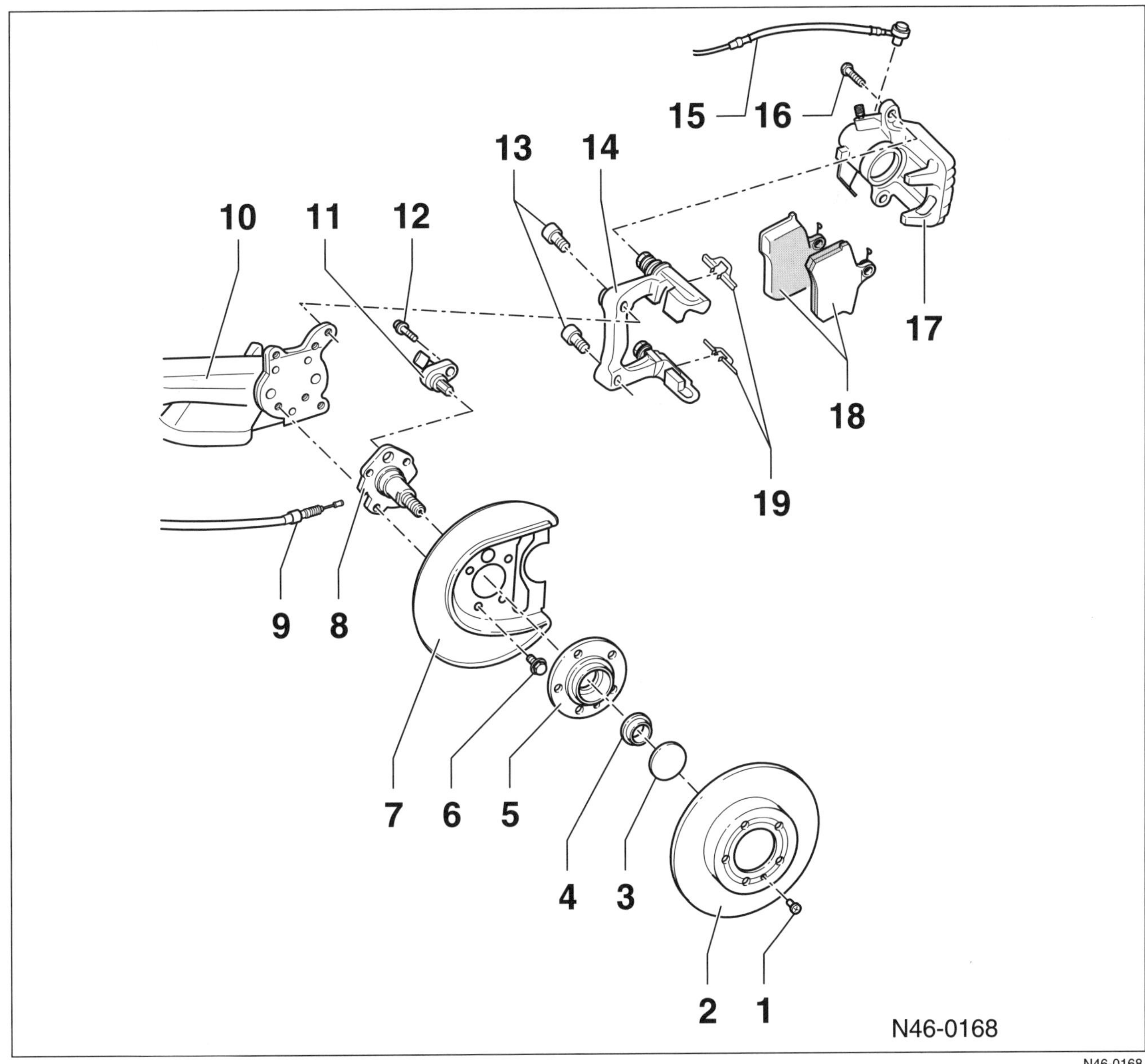

N46-0168

Fig. 8. Rear disc brake assembly.

1. **Screw**
   - Tighten to 4 Nm (35 in-lb)
2. **Brake disc**
   - Diameter: 232 mm (9.13 in.)
   - Thickness: 9 mm (0.354 in.)
   - Wear limit: 7 mm (0.275 in.)
   - When worn, always replace on both sides.
3. **Cap**
   - Removing and installing, see **42 Rear Suspension**
4. **Self-locking nut**
   - Tighten to 175 Nm (129 ft-lb)
   - Always replace after removing
5. **Wheel hub with wheel bearing and rotor**
   - Always replace after removing
   - Only replace as complete unit
   - Removing and installing, see **42 Rear Suspension**
6. **Bolt**
   - Tighten to 60 Nm (44 ft-lb)
   - With dished spring washer

(continued on following page)

(continued from previous page)

7. **Splash shield**
8. **Stub axle**
9. **Parking brake cable**
10. **Axle beam**
11. **ABS wheel speed sensor**
    - Before inserting sensor, clean installation hole inner surface and coat with grease (VW part no. G 000 650)
12. **Socket-head bolt**
    - Tighten to 8 Nm (71 in-lb)
13. **Socket-head bolt**
    - Tighten to 65 Nm (48 ft-lb)
14. **Brake carrier with guide pins and protective cap**
    - Supplied as replacement part assembled with sufficient grease on guide pins
    - If protective caps or guide pins are damaged use repair kit
    - Use grease packet supplied to lubricate guide pins.
15. **Brake hose with union and banjo bolt**
    - With seals
    - Tighten to 35 Nm (26 ft-lb)
    - Do not disconnect brake hose when changing brake pads
16. **Self-locking bolt**
    - Tighten to 35 Nm (26 ft-lb)
    - Always replace
17. **Brake caliper**
    - Adjust parking brake cable after maintenance or replacement.
    - Do not pull parking brake before adjusting it
18. **Brake pads**
    - Thickness: 12 mm (0.472 in.)
    - Checking thickness, see **0 Maintenance**
    - Always replace all pads on one axle at same time
19. **Pad retaining springs**
    - Always replace springs when changing pads

Rear brake pads, removing and installing

NOTE —
If re-using brake pads, mark pad position before removing. Reinstall brake pads in their original position to prevent uneven braking.

1. Raise car and support with jack stands or lift. See **0 Maintenance** for proper lifting procedure.

> ***WARNING —***
> *Observe all warnings and cautions associated with lifting vehicle in* **0 Maintenance**.

1. Remove rear wheels.
2. Remove retaining clip for parking brake cable. Press brake lever downward and unhook parking brake cable. See Fig. 9.

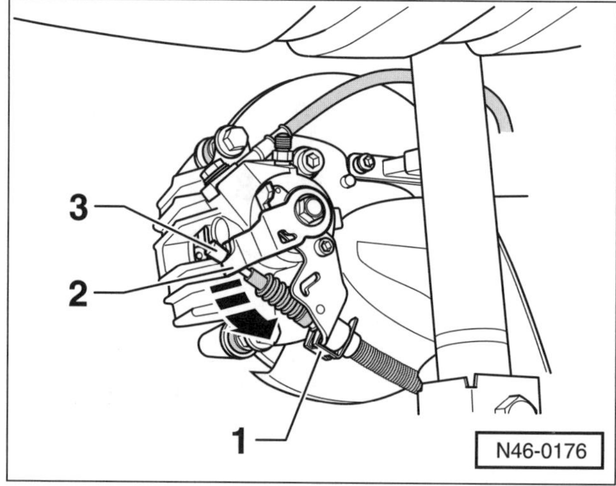

N46-0176

Fig. 9. Remove clip (**1**), press brake lever (**2**) in direction of **arrow** and unhook parking brake cable (**3**).

3. Remove bolts from brake caliper housing while counterholding guide pins. Remove brake caliper and hang up with wire. See Fig. 10.

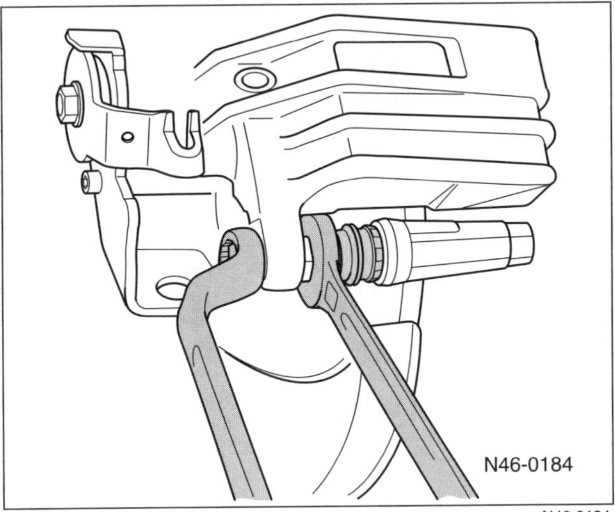

N46-0184

Fig. 10. Caliper mounting bolt being removed. Use wrench to counter-hold guide pin when removing mounting bolt.

> ***CAUTION —***
> - *Do not allow caliper to hang by the brake hose. The unsupported weight can stretch and damage the hose.*
> - *Do not disconnect the brake hose from the caliper when removing brake pads.*

4. Remove brake pads and pad retaining springs. See Fig. 11.

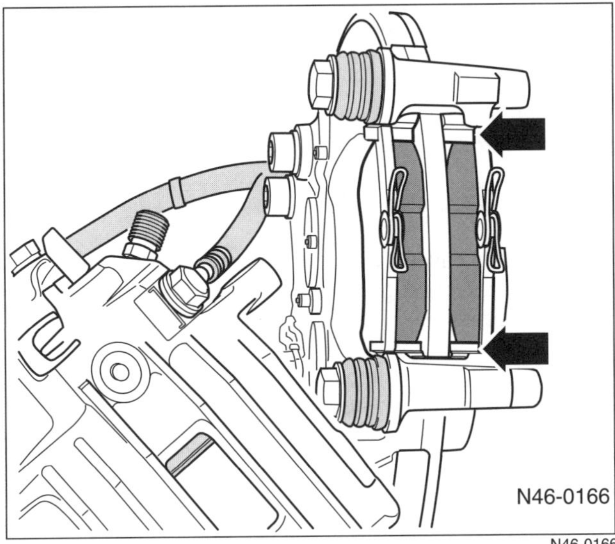

N46-0166

Fig. 11. Remove pads and retaining springs (**arrows**).

5. Clean brake caliper housing, especially bonding surface for brake pad. Bonding surfaces must be free of adhesive and grease residues.

6. Before installing new pads extract some of the brake fluid from the brake fluid reservoir.

> ***WARNING —***
> *Brake fluid is poisonous. Never siphon brake fluid by mouth.*

> ***CAUTION —***
> - *A full brake fluid reservoir may allow brake fluid to flow out and cause damage when pistons are pushed back.*
> - *Use a bleeder bottle or plastic bottle which is used only for brake fluid.*

7. Reset caliper's automatic adjustment mechanism by turning piston clockwise while pushing in. See Fig. 12.

> ***CAUTION —***
> - *If the piston is not reset correctly, or if the brake pedal is operated with the caliper removed, the automatic adjustment mechanism will be destroyed.*
> - *Always remove some brake fluid from the reservoir before resetting and pushing the caliper piston in. When the piston is pushed in, fluid is forced up into the reservoir.*

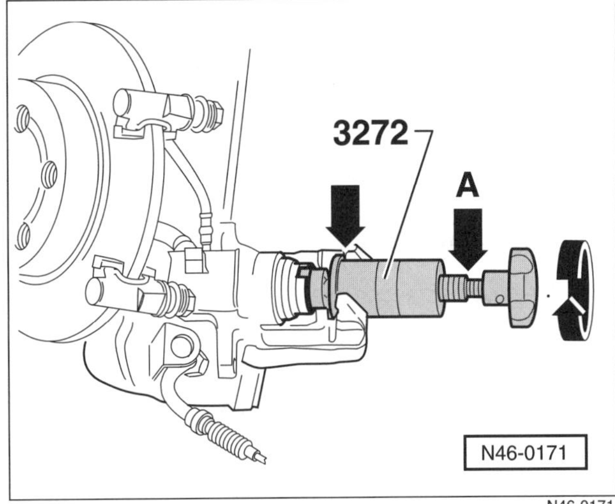

N46-0171

Fig. 12. Automatic adjustment mechanism being reset using Volkswagen special tool 3272. Turn piston clockwise (**rotational arrow**) while pushing piston in. An open-ended wrench can be used on flats (**A**) if necessary.

8. Pull protective foil off outer brake pad backing plate.

9. Insert brake pads and brake pad retaining springs into brake carrier.

10. Install brake caliper housing with new self-locking bolts.

> ***WARNING —***
> *Always replace the self-locking caliper mounting bolts with the ones in the repair kit.*

Tightening torque

- Brake caliper to brake carrier . . . . 35 Nm (26 ft-lb)

11. Connect parking brake cable to lever on caliper and install retaining clip.

12. Adjust parking brake if necessary, see **Parking brake, adjusting** given later.

> ***NOTE —***
> *Operate the foot brake first after adjusting the parking brake.*

13. Install rear wheels and lower vehicle.

14. Depress brake pedal firmly several times to seat brake pads to brake disc. Check brake fluid level and add as necessary.

PARKING BRAKE

The cable-operated parking brake mechanically actuates the rear caliper pistons independent of the hydraulic brake system. Because of the automatic rear wheel brake adjustment there is normally no need to adjust the parking brake. The parking brake must be adjusted only if the parking brake cables, brake calipers or brake discs are replaced.

Parking brake, adjusting

1. Remove center console extension, see **68 Body Interior Equipment**.

2. Raise car and support with jack stands or lift. See **0 Maintenance** for proper lifting procedure.

> ***WARNING —***
> *Observe all warnings and cautions associated with lifting vehicle in* **0 Maintenance**.

3. Release parking brake.

4. Firmly depress brake pedal once.

5. Pull parking brake lever to fourth notch.

6. Tighten parking brake cable adjusting nut until both rear wheels are difficult to turn by hand. See Fig. 13.

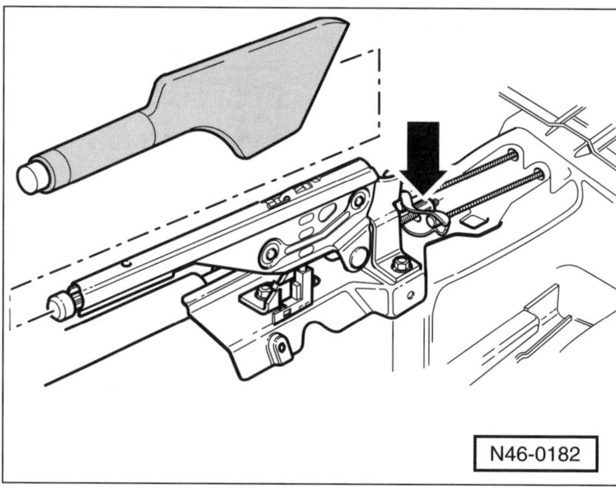

N46-0182

Fig. 13. Tighten adjustment nuts (**arrow**) until both rear wheel are difficult to turn by hand.

7. Release parking brake and check that both wheels turn freely. If necessary turn adjusting nut back slightly.

8. Install center console extension.

9. Lower vehicle.

Parking brake cables, removing and installing

1. Remove center console extension, see **68 Body Interior Equipment**.

2. Release parking brake.

3. Loosen parking brake adjustment nut (shown in Fig. 13) until parking brake cable can be unhooked from compensator.

4. Raise car and support with jack stands or lift. See **0 Maintenance** for proper lifting procedure.

> ***WARNING —***
> *Observe all warnings and cautions associated with lifting vehicle in* **0 Maintenance**.

5. Remove retaining clip for parking brake cable. Press brake lever downward and unhook parking brake cable as shown earlier in Fig. 9.

6. Unclip parking brake cable from retainers. See Fig. 14.

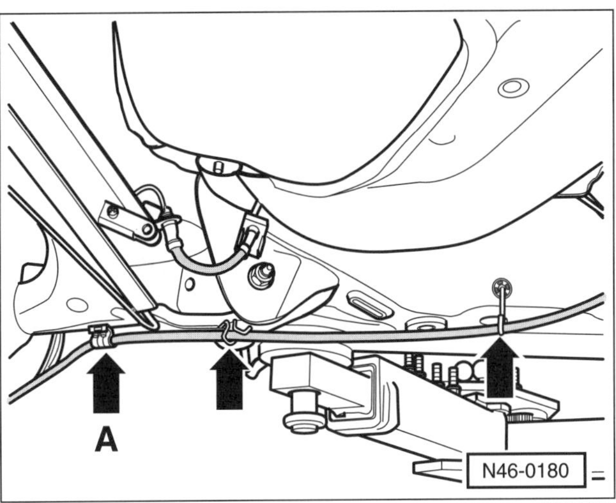

N46-0180

Fig. 14. Parking brake cable retainer on rear axle (**arrow A**) and additional retainers (**arrows**)

7. Pull parking brake cable out of guide tube. See Fig. 15.

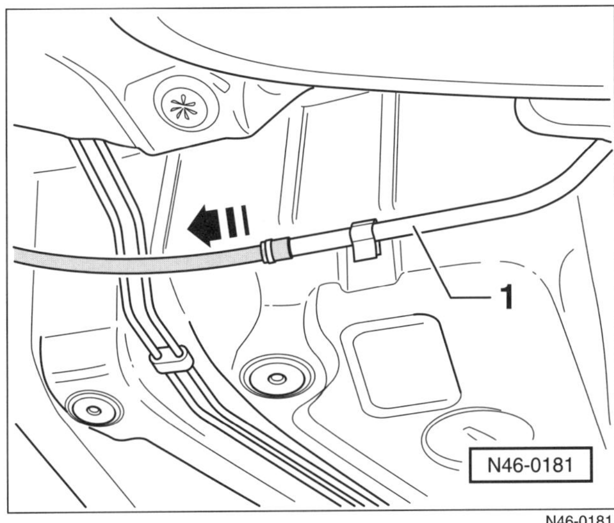

N46-0181

Fig. 15. Pull parking brake cable out of guide tube (**1**) in direction of **arrow**.

8. Begin installation by sliding parking brake cable into guide tube.

9. Connect parking brake cable to lever on caliper and install retaining clip. See Fig. 16.

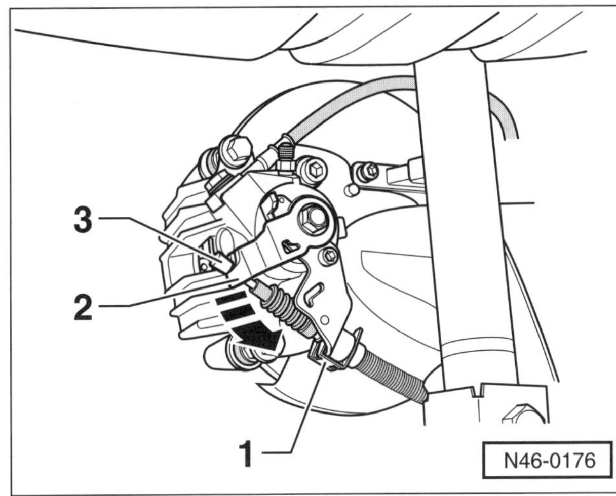

N46-0176

Fig. 16. Press brake lever (**2**) in direction of **arrow** and attach parking brake cable (**3**) and retaining clip (**1**).

10. Clip parking brake cable into retainer on rear axle.

NOTE —

Parking brake cable clamp ring must lie in middle of clip.

11. Hook parking brake cable into remaining retainers.

12. Hook parking brake cable into compensator at parking brake lever.

13. Install parking brake cable adjustment nut.

14. Adjust parking brake, see **Parking brake, adjusting** given earlier.

15. Lower vehicle.

16. Install center console extension.

Parking brake lever assembly

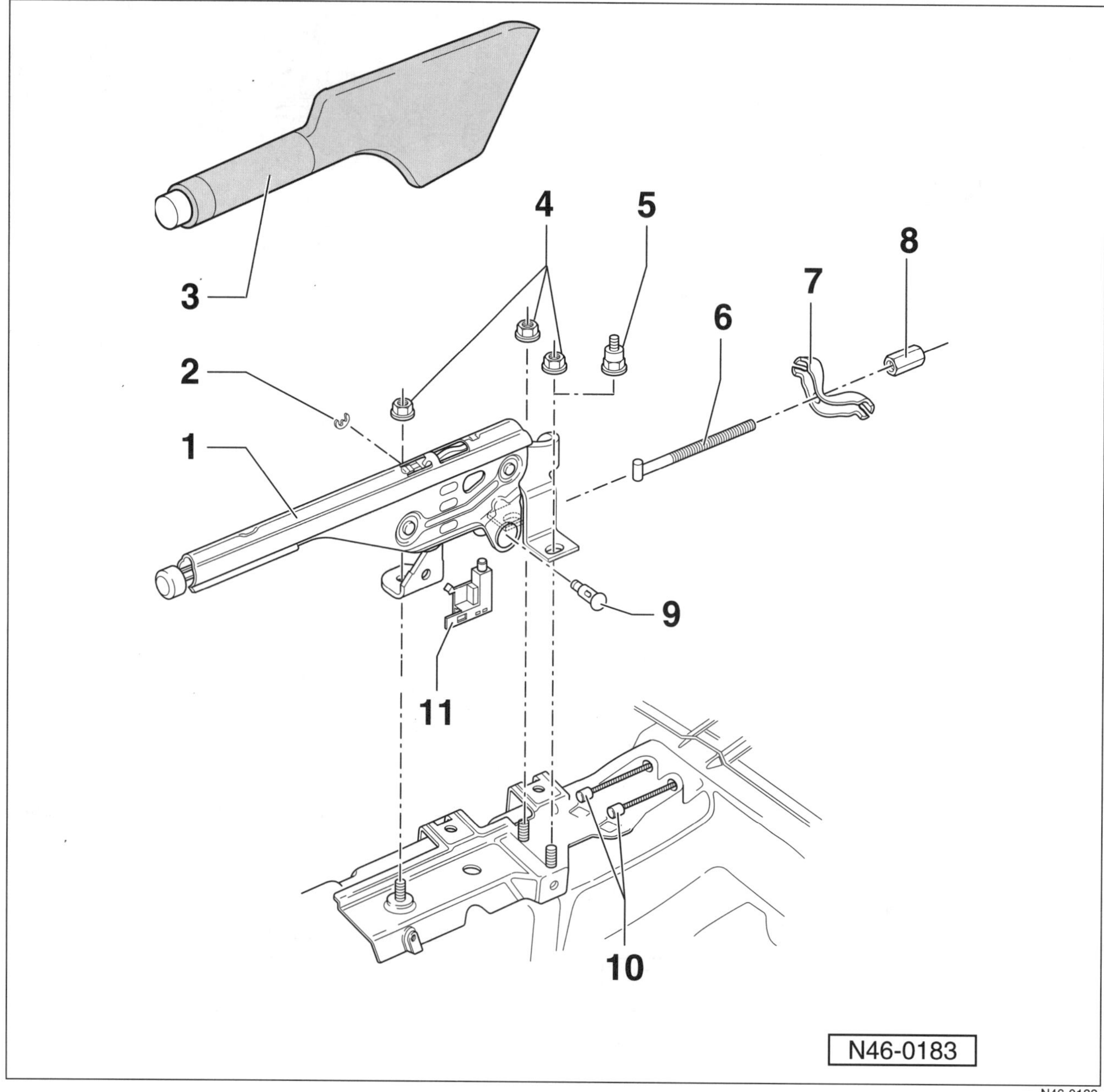

N46-0183

Fig. 17. Parking brake lever and related components.

1. **Parking brake lever**
   - Before removing remove center console
2. **Circlip**
3. **Parking brake lever trim**
   - Pull off toward front
4. **Nuts**
   - Tighten to 25 Nm (18 ft-lb)
5. **Adapter**
   - For vehicles with center armrest
6. **Pull rod**
7. **Compensator**
8. **Adjusting nut**
9. **Fulcrum pin**
   - Holds pull rod (item 6) in parking brake
10. **Parking brake cables**
11. **Parking brake warning light switch**

47 Brakes–Hydraulic System

GENERAL

This repair group covers service and repair to the hydraulic and vacuum-assist brake system components. Also included here is brake bleeding. Cars covered by this manual are equipped with front and rear disc brakes. Some cars are also equipped with anti-lock brakes (ABS).

> ***CAUTION —***
> - *This repair group does not cover the anti-lock braking system hydraulic unit (with integral master cylinder). For information on the ABS system see* **45 Anti-Lock Brakes (ABS)**.

Brake service precautions

The following warnings and cautions should be read before servicing the brake hydraulic system:

> ***WARNING —***
> - *A properly functioning brake system is essential to safe driving. If the red brake/parking warning light or the ABS warning light illuminates while driving, it is imperative that the system be given a thorough check, even if braking action still seems satisfactory. The brakes should be inspected regularly.*
> - *Brake fluid absorbs moisture from the air and must be replaced every two years. Use only new, approved brake fluid that complies with MVSS 116 DOT 4. Do not use silicone-based brake fluid (DOT 5). Even the smallest traces can cause severe corrosion in the brake system.*
> - *Brake fluid is poisonous. Wear safety glasses and rubber gloves when working with brake fluid. Prevent brake fluid from entering the bloodstream through cuts or scratches. Do not siphon brake fluid by mouth.*

> ***CAUTION —***
> - *Always disconnect battery negative (–) cable when working at or near pedal cluster.*
> - *Disconnecting the negative (–) battery cable may erase fault codes and basic settings in the engine management and automatic transmission control modules. Some driveability problems may be noticed until the system re-adapts to operating conditions. OBD II readiness codes, which may be required for emissions testing, may also be erased. Convenience electronics (alarm system, interior light control, power locks, mirrors, and windows) may need to be re-set using a VAG 1551/1552 or equivalent scan tool.*
> - *Before disconnecting the battery be sure to obtain the anti-theft radio code.*
> - *After replacing brake components, depress the brake pedal firmly several times to seat the brakes in their normal operating position. The pedal should be firm and at its normal height, if not, further work is required before driving vehicle.*
> - *Brake fluid is very damaging to paint.*

FRONT BRAKE CALIPER

Two types of front calipers are used on the cars covered by this manual. Repair procedures vary depending on caliper application. See the appropriate (FS III or FN 3) assembly view.

Front caliper application	
• 2.0L (AEG engine)	FS III
• 1.9L (ALH engine)	FS III
• 1.8L (APH engine)	FN 3

Front brake caliper (FS III) assembly

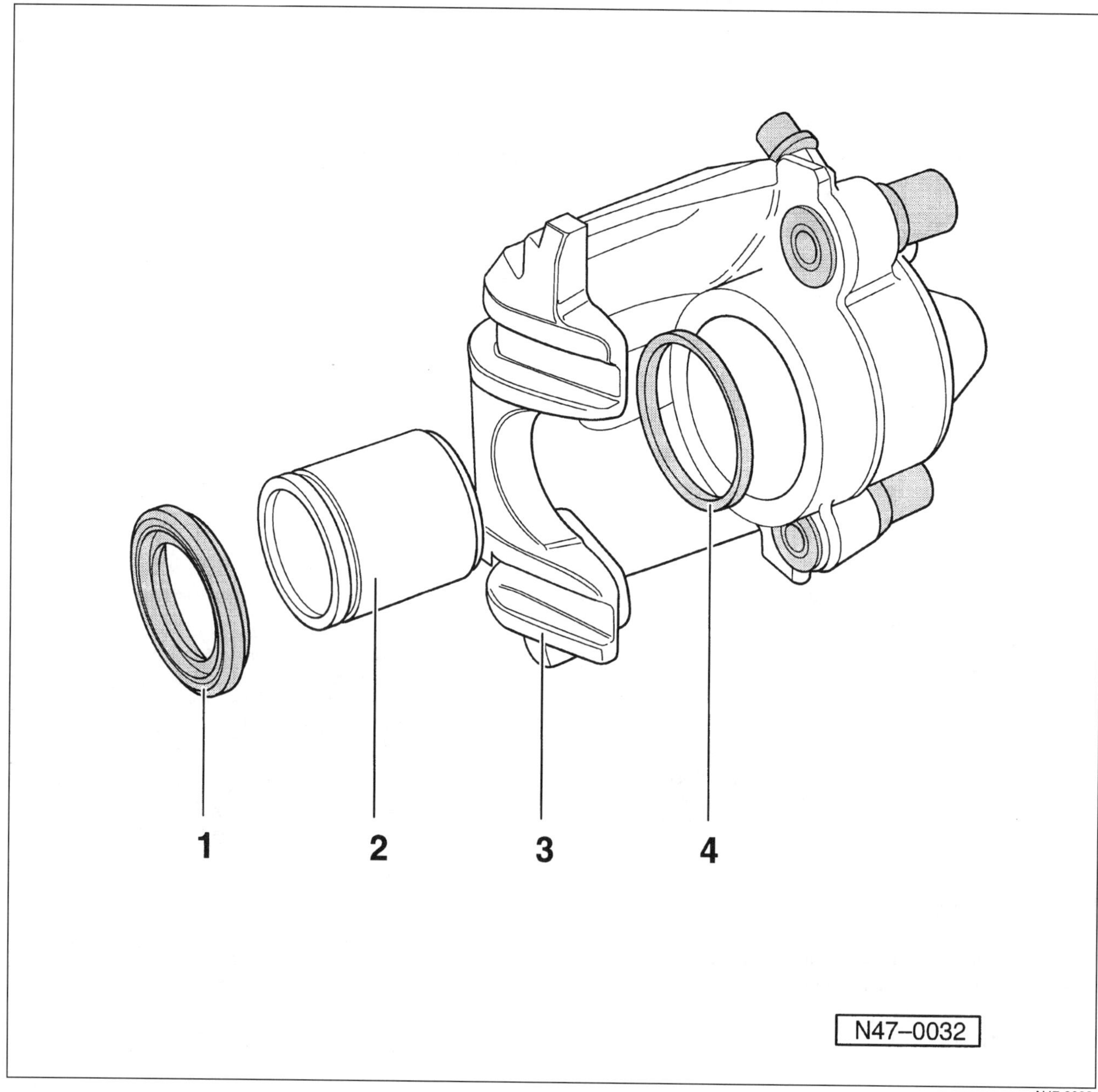

N47-0032

Fig. 1. FS III front brake caliper, piston and piston seals.

NOTE —
- *Install all parts in repair kit.*
- *New brake calipers are filled with brake fluid and are pre-bled.*
- *When assembling, apply a thin coat of grease (VW part no. G052 150 A2) to brake cylinders, pistons and seals.*

1. **Dust boot**
   - Do not damage when inserting piston
2. **Piston**
3. **Brake caliper housing**
4. **Piston seal**

Front brake caliper (FN 3) assembly

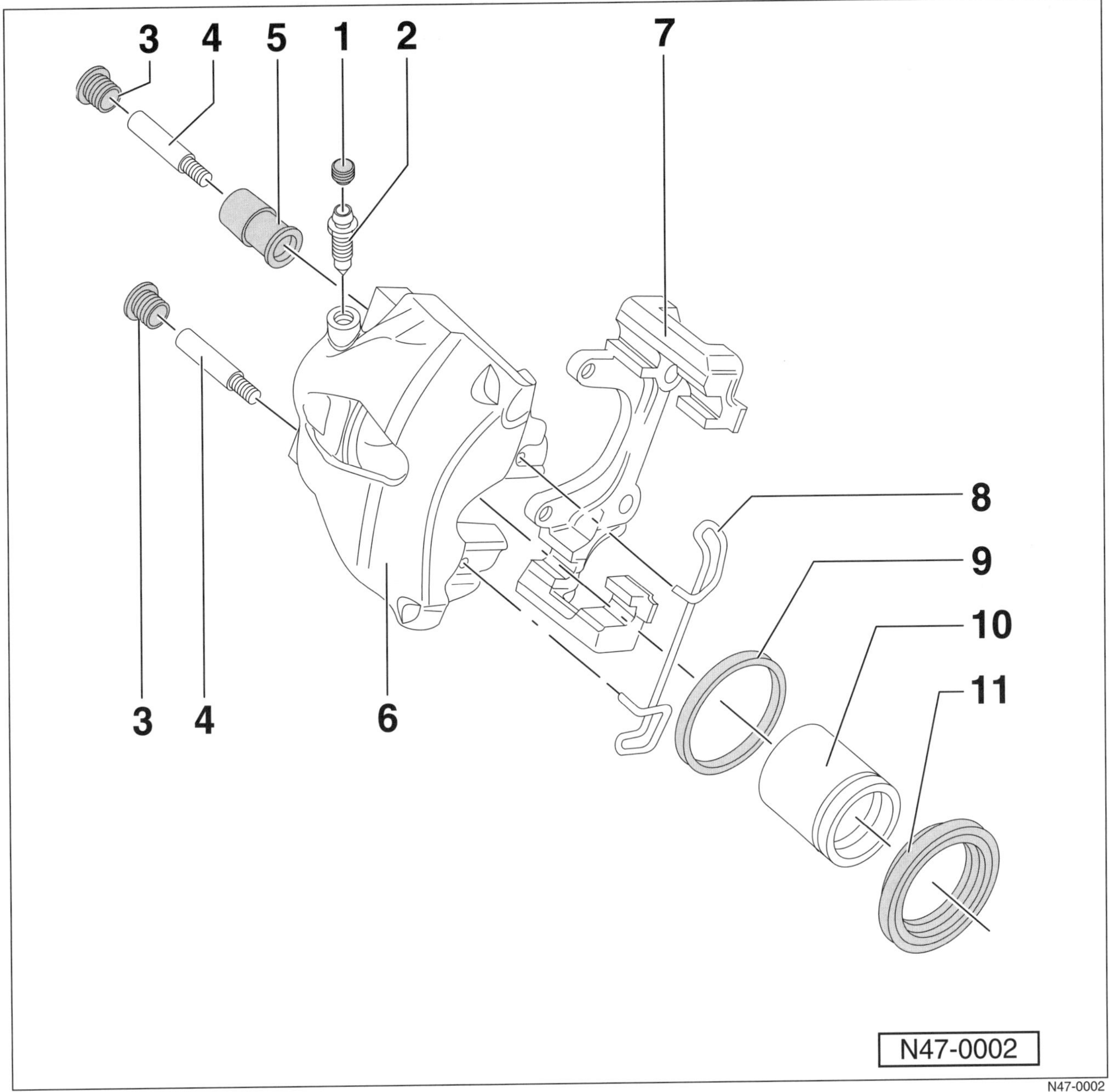

N47-0002

Fig. 2. FN 3 front brake caliper, piston and piston seals.

NOTE —

- *Install all parts in repair kit.*
- *New brake calipers are filled with brake fluid and are pre-bled.*
- *When assembling, apply a thin coat of grease (VW part no. G052 150 A2) to brake cylinders, pistons and seals.*

1. **Dust cap**
2. **Bleeder valve**
   - Apply thin coat of brake fluid to threads when installing
3. **Cap**
   - Insert in mounting bushing
4. **Guide pin**
   - Tighten to 25 Nm (18 ft-lb)

(continued on following page)

(continued from previous page)

5. **Mounting bushing**
   - Insert into brake caliper housing
6. **Brake caliper housing**
7. **Brake carrier**
8. **Retaining spring**
   - Insert with both ends in holes in brake caliper housing
9. **Piston seal**
10. **Piston**
    - Apply thin coat of brake fluid to piston before inserting
    - Piston diameter: 54 mm (2.125 in.)
11. **Dust boot**
    - Do not damage when inserting piston

Front caliper piston, removing and installing

1. Remove brake caliper and pads as described in **46 Brakes–Mechanical Components**.

2. Force piston out of brake caliper housing using compressed air. See Fig. 3.

V47-0406

Fig. 3. Use compressed air at **arrow** to force piston out of caliper.

> ***CAUTION —***
> - *Place a piece of wood in the recess to prevent damaging the piston.*
> - *Use only enough air pressure to force piston out.*

> ***WARNING —***
> *Always wear safety goggles when working with compressed air.*

3. Carefully remove piston seal using a plastic wedge. See Fig. 4.

> ***CAUTION —***
> *When removing, use care to ensure that the cylinder bore is not damaged.*

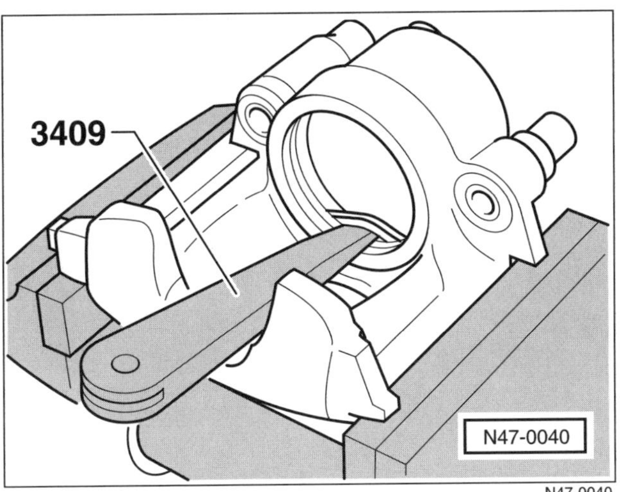

N47-0040

Fig. 4. Volkswagen special tool 3409 (wedge) being used to remove piston seal.

4. Clean caliper and piston with fresh brake fluid.

5. Install new piston seal in caliper.

6. Lubricate piston and cylinder bore lightly using grease (VW part no. G052 150 A2).

7. Install dust boot with outer sealing lip on piston. See Fig. 5.

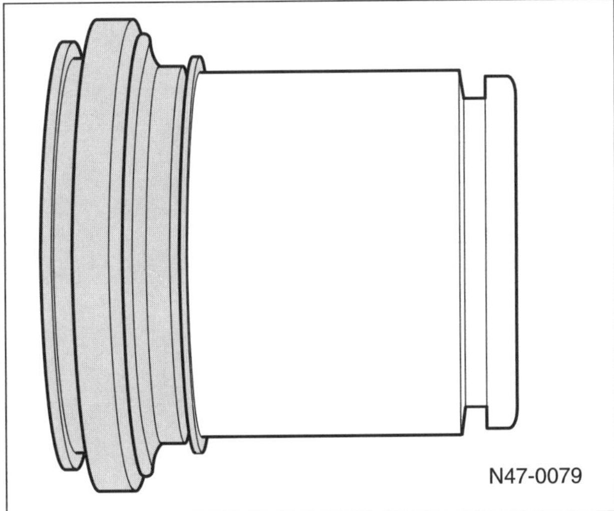

N47-0079

Fig. 5. Installation position of dust boot on piston.

8. Hold piston in front of caliper and insert inner sealing lip into grove in cylinder using a plastic wedge. See Fig. 6.

9. Press piston into brake caliper housing using piston resetting tool. See Fig. 7.

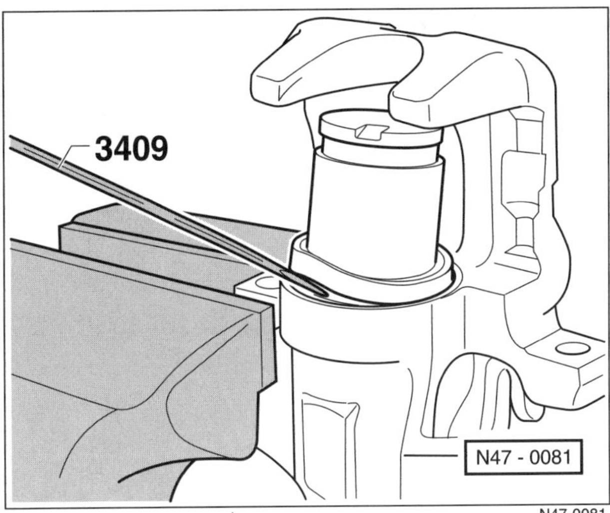

N47-0081

Fig. 6. Use wedge (VW 3409) to insert sealing lip into cylinder while installing piston.

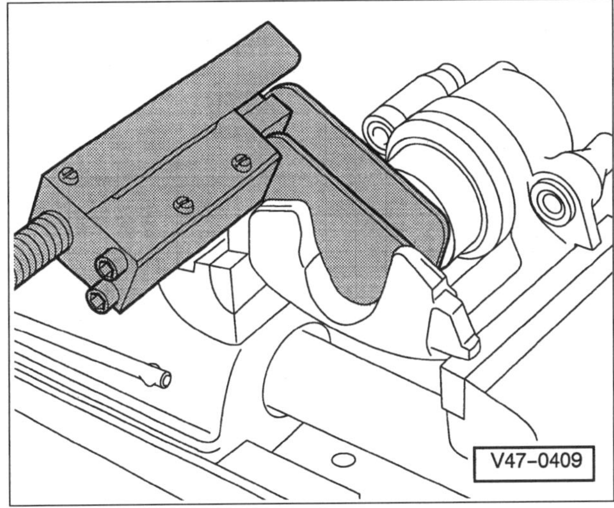

V47-0409

Fig. 7. Piston being pressed into brake caliper housing. Be sure that sealing lip of dust boot slips into the piston groove.

NOTE —
The outer sealing lip of the dust boot must slip into the piston groove.

10. Be sure to quality check your work, see **Quality Review** at the end of this repair group.

Rear brake caliper assembly

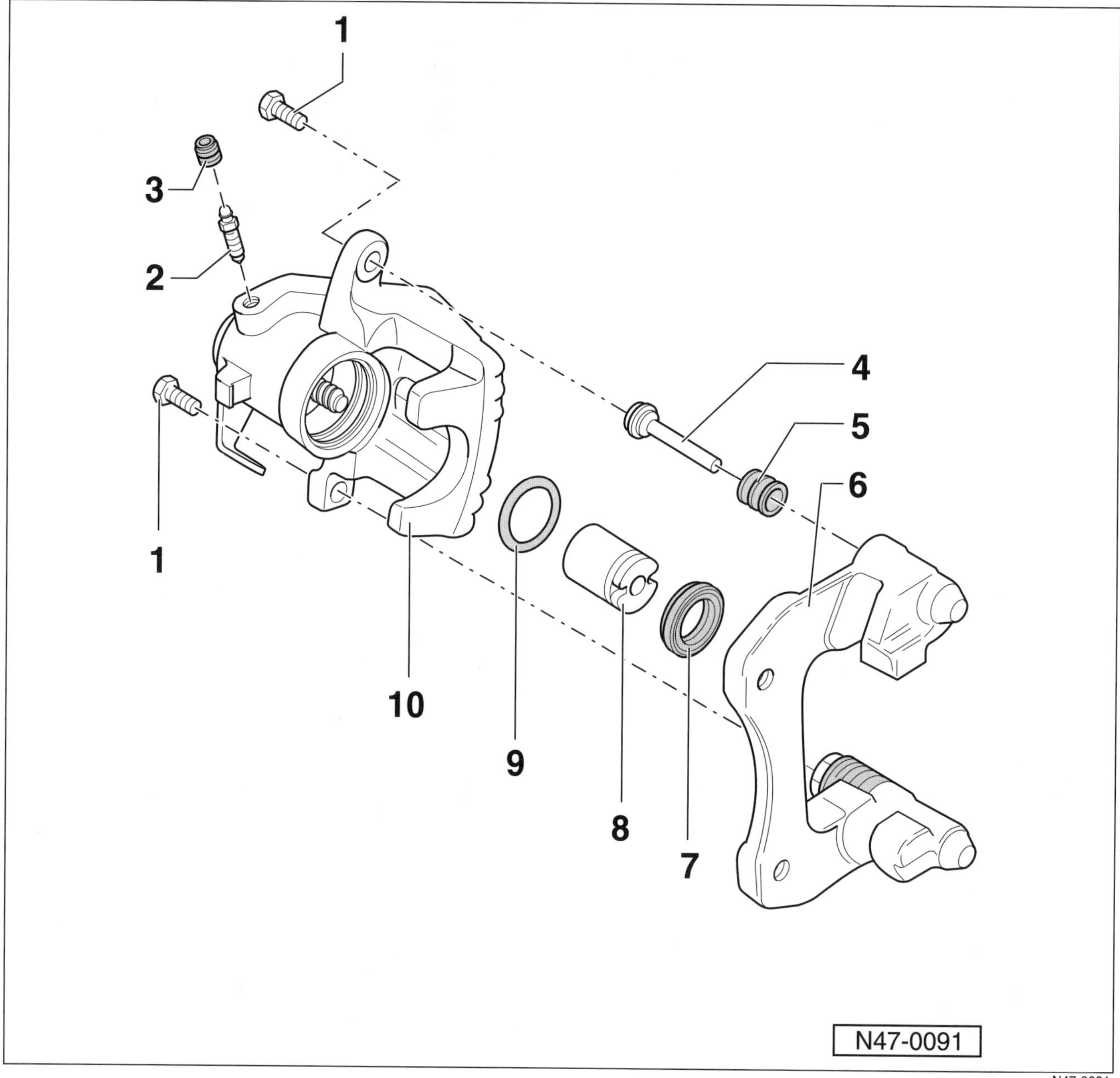

Fig. 8. Rear brake caliper.

N47-0091

NOTE —

- *Install all parts in repair kit.*
- *New brake calipers are filled with brake fluid and are pre-bled.*
- *When assembling, apply a thin coat of grease (VW part no. G052 150 A2) to brake cylinders, pistons and seals.*
- *When repairing, be sure to pre-bleed brake calipers (without brake pads) before installing, see* **Rear caliper piston, removing and installing**.

1. **Self-locking bolt**
   - Tighten to 30 Nm (22 ft-lb)
   - Always replace
   - When loosening and tightening, counter-hold on guide pin
2. **Bleeder screw**
   - Apply thin coat of grease (VW part no. G052 150 A2) to threads before installing
3. **Dust cap**

(continued form previous page)

4. **Guide pins**
   - Apply thin coat of grease (VW part no. G052 150 A2) before installing protective cap
5. **Protective cap**
   - Pull onto brake carrier and guide pin
6. **Brake carrier with guide pin and protective cap**
   - Replacement part is assembled with sufficient grease on guide pins.
   - If protective caps or guide pins are damaged, install repair kit. Use grease packet supplied to lubricate guide pins.
7. **Dust boot**
   - Pull outer sealing lip onto piston
8. **Piston with automatic adjustment**
   - Apply thin coat of grease (VW part no. G052 150 A2) before installing
9. **Piston seal**
10. **Brake caliper housing**
    - With parking brake cable lever
    - If fluid is leaking at parking brake cable lever, replace brake caliper housing
    - After repairing, pre-bleed caliper housing, see **Rear caliper piston, removing and installing**

Rear caliper piston, removing and installing

1. Remove piston from brake caliper housing by turning knurled wheel on piston resetting and removal tool counter-clockwise. See Fig. 9.

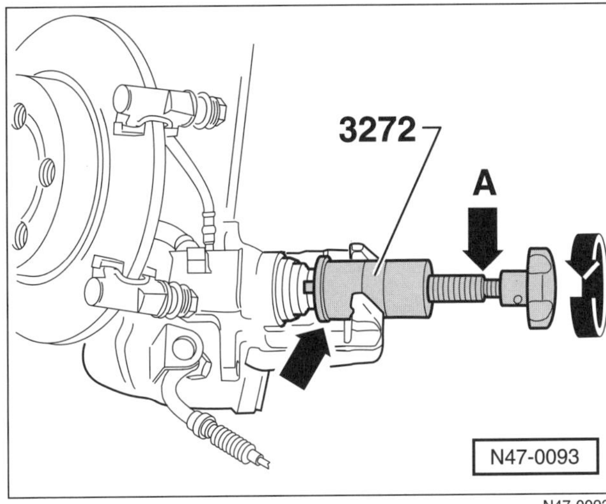

N47-0093

Fig. 9. Volkswagen special tool 3272 being used to remove rear caliper piston. Install tool with collar (**arrow**) positioned before the piston. If piston is difficult to move, use 13 mm wrench on flat spots (**arrow A**) of tool.

2. Remove seal using plastic wedge. See Fig. 10.

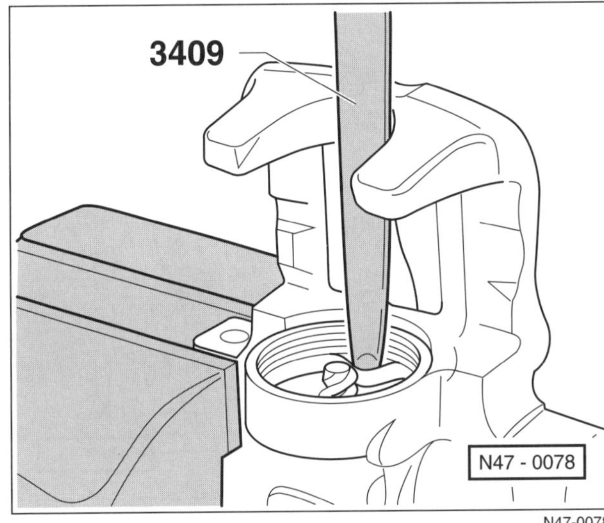

N47-0078

Fig. 10. Volkswagen special tool 3409 (wedge) being used to remove piston seal.

> ***CAUTION —***
> *When removing, use care to ensure that the cylinder bore is not damaged.*

3. Clean caliper and piston with fresh brake fluid.

4. Install new piston seal in caliper.

5. Lubricate piston and cylinder bore lightly using grease (VW part no. G052 150 A2).

6. Install dust boot with outer sealing lip on piston. See Fig. 11.

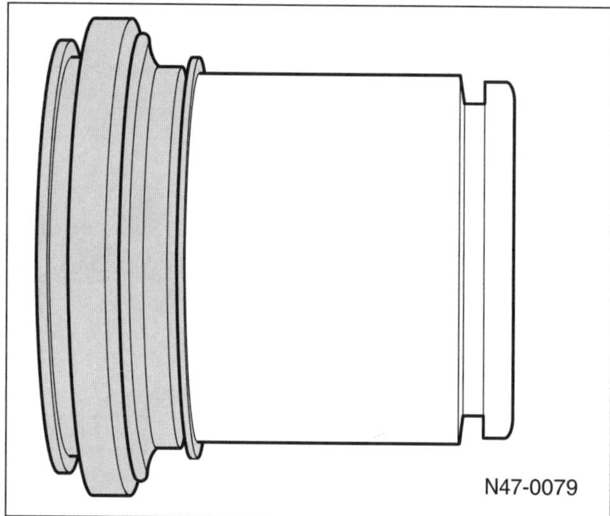

N47-0079

Fig. 11. Installation position of dust boot on piston.

7. Hold piston in front of caliper and insert inner sealing lip into grove in cylinder using a plastic wedge. See Fig. 12.

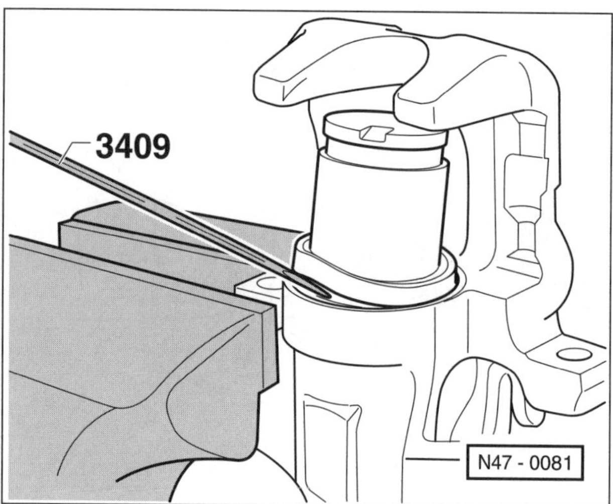

N47-0081

Fig. 12. Use wedge (VW 3409) to insert sealing lip into cylinder while installing piston.

8. Reset caliper's automatic adjustment mechanism by turning the piston clockwise while pushing piston in. See Fig. 13.

9. Pre-bleed caliper by opening bleeder screw and fill a standard bleeder bottle with brake fluid until bubble-free fluid flows from brake hose connection.

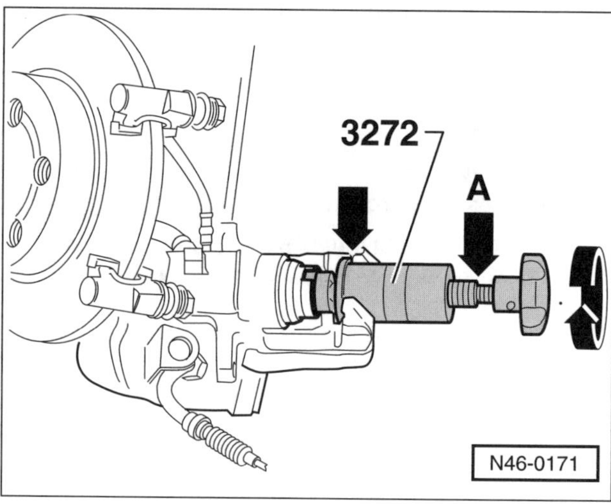

N46-0171

Fig. 13. Automatic adjustment mechanism being reset using Volkswagen special tool 3272. Turn piston clockwise (**rotational arrow**) while pushing piston in.

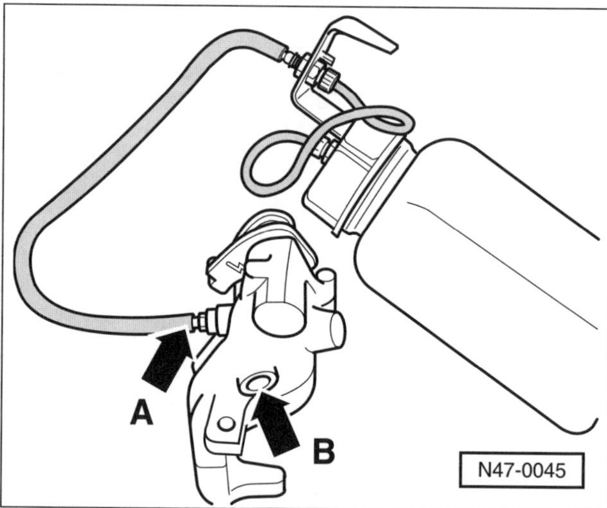

N47-0045

Fig. 14. Pre-bleed caliper by opening bleeder screw (**arrow A**) and fill bleeder bottle with brake fluid until bubble-free fluid flows from brake hose connection (**arrow B**).

> ***CAUTION—***
>
> - *If the piston is not reset correctly, or if the brake pedal is operated with the caliper removed, the automatic adjustment mechanism will be destroyed.*
> - *Always remove some brake fluid from the reservoir before resetting and pushing the caliper piston in. When the piston is pushed in, fluid is forced up into the reservoir.*

10. Close bleeder screw.

11. Be sure to quality check your work, see **Quality Review** at the end of this repair group.

Brake pressure regulator assembly

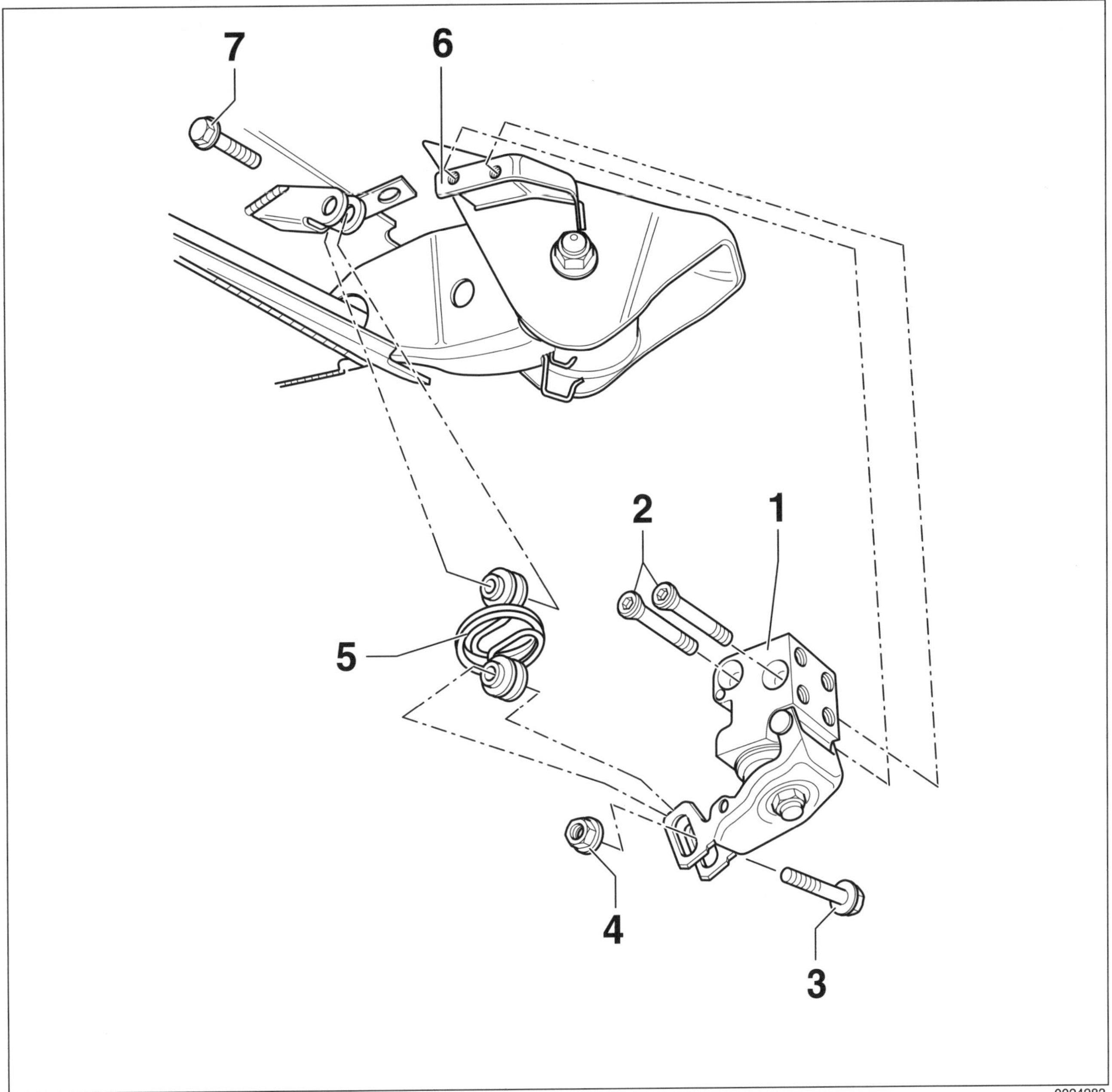

Fig. 15. Brake pressure regulator installed on the rear axle of non-ABS equipped cars.

1. **Brake pressure regulator**
2. **Socket-head bolt**
   - Tighten to 21 Nm (15 ft-lb)
3. **Bolt**
   - Tighten to 21Nm (15 ft-lb)
4. **Nut**
   - Tighten to 21 Nm (15 ft-lb)
5. **Spring**
6. **Mounting bracket**
7. **Bolt**
   - Tighten to 16 Nm (12 ft-lb)

Brake pressure regulator, checking

Cars without ABS have a brake pressure regulator mounted on a bracket attached to the rear axle. This load-sensing regulator is controlled from the rear axle by a spring. When the axle changes position, due to a heavy load or during hard braking, the pressure regulator varies the pressure to the rear brakes.

> ***NOTE —***
> *The brake pressure regulator should be checked and if necessary adjusted following repairs to the rear suspension, or when there is excessive rear brake wear.*

With the car resting on all four wheels and the fuel tank full, observe the pressure regulator while a helper depresses and quickly releases the brake pedal. The regulator should move slightly when the brake is quickly released. If not, the regulator is faulty and should be replaced.

> ***NOTE —***
> *For this check to be accurate, the car should be emptied of all cargo and occupants, except driver.*

Testing and adjusting the pressure-regulating function requires measuring brake system pressure at each wheel caliper using two pressure gauges. Because of the need for this specialized equipment, we recommend having this test performed by an authorized Volkswagen dealer.

BRAKE BLEEDING

The procedure given here applies to all vehicles covered in this manual with and without ABS.

The brake system can be bled using a pressure bleeder or manually using a helper. Pressure bleeding, if the equipment is available, is the fastest. Manual bleeding requires a helper, but is easy and requires no special tools.

> ***CAUTION —***
> - *Brake fluid absorbs moisture from the air and must be replaced every two years, see* **0 Maintenance**.
> - *Use only new, approved brake fluid that complies with MVSS 116 DOT 4. Do not use silicone-based brake fluid (DOT 5). Even the smallest traces can cause severe corrosion in the brake system.*
> - *Brake fluid is poisonous. Wear safety glasses and rubber gloves when working with brake fluid. Prevent brake fluid from entering the bloodstream through cuts or scratches. Do not siphon brake fluid by mouth.*
> - *Brake fluid is very damaging to paint. Immediately wipe up any brake fluid that spills on the vehicle.*
> - *The brake fluid level in the reservoir must not fall below the MIN mark during bleeding.*

> ***NOTE —***
> - *On non-ABS cars, the brake pressure regulator lever must be pressed toward the rear during rear brake bleeding.*
> - *Depress the brake pedal several times during the bleeding operation.*

Bleeding, with pressure bleeder

Pressure bleeding using Volkswagen special tool US1116 or equivalent is the preferred method of removing air from all brake systems because it does a more thorough purge.

1. Connect pressure bleeder with regulated compressed air supply to fluid reservoir according to manufacturer's instructions.

> ***CAUTION —***
> *Do not exceed filling pressure of 1 bar (14.5 psi) when filling brake fluid using pressure bleeder US 1116. The brake system will not be completely bled if excessive pressure is used.*

2. Connect hose from bleeder bottle to caliper/wheel cylinder bleeder screw and bleed brakes in following sequence:
   - Right rear caliper
   - Left rear caliper
   - Right front caliper
   - Left front caliper
3. Brake fluid should be allowed to flow from the bleeder valve/screw until it runs clear.

Bleeding, manually

1. Connect hose from bleeder bottle to brake bleeder screw at the right rear caliper or wheel cylinder.

> ***CAUTION —***
> *The brake fluid level in the reservoir must not fall below the MIN mark during bleeding.*

2. Have a helper pump the brake pedal several times and then hold pedal down.
3. Open bleeder screw at the caliper or wheel cylinder and collect fluid.
4. Close bleeder screw and then release brake pedal. Repeat operation until brake fluid runs clear and flows without air bubbles.
5. Repeat the above procedure at the remaining wheels, using the following sequence:
   - Left rear caliper
   - Right front caliper
   - Left front caliper

MASTER CYLINDER/BRAKE BOOSTER

Master cylinder/brake booster assembly

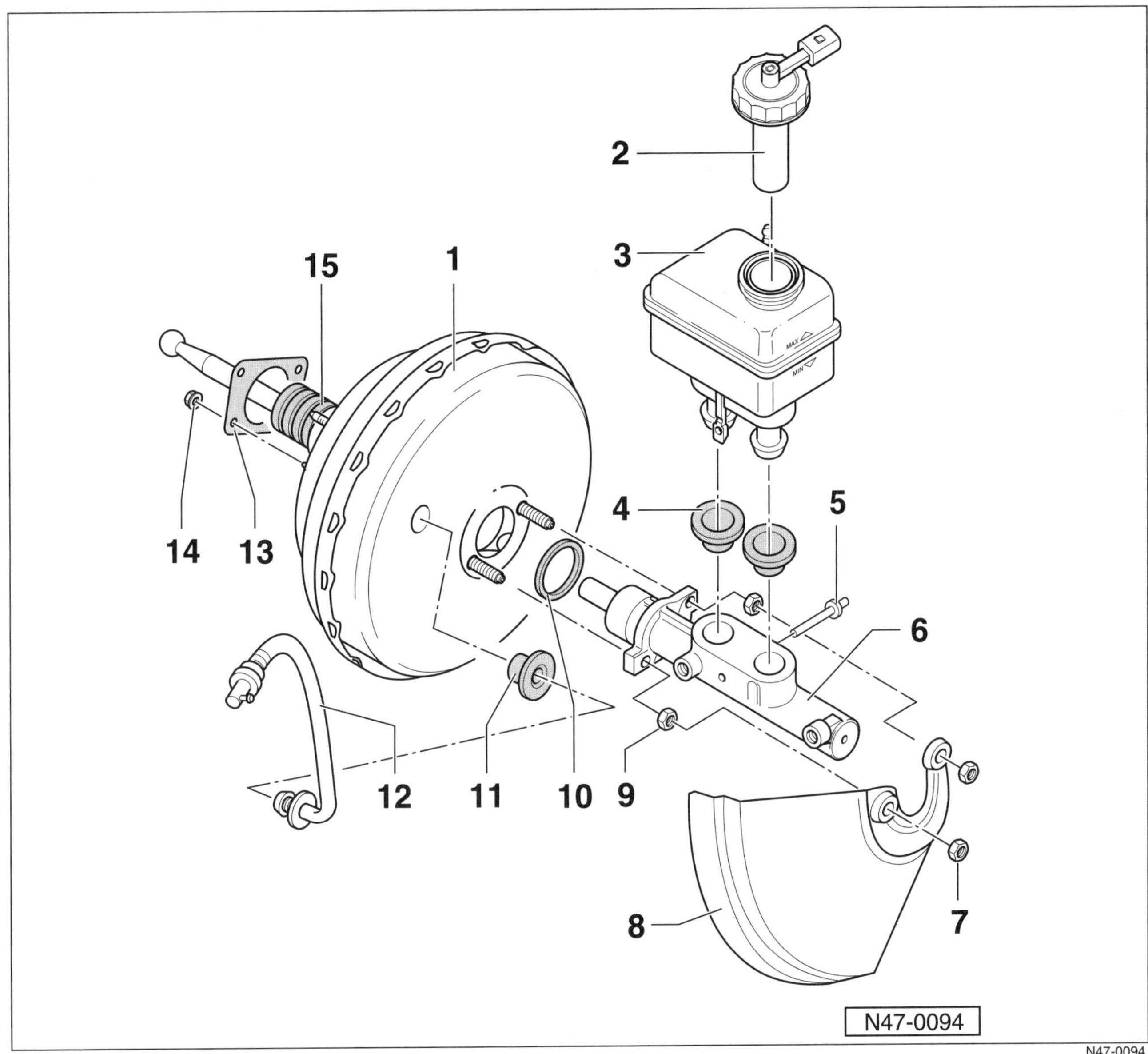

N47-0094

Fig. 16. Brake master cylinder with brake booster.

1. **Brake Booster**
   - Can be replaced separately from master cylinder
   - Gasoline engine: vacuum supplied by intake manifold
   - Diesel (ALH engine): pump supplies vacuum, **see** Ⓐ
   - Functional check:
     With engine off, depress brake pedal firmly several times (to exhaust vacuum in unit).
     Depress brake pedal with average foot pressure, hold and start engine. If brake booster is working properly, pedal will give slightly under foot.
   - If booster is not functioning replace complete brake booster
   - Check valve (in vacuum hose), **see** Ⓑ

2. **Cap**

3. **Brake fluid reservoir**

4. **Sealing plug**
   - Moisten with brake fluid and press into reservoir

5. **Retainer pin**
   - Install through brake master cylinder

6. **Brake master cylinder**
   - Cannot be repaired. If faulty, replace as complete unit.

(continued on following page)

(continued from previous page)

7. **Self-locking nut**
   - Tighten to 20 Nm (15 ft-lb)
   - Always replace
8. **Heat shield**
   - Only for vehicles with APH (1.8L) engine
9. **Self-locking nut**
   - Tighten to 20 Nm (15 ft-lb)
   - Always replace
10. **Seal**
    - Always replace
11. **Sealing plug**
12. **Vacuum hose**
    - Insert into brake booster
13. **Gasket**
    - For brake booster
14. **Self-locking nut**
    - Tighten to 20 Nm (15 ft-lb)
    - Always replace
15. **Boot**
    - Must be seated correctly or may cause air noise.

A Vacuum pump for brake booster (ALH engine), removing and installing

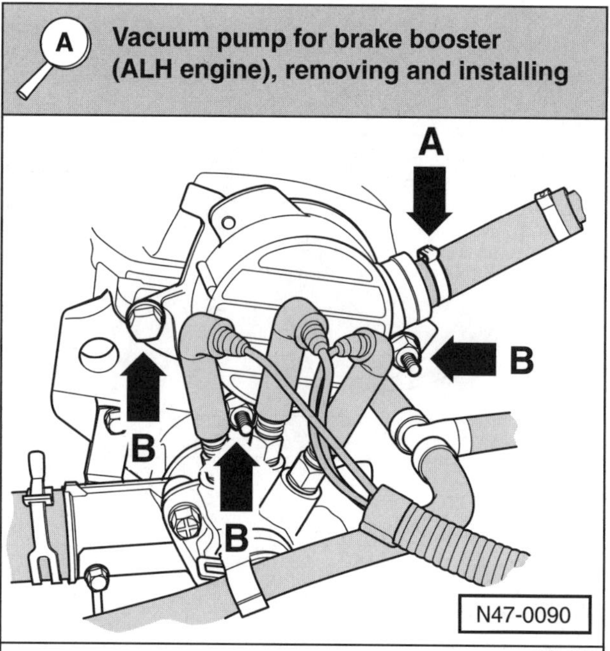

N47-0090

- **Remove retainer for wiring harness from vacuum pump.**
- **Loosen vacuum hose clamp (arrow A) and remove hose from pump.**
- **Remove bolts (arrow B) on flange and remove pump.**
- **When installing vacuum pump be sure that follower engages correctly with camshaft.**
- **Install bolts (arrows B) on cylinder head flange and secure vacuum hose with clamp (arrow A).**

B Vacuum check valve, checking

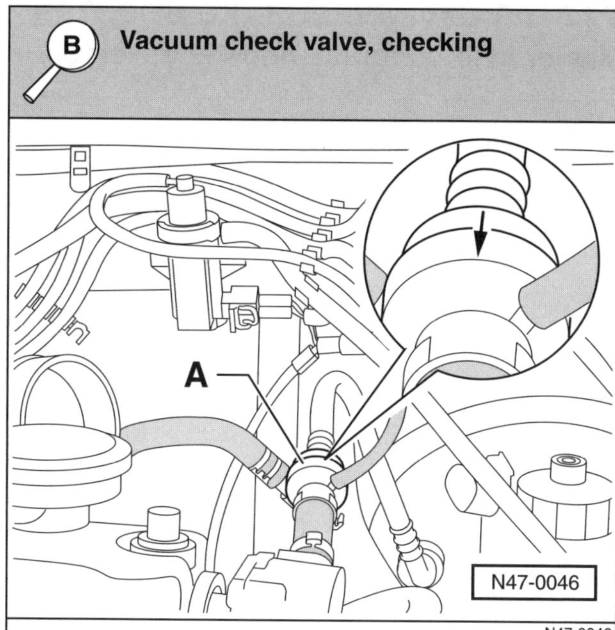

N47-0046

- **Air must pass through in direction of arrow.**
- **Check valve (A) must stay closed (no air passes through) if supplied from opposite direction.**

Brake master cylinder, removing and installing

1. Spread sufficient lint-free cloths in area of plenum chamber and on engine and transmission to catch any escaping brake fluid.

> ***WARNING —***
> - *Brake fluid is poisonous.*
> - *To draw off brake fluid from the reservoir, use a bleeder bottle which is used only for brake fluid. Never siphon brake fluid by mouth.*

2. Using bleeder bottle, draw off as much brake fluid as possible from brake fluid reservoir.
3. Clamp clutch master cylinder supply hose with special tool (VW 3094 or equivalent).
4. Remove clutch master cylinder supply hose from brake fluid reservoir.
5. Disconnect brake fluid level sensor wiring connector.
6. Disconnect brake lines on brake master cylinder and seal with plugs from repair kit, (VW part no. 1H0 698 311 A).

   NOTE —
   Volkswagen part numbers are given for reference only. Always consult with your Volkswagen Parts Department or aftermarket parts specialist for the latest parts information.

7. Remove nuts securing brake master cylinder to brake booster.
8. Carefully remove brake master cylinder from brake booster.
9. Install master cylinder in reverse order of removal, noting the following:
   - When connecting brake master cylinder and brake booster be sure that the push rod is correctly located in the master cylinder.
   - After installing, bleed brakes as described earlier. Bleed clutch, see **30 Clutch**.
10. Be sure to quality check your work, see **Quality Review** at the end of this repair group.

Brake booster, removing and installing

1. Disconnect battery ground (GND) strap from battery negative (–) terminal. See the **Cautions** at the beginning of this repair group regarding battery disconnection.

   NOTE —
   Be sure to have the anti-theft radio code on hand before disconnecting the battery.

Vehicles with manual transmission

2. Clamp clutch master cylinder supply hose with special tool (VW 3094 or equivalent).
3. Remove clutch master cylinder supply hose from brake fluid reservoir.

All vehicles

4. Remove ABS control module and hydraulic unit, see **45 Anti-lock Brakes (ABS)**.
5. Disconnect vacuum hose from brake booster.

Vehicles with Diesel TDI engine

6. Remove wiring harness retainer from vacuum pump.

All vehicles

7. Remove trim below instrument panel. See Fig. 17.

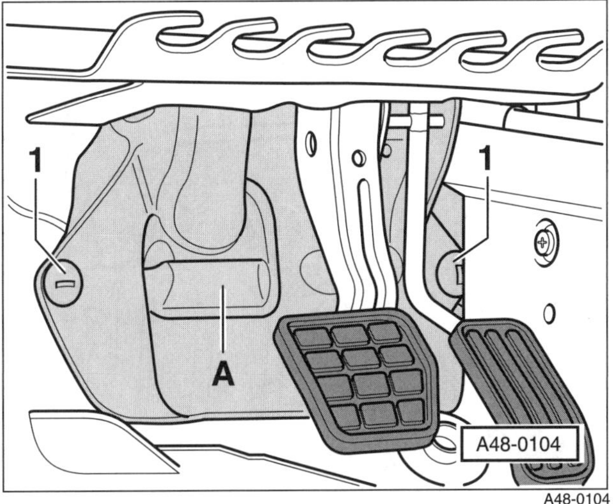

A48-0104

Fig. 17. Remove screws (**1**) and cover (**A**) on vehicles with TDI engine.

Vehicles with manual transmission

8. Remove connecting plate between clutch and brake pedals. See Fig. 18.

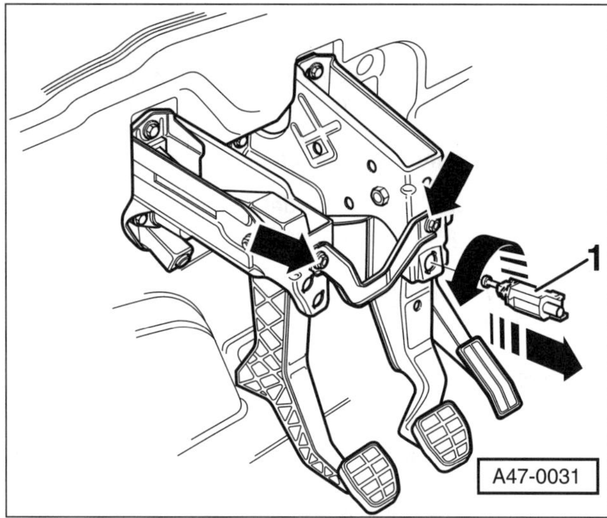

A47-0031

Fig. 18. On vehicles with manual transmission remove connecting plate between clutch and brake pedals. Remove brake light switch (**1**) by rotating and pulling out.

All vehicles

9. Remove brake light switch and separate brake pedal from brake booster.

10. Remove brake booster mounting nuts. See Fig. 19.

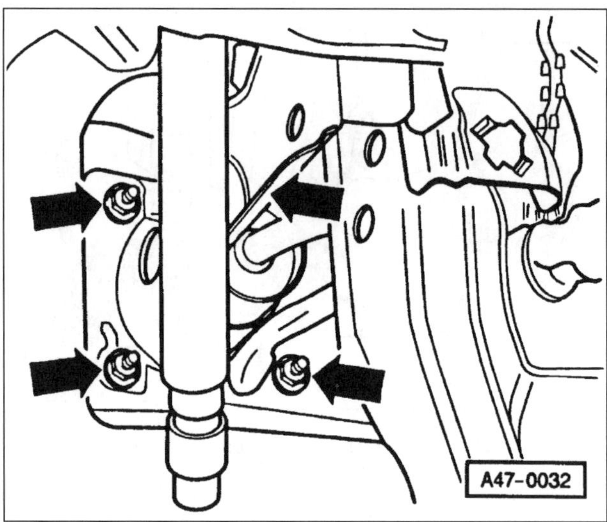

A47-0032

Fig. 19. Remove brake booster mounting nuts (**arrows**).

11. Guide brake booster with brake master cylinder out forward to remove.

12. Install brake master cylinder with brake booster in reverse order of removal noting the following:

    - Adjust brake light switch see **96 Lights, Accessories–Interior**.

13. Be sure to quality check your work, see **Quality Review** below.

QUALITY REVIEW

When you have finished working under the hood and around other areas of the vehicle, it is advisable to take a moment to quality check or review your work. This helps to insure that the operation or repair has been completed properly with all affected systems functioning within normal parameters. These may include the following:

- During the final road test make at least one controlled stop to test the brakes. On ABS equipped cars the brake pedal should be felt to pulsate (ABS operation).
- Ensure that all cable ties and clamps that were removed as part of the repair are replaced.
- Ensure that all fasteners and hardware were replaced and torqued as specified.
- Check and adjust brake fluid level.
- Be careful not to spill brake fluid as it can damage painted surfaces. Wipe up any spills immediately.
- Make sure that all other components involved in the repair are positioned correctly, properly torqued and function properly.
- Make sure that all tools, shop cloths, fender covers and protective tapes are removed before closing the hood.
- Clean grease and fingerprints from painted surfaces, steering wheel and shifter.

48 Steering

GENERAL

Power assisted rack and pinion steering is standard on all New Beetles. A vane type pump driven by the ribbed V-belt provides hydraulic pressure to the steering gear. Service of the steering gear, including repair of housing seal leaks is by replacement only. The power steering gear is available only as a complete assembly.

Special tools, equipment and procedures are required for most steering repair and component replacement. In addition, front wheel alignment is almost always disturbed when steering tie rods or steering gear are removed or replaced.

> ***WARNING —***
> - *Do not re-use any fasteners that are worn or deformed in normal use. Most fasteners are designed to be used only once and become unreliable and may fail when used a second time. This includes, but is not limited to, nuts, bolts, washers, circlips, cotter pins, self-locking nuts and bolts. For replacements, always use new parts.*
> - *Do not reinstall bolts and nuts coated with undercoating wax as correct tightening torque cannot be ensured. Always clean the threads of removed bolts and nuts that are to be re-used with a suitable solvent before installation. Ensure that new parts are clean.*

> ***WARNING —***
> - *Do not use standard nuts and bolts in place of green colored parts. The green color denotes a special anti-corrosion process known as "dacromet" or "delta-tone". Torque specifications are given based on use of these parts only.*
> - *Always replaced rusted or corroded bolts, nuts and washers even if not specifically indicated.*
> - *DO NOT attempt to straighten or weld suspension struts, wheel bearing housings, control arms or any other wheel locating or load bearing components of the front suspension.*

> ***CAUTION —***
> *Disconnecting the negative (–) battery cable may erase fault codes and basic settings in the engine management and automatic transmission control modules. Some driveability problems may be noticed until the system re-adapts to operating conditions. OBD II readiness codes, which may be required for emissions testing, may also be erased. Convenience electronics (alarm system, interior light control, power locks, mirrors, and windows) may need to be re-set using a VAG 1551/1552 or equivalent scan tool.*

Special precautions for airbag equipped vehicles

Airbag systems can enhance passenger safety in the event of a collision. To accomplish this task, they rely on sensitive electronic circuits and fast-acting deployment devices. Special service precautions must be followed to prevent possible serious bodily injury to the repair technician and others involved in the handling and storage of airbag components and to insure proper operation in the event of a collision.

> ***WARNING —***
>
> - *Before working on any airbag, steering wheel or steering column component, always* ***disconnect the battery first.***
> - *No waiting time is required after disconnecting the battery.*
> - *Airbags are inflated by an explosive device. Handled improperly or without adequate safeguards and training, the system can be very dangerous. Special precautions must be observed prior to any work at or near the steering wheel and steering column, including the pedal assembly.*
> - *The airbag is a vehicle safety system. To guard against personal injury or airbag system failure, only trained Volkswagen service technicians should test, disassemble or service the airbag system.*
> - *Airbag units that have been dropped onto a hard surface must not be installed. Always replace any airbag system component that has been mechanically or physically damaged (example: dented or cracked).*
> - *Make sure that no one is in the passenger compartment when connecting the battery Ground (GND) strap to the battery negative (–) terminal.*
> - *A technician must be electrostatically discharged before picking up or touching any airbag unit. This is accomplished by touching a suitable metal ground such as a water or heating pipe or metal frame. If in the vehicle, this is accomplished by touching a suitable chassis ground such as a door latch or striker.*
> - *Install new airbag unit as soon as the unit is removed from the packaging. Reinstall in packaging if work will not be completed immediately.*
> - *Do not leave any undeployed airbag unit unattended. If work is interrupted, store airbag unit in a secure location where it cannot be disturbed.*
> - *Undeployed airbag units that have been replaced must only be stored and shipped in packaging designed specifically for the purpose such as that found with the replacement unit.*
> - *Undeployed airbag units that have been replaced must be properly identified as such.*

> ***WARNING —***
>
> - *The storage and transportation of airbag units must be in accordance with all applicable federal, state and local rules and regulations.*
> - *Airbag units that have been removed during the course of repairs must be stored with the padded side facing up and in a secure location where it cannot be disturbed.*
> - *Observe all cautions, warnings and notes before starting repairs involving airbag systems.*

STEERING WHEEL WITH AIRBAG

All New Beetles designed for North American markets are equipped with multiple airbags. The driver's airbag unit is installed in the center area of the steering wheel. Because removal of the steering wheel is often required for repairs to the steering column, the driver's airbag unit will be covered in this section. For further details on the airbag unit, see **69 Seatbelts, Airbags.**

Airbag unit in steering wheel, assembly

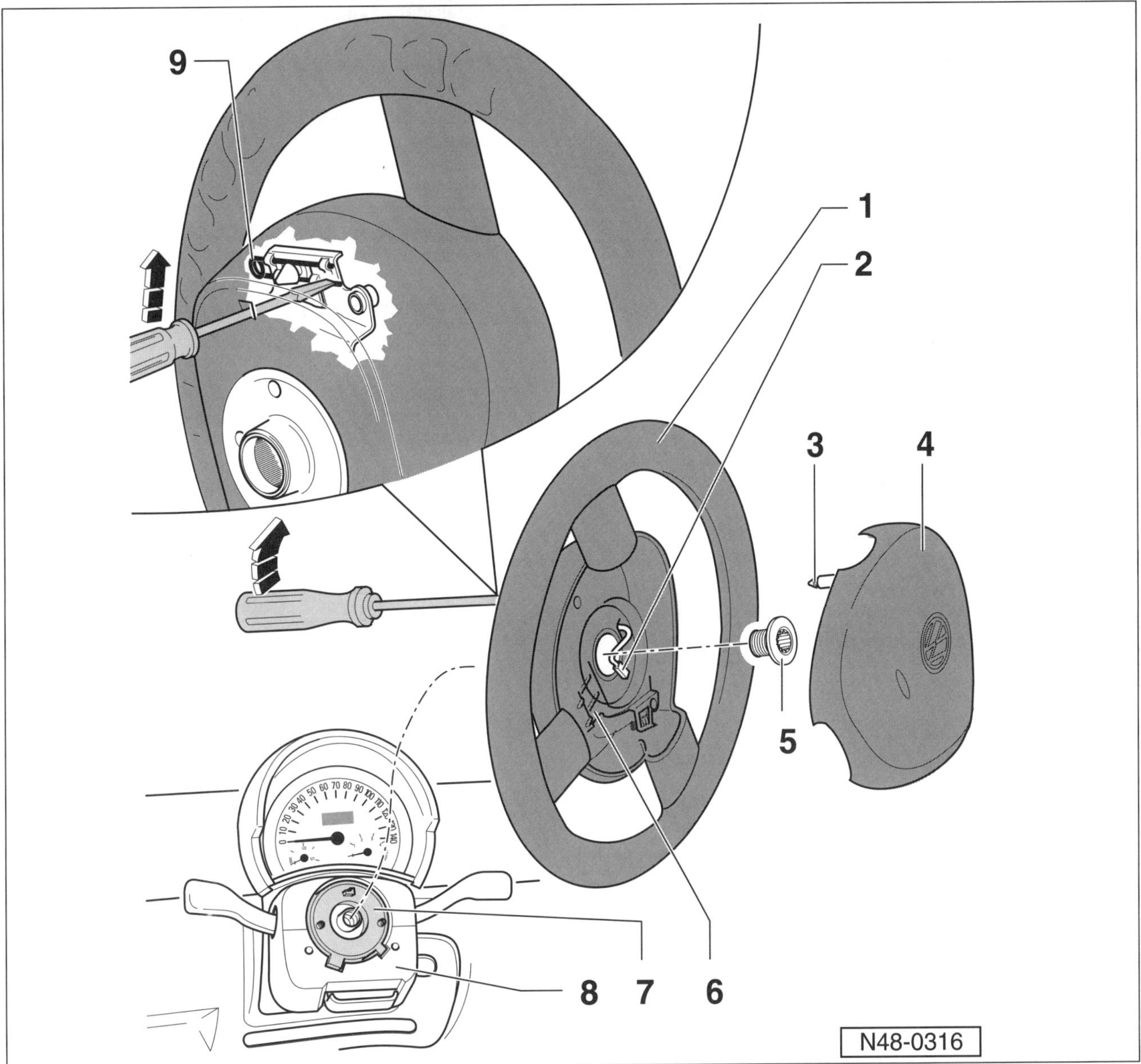

N48-0316

Fig. 1. Steering wheel shown with airbag and related components.

1. **Steering wheel**
2. **Harness connector for airbag**
3. **Locking lugs**
   - Release from rear of steering wheel
4. **Airbag unit**
5. **Bolt, multi-point socket-head**
   - Tighten to 50 Nm (37 ft-lb) with locking compound
   - Can be reused up to 5 times
   - Mark with center punch after each installation
6. **Securing plate**
7. **Spiral spring with slip ring**
8. **Steering column trim**
9. **Spring clip**

Airbag unit in steering wheel, removing

Removal of the steering wheel airbag unit is accomplished by inserting a tool into openings in the dashboard side of the steering wheel.

1. Disconnect battery ground (GND) strap from battery negative (–) terminal. See the **Cautions** at the beginning of this repair group regarding battery disconnection.

   NOTE —
   Be sure to have the anti-theft radio code on hand before disconnecting the battery.

2. Remove instrument cluster, see **70 Trim–Interior**.
3. Release steering column adjustment.
4. Turn steering wheel until a spoke is vertical. Extend steering wheel fully and move to uppermost position.
5. Secure steering column adjustment.
6. Using a screwdriver approximately 175 mm (7 in.) long, insert approximately 45 mm (1¾ in.) from reverse side into hole on dashboard side of steering wheel hub.

   NOTE —
   If a screwdriver with a very short handle is used, it is possible to eliminate step 2 and leave the instrument cluster in place.

7. Press screwdriver in direction of arrow to press back spring clip (Fig. 1, item 9) and release locking lug (Fig. 1, item 3) of airbag unit.
8. Turn steering wheel back ½ turn (180°) and release second locking lug on opposite side.
9. Turn steering wheel to center position (wheels straight ahead).
10. Disconnect harness connector from airbag unit.
11. Place removed airbag unit in a secure location with padding side facing up.

Airbag unit in steering wheel, installing

1. Install instrument cluster, if applicable.
2. Reconnect harness connector for airbag unit.
3. Position airbag unit on steering wheel and snap into place.

   NOTE —
   Airbag unit locking lugs must be heard and felt to snap into place.

4. Switch ignition on.

   WARNING —
   - *Make sure the passenger compartment is not occupied before connecting the battery Ground (GND) strap.*
   - *Observe all cautions, warnings and notes when completing repairs involving airbag systems.*

5. Connect battery ground (GND) strap to battery negative (–) terminal.

Steering wheel, assembly

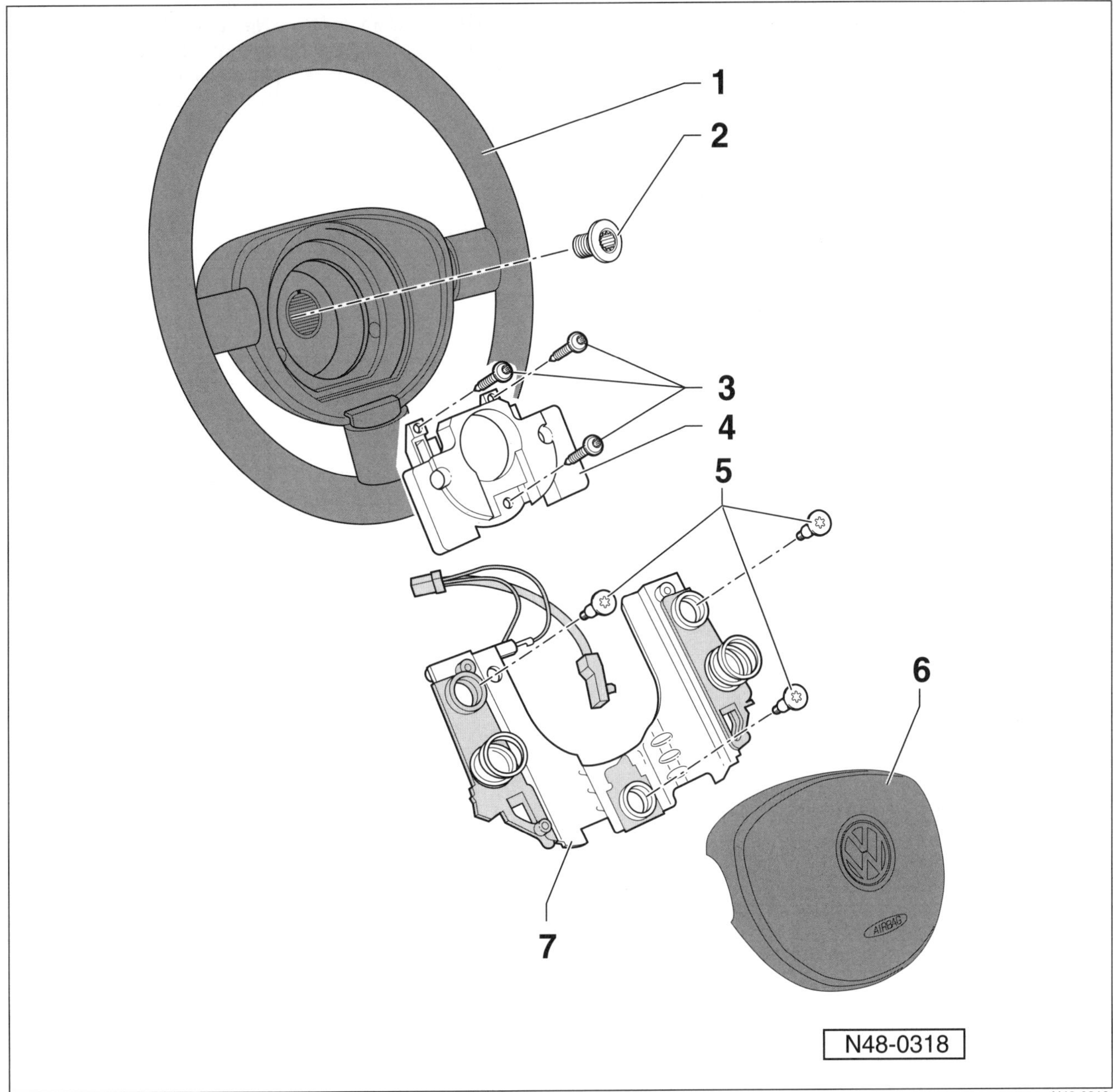

Fig. 2. Three spoke steering wheel and related components.

1. **Steering wheel**
   - Installed position, **see** Ⓐ
2. **Bolt, multi-point socket-head**
   - Tighten to 50 Nm (37 ft-lb) with locking compound
   - Can be reused up to 5 times
   - Mark with center punch after each installation
3. **Bolts, Torx®**
4. **Vibration damper**
   - Installed on vehicles equipped with ALH engine and automatic transmission
5. **Bolts, Torx®**
   - Tighten to 5 Nm (44 in-lb)
6. **Airbag unit**
7. **Securing plate**

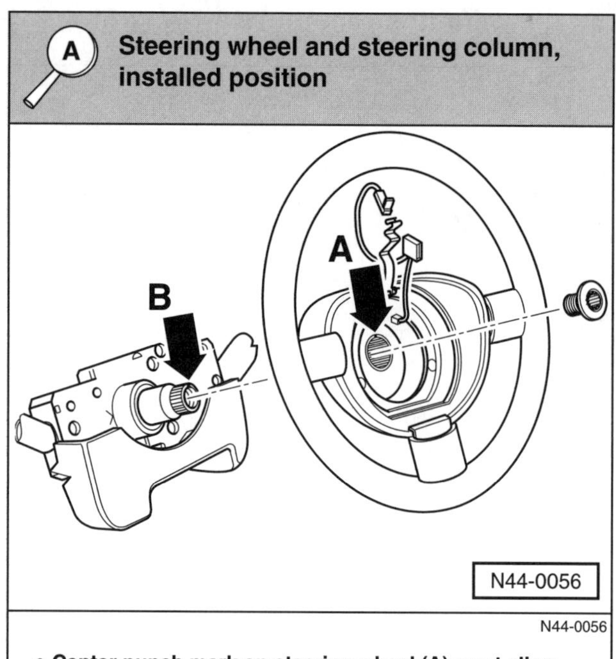

N44-0056

- **Center punch mark on steering wheel (A) must align with center punch mark on steering column (B).**
- **Replacement steering columns do not have center punch marks.**

STEERING COLUMN

Standard equipment on the New Beetle includes a steering column that is height adjustable and telescopic. Defective steering columns must be replaced as a complete assembly as no internal repair parts are available from Volkswagen. The steering column and related components are shown in Fig. 3.

Steering column, assembly

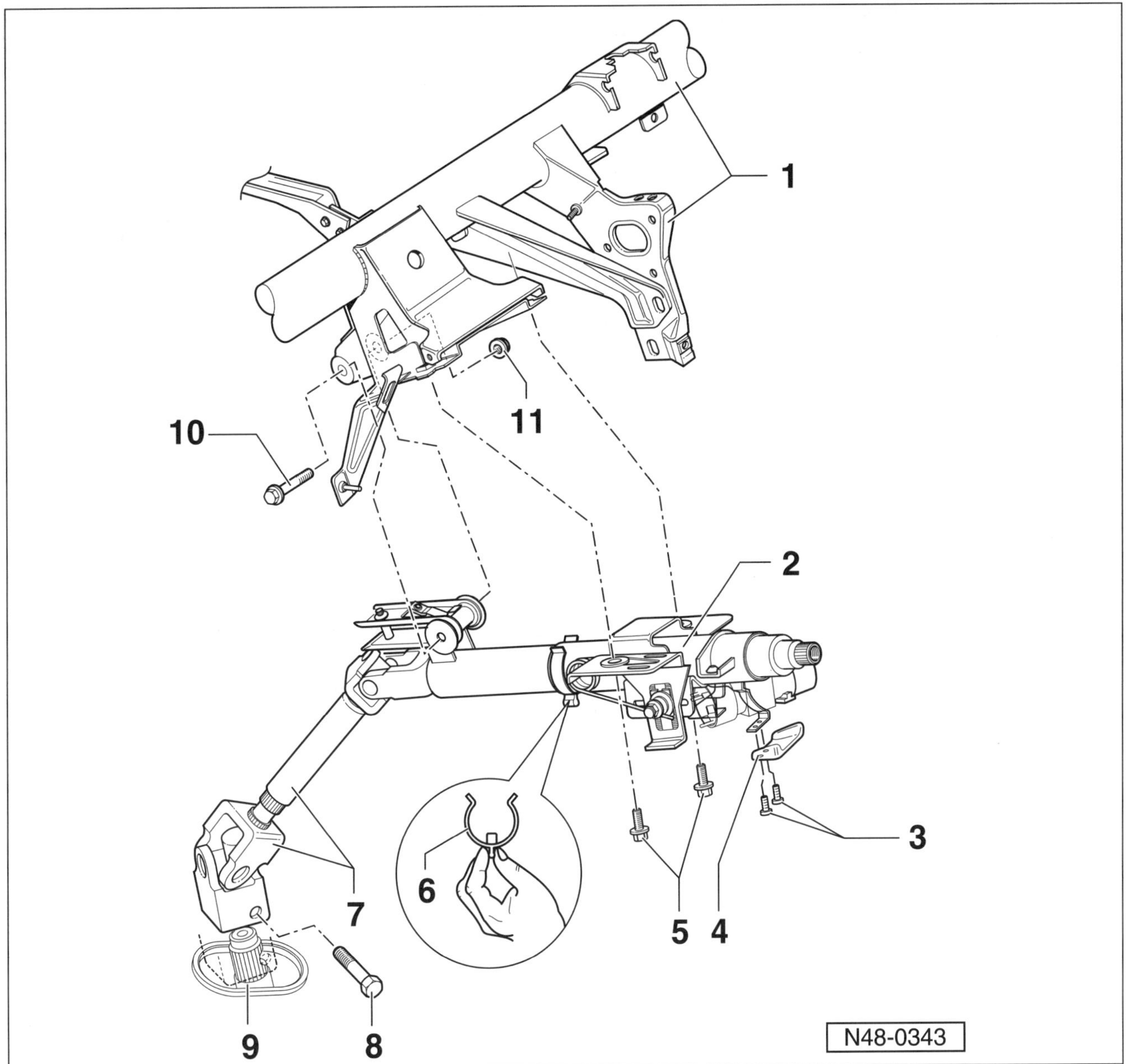

N48-0343

Fig. 3. Steering column and attachment points to body crossmember.

1. **Crossmember for steering column**
2. **Steering column**
   - Secure steering column before removal, **see** Ⓐ
   - Check for damage, **see** Ⓑ
3. **Bolts**
4. **Handle**
   - Lock/unlock column adjustment
5. **Bolts**
   - Tighten to 25 Nm (18 ft-lb)
6. **Transportation securing device**
   - Remove after column has been installed into vehicle
7. **Steering column universal joint shaft**
8. **Bolt**
   - Tighten to 20 Nm (15 ft-lb) + 1/4-turn (90°)
9. **Steering gear pinion shaft**
10. **Bolt**
11. **Nut**
    - Tighten to 10 Nm (7 ft-lb)

A Steering column, securing before removing

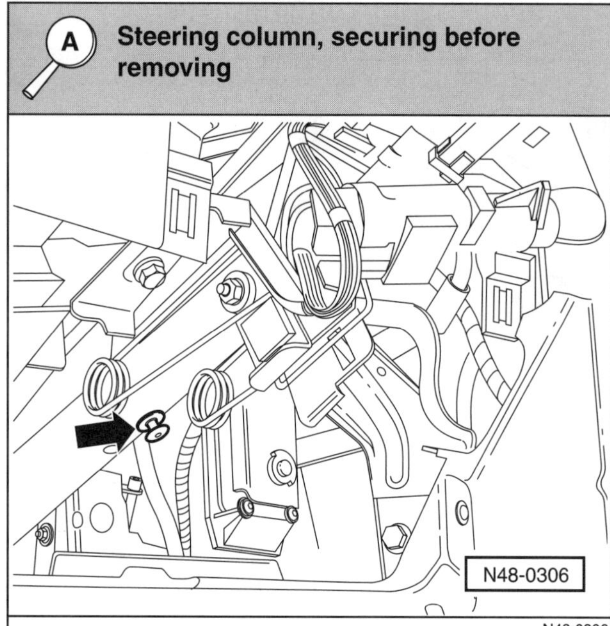

N48-0306

- Assembly aid is required to prevent upper and lower sections of steering column from pulling apart during removal.
- Splined sections can separate and cause rattling noises unless installed in original positions.
- Push or pull steering column slightly to align holes and insert suitable clip or pin into hole (arrow).

B Steering column, inspecting for damage

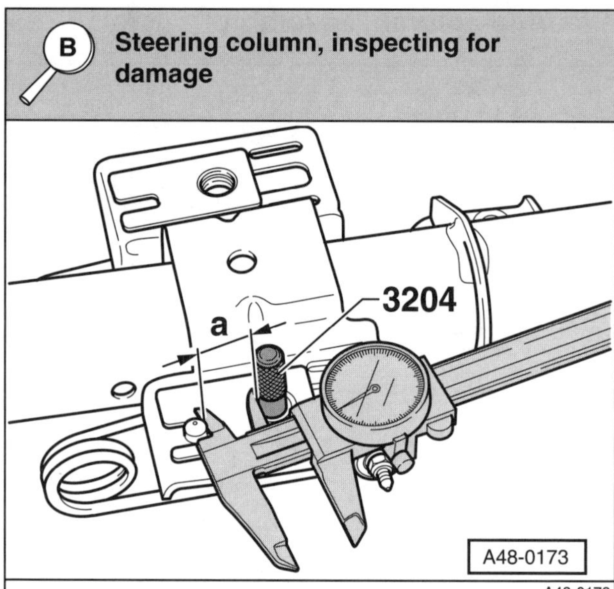

A48-0173

- Visually inspect for damage.
- Disconnect steering column universal joint shaft and check for smooth operation (without binding) of steering shaft.
- Check that steering column can be adjusted for full range of height and telescopic adjustment.
- Check gap (a) with alignment pin inserted in hole. Maximum distance from edge to edge is 23 mm (0.906 in).

Steering lock housing, removing

> ***WARNING —***
> *Observe all cautions, warnings and notes before starting repairs involving airbag systems.*

1. Steer the wheels to the straight ahead position.
2. Disconnect battery ground (GND) strap from battery negative (–) terminal. See the **Cautions** at the beginning of this repair group regarding battery disconnection.

   NOTE —
   Be sure to have the anti-theft radio code on hand before disconnecting the battery.

3. Remove airbag unit in steering wheel as described earlier.
4. Remove steering wheel as described earlier.
5. Remove adjustment handle and lower and upper trim. See Fig. 4.

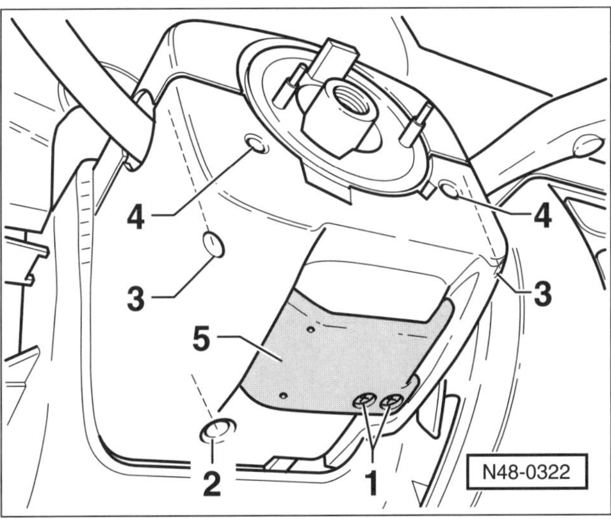

N48-00322

Fig. 4. Steering column as seen from below. Remove handle screws (**1**), handle (**5**), and securing screws (**2**), (**3**), (**4**).

6. Unplug harness connector and release locking lugs on spiral spring/slip ring and pull off. See Fig. 5.

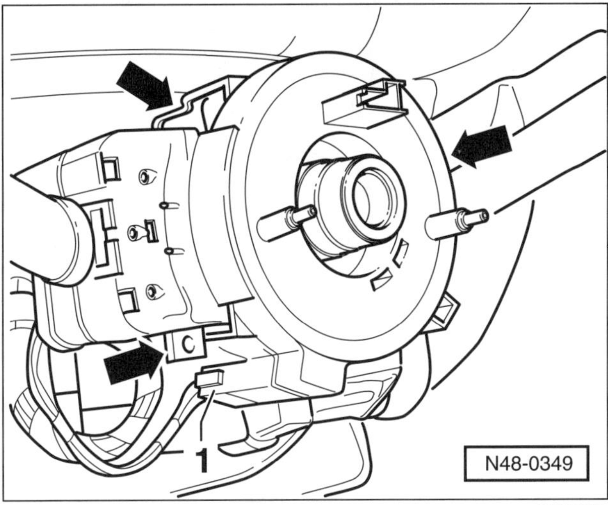

N48-0349

Fig. 5. Remove spiral spring/slip ring by releasing lugs (**arrows**) and unplugging harness connector (**1**).

7. Remove securing bolt for steering column switch, unplug switch assembly and slide off steering column. See Fig. 6.

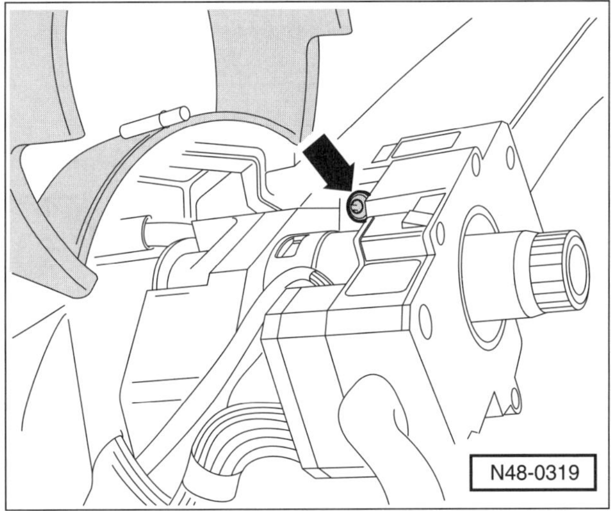

N48-0319

Fig. 6. Remove steering column switch securing bolt (**arrow**) and slide switch assembly off column.

8. Remove plastic cover over shear bolts. See Fig. 7.

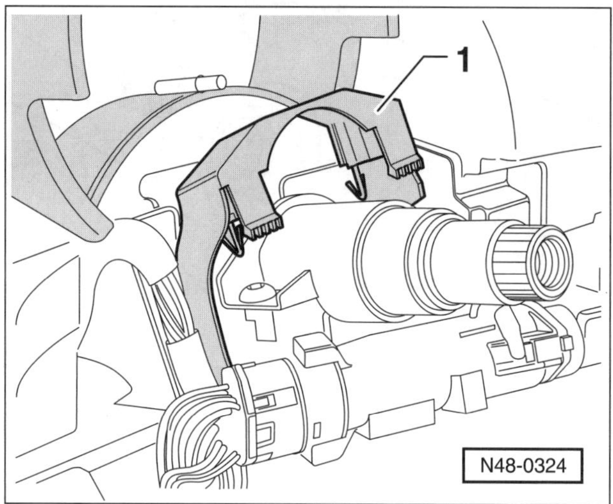

N48-0324

Fig. 7. Unclip plastic cover (**1**) over shear bolts and pull up to remove.

9. On vehicles with automatic transmission, unhook shift lock cable by placing shift lever in park, and turning ignition key to the on position. Press wire clip upward or downward (depending on installed position) while pulling out on locking cable. See Fig. 8.

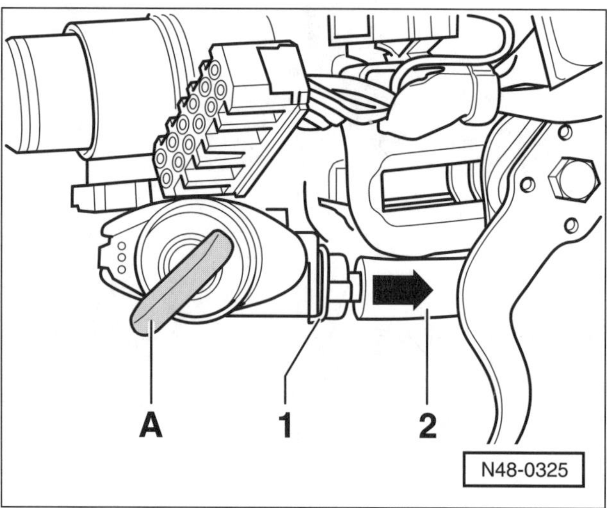

N48-0325

Fig. 8. Side view of ignition lock showing wire clip (**1**). Pull cable forward (**arrow**) to release.

10. Cut off shear head bolts using a suitable sharp chisel. See Fig. 9.

11. Unplug harness connector on ignition switch and slide lock housing off of column.

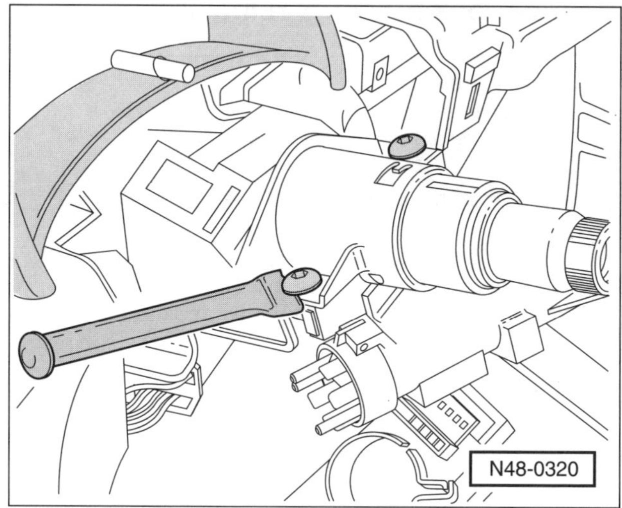

N48-0320

Fig. 9. Chisel off both shear bolts to remove them.

Steering lock housing, installing

1. Install lock housing onto steering column with new shear bolts. Bolts are correctly torqued when hex head on bolt shears off.

2. Install plastic cover over shear bolts.

3. On vehicles with automatic transmission, connect shift lock cable by placing shift lever in park, and turning ignition key to the on position. Slide locking cable onto steering lock housing until wire clip engages. See Fig. 10.

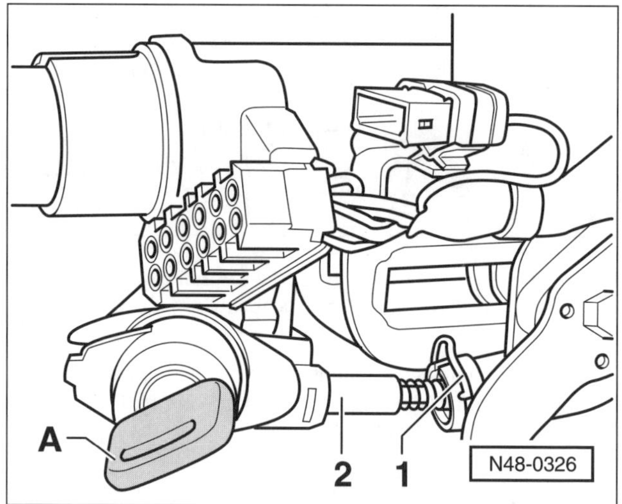

N48-0326

Fig. 10. Side view of ignition lock showing key (**A**). Slide shift lock cable (**2**) onto housing until wire clip (**1**) engages.

4. Install steering column switch assembly.

5. Install spiral spring/slip ring.

6. Temporarily install steering wheel and adjust distance between spiral spring/slip ring and steering wheel. Adjustment is made by sliding switch assembly on steering column and locking in place with securing screw. See Fig. 11.

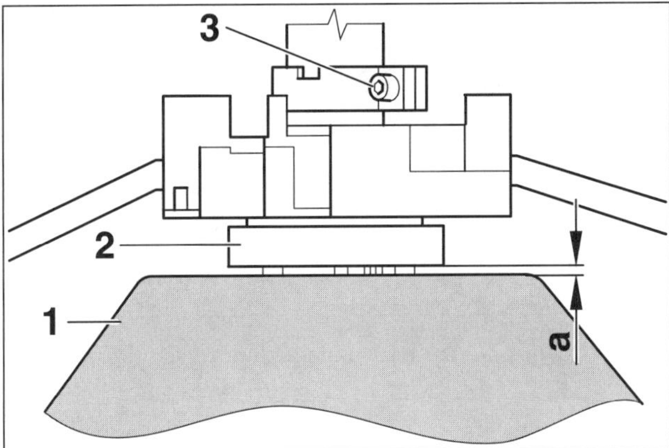

Fig. 11. Temporarily install steering wheel (**1**) and adjust gap (**a**) by sliding spiral spring/slip ring (**2**) and switch assembly. Tighten securing screw (**3**) when proper gap is obtained.

Specification

- Clearance between steering wheel and spiral spring/slipring . . . . approx. 2½ mm (0.1 in)

7. Remove steering wheel and install steering column trim.

8. Remainder of installation is the reverse of removal.

Tightening torque

- Steering wheel bolt . . . . 50 Nm (37 ft-lb)

> ***WARNING —***
> *Observe all cautions, warnings and notes when completing repairs involving airbag systems.*

Ignition lock cylinder and switch, removing and installing

> ***WARNING —***
> *Observe all cautions, warnings and notes before starting repairs involving airbag systems.*

1. Disconnect battery ground strap.

2. Remove airbag unit and steering wheel as described earlier.

3. Remove upper and lower steering column trim as described earlier.

4. Insert ignition key into lock cylinder and turn to ignition **ON** position.

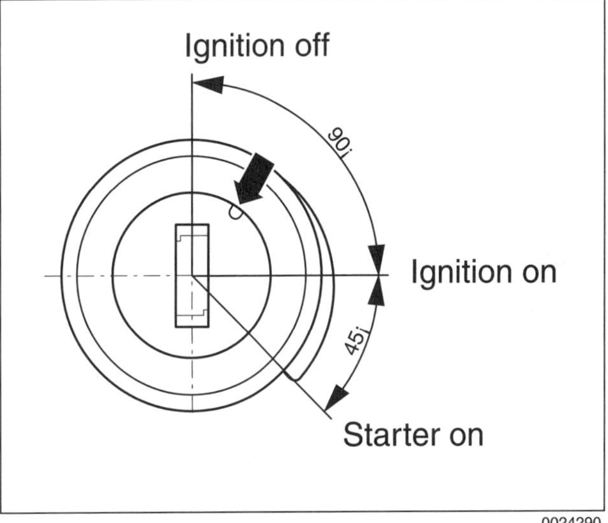

Fig. 12. Insert wire tool into opening (**arrow**) to remove lock cylinder.

5. Insert a wire tool approximately 1.2 mm (0.047 in) in diameter into the opening in the face of the lock cylinder. See Fig. 12.

> ***NOTE —***
> *A large paper clip or a 3/64 inch drill bit are suitable for inserting into lock cylinder opening.*

6. Release lock cylinder by gently pulling on key while pushing in on wire tool. See Fig. 13.

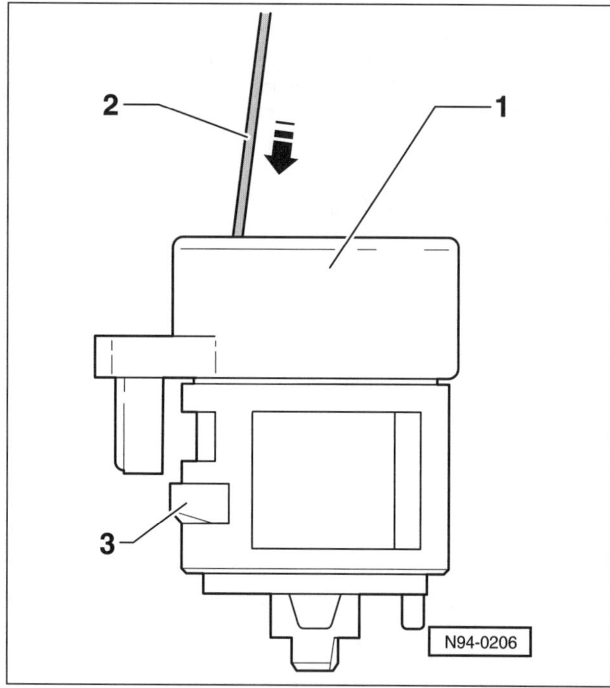

N94-0206

Fig. 13. Remove ignition lock cylinder by pushing in (**arrow**) on wire tool (**2**) while pulling gently on key. Wire tool (**2**) will release locking tab (**3**) and allow lock cylinder to slide out.

7. Disconnect harness connector from ignition switch.

8. Remove sealant (paint) from threaded holes of ignition switch securing screws. See Fig. 14.

9. Carefully remove two ignition switch securing screws and pull ignition switch out from steering lock housing.

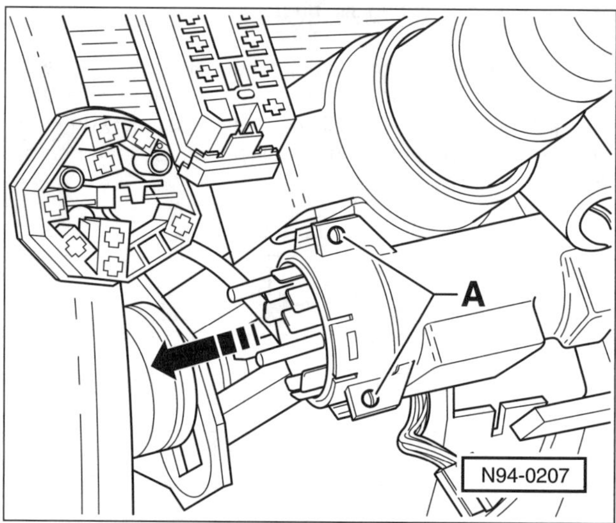

N94-0207

Fig. 14. Remove screws (**A**) and remove switch in direction of **arrow**.

> ***NOTE —***
> - *When installing ignition/starter lock switch ensure that it is in the same position as the lock cylinder, e.g. "ignition on".*
> - *Be sure to use locking compound on ignition switch securing screws when installing.*

10. Install ignition lock cylinder by inserting key into lock cylinder and turning key into the same position used on removal.

11. Insert wire tool into opening and slide assembly fully into ignition lock housing until seated.

12. Remove wire tool and check for smooth operation of ignition lock and cylinder.

13. Installation is reverse of removal for remaining components.

> ***WARNING —***
> *Observe all cautions, warnings and notes when completing repairs involving airbag systems.*

Steering column crossmember, assembly

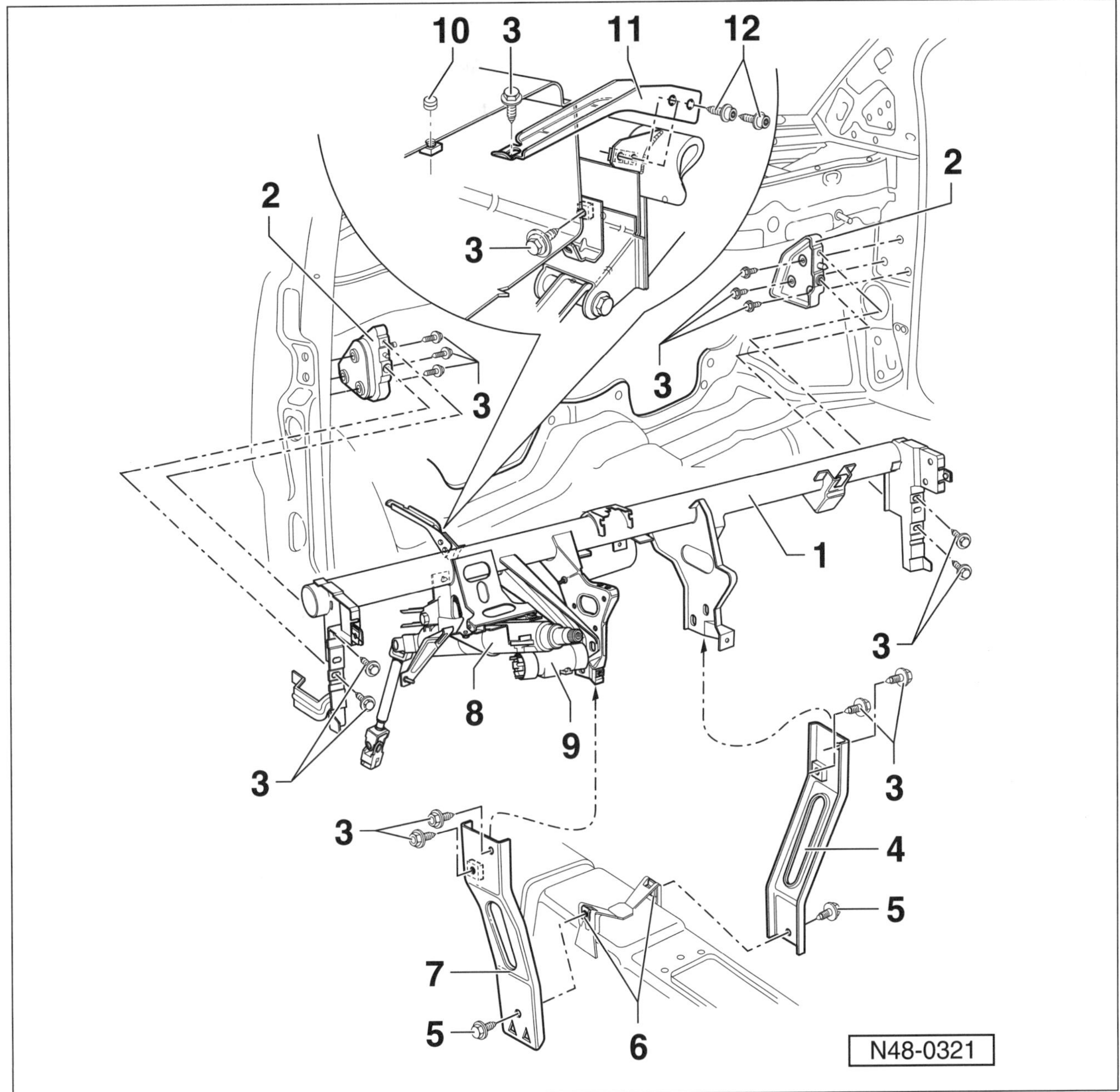

Fig. 15. Steering column crossmember and related components.

1. **Steering column crossmember**
2. **Adjustment brackets**
3. **Hex bolts**
   - Tighten to 25 Nm (18 ft-lb)
4. **Support, right**
5. **Bolts**
6. **Speed nuts**
7. **Support, left**
8. **Steering column assembly**
9. **Steering lock housing**
10. **Sealing plug**
11. **Support for bulkhead**
12. **Bolts**
    - Tighten to 8 Nm (71 in-lb)

POWER STEERING GEAR

The power rack and pinion steering gear is not serviceable, malfunctioning units must be replaced. An exploded view of the power steering gear is shown in Fig. 16.

Specifications

- Special steering rack grease . . . . AOF 063 000 04
- Power steering hydraulic oil . . . . .G 002 000
- Power steering hydraulic oil quantity . . . . .0.7-0.9 L (11.8-15.2 oz.)

NOTE —
Volkswagen part numbers are given for reference only! Always consult with your Volkswagen Parts Department or aftermarket parts specialist for the latest parts information.

Tightening torque

- Power steering gear to subframe always replace (M8) . . . 20Nm (15 ft-lb) + ¼ turn (90°)
- Subframe to body always replace (M14) . 100 Nm (74 ft-lb) + ¼ turn (90°)
- Universal joint to steering gear pinion always replace (M8) . . . . 30 Nm (22 ft-lb)
- Return line banjo bolt (M16). . . . . 45 Nm (33 ft-lb)
- Pressure hose banjo bolt (M14) . . . . . 40 Nm (30 ft-lb)
- Pendulum support to transmission always replace (M8) . . . 40 Nm (30 ft-lb) + ¼ turn (90°)
- Tie rod end to wheel bearing housing always replace (M12) . . . . 45 Nm (33 ft-lb)

Power steering gear, assembly

The following numbered list applies to Fig. 16.

1. **Tie rod end**
2. **Nut**
   - Tighten to 50 Nm (37 ft lb)
3. **Clamp**
   - Always replace
4. **Boot**
   - Must not be twisted while adjusting toe
   - Remove steering gear to replace
5. **Clamp**
   - Always replace
6. **Tie rod**
   - Tighten to 75 Nm (55 ft-lb)
   - Replacement parts are supplied preset
   - Check vehicle alignment if replaced
7. **Bolts**
   - Tighten to 22 Nm (16 ft-lb)
8. **Gasket**
9. **Hydraulic pressure hose**
10. **Banjo bolt**
    - Tighten to 45 Nm (33 ft-lb)
11. **Banjo bolt**
    - Tighten to 40 Nm (30 ft-lb)
12. **Seals**
    - Always replace

Power steering gear, assembly

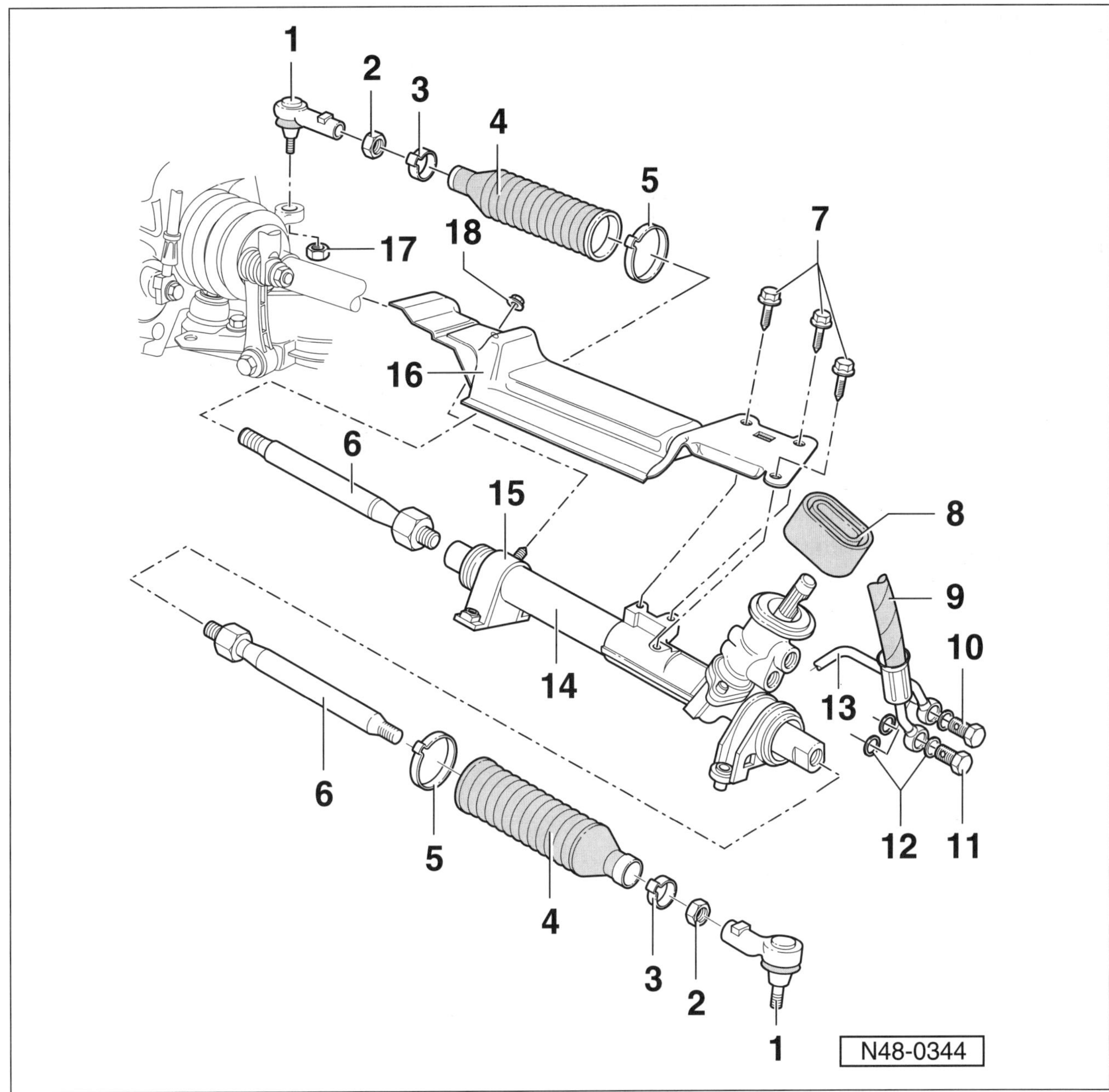

N48-0344

Fig. 16. Power steering gear with related steering components.

(continued from previous page)

13. Hydraulic return line

14. Power steering gear
- Center before installing, **see** (A)

15. Mounting bracket with rubber bushing
- Replace if threads in welded nut are damaged

16. Heat shield

17. Nut, self-locking
- Tighten to 45 Nm (33 ft-lb)

18. Nut
- Tighten to 22 Nm (16 ft-lb)

(A) Power steering rack, determining center position

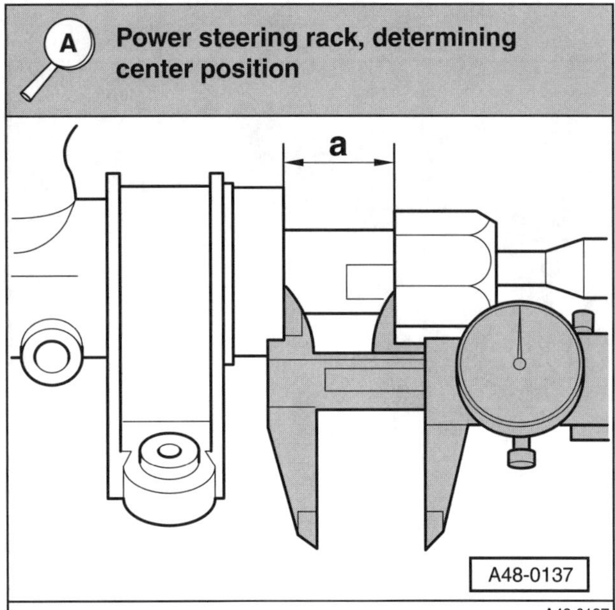

A48-0137

- Center position must be identified before installation.
- Slide rack until dimension (a) is obtained.
- Dimension (a) = 30.5 mm (1.20 in).

Power steering fluid reservoir, assembly

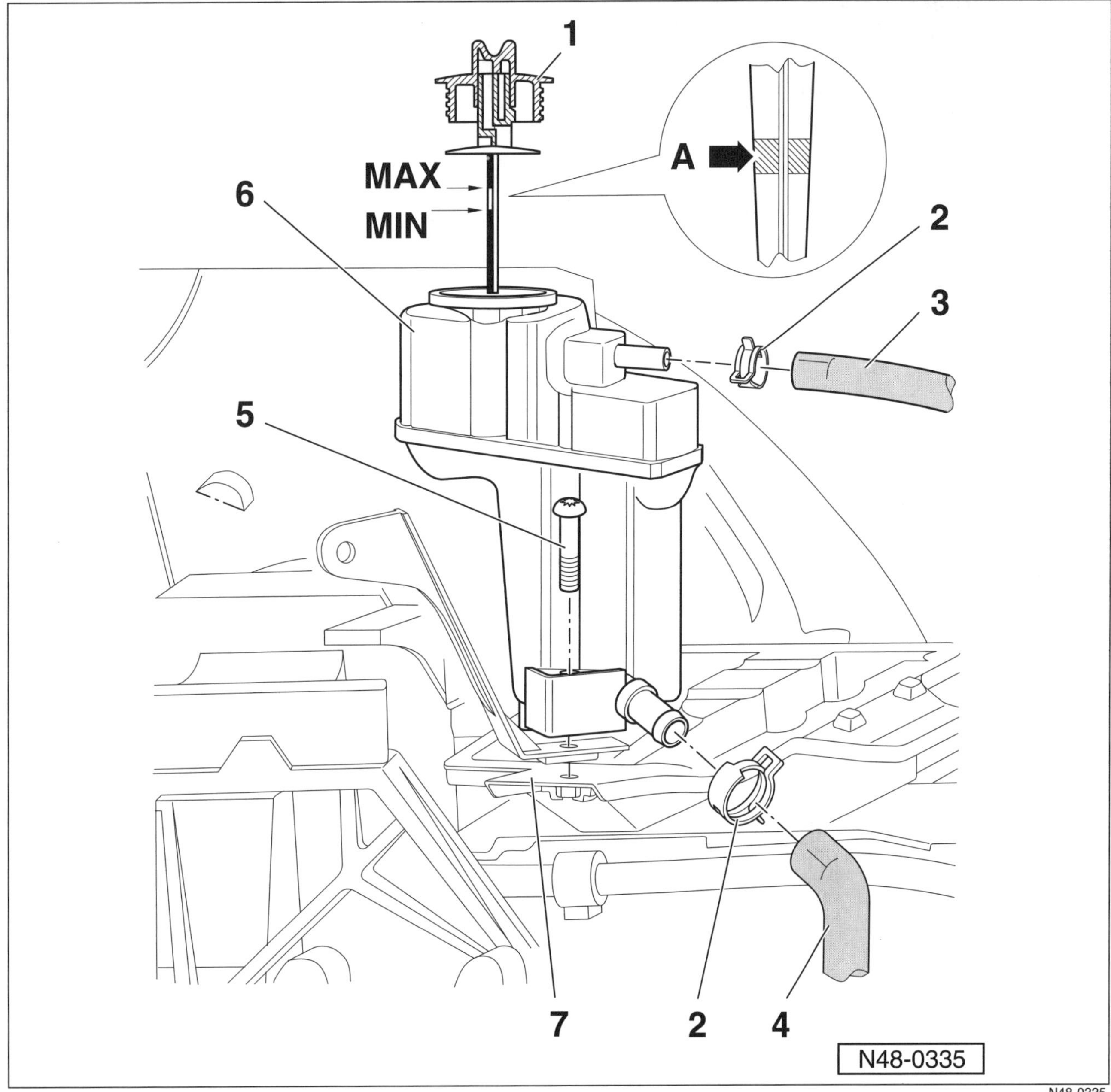

N48-0335

Fig. 17. Power steering fluid reservoir shown with related components.

1. **Cap with dip stick**
   - Twist to open using suitable tool as required
   - Screw cap on fully to check oil level
   - Oil level with engine warm, approx. 50°C (122°F): between **MIN** and **MAX** marks (**arrow A**)
   - Oil level with engine cold: not over **MIN** marking
2. **Spring clamp**
3. **Return hose**
4. **Suction hose**
5. **Bolt**
   - Tighten to 10 Nm (7 ft-lb)
6. **Reservoir**
7. **Battery tray**

POWER STEERING HYDRAULIC HOSES

Power steering hoses (ALH engine with A/C)

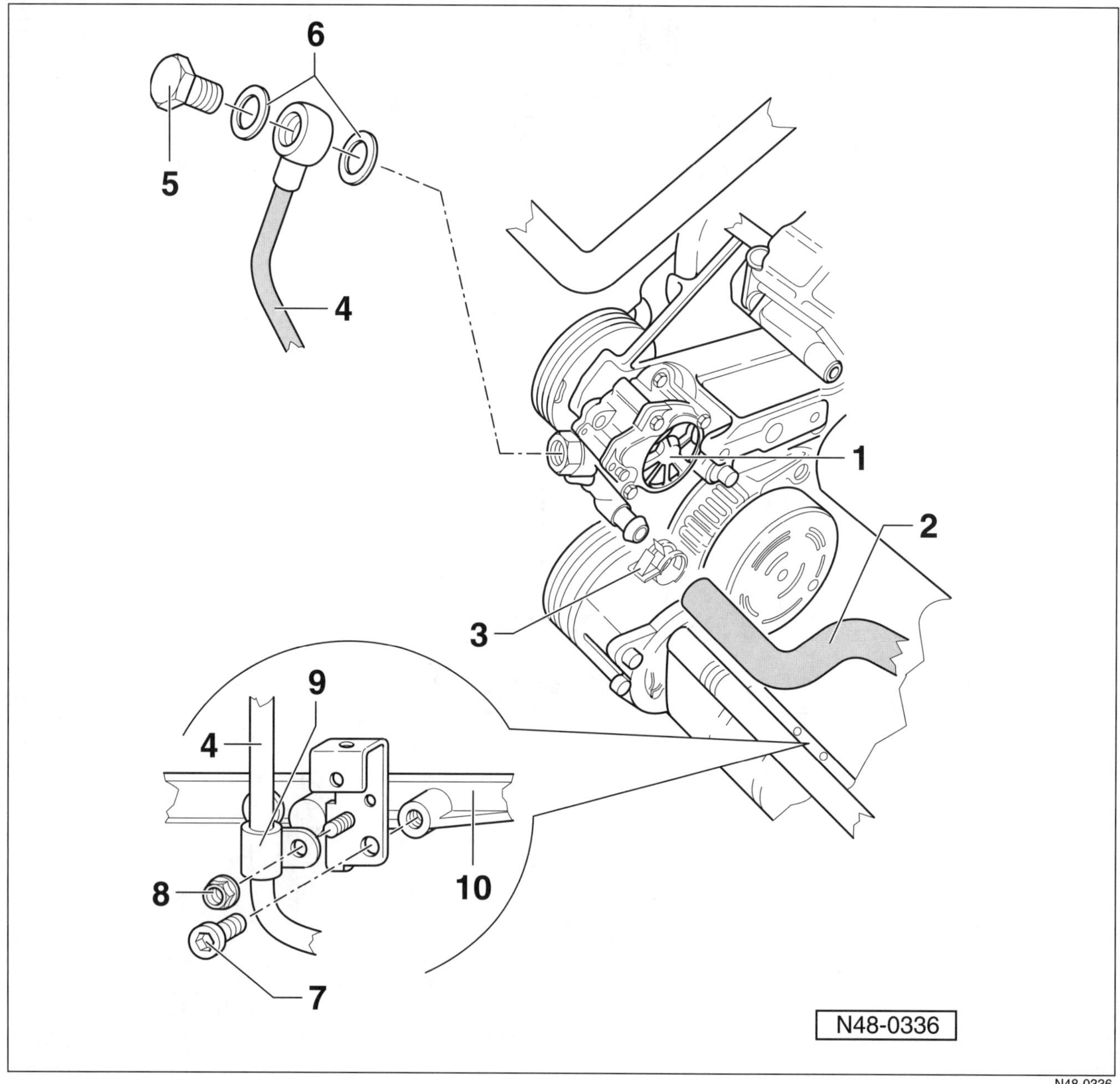

Fig. 18. Power steering hose detail on ALH engines equipped with A/C.

1. **Power steering pump**
   - Fill with oil before installing
2. **Suction hose**
3. **Spring clamp**
4. **Pressure hose assembly**
5. **Banjo bolt**
   - Tighten to 38 Nm (28 ft-lb)
6. **Seals**
   - Always replace
7. **Bolt**
   - Tighten to 40 Nm (30 ft-lb)
8. **Nut**
   - Tighten to 22 Nm (16 ft-lb)
9. **Mounting bracket**
10. **Cylinder block**

Power steering hoses (ALH and AEG engines without A/C)

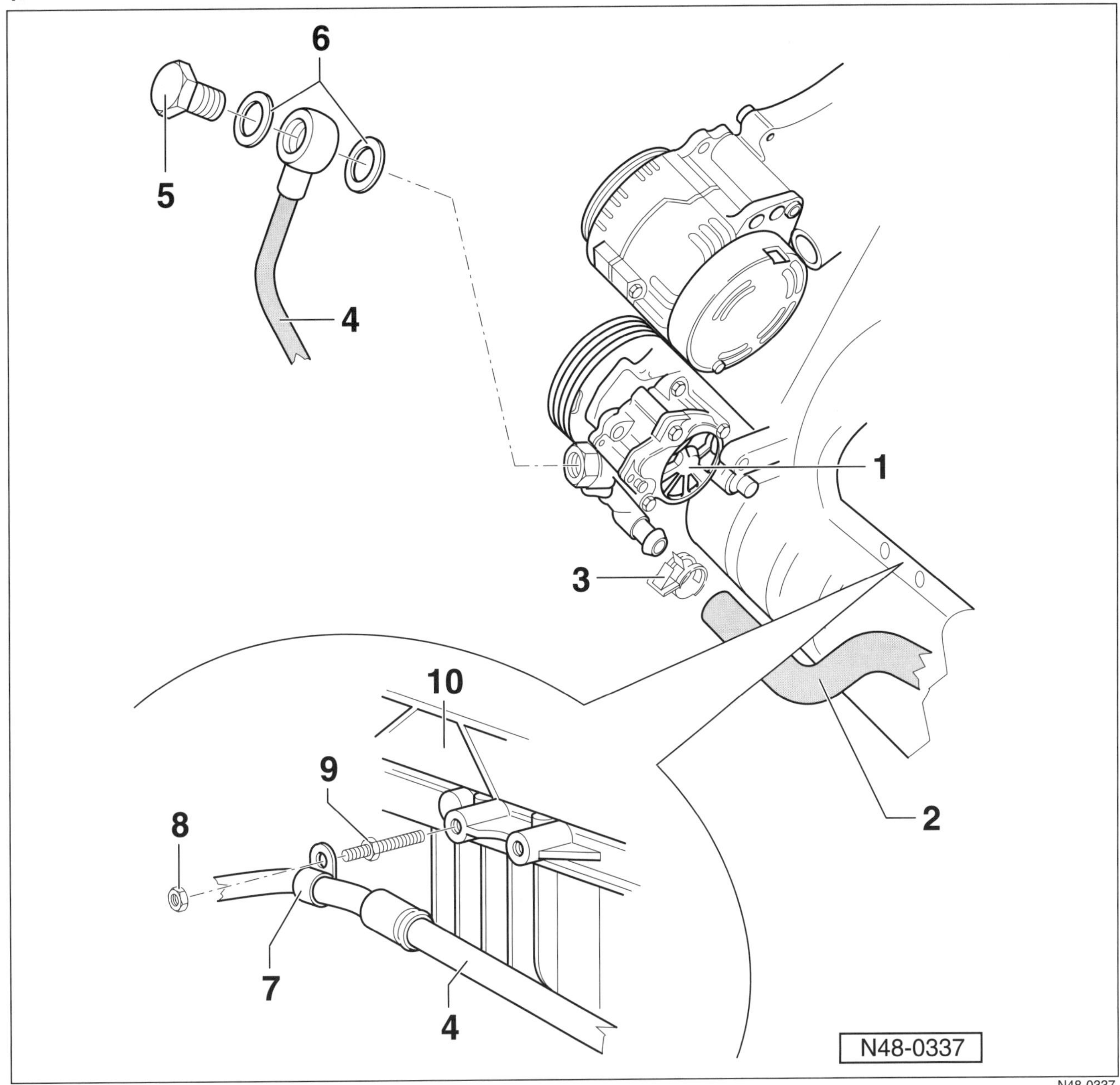

N48-0337

Fig. 19. Power steering hose detail on ALH and AEG engines not equipped with A/C.

1. **Power steering pump**
   - Fill with oil before installing
2. **Suction hose**
3. **Spring clamp**
4. **Pressure hose assembly**
5. **Banjo bolt**
   - Tighten to 38 Nm (28 ft-lb)
6. **Seals**
   - Always replace
7. **Mounting bracket**
8. **Nut**
   - Tighten to 22 Nm (16 ft-lb)
9. **Bolt**
   - Tighten to 40 Nm (30 ft-lb)
10. **Cylinder block**

Power steering hoses (AEG engine with A/C)

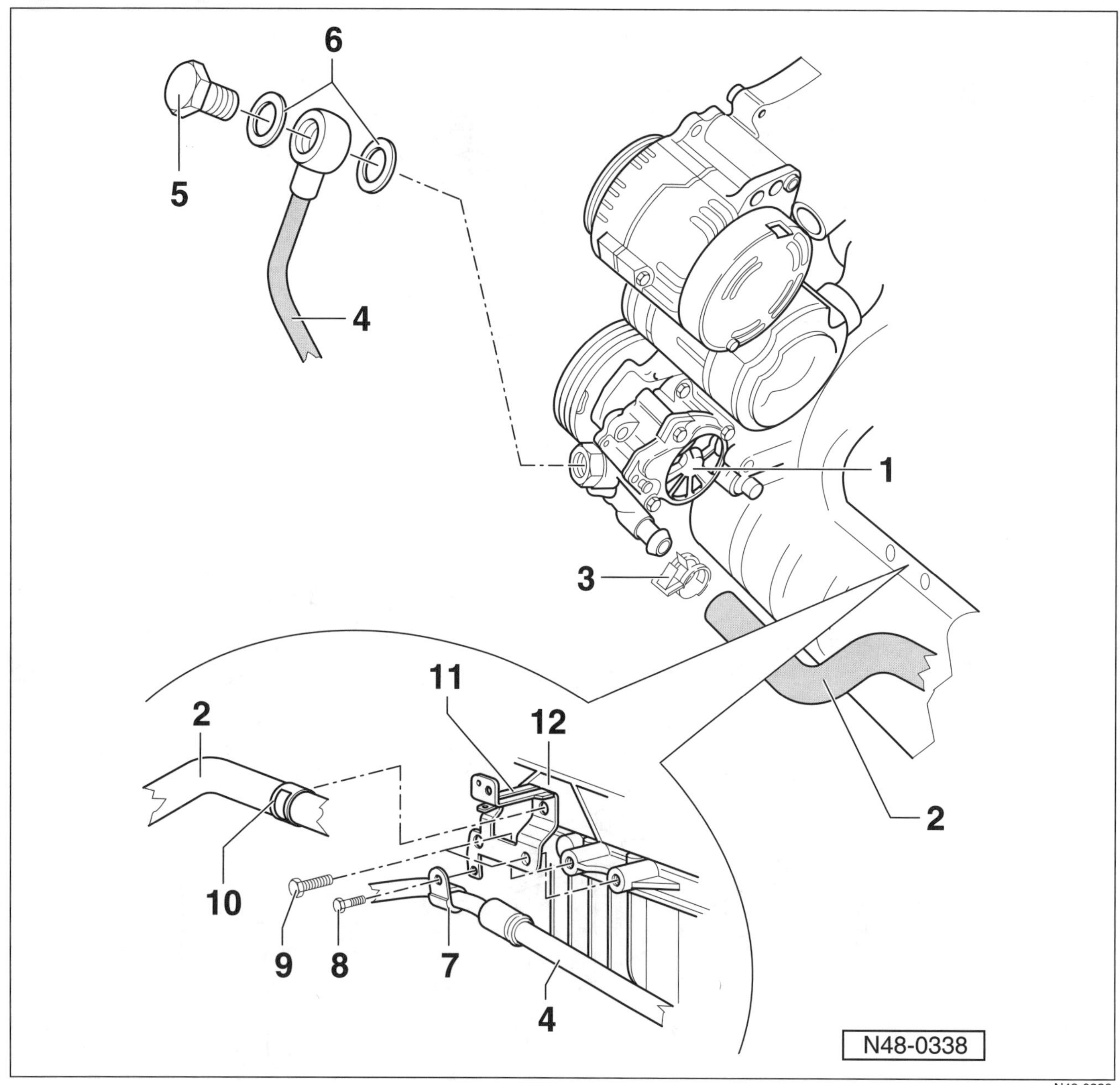

N48-0338

Fig. 20. Power steering hose detail on AEG engines equipped with A/C.

1. **Power steering pump**
   - Fill with oil before installing
2. **Suction hose**
3. **Spring clamp**
4. **Pressure hose assembly**
5. **Banjo bolt**
   - Tighten to 38 Nm (28 ft-lb)
6. **Seals**
   - Always replace
7. **Mounting bracket**
8. **Bolt**
   - Tighten to 22 Nm (16 ft-lb)
9. **Bolt**
   - Tighten to 40 Nm (30 ft-lb)
10. **Spring clamp**
11. **Mounting bracket**
12. **Cylinder block**

Pressure hose, mounting to manual transmission

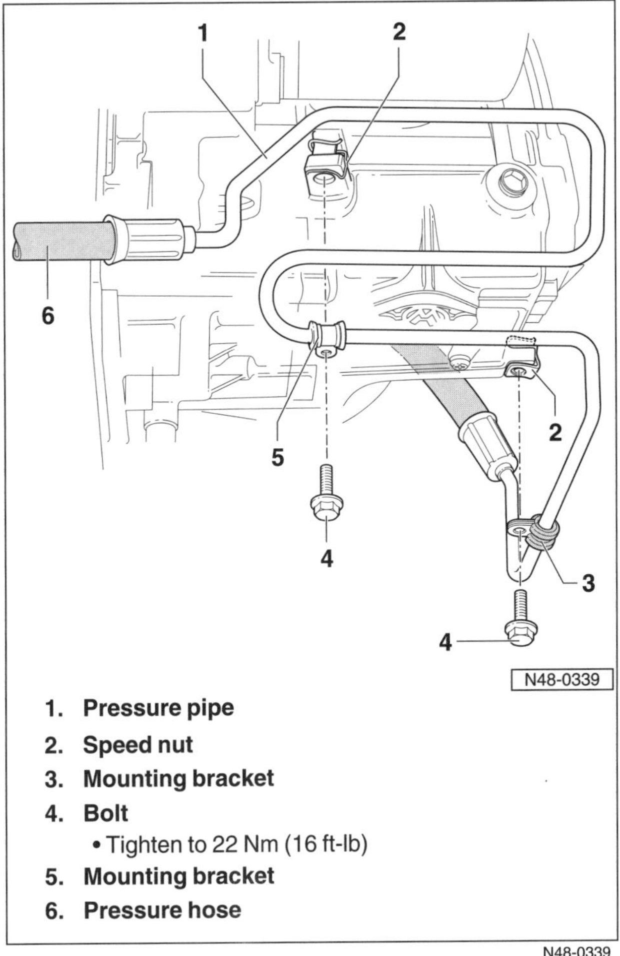

Fig. 21. Power steering pressure hose assembly mounting detail on vehicles equipped with manual transmissions.

Pressure hose, mounting to automatic transmission

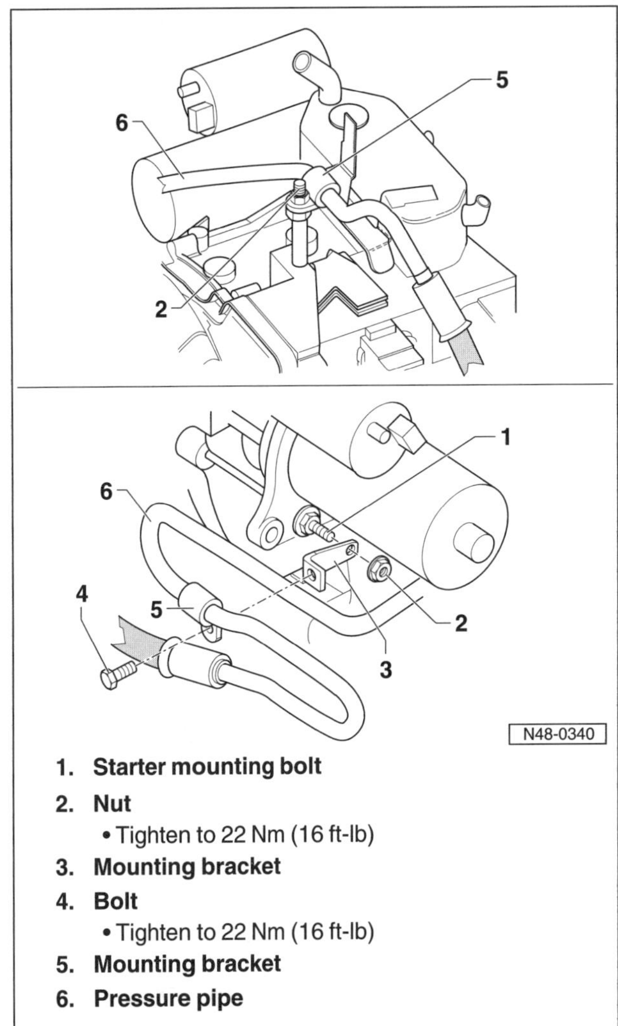

Fig. 22. Power steering pressure hose assembly mounting detail on vehicles equipped with automatic transmissions.

POWER STEERING PUMP

Different power steering pump positions and belt routings are used on the New Beetles depending on engine type and equipment level. For vehicles with power steering pump mounted lower on the bracket see Fig. 23. For vehicles with power steering pump mounted higher on the bracket see Fig. 24.

Specification

- Power steering pump pressures at idle
  AEG engine vehicles . . . . . 85-95 bar (1233-1378 psi)
  ALH engine vehicles. . . . . 96-105 bar (1392-1523 psi)

Power steering pump assembly, (pump in lower mounting bracket)

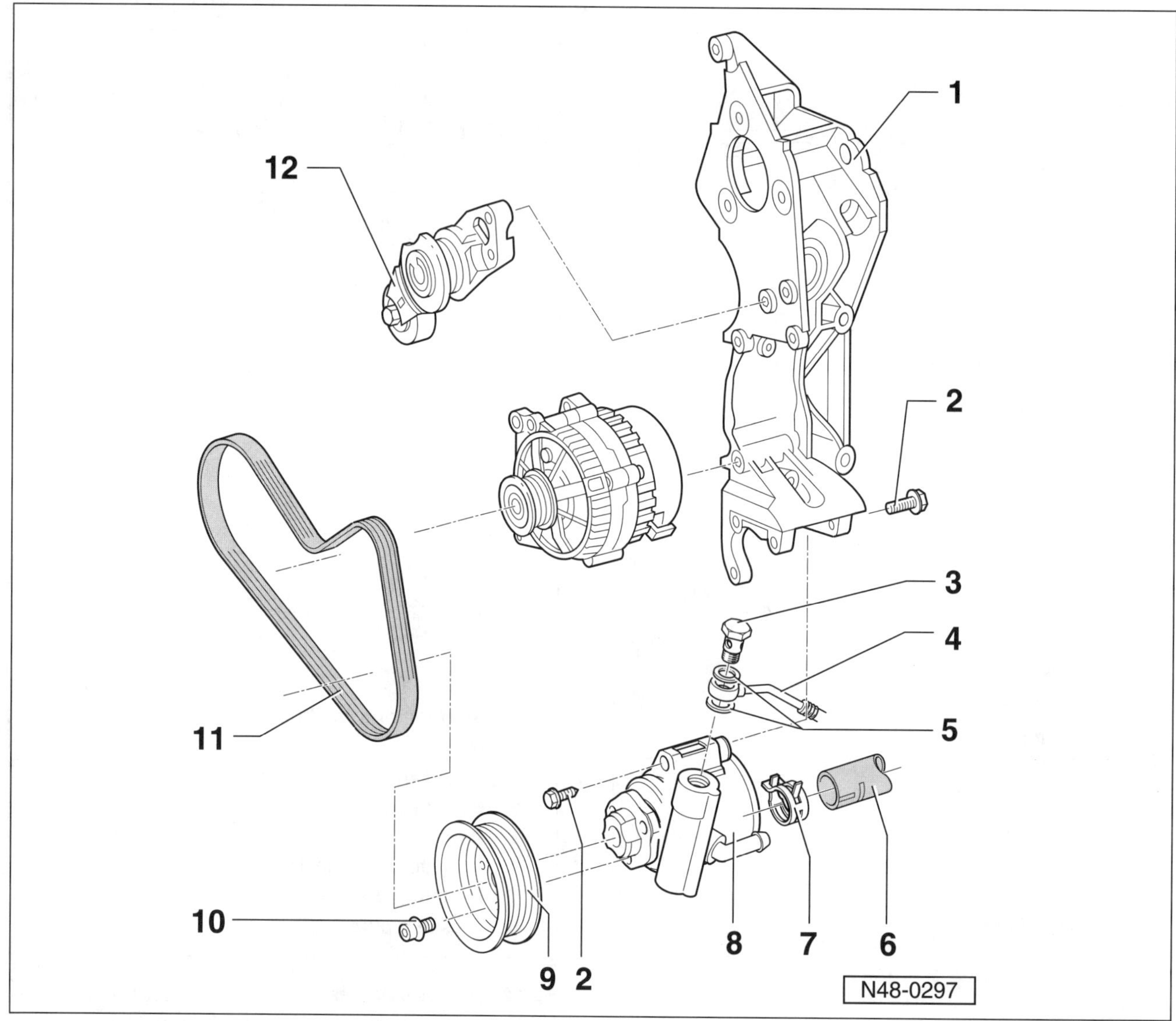

Fig. 23. Power steering pump and components mounted to lower section of bracket.

1. **Bracket (ALH shown, AEG similar)**
2. **Bolts**
   - Tighten to 25 Nm (18 ft-lb)
3. **Banjo bolt**
   - Tighten to 38 Nm (28 ft-lb)
4. **Pressure hose assembly**
5. **Seals**
   - Always replace
6. **Suction hose**
7. **Spring clamp**
8. **Power steering pump**
   - Fill with oil before installing
9. **Belt pulley**
10. **Bolt**
    - Tighten to 25 Nm (18 ft-lb)
11. **Ribbed V-belt**
    - Using a crayon or marker, mark the direction of travel before removing the ribbed belt
    - Reinstalling a used belt in the opposite direction could damage the belt
    - Make sure belt is correctly seated in the pulleys when installing
12. **Ribbed V-belt tensioner**

Power steering pump assembly, (pump in upper mounting bracket)

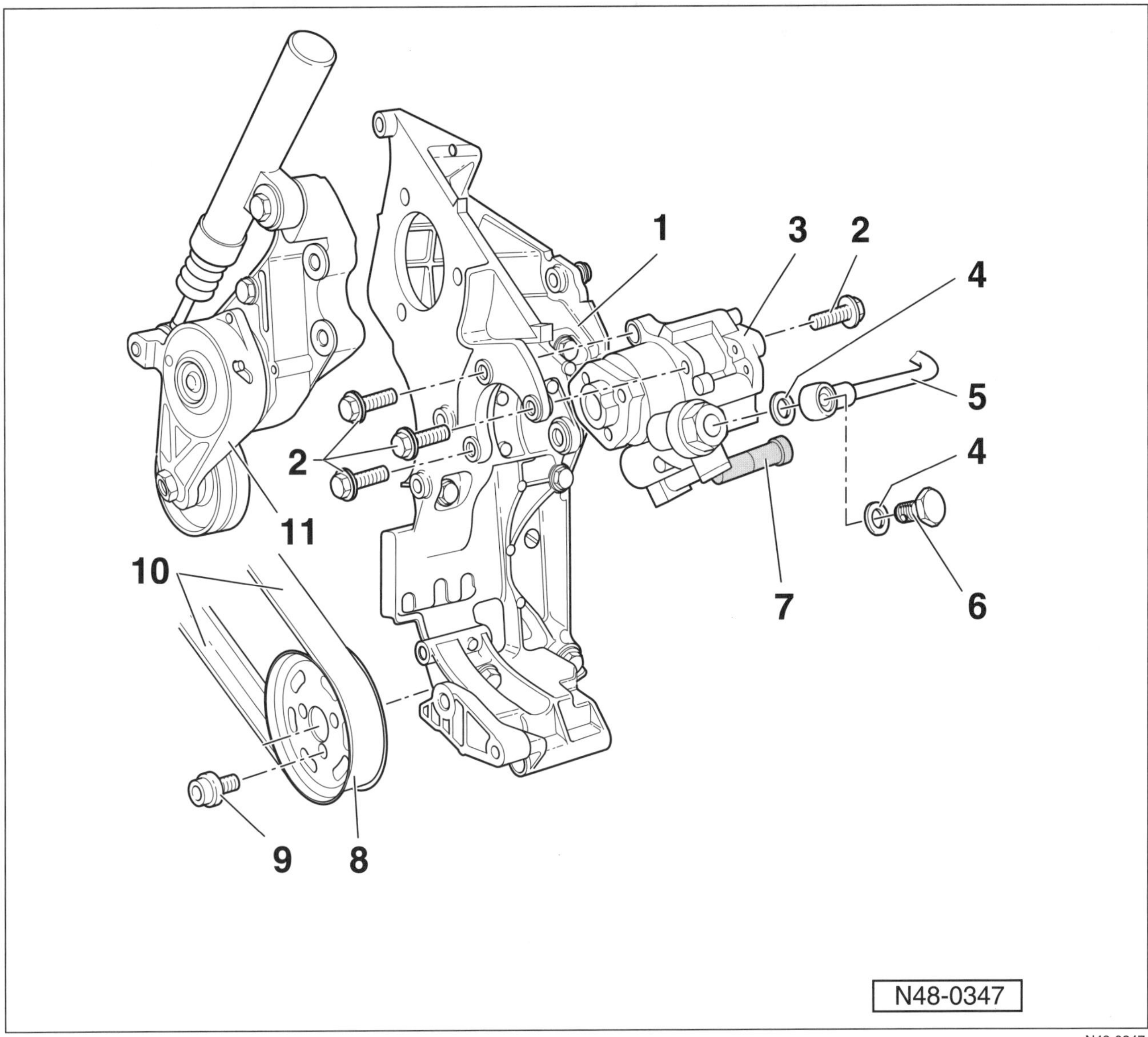

N48-0347

Fig. 24. Power steering components mounted to upper section of bracket.

1. **Bracket (ALH shown, AEG similar)**
2. **Bolts**
   - Tighten to 25 Nm (18 ft-lb)
3. **Power steering pump**
   - Fill with oil before installing
4. **Seals**
   - Always replace
5. **Pressure hose assembly**
6. **Banjo Bolt**
   - Tighten to 38 Nm (28 ft-lb)
7. **Suction hose**
8. **Belt pulley**
9. **Bolt**
   - Tighten to 25 Nm (18 ft-lb)
10. **Ribbed V-belt**
    - Using a crayon or marker, mark the direction of travel before removing the ribbed belt
    - Reinstalling a used belt in the opposite direction could damage the belt
    - Make sure belt is correctly seated in the pulleys when installing
11. **Ribbed V-belt tensioner**

QUALITY REVIEW

When you have finished working under the hood and around other areas of the vehicle, it is advisable to take a moment to quality check or review your work. This helps to insure that the operation or repair has been completed properly with all affected systems functioning within normal parameters. These may include the following:

- Ensure that all cable ties and clamps that were removed as part of the repair are replaced.
- Ensure that all fasteners and hardware were replaced and torqued as specified.
- Make sure that all other components involved in the repair are positioned correctly, properly torqued and function properly.
- Check and adjust all applicable fluid levels.
- Make sure that there are no fluid leaks.
- Align suspension if components were removed or repaired that would affect settings.
- Make sure that all tools, shop cloths, fender covers and protective tapes are removed before closing the hood.
- Clean grease and fingerprints from painted surfaces, steering wheel and shifter.
- Unlock anti-theft radio and reset the clock.

50 Body–Front

GENERAL

This repair group covers the front body section, front fender and radiator support removal and installation. The radiator support can be removed from the car as one unit to facilitate repairs, such as engine removal.

> ***WARNING —***
> *Disconnecting the negative (–) battery cable may erase fault codes and basic settings in the engine management and automatic transmission control modules. Some driveability problems may be noticed until the system re-adapts to operating conditions. OBD II readiness codes, which may be required for emissions testing, may also be erased. Convenience electronics (alarm system, interior light control, power locks, mirrors, and windows) may need to be re-set using a VAG 1551/1552 or equivalent scan tool.*

NOTE —
Volkswagen refers to the radiator support as a lock carrier.

FRONT BODY COMPONENTS

The front fenders are both part of the front clip which must be removed as a complete assembly. See Fig. 1.

Front body assembly

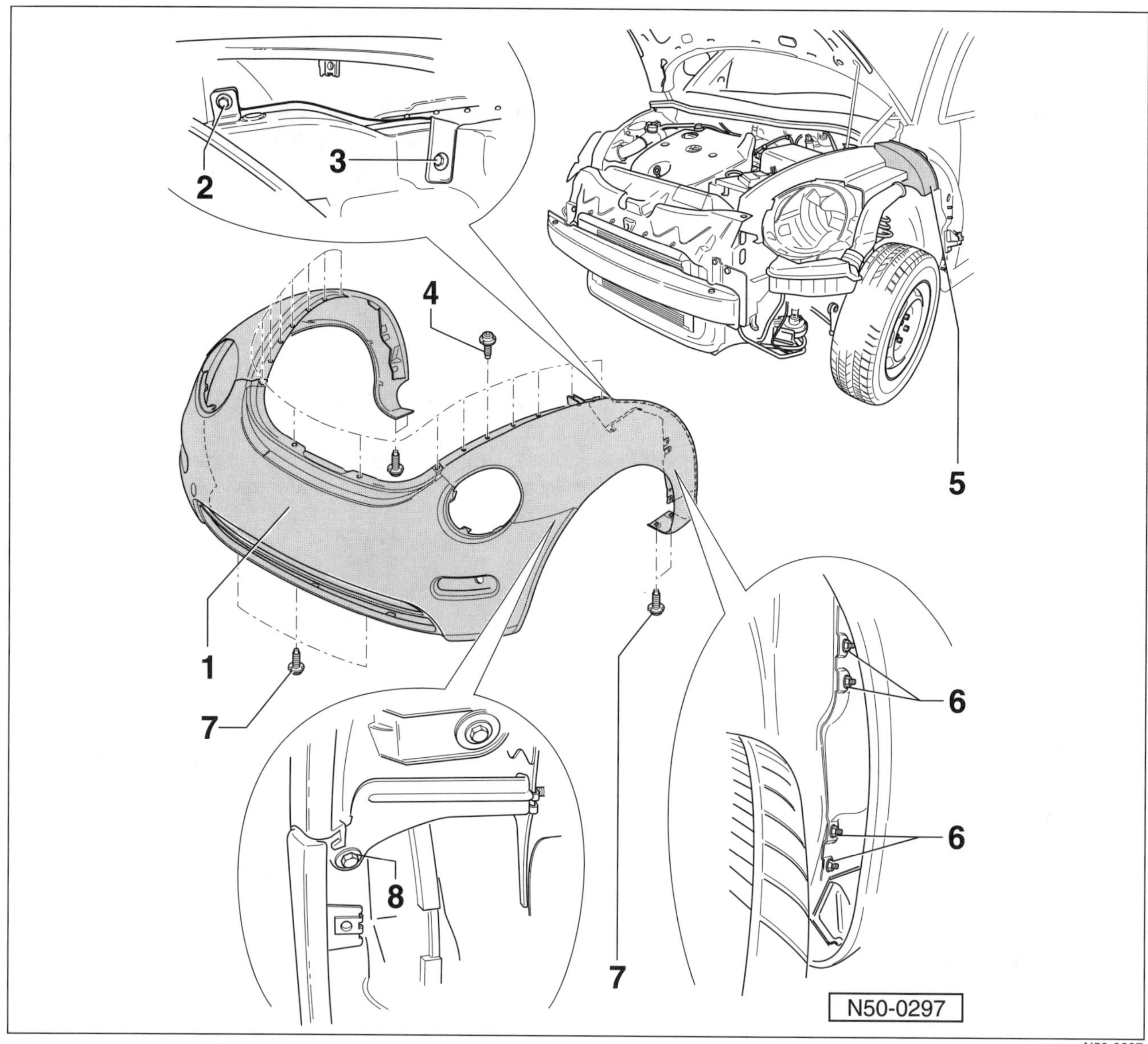

N50-0297

Fig. 1. Front body assembly with fenders must be removed as a complete unit.

1. **Front clip**
   - Use of low-tack tape on front quarter panels above fender mounting point is recommended to prevent damage
   - Before removing front clip, remove headlight assembly, see **94 Lights, Accessories–Exterior**
   - Removing:
     Remove wheel housing liner, see **66 Body–Exterior Equipment**
     Remove wheel housing bolts (items 2, 3, and 8)
     Remove nuts (item 6)
     Remove screws (items 4 and 7)
     Disconnect fog light harness connectors
     Using a helper, pull front clip outward slightly on left and right and forward off vehicle
   - Before installing screws on fender, fit a zinc intermediate piece (VW part no. AKL 381 035 50) to each bolt position contact area

NOTE —

Volkswagen part numbers are given for reference only. Always consult with your Volkswagen Parts Department or aftermarket parts specialist for the latest parts information.

2. **Bolt**
   - With nut
   - Tighten to 6 Nm (53 in-lb)

(continued from previous page)

3. **Combi bolt**
   - Tighten to 6 Nm (53 in-lb)
4. **Screw**
   - Qty. 18
   - Tighten to 6 Nm (53 in-lb)
   - Install with locking compound
5. **Foam cushion**
   - When installing the front clip, ensure the foam cushion is installed as shown on both sides
6. **Hex nut**
   - Tighten to Nm (53 in-lb)
7. **Screw**
   - Tighten to 7.5 Nm (66 in-lb)
   - Qty. 7
   - Install with locking compound
8. **Bolt**
   - With nut
   - Tighten to 6 Nm (53 in-lb)

Front fender assembly

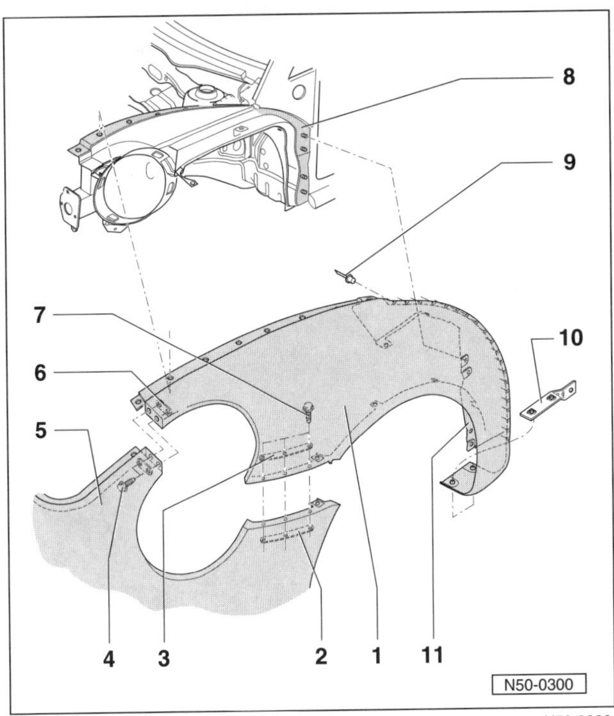

N50-0300

Fig. 2. Front fender and related components.

1. **Fender**
   - Remove with front clip as complete assembly
   - Before installing screws on fender, fit a zinc intermediate piece (VW part no. AKL 381 035 50) to each bolt position contact area
2. **Backing piece**
   - With weld nuts
3. **Reinforcement**
   - With holes
4. **Bolts**
   - Tighten to 4.5 ± 0.5 Nm (39 ± 4.5 in-lb)
5. **Front bumper cover**
6. **Reinforcement**
   - With weld nuts
7. **Bolts**
   - Tighten to 4.5 ± 0.5 Nm (39 ± 4.5 in-lb)
8. **Abrasion protection**
   - Check condition, replace if necessary
9. **Pop rivet**
   - Qty. 19
10. **Bracket**
    - Bolted to front of floor pan member
11. **Close out panel**
    - Riveted to fender

Lock carrier, removing and installing

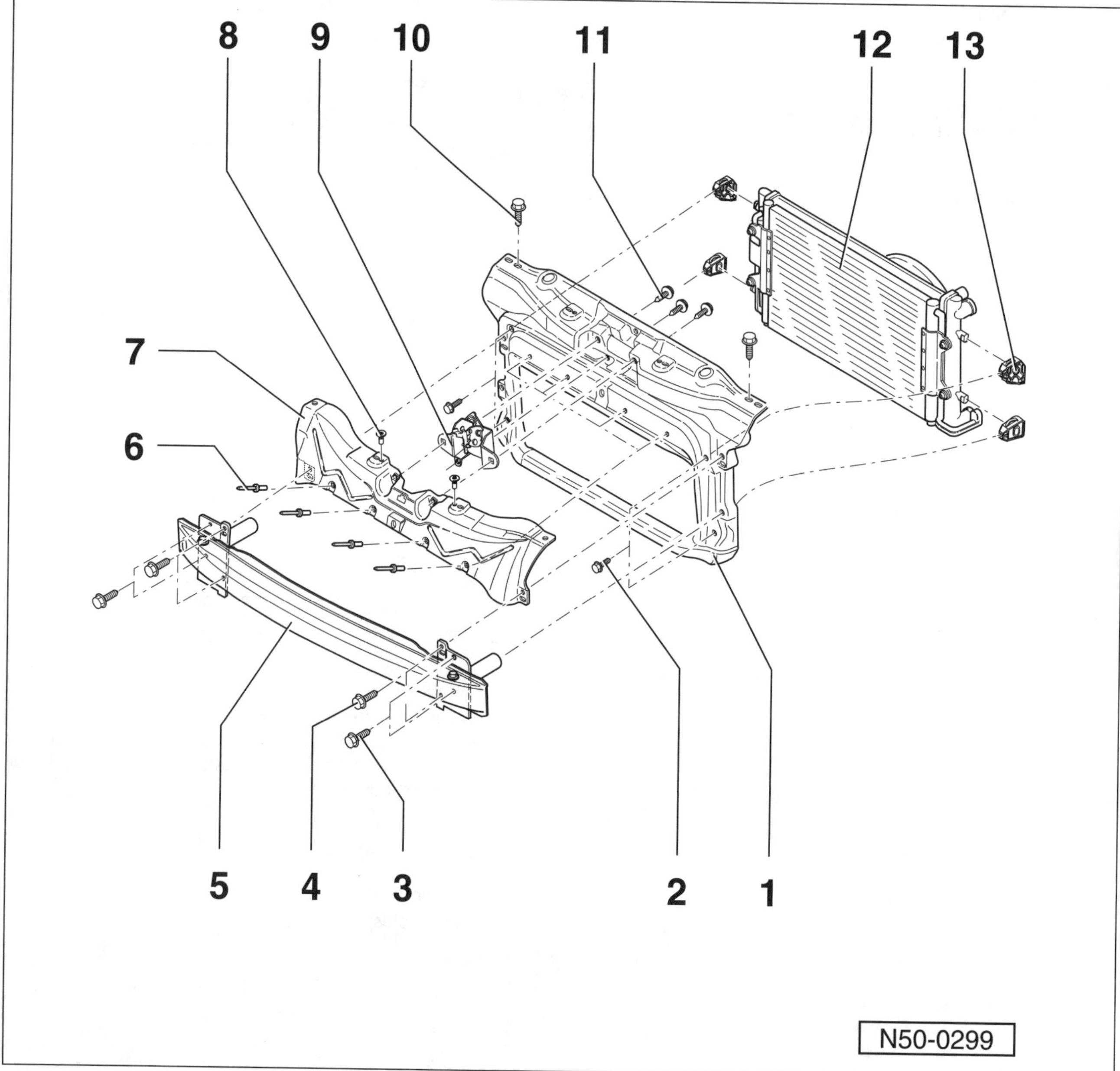

N50-0299

Fig. 3. Front lock carrier (radiator support) and related components.

1. **Lock carrier with attachments**
   - Removing:
     Remove front clip
     Disconnect bowden cable and harness connectors on lock
     Remove bolts (items 3 and 4) and bumper support (item 5)
     Unbolt radiator and condenser from lock carrier and secure in engine compartment
     Remove bolts (item 10)
     Remove lock carrier with connecting panel and hood lock
   - Align lock carrier to floor pan members when installing

2. **Bolt**
   - Qty. 4
   - Tighten to 6 Nm (53 in-lb)
   - For radiator support

3. **Bolt**
   - Qty. 4
   - Tighten to 30 Nm (22 ft-lb)

4. **Bolt**
   - Qty. 4
   - Tighten to 9 Nm (80 in-lb)

(continued from previous page)

5. **Bumper carrier**
   - With impact absorber
6. **Pop rivet**
   - Qty. 4
7. **Connecting panel**
   - Fastened to lock carrier with blind rivets
8. **Blind rivet nut**
   - Qty. 2
9. **Hood lock**
   - Removing and installing, see **55 Hood and Lids**
10. **Bolt**
    - Tighten to 20 Nm (15 ft-lb)
11. **Bolt (self-locking)**
    - Tighten to 12 Nm (9 ft-lb)
    - When reusing: clean bolt threads with a wire brush and nut threads with thread chaser; coat bolt with locking fluid (VW part no. D 185 400 A 2)
12. **Radiator and condenser**
13. **Bracket**

Lock carrier, service position

The lock carrier can be moved forward to allow easier access for various service procedures.

1. Remove front clip as described earlier.
2. Remove front bumper, see **63 Bumpers**.
3. Disconnect bowden cable on hood lock.
4. Remove one lock carrier mounting bolt from each floor pan member and install VW special tool 3411 (guide rods), or equivalent. See Fig. 4.

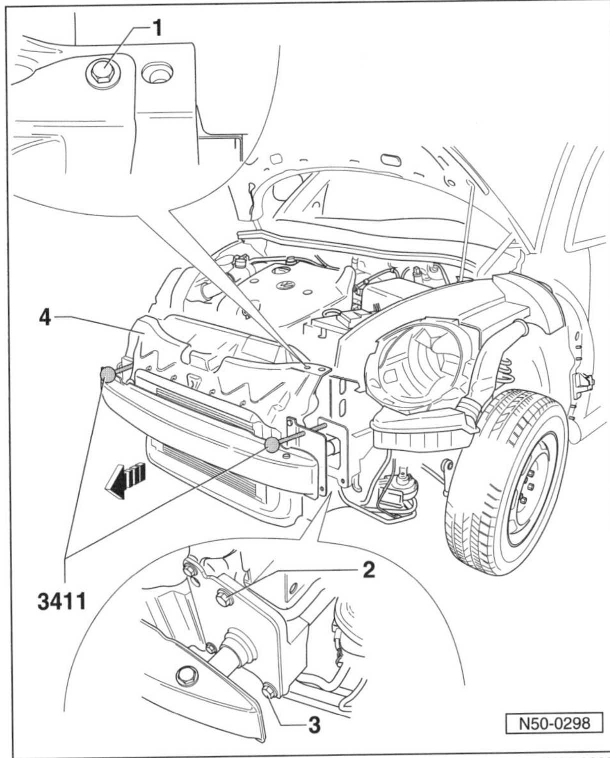

N50-0298

Fig. 4. Remove one mounting bolt (**2**) from each side of lock carrier and install VW special tool 3411. Remove bolts (**1** and **3**) and pull lock carrier forward.

5. Remove remaining lock carrier mounting bolts and pull lock carrier forward.

FRONT NOISE INSULATION

Gasoline and diesel equipped vehicles have different lower sound absorption panels (belly pans) as shown in Fig. 5 and Fig. 6. Fig. 7 shows the plenum close out panel with removal and installation notes.

Noise insulation (gasoline engines)

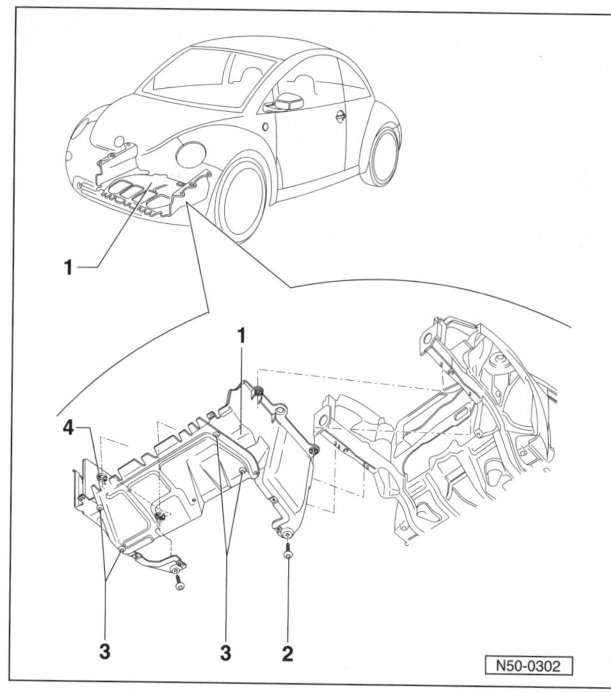

N50-0302

Fig. 5. Noise insulation assembly (**1**) bolted to lock carrier in gasoline equipped vehicles. Mounting hardware also shown (**2**, **3**, and **4**).

Noise insulation (diesel engines)

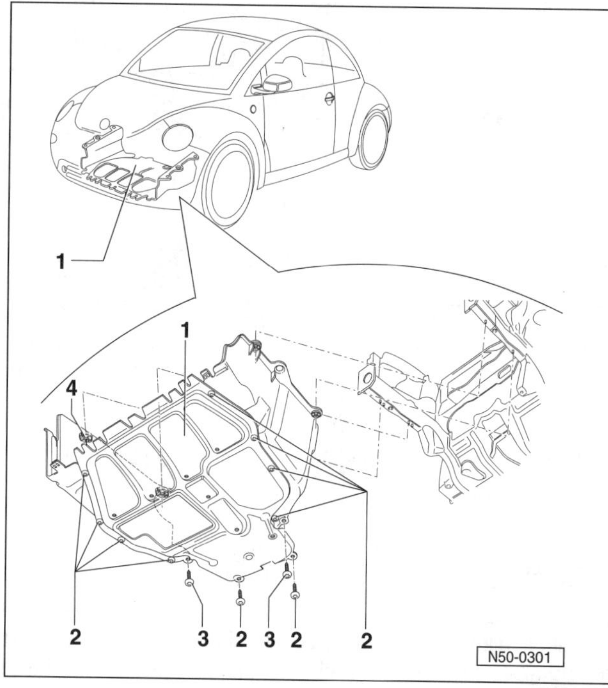

N50-0301

Fig. 6. Noise insulation assembly (**1**) bolted to lock carrier in diesel equipped vehicles. Mounting hardware also shown (**2**, **3**, and **4**).

Plenum close-out panel, removing and installing

1. Remove windshield wiper arms.
2. Remove seal from front edge of close-out panel.
3. Remove plastic plenum cover panel (outer).
4. If necessary, remove engine components from front of close-out panel.
5. Remove mounting bolt and bracket nut, then remove bracket. See Fig. 7.

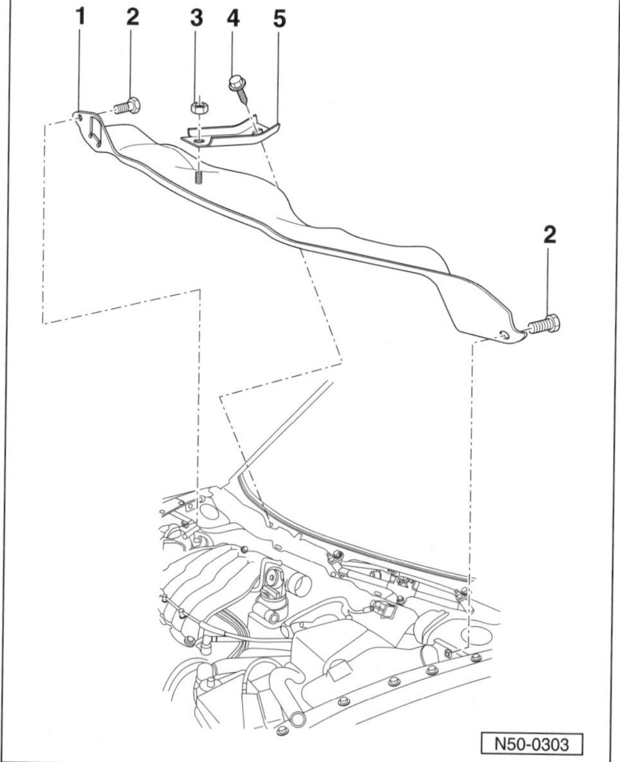

N50-0303

Fig. 7. Remove bolt (**4**), nut (**3**), and bracket (**5**). Then remove bolts (**2**) and close-out panel (**1**).

6. Remove mounting bolts on outer edges of close-out panel and remove panel.
7. Installation is reverse of removal.

53 Body–Rear

GENERAL

The rear clip may be removed as a complete unit. It will be necessary to have a helper when pulling the assembly away from the car.

> ***NOTE —***
> *Use of low-tack tape on rear quarter panels above fender mounting point is recommended to prevent damage to paint.*

REAR FENDER COMPONENTS

Fig. 1 shows an exploded view of the rear fender and related components. The following numbered list with removal and installation notes applies to Fig. 1.

1. **Fender**
   - Removing:
     Remove wheel housing liner, see **66 Body–Exterior Equipment**
     Remove taillight cluster, see **94 Lights, Accessories–Exterior**
     Remove fuel tank door (right only), see **55 Hood and Lids**
     Remove bolts (items 3 and 6)
     Remove bolt (item 2), nut (item 13) and bracket (item 11)
     Take out screws (item 9) and remove fender
   - Before installing screws on fender, fit a zinc intermediate piece (VW part no. AKL 381 035 50) to each bolt position contact area

   > ***NOTE —***
   > *Volkswagen part numbers are given for reference only. Always consult with your Volkswagen Parts Department or aftermarket parts specialist for the latest parts information.*

2. **Bolt**
   - Tighten to 4 ± 0.5 Nm (35 ± 4.5 in-lb)
3. **Bolt**
   - Tighten to 4 ± 0.5 Nm (35 ± 4.5 in-lb)
4. **Reinforcement**
   - With holes
5. **Bumper cover, rear**
   - Removing, see **63 Bumpers**
6. **Bolt**
   - Tighten to 4 ± 0.5 Nm (35 ± 4.5 in-lb)
7. **Reinforcement**
   - With holes
8. **Reinforcement**
   - With welded nuts

(continued on following page)

Rear fender, assembly overview

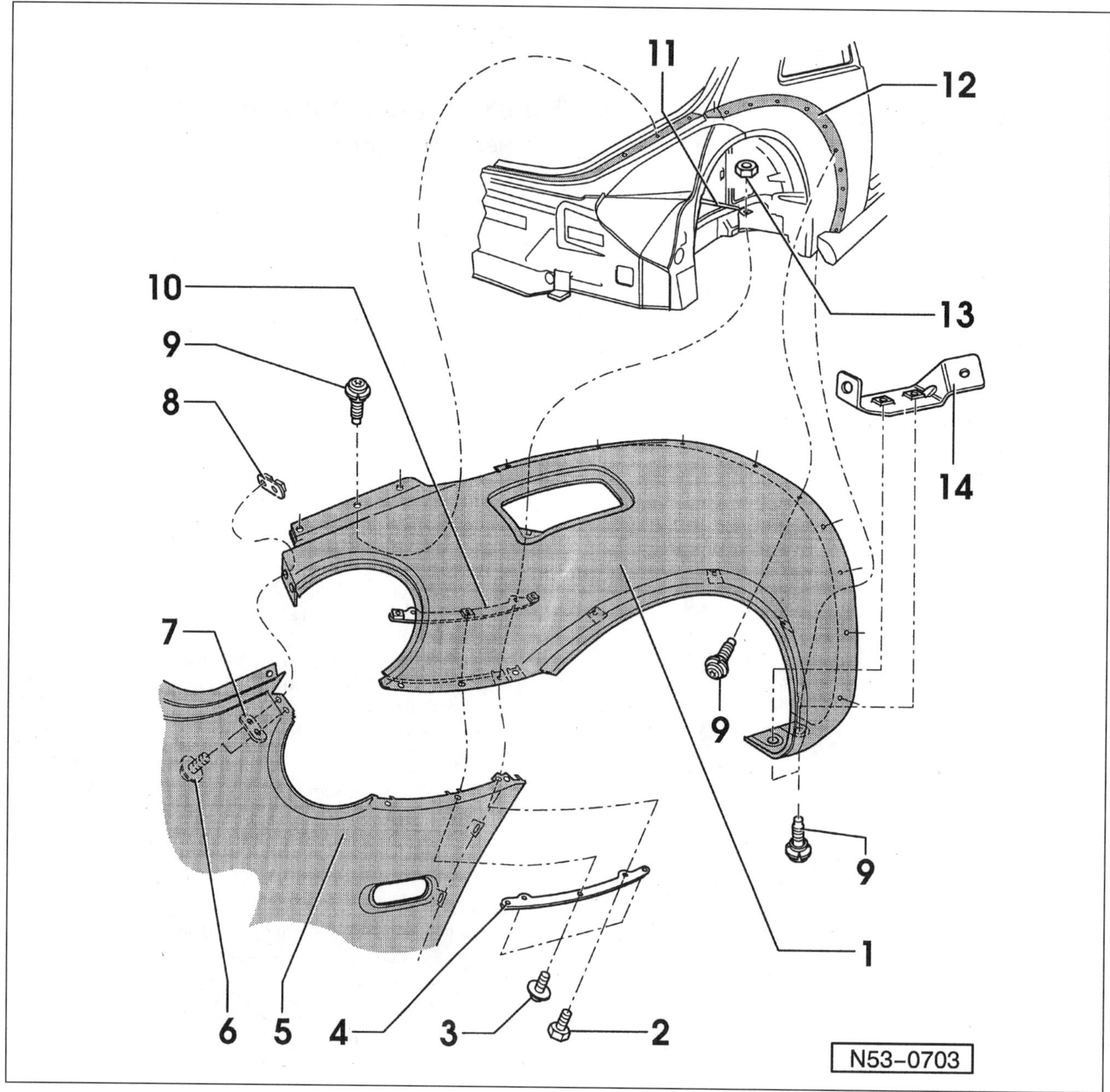

N53-0703

Fig. 1. Rear fender and related hardware.

9. **Screw**
   - Tighten to 6.0 Nm (53 in-lb)
   - Qty. 9
   - Install with locking compound
10. **Reinforcement**
    - With weld nuts
11. **Bracket**
    - Bolted to front of floor pan member
12. **Abrasion protection**
13. **Nut**
14. **Bracket**
    - Bolted to front of floor pan member

55 Hood and Lids

GENERAL

The front hood and rear hatch are easily removed with the aid of a helper. Where applicable, the support strut(s) should first be disconnected. See Fig. 1. Be sure to mark the lid location in reference to the hinges for proper alignment during installation.

0024286

Fig. 1. After prying off strut retaining clip with screwdriver, as shown, remove strut from ball stud.

Front Hood

Hood assembly

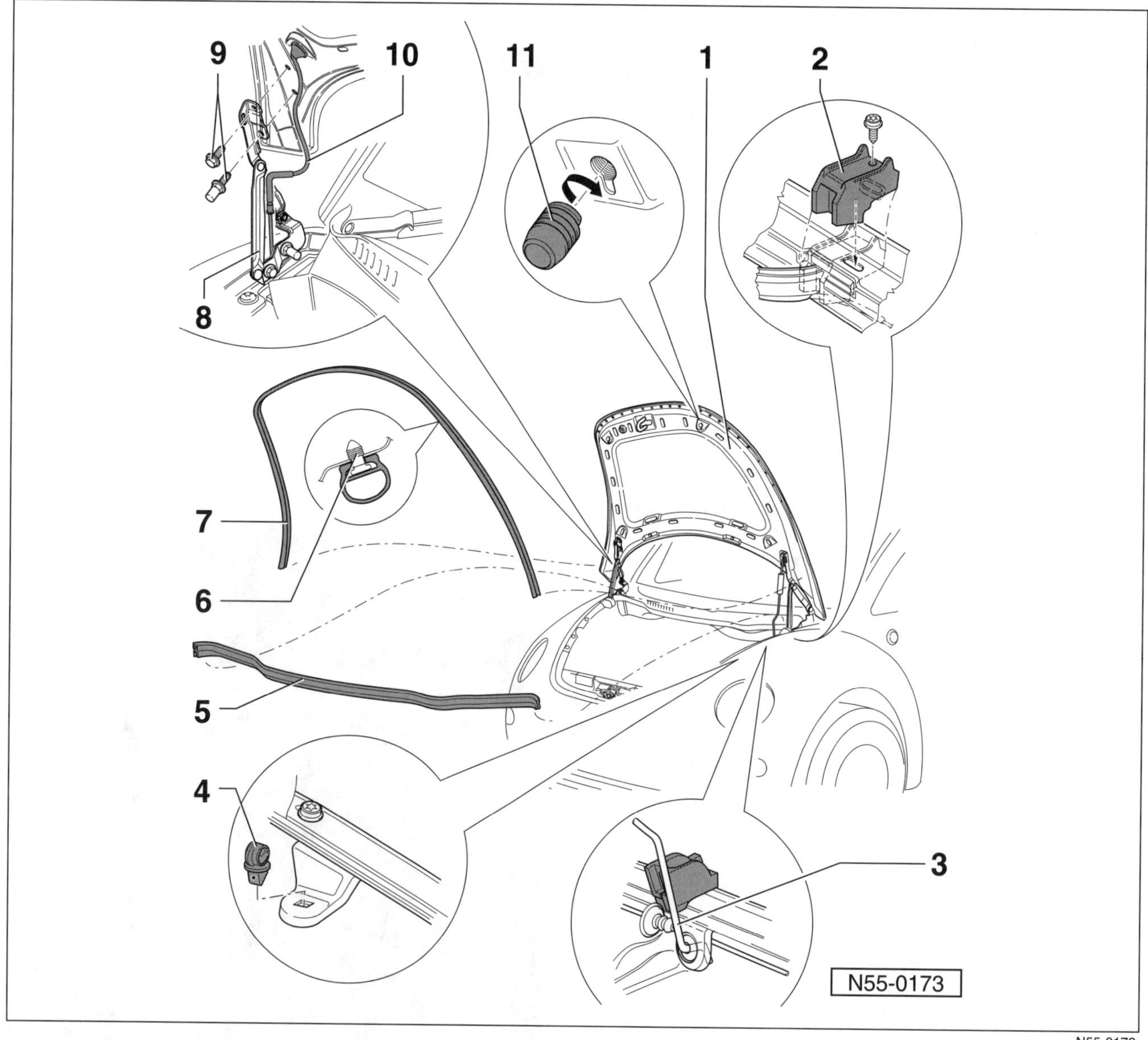

N55-0173

Fig. 2. Front hood assembly.

1. **Hood**
   - Removing:
     Remove windshield washer hoses and jets
     Take out bolts (item 9) and remove hood
2. **Cushion**
3. **Hood support**
4. **Clip**
5. **Plenum seal**
   - Pushed onto flange
6. **Clip**
7. **Seal**
8. **Hinge**
   - Hood can be aligned between fenders by moving hinges within the slotted holes
   - After installation or adjusting, treat hinges and bolts with corrosion protection
9. **Bolt**
   - Tighten to 23 Nm (17 ft-lb)
10. **Hose - windshield washer**
    - Removing, see **92 Wipers and Washers**
11. **Rubber stop**
    - Adjust hood height to fenders using rubber stops

Hood release cable assembly

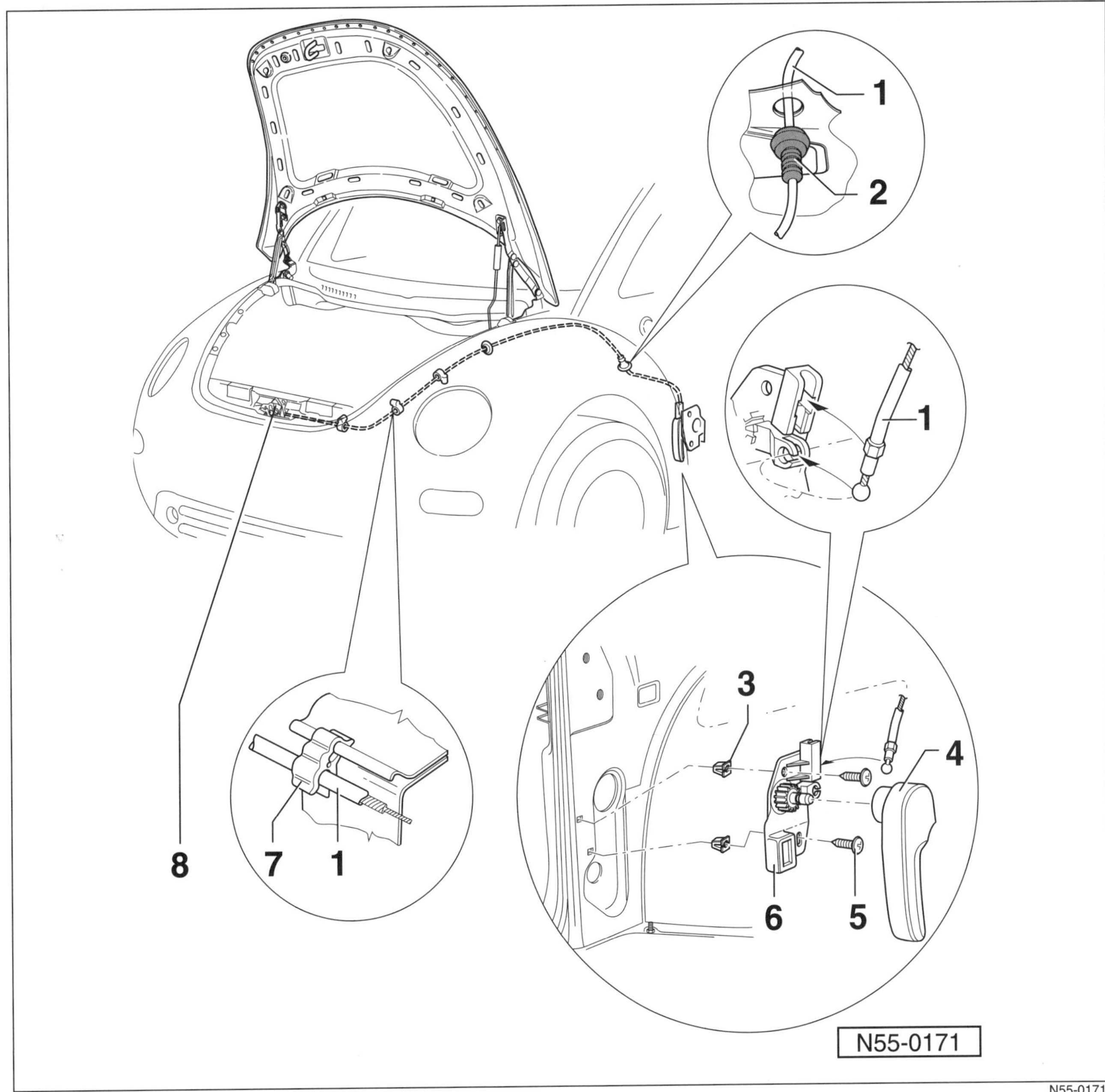

Fig. 3. Hood release cable and related hardware.

1. **Hood release (bowden) cable**
   - Removing:
     Remove release lever (item 4)
     Remove cable from clip at lock (item 8) and engine compartment (item 7)
     Remove lower A-pillar trim, see **70 Trim–Interior**
     Tie string (approx. 39 in.) to cable at hood release and pull cable out at release lever end
   - Use the same string to pull new cable into place
2. **Grommet**
3. **Spreader nut**
4. **Release lever**
   - Removing and installing, see Ⓐ
5. **Self-tapping screw**
6. **Lever bracket**
   - Cable attached
7. **Cable clip**
8. **Hood lock**

Release lever, removing and installing

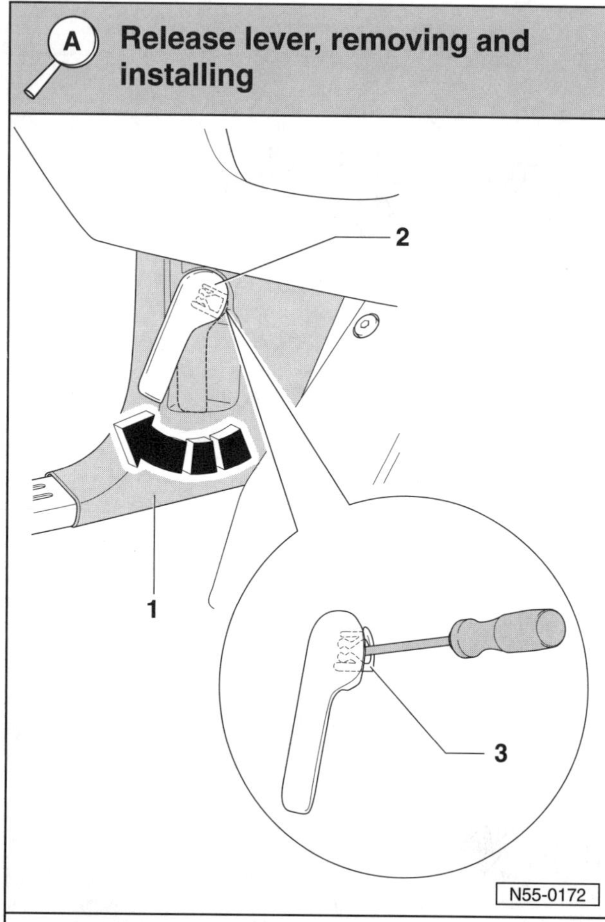

N55-0172

- Pull back release lever (1) approx. 2 cm (0.8 in.)
- Insert small screwdriver into gap between release lever and clip (3)
- Pull release lever again and remove clip from release lever (clip falls behind trim)
- To install, push clip (3) completely into release lever and press release lever onto bracket
- Check operation of release lever

Hood lock assembly

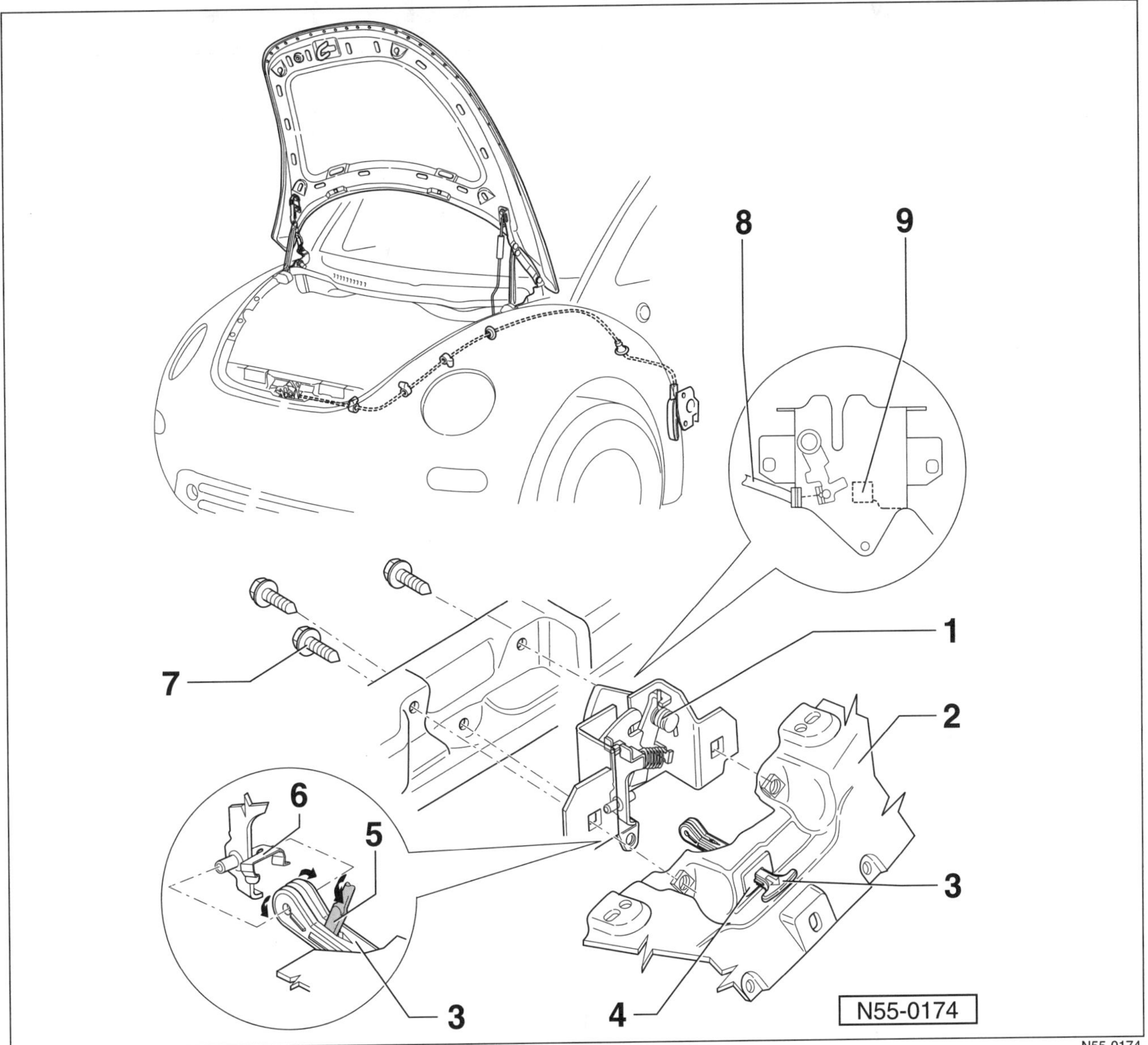

Fig. 4. Hood lock assembly.

1. **Hood lock**
   - Adjust with slotted mounting holes
   - Removing:
     Flip up clip (item 6)
     Press clevis arms of release lever (item 3) apart with a screwdriver (item 5) and remove release lever
     Remove screws (item 7)
     Remove hood release cable (item 8) and separate micro switch connection for anti-theft alarm (item 9), if applicable
2. **Connecting panel**
   - Fastened to lock carrier with blind rivets
3. **Release lever**
4. **Clip**
5. **Screwdriver (assembly aid)**
6. **Clip**
7. **Bolt (self-locking)**
   - Tighten to 12 Nm (9 ft lb)
   - When reusing: clean bolt threads with a wire brush and nut threads with thread cleaning tap; coat bolt with locking fluid (VW part no. D185 400 A2, or equivalent)
8. **Bowden cable**
9. **Micro switch**

REAR LIDS

Rear hatch assembly

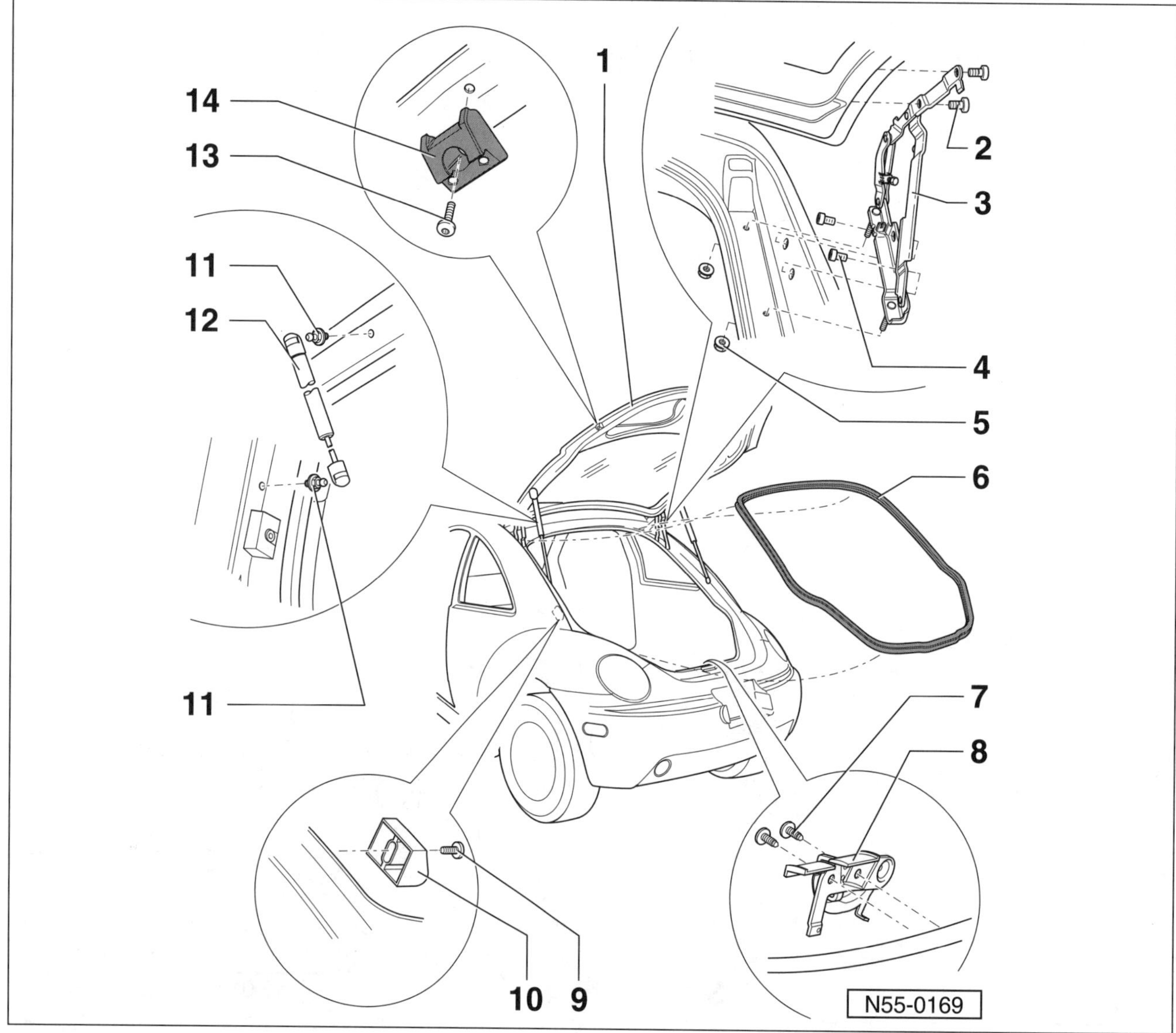

N55-0169

Fig. 5. Rear hatch and related hardware.

1. **Rear hatch**
2. **Bolt**
   - Tighten to 20 Nm (15 ft-lb)
3. **Hinge**
4. **Bolt**
   - Tighten to 8 Nm (71 in-lb)
5. **Nut**
   - Tighten to 8 Nm (71 in-lb)
6. **Gasket**
7. **Bolt**
   - Tighten to 23 Nm (17 ft-lb)
8. **Lock plate**
   - Adjusting - within oversized holes
9. **Bolt**
   - Tighten to 10 Nm (89 in-lb)
10. **Adjustment buffer**
11. **Ball stud**
    - Tighten to 21 Nm (15 ft-lb)
12. **Gas-filled strut**
    - Removing and installing, see Fig. 1.
13. **Bolt**
    - Tighten to 10 Nm (89 in-lb)
14. **Rubber cushion**

Rear hatch, adjusting

1. Install hinge without rear hatch.
   - When hinge is in closed position, set screw must just touch contact stop without pressure. See Fig. 6.

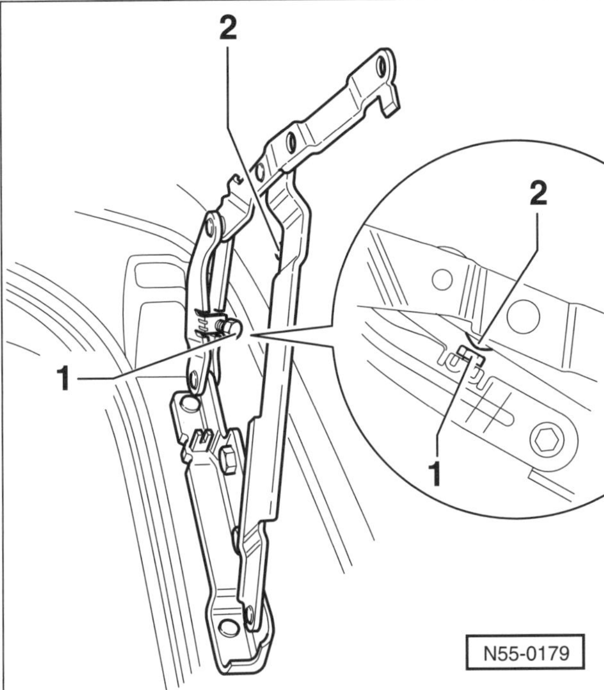

N55-0179

Fig. 6. With hinge in closed position, set screw (**1**) must just touch contact stop (**2**).

2. Turn hinge set screw on both sides 1.5 - 3 mm (0.05 - 0.15 in.) to pre-tension hinge.
3. Install rear hatch.
4. Install rubber grommet on both sides of rear hatch.
5. Install adjustment buffer in channel loosely, to aid adjustment. See Fig. 7.
6. Slide buffer up to top position.
7. Close rear hatch completely and open again.

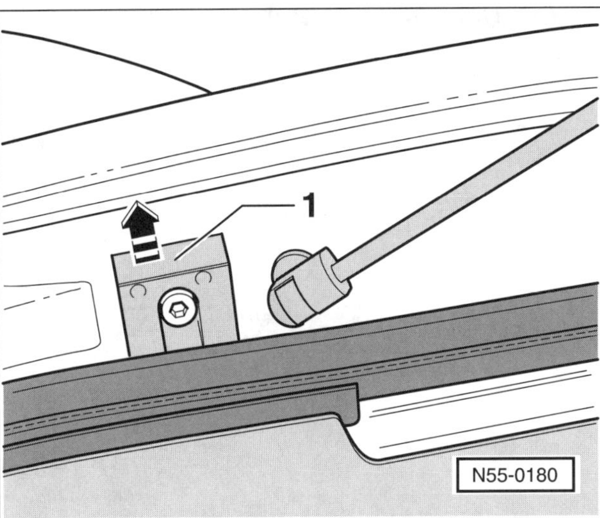

N55-0180

Fig. 7. Install adjustment buffer (**1**) loosely to allow for adjustment. Move buffer to top position (**arrow**), close and open rear hatch.

8. Slide adjustment buffer up 1 to 2 mm. See Fig. 8.

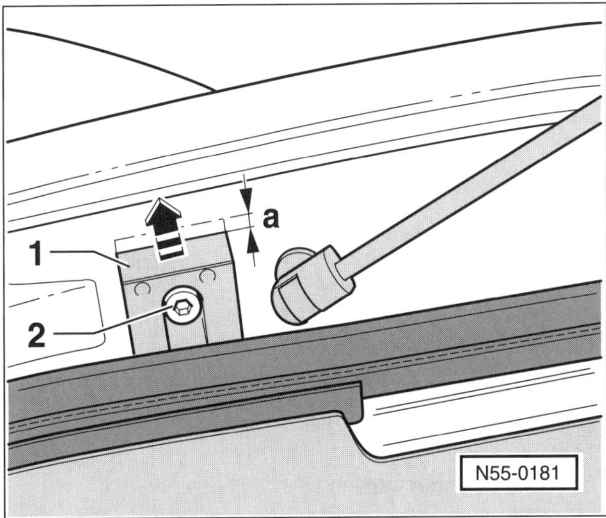

N55-0181

Fig. 8. Move adjustment buffer (**1**) up 1 to 2 mm (dimension **a**). Tighten bolt (**2**) and check that rear hatch closes properly.

9. Check that rear hatch closes without too much force and doesn't have any up or down movement when in locked position. When unlocking, the lid will pop up slightly due to pre-tension on hinge.

Tightening torque
- Rear hatch adjustment buffer . . . . 10 Nm (89 in-lb)

Rear hatch lock assembly

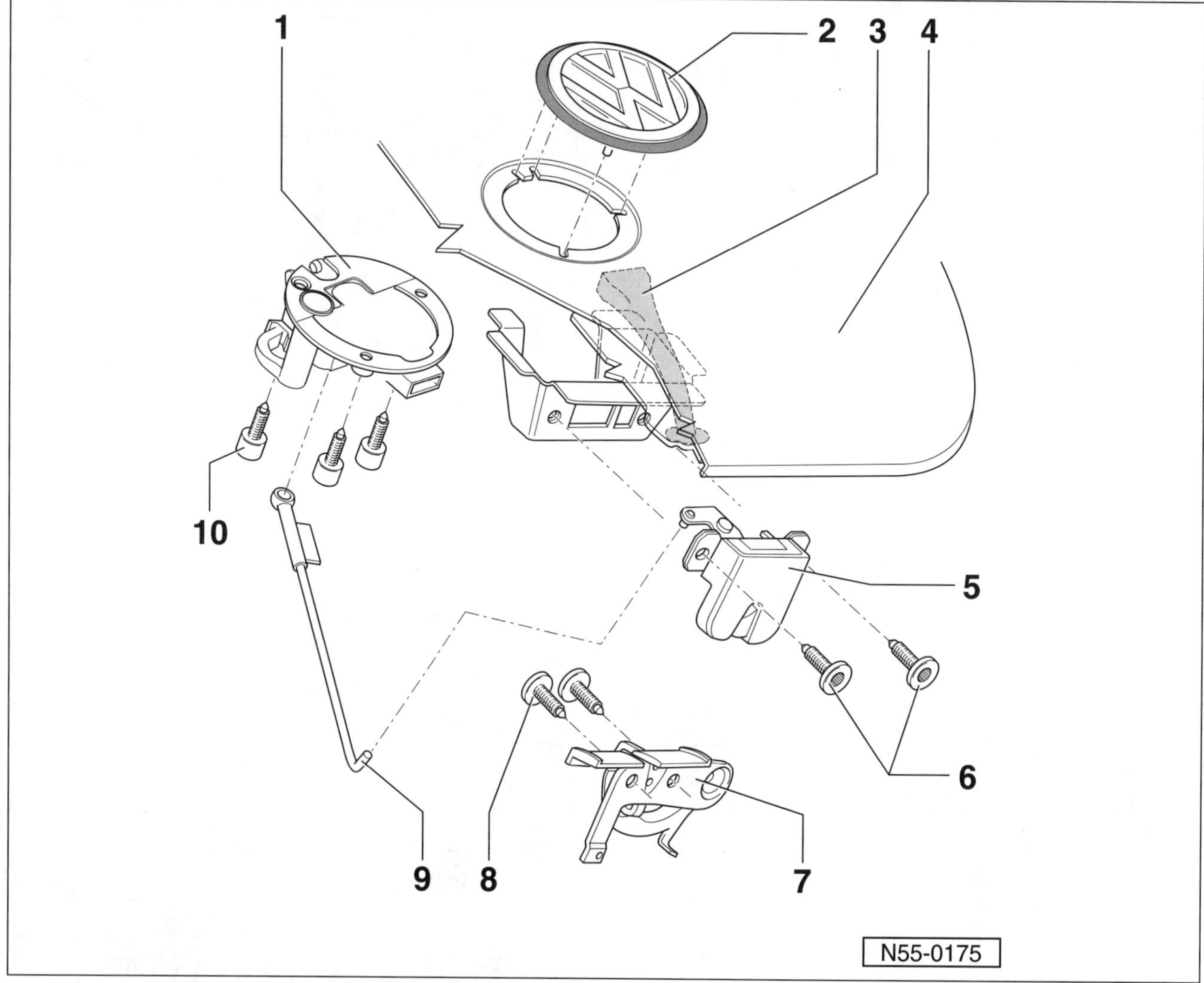

N55-0175

Fig. 9. Rear hatch lock and related components.

1. **Lock cylinder carrier**
   - The lock cylinder can only be removed with the carrier
2. **VW emblem**
   - Assemble with carrier
   - Remove with lock cylinder carrier
3. **Water drain channel (rubber)**
   - Fasten to carrier with tie wrap

> ***CAUTION —***
> *Ensure the rubber drain channel is routed correctly, otherwise water will drain into lock and trunk.*

4. **Rear hatch**
5. **Lock**
   - Removing:
     Remove rear hatch trim, see **70 Trim–Interior**
     Disconnect connector on lock
     Unclip operating rod and remove lock from rear hatch
6. **Bolt**
   - Tighten to 23 Nm (17 ft-lb)
7. **Lock plate**
   - Adjust - within slotted holes
   - Removing:
     Remove lock carrier trim, see **70 Trim–Interior**
     Remove bolts (item 8)
8. **Bolt**
   - Tighten to 23 Nm (17 ft-lb)
9. **Operating rod**
10. **Bolt**
    - Tighten to 6 Nm (53 in-lb)

Rear lock cylinder carrier (power), removing and installing

1. Remove rear hatch trim, see **70 Trim–Interior**.
2. Unplug harness connectors and release from any retaining clips.
3. Unclip operating rod for lock carrier. See Fig. 10.

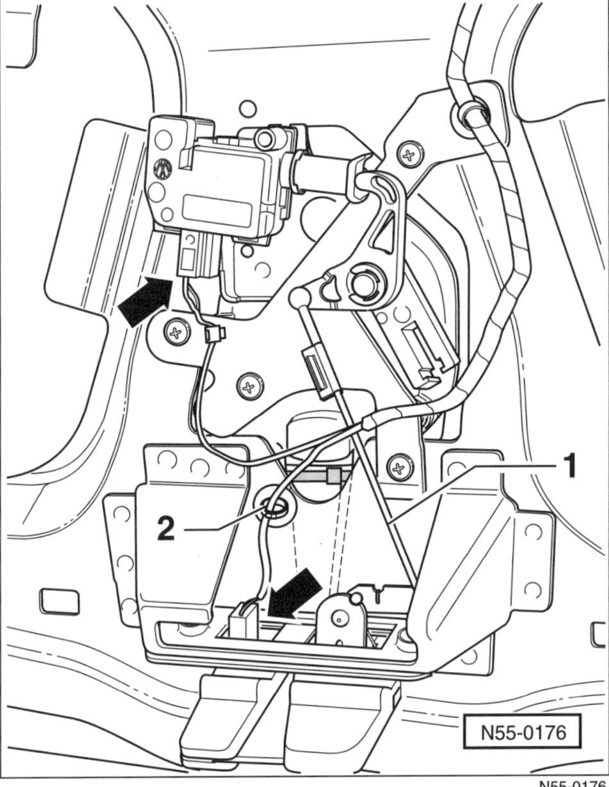

N55-0176

Fig. 10. Unplug harness connectors (**arrows**) and release from retaining clip (**2**). Unclip operating rod (**1**).

4. Remove mounting screws and electrical wire support panel. See Fig. 11.
5. Remove lock carrier mounting bolts and cut tie wrap on water drain channel. See Fig. 12.
6. Pull lock cylinder carrier off rear hatch and then away from outer hand grip.
7. Assembly is the reverse of removal, noting the following:
   - Replace tie wrap for water drain channel and clips to fasten wire harness.

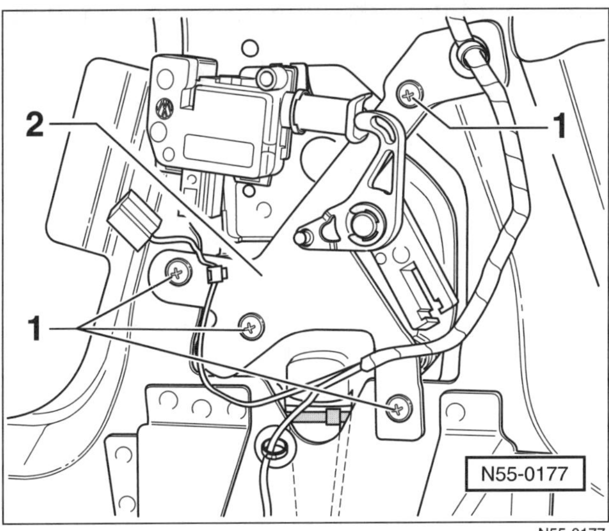

N55-0177

Fig. 11. Remove mounting screws (**1**) and electrical wire support panel (**2**).

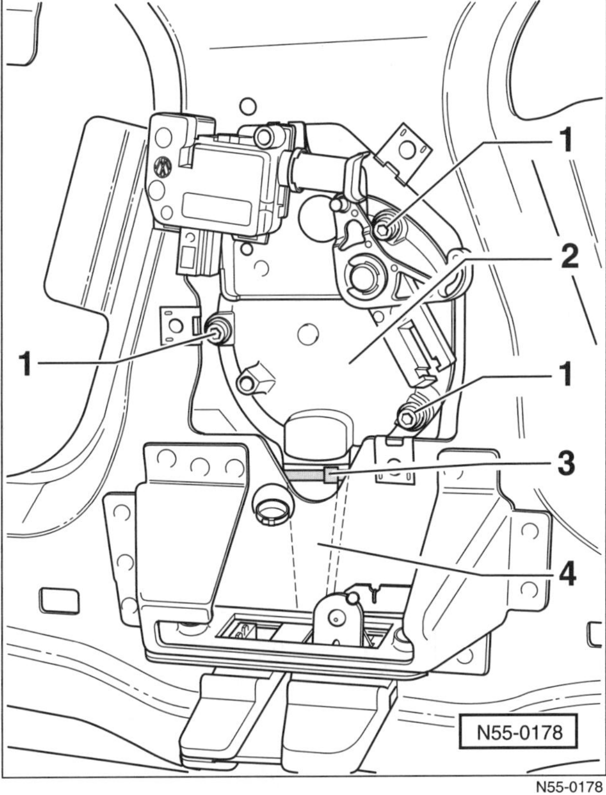

N55-0178

Fig. 12. Remove mounting bolts (**1**), cut tie wrap (**3**) and remove lock carrier (**2**).

Fuel tank filler lid, removing and installing

1. Remove right tail light, see **94 Lights, Accessories–Exterior**.

2. Remove filler cap.

3. Pull retaining ring (behind the sealing lip) out of rubber cup. Remove mounting screw in lower corner of fuel fill shroud. See Fig. 13.

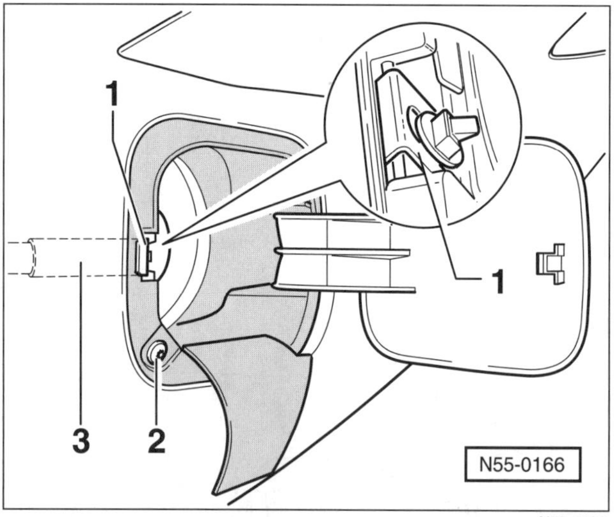

N55-0166

Fig. 13. Pull retaining ring (**1**) out of rubber cup (**3**) and remove screw (**2**).

4. Lift fuel tank filler lid and remove from rear. See Fig. 14.

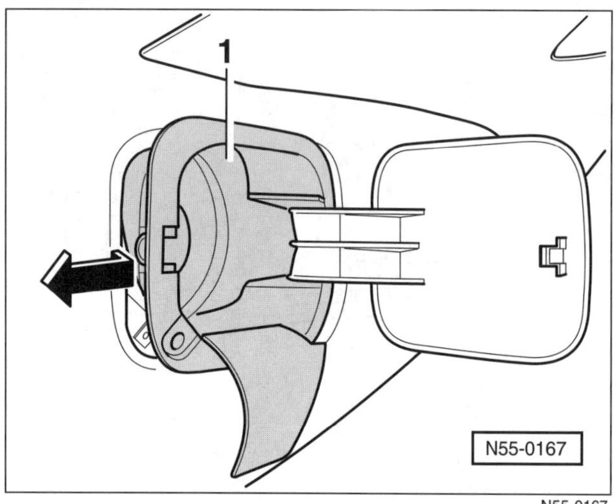

N55-0167

Fig. 14. Lift fuel tank filler lid with shroud (**1**) and remove from the back (**arrow**).

5. Install fuel tank filler lid in reverse order of removal.

Fuel fill lid actuator, removing and installing

> ***NOTE —***
> *The actuator for the fuel fill lid release is located on a bracket on the right wheel housing.*

1. Remove luggage compartment trim on right side, see **70 Trim–Interior**.

2. Remove harness connector from fuel door actuator motor.

3. Disconnect release cable at retaining bracket. See Fig. 15.

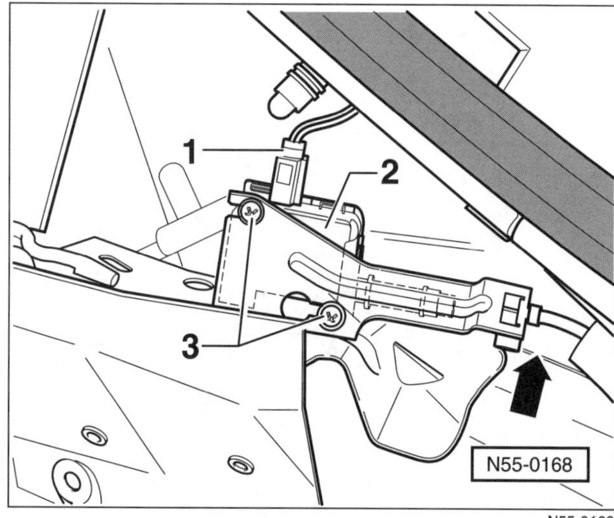

N55-0168

Fig. 15. Remove harness connector (**1**), release cable from bracket (**arrow**), mounting screws (**3**) and motor (**2**).

4. Remove actuator mounting screws, remove motor from bracket and disconnect cable at motor.

5. Installation is reverse of removal.

6. Check for proper operation of fuel fill lid actuator.

57 Doors

GENERAL

This repair group covers removal and installation of the door assemblies, the door glass and window regulators, and service to the door lock assemblies including the central locking system. Special tools and equipment are required for some operations. For removal of door panels see **70 Trim–Interior**.

> ***WARNING —***
> *Disconnecting the negative (–) battery cable may erase fault codes and basic settings in the engine management and automatic transmission control modules. Some driveability problems may be noticed until the system re-adapts to operating conditions. OBD II readiness codes, which may be required for emissions testing, may also be erased. Convenience electronics (alarm system, interior light control, power locks, mirrors, and windows) may need to be re-set using a VAG 1551/1552 or equivalent scan tool.*

Power windows

Models equipped with power windows feature the ability to raise and lower both front windows by using the key in the front door lock. By holding the key in the locked position for more than 1 second, either window that was in the down position will be raised to the closed position in addition to locking the vehicle. This feature is known as convenience close.

As a ventilation aid in hot weather, both front windows can be lowered. By holding the key in the unlock position for more than 2 seconds, both front windows will be lowered at the same time in addition to unlocking the vehicle.

Power windows also feature pinch protection and one-touch up and one-touch down operation. The power windows will remain functional for approximately 10 minutes after the ignition is shut off provided that a door is not opened. The one-touch up feature is deactivated when the ignition is switched off.

Central locking

All models are equipped with central locking that is activated by insertion of the key into an outside door, by activation of a locking switch from within, or by the keyless remote.

When opening a locked vehicle from the outside with the key, there are two options. If the key is turned once, only that particular door will unlock. If the key is quickly turned twice, both doors will be unlocked. This safety feature is known as selective unlocking.

DOORS

The doors of the New Beetle are designed with a split hinge. The hinge pin is locked by a grub screw that allows the hinge to slide apart once removed. After disconnecting the appropriate electrical connectors and the door check, the complete door can be easily removed from the vehicle as required. For an overview of the door hinges, latches and related components, see Fig. 1. Most of the internal components of the doors including the window regulators and window glass are assembled into a modular assembly known as a door assembly carrier. For an overview of the window glass and related components see Fig. 30.

Door, assembly

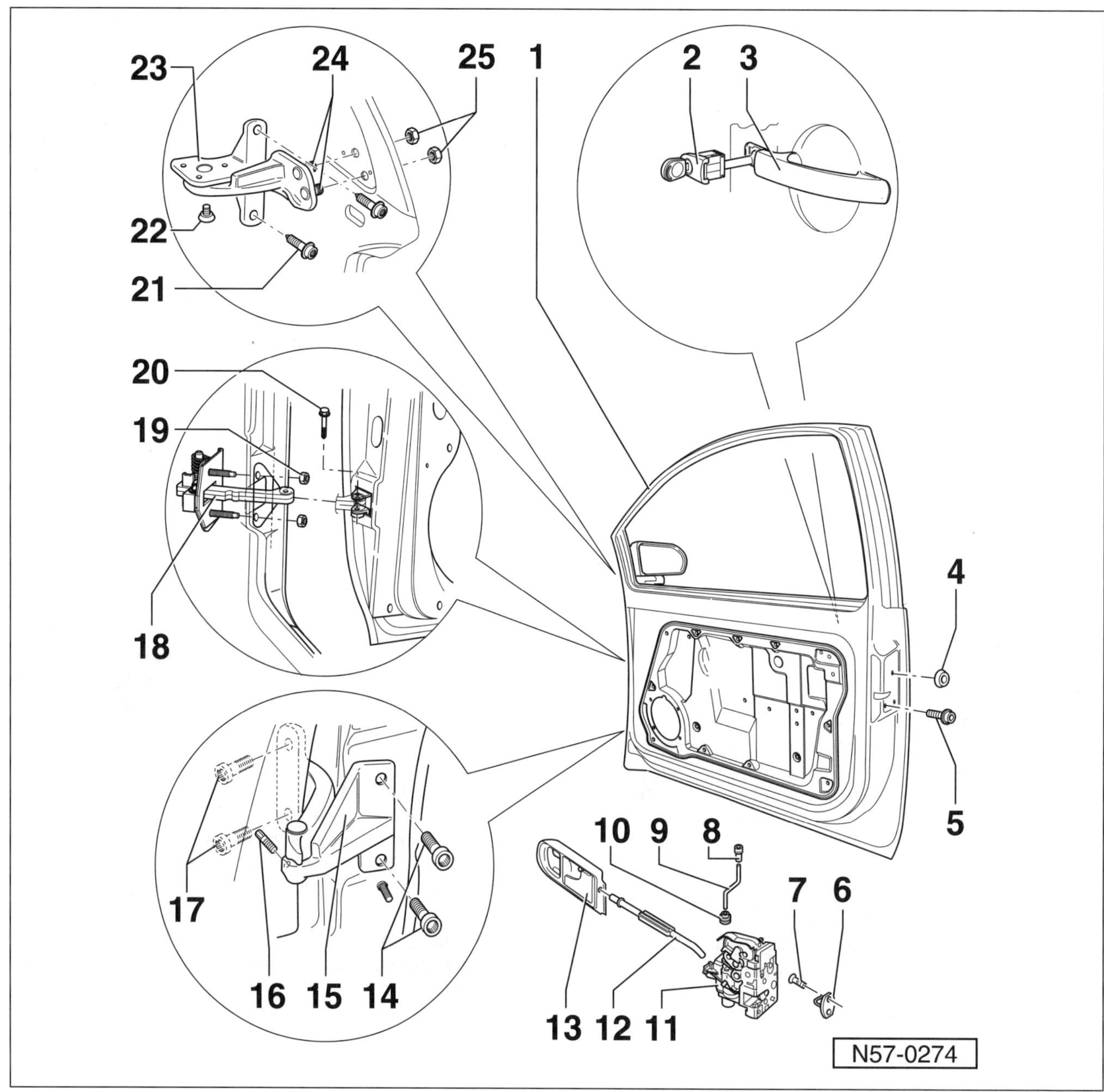

N57-0274

Fig. 1. Door hinges, latches and related components shown for the right side. Left side is similar.

1. **Door assembly**
2. **Lock cylinder housing**
3. **Door handle**
4. **Sealing plug**
5. **Bolt**
   - Tighten to 20 Nm (15 ft-lb)
   - Install with locking compound
6. **Striker plate**
7. **Bolt**
   - Tighten to 20 Nm (15 ft-lb)
8. **Locking button**
9. **Locking rod**
10. **Rubber boot**
11. **Door lock assembly**
12. **Interior release cable**

(continued from previous page)

13. Interior release handle

14. Lower hinge bolt, body side
- Tighten to 20 Nm (15 ft-lb) + ¼ turn (90°)
- Always replace bolt after loosening

15. Lower door hinge
- Split design allows door removal
- Always replace bolts after loosening

16. Grub screw
- Secures split hinge sections
- Concealed under plastic cap
- Tighten to 13 Nm (10 ft-lb)

17. Lower hinge bolt, door side
- Tighten to 20 Nm (15 ft-lb) + ¼ turn (90°)
- Always replace bolts after loosening

18. Door check assembly

19. Nut
- Tighten to 9 Nm (80 in-lb)

20. Pin
- Tighten 4.5 Nm (39 in-lb)

21. Upper hinge bolt, body side
- Tighten to 20 Nm (15 ft-lb) + ¼ turn (90°)
- Always replace bolts after loosening

22. Bolt
- Tighten to 27 Nm (20 ft-lb)

23. Upper door hinge
- Split design allows door removal
- Always replace bolts after loosening

24. Upper hinge bolt, door side
- Always replace bolt after loosening

25. Nut
- Tighten to 20 Nm (15 ft-lb) + ¼ turn (90°)
- Always replace bolt after loosening

Door, removing and installing

1. Remove screws from mirror hinge cover and swing hinge cover out from rear to remove. See Fig. 2.

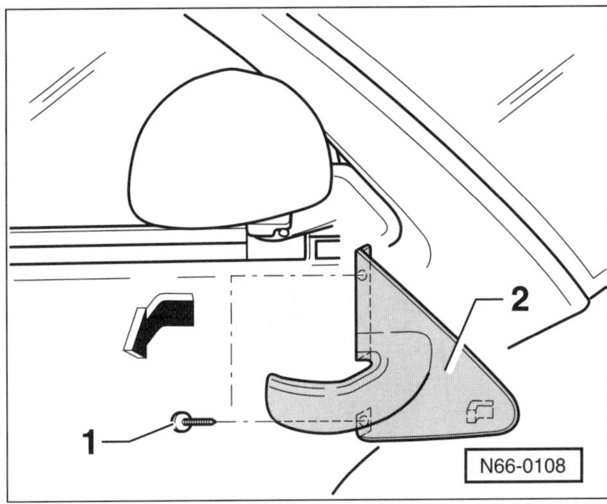

Fig. 2. Mirror hinge cover (**2**) and attaching screws (**1**). Pull rear of cover out (**arrow**) to remove.

2. Remove hood release lever, left side, as required, see **55 Hoods and Lids**.

3. Remove lower A-pillar trim, see **70 Body–Interior Trim.**

4. Disconnect multi-pin harness connectors and harness cover on lower A-pillar. See Fig. 3.

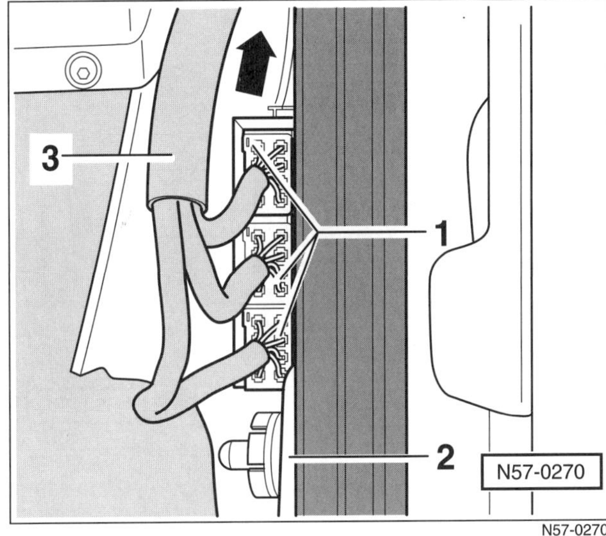

Fig. 3. Lower A-pillar shown with trim removed. Disconnect connectors (**1**) and (**2**) and remove cover (**3**).

5. Remove wiring harness boot at A-pillar and carefully work wiring harness connectors through opening. See Fig. 4.

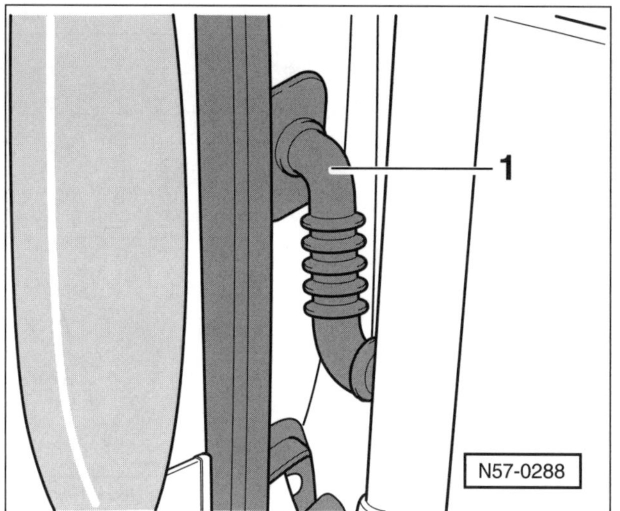

N57-0288

Fig. 4. Remove wiring harness boot (**1**) at A-pillar and pull harness connectors through opening.

> **CAUTION—**
> *Do not close door with harness connectors between door and A-pillar. They will be crushed.*

6. Remove pin from door check. See Fig. 5.

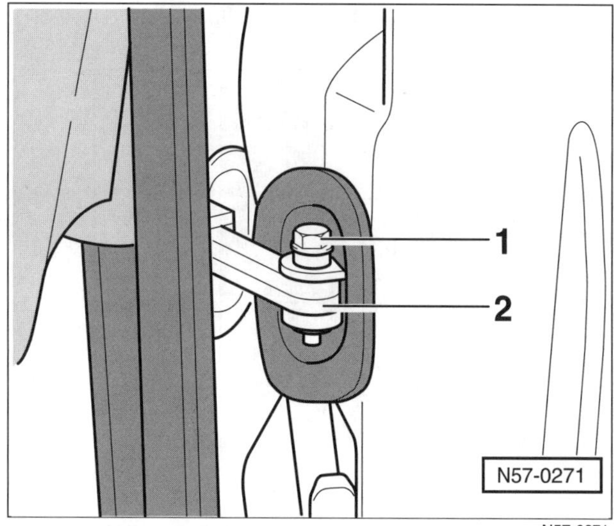

N57-0271

Fig. 5. Remove pin (**1**) from door check (**2**).

7. Apply textile reinforced adhesive tape (duct tape or equivalent) to fender to prevent paint damage at lower hinge area during removal. See Fig. 6.

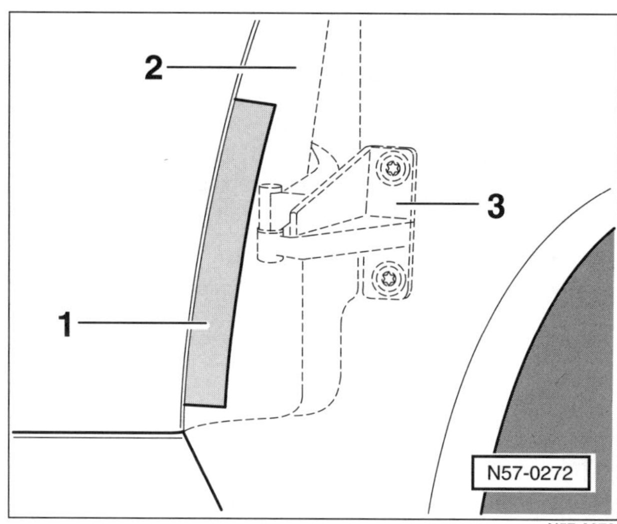

N57-0272

Fig. 6. Layer of duct tape (**1**) applied to fender (**2**) in area of lower hinge (**3**) will minimize risk of paint damage when door is removed.

8. Remove plastic cap from grub screw at lower hinge and remove grub screw. See Fig. 7.

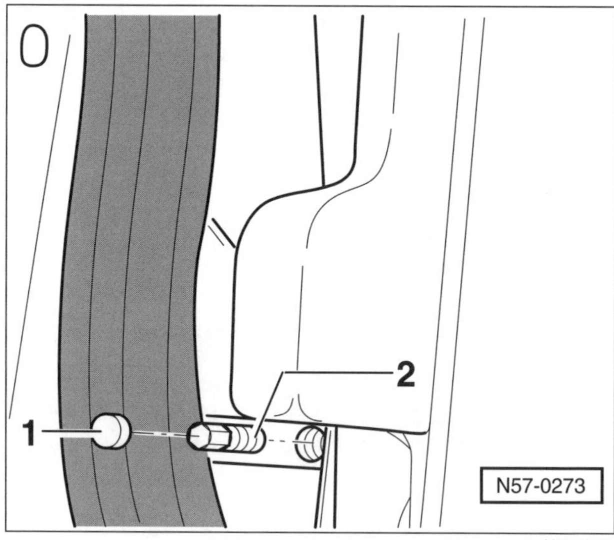

N57-0273

Fig. 7. Plastic cap (**1**) and grub screw (**2**) on lower hinge.

9. Remove grub screw from upper hinge. See Fig. 8.

10. Carefully lift door upward and out of hinge brackets.

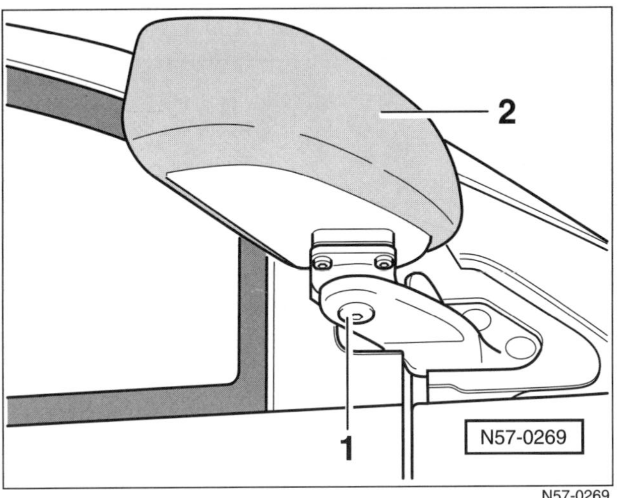

N57-0269

Fig. 8. Grub screw (**1**) on upper hinge. Mirror assembly (**2**) stays on the door.

NOTE —
To prevent damage, it is advisable to have a helper guide the door off the hinges while it is being lifted.

11. Place removed door on suitable padding to protect paint from damage. If stored vertically, also protect the lower edges.

12. Installation is the reverse of removal.

Tightening torques
- Lower grub screw . . . . 15 Nm (11 ft-lb)
- Upper grub screw . . . . 27 Nm (20 ft-lb)
- Door check pin . . . . 4.5 Nm (39 in-lb)

Door, adjusting

To correct door adjustment, loosen hinges. Attempting to correct door adjustment by measures such as raising the door upward without loosening the hinges generally have no effect and only distort the door and/or the A-pillar making further adjustment impossible. For door hinge details, see Fig. 9 and Fig. 10.

Door hinge, upper, assembly

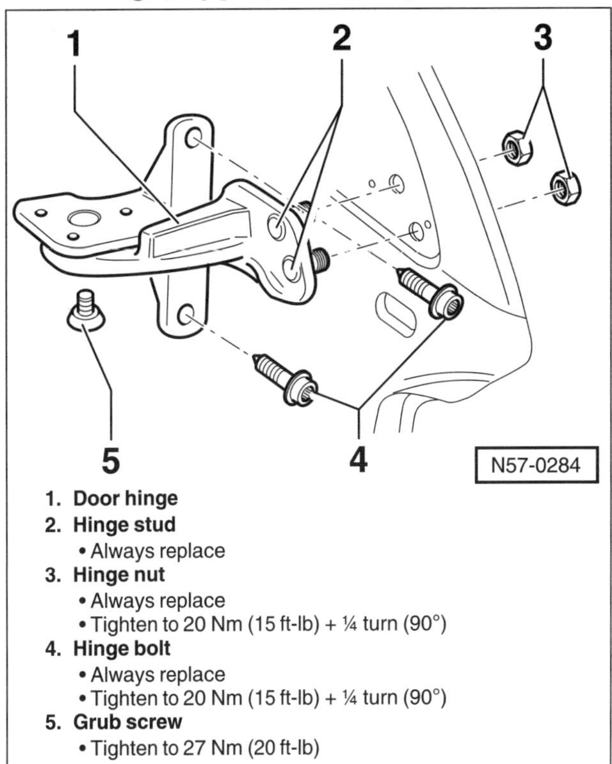

1. **Door hinge**
2. **Hinge stud**
   - Always replace
3. **Hinge nut**
   - Always replace
   - Tighten to 20 Nm (15 ft-lb) + ¼ turn (90°)
4. **Hinge bolt**
   - Always replace
   - Tighten to 20 Nm (15 ft-lb) + ¼ turn (90°)
5. **Grub screw**
   - Tighten to 27 Nm (20 ft-lb)

N57-0284

Fig. 9. Upper door hinge details.

Door hinge, lower, assembly

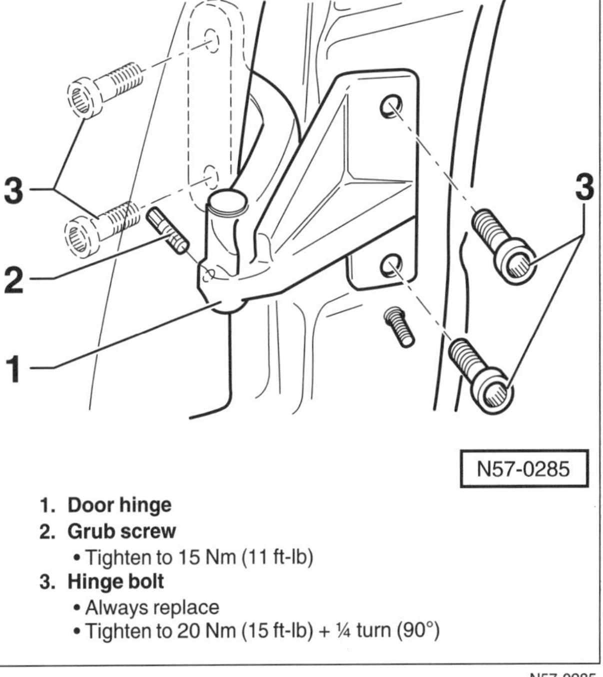

1. **Door hinge**
2. **Grub screw**
   - Tighten to 15 Nm (11 ft-lb)
3. **Hinge bolt**
   - Always replace
   - Tighten to 20 Nm (15 ft-lb) + ¼ turn (90°)

N57-0285

Fig. 10. Lower door hinge details.

Door handle and lock, assembly

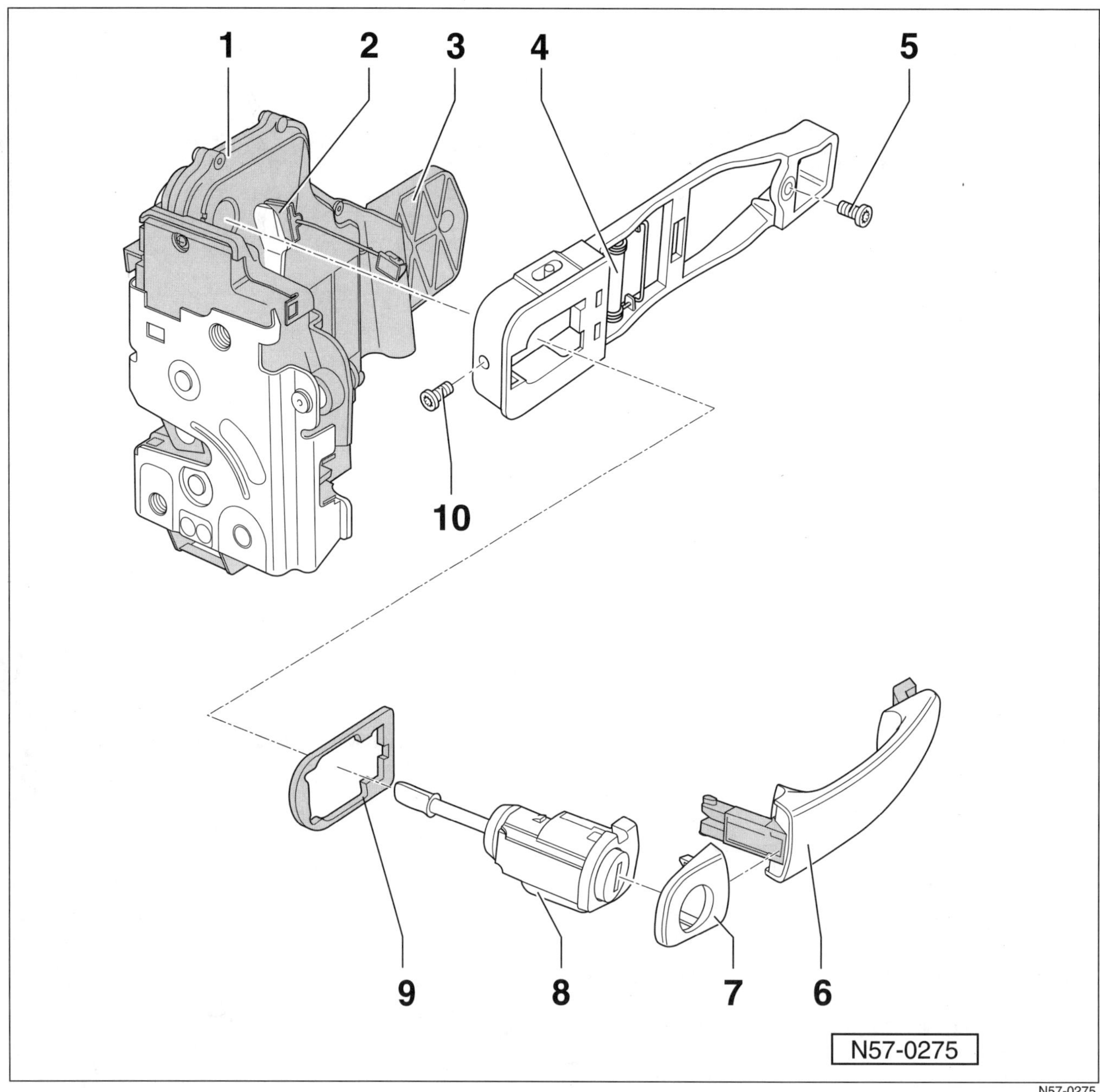

N57-0275

Fig. 11. Right side door lock, outside door handle and related components. Left side is similar.

1. **Door lock**
   - The door lock can only be removed with the carrier assembly
2. **Cable**
   - Outside door handle release
3. **Retaining bracket**
   - Bolted and riveted to carrier assembly and door lock
4. **Support plate**
5. **Screw, polygon socket**
   - Requires special socket insert tool T10011 or equivalent, **see** Ⓐ
   - Tighten to 8.5 Nm (76 in-lb)
6. **Door handle, outside**
7. **Lock cylinder cover (trim)**
8. **Lock cylinder housing**
   - Only supplied with lock cylinder and keys.

(continued from previous page)

9. Gasket

- Plastic

10. Screw, polygon socket

- Requires special socket insert tool T10011 or equivalent, **see** (A)
- Socket insert T 10011
- 8.5 Nm (76 in. lb)
- Loosening this screw releases the lock cylinder housing, allowing it to be pulled out of support plate.
- Loosen only, do not remove.

> ***CAUTION—***
> *Loosen polygon socket screw only. If screw is removed, the door lock must be removed to realign.*

(A) Special polygon driver tool for door repairs

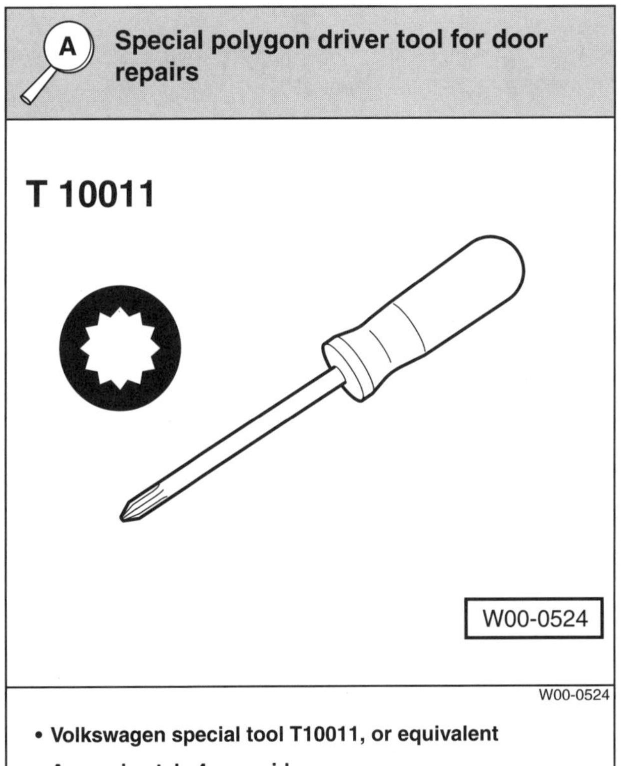

W00-0524

- **Volkswagen special tool T10011, or equivalent**
- **Approximately 4 mm wide**

Lock cylinder housing, removing

1. Carefully pry out sealing plug. See Fig. 12.

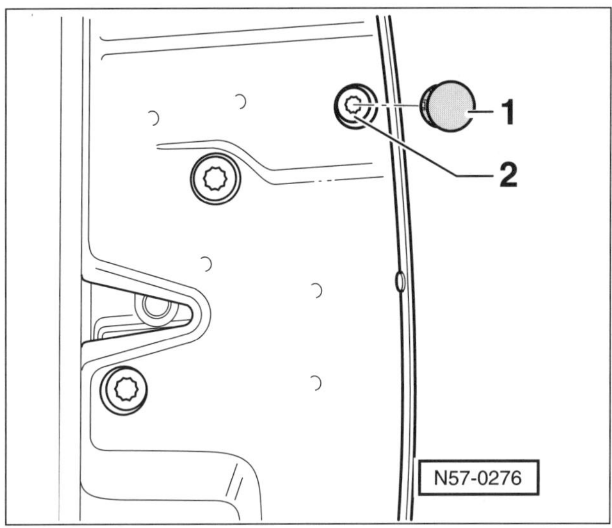

N57-0276

Fig. 12. Carefully pry out sealing plug (**1**) to access polygon socket screw (**2**).

2. Pull door handle open and hold.
3. Loosen ,polygon socket screw to the stop with Volkswagen special tool T10011 or equivalent to release lock cylinder housing. Lock cylinder housing is released before screw comes out. See Fig. 13.

> ***CAUTION—***
> *Loosen polygon socket screw only. If screw is removed, the door lock must be removed to reinstall.*

NOTE—
The door handle will remain open on its own if the polygon socket screw is loosened properly.

4. Pull lock cylinder housing straight out.

NOTE—
Inserting the key into lock cylinder aids in removing the lock cylinder housing.

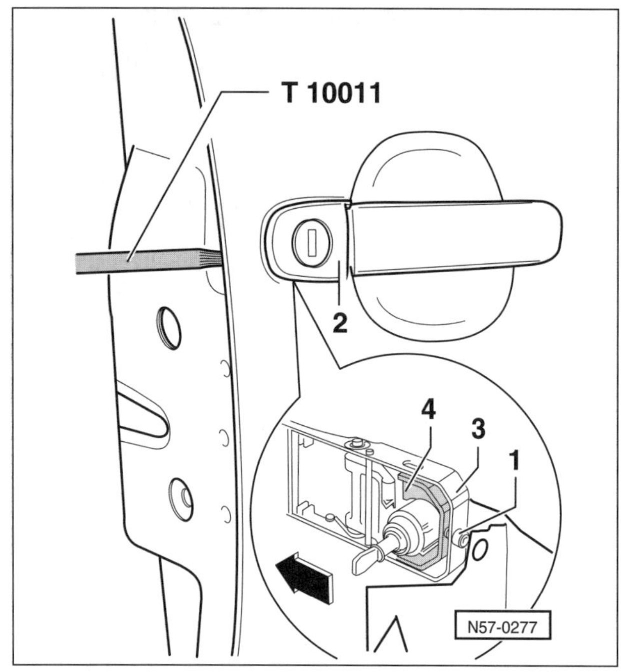

N57-0277

Fig. 13. Volkswagen special tool T10011 shown loosening polygon socket screw (**1**). Lock cylinder housing (**2**) is released when tensioning plate (**4**) moves within support plate (**3**) in direction of **arrow**.

Lock cylinder housing, installing

1. Ensure that door handle has remained opened from the removal procedure.
2. Carefully install lock cylinder housing into opening in door.
3. Tighten polygon socket screw. As screw is tightened, an audible noise should be heard indicating correct seating of lock cylinder housing and tensioning of door handle spring. See Fig. 14.
4. Operate key and door handle to ensure correct operation.
5. Reinstall sealing plug.

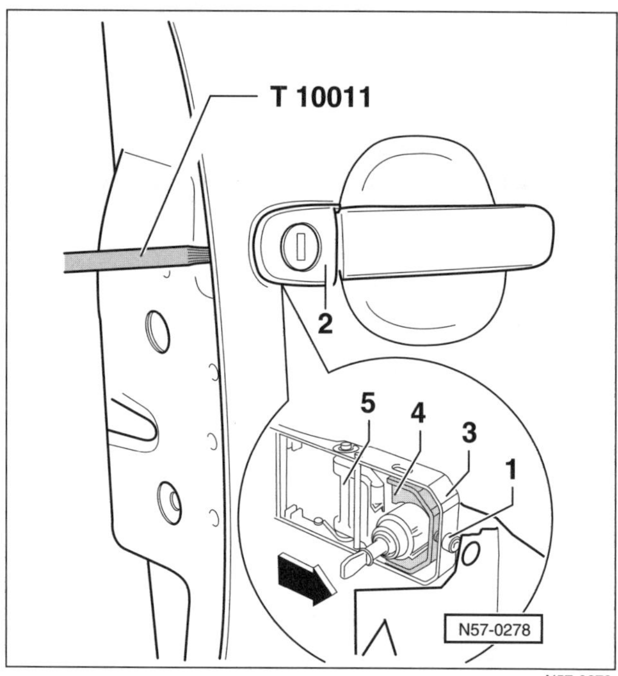

N57-0278

Fig. 14. Volkswagen special tool T10011 shown tightening polygon socket screw (**1**). Lock cylinder housing (**2**) is secured when tensioning plate (**4**) moves within support plate (**3**) in direction of arrow. Door handle lever (**5**) is also released.

Door handle, removing

1. Remove lock cylinder as given earlier.
2. Remove cable clip from door handle lock release with a pick or a small screwdriver. See Fig. 15.

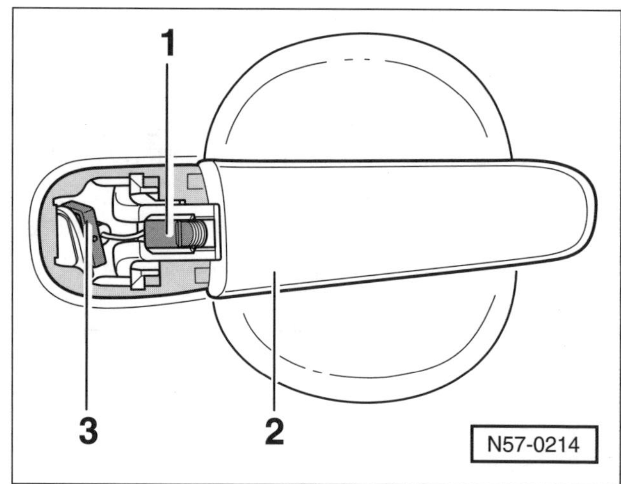

N57-0214

Fig. 15. Outside door handle (**2**) shown with lock cylinder housing removed. Pry out cable clip (**1**) with a pick or screwdriver. When installing door handle, do not pull lock operating lever (**3**).

3. Swing rear of door handle out of door, pivoting from front of handle.

> ***NOTE —***
> *By pivoting door handle out, door handle spring is tensioned and locked. After door handle is installed, spring tension is released.*

Door handle, installing

> ***NOTE —***
> *Replacement door handles are supplied finished in primer only and must be painted prior to installation.*

1. Slip front of door handle into door opening and swing rear of door handle into position against door.

2. Snap cable clip into slot in door handle taking care not to pull cable tight.

> ***NOTE —***
> *When installing cable clip, do not pull lock operating lever while pushing on door handle.*

3. Install lock cylinder housing.

Door lock, removing

The window regulator, door glass, door speaker and door lock are secured to the door assembly carrier. The door lock can only be removed with the door assembly carrier.

> ***NOTE —***
> *Window glass must be operable in order to remove door assembly carrier. Any malfunction that prevents the windows (manual or power) from being lowered must be corrected before proceeding.*

1. Remove door trim panel. **See 70 Trim–Interior.**

2. Remove lock cylinder housing as given earlier.

3. Remove cable clip from door handle. See Fig. 16.

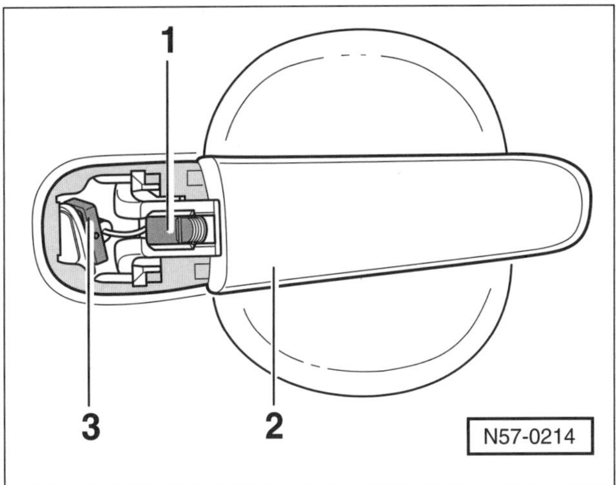

N57-0214

Fig. 16. Pry out cable clip (**1**) with a pick or screwdriver.

4. Pry out sealing plugs in door assembly carrier to gain access to window glass securing bolts. See Fig. 17.

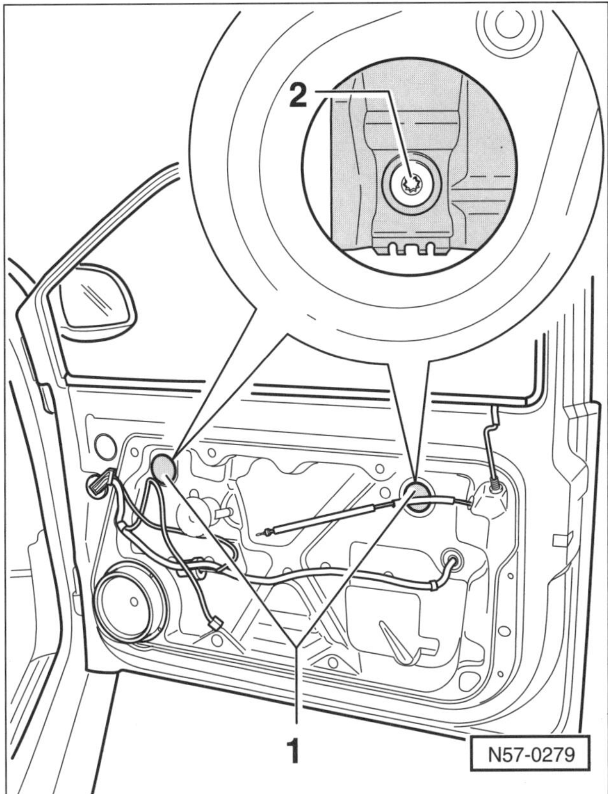

N57-0279

Fig. 17. Passenger side door shown with trim panel removed. Remove rubber sealing plugs (**1**) to access window glass securing bolts (**2**).

5. Lower window until window glass securing bolts are accessible.

6. Loosen window glass securing bolts and carefully press glass securing clamps apart.

7. Push window glass upward in the track. Secure the window glass in up position with strips of suitable adhesive tape stuck to inside glass, looped over door frame and stuck to the outside glass.

8. Remove hood release lever on left side, as required. **See 55 Hoods and Lids**.

9. Remove lower A-pillar trim. **See 70 Body–Interior Trim.**

10. Disconnect multi-pin harness connectors and harness cover on lower A-pillar. See Fig. 18.

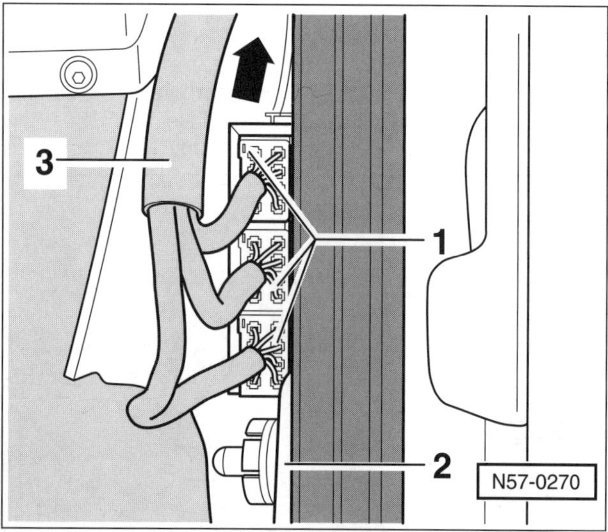

N57-0270

Fig. 18. Lower A-pillar (**2**) shown with trim removed. Disconnect harness connectors (**1**) and move harness (**3**) to side.

11. Remove wiring harness boot at A-pillar and carefully work wiring harness connectors through opening. See Fig. 19.

> ***CAUTION—***
> *Do not close door with harness connectors between door and A-pillar. They will be crushed.*

12. Disconnect harness connector for mirror. See Fig. 20.

13. Disconnect wiring harness guide panel. See Fig. 20.

14. Guide wiring harness with boot through door frame.

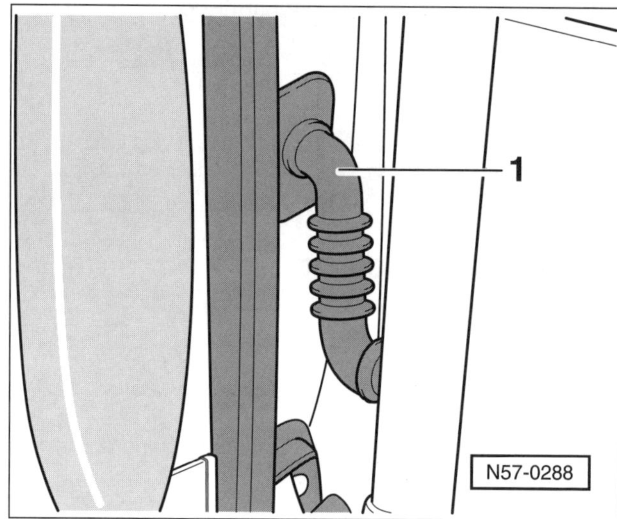

N57-0288

Fig. 19. Remove wiring harness boot (**1**) at A-pillar and pull harness connectors through opening.

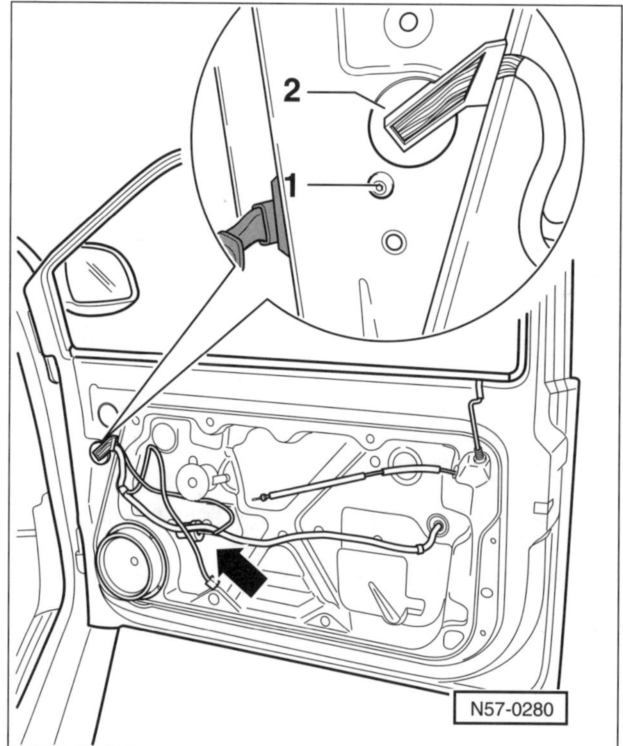

N57-0280

Fig. 20. Guide panel (**2**) is released by removing screw (**1**). Disconnect harness connector (**arrow**).

15. Remove door lock mounting bolts.See Fig. 21.

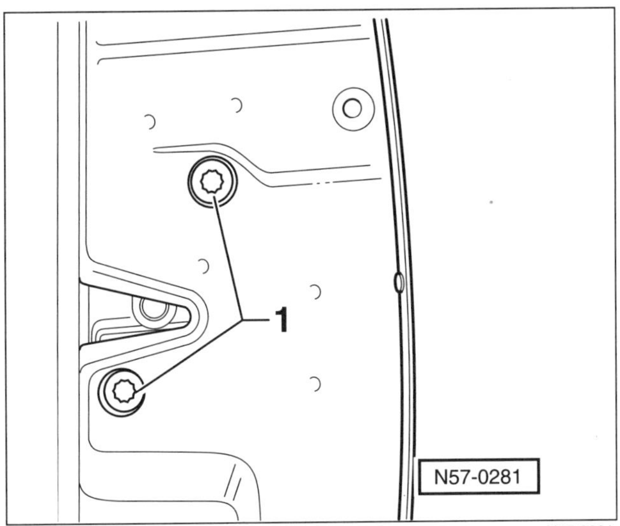

N57-0281

Fig. 21. Door lock mounting bolts (**1**) on edge of door.

16. Remove door assembly carrier bolts in sequence. See Fig. 22.

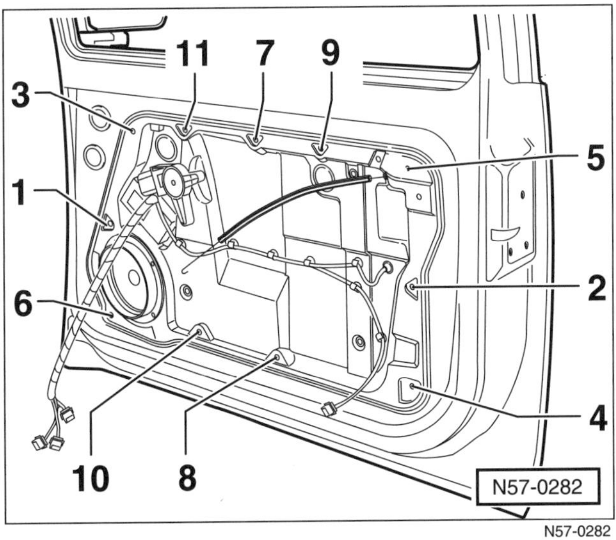

N57-0282

Fig. 22. Door assembly carrier shown ready for removal. Remove bolts in the order shown.

17. Pull top of door assembly carrier from door, lift and pull out of door toward hinges.

18. Turn assembly carrier and pull connector off door lock.

19. Drive out door lock securing clips with a drift. See Fig. 23.

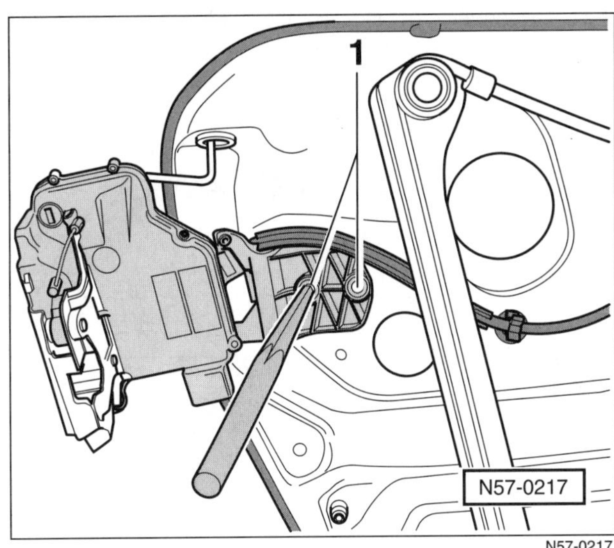

N57-0217

Fig. 23. Drive out clips (**1**) securing door lock to assembly carrier.

20. Disconnect inside release cable from clip on assembly carrier and carefully pry door lock off assembly carrier using a screwdriver. See Fig. 24.

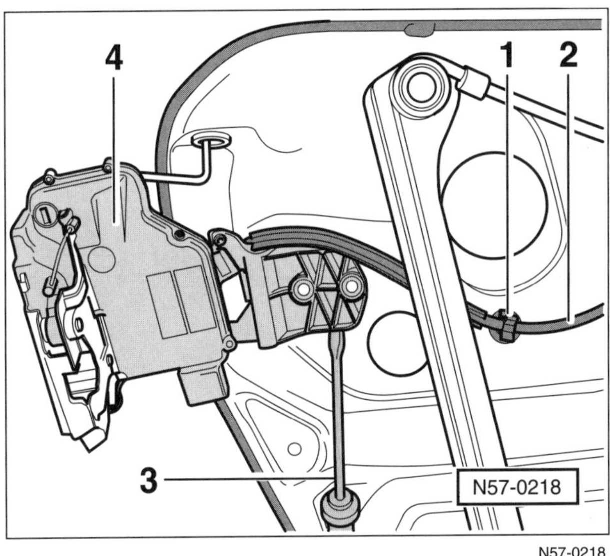

N57-0218

Fig. 24. Disconnect inside release cable (**2**) from clip (**1**) and pry retaining bracket for door lock (**4**) off carrier with a screwdriver (**3**).

NOTE—

The rdoor lock etaining bracket is a separate part. It is not part of the items supplied with the door lock. It is secured to the door lock with a bolt and a pop rivet.

21. Disconnect door lock rod and inside release cable. See Fig. 25.

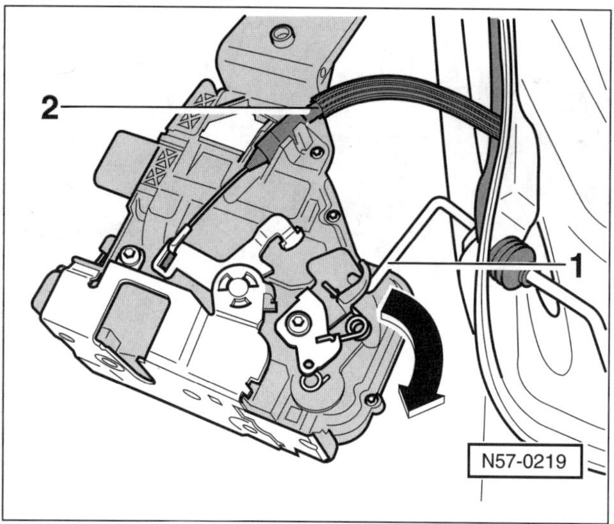

N57-0219

Fig. 25. Disconnect door lock rod (**1**) by turning door lock in direction of arrow. Unsnap inside release cable (**2**) and remove from eyelet in lever.

Door lock, installing

1. Prepare door lock assembly. See Fig. 26.

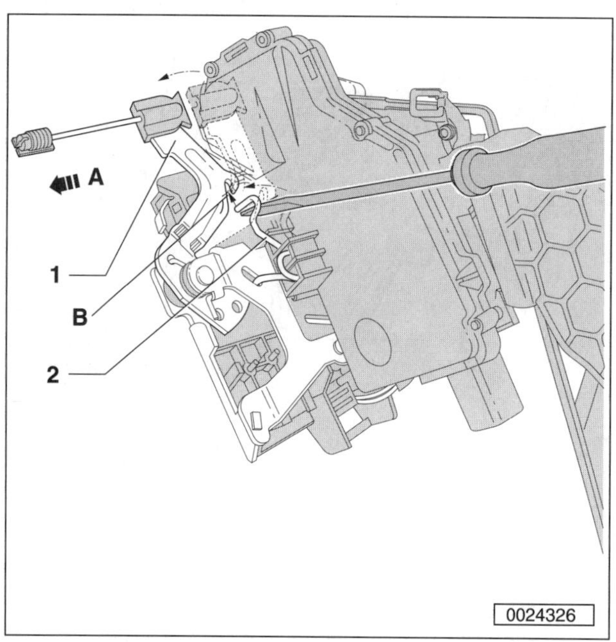

0024326

Fig. 26. Pull lock operating lever (**1**) in direction of arrow **A**. Hook spring (**2**) into slot on operating lever, arrow **B**.

NOTE —

Connecting the operating lever activates the lock. Incorrect attachment of the outside handle cable is prevented.

2. Attach door lock rod and inside release cable.
3. Attach door lock to door assembly carrier.
4. Insert assembly carrier in door.
5. Loosely install all door carrier assembly bolts and then tighten bolts in sequence. See Fig. 22.

Tightening torque

- Door carrier assembly bolts (M6) . . . . . 8 Nm (71 ft-lb)
- Window glass securing bolts, ... 10 Nm (89 in-lb)

6. Carefully release adhesive tape securing window glass and guide glass down into securing clamps.
7. Adjust window glass in securing clamps and tighten. See Fig. 27.

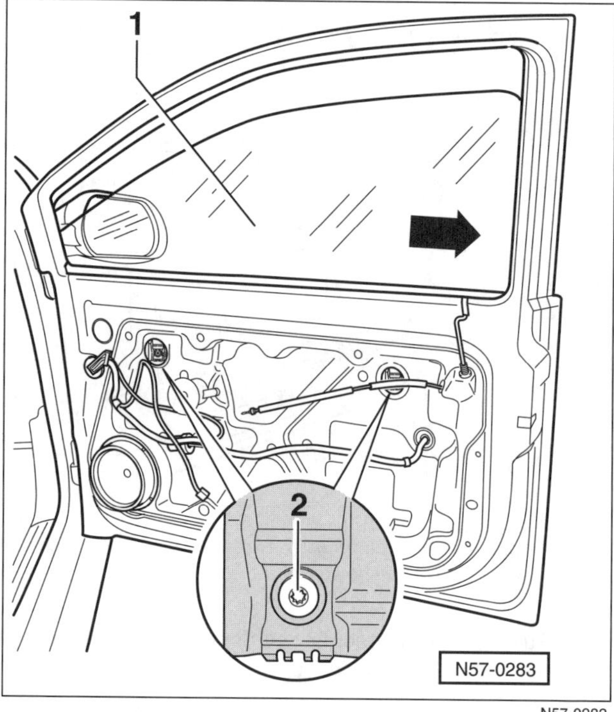

N57-0283

Fig. 27. Gently press window (**1**) in direction of arrow and tighten securing clamp bolts (**2**).

8. Remainder of installation is the reverse of disassembly.
9. Check operation of window before final installation of door trim panel.

Lock button, left door, removing and installing

> ***CAUTION—***
> *Failure to follow this procedure may result in loosening of the locking rods in the doors requiring complete disassembly to repair.*

1. Remove lock button by turning ½ turn (180°) counter-clockwise.

2. Pull lock button upward and off. See Fig. 28.

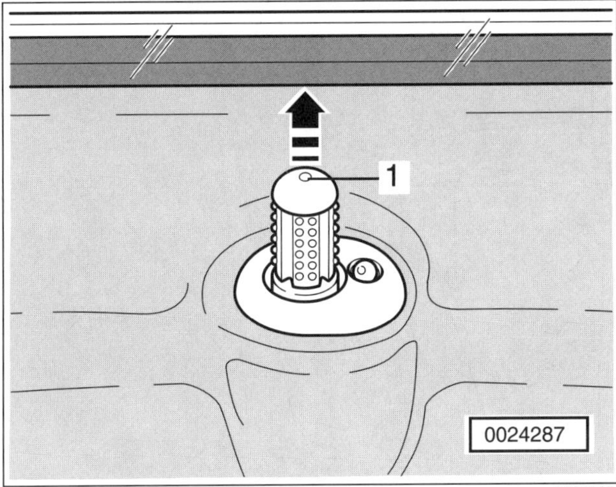

Fig. 28. Lock button shown with index (**1**) mark turned to the inside. Pull up to remove.

3. Install lock button on lock rod with index mark (small dot on top) toward vehicle interior. See Fig. 29.

4. Push lock button onto lock rod until fluted section is flush with door trim.

5. Turn lock button ½ turn (180°) counter-clockwise.

> ***NOTE—***
> *Lock button in the locked position can be flush with the door trim panel to approximately 2 mm (0.078 in.) above door trim panel.*

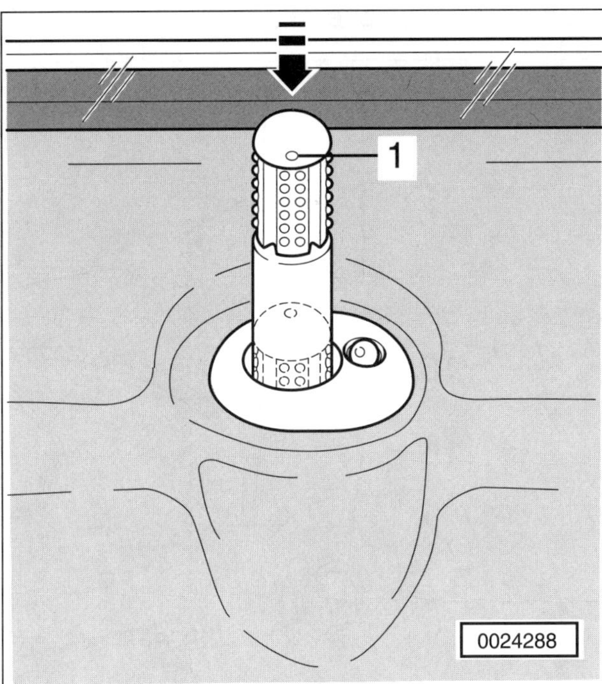

Fig. 29. Lock button shown with index mark (**1**) turned to the inside. Push button down and turn (180°). Turn left side counter-clockwise to install. Turn right side clockwise to install.

Lock button, right door, removing and installing

> ***CAUTION—***
> *Failure to follow this procedure may result in loosening of the locking rods in the doors requiring complete disassembly to repair*

1. Remove lock button by turning ½ turn (180°) clockwise.

2. Pull lock button upward and off. See Fig. 28.

3. Install lock button on lock rod with index mark (small dot on top) toward vehicle interior. See Fig. 29.

4. Push lock button onto lock rod until fluted section is flush with door trim.

5. Turn lock button ½ turn (180°) clockwise.

> ***NOTE—***
> *Lock button in the locked position can be flush with the door trim panel to approximately 2 mm (0.078 in.) above door trim panel.*

Door window, assembly

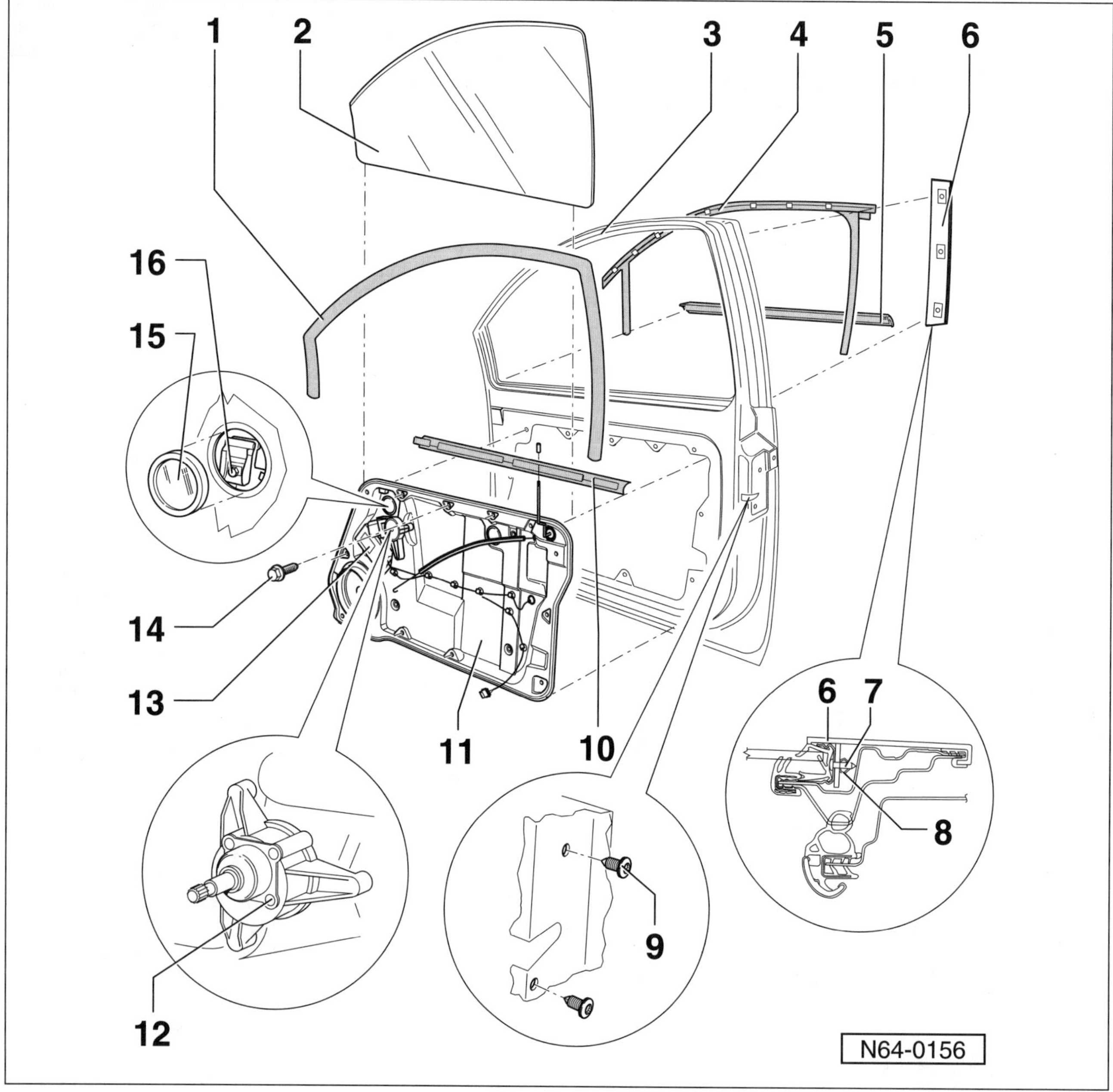

N64-0156

Fig. 30. Door window glass and related components shown for the right side. Left side is similar

1. **Window channel, inner**
   - Pushed into door frame opening
2. **Door window glass**
3. **Door assembly**
4. **Window channel, outer**
   - Pushed into door frame opening
5. **Window slot seal, outer**
   - Pushed onto door frame
6. **Trim**
7. **Screw**
8. **Spring clip**
9. **Bolt**
   - Tighten to 20 Nm (15 ft-lb)
   - Install with locking compound
10. **Window slot seal, inner**
    - Pushed onto door frame

(continued from previous page)

11. Door assembly carrier
- Window regulator is part of assembly carrier

12. Crank drive for manually window regulator
- Fastened to assembly carrier form the back with bolt

13. Door control module with motor for window regulator (J386 and V15)
- Bolted to assembly carrier from the back

14. Bolt
- Tighten to 8 Nm (71 in-lb)

15. Rubber sealing plug

16. Bolt
- Tighten to 10 Nm (89 in-lb)

Door window glass, removing

NOTE —
Window glass must be operable in order to remove door assembly carrier. Any malfunction that prevents the windows (manual or power) from being lowered must be corrected before proceeding.

1. Remove door trim panel. **See 70 Trim–Interior.**

2. Remove lock cylinder housing as given earlier.

3. Remove cable clip from door handle. See Fig. 31.

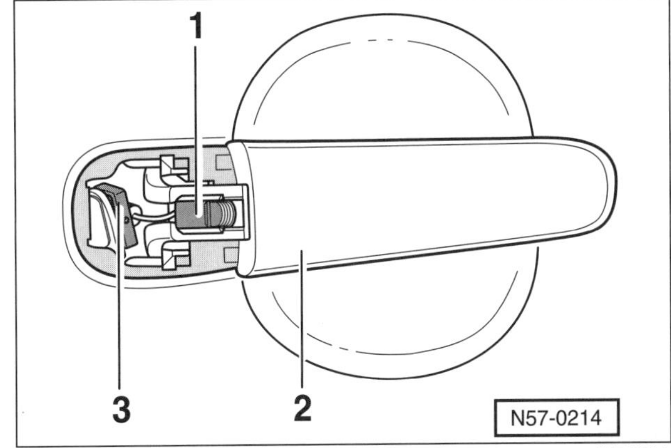

N57-0214

Fig. 31. Pry out cable clip (**1**) with a pick or screwdriver.

4. Pry out sealing plugs in door assembly carrier to gain access to window glass securing bolts. See Fig. 32.

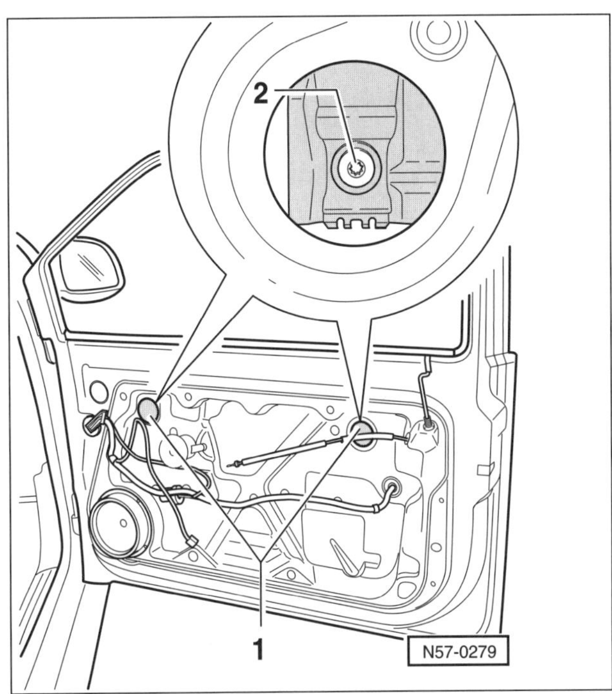

N57-0279

Fig. 32. Passenger side door shown with trim panel removed. Remove rubber sealing plugs (**1**) to access window glass securing bolts (**2**).

5. Lower window until window glass securing bolts are accessible.

6. Loosen window glass securing bolts and carefully press glass securing clamps apart.

NOTE —
If glass is being replaced due to breakage, remove door assembly carrier as given earlier and remove all broken shards of glass to prevent rattling noises in door.

7. Carefully lower the window regulator.

8. Lift the window glass up and pivot forward. See Fig. 33.

N64-0157

Fig. 33. Remove door window glass by lifting up while tilting forward (**arrow**).

9. Place removed window glass in a secure location.

Door window glass, installing

1. Slide forward part of window glass into opening and pivot glass downward, reversing the removal procedure.

2. Raise window regulator until window glass securing bolts are visible in access holes on door assembly carrier.

3. Guide glass down into securing clamps and adjust window glass in securing clamps and tighten. See Fig. 34.

4. Remainder of installation is the reverse of disassembly.

5. Check operation of window before final installation of door trim panel.

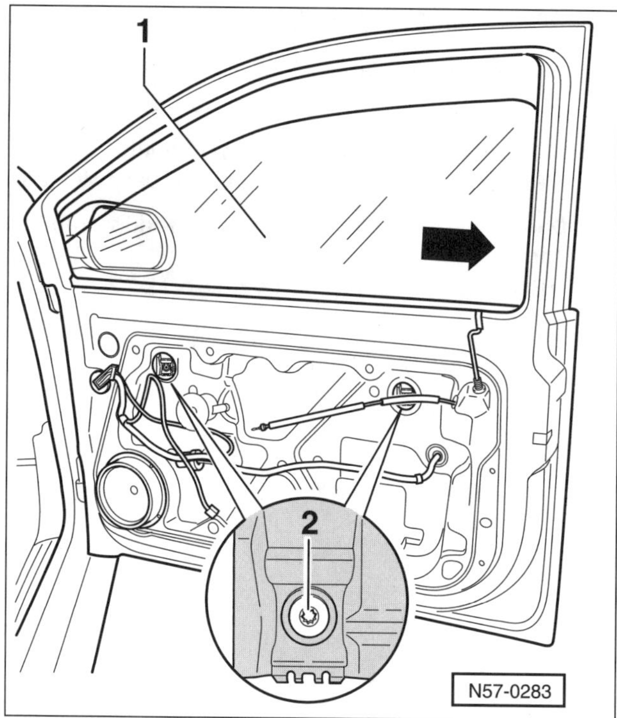

N57-0283

Fig. 34. Gently press window (**1**) in direction of **arrow** and tighten securing clamp bolts (**2**).

Tightening torque
- Window glass securing bolts . . . . 10 Nm (89 in-lb)

COMFORT SYSTEM

New Beetles are equipped with central locking, anti-theft alarm system, keyless remote system and power mirrors as standard. Electrically operated power windows are available as an option. This combination of inter-connected systems is known as the Comfort System. See Fig. 35.

NOTE —
- *The comfort system features built-in diagnostic circuitry that detects and stores Diagnostic Trouble Code (DTC) information. When the system detects a fault, a DTC is generated and stored in the comfort system central control module memory. This may result in failure of the system to operate properly. Proper diagnosis of fault codes can be accessed through the data link connector using Volkswagen scan tool VAG 1551/1552 or equivalent.*
- *Additional diagnostic information is available in a data-stream format to aid in troubleshooting. This valuable information can only be accessed by scan tools such as the Volkswagen VAG 1551/1552 or equivalent. Evaluation and interpretation of this information fall outside the scope of this service manual.*

Comfort system, component overview

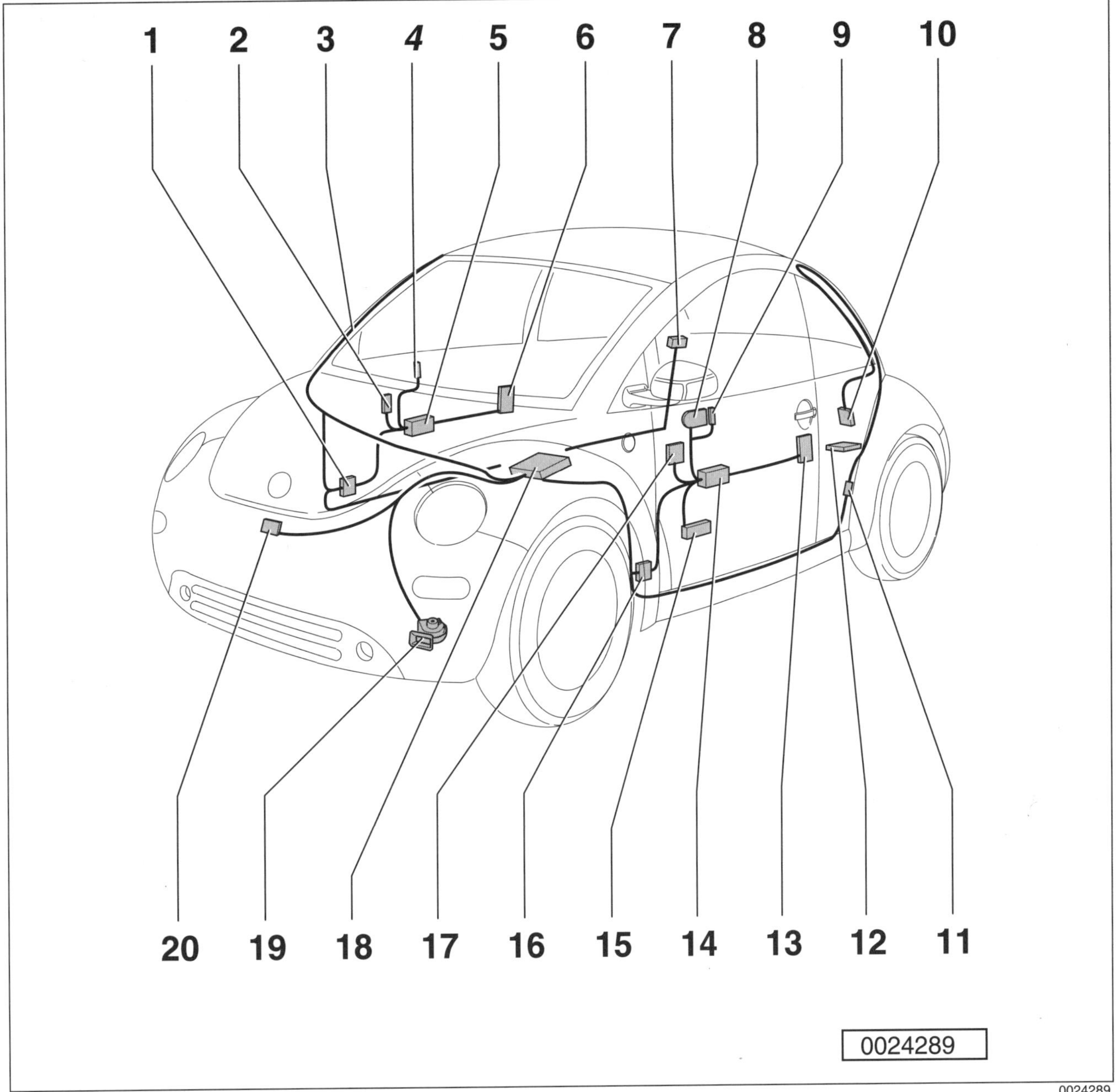

0024289

Fig. 35. Overview of major components of central locking, power windows, anti-theft alarm and keyless remote system.

1. **Connector station (T10l)**
   - Color: black
   - Location: right side lower A-pillar
2. **Switch, right power window (E107)**
   - Location: right front door panel
3. **Antenna wire (R47)**
   - Comfort system remote receiving
   - Location: upper A-pillar
   - U.S. market cars located in left A-pillar
4. **Switch, central locking (E198)**
   - Location: right front door
5. **Door control module with motor for window regulator, right (J387 and V148)**
   - Operating functions: power windows, central locking
   - Linked to central control module via CAN-bus
   - Integrated into right side power window motor

(continued on following page)

(continued from previous page)

6. **Lock unit, front door (F122)**
    - Location: inside right front door, secured to door assembly carrier
7. **Motor, fuel tank filler flap (V155)**
    - Location: inside vehicle above right rear wheel housing
8. **Switch, mirror adjustment (E43 & E48)**
    - Adjustment switch (E43)
    - Selector switch (E48)
    - Location: Left front door trim panel
9. **Switch, central locking (E150)**
    - Location: left front door
10. **Lock unit, rear hatch (V151)**
    - Location: inside rear hatch
11. **Harness connector (T5)**
    - Color: black
    - Location: inside vehicle above left rear wheel housing
12. **Rear hatch striker plate**
13. **Lock unit, left door (F220)**
    - Location: inside left front door, secured to door assembly carrier.
14. **Door control module with motor for window regulator, left (J386 and V147)**
    - Operating functions: power windows, central locking, power mirrors
    - Linked to central control module via CAN-bus
    - Location: integrated into left side power window motor
15. **Switch, rear hatch release (E188) and fuel tank filler flap release (E204)**
    - Location: in left door panel
16. **Connector station (T10k)**
    - Color: black
    - Location: left side lower A pillar
17. **Switch, left and right power windows (E40 & E81)**
    - Location: left front door panel
18. **Comfort system central control module (J393)**
    - Operating functions: keyless remotes, anti-theft alarm, interior lights, electrical system interface
    - Linked to door control modules via CAN-bus
    - Location: under instrument panel, left of steering column.
19. **Horn, anti-theft alarm (H8)**
    - Location: In right side of air plenum accessible from engine compartment.
20. **Switch, hood alarm (F120)**
    - Location: in hood lock carrier

Keyless remote control

A battery-powered keyless remote transmitter is standard with each New Beetle. Up to 4 keyless remotes can be purchased and programmed into the system. See Fig. 36.

The four functions of the keyless remote transmitter are:

- Lock the vehicle and arm the alarm.
- Unlock the vehicle and disarm the alarm.
- Disarm the alarm and open the trunk or hatch. The system will rearm when the trunk or hatch is closed if the alarm system had previously been armed.
- Red panic button to trigger the alarm at any time.

The selective unlock feature of the central locking and the convenience close feature of the power windows do not function with the keyless remote system.

As a security feature, if the vehicle has been unlocked using the keyless remote transmitter and a door is not opened within approximately 30 seconds, the system will re-lock all of the doors and re-arm the alarm system.

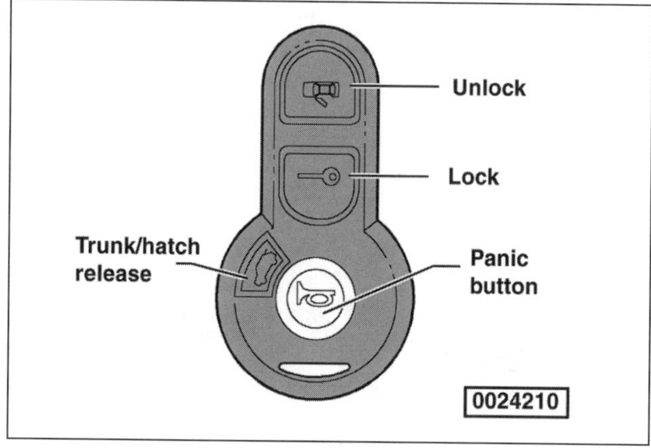

0024210

Fig. 36. Four function keyless remote transmitter.

Quality Review

When you have finished working on the vehicle, it is advisable to take a moment to quality check or review your work. This helps to insure that the operation or repair has been completed properly with all affected systems functioning within normal parameters. These may include the following:

- Ensure that all cable ties and clamps that were removed as part of the repair are replaced.
- Ensure that all fasteners and hardware were replaced and torqued as specified.
- Make sure that all other components involved in the repair are positioned correctly and function properly.
- Make sure that all tools, shop cloths, fender covers and protective tapes are removed before closing the hood.
- Clean grease and fingerprints from painted surfaces, steering wheel and shifter.
- Unlock anti-theft radio and reset the clock.

63 Bumpers

GENERAL

The bumpers consist of a cross-member that is bolted directly to the body structure. The front bumper cover is part of the front end assembly (front clip) and must be removed with the fenders attached, see **50 Body–Front**. The rear bumper cover can be removed without the fenders as shown later, however it may be easier to remove the entire rear clip (bumper cover and fenders) as an assembly.

BUMPERS, SERVICING

Fig. 1 shows an exploded view of the front bumper assembly and Fig. 2 shows the rear bumper assembly.

Front bumper assembly

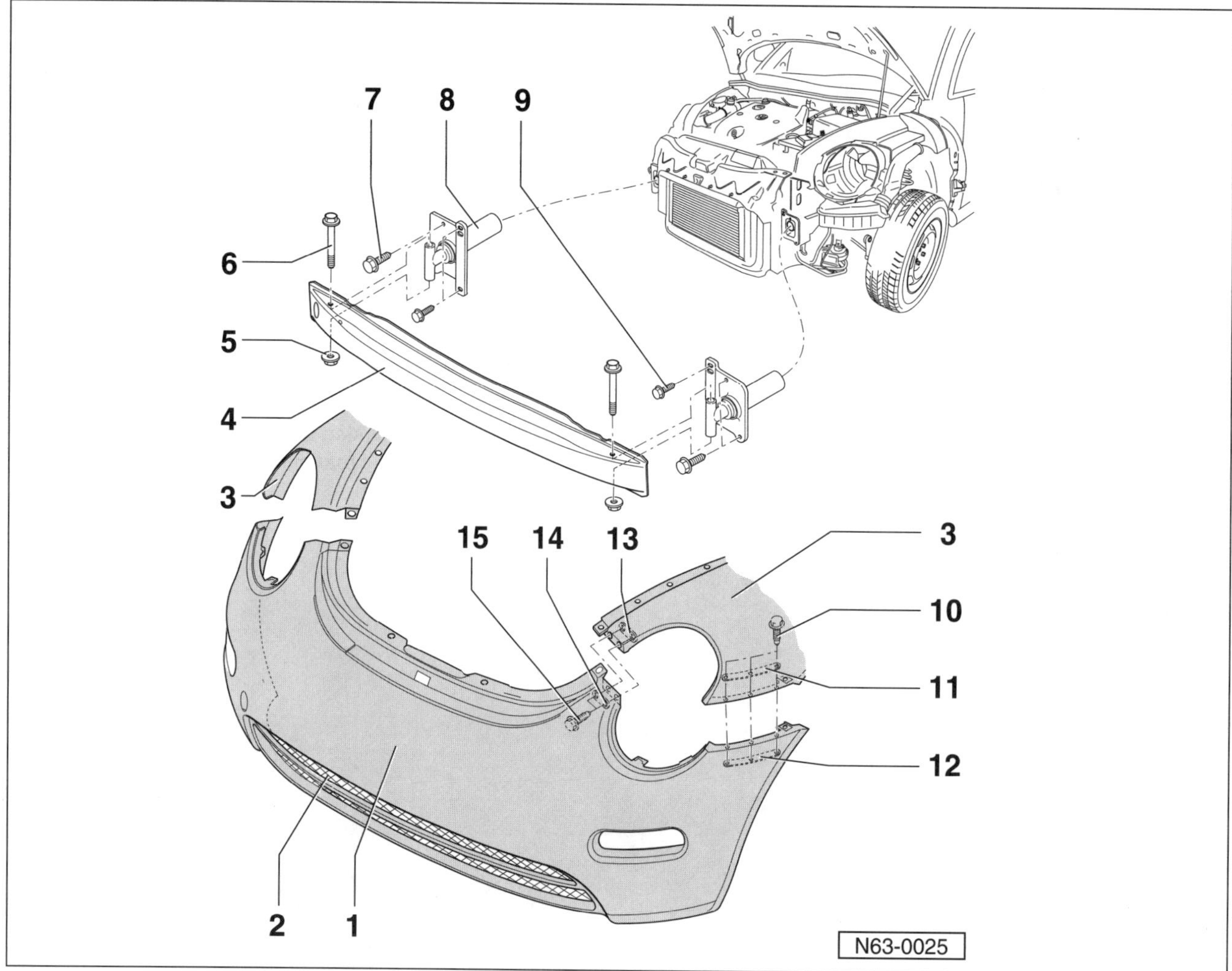

N63-0025

Fig. 1. Front bumper assembly.

1. **Bumper cover**
   - Remove as complete assembly with fenders, see **50 Body–Front**
2. **Grille**
   - Clipped into bumper cover
   - Shown without fog lights
3. **Fender**
4. **Bumper impact beam**
5. **Nut**
   - Tighten to 90 Nm (66 ft-lb)
6. **Bolt**
7. **Bolt**
   - Qty. 4
   - Tighten to 30 Nm (22 ft-lb)
8. **Impact damper**
9. **Bolt**
   - Qty. 4
   - Tighten to 6 Nm (53 in-lb)
10. **Bolt**
    - Qty. 4
    - Tighten to 4.5 ± 0.5 Nm (39 ± 4.5 in-lb)
11. **Reinforcement**
    - Qty. 2
12. **Reinforcement**
    - Qty. 2
13. **Reinforcement**
    - Qty. 2
14. **Reinforcement**
    - Qty. 2
15. **Bolt**
    - Qty. 2
    - Tighten to 6 Nm (53 in-lb)

Rear bumper assembly

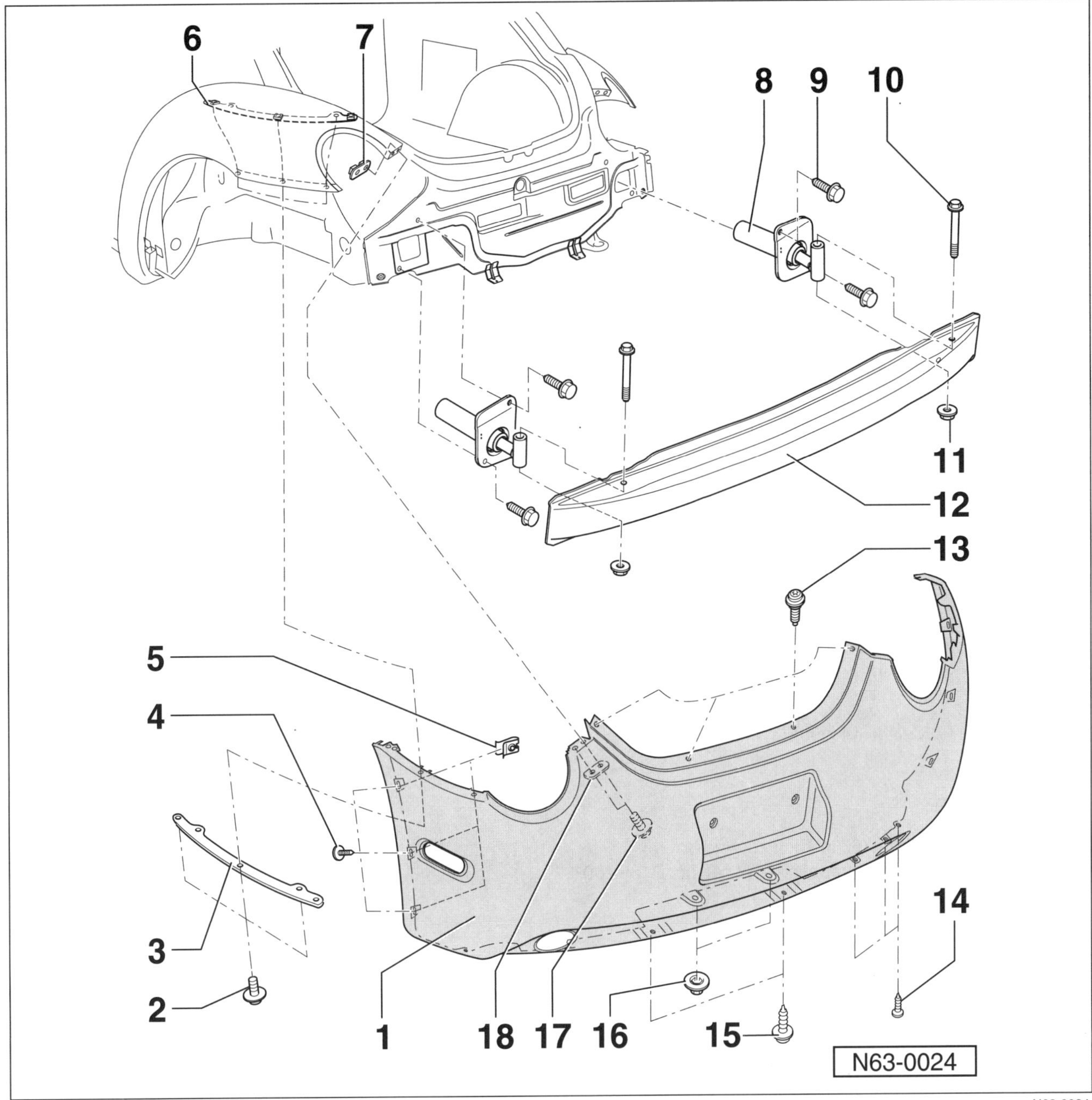

Fig. 2. Rear bumper assembly.

1. **Bumper cover**
   - Removing:
     Loosen cover in area of wheel housing liner, see **66 Body–Exterior Equipment**
     Remove tail light assemblies, see **94 Lights, Accessories–Exterior**
     Disconnect harness connector for licence plate light (below left tail light)
     Remove bolts (items 14, 15) and spring nut (item 16)
     Remove bolts (item 2)
     Pull cover off guides

2. **Bolt**
   - Qty. 6
   - Tighten to 4.5 ± 0.5 Nm (39 ± 4.5 in-lb)

3. **Reinforcement**
   - Qty. 2

4. **Bolt**
   - Qty. 6
   - Tighten to 1.5 Nm (13 in-lb)

(continued on following page)

(continued from previous page)

5. **Speed nut**
    - Qty. 6
6. **Reinforcement**
    - With weld nuts
    - Qty. 2
7. **Reinforcement**
    - With weld nuts
    - Qty. 2
8. **Impact damper**
9. **Bolt**
    - Qty. 4
    - Tighten to 30 Nm (22 ft-lb)
10. **Bolt**
    - Qty. 2
11. **Nut**
    - Qty. 2
    - Tighten to 90 Nm (66 ft-lb)
12. **Bumper impact beam**
13. **Bolt**
    - Qty. 4
    - Tighten to 6 Nm (53 in-lb)
    - Install with locking compound (VW part no. D185 400 A2, or equivalent)
14. **Bolt**
    - Tighten to 1.2 Nm (14 in-lb)
    - Qty. 3
15. **Bolt**
    - Qty. 2
    - Tighten to 7.5 Nm (66 in-lb)
    - Install with locking compound (VW part no. D185 400 A2, or equivalent)
16. **Speed nut**
    - Qty. 2
17. **Bolt**
    - Qty. 2
    - Tighten to 6 Nm (53 in-lb)
18. **Reinforcement**
    - Qty. 2

66 Body–Exterior Equipment

GENERAL

This repair group covers various exterior equipment including side-view mirrors, wheel housing liners, and roof moldings.

SIDE-VIEW MIRROR

Mirror glass and housing, removing and installing

> ***WARNING —***
> *Use protective eye wear and gloves.*

1. Protect bottom mirror housing edge from paint damage with reinforced tape.
2. Pivot top of mirror into housing.
3. Press off mirror from tab in housing. See Fig. 1. Remove harness connector for heated mirror (as applicable).
4. Use screwdriver to release housing retaining clip on top of actuator bracket. See Fig. 2.
5. Pull mirror housing upward off mirror carrier.

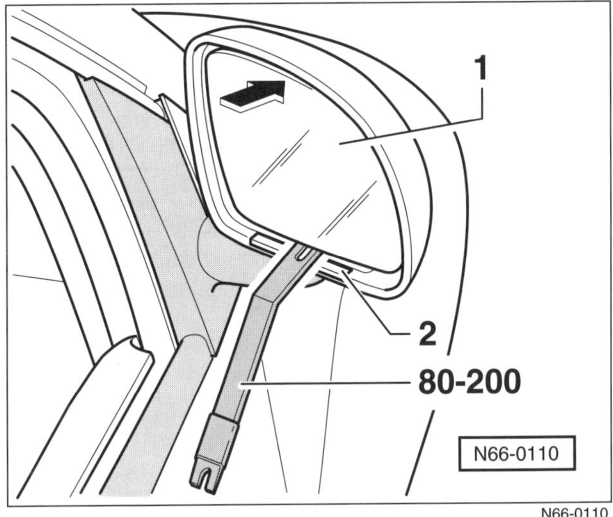

N66-0110

Fig. 1. Pivot mirror (**1**) in direction of **arrow** and use VW special tool 80-200 to pry mirror from tab in housing. Protective tape is applied to bottom edge of housing (**2**) to protect paint.

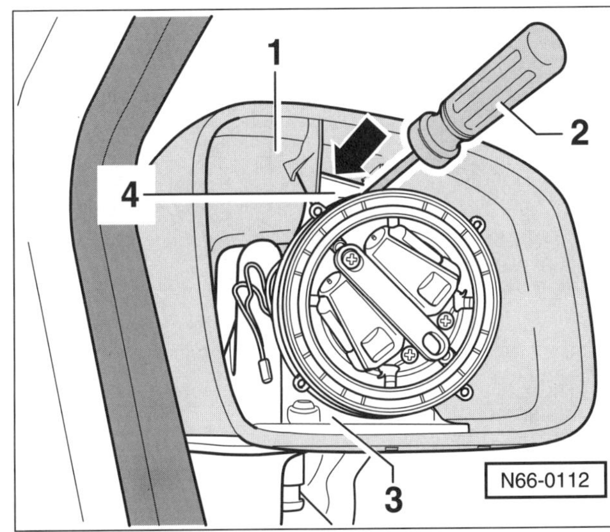

N66-0112

Fig. 2. Press screwdriver (**2**) in direction of **arrow** to release housing retaining clip (**4**). Pull mirror housing (**1**) upward off mirror carrier (**3**).

66

Side-view mirror assembly, removing and installing

1. Remove front door trim, see **70 Trim–Interior**.

2. Disconnect harness connectors in door. See Fig. 3.

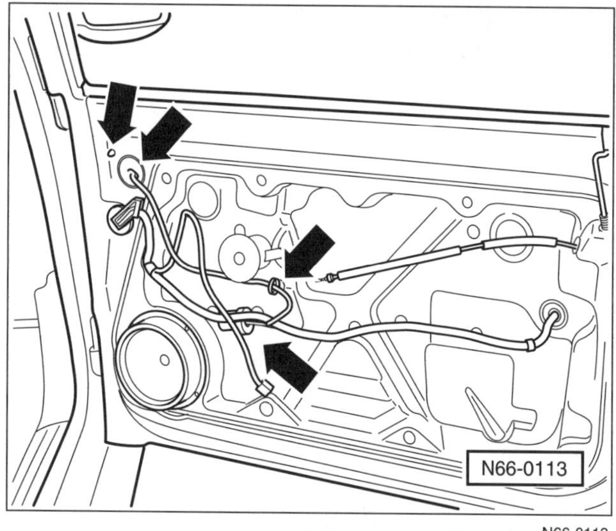

N66-0113

Fig. 3. Door harness connectors (**arrows**).

> ***NOTE —***
> *Position wire connector with adhesive strip so it won't catch in door.*

3. Remove hinge cover. See Fig. 4.

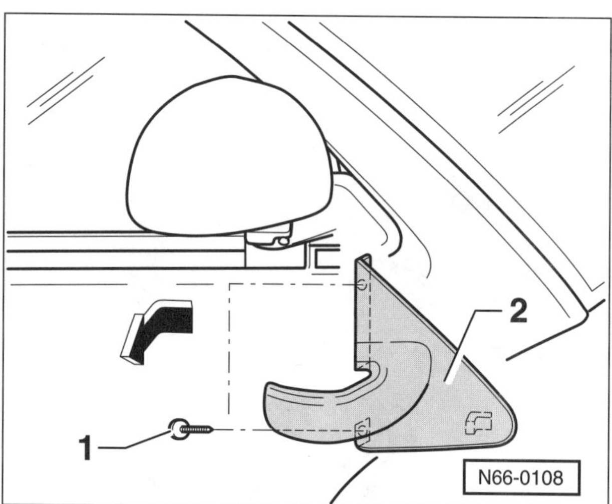

N66-0108

Fig. 4. Remove screws (**1**) and pull off hinge cover (**2**) from the rear (**arrow**).

> ***NOTE —***
> *Hinge cover bolts are accessible after opening the door.*

4. Remove mirror assembly mounting screws and remove mirror from door hinge. See Fig. 5.

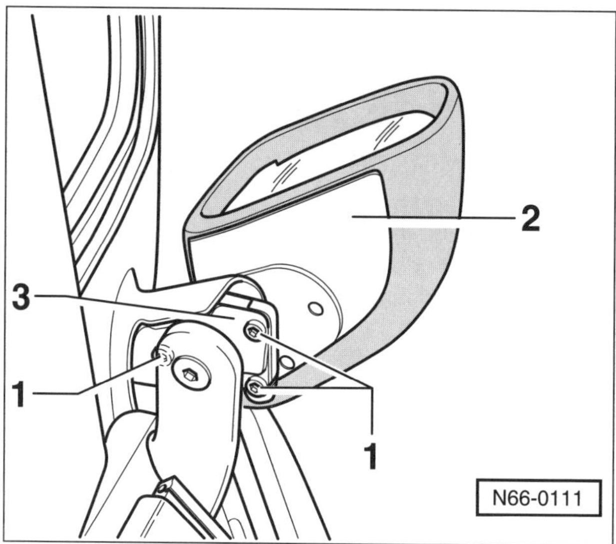

N66-0111

Fig. 5. Remove mounting screws (**1**) and remove mirror (**2**) from hinge (**3**).

> ***NOTE —***
> *Electrical wires for mirror are routed through door opening.*

5. Reinstall in reverse sequence.

Tightening torque

- Mirror assembly to hinge . . . . 10 Nm (89 in-lb)

---

6. When installing mirror assembly, ensure electrical wire in window channel is routed correctly, otherwise window can catch on the wire when opening and closing window.

7. Check operation of power mirror.

WHEEL HOUSING

Front wheel housing liner assembly

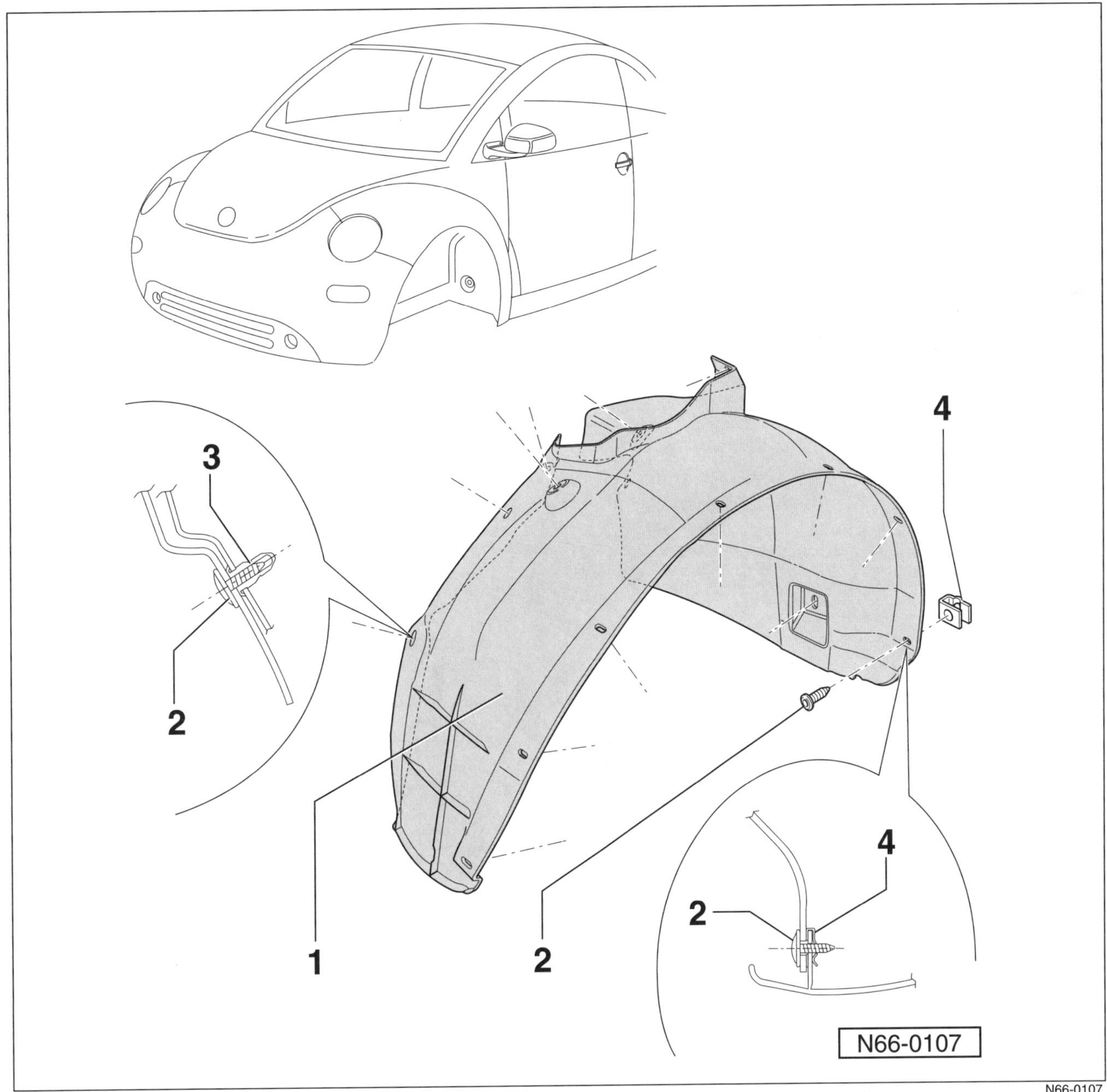

N66-0107

Fig. 6. Front wheel housing liner and related hardware.

1. **Wheel housing liner**
   - Removal:
     Remove wheel
     (when installing tighten lug bolts to 102 Nm (75 ft-lb)
     Remove screws (item 2)–(qty. 12) and remove wheel housing liner

2. **Screw**

3. **Spreader nut**

4. **Speed nut**
   - On bumper cover

Rear wheel housing liner

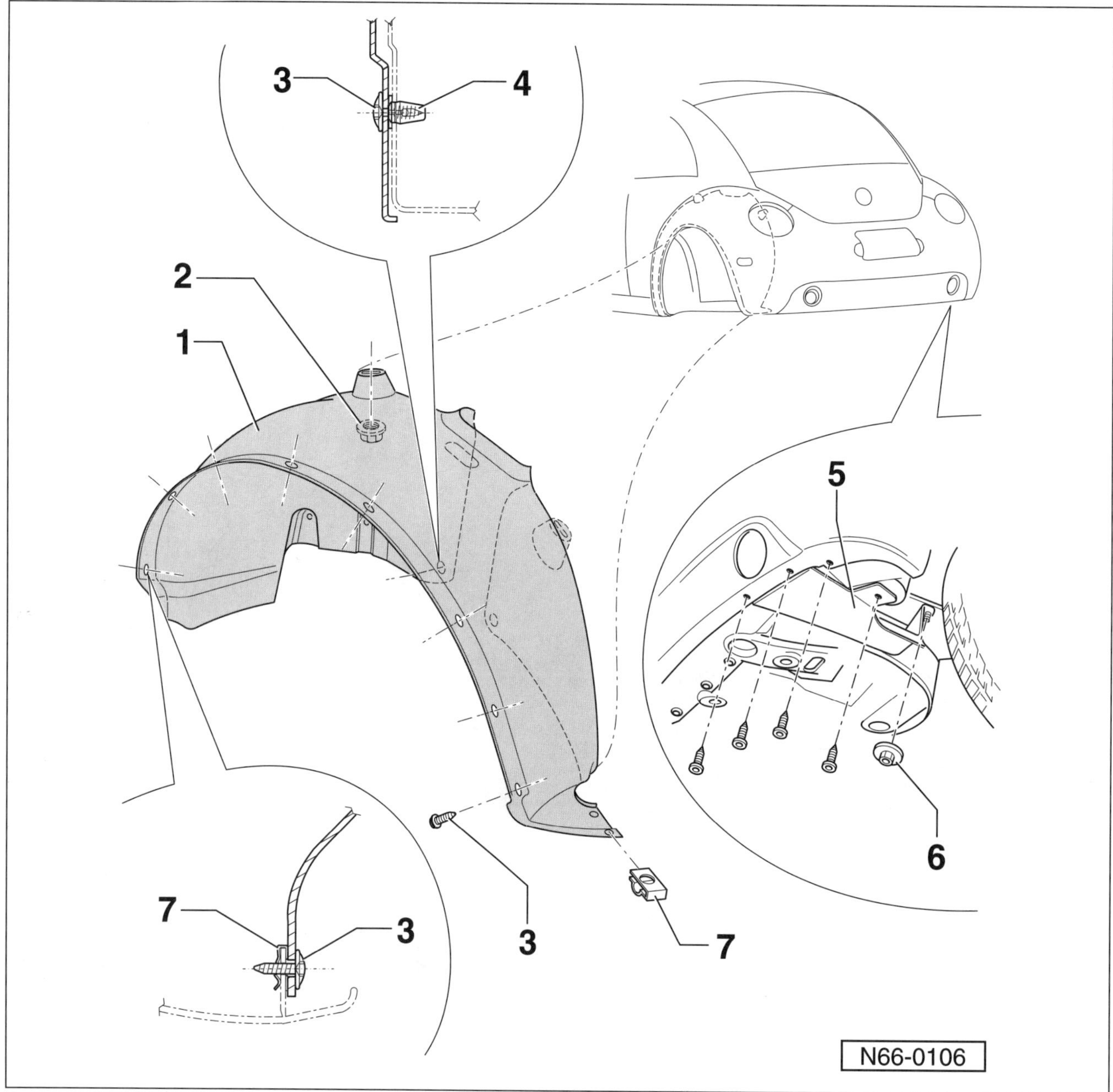

N66-0106

Fig. 7. Rear wheel housing liner and related hardware.

NOTE —
Wheel housing liners may differ slightly depending on equipment, with regard to position and number of mounting elements.

1. **Wheel housing liner**
   - Removal:
     Remove wheel
     (when installing tighten lug bolts to 102 Nm (75 ft-lb)
     Remove screws (qty. 7) and wheel house liner
2. **Hex nut**
   - Tighten to 1 ± 0.3 Nm (9 ± 3 in-lb)
3. **Screw**
4. **Spreader nut**
5. **Cover**
   - Right side only
6. **Speed nut**
7. **Speed nut**
   - On bumper cover or fender

ROOF MOLDINGS

Roof moldings, overview

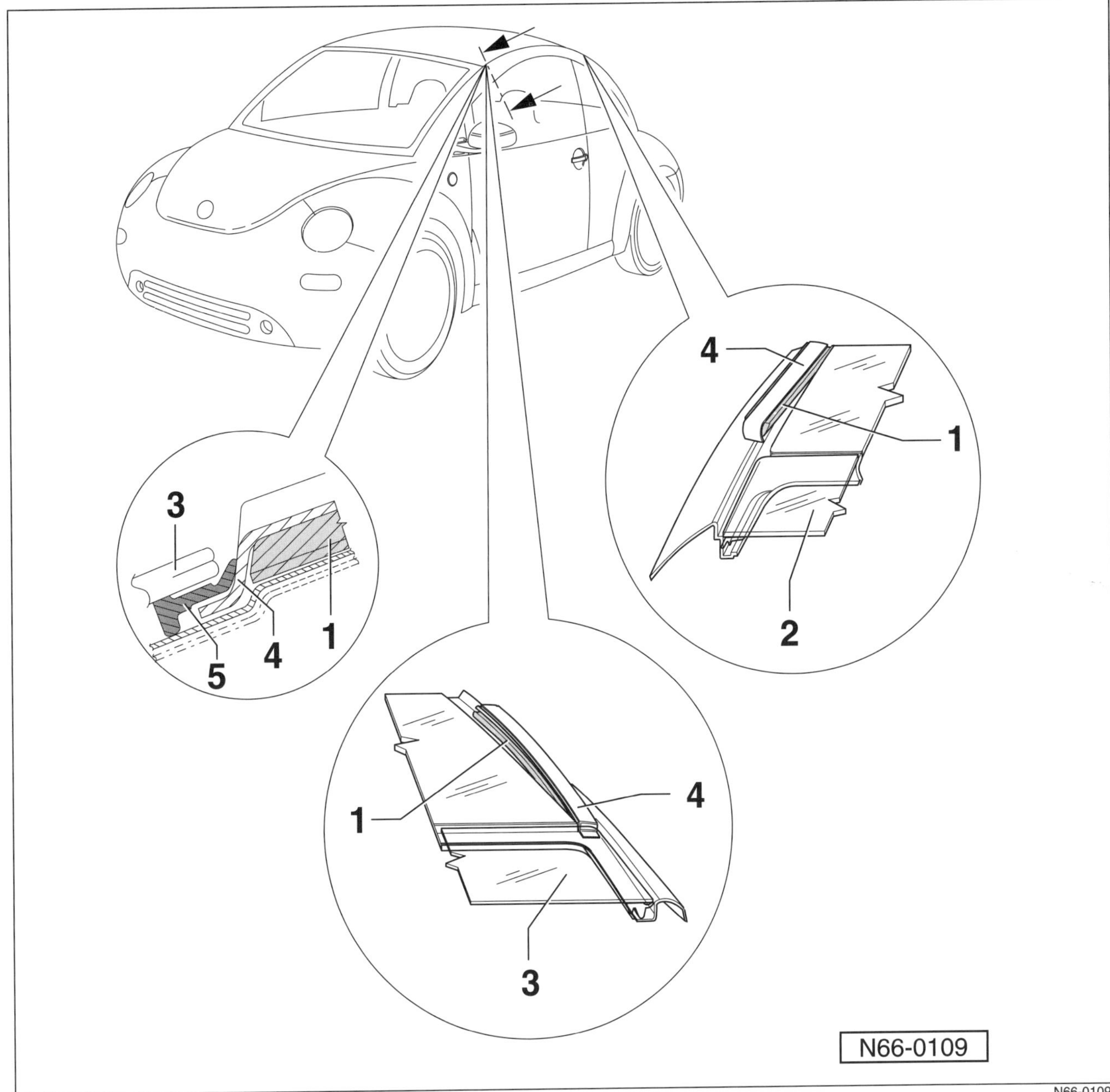

Fig. 8. Details of various roof moldings on New Beetle.

1. **Roof molding**
   - With cover strip (item 4).
   - Do not bend roof molding
   - Starting at windshield, carefully pry off with soft plastic wedge
   - Place roof molding on rear end of roof channel and press in from rear to front stop
2. **Rear window**
3. **Windshield**
4. **Cover strip**
   - Installing:
     Insert cover strip into pocket of roof molding onto stop, then press into roof channel
5. **Sealing lip**
   - Component part of pre-coating

69 Seatbelts, Airbags

GENERAL

This repair group covers emergency tensioning (pyrotechnic) seat belt assemblies and airbag system components. This repair group does not cover airbag system or pyrotechnic seat belt fault diagnosis or repair. Service and repair to these systems requires special test equipment, knowledge and training and should only be carried out by an authorized Volkswagen Dealer. Before starting repairs involving these systems, always read and observe all warnings, cautions and notes.

> ***WARNING —***
> *Disconnecting the negative (–) battery cable may erase fault codes and basic settings in the engine management and automatic transmission control modules. Some driveability problems may be noticed until the system re-adapts to operating conditions. OBD II readiness codes, which may be required for emissions testing, may also be erased. Convenience electronics (alarm system, interior light control, power locks, mirrors, and windows) may need to be re-set using a VAG 1551/1552 or equivalent scan tool.*

SEATBELTS

Volkswagen New Beetles use an inertia reel-type lap/shoulder belt combination to restrain the front seat passengers. In addition, these belts are self-tensioning through the use of a pyrotechnic device. Deployment of the pyrotechnic tensioner is by means of either a mechanical trigger or in conjunction with the airbag system. Rear seat passengers are protected by an inertia reel-type lap/shoulder belt combination. A warning light in the instrument cluster illuminates when the ignition is first switched on as a reminder to buckle up. See Fig. 1.

0024312

Fig. 1. Seat belt warning light (**arrow**) will be illuminated when ignition is switched on. It will stay illuminated for approximately 6 seconds and then go out if the seatbelt is not buckled. It will not come on at any other time.

Special precautions for pyrotechnic seatbelt equipped vehicles

Emergency tensioning front seat belt systems can enhance passenger safety in the event of a collision provided that the seat belts are used. Special service precautions must be followed to prevent possible serious bodily injury to the repair technician and others involved in the handling and storage of pyrotechnic seatbelt components and to insure proper operation in the event of a collision.

69

WARNING —
- *Before working on pyrotechnic seatbelt components linked to airbag systems,* ***disconnect the battery first.***
- *Pyrotechnic seat belts are activated by an explosive device. Handled improperly or without adequate safeguards and training, the system can be very dangerous. Special precautions must be observed when working on or near the seatbelts.*
- *Seat belts are vehicle safety systems. To guard against personal injury or system failure, only trained Volkswagen service Technicians should test, disassemble or service the pyrotechnic seat belt systems.*
- *Install new seatbelt unit as soon as the unit is removed from the packaging. Reinstall in packaging if work will not be completed immediately.*
- *Do not leave any pyrotechnic seatbelt unit unattended. If work is interrupted, store seatbelt unit in a secure location where it cannot be disturbed.*
- *The storage and transportation of airbag units must be in accordance with all applicable Federal, State and Local rules and regulations.*
- *Observe all cautions, warnings and notes before starting repairs involving airbag systems.*
- *Belt tensioners that have been deployed can be disposed of as normal scrap.*
- *Do not use tools with a hammer-type action to disassemble the belt tensioner.*
- *The pyrotechnic seatbelt propellant has no expiration date, and it has an unlimited, maintenance-free life.*
- *The belt tensioner unit must not be exposed to grease, cleaning solutions or similar substances.*
- *Belt tensioner units must not be exposed to temperatures above 100°C (212°F), even for short periods.*
- *Belt tensioner components may not be opened or repaired; always use new parts.*
- *Belt tensioner units which have been dropped on the must not be installed into a vehicle.*
- *Belt tensioner units that show evidence of mechanical or physical damaged (dents, cracks) must be replaced.*
- *Pyrotechnic seatbelt units which have not been deployed should be marked and returned to the manufacturer for disposal using original seatbelt shipping container.*

Seatbelts, inspecting

Any time that a New Beetle is involved in an accident, all of the seatbelts should be checked for damage and proper operation.

WARNING —
After every accident the seat belt system must be inspected systematically. If damage is found when inspecting the check points, the customer must be advised regarding the necessity of replacing the seatbelts.

Webbing (belt material), checking

- Pull belt completely out.
- Inspect webbing for dirt and soiling; wash as needed using a mild soap solution.
- Inspect for damage according to Fig. 2. Fig. 3. or Fig. 4.

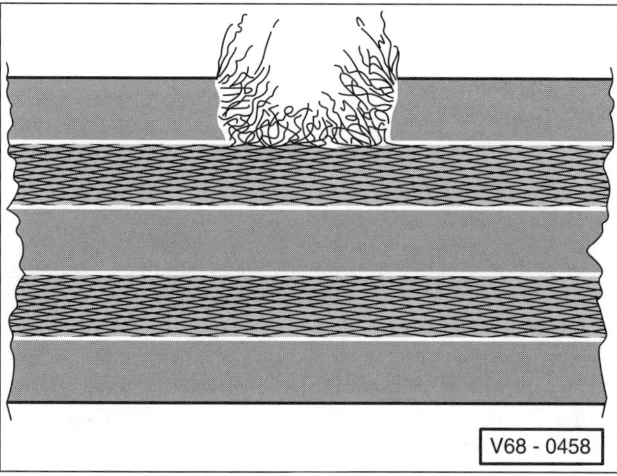

V68-0458

Fig. 2. Seatbelt webbing showing example of cuts, chafing and tears. If vehicle was in an accident replace complete seatbelt assembly with buckle. If vehicle was not in an accident and damage is from other sources, it is ok to replace only the belt.

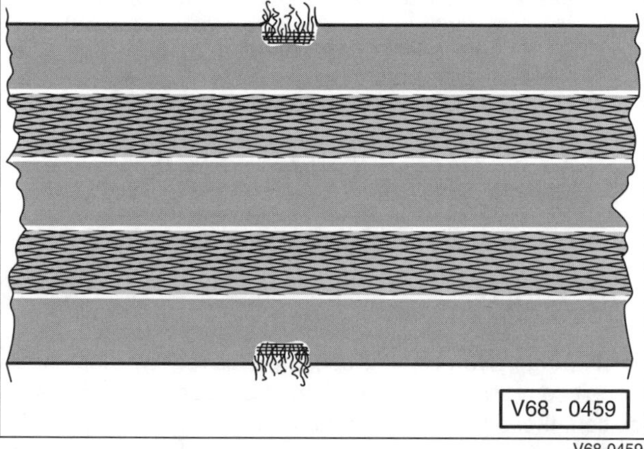

V68-0459

Fig. 3. Seatbelt webbing showing example of torn edges. If vehicle was in an accident replace complete seatbelt assembly with buckle. If vehicle was not in an accident and damage is from other sources, it is permissible to replace only the belt.

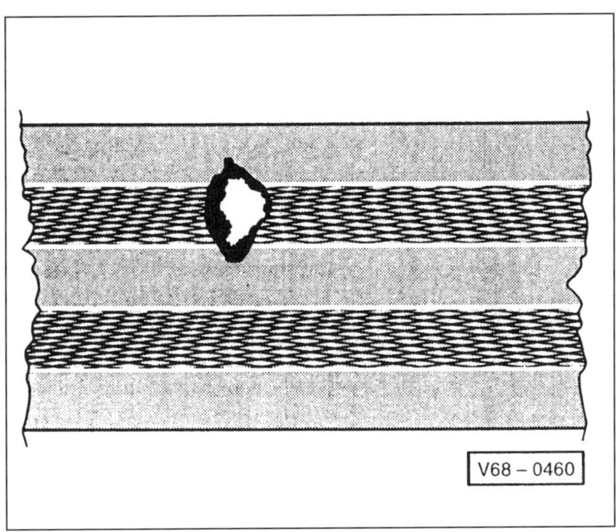

V68-0460

Fig. 4. Seatbelt webbing showing example of burns from cigarettes etc. It is permissible to replace only the belt in this case.

Inertia reel, checking

- Pull belt out of reel with a firm and sudden jerk. Seatbelt should lock immediately.
- Road test from 20 kph (12 mph) by applying brakes suddenly to simulate an emergency stop. Seatbelt should lock immediately.
- If belt does not lock, check mounting position and correct as necessary.
- If belt does not lock and mounting is in order, replace complete seatbelt assembly.

> ***WARNING —***
> *For safety reasons, the road test should be done on a traffic-free stretch of road or parking lot to ensure safety to the vehicle and driver as well as other vehicles and pedestrians.*

Belt buckle latch, checking

- Inspect belt latch and buckle for cracks and breaks.
- If there is any indication of cracking or breakage, replace complete seatbelt assembly
- Inspect belt latch and buckle for proper operation by inserting latch into buckle a minimum of 5 times. Latch should engage buckle firmly and securely with an audible clicking sound and should not pull apart.
- If latch and buckle do not engage smoothly or firmly, or come apart when pulled, replace complete seatbelt assembly.

Belt buckle release, checking

- Engage latch and buckle with no tension on the belt (slack) and push release button a minimum of 5 times. Latch must spring out of belt buckle on its own.
- If latch fails to spring out of belt buckle, replace complete seatbelt assembly.

Belt guides and latch tongue, checking

- Inspect plastic guides for deformation, scoring and fractures due to accident. Do not confuse smooth wear marks which are normal due to frequent use.
- If deformation, scoring or fractures are present, replace complete seatbelt assembly.

Seatbelt mounting components and anchorage points, checking

- Check latch and bracket for deformation and/or stretching.
- Check function of height adjuster.
- Check anchorage points on B-pillar, seat and floor for distortion, damage and proper torque.
- If distortion or damage is present, repair or replace components as required. Torque fasteners to specification.

Automatic retractor mechanism, checking

- Check retractor mechanism for smooth operation when seatbelt is pulled out and smooth operation when belt is reeled in.
- Ensure that seatbelts equipped with child seat feature operate properly when seatbelt is pulled completely out.
- Ensure that seatbelt is not twisted.
- If retractor mechanism does not operate properly, replace seat belt retractor.
- If front pyrotechnic seatbelts do not retract, they have been deployed and are no longer usable. They must be replaced.

Front pyrotechnic seatbelt, assembly

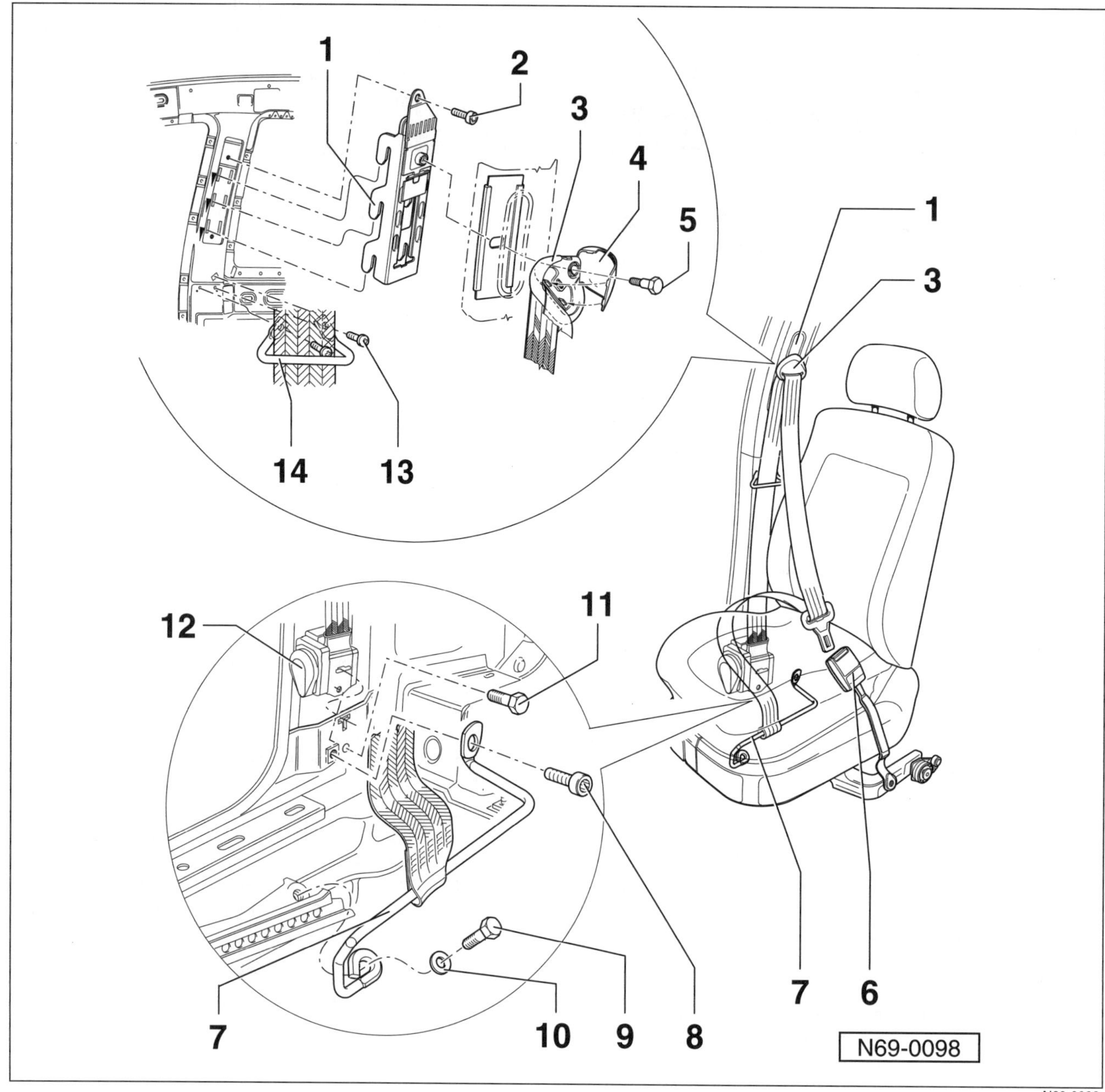

Fig. 5. Front pyrotechnic seatbelt tensioner shown with related components.

> ***WARNING —***
> *Observe all cautions, warnings and notes before starting repairs involving airbag systems.*

> ***CAUTION —***
> *Before starting any body disassembly, straightening or other body repair work, the belt tensioning units must be removed.*

1. **Belt height adjuster**
   - To remove height adjustment mechanism, first remove trim on top of B-pillar
2. **Screw**
   - Tighten to 23 Nm (17 ft-lb)
3. **Belt relay/guide**
4. **Belt relay/guide cover**

(continued from previous page)

5. **Bolt**
    - Tighten to 40 Nm (30 ft-lb)
6. **Front belt buckle (latch)**
7. **Anchor rail, lower**
8. **Bolt**
    - Tighten to 23 Nm (17 ft-lb)
9. **Bolt**
    - Tighten to 40 Nm (30 ft-lb)
10. **Washer**
11. **Bolt**
    - Tighten to 40 Nm (30 ft-lb)
    - Loosen bolt to prevent belt tensioner from deploying during repairs (safe mode)
    - Tighten bolt to return tensioner to operational condition after repairs
12. **Seat belt with pyrotechnic belt tensioner**
    - 2 different pyrotechnic seatbelt tensioners are installed depending on vehicle production date
    - Mechanically activated (m.y. 1998)
    - Electrically deployed via airbag system (m.y. 1999)
    - After an accident in which one or both belt tensioners have been deployed (triggered), both seat belts must be replaced (the belts will no longer retract)
    - The disposal of old components that have not been deployed (triggered) is done by the manufacturer
    - To remove, first remove quarter panel trim
    - Retaining tabs determine position of belt reel in mount
13. **Screws**
    - Tighten to 1.5 Nm (13 in-lb)
14. **Belt guide**

Rear seat belts, assembly

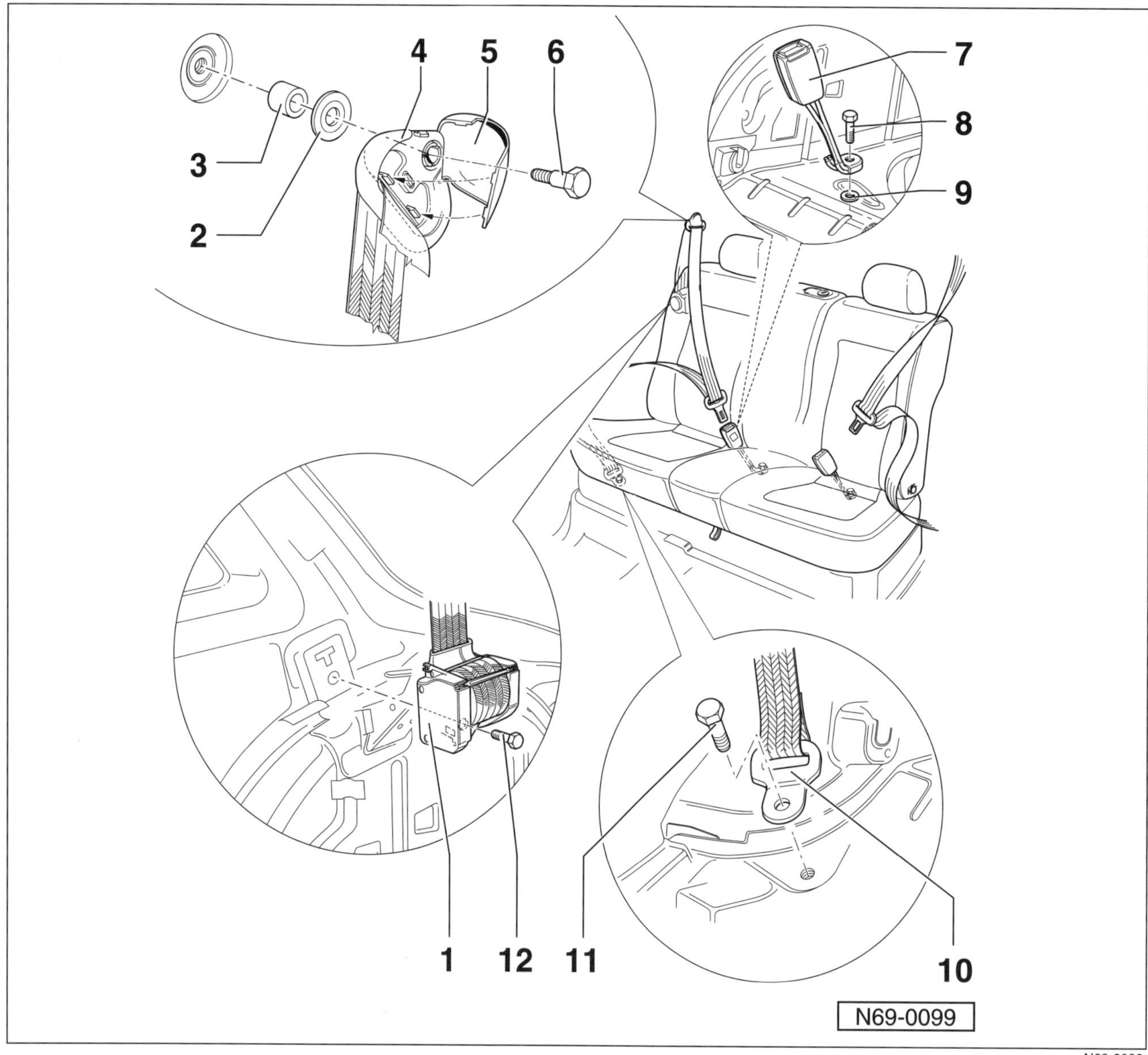

N69-0099

Fig. 6. Rear seatbelt assemblies shown with related components.

1. **Belt inertia reel**
   - Retaining tabs determine position of belt reel in mount
   - To remove, first remove quarter panel trim, then remove belt inertia reel (item 1), belt relay (item 4), and lower anchorage (item 10)
2. **Special washer**
3. **Spacer sleeve**
4. **Belt relay/guide**
5. **Belt relay/guide cover**
6. **Bolt**
   - Tighten to 40 Nm (30 ft-lb)
7. **Belt buckle (latch)**
8. **Bolt**
   - Tighten to 40 Nm (30 ft-lb)
9. **Sealing washer**
10. **Lower anchorage**
11. **Bolt**
    - Tighten to 40 Nm (30 ft-lb)
12. **Bolt**
    - Tighten to 40 Nm (30 ft-lb)

AIRBAGS

Diagnostics, component testing and repair of the airbag system should only be carried out by properly trained Volkswagen technicians using specialized test equipment.

When the ignition key is turned on, the airbag warning light will illuminate for approximately 5 seconds. See Fig. 7. The illuminated light indicates the self-test of the air bag electronic control module, and all of the related electronic components. If all monitored systems are operating normally, the light will go out. If the warning light does not go out after approximately 5 seconds, or if it comes on at any time while driving, the system has detected a fault and will not operate. In this case, the vehicle should be inspected by an authorized Volkswagen Dealer.

0024314

Fig. 7. Airbag warning light is shown at **arrow**.

If the vehicle has been involved in an accident where the airbag was deployed, Volkswagen specifies that the following components must be replaced:

- All airbag units that have been deployed
- Passenger side airbag support
- Airbag control module and sensors
- Airbag spiral spring/slip ring
- Deployed front seatbelt tensioners

In addition, the following must also be replaced if necessary:

- All damaged components including, but not limited to, seat frames, covers and rear seatbelts

In the event of an accident where the airbags have not been deployed, observe the airbag system warning light. If the airbag system warning light does not indicate a fault, it is not necessary to replace any airbag components.

Special precautions for airbag equipped vehicles

Special service precautions must be followed to prevent possible serious bodily injury to the repair technician and others involved in the handling and storage of airbag components and to insure proper operation in the event of a collision. For an overview of the airbag system. See Fig. 8.

WARNING —

- *Before working on any airbag, steering wheel or steering column component, always* ***disconnect the battery first.***
- *No waiting time is required after disconnecting the battery. Airbag systems can be worked on immediately.*
- *Airbags are inflated by an explosive device. Handled improperly or without adequate safeguards and training, the system can be very dangerous. Special precautions must be observed prior to any work at or near the steering wheel and steering column including the pedal assembly.*
- *The airbag is a vehicle safety system. To guard against personal injury or airbag system failure, only factory trained Volkswagen service technicians should test, disassemble or service the airbag system.*
- *Airbag units that have been dropped onto a hard surface must not be installed. Always replace any airbag system component that has been mechanically or physically damaged (example: dented or cracked).*
- *Make sure that no one is in the passenger compartment when connecting the battery Ground (GND) strap.*
- *A technician must be electrostatically discharged before picking up or touching any airbag unit. This is accomplished by touching a suitable metal ground such as a water or heating pipe or metal frame. If in the vehicle, this is accomplished by touching a suitable chassis ground such as a door latch or striker.*
- *Install new airbag unit as soon as the unit is removed from the packaging. Reinstall in packaging if work will not be completed immediately.*
- *Do not leave any undeployed airbag unit unattended. If work is interrupted, store airbag unit in a secure location where it cannot be disturbed.*
- *Undeployed airbag units that have been replaced must only be stored and shipped in packaging designed specifically for the purpose, such as packaging found with the replacement unit.*
- *Undeployed airbag units that have been replaced must be properly identified as such.*
- *The storage and transportation of airbag units must be in accordance with all applicable Federal, State and Local rules and regulations.*
- *Airbag units that have been removed during the course of repairs must be stored with the padded side facing up and in a secure location where it cannot be disturbed.*
- *Observe all cautions, warnings and notes before starting repairs involving airbag systems.*

Airbag system, overview

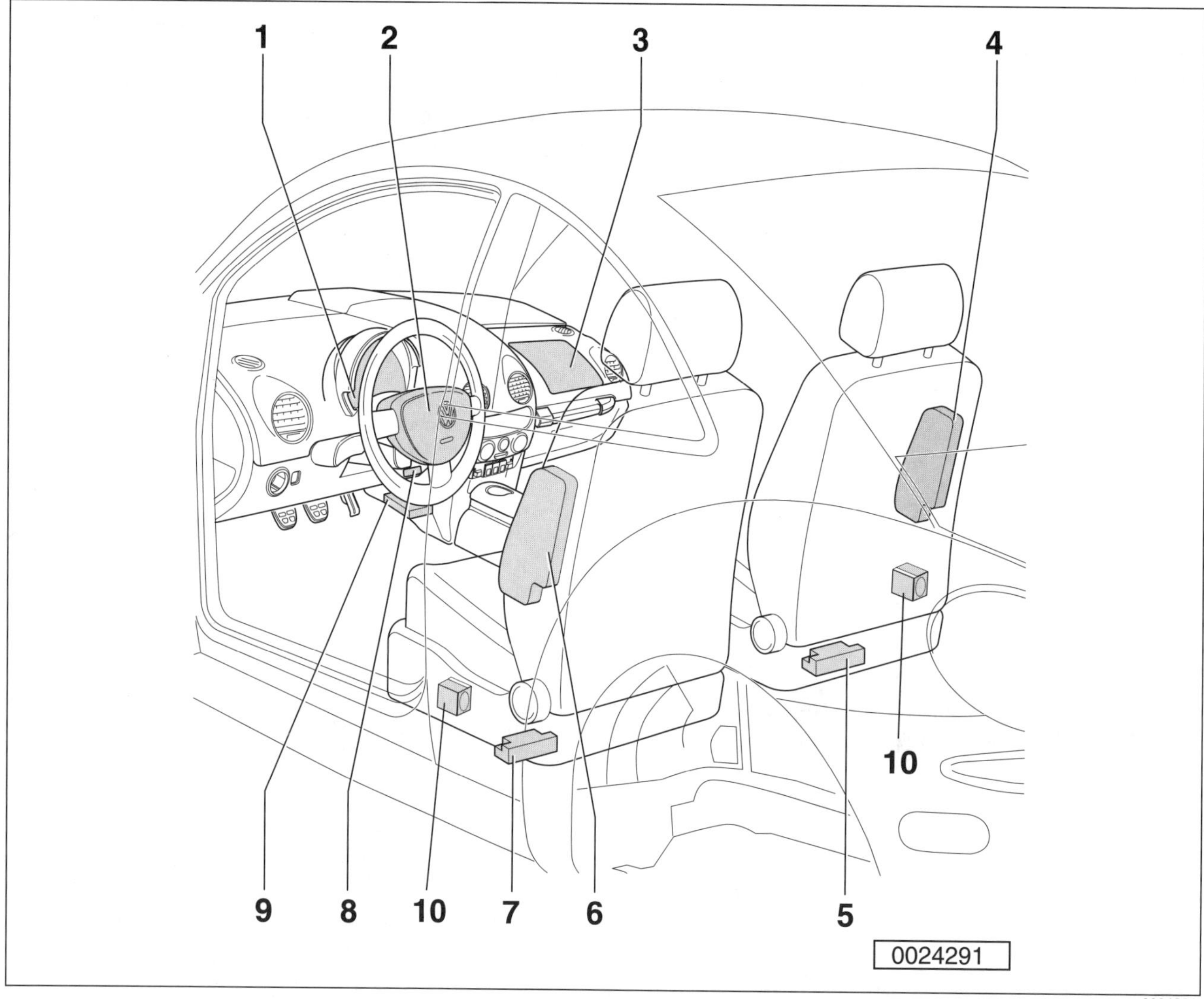

0024291

Fig. 8. Airbag system shown with related components including seatbelt tensioners where applicable.

1. **Airbag Malfunction Indicator Lamp (K75)**
    - Location: in instrument cluster
2. **Airbag unit, driver's side**
    - Location: in steering wheel
3. **Airbag unit, front passenger**
    - Location: in padded dash, right side
4. **Airbag unit, side, front passenger**
    - Location: in right front seat backrest frame
5. **Impact sensor, side airbag, front passenger**
    - Location: bolted to right front floor crossmember under passenger seat
6. **Airbag unit, side, driver**
    - Location: in left front seat backrest frame
7. **Impact sensor, side airbag, front passenger**
    - Location: bolted to left front floor crossmember under driver seat
8. **Data Link Connector, DLC**
    - Location: left lower side of instrument panel
9. **Airbag Control Module (J234)**
    - Location: on tunnel under center console
    - If replacing any airbag unit or airbag control module, consult your authorized Volkswagen Dealer's Parts Department for the proper registration procedure
10. **Pyrotechnic belt tensioner**
    - Electrically deployed via airbag system (m.y. 1999)
    - Mechanically activated, not part of airbag system (m.y. 1998)
    - Location: bottom of B-pillar

Airbag control module

The airbag control module is mounted to the floor on the tunnel near the base of the bulkhead. See Fig. 10. Most service and repair to the airbag system requires the use of a scan tool such as the Volkswagen VAG 1551/1552 or equivalent. Access for diagnosis is via the Data Link Connector (DTC) including coding of replacement control modules. See Fig. 9. Replacement airbag control modules are shipped uncoded and will not function when installed. Because of the specialized nature of these repairs, servicing should be referred to an authorized Volkswagen Dealer or qualified independent repair shop. Proper airbag control module coding is derived from the airbag control module part number as reported by the scan tool. For a listing of possible airbag control module codings, refer to **Table a**. Always verify vehicle equipment when installing and coding a new airbag control module.

Table a. Airbag control module coding

Vehicle equipment	Index	Airbag Control Module Code Number
Driver and passenger airbags	F	00070
Driver and passenger airbags and driver and passenger side airbags	AQ	16721

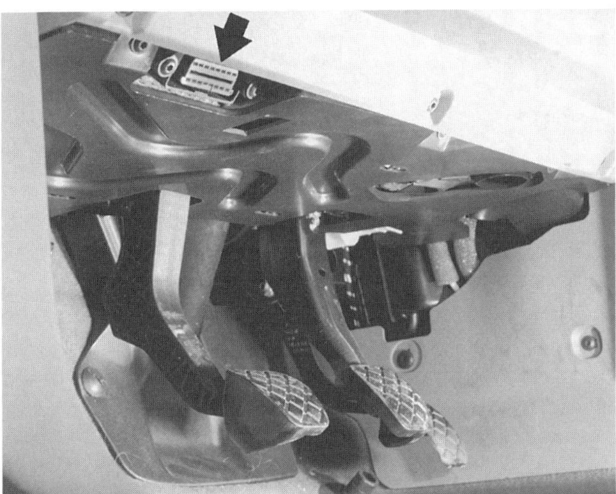

0024272

Fig. 9. Data Link Connector (DLC), (**arrow**) under left lower side of instrument panel.

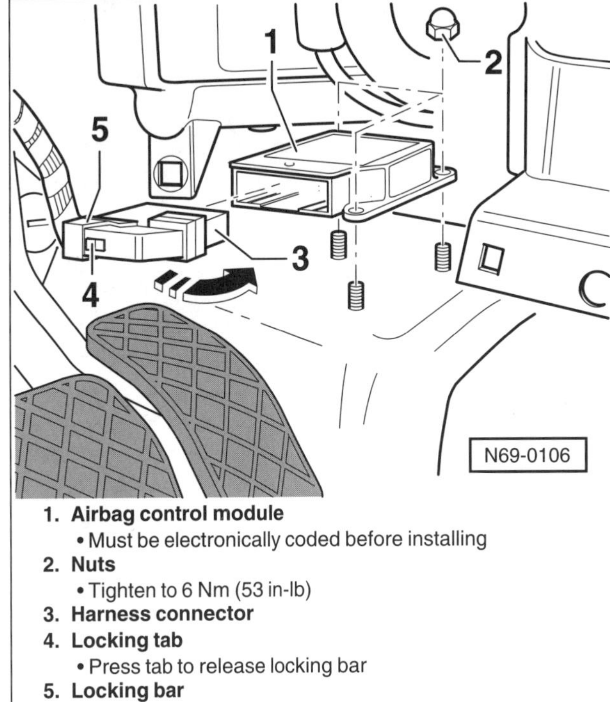

1. **Airbag control module**
   - Must be electronically coded before installing
2. **Nuts**
   - Tighten to 6 Nm (53 in-lb)
3. **Harness connector**
4. **Locking tab**
   - Press tab to release locking bar
5. **Locking bar**
   - Swing in direction of arrow to release harness connector

N69-0106

Fig. 10. Airbag control module mounting position on tunnel.

> ***WARNING —***
> - *Observe all cautions, warnings and notes before starting repairs involving airbag systems.*
> - *Disconnect battery Ground (GND) strap before disconnecting or removing the airbag control module.*

Airbag unit in steering wheel, assembly

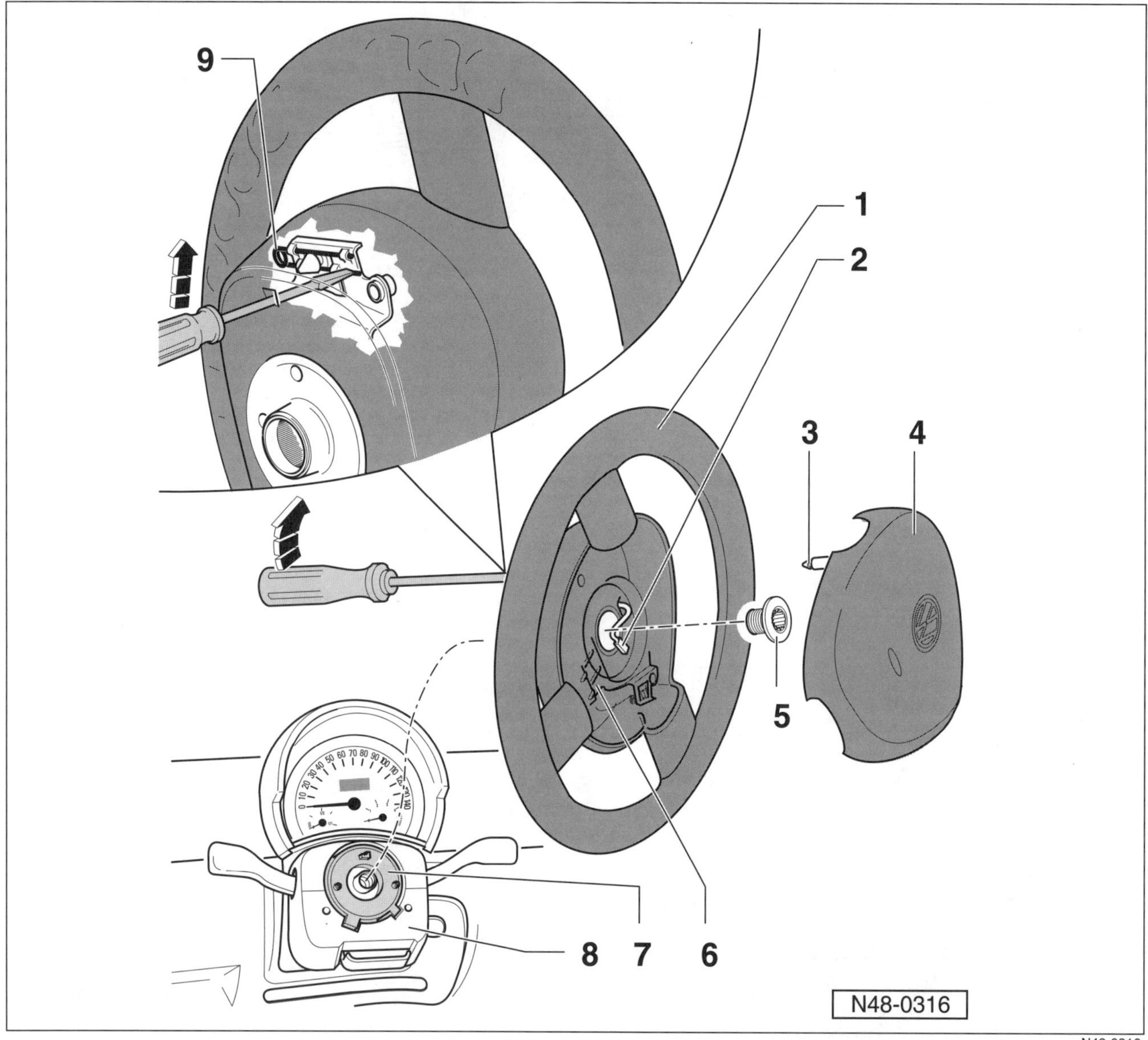

N48-0316

Fig. 11. Steering wheel shown with airbag and related components.

> ***WARNING —***
> - *Observe all cautions, warnings and notes before starting repairs involving airbag systems.*
> - *Observe all cautions, warnings and notes when completing repairs involving airbag systems.*

1. **Steering wheel**
2. **Harness connector for airbag**
3. **Locking lugs**
   - Release from rear of steering wheel
4. **Airbag unit**
5. **Bolt, multi-point socket-head**
   - Tighten to 50 Nm (37 ft-lb) with locking compound
   - Can be reused up to 5 times
   - Mark with center punch after each installation
6. **Securing plate**
7. **Spiral spring with slip ring**
8. **Steering column trim**
9. **Spring clip**

Airbag unit in steering wheel, removing

Removal of the steering wheel airbag unit is accomplished by inserting a tool into openings in the dashboard side of the steering wheel.

> ***WARNING —***
> *Observe all cautions, warnings and notes before starting repairs involving airbag systems.*

1. Disconnect battery ground strap.
2. Remove instrument cluster, see **90 Instruments**.
3. Release steering column adjustment lever.
4. Turn steering wheel until a spoke is vertical. Extend steering wheel fully and move to uppermost position.
5. Secure steering column adjustment lever.
6. Using a screwdriver approximately 175 mm (7 in.) long, insert approximately 45 mm (1¾ in.) from reverse side into hole on dashboard side of steering wheel hub. See Fig. 11.

   NOTE —
   If a screwdriver with a very short handle is used, it is possible to eliminate step 2 and leave the instrument cluster in place.

7. Press screwdriver in direction of arrow to press back spring clip (item 9, Fig. 11.) and release locking lug (item 3, Fig. 11.) of airbag unit.
8. Turn steering wheel back ½ turn (180°) and release second locking lug on opposite side.
9. Turn steering wheel to center position (wheels straight ahead).
10. Disconnect harness connector from airbag unit.
11. Place the removed airbag unit in a secure location with the padding side facing up.

Airbag unit in steering wheel, installing

1. Install instrument cluster as required.
2. Reconnect harness connector for airbag unit.
3. Position airbag unit on steering wheel and snap into place.

   NOTE —
   Airbag unit locking lugs must be heard and felt to snap into place.

4. Switch ignition on.

> ***CAUTION —***
> *Make sure the passenger compartment is not occupied before connecting the battery Ground (GND) strap.*

> ***WARNING —***
> *Observe all cautions, warnings and notes when completing repairs involving airbag systems.*

5. Connect battery ground strap.

Airbag spiral spring/slip ring, removing and installing

> ***WARNING —***
> *Observe all cautions, warnings and notes before starting repairs involving airbag systems.*

1. Turn the wheels to the straight ahead position.
2. Disconnect battery ground strap.
3. Remove airbag unit in steering wheel as described earlier.
4. Remove steering wheel as described earlier.
5. Remove steering column adjustment lever and lower and upper steering column switch trim. See Fig. 12.

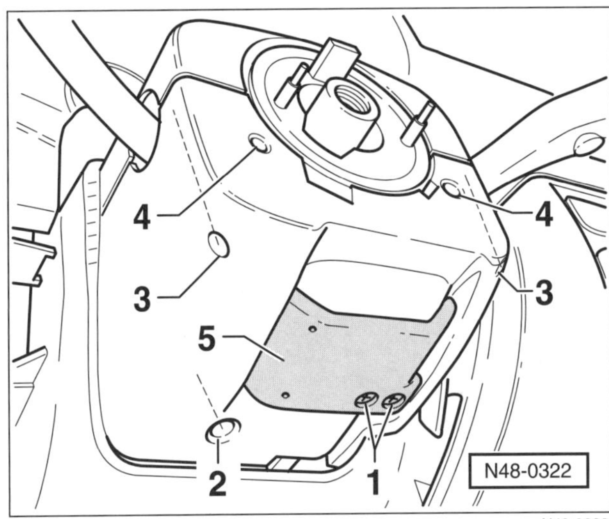

N48-0322

Fig. 12. Steering column as seen from below. Remove screws (**1**), lever (**5**), and securing screws (**2**), (**3**), (**4**).

6. Unplug harness connector and release locking lugs on spiral spring/slip ring and pull off. See Fig. 13.

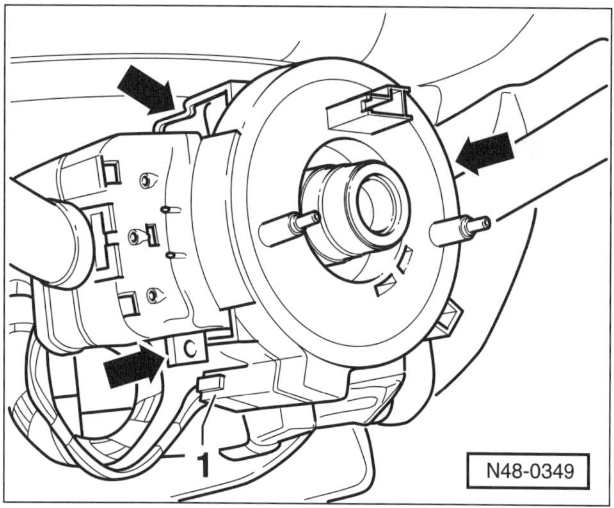

N48-0349

Fig. 13. Remove spiral spring/slip ring by releasing lugs (**arrows**) and unplugging harness connector (**1**).

7. Installation is the reverse of removal.

> ***WARNING —***
> *Observe all cautions, warnings and notes when completing repairs involving airbag systems.*

Side airbag units

Both driver's and passenger's front seats are equipped with airbags mounted in the seat backrest frames. These airbags are designed to deploy under certain side impact conditions and are triggered by separate sensors mounted to the front floor crossmembers under the front seats. Before removing the front seats, a special safety harness must be installed to prevent accidental deployment of the airbag units. See Fig. 14.

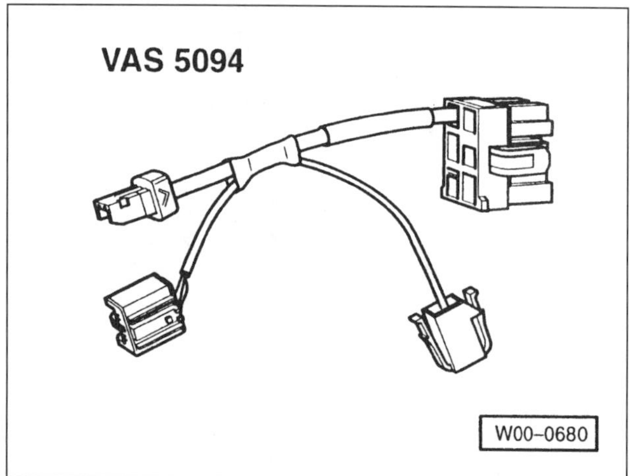

W00-0680

Fig. 14. Special tool VAS 5094 must be installed on seats before removal or repairs.

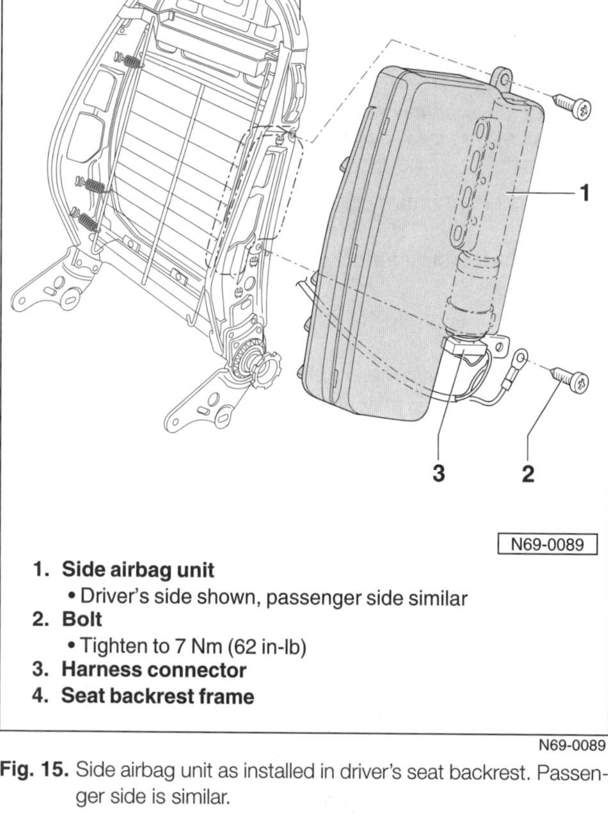

1. **Side airbag unit**
   - Driver's side shown, passenger side similar
2. **Bolt**
   - Tighten to 7 Nm (62 in-lb)
3. **Harness connector**
4. **Seat backrest frame**

N69-0089

Fig. 15. Side airbag unit as installed in driver's seat backrest. Passenger side is similar.

> ***WARNING —***
> - *Observe all cautions, warnings and notes before starting and when completing repairs involving airbag system.*
> - *Volkswagen of America specifically warns against the installation of aftermarket upholstery on any vehicle equipped with side airbags. The factory-installed upholstery is designed to separate in specific places at specific rates, and in specific directions. Installation of non-factory upholstery including, but not limited to, "beads" and "sheepskins", may cause seat mounted airbags to deploy when they are not supposed to; fail to deploy when they should; or to deploy in some manner other than designed. This is a safety hazard and could result in serious injury or death to occupants of the vehicle.*

Impact sensor, side airbag, overview

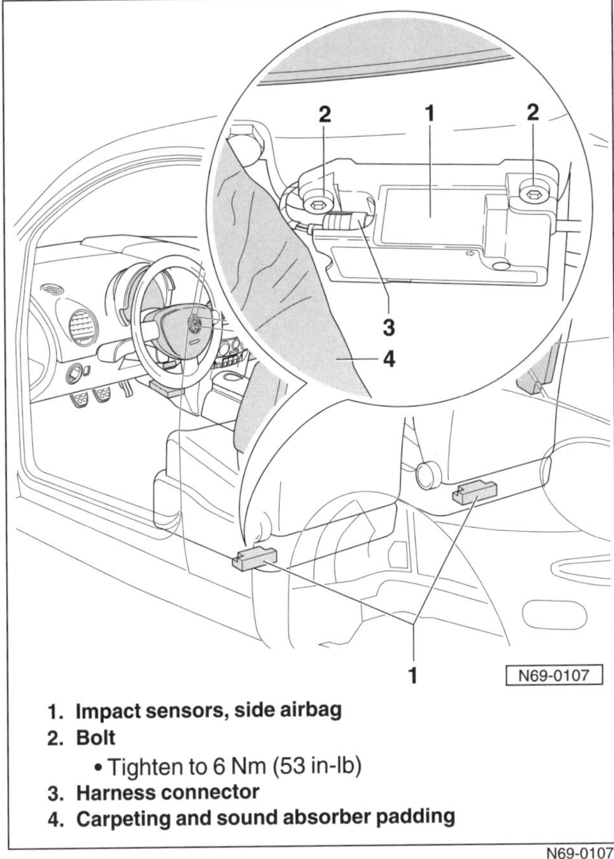

Fig. 16. Impact sensors for side airbags shown in position on the floor crossmember under the seats.

Airbag unit, front passenger, assembly

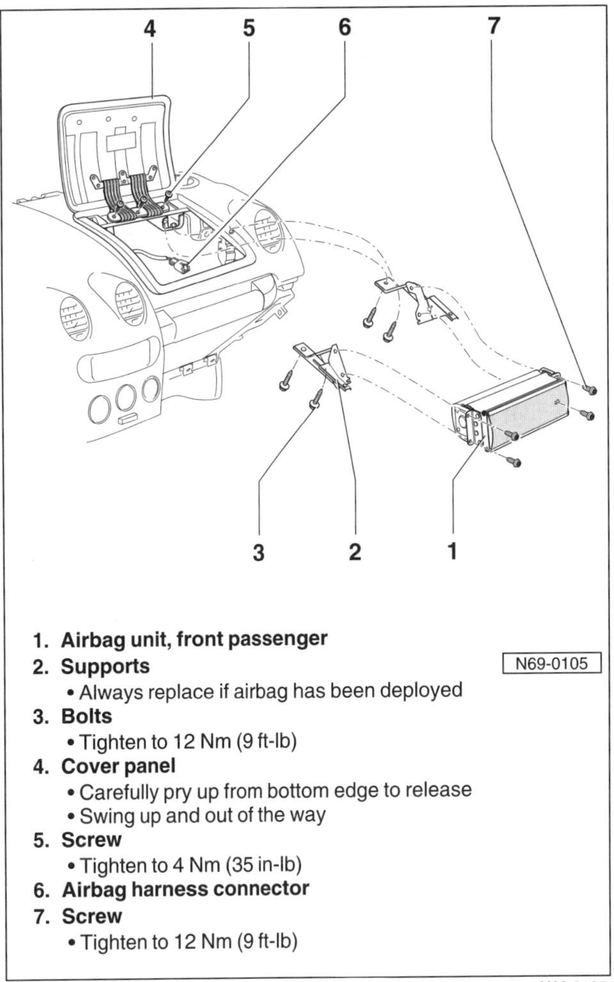

4
5
6
7
3
2
1
N69-0105
1. Airbag unit, front passenger
2. Supports
• Always replace if airbag has been deployed
3. Bolts
• Tighten to 12 Nm (9 ft-lb)
4. Cover panel
• Carefully pry up from bottom edge to release
• Swing up and out of the way
5. Screw
• Tighten to 4 Nm (35 in-lb)
6. Airbag harness connector
7. Screw
• Tighten to 12 Nm (9 ft-lb)
N69-0105

Fig. 17. Airbag and related components for front seat passenger.

QUALITY REVIEW

When you have finished working under the hood and around other areas of the vehicle, it is advisable to take a moment to quality check or review your work. This helps to insure that the operation or repair has been completed properly with all affected systems functioning within normal parameters. These may include the following:

- Ensure that all cable ties and clamps that were removed as part of the repair are replaced.
- Ensure that all fasteners and hardware were replaced and torqued as specified.
- Make sure that all other components involved in the repair are positioned correctly, properly torqued and function properly.
- Make sure that all tools, shop cloths, fender covers and protective tapes are removed before closing the hood.
- Clean grease and fingerprints from painted surfaces, steering wheel, upholstery and shifter.
- Make sure that seatbelt and airbag warning lights function correctly.
- Unlock anti-theft radio and reset clock.

70 Trim–Interior

GENERAL

This repair group covers interior equipment and trim panels, including center console and instrument panel removal. For interior lights and accessories see **96 Lights, Accessories–Interior**.

CENTER CONSOLE

Center console, removing and installing

1. Pull up parking brake lever and use a screwdriver to disengage trim around lever. Pull trim forward to remove. See Fig. 1.

2. Manual transmission vehicles:
   - Carefully pry shift boot out from center console.
   - Turn shift boot inside out to expose retaining clamp.
   - Remove retaining clamp and shift knob with shift boot, see **34 Manual Transmission**.

3. For automatic transmission vehicles, see **37 Automatic Transmission** for removing selector lever position display and related components.

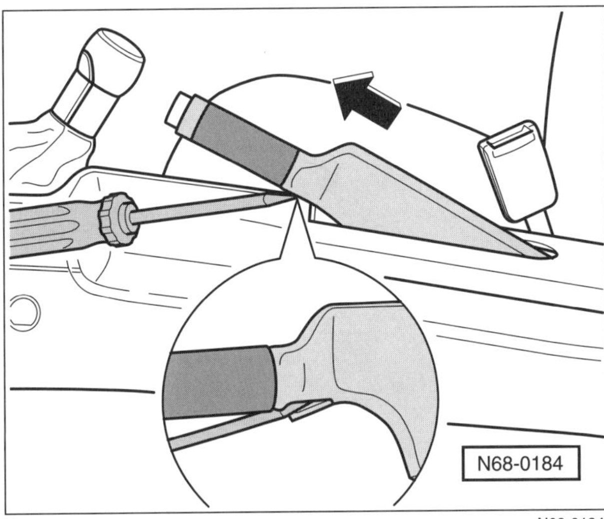

N68-0184

Fig. 1. Use a screwdriver to release parking brake lever trim and pull trim forward (**arrow**).

4. For a guide to center console components, refer to Fig. 2.

70

Center console assembly

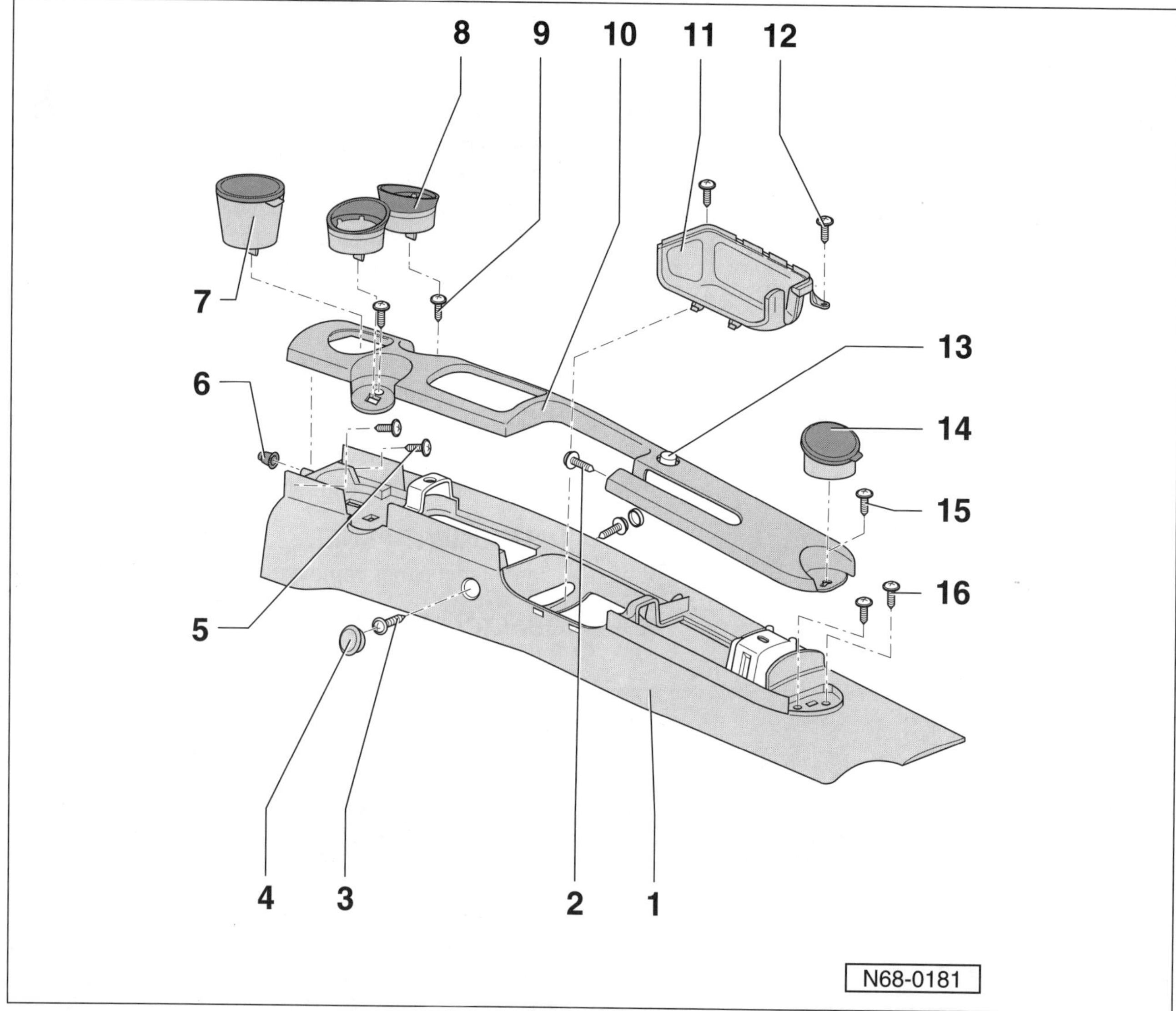

N68-0181

Fig. 2. Center console components.

1. **Center console**
2. **Bolt**
3. **Screw**
   - Qty. 2
4. **Cover**
   - Qty. 2
5. **Screw**
   - Qty. 2
6. **Rubber grommet**
7. **Ashtray**
8. **Cupholder**
   - Qty. 2
9. **Screw**
   - Qty. 2
10. **Cover**
11. **Center console insert**
12. **Screw**
    - Qty. 2
13. **Cigarette lighter**
14. **Ashtray**
15. **Screw**
16. **Screw**
    - Qty. 2

Center console, removing and installing (continued)

5. Remove ashtrays (items 7 and 14, Fig. 2.), if applicable, and cupholders (item 8, Fig. 2.) by pulling upward out of center console.

6. Remove center console cover mounting hardware (items 9, 2, and 15, Fig. 2.)

7. Remove console cover and disconnect harness connector for cigarette lighter/12V accessory outlet.

> ***WARNING —***
> - *Disconnect the battery Ground strap (GND) from negative (–) battery terminal before working on the electrical system.*
> - *Disconnecting the negative (–) battery cable may erase fault codes and basic settings in the engine management and automatic transmission control modules. Some driveability problems may be noticed until the system re-adapts to operating conditions. OBD II readiness codes, which may be required for emissions testing, may also be erased. Convenience electronics (alarm system, interior light control, power locks, mirrors, and windows) may need to be re-set using a VAG 1551/1552 or equivalent scan tool.*

8. Remove center console insert mounting screws and insert (items 12 and 11, Fig. 2.)

9. Pry off covers on either side of console and remove screws (items 4 and 3, Fig. 2.)

10. Remove remaining console mounting screws (items 5 and 16, Fig. 2.)

11. Lift center console from rear and carefully pull upward over shift lever.

12. Installation is reverse of removal, noting the following:
    - After connecting battery, check all vehicle equipment (radio, clock, power windows) for proper operation.
    - After connecting battery, the readiness code for the ECM will need to be re-set using VAG 1551/1552 scan tool or equivalent.

INTERIOR EQUIPMENT

Glove box, removing

1. Carefully pry off right side instrument panel cover at mounting clips.

2. Remove glove box mounting screw behind right side cover. See Fig. 3.

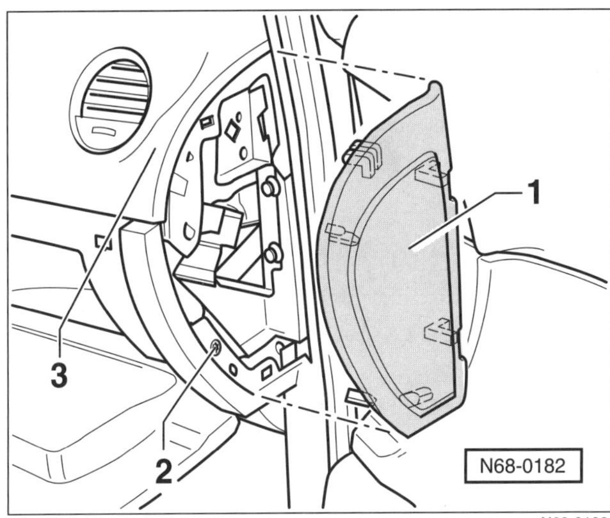

N68-0182

Fig. 3. Pry off right side trim panel (**1**) and remove screw (**2**).

3. Pry off switch console covers and remove mounting screws. Pull switch console down from bracket. See Fig. 4.

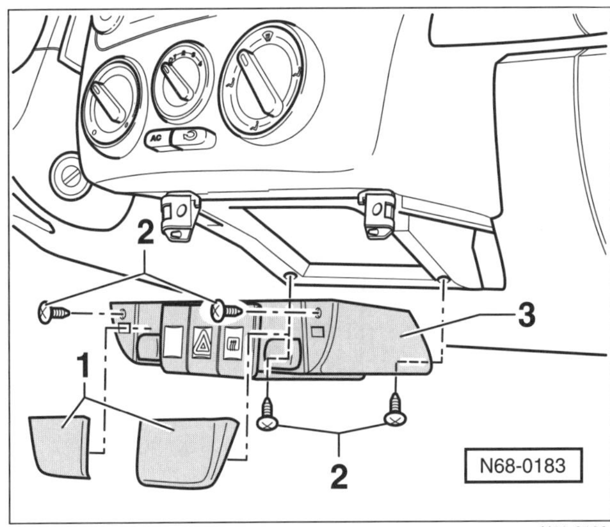

N68-0183

Fig. 4. Pry off covers (**1**), remove screws (**2**) and switch console (**3**).

4. Remove the glovebox retaining screws and the glove box. See Fig. 5.

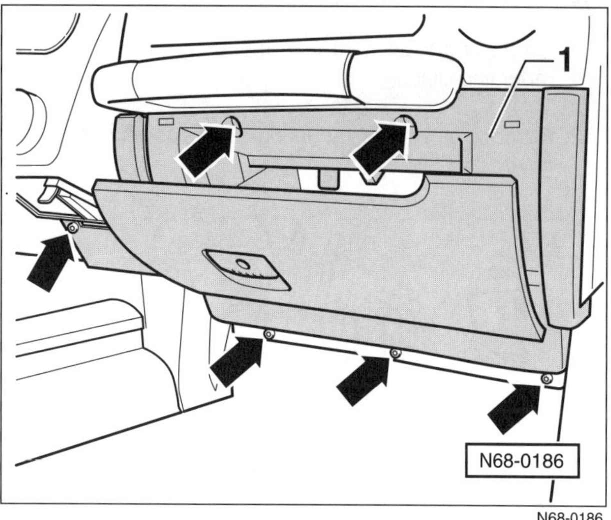

N68-0186

Fig. 5. Remove retaining screws (**arrows**) and glove box (**1**).

5. Disconnect harness connector for glove box light.

Hold strap, removing

1. Pry hold strap cover off with screwdriver and pull down.

2. Remove hold strap mounting screws and take off strap. See Fig. 6.

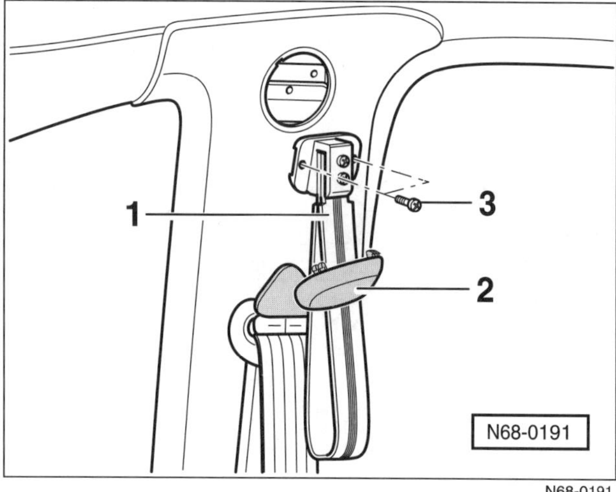

N68-0191

Fig. 6. Pry off cover (**2**) remove screws (**3**) and holding strap (**1**).

Inside rear view mirror, removing

1. Pull rear edge of mirror mount trim down from headliner and unhook trim at front edge. See Fig. 7.

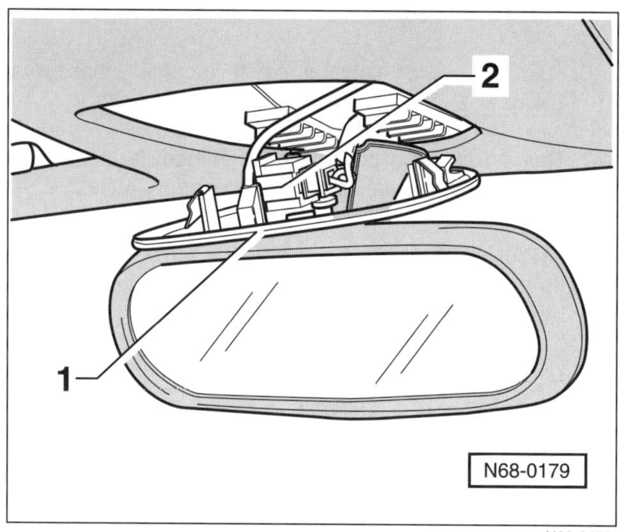

N68-0179

Fig. 7. Pry rear edge of trim (**1**) down and unhook at front edge. Disconnect harness connector (**2**).

2. Disconnect harness connector for interior light from mirror mount.

3. Press mirror downward at an angle off retaining plate (spring clip in mirror base). See Fig. 8.

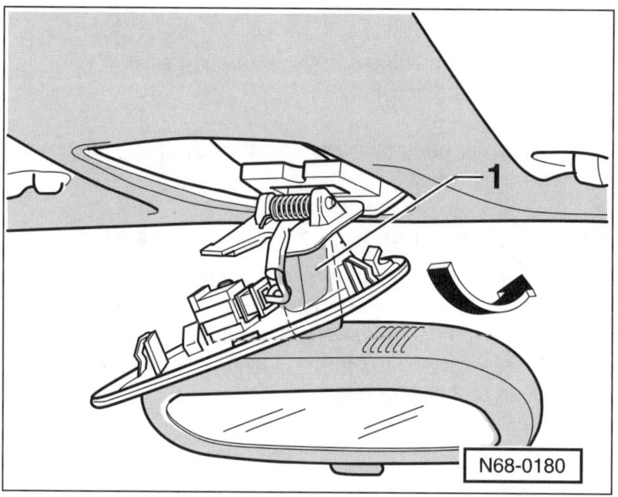

N68-0180

Fig. 8. Rotate mirror (**1**) downward (**arrow**) at an angle and release from retaining plate.

Instrument panel handle, removing

1. Pull off handle mount covers.

2. Remove mounting screws and pull handle out of instrument panel. See Fig. 9.

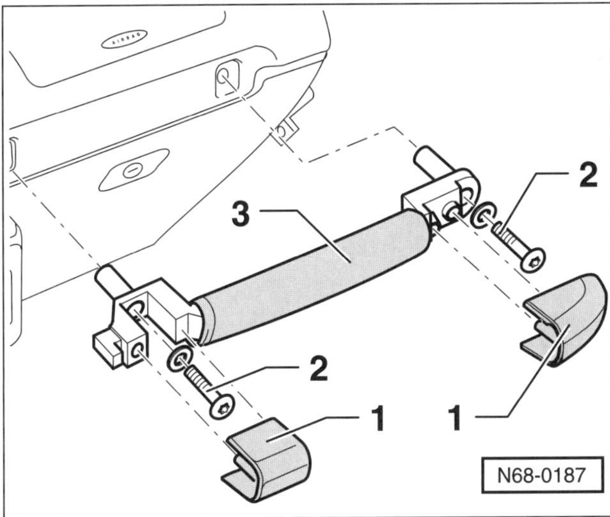

N68-0187

Fig. 9. Remove covers (**1**), screws (**2**) and handle (**3**).

Tightening torque

• Handle to instrument panel . . . . 8 Nm (71 in-lb)

Roof handle, removing

1. Fold handle down.

2. Pry cover up with screwdriver. Remove mounting screws and handle.

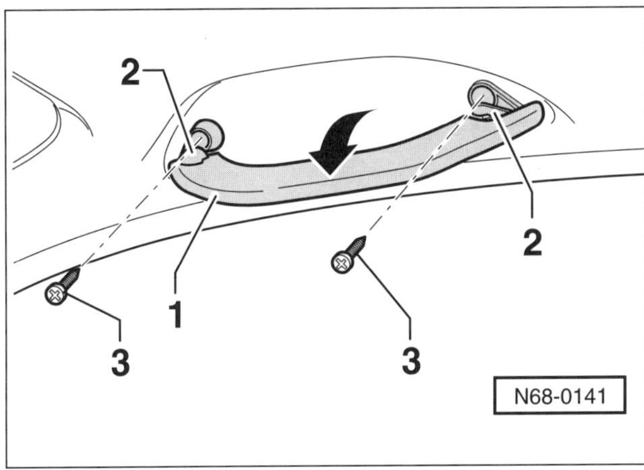

N68-0141

Fig. 10. Fold handle (**1**) down, pry open caps (**2**) and remove screws (**3**).

Sun visor, removing

1. Release sun visor from inner mount (item 2, Fig. 11.)

2. Pry off cover cap and remove mounting screw (items 5 and 6, Fig. 11.)

3. Swing sun visor outer mount (item 4, Fig. 11.) down from roof and separate harness connector (item 3, Fig. 11.)

4. Pry off inner mount cover cap (item 7, Fig. 11.)

5. Remove inner mount screws and mount (items 8 and 2, Fig. 11.)

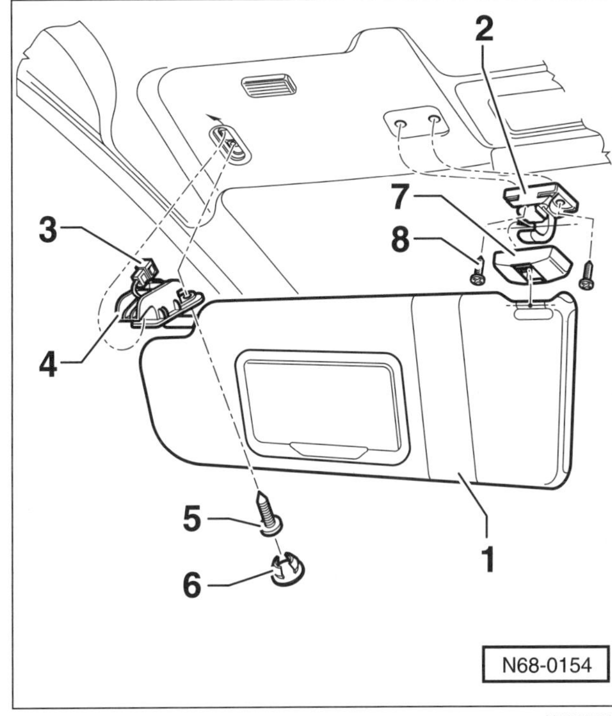

N68-0154

Fig. 11. Sun visor and related mounting hardware.

TRIM PANELS

Details of the interior trim panels are shown in Fig. 12 through Fig. 15. Unless otherwise noted, installation is the reverse of removal.

It is advisable to use a special non-marring trim removal tool (plastic bone) to pry various trim panels out without damaging paint or other adjacent panels.

A-pillar upper trim, removing

1. Pull door inner seal off A-pillar.
2. Starting at top, unclip trim from A-pillar. Lift up to remove.
3. Disconnect harness connector for speaker.
4. Before installing trim, check clips on A-pillar and replace as necessary. See Fig. 12.
5. After installing trim, make sure door seal is seated correctly.

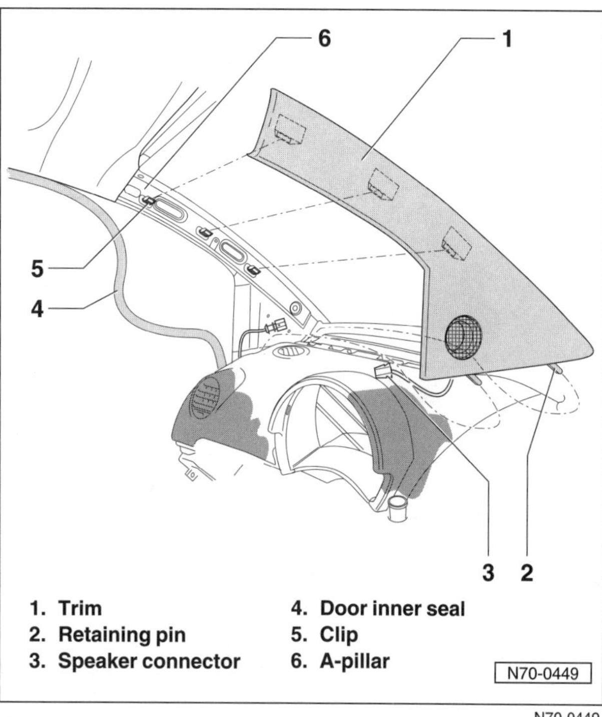

N70-0449

Fig. 12. A-pillar upper trim on left side.

A-pillar lower trim, removing

1. Remove hood release lever as described in **55 Hoods and Lids**.
2. Unclip top part of A-pillar lower trim and release bottom from sill panel trim. See Fig. 13.

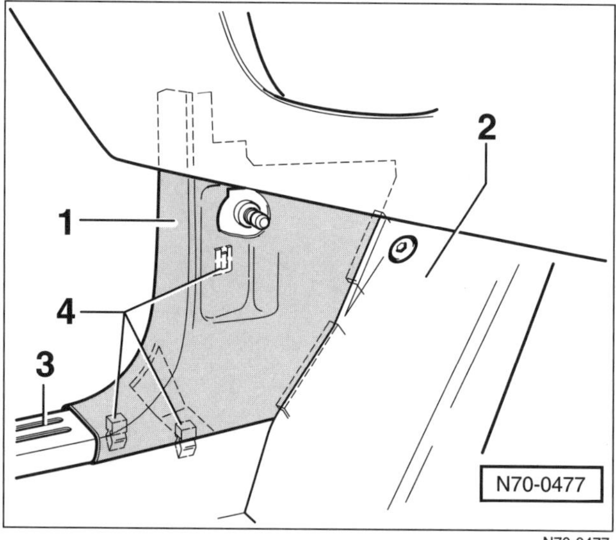

N70-0477

Fig. 13. Unclip top of trim (**1**) first, then unclip from sill (**3**). Driver's side trim is also inserted into cover for foot support (**2**).

B-pillar trim, removing

1. Remove rear side panel as described later.
2. Remove D-ring for front seat belt, see **69 Seatbelts, Airbags**.
3. Pull inner door seal off B-pillar.
4. Pry off hold strap cover and remove hold strap as described earlier.
5. Pry B-pillar trim off at sides and then in center. See Fig. 14.
6. Before installing B-pillar trim check condition of retaining clips and replace as necessary.

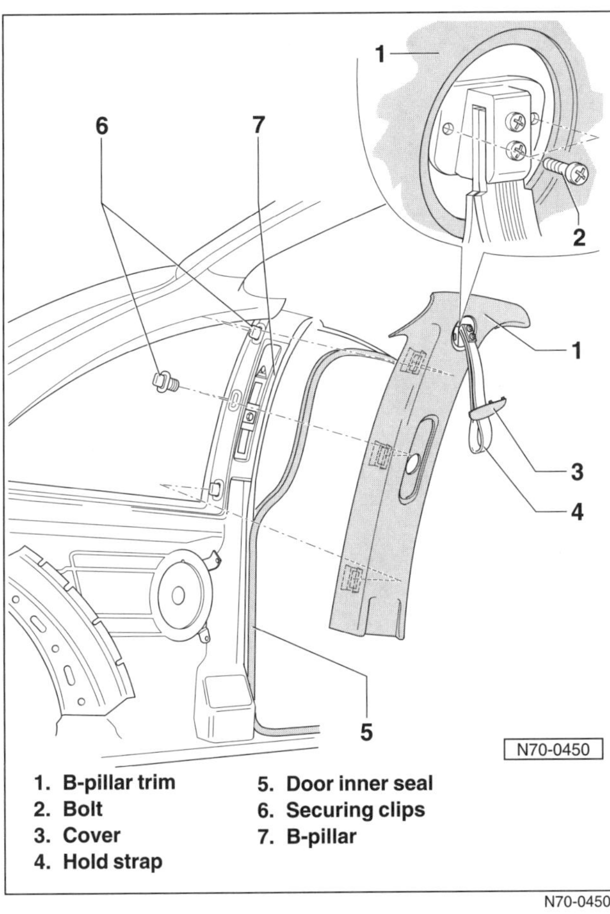

N70-0450

Fig. 14. B-pillar trim and mounting hardware.

C-pillar trim, removing

1. Remove side panel trim as described later.
2. Remove D-ring for front and rear seat belts, see **69 Seatbelts, Airbags**.
3. Remove B-pillar trim as described earlier.
4. Pull center rear trim strip (clipped on) downward off roof frame.
5. Remove C-pillar trim mounting screw and pull trim off from top. See Fig. 15.
6. Before installing C-pillar trim check condition of retaining clips and replace as necessary.

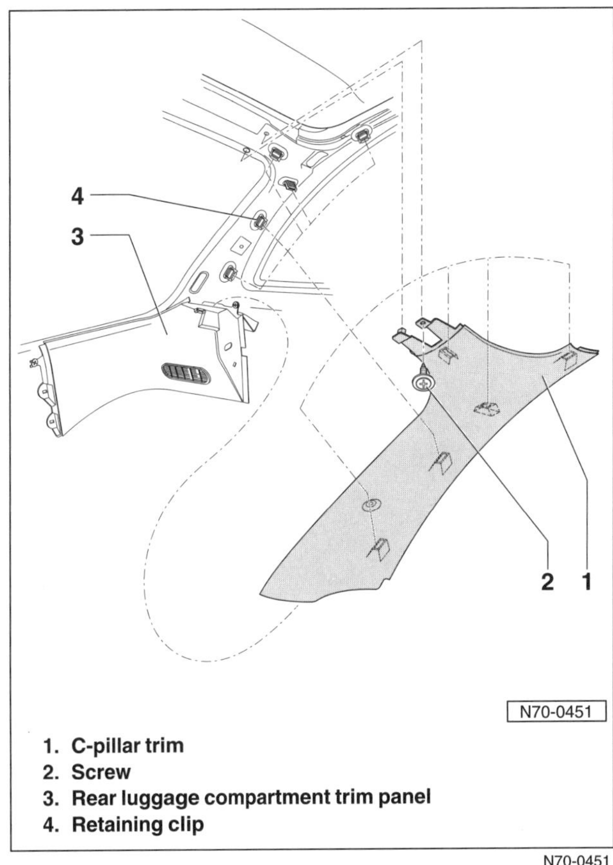

N70-0451

Fig. 15. C-pillar trim and mounting hardware.

Rear side panel, removing

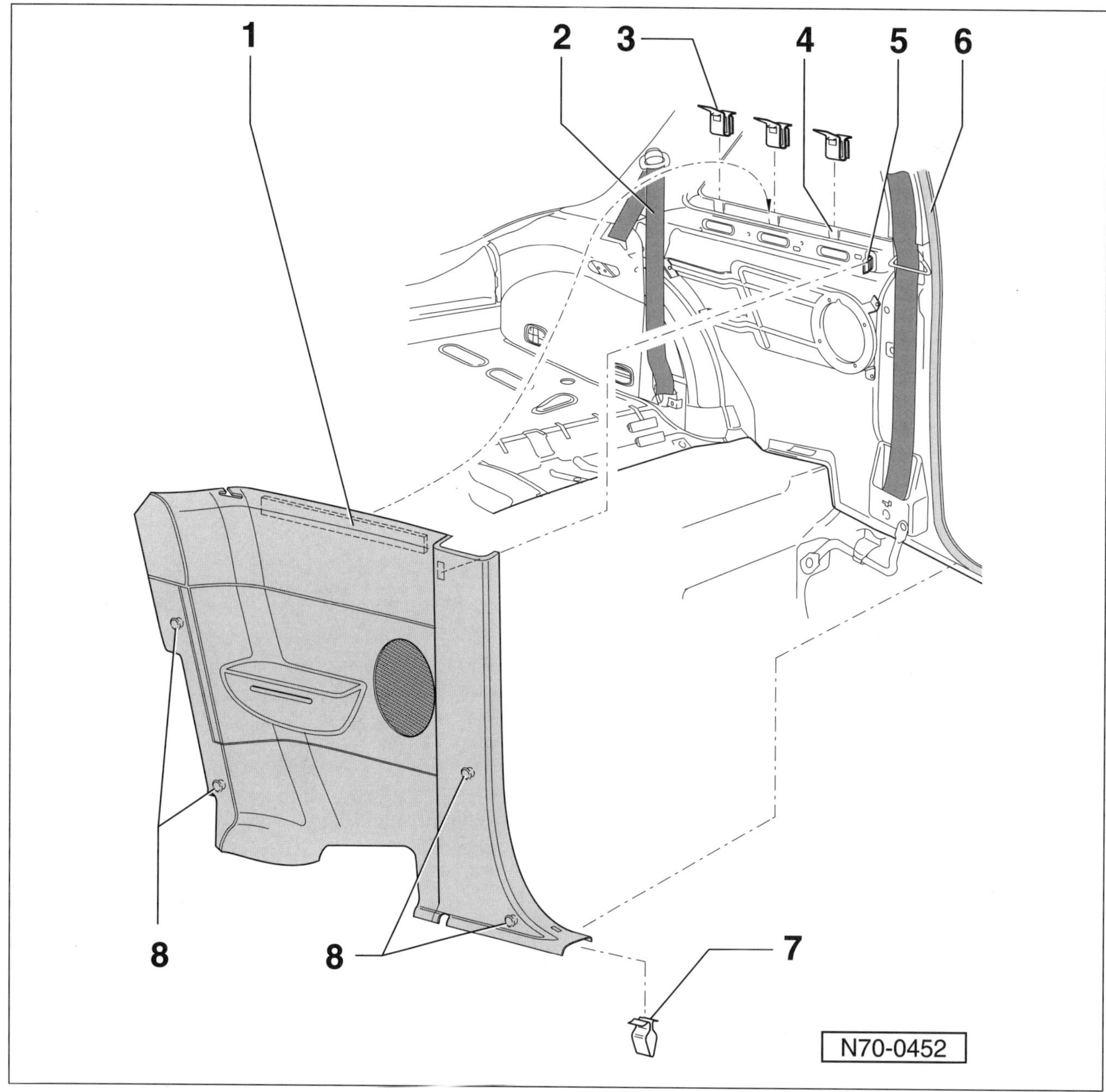

N70-0452

Fig. 16. Rear side panel.

1. **Rear side panel**
   - Removing:
     Remove rear seat cushion and backrest
     Pull off inner door seal from lower B-pillar
     Pull trim out of clips (items 8 and 5)
     Lift out of clips (item 7)
2. **Seat belt with tensioner**
3. **Clip**
   - Attached to side window flange
   - May be necessary to attach to window flange for side panel installation
4. **Securing point**
   - For clips (item 3)
5. **Clip**
   - Check for damage and replace if necessary
6. **Inner door seal**
   - Check for proper position after installing side panel
7. **Clip**
8. **Clip**

Door panel assembly

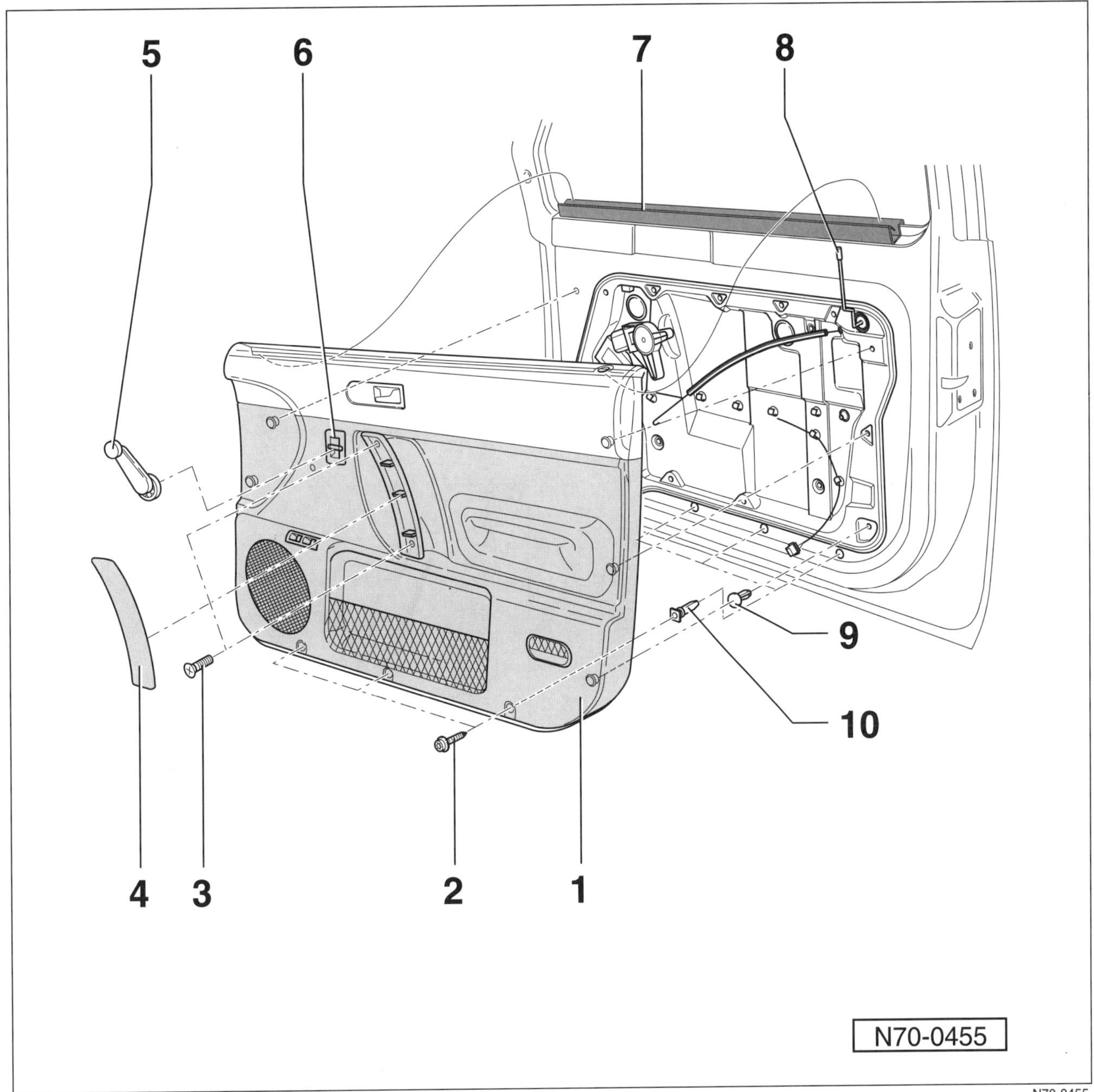

N70-0455

Fig. 17. Door panel and related mounting hardware.

1. **Door panel**
2. **Screw**
   - Qty. 3
3. **Screw**
   - Qty. 3
4. **Handle cover**
5. **Window crank**
   - For manual windows
6. **Window switch**
   - For power windows
7. **Window inner slot seal**
8. **Locking knob**
9. **Clip**
   - Qty. 3
10. **Screw**
    - Qty. 3

Door panel, removing and installing

It is advisable to use a special non-marring trim removal tool (plastic bone) to pry various trim panels out without damaging paint or other adjacent panels.

> ***WARNING —***
> - *Disconnect the battery ground strap (GND) from negative (–) battery terminal before working on the electrical system.*
> - *Disconnecting the negative (–) battery cable may erase fault codes and basic settings in the engine management and automatic transmission control modules. Some driveability problems may be noticed until the system re-adapts to operating conditions. OBD II readiness codes, which may be required for emissions testing, may also be erased. Convenience electronics (alarm system, interior light control, power locks, mirrors, and windows) may need to be re-set using a VAG 1551/1552 or equivalent scan tool.*

NOTE —
Be sure to have the anti-theft radio code on hand before disconnecting the battery.

1. Carefully pry off door handle trim. See Fig. 18.

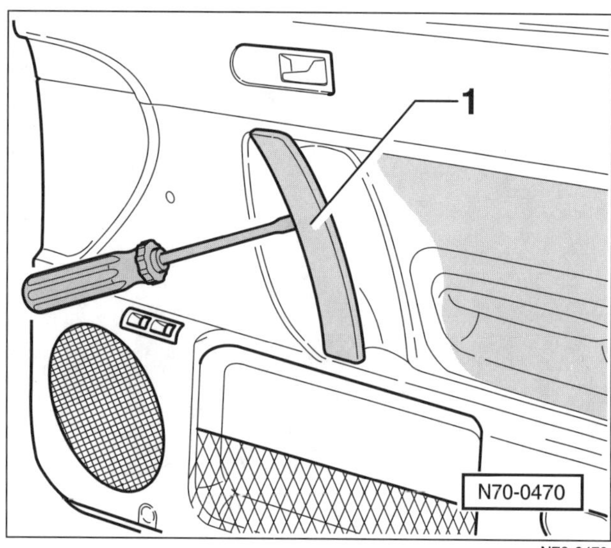

N70-0470

Fig. 18. Carefully pry off door handle trim.

2. On cars with manual windows, slide spacer behind window crank handle forward (retaining clip will be unlocked) and pull window crank off shaft. See Fig. 19.

3. Remove door panel mounting screws and unclip door panel at sides. See Fig. 20.

4. Lift door trim upward off window slot.

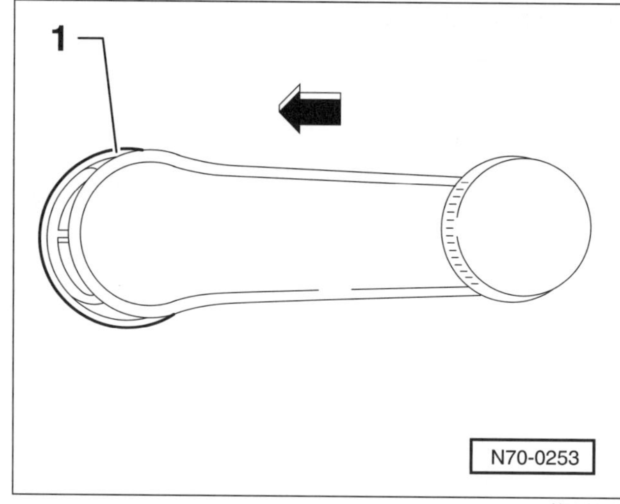

N70-0253

Fig. 19. On cars with manual windows, slide spacer (**1**) forward (**arrow**) to release retaining clip and pull window crank off shaft.

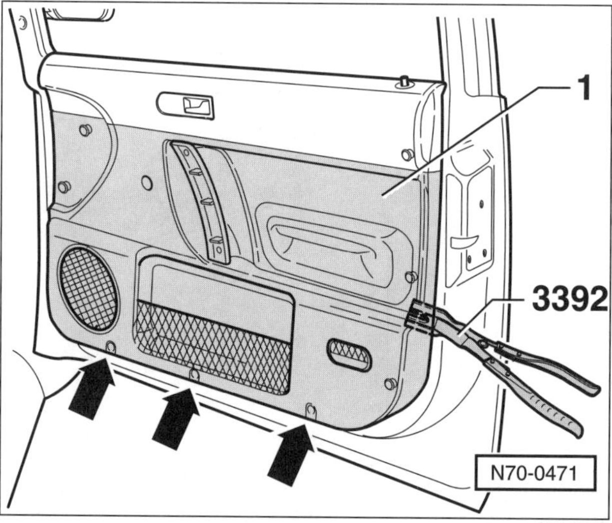

N70-0471

Fig. 20. Remove mounting screws (**arrows**) and unclip door panel at sides with VW special tool 3392, or equivalent. Lift door panel upward out of window slot.

5. Unclip cable guide from door latch with screwdriver, pull cable out from retainer and unhook cable hook. See Fig. 21.

6. Disconnect harness connectors from door panel switches.

7. Install door panel in reverse order of removal, noting the following:
   - Check door trim clips before installing and replace if necessary.
   - After connecting battery, check operation of vehicle equipment (radio, clock, power windows).

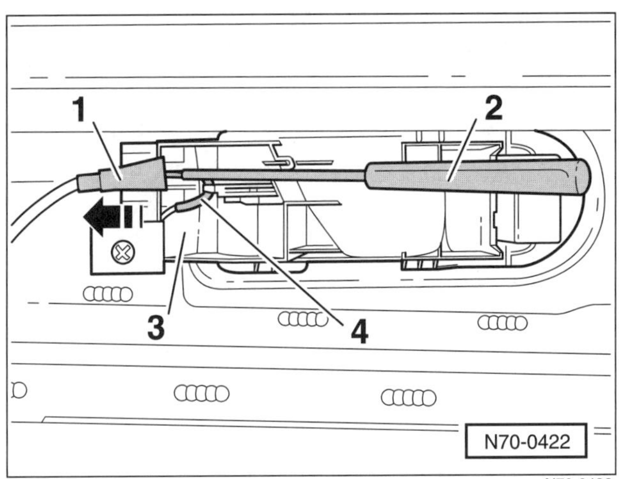

N70-0422

Fig. 21. Unclip cable guide (**1**) with screwdriver (**2**), pull out from retainer (**3**) in direction of **arrow** and unhook cable hook (**4**).

Driver side footwell cover, removing

1. Remove footwell cover mounting screws.

2. Pull footwell cover to rear off retainers. See Fig. 22.

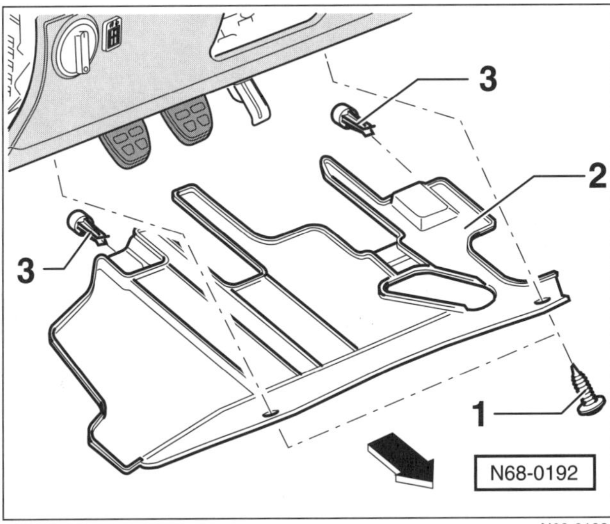

N68-0192

Fig. 22. Remove screws (**1**) and pull footwell cover (**2**) off retainers (**3**).

Inner plenum covers, removing

The inner section of the plenum is accessed through the top covers of the dashboard. The Engine Control Module (ECM), the automatic Transmission Control Module (TCM) and the dust and pollen filter are located in the inner plenum.

1. Remove center plenum cover. See Fig. 23.

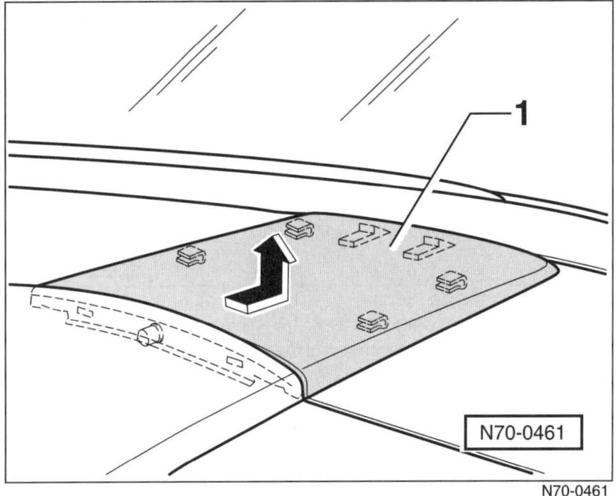

N70-0461

Fig. 23. Push center cover (**1**) forward and lift out (**arrow**) from instrument panel.

2. Remove retaining screws in center of plenum. See Fig. 24.

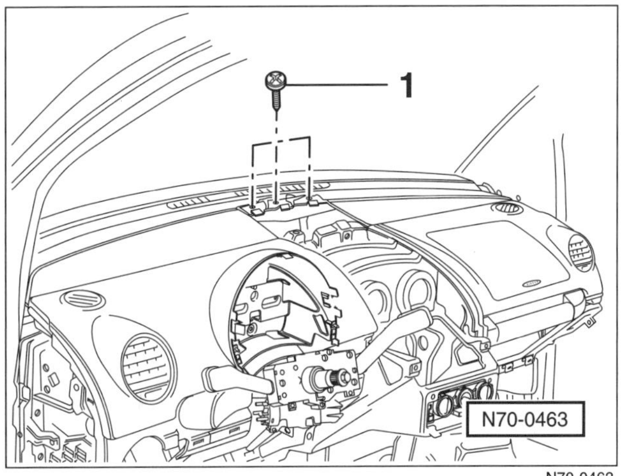

N70-0463

Fig. 24. Remove screws (**1**) in center of plenum.

3. Lift left side plenum panel cover and pull towards center of car to release from retainer in A-pillar. See Fig. 25.

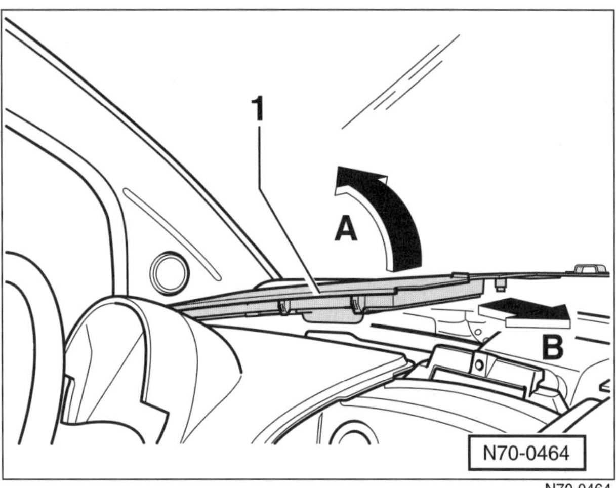

N70-0464

Fig. 25. Lift left side plenum cover (**1**) in direction of **arrow A** and pull out toward center of car (**arrow B**).

4. Lift right side plenum panel cover and pull towards center of car to release from retainer in A-pillar. See Fig. 26.

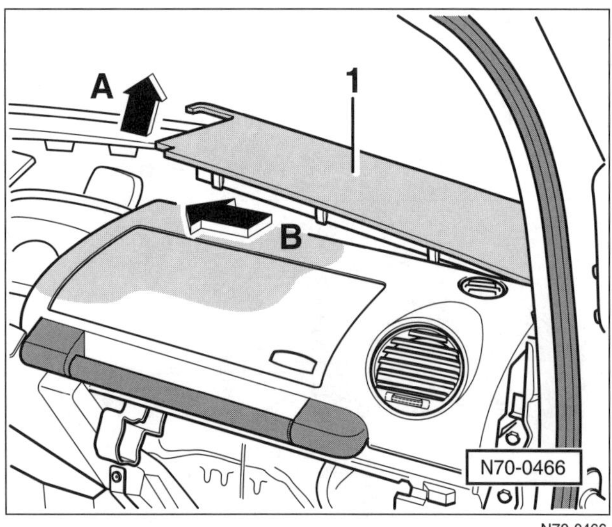

N70-0466

Fig. 26. Lift right side plenum cover (**1**) in direction of **arrow A** and pull out toward center of car (**arrow B**)

5. Remove mounting bolts from right and/or left close-out panel and pull panels upward out of plenum to remove. See Fig. 27.

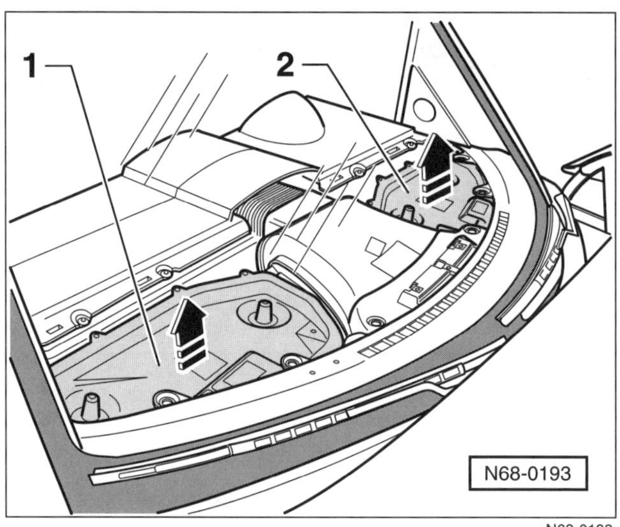

N68-0193

Fig. 27. Remove mounting bolts and pull up close out panels (**1** and/or **2**) to remove.

Rear compartment trim panel, removing

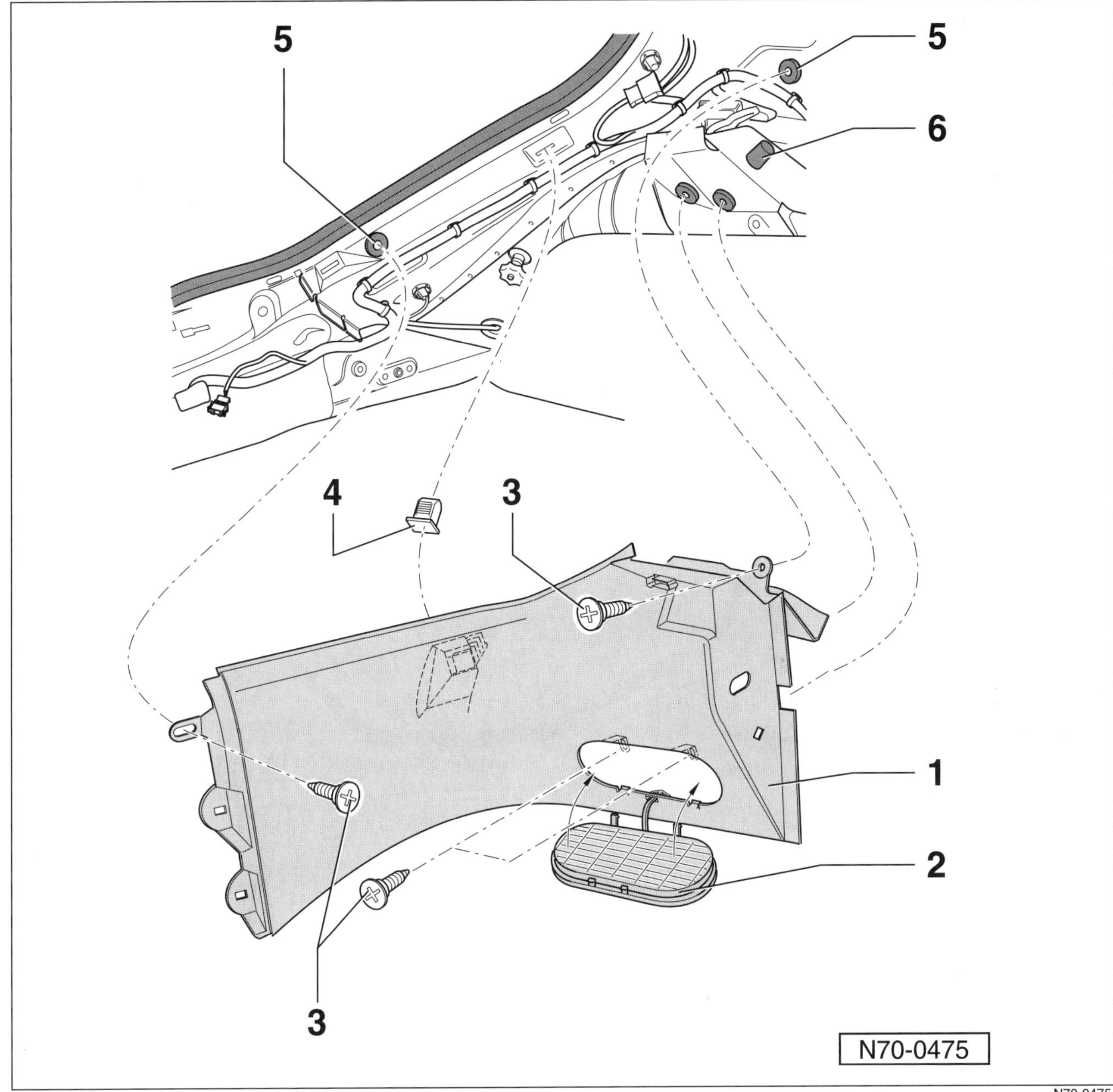

N70-0475

Fig. 28. Rear compartment trim panel and related hardware.

1. **Rear compartment trim panel**
   - Removing:
     Remove lock carrier trim as described later
     Remove side panel trim as described earlier
     Remove C-pillar trim as described earlier
     Unclip air grille (item 2)
     Remove screws (item 3) and pull trim panel toward front of vehicle
2. **Air grille**
3. **Screws**
   - Qty. 4
4. **Clip**
5. **Expanding nut**
6. **Rubber buffer**

Rear lock carrier trim, removing

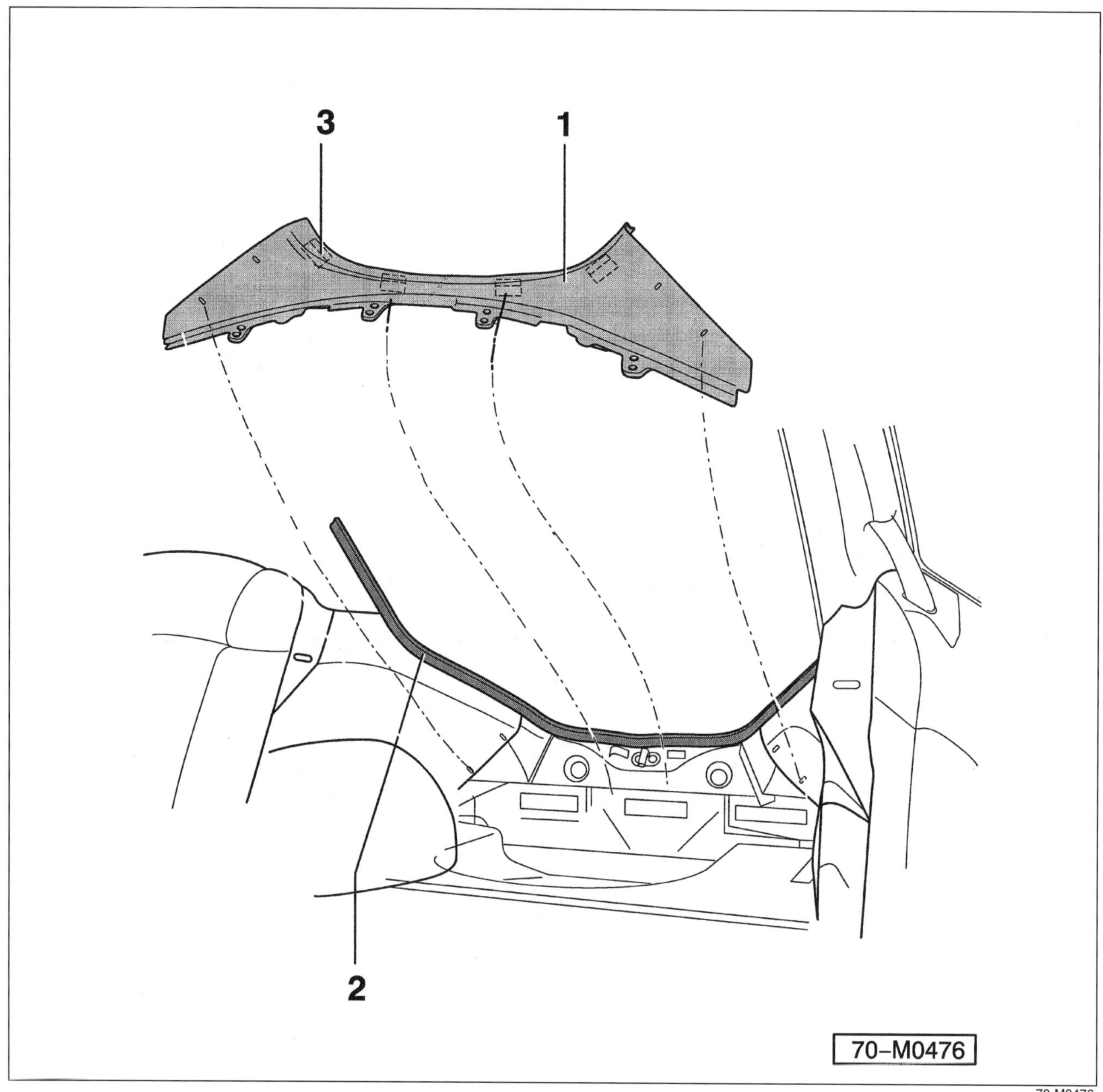

70-M0476

Fig. 29. Rear lock carrier trim.

1. **Lock carrier trim**
   - Pull upward off lock carrier panel
2. **Rear compartment seal**
   - Check for proper fit after installing trim
3. **Clip**
   - Check for damage and replace as necessary

Rear hatch lower trim, removing

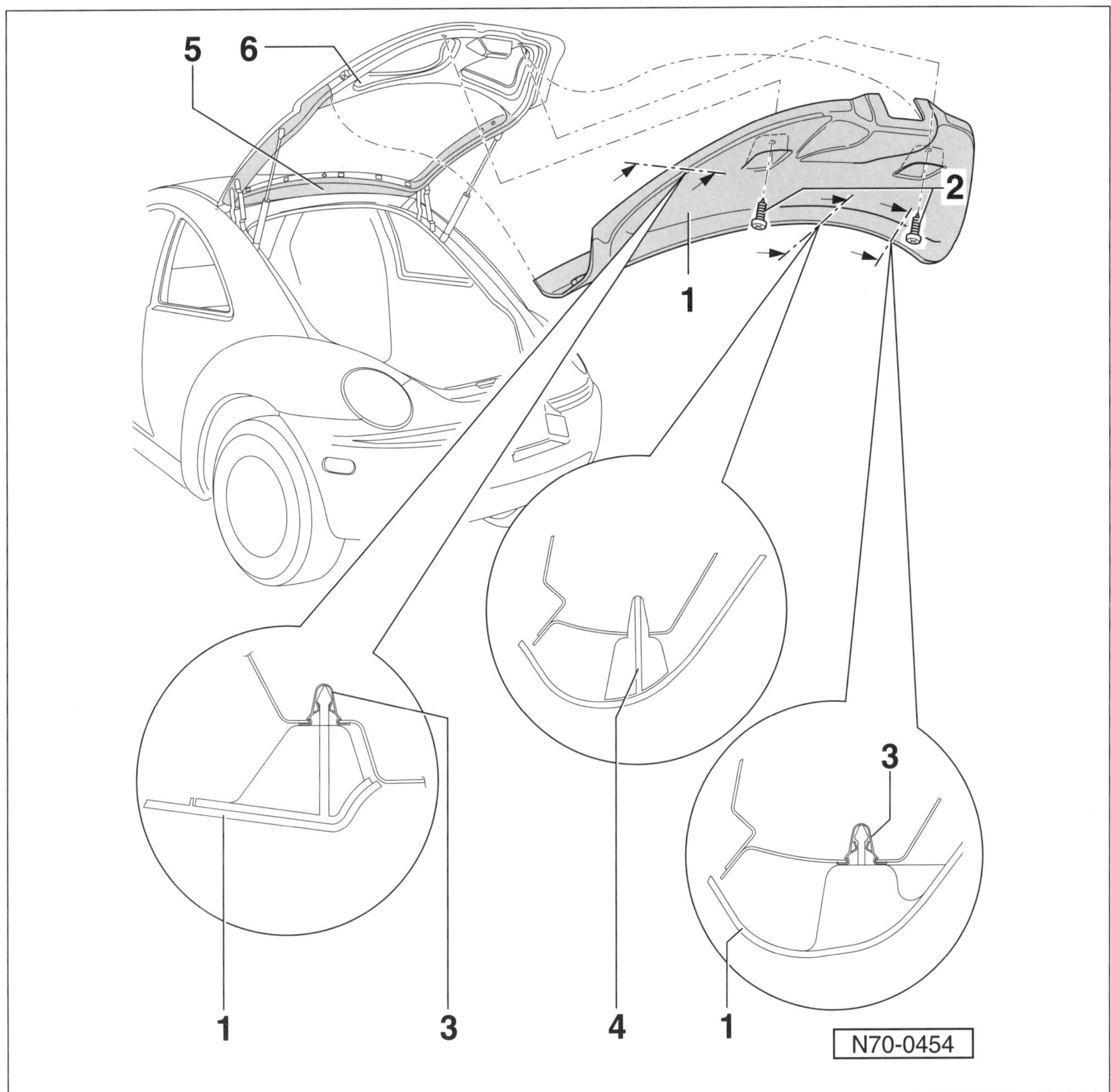

Fig. 30. Rear hatch lower trim and related mounting hardware.

1. **Rear hatch lower trim**
   - Removing:
     Remove screws (item 2)
     Unclip lower trim from rear hatch and upper trim
2. **Screws**
   - Qty. 2
3. **Clips**
   - Check for damage and replace as necessary
4. **Stud**
5. **Rear lid upper trim**
6. **Rear lid**

Rear hatch upper trim, removing

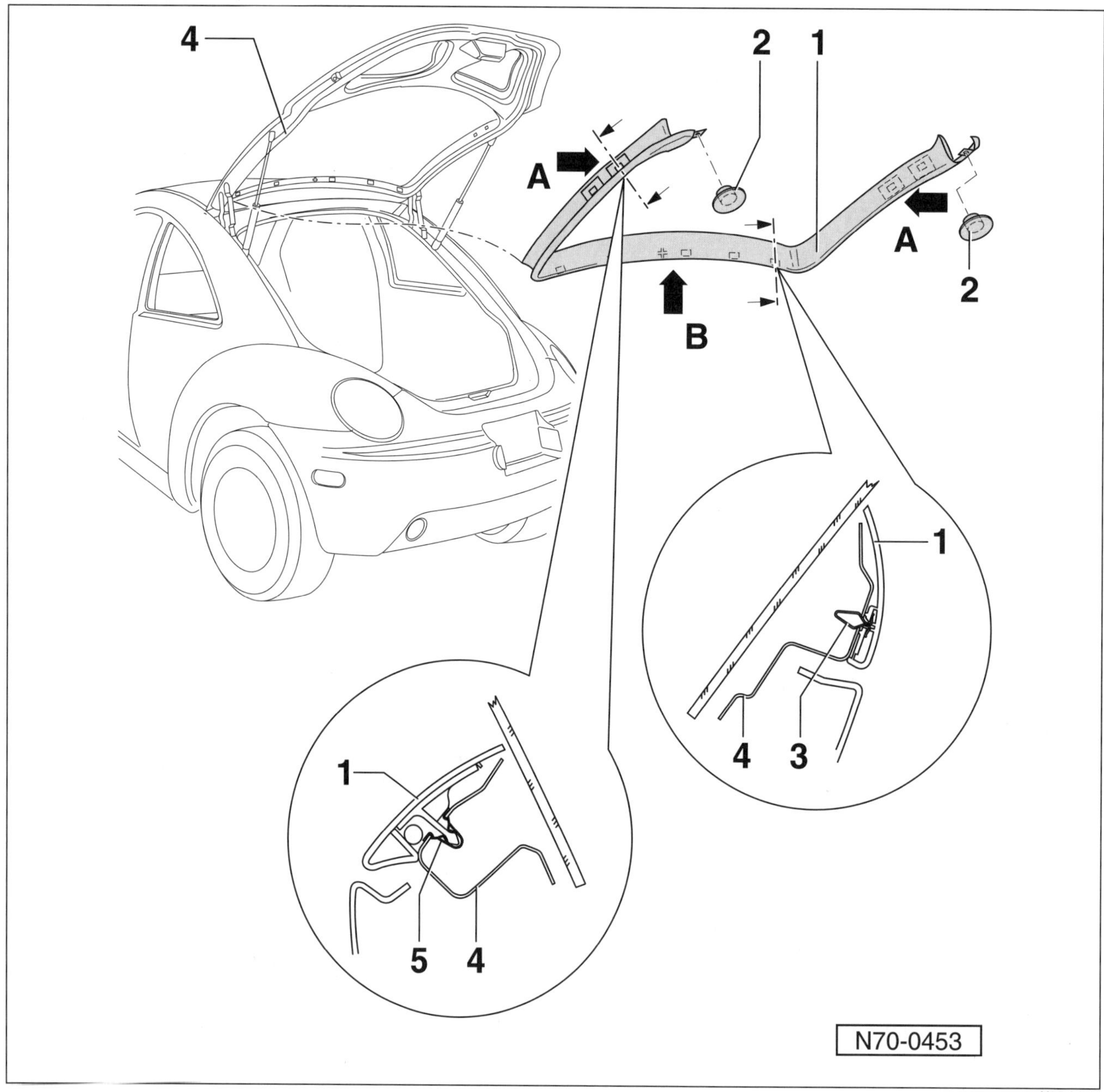

N70-0453

Fig. 31. Rear hatch upper trim and related mounting hardware.

1. **Rear hatch upper trim**
   - Removing:
     Remove rear hatch lower trim as described earlier
     Pry out plug (item 2)
     Unclip trim at sides (**arrow A**) and then top (**arrow B**)
2. **Plug**
3. **Clip**
   - Slide into trim
   - Check for damage and replace as necessary
4. **Rear lid**
5. **Clip**
   - For mounting stud to trim
   - Check for damage and replace as necessary

Sill panel trim, removing

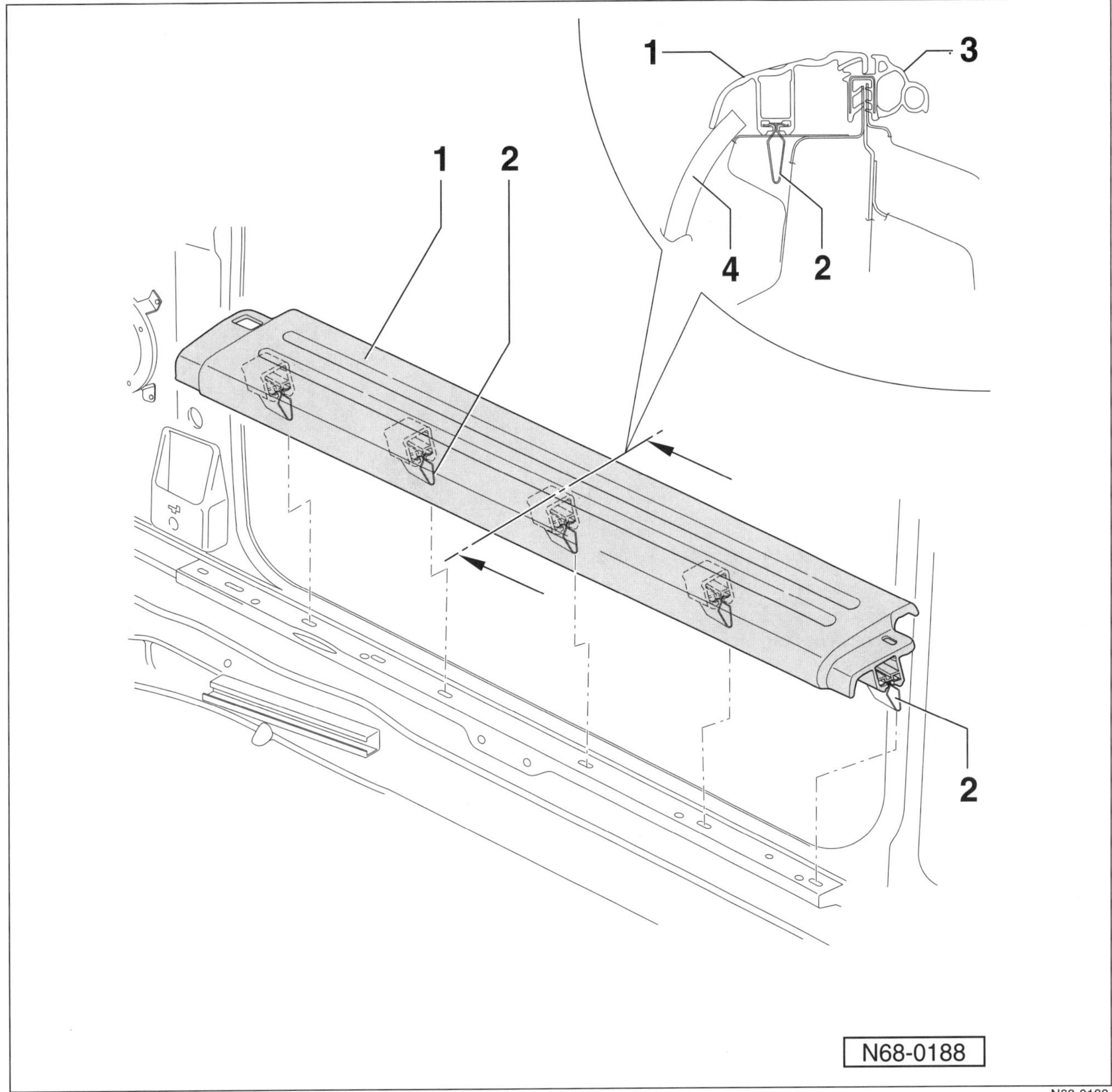

N68-0188

Fig. 32. Sill panel trim with cross-section view.

1. **Sill panel trim**
   - Removing:
     Remove lower A-pillar and side panel trim as described earlier
     Unclip sill panel trim by pulling upward
2. **Clip**
   - Qty. 5
   - Check for damage and replace as necessary
3. **Door inner seal**
   - Make sure seal is seated correctly after installing sill panel trim
4. **Carpet**

Steering column lower trim, removing

1. Pry off trim covers from lower switch housing and remove mounting screws. See Fig. 33.

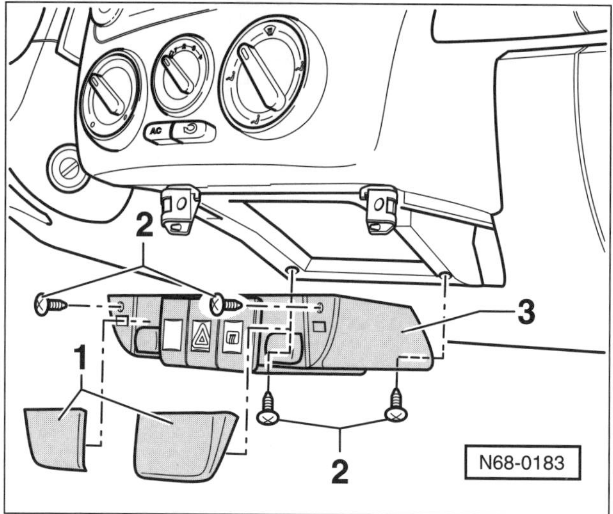

N68-0183

Fig. 33. Pry off trim covers (**1**), remove mounting screws (**2**) and lower switch housing (**3**).

2. Remove lower switch housing from bracket and disconnect harness connectors on switches.

3. Release fuse box cover on left side of instrument panel from retaining clips. Remove mounting screws. See Fig. 34.

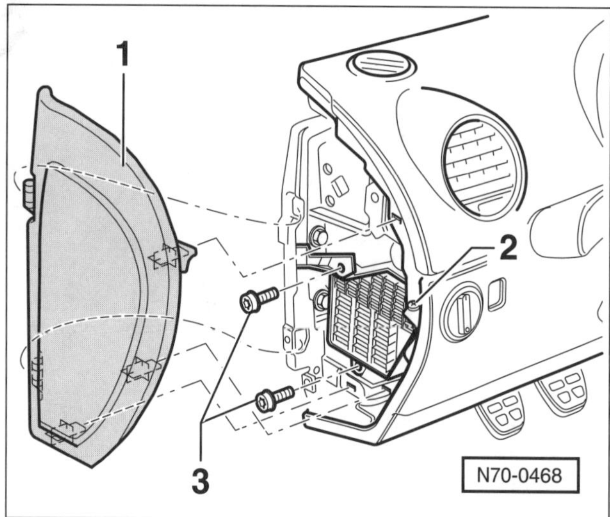

N70-0468

Fig. 34. Remove fuse box cover (**1**) and screws (**2** and **3**).

4. Turn light switch knob to "0" position.

5. Push light switch knob in and turn to right.

6. Pull light switch out of instrument panel and disconnect harness connectors. See Fig. 35.

7. Unclip instrument illumination control switch and disconnect harness connector.

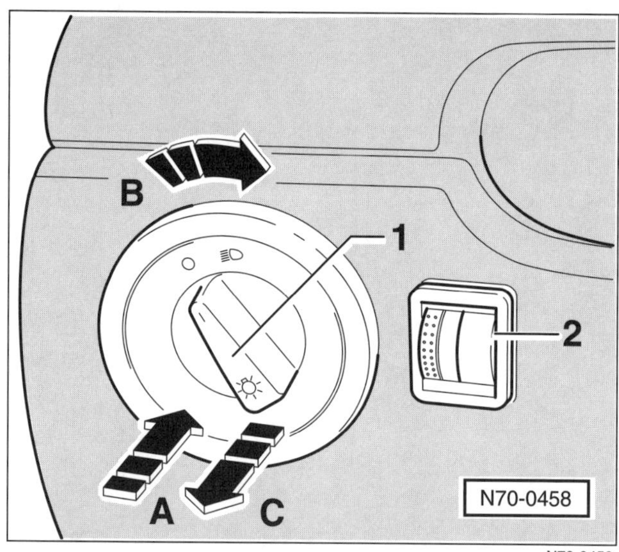

N70-0458

Fig. 35. Turn light switch to "0" position, push knob in (**arrow A**), turn to right (**arrow B**) and pull out (**arrow C**). Unclip and remove instrument dimmer switch (**2**).

8. Remove screw under cap on left side of glove box. See Fig. 36.

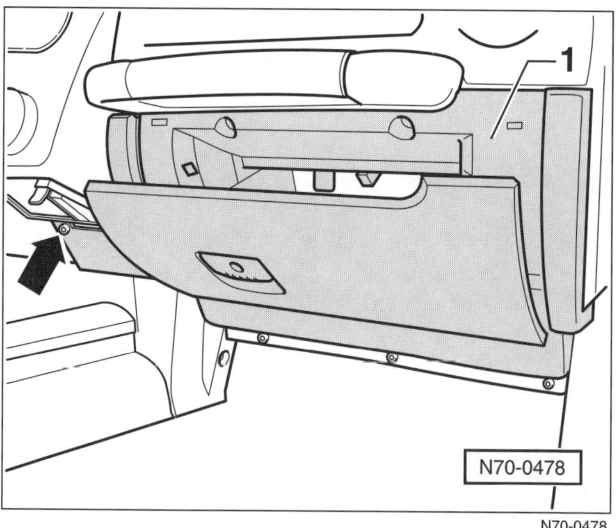

N70-0478

Fig. 36. Pry off cap and remove screw (**arrow**) on left side of glove box.

9. Remove screws from steering column lower trim. Unclip top of trim and remove from instrument panel.

10. Remove kneebar mounting screws and kneebar. See Fig. 37.

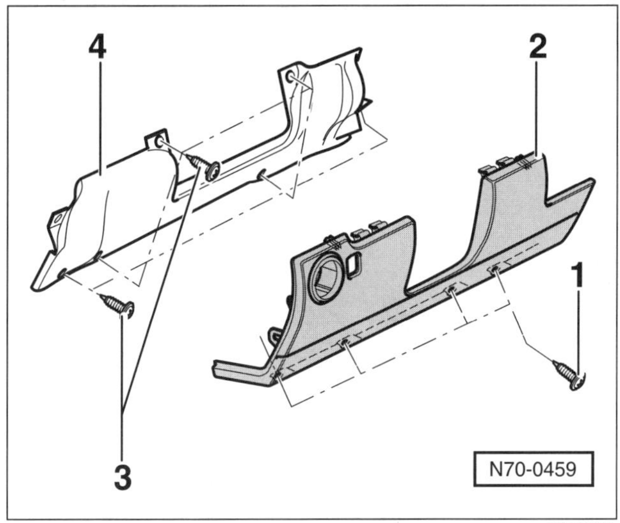

N70-0459

Fig. 37. Remove trim screws (**1**), trim panel (**2**), kneebar screws (**3**) and kneebar (**4**).

Trim below instrument panel, removing

1. Remove center console as shown earlier.

2. Remove screws on left side of trim panel. See Fig. 38.

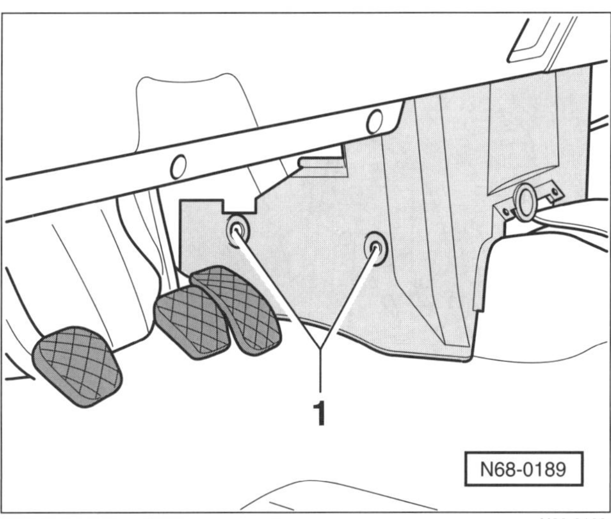

N68-0189

Fig. 38. Remove screws on left side of trim panel.

3. Remove screw on right side of trim panel and pull panel toward rear to remove. See Fig. 39.

N68-0190

Fig. 39. Remove screw (**1**) and pull trim panel (**2**) toward rear (**arrow**).

INSTRUMENT PANEL

Instrument panel, removing and installing

> ***WARNING —***
>
> *• Disconnect the battery Ground strap (GND) from negative (–) battery terminal before working on the electrical system.*
>
> *• Disconnecting the negative (–) battery cable may erase fault codes and basic settings in the engine management and automatic transmission control modules. Some driveability problems may be noticed until the system re-adapts to operating conditions. OBD II readiness codes, which may be required for emissions testing, may also be erased. Convenience electronics (alarm system, interior light control, power locks, mirrors, and windows) may need to be re-set using a VAG 1551/1552 or equivalent scan tool.*

NOTE —

• Be sure to have the anti-theft radio code on hand before disconnecting the battery.

• Removal of the instrument panel requires removing the radio. Volkswagen special tool 3344A is necessary for removing the factory radio.

1. Remove steering wheel and driver's airbag unit as described in **48 Steering** and **69 Seatbelts, Airbags**.
2. Remove screws holding upper steering column switch trim in place and remove trim. See Fig. 40.

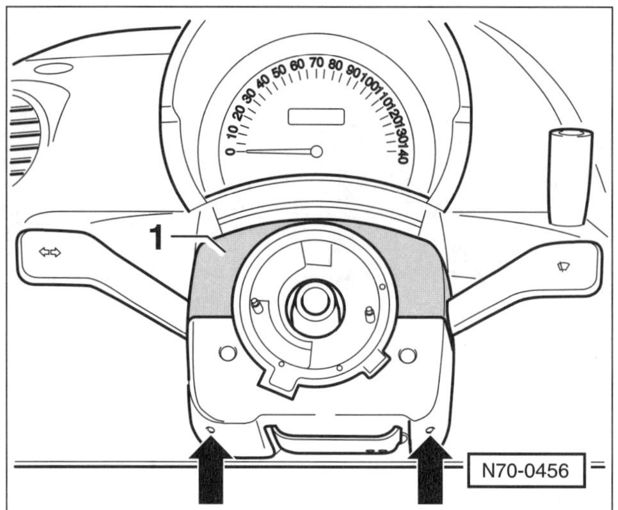

N70-0456

Fig. 40. Remove screws (**arrows**) and upper steering column switch trim (**1**).

3. Remove screws from lower steering column switch trim.

4. Release steering wheel height adjustment lever.

5. Remove lower steering column switch trim. See Fig. 41.

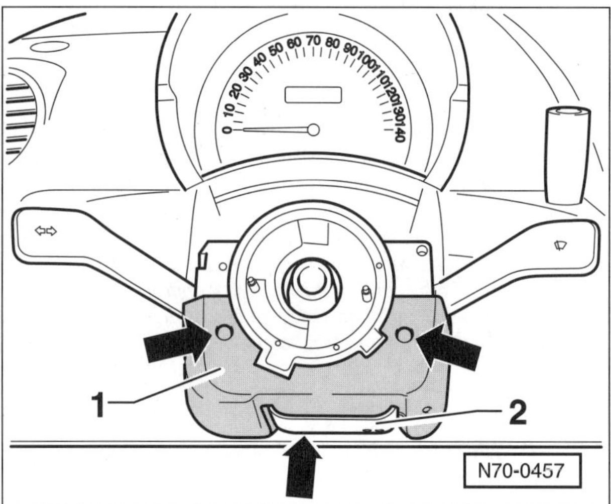

N70-0457

Fig. 41. Remove screws (**arrows**), release height adjustment handle (**2**) and remove lower steering column switch trim (**1**).

NOTE —

Remove the height adjustment handle (two screws) for easier removal of the lower trim.

6. Remove bolt behind steering column switch assembly.

7. Disconnect harness connectors from steering column switch assembly.

8. Remove steering column switch assembly. See Fig. 42.

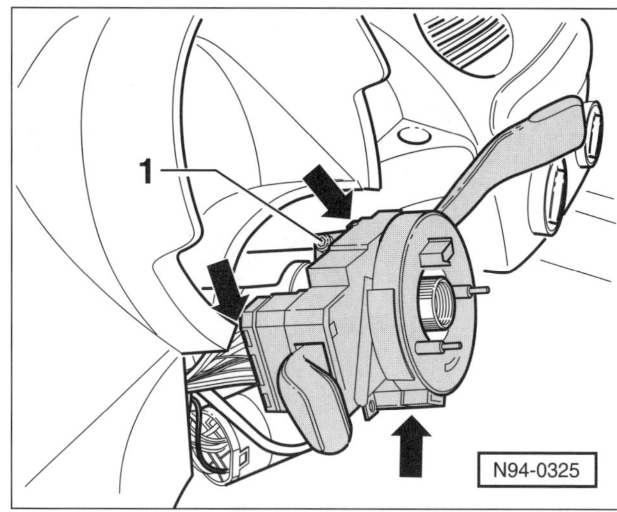

N94-0325

Fig. 42. Remove bolt (**1**) and disconnect harness connectors (**arrows**).

9. Remove driver side footwell cover as shown earlier in Fig. 22.

10. Remove right side instrument panel cover and mounting screw for glovebox trim. See Fig. 43.

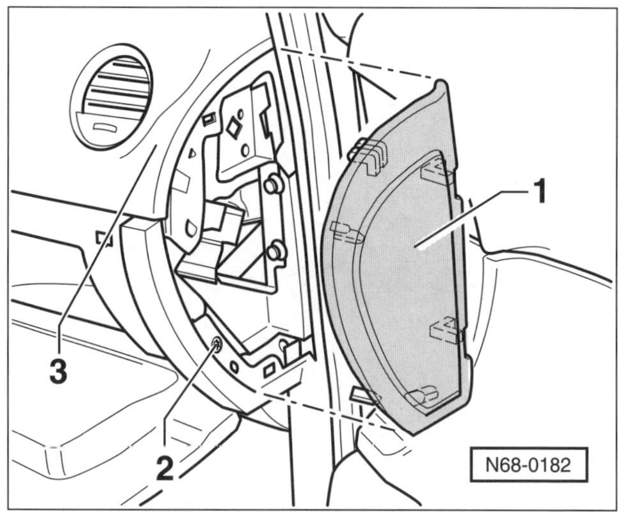

N68-0182

Fig. 43. Remove cover (**1**) and mounting screw (**2**).

11. Remove lower switch housing as shown earlier in Fig. 33.

12. Remove inner plenum covers from top of instrument panel. See **Inner plenum covers, removing**, given earlier.

13. Slide Volkswagen radio release special tools 3344A into slots until they engage. See Fig. 44.

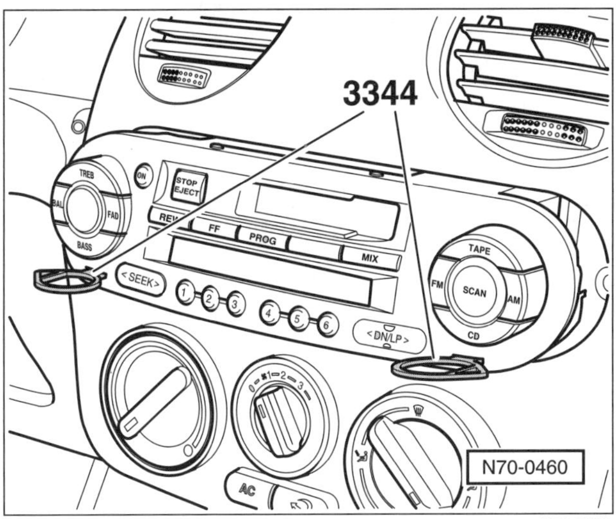

N70-0460

Fig. 44. Volkswagen special tools being used to remove radio.

14. Pull radio out of instrument panel using grip rings of release tools and disconnect harness connectors on back of radio.

NOTE —

- *Do not push the radio release tool 3344A to the side or tilt it.*
- *Press the locating tabs on the side of the radio inward to remove the release tools.*
- *Do not install radio with release tools in place.*

15. For vehicles without radio, remove radio block-off trim.

16. Remove center air outlet console mounting screws and console. See Fig. 45.

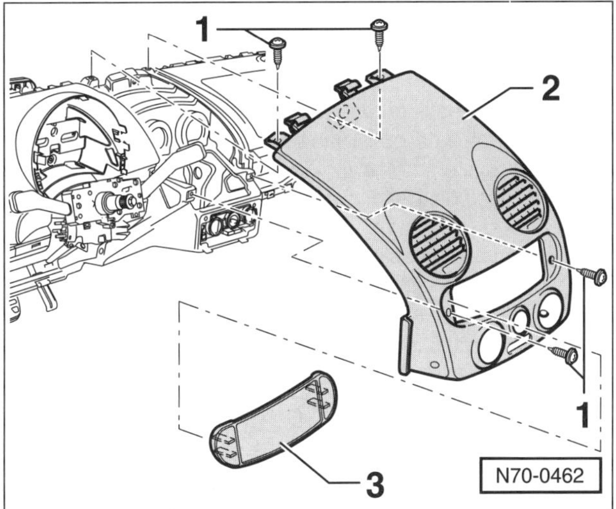

N70-0462

Fig. 45. Remove block-off plate (**3**), if applicable, or radio, screws (**1**), and console (**2**).

17. Remove air duct from center of instrument panel. See Fig. 46.

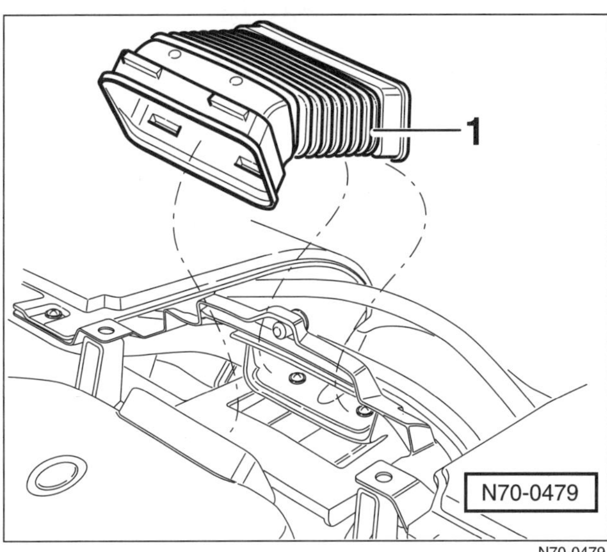

N70-0479

Fig. 46. Remove air duct (**1**) from center of instrument panel.

18. Remove mounting screws for heating and ventilation control unit. Press control unit with attached cables under instrument panel. See Fig. 47.

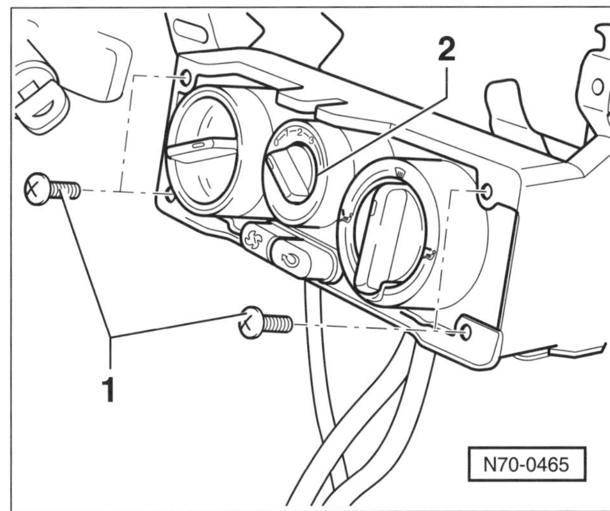

N70-0465

Fig. 47. Remove screws (**1**) and press heating and ventilation control unit (**2**) with attached cables under instrument panel.

19. Remove glovebox and disconnect harness connector for light, see **Glove box, removing**.

20. Remove fuse box cover on left side of dash and mounting screws as shown earlier in Fig. 34.

21. Remove light switch and instrument dimmer switch as shown in Fig. 35.

22. Remove lower steering column trim panel and kneebar as shown in Fig. 37.

23. Remove mounting screws on top of instrument panel. See Fig. 48.

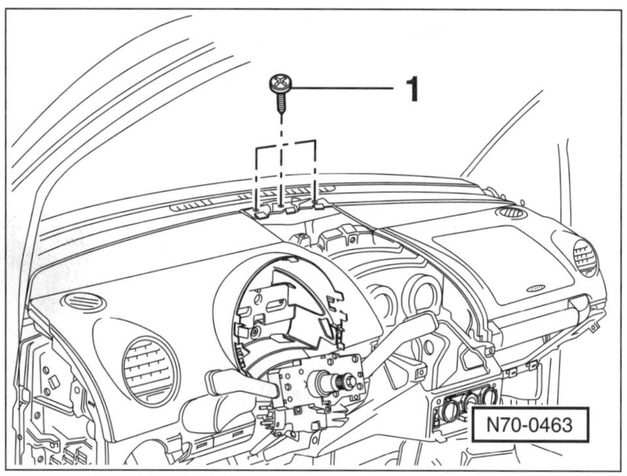

N70-0463

Fig. 48. Remove screws (**1**).

24. Unclip trim from instrument cluster, remove cluster mounting screws and cluster. Disconnect multi-pin connector on back of cluster. See Fig. 49.

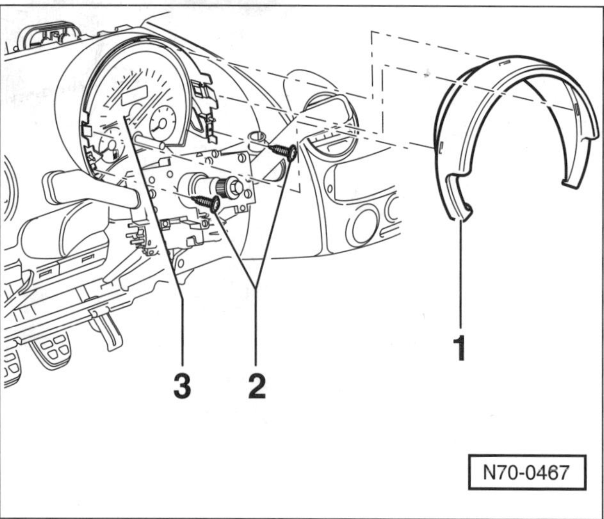

N70-0467

Fig. 49. Unclip trim (**1**), remove screws (**2**) and instrument cluster (**3**).

25. Remove glovebox retaining frame (item 6, Fig. 50.)

26. Remove instrument panel mounting screws. See Fig. 50.

27. Remove instrument panel from crossmember.

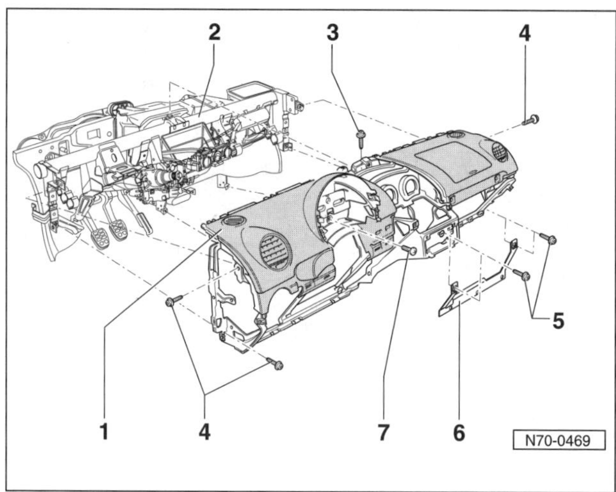

N70-0469

Fig. 50. Remove screws (**5**, **3**, **4**, and **7**) and glovebox retaining frame (**6**). Remove instrument panel from cross-member (**2**).

28. Install instrument panel in reverse order of removal, noting the following:
    - Always replace steering wheel mounting bolt when installing steering wheel.
    - After connecting battery check operation of vehicle equipment (radio, clock, power windows).
    - After connecting battery, readiness code for the ECM will need to be re-set using VAG 1551/1552 scan tool or equivalent.
    - If airbag malfunction indicator lamp (MIL) signals a malfunction after installing instrument panel, the Diagnostic Trouble Code (DTC) memory must be erased and checked again with VAG 1551/1552 scan tool or equivalent.

QUALITY REVIEW

When you have finished working under the hood and around other areas of the vehicle, it is advisable to take a moment to quality check or review your work. This helps to insure that the operation or repair has been completed properly with all affected systems functioning within normal parameters. These may include the following:

- Ensure that all cable ties and clamps that were removed as part of the repair are replaced.
- Ensure that all fasteners and hardware were replaced and torqued as specified.
- Make sure that all other components involved in the repair are positioned correctly, properly torqued and function properly.
- Make sure that all tools, shop cloths, fender covers and protective tapes are removed.
- Clean grease and fingerprints from painted surfaces, steering wheel, upholstery and shifter.
- Make sure that seatbelt and airbag warning lights function correctly.
- Unlock anti-theft radio and reset the clock.

72 Seats

FRONT SEATS

Both driver and passenger front seats are equipped with airbags mounted in the seat backrest frames. These airbags are designed to deploy under certain side impact conditions and are triggered by separate sensors mounted to the front floor crossmembers under the front seats. Before removing the front seats, a safety device (VAS 5094) must be installed to prevent accidental deployment of the airbag units.

> ***WARNING —***
> - *Observe all cautions, warnings and notes before starting repairs involving airbag systems, see* **69 Seatbelts, Airbags**.
> - *Volkswagen of America specifically warns against the installation of aftermarket upholstery on any vehicle equipped with side airbags. The factory-installed upholstery is designed to separate in specific places at specific rates, and in specific directions. Installation of non-factory upholstery including, but not limited to, "beads" and "sheepskins", may cause seat mounted airbags to deploy when they are not supposed to; fail to deploy when they should; or to deploy in some manner other than designed. This is a safety hazard and could result in serious injury or death to occupants of the vehicle.*

Front seat, removing and installing

1. Disconnect the battery ground (–) strap before working on the electrical system.

> ***CAUTION —***
> *Disconnecting the negative (–) battery cable may erase fault codes and basic settings in the engine management and automatic transmission control modules. Some driveability problems may be noticed until the system re-adapts to operating conditions. OBD II readiness codes, which may be required for emissions testing, may also be erased. Convenience electronics (alarm system, interior light control, power locks, mirrors, and windows) may need to be re-set using a VAG 1551/1552 or equivalent scan tool.*

NOTE —
- *The removal and installation procedures may have to be modified slightly depending on equipment variations.*
- *Obtain the radio code before disconnecting the battery.*

2. Slide seat forward.

3. Remove screw cover (**1**) and screw (**2**). See Fig. 1.

NOTE —
The items in parenthesis for steps 3 through 8 refer to Fig. 1.

4. Unclip cover strip (**3**) from inner seat rail (**arrow A**) and remove toward rear (**arrow B**).

5. Remove screw cover (**4**) and screw (**5**).

6. Unclip cover strip (**6**) from outer seat rail (**arrow C**) and remove toward rear (**arrow D**).

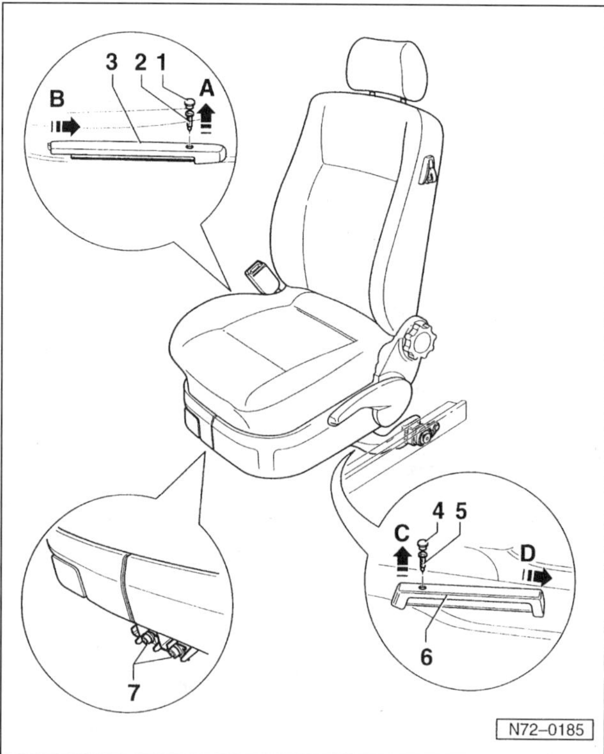

Fig. 1. Front seat with removal and installation details.

7. Slide seat to rear.

8. Remove retaining bolts (**7**). See Fig. 1.

Tightening torque
- Front seat retaining bolts . . . . 23 Nm (17 ft-lb)

9. Separate side airbag wiring harness connector (**1**) at seat connector station (**2**). See Fig. 2.

NOTE —
The items in parenthesis for steps 9 through 11 refer to Fig. 2.

WARNING —
Before disconnecting the side airbag connector for the seat, a technician must discharge him/herself electrostatically by briefly touching door striker or vehicle body.

10. Separate connector (**3**) for seat heating (as applicable) and seat adjustment connector (as applicable).

11. Insert connector (**4**) of special tool VAS 5094 into connector housing (**5**).

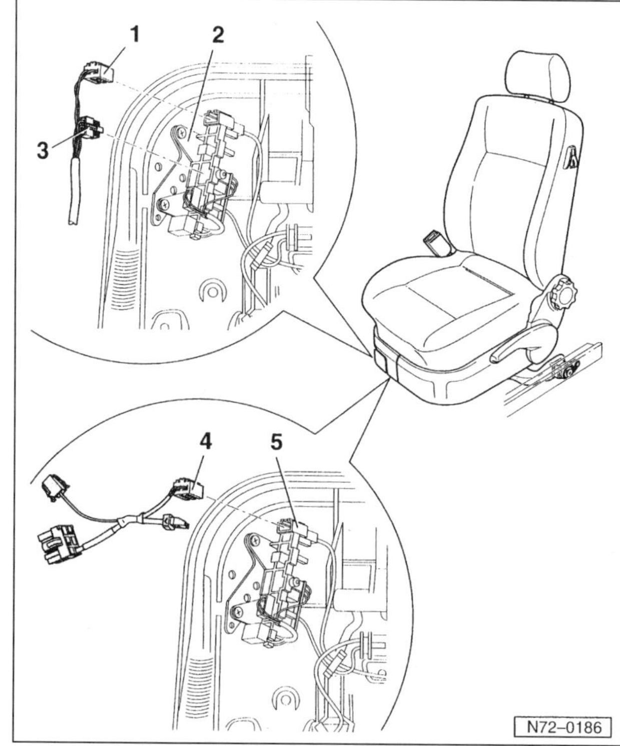

Fig. 2. Special tool VAS 5094 (**4**) must be installed on seats to prevent accidental discharge of the side airbag.

WARNING —
Failure to install VAS 5094 could result in deployment of the side airbag.

12. Slide seat out of guide rails.

13. Install in reverse order of removal, noting the following:
    - After all components are installed, switch ignition on.
    - Connect battery ground strap.

WARNING —
Make sure the passenger compartment is not occupied before connecting the battery ground strap.

- After connecting the battery ground (–), ensure proper operation of vehicle equipment (radio, clock, power windows).

Front backrest, removing and installing

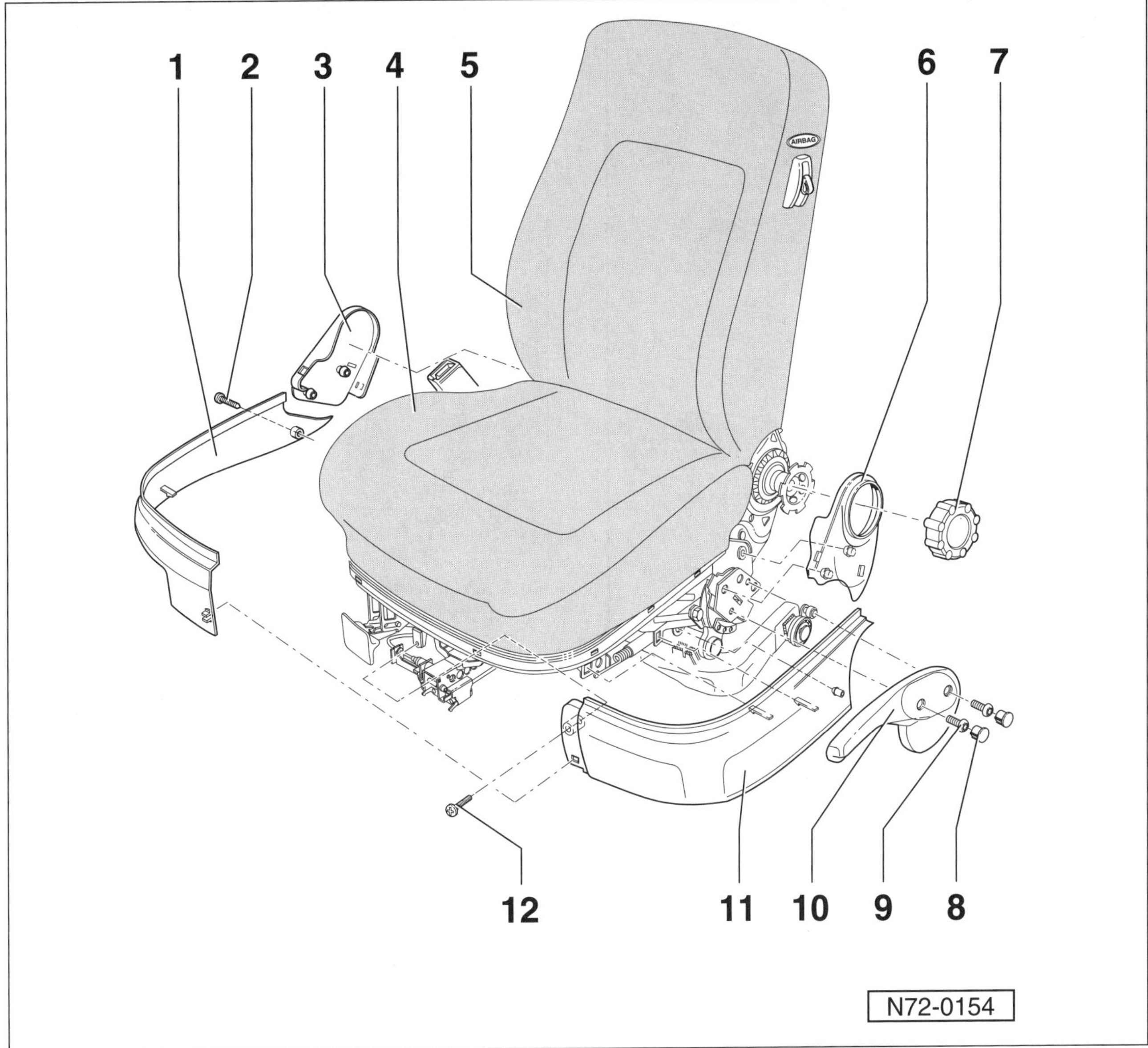

N72-0154

Fig. 3. Front seat with notes on removal of backrest.

1. **Seat trim, right**
2. **Screw**
3. **Cover**
4. **Seat**
5. **Backrest**
   - Removal:
     Remove seat from vehicle
     Remove adjusting knob (item 7)
     Remove adjusting lever (item 10)
     Remove trim (items 1 and 11)
     Unclip and remove covers (item 3 and 6)
     For remainder of removal procedure see Ⓐ
6. **Cover**
7. **Adjusting knob (backrest)**
8. **Cap**
   - Qty. 2
9. **Screw**
   - Qty. 2
10. **Adjusting lever (seat height)**
11. **Seat trim, left**
12. **Screw**

Front backrest, removing and installing (continued)

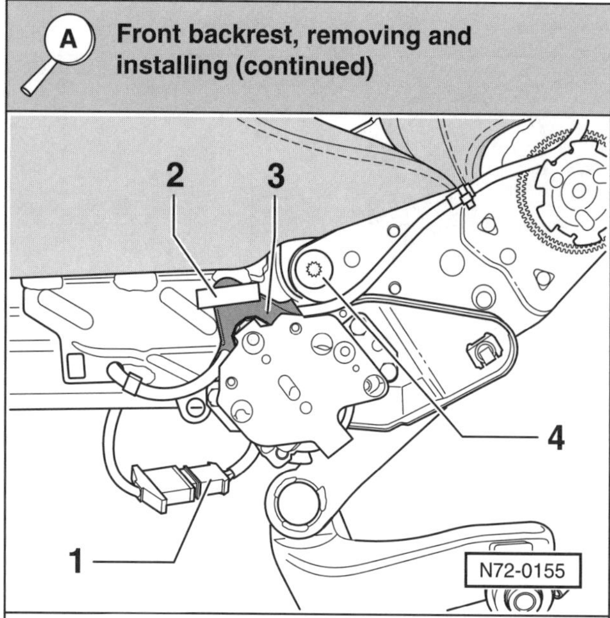

N72-0155

- **Unclip wiring guides under seat.**
- **Disconnect wiring connector (1) for backrest heating, if equipped.**
- **Pry out retaining clip (2) and remove guide for side air-bag wiring.**
- **Remove bolts (4) from both sides of seat and take off backrest.**
- **When installing, bolts (4) must be secured with thread locking compound and tightened to 20 Nm (15 ft-lb).**

Head restraint guides, removing

1. Remove head restraint from backrest by pulling the restraint up until it stops. Then, press the release button on the guide while pulling the head restraint up and out. See Fig. 4.

B1B-069C

Fig. 4. Press button (**arrow**) while pulling headrest up and out from seat backrest.

2. Push backrest cushion down below head restraint guide and release retaining tab with screwdriver or mandrel. See Fig. 5.

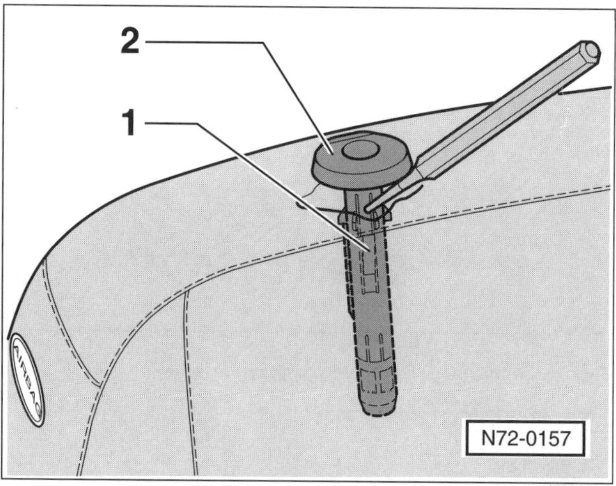

N72-0157

Fig. 5. Push backrest cushion down below guide (**2**) and release retaining tab (**1**) with screwdriver.

3. Pull out backrest guide.

Front backrest frame assembly

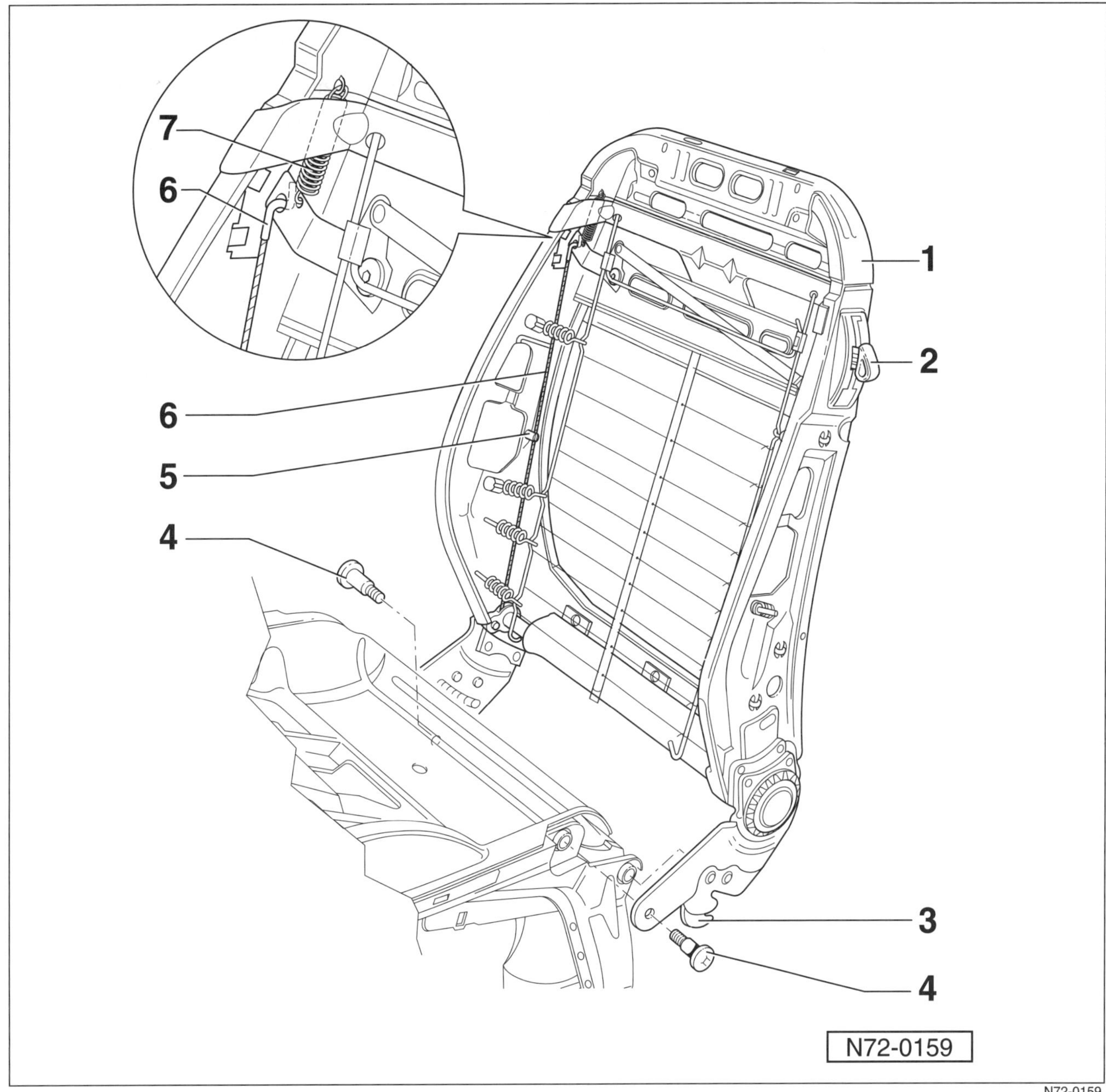

N72-0159

Fig. 6. Front seat backrest with detail of release mechanism.

1. **Backrest frame**
2. **Release lever**
3. **Locking hook**
4. **Mounting bolt**
   - Tighten to 20 Nm (15 ft-lb)
   - Install with locking compound
5. **Cable guide**
6. **Cable**
7. **Spring**

Front seat adjustment cable, removing and installing

The front seat adjustment cable allows the seat to be moved forward or backward using the lever on the lower front corner of the seat.

1. Remove seat as described earlier.

2. Remove retaining clip and lock pin from bracket under seat. See Fig. 7.

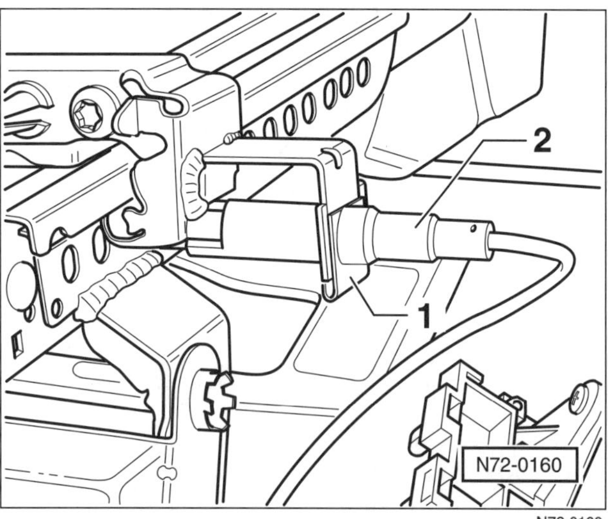

N72-0160

Fig. 7. Remove clip (**1**) and lock pin (**2**) from bracket under seat.

3. Press lock pin into cable housing and unhook cable at bolt on operating lever. See Fig. 8.

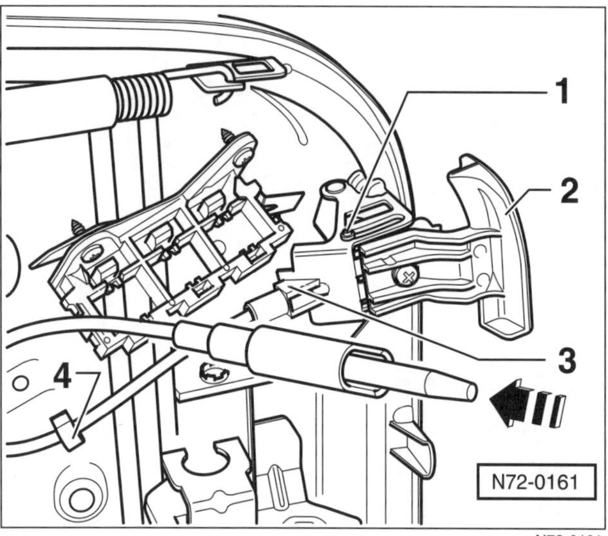

N72-0161

Fig. 8. Press lock pin in (**arrow**) and unhook cable at bolt (**1**) in operating lever (**2**). Press out bolt (**1**), unclip mount (**3**) and cable guide (**4**).

4. Press out bolt and unclip adjustment lever mount. Refer to Fig. 8.

5. Unclip cable guide from seat frame and remove cable.

6. Installation is reverse of removal, noting the following:
   - Press lock pin housing in up to stop in bracket and position lock pin in opening below bracket. See Fig. 9.
   - Install lock pin retaining clip.

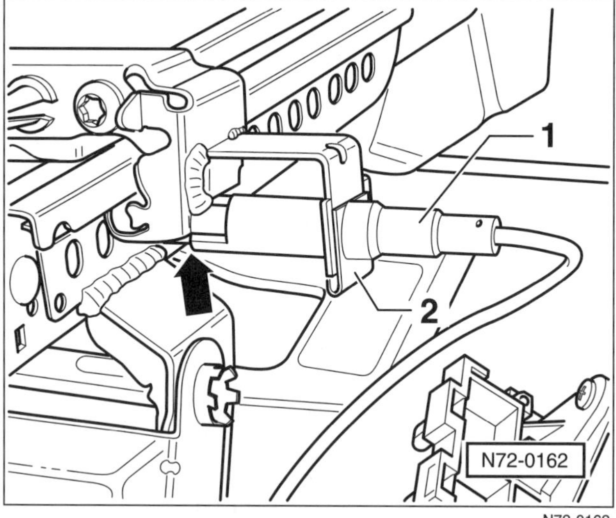

N72-0162

Fig. 9. Press lock pin housing (**1**) in up to stop in bracket (**2**) while properly locating lock pin in hole (**arrow**).

REAR SEATS

Seat cushion, removing and installing

1. Lift seat cushion and pull forward.

2. Unhook seat retaining rods from retainers. See Fig. 10.

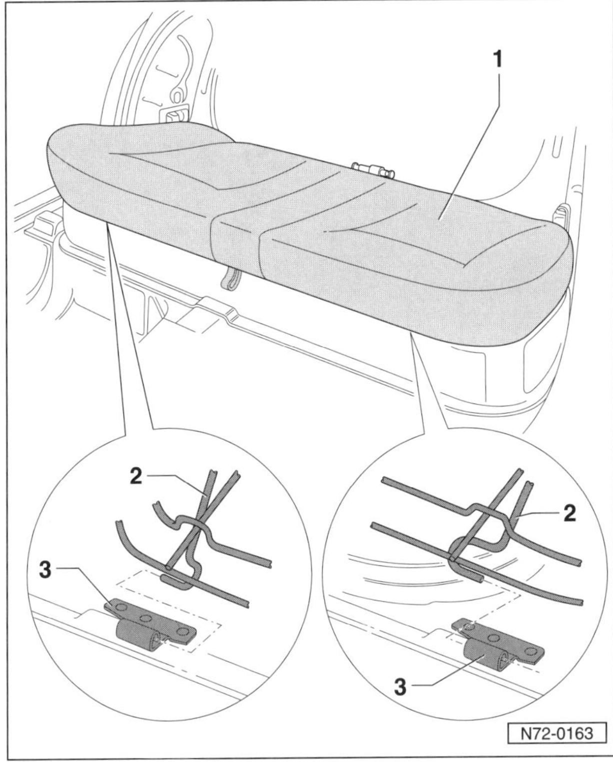

N72-0163

Fig. 10. Unhook rods (**2**) from retainers (**3**) to remove rear seat cushion.

3. To install, hook rods into retainers, fold seat cushion back and push down at front.

Seatback, removing and installing

1. Remove bolts from retainer at rear center of seatback. See Fig. 11.

Tightening torque
- Seatback retainer bolts . . . . 20 Nm (15 ft-lb)

2. Fold bottom seat cushion forward.

3. Fold backrest down.

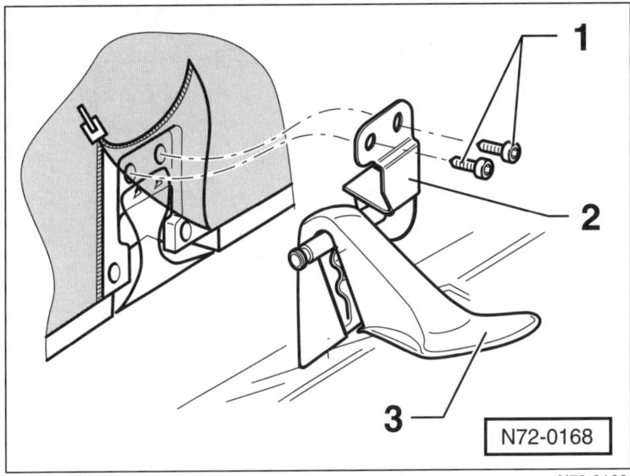

N72-0168

Fig. 11. Remove bolts (**1**) from retainer (**2**) at seatback center.

4. Using a screwdriver, press back seatback retaining hooks on right and left sides and pull seatback up out of mount. See Fig. 12.

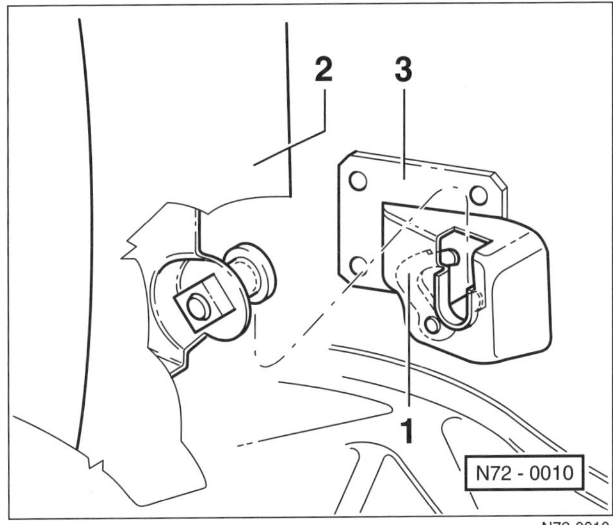

N72-0010

Fig. 12. Use a screwdriver to press back retaining hooks (**1**) and pull seatback (**2**) up and out of mount (**3**).

5. Installation is reverse of removal.

Seatback release mechanism assembly

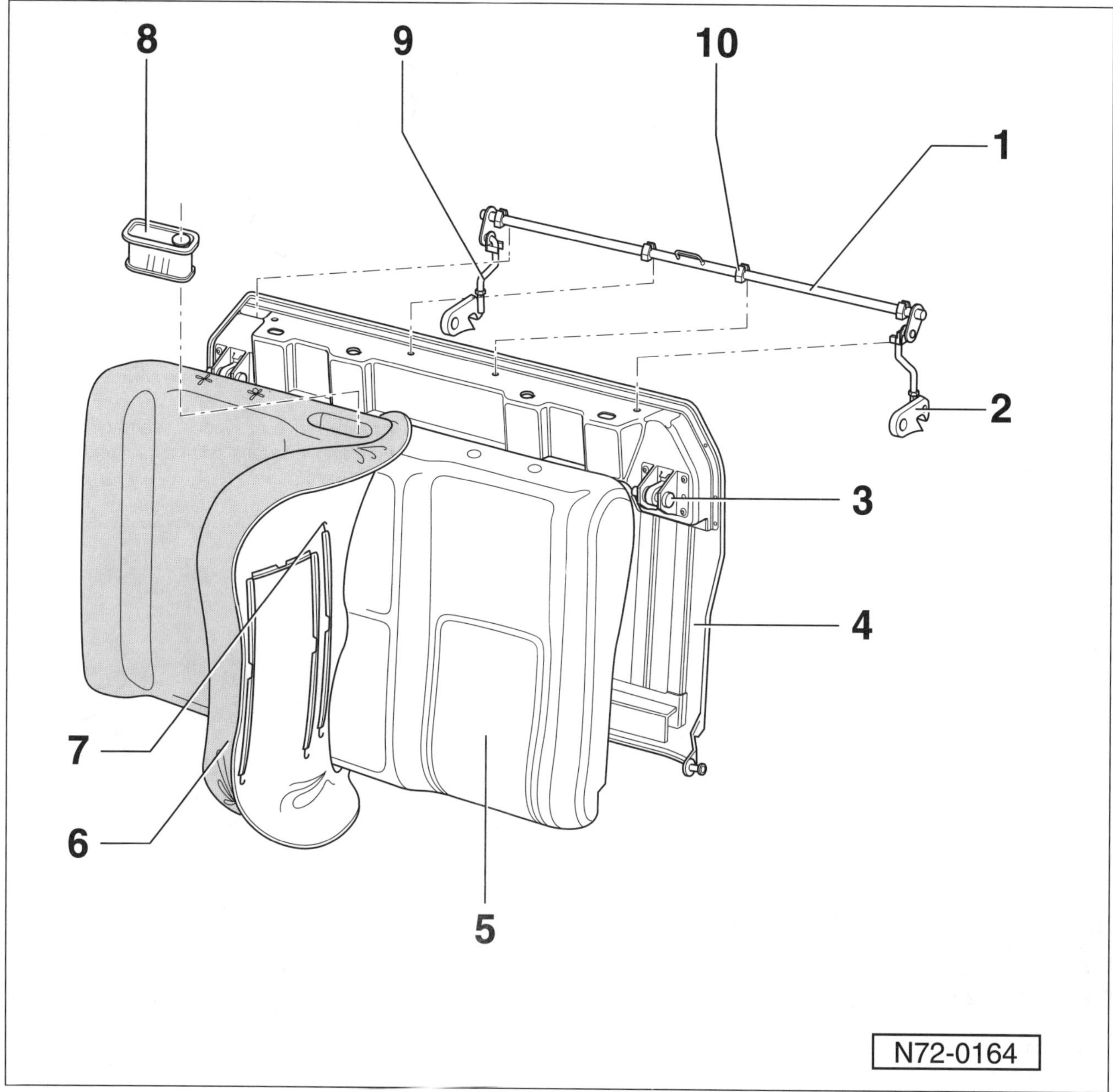

N72-0164

Fig. 13. Seatback release mechanism and related hardware.

1. **Release rod**
2. **Lock hook**
3. **Lock pin**
4. **Rear panel**
5. **Padding**
6. **Cover**
7. **Padding wire**
8. **Release button**
9. **Relay rod**
10. **Clip**

80 Heating and Ventilation

GENERAL

This section primarily applies to vehicles without air conditioning (A/C). For those vehicles with A/C, the refrigerant must first be discharged using specialized equipped before working on most of the heating and ventilation components, see **87 Air Conditioning**.

> ***WARNING —***
> *The cooling system is pressurized when the engine is warm. Wear gloves and other protection and carefully release system pressure if necessary, before performing repairs.*

> ***CAUTION —***
> *Disconnecting the negative (–) battery cable may erase fault codes and basic settings in the engine management and automatic transmission control modules. Some driveability problems may be noticed until the system re-adapts to operating conditions. OBD II readiness codes, which may be required for emissions testing, may also be erased. Convenience electronics (alarm system, interior light control, power locks, mirrors, and windows) may need to be re-set using a VAG 1551/1552 or equivalent scan tool.*

HEATING AND VENTILATION CONTROLS

For an overview of the major heating and ventilation system components, see Fig. 1.

Passenger compartment components, overview

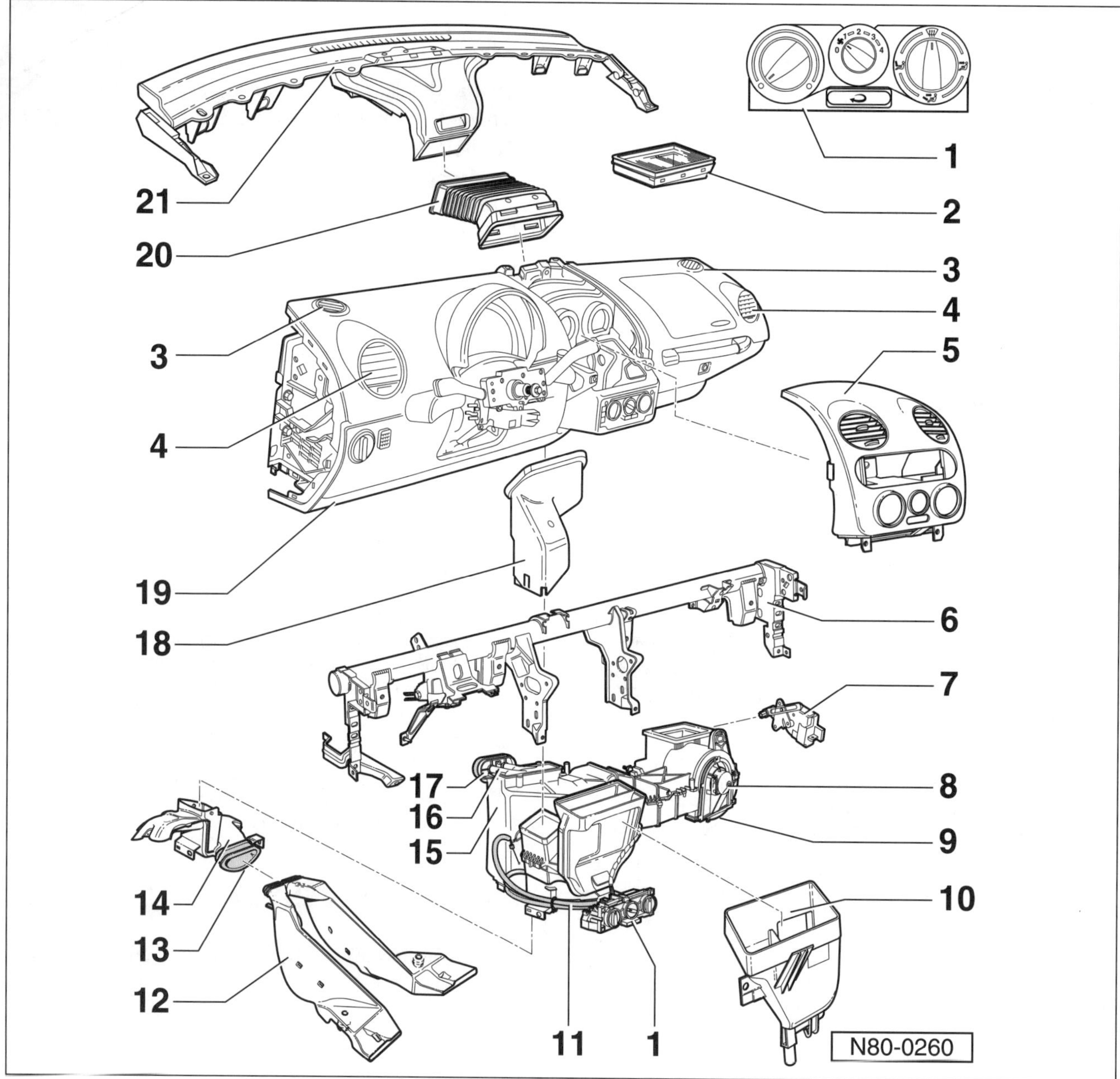

N80-0260

Fig. 1. Major components related to the heating and ventilation system located in the passenger compartment.

1. **Heating and ventilation controls**
   - With blower fan switch (E9)
   - With recirculation switch (E184)
2. **Dust and pollen filter**
   - Covers outside air inlet to passenger compartment
   - Filters all incoming air
3. **Side window air outlet, see Ⓐ**
4. **Side air outlets, see Ⓑ**
5. **Center air outlet console**
6. **Instrument panel cross member, see Ⓒ**
7. **Servo motor for recirculation door (V154)**
8. **Blower fan (V2)**
9. **Blower fan series resistance pack (N24)**
   - With thermal fuse
10. **Intermediate duct**

(continued from previous page)

11. Cables
- Color code yellow - air distribution control knob to central flap
- Color code green - air distribution control knob to footwell/defrost flap
- Color code beige - temperature control knob to temperature flap

12. Rear footwell duct

13. Gasket

14. Connecting duct

15. Heater assembly

16. Heater core

17. Heater core/bulkhead seal
- Note installed position

18. Defroster duct

19. Instrument panel

20. Center air outlet duct

21. Defroster air outlet panel

A Side window fixed air vents, removing and installing

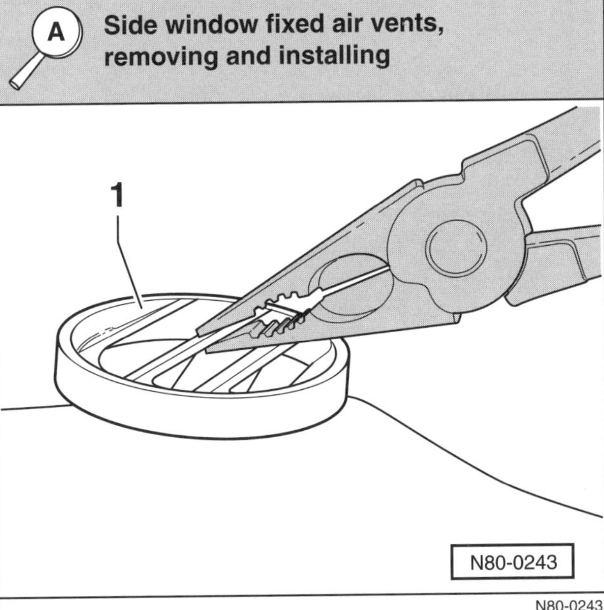

N80-0243

- **Protect vanes of vent before removing.**
- **Apply cloth tape to the pliers or vanes or use needle nose pliers with plastic or rubber protective jaws.**
- **Carefully remove air outlet (1) by pulling out with needle nose pliers.**
- **Snap into place to install.**

B Side window movable air vents, removing and installing

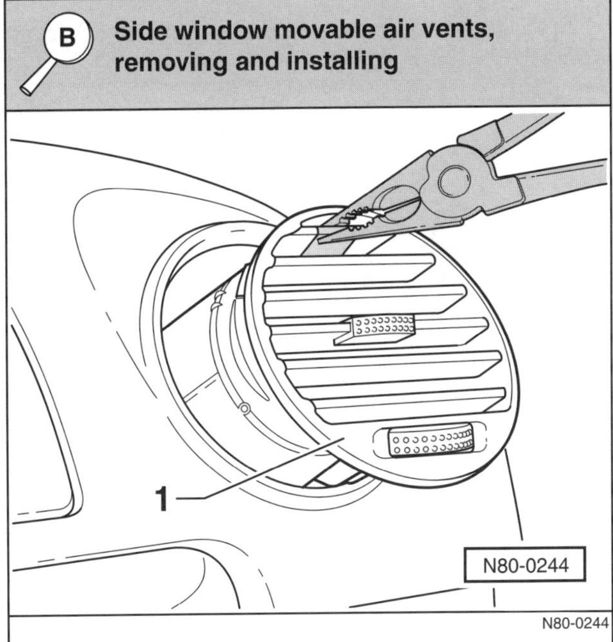

N80-0244

- **Protect vanes of vent before removing.**
- **Apply cloth tape to the pliers or vanes or use needle nose pliers with plastic or rubber protective jaws.**
- **Carefully remove air outlet (1) by pulling out with needle nose pliers.**
- **Snap into place to install.**

C Instrument panel crossmember, loosening and tightening

N80-0251

- **Remove securing bolts (arrows). Tightening torque: 25 Nm (18 ft-lb)**
- **To access or remove heating and ventilation unit, lift cross member in direction of (arrow A) and support unit.**
- **To prevent damage to the steering column, work should be done with aid of another technician.**
- **If removed component(s) are not to be reinstalled immediately, re-secure the cross member to the bulkhead.**
- **Any wiring harnesses released from their retainers must be secured again at the same point, using the same method of securing.**

Heating and ventilation controls, removing and installing

1. Remove center air outlet console as described later.
2. Remove mounting screws and lift controls from opening in dash. See Fig. 2.

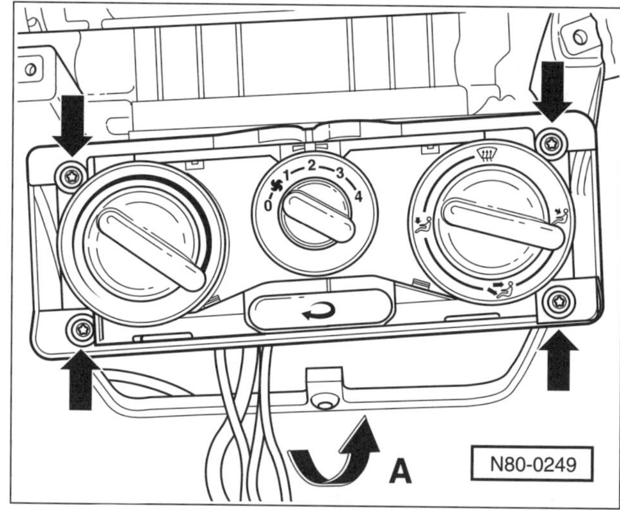

N80-0249

Fig. 2. Heating and ventilation controls shown with air outlet console removed. After removing securing screws (**arrows**), lift controls down and out (**arrow A**).

3. Unclip cables and detach from controls.
4. Disconnect harness connector and remove controls.
5. Before installing controls, check operation of cables. Replace cables with damage or stiff/binding operation. See Fig. 3.

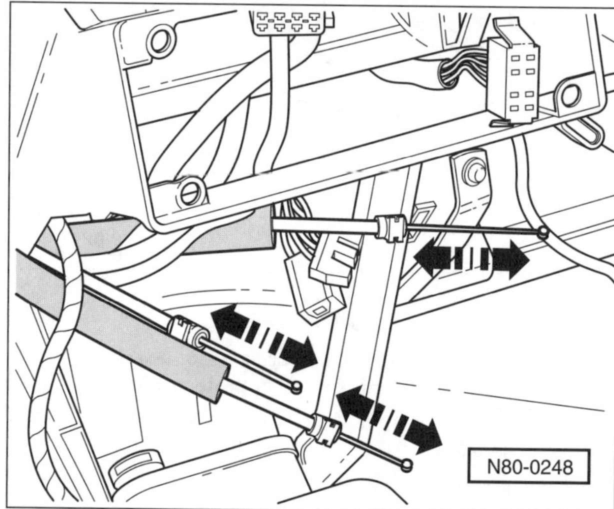

N80-0248

Fig. 3. Check control cable operation with controls removed. Move cables in and out (**arrows**) several times.

6. Attach color coded cable to correct actuating arm. See Fig. 4.

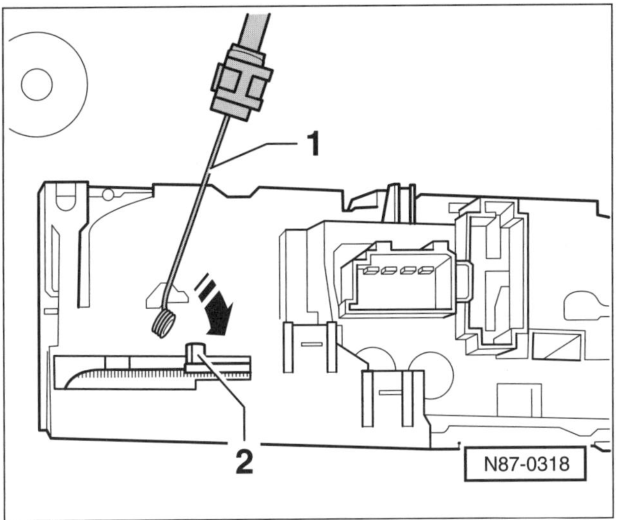

Fig. 4. Attach cable (**1**) to actuating arm (**2**).

7. Snap each cable into appropriate retainer. See Fig. 5.

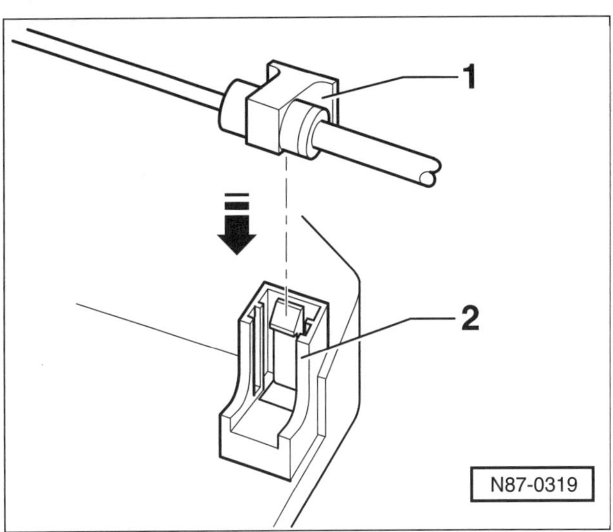

Fig. 5. Press cable (**1**) fully into retainer (**2**) until it engages.

8. Install harness connector.

9. Fit controls into instrument panel opening and install mounting screws.

10. Adjust cables as needed.

Heating and ventilation controls, assembly

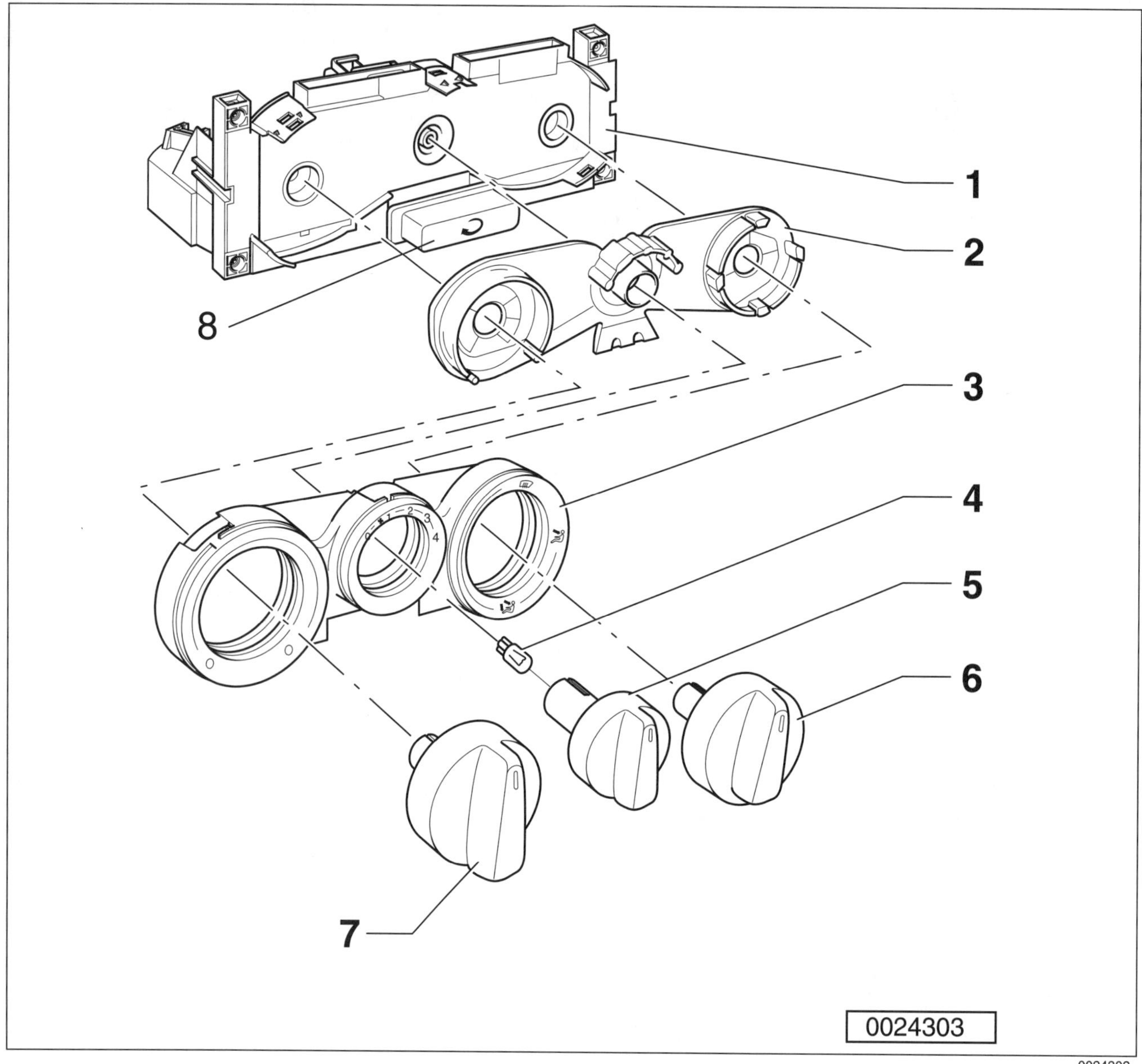

0024303

Fig. 6. Exploded view of heating and ventilation controls.

1. **Heating and ventilation controls)**
   - With blower fan switch (E9)
   - With recirculation switch (E184)
2. **Illumination filter ring**
3. **Trim panel**
4. **Fresh air control lever light (L16)**
   - Clear bulb 12V, 1.2W
5. **Rotary control knob**
   - For blower fan speed
   - Removing: use pliers with suitable plastic or rubber protection on jaws
6. **Rotary control knob**
   - For air distribution
   - Removing: Use pliers with suitable plastic or rubber protection on jaws
7. **Rotary control knob**
   - For interior temperature regulation
   - Removing: Use pliers with suitable plastic or rubber protection on jaws
8. **Recirculation switch (E184)**
   - Integral with controls

Heating and ventilation controls, adjusting

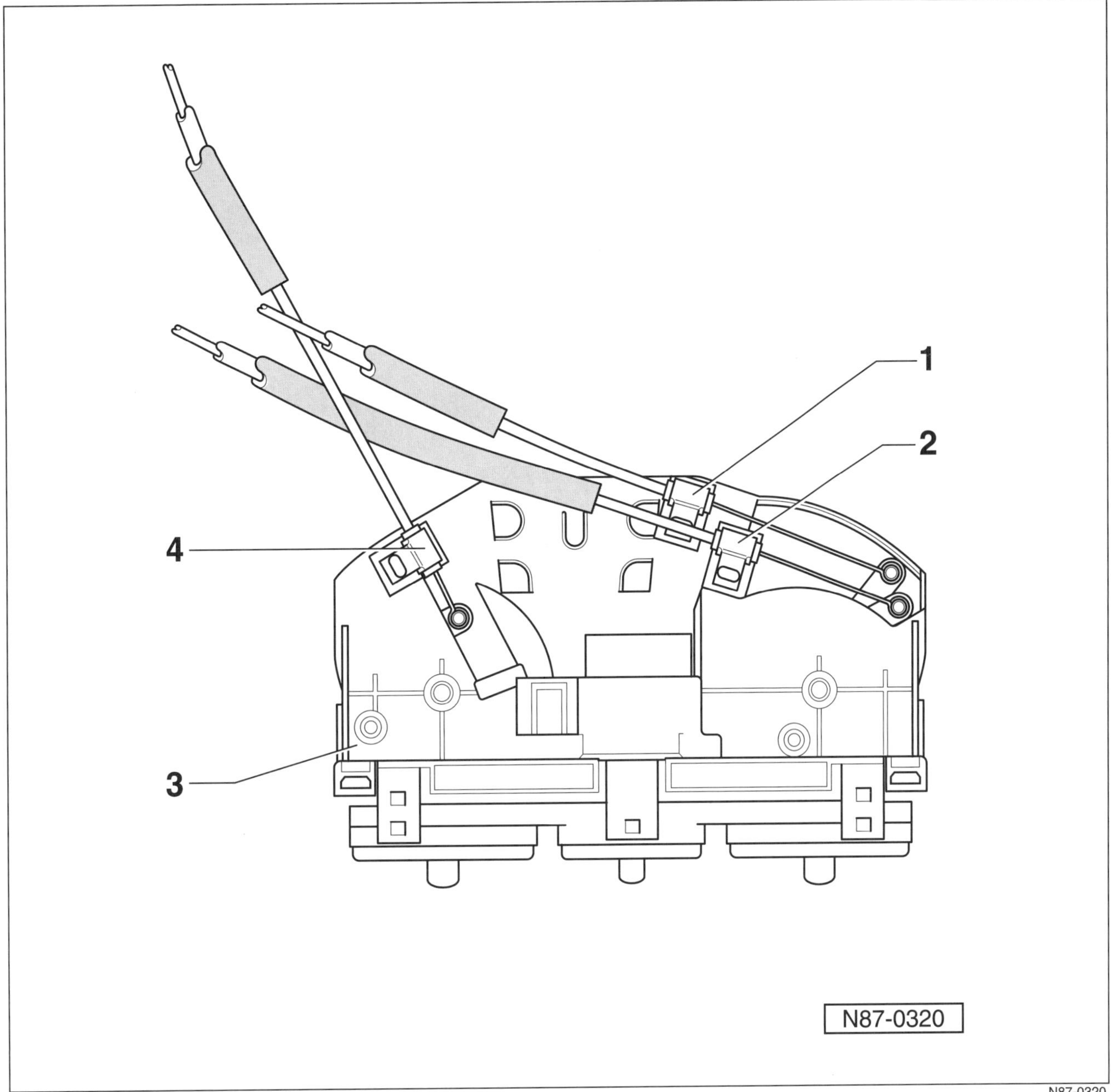

N87-0320

Fig. 7. Heating and ventilation control shown with assembled control cables.

1. **Central flap cable**
   - From air distribution rotary control to central flap
   - Cable sleeve color code: Yellow
   - Adjusting, **see** Ⓐ
2. **Footwell/defrost flap cable**
   - From air distribution rotary control to footwell/defrost flap
   - Cable sleeve color code: Green
   - Adjusting, **see** Ⓑ
3. **Heating and ventilation controls**
   - First attach cables to removed controls then to appropriate levers
   - All air flaps must be heard to move onto end stops when operating controls
4. **Temperature flap cable**
   - From temperature rotary control to temperature flap
   - Cable sleeve color code: Beige
   - Adjusting, **see** Ⓒ

(A) Temperature flap cable, installing and adjusting

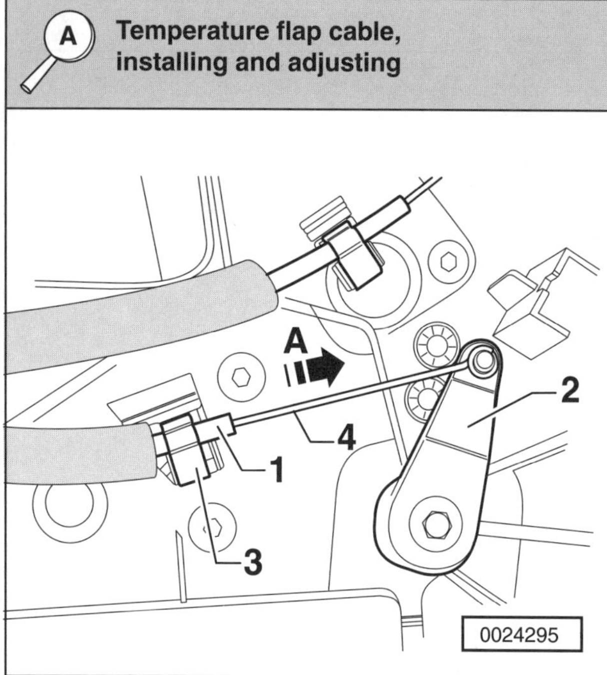

0024295

- Cable sleeve color code: beige.
- Install/adjust with controls installed and connecting duct removed.
- Turn temperature rotary control knob fully counter-clockwise against stop.
- Attach center wire of cable (4) to the temperature flap lever (2).
- Push temperature flap lever (2) against stop (arrow A) and secure outer cable (1) with clip (3).
- Turn temperature rotary control knob fully to left and right against stops.
- When turning the rotary control knob both end stops must be reached.

(B) Footwell/defrost flap cable, installing and adjusting

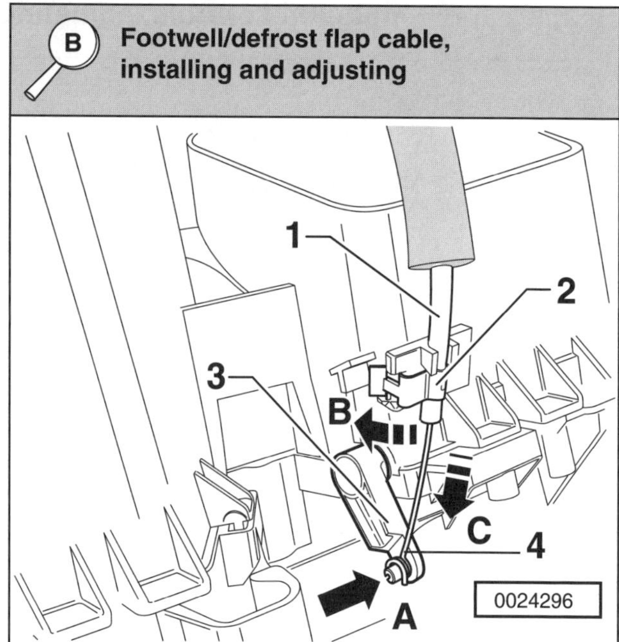

0024296

- Cable sleeve color code: green
- Install/adjust with controls installed.
- Turn air distribution rotary control knob fully counter-clockwise against stop.
- Attach center wire of cable (4) to the footwell/defrost flap lever (3) at arrow (A).
- Press footwell/defrost flap lever against stop (arrow C) and secure outer cable (1) with clip (2) (arrow B).
- Turn air distribution rotary control knob fully to left and right against stops.
- When turning the rotary control knob both end stops must be reached.

Central flap cable, installing and adjusting

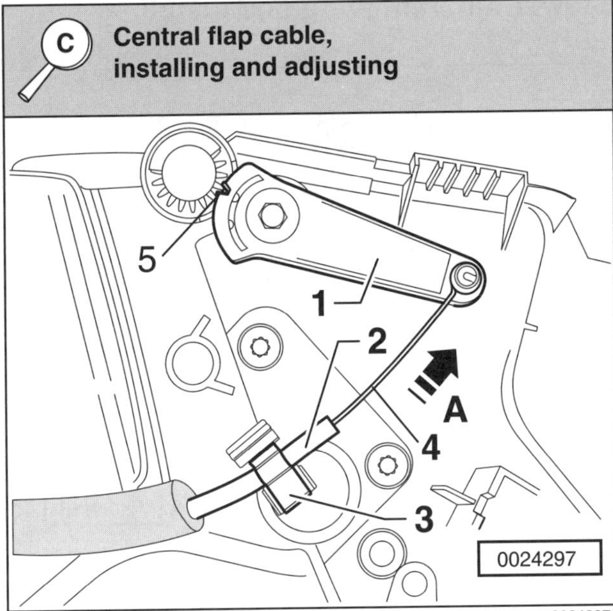

0024297

- **Cable sleeve color code: yellow.**
- **Install/adjust with controls installed, connecting duct removed and flap lever correctly indexed (5).**
- **Turn air distribution rotary control knob fully counter-clockwise against stop.**
- **Attach center wire of cable (4) to the central flap lever (1).**
- **Press central flap lever against stop (arrow A) and attach outer cable (2) with clip (3).**
- **Turn air distribution rotary control knob fully to left and right against stops.**
- **When turning the rotary control knob both end stops must be reached.**

HEATING AND VENTILATION COMPONENTS

Dust and pollen filter, removing and installing

The dust and pollen filter is located near the right forward corner of the instrument panel at the base of the windshield. It is covered by trim panels removed from the interior of the vehicle. See Fig. 8.

1. Push center dashboard cover forward and lift up to remove.

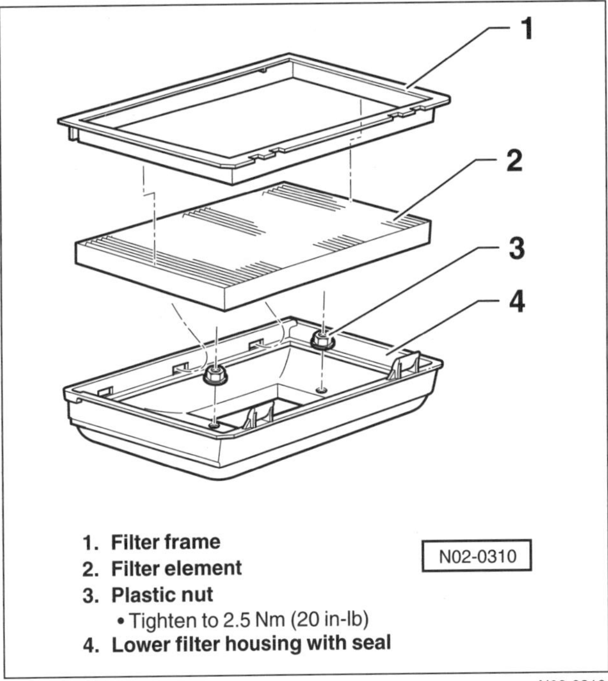

N02-0310

Fig. 8. Exploded view of dust and pollen filter assembly as found on New Beetles.

2. Remove securing screws and lift right side plenum panel cover up while carefully releasing from clips along front and rear edges. See Fig. 9.

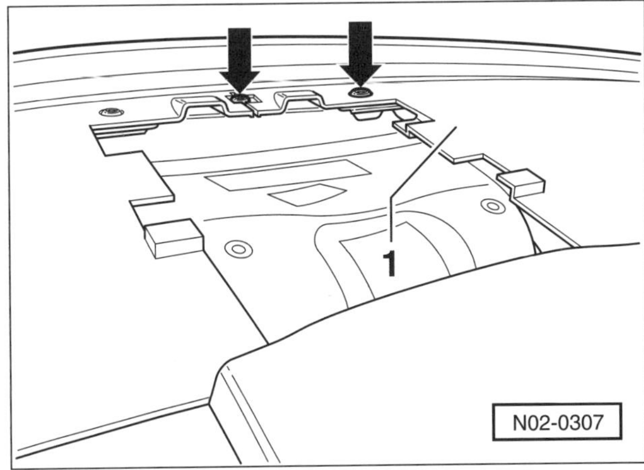

N02-0307

Fig. 9. Remove screws (**arrows**) from right side plenum panel cover (**1**).

3. Pull right side plenum panel cover toward center of vehicle and out of retainer in A-pillar to remove.

4. Remove screws and lift right side air plenum close-out panel from air plenum. See Fig. 10.

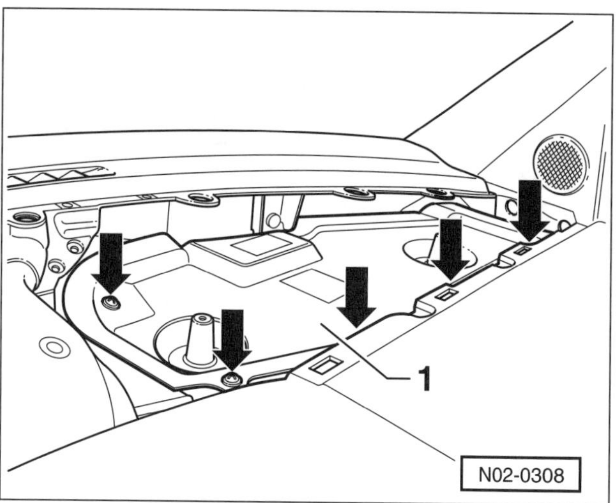

N02-0308

Fig. 10. Remove screws (**arrows**) from air plenum close-out panel to remove.

5. Remove rubber grommet above filter element.

6. Press tabs of filter housing (not the filter frame) towards the rear of the vehicle and lift the filter element with the frame up and out. See Fig. 11.

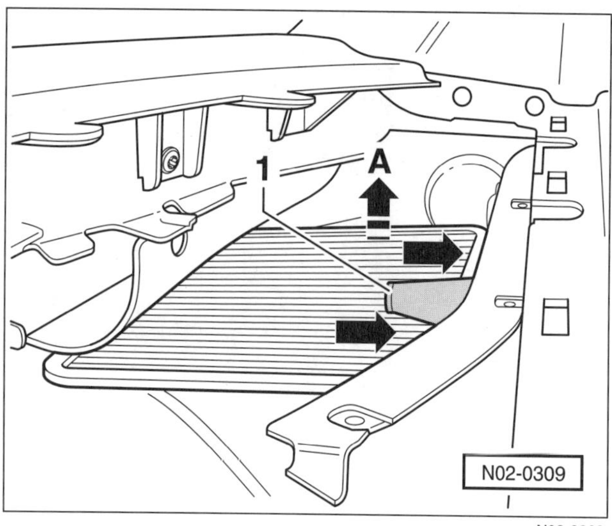

N02-0309

Fig. 11. Remove rubber grommet (**1**) and press tabs (**arrows**) on filter frame to the rear while lifting up (**arrow A**) on filter element and frame.

7. Install new filter element into frame. Make sure the ends of the frame fit into the first fold of filter element.

8. Press frame with filter into housing and snap into retainers.

9. Install remaining components in the reverse of removal.

HEATING AND VENTILATION COMPONENTS

Blower fan, removing and installing

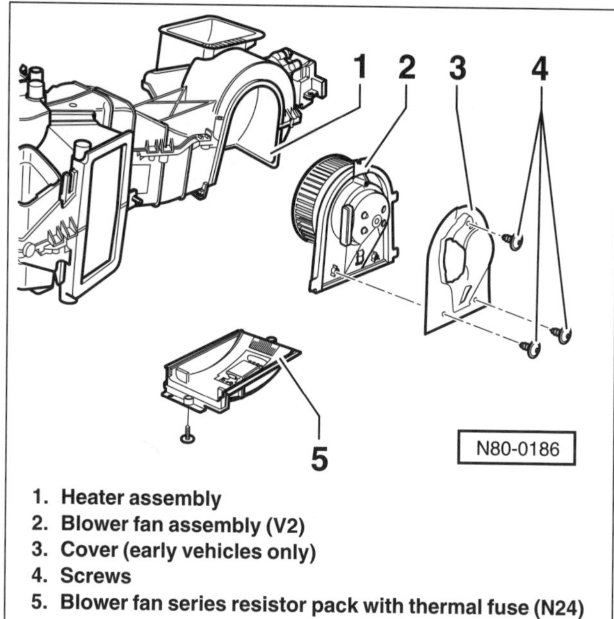

1. **Heater assembly**
2. **Blower fan assembly (V2)**
3. **Cover (early vehicles only)**
4. **Screws**
5. **Blower fan series resistor pack with thermal fuse (N24)**

N80-0186

Fig. 12. Blower fan with related mounting components.

1. Remove glove box, see **70 Trim–Interior**

2. Remove screws (4) and cover (3) where applicable.

NOTE —

The numbers in parenthesis in the procedure steps refer to Fig. 12.

3. Remove lower cover containing series resistor pack (5) and disconnect harness connector.

4. Disconnect harness connector from blower fan (2).

5. Pull blower fan out and downward.

6. Installation is the reverse of removal.

Center air outlet console, removing and installing

1. Remove radio, see **91 Radio**.

2. Push center cover forward and lift up to remove as shown earlier. Refer to Fig. 9.

3. Unclip and remove covers on lower switch console ends. See Fig. 13.

4. Unscrew and remove lower switch console cover.

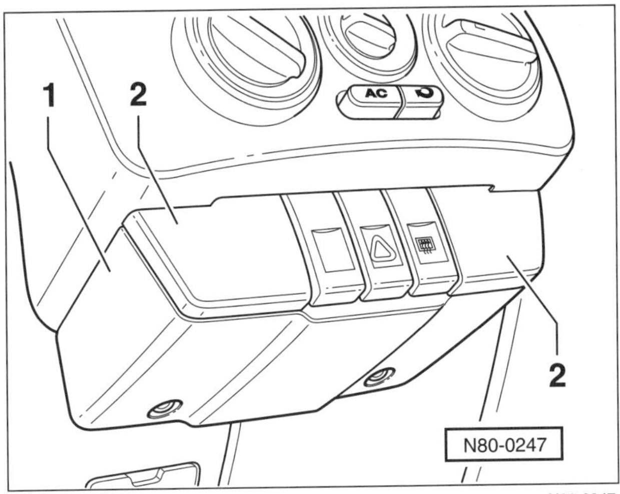

N80-0247

Fig. 13. Unclip and remove covers (**2**) and unscrew and remove switch console cover (**1**).

5. Remove securing screws and remove center air outlet console. See Fig. 14.

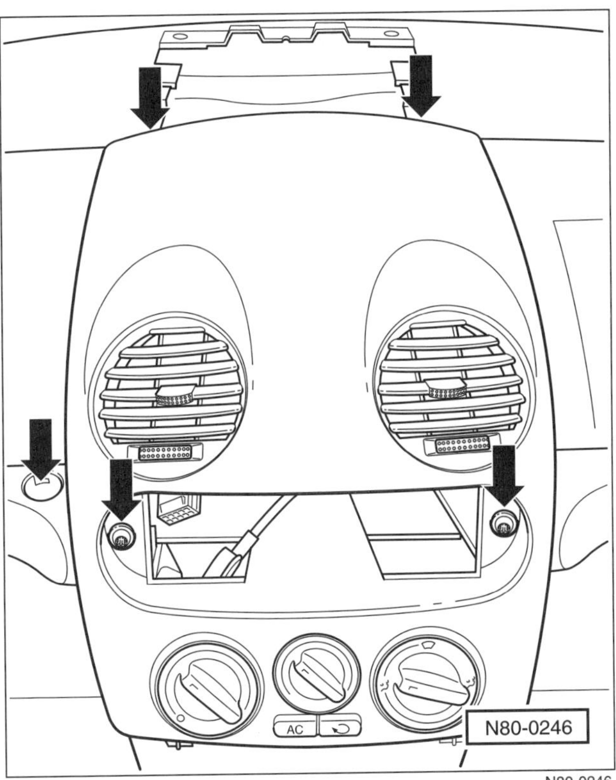

N80-0246

Fig. 14. Remove screws (**arrows**) to allow removal of center air outlet console.

Connecting duct, assembly

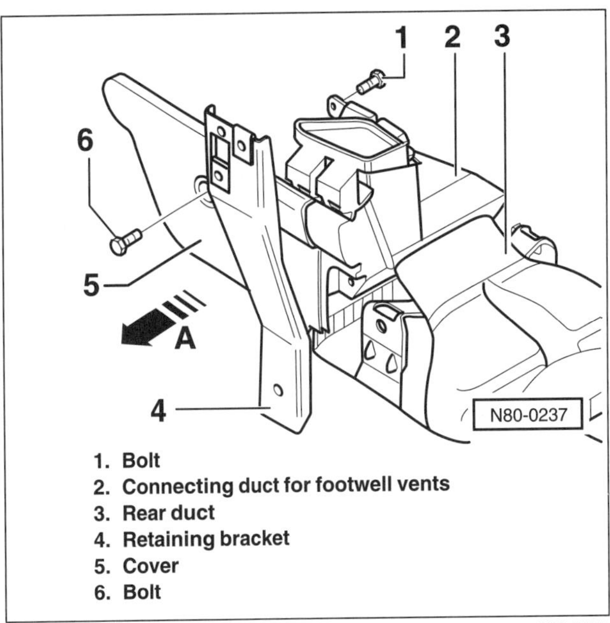

1. **Bolt**
2. **Connecting duct for footwell vents**
3. **Rear duct**
4. **Retaining bracket**
5. **Cover**
6. **Bolt**

N80-0237

Fig. 15. Connecting duct for footwell vents and related hardware.

Defroster air outlet panel, assembly

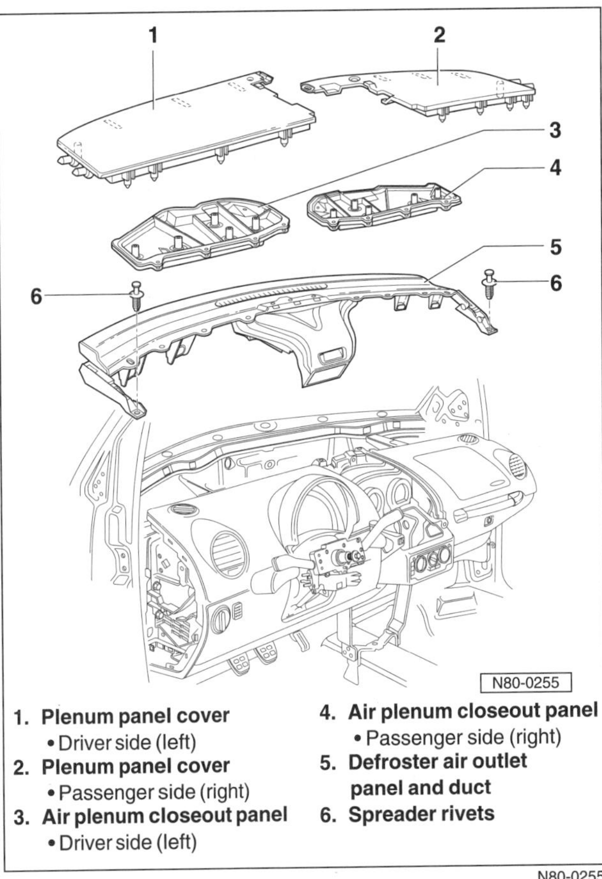

1. **Plenum panel cover**
   - Driver side (left)
2. **Plenum panel cover**
   - Passenger side (right)
3. **Air plenum closeout panel**
   - Driver side (left)
4. **Air plenum closeout panel**
   - Passenger side (right)
5. **Defroster air outlet panel and duct**
6. **Spreader rivets**

N80-0255

Fig. 16. Defroster air outlet panel with related panels and covers.

Heater assembly, overview

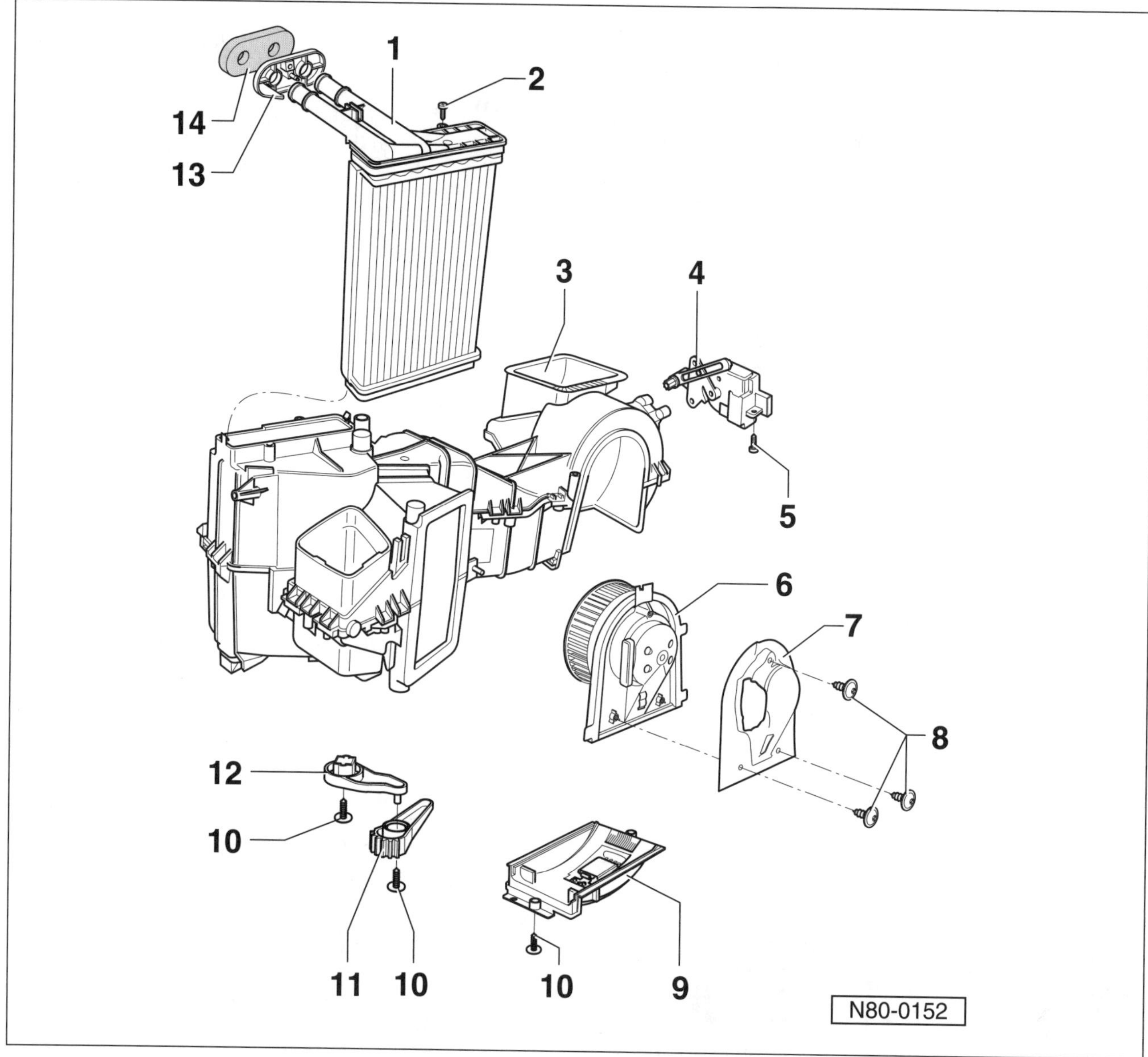

N80-0152

Fig. 17. Heater core shown with housing and major related components.

1. **Heater core**
   - Drain coolant before removal
   - Always use new coolant after replacement
   - Secured to housing with retainer clips
2. **Screw, self-tapping**
   - Use if retainer clips break
3. **Air distribution housing**
   - With air distribution flaps
4. **Servo motor for recirculation flap (V154)**
5. **Screw, self-tapping**
6. **Blower fan (V2)**
7. **Cover**
8. **Screw, self-tapping**
9. **Series resistor pack (N24)**
10. **Screw, self-tapping**
11. **Central flap lever**
    - Installed position, **see** Ⓐ
12. **Temperature flap lever**
13. **Base plate**
14. **Heater core bulkhead seal**
    - Installed position, **see** Ⓑ

A Central flap lever, installing and adjusting

N80-0198

N80-0198

- Central flap pinion shaft has an index mark.
- Install the lever so that index notches on lever and pinion shaft are aligned (arrows).

B Heater core bulkhead seal, installed position

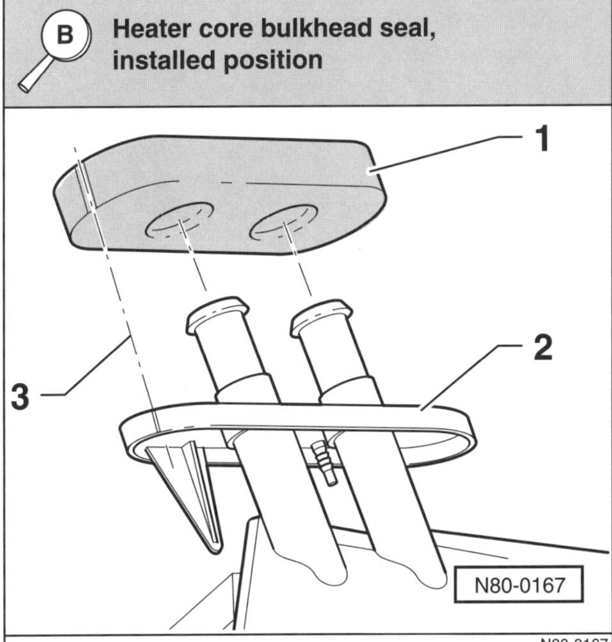

N80-0167

- Seal between heater core and bulkhead has a positioning mark on the side.
- Install seal (1) so that the notches on the seal and notches on the base plate (2) are aligned (3).

Recirculation flap servo, removing and installing

1. Remove glove box, see **70 Trim–Interior**.
2. Disconnect harness connector from flap servo.
3. Remove securing screw and swing motor downwards. See Fig. 18.

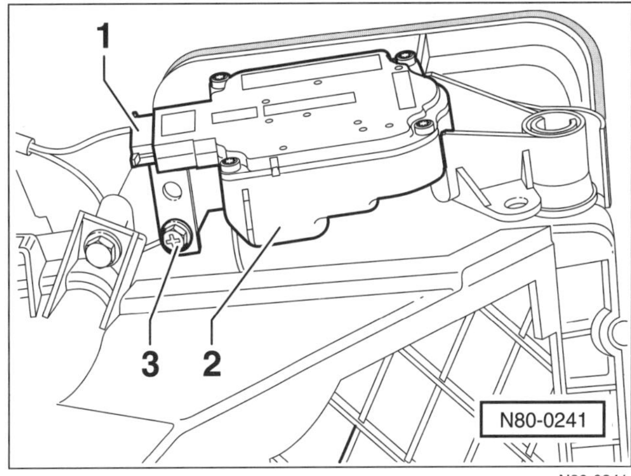

N80-0241

Fig. 18. Recirculation flap servo (**2**) shown in installed position. Unplug harness connector (**1**) and remove securing screw (**3**).

4. Disconnect motor from recirculation flap lever.
5. Before installing a new servo, attach harness connector to the new servo and switch on ignition.

NOTE —
Replacement servos are supplied with operating levers in the "recirculation" position.

6. Operate switch for recirculation flap and observe lever position.
7. When center position of travel is reached, quickly unplug the harness connector and switch off ignition.
8. Install servo onto recirculation flap shaft.

NOTE —
If it is difficult to align and fit the servo to the recirculation flap shaft, remove the blower fan and position the flap and shaft as required.

9. When servo has been installed onto recirculation flap shaft, move motor into mounting position and install securing screw. See Fig. 19.

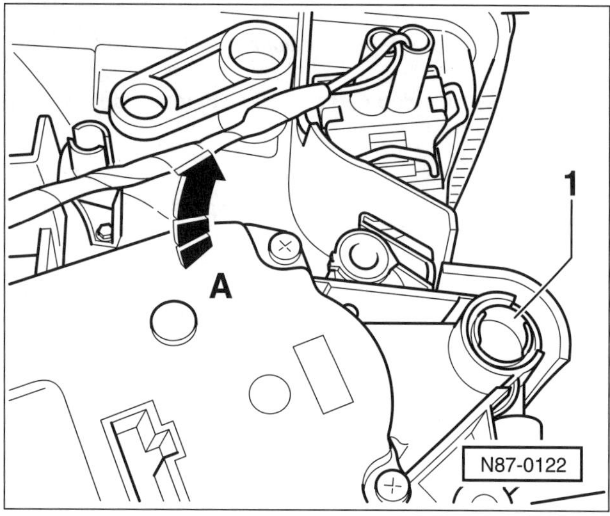

N87-0122

Fig. 19. When servo is installed onto recirculation flap shaft (**1**), move servo in direction of arrow (**A**) to installed position and secure with mounting screw.

10. Install harness connector.

11. Install glove box and remainder of removed components.

QUALITY REVIEW

When you have finished working under the hood and around other areas of the vehicle, it is advisable to take a moment to quality check or review your work. This helps to insure that the operation or repair has been completed properly with all affected systems functioning within normal parameters. These may include the following:

- Ensure that all cable ties and clamps that were removed as part of the repair are replaced.
- Ensure that all fasteners and hardware were replaced and torqued as specified.
- Make sure that all other components involved in the repair are positioned correctly, properly torqued and function properly.
- Make sure that all tools, shop cloths, fender covers and protective tapes are removed before closing the hood.
- Clean grease and fingerprints from painted surfaces, steering wheel, upholstery and shifter.
- Make sure that warm/hot air is delivered by the appropriate air vents when the heater is switched on.
- Unlock anti-theft radio and reset the clock.

87 Air Conditioning

TABLES

GENERAL

This section covers the Air Conditioning (A/C) refrigerant system and related components. Service and adjustment to the ventilation control cables is covered in **80 Heating and Ventilation.**

> ***CAUTION —***
> *Disconnecting the negative (–) battery cable may erase fault codes and basic settings in the engine management and automatic transmission control modules. Some driveability problems may be noticed until the system re-adapts to operating conditions. OBD II readiness codes, which may be required for emissions testing, may also be erased. Convenience electronics (alarm system, interior light control, power locks, mirrors, and windows) may need to be re-set using a VAG 1551/1552 or equivalent scan tool.*

The refrigerant system of the New Beetle is designed to work only with a refrigerant known generally as R-134a. In this section, the refrigerant will always be referred to as R-134a, however, this chemical is marketed and sold under several trade designations such as: Tetrafluoroethane, CH_2F CF_3, H-KW 134a, SUVA® 134a, and ARCTON® 134a.

Other refrigerants may be available in the marketplace, however, Volkswagen specifically recommends that no other refrigerant be used. Serious damage will usually result and performance will be reduced.

Special precautions for A/C systems

New Beetle air conditioning systems are filled with refrigerant R-134a under pressure. The unique characteristics of this chemical necessitate special servicing and handling procedures which may be governed by Federal, State, Provincial and Local regulations.

> ***WARNING —***
> - *Work in a well ventilated area. Refrigerant gases are heavier than air, displace oxygen and may cause suffocation in areas of poor air circulation, for example under the vehicle.*
> - *Pressurized R134a refrigerant in the presence of oxygen may form a combustible mixture. Never introduce compressed air into any R-134a container (full or empty), capped off A/C component, or piece of service equipment.*

87

WARNING —

- *As of January 1, 1992 any person who services a motor vehicle air conditioner in the USA MUST, by law, be properly trained and certified and use approved refrigerant recycling equipment. Technicians must complete an EPA approved recycling course to be certified.*
- *State, Provincial and Local governments may have additional requirements regarding air conditioning servicing. Always comply with all applicable laws and regulations.*
- *The A/C system is filled with refrigerant gas which is under pressure.*
- *Avoid breathing refrigerant vapors. Exposure may irritate eyes, nose and throat.*
- *Always be careful that refrigerant does not come in contact with your skin. Always wear hand and eye protection (gloves and goggles) when working around the A/C system. If refrigerant has come in contact with your skin or eyes:*
  - *Do not rub skin or eyes.*
  - *Immediately flush with cool water for 15 minutes.*
  - *Rush to a doctor or hospital.*
  - *Do not attempt to treat yourself.*
- *Keep refrigerant containers stored below 50°C (122°F) and use care to avoid dropping.*
- *DO NOT warm refrigerant containers with an open flame. If refrigerant needs to be warmed, place bottom of tank in warm water.*
- *Do not expose any component of the A/C system to high temperatures above 80°C (176°F) or open flames. Excessive heat will cause system pressure increases which could burst the system.*
- *Switch on exhaust/ventilation systems when working on the refrigerant system.*
- *Keep refrigerant away from open flames. Poisonous gas will be produced if it burns. Do not smoke when refrigerant gases are present for the same reason.*
- *Electric welding near refrigerant hoses causes R-134a to decompose from ultraviolet light. Discharge system before electric welding.*
- *Always use an Underwriter's Laboratory (UL) approved refrigerant recovery/recycling/recharging unit such as Kent-Moore ACR4, or equivalent, whenever servicing an R-134a A/C system.*
- *Do not steam clean condensers or evaporators. Use only cold water or compressed air on the outside of the component.*

CAUTION —

- *Refrigerant oils used for the R-134a system and R-12 (FREON®) systems are NOT compatible. Use only the specified synthetic oil (Polyalkylene Glycol/PAG) for the R-134a refrigerant system. DO NOT use R-12 system oil in an R-134a system or R-134a system oil in an R-12 system. If the refrigerant oils are mixed, system contamination will occur and compressor failure may result.*
- *R-134a refrigerant system oil (PAG oil) absorbs moisture very rapidly. Moisture combines with the refrigerant to form acids which will damage the system. Use only the specified oil from a sealed container and ALWAYS reseal oil container immediately after use. DO NOT use oil if it has become contaminated with moisture.*
- *Only use R-134a in New Beetle A/C systems. Never use substitute or "drop-in" replacement refrigerants. Vehicle safety will be compromised and severe damage to vehicle and servicing equipment will result.*
- *Immediately plug open connections on A/C components to prevent dirt and especially moisture contamination. Likewise, DO NOT remove new components from packaging until ready to install. Immediately tighten component connections after installation.*
- *Always use separate refrigerant recovery/recycling/recharging servicing equipment for R-12 and R-134a systems. DO NOT use one piece of equipment for both R-12 and R-134a systems. The residual traces of refrigerant will contaminate and damage the equipment. Servicing equipment includes recovery/recycling/recharging unit, charging station, vacuum pump, manifold gauges, etc. Use only equipment designed to meet Society of Automotive Engineers (SAE) standards.*
- *R-134a and R-12 systems use different size service fittings. NEVER use adaptors to convert an R-12 fitting to R-134a size or R-134a fitting to R-12 size.*
- *R-134a and R-12 A/C components including compressor, hoses, O-rings, evaporator, condenser, receiver-drier, etc. are NOT interchangeable. Components of the R-134a system are identified by lettering (R-134a) or by a green label (or stripe). In addition a label on the upper radiator support identifies which type refrigerant is used. Use only the correct system component for each refrigerant type.*
- *Discharge A/C system before removing any A/C system component.*
- *Always replace damaged and/or leaking A/C system components. Do not attempt repair by soldering or welding.*
- *Always reinstall caps over A/C service valves.*

> ***CAUTION —***
> - *Always replace O-rings, DO NOT reuse. Use only the correct size and type of O-rings specified for use with R-134a refrigerant. Lubricate O-ring with refrigerant oil before installing.*
> - *Work area must be extremely clean when working on A/C system components.*

A/C refrigerant circuit

Fig. 1 shows the basic schematic layout of the air conditioning system found in the New Beetle. The variable displacement compressor compresses the R-134a refrigerant and moves it from the discharge port in a gaseous state to the condenser. The condenser is mounted in the front of the vehicle where air from the radiator fans or the motion of the vehicle passes through it. The motion of the air removes the heat from the refrigerant and a change of state from gas to liquid occurs. The liquid refrigerant flows to the receiver-drier where it is temporarily stored and a desiccant removes any moisture. The refrigerant then moves past a sight glass (early vehicles only) and a high pressure service port to the expansion valve unit. The expansion valve has a small internal orifice which sprays the liquid refrigerant into the evaporator. The resulting change of state from liquid to gas and the associated pressure drop causes the evaporator to become cold. Air from inside the passenger compartment is passed over the evaporator by a fan where it gives up its heat and becomes cold. It is then distributed through the vent system. The gaseous refrigerant passes back through a port on the expansion valve, past a low pressure service port and damper and finally back to the suction side of the compressor to be compressed again. See Fig. 1.

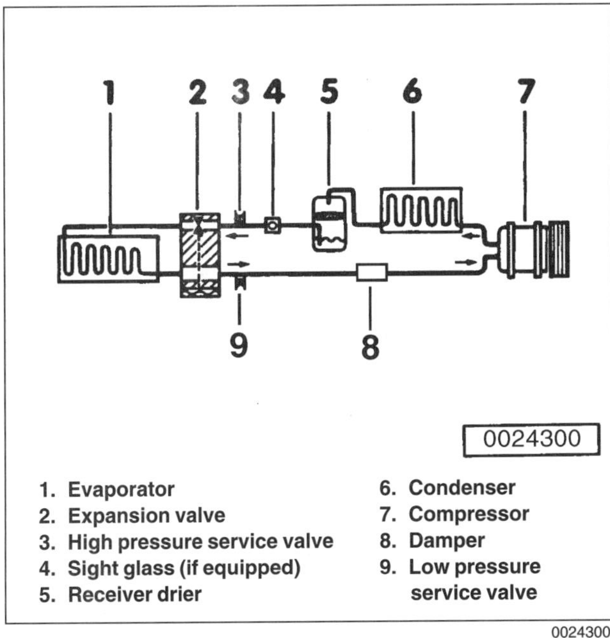

0024300

Fig. 1. New Beetle air conditioning refrigerant system schematic. Arrows indicate direction of refrigerant flow.

Several other components are used to control and protect the system in addition to those mentioned above. The compressor runs when needed by means of an electro-magnetic clutch which is in turn controlled by several relays. A pressure switch in the refrigerant line also controls operation of the compressor clutch and the radiator cooling fans. A pressure relief valve is mounted to the compressor cylinder head plate. Switches for operation are mounted within easy reach of the driver and fuses and relays are mounted under the instrument panel.

A/C REFRIGERANT SYSTEM

The air conditioning system is comprised of components that can be grouped into several areas. This heading covers those components that are used to handle and contain the R-134a refrigerant. See Fig. 2.

> ***WARNING —***
> *Observe all cautions, warnings and notes before starting repairs involving air conditioning systems.*

NOTE —
Volkswagen identifies electrical components by a letter and/or a number in the electrical schematics. See **97 Wiring Diagrams, Fuses and Relays**. *These electrical identifiers are listed in parenthesis as an aid to electrical troubleshooting.*

A/C refrigerant system, component overview

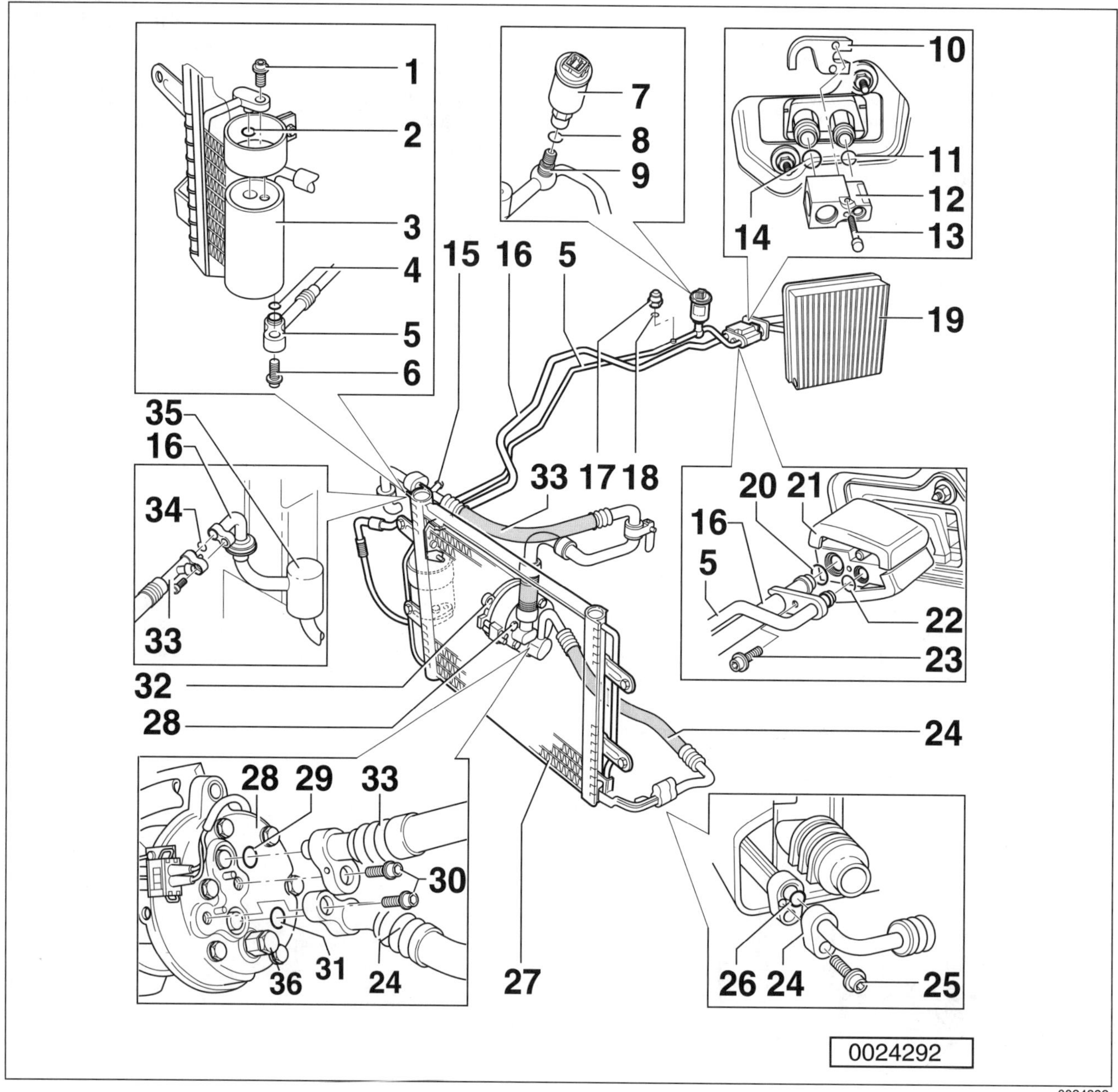

0024292

Fig. 2. A/C system components as installed in New Beetles.

1. **Sealing plug**
    - Tighten to 15 Nm (11 ft-lb)
2. **O-ring, see** Ⓐ
    - Always replace
    - 7.6 mm x 1.82 mm
3. **Receiver drier, see** Ⓑ
    - Location: attached to right side of condenser
4. **O-ring**
    - Always replace
    - 7.6 mm x 1.82 mm
5. **Liquid refrigerant line**
    - Location: between receiver drier outlet and expansion valve inlet
6. **Bolt**
    - Tighten to 15 Nm (11 ft-lb)

(continued from previous page)

7. **A/C pressure switch (F129), see Ⓒ**
   - Location: liquid refrigerant line near expansion valve
   - Switch can be removed without discharging refrigerant system
8. **O-ring**
   - Always replace
   - 7.6 mm x 1.82 mm
9. **Threaded fitting**
   - Location: in liquid refrigerant line
10. **Reinforcement plate**
11. **O-ring**
   - Always replace
   - 7.6 mm x 1.82 mm
12. **Expansion valve**
   - Location: near bulkhead on right side of engine compartment
13. **Bolt**
   - Tighten to 8 Nm (71 in-lb)
14. **O-ring**
   - Always replace
   - 14.0 mm x 1.82 mm
15. **Low pressure service valve port**
   - Location: low pressure refrigerant line II near top of condenser
   - Only use Kent Moore ACR4 or equivalent
16. **Low pressure refrigerant line I**
   - Location: outlet side of expansion valve
17. **High pressure service valve port**
   - Location: liquid refrigerant line near expansion valve
   - Only use Kent Moore ACR4 or equivalent
18. **O-ring**
   - Always replace
   - 7.6 mm x 1.82 mm
19. **Evaporator**
   - Location: in heater/evaporator housing
20. **O-ring**
   - Always replace
   - 17.0 mm x 1.85 mm
21. **Insulation**
   - Location: wrapped around expansion valve
22. **O-ring**
   - Always replace
   - 8.13 mm x 1.78 mm
23. **Bolt**
   - Tighten to 8 Nm (71 in-lb)
24. **High pressure refrigerant line**
   - Location: discharge side of compressor to condenser
25. **Bolt**
   - Tighten to 15 Nm (11 ft lb)
26. **O-ring**
   - Always replace
   - 7.6 mm x 1.82 mm
27. **Condenser**
   - Location: ahead of radiator
28. **Compressor**
   - Location: attached to mounting bracket on engine
   - Type: Sanden SD7-V16 automatic variable displacement
   - Replacement compressors are filled with the total system refrigerant oil quantity
29. **O-ring**
   - Always replace
   - 14.3 mm x 2.4 mm
30. **Bolt**
   - Tighten to 20 Nm (15 ft-lb)
31. **O-ring**
   - Always replace
   - 7.6 mm x 1.82 mm
32. **A/C compressor clutch (N25)**
   - Location: attached to front of A/C compressor
   - Type: Sanden
   - Switch can be removed without discharging refrigerant system
33. **Low pressure refrigerant line II**
   - Location: suction side of compressor
   - Engine code AEG shown, ALH similar
34. **O-ring**
   - Always replace
   - 14.3 mm x 2.4 mm
35. **Damper**
   - Location: built into low pressure line I (item 16)
36. **Pressure relief valve, see Ⓓ**
   - Location: on compressor cylinder head plate

A O-rings

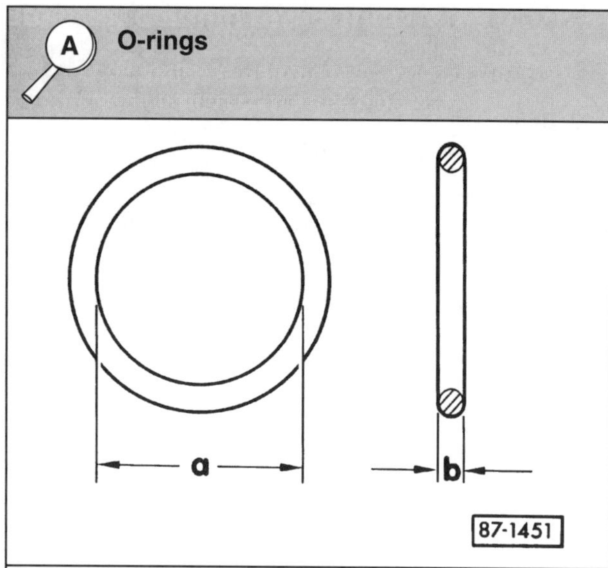

87-1451

- Note inner diameter (a) and thickness (b).
- Lubricate with PAG oil before installing.
- Always replace during repairs, never reuse.
- Only use O-rings that are compatible with R-134a.
- May be color coded green, red, violet or black.

B Receiver drier

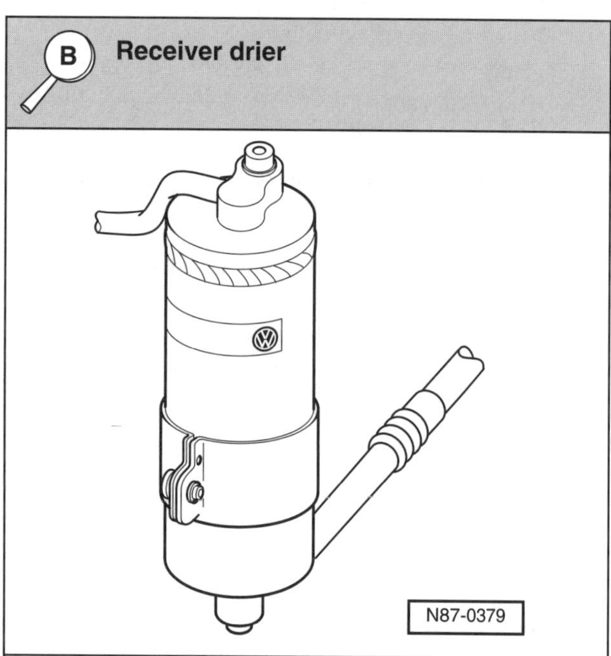

N87-0379

- Reservoir for liquid refrigerant.
- Contains desiccant to absorb moisture from refrigerant.
- Must have green identification markings to indicate compatibility with R-134a.
- Never use R-12 FREON parts.
- To ensure optimum system operation, always replace every time refrigerant system is opened.

C A/C pressure switch

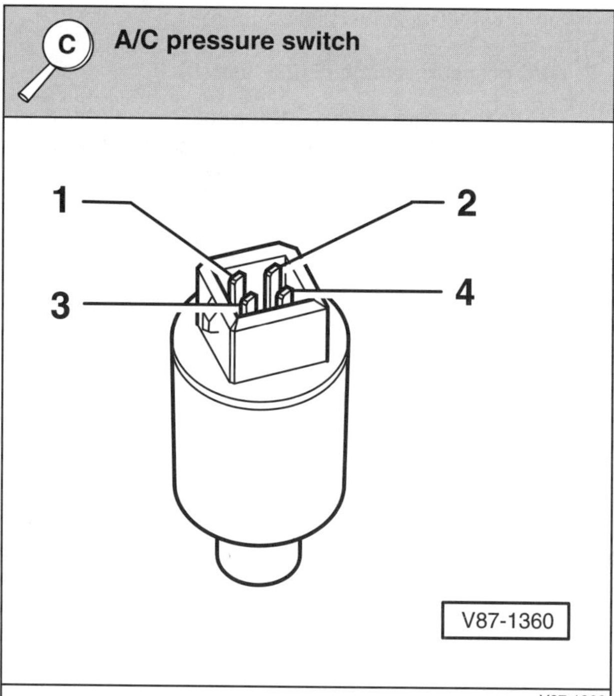

V87-1360

- Can be replaced without discharging refrigerant due to schraeder valve in threaded fitting.
- Switches A/C clutch off when refrigerant pressure exceeds 32 bar (464 psi) and resets when pressure drops to 24 bar (348 psi).
- Switches A/C clutch off when refrigerant pressure falls below 1.2 bar (17.4 psi).
- Switches radiator coolant fan to second speed when pressure reaches 16 bar (232 psi).
- Terminals 1 and 2 switch A/C clutch.
- Terminals 3 and 4 switch radiator coolant fan.

D Pressure relief valve

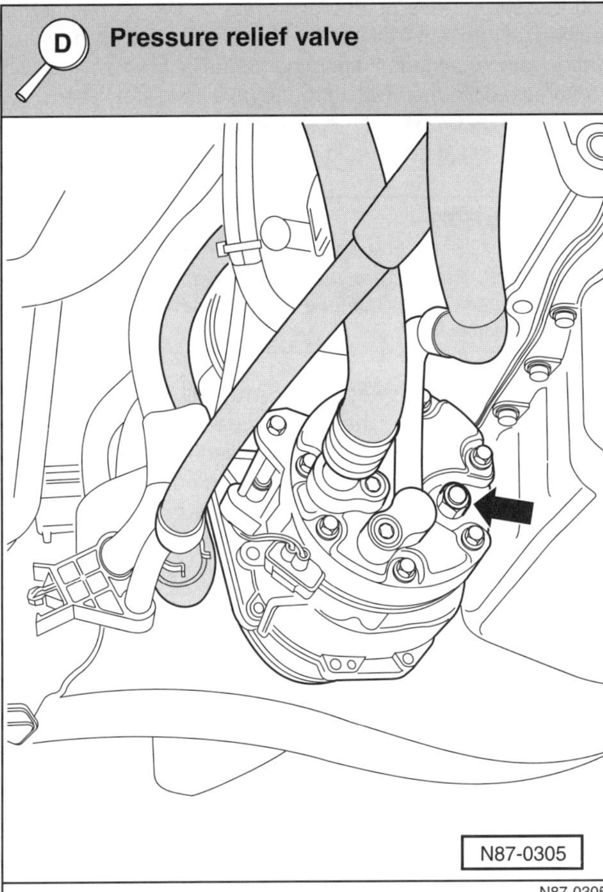

N87-0305

- **Protects refrigerant circuit from over-pressure.**
- **Opens to vent pressures over 40 bar (580 psi) and then closes to prevent total refrigerant loss.**
- **Adhesive plate (arrow) is pushed out if valve has opened.**

A/C refrigerant R-134a

Refrigerant R-134a as used in automotive applications has performance similar to FREON® (R-12) but is understood at this time to be environmentally safer. Refrigerant R-134a has the following characteristics:

- Colorless and is invisible as a gas.
- R-134a when viewed through the sight glass may appear milky due to the mixture of refrigerant and lubricating oil (PAG oil).
- Escaped R-134a gases are heavier than air and will gather first in low places, such as under the car.
- R-134a refrigerant gas displaces oxygen and may cause suffocation in low areas or areas of poor air circulation.
- Refrigerant R-134a will deteriorate some plastics. Therefore, when making system repairs, use only genuine VW replacement parts or parts which are specified for use with R-134a refrigerant.
- R-134a in an enclosed container will have a specific temperature/pressure relationship.
- Refrigerant R-134a is not poisonous in any state (liquid or gas) and is safe when used properly.
- Refrigerant R-134a, in its pure state, is chemically stable and will not attack iron, copper, brass or aluminum. However, the mixture of R-134a and PAG oil may deteriorate certain metals (copper). Therefore, when making system repairs, use only genuine VW replacement parts or parts which are specified for use with R-134a refrigerant.
- Liquid R-134a refrigerant will absorb only very minute quantities of moisture. However, R-134a vapor can absorb large amounts of moisture.
- R-134a refrigerant is not flammable.
- DO NOT exceed maximum rated capacity of refrigerant stored in containers.
- Use halogen leak detector Hitec HI400A-TEL or equivalent to check for R-134a system leaks. This tool can also be used to detect leaks in R-12 systems. Many currently available R-12 leak detectors cannot detect R-134a refrigerant leaks.

Refrigerant oil, PAG

A special Polyalkylene Glycol (PAG) synthetic oil is used in R-134a systems. This oil is NOT compatible with mineral based oils used in older R-12 systems. Refer to **Special precautions for A/C systems**. For specifications and quantity, see **Table a**.

Table a. A/C system capacities

Fluid & Specification	Quantity
Refrigerant, R-134a	700 g + 50 g (24.7 + 1.8 oz.)
Oil, PAG, SP-10 (G 052 154 A2)	135 cc (4.6 oz.)

NOTE —

- *Volkswagen part numbers are given for reference only. Always consult with your Volkswagen Parts Department or aftermarket parts specialist for the latest parts information.*
- *A label on the lock carrier in the engine compartment indicates the refrigerant type and capacity and should be consulted before starting any servicing or repairs.*

Refrigerant lines and hoses

Lines and hoses are fastened together with threaded couplings and fittings. They are retained to the bodywork or components with specially isolated hose clamps. During servicing, all couplings, fittings and related fasteners must be torqued to specification.

A/C refrigerant system, replacing components

Replacement A/C compressors, evaporators and condensers supplied by the authorized Volkswagen dealer parts departments are filled with Nitrogen. If gas (Nitrogen) does not escape when component is first opened, the component may be faulty (leaking), do not install. Additionally, replacement A/C compressors are filled with the total refrigerant oil quantity needed for the entire refrigerant system.

Always replace the receiver drier whenever the refrigerant system has been left open. Install immediately after opening to prevent moisture contamination of drier desiccant. Moreover, keep refrigerant system and other replacement components sealed for as long as possible to minimize the chance of dirt and moisture contamination. Even the slightest amount of trapped moisture can freeze within the system causing blockage and erratic performance. Always plug any open refrigerant line connections to prevent dirt and moisture contamination during the repair especially if the repair will not be completed immediately.

If the system has been discharged due to a damaged or leaking component (refrigerant hose/line, compressor, evaporator, condenser, etc.), flush the refrigerant system first with compressed air, then with nitrogen (available locally) and collect the oil that runs out. This will remove the refrigerant oil which may be saturated with moisture.

CAUTION —
DO NOT flush R-134a refrigerant system with R-11. R-11 is not compatible with refrigerant R-134a and PAG oil and will cause total system contamination!

If the compressor is not replaced after flushing the system, fill the compressor with the correct type and quantity of refrigerant oil for the total system as specified in **Table a**. If a new Sanden compressor is used, do not add any additional oil as the total amount of oil required is already in the compressor. Refrigerant oil is distributed in most major parts of the refrigerant system. For approximate capacities, see **Table b**.

Table b. Refrigerant oil distribution

Component	Approximate amount of oil in component - % of total
Compressor	67.5 cc (2.3 oz) - 50%
Condenser	13.5 cc (0.46 oz) - 10%
Suction line	13.5 cc (0.46 oz) - 10%
Discharge line	--
Evaporator	27 cc (0.92 oz) - 20%
Receiver-drier	13.5 cc (0.46 oz) - 10%

WARNING —
Dispose of contaminated refrigerant oil following laws governing hazardous waste disposal. Do not combine any refrigerant oil with any other old oils such as engine oil or transmission fluid unless approved by the appropriate governing body.

Condenser assembly, overview

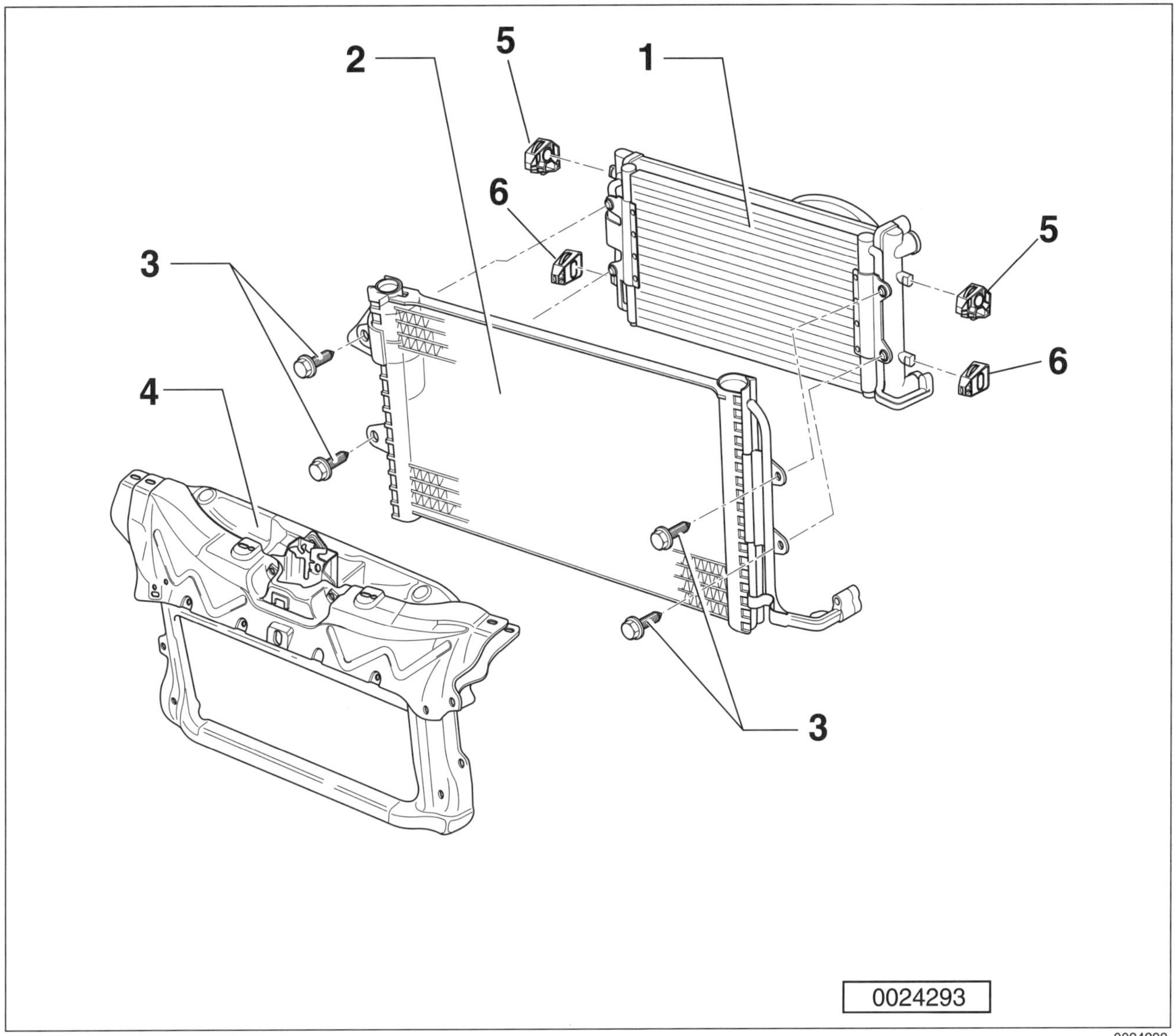

0024293

Fig. 3. A/C condenser shown with related mounting components.

> ***WARNING —***
> *Observe all cautions, warnings and notes before starting repairs involving air conditioning systems.*

1. **Radiator**
   - Drain coolant before removal
   - Always use new coolant after replacement
2. **Condenser**
   - Discharge and recover refrigerant before removal
   - Disconnect refrigerant lines at condenser
   - Seal open refrigerant lines immediately
   - Inspect for bent and obstructed fins and physical damage before installing
   - Always replace O-rings for refrigerant lines
3. **Bolt**
   - Tighten to 8 Nm (71 in-lb)
4. **Lock carrier**
   - Bring into service position for condenser removal
5. **Bracket**
   - For radiator, upper
   - Note installation position
6. **Bracket**
   - For radiator, lower
   - Note installation position

Evaporator/heater assembly, overview

The A/C evaporator and the heater core are encased in a multi-piece housing inside the vehicle. See Fig. 4. Access is from the interior and requires A/C refrigerant discharge and removal of the instrument panel and instrument panel cross-member. See **70 Trim–Interior**.

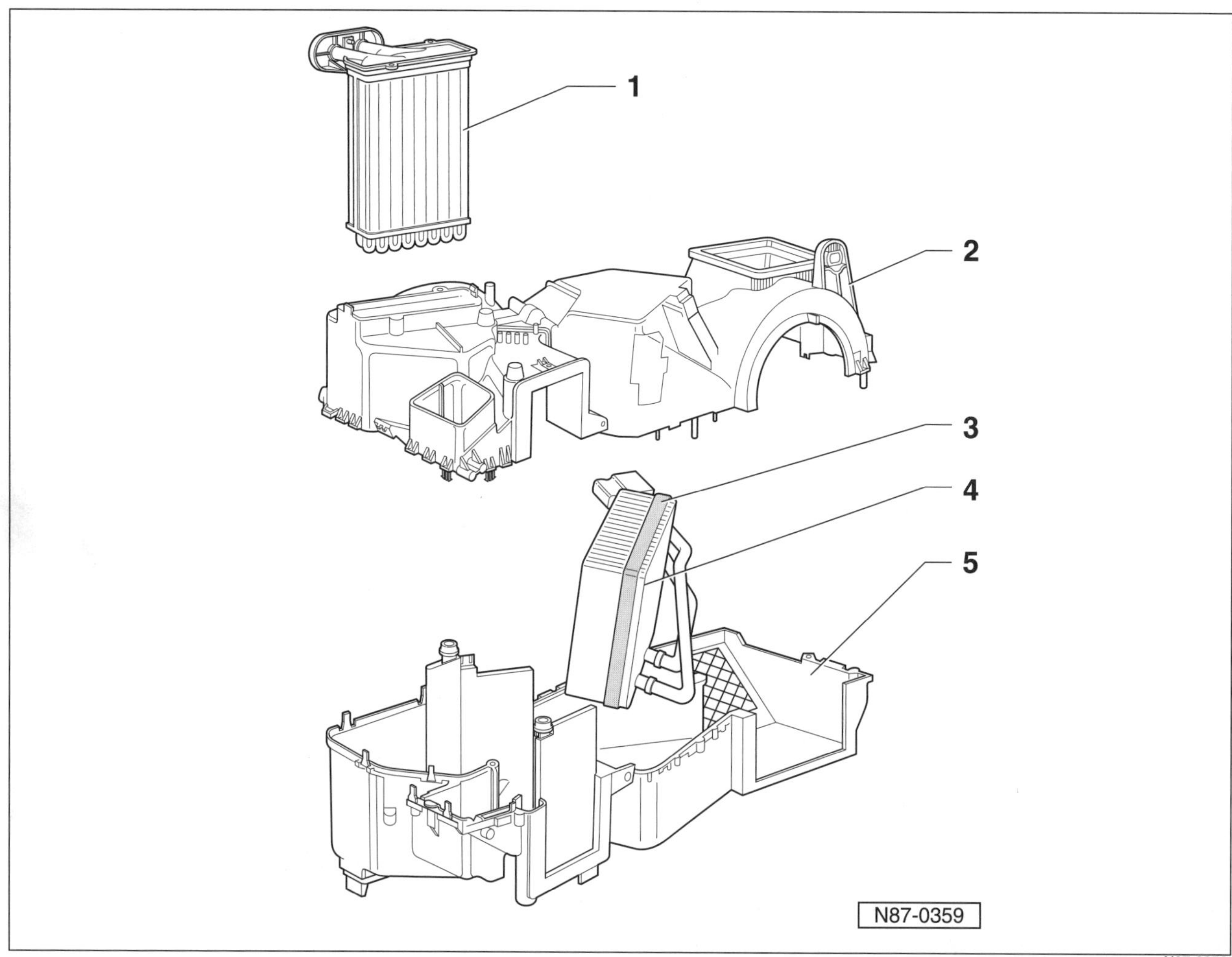

N87-0359

Fig. 4. A/C evaporator shown with heater core and housing.

> ***WARNING —***
> *Observe all cautions, warnings and notes before starting repairs involving air conditioning systems.*

NOTE —
Availability of individual air conditioning components may be limited. Complete assemblies may be required.

1. **Heater core**
   - Drain coolant before removal
   - Always use new coolant after replacement
2. **Housing, upper section**
   - With fresh/recirculating air flap
3. **Evaporator seal**
   - Install seal to top and sides only, not to bottom
   - Secure with glue
   - Condensate MUST be free to drain out from the bottom of the housing under the evaporator.
4. **Evaporator**
   - Discharge and recover refrigerant before removal
   - Disconnect refrigerant lines at expansion valve
   - Seal open refrigerant lines immediately
   - Inspect for bent and obstructed fins and physical damage before installing
   - Always replace O-rings for refrigerant lines
5. **Housing, lower section**

A/C system odor, checking

An unpleasant smell or "musty" odor can be emitted from any automotive air conditioning system under certain conditions. Many times this "musty" odor is caused by residual condensate in and around the A/C evaporator mixing with airborne pollutants. This environment is suitable for the formation and growth of bacteria and/or fungi which can cause undesirable odors. Condensation is normally formed as part of the air conditioning process and must be allowed to flow out of the system.

To minimize the growth of bacteria and/or fungi, there are several steps that can be performed:

- Water drain(s) in the bottom of the plenum chamber(s) under the hood must be open and free of any debris.
- The bulkhead between the engine compartment and the passenger compartment must be sealed along with any cable grommets passing through the bulkhead.
- The evaporator water (condensate) drain must open freely. This valve is located behind the bulkhead insulation.

If the above steps fail to correct an odor problem, professional preparation and treatment using a commercially available product such as Airsept Air Conditioning Treatment™ should be performed. Special tools, equipment and training are required to properly apply Airsept™ Products. These procedures are outside the scope of this repair manual.

A/C REFRIGERANT SYSTEM SERVICING

In accordance with SAE and industry standards, New Beetle air conditioners are equipped with service fittings that accept standard R-134a charging equipment. Connecting gauges to the refrigerant system and measuring the various pressures during operation is a valuable and accurate way to troubleshoot. The pressures and associated temperatures in the A/C system will vary depending on engine speed (rpm), coolant fan speed, engine coolant temperature, A/C clutch engagement, outside temperature, humidity, etc. and can give an accurate indication of system performance.

> ***WARNING —***
> *Observe all cautions, warnings and notes before starting repairs involving air conditioning systems.*

A/C refrigerant system, testing with pressure gauges

Due to the constant temperature/pressure relationship of refrigerant R-134a, approximate high side and low side system temperature can be determined based on system pressures, see **Table c**.

Table c. R-134a temperature/pressure relationship

Temperature in °C (°F)	Pressure in bar (psi)
-30 (-22)	0.0 (0.0)
-20 (-4)	0.3 (4.4)
-10 (14)	1.0 (14.5)
0 (32)	1.9 (27.5)
10 (50)	3.1 (45.0)
20 (68)	4.7 (68.2)
30 (86)	6.7 (97.2)
40 (104)	9.1 (132.0)
50 (122)	12.2 (177.0)
60 (140)	15.8 (229.0)
70 (158)	20.2 (293.0)

Commercially available manifold gauge sets are specifically calibrated for R-134a and should be connected to the system according to the manufacturers instructions. All commercially available refrigerant recovery, recycling and recharging equipment also have gauges that are appropriate for R-134a and are suitable for system testing.

Pressure and temperature measurements should be made using the following conditions:

- Engine running at 1,500 rpm with A/C switched on.
- Blower fan control set to highest speed.
- A/C temperature control set to maximum cooling and recirculation switched on.
- All passenger compartment air outlets open fully.

For pressure and temperature specifications of the various components, see **Table d**.

Table d. Pressure and temperature specifications[a]

Component	Refrigerant state	Approximate pressure	Approximate temperature
Evaporator, inlet to outlet	Vapor to gas	1.2 bar (17.4 psi)[b]	-7°C (19°F)[c]
Low pressure service valve port	Gas		-1°C (30°F)
Compressor, low pressure (suction) side	Gas		
Compressor, high pressure (discharge) side	Gas	14 bar (203 psi)	65°C (149°F)
Condenser	Gas to vapor to liquid		55°C (131°F) at outlet
Receiver drier	Liquid		55°C (131°F)
Sight glass (where equipped)	Liquid		
High pressure service valve port	Liquid		
Expansion valve	Liquid to vapor	Inlet: 14 bar (203 psi) Outlet: 1.2 bar (17.4 psi)	Inlet: 55°C (131°F) Outlet: -7°C (19°F)

a. Pressure and temperature specifications are based on: 1) Engine speed at 1,500 rpm, 2) Blower fan set to high speed, 3) A/C controls set to maximum cooling.

b. Pressure maintained in the refrigerant system by the variable displacement compressor despite variables in temperature, load and engine speeds (RPM).

c. Temperature maintained in the refrigerant system by the variable displacement compressor despite variable in temperature, load and engine speeds (RPM).

A/C refrigerant system, discharging and charging

Before starting repairs involving opening of the refrigerant system, the refrigerant must first be removed. It is not permissible to vent the refrigerant into the atmosphere for environmental, legal and economic reasons. In addition, due to the lack of a sight glass in most vehicles, a measured amount of refrigerant must be installed to insure that the system is fully charged. Equipment suitable for this purpose is available from several manufacturers. See Fig. 5. All refrigerant servicing equipment attaches to the high and low pressure service valve ports, but exact connection details and operation may differ slightly between individual equipment manufacturers. Always follow the equipment manufacturer's instructions regarding connections to the vehicle. See Fig. 6.

After discharging and recovering the refrigerant, proceed with repairs as required. Do not leave the refrigerant system open. Seal openings to keep dirt and especially moisture from entering. When repairs have been completed, the system must be evacuated for a minimum of 30 minutes. This will "pull the system down" by creating a vacuum. It will remove all traces of the old refrigerant ensuring an accurate recharge. More importantly, however, it will remove any moisture that may have entered the system.

When the system has been repaired and properly evacuated, add refrigerant oil if required and recharge according to the equipment manufacturers instructions. Consult the A/C system capacities table given earlier.

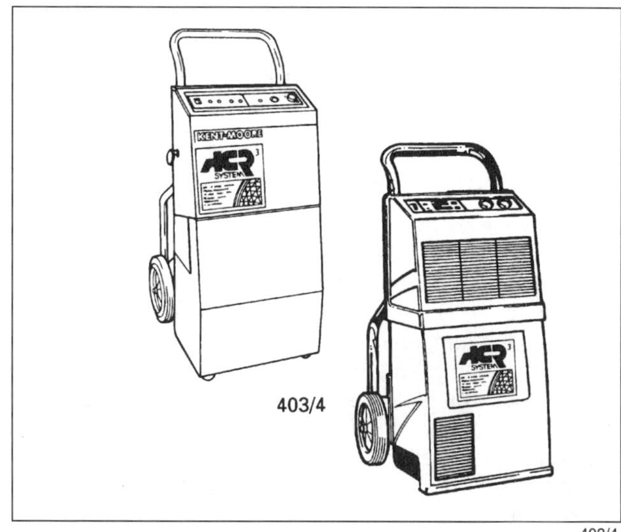

403/4

Fig. 5. Front view of typical R-134a equipment used for discharging, (recovery), recharging and recycling as supplied by Kent-Moore.

After the system has been recharged, switch on the ignition, but do not start the engine. Switch on the A/C and manually rotate the A/C compressor approximately 10 turns before starting the engine to insure adequate compressor lubrication. Start the engine with the A/C switched OFF. After idle speed has stabilized, switch A/C ON and let the engine idle with the compressor running for a minimum of two minutes before raising engine speed. This will allow the refrigerant oil to properly circulate to all parts of the system.

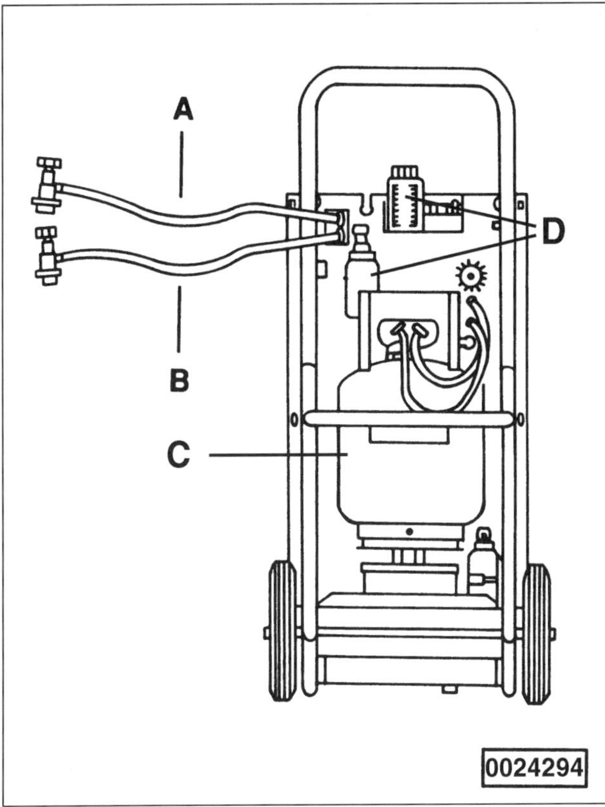

0024294

Fig. 6. Rear view of R-134a equipment supplied by Kent-Moore. High pressure hose (**A**) is color coded red and low pressure hose (**B**) is color coded blue. Equipment also has a built-in tank for R-134a (**C**) and provisions for adding PAG oil (**D**).

A/C refrigerant system, flushing

Certain circumstances may require complete removal of the refrigerant and refrigerant oil. This process is known as flushing and is accomplished with nitrogen and compressed air. Compressed nitrogen with regulators and adapters are available locally. Flushing is usually needed under the following conditions:

- Refrigerant oil is dark and viscous (thick) or shows metallic particles.
- Too much refrigerant oil is known to be in the system following compressor replacement.
- Unclear or do not know how much refrigerant oil is in the system.
- Moisture, dirt or other impurities have entered the refrigerant system, (i.e. following an accident).
- Unable to pull a constant vacuum during evacuation of a leak-free system due to excessive moisture in the system.
- Refrigerant system has been open longer than the time required for normal repairs, (i.e. following an accident).
- Based on temperature and pressure measurements, system is diagnosed with moisture contamination.
- Compressor is replaced due to noises or internal damage.

If flushing the system, observe the following points:

- When using compressed nitrogen always use a pressure regulator and the proper adaptor hoses and fittings (available locally).
- During flushing, use existing exhaust/ventilation systems to draw off the gas mixture escaping from the A/C system.
- Use compressed air and nitrogen (available locally) to remove moisture, impurities and old refrigerant oil from A/C refrigerant system.
- First blow out old refrigerant oil and dirt with compressed air, then dry components with nitrogen.
- DO NOT blow compressed air and nitrogen through the compressor or expansion valve. Only blow compressed air and nitrogen through disconnected, free flowing components (i.e. disconnected hose, condenser, evaporator, etc.)
- DO NOT blow compressed air and nitrogen into a capped off A/C component. Pressurized R-134a refrigerant in the presence of oxygen may form a combustible mixture.
- Always flush components in opposite direction of refrigerant flow.
- Flush evaporator through the low pressure line with the high pressure line removed.
- If any component has dark thick deposits that cannot be removed with compressed air, replace component.
- Thin light gray deposits in refrigerant lines and hoses are normal and do not impair the function of the system.
- Always replace receiver drier and restrictor after flushing.
- Dispose of contaminated refrigerant (PAG) oil following laws governing hazardous waste disposal. Do not combine PAG oil with any other old oils such as engine oil or transmission fluid.

> ***WARNING —***
> - *DO NOT flush R-134a refrigerant system with R-11. R-11 is not compatible with R-134a refrigerant and PAG oil and will cause total system contamination.*
> - *DO NOT blow compressed air and nitrogen through the compressor or expansion valve. Only blow compressed air and nitrogen through disconnected, free flowing components (i.e. disconnected hose, condenser, evaporator, etc.).*
> - *DO NOT blow compressed air and nitrogen into a capped off A/C component. Pressurized R-134a refrigerant in the presence of oxygen may form a combustible mixture.*

A/C refrigerant system, checking for leaks

If it is determined that the refrigerant system is low on refrigerant and the source of the leak is not readily apparent, use of a halogen leak detector may help in locating the leak. See Fig. 7.

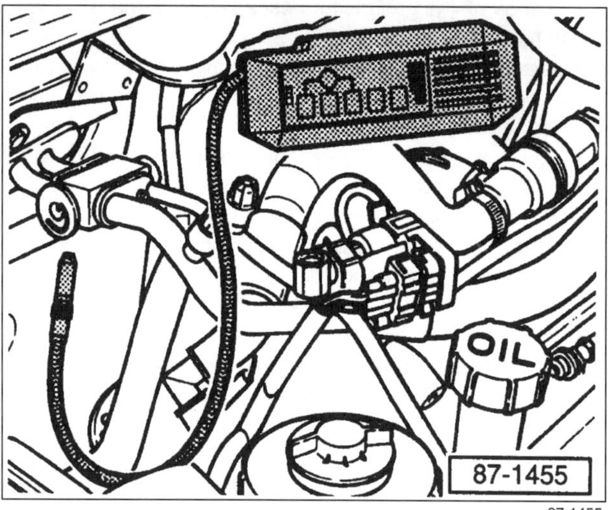

87-1455

Fig. 7. Leak detector such as the Hitec HI400A-TEL (shown) or equivalent, being used to check for refrigerant leaks. Always follow the leak detector manufacturer's instructions.

> ***NOTE —***
> - *Refrigerant gas dissipates very quickly. To make the job easier, avoid drafty or windy areas when checking for leaks.*
> - *If the refrigerant system is discharged (empty), it is permissible to temporarily recharge the system with approx. 100 g (3.5 oz) of refrigerant in order to check for leaks. When the source of the leak is found, this refrigerant must be recovered from the system before repairs are started.*

In some instances, very small leaks may not be readily apparent due to location or other circumstances. In these situations, commercially available refrigerant dye may be useful in locating the source of the leak.

A/C, HEATING AND VENTILATION CONTROLS

An exploded view of the heating and ventilation components in the passenger compartment for vehicles equipped with air conditioning is shown in Fig. 8.

> ***NOTE —***
> *For vehicles without air conditioning, see* **80 Heating and Ventilation**.

> ***WARNING —***
> *Observe all cautions, warnings and notes before starting repairs involving air conditioning systems.*

The following numbered list applies to Fig. 8.

1. **A/C, heating and ventilation controls**
   - With A/C switch (E35)
   - With blower fan switch (E9)
   - With recirculation switch (E184)
2. **Dust and pollen filter**
   - Covers outside air inlet to passenger compartment
   - Cleans all incoming air
3. **Side window air outlet**
4. **Side air outlets**
5. **Center air outlet console**
6. **Instrument panel cross member**
7. **Servo motor for recirculation door (V154)**
8. **Blower fan (V2)**
9. **Blower fan series resistance pack (N24)**
   - With thermal fuse
10. **Intermediate duct**
11. **Control cables**
    - Color code yellow - air distribution control knob to central flap
    - Color code green - air distribution control knob to footwell/defrost flap
    - Color code beige - temperature control knob to temperature flap
12. **Rear footwell duct**
13. **Gasket**
14. **Connecting duct**
15. **Evaporator/heater assembly**
    - Refrigerant system must be discharged before removing.

A/C passenger compartment components, overview

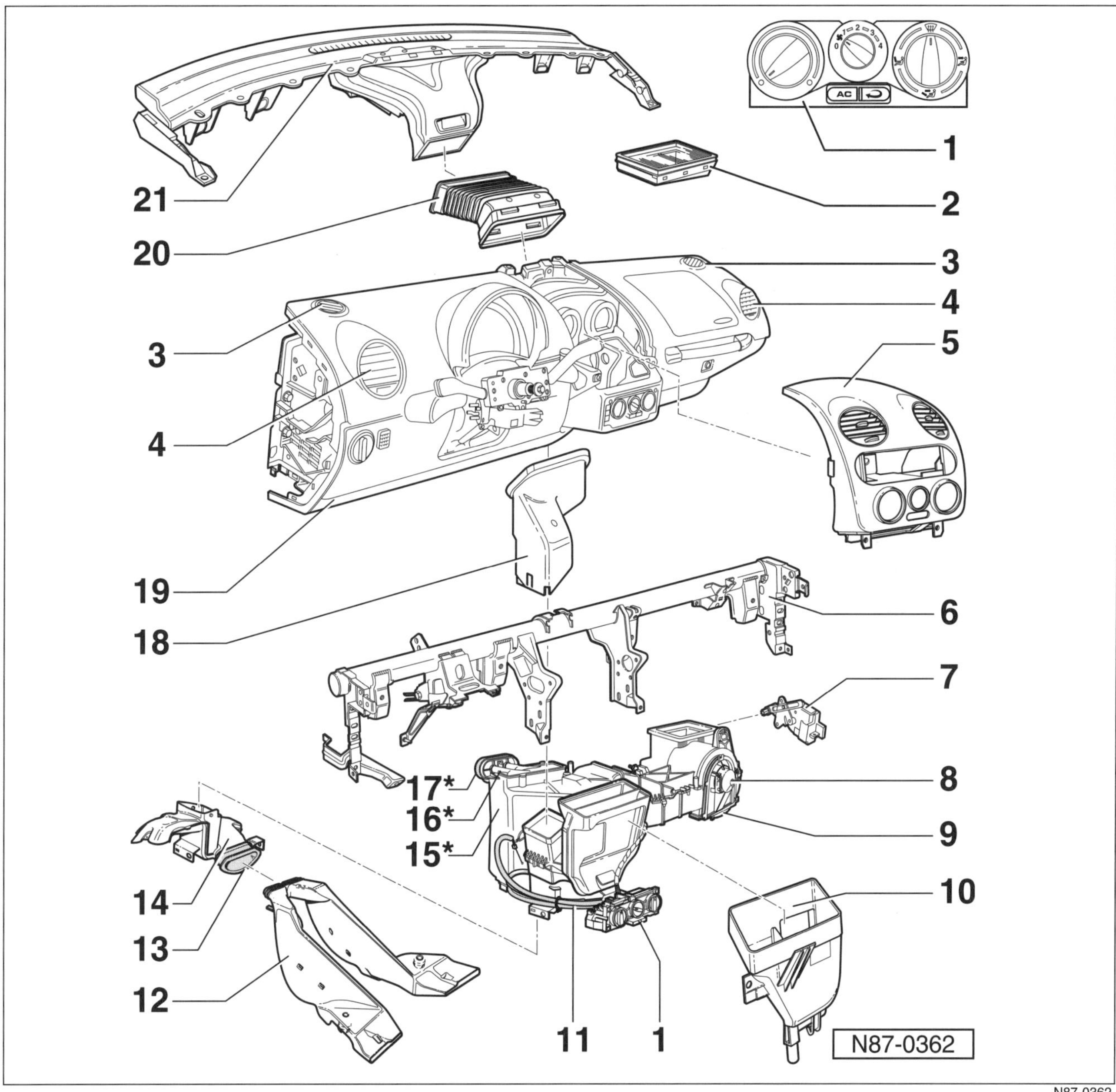

N87-0362

Fig. 8. Major components related to the A/C system located in the passenger compartment. Components identified with an asterisk (*) cannot be removed until refrigerant system is discharged.

16. Heater core

- Refrigerant system must be discharged before removing.

17. Heater core/bulkhead seal

- Refrigerant system must be discharged before removing.
- Note installed position

18. Defroster duct

19. Instrument panel

20. Center air outlet duct

21. Defroster air outlet panel

A/C, heating and ventilation controls, removing and installing

> ***WARNING —***
> *Observe all cautions, warnings and notes before starting repairs involving air conditioning systems.*

1. Remove center air outlet console, see **80 Heating and Ventilation**
2. Remove mounting screws and lift controls from opening in dash. See Fig. 9.

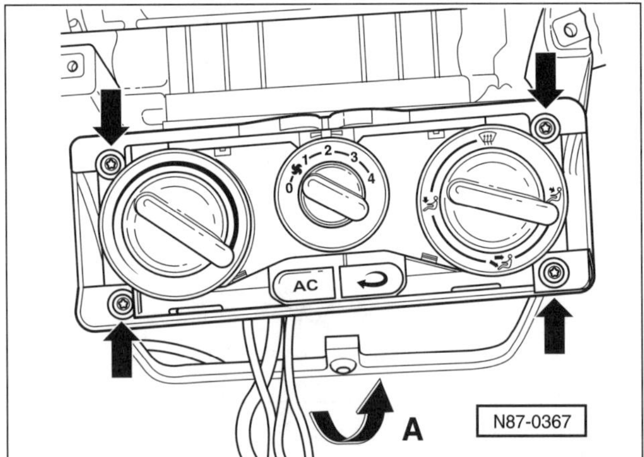

N87-0367

Fig. 9. A/C, heating and ventilation controls shown with air outlet console removed. After removing securing screws (**arrows**), pull controls down and out (**arrow A**).

3. Unclip cables and detach from controls.
4. Disconnect electrical connector and remove controls.
5. Before installing controls, check operation of cables. Replace cables with damage or stiff/binding operation. See Fig. 10.

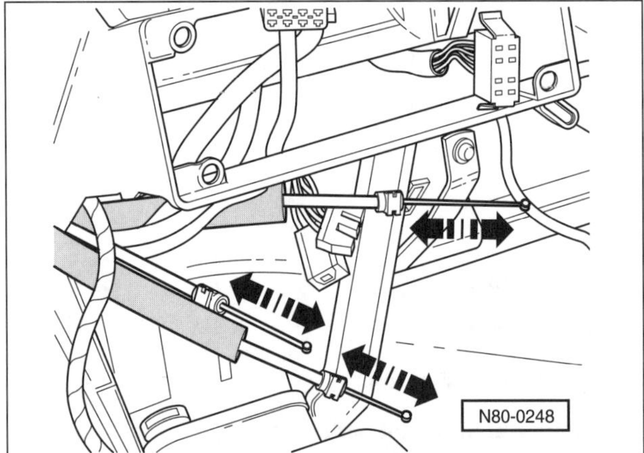

N80-0248

Fig. 10. Check control cable operation with controls removed. Move cables in and out (**arrows**) several times.

6. Attach color coded cable to correct actuating arm. See Fig. 11.

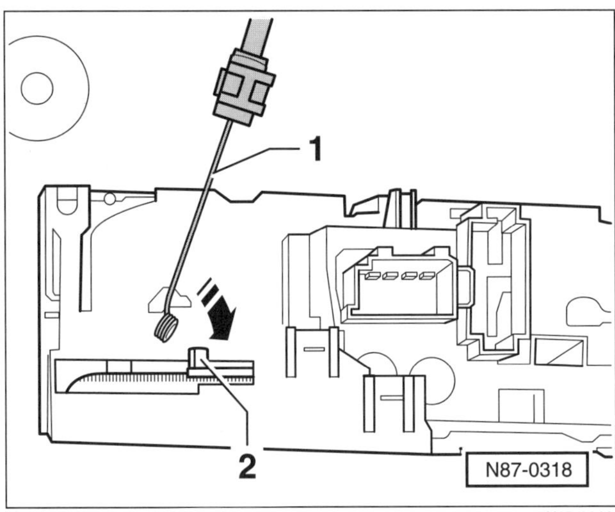

N87-0319

Fig. 11. Attach cable (**1**) to actuating arm (**2**).

7. Snap each cable into appropriate retainer. See Fig. 12.

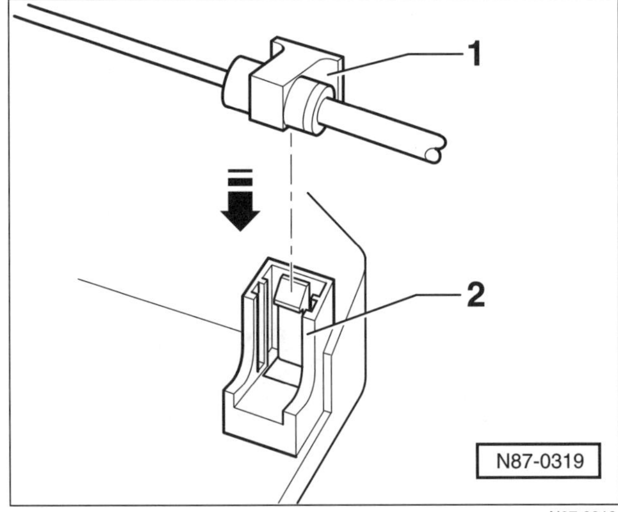

N87-0319

Fig. 12. Press cable (**1**) fully into retainer (**2**) until it engages.

8. Install electrical connector.
9. Fit controls into instrument panel opening and install mounting screws.
10. Adjust cables as needed.

A/C, heating and ventilation controls, assembly

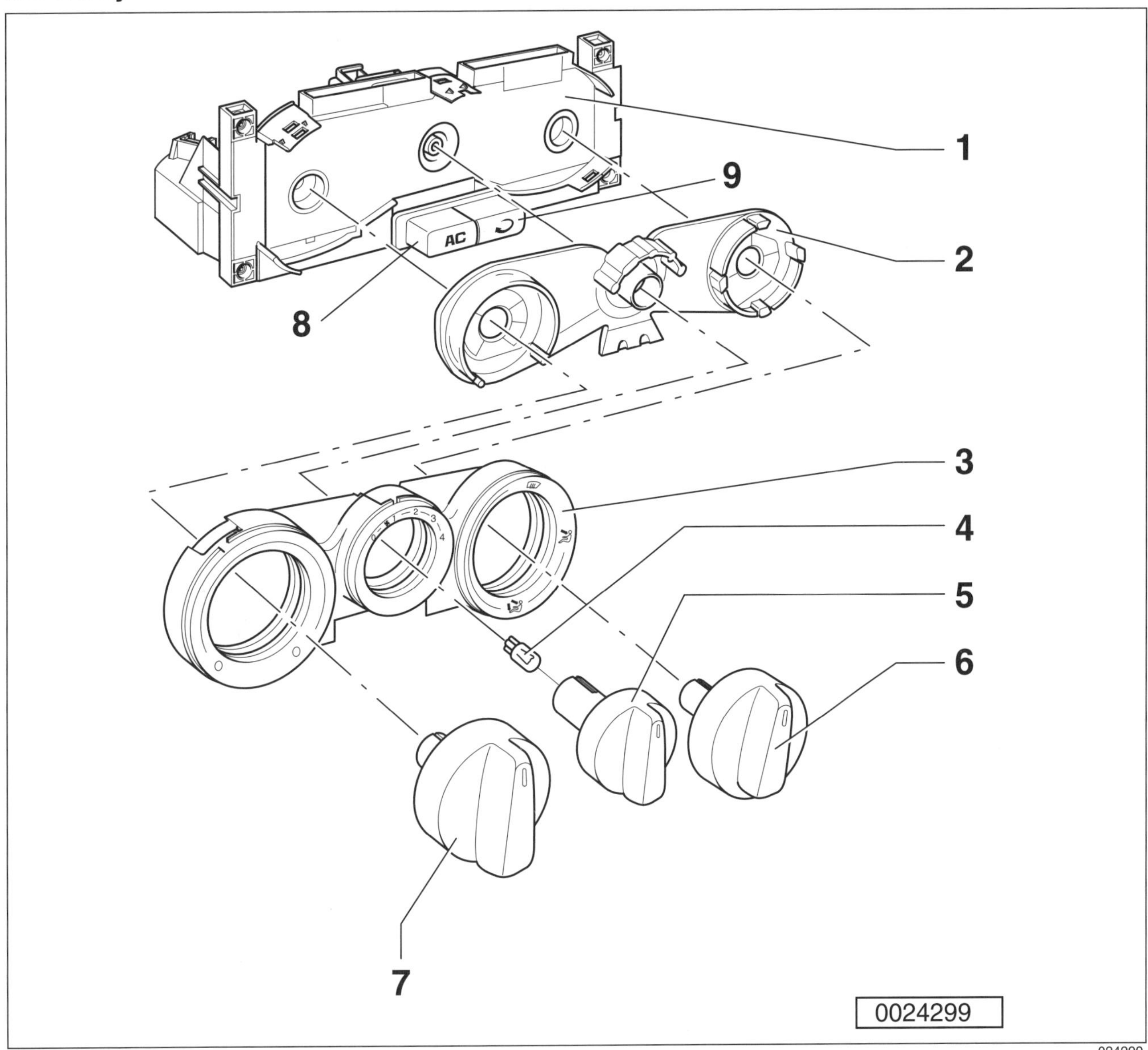

Fig. 13. Exploded view of A/C, heating and ventilation controls

1. **A/C, heating and ventilation controls**
   - With A/C switch (E35)
   - With blower fan switch (E9)
   - With recirculation switch (E184)
2. **Illumination filter ring**
3. **Trim panel**
4. **Fresh air control lever light (L16)**
   - Clear bulb 12V, 1.2W
5. **Rotary control knob**
   - For blower fan speed
   - Removing: use pliers with suitable plastic or rubber protection on jaws
6. **Rotary control knob**
   - For air distribution
   - Removing: Use pliers with suitable plastic or rubber protection on jaws
7. **Rotary control knob**
   - For interior temperature regulation
   - Removing: Use pliers with suitable plastic or rubber protection on jaws
8. **A/C switch (E35)**
   - Integral with controls
9. **Recirculation switch (E184)**
   - Integral with controls

A/C, heating and ventilation controls, adjusting

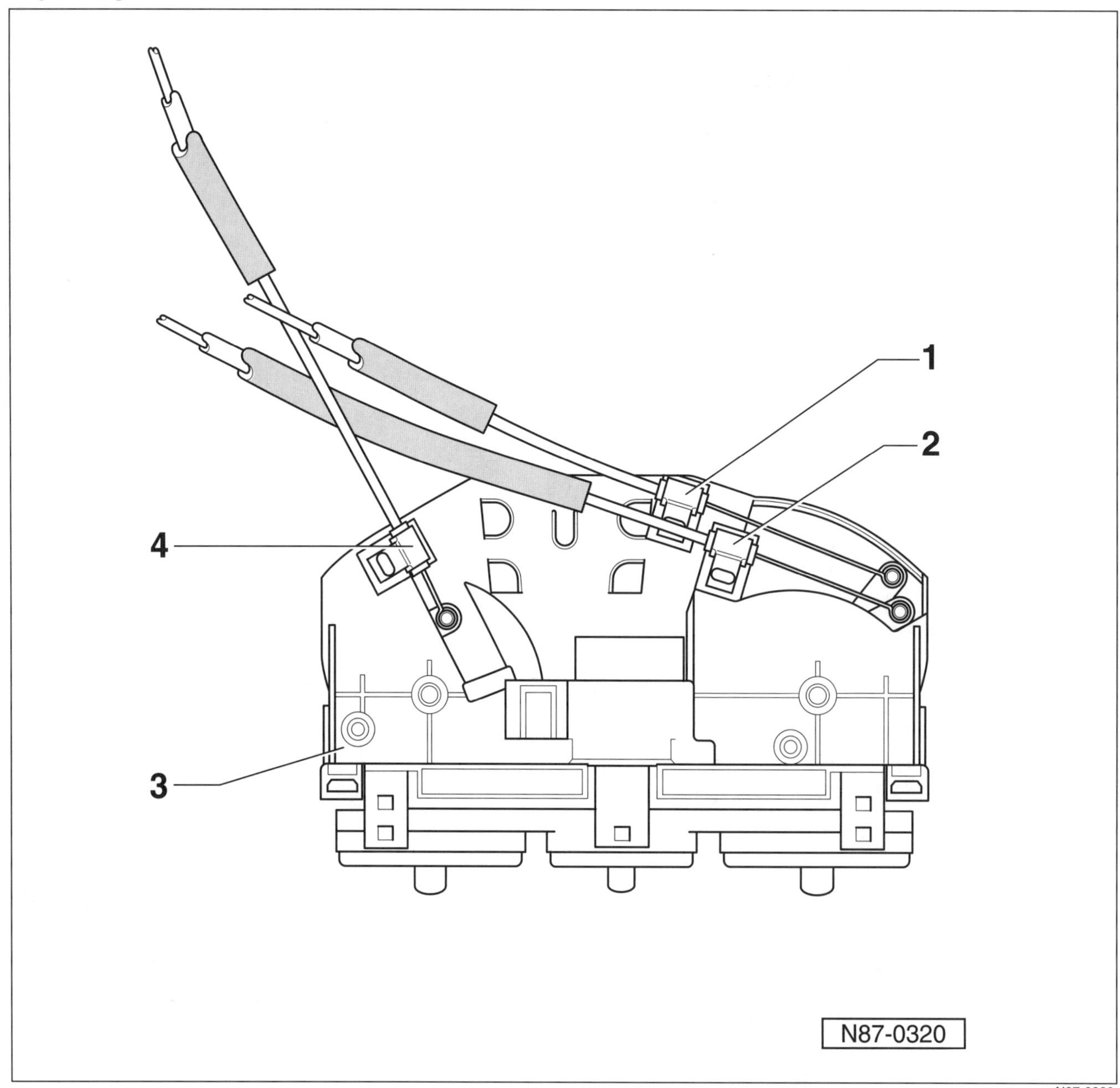

N87-0320

Fig. 14. A/C, heating and ventilation control shown with assembled control cables.

1. **Central flap cable**
   - From air distribution rotary control to central flap
   - Cable sleeve color code: Yellow
   - Adjusting, **see** Ⓐ
2. **Footwell/defrost flap cable**
   - From air distribution rotary control to footwell/defrost flap
   - Cable sleeve color code: Green
   - Adjusting, **see** Ⓑ
3. **A/C, heating and ventilation controls**
   - First attach cables to removed controls then to appropriate levers
   - All air flaps must be heard to move onto end stops when operating controls
4. **Temperature flap cable**
   - From temperature rotary control to temperature flap
   - Cable sleeve color code: Beige
   - Adjusting, **see** Ⓒ

(A) Temperature flap cable, installing and adjusting

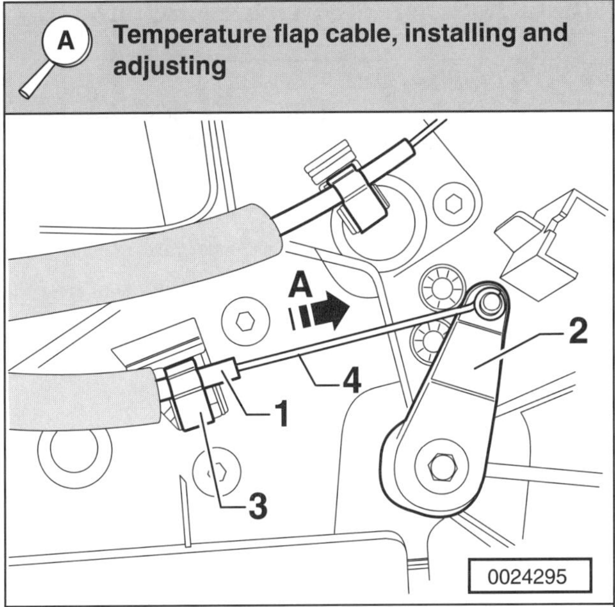

0024295

- Cable sleeve color code: beige.
- Install/adjust with controls installed and connecting duct removed.
- Turn temperature rotary control knob fully counter-clockwise against stop.
- Attach center wire of cable (4) to the temperature flap lever (2).
- Push temperature flap lever (2) against stop (arrow A) and secure outer cable (1) with clip (3).
- Turn temperature rotary control knob fully to left and right against stops.
- When turning the rotary control knob both end stops must be reached.

(B) Footwell/defrost flap cable, installing and adjusting

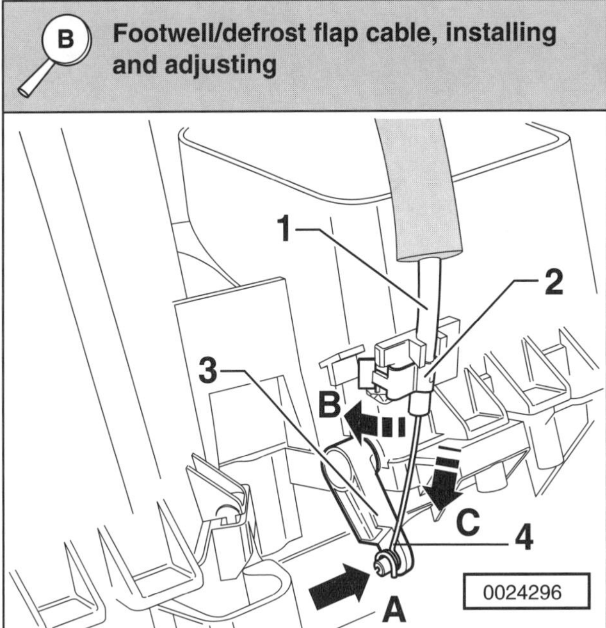

0024296

- Cable sleeve color code: green.
- Install/adjust with controls installed.
- Turn air distribution rotary control knob fully counter-clockwise against stop.
- Attach center wire of cable (4) to the footwell/defrost flap lever (3) at arrow (A).
- Press footwell/defrost flap lever against stop (arrow C) and secure outer cable (1) with clip (2) (arrow B).
- Turn air distribution rotary control knob fully to left and right against stops.
- When turning the rotary control knob both end stops must be reached.

Central flap cable, installing and adjusting

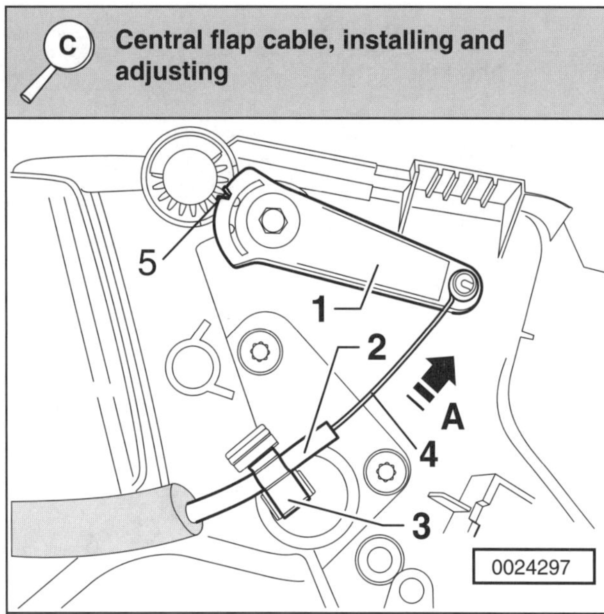

0024297

- **Cable sleeve color code: yellow.**
- **Install/adjust with controls installed, connecting duct removed and flap lever correctly indexed (5).**
- **Turn air distribution rotary control knob fully counter-clockwise against stop.**
- **Attach center wire of cable (4) to the central flap lever (1).**
- **Press central flap lever against stop (arrow A) and attach outer cable (2) with clip (3).**
- **Turn air distribution rotary control knob fully to left and right against stops.**
- **When turning the rotary control knob both end stops must be reached.**

A/C COMPONENTS, UNDERHOOD

> ***WARNING —***
> *Observe all cautions, warnings and notes before starting repairs involving air conditioning systems.*

NOTE —
Components identified with an asterisk (*) can only be removed after discharging the refrigerant.

The following numbered list applies to Fig. 15.

1. **Damper**
2. **Low pressure refrigerant line II**
   - Engine code AEG version shown
3. **Low pressure refrigerant line I**
4. **Ambient air temperature switch (F38)**
   - Switches off A/C clutch (N25) at low ambient air temperatures to prevent damage
   - Switches clutch off at -1°C (30°F)
   - Switches back on at 7°C (45°F)
5. **Liquid refrigerant line**
6. **High pressure service valve port**
7. **A/C pressure switch (F129)**
8. **Expansion valve**
9. **Evaporator water drain valve**
   - Location: Under insulation flap on bulkhead
   - Checking, **see** Ⓐ
10. **A/C thermal cut-out switch (F163)**
    - Switches off A/C clutch (N25) at excessively high coolant temperature
    - Switches clutch off at 119°C (246°F)
    - Switches clutch back on at 112°C (234°F)
11. **Coolant fan control module (J293)**
    - Location: lower left side of engine compartment near radiator
    - Controls all A/C clutch functions and A/C related radiator fan functions

A/C components, underhood overview

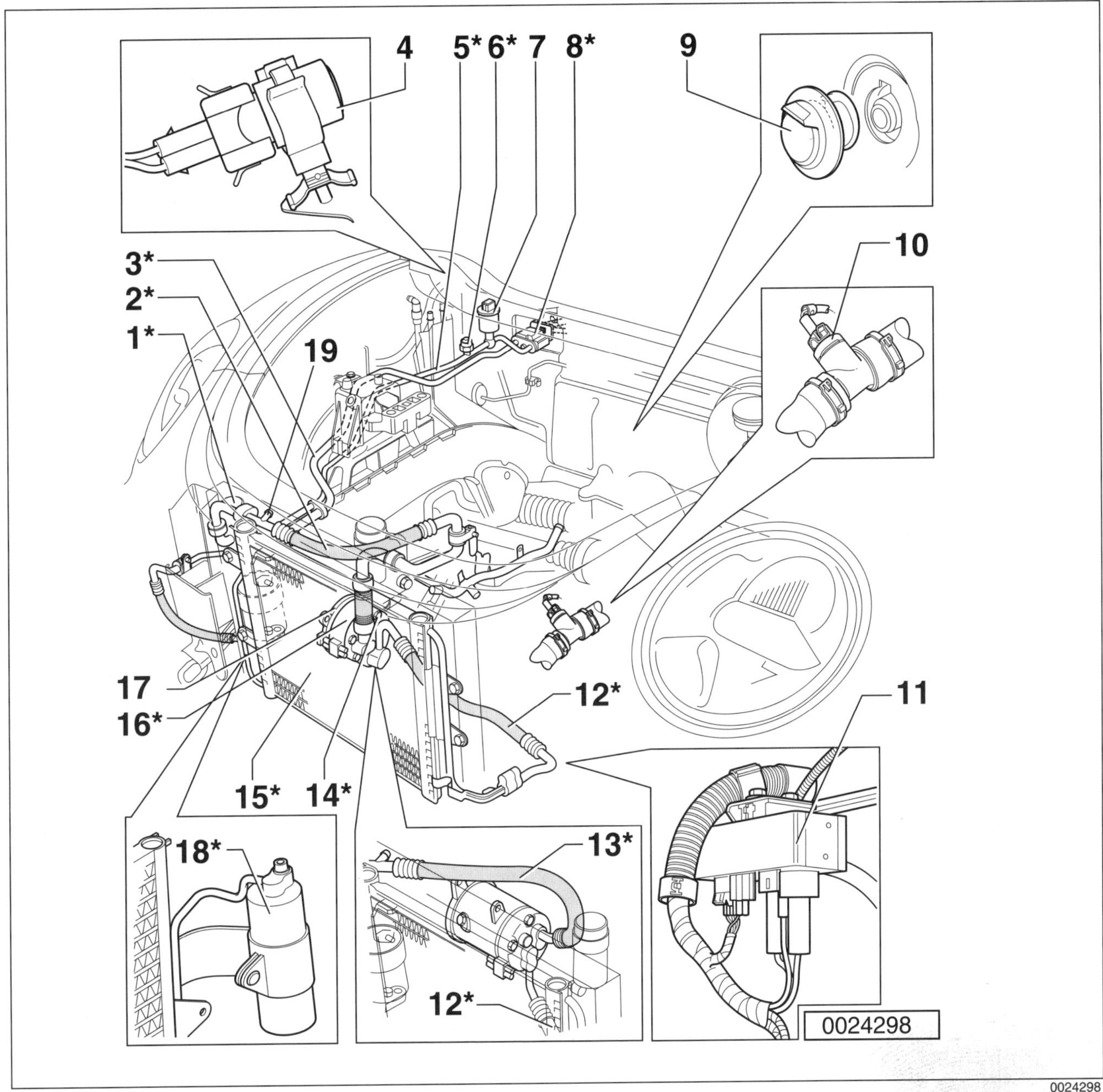

Fig. 15. A/C components in the engine compartment in addition to those directly associated with the refrigerant system. Components identified with an asterisk (*) can only be removed after discharging refrigerant.

12. **High pressure refrigerant line**
13. **Low pressure refrigerant line II**
    - Engine code ALH version shown
14. **Pressure relief valve**
15. **Condenser**
16. **Compressor**
17. **A/C compressor clutch (N25)**
18. **Receiver drier**
19. **High pressure service valve port**

Evaporator water drain valve, checking

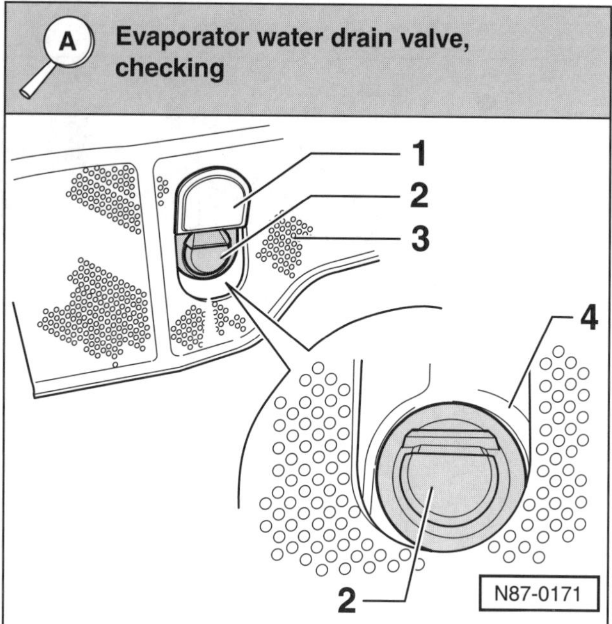

N87-0171

- Fold cover (1) in bulkhead insulation mat (3) upwards.
- Remove drain valve (2) from opening in bulkhead (4).
- The water drain valve flap and body must not be stuck together.
- Insulation mat must not be deformed or damaged in the area of water drain valve.
- The opening in the drain valve body must point downwards with the flap hinge at the top.
- When the insulation cover (1) is closed it must be flush with the insulation matting (3). If the insulation cover (1) is pushed in too far, the water drain valve flap can become jammed.

Mounting bracket assembly (AEG engine)

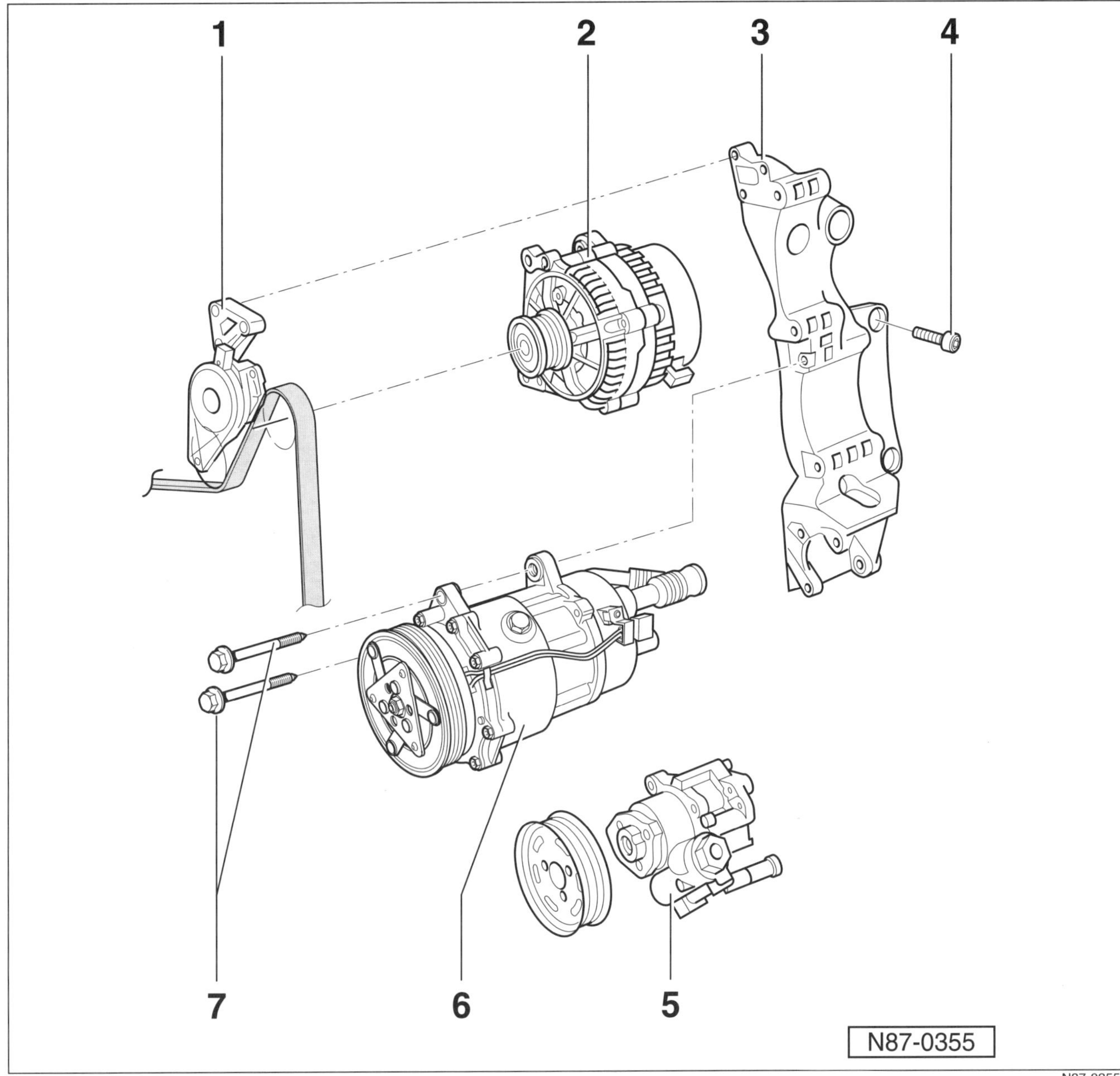

N87-0355

Fig. 16. Mounting bracket and related components for A/C equipped AEG engines.

1. **Tensioning roller, ribbed V-belt**
2. **Generator (GEN) and pulley**
3. **Bracket**
   - Compressor bracket and related components can be removed and installed without having to open the refrigerant circuit
   - Mounting for generator, A/C compressor and power steering pump
   - Remove compressor from bracket, swing away and secure in engine compartment with wire
4. **Bolts**
   - Tighten to 50 Nm (37 ft-lb)
5. **Power steering pump**
6. **A/C compressor**
7. **Bolts**
   - Tighten to 45 Nm (33 ft-lb)

Mounting bracket assembly (ALH engine)

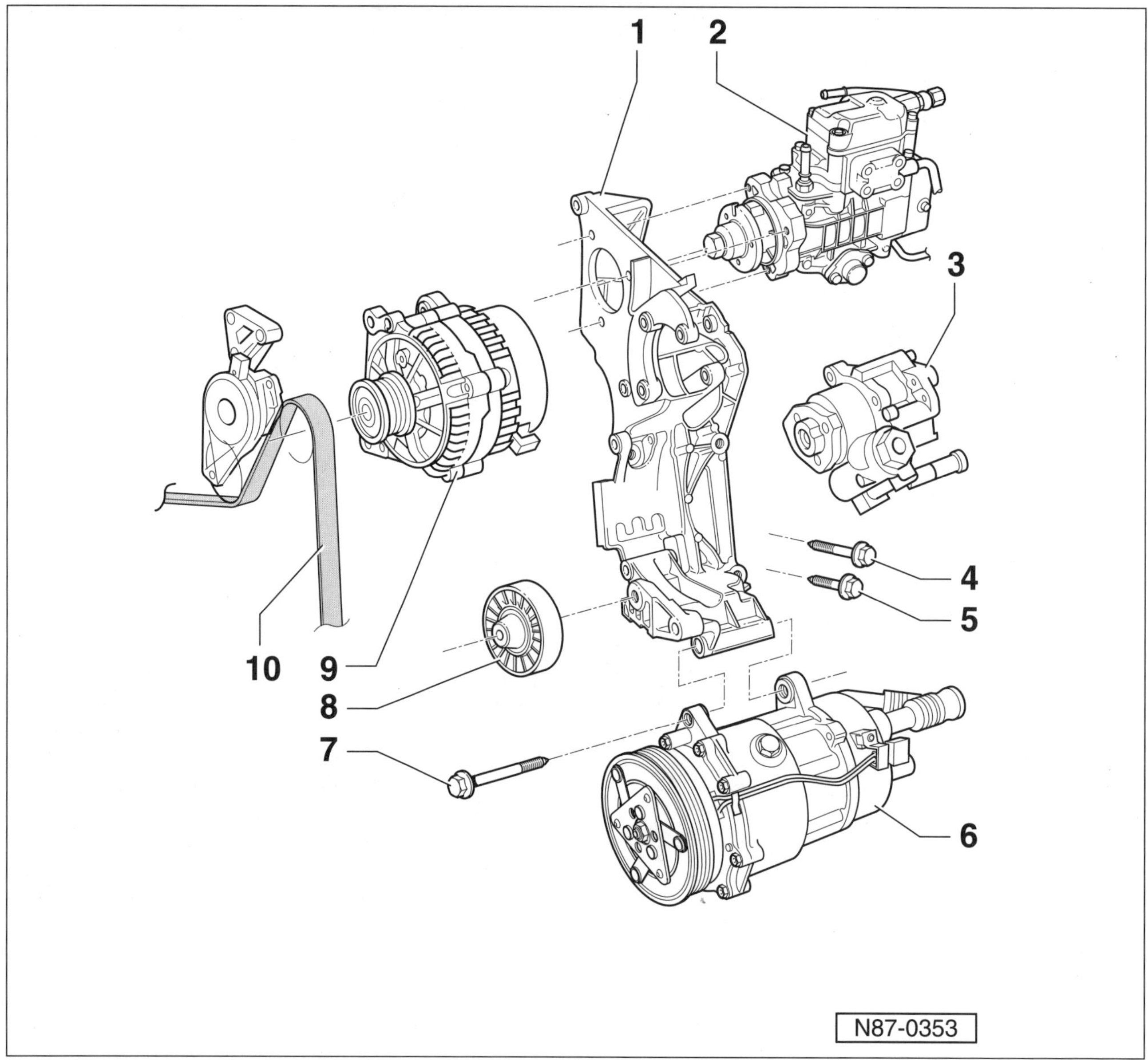

N87-0353

Fig. 17. Mounting bracket and related components for A/C equipped ALH (TDI) engines.

1. **Bracket**
   - The compressor bracket and related components can be removed and installed without having to open the refrigerant circuit.
   - Mounting for generator, compressor, power steering pump, diesel injection pump.
   - Remove compressor from bracket, swing away and secure in engine compartment with wire.
2. **Diesel injection pump**
3. **Power steering pump**
4. **Bolts**
   - Tighten to 45 Nm (33 ft-lb)
5. **Bolts**
   - Tighten to 45 Nm (33 ft-lb)
6. **Compressor**
7. **Bolt**
   - Tighten to 45 Nm (33 ft-lb)
8. **Idler pulley, see** Ⓐ
9. **Generator (GEN) and pulley**
10. **Ribbed V-belt**
    - Routing, **see** Ⓑ

A Idler pulley, assembly

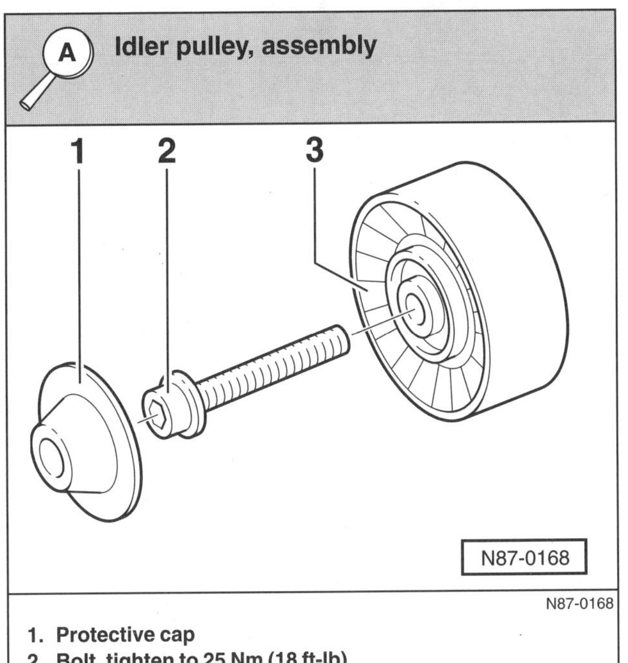

N87-0168

1. Protective cap
2. Bolt, tighten to 25 Nm (18 ft-lb)
3. Idler roller with bearings

B Ribbed V-belt, routing

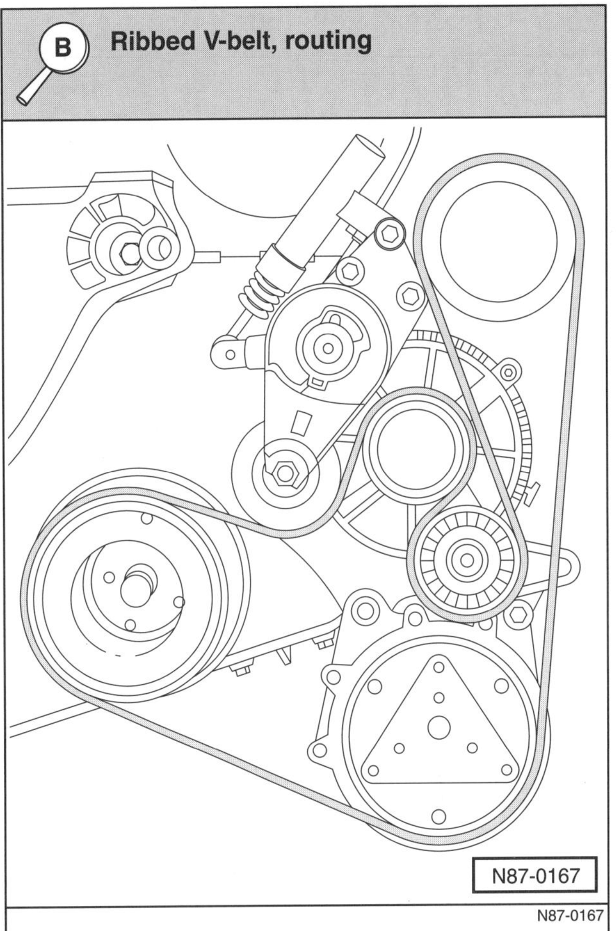

N87-0167

- Always mark the running direction before removing and install in the same direction.
- When installing the belt ensure it is correctly seated in the pulley.

A/C compressor overview

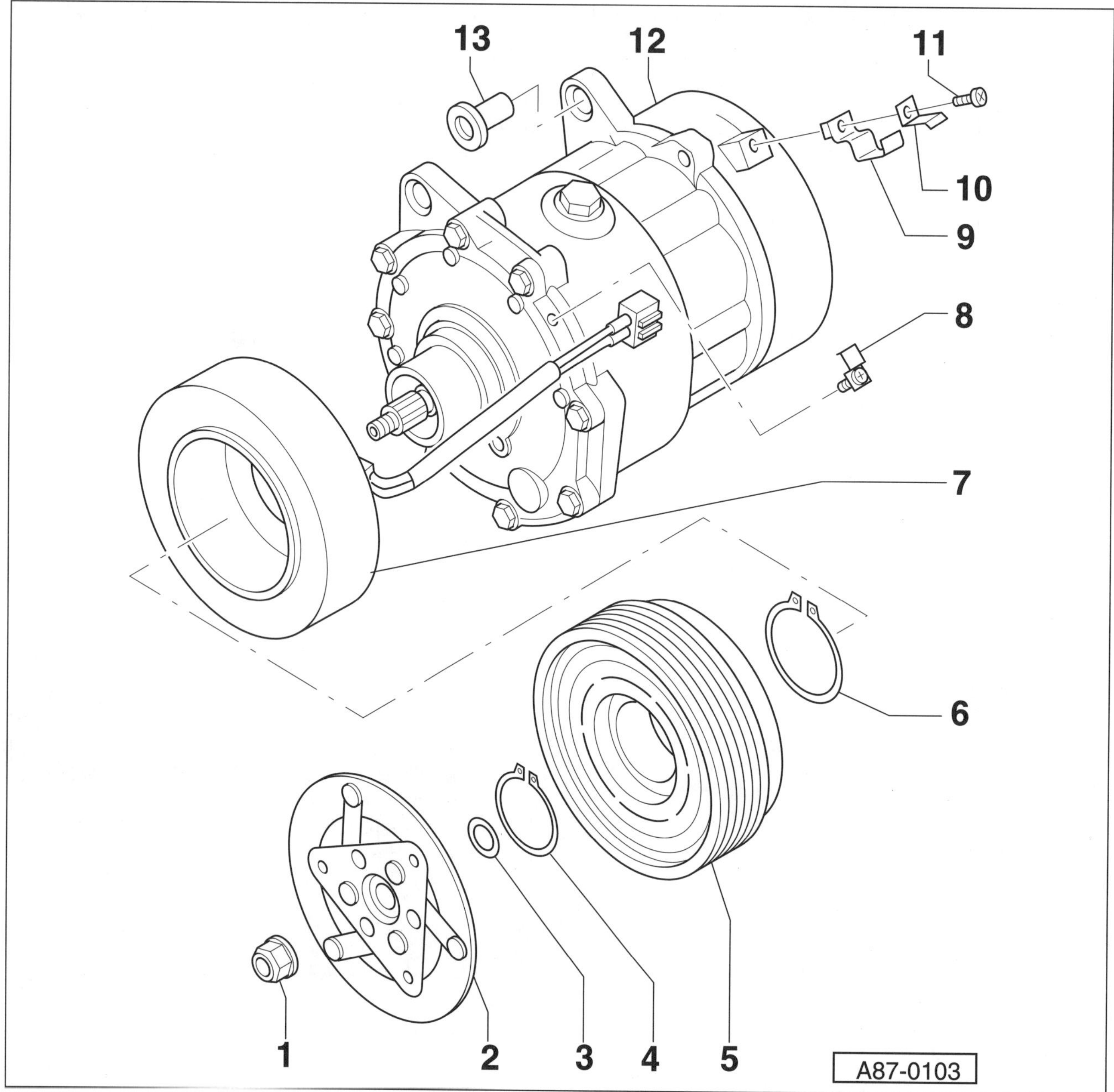

A87-0103

Fig. 18. A/C compressor shown with related clutch components.

> ***WARNING —***
> *Observe all cautions, warnings and notes before starting repairs involving air conditioning systems.*

1. **Nut, self locking**
   - Always replace
   - Tighten to 15 Nm (11 ft-lb)
2. **Clutch plate**
3. **Shims**
   - Used to adjust gap between clutch plate and pulley, **see** Ⓐ
4. **Circlip**
   - Always replace
   - Note installation position: flat side faces compressor
   - Ensure correct seating in groove

(continued from previous page)

5. **Clutch pulley**
   - Refrigerant circuit does not need to be discharged to service A/C clutch.
   - If A/C clutch is to be serviced without removing compressor, remove intercooler first (ALH engine).
6. **Circlip**
   - Always replace
   - Note installation position: flat side faces compressor
   - Ensure correct seating in groove
7. **Clutch coil**
   - Thermo-fuse integrated into the clutch coil protects the A/C clutch in the event of overheating due to a binding compressor. The clutch coil circuit is interrupted.
   - Note installation position: locking tab on coil into recess on compressor, **see** (B)
8. **Wiring harness securing clip**
   - With screw
9. **Terminal connector securing clip**
10. **Terminal connector securing clip**
11. **Screw**
12. **Compressor**
13. **Threaded bushing**

(A) Clutch plate gap, checking

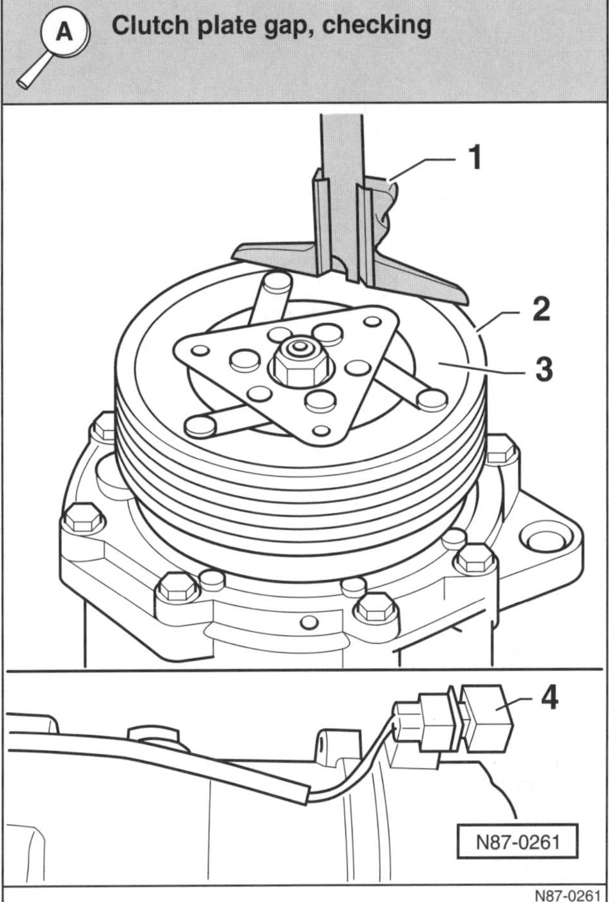

N87-0261

- **Gap between clutch plate and clutch pulley when clutch is not energized: 0.4 - 0.8 mm (0.015 - 0.032 in).**
- **Using depth gauge (1), measure gap between top of clutch plate (3) and clutch pulley (2) at three equally spaced locations. Measurements must not deviate from each other.**
- **If gap between clutch plate and clutch pulley is not within specification, remove clutch plate and add or remove shims as needed.**
- **When installing, ensure that wiring harness and harness connector (4) are secured under securing clips.**

Clutch coil, installed position

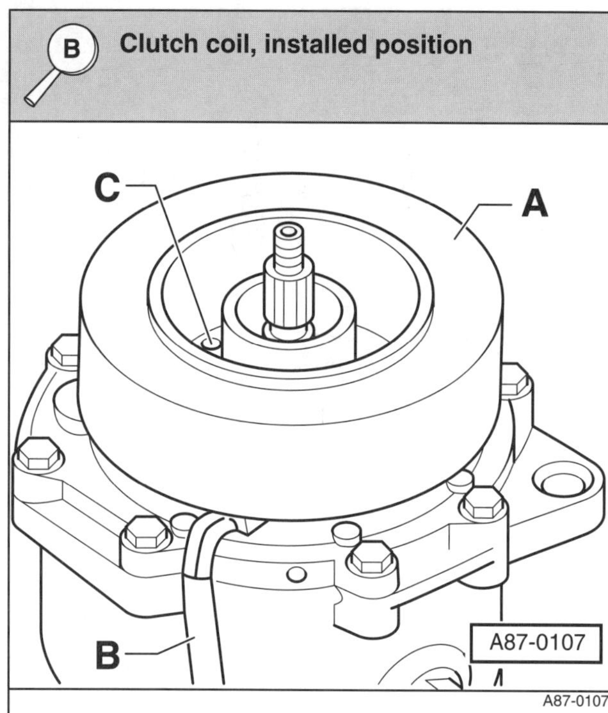

A87-0107

- **Install coil (A) onto compressor.**
- **Locate locking tab on coil and position into recess (C) in face of compressor.**
- **Ensure proper routing of coil wiring harness (B).**

QUALITY REVIEW

When you have finished working under the hood and around other areas of the vehicle, it is advisable to take a moment to quality check or review your work. This helps to insure that the operation or repair has been completed properly with all affected systems functioning within normal parameters. These may include the following:

- Ensure that all cable ties and clamps that were removed as part of the repair are replaced.
- Ensure that all fasteners and hardware were replaced and torqued as specified.
- Make sure that all other components involved in the repair are positioned correctly, properly torqued and function properly.
- Make sure that all tools, shop cloths, fender covers and protective tapes are removed before closing the hood.
- Clean grease and fingerprints from painted surfaces, steering wheel, upholstery and shifter.
- Make sure that cold air is delivered by the appropriate air vents when the A/C is switched on.
- Make sure that warm/hot air is delivered by the appropriate air vents when the heater is switched on.
- Make sure that all valves on charging system equipment are closed or positioned as the manufacturer specifies.
- Unlock anti-theft radio and reset the clock.

9 Electrical System

GENERAL

This group covers a brief description of the principal parts of the electrical system. Also covered here is general electrical system troubleshooting.

Voltage and polarity

Volkswagen electrical systems are 12-volt direct current (DC) negative-ground systems. A voltage regulator controls the output of the alternator to approximately 13.5 volts. All circuits are grounded by direct or indirect connection to the negative (–) terminal of the battery. A number of ground connections throughout the car connect the wiring harness to chassis ground. These circuits are completed by the battery cable or ground strap between the body and the battery negative (–) terminal.

Electrical system safety precautions

Please read the following warnings and cautions before doing any work on your electrical system.

> ***WARNING —***
> - *Ignition systems operate in a dangerous voltage range that could prove to be fatal if exposed terminals or live parts are contacted. Use extreme caution when working on a vehicle with the ignition on or the engine running.*
> - *On cars equipped with Airbags, special precautions apply to any electrical system testing or repair. The airbag unit is an explosive device and must be handled with extreme care. Before starting any work on an airbag equipped car, refer to the warnings and cautions in* **69 Seatbelts, Airbags**.
> - *Before operating the starter without starting the engine (as when making a compression test), disable ignition system as described in* **28a Ignition System**.

> ***CAUTION —***
> - *Always switch the ignition off and disconnect the negative (–) battery cable before removing any electrical components.*
> - *Before disconnecting battery be sure to obtain radio anti-theft code.*
> - *Connect and disconnect ignition system wires, multiple connectors, and ignition test equipment leads only while the ignition is switched off.*
> - *Do not disconnect battery while the engine is running. Never reverse the battery terminal connections. Even a momentary wrong connection can damage the alternator or electrical components. If the polarity markings on the battery are not visible, confirm the polarity of battery using a voltmeter.*
> - *Always remove the battery cables before quick-charging the battery. Never use a quick-charger as a booster for starting the car. Do not exceed 16.5 volts at the battery.*
> - *Many solid-state modules operate on very low current and can be permanently damaged if exposed to static discharge. Always handle the modules using proper static prevention equipment and techniques.*
> - *Always switch a test meter to the appropriate function and range before making test connections.*
> - *Disconnect the battery before doing any electric welding on the car.*
> - *Do not wash the engine while it is running, or anytime the ignition is switched on.*
> - *Do not try to start the engine of a car which has been heated above 176°F (80°C), (for example, in a paint drying booth) until allowing it to cool to normal temperature.*

Electrical test equipment

Many of the electrical tests described in this manual call for measuring voltage, current or resistance using a digital multimeter (DMM). DMMs are preferred for precise measurements and for electronics work because they are generally more accurate than analog meters. The DMM is also safe for most solid state components whereas an analog meter can damage some components.

An LED test light is a safe, inexpensive tool that can be used to perform many simple electrical tests that would otherwise require a multimeter. The LED indicates when voltage is present between any two test-points in a circuit.

> ***CAUTION —***
> - *Choose test equipment carefully. Use a meter with at least 10 megohm input impedance, or an LED test light. An analog meter (swing-needle) or a test light with a normal incandescent bulb may draw enough current to damage sensitive electronic components.*
> - *An analog meter must not be used to measure resistance on solid state components such as control units or time delay relays.*
> - *Always disconnect the battery before making resistance (ohm) measurements on the circuit.*

Wiring diagrams, fuses and relays

Nearly all parts of the wiring harness connect to components of the electrical system with keyed, push-on connectors that lock into place. Notable exceptions are the heavy battery cables and the alternator wiring.

With the exception of the charging system, all electrical power is routed from the ignition switch or the battery through the fuse panel, located in the passenger compartment behind the driver side left knee bar. Fuses prevent excessive current from damaging components and wiring. Fuses are color coded to indicate their different current capacities. Most relays are electromechanical switches that operate on low current to switch a high-current circuit on and off.

The wiring diagrams shown in **97 Wiring Diagrams, Fuses and Relays** are organized according to model year and engine type, with complete diagrams for each year.

ELECTRICAL TROUBLESHOOTING

Four things are required for current to flow in any electrical circuit: a voltage source, wires or connections to transport the voltage, a consumer or device that uses the electricity, and a connection to ground or a return to the voltage source. Most problems can be found using only a digital multimeter (volt/ohm/amp meter) to check for voltage supply, for breaks in the wiring (infinite resistance/no continuity), or for a path to ground that completes the circuit.

Electric current is logical in its flow, always moving from the voltage source toward ground. Keeping this in mind, electrical faults can be located through a process of elimination. When troubleshooting a complex circuit, separate the circuit into smaller parts. Be sure to analyze the problem. Use the wiring diagrams to determine the most likely cause of the problem. Get an understanding of how the circuit works by following the circuit from ground back to the power source.

> ***CAUTION —***
> *When making test connections at connectors and components, use care to avoid spreading or damaging the connectors or terminals. Some electrical tests may require jumper wires to bypass components. When connecting jumper wires, use blade connectors at the wire ends that match the size of the terminal being tested. The small internal contacts are easily spread apart, and this can cause intermittent or faulty connections that can lead to more problems.*

Voltage and ground, checking

Checking for the presence of voltage or ground is usually the first step in troubleshooting a problem circuit. For example, if a parking light does not work, a check for voltage at the bulb socket will quickly determine if the circuit is functioning properly or if the bulb itself is faulty. If voltage and ground are found at the socket, then the bulb is most likely faulty.

Another valuable troubleshooting technique is a voltage drop test. This is a good test to perform if current is flowing through the circuit but the circuit is not operating correctly. Sluggish wipers or dim headlights are examples of this. A voltage drop test will help to pinpoint a corroded ground strap or a faulty switch. Normally, there should be less than 1 volt drop across most wires or closed switches. A voltage drop across a connector or short cable should not exceed 0.5 volts.

A voltage drop is caused by higher than normal resistance in a circuit. This additional resistance actually decreases or stops the flow of current. Some common sources of voltage drops are faulty wires or switches, dirty or corroded connections or contacts, and loose or corroded ground wires and ground connections.

A voltage drop can be checked only when current is flowing through the circuit, such as by operating the starter motor or turning on the headlights. Making a voltage drop test requires measuring the voltage in the circuit and comparing it to what the voltage should be. Since these measurements are usually small, a digital voltmeter should be used to ensure accurate readings. If a voltage drop is suspected, turn the circuit on and measure the voltage at the circuit's load.

NOTE —

- *A voltage drop test is generally more accurate than a simple resistance check because the resistances involved are often too small to measure with most ohmmeters. For example, a resistance as small as 0.02 ohms would result in a 3 Volt drop in a typical 150 amp starter circuit (150 amps x 0.02 ohms = 3 volts).*
- *Keep in mind that voltage with the key on and voltage with the engine running are not the same. With the ignition on and the engine off (battery voltage), voltage should be approximately 12.6 volts. With the engine running (charging voltage), voltage should be approximately 14.0 volts. Measure voltage at the battery with the ignition on and then with the engine running to get exact measurements.*

Voltage, measuring

1. Set voltage meter to 20V DC scale and connect negative lead to a reliable ground point on car.
2. Connect voltmeter positive lead to the point in the circuit you wish to measure. See Fig. 1.
3. If a reading is obtained, there is voltage at that point in the circuit. The voltage reading should not deviate more than 1 volt from voltage at battery. If the voltage is less than this, there is probably a fault in the circuit, such as a corroded connector or a loose ground wire.

Voltage drop, testing

1. Connect digital voltmeter positive lead to positive (+) connector of component to be tested.
2. Connect voltmeter negative lead to the negative (–) connector of component being tested. See Fig. 2.

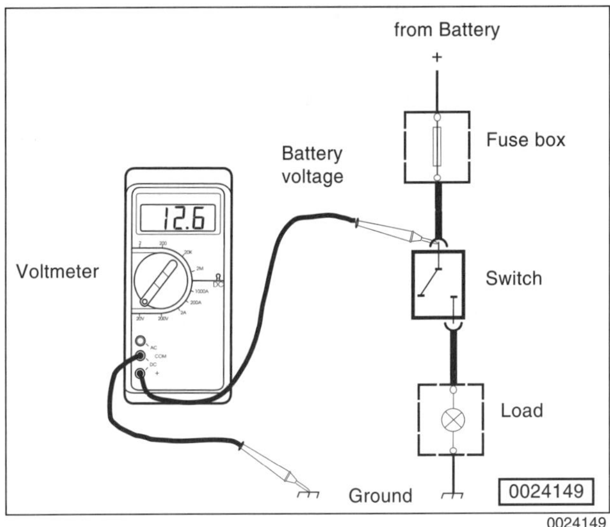

0024149

Fig. 1. Voltmeter being used to check for voltage.

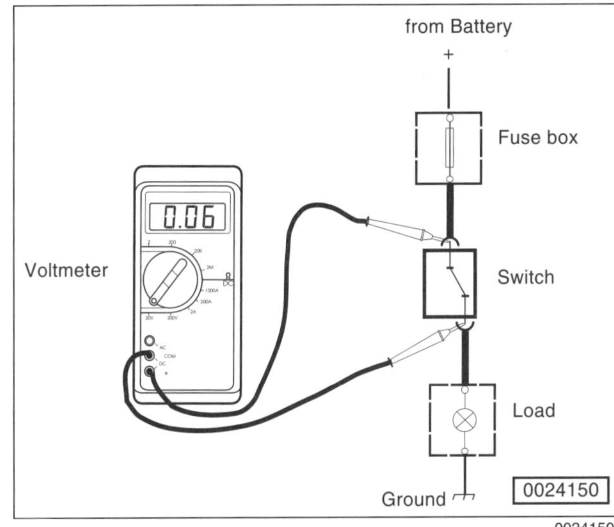

0024150

Fig. 2. Voltmeter being used to check for voltage drop across switch.

3. With power on and circuit working, meter shows the voltage drop (difference between the two points). This value should not exceed 1 volt.

NOTE —

The maximum voltage drop in an automotive circuit, as recommended by the Society of Automotive Engineers (SAE), is as follows: 0 Volts for small wire connections; 0.1 Volts for high current connections; 0.2 Volts for high current cables; and 0.3 Volts for switch or solenoid contacts. On longer wires or cables, the drop may be slightly higher. In any case, a voltage drop of more than 1.0 Volt usually indicates a problem.

Continuity, checking

The continuity test can be used to check the basic integrity of a circuit or switch. Because most automotive circuits are designed to have little or no resistance, a circuit or part of a circuit can be easily checked for faults using an ohmmeter. An open circuit or a circuit with high resistance will not allow current to flow. A circuit with little or no resistance allows current to flow easily.

> ***CAUTION —***
> *Do not use an analog (swing-needle) ohmmeter to check circuit resistance or continuity on any electronic (solid-state) components. The internal power source used in most analog meters can damage solid state components. Use only a high quality digital ohmmeter having high input impedance when checking electronic components.*

When checking continuity, the ignition should be off. On circuits that are powered at all times, the battery should be disconnected. Using the appropriate wiring diagram, a circuit can be easily tested for faulty connections, wires, switches, relays, and engine sensors by checking for continuity. Fig. 3 shows a continuity test being made on a brake light switch.

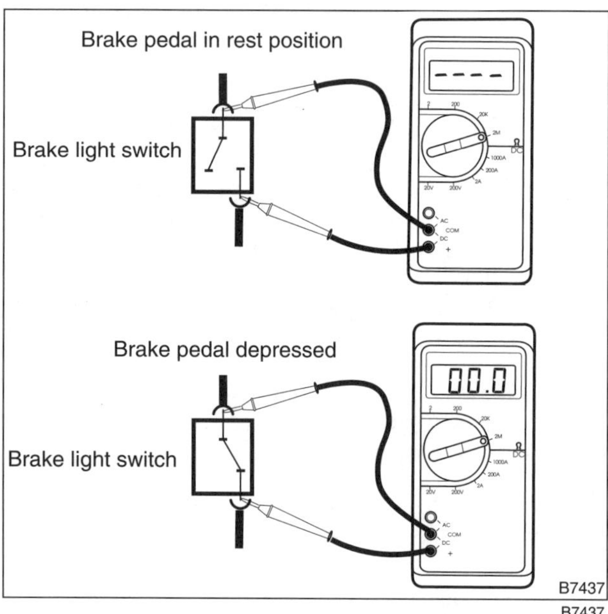

B7437

Fig. 3. Brake light switch being tested for continuity (battery disconnected). With brake pedal in rest position (switch open) there is no continuity (infinite ohms). With the pedal depressed (switch closed) there is continuity (zero ohms).

Short circuits, checking

A short circuit is exactly what the name implies. The circuit takes a shorter path than it was designed to take. The most common short that causes problems is a short to ground where the insulation on a positive (+) wire wears away and the metal wire is exposed. When the wire rubs against a metal part of the car or other ground source, the circuit is shorted to ground. If the exposed wire is live (positive battery voltage), the direct current flow to ground will blow a fuse or damage an unfused circuit.

> ***CAUTION —***
> - *On circuits protected with large fuses (25 amp and greater), the wires or circuit components may be damaged before the fuse blows. Always check for damage before replacing fuses of this rating.*
> - *When replacing blown fuses, use only fuses having the correct rating. Always confirm the correct fuse rating printed on the fuse panel cover.*

Short circuit test with voltmeter

1. Remove blown fuse from circuit.
2. Disconnect harness connector from circuit load or consumer.
3. Using a voltmeter, connect test leads across fuse terminals. See Fig. 4. Make sure power is present in circuit. If necessary, turn key on.

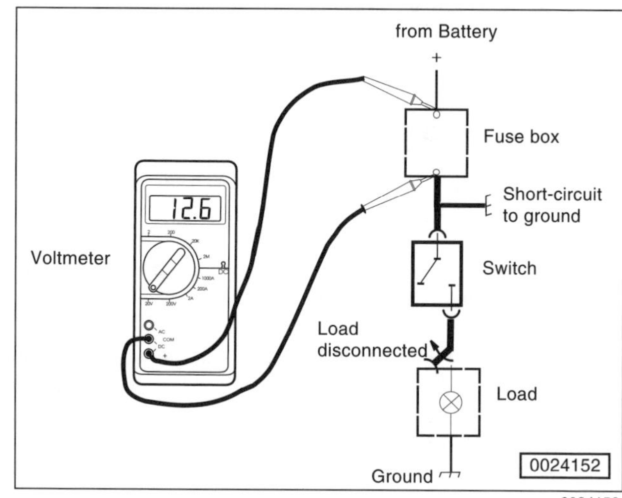

0024152

Fig. 4. Voltmeter being used to find short circuit.

4. If voltage is indicated at voltmeter, there is a short to ground somewhere in the circuit.
5. If voltage is not indicated, work from wire harness nearest to fuse panel and move or wiggle wires while observing meter. Continue to move down harness until meter displays a reading. This is the location of the short to ground.
6. Inspect wire harness at this point for any faults. If no faults are visible, carefully slice open harness cover or wire insulation for further inspection. Repair any faults found.

90 Instruments

TABLES

GENERAL

An electronic speedometer with an LCD digital odometer display is used on all models. The speedometer receives an electronic signal from a Hall sender on the transmission. Mileage is permanently held in memory and will be retained if power to the instrument cluster is interrupted.

Individual components for the instrument cluster are not available from Volkswagen and therefore disassembly of the cluster is not recommended. The illumination for the instrument cluster is provided by several blue light emitting diodes (LEDs) that are not serviceable. Remanufactured instrument cluster assemblies are available through the Volkswagen parts department.

NOTE —
Some versions of the instrument cluster may use a miniature light bulb to provide illumination for certain displays. These bulbs are replaceable separately.

CAUTION —
Disconnecting the negative (–) battery cable may erase fault codes and basic settings in the engine management and automatic transmission control modules. Some driveability problems may be noticed until the system re-adapts to operating conditions. OBD II readiness codes, which may be required for emissions testing, may also be erased. Convenience electronics (alarm system, interior light control, power locks, mirrors, and windows) may need to be re-set using a VAG 1551/1552 or equivalent scan tool.

INSTRUMENT CLUSTER

NOTE —
- *Vehicles with manual transmission have the trip odometer display.*
- *Vehicles with automatic transmission have trip odometer display and gear selector lever position display.*

Malfunction recognition and display

The instrument cluster has On-Board Diagnostic (OBD) capability, which is an aid to troubleshooting.

If the instrument cluster control module detects a malfunction with the odometer or speedometer that is non-repairable, then “dEF” will appear in the trip recorder display. Replacement of the instrument cluster will be necessary.

If the instrument cluster control module detects a malfunction and nothing is displayed on the trip recorder display, carry out the following work before removing the instrument cluster:

1. Check DTC memory with VAG1551/1552 or equivalent scan tool .
2. Read service interval display values and odometer reading with VAG1551/1552 or equivalent scan tool and note the values.

If the malfunction indicates that the instrument cluster requires replacement, the recorded values can be entered in the new instrument cluster.

Instrument cluster, removing and installing

> ***WARNING —***
> - *Special safety precautions apply to vehicles equipped with airbags.*
> - *Refer to airbag* ***CAUTIONS*** *and* ***WARNINGS*** *in* **69 Seatbelts, Airbags**.

> ***CAUTION —***
> - *Disconnect battery ground (GND) strap from battery negative (–) terminal.*
> - *Be sure to have the anti-theft radio code on hand before disconnecting the battery.*
> - *Disconnecting the negative (–) battery cable may erase fault codes and basic settings in the engine management and automatic transmission control modules. Some driveability problems may be noticed until the system re-adapts to operating conditions. OBD II readiness codes, which may be required for emissions testing, may also be erased. Convenience electronics (alarm system, interior light control, power locks, mirrors, and windows) may need to be re-set using a VAG 1551/1552 or equivalent scan tool.*
> - *See* **Malfunction recognition and display** *given earlier before removing instrument cluster.*

NOTE —
For ease of illustration the steering wheel is not shown in the following illustrations. It is not necessary to remove the steering wheel to remove the instrument cluster.

1. Release steering wheel position lock, pull steering wheel out completely and lock again in lowest position.
2. Pull trim ring from instrument cluster mounting clips. See Fig. 1.
3. Remove instrument cluster mounting screws. See Fig. 2.
4. Tilt instrument cluster slightly toward passenger compartment.
5. Disconnect harness connectors at rear of instrument cluster.
6. Remove instrument cluster.
7. Installation is reverse of removal. After completing installation check function of instrument cluster.

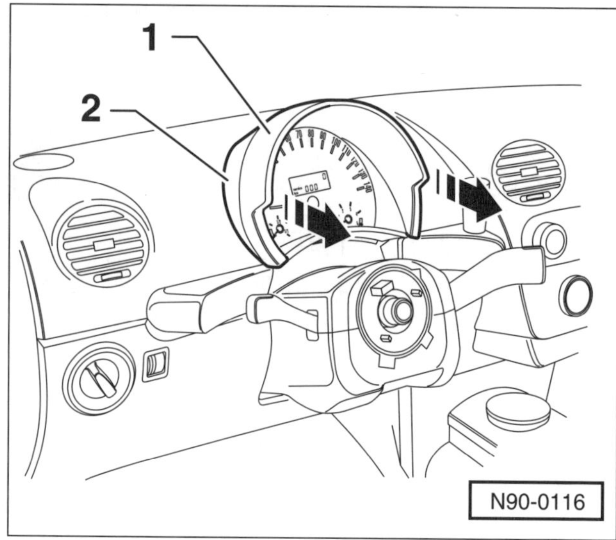

N90-0116

Fig. 1. Release trim ring (**1**) from instrument cluster mounting (**2**) clips by pulling in direction of **arrows**.

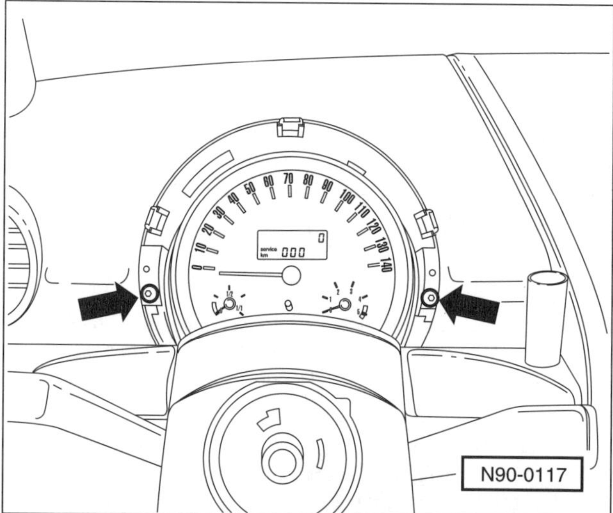

N90-0117

Fig. 2. Remove instrument cluster mounting screws (**arrows**).

NOTE —
- *Due to the large number of instrument cluster variations it always advisable to order a replacement cluster using the part number on the back of the cluster.*
- *Replacement clusters can have the odometer mileage adjusted to match the mileage of the original cluster. Because of the specialized nature of these repairs, servicing should be referred to an authorized Volkswagen dealer or qualified independent repair shop.*
- *If the instrument cluster has been replaced because it was faulty, and a functional check does not display a malfunction the instrument cluster will need to be coded with VAG 1551/1552 scan tool or equivalent, see* **Table a**.

Table a. Instrument cluster coding values

Digit position					Equipment variation
1	2	3	4	5	
0	1				Brake pad wear indicator (only)
0	2				Seat belt warning, active (only)
0	3				Brake pad wear indicator and seat belt warning, active (both)
		2			USA market (US)
		3			Canada market (CDN)
			4		4-cylinder
			5		5-cylinder
			6		6-cylinder
					Code number for number of impulses from vehicle speed sensor to read 1 mile:
				1	4358
				2	3538
				3	4146

Multi-pin connector terminal assignment

NOTE —
- *The instrument cluster must not be disassembled.*
- *For troubleshooting specific systems and circuits see* **Wiring Diagrams, Fuses and Relays**.

The back of the instrument cluster has a blue and a green 32-pin connector, see Fig. 3. **Table b** and **Table c** identify the various terminals for these connectors.

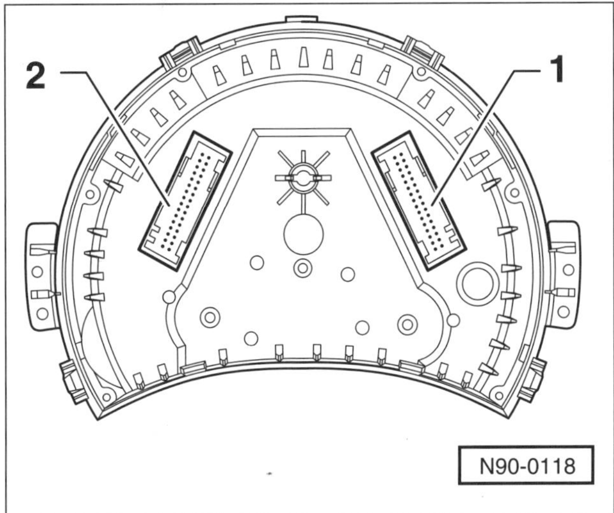

N90-0118

Fig. 3. Blue (**1**) and green (**2**) 32-pin connectors on back of instrument cluster

Table b. Instrument cluster 32-pin connector (blue) terminal identification

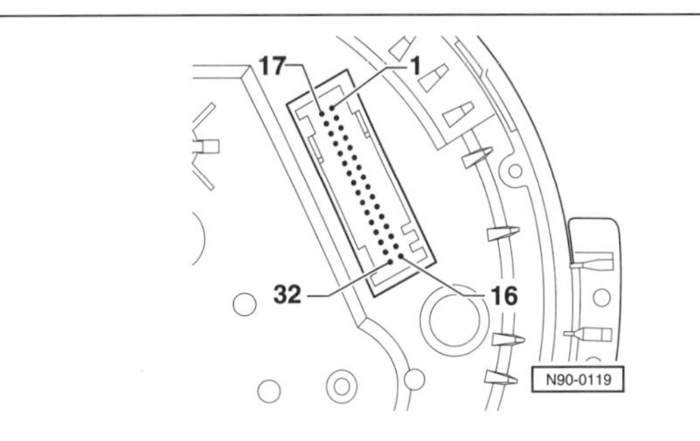

Terminal	Circuit
1	Terminal 15, positive
2	Right turn signal indicator light (K94)
3	Output signal 1 from electronic speedometer
4	Open
5	Fuel gauge (G1)
6	Airbag
7	Terminal 31, sender Ground (GND)
8	Engine coolant temperature gauge (G3)
9	Terminal 31, Ground (GND)
10	Oil pressure switch (F1)
11	RPM signal
12	Generator warning light (K2), terminal 61
13	Glow plug indicator light (K29) (Diesel only)
14	Rear fog light indicator light (K13)
15	Open
16	Warning light for rear lid unlocked (K116)
17	Headlight high beam indicator light (K1), terminal 56a
18	Left turn signal indicator light (K65)
19	ABS warning light (K47)
20	Instrument cluster illumination, terminal 58b
21	Signal for open driver's door
22	Engine Coolant Level (ECL) sensor (G32)
23	Terminal 30, (B+)
24	Terminal 31, Ground (GND)
25	On-Board Diagnostic (K-wire)
26	Parking light right
27	Parking light left
28	Speedometer Vehicle Speed Sensor (VSS) (G22)
29	Warning light for brake system
30	S-contact
31	Seat belt warning system
32	Malfunction Indicator Light (MIL)

Table c. Instrument cluster 32-pin connector (green) terminal identification

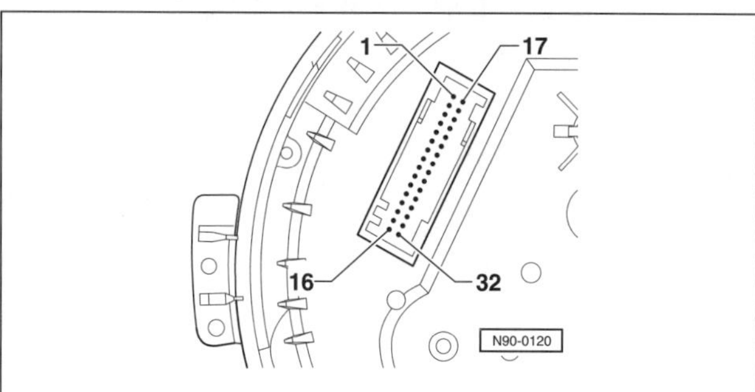

Terminal	Circuit
1	Open
2	Reading coil for immobilizer 1 (where applicable)
3	Open
4	Open
5	W-wire
6	Low level washer fluid
7	Brake pad wear
8	External buzzer
9	External gong (e.g. for seat belt warning system)
10	Fuel reserve warning (certain countries only)
11	Signal for vehicle stationary
12	Air conditioning system cut-off
13	Parking brake indicator light (K14)
14	Warning light for traction control/vehicle stability
15	Malfunction light for electric accelerator mechanism
16	Open
17	Reading coil for immobilizer 2 (where applicable)
18	Open
19	Open
20	Open
21	Open
22	Open
23	Open
24	Open
25	Open
26	Open
27	Open
28	Open
29	Open
30	Output signal 2 from electronic speedometer
31	Selector lever display
32	Open

91 Radio

TABLES

GENERAL

This section covers the Volkswagen factory installed stereo radio sound systems. For specific circuit tracing, it is necessary to see **97 Wiring Diagrams, Fuses and Relays**.

> ***CAUTION —***
> *Disconnecting the negative (–) battery cable may erase fault codes and basic settings in the engine management and automatic transmission control modules. Some driveability problems may be noticed until the system re-adapts to operating conditions. OBD II readiness codes, which may be required for emissions testing, may also be erased. Convenience electronics (alarm system, interior light control, power locks, mirrors, and windows) may need to be re-set using a VAG 1551/1552 or equivalent scan tool.*

> ***WARNING —***
> - *Be sure to have the anti-theft radio code on hand before disconnecting the battery.*
> - *Before working on any part of the electrical system, always disconnect the battery ground strap first.*

Radio reception

Radio stations send out electromagnetic signals from transmitting towers. When these signals move past an automobile, a small electrical impulse is induced in the antenna and sent to the radio for detection and amplification. The radio takes these small electrical impulses and converts them to a level sufficient to operate a speaker.

> ***CAUTION —***
> - *The radio is wired to the vehicle alarm system. If the alarm system is armed, removing the radio will activate the alarm even if the proper tools are used. Do not attempt to remove the radio without disarming the alarm.*
> - *The factory installed connectors are designed for genuine Volkswagen radios. If installing a different radio, remember that the radio may not fit properly into the space provided, the electrical connections may not be compatible and different terminals may be needed.*
> - *Keep in mind that factory installed radios are electronically linked to the ignition, alarm and data link circuits.*

AM (amplitude modulation) radio signals travel in two ways; ground waves and sky waves. Ground waves travel through the air and follow the curve of the earth. Sky waves spread up into the sky until they reach the ionosphere where they are reflected back to earth. Depending on the power of the transmitting station, this reflection or “skip”, enables AM radio waves to travel great distances. FM (frequency modulation) radio waves are not reflected by the atmosphere and travel in what is known as “line of sight”. Therefore, FM broadcasts do not travel as far as AM broadcasts.

Radio reception will be affected by the height of the transmitting antenna, station power and conditions between radio stations and the vehicle radio. Radio signals are also affected by the weather, mountains, buildings, tunnels and other barriers. Best reception is when the vehicle antenna can “see” the station's transmitting antenna. That is, however, rarely the case. Normally, the signal picked up by the vehicle antenna has been reflected by many solid objects. This makes the transmission path longer or shorter and delays or weakens the signal.

Several impediments can prevent optimum radio reception in any vehicle and can include:

Fading

- Signal fading is typical on AM when driving through an underpass or near large buildings or objects. FM does not tend to fade as much as AM. In the same location where AM fades, FM may come in strong and clear because the shorter radio waves are reflected by metal objects such as buildings and bridges.

Flutter-fence effect

- In weak FM reception areas you may hear short pops of hissing background noise with otherwise good reception of the radio program. This "flutter" noise is like the sound burst that occurs when passing poles or posts close to the side of the road. This flutter effect may cause the stereo indicator to flicker because the signal has fallen below the minimum level to operate the stereo decoder. In even more remote areas such as in the desert or in hilly or mountain areas, it may not be possible to receive some AM or FM radio stations at all.

Multi-Path Cancellation

- Flutter and distortion is also caused by a mixing of several signals coming from different directions as a result of reflection from various objects. Mixing or cancellation effects often happen in cities even when close to the radio station transmitting towers and when transmitting towers are in close proximity to each other.

Interference

- Ignition or accessory interference, flutter, distortion and background noise can be caused by the ignition system or electrical accessories in the vehicle. In addition to internal sources, noise can also be caused by outside sources such as electrical power lines, other radio wave transmitters and other vehicles.

Interference suppression

The majority of the electrical consumers in the vehicle have radio suppression built in. All vehicles also include additional suppression measures in the following areas and components:

- Coolant fans (V7)
- Windshield wiper motor (V)
- Ground (GND) strap from left wheel housing to fender

RADIO SYSTEM

Radio system, description

The radio system consists of a radio head and cassette tape player with bass loudspeakers (woofers) in the front doors and rear side panels. Domed treble loudspeakers (tweeters) are installed in each A-pillar. The system also includes an amplified roof mounted antenna. See Fig. 1.

A 6-Disc CD changer is available as optional equipment, and (if equipped) is located in left side of the luggage compartment behind the rear seat. All vehicles are pre-wired from the factory for this unit only.

Volkswagen New Beetle radios are capable of communicating with scan tool VAG 1551/1552 through the Data Link Connector (DLC). Radios can store Diagnostic Trouble Codes, (DTCs), and must be coded via the scan tool in order to function properly. The correct code varies depending on the type of vehicle, the type of antenna and the CD changer, if applicable.

NOTE —
Radio malfunctions and equipment changes requiring the use of scan tool VAG 1551/1552 should be handled by an authorized Volkswagen dealer or other qualified repair facility.

CAUTION —
Observe all cautions and warnings in **9 Electrical System** *before starting repairs involving the electrical system.*

NOTE —
- *Before troubleshooting or servicing, the technician must be familiar with the function and operation of the radio system. Read the radio owner's manual and review all radio, tape player and CD changer functions.*
- *Only factory approved accessory radios and radio equipment (available from Volkswagen of America, Inc.) should be installed. This ensures proper installation and minimizes risk of damaging vehicle electrical system and On-Board Diagnostic functions.*

Radio system, overview

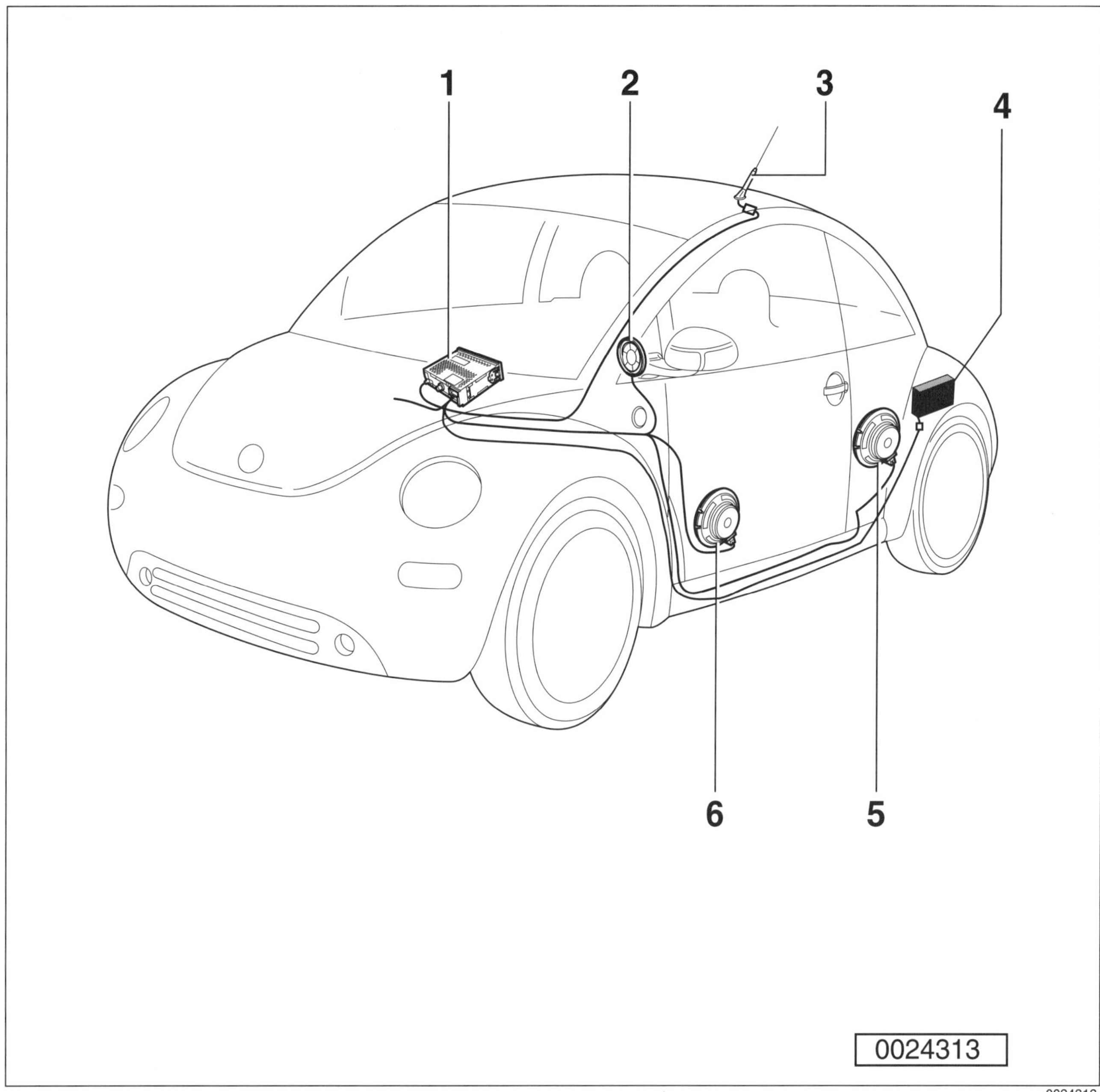

0024313

Fig. 1. Major components of the radio system showing the optional CD changer. Left side speakers are shown. Right side speakers are the same.

1. **Radio head unit**
   - Location: in center console
   - AM/FM receiver
   - Cassette player
   - Equipped to control optional CD changer
2. **Domed treble speaker (tweeter), see** Ⓐ
   - Location: base of A-pillar
3. **Amplified antenna**
   - Location: center rear of roof
4. **CD changer (optional equipment)**
   - Location: left rear area of luggage compartment
   - Factory pre-wired for VW supplied changers only
5. **Bass speaker (woofer), see** Ⓑ
   - Location: rear side panel
   - Diameter: 168 mm (approx. 6 5/8 in)
6. **Bass speaker (woofer), see** Ⓑ
   - Location: front door panel
   - Diameter: 168 mm (approx. 6-5/8 in)

A Domed treble speaker (tweeter), replacing

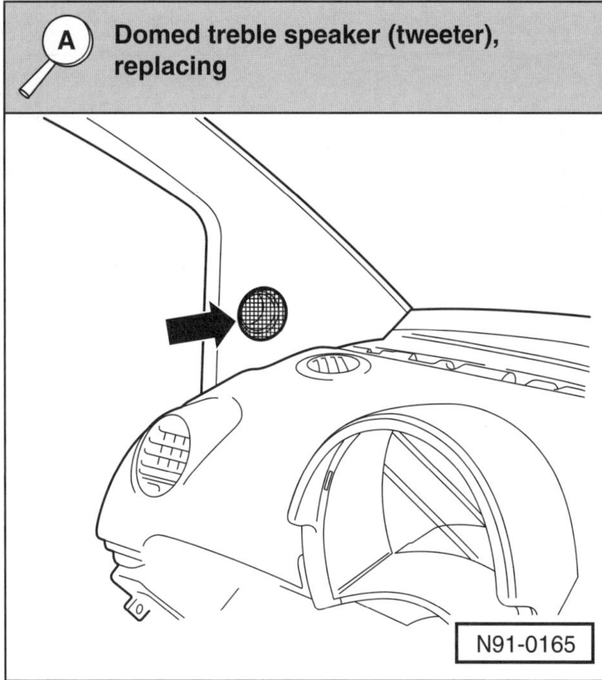

N91-0165

- The domed treble (tweeter) speakers (arrow) in the front A-pillars are permanently attached to the interior A-pillar trim cover.
- To replace a domed treble loudspeaker, the entire A-pillar trim cover must be replaced.

B Bass speaker (woofer), front and rear, replacing

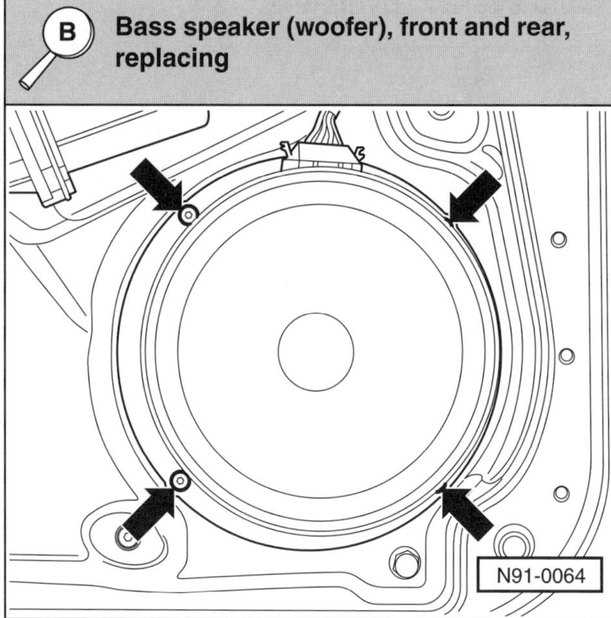

N91-0064

- Remove door trim panel or rear trim panel.
- Disconnect harness connector.
- Carefully drill out rivets (arrows) and remove speaker.
- To prevent corrosion, make sure that all metal particles from drilling are removed from inside the door.
- If the paint on door frame is damaged during drilling, touch-up immediately.
- Secure new speaker with pop rivets of proper length and diameter.
- Do not forget rubber ring between door trim and loudspeaker when reinstalling door trim panel.

Radio head unit, removing and installing

> ***CAUTION —***
> *Observe all cautions and warnings in* **9 Electrical System** *before starting repairs involving the electrical system.*

1. Slide Volkswagen radio release tools 3344A into radio release slots until they engage the release mechanism. See Fig. 2.

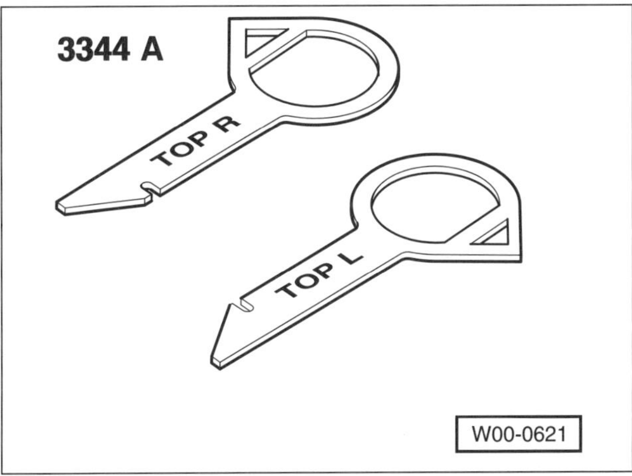

W00-0621

Fig. 2. The radio release tool 3344A consists of two identical parts. Tool 3344A is approximately 20 mm longer than the earlier 3344 version.

2. Pull radio out of instrument panel using grip rings of release tools. See Fig. 3.

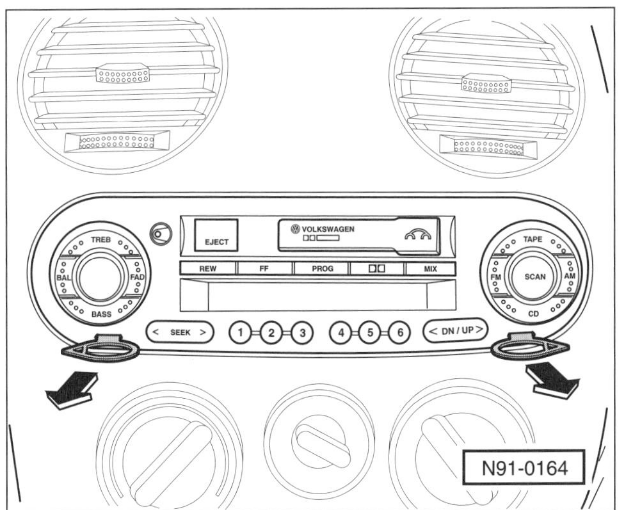

N91-0164

Fig. 3. Radio release tools shown in proper position to remove radio (**arrows**).

NOTE —

- *The radio release tool 3344A must not be pushed to the side or tilted. Pull straight out.*
- *Remove release tools before reinstalling radio head unit.*
- *To remove the release tools from the radio the locating lugs on the side of the radio must be pressed inward.*

3. Remove antenna connector and harness connectors on back of radio head unit.
4. To install radio head unit, remove release tools.
5. Connect harness and antenna connectors to radio head unit.
6. Carefully slide radio head unit straight into instrument panel until it engages properly in assembly frame in center console.
7. If new (or exchange) radio head unit has been installed, be sure to leave new radio code card in vehicle.

Radio anti-theft system, description

All factory installed and supplied radios are equipped with an electronic anti-theft system. The anti-theft system is activated and electronically de-activates (locks) the radio as soon as any of the following occur:

- Voltage supply (terminal 30) drops below a predetermined voltage value.
- The radio unit is disconnected from voltage supply (terminal 30) such as when removing radio head unit or if the fuse blows.
- Vehicle battery has been disconnected.

A radio which is locked by the electronic anti-theft system has the word “SAFE” in the display window when the radio is switched on. After 3 seconds, the word “SAFE” will be replaced by the number “1000” indicating readiness to unlock.

In addition to electronic anti-theft locking, the radio is linked to the alarm system. The alarm horn will sound if the alarm has been set and the radio is removed.

Radio anti-theft system, unlocking

If the radio has been electronically locked as described above, it can be unlocked using the following procedure. The radio will only work if the correct code number for the anti-theft system is entered. The anti-theft code can be found along with the radio number on the radio card provided with the vehicle.

NOTE —
For security reasons, the radio card should not be left in the vehicle. Ask the customer for the code before starting repairs. Never leave the radio card in the car.

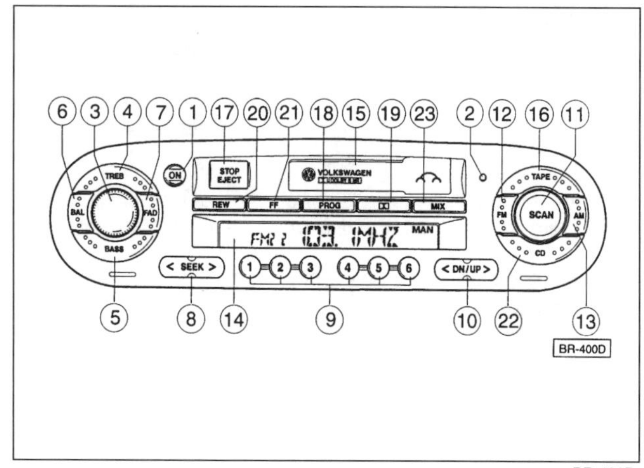

BR-400D

Fig. 4. Sound System radio head unit showing controls. Several circled numbers are referenced in text.

To unlock the radio anti-theft feature, perform the following steps:

1. Obtain correct anti-theft code number from radio card.

2. Switch radio on (**1**).

   NOTE —
   Numbers in parenthesis in procedure steps refer to Fig. 4.

3. "SAFE" will appear in the display window (**14**). After 3 seconds, the number "1000" will appear in the display window.

4. Use station preset buttons 1 to 4 (**9**) to enter 4 digit code number.
   - Press preset button 1 to enter first digit in code number, preset button 2 for second digit and so on.
   - To enter code number, press applicable button repeatedly until desired number appears on display.
   - The value range for each of the 4 digits is between 0 and 9.
   - If a button is pressed beyond desired number, sequence will start over at 1 after 9 is pressed.

5. When entire code is entered, press right side of "Seek" button (**8**) for about 2 seconds, until audible signal is heard.
   - If wrong code was accidentally entered, display window will show "SAFE"; flashing at first and then remaining on.
   - Coding procedure may be repeated a second time (the number of coding attempts will be shown on display window). If wrong code is entered again, radio will be disabled for an hour. If this happens, leave radio ON and key in ignition for one hour. After the hour has elapsed, you will have two more attempts to unlock system. Unsuccessful attempts will cause the cycle to be repeated.
   - The cycle is: 2 attempts, 1 hour locked.

Radio anti-theft system, first activation

On new radios the anti-theft coding is not active. The electronic anti-theft system only becomes active after entering the correct code number factory assigned to that particular unit. If the radio is disconnected from the voltage supply before the anti-theft system is activated, it will not electronically lock. Radio head units that have not had the anti-theft system activation done initially will not have the blinking LED (**2**) when the key is removed. Note the following points:

- Each radio is assigned a unique code.
- If the radio has been replaced, the new code must be used.
- The customer must be informed that the code number has changed.

Perform steps in the exact order given below. Numbers in parenthesis refer to Fig. 4.

1. Obtain correct anti-theft code number from radio card.

2. Switch radio on (**1**).

3. "SAFE" will appear in the display window (**14**). After 3 seconds, the number "1000" will appear in display window.

4. Use station preset buttons 1 to 4 (**9**) to enter 4 digit code number.
   - Press preset button 1 to enter first digit in the code number, preset button 2 for second digit and so on.
   - To enter code number, press applicable button repeatedly until desired number appears on display.
   - Value range for each of the 4 digits is between 0 and 9.
   - If a button is pressed beyond the desired number, sequence will start over at 1 after 9 is pressed.

5. When entire code is entered, press right side of "Seek" button (**8**) for about 2 seconds, until audible signal is heard.
   - If a wrong code was accidentally entered, display window will show "SAFE"; flashing at first and then remaining on.
   - Coding procedure may be repeated a second time (the number of coding attempts will be shown on the display window). If wrong code is entered again, radio will be disabled for an hour. If this happens, leave radio ON and key in the ignition for one hour. After the hour has elapsed, you will have two more attempts to unlock system. Unsuccessful attempts will cause cycle to be repeated.
   - The cycle is: 2 attempts, 1 hour locked.

Radio head unit, coding

The radio is controlled by a microprocessor which has extensive On-Board Diagnostic (OBD) capability. To take full advantage of the OBD capabilities, the head unit must be coded to match the equipment level of the vehicle. Since all New Beetle sound systems are alike except for the addition of an optional CD changer, there are only 2 possible codes available at this time. Failure to code the radio head upon the addition of a CD changer will prevent it from being included in the On-Board Diagnostics, however, it will operate properly. Conversely, failure to change the code after removing a CD changer will cause erroneous DTCs to be stored in the radio head unit memory. Access to the radio head unit is via the Data Link Connector (DLC). Because of the specialized nature of these repairs, coding should be referred to an authorized Volkswagen Dealer or qualified independent repair shop. See **Table a**.

Table a. Radio head unit codes

System	Radio head unit code
Without CD changer	06401
With CD changer	06403

Table b lists the terminal assignments for the multi-pin connector on the back of the radio.

Table b. Radio head unit terminal assignments

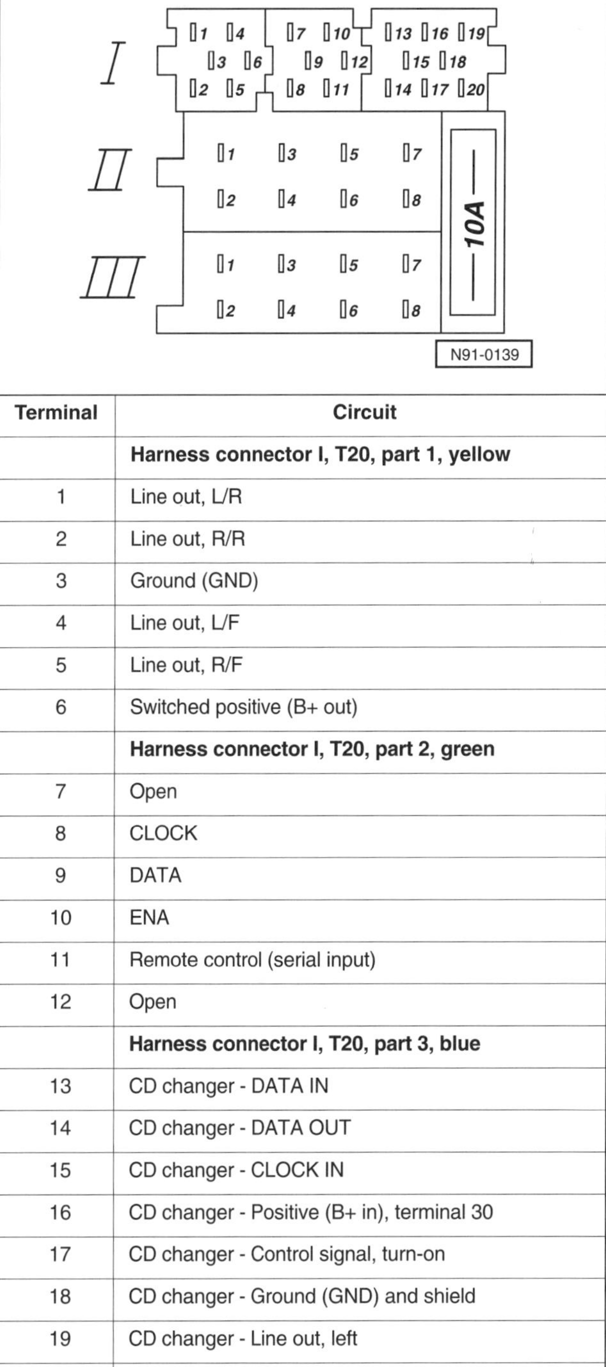

Terminal	Circuit
	Harness connector I, T20, part 1, yellow
1	Line out, L/R
2	Line out, R/R
3	Ground (GND)
4	Line out, L/F
5	Line out, R/F
6	Switched positive (B+ out)
	Harness connector I, T20, part 2, green
7	Open
8	CLOCK
9	DATA
10	ENA
11	Remote control (serial input)
12	Open
	Harness connector I, T20, part 3, blue
13	CD changer - DATA IN
14	CD changer - DATA OUT
15	CD changer - CLOCK IN
16	CD changer - Positive (B+ in), terminal 30
17	CD changer - Control signal, turn-on
18	CD changer - Ground (GND) and shield
19	CD changer - Line out, left
20	CD changer - Line out, right

(continued on following page)

Table b. Radio head unit terminal assignments

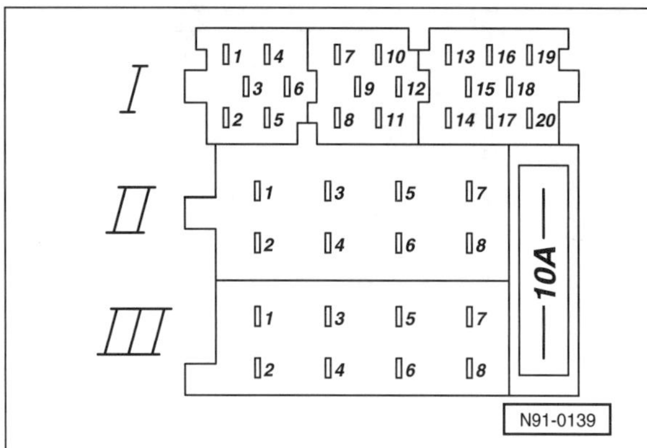

Terminal	Circuit
	Harness connector II, T8a, brown
1	R/R speaker +
2	R/R speaker -
3	R/F speaker +
4	R/F speaker -
5	L/F speaker +
6	L/F speaker -t
7	L/R speaker +
8	L/R speaker -
	Harness connector III, T8, black
1	Signal for anti-theft alarm
2	Open
3	Data Link Connector (DLC), K wire
4	Ignition switch, S contact
5	Battery positive (B+), terminal 30
6	Illumination, terminal 58b
7	Battery positive (B+), terminal 30
8	Battery ground, (GND), terminal 31

NOTE —

Harness connector I, T20, part 1 (yellow) and part 2 (green) are not used at this time.

Amplified antenna, roof mounted

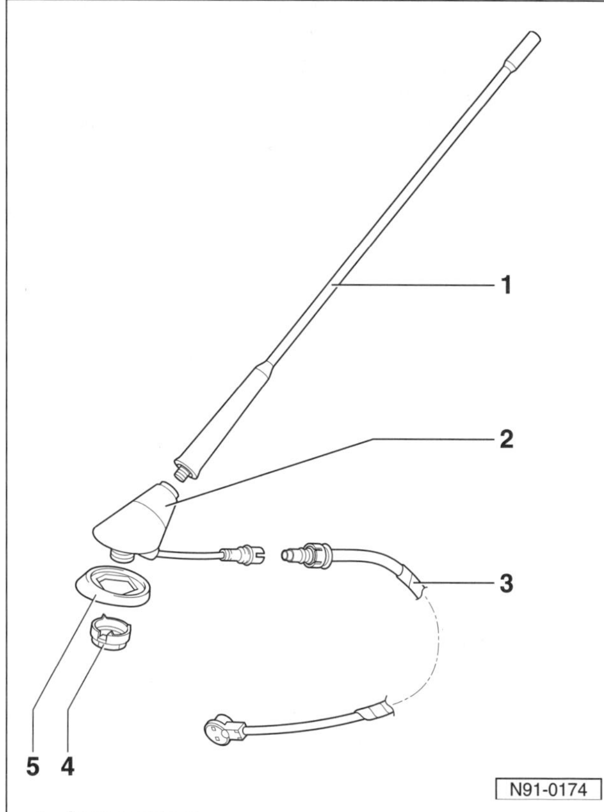

1. **Antenna mast**
2. **Antenna base**
   - With amplifier
   - Lower molded headliner at rear to access base
3. **Antenna cable**
   - From roof antenna to radio head unit
   - Current to operate the amplifier is supplied from the radio head unit through the center coaxial conductor. No separate 12 volt power lead is used.
4. **Nut with serrated washer**
   - Special M14 nut with attached serrated grounding washer
   - Serrated washer is attached to nut with plastic ring
   - Apply contact grease to inside of roof in area of the serrated washer to insure good electrical grounding
   - Tighten to: 7 Nm (62 in lb)
5. **Gasket**
   - Ensure correct positioning to provide water tight seal.

N91-0174

Fig. 5. Roof mounted amplified antenna shown with related components. Roof mounting provides optimal reception.

CAUTION —

Observe all cautions and warnings in **9 Electrical System** *before starting repairs involving the electrical system.*

CD CHANGER

With the increased popularity of compact discs (CDs), the addition of a player is a common option. As a result of this popularity, all New Beetles are factory wired for an optional 6 disc CD changer. Only genuine Volkswagen supplied changers are compatible with the radio head unit and the additional wiring. Installed location is in the left rear area of the luggage compartment just behind the rear seat. See Fig. 6.

0024308

Fig. 6. CD changer shown properly installed behind rear seat in the left side of luggage compartment.

CD changer installing

The following describes the factory approved service installation of Volkswagen CD changers into New Beetles models from model year 1998 equipped with Volkswagen sound system radios.

NOTE—
Always confirm CD changer and radio compatibility with your Volkswagen parts department or aftermarket parts specialist.

- *Carefully review all of the following instructions before proceeding with installation.*
- *Never install CD changer in a location, position, or manner other than specified by these instructions.*

> ***CAUTION—***
> *Observe all cautions and warnings in* **9 Electrical System** *before starting repairs involving the electrical system.*

1. Remove all items from luggage compartment. Lift luggage compartment carpet to expose floor of compartment. See Fig. 7.

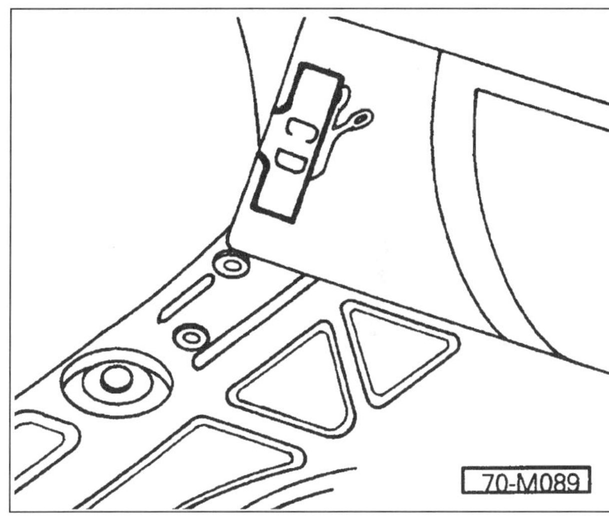

70-M089

Fig. 7. Floor of luggage compartment with carpet pulled back.

2. Note location of three CD changer bracket mounting holes on the luggage compartment floor. See Fig. 8.

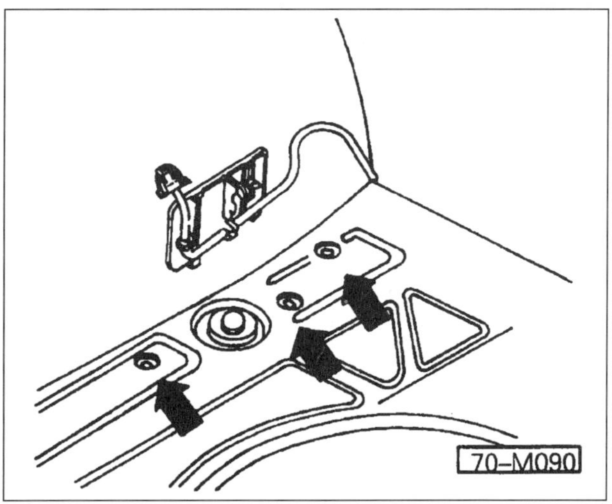

70-M090

Fig. 8. Changer mounting bracket hole (**arrows**) in floor of luggage compartment.

3. Locate CD changer cable on left side of luggage compartment. There are 2 versions. For early production, see Fig. 9. For later production, see Fig. 10.

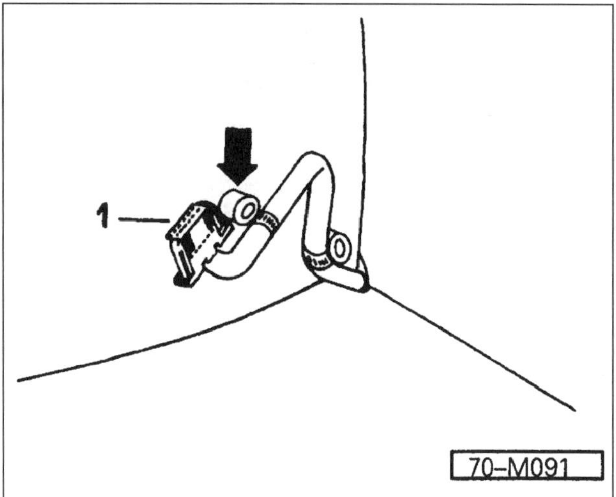

70-M091

Fig. 9. Cable version 1: secured by a clip on left side of luggage compartment. Remove clip (**arrow**) and fold back connector (**1**).

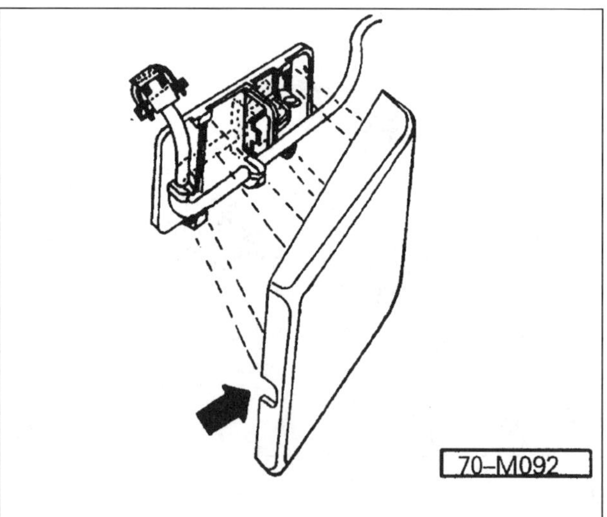

70-M092

Fig. 10. Cable version 2: secured inside cover. Unclip cover (**arrow**) and pull out harness connector.

4. Locate cut markings on underside of luggage compartment carpet and carefully cut out marked area. See Fig. 11.

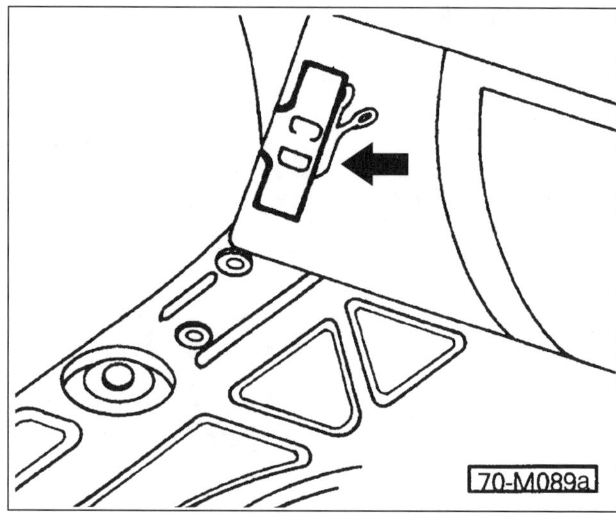

70-M089a

Fig. 11. Cut luggage compartment carpet along marked area (**arrow**).

5. Refit luggage compartment carpet. See Fig. 12.

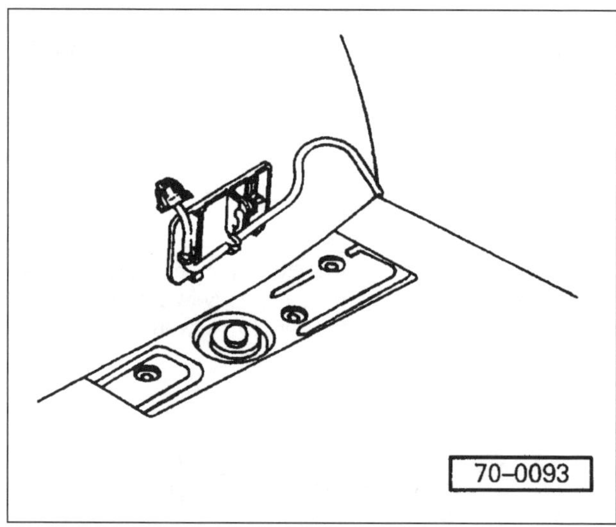

70-0093

Fig. 12. Luggage compartment carpet shown back in place with cutout for mounting bracket.

6. Mount CD changer bracket to floor using supplied screws. See Fig. 13.

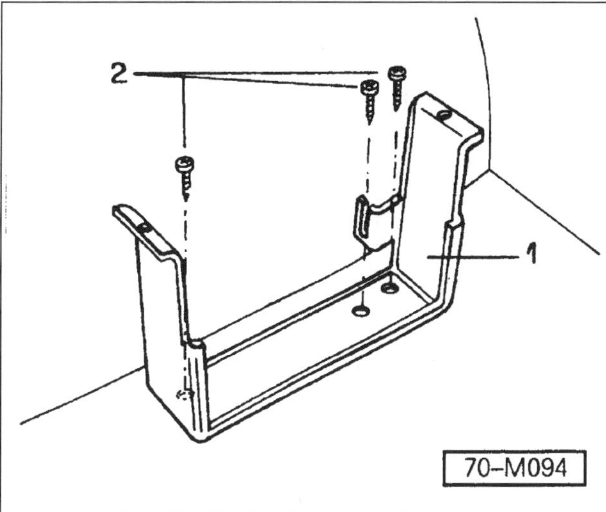

70-M094

Fig. 13. CD changer mounting bracket (**1**) shown in position with securing screws (**2**).

Tightening torque

• CD changer bracket screws . . . . 4.5 Nm (39 in-lb)

7. Check CD changer angle of installation switches. Both switches must be in vertical (V) position for this application. Switches are located on the side and bottom of the CD changer. See Fig. 14.

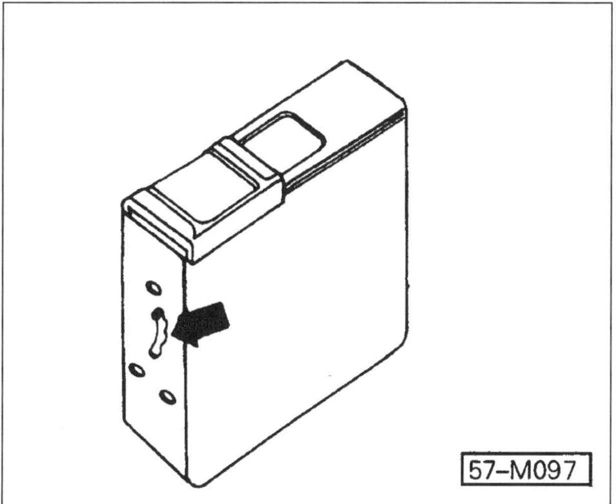

57_M097

Fig. 14. Side mounted position switch (**arrow**) must be set to **V**. Bottom switch arrangement is similar and must also be set to **V**.

8. If switches need to be reset, loosen securing screws, slide both switches to "V" position and tighten screws.

Tightening torque

• CD changer position switch screw . . . . 2 Nm (18 in-lb)

NOTE —

- *CD playback will skip if switches are not set correctly.*
- *Always check and/or set switches before installation.*
- *Switches must move completely to their end positions.*

9. Cover position switch openings with adhesive seals (if supplied).

10. Attach support brackets to CD changer. See Fig. 15.

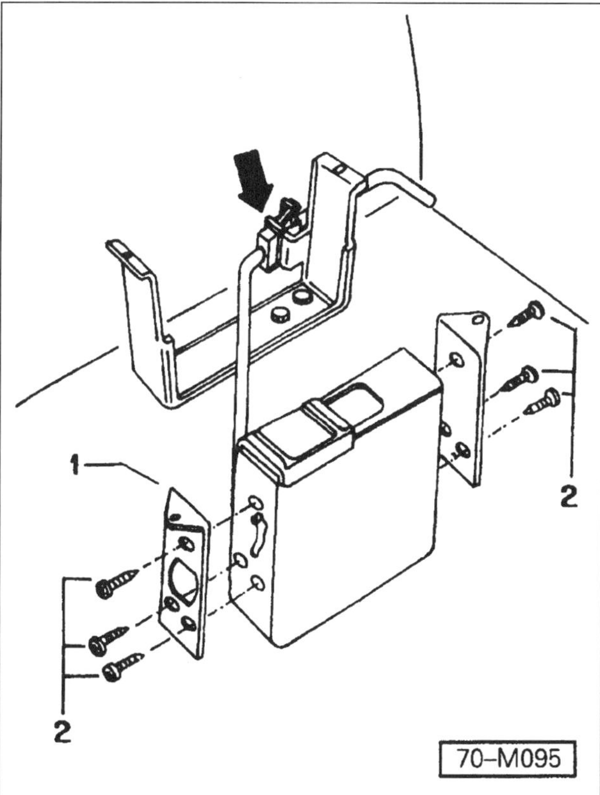

70-M095

Fig. 15. Attach support brackets (**1**) with screws (**2**) to CD changer as shown. Harness connector (**arrow**) shown connected and attached to support tab.

Tightening torque

• CD changer to support bracket . . . . . . 3 Nm (27 in-lb)

11. Route harness connector from CD changer and connect to vehicle harness connector. Clip connector into support tab on CD changer bracket.

12. Slide CD changer into bracket from top making sure that cable connector is secured in support tab.

13. Install protective cover around CD changer and secure bracket and cover with screws from the top. See Fig. 16.

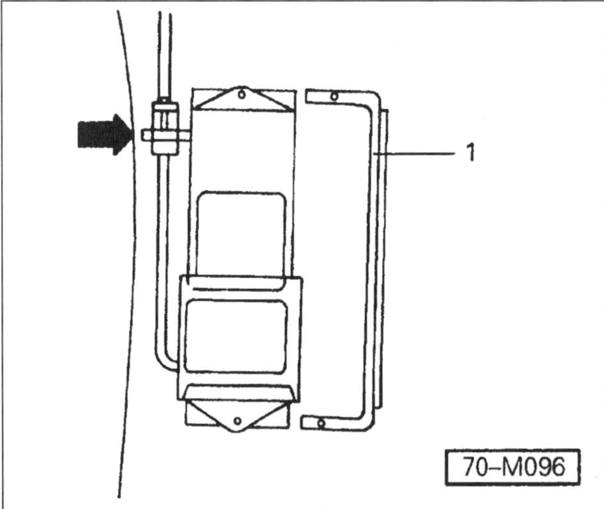

70-M096

Fig. 16. Top view of CD changer showing protective cover (**1**) and harness connector secured into support tab (**arrow**).

> ***NOTE —***
> *Early CD changer kits supplied by Volkswagen did not include protective cover.*

Tightening torque
- CD changer to mounting bracket . . . . . 3 Nm (27 in-lb)

---

14. Code radio head unit for addition of CD changer with VAG 1551/1552 scan tool or equivalent.

15. Quality check operation on CD changer and radio.

> ***NOTE —***
> *Refer to sound system owner's manual for operating instructions.*

QUALITY REVIEW

When you have finished working inside the vehicle, it is advisable to take a moment to quality check or review your work. This helps to insure that the operation or repair has been completed properly with all affected systems functioning within normal parameters. These may include the following:

- Ensure that all cable ties and clamps that were removed as part of the repair are replaced.
- Ensure that all fasteners and hardware were replaced and torqued as specified.
- Make sure that all other components involved in the repair are positioned correctly, properly torqued and function properly.
- Make sure that all tools, shop cloths, fender covers and protective tapes are removed before closing the hood.
- Clean grease and fingerprints from painted surfaces, steering wheel, upholstery and shifter.
- Place all items removed for installation of CD changer back into luggage compartment.
- Unlock anti-theft radio and reset the clock.
- Restore radio station selections to radio memory as required.

92 Wipers and Washers

GENERAL

The front windshield wipers are operated by the wiper switch on the steering column. There is a small lever on the top of the wiper switch which adjusts the interval when the wipers are in delay mode. Pulling the wiper switch back toward the passenger compartment operates the washer and the wipers automatically.

Some vehicles are equipped with heated washer nozzles which do not have a seperate switch and are automatically activated (with ignition switched on) depending on outside temperature.

WIPERS AND WASHERS

CAUTION —

- *Worn or dirty wiper blades will reduce visibility, making driving hazardous. Clean blades regularly to remove road film and car wash wax build-up. Use an alcohol based cleaning solution and a lint free cloth to wipe along the rubber blade.*
- *Clean all inside and outside glass regularly. Use an alcohol based cleaning solution and wipe dry with a lint free cloth.*
- *Do not use the wiper/washer in freezing weather without first warming the windshield with the defroster. Otherwise the washer solution may freeze on the windshield and obscure your vision.*
- *To prevent scratching the glass avoid running the wiper blades over a dry windshield. A scratched windshield will reduce visibility and increase glare.*

Rubber wiper inserts, replacing

1. Free end of wiper insert from retaining hooks by squeezing metal strip in insert with pliers.

2. Slide rubber insert from retaining hooks.

3. Slide rubber insert into lower retaining hooks of wiper blade.

NOTE —
If necessary, transfer metal strips from old insert to new insert. Notches in metal strips must face rubber and engage rubber lugs in groove.

4. Squeeze metal strips at open end of rubber insert using pliers and install insert into hooks so that hook engages rubber retaining slot on insert. See Fig. 1.

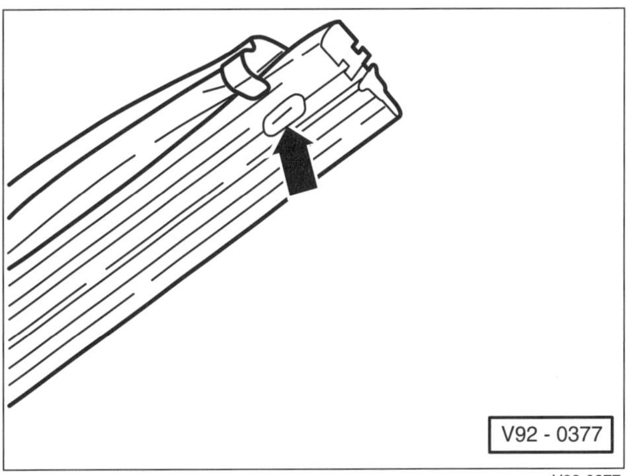

V92-0377

Fig. 1. Install rubber insert so that hook engages rubber retaining slot (**arrow**).

Windshield wiper assembly

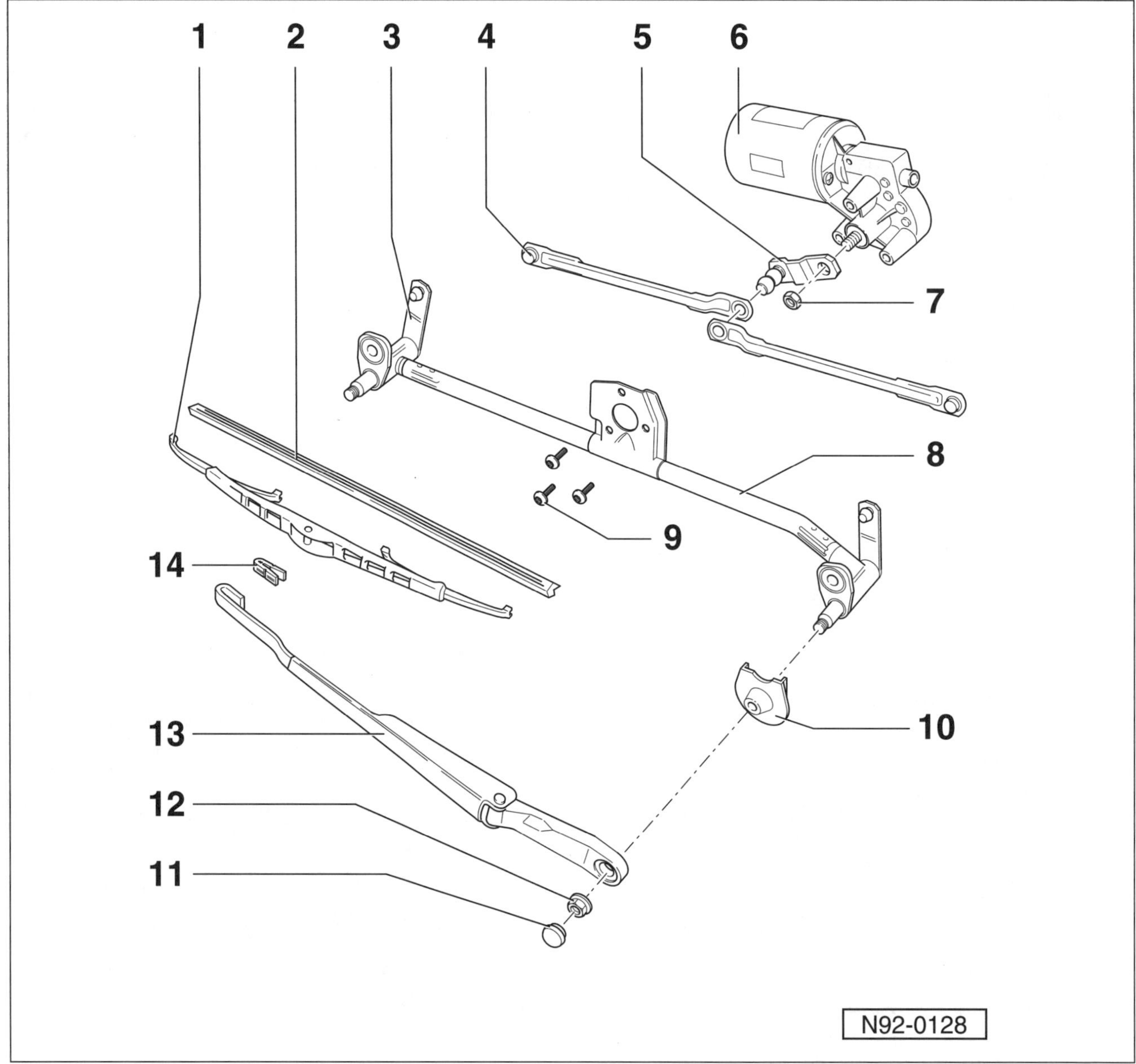

N92-0128

Fig. 2. Windshield wiper assembly.

1. **Wiper blade**
   - Adjusting park position, **see** Ⓐ
2. **Wiper blade rubber**
3. **Connecting lever**
4. **Connecting rod**
5. **Crank**
6. **Wiper motor**
7. **Hex nut M8**
   - Tighten to 20 Nm (15 ft-lb)
8. **Wiper frame**
9. **Securing bolts M6**
   - Tighten to 5 Nm (44 in-lb)
10. **Protective sleeve**
11. **Cover cap**
12. **Hex nut M8**
    - Tighten to 20 Nm (15 ft-lb)
13. **Wiper arm**
14. **Retaining clip**

(A) Wiper blade park position, adjusting

0024301

- **Align wiper blades so they are 20 mm (¾ in.) from lower edge of windshield (arrows a).**
- **Distance between arrows b = 20 to 30 mm (¾ to 1-3/16 in.)**

Wiper motor, removing and installing

1. Make sure the wiper arms are in park position. Only then can wiper arm end position be correctly set when reinstalling.

2. Disconnect battery ground (GND) strap from battery negative (–) terminal.

   NOTE —
   Be sure to have the anti-theft radio code on hand before disconnecting the battery.

   CAUTION —
   Disconnecting the negative (–) battery cable may erase fault codes and basic settings in the engine management and automatic transmission control modules. Some driveability problems may be noticed until the system re-adapts to operating conditions. OBD II readiness codes, which may be required for emissions testing, may also be erased. Convenience electronics (alarm system, interior light control, power locks, mirrors, and windows) may need to be re-set using a VAG 1551/1552 or equivalent scan tool.

3. Pry off wiper arm mounting nut cover caps using screwdriver.

4. Loosen wiper arm mounting nuts and move wiper arms slightly until they release.

5. Remove wiper arm mounting nuts and wiper arms.

6. Pull up plenum panel rubber gasket and remove. Carefully pry cowl panel upward and off. See Fig. 3.

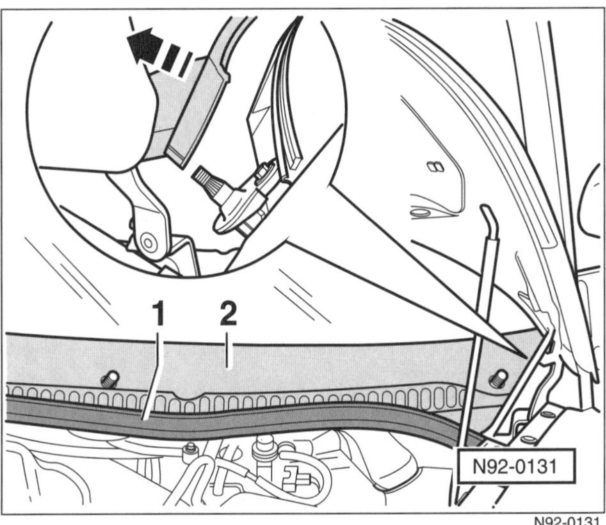

N92-0131

Fig. 3. Pull off rubber gasket (**1**) and carefully pry off cowl panel (**2**).

NOTE —
The cowl panel is attached to a window guide underneath the windshield.

7. Remove plenum close-out panel mounting screws and pull close-out panel slightly forward. See Fig. 4. See also **50 Body–Front**, **Plenum close-out panel, removing and installing**.

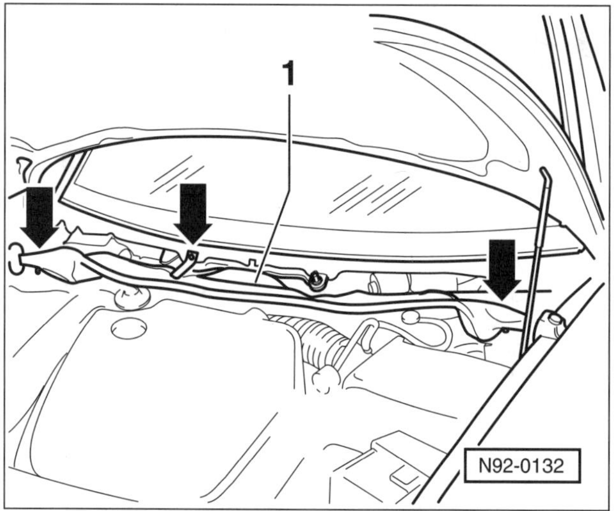

Fig. 4. Remove hex screws (**arrows**) and pull plenum panel forward.

8. Remove wiper motor assembly mounting bolts and washers. See Fig. 5.

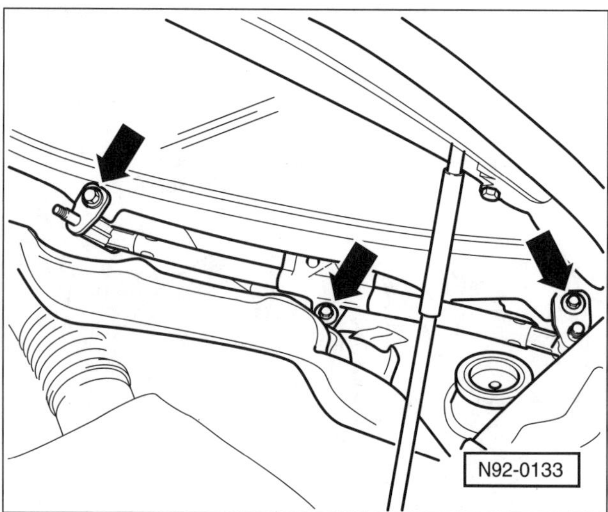

Fig. 5. Remove wiper assembly mounting bolts (**arrows**).

9. Disconnect harness connector from wiper motor.

10. Remove complete wiper assembly.

11. Pry connecting rods off wiper motor crank using large screwdriver.

12. Unbolt wiper motor-to-frame mounting bolts. See Fig. 6.

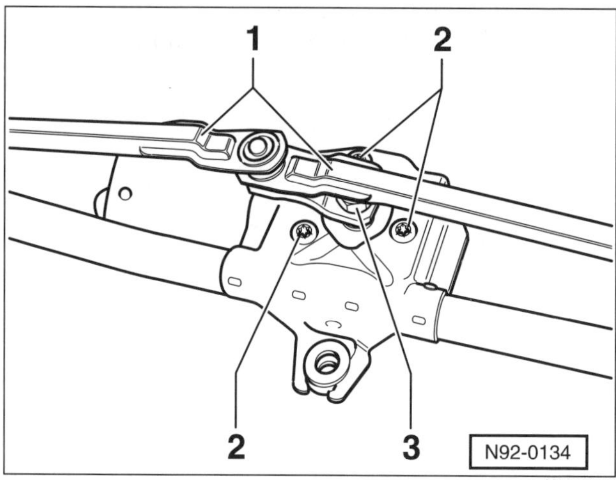

Fig. 6. Pry off connecting rods (**1**), remove motor-to-frame mounting bolts (**2**), and nut for crank arm (**3**).

13. Remove wiper motor from wiper frame.

14. Remove crank arm nut and crank arm.

15. Begin installation by connecting harness connector to wiper motor and operating wiper switch briefly to ensure that motor is in park position.

16. Disconnect harness connector again and install wiper motor-to-frame mounting bolts.

Tightening torque

- Wiper motor to frame . . . . 8 Nm (71 in-lb)

17. Install crank and align so that connecting rods are in line. See Fig. 7.

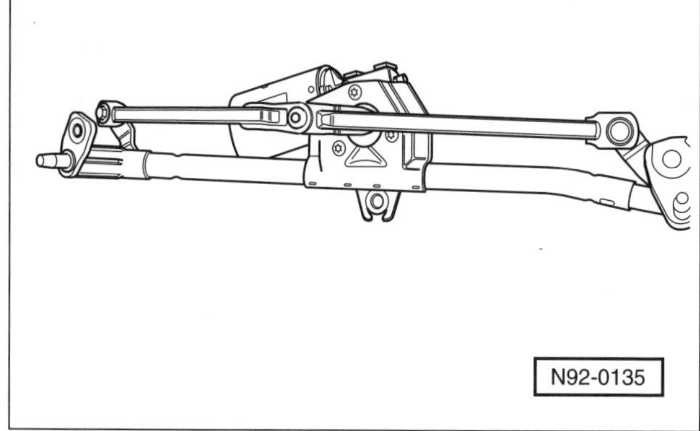

Fig. 7. Install wiper motor crank so that wiper arms line up as shown.

18. Tighten crank arm nut and press rods back onto crank.

Tightening torque

- Wiper motor crank arm nut. . . . . 20 Nm (15 ft-lb)

Windshield washer system overview

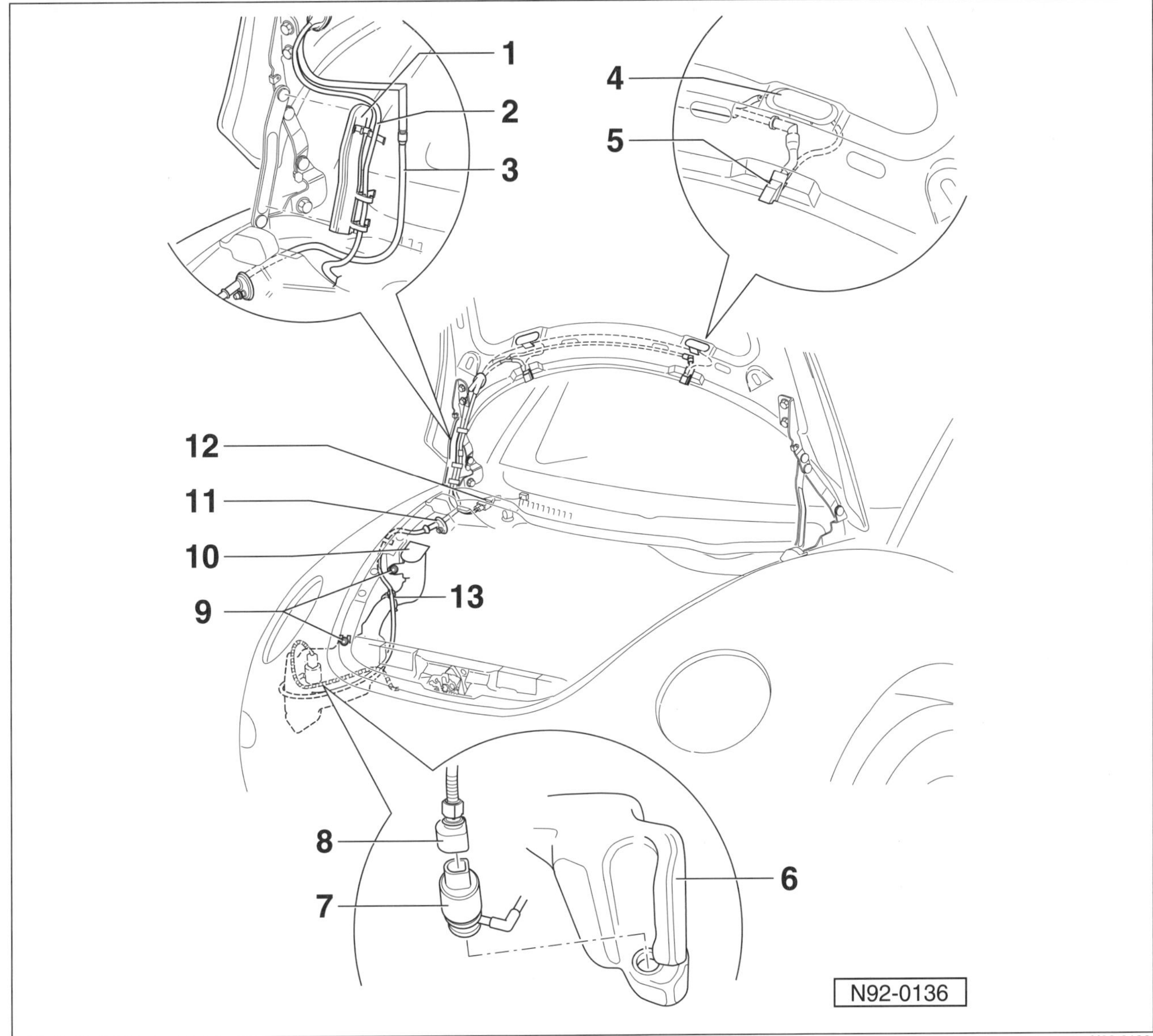

Fig. 8. Windshield washer system and related components.

1. **Securing clip**
2. **Wiring harness for heated washer jets**
   - Optional equipment
   - Disconnecting, **see** (A)
3. **Hose**
4. **Cover cap**
   - With connectors for heated washer nozzles
5. **Jets**
   - Removing, **see** (B)
   - Checking, **see** (C)
6. **Windshield washer system reservoir**
   - Removing: remove right front wheel housing liner
7. **Windshield washer system pump**
   - Pull pump upward off rubber grommet
8. **Harness connector**
9. **Securing bolts**
   - Tighten to 5 Nm (44 in-lb)
10. **Container cap**
11. **Transfer piece**
12. **Harness connector for heated washer nozzles**
13. **Hose clip**

A Heated washer nozzle, disconnecting harness connector

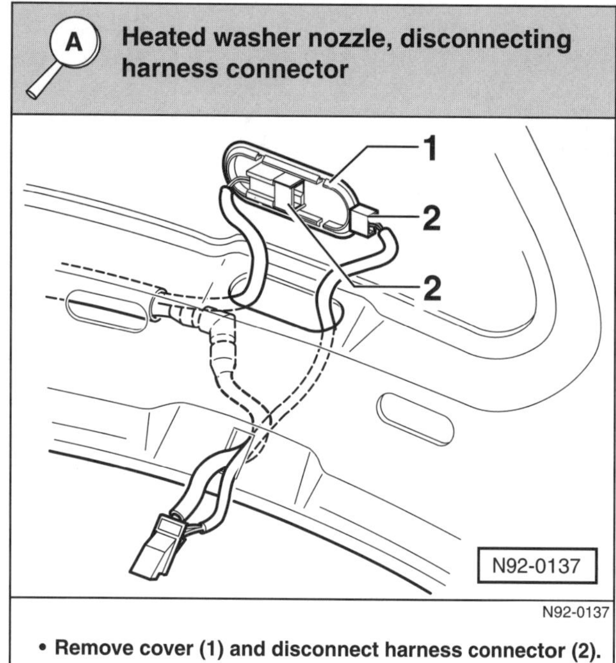

N92-0137

- Remove cover (1) and disconnect harness connector (2).

B Windshield washer jets, removing

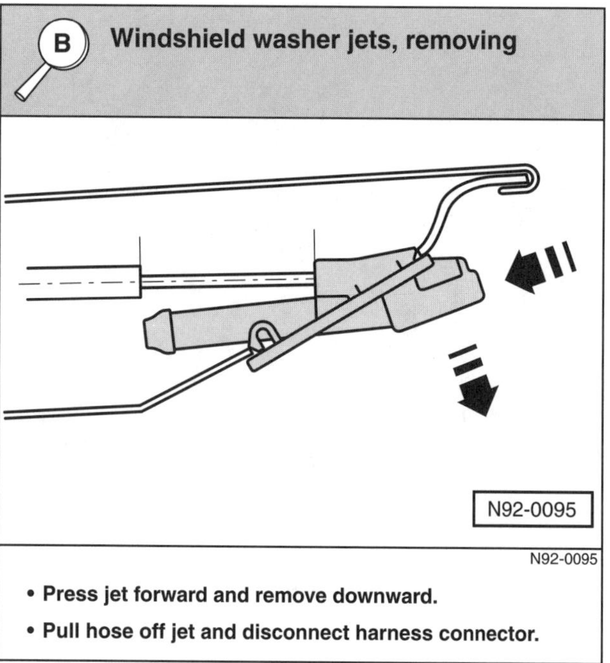

N92-0095

- Press jet forward and remove downward.
- Pull hose off jet and disconnect harness connector.

C Windshield washer system jets, checking

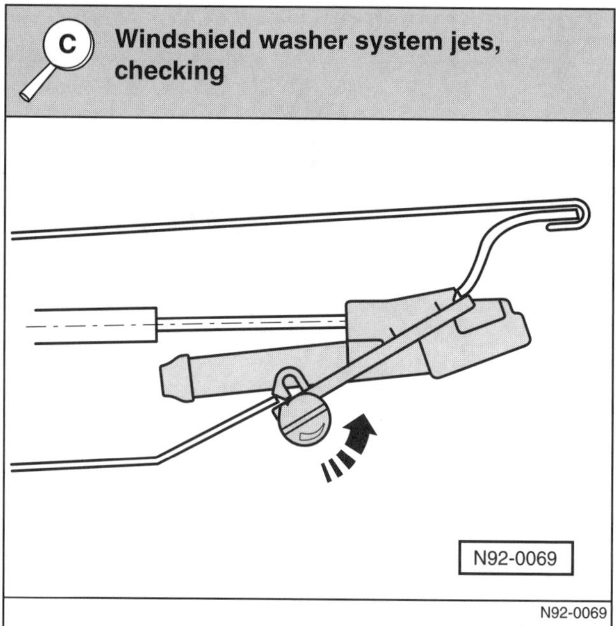

N92-0069

- The washer jets are preset but small height adjustments can be made.
- Using screwdriver, turn eccentric on spray jet in direction of arrow to move spray field on windshield upward.
- The spray jets must not be cleaned opposite to direction of spray, e.g. blown through from front.

94 Lights, Accessories–Exterior

GENERAL

This repair group covers removal, installation and replacing of the exterior lights and bulbs.

> ***CAUTION —***
> - *Before working on the electrical system disconnect battery ground (GND) strap from battery negative (–) terminal.*
> - *Be sure to have the anti-theft radio code on hand before disconnecting the battery.*
> - *Disconnecting the negative (–) battery cable may erase fault codes and basic settings in the engine management and automatic transmission control modules. Some driveability problems may be noticed until the system re-adapts to operating conditions. OBD II readiness codes, which may be required for emissions testing, may also be erased. Convenience electronics (alarm system, interior light control, power locks, mirrors, and windows) may need to be re-set using a VAG 1551/1552 or equivalent scan tool.*

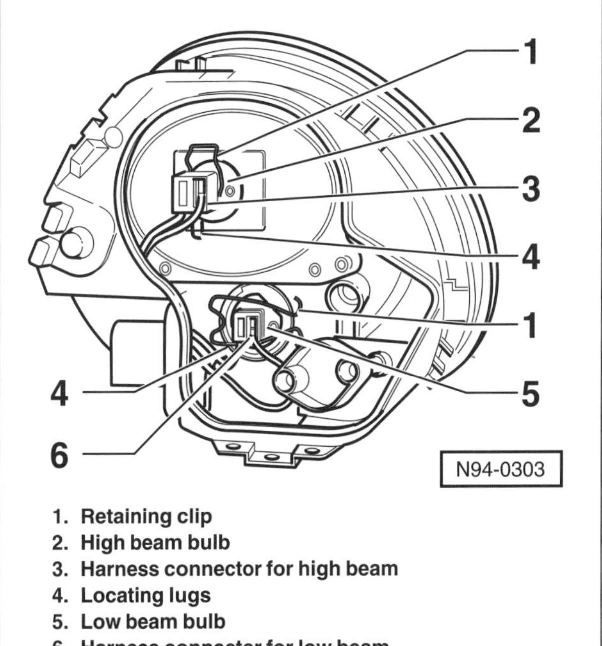

Fig. 1. Rear view of headlight assembly.

FRONT LIGHTS

Headlight bulb, replacing

1. Remove headlight assembly as described later.
2. Remove cover on rear of headlight assembly.
3. Disconnect harness connector from bulb.
4. Push spring retaining clip over locating lugs and move clip to side. See Fig. 1.
5. Pull bulb out from reflector.

> ***CAUTION —***
> *Do not touch the glass portion of the bulb with bare hands. The moisture and/or grease from fingers that evaporates on the bulb during operation, can cause the glass to cloud over.*

6. Insert new bulb so lugs on laminated plate align with grooves in reflector.
7. After installing new bulb check headlight aim as described later.

Headlights, component overview

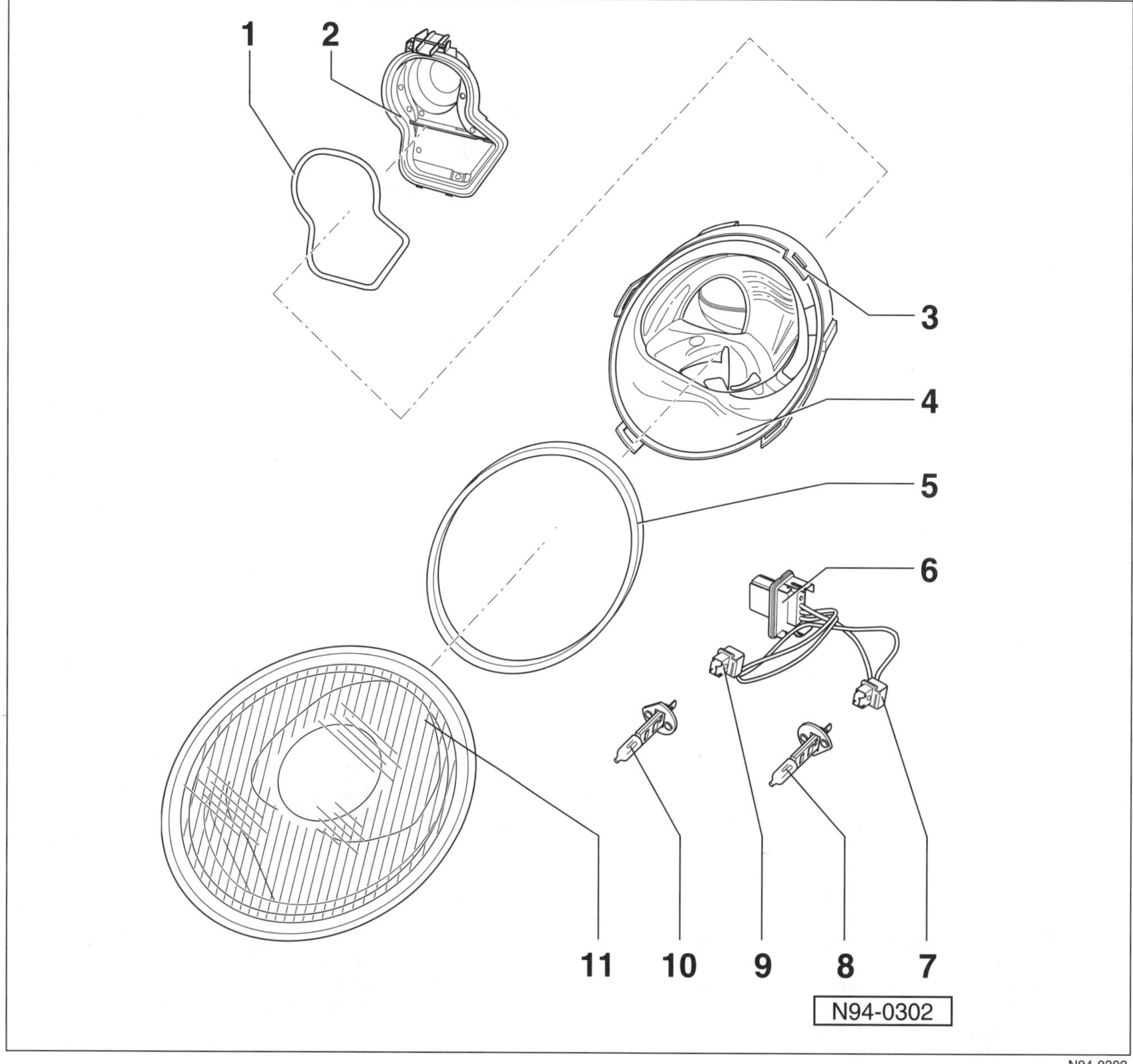

N94-0302

Fig. 2. Headlight assembly.

1. **Gasket**
   - Replace if damaged
2. **Cover**
3. **Retaining pockets**
   - Qty. 4
4. **Headlight housing**
5. **Gasket**
   - Replace if damaged
6. **Harness connector**
   - Clipped into headlight housing
7. **Harness connector for high beam bulb**
8. **High beam bulb**
   - H1 12 V, 60 Watt
9. **Harness connector for low beam bulb**
10. **Low beam bulb**
    - H7 12 V, 55 Watt
11. **Headlight glass**
    - Replace if gasket is faulty
    - Unclip retaining pocket tabs to remove

Headlights, removing and installing

1. Push up headlight release lever. See Fig. 3.

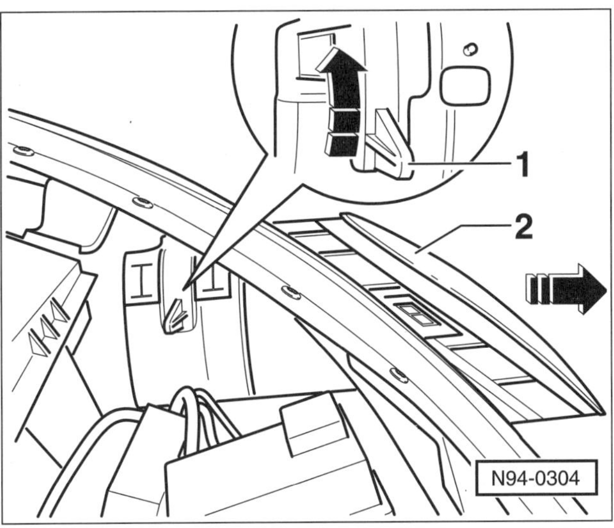

N94-0304

Fig. 3. Push up headlight release lever (**1**) and pull headlight forward. Driver side shown, passenger side is similar.

2. Pull headlight housing slightly forward enough to disconnect harness connectors from headlight.
3. Pull headlight housing out forward.
4. Begin installation by connecting harness connectors to headlight.
5. Insert headlight into guide tracks in fender and push inward. See Fig. 4.

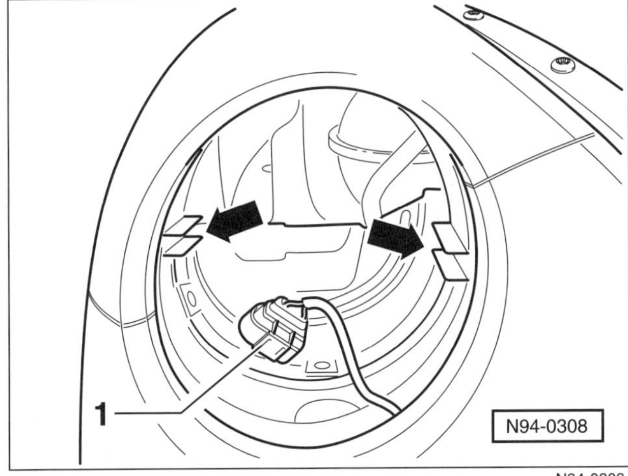

N94-0308

Fig. 4. Insert headlined into guide tracks (**arrows**) and push into fender.

6. Push down headlight release lever to lock headlight.
7. Check headlight aim.

Headlight aim, adjusting

Adjusting the headlights is best accomplished with a headlight adjusting unit. The height and lateral adjustment screws are shown in Fig. 5.

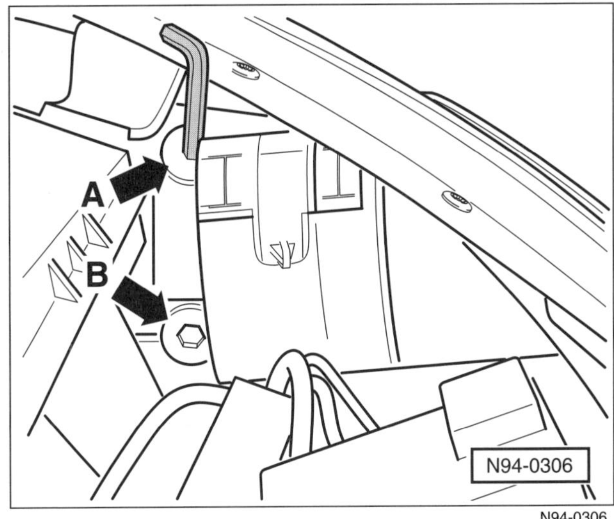

N94-0306

Fig. 5. Height adjustment (**A**) and lateral adjustment (**B**) on driver side headlight. Passenger side is oriented the same way.

Front turn signal and side marker lights

1. Remove screw cover and securing screw for lens
2. Pull turn signal out forward and disconnect harness connector.
3. Slide turn signal retaining tab into fender cut-out. See Fig. 6.

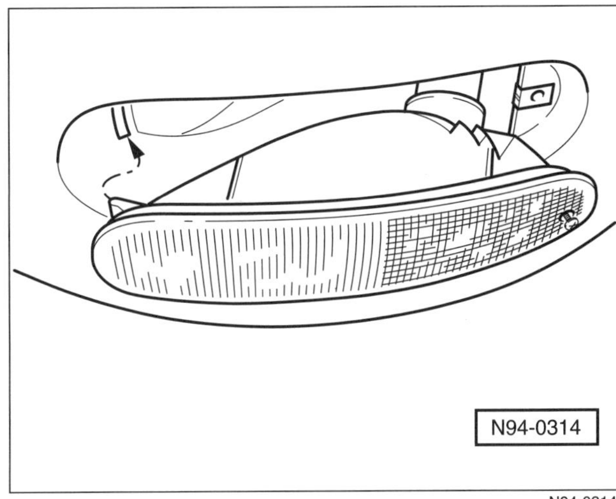

N94-0314

Fig. 6. Slide turn signal retaining tab into fender cut-out (**arrow**) when installing.

4. To replace bulb, turn bulb holder counterclockwise and pull out from housing. See Fig. 7.

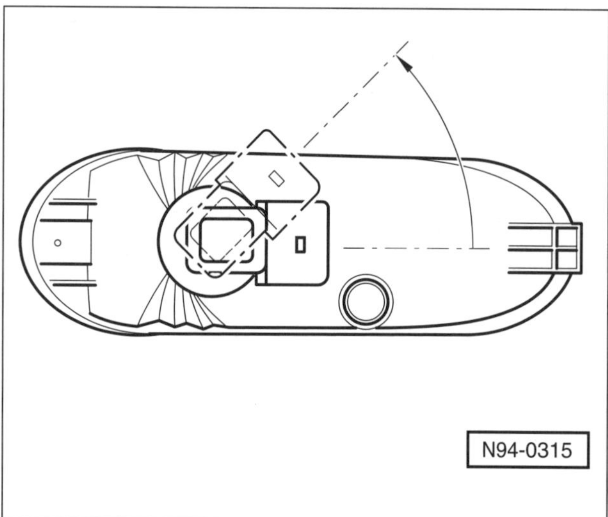

N94-0315

Fig. 7. Turn bulb holder in direction of **arrow** and pull out from housing.

5. Remove bulb from holder and replace.

> ***CAUTION—***
> *Do not touch the glass portion of the bulb with bare hands. The moisture and/or grease from fingers that evaporates on the bulb during operation, can cause the glass to cloud over.*

Fog light bulb, replacing

1. Pull harness connector off fog light rear cap.

2. Turn rear cap counterclockwise and pull down.

3. Disconnect unsheilded (ground) wire for fog light bulb. See Fig. 8.

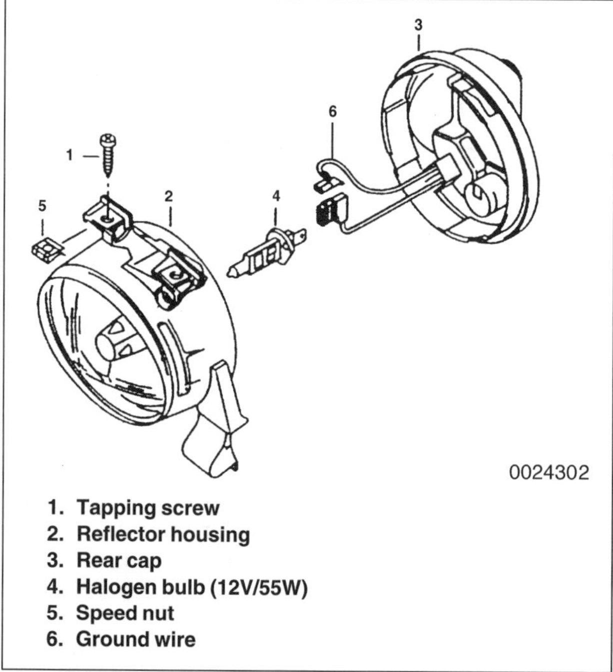

1. **Tapping screw**
2. **Reflector housing**
3. **Rear cap**
4. **Halogen bulb (12V/55W)**
5. **Speed nut**
6. **Ground wire**

0024302

Fig. 8. Fog light assembly.

4. Squeeze top of bulb retaining clip and rotate downward to release bulb from reflector housing.

5. Remove rear cap with bulb and replace bulb.

> ***CAUTION—***
> *Do not touch the glass portion of the bulb with bare hands. The moisture and/or grease from fingers that evaporates on the bulb during operation, can cause the glass to cloud over.*

6. Install in reverse order of removal.

REAR LIGHTS

Taillight assembly

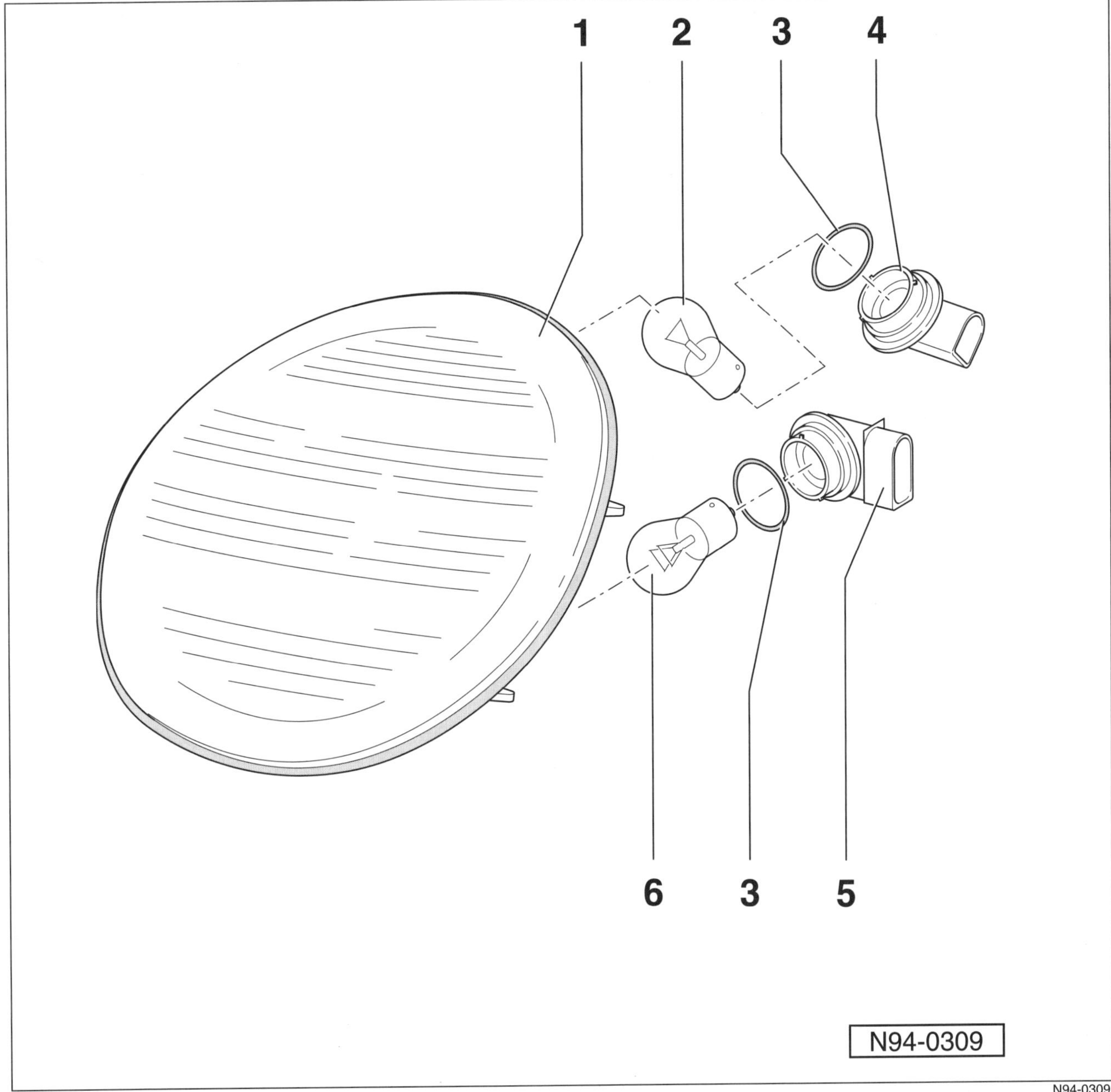

Fig. 9. Taillight assembly.

1. **Taillight housing**
   - Replace if gasket is faulty
2. **Turn signal bulb**
   - 12V/21W
3. **O-ring**
   - Replace if damaged
4. **Bulb holder for turn signal**
5. **Bulb holder for brake light and taillight**
6. **Dual filament bulb for brake light and taillight**
   - 12V/21W/5W

Taillights, removing and installing

1. Remove rear lock carrier trim, see **70 Trim–Interior**.
2. Reach behind quarter panel trim and unscrew knurled taillight mounting nut. Make sure washer and spacer do not fall down. See Fig. 10.

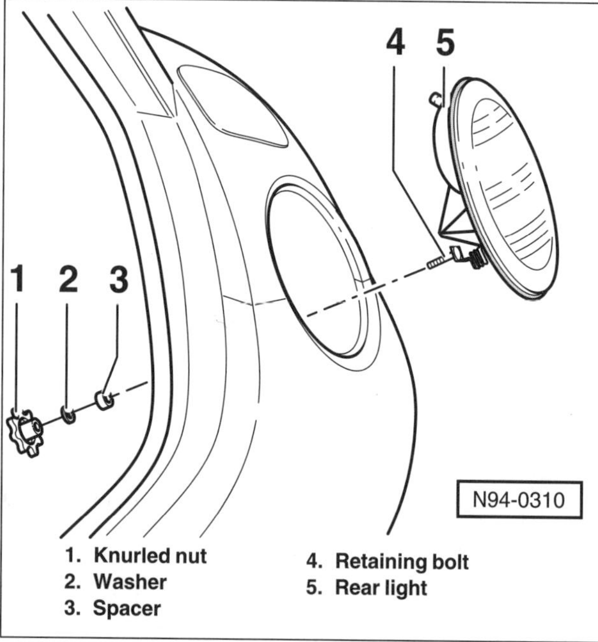

N94-0310

Fig. 10. Taillight assembly.

NOTE—

It may be necessary to remove the rear compartment trim panel(s) to access taillight knurled nut, see **70 Trim–Interior**.

3. Remove taillight and disconnect harness connector.
4. When installing, line up tab on outer edge of taillight to cut-out in fender.

Taillight bulbs, replacing

The procedure for removing and installing turn signal light bulbs is the same as that for brake light and taillight bulbs. Only the procedure for brake light and taillight bulbs is described here.

1. Remove taillight as described above.
2. Turn bulb holder counterclockwise and remove from housing. See Fig. 11.
3. Remove bulb from holder.

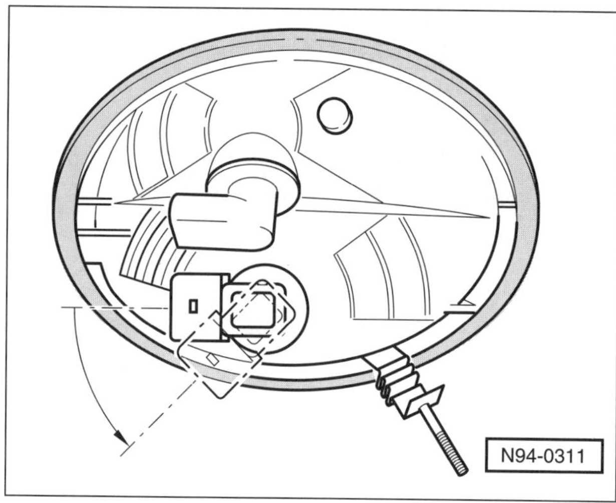

N94-0311

Fig. 11. Turn taillight bulb holder in direction of **arrow** to remove.

CAUTION—

Do not touch the glass portion of the bulb with bare hands. The moisture and/or grease from fingers that evaporates on the bulb during operation, can cause the glass to cloud over.

Rear side marker lights

1. Remove rear inner wheel housing liner, see **66 Body Exterior Equipment**.
2. On inner side of bumper, carefully press retainer clip and remove side marker housing. See Fig. 12.

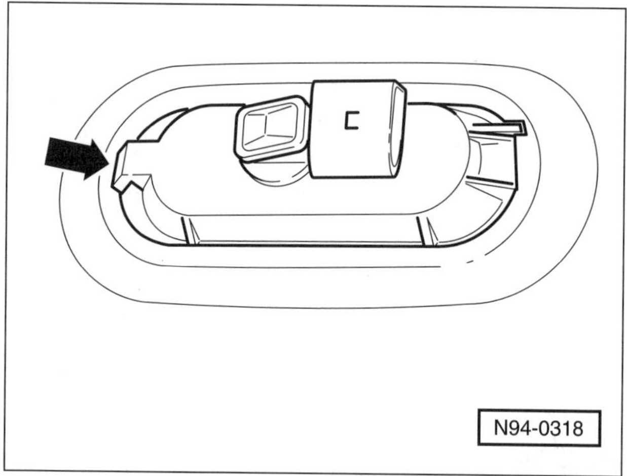

N94-0318

Fig. 12. Press retaining clip in direction of **arrow** to remove marker light.

3. Disconnect harness connector.

4. To install, insert side marker light into bumper and click in place, make sure locating tab is seated correctly in cutout.

5. To remove rear side marker light bulb, turn bulb holder counterclockwise and pull out from housing. See Fig. 13.

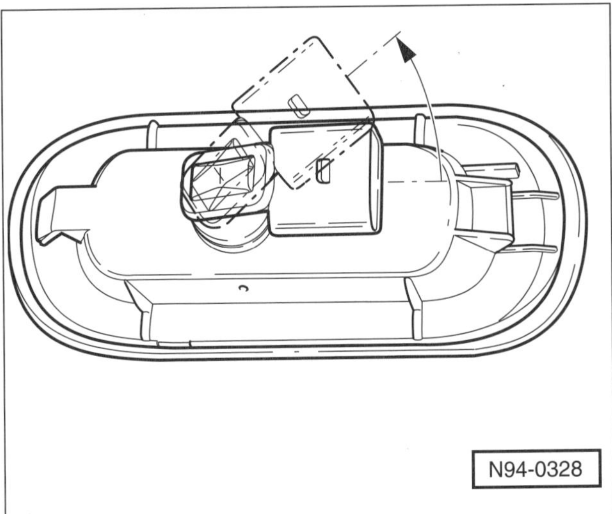

N94-0328

Fig. 13. Turn bulb holder in direction of **arrow** to remove.

6. Pull out bulb (12V/5W), do not turn.

> ***CAUTION—***
> *Do not touch the glass portion of the bulb with bare hands. The moisture and/or grease from fingers that evaporates on the bulb during operation, can cause the glass to cloud over.*

Back-up lights

1. Remove retaining nuts from inside rear bumper. See Fig. 14.

2. Remove back-up lights toward rear and disconnect harness connector from back-up lights.

3. To remove bulb, turn bulb holder counterclockwise and pull out from housing.

> ***CAUTION—***
> *Do not touch the glass portion of the bulb with bare hands. The moisture and/or grease from fingers that evaporates on the bulb during operation, can cause the glass to cloud over.*

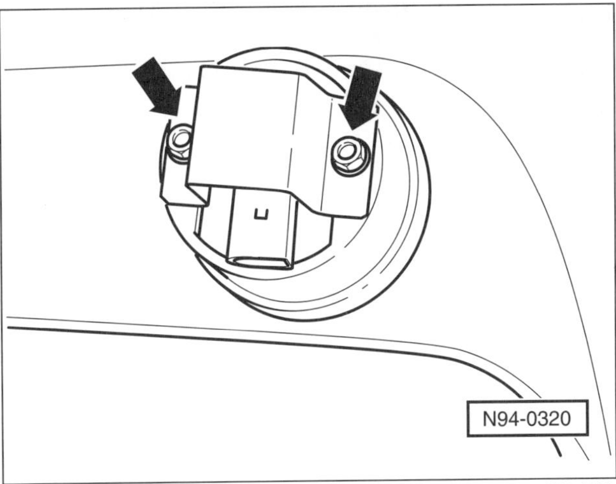

N94-0320

Fig. 14. Remove back-up light retaining nuts (**arrows**) from inside rear bumper.

Center brake light

1. Remove rear trim cover, see **70 Trim–Interior**.

2. Unscrew mounting screws for center brake light. See Fig. 15.

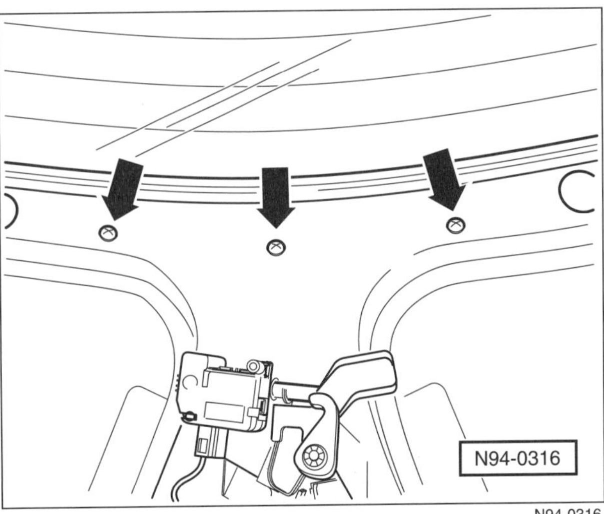

N94-0316

Fig. 15. Unscrew center brake light mounting screws (**arrows**).

3. Remove brake light upward and disconnect harness connector.

4. Installation is reverse of removal.

License plate light

1. Carefully pry out license plate light with suitable tool, until retaining tab releases. See Fig. 16.

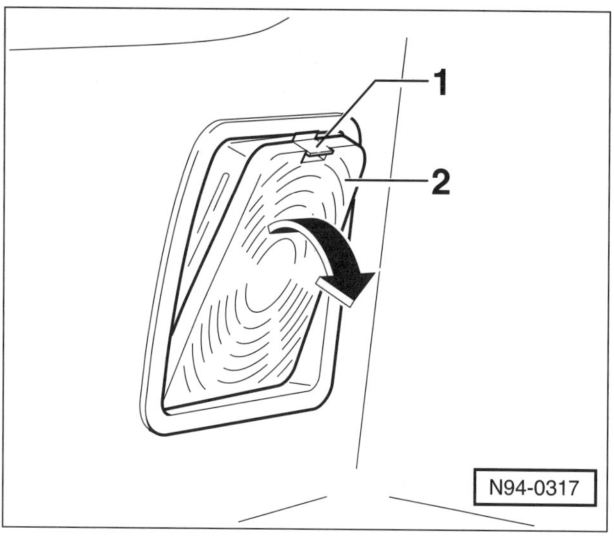

N94-0317

Fig. 16. Pry out license plate light (**2**) until retaining tab (**1**) releases.

2. Remove license plate light and disconnect harness connector.

3. To remove bulb, turn bulb holder counterclockwise and pull out from housing.

> ***CAUTION —***
> *Do not touch the glass portion of the bulb with bare hands. The moisture and/or grease from fingers that evaporates on the bulb during operation, can cause the glass to cloud over.*

QUALITY REVIEW

When you have finished working under the hood and around other areas of the vehicle, it is advisable to take a moment to quality check or review your work. This helps to insure that the operation or repair has been completed properly with all affected systems functioning within normal parameters. These may include the following:

- Ensure that all cable ties and clamps that were removed as part of the repair are replaced.
- Ensure that all fasteners and hardware were replaced and torqued as specified.
- Make sure that all other components involved in the repair are positioned correctly, properly torqued and function properly.
- Make sure that all tools, shop cloths, fender covers and protective tapes are removed before closing the hood.
- Clean grease and fingerprints from painted surfaces, steering wheel, upholstery and shifter.
- Unlock anti-theft radio and reset the clock.
- Check operation of all exterior lights with a helper if necessary.

96 Lights, Accessories–Interior

GENERAL

This section covers electrical light switches and accessories located in the passenger compartment. Items such as radio, heating and A/C that require detailed coverage have their own repair groups. See **97 Wiring Diagrams, Fuses and Relays** for additional information.

> ***CAUTION —***
> - *Before working on electrical system disconnect negative (–) battery cable.*
> - *Before disconnecting battery be sure to obtain radio anti-theft code.*

INTERIOR LIGHTS AND SWITCHES

> ***NOTE —***
> - *The luggage compartment light switch is integrated into the trunk lock and cannot be replaced separately. If the luggage compartment light switch is faulty the complete trunk lock must be replaced, see* **70 Trim–Interior**.
> - *The door contact switch is integrated into the door lock and cannot be replaced individually. The complete door lock must be replaced if the door contact switch is faulty, see* **70 Trim–Interior**.
> - *For steering column switches, see* **48 Steering**.

Light switch, removing and installing

1. Turn rotary knob of light switch to "0" position.

2. Press rotary knob inward and turn slightly to right. See Fig. 1.

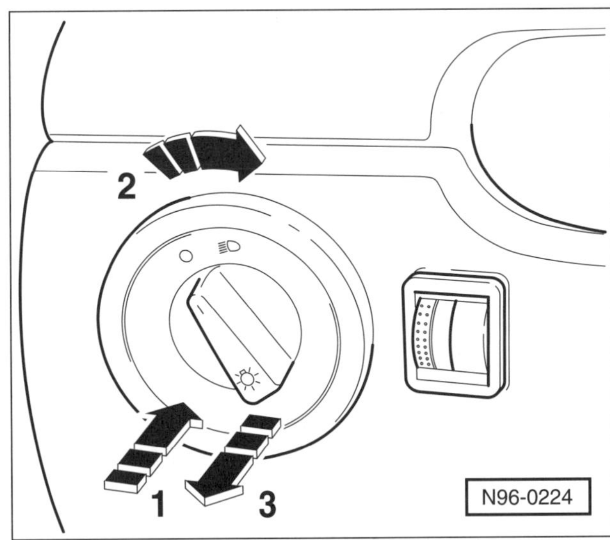

N96-0224

Fig. 1. Turn light switch to "0" position, press knob inward (**arrow 1**), turn slightly to right (**arrow 2**), pull on knob to remove (**arrow 3**).

3. Hold rotary knob in this position, pull on rotary knob and remove light switch from instrument panel.

4. Disconnect harness connector.

5. To install, first connect harness connector.

6. Hold light switch and press rotary knob inward and turn slightly to left. See Fig. 2.

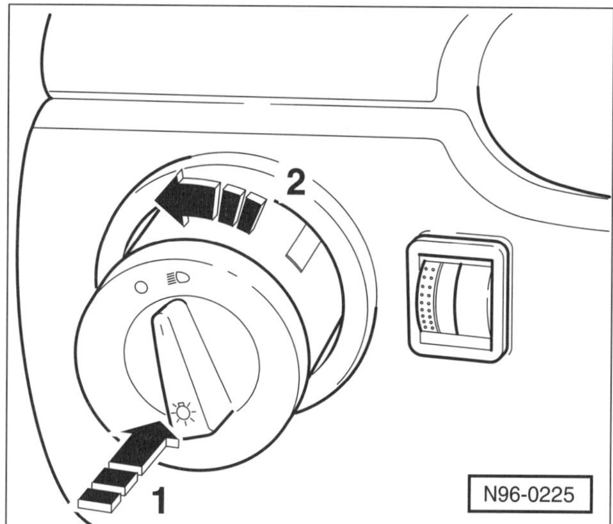

N96-0225

Fig. 2. To install light switch, press knob inward (**arrow 1**), turn slightly to left (**arrow 2**) and slide into instrument panel.

7. Hold rotary knob in this position and slide light switch into instrument panel.

8. Turn rotary knob to "0" position, release and engage switch.

Instrument panel light dimmer switch, removing and installing

1. Place screwdriver behind switch housing and pry switch carefully out of locking device. See Fig. 3.

2. Disconnect harness connector.

3. To install, first connect harness connector.

4. Insert switch into locking device and engage.

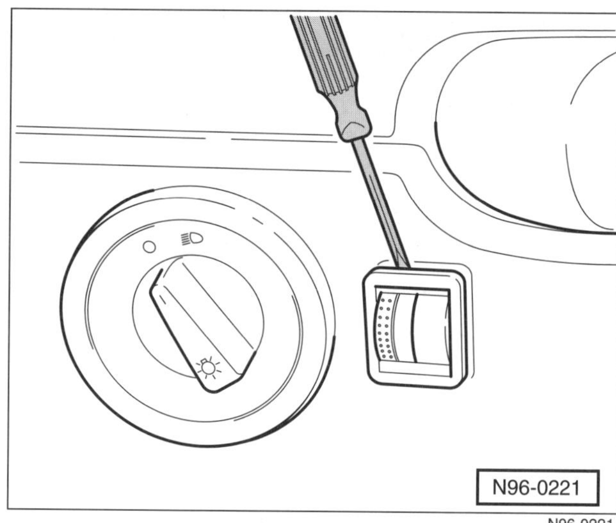

N96-0221

Fig. 3. Dimmer switch being removed from instrument panel.

Mirror adjustment switch, removing and installing

1. Remove interior door trim, see **70 Trim–Interior**.

2. Disconnect harness connector from switch.

3. Pry mounting frame outward on long side of switch and remove switches from mounting frame. See Fig. 4.

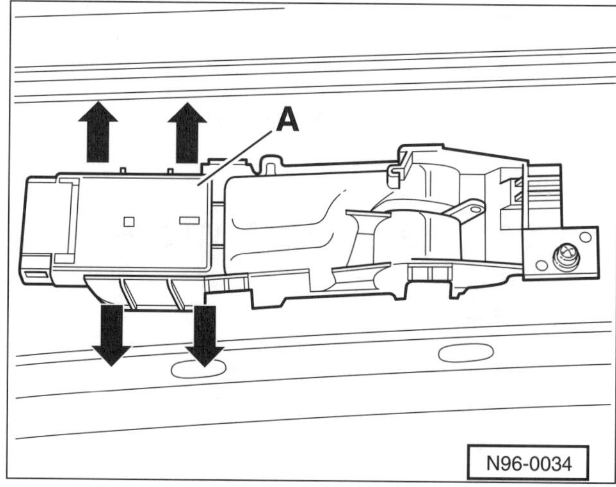

N96-0034

Fig. 4. Pry mounting frame outward (**arrows**) to remove mirror adjustment switch (**A**).

4. To install, insert switch in mounting frame and engage.

5. Connect harness connector.

6. Install interior door trim.

Interior lock switch–passenger side, removing and installing

1. Remove interior door trim, see **70 Trim–Interior**.
2. Disconnect harness connector from switch.
3. Release switch housing by pressing sideways out from locking device in mounting frame and remove. See Fig. 5.

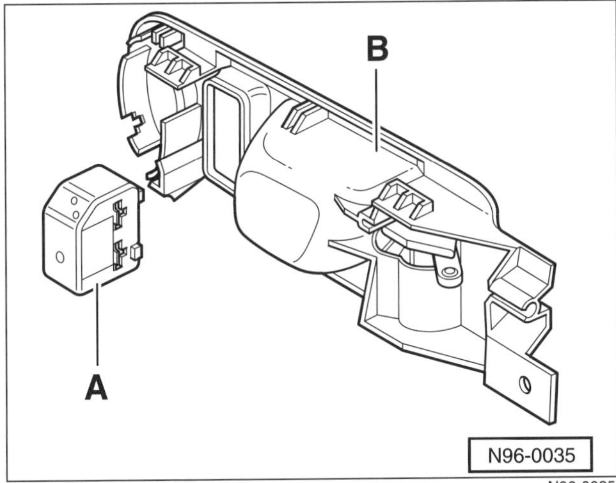

Fig. 5. Release interior lock switch housing (**A**) by pressing sideways out from mounting frame locking device (**B**).

4. To install, first connect harness connector.
5. Insert switch in recess of mounting frame and engage.
6. Install door trim.

Remote fuel tank door/rear lid unlock switch, removing and installing

NOTE —
The switches for remote/fuel tank door and remote unlock rear trunk lid cannot be removed separately. The complete switch unit must be removed and replaced, if necessary.

1. Remove interior door trim, see **70 Trim–Interior**.
2. Disconnect harness connector from switch.
3. Release switch housing by pressing sideways on locking tabs and remove from door trim. See Fig. 6.

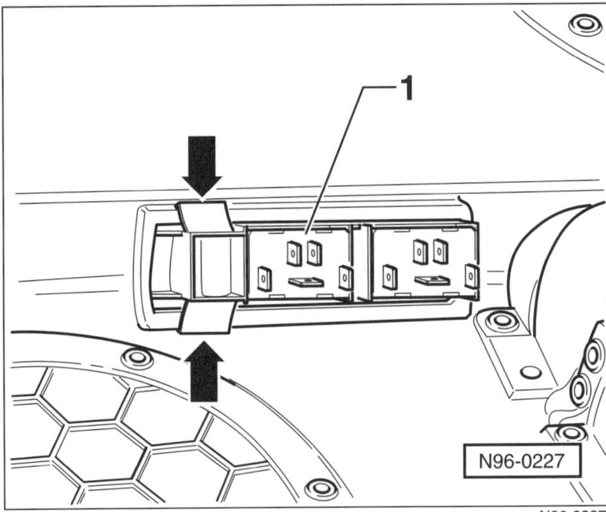

Fig. 6. Release remote fuel tank door/rear lid switch housing (**1**) by pressing sideways on locking tabs (**arrows**) and remove from door trim.

4. To install, insert switch into door trim and engage.
5. Connect harness connector.
6. Install door trim.

Instrument panel switches–center, removing and installing

NOTE —
- *Removing and installing is the same procedure for all switches. Only the hazard warning light switch is described here.*
- *The switch must be pulled out from the instrument panel in order to disconnect harness connector.*
- *A wooden or plastic wedge should be used to prevent damage to plastic trim and adjacent switches.*

1. Protect instrument panel and adjacent switches with adhesive tape if necessary.

2. Press in adjacent switch and carefully pry out switch using flat plastic wedge or screwdriver. See Fig. 7.

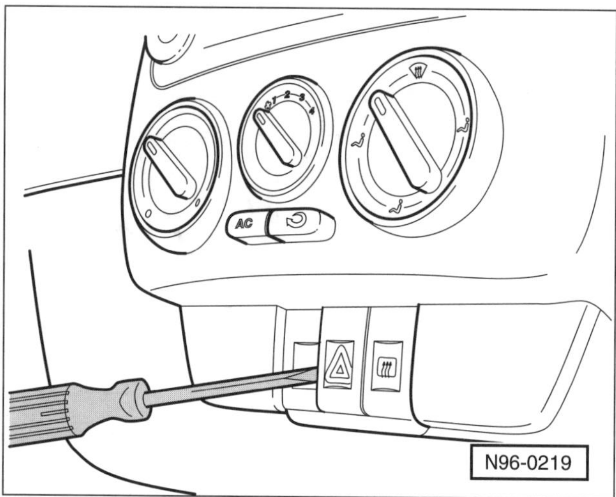

N96-0219

Fig. 7. Hazard warning light switch being pried out of instrument panel.

3. Release connections and disconnect harness connector from applicable switch.

4. To install, first connect harness connector.

5. Insert switch into mounting and engage properly.

Interior light, removing and installing

1. Carefully pry lens out from bottom of interior mirror and remove. See Fig. 8.

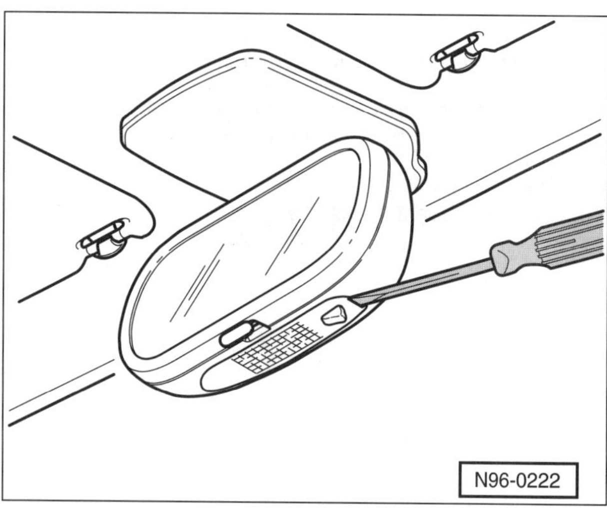

N96-0222

Fig. 8. Pry interior light lens out from bottom of mirror.

2. Disconnect harness connector from light.

3. Replace 12V/3W bulb, if necessary.

4. To install, connect harness connector to interior light.

5. Insert lens and engage properly.

Glove compartment light, removing and installing

1. Insert screwdriver behind lens and carefully pry lens out. See Fig. 9.

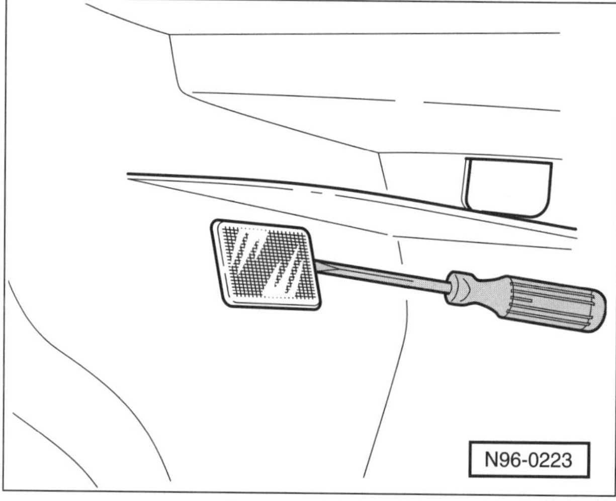

N96-0223

Fig. 9. Glove compartment light being removed.

2. Remove lens with bulb holder.

3. Disconnect harness connector from light.

4. Replace 12V/3W bulb, if necessary.

5. To install, first connect harness connector.

6. Insert lens with bulb holder into glove compartment and engage properly.

> ***NOTE—***
> *After working on the glove compartment light, ensure that the light does not stay on when the glove compartment door is closed.*

Make-up mirror light, removing and installing

> ***NOTE—***
> *The procedures for removing left make-up-mirror light and right make-up mirror light are identical.*

1. Insert screwdriver behind lens and carefully pry lens out. See Fig. 10.

2. Remove lens with bulb holder.

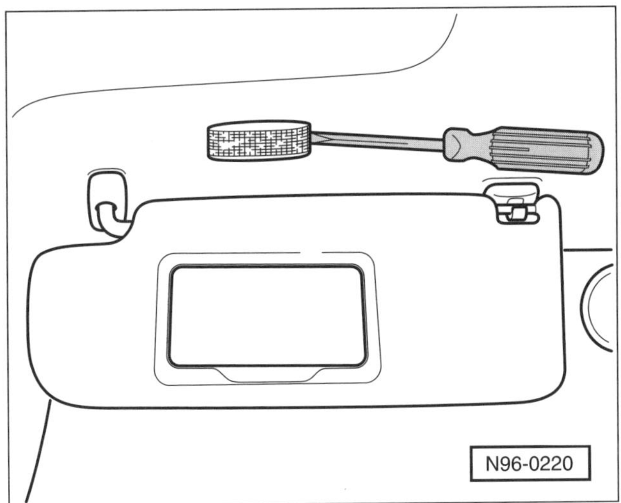

Fig. 10. Make-up mirror light being removed.

3. Disconnect harness connector.

4. Replace 12V/3W bulb, if necessary.

5. To install, first connect harness connector.

6. Insert lens with bulb holder into headliner and engage properly.

Luggage compartment light, removing and installing

1. Insert screwdriver behind lens and carefully pry lens out. See Fig. 11.

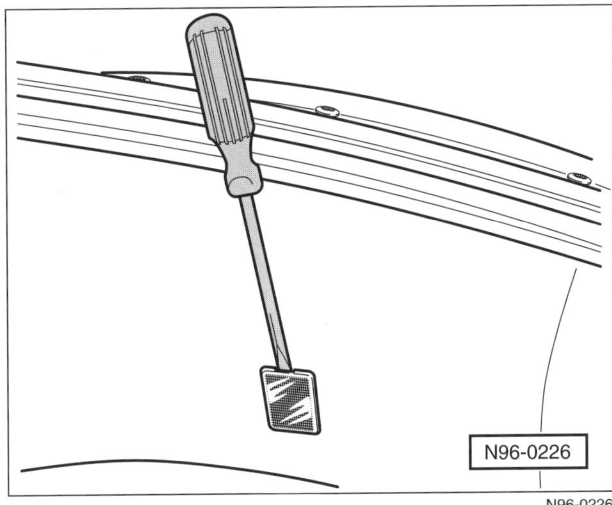

Fig. 11. Luggage compartment light being removed.

2. Remove lens with bulb holder.

3. Disconnect harness connector from light.

4. Replace 12V/3W bulb, if necessary.

5. To install, connect harness connector.

6. Insert lens with bulb holder into mounting and engage properly.

NOTE —
After working on the luggage compartment light ensure that the light does not stay on when the rear hatch is closed.

Brake light switch, removing and adjusting

The brake light switch is located above brake pedal in pedal bracket.

CAUTION —
Shut off engine and apply parking brake before removing brake light switch.

NOTE —
- *It is necessary to first remove brake light switch to adjust it.*
- *Once removed, the brake light switch plunger should extend fully out. If not, switch is defective.*

1. Remove brake light switch by rotating it 90° clockwise.

2. Press brake pedal down as far as possible by hand.

3. Guide brake light switch through pedal bracket opening until plunger contacts brake pedal.

4. Lock in position by turning 90° counter-clockwise.

5. Release brake pedal and check function of brake lights.

QUALITY REVIEW

When you have finished working under the hood and around other areas of the vehicle, it is advisable to take a moment to quality check or review your work. This helps to insure that the operation or repair has been completed properly with all affected systems functioning within normal parameters. These may include the following:

- Ensure that all cable ties and clamps that were removed as part of the repair are replaced.
- Ensure that all fasteners and hardware were replaced and torqued as specified.
- Make sure that all other components involved in the repair are positioned correctly, properly torqued and function properly.
- Make sure that all tools, shop cloths, fender covers and protective tapes are removed before closing the hood.
- Clean grease and fingerprints from painted surfaces, steering wheel, upholstery and shifter.

97 Wiring Diagrams, Fuses and Relays

TABLES

GENERAL

This section contains wiring diagrams for 1998 through 1999 m.y. New Beetles. Also included here are the fuse and relay positions and the ground locations.

> ***WARNING —***
> *Special airbag precautions apply to any electrical system testing or repair. the airbag unit is an explosive device and must be handled with extreme care. Before starting any work on the vehicle, refer to the warnings and cautions in* **69 Seatblets, Airbags**.

> ***CAUTION —***
> - *Before working on the elctrical system always switch the ignition off and disconnect battery ground strap from battery negative (–) terminal.*
> - *Be sure to have the anti-theft radio code on hand before disconnecting the battery.*
> - *Disconnecting the negative (–) battery cable may erase fault codes and basic settings in the engine management and automatic transmission control modules. Some driveability problems may be noticed until the system re-adapts to operating conditions. OBD II readiness codes, which may be required for emissions testing, may also be erased.*
> - *Always switch test meter to the appropriate function and range before making test connections.*

> ***NOTE —***
> *The Society of Automotive Engineers (SAE) has implemented standardized terms for automotive components, including alternator which should always be referred to as a generator.*

FUSES AND RELAYS

Fuse panels

The central electric panel (fuse panel) is located behind an acces panel on left edge of the instrument panel. It contains both standard size fuses and mini-fuses. The use of mini-fuses allows protection of individual circuits.

There is also a main fuse box located on top of the battery in the engine compartment. It contains special fuses for high current applications and prevents the main wiring harness in the event of a short circuit. See Fig. 1. To access these fuses, squeeze tabs of plastic fuse cover and pull upward.

NOTE —
Volkswagen identifies electrical components by a letter and/or a number in the electrical schematics. These electrical identifiers are listed in parenthesis as an aid to electrical troubleshooting.

Main fuse box on top of battery

- Standard fuse applications
  - Coolant fan, single speed (S180) 30A
  - ABS (S179). 30A
  - ABS (S178). 30A
- Metal fuse applications
  - Generator (S177) 150A
  - Vehicle electrical system (S176). 110A
  - Coolant fan, two-speed (S164) 40A
  - Fuel pump relay or glow plug relay (S163) 50A
  - Secondary air injection relay or coolant pre-heating relays (S162). 50A

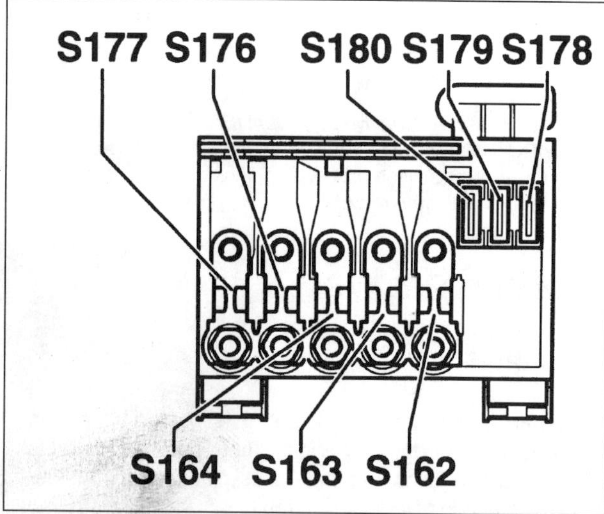

0024315

Fig. 1. Main fuse box on top of battery with fuse identification.

WARNING —
Metal fuses in the main fuse box should be changed by an authorized Volkswagen service professional.

The fuses in the central electric panel are identified in **Table a**.

NOTE —
- *Fuse application and amperage may vary depending on equipment level.*
- *All fuses are identified in the wiring diagrams with the prefix of S, i.e. fuse #4 is S4.*
- *"RES" in the central electric panel refers to reserve, or places for spare fuses.*

Fuse colors and amperage

- Green 30A
- White 25A
- Yellow 20A
- Blue 15A
- Red. 10A
- Brown 7.5A
- Beige 5A
- Violet 3A

Table a. Fuse identification

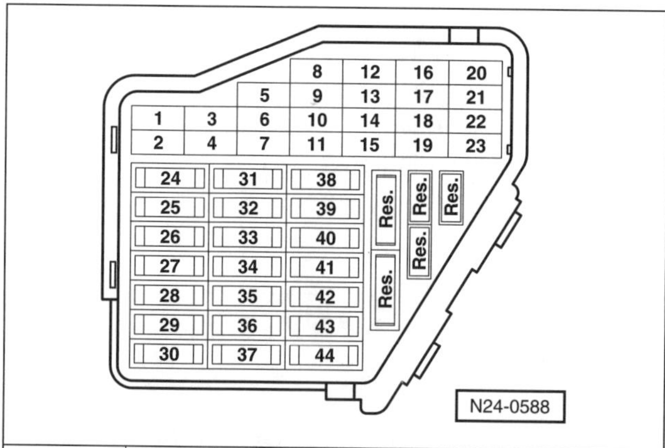

Position	Description	Amperage
1	Heated washer nozzles, mirrors	10
2	Turn signal system	10
3	Illumination	5
4	License plate light	5
5	Comfort system	7.5
6	Central locking system	5
7	Back-up lights	10
8	Telephone system (future option)	5
9	ABS	5
10	Engine control, gasoline	10
11	Instrument cluster, shift lock	5
12	B+ (battery positive voltage) for DLC	7.5
13	Brake lights	10
14	Interior lights, with central locking Interior lights, only	10 5
15	Instrument cluster, automatic trans.	5
16	A/C clutch	10
17	Door lock heater (future option)	7.5
18	High beam right	10
19	High beam left	10
20	Low beam right	10
21	Low beam left	10
22	Tail and side marker lights, right	5

Table a. Fuse identification

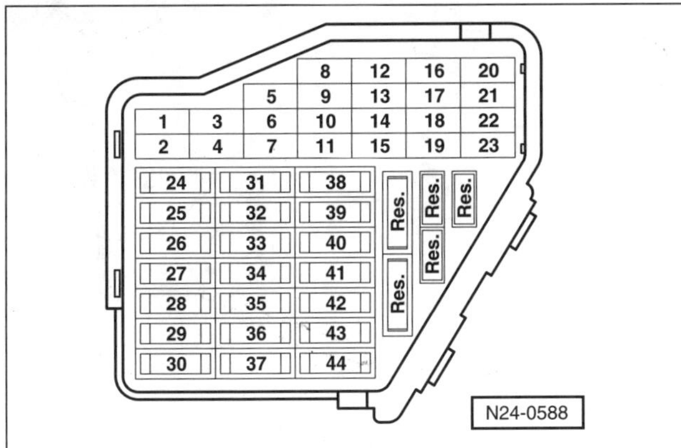

Position	Description	Amperage
23	Tail and side marker lights, left	5
24	Wiper system, washer pump	20
25	Fresh air blower	25
26	Rear window defogger	20
27	Daytime running lights	10
28	Fuel pump, gasoline	15
29	Engine control, gasoline Engine control, diesel	15 10
30	Sunroof	20
31	Automatic tranmission	20
32	Engine control, injectors, gasoline Engine control, injectors, diesel	10 15
33	Headlight washer system	20
34	Engine control	10
35	Trailer socket	30
36	Fog lights	15
37	Radio system	10
38	Luggage compartment light, central locking system	15
39	Emergency flasher system	15
40	Dual horn	20
41	Cigarette lighter	15
42	Radio system	25
43	Engine control	10
44	Heated seats	15

NOTE —

Fuses number 23 through 44 are identified in the wiring diagrams with an additional prefix of 2, i.e. fuse #40 is S240.

- *Some fuse or relay positions may be empty if equipment is not installed in vehicle.*

Relay positions

The relay panel is located under the left side of the instrument panel. There are three fuse positions on the relay panel which are identified in **Table b**. The relays are also identified in **Table b**.

Table b. Relay panel identification

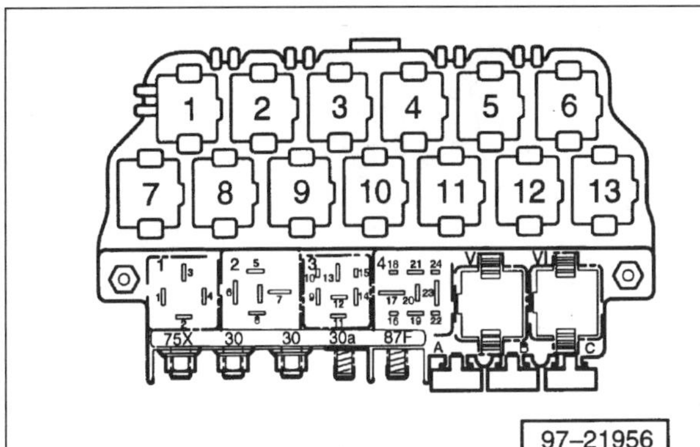

Position	Description	Number on relay
	Lower relay panel	
1	Dual horn relay	204
2	Load reduction relay	213
3	open	
4	Fuel pump relay	208
V	Wiper/Washer intermittent relay	377
VI	Wiper/Washer intermittent relay	377
	Fuses on lower relay panel	
A	Fuse for power windows (red connector)	-
B	open	-
C	Fuse for heated seats (black connector)	-
	Relays on upper (auxiliary) relay panel	
1	Fog light relay	381
2	Rear lid remote unlock motor relay	79
3	Anti-theft starter lock relay	186
4	Starter lock out relay (clutch)	53
5	open	-
6	Radio speaker/telephone change-over relay (future option)	-
7	open	
8	Daytime running lights change-over relay	173
9	open	-
10	Glow plug relay	180
11	Park/Nuetral position relay	175
12	Power supply (terminal 30b, B+) relay	109
13	Coolant fan control relay	53

GROUND LOCATIONS

Various ground locations are identified in Fig. 2, 3, and 4. Be sure to inspect these for clean tight connections when troubleshooting electrical problems.

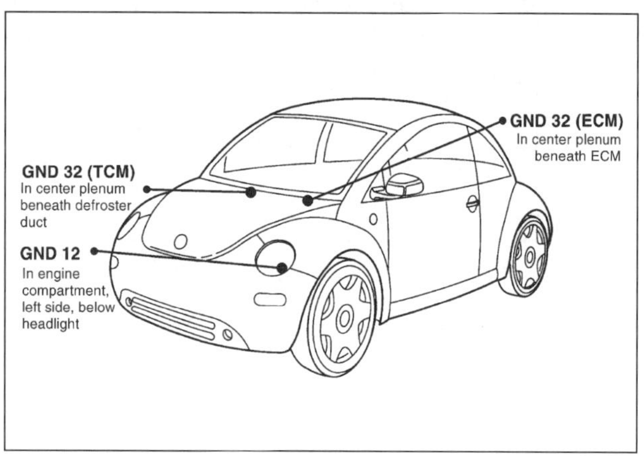

Fig. 2. Ground locations in the engine compartment.

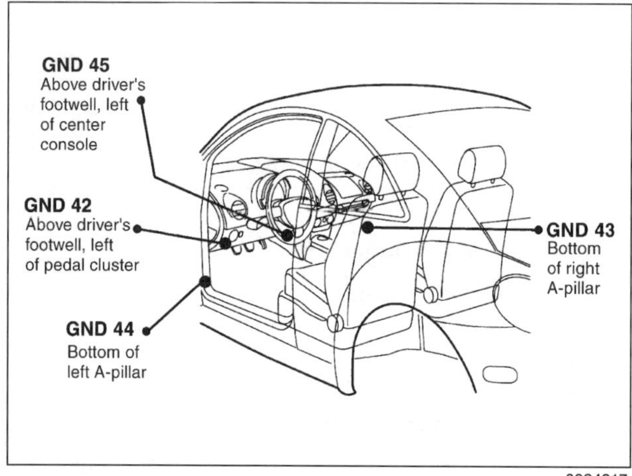

Fig. 3. Ground locations inside vehicle.

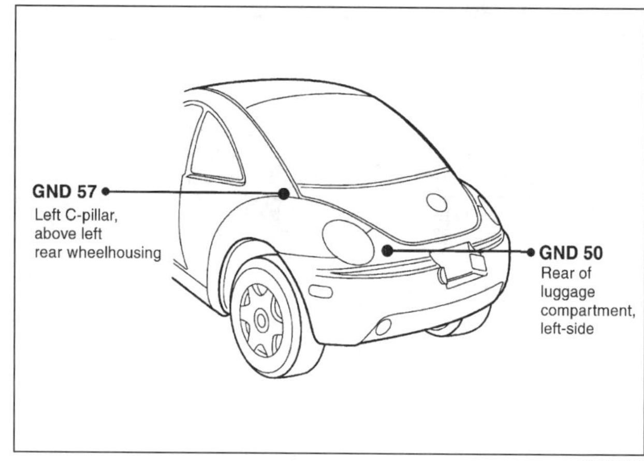

Fig. 4. Ground locations in rear of vehicle.

USING WIRING DIAGRAMS

The wiring diagrams are oriented on the pages in a 2-up horizontal format in order to facilitate easier tracking of the various circuits which frequently run across several pages.

Please take a few minutes to review the next few pages as the information has been updated for this latest Volkswagen platform.

This electrical wiring diagram section has been organized based on the way the electrical wiring diagrams were originally distributed. Each wiring diagram page appears in its original and complete form, including original page numbers or technical bulletin numbers. In addition, every page contains a unique Repair Manual page number to facilitate indexing and easy access to individual circuits.

The electrical wiring diagram section has several comprehensive indexes designated by model year and identified by black page tabs. These indexes list the various components and electrical systems on a particular vehicle model, or systems that are common to all models. The actual wiring diagrams themselves follow the indexes.

The diagram below shows important wiring diagram information.

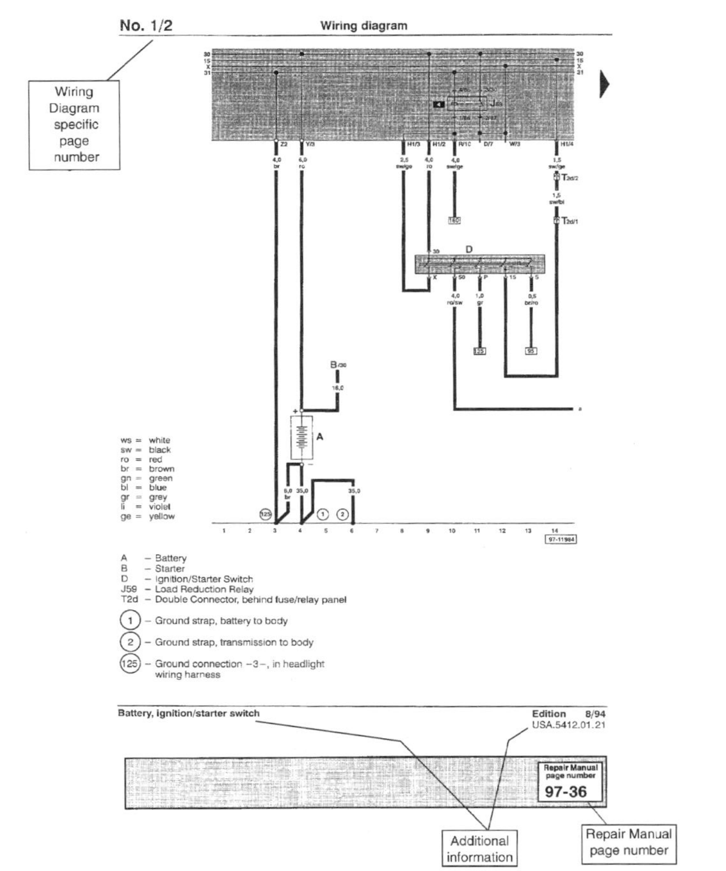

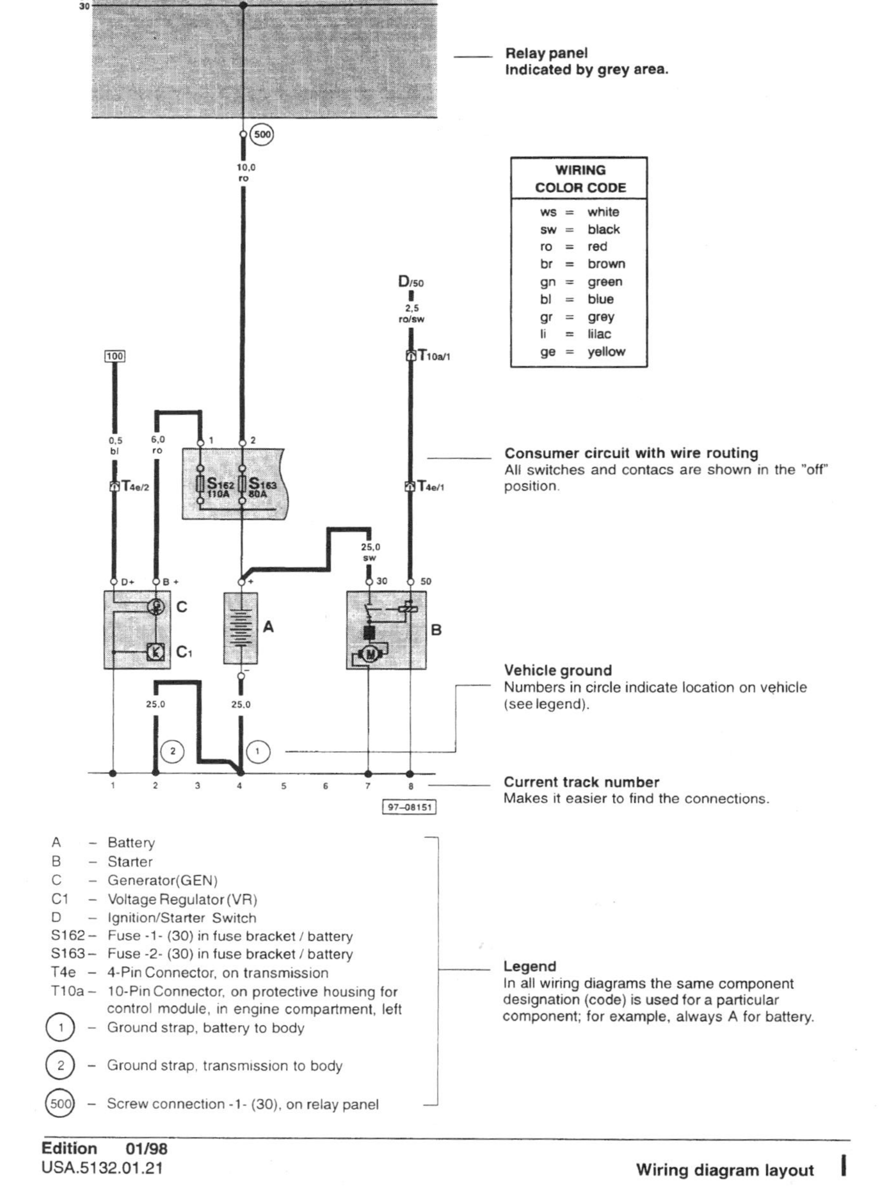

Relay panel
Indicated by grey area.
WIRING COLOR CODE
ws = white
sw = black
ro = red
br = brown
gn = green
bl = blue
gr = grey
li = lilac
ge = yellow
Consumer circuit with wire routing
All switches and contacs are shown in the "off" position.
Vehicle ground
Numbers in circle indicate location on vehicle (see legend).
Current track number
Makes it easier to find the connections.
97-08151
Legend
In all wiring diagrams the same component designation (code) is used for a particular component; for example, always A for battery.

A – Battery
B – Starter
C – Generator(GEN)
C1 – Voltage Regulator (VR)
D – Ignition/Starter Switch
S162 – Fuse -1- (30) in fuse bracket / battery
S163 – Fuse -2- (30) in fuse bracket / battery
T4e – 4-Pin Connector, on transmission
T10a – 10-Pin Connector, on protective housing for control module, in engine compartment, left
(1) – Ground strap, battery to body
(2) – Ground strap, transmission to body
(500) – Screw connection -1- (30), on relay panel

Edition 01/98
USA.5132.01.21

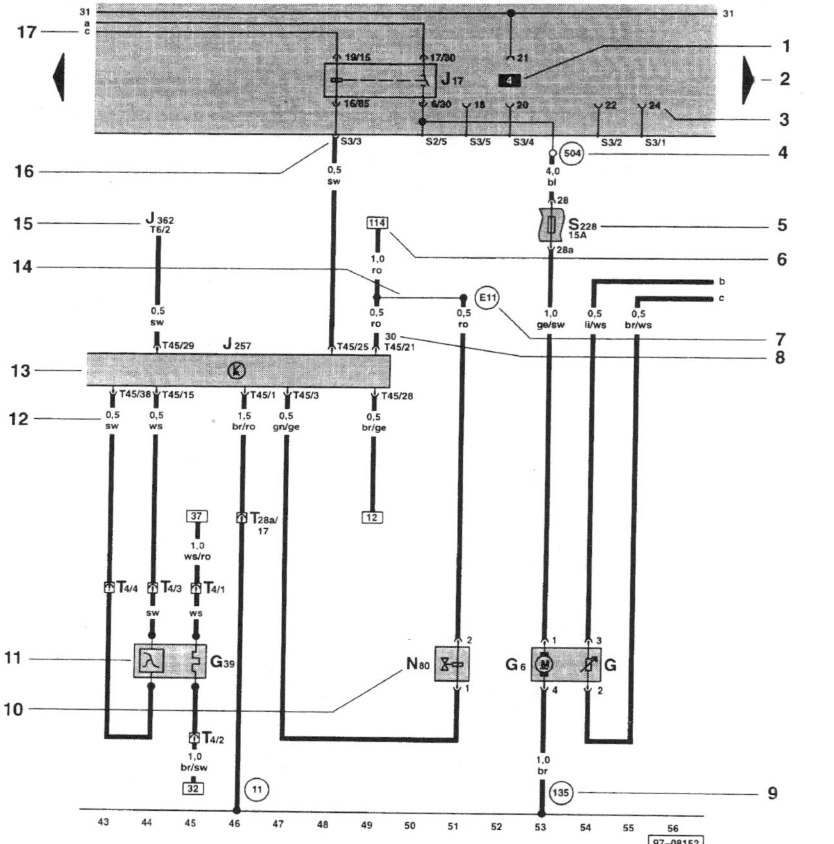

1 – **Relay location number**
Indicates location on relay panel.

2 – **Arrow**
Indicates wiring circuit is continued on the previous and/or next page.

3 – **Connection designation – relay control module on relay panel**
Shows the individual terminals in a multi-point connector.
For example: contact 24 on terminal **4** on relay panel.

4 – **Diagram of threaded pin on relay panel**
White circle shows a detachable connection.

5 – **Fuse designation**
For example: S228 = Fuse number 228, 15 amps, in relay panel

6 – **Reference of wire continuation (current track number)**
Number in frame indicates current track where wire is continued.

7 – **Wire connection designation in wiring harness**
Location of wire connections are indicated in the legend.

8 – **Terminal designation**
Designation which appears on actual component and/or terminal number of a multi-point connector

9 – **Ground connection designation in wire harness**
Locations of ground connections are indicated in legend.

10 – **Component designation**
Use legend at bottom of page to identify the component code.

11 – **Component symbols (see Symbols used in wiring diagrams)**

12 – **Wire cross-section size (in mm^2) and wire colours**
Abbreviations are explaining in colour chart beside the wiring diagram.

13 – **Component symbol with open drawing side**
Indicated component is continued on another wiring diagram. The number of corresponding wiring diagram can taken from list of contents.

14 – **Internal connections (thin lines)**
These connections are **not** wires. Internal connections are current carrying and are listed to allow tracing of current flow inside components and wiring harness.

15 – **Reference of continuation of wire to component**
For example: Control module for anti-theft immobilizer J362 on 6-Pin Connector, terminal 2

16 – **Relay panel connectors**
Shows wiring of multi-point or single connectors on relay panel
For example: S3/3 – Multi-point connector S3, terminal 3

17 – **Reference of internal connection continuation**
Letters indicate where connection continues on the previous and/or next page.

Wiring diagram terminal (circuit) identification

Several wiring circuits in the vehicle's electrical system are identified with a number or letter designation. These circuits are identified the same in all wiring diagrams and are most commonly shown near the top of each page in the fuse/relay panel portion of the wiring diagram. The circuit designations may also be used to identify switch connector terminals (switch circuits). Following are the most common numbered/lettered circuits:

Terminal (circuit) 1-	Ignition coil/ignition distributor low voltage (typically used as an Engine Speed (RPM) signal for the tachometer)
Terminal (circuit) 15-	Switched Battery Positive Voltage (B+) from ignition/starter switch
Terminal (circuit) 30-	Battery Positive Voltage (B+), hot at all times
Terminal (circuit) 31-	Ground (GND)
Terminal (circuit) 50-	Starter control; switched B+ from ignition/starter switch
Terminal (circuit) 56-	Switched headlight B+ from light switch
Terminal (circuit) 58-	Switched parking light, taillight, illumination B+ from light switch
Terminal (circuit) S (SU)-	Key in ignition circuit; switched B+ from ignition/starter switch
Terminal (circuit) X-	Load reduction circuit; switched B+ from load reduction relay

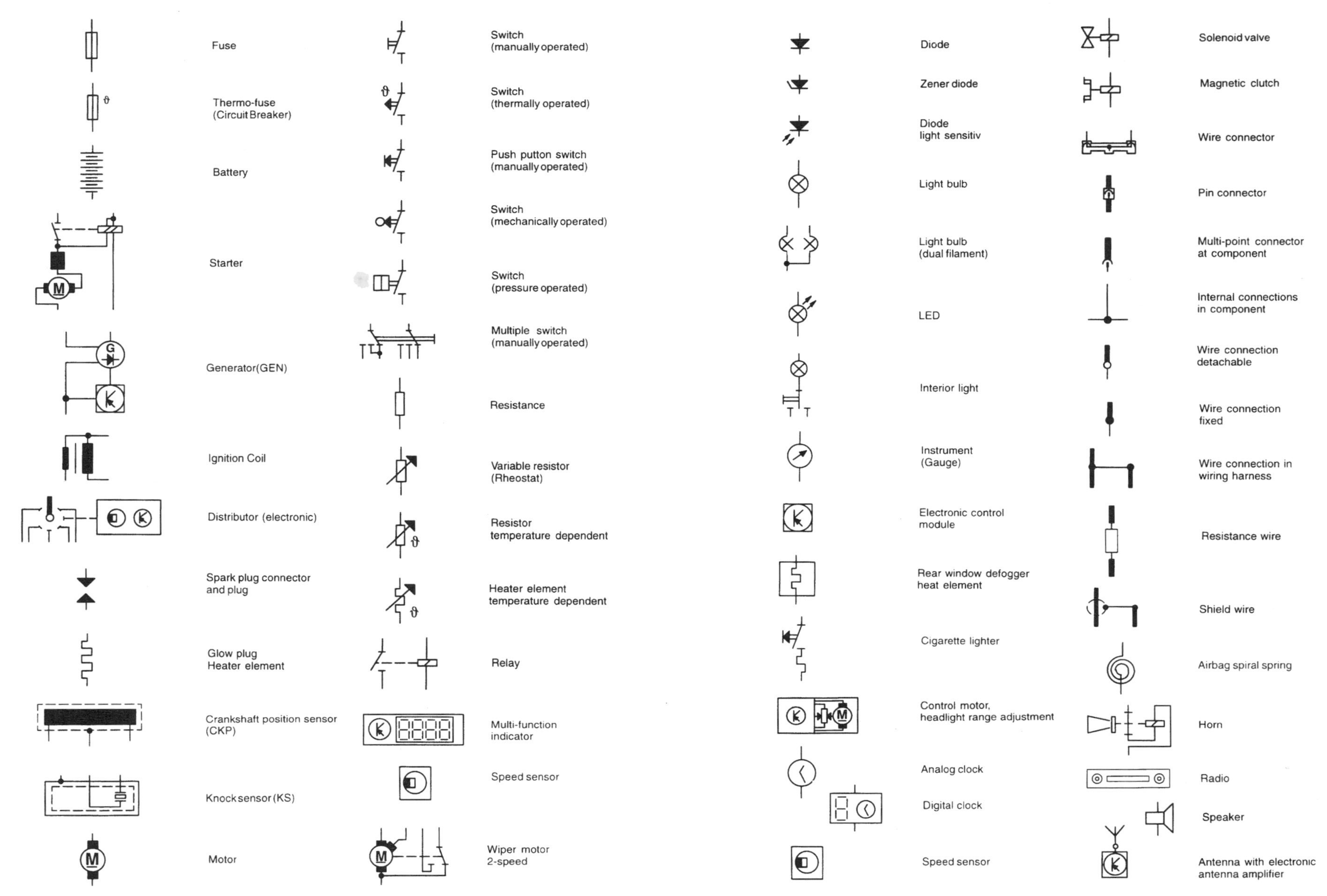
Fuse
Thermo-fuse
(Circuit Breaker)
Battery
Starter
Generator(GEN)
Ignition Coil
Distributor (electronic)
Spark plug connector
and plug
Glow plug
Heater element
Crankshaft position sensor
(CKP)
Knock sensor (KS)
Motor
Switch
(manually operated)
Switch
(thermally operated)
Push putton switch
(manually operated)
Switch
(mechanically operated)
Switch
(pressure operated)
Multiple switch
(manually operated)
Resistance
Variable resistor
(Rheostat)
Resistor
temperature dependent
Heater element
temperature dependent
Relay
Multi-function
indicator
Speed sensor
Wiper motor
2-speed
Diode
Zener diode
Diode
light sensitiv
Light bulb
Light bulb
(dual filament)
LED
Interior light
Instrument
(Gauge)
Electronic control
module
Rear window defogger
heat element
Cigarette lighter
Control motor,
headlight range adjustment
Analog clock
Digital clock
Speed sensor
Solenoid valve
Magnetic clutch
Wire connector
Pin connector
Multi-point connector
at component
Internal connections
in component
Wire connection
detachable
Wire connection
fixed
Wire connection in
wiring harness
Resistance wire
Shield wire
Airbag spiral spring
Horn
Radio
Speaker
Antenna with electronic
antenna amplifier

Symbols used in wiring diagrams

Electrical Wiring Diagram Index

Standard equipment, from Jan. 1998

	Wiring Diagram page number	Repair Manual page number
● **New Beetle Standard Equipment, from January 1998**	1/1	97-19
– Battery, load reduction relay, fuses in fuse bracket/battery	1/2	97-20
– Ignition/starter switch, lock relay for starter (theft warning system), locking relay for starter (clutch pedal switch)	1/3	97-21
– Instrument cluster, warning buzzer for light switched on, generator (GEN) warning light	1/4	97-22
– Instrument cluster, tachometer, low fuel level warning light, odometer display	1/5	97-23
– Instrument cluster, brake fluid level warning switch, turn signal indicator lights, headlight high beam indicator light, rear fog light indicator light	1/6	97-24
– Turn signal switch, headlight dimmer/flasher switch	1/7	97-25
– Emergency flasher switch with turn signal relay, right low and high beam headlights, light for turn signal and sidemarker, front, right	1/8	97-26
– Brake light switch, back-up light switch, left back-up light, left brake/tail light, high-mount brake light, side blinker	1/9	97-27
– Luggage compartment light, right rear turnsignal light, right back-up light, right brake/tail light, sidemarker light, right, rear	1/10	97-28
– Data Link Connector (DLC), radio connection	1/11	97-29
– Ashtray light, cigarette lighter, cigarette lighter light, motor for fuel tank lid unlock, switch for remote/fuel tank door	1/12	97-30
– Light switch, left rear fog light	1/13	97-31
– Dual horns, instrument light dimmer switch, glove compartment light, license plate light	1/14	97-32
– Fresh air blower, fresh air blower switch	1/15	97-33
– Heated rear window, rear window defogger switch, parking brake warning light switch daytime running lights change-over relay	1/16	97-34
– Windshield wiper/washer switch, windshield wiper motor, windshield wiper/washer intermittent relay,	1/17	97-35

2.0L engine (code AEG), without cruise control, from Jan. 1998

	Wiring Diagram page number	Repair Manual page number
● **New Beetle (2,0L-Engine – Motronic Multiport Fuel Injection (MFI)/85 kW), code AEG, (without cruise control) from January 1998**	2/1	97-37
– Starter, generator (GEN)	2/2	97-38
– Motronic engine control module (ECM), ignition system	2/3	97-39
– Motronic engine control module (ECM), throttle valve control module camshaft position (CMP) sensor, engine coolant temperature (ECT) sensor	2/4	97-40
– Motronic engine control module (ECM), engine speed (RPM) sensor, knock sensor (KS) 1, knock sensor (KS) 2	2/5	97-41
– Motronic engine control module (ECM), fuel injectors, heated oxygen sensor (HO2S) 2, positive crankcase ventilation (PCV) heating element	2/6	97-42
– Heated oxygen sensor (HO2S), mass air flow (MAF) sensor, evaporative emission (EVAP) canister purge regulator valve, secondary air injection (AIR) system	2/7	97-43
– Motronic engine control module (ECM), diagnosis pump for fuel system, secondary air injection solenoid valve	2/8	97-44
– Oil pressure switch, fuel pump (FP), fuel pump (FP) relay, engine coolant level sensor, speedometer vehicle speed sensor	2/9	97-45
– Instrument cluster, fuel gauge, engine coolant temperature (ECT) gauge, tachometer, generator (GEN) warning light, oil pressure warning light	2/10	97-46

1.9L engine (code ALH) from Jan. 1998

1998 additional electrical wiring diagrams

Electrical Wiring Diagram Index

2.0L engine (code AEG), without cruise control, from Aug. 1998

	Wiring Diagram page number	Repair Manual page number
● **New Beetle (2,0L-Engine – Motronic Multiport Fuel Injection (MFI)/85 kW), code AEG,** (without cruise control) from August 1998	19/1	97-135
– Starter, generator (GEN))	19/2	97-136
– Motronic engine control module (ECM), ignition system	19/3	97-137
– Motronic engine control module (ECM), throttle valve control module camshaft position (CMP) sensor, engine coolant temperature (ECT) sensor	19/4	97-138
– Motronic engine control module (ECM), engine speed (RPM) sensor, knock sensor (KS) 1, knock sensor (KS) 2	19/5	97-139
– Motronic engine control module (ECM), fuel injectors, heated oxygen sensor (HO2S) 2, positive crankcase ventilation (PCV) heating element	19/6	97-140
– Heated oxygen sensor (HO2S), mass air flow (MAF) sensor, evaporative emission (EVAP) canister purge regulator valve, secondary air injection (AIR) system	19/7	97-141
– Motronic engine control module (ECM), diagnosis pump for fuel system, secondary air injection solenoid valve	19/8	97-142
– Oil pressure switch, fuel pump (FP), fuel pump (FP) relay, engine coolant level sensor, speedometer vehicle speed sensor	19/9	97-143
– Instrument cluster, fuel gauge, engine coolant temperature (ECT) gauge, tachometer, generator (GEN) warning light, oil pressure warning light	19/10	97-144

Standard equipment from Aug. 1998

	Wiring Diagram page number	Repair Manual page number
● **New Beetle Standard Equipment, from August 1998**	21/1	97-159
– Battery, load reduction relay, fuses in fuse bracket/battery	21/2	97-160
– Ignition/starter switch, lock relay for starter (theft warning system), locking relay for starter (clutch pedal switch)	21/3	97-161
– Instrument cluster, warning buzzer for light switched on, generator (GEN) warning light	21/4	97-162
– Instrument cluster, tachometer, low fuel level warning light, odometer display	21/5	97-163
– Instrument cluster, brake fluid level warning switch, turn signal indicator lights, headlight high beam indicator light, rear fog light indicator light	21/6	97-164
– Turn signal switch, headlight dimmer/flasher switch	21/7	97-165
– Emergency flasher switch with turn signal relay, right low and high beam headlights, light for turn signal and sidemarker, front, right	21/8	97-166
– Brake light switch, back-up light switch, left back-up light, left brake/tail light, high-mount brake light, side blinker lights	21/9	97-167
– Luggage compartment light, right rear turnsignal light, right back-up light, right brake/tail light, sidemarker light, right, rear	21/10	97-168
– Data Link Connector (DLC), radio connection	21/11	97-169
– Ashtray light, cigarette lighter, cigarette lighter light, motor for fuel tank lid unlock, switch for remote/fuel tank door	21/12	97-170
– Light switch, left rear fog light	21/13	97-171
– Dual horns, instrument light dimmer switch, glove compartment light, license plate light	21/14	97-172
– Fresh air blower, fresh air blower switch	21/15	97-173
– Heated rear window, rear window defogger switch, parking brake warning light switch daytime running lights change-over relay	21/16	97-174
– Windshield wiper/washer switch, windshield wiper motor, windshield wiper/washer intermittent relay,	21/17	97-175

1999 additional electrical wiring diagrams

NOTE —

For 1999 m.y. 1.9L engine (code ALH), use the wiring diagrams for 1.9L engine (code ALH) from Jan. 1998 on Repair Manual page number 97-13 as a reference. As of the editiorial closing date of this manual specific electrical wiring diagrams for the 1999 m.y. 1.9L engine (code ALH) were not available from Volkswagen.

THIS PAGE INTENTIONALLY LEFT

BLANK

New Beetle – Standard Equipment,

from January 1998

97-21956

Relay location on the thirteen position auxiliary relay panel, above relay panel:

- **3** Lock relay for starter (theft warning system) (185)
- **4** Lock relay for starter (clutch pedal switch) (53)
- **8** Daytime Running Lights Change-over Relay (173)

Relay panel:

- **1** Dual Horn Relay (53)
- **2** Load Reduction Relay (100)
- **4** Fuel Pump (FP) Relay (409)
- **V** Wiper/Washer Intermittent Relay (377)
- **VI** Wiper/Washer Intermittent Relay (377)

Note: Number in parentheses indicates production control number stamped on relay housing.

Fuse colors
30 A – green
25 A – white
20 A – yellow
15 A – blue
10 A – red
7,5 A – brown
5 A – beige

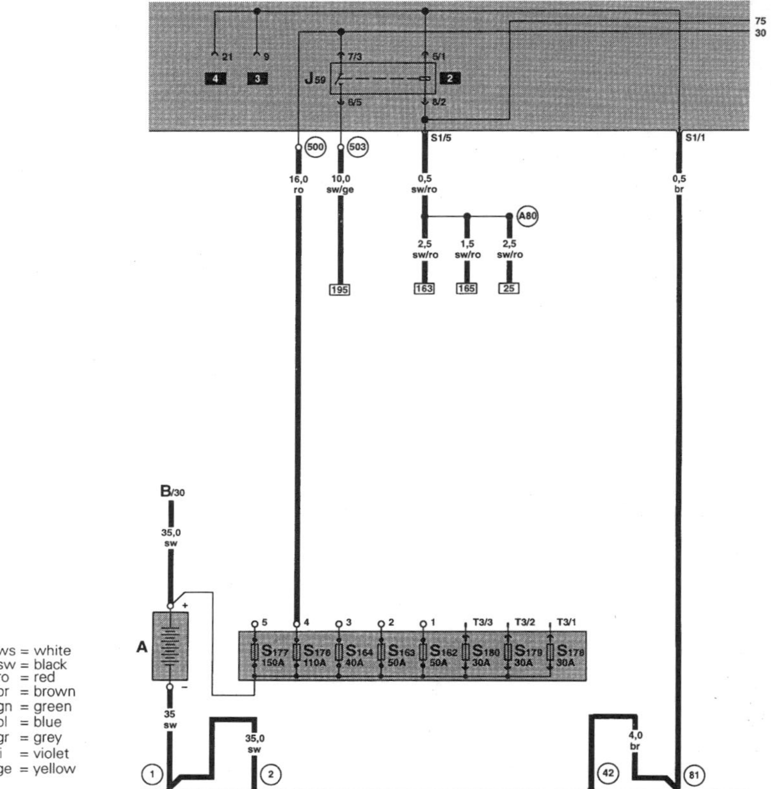

ws = white
sw = black
ro = red
br = brown
gn = green
bl = blue
gr = grey
li = violet
ge = yellow

A – Battery
B – Starter
J59 – Load Reduction Relay
S162 – Fuse -1- in fuse bracket/battery
S163 – Fuse -2- in fuse bracket/battery
S164 – Fuse -3- in fuse bracket/battery
S176 – Fuse -4- (30), in fuse bracket/battery
S177 – Fuse -5- (30), in fuse bracket/battery
S178 – Fuse -6- (30), in fuse bracket/battery
S179 – Fuse -7- (30), in fuse bracket/battery
S180 – Fuse -8- (30), in fuse bracket/battery

(1) – Ground strap, battery to body
(2) – Ground strap, transmission to body

(42) – Ground connection, beside steering column
(81) – Ground connection -1-, in instrument panel wiring harness
(500) – Threaded connection -1- (30) on the relay plate
(503) – Threaded connection -1- (75x) on the relay plate
(A80) – Connector -1- (X), in instrument panel wiring harness

Battery, load reduction relay, fuses in fuse bracket/battery

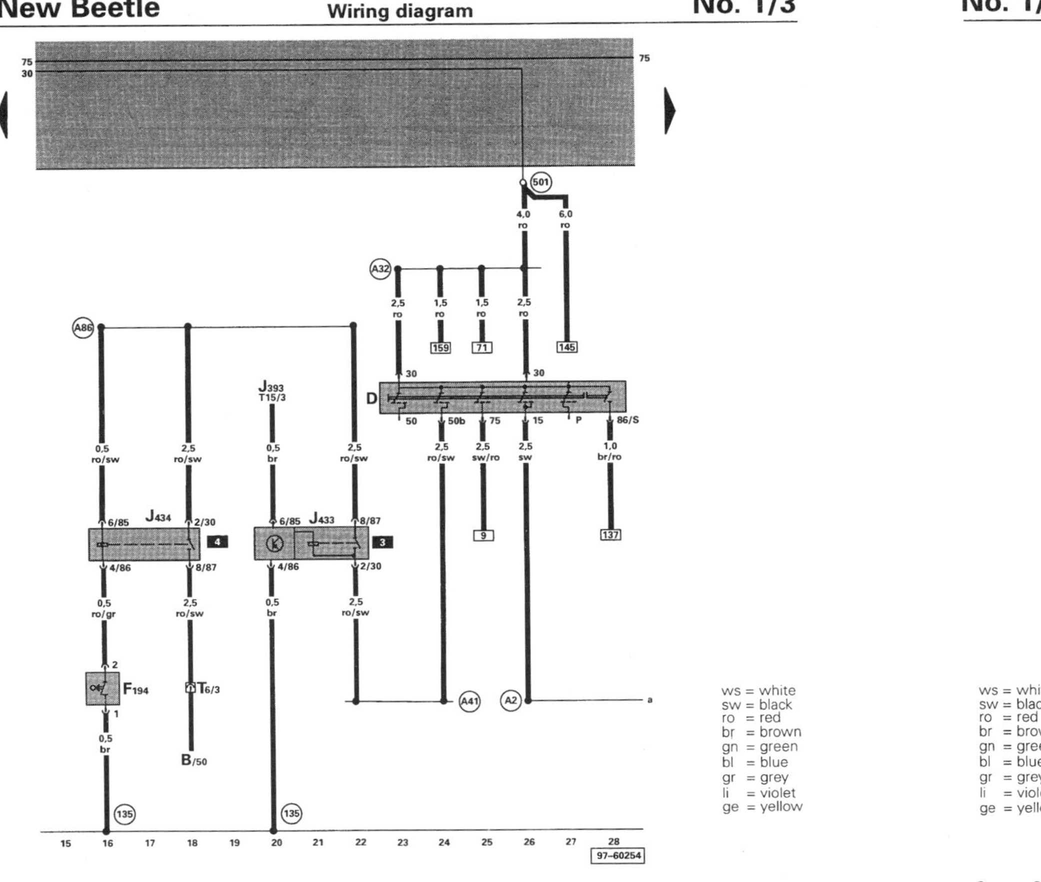

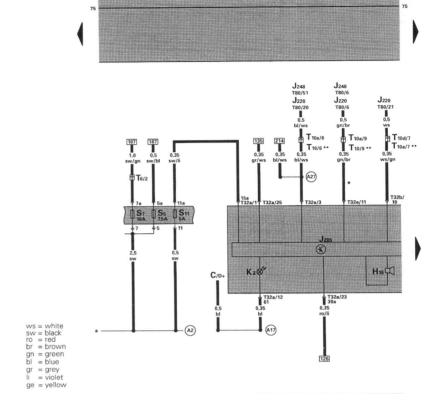

ws = white
sw = black
ro = red
br = brown
gn = green
bl = blue
gr = grey
li = violet
ge = yellow

B – Starter
D – Ignition/Starter Switch
F194 – Clutch Pedal Position (CPP) Switch
J393 – Central control module for comfort system
J433 – Lock relay for starter (theft warning system) (185), on the thirteen position relay panel
J434 – Locking relay for starter (clutch pedal switch)
T6 – 6-Pin Connector, red, behind instrument panel, left
T15 – 15-Pin Connector, on Central control module for comfort system

(135) – Ground connection -2-, in instrument panel wiring harness
(501) – Threaded connection -2- (30) on the relay plate

(A2) – plus connection (15), in instrument panel wiring harness
(A32) – plus connection (30), in instrument panel wiring harness
(A41) – plus connection (50), in instrument panel wiring harness
(A86) – Conenction (50a), in instrument panel wiring harness

Edition 09/98
USA.5132.05.21

Ignition/starter switch, lock relay for starter (theft warning system), locking relay for starter (clutch pedal switch)

ws = white
sw = black
ro = red
br = brown
gn = green
bl = blue
gr = grey
li = violet
ge = yellow

C – Generator (GEN)
H16 – Warning buzzer for light switched on
J220 – Motronic Engine Control Module (ECM), behind instrument panel, left
J248 – Diesel Direct Fuel Injection (DFI) Engine Control Module (ECM), behind instrument panel, left
J285 – Control module with indicator unit in instrument panel insert
K2 – Generator (GEN) Warning Light
S5 – Fuse 5 in fuse holder
S7 – Fuse 7 in fuse holder
S11 – Fuse 11 in fuse holder
T6 – 6-Pin Connector, brown, behind instrument panel, left
T10 – 10-Pin Connector, white, behind instrument panel, left
T10a – 10-Pin Connector, orange, behind instrument panel, left
T10d – 10-Pin Connector, green, behind instrument panel, left
T32a – 32-Pin Connector, blue, on instrument cluster
T32b – 32-Pin Connector, green, on instrument cluster
T80 – Connector, 80 point, on Engine Control Module (ECM)

(A2) – plus connection (15), in instrument panel wiring harness
(A17) – wire connection (61), in instrument panel wiring harness
(A27) – wire Connection (vehicle speed signal), in instrument panel wiring harness
* – speed signal from engine control module
** – early vehicles only

Instrument cluster, waming buzzer for light swiched on, generator (GEN)

Edition 09/98
USA.5132.05.21

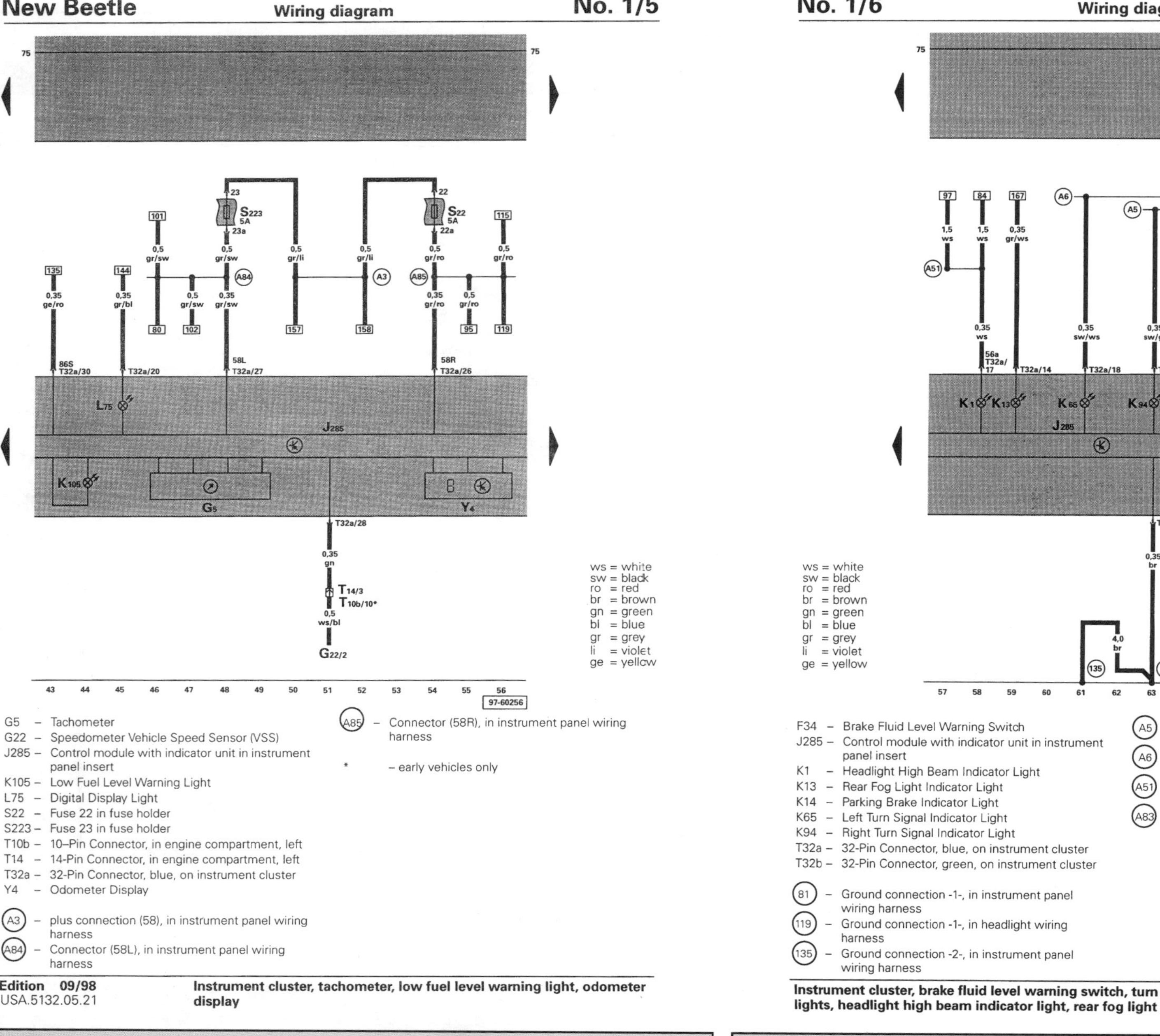

ws = white
sw = black
ro = red
br = brown
gn = green
bl = blue
gr = grey
li = violet
ge = yellow

G5 – Tachometer
G22 – Speedometer Vehicle Speed Sensor (VSS)
J285 – Control module with indicator unit in instrument panel insert
K105 – Low Fuel Level Warning Light
L75 – Digital Display Light
S22 – Fuse 22 in fuse holder
S223 – Fuse 23 in fuse holder
T10b – 10-Pin Connector, in engine compartment, left
T14 – 14-Pin Connector, in engine compartment, left
T32a – 32-Pin Connector, blue, on instrument cluster
Y4 – Odometer Display

(A3) – plus connection (58), in instrument panel wiring harness
(A84) – Connector (58L), in instrument panel wiring harness
(A85) – Connector (58R), in instrument panel wiring harness

* – early vehicles only

Edition 09/98
USA.5132.05.21

Instrument cluster, tachometer, low fuel level warning light, odometer display

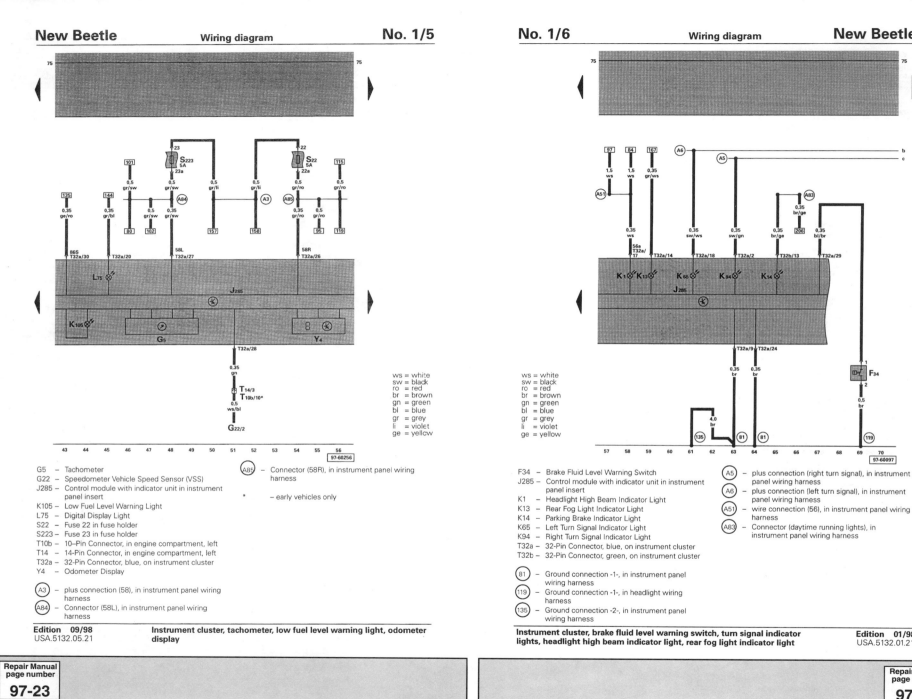

ws = white
sw = black
ro = red
br = brown
gn = green
bl = blue
gr = grey
li = violet
ge = yellow

F34 – Brake Fluid Level Warning Switch
J285 – Control module with indicator unit in instrument panel insert
K1 – Headlight High Beam Indicator Light
K13 – Rear Fog Light Indicator Light
K14 – Parking Brake Indicator Light
K65 – Left Turn Signal Indicator Light
K94 – Right Turn Signal Indicator Light
T32a – 32-Pin Connector, blue, on instrument cluster
T32b – 32-Pin Connector, green, on instrument cluster

(81) – Ground connection -1-, in instrument panel wiring harness
(119) – Ground connection -1-, in headlight wiring harness
(135) – Ground connection -2-, in instrument panel wiring harness

(A5) – plus connection (right turn signal), in instrument panel wiring harness
(A6) – plus connection (left turn signal), in instrument panel wiring harness
(A51) – wire connection (56), in instrument panel wiring harness
(A83) – Connector (daytime running lights), in instrument panel wiring harness

Instrument cluster, brake fluid level warning switch, turn signal indicator lights, headlight high beam indicator light, rear fog light indicator light

Edition 01/98
USA.5132.01.21

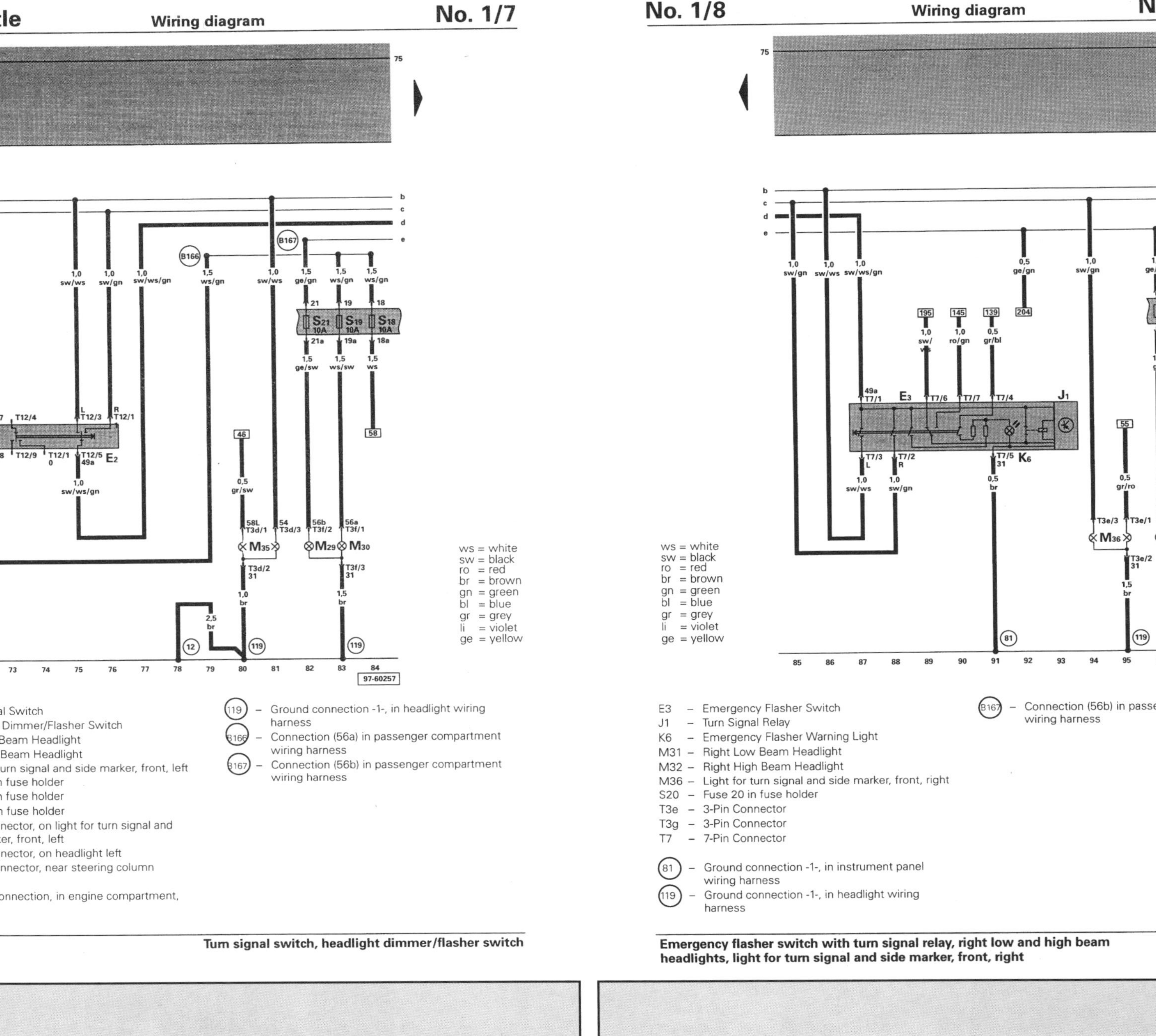

ws = white
sw = black
ro = red
br = brown
gn = green
bl = blue
gr = grey
li = violet
ge = yellow

E2 – Turn Signal Switch
E4 – Headlight Dimmer/Flasher Switch
M29 – Left Low Beam Headlight
M30 – Left High Beam Headlight
M35 – Light for turn signal and side marker, front, left
S18 – Fuse 18 in fuse holder
S19 – Fuse 19 in fuse holder
S21 – Fuse 21 in fuse holder
T3d – 3-Pin Connector, on light for turn signal and side marker, front, left
T3f – 3-Pin Connector, on headlight left
T12 – 12-Pin Connector, near steering column

(12) – Ground connection, in engine compartment, left

(119) – Ground connection -1-, in headlight wiring harness

(B166) – Connection (56a) in passenger compartment wiring harness

(B167) – Connection (56b) in passenger compartment wiring harness

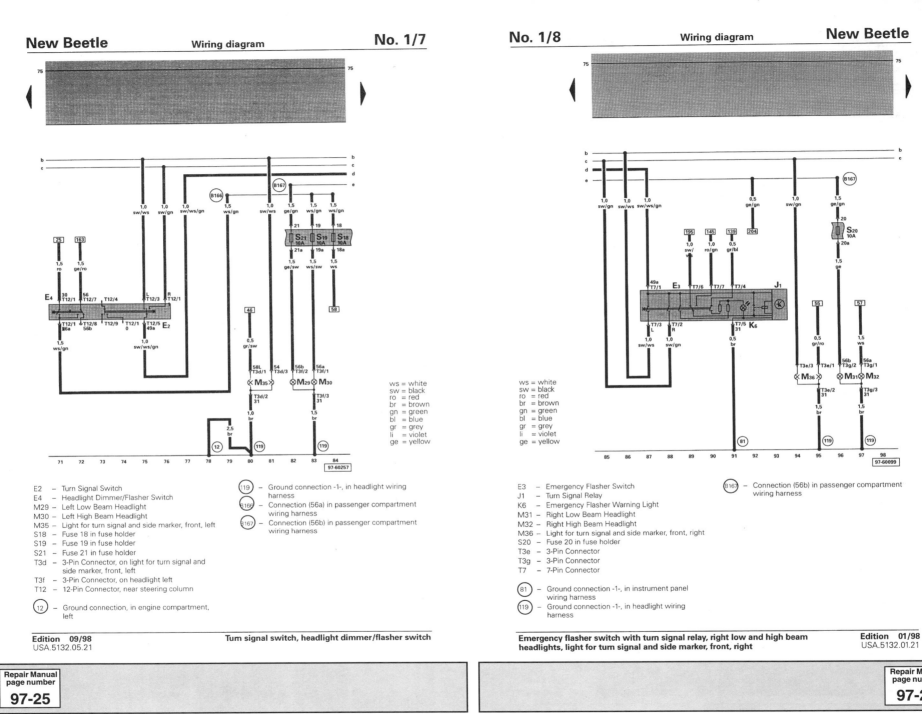

ws = white
sw = black
ro = red
br = brown
gn = green
bl = blue
gr = grey
li = violet
ge = yellow

E3 – Emergency Flasher Switch
J1 – Turn Signal Relay
K6 – Emergency Flasher Warning Light
M31 – Right Low Beam Headlight
M32 – Right High Beam Headlight
M36 – Light for turn signal and side marker, front, right
S20 – Fuse 20 in fuse holder
T3e – 3-Pin Connector
T3g – 3-Pin Connector
T7 – 7-Pin Connector

(81) – Ground connection -1-, in instrument panel wiring harness

(119) – Ground connection -1-, in headlight wiring harness

(B167) – Connection (56b) in passenger compartment wiring harness

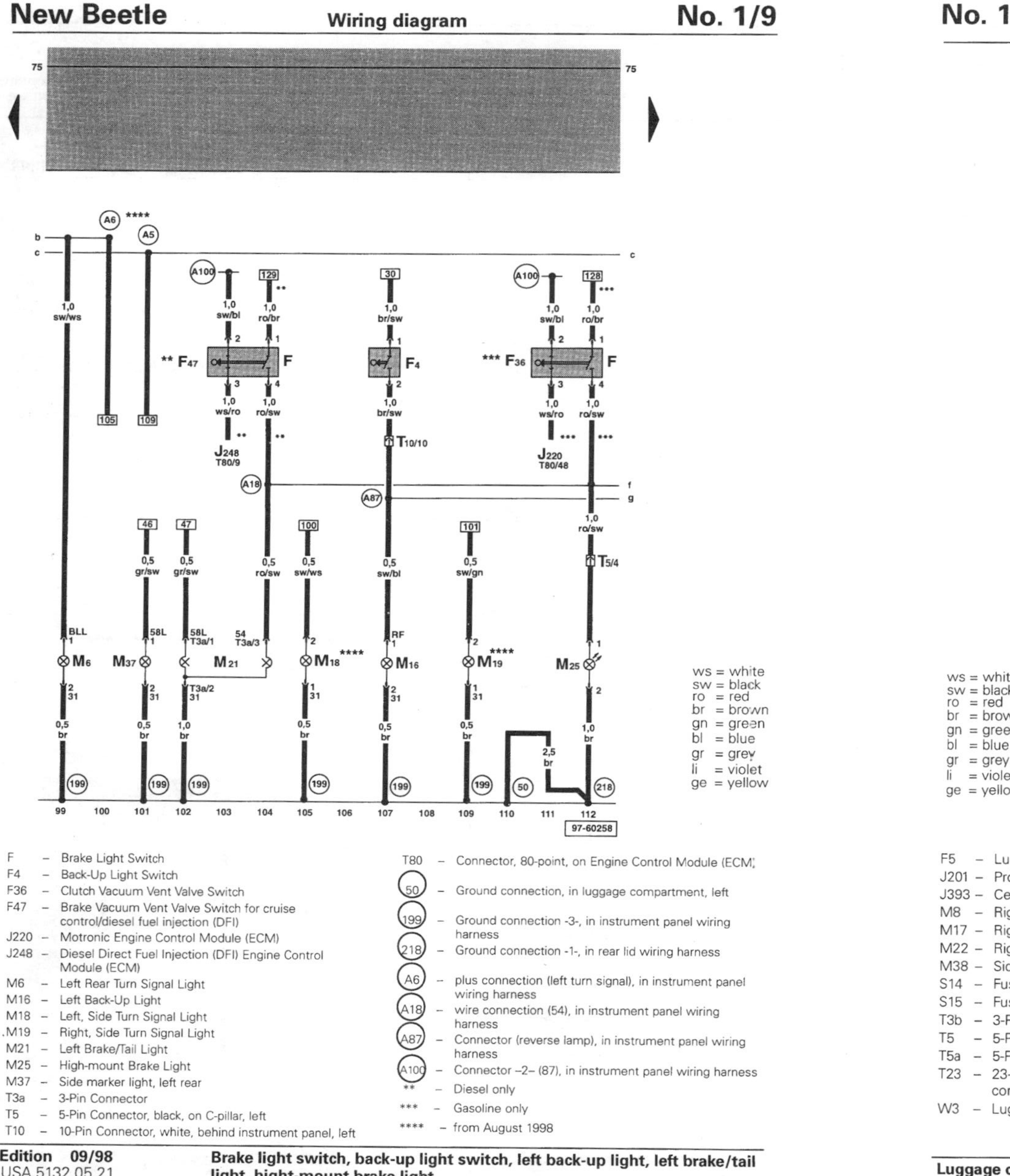

F – Brake Light Switch
F4 – Back-Up Light Switch
F36 – Clutch Vacuum Vent Valve Switch
F47 – Brake Vacuum Vent Valve Switch for cruise control/diesel fuel injection (DFI)
J220 – Motronic Engine Control Module (ECM)
J248 – Diesel Direct Fuel Injection (DFI) Engine Control Module (ECM)
M6 – Left Rear Turn Signal Light
M16 – Left Back-Up Light
M18 – Left, Side Turn Signal Light
M19 – Right, Side Turn Signal Light
M21 – Left Brake/Tail Light
M25 – High-mount Brake Light
M37 – Side marker light, left rear
T3a – 3-Pin Connector
T5 – 5-Pin Connector, black, on C-pillar, left
T10 – 10-Pin Connector, white, behind instrument panel, left
T80 – Connector, 80-point, on Engine Control Module (ECM)
(50) – Ground connection, in luggage compartment, left
(199) – Ground connection -3-, in instrument panel wiring harness
(218) – Ground connection -1-, in rear lid wiring harness
(A6) – plus connection (left turn signal), in instrument panel wiring harness
(A18) – wire connection (54), in instrument panel wiring harness
(A87) – Connector (reverse lamp), in instrument panel wiring harness
(A100) – Connector -2- (87), in instrument panel wiring harness
** – Diesel only
*** – Gasoline only
**** – from August 1998

ws = white
sw = black
ro = red
br = brown
gn = green
bl = blue
gr = grey
li = violet
ge = yellow

Edition 09/98
USA.5132.05.21

Brake light switch, back-up light switch, left back-up light, left brake/tail light, hight-mount brake light

F5 – Luggage Compartment Light Switch
J201 – Protection Diode (* not on early vehicles)
J393 – Central control module for comfort system
M8 – Right Rear Turn Signal Light
M17 – Right Back-Up Light
M22 – Right Brake/Tail Light
M38 – Side marker light, right rear
S14 – Fuse 14 in fuse holder
S15 – Fuse 15 in fuse holder
T3b – 3-Pin Connector
T5 – 5-Pin Connector, black, on C-pillar, left
T5a – 5-Pin Connector, black, in rear lid
T23 – 23-Pin Connector, on Central control module for comfort system
W3 – Luggage compartment Light
(98) – Ground connection, in rear lid wiring harness
(199) – Ground connection -3-, in instrument panel wiring harness
(218) – Ground connection -1-, in rear lid wiring harness
(A5) – plus connection (right turn signal), in instrument panel wiring harness
(A18) – wire connection (54), in instrument panel wiring harness
(A40) – plus connection -1- (30), in instrument panel wiring harness
(A87) – Connector (reverse lamp), in instrument panel wiring harness
(B128) – Connector (Luggage compartment lamp) in wiring harness interior

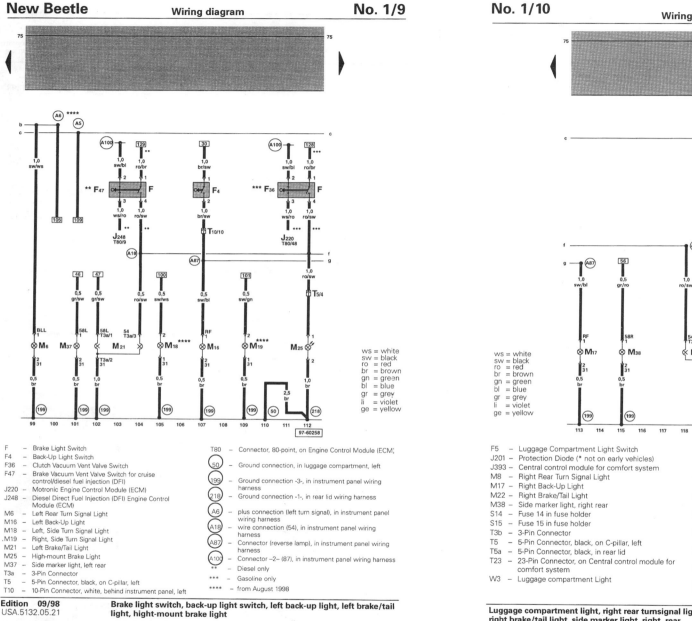

ws = white
sw = black
ro = red
br = brown
gn = green
bl = blue
gr = grey
li = violet
ge = yellow

Luggage compartment light, right rear turnsignal light, right back-up light, right brake/tail light, side marker light, right, rear

Edition 09/98
USA.5132.05.21

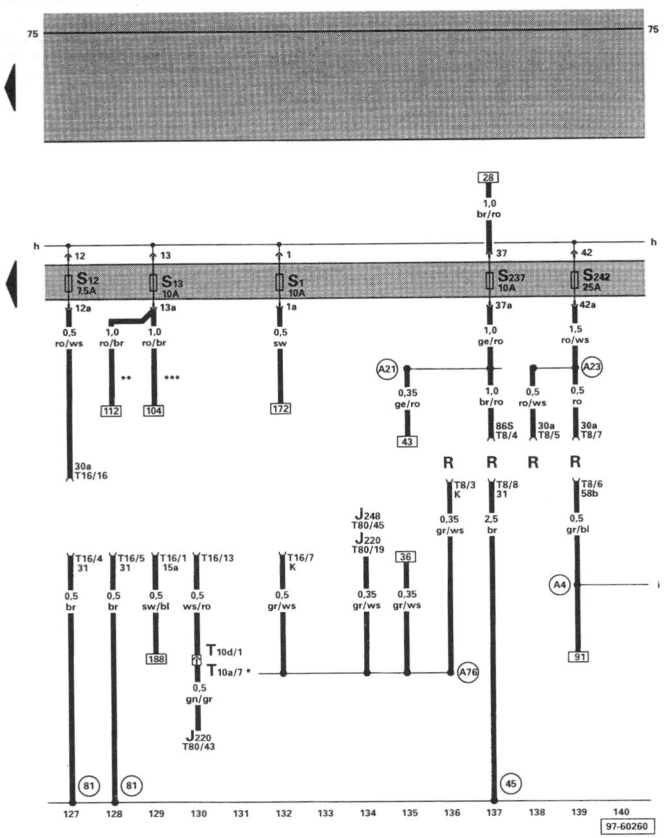

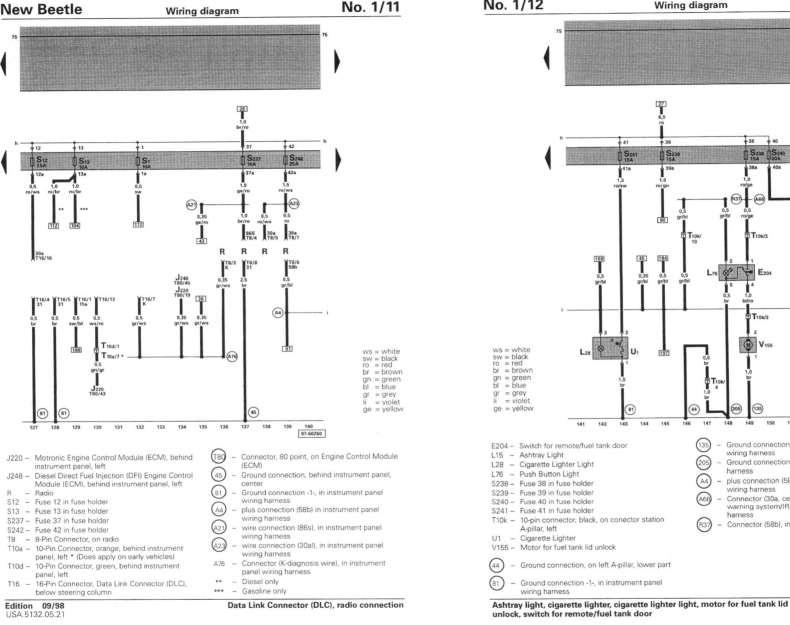

ws = white
sw = black
ro = red
br = brown
gn = green
bl = blue
gr = grey
li = violet
ge = yellow

J220 – Motronic Engine Control Module (ECM), behind instrument panel, left
J248 – Diesel Direct Fuel Injection (DFI) Engine Control Module (ECM), behind instrument panel, left
R – Radio
S12 – Fuse 12 in fuse holder
S13 – Fuse 13 in fuse holder
S237 – Fuse 37 in fuse holder
S242 – Fuse 42 in fuse holder
T8 – 8-Pin Connector, on radio
T10a – 10-Pin Connector, orange, behind instrument panel, left * (Does apply on early vehicles)
T10d – 10-Pin Connector, green, behind instrument panel, left
T16 – 16-Pin Connector, Data Link Connector (DLC), below steering column

(T80) – Connector, 80 point, on Engine Control Module (ECM)
(45) – Ground connection, behind instrument panel, center
(81) – Ground connection -1-, in instrument panel wiring harness
(A4) – plus connection (58b) in instrument panel wiring harness
(A21) – wire connection (86s), in instrument panel wiring harness
(A23) – wire connection (30al), in instrument panel wiring harness
A76 – Connector (K-diagnosis wire), in instrument panel wiring harness
** – Diesel only
*** – Gasoline only

Data Link Connector (DLC), radio connection

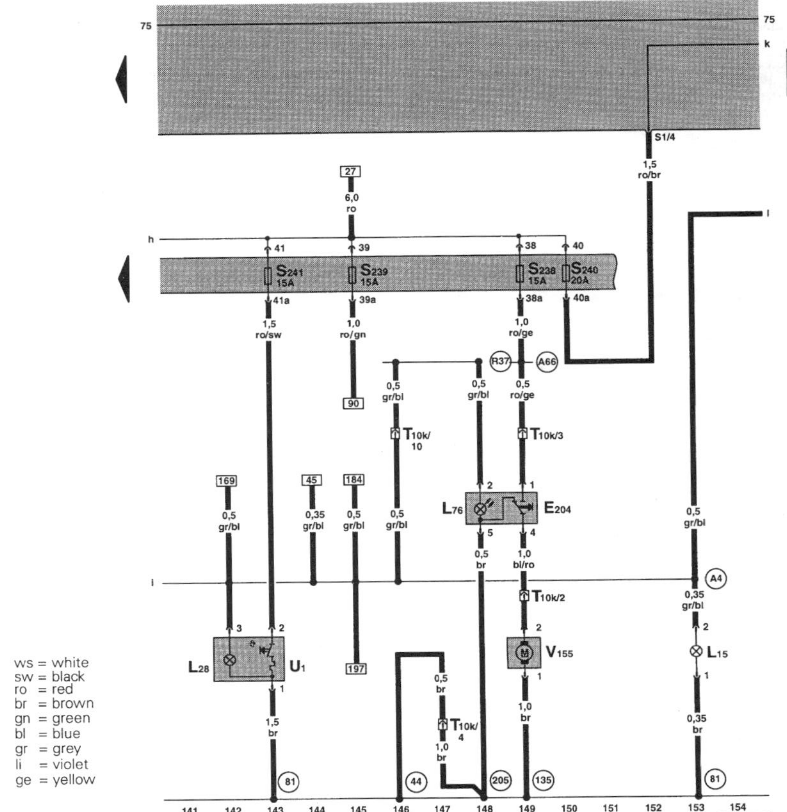

ws = white
sw = black
ro = red
br = brown
gn = green
bl = blue
gr = grey
li = violet
ge = yellow

E204 – Switch for remote/fuel tank door
L15 – Ashtray Light
L28 – Cigarette Lighter Light
L76 – Push Button Light
S238 – Fuse 38 in fuse holder
S239 – Fuse 39 in fuse holder
S240 – Fuse 40 in fuse holder
S241 – Fuse 41 in fuse holder
T10k – 10-pin connector, black, on conector station A-pillar, left
U1 – Cigarette Lighter
V155 – Motor for fuel tank lid unlock

(44) – Ground connection, on left A-pillar, lower part
(81) – Ground connection -1-, in instrument panel wiring harness

(135) – Ground connection -2-, in instrument panel wiring harness
(205) – Ground connection, in driver's door wiring harness
(A4) – plus connection (58b) in instrument panel wiring harness
(A66) – Connector (30a, central locking/anti-theft warning system/IR), in instrument panel wiring harness
(R37) – Connector (58b), in driver's door wiring harness

Ashtray light, cigarette lighter, cigarette lighter light, motor for fuel tank lid unlock, switch for remote/fuel tank door

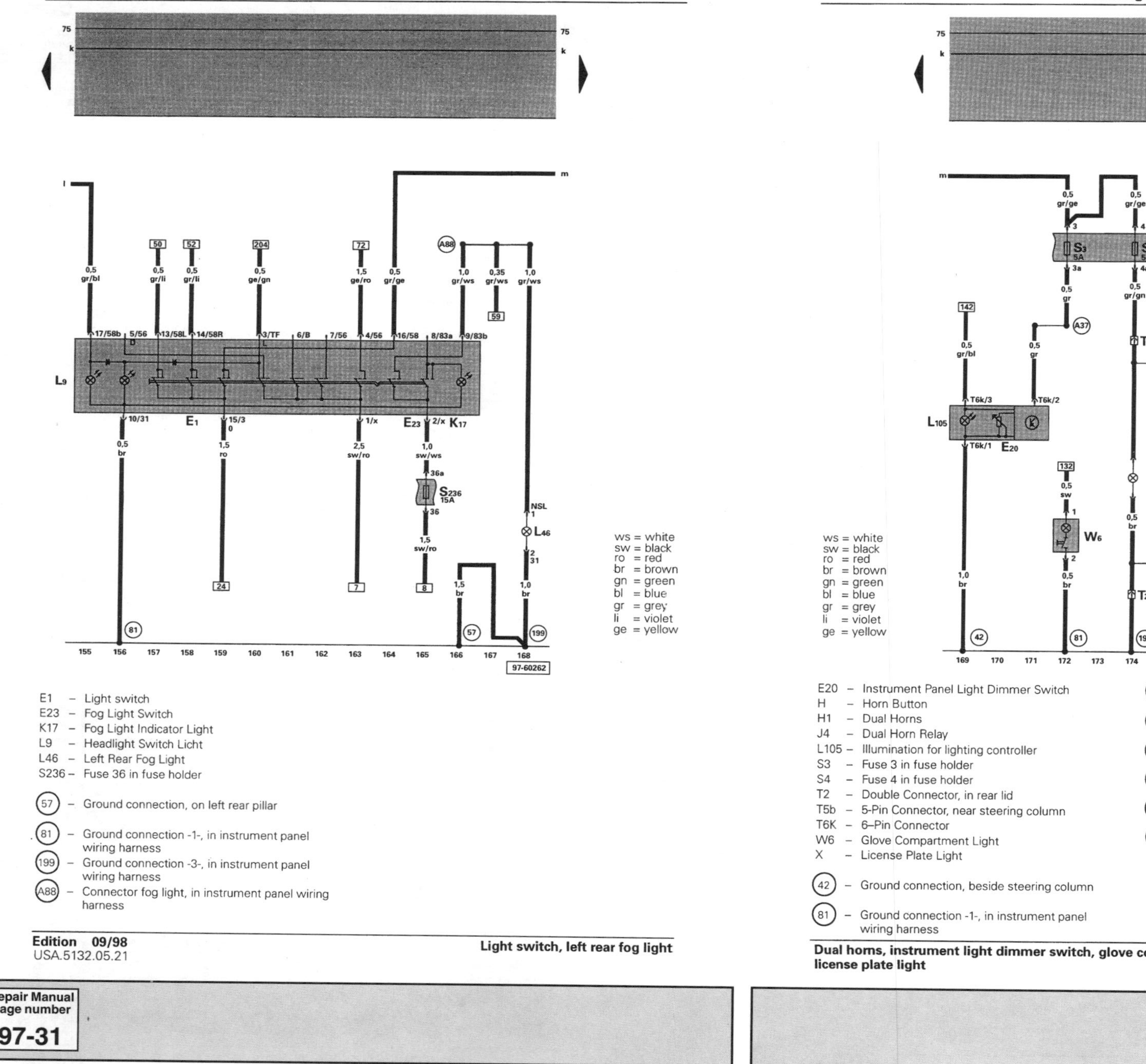

No. 1/13

ws = white
sw = black
ro = red
br = brown
gn = green
bl = blue
gr = grey
li = violet
ge = yellow

- E1 – Light switch
- E23 – Fog Light Switch
- K17 – Fog Light Indicator Light
- L9 – Headlight Switch Licht
- L46 – Left Rear Fog Light
- S236 – Fuse 36 in fuse holder
- (57) – Ground connection, on left rear pillar
- (81) – Ground connection -1-, in instrument panel wiring harness
- (199) – Ground connection -3-, in instrument panel wiring harness
- (A88) – Connector fog light, in instrument panel wiring harness

Light switch, left rear fog light

No. 1/14

ws = white
sw = black
ro = red
br = brown
gn = green
bl = blue
gr = grey
li = violet
ge = yellow

- E20 – Instrument Panel Light Dimmer Switch
- H – Horn Button
- H1 – Dual Horns
- J4 – Dual Horn Relay
- L105 – Illumination for lighting controller
- S3 – Fuse 3 in fuse holder
- S4 – Fuse 4 in fuse holder
- T2 – Double Connector, in rear lid
- T5b – 5-Pin Connector, near steering column
- T6K – 6–Pin Connector
- W6 – Glove Compartment Light
- X – License Plate Light
- (42) – Ground connection, beside steering column
- (81) – Ground connection -1-, in instrument panel wiring harness
- (119) – Ground connection -1-, in headlight wiring harness
- (199) – Ground connection -3-, in instrument panel wiring harness
- (218) – Ground connection -1-, in rear lid wiring harness
- (A37) – wire connection (58a), in instrument panel wiring harness
- (C80) – wire connection (58b), in wiring harness headlamp
- (W11) – wire connection (58), in rear lid wiring harness

Dual horns, instrument light dimmer switch, glove compartment light, license plate light

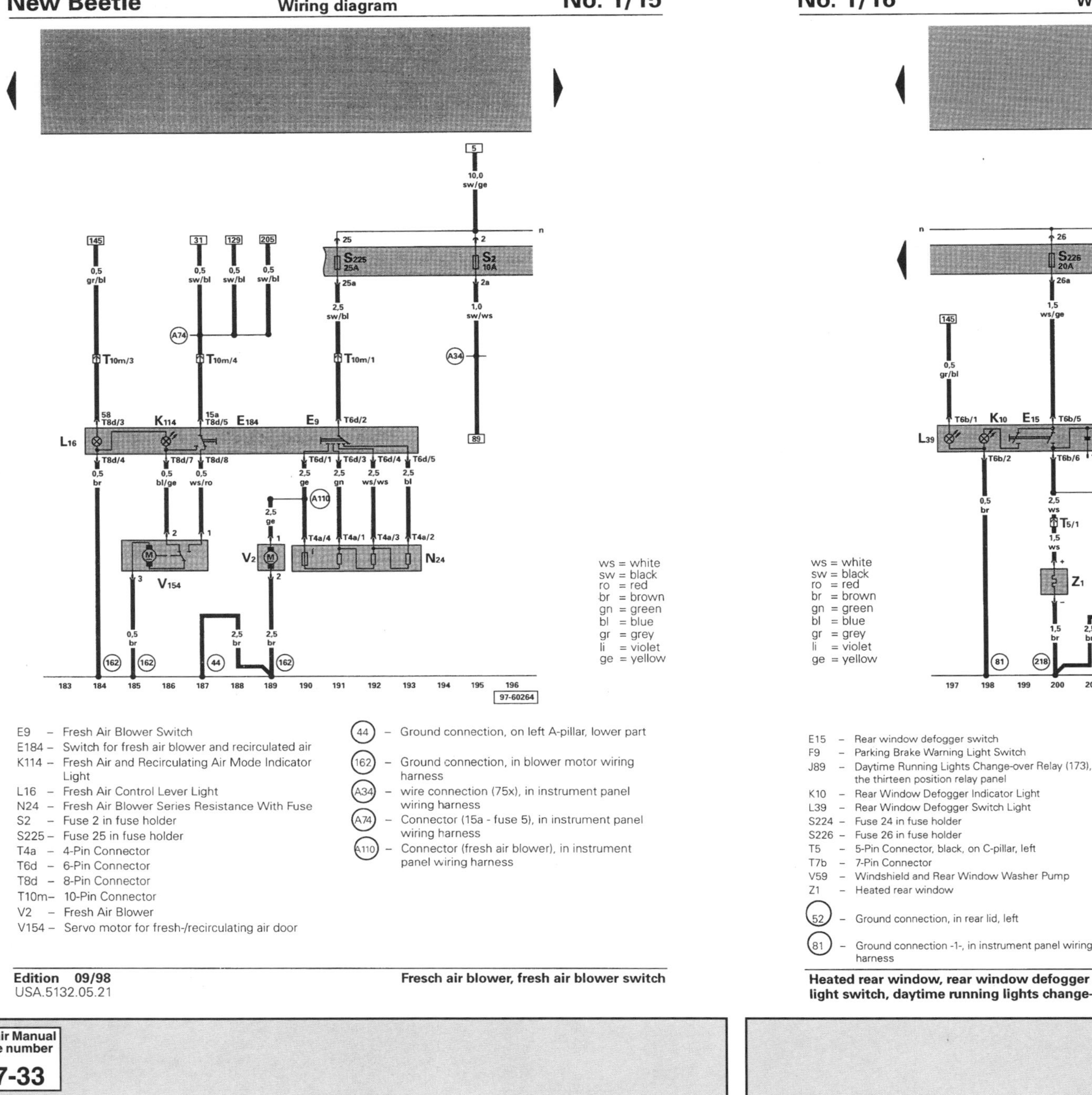

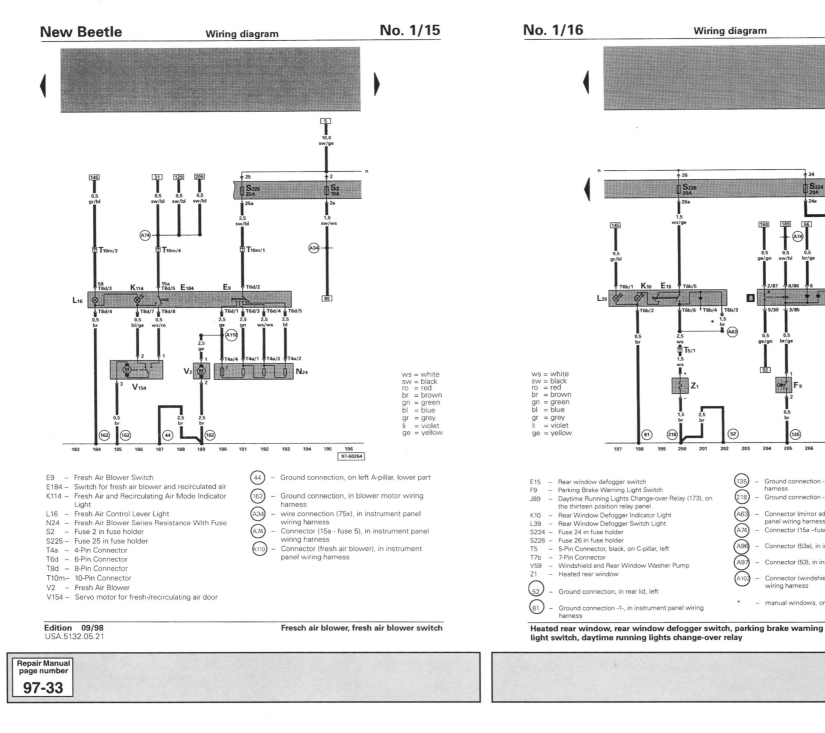

ws = white
sw = black
ro = red
br = brown
gn = green
bl = blue
gr = grey
li = violet
ge = yellow

E9 – Fresh Air Blower Switch
E184 – Switch for fresh air blower and recirculated air
K114 – Fresh Air and Recirculating Air Mode Indicator Light
L16 – Fresh Air Control Lever Light
N24 – Fresh Air Blower Series Resistance With Fuse
S2 – Fuse 2 in fuse holder
S225 – Fuse 25 in fuse holder
T4a – 4-Pin Connector
T6d – 6-Pin Connector
T8d – 8-Pin Connector
T10m – 10-Pin Connector
V2 – Fresh Air Blower
V154 – Servo motor for fresh-/recirculating air door

(44) – Ground connection, on left A-pillar, lower part
(162) – Ground connection, in blower motor wiring harness
(A34) – wire connection (75x), in instrument panel wiring harness
(A74) – Connector (15a - fuse 5), in instrument panel wiring harness
(A110) – Connector (fresh air blower), in instrument panel wiring harness

Fresch air blower, fresh air blower switch

ws = white
sw = black
ro = red
br = brown
gn = green
bl = blue
gr = grey
li = violet
ge = yellow

E15 – Rear window defogger switch
F9 – Parking Brake Warning Light Switch
J89 – Daytime Running Lights Change-over Relay (173), on the thirteen position relay panel
K10 – Rear Window Defogger Indicator Light
L39 – Rear Window Defogger Switch Light
S224 – Fuse 24 in fuse holder
S226 – Fuse 26 in fuse holder
T5 – 5-Pin Connector, black, on C-pillar, left
T7b – 7-Pin Connector
V59 – Windshield and Rear Window Washer Pump
Z1 – Heated rear window

(52) – Ground connection, in rear lid, left
(81) – Ground connection -1-, in instrument panel wiring harness
(135) – Ground connection -2-, in instrument panel wiring harness
(218) – Ground connection -1-, in rear wiring harness
(A63) – Connector (mirror adjustment/ –heated) in instrument panel wiring harness
(A74) – Connector (15a –fuse 5), in instrument panel
(A96) – Connector (53a), in instrument panel wiring harness
(A97) – Connector (53), in instrument panel wiring harness
(A102) – Connector (windshield wiper), in instrument panel wiring harness
* – manual windows, only

Heated rear window, rear window defogger switch, parking brake warning light switch, daytime running lights change-over relay

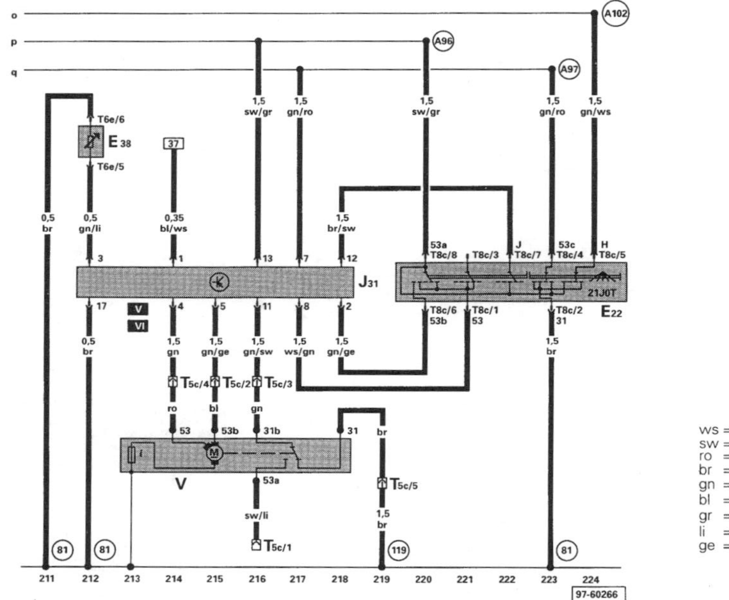

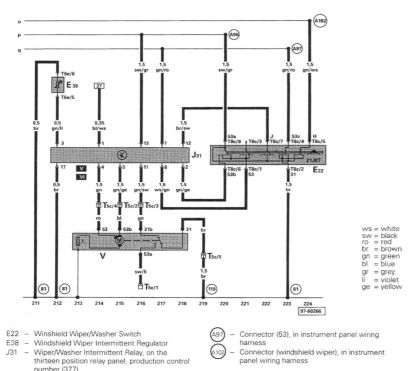

ws = white
sw = black
ro = red
br = brown
gn = green
bl = blue
gr = grey
li = violet
ge = yellow

E22 – Winshield Wiper/Washer Switch
E38 – Windshield Wiper Intermittent Regulator
J31 – Wiper/Washer Intermittent Relay, on the thirteen position relay panel, production control number (377)
T5c – 5-Pin Connector, on Windshield Wiper Motor
T6e – 6-Pin Connector, near steering column
T8c – 8-Pin Connector
V – Windshield Wiper Motor

(81) – Ground connection -1-, in instrument panel wiring harness
(119) – Ground connection -1-, in headlight wiring harness
(A96) – Connector (53a), in instrument panel wiring harness
(A97) – Connector (53), in instrument panel wiring harness
(A102) – Connector (windshield wiper), in instrument panel wiring harness

Edition 09/98
USA.5132.05.21

Windshield wiper/washer switch, windshield wiper motor, windshield wiper/washer intermittent relay

THIS PAGE INTENTIONALLY LEFT

BLANK

2,0L-Engine – Motronic Multiport Fuel Injection (MFI)/85 kW, code AEG, (without cruise control)

from January 1998

97-21956

Relay location on the thirteen position auxiliary relay panel, above relay panel:

Relay panel:

2 Load Reduction Relay (213), (18)

4 Fuel Pump Relay (409)

Note: Number in parentheses indicates production control number stamped on relay housing.

Fuse colors

30 A – green
25 A – white
20 A – yellow
15 A – blue
10 A – red
7,5 A – brown
5 A – beige

ws = white
sw = black
ro = red
br = brown
gn = green
bl = blue
gr = grey
li = violet
ge = yellow

A – Battery
B – Starter
C – Generator (GEN)
C1 – Voltage Regulator (VR)
D – Ignition/Starter Switch
E1 – Light Switch
J59 – Load Reduction Relay
J434 – Locking relay for starter (clutch pedal switch)
S163 – Fuse -2- (50)in fuse bracket/battery
S176 – Fuse -4- (30), in fuse bracket/battery
S177 – Fuse -5- (30), in fuse bracket/battery
S162 – Fuse -1- (30), in fuse bracket/battery
T2 – Double Connector
T4 – 4-Pin Connector, in engine compartment left
T6 – 6-Pin Connector, brown, behind instrument panel, left

(500) – Threaded connection -1- (30) on the relay plate
(501) – Threaded connection -2- (30) on the relay plate
(502) – Threaded connection -1- (30a) on the relay plate
(A17) – wire connection (61), in instrument panel wiring harness
(A32) – plus connection (30), in instrument panel wiring harness

Starter, generator (GEN)

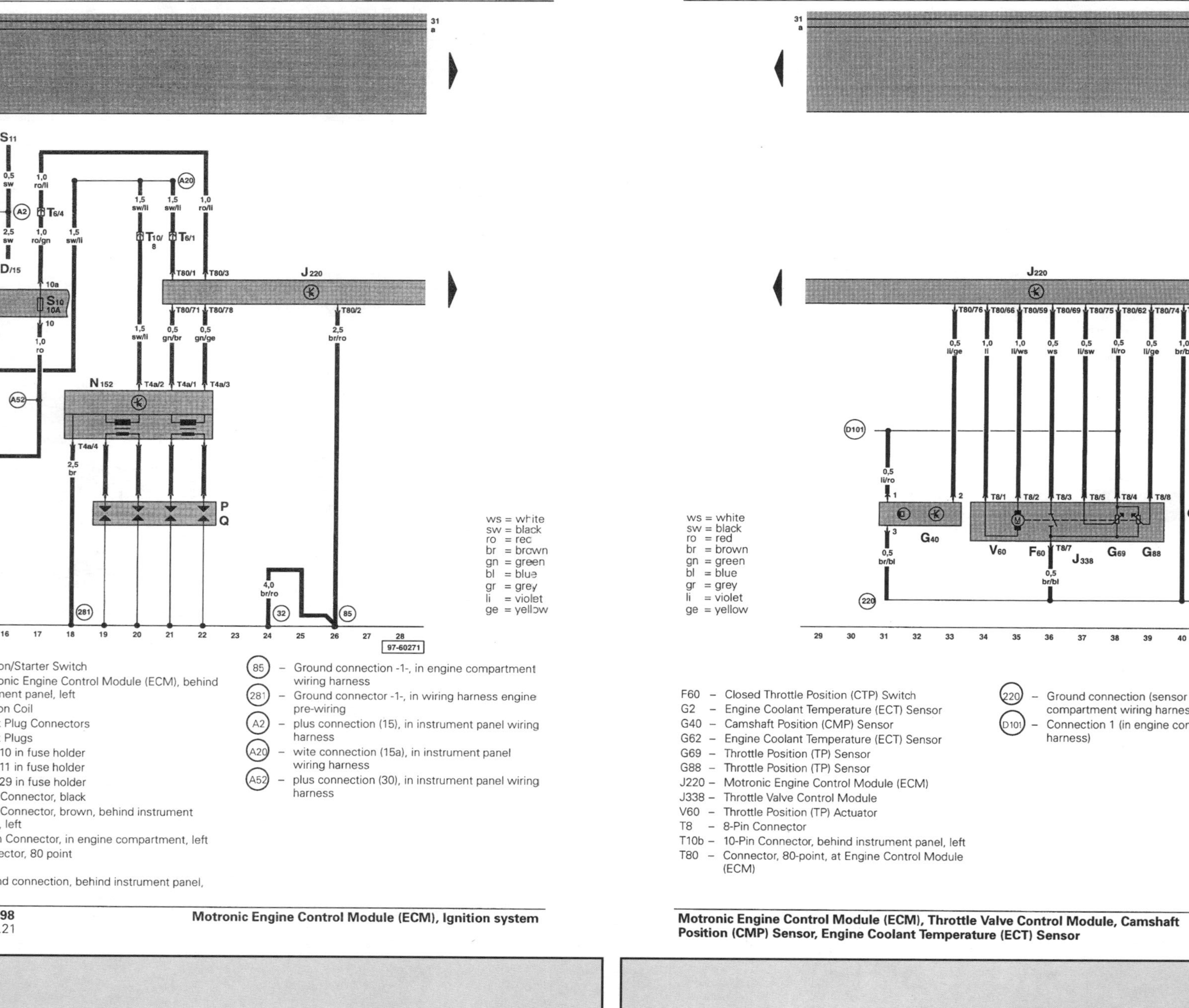

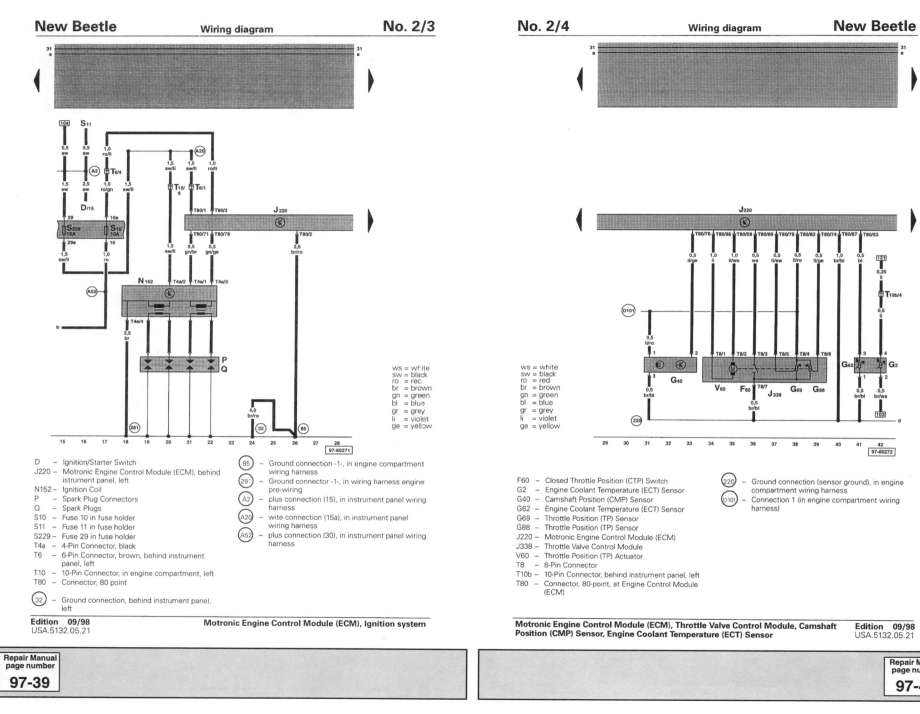

ws = white
sw = black
ro = red
br = brown
gn = green
bl = blue
gr = grey
li = violet
ge = yellow

D – Ignition/Starter Switch
J220 – Motronic Engine Control Module (ECM), behind istrument panel, left
N152 – Ignition Coil
P – Spark Plug Connectors
Q – Spark Plugs
S10 – Fuse 10 in fuse holder
S11 – Fuse 11 in fuse holder
S229 – Fuse 29 in fuse holder
T4a – 4-Pin Connector, black
T6 – 6-Pin Connector, brown, behind instrument panel, left
T10 – 10-Pin Connector, in engine compartment, left
T80 – Connector, 80 point

(32) – Ground connection, behind instrument panel, left

(85) – Ground connection -1-, in engine compartment wiring harness
(281) – Ground connector -1-, in wiring harness engine pre-wiring
(A2) – plus connection (15), in instrument panel wiring harness
(A20) – wite connection (15a), in instrument panel wiring harness
(A52) – plus connection (30), in instrument panel wiring harness

Motronic Engine Control Module (ECM), Ignition system

F60 – Closed Throttle Position (CTP) Switch
G2 – Engine Coolant Temperature (ECT) Sensor
G40 – Camshaft Position (CMP) Sensor
G62 – Engine Coolant Temperature (ECT) Sensor
G69 – Throttle Position (TP) Sensor
G88 – Throttle Position (TP) Sensor
J220 – Motronic Engine Control Module (ECM)
J338 – Throttle Valve Control Module
V60 – Throttle Position (TP) Actuator
T8 – 8-Pin Connector
T10b – 10-Pin Connector, behind instrument panel, left
T80 – Connector, 80-point, at Engine Control Module (ECM)

(220) – Ground connection (sensor ground), in engine compartment wiring harness
(D101) – Connection 1 (in engine compartment wiring harness)

Motronic Engine Control Module (ECM), Throttle Valve Control Module, Camshaft Position (CMP) Sensor, Engine Coolant Temperature (ECT) Sensor

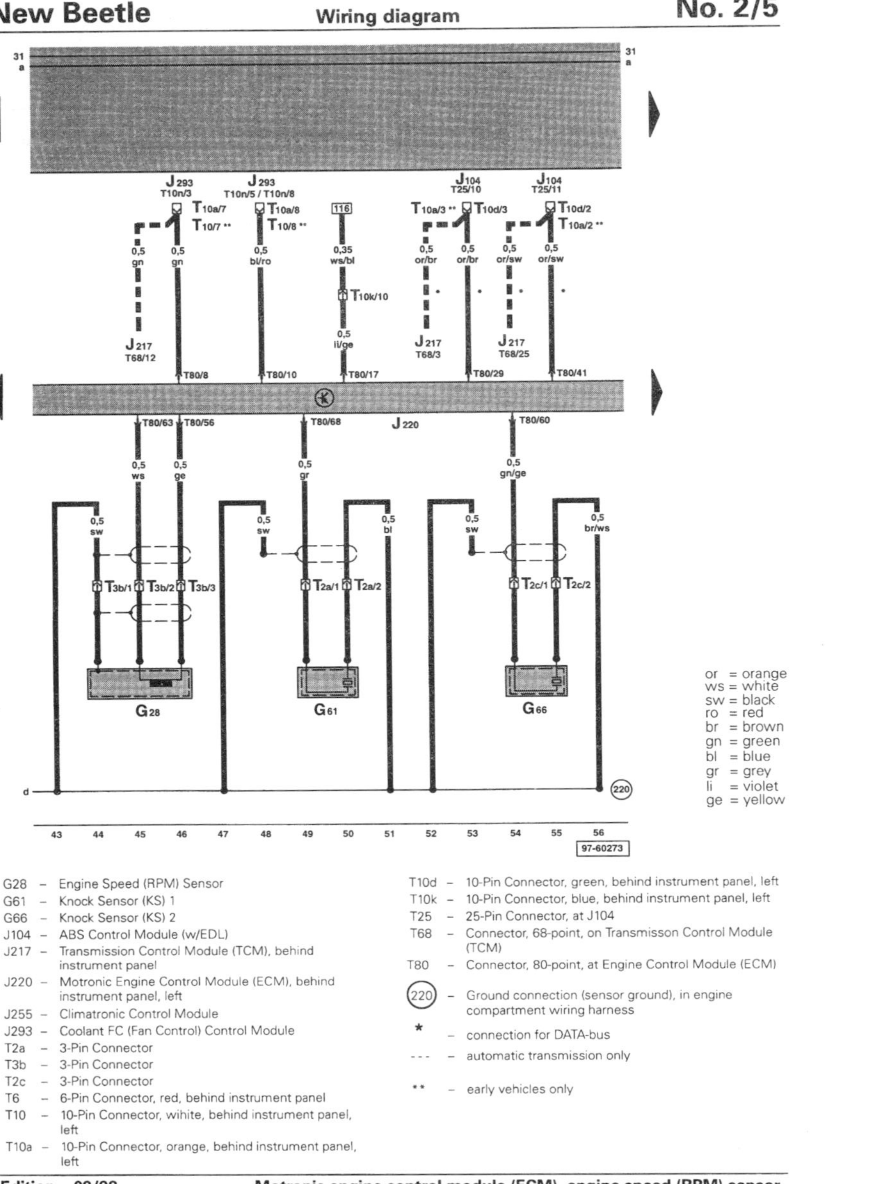

or = orange
ws = white
sw = black
ro = red
br = brown
gn = green
bl = blue
gr = grey
li = violet
ge = yellow

G28 – Engine Speed (RPM) Sensor
G61 – Knock Sensor (KS) 1
G66 – Knock Sensor (KS) 2
J104 – ABS Control Module (w/EDL)
J217 – Transmission Control Module (TCM), behind instrument panel
J220 – Motronic Engine Control Module (ECM), behind instrument panel, left
J255 – Climatronic Control Module
J293 – Coolant FC (Fan Control) Control Module
T2a – 3-Pin Connector
T3b – 3-Pin Connector
T2c – 3-Pin Connector
T6 – 6-Pin Connector, red, behind instrument panel
T10 – 10-Pin Connector, wihite, behind instrument panel, left
T10a – 10-Pin Connector, orange, behind instrument panel, left
T10d – 10-Pin Connector, green, behind instrument panel, left
T10k – 10-Pin Connector, blue, behind instrument panel, left
T25 – 25-Pin Connector, at J104
T68 – Connector, 68-point, on Transmisson Control Module (TCM)
T80 – Connector, 80-point, at Engine Control Module (ECM)
(220) – Ground connection (sensor ground), in engine compartment wiring harness
* – connection for DATA-bus
- - - – automatic transmission only
** – early vehicles only

Edition 09/98
USA.5132.05.21

Motronic engine control module (ECM), engine speed (RPM) sensor, knock sensor (KS) 1, knock sensor (KS) 2

97-60274

ws = white
sw = black
ro = red
br = brown
gn = green
bl = blue
gr = grey
li = violet
ge = yellow

G108 – Heated Oxygen Sensor (HO2S) 2 brown
J220 – Motronic Engine Control Module (ECM), behind instrument panel, left
N30 – Cylinder 1 Fuel Injector
N31 – Cylinder 2 Fuel Injector
N32 – Cylinder 3 Fuel Injector
N33 – Cylinder 4 Fuel Injector
N79 – Positive Crankcase Ventilation (PCV) Heating Element
S232 – Fuse 32 in fuse holder
S234 – Fuse 34 in fuse holder
T4b – 4-Pin Connector, black, in engine compartment, left
T6 – 6-Pin Connector, red, behind instrument panel, left
T10 – 10-Pin Connector, white, behind instrument panel, left
T10a – 10-Pin Connector, orange, behind instrument panel, left
T10b – 10-Pin Connector, in engine compartment, left
T16 – 16-Pin Connector, Data Link Connector (DLC), below steering column
T80 – 80-Pin Connector, at Engine Control Module (ECM)
(85) – Ground connection -1-, in engine compartment wiring harness
(A76) – Connector (K-diagnosis wire), in instrument panel wiring harness
(D140) – Connector (injectors), in wiring harness, engine pre-wiring
(B146) – Plus connector -1- (87), in wiring harness interior
* – early vehicles only

Motronic engine control module (ECM), fuel injectors, heated oxygen sensor (HO2S) 2, positive crankcase ventilation (PCV) heating element

Edition 09/98
USA.5132.05.21

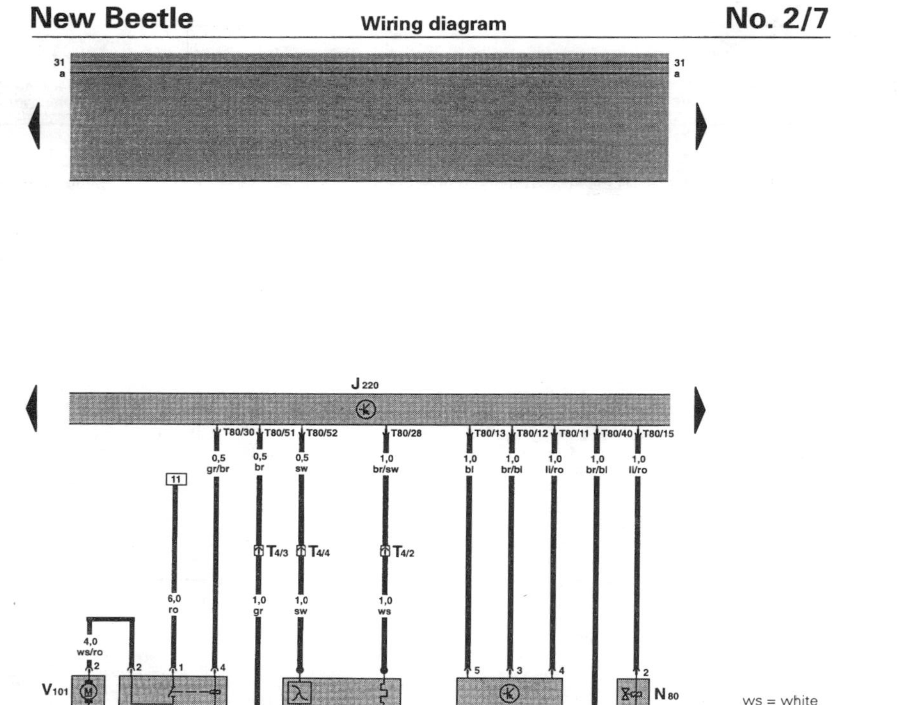

ws = white
sw = black
ro = red
br = brown
gn = green
bl = blue
gr = grey
li = violet
ge = yellow

G39 – Heated Oxygen Sensor (HO2S), black
G70 – Mass Air Flow (MAF) Sensor
J220 – Motronic Engine Control Module (ECM), behind instrument panel, left
J299 – Secondary Air Injection (AIR) Pump Relay, in engine compartment, left
N80 – Evaporative Emission (EVAP) Canister Purge Regulator Valve
V101 – Secondary Air Injection (AIR) Pump Motor
T4 – 4-Pin Connector, brown
T80 – 80-Pin Connector

(12) – Ground connection, in engine compartment, left
(E30) – Connector (87a), in wiring harness engine

Heated oxygen sensor (HO2S), mass air flow (MAF) sensor, evaporative emission (EVAP) canister purge regulator valve, secondary air injection (AIR) system

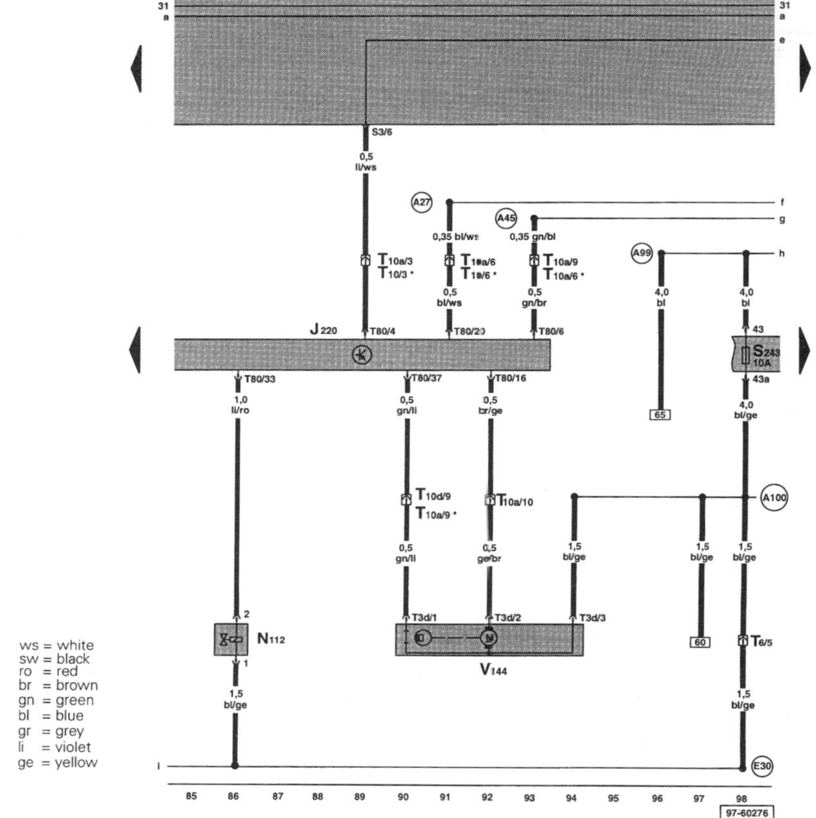

ws = white
sw = black
ro = red
br = brown
gn = green
bl = blue
gr = grey
li = violet
ge = yellow

J220 – Motronic Engine Control Module (ECM), behind instrument panel, left
N112 – Secondary Air Injection (AIR) Solenoid Valve
S243 – Fuse 43 in fuse holder
V144 – Leak Detection Pump (LDP)
T3d – 3-Pin Connector
T6 – 6-Pin Connector, red, behind instrument panel, left
T10 – 10-Pin Connector,white, behind instrument panel, left
T10a – 10-Pin Connector,orange, behind instrument panel, left
T10d – 10-Pin Connector, green, behind instrument panel, left
T80 – Connector, 80-point, at Engine Control Module (ECM)

(A27) – wire Connection (vehicle speed signal), in instrument panel wiring harness
(A45) – wire connection (RPM-signal), in instrument panel wiring harness
(A99) – Connector -1- (87), in instrument panel wiring harness
(A100) – Connector -2- (87), in instrument panel wiring harness
(E30) – Connector (87a), in wiring harness engine
* – early vehicles only

Motronic engine control module (ECM), diagnosis pump for fuel system, secondary air injection solenoid valve

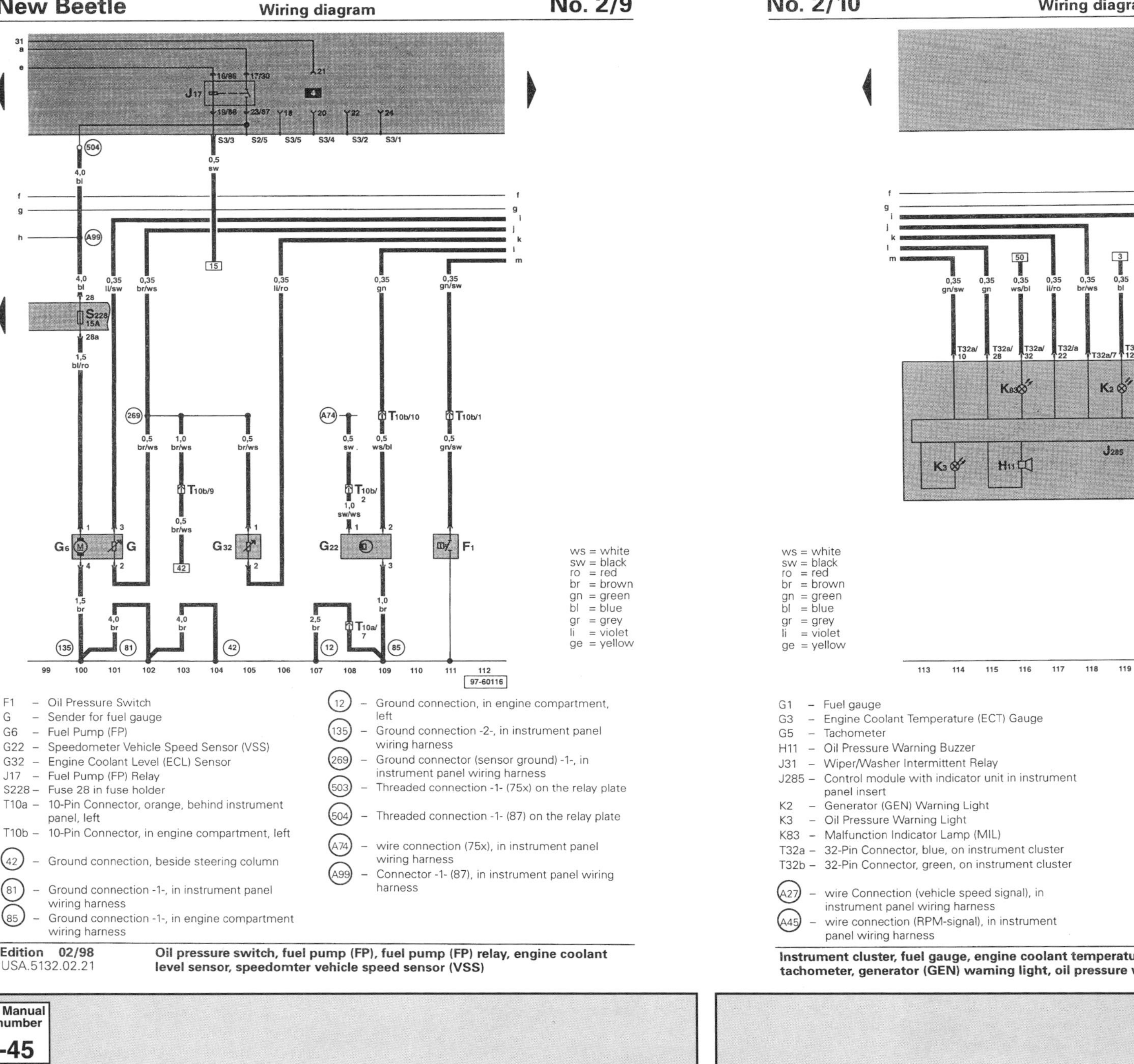

ws = white
sw = black
ro = red
br = brown
gn = green
bl = blue
gr = grey
li = violet
ge = yellow

F1 – Oil Pressure Switch
G – Sender for fuel gauge
G6 – Fuel Pump (FP)
G22 – Speedometer Vehicle Speed Sensor (VSS)
G32 – Engine Coolant Level (ECL) Sensor
J17 – Fuel Pump (FP) Relay
S228 – Fuse 28 in fuse holder
T10a – 10-Pin Connector, orange, behind instrument panel, left
T10b – 10-Pin Connector, in engine compartment, left
(42) – Ground connection, beside steering column
(81) – Ground connection -1-, in instrument panel wiring harness
(85) – Ground connection -1-, in engine compartment wiring harness
(12) – Ground connection, in engine compartment, left
(135) – Ground connection -2-, in instrument panel wiring harness
(269) – Ground connector (sensor ground) -1-, in instrument panel wiring harness
(503) – Threaded connection -1- (75x) on the relay plate
(504) – Threaded connection -1- (87) on the relay plate
(A74) – wire connection (75x), in instrument panel wiring harness
(A99) – Connector -1- (87), in instrument panel wiring harness

Edition 02/98
USA.5132.02.21

Oil pressure switch, fuel pump (FP), fuel pump (FP) relay, engine coolant level sensor, speedomter vehicle speed sensor (VSS)

ws = white
sw = black
ro = red
br = brown
gn = green
bl = blue
gr = grey
li = violet
ge = yellow

G1 – Fuel gauge
G3 – Engine Coolant Temperature (ECT) Gauge
G5 – Tachometer
H11 – Oil Pressure Warning Buzzer
J31 – Wiper/Washer Intermittent Relay
J285 – Control module with indicator unit in instrument panel insert
K2 – Generator (GEN) Warning Light
K3 – Oil Pressure Warning Light
K83 – Malfunction Indicator Lamp (MIL)
T32a – 32-Pin Connector, blue, on instrument cluster
T32b – 32-Pin Connector, green, on instrument cluster
(A27) – wire Connection (vehicle speed signal), in instrument panel wiring harness
(A45) – wire connection (RPM-signal), in instrument panel wiring harness

Instrument cluster, fuel gauge, engine coolant temperature (ECT) gauge, tachometer, generator (GEN) waming light, oil pressure waming light

Edition 09/98
USA.5132.05.21

1,9L-Engine – Turbo Diesel Fuel Injection (DFI)/66 kW, code ALH,

from January 1998

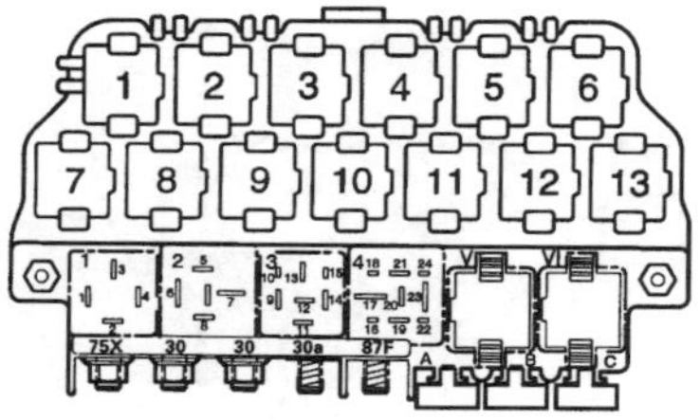

97-21956

Relay location on the thirteen position auxiliary relay panel, above relay panel:

10 Glow Plug Relay (180)

12 Power Suppy (Terminal 30, B+) Relay (109))

Relay panel:

2 Load Reduction Relay (213)

Note: Number in parentheses indicates production control number stamped on relay housing.

Fuse colors
30 A – green
25 A – white
20 A – yellow
15 A – blue
10 A – red
7,5 A – brown
5 A – beige

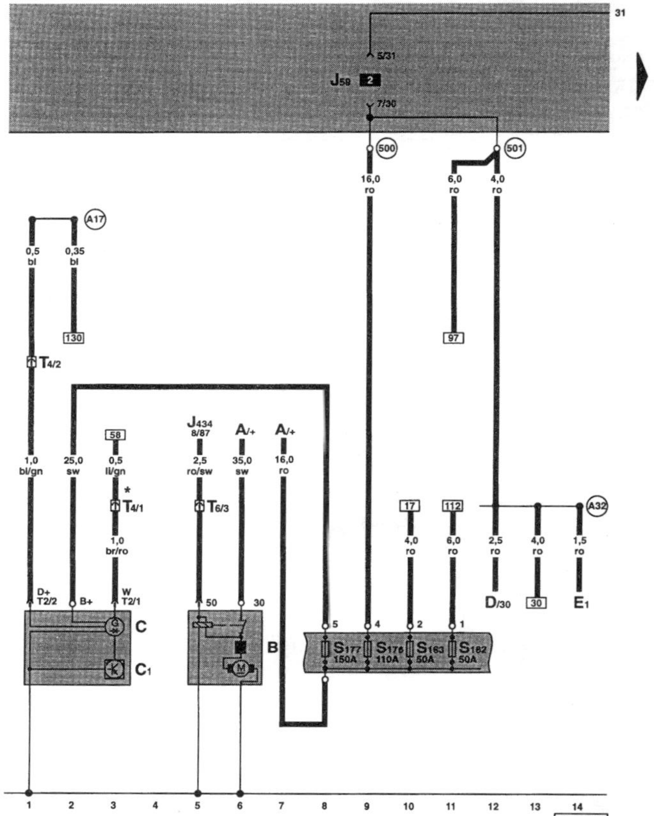

97-21932

ws = white
sw = black
ro = red
br = brown
gn = green
bl = blue
gr = grey
li = violet
ge = yellow

A – Battery
B – Starter
C – Generator (GEN)
C1 – Voltage Regulator (VR)
D – Ignition/Starter Switch
E1 – Light switch
J59 – Load Reduction Relay
J434 – Locking relay for starter (clutch pedal switch)
S162 – Fuse -1- in fuse bracket/battery
S163 – Fuse -2- in fuse bracket/battery
S176 – Fuse -4- (30), in fuse bracket/battery
S177 – Fuse -5- (30), in fuse bracket/battery
T2 – Double Connector
T4 – 4-Pin Connector, in engine compartment, left
T6 – 6-Pin Connector, red, behind instrument panel, left

(500) – Threaded connection -1- (30) on the relay plate
(501) – Threaded connection -2- (30) on the relay plate
(A17) – wire connection (61), in instrument panel wiring harness
(A32) – plus connection (30), in instrument panel wiring harness
* – manual transmission only

Starter, generator (GEN)

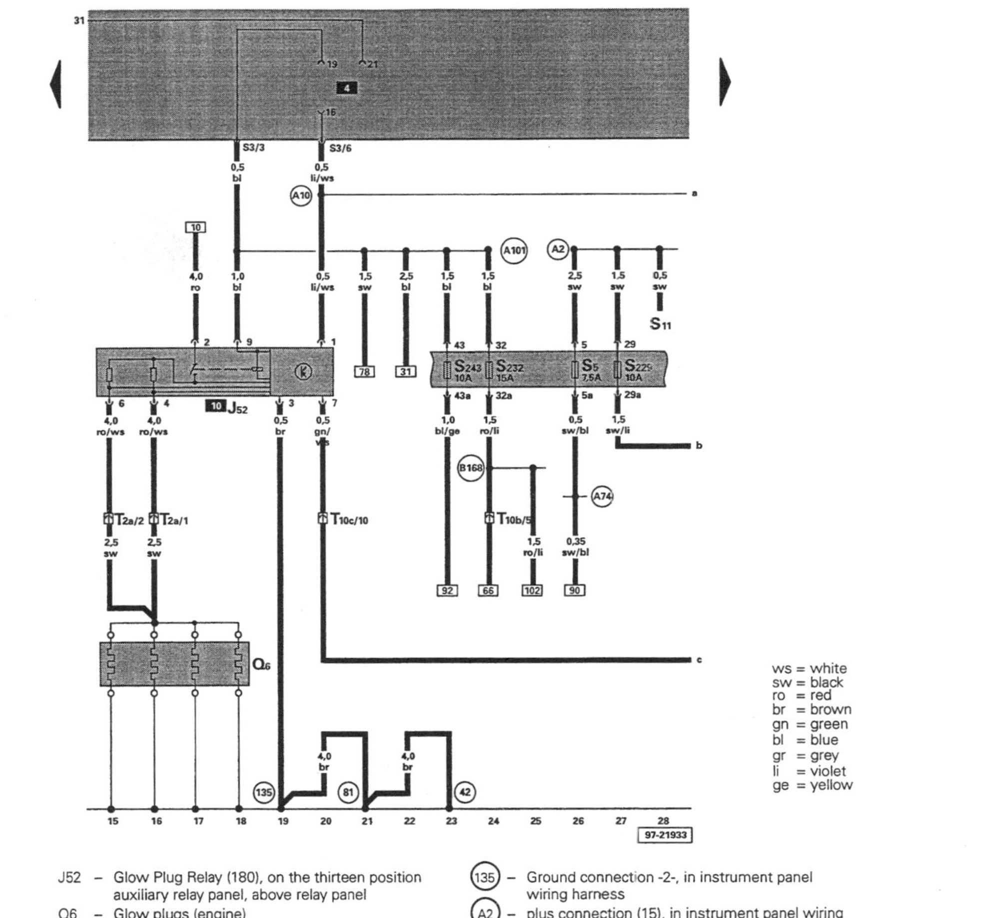

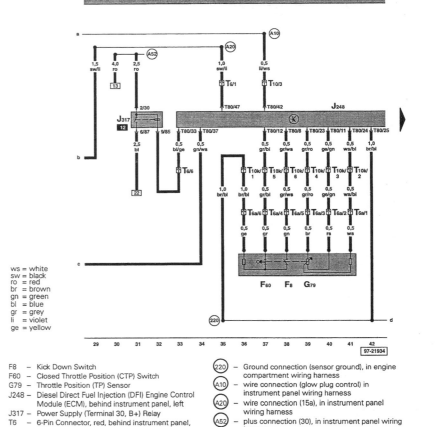

ws = white
sw = black
ro = red
br = brown
gn = green
bl = blue
gr = grey
li = violet
ge = yellow

J52 – Glow Plug Relay (180), on the thirteen position auxiliary relay panel, above relay panel
Q6 – Glow plugs (engine)
S5 – Fuse 5 in fuse holder
S11 – Fuse 11 in fuse holder
S229 – Fuse 29 in fuse holder
S232 – Fuse 32 in fuse holder
S243 – Fuse 43 in fuse holder
T2a – Double Connector, in engine compartment, left
T10b – 10-Pin Connector, in engine compartment, left
T10c – 10-Pin Connector, blue, behind instrument panel, left
(42) – Ground connection, beside steering column
(81) – Ground connection -1-, in instrument panel wiring harness
(135) – Ground connection -2-, in instrument panel wiring harness
(A2) – plus connection (15), in instrument panel wiring harness
(A10) – wire connection (glow plug control) in instrument panel wiring harness
(A74) – Connector (15a - fuse 5), in instrument panel wiring harness
(A101) – Connector -3- (87), in instrument panel wiring harness
(B168) – Connection (86), in passenger compartment wiring harness

Edition 07/98
USA.5132.03.21

Glow plugs (engine), glow plug relay

ws = white
sw = black
ro = red
br = brown
gn = green
bl = blue
gr = grey
li = violet
ge = yellow

F8 – Kick Down Switch
F60 – Closed Throttle Position (CTP) Switch
G79 – Throttle Position (TP) Sensor
J248 – Diesel Direct Fuel Injection (DFI) Engine Control Module (ECM), behind instrument panel, left
J317 – Power Supply (Terminal 30, B+) Relay
T6 – 6-Pin Connector, red, behind instrument panel, left
T6a – 6-Pin Connector, behind instrument panel, left
T10 – 10-Pin Connector, white, behind instrument panel, left
T10k – 10-Pin Connector, blue, behind instrument panel, left
T80 – Connector, 80 point, at Diesel Direct Fuel Injection (DFI) Engine Control Module (ECM)
(220) – Ground connection (sensor ground), in engine compartment wiring harness
(A10) – wire connection (glow plug control) in instrument panel wiring harness
(A20) – wire connection (15a), in instrument panel wiring harness
(A52) – plus connection (30), in instrument panel wiring harness

Diesel direct fuel injection (DFI) engine control module (ECM), power supply (terminal 30, B+) relay, kick down switch, throttle position (TP) sensor

Edition 01/98
USA.5132.01.21

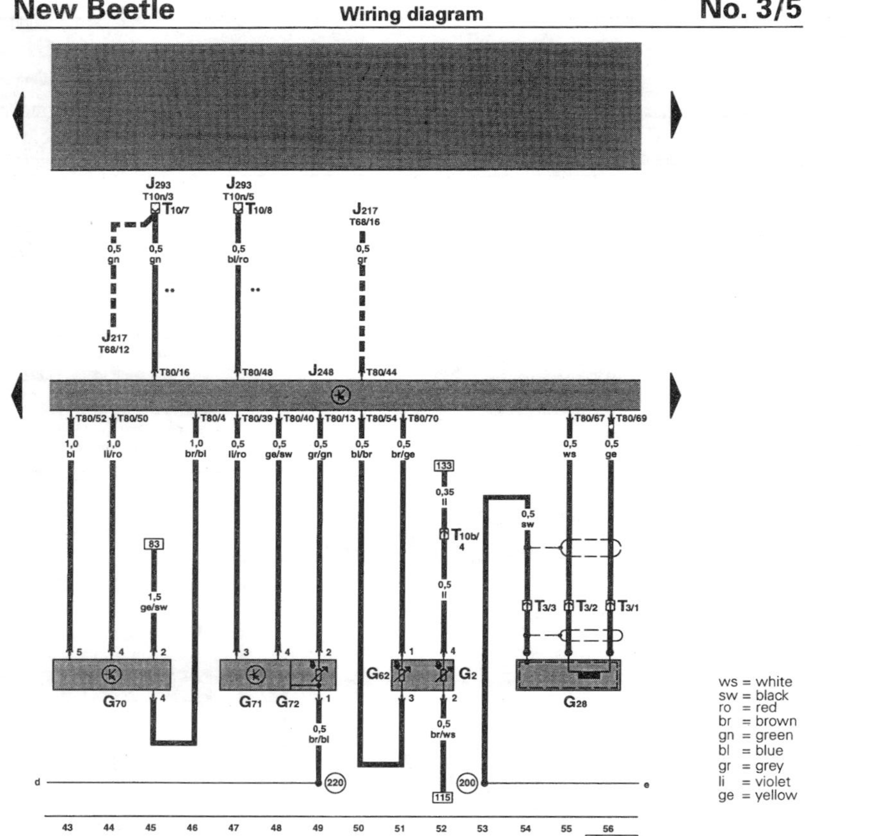

ws = white
sw = black
ro = red
br = brown
gn = green
bl = blue
gr = grey
li = violet
ge = yellow

G2 – Engine Coolant Temperature (ECT) Sensor
G28 – Engine Speed (RPM) Sensor
G62 – Engine Coolant Temperature (ECT) Sensor
G70 – Mass Air Flow (MAF) Sensor
G71 – Manifold Absolute Pressure (MAP) Sensor
G72 – Intake Air Temperature (IAT) Sensor
J217 – Transmission Control Module (TCM), behind instrument panel, center
J248 – Diesel Direct Fuel Injection (DFI) Engine Control Module (ECM), behind instrument panel, left
J293 – Coolant FC (Fan Control) Control Module
T3 – 3-Pin Connector, on engine, front
T10 – 10-Pin Connector, white, behind instrument panel, left
T10b – 10-Pin Connector, in engine compartment, left
T10n – 10-Pin Connector, on J293
T68 – 68-Pin Connector, on Transmission Control Module (TCM)
T80 – Connector, 80 point
(200) – Ground connection (shielding), in engine compartment wiring harness
(220) – Ground connection (sensor ground), in engine compartment wiring harness
** – Connection A/C
- - - automatic transmission only

Diesel direct fuel injection (DFI) engine control module (ECM), mass air flow (MAF) sensor, engine speed (RPM) sensor

ws = white
sw = black
ro = red
br = brown
gn = green
bl = blue
gr = grey
li = violet
ge = yellow

G80 – Needle Lift Sensor
G81 – Fuel Temperature Sensor
G149 – Modulating Piston Displacement Sensor
J217 – Transmission Control Module (TCM), behind instrument panel, center
J248 – Diesel Direct Fuel Injection (DFI) Engine Control Module (ECM), behind instrument panel, left
N146 – Quantity Adjuster
T2b – Double Connector, behind instrument panel, left
T2c – Double Connector, on engine, front
T10a – 10-Pin Connector, orange, behind instrument panel, left
T10f – 10-Pin Connector, on engine, front
T68 – 68-Pin Connector, on Transmission Control Module (TCM)
T80 – Connector, 80 point
(200) – Ground connection (shielding), in engine compartment wiring harness
(F25) – Wire connection -1-, in Diesel Direct Fuel Injection (DFI) system wiring harness
* – manual transmission only
*** – connection DATA-Bus
- - - automatic transmission only

Diesel direct fuel injection (DFI) engine control module (ECM), needle lift sensor, fuel temperature sensor, modulating piston displacement sensor

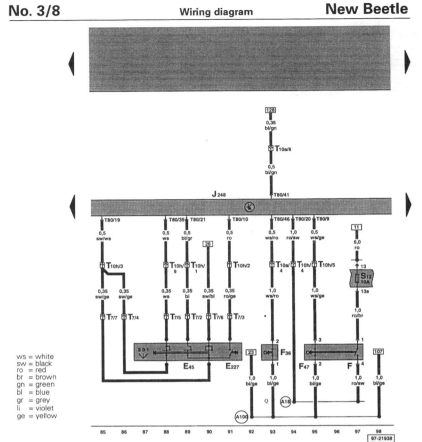

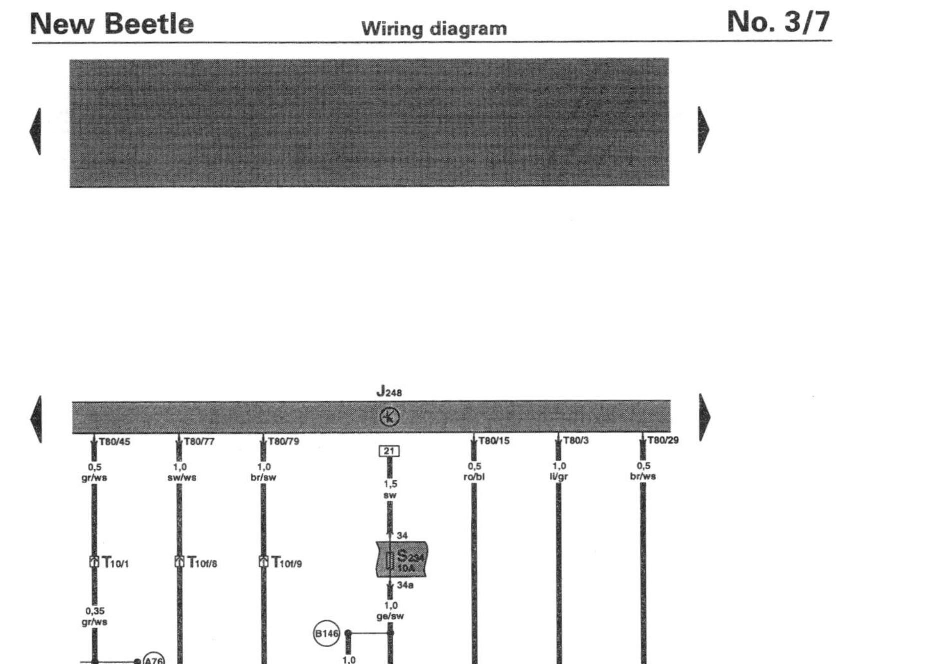

ws = white
sw = black
ro = red
br = brown
gn = green
bl = blue
gr = grey
li = violet
ge = yellow

J248 – Diesel Direct Fuel Injection (DFI) Engine Control Module (ECM), in plenum chamber, left
N18 – EGR Vacuum Regulator Solenoid Valve
N75 – Wastegate Bypass Regulator Valve
N108 – Cold Start Injector
N109 – Fuel Cut-off Valve
N239 – Change-over valve for intake manifold flap
S234 – Fuse 34 in fuse holder
T10 – 10-Pin Connector, white, behind instrument panel, left
T10b – 10-Pin Connector, in engine compartment, left
T10f – 10-Pin Connector, on engine, front
T16 – 16-Pin Connector, Data Link Connector (DLC), below steering column
T80 – Connector, 80 point

(A76) – Connector (K-diagnosis wire), in instrument panel wiring harness
(B146) – Plus connector -1- (87), in wiring harness interior
(E30) – Connector (87a), in wiring harness engine

Edition 01/98
USA.5132.01.21

Diesel direct fuel injection (DFI) engine control module (ECM), EGR vacuum regulator solenoid valve, cold start injector, fuel cut-off valve

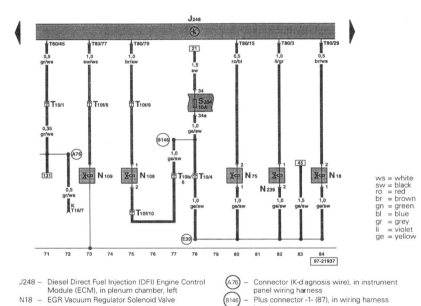

ws = white
sw = black
ro = red
br = brown
gn = green
bl = blue
gr = grey
li = violet
ge = yellow

E45 – Cruise Control Switch (if equipped)
E227 – Button for cruise control (set), (if equipped)
F – Brake Light Switch
F36 – Clutch Vacuum vent Valve Switch
F47 – Brake Vacuum Vent Valve Switch for cruise control/diesel fuel injection (DFI)
J248 – Diesel Direct Fuel Injection (DFI) Engine Control Module (ECM), behind instrument panel, left
S13 – Fuse 13 in fuse holder
T7 – 7-Pin Connector, near steering column
T10a – 10-Pin Connector, orange, behind instrument panel, left
T10h – 10-Pin Connector, black, behind instrument panel, left
T80 – Connector, 80 point

(A18) – wire connection (54), in instrument panel wiring harness
(A100) – Connector -2- (87), in instrument panel wiring harness
• – manual transmission only

Diesel direct fuel injection (DFI) engine control module (ECM), cruise control switch, brake light switch, clutch vacuum vent valve switch

Edition 01/98
USA.5132.01.21

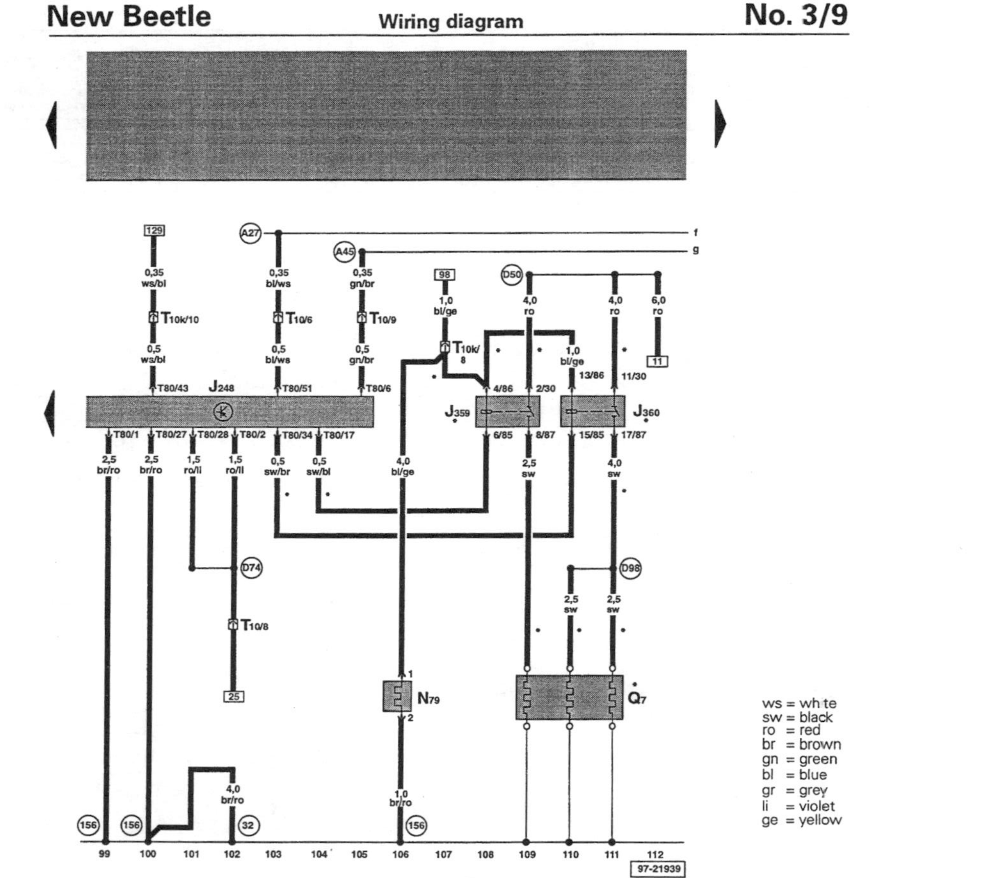

ws = white
sw = black
ro = red
br = brown
gn = green
bl = blue
gr = grey
li = violet
ge = yellow

J248 – Diesel Direct Fuel Injection (DFI) Engine Control Module (ECM), behind instrument panel, left
J359 – Relay for preheating coolant, low heat output, in engine compartment
J360 – Relay for preheating coolant, high heat output, in engine compartment
N79 – Positive Crankcase Ventilation (PCV) Heating Element
Q7 – glow plugs (coolant)
T10 – 10-Pin Connector, white, behind instrument panel, left
T10k – 10-Pin Connector, blue, behind instrument panel, left
T80 – Connector, 80 point

(32) – Ground connection, behind instrument panel, left

(156) – Ground connection, in Diesel Direct Fuel Injection (DFI) wiring harness
(A27) – wire Connection (vehicle speed signal), in instrument panel wiring harness
(A45) – wire connection (RPM-signal), in instrument panel wiring harness
(D50) – plus connection (30), in engine compartment wiring harness
(D74) – wire connection (86), in engine compartment wiring harness
(D98) – Wire connection (glow plugs), in engine compartment wiring harness

* – manual transmission only

Diesel direct fuel injection (DFI) engine control module (ECM), relay for preheating coolant, glow plugs (coolant)

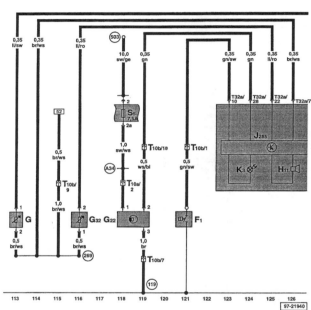

ws = white
sw = black
ro = red
br = brown
gn = green
bl = blue
gr = grey
li = violet
ge = yellow

F1 – Oil Pressure Switch
G – Sender for fuel gauge
G22 – Speedometer Vehicle Speed Sensor (VSS)
G32 – Engine Coolant Level (ECL) Sensor
H11 – Oil Pressure Warning Buzzer
J285 – Control module with indicator unit in instrument panel insert
K3 – Oil Pressure Warning Light
S2 – Fuse 2 in fuse holder
T10a – 10-Pin Connector, orange, behind instrument panel, left
T10b – 10-Pin Connector, in engine compartment, left
T32a – 32-Pin Connector, blue, on instrument cluster

(119) – Ground connection -1-, in headlight wiring harness

(269) – Ground connector (sensor ground) -1-, in instrument panel wiring harness
(503) – Threaded connection -1- (75x) on the relay plate
(A34) – wire connection (75x), in instrument panel wiring harness

Sender for fuel gauge, engine coolant level (ECL) sensor, speedometer vehicle speed sensor (VSS), visual and acoustical oil pressure control

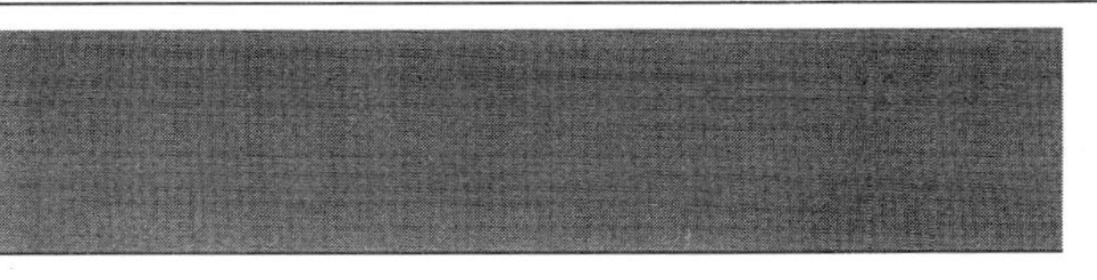

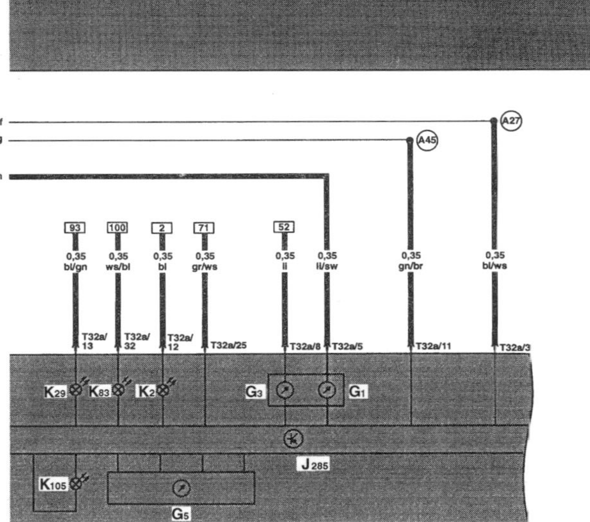

ws = white
sw = black
ro = red
br = brown
gn = green
bl = blue
gr = grey
li = violet
ge = yellow

G1 – Fuel gauge
G3 – Engine Coolant Temperature (ECT) Gauge
G5 – Tachometer
J285 – Control module with indicator unit in instrument panel insert
K2 – Generator (GEN) Warning Light
K83 – Exhaust Warning Light
K29 – Glow Plug Indicator Light
K105 – Low Fuel Level Warning Light
T32a – 32-Pin Connector, blue, on instrument cluster

(A27) – wire Connection (vehicle speed signal), in instrument panel wiring harness
(A45) – wire connection (RPM-signal), in instrument panel wiring harness

THIS PAGE INTENTIONALLY LEFT BLANK

Automatic transmission,

from January 1998

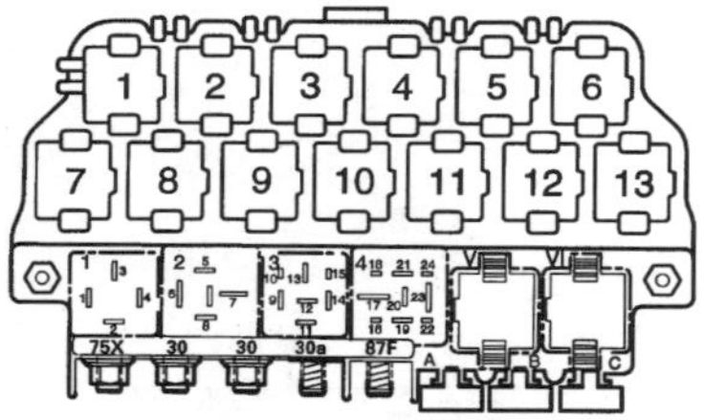

1 2 3 4 5 6
7 8 9 10 11 12 13
75X 30 30 30a 87F A B C

97–21956

Relay location on the thirteen position auxiliary relay panel, above relay panel:

11 Park/Neutral Position (PNP) Relay (175)

Relay panel:

Note: Number in parentheses indicates production control number stamped on relay housing.

Fuse colors

30 A – green
25 A – white
20 A – yellow
15 A – blue
10 A – red
7,5 A – brown
5 A – beige

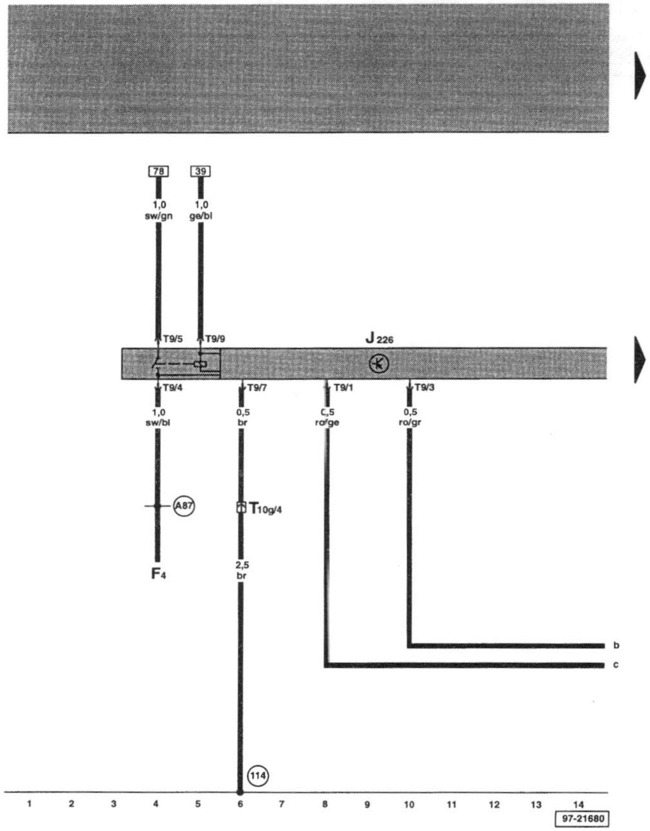

78 39
1,0 sw/gn 1,0 ge/bl
T9/5 T9/9
J 226
T9/4 T9/7 T9/1 T9/3
1,0 sw/bl 0,5 br 0,5 ro/ge 0,5 ro/gr
A87 T10g/4
F4 2,5 br
b c
114
1 2 3 4 5 6 7 8 9 10 11 12 13 14
97-21680

ws = white
sw = black
ro = red
br = brown
gn = green
bl = blue
gr = grey
li = violet
ge = yellow

F4 – Back-Up Light Switch
J226 – Park/Neutral Position (PNP) Relay (175), on the thirteen position auxiliary relay panel
T9 – 9-Pin Connector
T10g – 10-Pin Connector, grey, behind instrument panel, left
(114) – Ground connection, in automatic transmission wiring harness
(A87) – Connector (reverse lamp), in instrument panel wiring harness

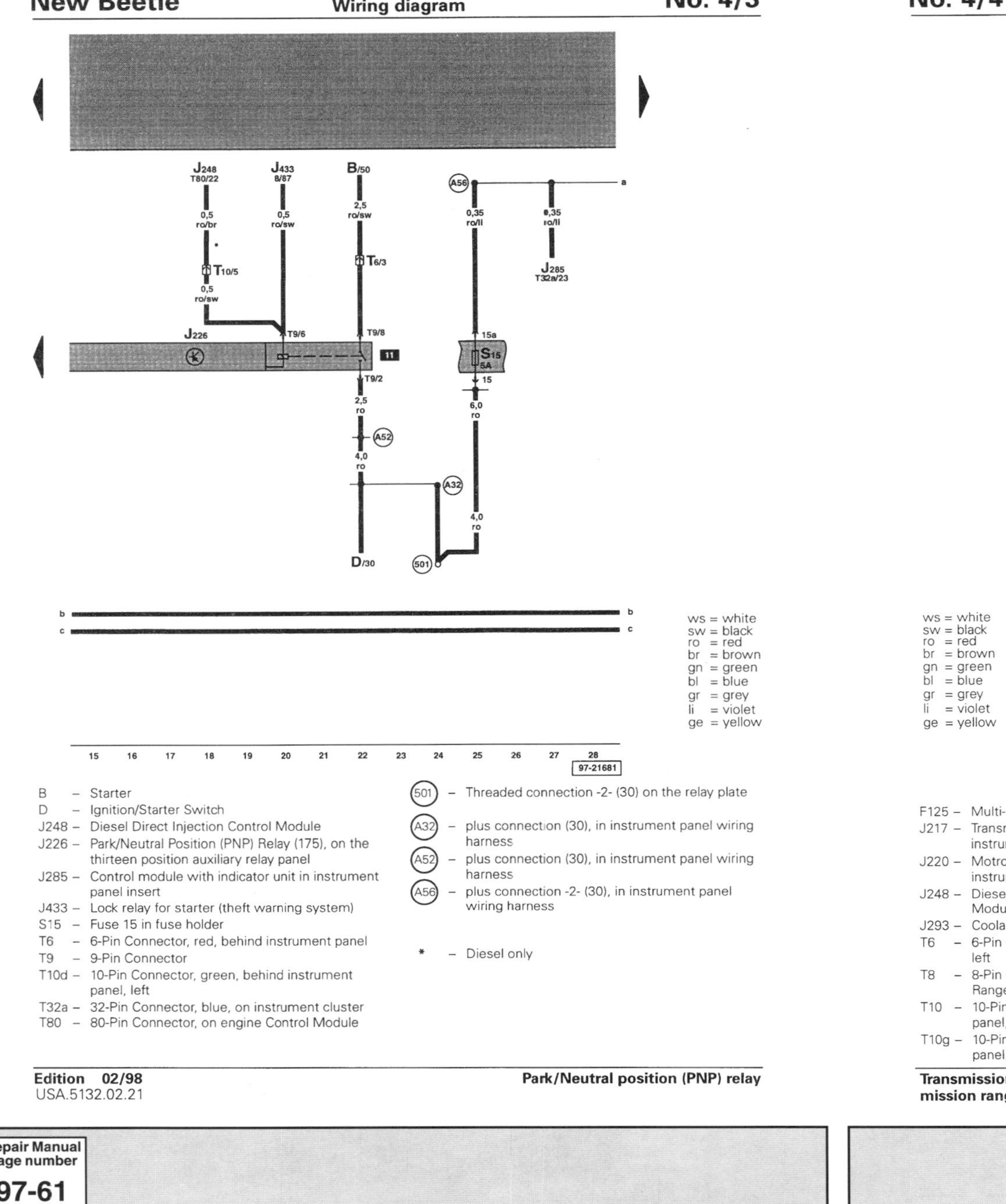

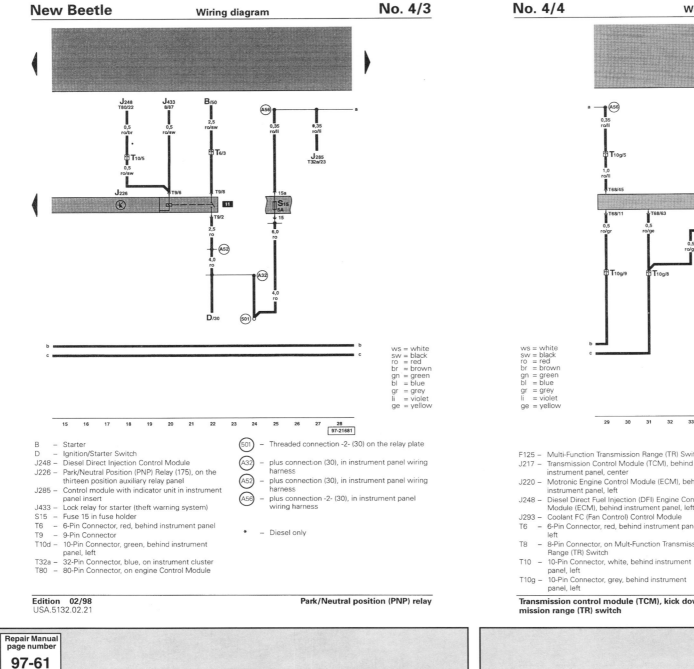

ws = white
sw = black
ro = red
br = brown
gn = green
bl = blue
gr = grey
li = violet
ge = yellow

- B – Starter
- D – Ignition/Starter Switch
- J248 – Diesel Direct Injection Control Module
- J226 – Park/Neutral Position (PNP) Relay (175), on the thirteen position auxiliary relay panel
- J285 – Control module with indicator unit in instrument panel insert
- J433 – Lock relay for starter (theft warning system)
- S15 – Fuse 15 in fuse holder
- T6 – 6-Pin Connector, red, behind instrument panel
- T9 – 9-Pin Connector
- T10d – 10-Pin Connector, green, behind instrument panel, left
- T32a – 32-Pin Connector, blue, on instrument cluster
- T80 – 80-Pin Connector, on engine Control Module
- (501) – Threaded connection -2- (30) on the relay plate
- (A32) – plus connection (30), in instrument panel wiring harness
- (A52) – plus connection (30), in instrument panel wiring harness
- (A56) – plus connection -2- (30), in instrument panel wiring harness
- * – Diesel only

Park/Neutral position (PNP) relay

ws = white
sw = black
ro = red
br = brown
gn = green
bl = blue
gr = grey
li = violet
ge = yellow

- F125 – Multi-Function Transmission Range (TR) Switch
- J217 – Transmission Control Module (TCM), behind instrument panel, center
- J220 – Motronic Engine Control Module (ECM), behind instrument panel, left
- J248 – Diesel Direct Fuel Injection (DFI) Engine Control Module (ECM), behind instrument panel, left
- J293 – Coolant FC (Fan Control) Control Module
- T6 – 6-Pin Connector, red, behind instrument panel, left
- T8 – 8-Pin Connector, on Mult-Function Transmission Range (TR) Switch
- T10 – 10-Pin Connector, white, behind instrument panel, left
- T10g – 10-Pin Connector, grey, behind instrument panel, left
- T10n – 10 -Pin Connector, at Coolant Fan Control (FC) Module
- T16 – 16-Pin Connector, Data Link Connector (DLC), below steering column
- T68 – 68-Pin Connector
- T80 – Connector, 80 point, on Engine Control Module (ECM)
- (32) – Ground connection, behind instrument panel, left
- (114) – Ground connection, in automatic transmission wiring harness
- (A56) – plus connection -2- (30), in instrument panel wiring harness
- (A76) – Connector (K-diagnosis wire), in instrument panel wiring harness

Transmission control module (TCM), kick down switch, multi-function transmission range (TR) switch

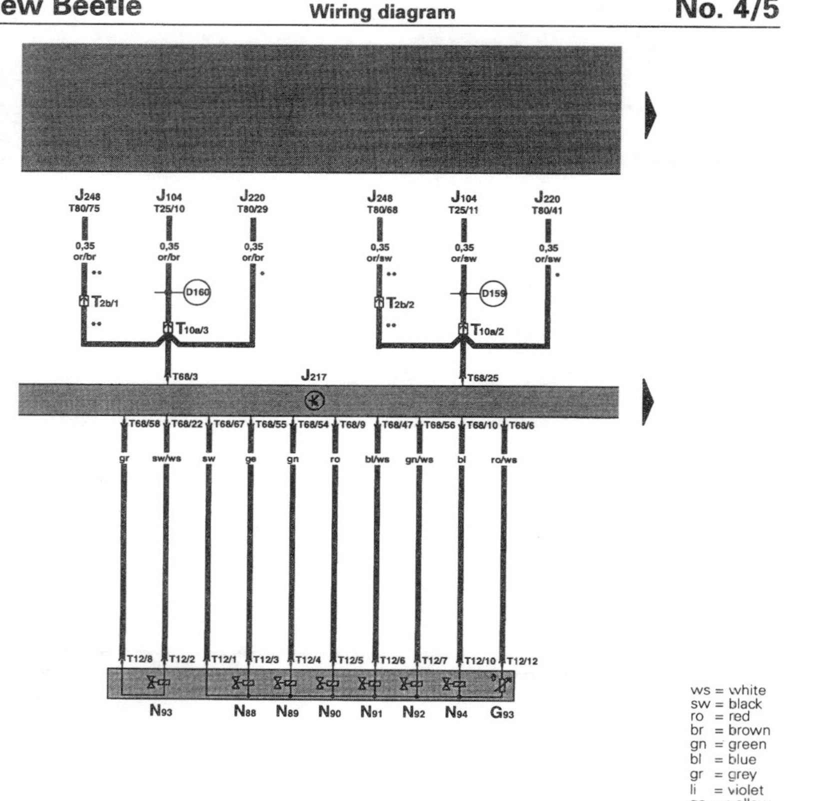

ws = white
sw = black
ro = red
br = brown
gn = green
bl = blue
gr = grey
li = violet
ge = yellow

G93 – Transmission Fluid Temperature Sensor
J104 – ABS Control Module (w/EDL)
J217 – Transmission Control Module (TCM), behind instrument panel, center
J220 – Motronic Engine Control Module (ECM), behind instrument panel, left
J248 – Diesel Direct Fuel Injection (DFI) Engine Control Module (ECM), behind instrument panel, left
N88 – Solenoid Valve 1
N89 – Solenoid Valve 2
N90 – Solenoid Valve 3
N91 – Solenoid Valve 4
N92 – Solenoid Valve 5
N93 – Solenoid Valve 6
N94 – Solenoid Valve 7
T2b – Double Connector (Diesel only)
T10a – 10-Pin Connector, orange, behind instrument panel, left
T12 – 12-Pin Connector
T25 – 25-Pin Connector, on ABS Control Module (w/EDL)
T68 – 68-Pin Connector
T80 – Connector, 80 point, on Engine Control Module (ECM)
(D159) – CAN - bus High, in engine wiring harness
(D160) – CAN - bus Low, in engine wiring harness
* – Gasoline only
** – Diesel only

Transmission control module, solenoid valves, transmission fluid temperature sensor

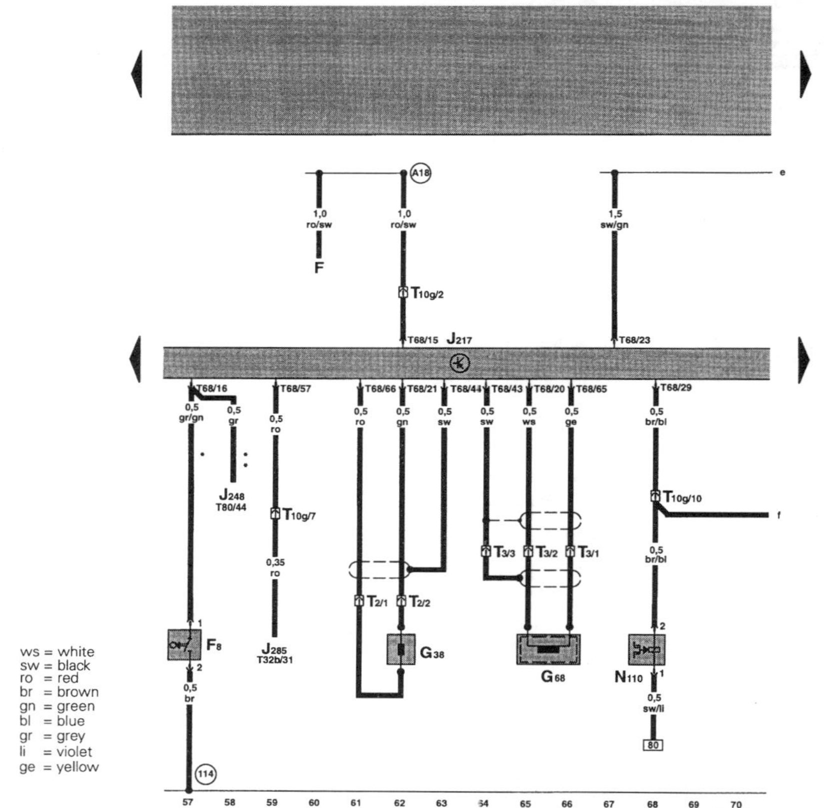

ws = white
sw = black
ro = red
br = brown
gn = green
bl = blue
gr = grey
li = violet
ge = yellow

F – Brake Light Switch
F8 – Kick-Down Switch
G38 – Transmission Vehicle Speed Sensor
G68 – Vehicle Speed Sensor (VSS)
J217 – Transmission Control Module (TCM), behind instrument panel, center
J248 – Diesel Direct Fuel Injection (DFI) Engine Control Module (ECM)
J285 – Control module with indicator unit in instrument panel insert
N110 – Shift Lock Solenoid
T2 – Double-Connector
T3 3-Pin Connector, on transmission
T10g – 10-Pin Connector, grey, behind instrument panel, left
T32b – 32-Pin Connector, blue, on instrument cluster
T68 – 68-Pin Connector
T80 – 80-Pin Connector
(114) – Ground connection in automatic transmission wiring harness
(A18) – wire connection (54), in instrument panel wiring harness
* – Gasoline only
** – Diesel only

Transmission control module (TCM), vehicle speed sensor, warning light for selector lever position P/N

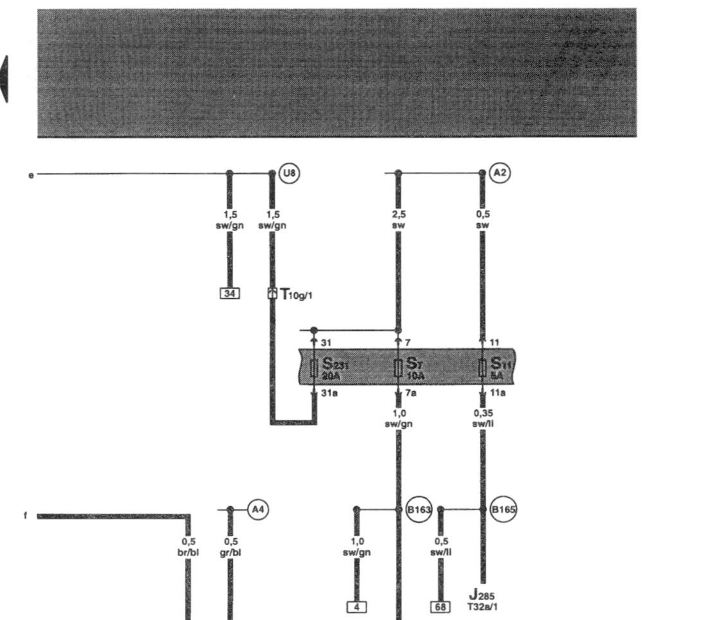

ws = white
sw = black
ro = red
br = brown
gn = green
bl = blue
gr = grey
li = violet
ge = yellow

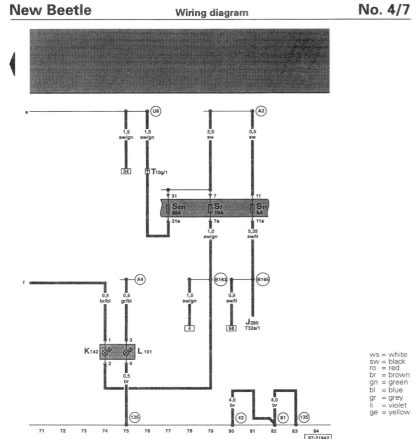

J285 – Control module with indicator unit in instrument panel insert
K142 – Warning light for selector lever position P/N
L101 – Illumination for selector lever scale
S7 – Fuse 7 in fuse holder
S11 – Fuse 11 in fuse holder
S231 – Fuse 31 in fuse holder
T10g – 10-Pin Connector, grey, behind instrument panel, left
T32a – 32-Pin Connector, blue, on instrument cluster

(42) – Ground connection, beside steering column

(81) – Ground connection -1-, in instrument panel wiring harness
(135) – Ground connection -2-, in instrument panel wiring harness

(A2) – plus connection (15), in instrument panel wiring harness
(A4) – plus connection (58b), in instrument panel wiring harness
(B163) – Plus connector -1- (15), in wiring harness interior
(B165) – Plus connector -2- (15), in wiring harness interior
(U8) – Connector (15a), in automatic transmission wiring harness

Edition 01/98
USA.5132.01.21

Warning light for selector lever position P/N, illumination for selector lever scale

THIS PAGE INTENTIONALLY LEFT

BLANK

Anti-lock brake system (ABS) with electronic differential lock (EDL),

from January 1998

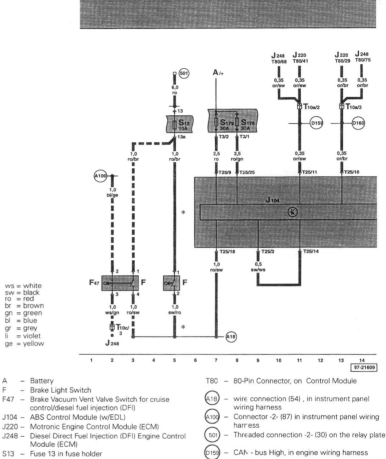

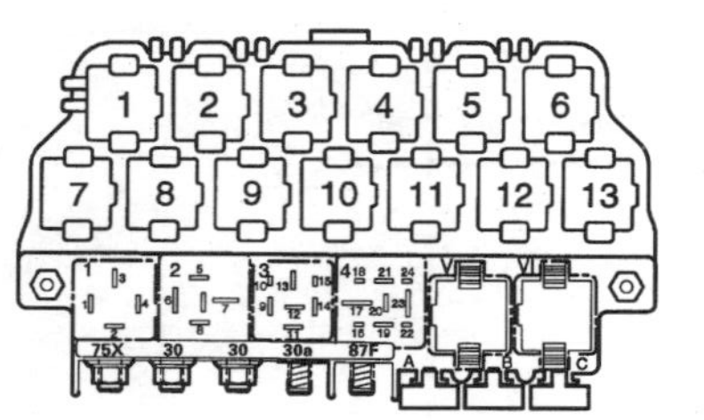

Fuse colors

30 A – green
25 A – white
20 A – yellow
15 A – blue
10 A – red
7,5 A – brown
5 A – beige

ws = white
sw = black
ro = red
br = brown
gn = green
bl = blue
gr = grey
li = violet
ge = yellow

97-21609

- A – Battery
- F – Brake Light Switch
- F47 – Brake Vacuum Vent Valve Switch for cruise control/diesel fuel injection (DFI)
- J104 – ABS Control Module (w/EDL)
- J220 – Motronic Engine Control Module (ECM)
- J248 – Diesel Direct Fuel Injection (DFI) Engine Control Module (ECM)
- S13 – Fuse 13 in fuse holder
- S178 – Fuse -6- (30), in fuse bracket/battery
- S179 – Fuse -7- (30), in fuse bracket/battery
- T3 – 3-Pin Connector,
- T10a – 10-Pin Connector, orange, behind instrument panel,left
- T10c – 10-Pin Connector, blue, behind instrument panel, left
- T25 – 25-Pin Connector
- T80 – 80-Pin Connector, on Control Module
- (A18) – wire connection (54) , in instrument panel wiring harness
- (A100) – Connector -2- (87) in instrument panel wiring harness
- (501) – Threaded connection -2- (30) on the relay plate
- (D159) – CAN - bus High, in engine wiring harness
- (D160) – CAN - bus Low, in engine wiring harness
- - - - Diesel only
- * – Gasoline only

ABS control module, brake light switch light switch

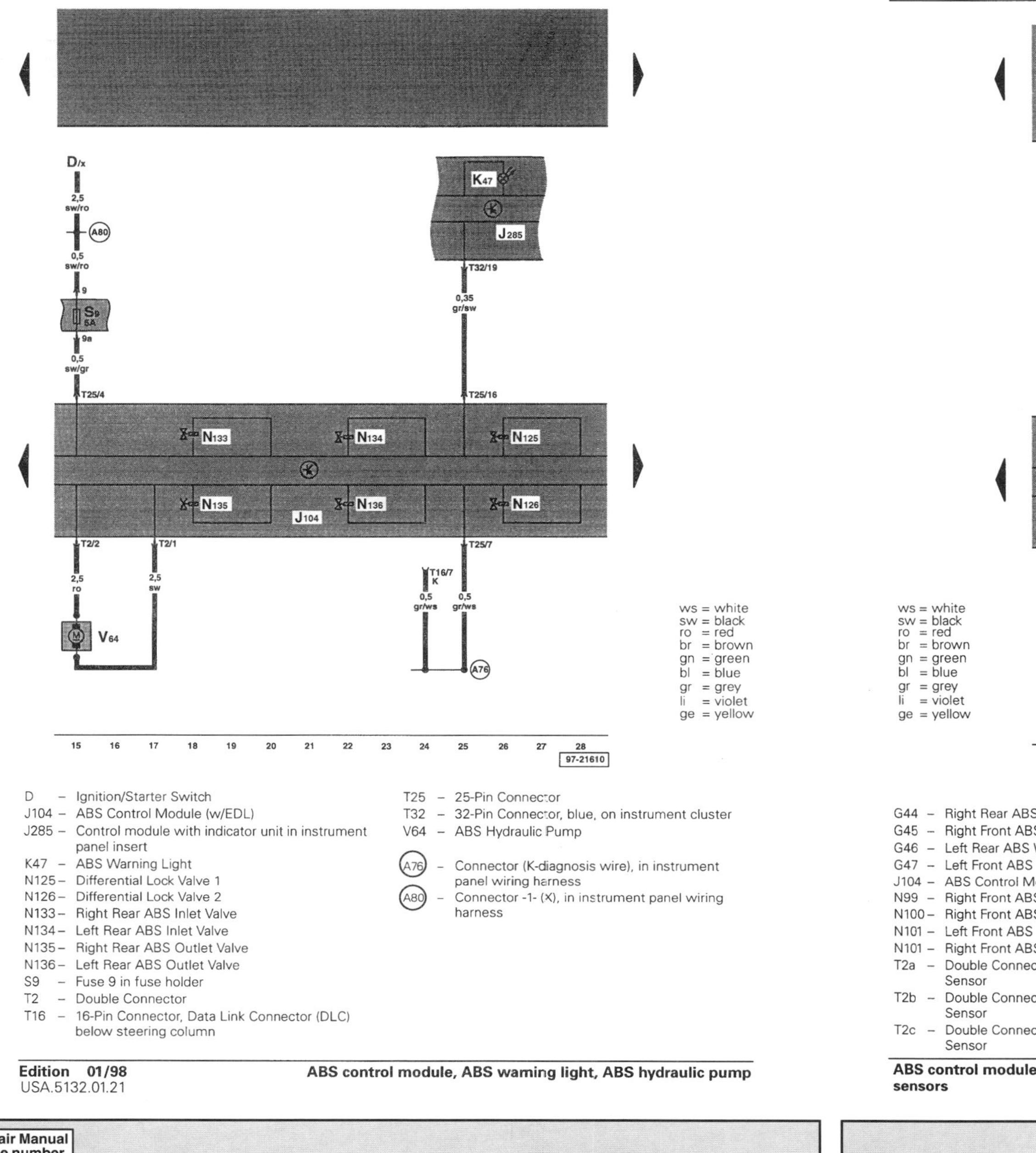

ws = white
sw = black
ro = red
br = brown
gn = green
bl = blue
gr = grey
li = violet
ge = yellow

- D – Ignition/Starter Switch
- J104 – ABS Control Module (w/EDL)
- J285 – Control module with indicator unit in instrument panel insert
- K47 – ABS Warning Light
- N125 – Differential Lock Valve 1
- N126 – Differential Lock Valve 2
- N133 – Right Rear ABS Inlet Valve
- N134 – Left Rear ABS Inlet Valve
- N135 – Right Rear ABS Outlet Valve
- N136 – Left Rear ABS Outlet Valve
- S9 – Fuse 9 in fuse holder
- T2 – Double Connector
- T16 – 16-Pin Connector, Data Link Connector (DLC) below steering column
- T25 – 25-Pin Connector
- T32 – 32-Pin Connector, blue, on instrument cluster
- V64 – ABS Hydraulic Pump
- (A76) – Connector (K-diagnosis wire), in instrument panel wiring harness
- (A80) – Connector -1- (X), in instrument panel wiring harness

ABS control module, ABS warning light, ABS hydraulic pump

ws = white
sw = black
ro = red
br = brown
gn = green
bl = blue
gr = grey
li = violet
ge = yellow

- G44 – Right Rear ABS Wheel Speed Sensor
- G45 – Right Front ABS Wheel Speed Sensor
- G46 – Left Rear ABS Wheel Speed Sensor
- G47 – Left Front ABS Wheel Speed Sensor
- J104 – ABS Control Module (w/EDL)
- N99 – Right Front ABS Inlet Valve
- N100 – Right Front ABS Outlet Valve
- N101 – Left Front ABS Inlet Valve
- N101 – Right Front ABS Inlet Valve
- T2a – Double Connector, on Rear Right ABS Wheel Sensor
- T2b – Double Connector, on Front Right ABS Wheel Sensor
- T2c – Double Connector, on Rear Left ABS Wheel Sensor
- T2d – Double Connector, on Front Left ABS Wheel Sensor
- T25 – 25-Pin Connector, at ABS Control Module
- (12) – Ground connection, in engine compartment, left
- (132) – Ground connection -3-, in engine compartment wiring harness
- (D146) – Connector(speed sensor rear, left +), in wiring harness engine compartment
- (D147) – Connector(speed sensor rear, left –), in wiring harness engine compartment
- (D148) – Connector(speed sensor rear, right +), in wiring harness engine compartment
- (D149) – Connector(speed sensor rear, right –), in wiring harness engine compartment

ABS control module, ABS inlet valves, ABS outlet valves, ABS wheel speed sensors

Airbag systems,

from January 1998

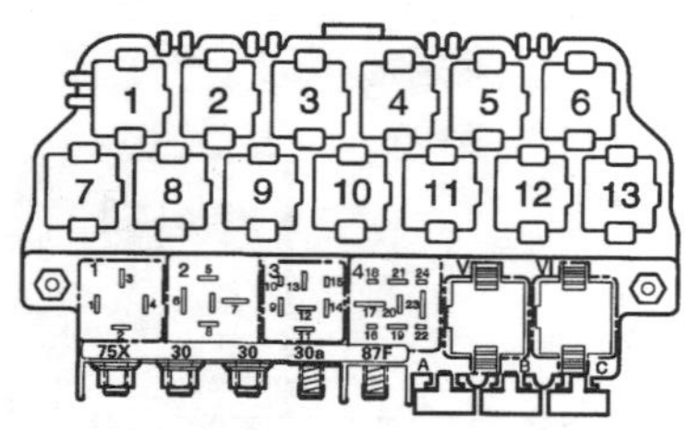

Fuse colors
30 A – green
25 A – white
20 A – yellow
15 A – blue
10 A – red
7,5 A – brown
5 A – beige

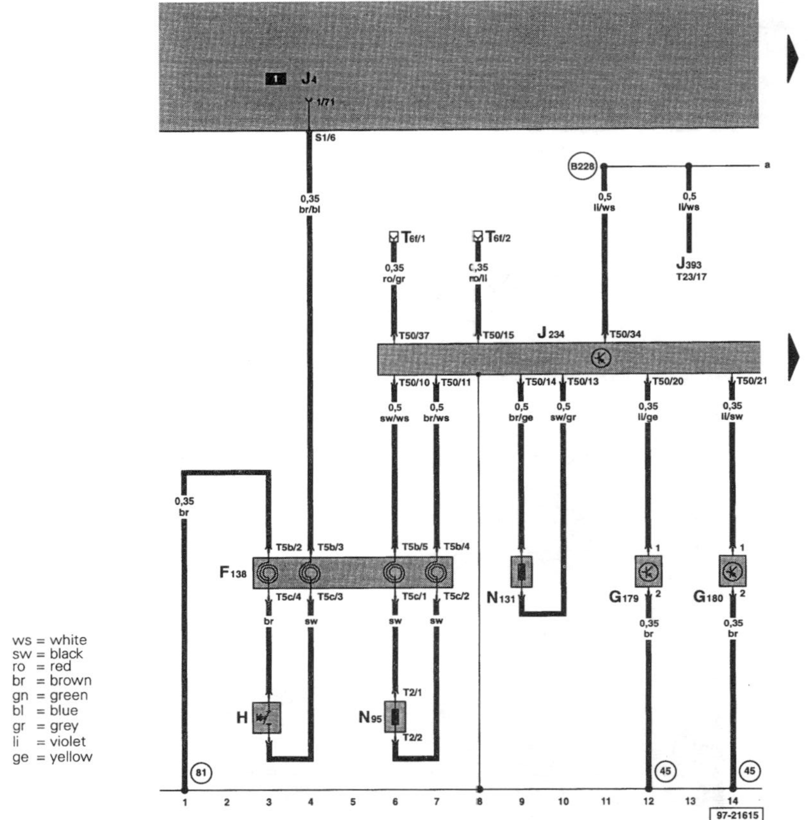

ws = white
sw = black
ro = red
br = brown
gn = green
bl = blue
gr = grey
li = violet
ge = yellow

F138 – Airbag Spiral Spring/Return Spring With Slip Ring
G179 – Crash sensor for side airbag, driver's side
G180 – Crash sensor for side airbag, passenger side
H – Horn Button
J4 – Dual Horn Relay
J234 – Airbag Control Module, behind console
J393 – Central control module for comfort system
N95 – Driver's Side Airbag Igniter
N131 – Passenger's Side Airbag Igniter 1
T2 – Double Connector, yellow, on Airbag Igniter
T5b – 5-Pin Connector, yellow, near steering column on Airbag Spiral Spring/Return Spring
T5c – 5-Pin Connector, black, near steering column on Airbag Spiral Spring/Return Spring
T6f – 6-Pin Connector, below passenger's seat, red
T23 – 23-Pin Connector, on Central control module for comfort system
T50 – 50-Pin Connector
(45) – Ground connection, behind instrument panel, center
(81) – Ground connection -1-, in instrument panel wiring harness
(B228) – wire connection (crash), in instrument panel wiring harness

Airbag control module, airbag spiral spring, igniters for front airbags, crash sensors for side airbags

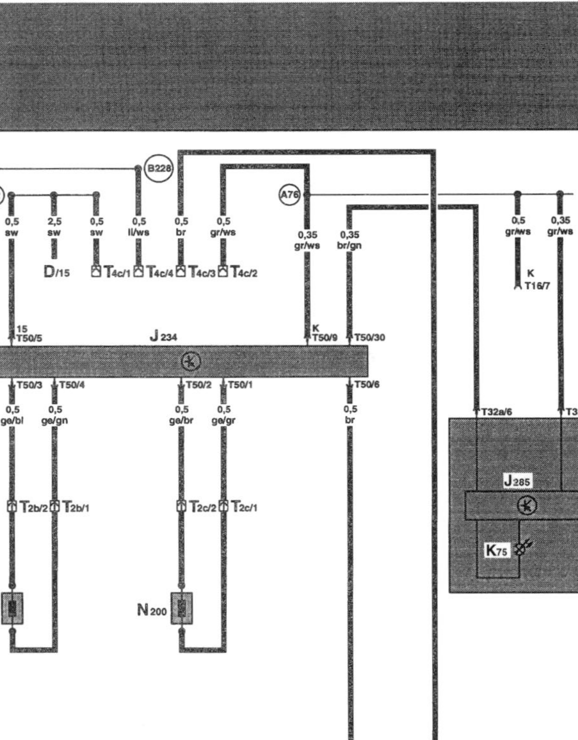

ws = white
sw = black
ro = red
br = brown
gn = green
bl = blue
gr = grey
li = violet
ge = yellow

- D – Ignition/Starter Switch
- J234 – Airbag Control Module, behind console
- J285 – Control module with indicator unit in instrument panel insert
- K75 – Airbag Malfunction Indicator Lamp (MIL)
- N199 – Igniter for side airbag, driver's side
- N200 – Igniter for side airbag, passenger side
- T2b – Double Connector
- T2c – Double Connector
- T4c – 4-Pin Connector
- T16 – 16-Pin Connector, Data Link Connector (DLC) below steering column
- T32a – 32-Pin Connector, blue, on instrument cluster
- T32b – 32-Pin Connector, green, on instrument cluster
- T50 – 50-Pin Connector

- (45) – Ground connection, behind instrument panel, center
- (135) – Ground connection -2-, in instrument panel wiring harness
- (A2) – plus connection (15), in instrument panel wiring harness
- (A76) – Connector (K-diagnosis wire), in instrument panel wiring harness
- (B228) – wire connection (crash), in instrument panel wiring harness

Edition 01/98
USA.5132.01.21

Airbag control module, igniter for side airbag, airbag malfunction indicator lamp (MIL)

THIS PAGE INTENTIONALLY LEFT BLANK

Radio system,

from January 1998

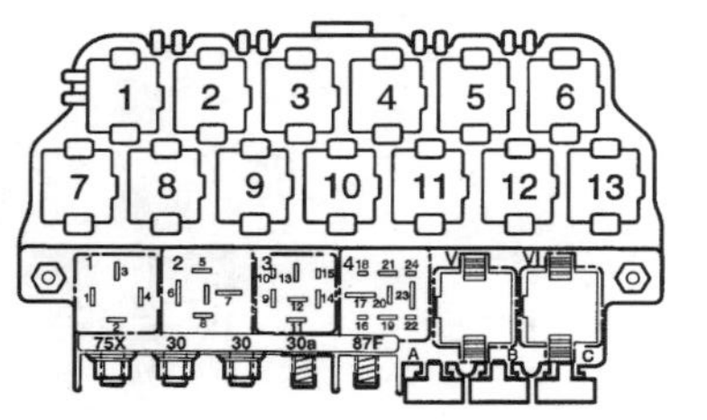

Fuse colors
30 A – green
25 A – white
20 A – yellow
15 A – blue
10 A – red
7,5 A – brown
5 A – beige

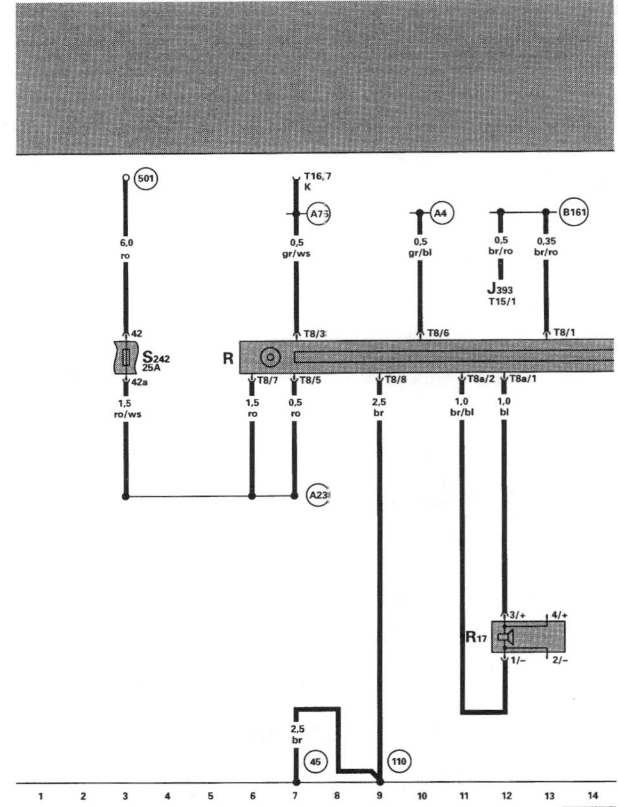

ws = white
sw = black
ro = red
br = brown
gn = green
bl = blue
gr = grey
li = violet
ge = yellow

J393 – Central control system for comfort system
R – Radio
R17 – Right Rear Woofer, in right rear door
S242 – Fuse 42 in fuse holder
T8 – 8-Pin Connector, black, on radio
T8a – 8-Pin Connector, brown, on radio
T15 – 15-Pin Connector, on Central control module for comfort system
T16 – 16–Pin Connector, Data Link Connector (DLC), below steering column
(45) – Ground connection, behind instrument panel, center
(110) – Ground connection -2-, in instrument panel wiring harness
(501) – Screw Connection -2- (30), on relay panel

(A4) – plus connection (58b), in instrument panel wiring harness
(A23) – wire connection (30al), in instrument panel wiring harness
(A76) – Connector (K–diagnosis wire), in instrument panel wiring harness
(B161) – connection (Alarm system), in wiring harness, interior

Radio, right rear speaker

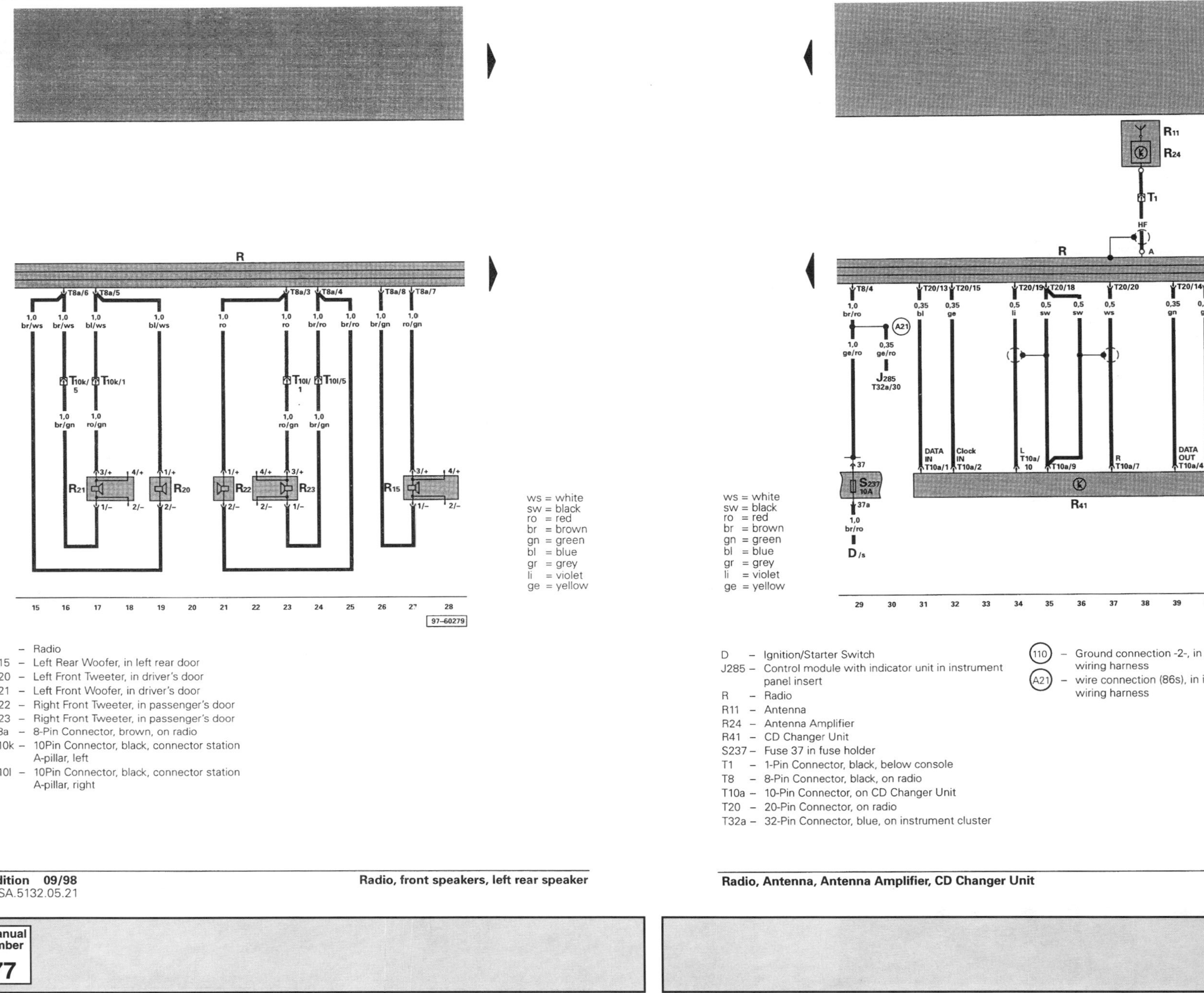

ws = white
sw = black
ro = red
br = brown
gn = green
bl = blue
gr = grey
li = violet
ge = yellow

R – Radio
R15 – Left Rear Woofer, in left rear door
R20 – Left Front Tweeter, in driver's door
R21 – Left Front Woofer, in driver's door
R22 – Right Front Tweeter, in passenger's door
R23 – Right Front Tweeter, in passenger's door
T8a – 8-Pin Connector, brown, on radio
T10k – 10Pin Connector, black, connector station A-pillar, left
T10l – 10Pin Connector, black, connector station A-pillar, right

ws = white
sw = black
ro = red
br = brown
gn = green
bl = blue
gr = grey
li = violet
ge = yellow

D – Ignition/Starter Switch
J285 – Control module with indicator unit in instrument panel insert
R – Radio
R11 – Antenna
R24 – Antenna Amplifier
R41 – CD Changer Unit
S237 – Fuse 37 in fuse holder
T1 – 1-Pin Connector, black, below console
T8 – 8-Pin Connector, black, on radio
T10a – 10-Pin Connector, on CD Changer Unit
T20 – 20-Pin Connector, on radio
T32a – 32-Pin Connector, blue, on instrument cluster

(110) – Ground connection -2-, in instrument panel wiring harness
(A21) – wire connection (86s), in instrument panel wiring harness

Air conditioning,

from January 1998

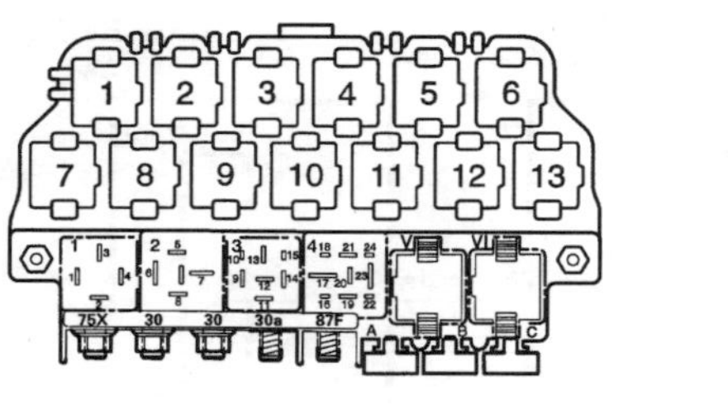

Fuse colors
30 A – green
25 A – white
20 A – yellow
15 A – blue
10 A – red
7,5 A – brown
5 A – beige

Edition 01.98
USA.5132.01.21

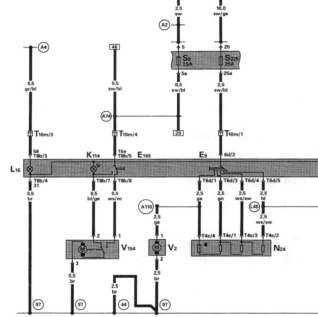

ws = white
sw = black
ro = red
br = brown
gn = green
bl = blue
gr = grey
li = violet
ge = yellow

97-60280

D – Ignition/Starter Switch
E9 – Fresh Air Blower Switch
E159 – Fresh Air/Recirculating Flap Switch
K114 – Fresh Air and Recirculating Air Mode Indicator Light
L16 – Fresh Air Control Lever Light
N24 – Fresh Air Blower Series Resistance With Fuse
S5 – Fuse 5 in fuse holder
S225 – Fuse 25 in fuse holder
T4c – 4-Pin Connector
T6d – 6-Pin Connector
T8b – 6-Pin Connector
T10m – 10-Pin Connector
V2 – Fresh Air Blower
V154 – Servo motor for fresh-/recirculating air door

(44) – Ground connection, on left A-pillar, lower part
(97) – Ground connection -1-, in A/C wiring harness
(503) – Screw Connection (75x), on relay panel
(A2) – plus connection (15), in instrument panel wiring harness
(A4) – plus connection (58b), in instrument panel wiring harness
(A74) – Connector (15a - fuse 5), in instrument panel wiring harness
(A110) – Connection (fresh air blower), in instrument panel wiring harness
(L45) – Wire connection, in A/C wiring harness

Fresh air blower, fresh air blower switch, fresh air/recirculating flap switch, fresh air blower series resistance with fuse

Edition 09/98
USA.5132.05.21

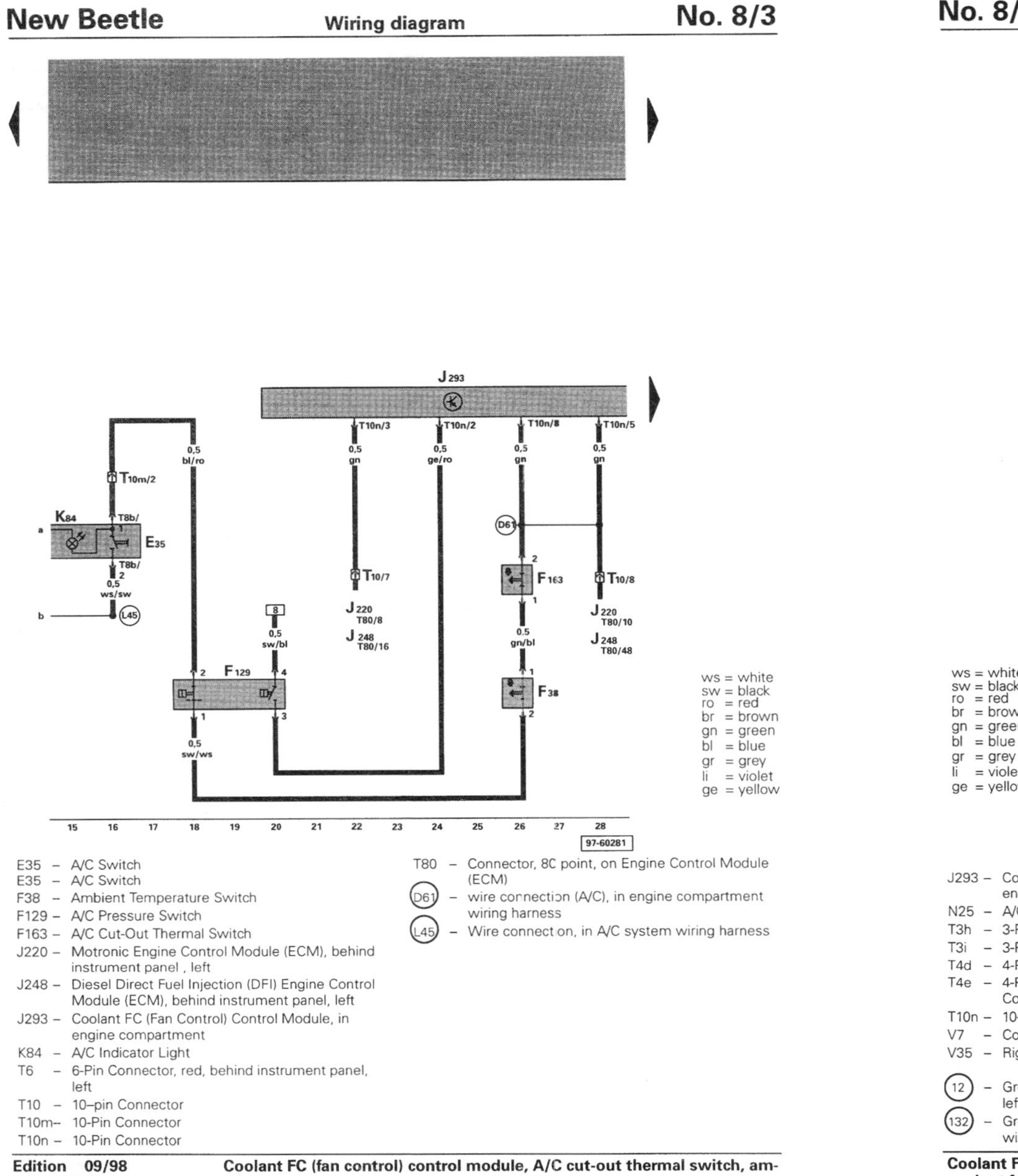

ws = white
sw = black
ro = red
br = brown
gn = green
bl = blue
gr = grey
li = violet
ge = yellow

- E35 – A/C Switch
- E35 – A/C Switch
- F38 – Ambient Temperature Switch
- F129 – A/C Pressure Switch
- F163 – A/C Cut-Out Thermal Switch
- J220 – Motronic Engine Control Module (ECM), behind instrument panel, left
- J248 – Diesel Direct Fuel Injection (DFI) Engine Control Module (ECM), behind instrument panel, left
- J293 – Coolant FC (Fan Control) Control Module, in engine compartment
- K84 – A/C Indicator Light
- T6 – 6-Pin Connector, red, behind instrument panel, left
- T10 – 10-pin Connector
- T10m – 10-Pin Connector
- T10n – 10-Pin Connector
- T80 – Connector, 8C point, on Engine Control Module (ECM)
- (D61) – wire connection (A/C), in engine compartment wiring harness
- (L45) – Wire connection, in A/C system wiring harness

Edition 09/98
USA.5132.05.21

Coolant FC (fan control) control module, A/C cut-out thermal switch, ambient temperature sensor, A/C indicator light

ws = white
sw = black
ro = red
br = brown
gn = green
bl = blue
gr = grey
li = violet
ge = yellow

- J293 – Coolant FC (Fan Control) Control Module, in engine compartment
- N25 – A/C Clutch
- T3h – 3-Pin Connector, in engine compartment
- T3i – 3-Pin Connector, in engine compartment
- T4d – 4-Pin Connector, near A/C Clutch
- T4e – 4-Pin Connector, on Coolant FC (Fan Control) Control Module
- T10n – 10-Pin Connector
- V7 – Coolant Fan
- V35 – Right Coolant Fan
- (12) – Ground connection, in engine compartment, left
- (132) – Ground connection -3-, in engine compartment wiring harness
- (D106) – wire connection -4-, in engine compartment wiring harness
- (D107) – wire connection -5-, in engine compartment wiring harness

Coolant FC (fan control) control module, A/C clutch, coolant fan, right coolant fan

Edition 01/98
USA.5132.01.21

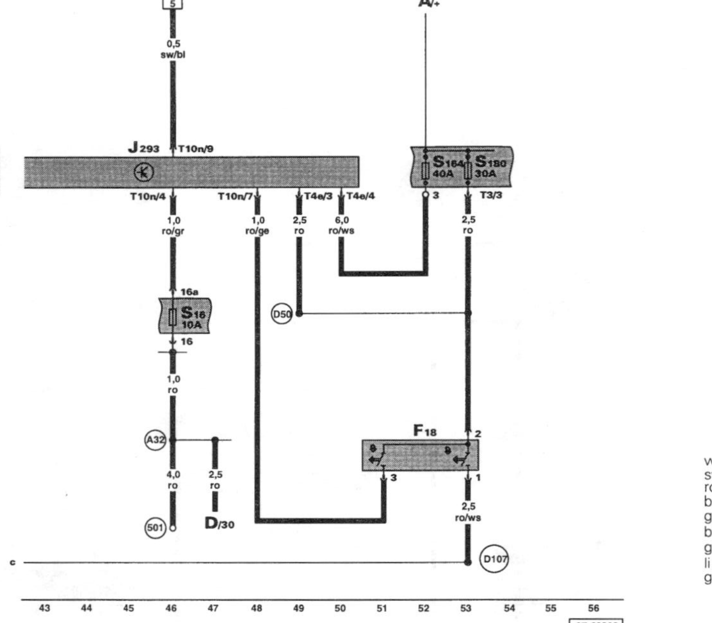

ws = white
sw = black
ro = red
br = brown
gn = green
bl = blue
gr = grey
li = violet
ge = yellow

A – Battery
D – Ignition/Starter Switch
F18 – Coolant Fan Control (FC) Thermal Switch
J293 – Coolant FC (Fan Control) Control Module
S16 – Fuse 16 in fuse holder
S164 – Fuse -3- in fuse bracket/battery
S180 – Fuse -8- (30), in fuse bracket/battery
T4e – 4-Pin Connector, on Coolant FC (Fan Control) Control Module
T10n – 10-Pin Connector, on Coolant FC (Fan Control) Control Module
(501) – Threaded connection -2- (30), on the relay plate
(A32) – plus connection (30), in instrument panel wiring harness
(D50) – plus connection (30), in engine compartment wiring harness
(D107) – wire connection -5-, in engine compartment wiring harness

Edition 09/98 **Coolant fan control (FC) module, coolant fan control (FC) thermal switch**
USA.5132.05.21

THIS PAGE INTENTIONALLY LEFT BLANK

Comfort system, with anti-theft alarm system, (vehicles with power windows)

from January 1998

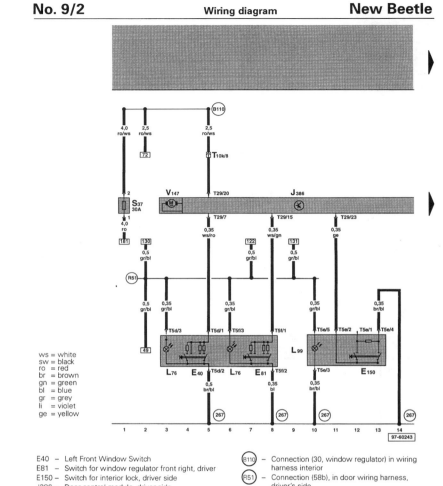

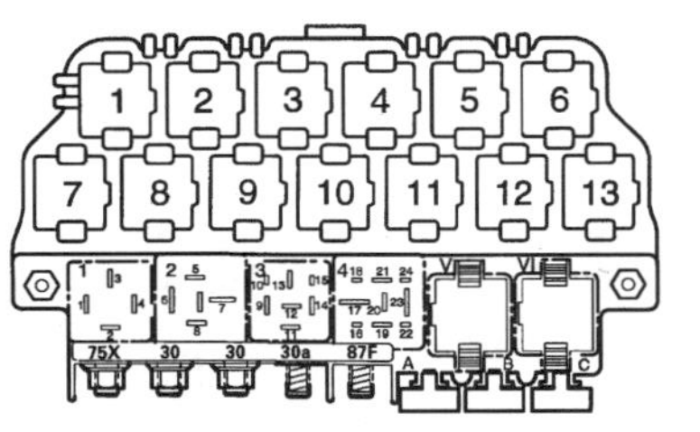

Fuse colors

30 A – green
25 A – white
20 A – yellow
15 A – blue
10 A – red
7,5 A – brown
5 A – beige

Edition 07/98
USA.5132.03.21

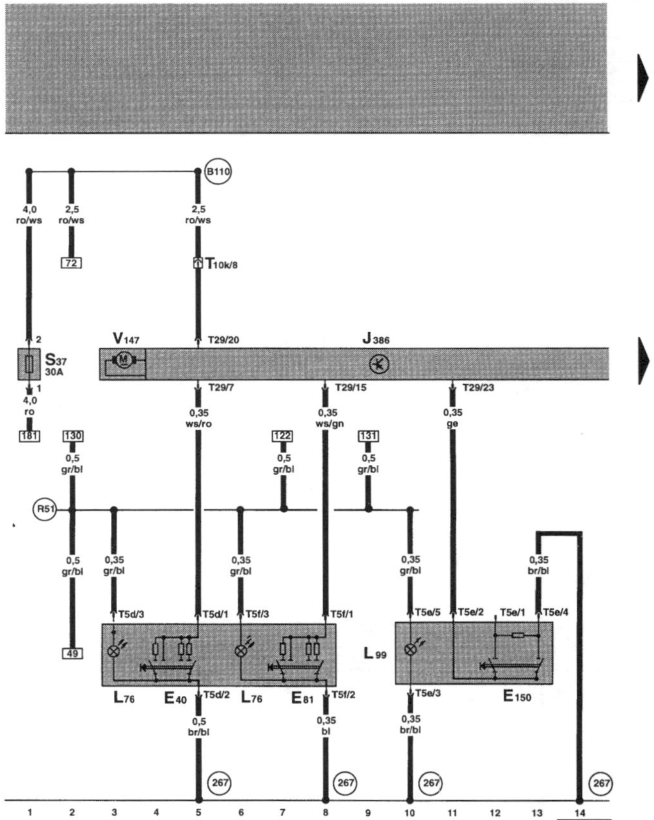

ws = white
sw = black
ro = red
br = brown
gn = green
bl = blue
gr = grey
li = violet
ge = yellow

E40 – Left Front Window Switch
E81 – Switch for window regulator front right, driver
E150 – Switch for interior lock, driver side
J386 – Door control module, driver side
L76 – Push Button Light
L99 – Lighting for switch interior lock
S37 – Power Window Fuse, on relay panel
T5d – 5-Pin Connector, brown
T5f – 5-Pin Connector, black
T5e – 5-Pin Connector, black
T10k – 10-Pin Connector, black, on A-Pillar left
T29 – 29-Pin Connector, on Door control module
V147 – Motor for window regulator, driver side

(267) – Ground connector -2-, in wiring harness door cable

(B110) – Connection (30, window regulator) in wiring harness interior
(R51) – Connection (58b), in door wiring harness, driver's side

Door control module (driver side), left front window switch, switch for window regulator front right (driver), switch for interior lock (driver side)

Edition 09/98
USA.5132.05.21

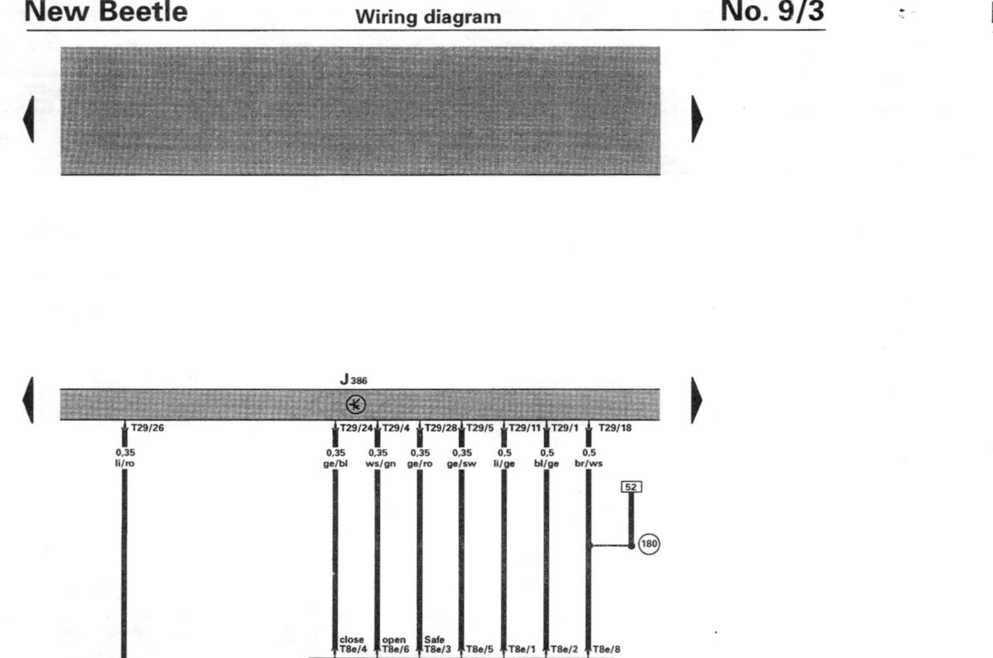

ws = white
sw = black
ro = red
br = brown
gn = green
bl = blue
gr = grey
li = violet
ge = yellow

F220 – Lock unit for central locking, driver side
J386 – Door control module, driver side
K133 – Warning light for central locking -SAFE-
T8e – 8-Pin Connector, on Lock unit for central locking, driver side
T29 – 29-Pin Connector, on Door control module

(180) – Ground connection –2–, in central locking system wiring harness
(267) – Ground connector -2-, in wiring harness door cable

Edition 08/98
USA.5132.04.21

Door control module (driver side), lock unit for central locking (driver side)

ws = white
sw = black
ro = red
br = brown
gn = green
bl = blue
gr = grey
li = violet
ge = yellow

J386 – Door control module, driver side
T8 – 8-Pin Connector, in driver's door wiring
T10k – 10-Pin Connector, on A-Pillar left, black
T29 – 29-Pin Connector, on Door control module – driver side
V17 – Driver's Side Mirror Adjustment Motor
V149 – Motor for mirror adjustment, driver side

Z4 – Heated outside mirror, driver side

(44) – Ground connection, on left A-pillar, lower part

(205) – Ground connection, in driver's door wiring harness
(267) – Ground connector -2-, in wiring harness door cable

Door control module (driver side), driver's side mirror adjustment motor, motor for mirror adjustment (driver side), heated outside mirror (driver side)

Edition 09/98
USA.5132.05.21

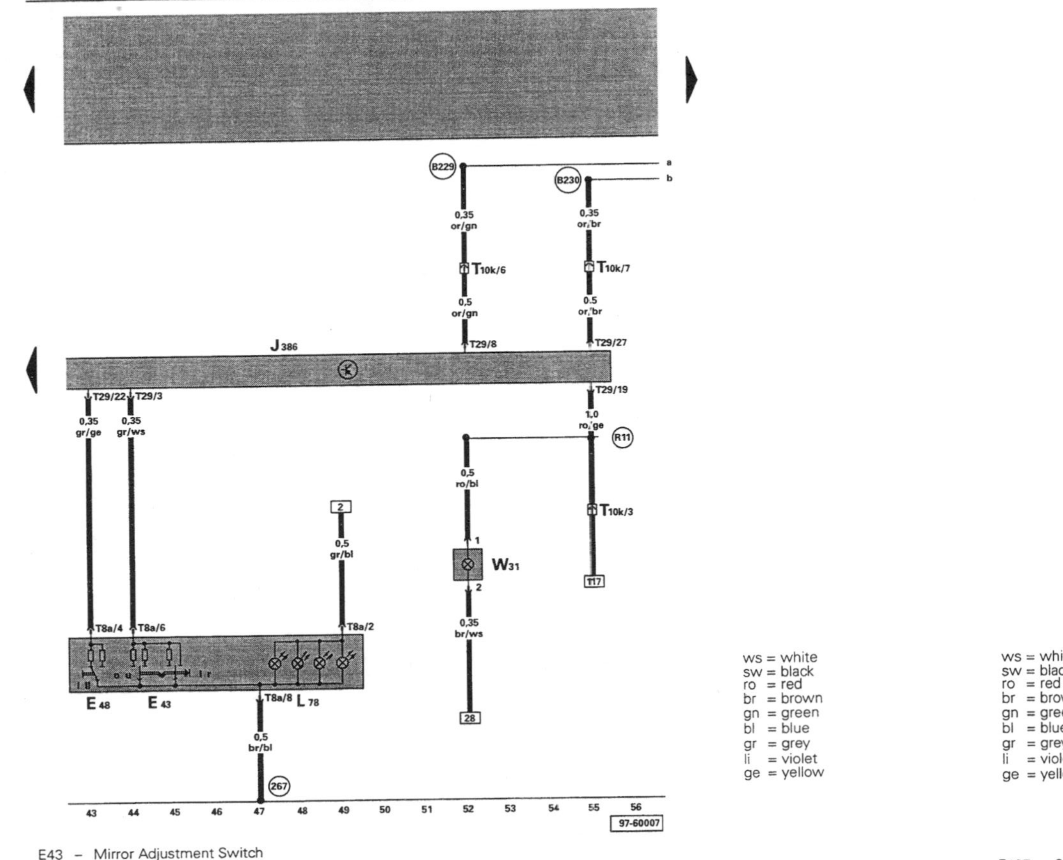

ws = white
sw = black
ro = red
br = brown
gn = green
bl = blue
gr = grey
li = violet
ge = yellow

E43 – Mirror Adjustment Switch
E48 – Mirror Selector Switch
J386 – Door control module, driver side
L78 – Mirror Adjusting Switch Light
T8a – 8-Pin Connector
T10k – 10-Pin Connector, on A-Pillar left, black
T29 – 29-Pin Connector, on Door control module
W31 – Entry light front, left

(267) – Ground connector -2-,in wiring harness door cable
(B229) – connection (High-Bus), in wiring harness, interior
(B230) – connection (Low-Bus), in wiring harness, interior
(R11) – plus connection -2- (30), in driver's door wiring harness

Door control module (driver side) mirror adjustment switch, mirror selector switch, door entry (courtesy) lights

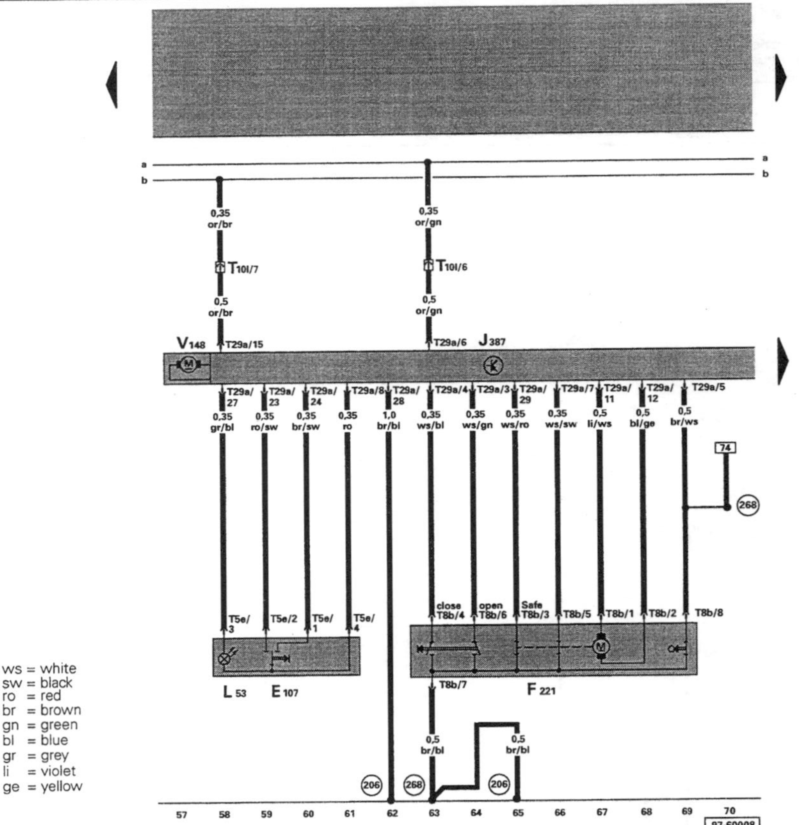

ws = white
sw = black
ro = red
br = brown
gn = green
bl = blue
gr = grey
li = violet
ge = yellow

E107 – Switch for window regulator, in passenger door
F221 – Lock unit for central locking, passenger side
J387 – Door control module, passenger side
T5e – 5-Pin Connector
T8b – 8-Pin Connector
T10l – 10-Pin Connector, black, on A-Pillar right
T29a – 29-Pin Connector, on Door control module
L53 – Power Window Switch Light
V148 – Motor for window regulator, passenger side

(206) – Ground connection, in passenger's door wiring harness
(268) – Ground connector -2-, in wiring harness door cable – passenger side

Door control module (passenger side), lock unit for central locking (passenger side), switch for window regulator (passenger side)

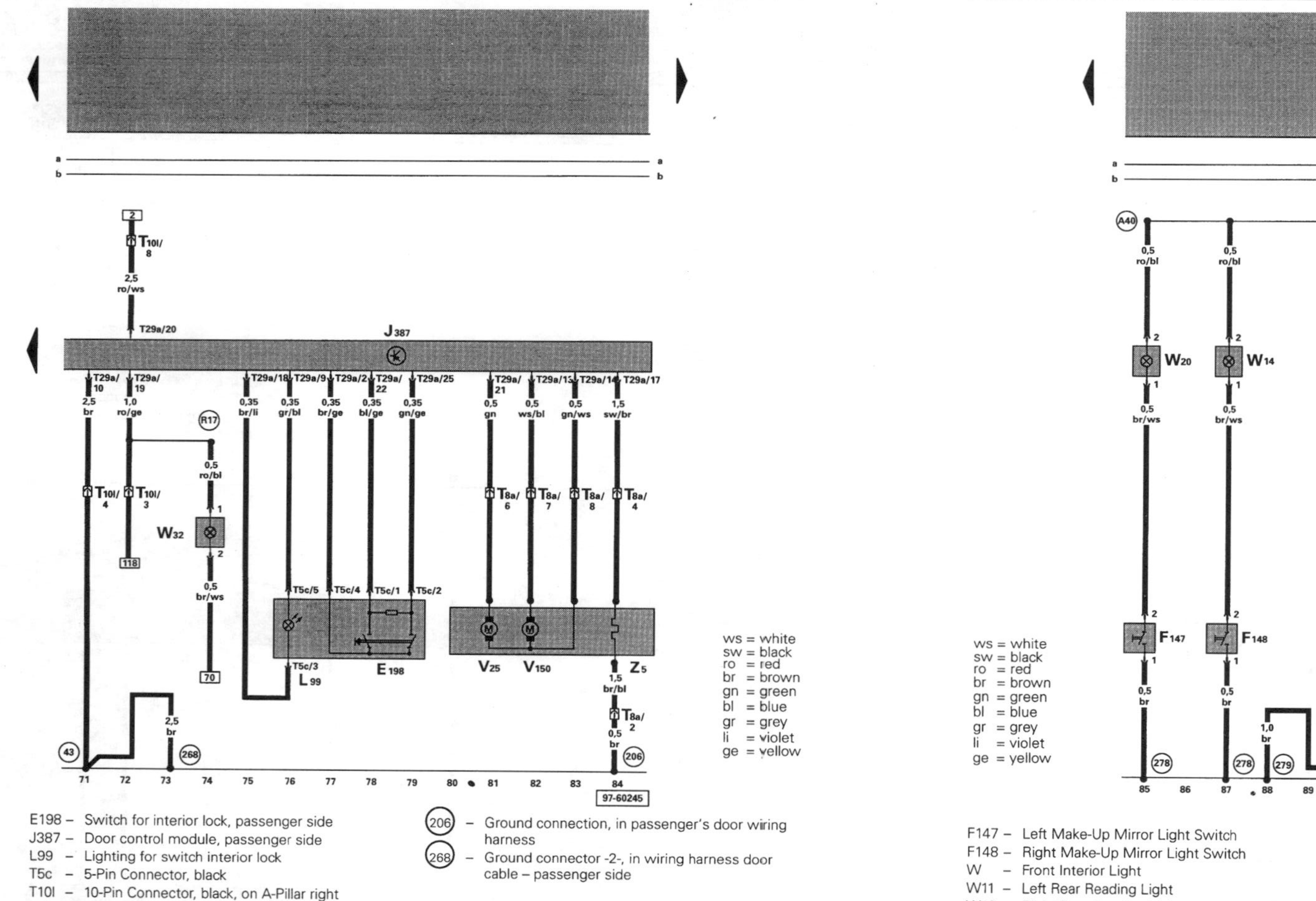

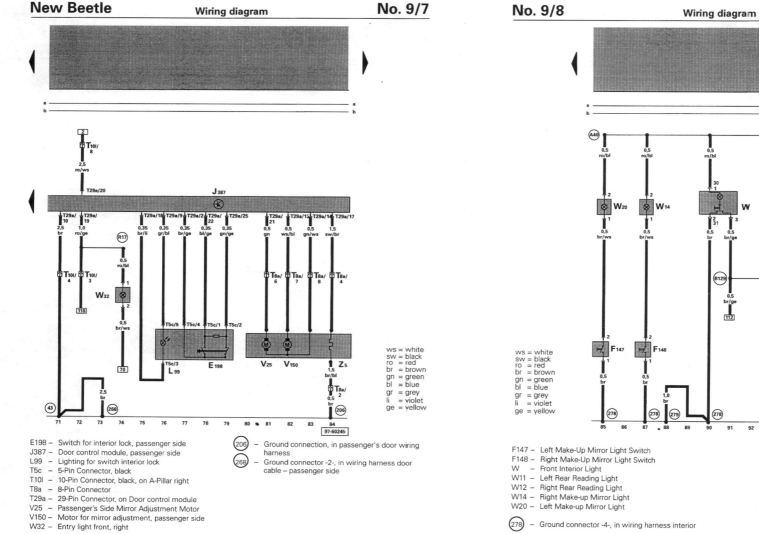

ws = white
sw = black
ro = red
br = brown
gn = green
bl = blue
gr = grey
li = violet
ge = yellow

E198 – Switch for interior lock, passenger side
J387 – Door control module, passenger side
L99 – Lighting for switch interior lock
T5c – 5-Pin Connector, black
T10l – 10-Pin Connector, black, on A-Pillar right
T8a – 8-Pin Connector
T29a – 29-Pin Connector, on Door control module
V25 – Passenger's Side Mirror Adjustment Motor
V150 – Motor for mirror adjustment, passenger side
W32 – Entry light front, right

Z5 – Heated outside mirror, passenger side

(R17) – Plus connection –2– (30), in passenger's door wiring harness
(43) – Ground connection, on right A-pillar, lower part
(206) – Ground connection, in passenger's door wiring harness
(268) – Ground connector -2-, in wiring harness door cable – passenger side

Edition 09/98
USA.5132.05.21

Door control module (passenger side), switch for interior lock (passenger side), passenger's side mirror adjustment motor, heated outside mirror

ws = white
sw = black
ro = red
br = brown
gn = green
bl = blue
gr = grey
li = violet
ge = yellow

F147 – Left Make-Up Mirror Light Switch
F148 – Right Make-Up Mirror Light Switch
W – Front Interior Light
W11 – Left Rear Reading Light
W12 – Right Rear Reading Light
W14 – Right Make-up Mirror Light
W20 – Left Make-up Mirror Light

(278) – Ground connector -4-, in wiring harness interior
(279) – Ground connector -5, in wiring harness interior
(A40) – plus connection -1- (30), in instrument cluster wiring harness
(B129) – Connector (interior light 3/L), in wiring harness interior

Front interior light, left rear reading light, right rear reading light, right make-up mirror light, left make-up mirror light

Edition 01/98
USA.5132.01.21

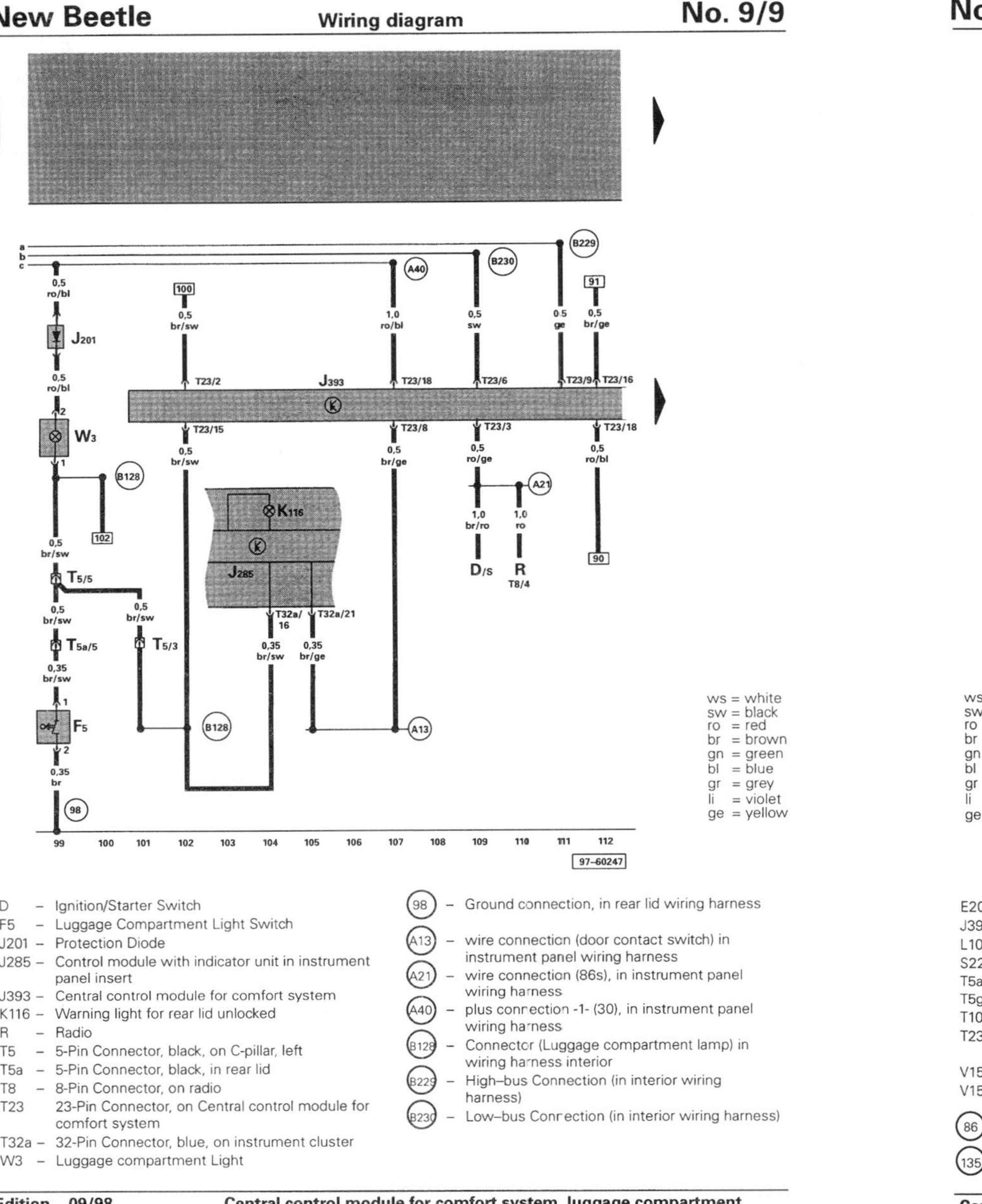

ws = white
sw = black
ro = red
br = brown
gn = green
bl = blue
gr = grey
li = violet
ge = yellow

D – Ignition/Starter Switch
F5 – Luggage Compartment Light Switch
J201 – Protection Diode
J285 – Control module with indicator unit in instrument panel insert
J393 – Central control module for comfort system
K116 – Warning light for rear lid unlocked
R – Radio
T5 – 5-Pin Connector, black, on C-pillar, left
T5a – 5-Pin Connector, black, in rear lid
T8 – 8-Pin Connector, on radio
T23 – 23-Pin Connector, on Central control module for comfort system
T32a – 32-Pin Connector, blue, on instrument cluster
W3 – Luggage compartment Light

(98) – Ground connection, in rear lid wiring harness
(A13) – wire connection (door contact switch) in instrument panel wiring harness
(A21) – wire connection (86s), in instrument panel wiring harness
(A40) – plus connection -1- (30), in instrument panel wiring harness
(B128) – Connector (Luggage compartment lamp) in wiring harness interior
(B229) – High–bus Connection (in interior wiring harness)
(B230) – Low–bus Connection (in interior wiring harness)

Edition 09/98
USA.5132.05.21

Central control module for comfort system, luggage compartment light, luggage compartment light switch

ws = white
sw = black
ro = red
br = brown
gn = green
bl = blue
gr = grey
li = violet
ge = yellow

E204 – Switch for remote/fuel tank door
J393 – Central control module for comfort system
L104 – Illumination for switch remote unlock
S228 – Fuse in fuse holder
T5a – 5-Pin Connector, black, in rear lid
T5g – 5-Pin Connector, brown, in rear lid
T10k – 10-Pin Connector, on A-Pillar left, black
T23 – 23-Pin Connector, on Central control module for comfort system
V151 – Motor for remote unlock rear lid
V155 – Motor for fuel tank lid unlock

(86) – Ground connection –1–, in rear wiring harness
(135) – Ground connection -2-, in instrument panel wiring harness
(267) – Ground connector -2-, in wiring harness door cable - driver side
(501) – Screw connection -2- (30), on relay panel
(A66) – Connector (30a, central locking/anti-theft warning system/IR) in instrument panel wiring harness

Central control module for comfort system, relay for motor remote unlock rear lid, switch for remote unlock, rear lid

Edition 09/98
USA.5132.05.21

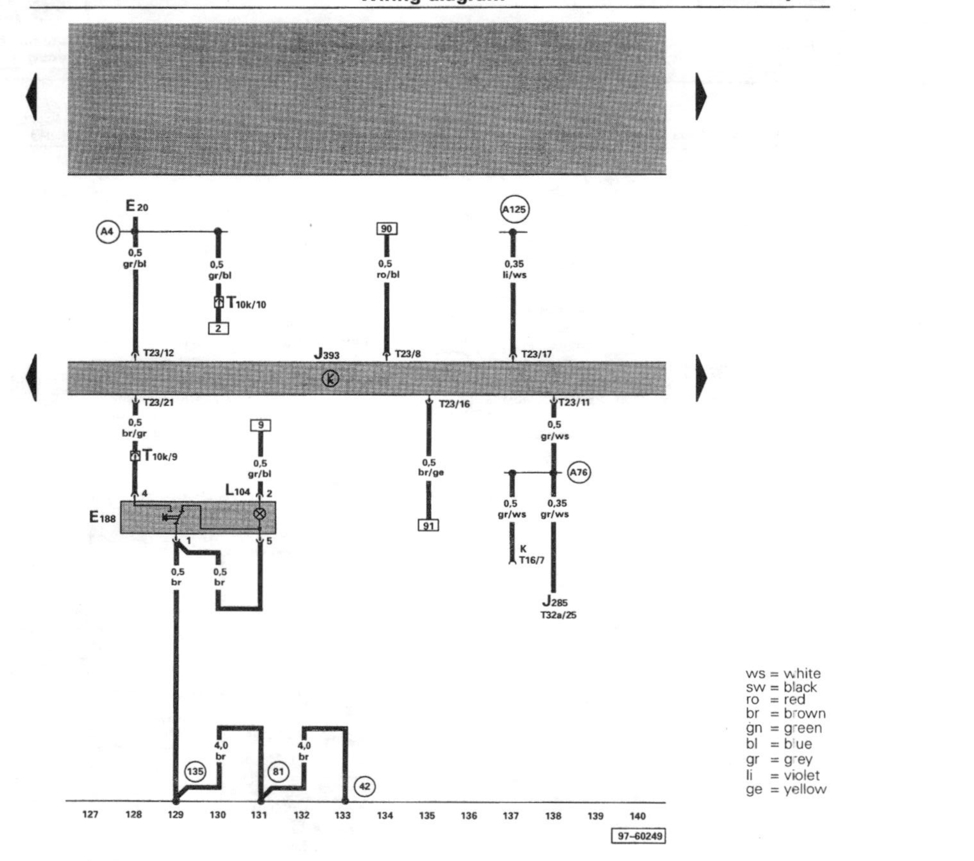

ws = white
sw = black
ro = red
br = brown
gn = green
bl = blue
gr = grey
li = violet
ge = yellow

E20 – Instrument Panel Light Dimmer Switch
E188 – Switch for remote unlock, rear lid
J285 – Control module with indicator unit in instrument panel insert
J393 – Central control module for comfort system
L104 – Illumination for switch remote unlock
T10k – 10-Pin Connector, on A-Pillar left, black
T23 23-Pin Connector, on Central control module for comfort system
T32a – 32-Pin Connector, blue, on instrument cluster

(42) – Ground connection, beside steering column

(81) – Ground connection -1-, in instrument panel wiring harness

(135) – Ground connection -2-, in instrument panel wiring harness

(A4) – plus connection (58b) in instrument panel wiring harness

(A76) – Connector (K–diagnosis wire) in instrument panel wiring harness

(A125) – wire connection (crash), in instrument panel wiring harness

Central control module for comfort system, switch for remote/fuel tank door, motor for fuel tank lid unlock

J393
T23/23 31 1,0 br
T23/1 1,0 sw/br
E15 T6b/3
T23/14 0,5 bl/ws
A27
1,0 br
T5a/3
2,5 br
42 279 98 218 52
141 142 143 144 145 146 147 148 149 150 151 152 153 154
97-60250

ws = white
sw = black
ro = red
br = brown
gn = green
bl = blue
gr = grey
li = violet
ge = yellow

E15 – Rear window defogger switch
J393 – Central control module for comfort system
T5a 5-Pin Connector, black, in rear lid
T5h 5-Pin Connector, brown, in rear lid
T6b 6-Pin Connector, on rear window defogger switch
T23 23-Pin Connector, on Central control module for comfort system

(42) – Ground connection, beside steering column

(52) – Ground connection, in rear lid, left

(98) – Ground connection, in rear lid wiring harness

(218) – Ground connection -1-, in rear lid wiring harness

(279) – Ground connector -5-, in wiring harness interior

(A27) – wire Connection (vehicle speed signal), in instrument panel wiring harness

Central control module for comfort system,

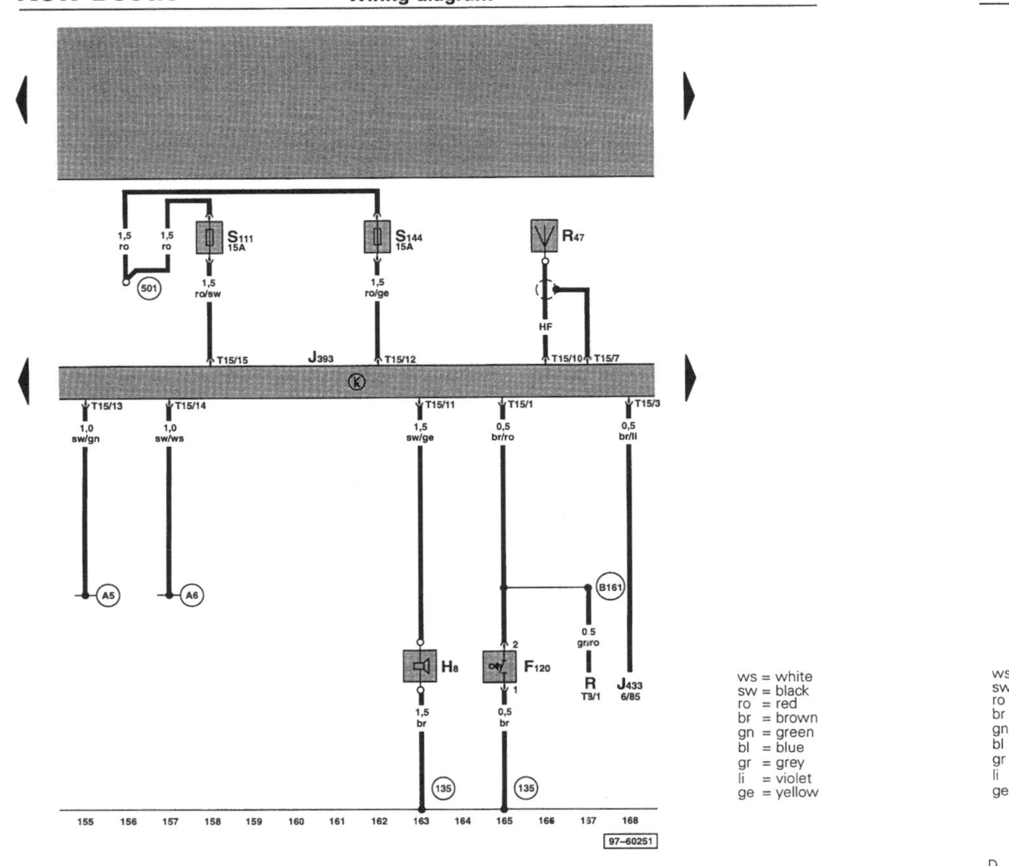

ws = white
sw = black
ro = red
br = brown
gn = green
bl = blue
gr = grey
li = violet
ge = yellow

F120 – Hood Alarm Switch
H8 – Alarm Horn
J393 – Central control module for comfort system
J433 – Locking relay for starter (clutch pedal switch)
R – Radio
R47 – Antenna wire for central locking and antitheft warning system
S111 – Alarm System and Anti-Theft Engine Disable Fuse
S144 – Fuse for central locking/anti-theft warning system
T8 – 8-Pin Connector, on radio
T15 – 15-Pin Connector, on Central control module for comfort system

(135) – Ground connection -2-, in instrument panel wiring harness
(501) – Threaded connection -1- (30) on the relay plate
(A5) – plus connection (right turn signal), in instrument panel wiring harness
(A6) – plus connection (left turn signal), in instrument panel wiring harness
(B161) – connection (Alarm system), in wiring harness, interior

Central control module for comfort system, hood alarm switch, alarm horn

ws = white
sw = black
ro = red
br = brown
gn = green
bl = blue
gr = grey
li = violet
ge = yellow

D – Ignition/Starter Switch
E139 – Sunroof Regulator
J245 – Power Sunroof Control Module
J393 – Central control module for comfort system
S6 – Fuse 6 in fuse holder
S230 – Fuse 30 in fuse holder
T6 – 6-Pin Connector
T23 – 23-Pin Connector

(135) – Ground connection -2-, in instrument panel wiring harness
(501) – Threaded connection -2- (30), on relay panel
(A2) – plus connection (15), in instrument panel wiring harness
(A32) – plus connection (30), in instrument panel wiring harness

Central control module for comfort system, power sunroof

Front foglights

from January 1998

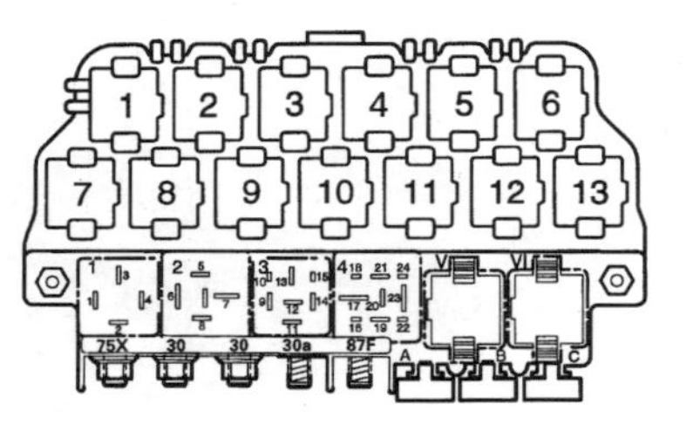

Fuse colors

30 A – green
25 A – white
20 A – yellow
15 A – blue
10 A – red
7.5 A – brown
5 A – beige

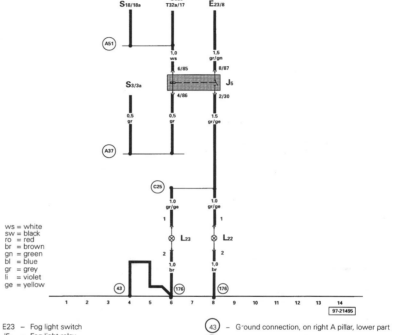

ws = white
sw = black
ro = red
br = brown
gn = green
bl = blue
gr = grey
li = violet
ge = yellow

97-21495

- E23 – Fog light switch
- J5 – Fog light relay
- J285 – Control module with indicator unit in instrument panel insert
- L22 – Left front foglight
- L23 – Right front foglight
- S3 – Fuse 3 in fuse holder
- S18 – Fuse 18 in fuse holder
- T32a – 32-Pin Connector, blue, on J285

- (43) – Ground connection, on right A pillar, lower part
- (176) – Ground connection, in right headlight wiring harness
- (A37) – wire connection (58a), in instrument panel wiring harness
- (A51) – wire connection (56), in instrument panel wiring harness
- (C25) – wire connection, fog lights, in front light wiring harness

Heated washer nozzles

from January 1998

97-21956

Fuse colors
30 A – green
25 A – white
20 A – yellow
15 A – blue
10 A – red
7,5 A – brown
5 A – beige

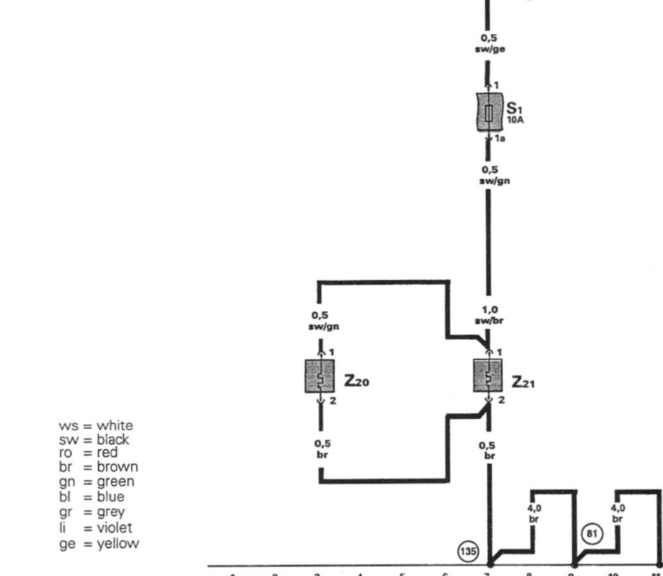

ws = white
sw = black
ro = red
br = brown
gn = green
bl = blue
gr = grey
li = violet
ge = yellow

S1 – Fuse 1 in fuse holder
Z20 – Left washer nozzle heater
Z21 – Right washer nozzle heater

(42) – Ground connection, beside steering column

(81) – Ground connection -1-, in instrument panel wiring harness

(135) – Ground connection -2-, in instrument panel wiring harness

(A80) – Connector -1- (X) in instrument panel wiring harness

Digital clock

from January 1998

97-21956

Fuse colors
30 A – green
25 A – white
20 A – yellow
15 A – blue
10 A – red
7,5 A – brown
5 A – beige

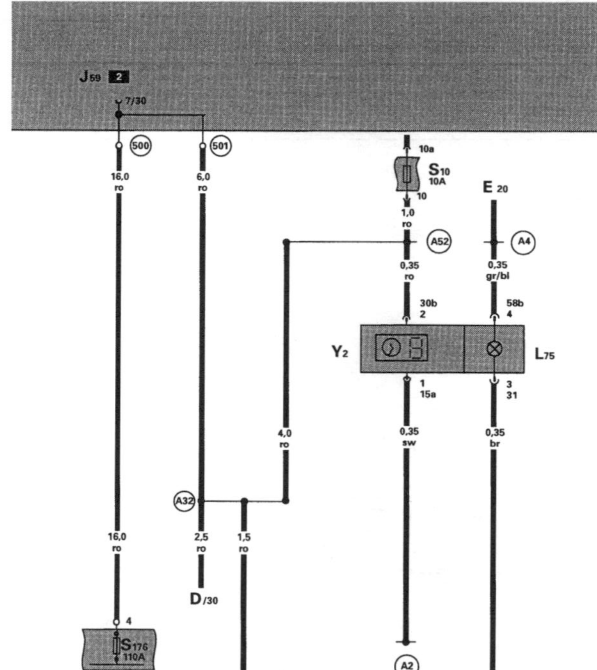

ws = white
sw = black
ro = red
br = brown
gn = green
bl = blue
gr = grey
li = violet
ge = yellow

D – Ignition/Starter Switch
E1 – Light Switch
E20 – Switches and instruments – lighting control
J59 – Load Reduction Relay
L75 – Light for digital display
S10 – Fuse in fuse box
S176 – Fuse -4- (30), in fuse bracket/battery
Y2 – Digital Clock

(A2) – Positive (+) connection (15), in instrument panel wiring harness
(A4) – Positive (+) connection (58b), in instrument panel wiring harness
(A32) – plus connection (30), in instrument panel wiring harness
(A52) – Positive connection (30), in instrument panel wiring harness

(81) – Ground connection -1-, in instrument panel wiring harness
(135) – Ground connection -2-, in instrument panel wiring harness
(500) – Threaded connection -1- (30), on the relay plate
(501) – Threaded connection -2- (30), on the relay plate

Digital clock, digital display light

Cruise control system (gasoline engine only)

from January 1998

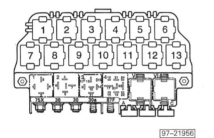

97-21956

Relay panel:

- **2** Load Reduction Relay (100)
- **4** Fuel Pump (FP) Relay (409)

Note: Number in parentheses indicates production control number stamped on relay housing.

Fuse colors

30 A – green
25 A – white
20 A – yellow
15 A – blue
10 A – red
7,5 A – brown
5 A – beige

J17 4, J59 2, S2/5, 23/87, 7/30, 504, 501, 500, D/15, A99, A2, S176, J220, S243 10A, S5 7,5A, S13 10A, T80/47, A20, 24, 17, 16, F, F47, A18, A100, T10c/6 *, T10h/4

97-60267

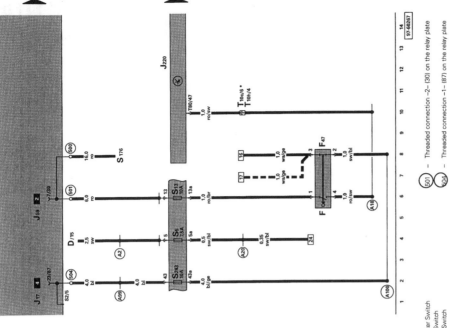

ws = white
sw = black
ro = red
br = brown
gn = green
bl = blue
gr = grey
li = violet
ge = yellow

D – Ignition/Starter Switch
F – Brake Light Switch
F47 – Brake Pedal Switch
J17 – Fuel Pump (FP) Relay
J59 – Load Reduction Relay
J220 – Motronic Engine Control Module (ECM)
S5 – Fuse 5 in fuse holder
S13 – Fuse 13 in fuse holder
S176 – Fuse -4- (30), in fuse bracket/battery
S243 – Fuse 43 in fuse holder
T10c – 10-Pin Connector, blue, behind instrument panel, left
T10h – 10-Pin Connector, black, behind instrument panel, left
T80 – Connector, 80 point

(500) – Threaded connection -1- (30) on the relay plate
(501) – Threaded connection -2- (30) on the relay plate
(504) – Threaded connection -1- (87) on the relay plate
(A2) – plus connection (15), in instrument panel wiring harness
(A18) – plus connection (54), in rear wiring harness
(A20) – wire connection (15a), in instrument panel wiring harness
(A99) – Connector -1- (87), in instrument panel
(A100) – Connector -2- (87), in instrument panel wiring harness
* – early vehicles only
--- Automatic transmission only

Brake light switch, brake pedal switch, fuel pump relay, Motronic engine control module

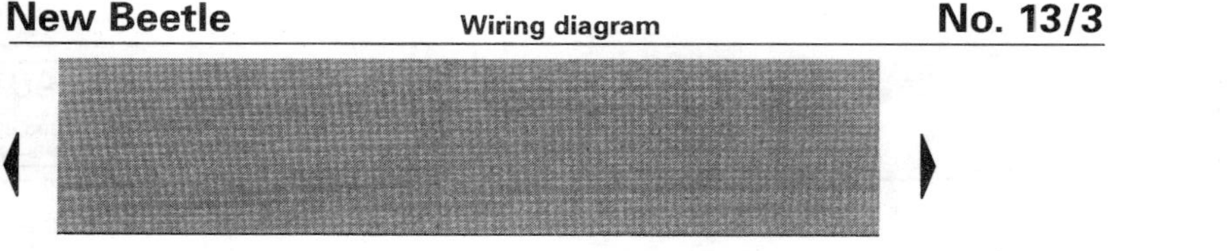

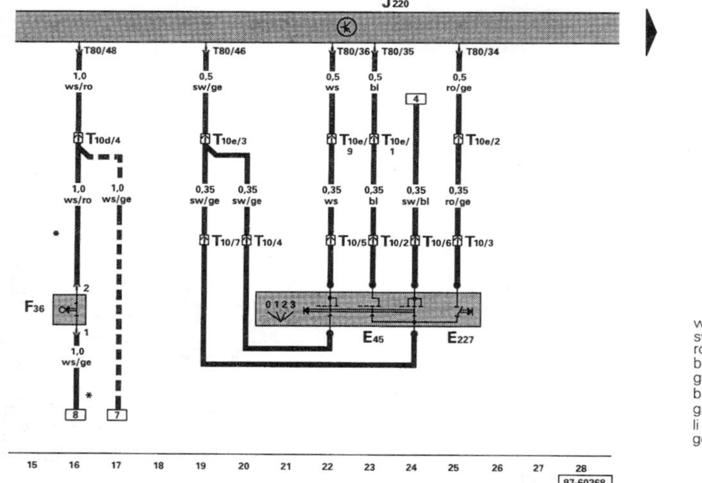

ws = white
sw = black
ro = red
br = brown
gn = green
bl = blue
gr = grey
li = violet
ge = yellow

E45 – Cruise Control Switch
E227 – Button for cruise control (set)
F36 – Clutch Vacuum Vent Valve Switch
J220 – Motronic Engine Control Module (ECM)
T10 – 10-pin connector, to right of steering column
T10d – 10-pin Connector, green, behind instrument panel, left
T10e – 10-pin Connector, black, behind instrument panel, left
T80 – 80-pin Connector, in Motronic Engine Control Module

(A100) – Connection 2 (87) (in instrument panel wiring harness)

* – Standard transmission only

– – – Automatic transmission only

Edition 09/98
USA.5132.05.21

Cruise control switch, button for cruise control, clutch vacuum vent valve switch, Motronic engine control module.

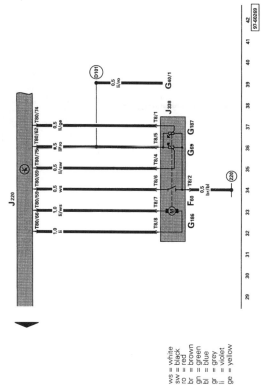

J220
T80/66 T80/59 T80/69 T80/75 T80/62 T80/74
1,0 li
1,0 li/ws
0,5 ws
0,5 li/sw
0,5 li/ro
0,5 li/ge
D101
0,5 li/ro
T8/8 T8/7 T8/6 T8/4 T8/5 T8/1
J338
G40/1
G186 F60 T8/2 G69 G187
0,5 br/bl
220
29 30 31 32 33 34 35 36 37 38 39 40 41 42
97-60269

ws = white
sw = black
ro = red
br = brown
gn = green
bl = blue
gr = grey
li = violet
ge = yellow

F60 – Closed Throttle Position (CTP) Switch
G40 – Camshaft Position (CMP) Sensor
G69 – Throttle Position (TP) Sensor
G186 – Throttle Drive (electronic throttle)
G187 – Throttle Drive Angle Sensor 1 (electronic throttle)
J220 – Motronic Engine Control Module
J338 – Throttle Valve Control Module
T8 – 8-pin Connector
T80 – 80-pin Connector, in Motronic Engine Control Module

(220) – Ground Connection, Sensor Ground (in engine compartment wiring harness)

(D101) – Connection 1 (in engine compartment wiring harness)

Closed throttle position, Camshaft position sensor, Throttle position sensor, Throttle drive (electronic), Throttle drive angle sensor 1.

Edition 09/98
USA.5132.05.21

Power outlets

from January 1998

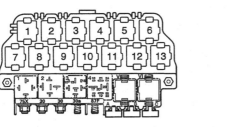

97-21956

Fuse colors
30 A – green
25 A – white
20 A – yellow
15 A – blue
10 A – red
7,5 A – brown
5 A – beige

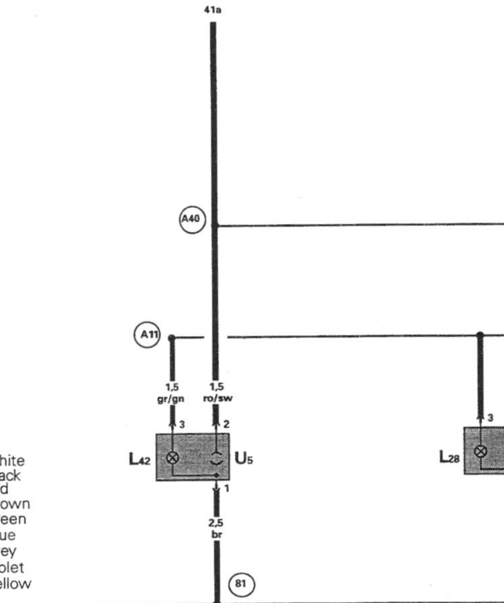

ws = white
sw = black
ro = red
br = brown
gn = green
bl = blue
gr = grey
li = violet
ge = yellow

L28 – Cigarette lighter light
L42 – Socket light bulb
S241 – Fuse 41 in fuse holder
U1 – Cigarette Lighter
U5 – 12 V socket
U19 – 12V outlet -3- (in luggage compartment)

(A11) – Positive (+) connection (58b), in instrument cluster wiring harness
(A40) – Positive connection -1- (30), in instrument panel wiring harness
(81) – Ground connection -1-, in instrument panel wiring harness

---- – from August 1998

12 V socket, cigarette lighter

Heated seats

from January 1998

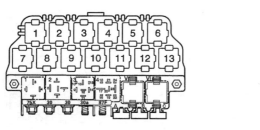

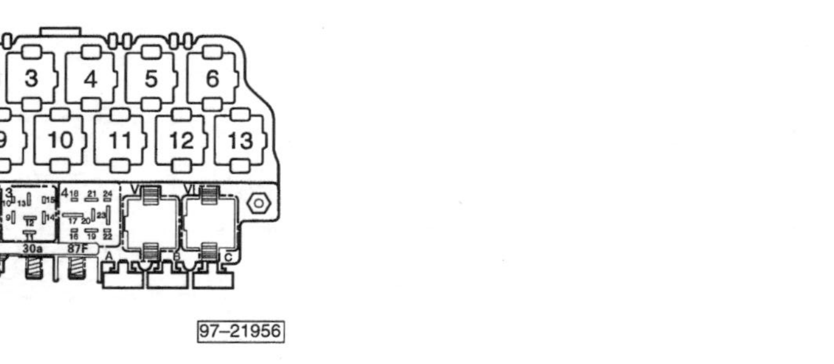

Fuse colors
30 A – green
25 A – white
20 A – yellow
15 A – blue
10 A – red
7,5 A – brown
5 A – beige

Edition 02.98
USA.5132.02.21

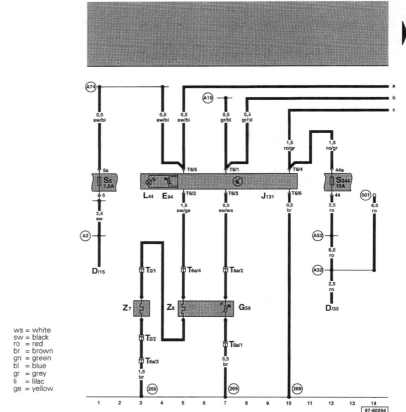

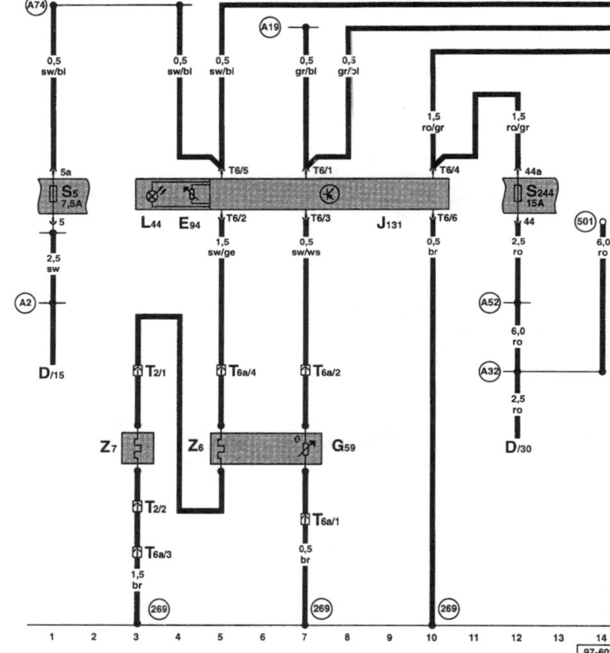

ws = white
sw = black
ro = red
br = brown
gn = green
bl = blue
gr = grey
li = lilac
ge = yellow

D – Ignition/Starter Switch
E94 – Adjuster for heated driver's seat
G59 – Driver's Heated Seat Temperature Sensor
J131 – Driver's Heated Seat Control Module
L44 – Heated Seat Switch Illumination Light
S5 – Fuse 5 in fuse holder
S244 – Fuse 44 in fuse holder
T2 – 2-Pin Connector, under driver's seat
T6 – 6-Pin Connector
T6a – 6-Pin Connector, green, below driver's seat
Z6 – Driver's Seat Heating Element
Z7 – Driver's Backrest Heating Element

(269) – Ground connection (sensor ground) -1-, in instrument panel wiring harness

(501) – Threaded connection -2- (30) on the relay plate

(A19) – wire connection (58d), in instrument panel wiring harness

(A74) – Connection (15a, fuse 5), in instrument panel wiring harness

(A32) – Plus connection (30), in instrument panel wiring harness

(A52) – Plus connector -4- (30), in instrument panel wiring harness

Driver's heated seat control module, driver's heated seat temperature sensor, driver's seat heating element

Edition 09/98
USA.5132.05.21

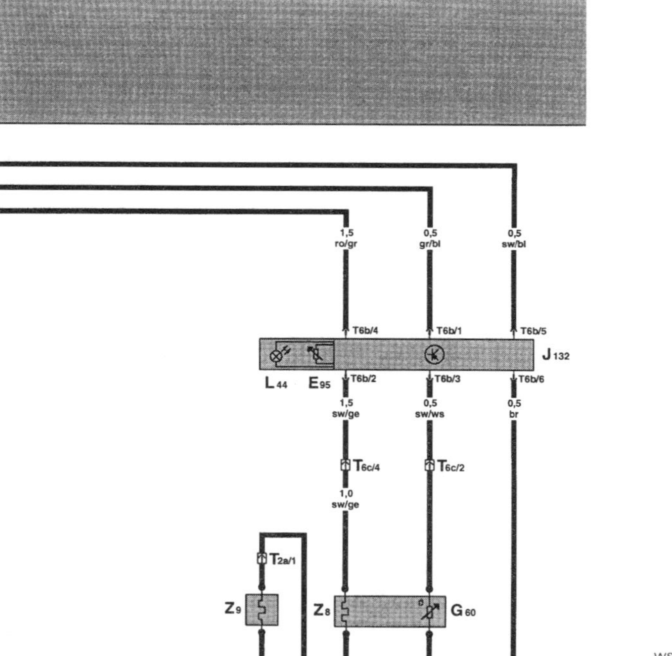

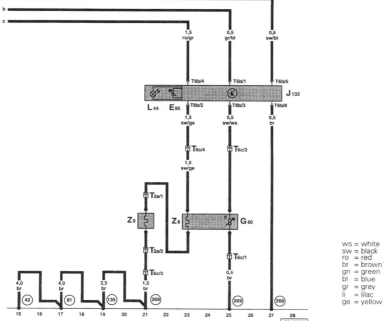

ws = white
sw = black
ro = red
br = brown
gn = green
bl = blue
gr = grey
li = lilac
ge = yellow

E95 – Adjuster for heated passenger seat
G60 – Passenger's Heated Seat Temperature Sensor
J132 – Passenger's Heated Seat Control Module
L44 – Heated Seat Switch Illumination Light
T2a – 2–Pin Connector, under passenger's seat
T6b – 6-Pin Connector
T6c – 6-Pin Connector, green, below passenger's seat
Z8 – Passenger's Seat Heating Element
Z9 – Passenger's Backrest Heating Element

(42) – Ground connection, beside steering column

(81) – Ground connection -1-, in instrument panel wiring harness

(269) – Ground connection (sensor ground) –1–, in instrument panel wiring harness

(135) – Ground connection -2-, in instrument panel wiring harness

Edition 09/98
USA.5132.05.21

Passenger's heated seat control module, passenger's heated seat temperature sensor, passenger's seat heating element, passenger's backrest heating element

THIS PAGE INTENTIONALLY LEFT BLANK

Comfort system, with anti-theft alarm system (vehicles with manual windows)

from January 1998

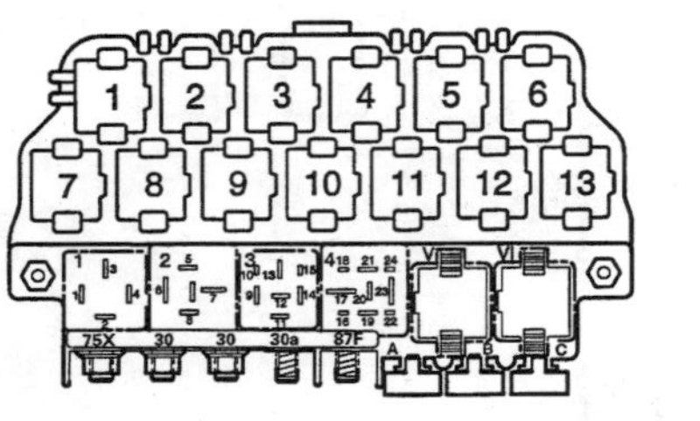

Fuse colors
30 A – green
25 A – white
20 A – yellow
15 A – blue
10 A – red
7,5 A – brown
5 A – beige

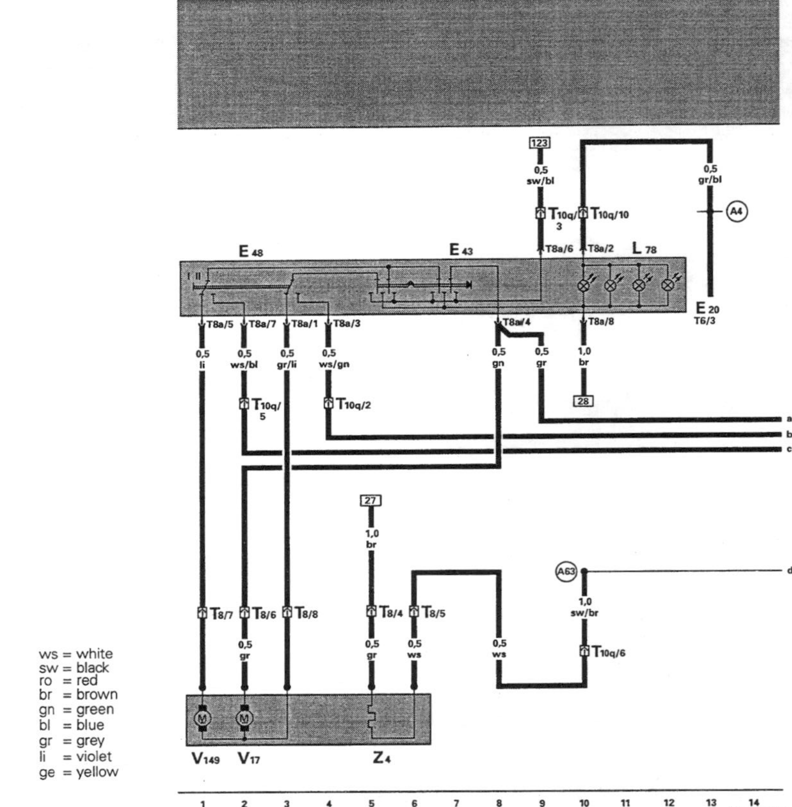

ws = white
sw = black
ro = red
br = brown
gn = green
bl = blue
gr = grey
li = violet
ge = yellow

E20 – Instrument/Switch Illumination Dimmer Switch
E43 – Mirror Adjustment Switch
E48 – Mirror Selector Switch
L78 – Mirror Adjusting Switch Illumination Bulb
V17 – Driver's Side Mirror Adjustment Motor
V149 – Driver's Side Mirror Adjustment Motor
Z4 – Driver's Side Heated Outside Mirror
T6 – 6-Pin Connector, on Instrument/Switch illumination Dimmer Switch
T8 – 8-pin Connector
T8a – 8-pin Connector
T10q – 10-Pin Connector, blue, on A-Pillar left

(A4) – Plus Connection (56b) (in instrument panel wiring harness)
(A63) – Mirror Adjustment /Heating Connection (in instrument panel wiring harness)

Instrument/Switch, illumination Dimmer Switch, Mirror Adjustment Switch, Mirror Selector Switch, Driver's Side Mirror Adjustment Motor.

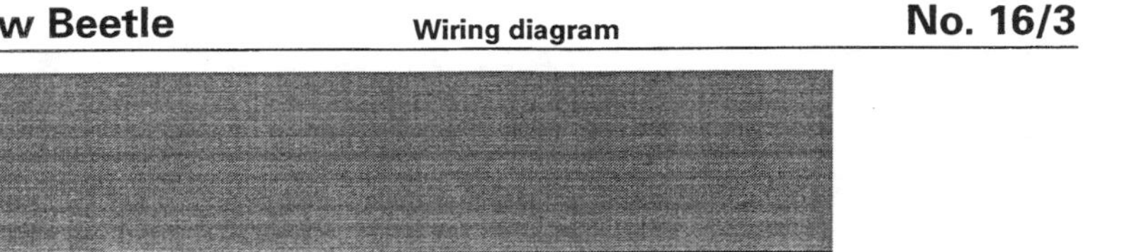

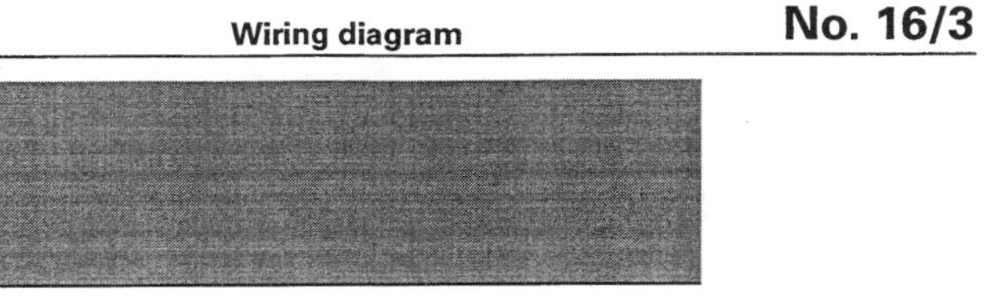

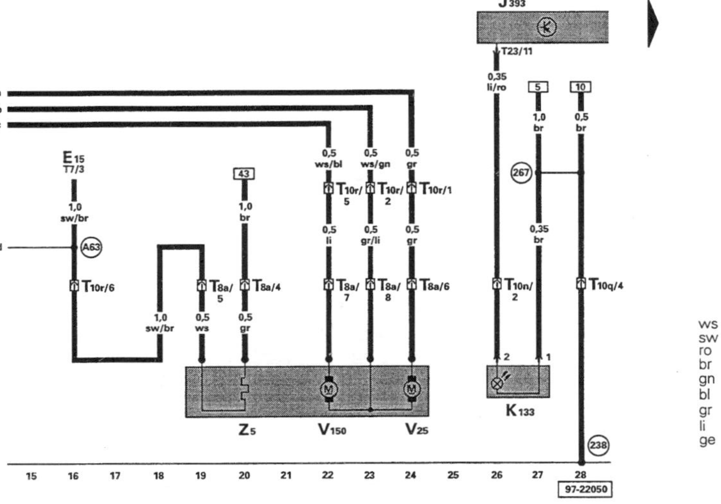

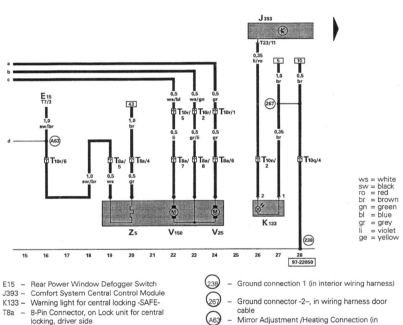

ws = white
sw = black
ro = red
br = brown
gn = green
bl = blue
gr = grey
li = violet
ge = yellow

E15 – Rear Power Window Defogger Switch
J393 – Comfort System Central Control Module
K133 – Warning light for central locking -SAFE-
T8a – 8-Pin Connector, on Lock unit for central locking, driver side
T10q – 10-Pin Connector, blue, on A-Pillar left
T10r – 10-Pin Connector, blue, on A-Pillar right
T10n – 10-Pin Connector, brown, on A-Pillar left
T23 – 23-Pin Connector
V25 – Passenger's Side Mirror Adjustment Motor
V150 – Passenger's Side Mirror Adjustment Motor
Z5 – Passenger's Side Heated Outside Mirror

(238) – Ground connection 1 (in interior wiring harness)
(267) – Ground connector -2–, in wiring harness door cable
(A63) – Mirror Adjustment /Heating Connection (in instrument panel wiring harness)

Edition 07/98
USA.5132.03.21

Rear Power Window Defogger Switch, Confort System Central Control Module, Warning light for central locking –SAFE–, Passenger's Side Mirror.

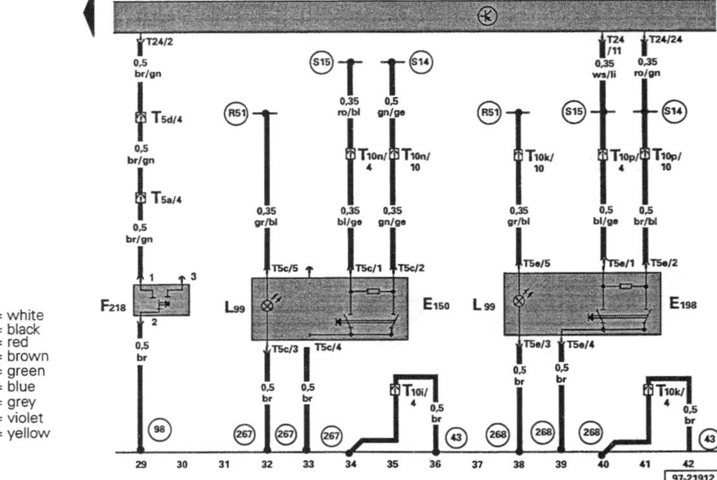

ws = white
sw = black
ro = red
br = brown
gn = green
bl = blue
gr = grey
li = violet
ge = yellow

E150 – Switch for interior lock, driver side
E165 – Rear Lid Release Switch
E198 – Passenger's Interior Lock Switch
F218 – Switch for central locking, trunk lid
J393 – Comfort System Central Control Module
L99 – Lighting for switch interior lock
T5a – 5–Pin Connector
T5c – 5-Pin Connector
T5d – 5-Pin Connector
T5e – 5-Pin Connector
T10i – 10-Pin Connector, black, on A-Pillar left
T10k – 10-Pin Connector, black, on A-Pillar left
T10n – 10-Pin Connector, brown, on A-Pillar left
T10p – 10-Pin Connector, brown, on A-Pillar right
T24 – 24-Pin Connector

(43) – Ground Connection (on right lower A–pillar)
(98) – Ground connection, in rear lid wiring harnnes
(267) – Ground connector -2-, in wiring harness door cable
(268) – Ground connector -2-, in wiring harness
(R51) – Connection (58b) (in driver's door wiring harness)
(S14) – Connection (open) (in central locking system wiring harness)
(S15) – Connection (closed) (in central locking system wiring harness)

Switch for interior lock, driver side, Passenger's Interior Lock Switch, Confort System System Central Control Module

Edition 07/98
USA.5132.03.21

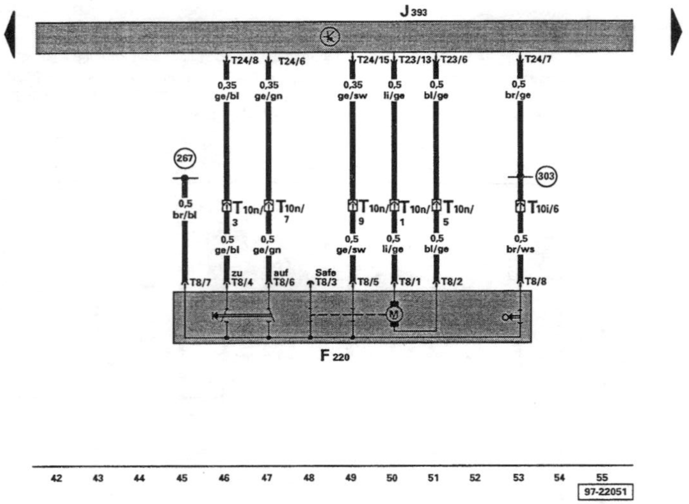

ws = white
sw = black
ro = red
br = brown
gn = green
bl = blue
gr = grey
li = violet
ge = yellow

F220 – Driver's Door Central Locking Actuator
J393 – Comfort System Central Control Module
T8 – 8-Pin Connector, on Lock unit for central locking, driver side
T10i – 10-Pin Connector, black, on A–Pillar left
T10n – 10-Pin Connector, brown, on A–Pillar left
T24 – 24-Pin Connector

(267) – Ground connector -2–, in wiring harness door cable
(303) – Ground Connection 3 (in passenger's door wiring harness)

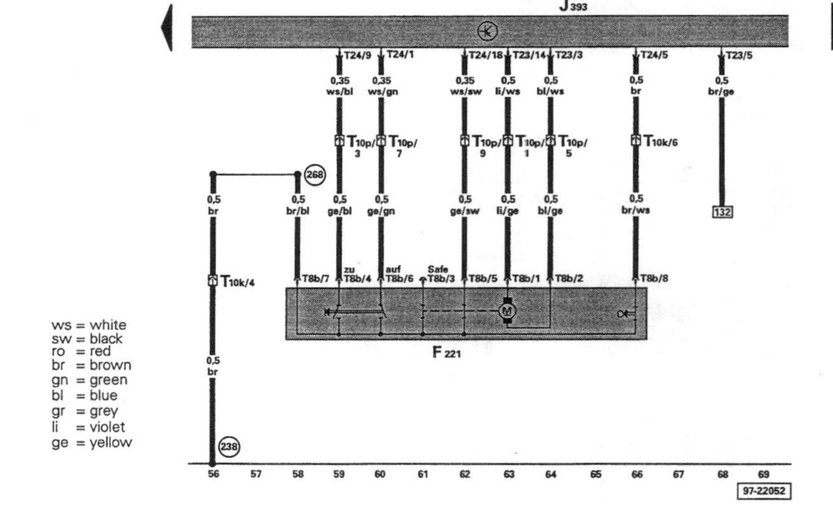

ws = white
sw = black
ro = red
br = brown
gn = green
bl = blue
gr = grey
li = violet
ge = yellow

F221 – Passenger's Door Central Locking Actuator
J393 – Comfort System Central Control Module
T8b – 8-Pin Connector
T10k – 10-Pin Connector, black, on A-Pillar left
T10p – 10-Pin Connector, brown, on A-Pillar right
T24 – 24-Pin Connector

(238) – Ground connection, on left A-pillar, lower part
(268) – Ground connection, in driver's door wiring harness

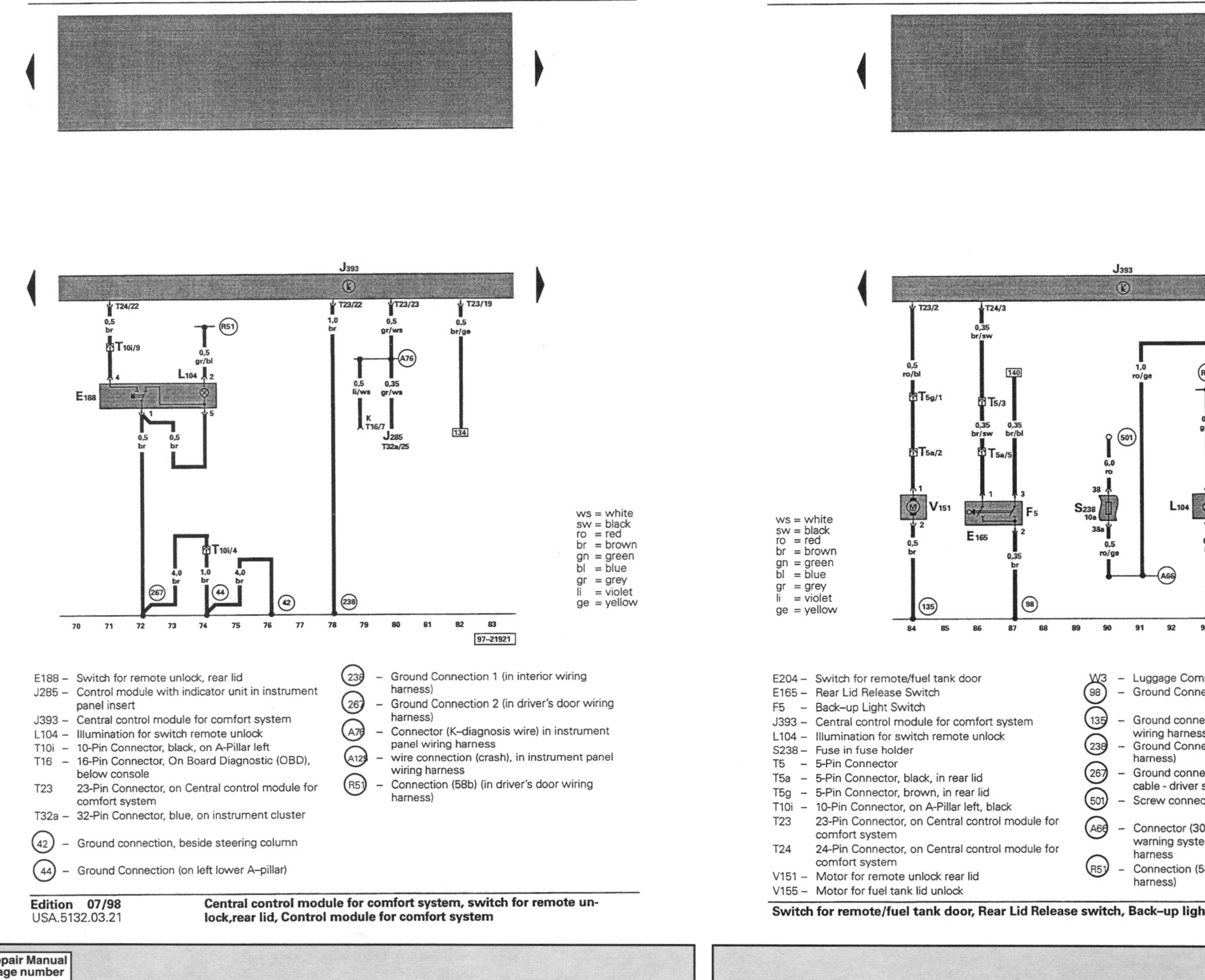

ws = white
sw = black
ro = red
br = brown
gn = green
bl = blue
gr = grey
li = violet
ge = yellow

E188 – Switch for remote unlock, rear lid
J285 – Control module with indicator unit in instrument panel insert
J393 – Central control module for comfort system
L104 – Illumination for switch remote unlock
T10i – 10-Pin Connector, black, on A-Pillar left
T16 – 16-Pin Connector, On Board Diagnostic (OBD), below console
T23 – 23-Pin Connector, on Central control module for comfort system
T32a – 32-Pin Connector, blue, on instrument cluster
(42) – Ground connection, beside steering column
(44) – Ground Connection (on left lower A–pillar)
(238) – Ground Connection 1 (in interior wiring harness)
(267) – Ground Connection 2 (in driver's door wiring harness)
(A76) – Connector (K–diagnosis wire) in instrument panel wiring harness
(A129) – wire connection (crash), in instrument panel wiring harness
(R51) – Connection (58b) (in driver's door wiring harness)

Edition 07/98
USA.5132.03.21

Central control module for comfort system, switch for remote unlock,rear lid, Control module for comfort system

ws = white
sw = black
ro = red
br = brown
gn = green
bl = blue
gr = grey
li = violet
ge = yellow

E204 – Switch for remote/fuel tank door
E165 – Rear Lid Release Switch
F5 – Back–up Light Switch
J393 – Central control module for comfort system
L104 – Illumination for switch remote unlock
S238 – Fuse in fuse holder
T5 – 5-Pin Connector
T5a – 5-Pin Connector, black, in rear lid
T5g – 5-Pin Connector, brown, in rear lid
T10i – 10-Pin Connector, on A-Pillar left, black
T23 – 23-Pin Connector, on Central control module for comfort system
T24 – 24-Pin Connector, on Central control module for comfort system
V151 – Motor for remote unlock rear lid
V155 – Motor for fuel tank lid unlock
W3 – Luggage Compartment Light
(98) – Ground Connection (in rear lid wiring harness)
(135) – Ground connection -2-, in instrument panel wiring harness
(238) – Ground Connection 1 (in interior wiring harness)
(267) – Ground connector -2-, in wiring harness door cable - driver side
(501) – Screw connection -2- (30), on relay panel
(A66) – Connector (30a, central locking/anti-theft warning system/IR) in instrument panel wiring harness
(R51) – Connection (58b) (in driver's door wiring harness)

Switch for remote/fuel tank door, Rear Lid Release switch, Back–up light Switch

Edition 07/98
USA.5132.03.21

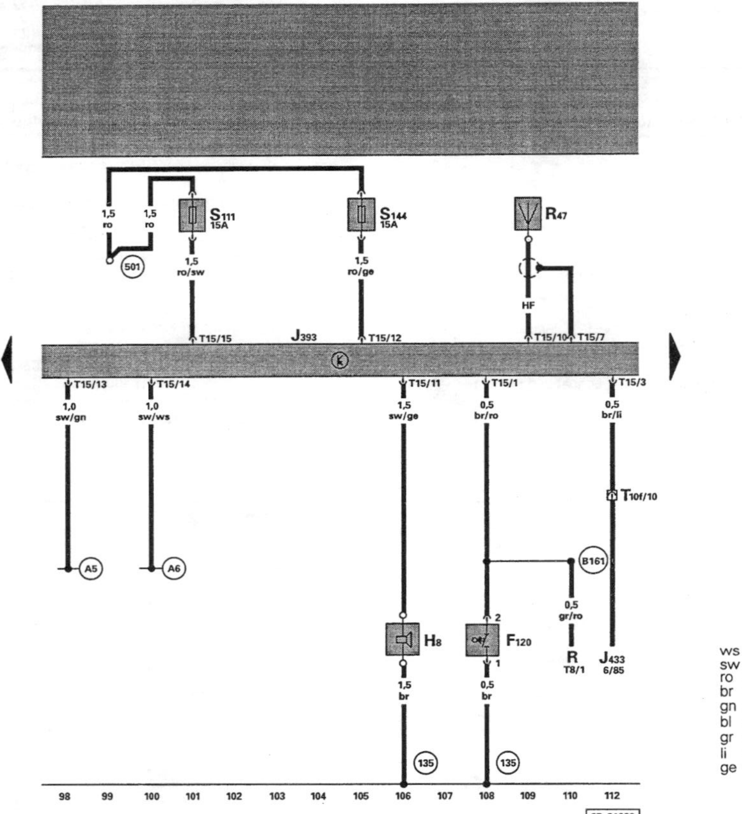

ws = white
sw = black
ro = red
br = brown
gn = green
bl = blue
gr = grey
li = violet
ge = yellow

- F120 – Hood Alarm Switch
- H8 – Alarm Horn
- J393 – Central control module for comfort system
- J433 – Locking relay for starter (clutch pedal switch)
- R – Radio
- R47 – Antenna wire for central locking and antitheft warning system
- S111 – Alarm System and Anti-Theft Engine Disable Fuse
- S144 – Fuse for central locking/anti-theft warning system
- T8 – 8-Pin Connector, on radio
- T10f – 10-Pin Connector
- T15 – 15-Pin Connector, on Central control module for comfort system

- (135) – Ground connection -2-, in instrument panle wiring harness
- (501) – Threaded connection -1- (30) on the relay plate
- (A5) – plus connection (right turn signal), in instrument panel wiring harness
- (A6) – plus connection (left turn signal), in instrument panel wiring harness
- (B161) – Anti-theft alarm connection (in interior wiring harness)

Central control module for comfort system, hood alarm switch, alarm horn

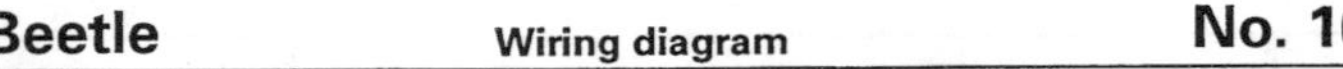

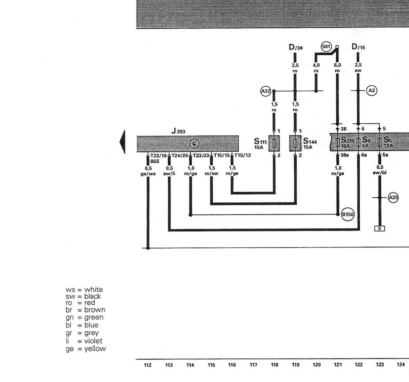

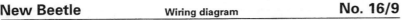

ws = white
sw = black
ro = red
br = brown
gn = green
bl = blue
gr = grey
li = violet
ge = yellow

- D – Ignition/Starter Switch
- J285 – Instrument Cluster Display Control Module
- J393 – Comfort System Central Control Module
- S5 – Fuse (in fuse/relay panel)
- S6 – Fuse (in fuse/relay panel)
- S111 – Alarm system and Anti–theft Engine Disable Fuse
- S144 – Central Locking/Alarm System Fuse
- S237 – Fuse 37 (in fuse holder)
- S238 – Fuse 38 (in fuse holder)
- T15 – 15–pin Connector
- T23 – 23–pin Connector
- T24 – 24–pin Connector
- T32 – 32–pin Connector, blue

- (501) – Bolted Connection 2 (30) (at relay panel)
- (A2) – Plus Connection (15) (in instrument panel wiring harness)
- (A20) – Connection (15a) (in instrument panel wiring harness)
- (A21) – Connection (86s) (in instrument panel wiring harness)
- (A32) – Plus Connection (30) (in instrument panel wiring harness)
- (B156) – Plus Connection 3 (15a) (in interior wiring harness)

Ignition/Starter Switch, Instrument Cluster Display Control Module, Comfort System Central Control Module.

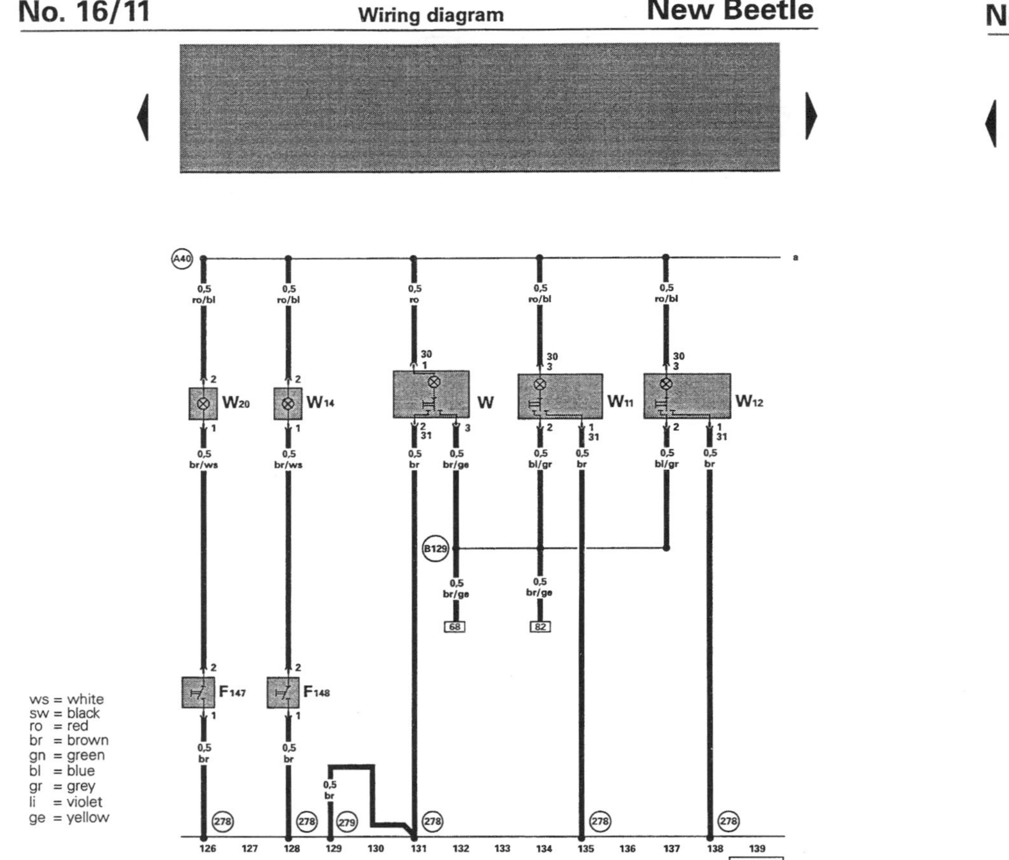

ws = white
sw = black
ro = red
br = brown
gn = green
bl = blue
gr = grey
li = violet
ge = yellow

F147 – Left Make-Up Mirror Light Switch
F148 – Right Make-Up Mirror Light Switch
W – Front Interior Light
W11 – Left Rear Reading Light
W12 – Right Rear Reading Light
W14 – Right Make-up Mirror Light
W20 – Left Make-up Mirror Light

(278) – Ground connector -4-, in wiring harness interior

(279) – Ground connector -5, in wiring harness interior

(A40) – plus connection -1- (30), in instrument cluster wiring harness

(B129) – Connector (interior light 3/L), in wiring harness interior

Front interior light, left rear reading light, right rear reading light, right make-up mirror light, left make-up mirror light

Edition 07/98
USA.5132.03.21

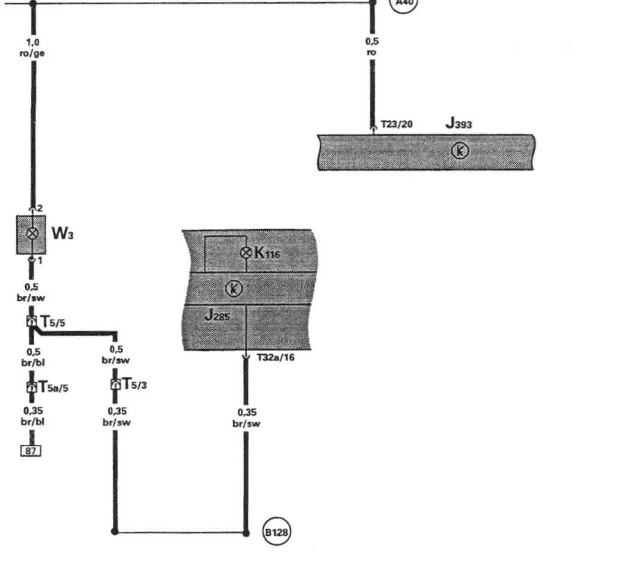

ws = white
sw = black
ro = red
br = brown
gn = green
bl = blue
gr = grey
li = violet
ge = yellow

J285 – Control module with indicator unit in instrument panel insert
J393 – Control module for comfort system
T5 – 5-Pin Connector, black, on C-pillar, left
K116 – Warning light for rear lid unlocked
T5a – 5-Pin Connector, black, in rear lid
T23 – 23-Pin Connector, on Central control module for comfort system
T32a – 32-Pin Connector, blue, on instrument cluster
W3 – Luggage compartment Light

(A13) – wire connection (door contact switch) in instrument panel wiring harness

(A21) – wire connection (86s), in instrument panel wiring harness

(A40) – plus connection -1-(30), in instrument cluster wiring harness

(B128) – Connector (Luggage compartment lamp) in wiring harness interior

Edition 07/98
USA.5132.03.21

Luggage compartment light, luggage compartment light switch

Digital clock with ambient temperature display and front interior light, rear reading lights. (vehicles with manual windows)

from August 1998

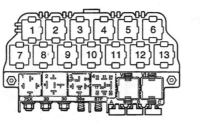

97-21956

Fuse colors
30 A – green
25 A – white
20 A – yellow
15 A – blue
10 A – red
7,5 A – brown
5 A – beige

Edition 08.98
USA.5132.04.21

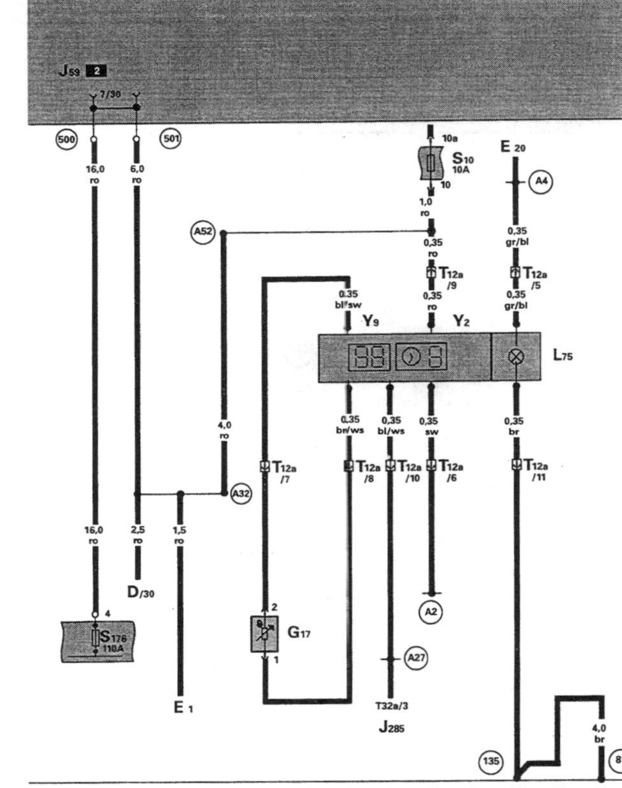

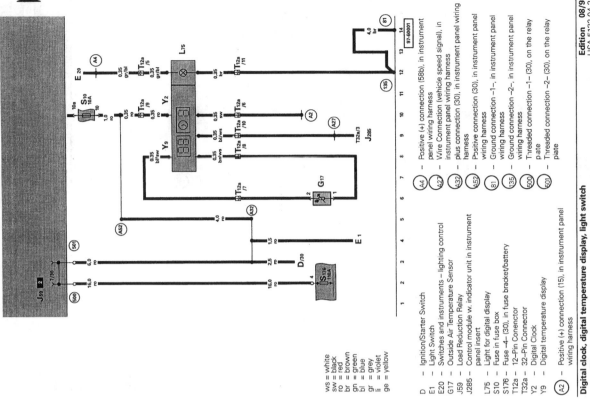

ws = white
sw = black
ro = red
br = brown
gn = green
bl = blue
gr = grey
li = violet
ge = yellow

D – Ignition/Starter Switch
E1 – Light Switch
E20 – Switches and instruments – lighting control
G17 – Outside Air Temperature Sensor
J59 – Load Reduction Relay
J285 – Control module w. indicator unit in instrument panel insert
L75 – Light for digital display
S10 – Fuse in fuse box
S176 – Fuse –4– (30), in fuse bracket/battery
T12a – 12–Pin Conenctor
T32a – 32–Pin Connector
Y2 – Digital Clock
Y9 – Digital temperature display

(A2) – Positive (+) connection (15), in instrument panel wiring harness
(A4) – Positive (+) connection (58b), in instrument panel wiring harness
(A27) – Wire Connection (vehicle speed signal), in instrument panel wiring harness
(A32) – plus connection (30), in instrument panel wiring harness
(A52) – Positive connection (30), in instrument panel wiring harness
(81) – Ground connection –1–, in instrument panel wiring harness
(135) – Ground connection –2–, in instrument panel wiring harness
(500) – Threaded connection –1– (30), on the relay plate
(501) – Threaded connection –2– (30), on the relay plate

Digital clock, digital temperature display, light switch

Edition 08/98
USA.5132.04.21

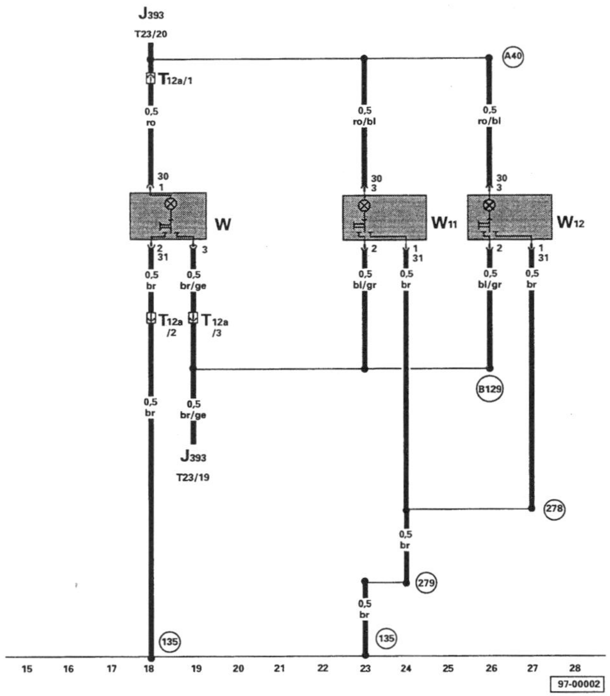

ws = white
sw = black
ro = red
br = brown
gn = green
bl = blue
gr = grey
li = violet
ge = yellow

97-00002

J393 – Central control module for comfort system
W – Front Interior Light
W11 – Left Rear Reading Light
W12 – Right Rear Reading Light
T23 – 23–Pin Connector, on Central control module for comfort system

(135) – Ground connection –2–, in instrument panel wiring harness

(278) – Ground connector -4-, in wiring harness interior

(279) – Ground connector -5, in wiring harness interior

(A40) – plus connection -1- (30), in instrument cluster wiring harness

(B129) – Connector (interior light 3/L), in wiring harness interior

Edition 08/98
USA.5132.04.21

Front interior light, left rear reading light, right rear reading light

THIS PAGE INTENTIONALLY LEFT BLANK

Digital clock with ambient temperature display and front interior light, rear reading lights. (vehicles with power windows)

from August 1998

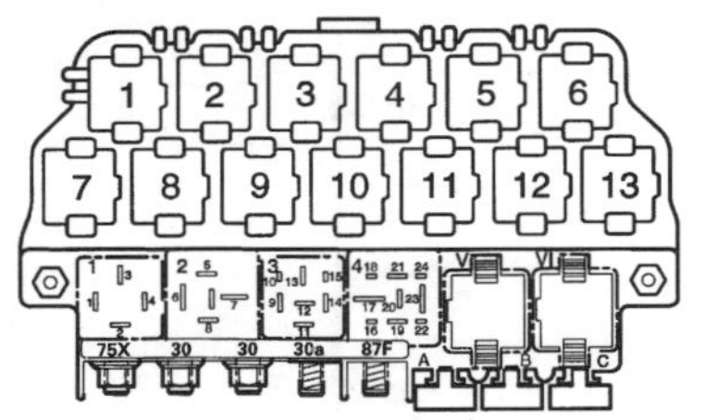

Fuse colors
30 A – green
25 A – white
20 A – yellow
15 A – blue
10 A – red
7,5 A – brown
5 A – beige

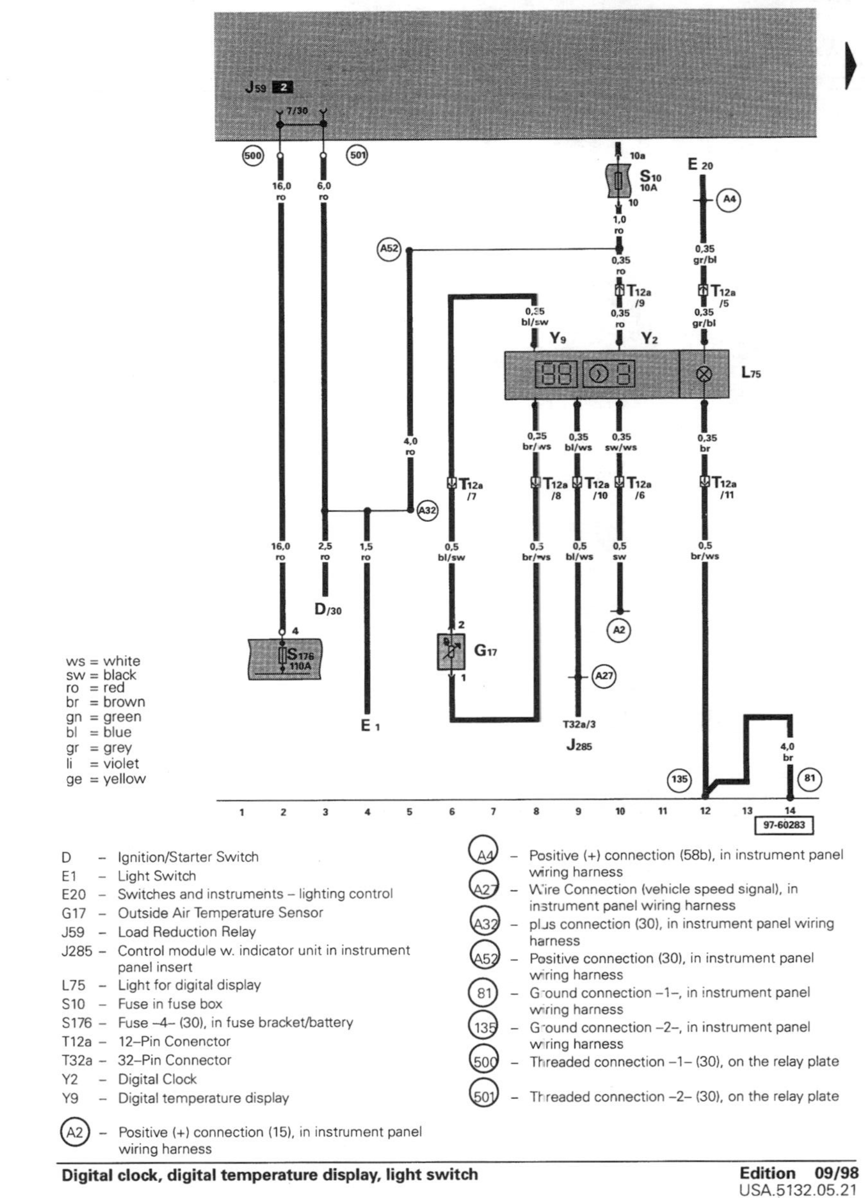

ws = white
sw = black
ro = red
br = brown
gn = green
bl = blue
gr = grey
li = violet
ge = yellow

D – Ignition/Starter Switch
E1 – Light Switch
E20 – Switches and instruments – lighting control
G17 – Outside Air Temperature Sensor
J59 – Load Reduction Relay
J285 – Control module w. indicator unit in instrument panel insert
L75 – Light for digital display
S10 – Fuse in fuse box
S176 – Fuse -4- (30), in fuse bracket/battery
T12a – 12-Pin Conenctor
T32a – 32-Pin Connector
Y2 – Digital Clock
Y9 – Digital temperature display

(A2) – Positive (+) connection (15), in instrument panel wiring harness
(A4) – Positive (+) connection (58b), in instrument panel wiring harness
(A27) – Wire Connection (vehicle speed signal), in instrument panel wiring harness
(A32) – plus connection (30), in instrument panel wiring harness
(A52) – Positive connection (30), in instrument panel wiring harness
(81) – Ground connection -1-, in instrument panel wiring harness
(135) – Ground connection -2-, in instrument panel wiring harness
(500) – Threaded connection -1- (30), on the relay plate
(501) – Threaded connection -2- (30), on the relay plate

Digital clock, digital temperature display, light switch

J393 – Central control module for comfort system
W – Front Interior Light
W11 – Left Rear Reading Light
W12 – Right Rear Reading Light
T23 – 23–Pin Connector, on Central control module for comfort system

(135) – Ground connection –2–, in instrument panel wiring harness

(278) – Ground connector -4-, in wiring harness interior

(279) – Ground connector -5, in wiring harness interior

(A40) – plus connection -1- (30), in instrument cluster wiring harness

(B129) – Connector (interior light 3/L), in wiring harness interior

ws = white
sw = black
ro = red
br = brown
gn = green
bl = blue
gr = grey
li = violet
ge = yellow

97–60004

THIS PAGE INTENTIONALLY LEFT
BLANK

2,0L-Engine – Motronic Multiport Fuel Injection (MFI)/85 kW, code AEG, (without cruise control)

from August 1998

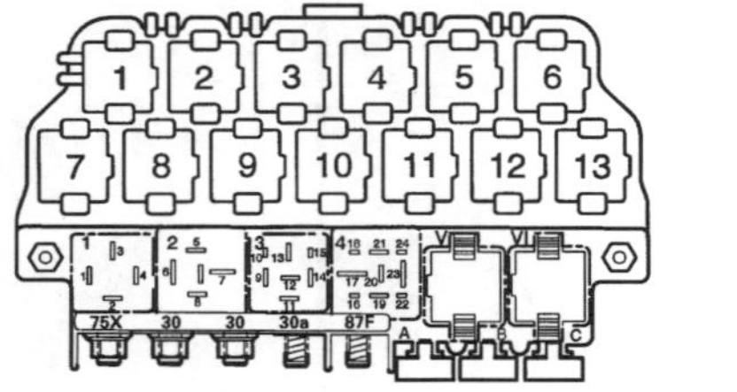

Relay location on the thirteen position auxiliary relay panel, above relay panel:

Relay panel:

2 Load Reduction Relay (213), (18)

4 Fuel Pump Relay (409)

Note: Number in parentheses indicates production control number stamped on relay housing

Fuse colors

30 A – green
25 A – white
20 A – yellow
15 A – blue
10 A – red
7,5 A – brown
5 A – beige

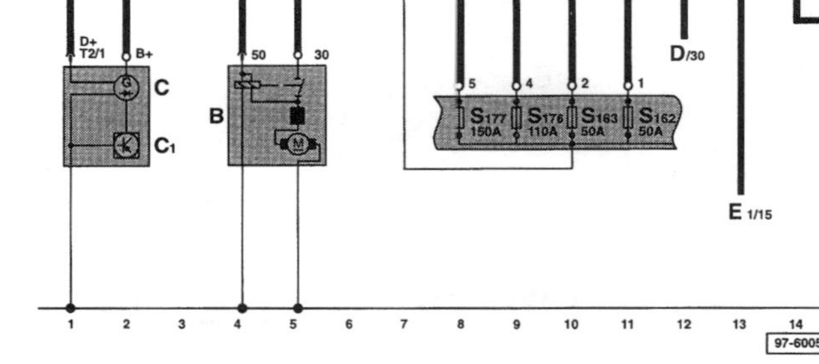

ws = white
sw = black
ro = red
br = brown
gn = green
bl = blue
gr = grey
li = violet
ge = yellow

A – Battery
B – Starter
C – Generator (GEN)
C1 – Voltage Regulator (VR)
D – Ignition/Starter Switch
E1 – Light Switch
J59 – Load Reduction Relay
J434 – Locking relay for starter (clutch pedal switch)
S162 – Fuse -1- in fuse bracket/battery
S163 – Fuse -2- (50)in fuse bracket/battery
S176 – Fuse -4- (30), in fuse bracket/battery
S177 – Fuse -5- (30), in fuse bracket/battery
T2 – Double Connector
T4 – 4-Pin Connector, in engine compartment left
T6 – 6-Pin Connector, brown, behind instrument panel, left

(500) – Threaded connection -1- (30) on the relay plate
(501) – Threaded connection -2- (30) on the relay plate
(502) – Threaded connection -1- (30a) on the relay plate
(A17) – wire connection (61), in instrument panel wiring harness
(A32) – plus connection (30), in instrument panel wiring harness

Starter, generator (GEN)

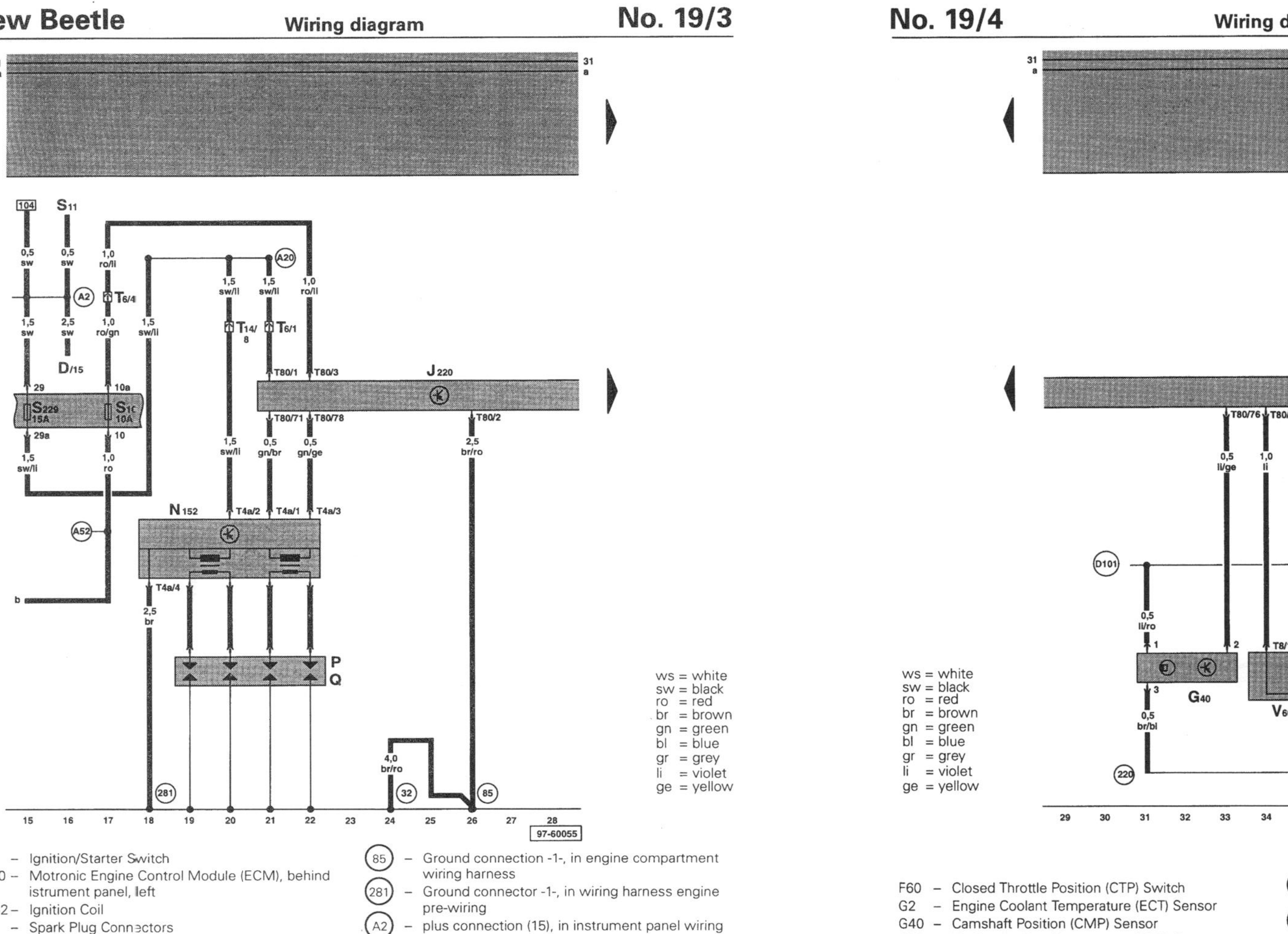

ws = white
sw = black
ro = red
br = brown
gn = green
bl = blue
gr = grey
li = violet
ge = yellow

D – Ignition/Starter Switch
J220 – Motronic Engine Control Module (ECM), behind istrument panel, left
N152 – Ignition Coil
P – Spark Plug Connectors
Q – Spark Plugs
S10 – Fuse 10 in fuse holder
S11 – Fuse 11 in fuse holder
S229 – Fuse 29 in fuse holder
T4a – 4-Pin Connector, black
T6 – 6-Pin Connector, brown, behind instrument panel, left
T14 – 14-Pin Connector, in engine compartment, left
T80 – Connector, 80 point

(32) – Ground connection, behind instrument panel, left

(85) – Ground connection -1-, in engine compartment wiring harness
(281) – Ground connector -1-, in wiring harness engine pre-wiring
(A2) – plus connection (15), in instrument panel wiring harness
(A20) – wire connection (15a), in instrument panel wiring harness
(A52) – plus connection (30), in instrument panel wiring harness

Motronic Engine Control Module (ECM), Ignition system

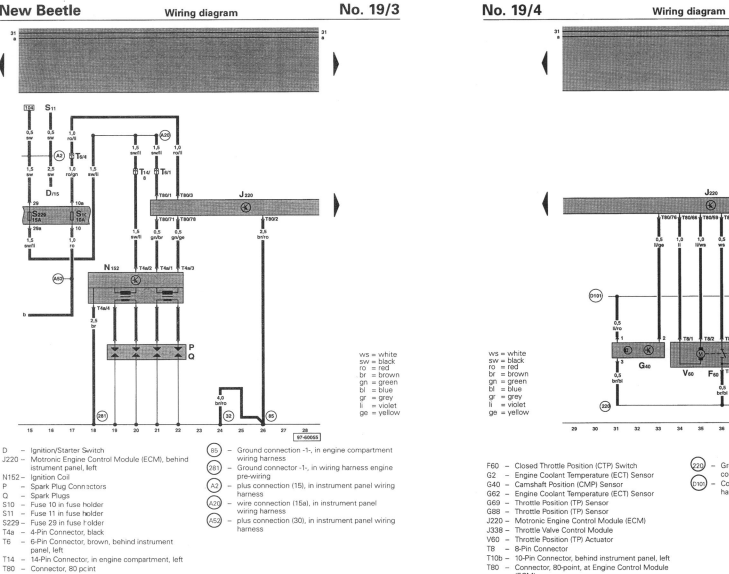

ws = white
sw = black
ro = red
br = brown
gn = green
bl = blue
gr = grey
li = violet
ge = yellow

F60 – Closed Throttle Position (CTP) Switch
G2 – Engine Coolant Temperature (ECT) Sensor
G40 – Camshaft Position (CMP) Sensor
G62 – Engine Coolant Temperature (ECT) Sensor
G69 – Throttle Position (TP) Sensor
G88 – Throttle Position (TP) Sensor
J220 – Motronic Engine Control Module (ECM)
J338 – Throttle Valve Control Module
V60 – Throttle Position (TP) Actuator
T8 – 8-Pin Connector
T10b – 10-Pin Connector, behind instrument panel, left
T80 – Connector, 80-point, at Engine Control Module (ECM)

(220) – Ground connection (sensor ground), in engine compartment wiring harness
(D101) – Connection 1 (in engine compartment wiring harness)

Motronic Engine Control Module (ECM), Throttle Valve Control Module, Camshaft Position (CMP) Sensor, Engine Coolant Temperature (ECT) Sensor

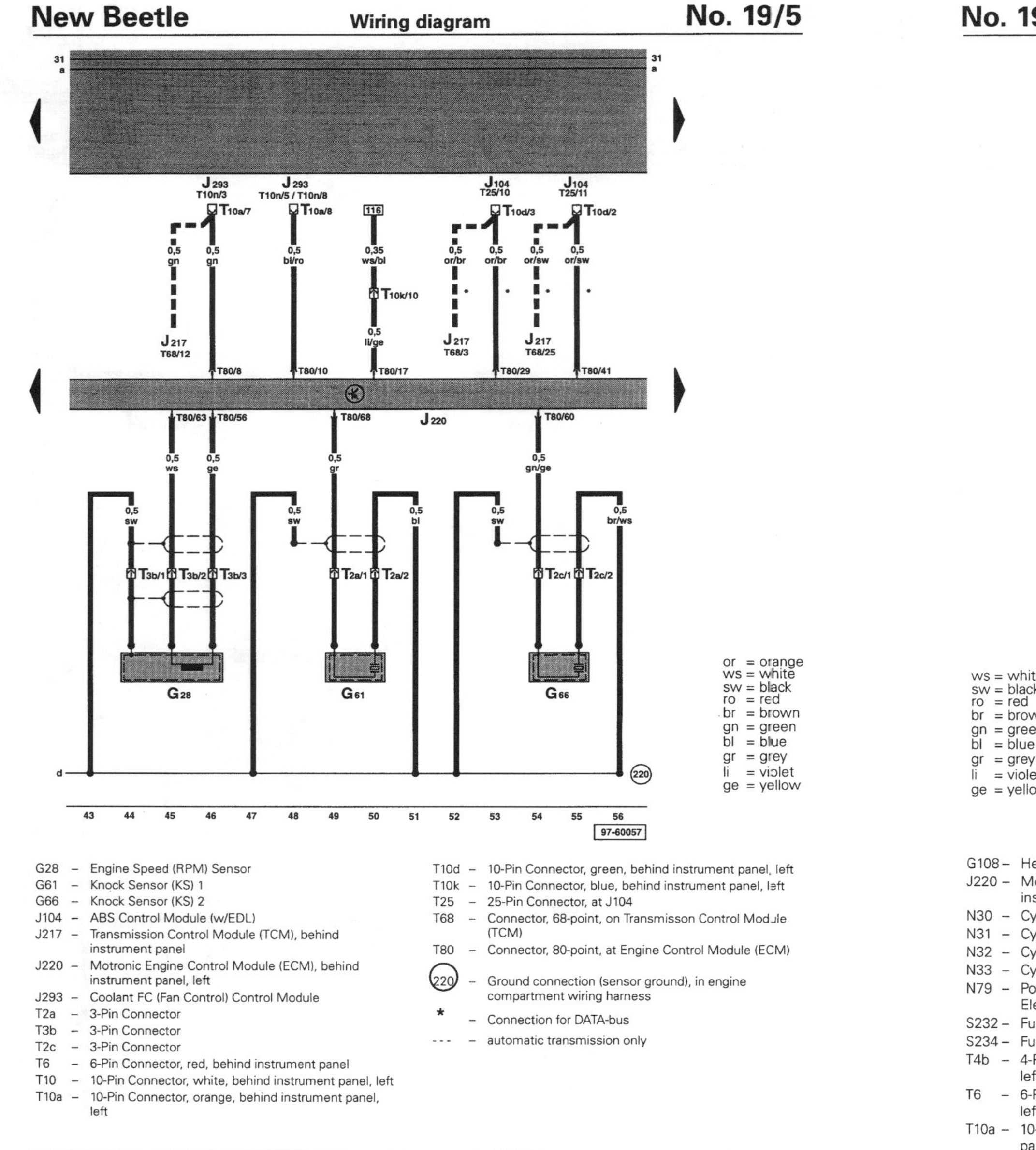

or = orange
ws = white
sw = black
ro = red
br = brown
gn = green
bl = blue
gr = grey
li = violet
ge = yellow

G28 – Engine Speed (RPM) Sensor
G61 – Knock Sensor (KS) 1
G66 – Knock Sensor (KS) 2
J104 – ABS Control Module (w/EDL)
J217 – Transmission Control Module (TCM), behind instrument panel
J220 – Motronic Engine Control Module (ECM), behind instrument panel, left
J293 – Coolant FC (Fan Control) Control Module
T2a – 3-Pin Connector
T3b – 3-Pin Connector
T2c – 3-Pin Connector
T6 – 6-Pin Connector, red, behind instrument panel
T10 – 10-Pin Connector, white, behind instrument panel, left
T10a – 10-Pin Connector, orange, behind instrument panel, left
T10d – 10-Pin Connector, green, behind instrument panel, left
T10k – 10-Pin Connector, blue, behind instrument panel, left
T25 – 25-Pin Connector, at J104
T68 – Connector, 68-point, on Transmisson Control Module (TCM)
T80 – Connector, 80-point, at Engine Control Module (ECM)
(220) – Ground connection (sensor ground), in engine compartment wiring harness
* – Connection for DATA-bus
- - - – automatic transmission only

Edition 09/98
USA.5132.05.21

Motronic engine control module (ECM), engine speed (RPM) sensor, knock sensor (KS) 1, knock sensor (KS) 2

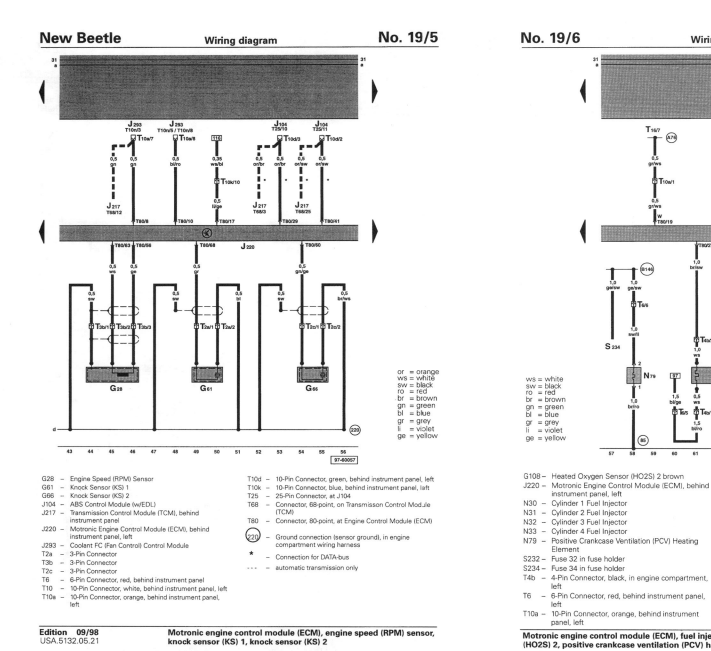

ws = white
sw = black
ro = red
br = brown
gn = green
bl = blue
gr = grey
li = violet
ge = yellow

97-60058

G108 – Heated Oxygen Sensor (HO2S) 2 brown
J220 – Motronic Engine Control Module (ECM), behind instrument panel, left
N30 – Cylinder 1 Fuel Injector
N31 – Cylinder 2 Fuel Injector
N32 – Cylinder 3 Fuel Injector
N33 – Cylinder 4 Fuel Injector
N79 – Positive Crankcase Ventilation (PCV) Heating Element
S232 – Fuse 32 in fuse holder
S234 – Fuse 34 in fuse holder
T4b – 4-Pin Connector, black, in engine compartment, left
T6 – 6-Pin Connector, red, behind instrument panel, left
T10a – 10-Pin Connector, orange, behind instrument panel, left
T10d – 10-Pin Connector, green, behind instrument panel, left
T14 – 14-Pin Connector, in engine compartment, left
T16 – 16-Pin Connector, Data Link Connector (DLC), below steering column
T80 – 80-Pin Connector, at Engine Control Module (ECM)
(85) – Ground connection -1-, in engine compartment wiring harness
(A76) – Connector (K-diagnosis wire), in instrument panel wiring harness
(D140) – Connector (injectors), in wiring harness, engine pre-wiring
(B146) – Flus connector -1- (87), in wiring harness interior

Motronic engine control module (ECM), fuel injectors, heated oxygen sensor (HO2S) 2, positive crankcase ventilation (PCV) heating element

Edition 09/98
USA.5132.05.21

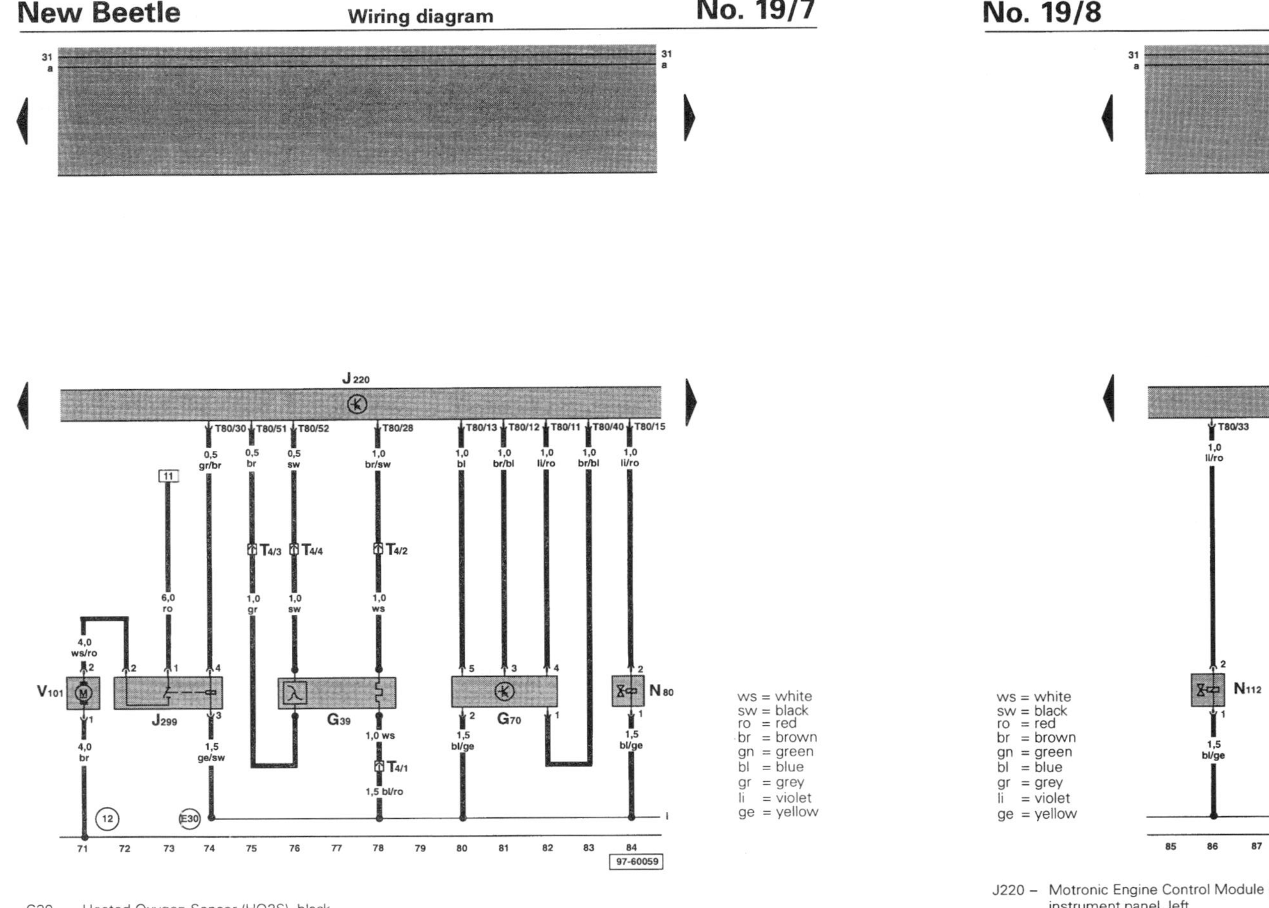

ws = white
sw = black
ro = red
br = brown
gn = green
bl = blue
gr = grey
li = violet
ge = yellow

G39 – Heated Oxygen Sensor (HO2S), black
G70 – Mass Air Flow (MAF) Sensor
J220 – Motronic Engine Control Module (ECM), behind instrument panel, left
J299 – Secondary Air Injection (AIR) Pump Relay, in engine compartment, left
N80 – Evaporative Emission (EVAP) Canister Purge Regulator Valve
V101 – Secondary Air Injection (AIR) Pump Motor
T4 – 4-Pin Connector, brown
T80 – 80-Pin Connector

(12) – Ground connection, in engine compartment, left
(E30) – Connector (87a), in wiring harness engine

Edition 09/98
USA.5132.05.21

Heated oxygen sensor (HO2S), mass air flow (MAF) sensor, evaporative emission (EVAP) canister purge regulator valve, secondary air injection (AIR) system

ws = white
sw = black
ro = red
br = brown
gn = green
bl = blue
gr = grey
li = violet
ge = yellow

J220 – Motronic Engine Control Module (ECM), behind instrument panel, left
N112 – Secondary Air Injection (AIR) Solenoid Valve
S243 – Fuse 43 in fuse holder
V144 – Leak Detection Pump (LDP)
T3d – 3-Pin Connector
T6 – 6-Pin Connector, red, behind instrument panel, left
T10a – 10-Pin Connector,orange, behind instrument panel, left
T10d – 10-Pin Connector, green, behind instrument panel, left
T80 – Connector, 80-point, at Engine Control Module (ECM)

(A27) – wire Connection (vehicle speed signal), in instrument panel wiring harness
(A45) – wire connection (RPM-signal), in instrument panel wiring harness
(A99) – Connector -1- (87), in instrument panel wiring harness
(A100) – Connector -2- (87), in instrument panel wiring harness
(E30) – Connector (87a), in wiring harness engine

Motronic engine control module (ECM), diagnosis pump for fuel system, secondary air injection solenoid valve

Edition 09/98
USA.5132.05.21

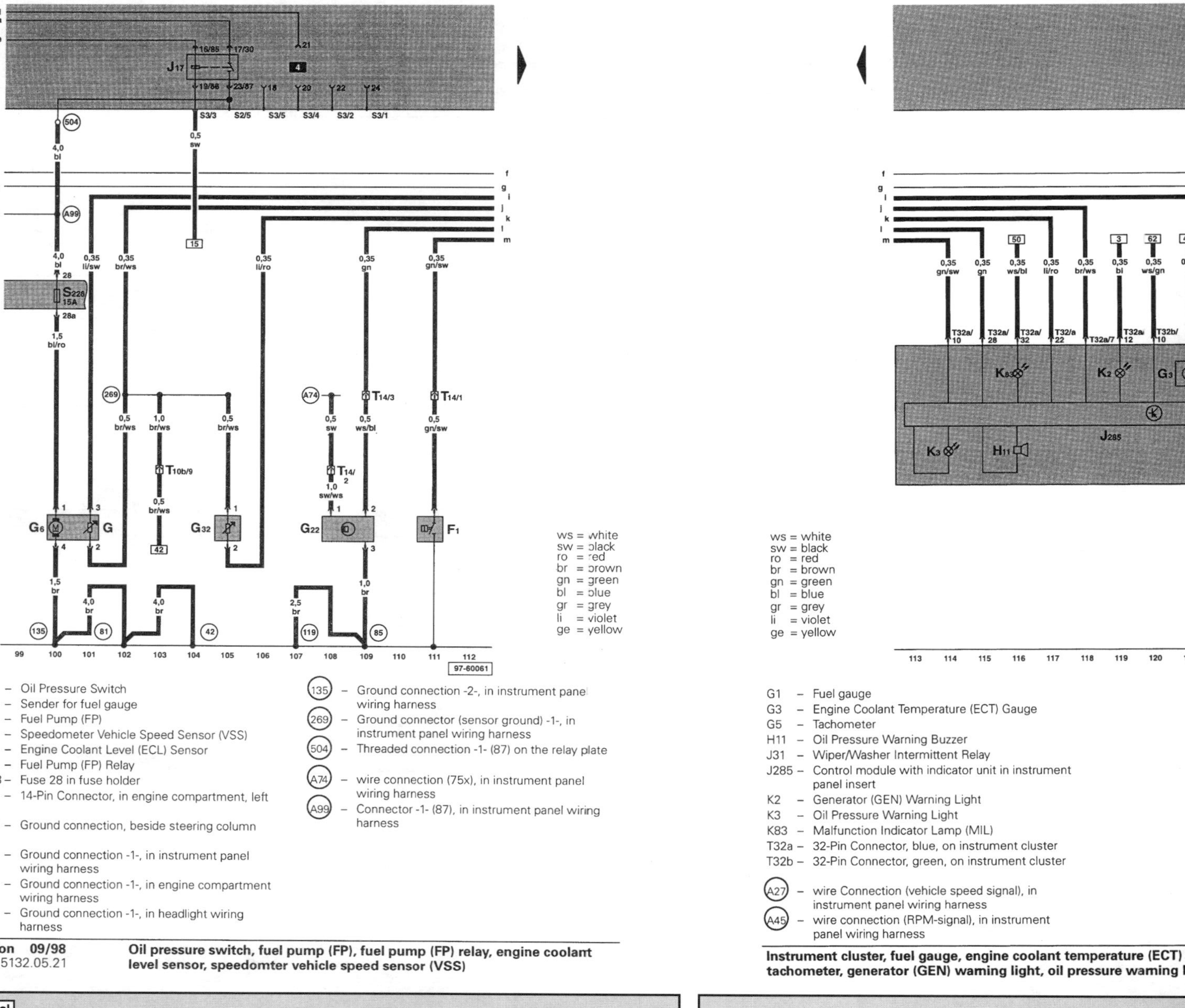

ws = white
sw = black
ro = red
br = brown
gn = green
bl = blue
gr = grey
li = violet
ge = yellow

F1 – Oil Pressure Switch
G – Sender for fuel gauge
G6 – Fuel Pump (FP)
G22 – Speedometer Vehicle Speed Sensor (VSS)
G32 – Engine Coolant Level (ECL) Sensor
J17 – Fuel Pump (FP) Relay
S228 – Fuse 28 in fuse holder
T14 – 14-Pin Connector, in engine compartment, left

(42) – Ground connection, beside steering column

(81) – Ground connection -1-, in instrument panel wiring harness

(85) – Ground connection -1-, in engine compartment wiring harness

(119) – Ground connection -1-, in headlight wiring harness

(135) – Ground connection -2-, in instrument panel wiring harness

(269) – Ground connector (sensor ground) -1-, in instrument panel wiring harness

(504) – Threaded connection -1- (87) on the relay plate

(A74) – wire connection (75x), in instrument panel wiring harness

(A99) – Connector -1- (87), in instrument panel wiring harness

Oil pressure switch, fuel pump (FP), fuel pump (FP) relay, engine coolant level sensor, speedomter vehicle speed sensor (VSS)

ws = white
sw = black
ro = red
br = brown
gn = green
bl = blue
gr = grey
li = violet
ge = yellow

G1 – Fuel gauge
G3 – Engine Coolant Temperature (ECT) Gauge
G5 – Tachometer
H11 – Oil Pressure Warning Buzzer
J31 – Wiper/Washer Intermittent Relay
J285 – Control module with indicator unit in instrument panel insert
K2 – Generator (GEN) Warning Light
K3 – Oil Pressure Warning Light
K83 – Malfunction Indicator Lamp (MIL)
T32a – 32-Pin Connector, blue, on instrument cluster
T32b – 32-Pin Connector, green, on instrument cluster

(A27) – wire Connection (vehicle speed signal), in instrument panel wiring harness

(A45) – wire connection (RPM-signal), in instrument panel wiring harness

Instrument cluster, fuel gauge, engine coolant temperature (ECT) gauge, tachometer, generator (GEN) waming light, oil pressure waming light

Comfort system, with anti-theft alarm system (vehicles with power windows)

from August 1998

97-21956

Fuse colors
30 A – green
25 A – white
20 A – yellow
15 A – blue
10 A – red
7,5 A – brown
5 A – beige

Edition 09/98
USA.5132.05.21

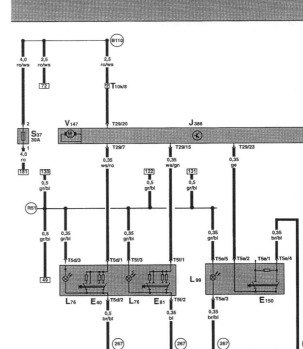

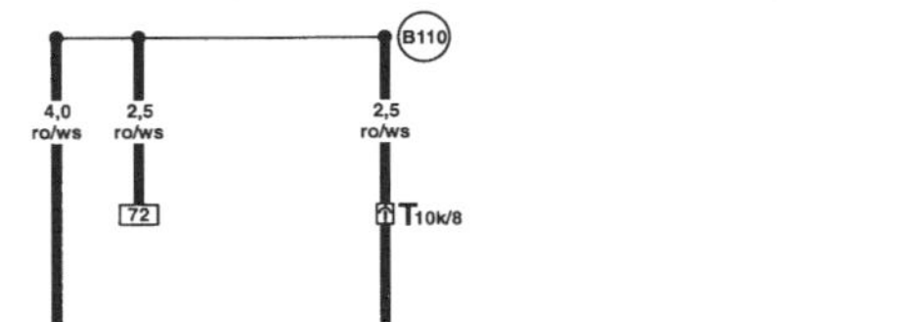
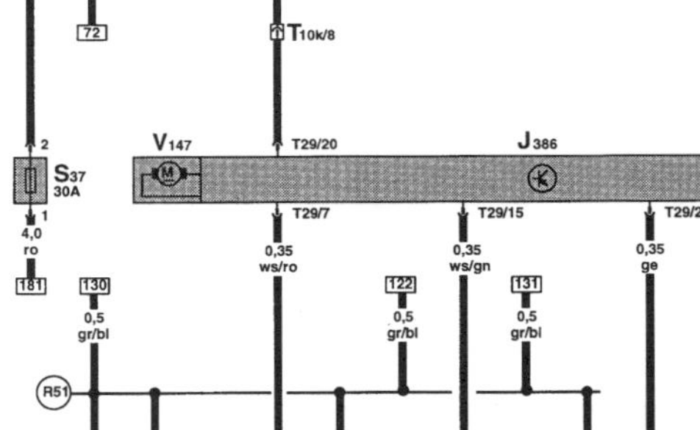

ws = white
sw = black
ro = red
br = brown
gn = green
bl = blue
gr = grey
li = violet
ge = yellow

E40 – Left Front Window Switch
E81 – Switch for window regulator front right, driver
E150 – Switch for interior lock, driver side
J386 – Door control module, driver side
L76 – Push Button Light
L99 – Lighting for switch interior lock
S37 – Power Window Fuse, on relay panel
T5d – 5-Pin Connector, brown
T5f – 5-Pin Connector, black
T5e – 5-Pin Connector, black
T10k – 10-Pin Connector, black, on A-Pillar left
T29 – 29-Pin Connector, on Door control module
V147 – Motor for window regulator, driver side

(267) – Ground connector -2-, in wiring harness door cable

(B110) – Connection (30, window regulator) in wiring harness interior
(R51) – Connection (58b), in door wiring harness, driver's side

Door control module (driver side), left front window switch, switch for window regulator front right (driver), switch for interior lock (driver side)

Edition 09/98
USA.5132.05.21

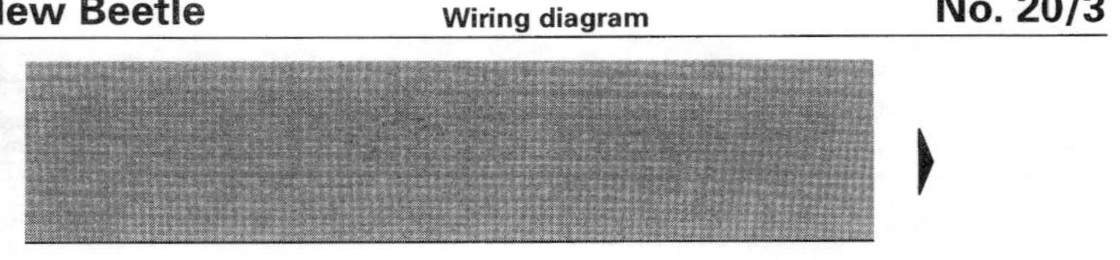

ws = white
sw = black
ro = red
br = brown
gn = green
bl = blue
gr = grey
li = violet
ge = yellow

F220 – Lock unit for central locking, driver side
J386 – Door control module, driver side
K133 – Warning light for central locking -SAFE-
T8e – 8-Pin Connector, on Lock unit for central locking, driver side
T29 – 29-Pin Connector, on Door control module

(180) – Ground connection –2–, in central locking system wiring harness
(267) – Ground connector -2–, in wiring harness door cable

Door control module (driver side), lock unit for central locking (driver side)

ws = white
sw = black
ro = red
br = brown
gn = green
bl = blue
gr = grey
li = violet
ge = yellow

J386 – Door control module, driver side
T8 – 8-Pin Connector, in driver's door wiring
T10k – 10-Pin Connector, on A-Pillar left, black
T29 – 29-Pin Connector, on Door control module – driver side
V17 – Driver's Side Mirror Adjustment Motor
V149 – Motor for mirror adjustment, driver side
Z4 – Heated outside mirror, driver side

(44) – Ground connection, on left A-pillar, lower part
(205) – Ground connection, in driver's door wiring harness
(267) – Ground connector -2-, in wiring harness door cable

Door control module (driver side), driver's side mirror adjustment motor, motor for mirror adjustment (driver side), heated outside mirror (driver side)

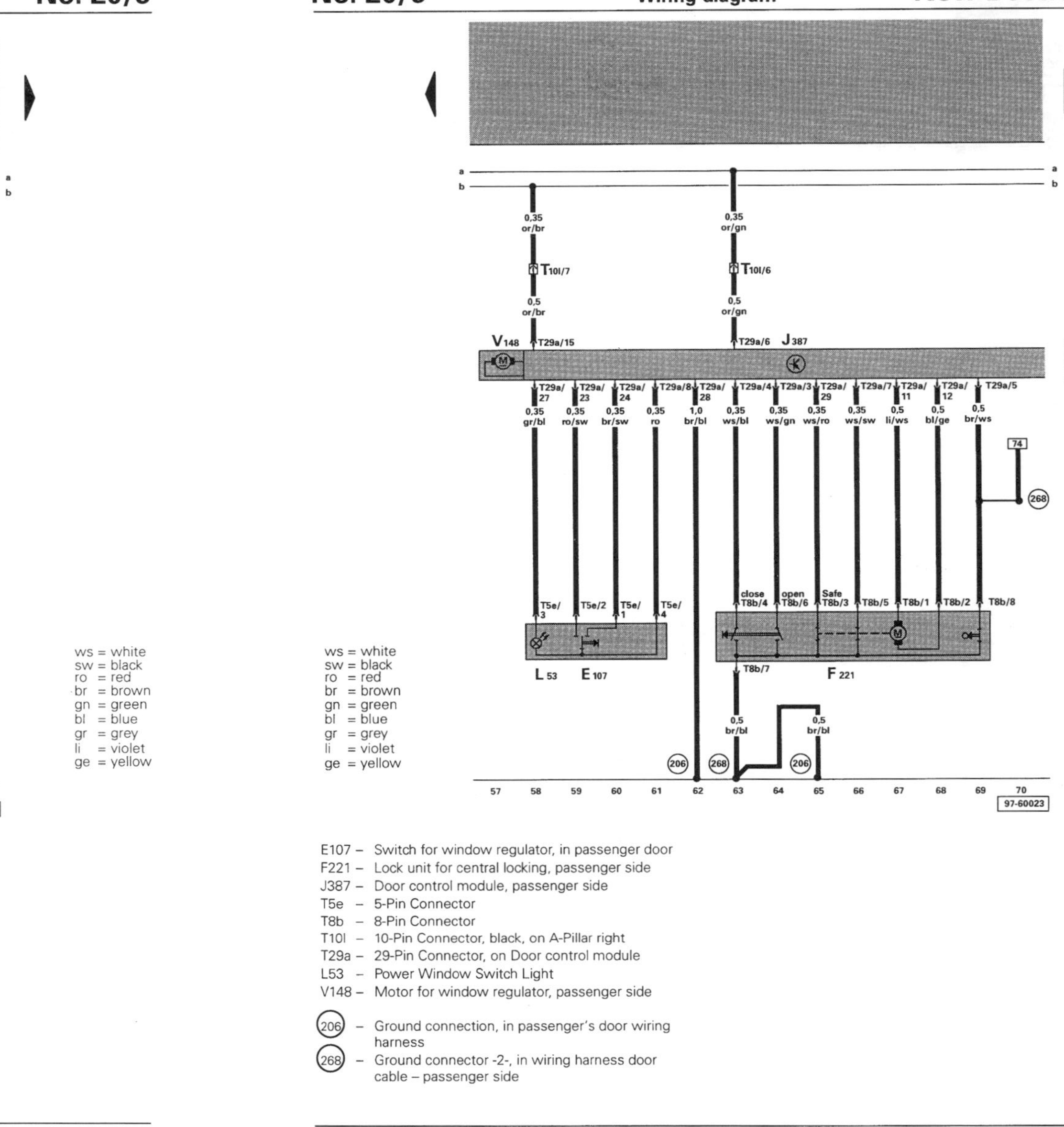

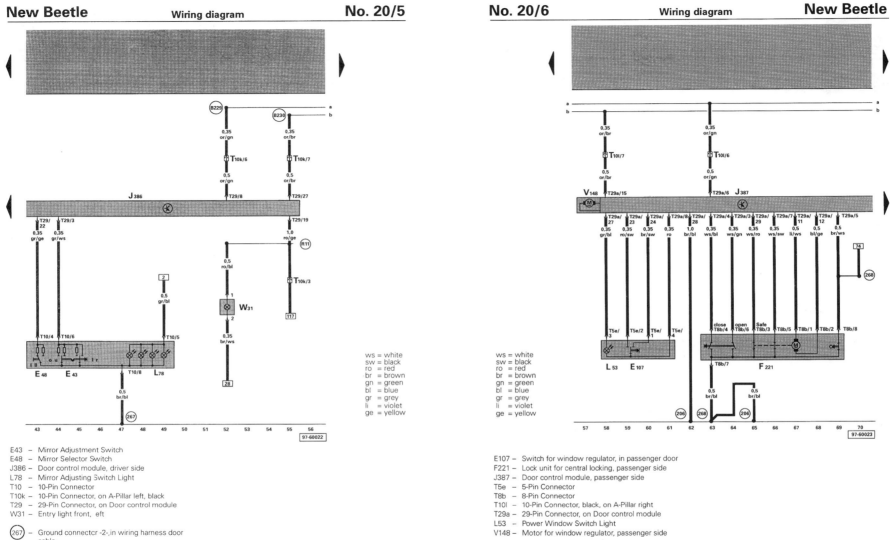

ws = white
sw = black
ro = red
br = brown
gn = green
bl = blue
gr = grey
li = violet
ge = yellow

E43 – Mirror Adjustment Switch
E48 – Mirror Selector Switch
J386 – Door control module, driver side
L78 – Mirror Adjusting Switch Light
T10 – 10-Pin Connector
T10k – 10-Pin Connector, on A-Pillar left, black
T29 – 29-Pin Connector, on Door control module
W31 – Entry light front, eft

(267) – Ground connector -2-,in wiring harness door cable
(B229) – connection (High-Bus), in wiring harness, interior
(B230) – connection (Low-Bus), in wiring harness, interior
(R11) – plus connection -2- (30), in driver's door wiring harness

Door control module (driver side) mirror adjustment switch, mirror selector switch, entry light front, left

ws = white
sw = black
ro = red
br = brown
gn = green
bl = blue
gr = grey
li = violet
ge = yellow

E107 – Switch for window regulator, in passenger door
F221 – Lock unit for central locking, passenger side
J387 – Door control module, passenger side
T5e – 5-Pin Connector
T8b – 8-Pin Connector
T10l – 10-Pin Connector, black, on A-Pillar right
T29a – 29-Pin Connector, on Door control module
L53 – Power Window Switch Light
V148 – Motor for window regulator, passenger side

(206) – Ground connection, in passenger's door wiring harness
(268) – Ground connector -2-, in wiring harness door cable – passenger side

Door control module (passenger side), lock unit for central locking (passenger side), switch for window regulator (passenger side)

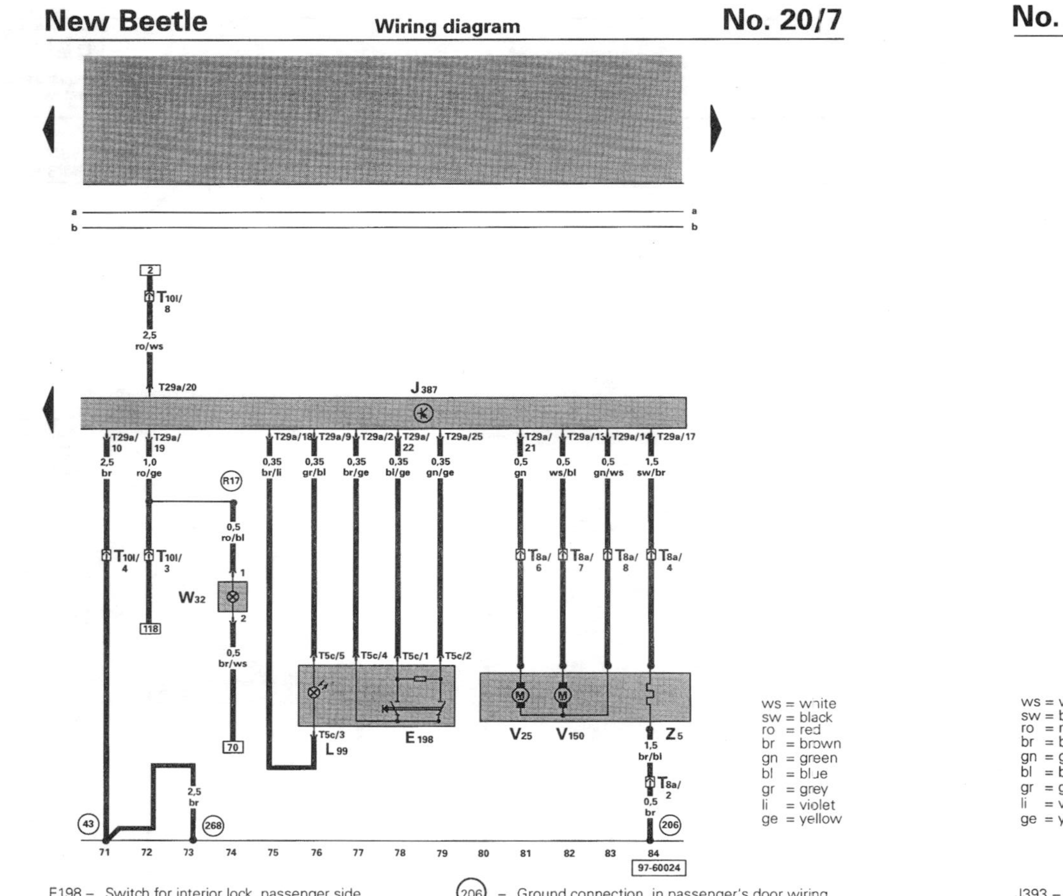

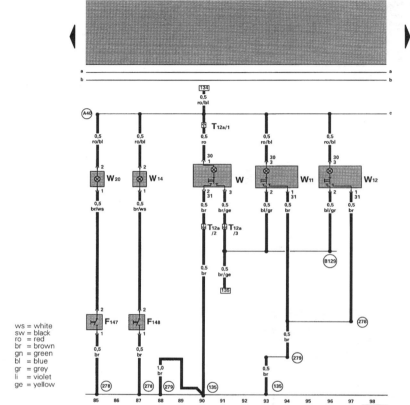

ws = white
sw = black
ro = red
br = brown
gn = green
bl = blue
gr = grey
li = violet
ge = yellow

E198 – Switch for interior lock, passenger side
J387 – Door control module, passenger side
L99 – Lighting for switch interior lock
T5c – 5-Pin Connector
T10l – 10-Pin Connector, black, on A-Pillar right
T8a – 8-Pin Connector
T29a – 29-Pin Connector, on Door control module
V25 – Passenger's Side Mirror Adjustment Motor
V150 – Motor for mirror adjustment, passenger side
W32 – Entry light front, right
Z5 - Heated outside mirror, passenger side
(R17) – Plus connection –2– (30), in passenger's door wiring harness
(Z5) – Heated outside mirror, passenger side
(43) – Ground connection, on right A-pillar, lower part
(206) – Ground connection, in passenger's door wiring harness
(268) – Ground connector -2-, in wiring harness door cable – passenger side

Door control module (pass. side), switch for interior lock (pass. side), pass. side mirror adjustment motor, heated outside mirror, entry light front, right

ws = white
sw = black
ro = red
br = brown
gn = green
bl = blue
gr = grey
li = violet
ge = yellow

J393 – Central control module for comfort system
F147 – Left Make-Up Mirror Light Switch
F148 – Right Make-Up Mirror Light Switch
W – Front Interior Light
W11 – Left Rear Reading Light
W12 – Right Rear Reading Light
W14 – Right Make-up Mirror Light
W20 – Left Make-up Mirror Light
T12a – 12–Pin Connector
T23 – 23–Pin Connector, on Central control module for comfort harness
(135) – Ground connection –2–, in instrument panel wiring harness
(278) – Ground connector -4-, in wiring harness interior
(279) – Ground connector -5, in wiring harness interior
(A40) – plus connection -1- (30), in instrument cluster wiring harness
(B129) – Connector (interior light 3/L), in wiring harness interior

Front interior light, left rear reading light, right rear reading light, right make-up mirror light, left make-up mirror light

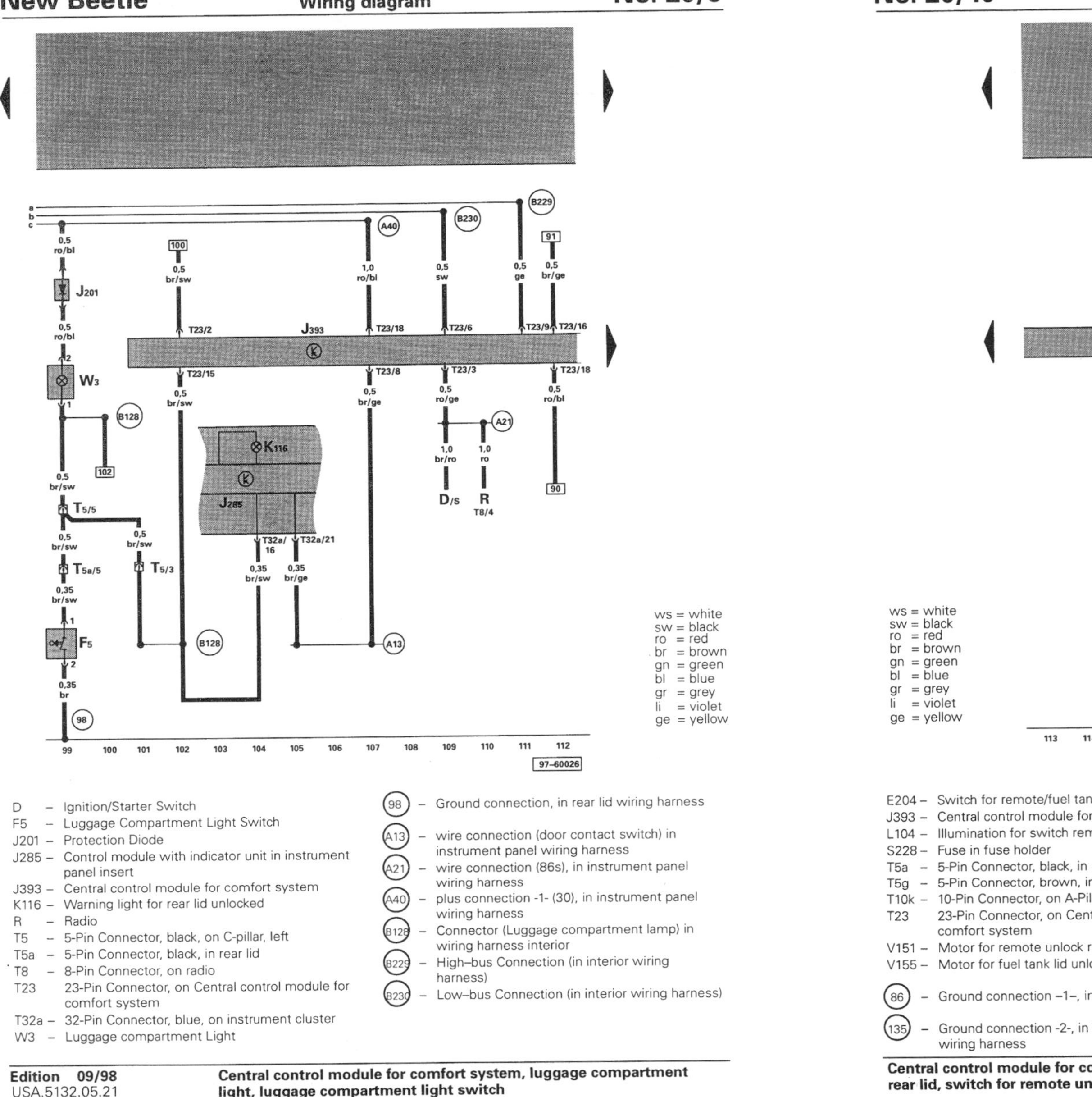

ws = white
sw = black
ro = red
br = brown
gn = green
bl = blue
gr = grey
li = violet
ge = yellow

- D – Ignition/Starter Switch
- F5 – Luggage Compartment Light Switch
- J201 – Protection Diode
- J285 – Control module with indicator unit in instrument panel insert
- J393 – Central control module for comfort system
- K116 – Warning light for rear lid unlocked
- R – Radio
- T5 – 5-Pin Connector, black, on C-pillar, left
- T5a – 5-Pin Connector, black, in rear lid
- T8 – 8-Pin Connector, on radio
- T23 23-Pin Connector, on Central control module for comfort system
- T32a – 32-Pin Connector, blue, on instrument cluster
- W3 – Luggage compartment Light

- (98) – Ground connection, in rear lid wiring harness
- (A13) – wire connection (door contact switch) in instrument panel wiring harness
- (A21) – wire connection (86s), in instrument panel wiring harness
- (A40) – plus connection -1- (30), in instrument panel wiring harness
- (B128) – Connector (Luggage compartment lamp) in wiring harness interior
- (B229) – High–bus Connection (in interior wiring harness)
- (B230) – Low–bus Connection (in interior wiring harness)

Central control module for comfort system, luggage compartment light, luggage compartment light switch

ws = white
sw = black
ro = red
br = brown
gn = green
bl = blue
gr = grey
li = violet
ge = yellow

- E204 – Switch for remote/fuel tank door
- J393 – Central control module for comfort system
- L104 – Illumination for switch remote unlock
- S228 – Fuse in fuse holder
- T5a – 5-Pin Connector, black, in rear lid
- T5g – 5-Pin Connector, brown, in rear lid
- T10k – 10-Pin Connector, on A-Pillar left, black
- T23 23-Pin Connector, on Central control module for comfort system
- V151 – Motor for remote unlock rear lid
- V155 – Motor for fuel tank lid unlock

- (86) – Ground connection –1–, in rear wiring harness
- (135) – Ground connection -2-, in instrument panel wiring harness
- (267) – Ground connector -2-, in wiring harness door cable - driver side
- (501) – Screw connection -2- (30), on relay panel
- (A66) – Connector (30a, central locking/anti-theft warning system/IR) in instrument panel wiring harness

Central control module for comfort system, relay for motor remote unlock rear lid, switch for remote unlock, rear lid

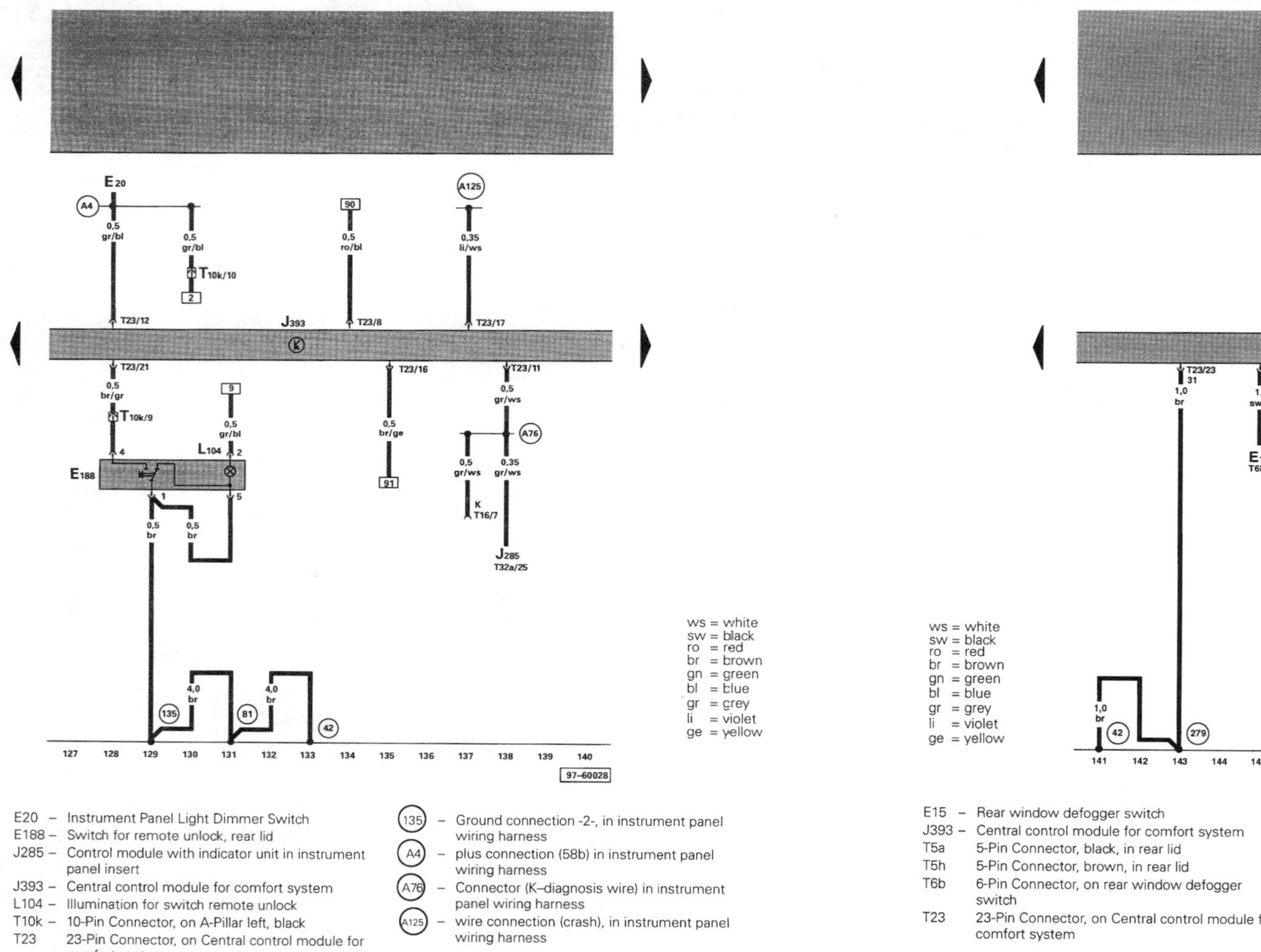

ws = white
sw = black
ro = red
br = brown
gn = green
bl = blue
gr = grey
li = violet
ge = yellow

E20 – Instrument Panel Light Dimmer Switch
E188 – Switch for remote unlock, rear lid
J285 – Control module with indicator unit in instrument panel insert
J393 – Central control module for comfort system
L104 – Illumination for switch remote unlock
T10k – 10-Pin Connector, on A-Pillar left, black
T23 23-Pin Connector, on Central control module for comfort system
T32a – 32-Pin Connector, blue, on instrument cluster

(42) – Ground connection, beside steering column

(81) – Ground connection -1-, in instrument panel wiring harness

(135) – Ground connection -2-, in instrument panel wiring harness

(A4) – plus connection (58b) in instrument panel wiring harness

(A76) – Connector (K–diagnosis wire) in instrument panel wiring harness

(A125) – wire connection (crash), in instrument panel wiring harness

Edition 09/98
USA.5132.05.21

Central control module for comfort system, switch for remote/fuel tank door, motor for fuel tank lid unlock

ws = white
sw = black
ro = red
br = brown
gn = green
bl = blue
gr = grey
li = violet
ge = yellow

E15 – Rear window defogger switch
J393 – Central control module for comfort system
T5a 5-Pin Connector, black, in rear lid
T5h 5-Pin Connector, brown, in rear lid
T6b 6-Pin Connector, on rear window defogger switch
T23 23-Pin Connector, on Central control module for comfort system

(218) – Ground connection -1-, in rear lid wiring harness

(279) – Ground connector -5-, in wiring harness interior

(A27) – wire Connection (vehicle speed signal), in instrument panel wiring harness

(42) – Ground connection, beside steering column

(52) – Ground connection, in rear lid, left

(98) – Ground connection, in rear lid wiring harness

Central control module for comfort system,

Edition 09/98
USA.5132.05.21

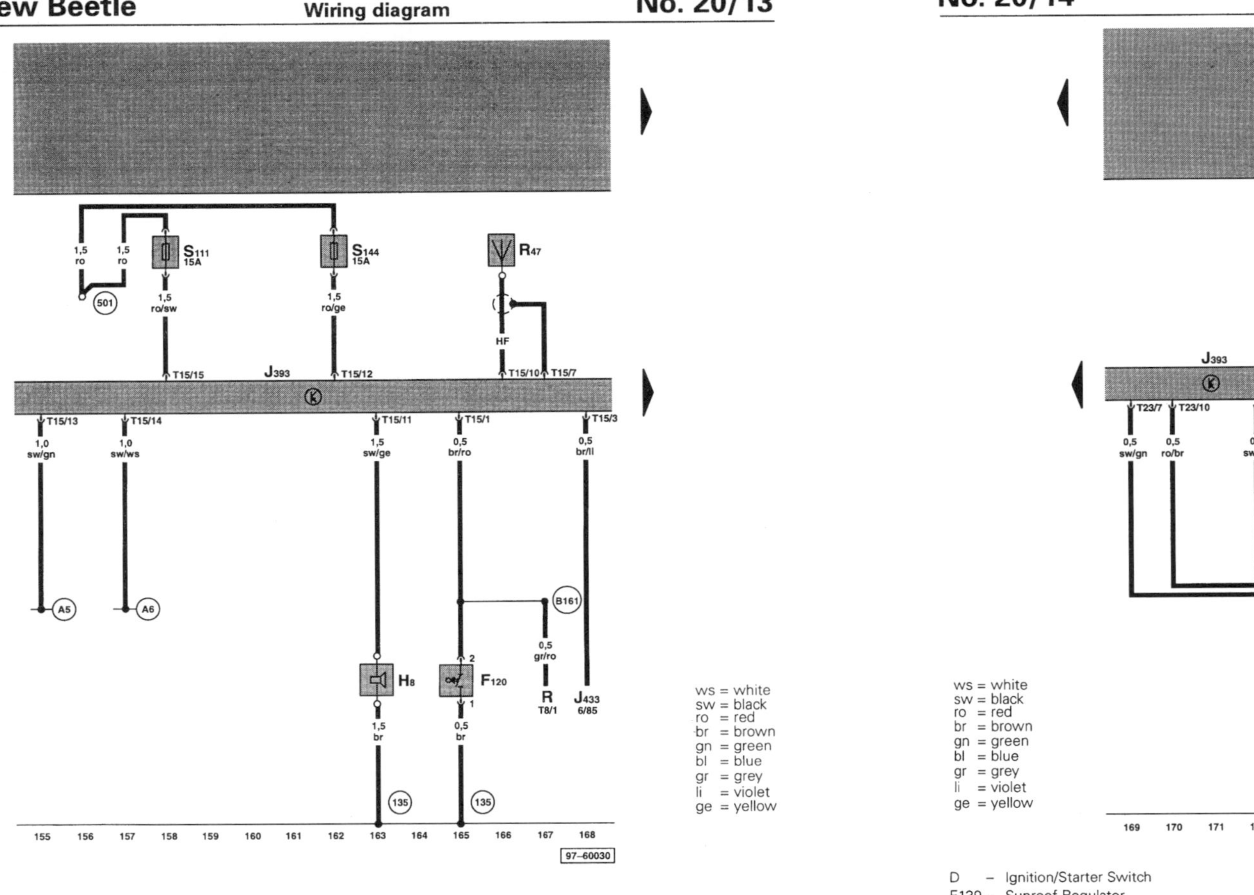

ws = white
sw = black
ro = red
br = brown
gn = green
bl = blue
gr = grey
li = violet
ge = yellow

F120 – Hood Alarm Switch
H8 – Alarm Horn
J393 – Central control module for comfort system
J433 – Locking relay for starter (clutch pedal switch)
R – Radio
R47 – Antenna wire for central locking and antitheft warning system
S111 – Alarm System and Anti-Theft Engine Disable Fuse
S144 – Fuse for central locking/anti-theft warning system
T8 – 8-Pin Connector, on radio
T15 – 15-Pin Connector, on Central control module for comfort system

(135) – Ground connection -2-, in instrument panel wiring harness
(501) – Threaded connection -1- (30) on the relay plate
(A5) – plus connection (right turn signal), in instrument panel wiring harness
(A6) – plus connection (left turn signal), in instrument panel wiring harness
(B161) – connection (Alarm system), in wiring harness, interior

Central control module for comfort system, hood alarm switch, alarm horn

ws = white
sw = black
ro = red
br = brown
gn = green
bl = blue
gr = grey
li = violet
ge = yellow

D – Ignition/Starter Switch
E139 – Sunroof Regulator
J245 – Power Sunroof Control Module
J393 – Central control module for comfort system
S6 – Fuse 6 in fuse holder
S230 – Fuse 30 in fuse holder
T6 – 6-Pin Connector
T23 – 23-Pin Connector

(135) – Ground connection -2-, in instrument panel wiring harness
(501) – Threaded connection -2- (30), on relay panel
(A2) – plus connection (15), in instrument panel wiring harness
(A32) – plus connection (30), in instrument panel wiring harness

Central control module for comfort system, power sunroof

New Beetle – Standard Equipment,

from August 1998

97–21956

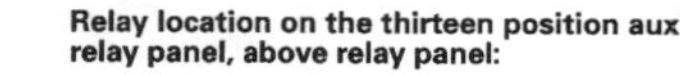

Relay location on the thirteen position auxiliary relay panel, above relay panel:

- **3** Lock relay for starter (theft warning system) (185)
- **4** Lock relay for starter (clutch pedal switch) (53)
- **8** Daytime Running Lights Change-over Relay (173)

Relay panel:

- **1** Dual Horn Relay (53)
- **2** Load Reduction Relay (100)
- **4** Fuel Pump (FP) Relay (409)
- **V** Wiper/Washer Intermittent Relay (377)
- **VI** Wiper/Washer Intermittent Relay (377)

Note: Number in parentheses indicates production control number stamped on relay housing.

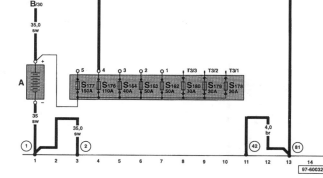

Fuse colors
30 A – green
25 A – white
20 A – yellow
15 A – blue
10 A – red
7,5 A – brown
5 A – beige

97-60032

ws = white
sw = black
ro = red
br = brown
gn = green
bl = blue
gr = grey
li = violet
ge = yellow

A – Battery
B – Starter
J59 – Load Reduction Relay
S162 – Fuse -1- in fuse bracket/battery
S163 – Fuse -2- in fuse bracket/battery
S164 – Fuse -3- in fuse bracket/battery
S176 – Fuse -4- (30), in fuse bracket/battery
S177 – Fuse -5- (30), in fuse bracket/battery
S178 – Fuse -6- (30), in fuse bracket/battery
S179 – Fuse -7- (30), in fuse bracket/battery
S180 – Fuse -8- (30), in fuse bracket/battery

(1) – Ground strap, battery to body

(2) – Ground strap, transmission to body

(42) – Ground connection, beside steering column

(81) – Ground connection -1-, in instrument panel wiring harness

(500) – Threaded connection -1- (30) on the relay plate

(503) – Threaded connection -1- (75x) on the relay plate

(A80) – Connector -1- (X), in instrument panel wiring harness

Battery, load reduction relay, fuses in fuse bracket/battery

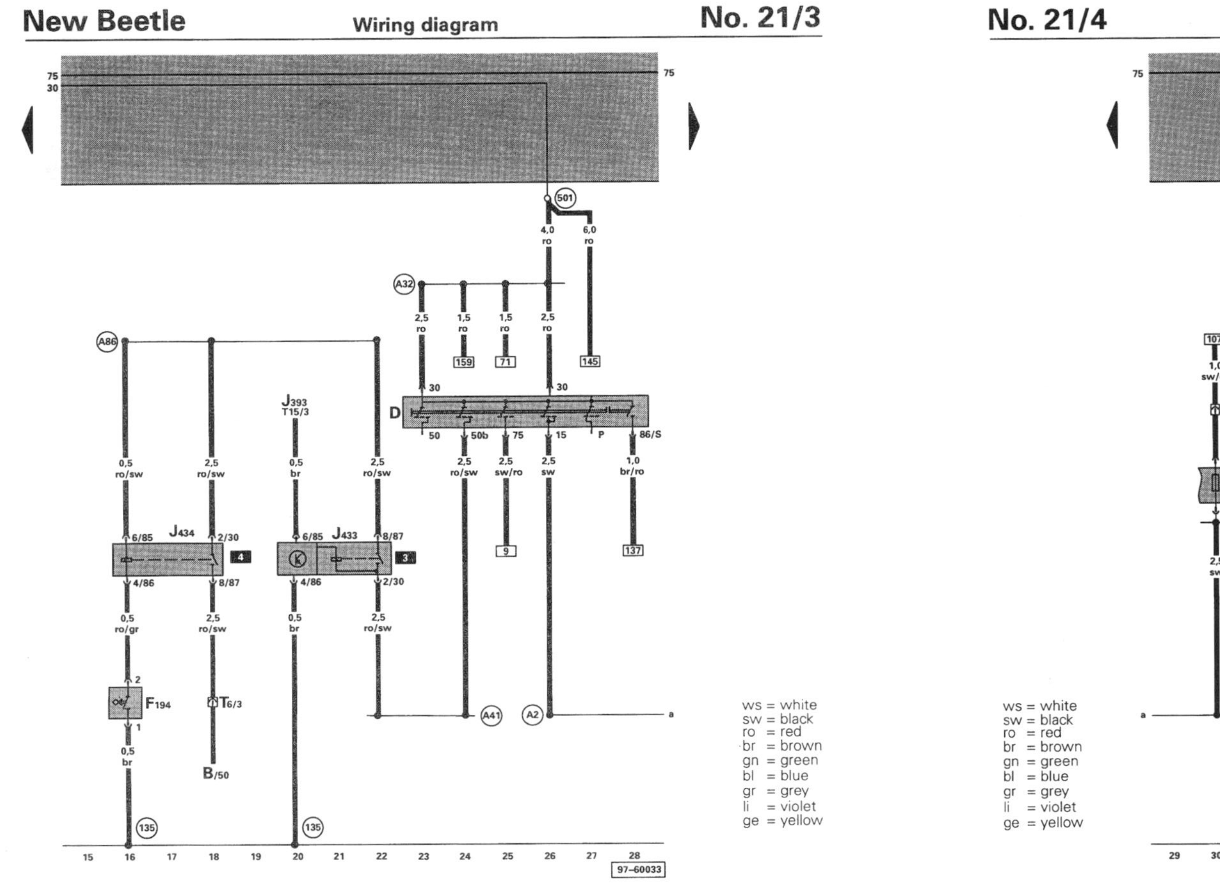

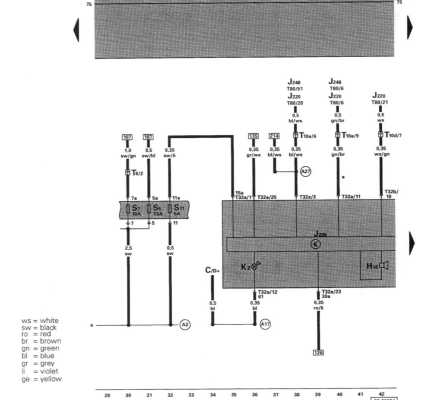

ws = white
sw = black
ro = red
br = brown
gn = green
bl = blue
gr = grey
li = violet
ge = yellow

97-60033

B – Starter
D – Ignition/Starter Switch
F194 – Clutch Pedal Position (CPP) Switch
J393 – Central control module for comfort system
J433 – Lock relay for starter (theft warning system) (185), on the thirteen position relay panel
J434 – Locking relay for starter (clutch pedal switch)
T6 – 6-Pin Connector, red, behind instrument panel, left
T15 – 15-Pin Connector, on Central control module for comfort system

(135) – Ground connection -2-, in instrument panel wiring harness
(501) – Threaded connection -2- (30) on the relay plate

(A2) – plus connection (15), in instrument panel wiring harness
(A32) – plus connection (30), in instrument panel wiring harness
(A41) – plus connection (50), in instrument panel wiring harness
(A86) – Conenction (50a), in instrument panel wiring harness

Edition 09/98
USA.5132.05.21

Ignition/starter switch, lock relay for starter (theft warning system), locking relay for starter (clutch pedal switch)

ws = white
sw = black
ro = red
br = brown
gn = green
bl = blue
gr = grey
li = violet
ge = yellow

97-60034

C – Generator (GEN)
H16 – Warning buzzer for light switched on
J220 – Motronic Engine Control Module (ECM), behind instrument panel, left
J248 – Diesel Direct Fuel Injection (DFI) Engine Control Module (ECM), behind instrument panel, left
J285 – Control module with indicator unit in instrument panel insert
K2 – Generator (GEN) Warning Light
S5 – Fuse 5 in fuse holder
S7 – Fuse 7 in fuse holder
S11 – Fuse 11 in fuse holder
T6 – 6-Pin Connector, brown, behind instrument panel, left
T10d – 10-Pin Connector, green, behind instrument panel, left

T10a – 10-Pin Connector, orange, behind instrument panel, left
T32a – 32-Pin Connector, blue, on instrument cluster
T32b – 32-Pin Connector, green, on instrument cluster
T80 – Connector, 80 point, on Engine Control Module (ECM)

(A2) – plus connection (15), in instrument panel wiring harness
(A17) – wire connection (61), in instrument panel wiring harness
(A27) – wire Connection (vehicle speed signal), in instrument panel wiring harness
* – speed signal from engine control module

Instrument cluster, warning buzzer for light swiched on, generator (GEN)

Edition 09/98
USA.5132.05.21

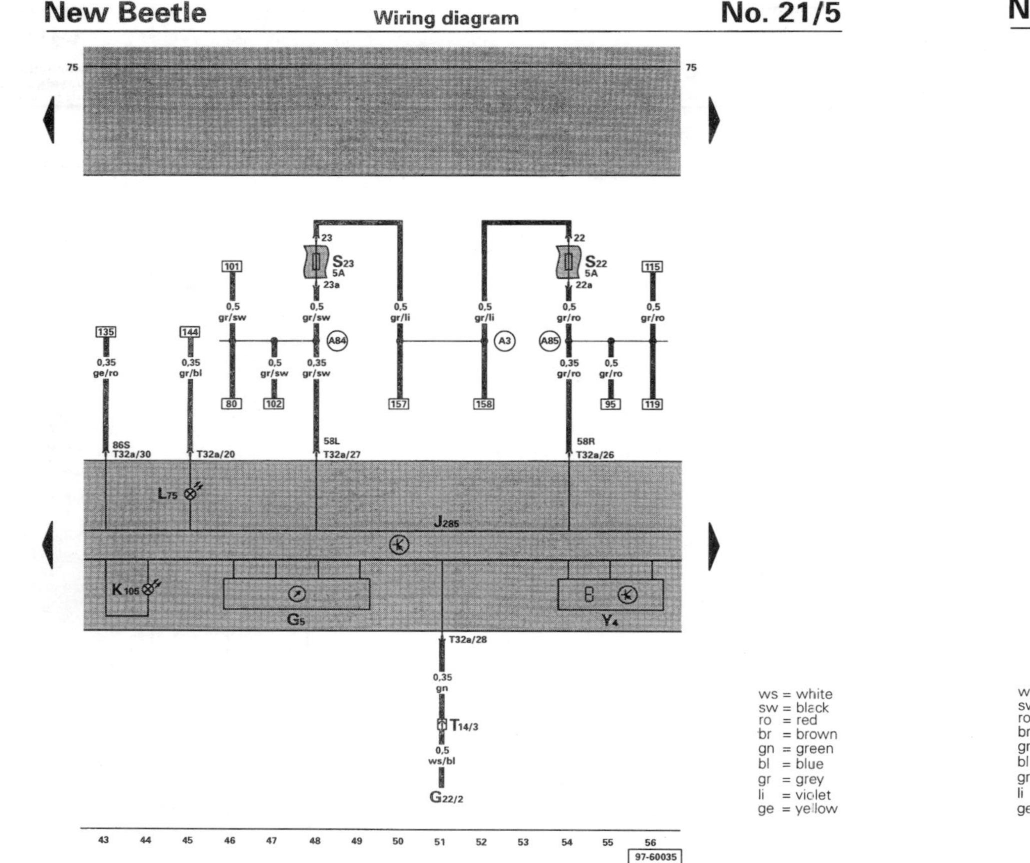

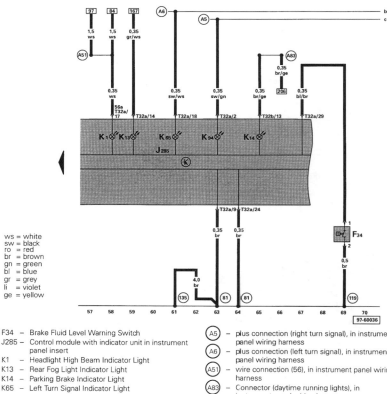

ws = white
sw = black
ro = red
br = brown
gn = green
bl = blue
gr = grey
li = violet
ge = yellow

G5 – Tachometer
G22 – Speedometer Vehicle Speed Sensor (VSS)
J285 – Control module with indicator unit in instrument panel insert
K105 – Low Fuel Level Warning Light
L75 – Digital Display Light
S22 – Fuse 22 in fuse holder
S23 – Fuse 23 in fuse holder
T14 – 14-Pin Connector, in engine compartment, left
T32a – 32-Pin Connector, blue, on instrument cluster
Y4 – Odometer Display

(A3) – plus connection (58), in instrument panel wiring harness
(A84) – Connector (58L), in instrument panel wiring harness
(A85) – Connector (58R), in instrument panel wiring harness

Instrument cluster, tachometer, low fuel level warning light, odometer display

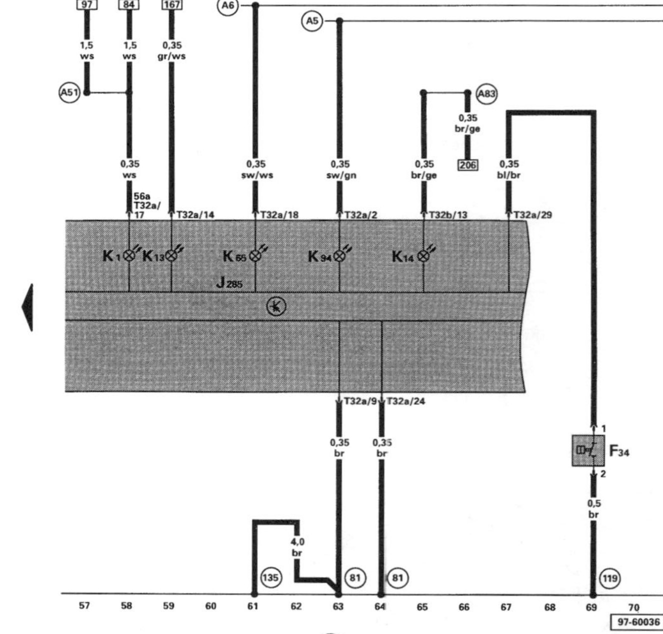

ws = white
sw = black
ro = red
br = brown
gn = green
bl = blue
gr = grey
li = violet
ge = yellow

F34 – Brake Fluid Level Warning Switch
J285 – Control module with indicator unit in instrument panel insert
K1 – Headlight High Beam Indicator Light
K13 – Rear Fog Light Indicator Light
K14 – Parking Brake Indicator Light
K65 – Left Turn Signal Indicator Light
K94 – Right Turn Signal Indicator Light
T32a – 32-Pin Connector, blue, on instrument cluster
T32b – 32-Pin Connector, green, on instrument cluster

(81) – Ground connection -1-, in instrument panel wiring harness
(119) – Ground connection -1-, in headlight wiring harness
(135) – Ground connection -2-, in instrument panel wiring harness

(A5) – plus connection (right turn signal), in instrument panel wiring harness
(A6) – plus connection (left turn signal), in instrument panel wiring harness
(A51) – wire connection (56), in instrument panel wiring harness
(A83) – Connector (daytime running lights), in instrument panel wiring harness

Instrument cluster, brake fluid level warning switch, turn signal indicator lights, headlight high beam indicator light, rear fog light indicator light

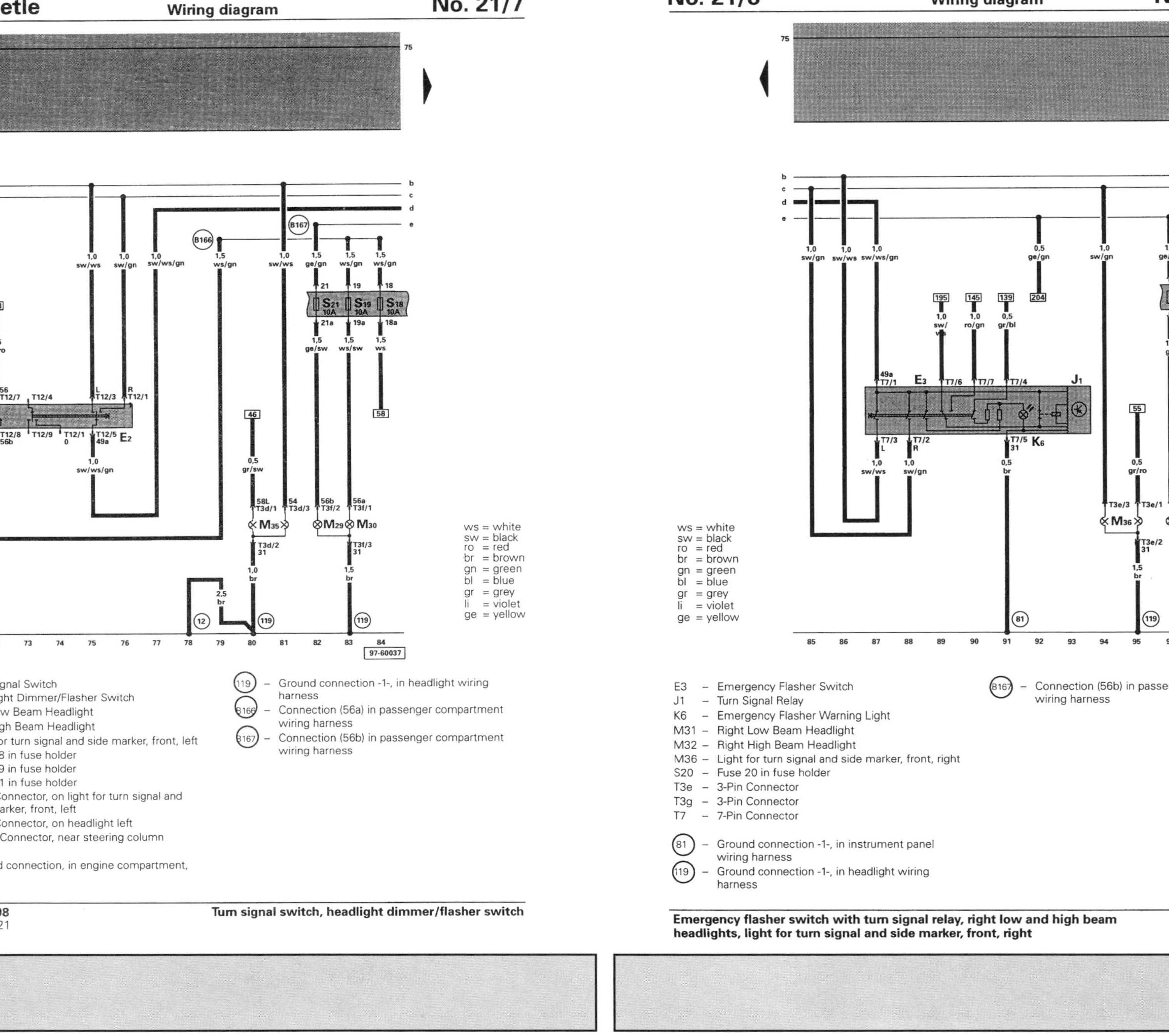

ws = white
sw = black
ro = red
br = brown
gn = green
bl = blue
gr = grey
li = violet
ge = yellow

E2 – Turn Signal Switch
E4 – Headlight Dimmer/Flasher Switch
M29 – Left Low Beam Headlight
M30 – Left High Beam Headlight
M35 – Light for turn signal and side marker, front, left
S18 – Fuse 18 in fuse holder
S19 – Fuse 19 in fuse holder
S21 – Fuse 21 in fuse holder
T3d – 3-Pin Connector, on light for turn signal and side marker, front, left
T3f – 3-Pin Connector, on headlight left
T12 – 12-Pin Connector, near steering column

(12) – Ground connection, in engine compartment, left

(119) – Ground connection -1-, in headlight wiring harness
(B166) – Connection (56a) in passenger compartment wiring harness
(B167) – Connection (56b) in passenger compartment wiring harness

Edition 09/98
USA.5132.05.21

Turn signal switch, headlight dimmer/flasher switch

ws = white
sw = black
ro = red
br = brown
gn = green
bl = blue
gr = grey
li = violet
ge = yellow

E3 – Emergency Flasher Switch
J1 – Turn Signal Relay
K6 – Emergency Flasher Warning Light
M31 – Right Low Beam Headlight
M32 – Right High Beam Headlight
M36 – Light for turn signal and side marker, front, right
S20 – Fuse 20 in fuse holder
T3e – 3-Pin Connector
T3g – 3-Pin Connector
T7 – 7-Pin Connector

(81) – Ground connection -1-, in instrument panel wiring harness
(119) – Ground connection -1-, in headlight wiring harness

(B167) – Connection (56b) in passenger compartment wiring harness

Emergency flasher switch with turn signal relay, right low and high beam headlights, light for turn signal and side marker, front, right

Edition 09/98
USA.5132.05.21

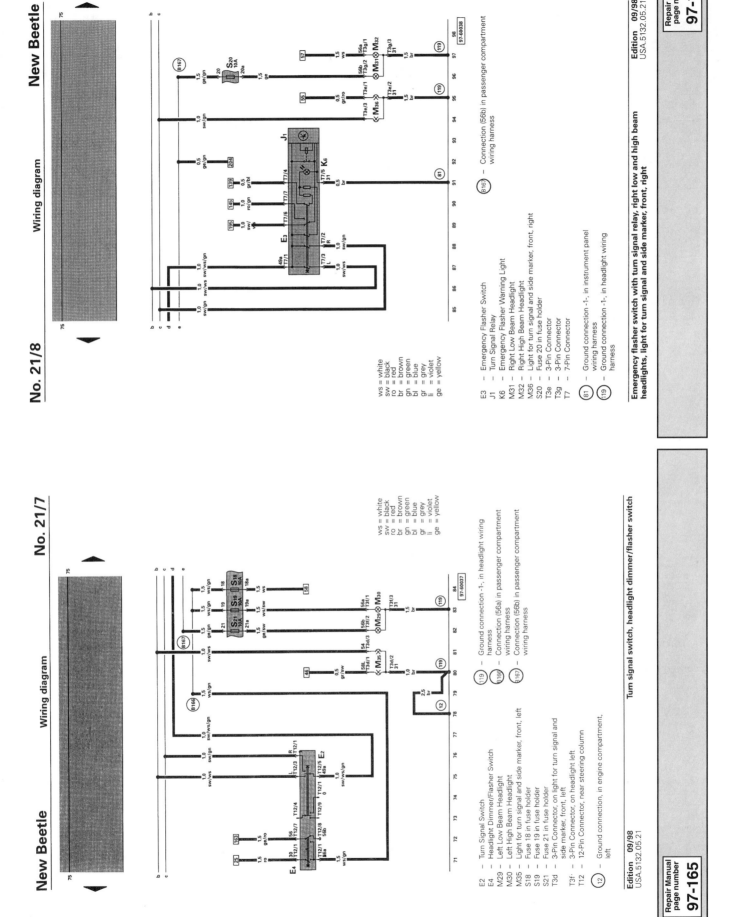

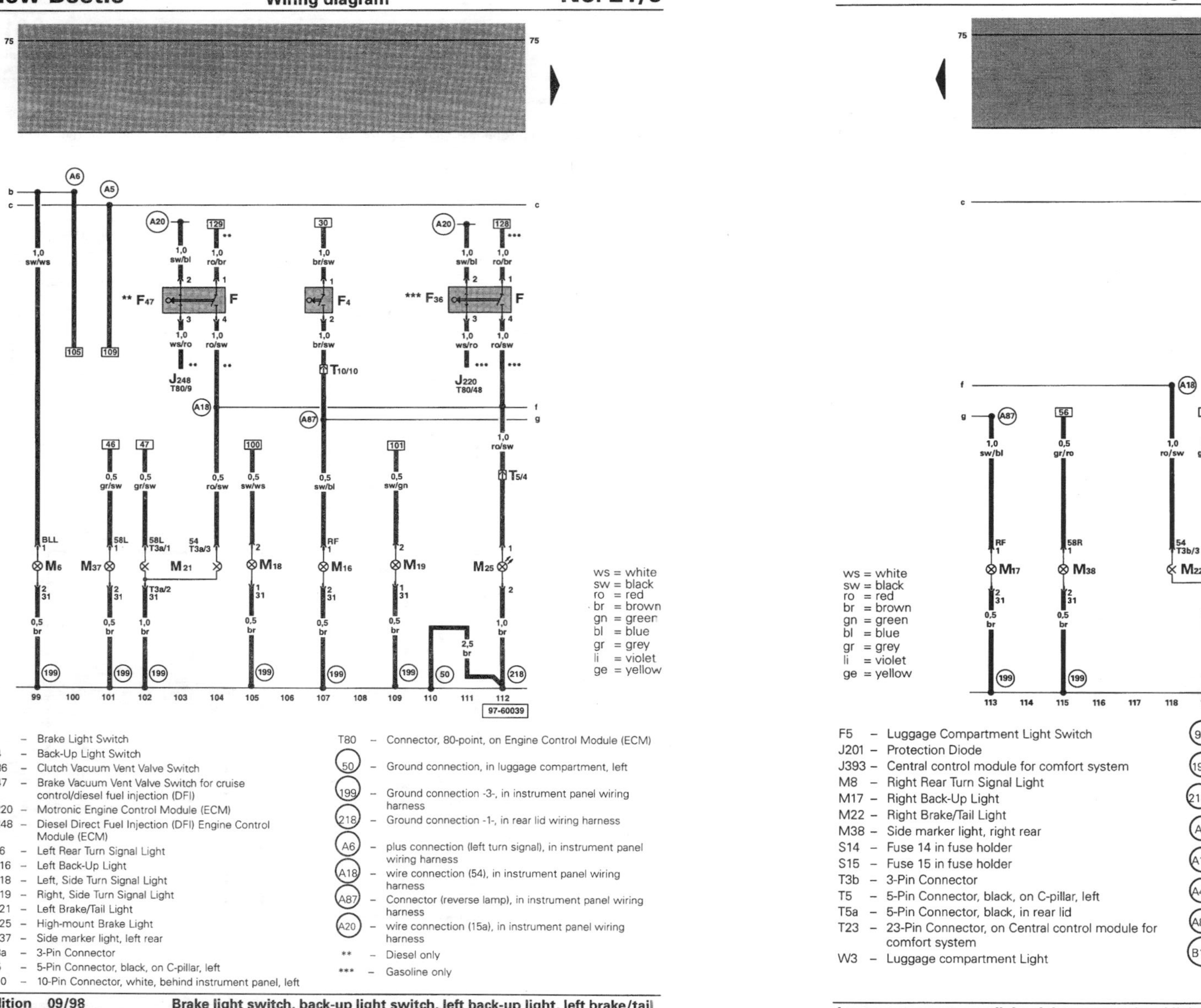

ws = white
sw = black
ro = red
br = brown
gn = green
bl = blue
gr = grey
li = violet
ge = yellow

F – Brake Light Switch
F4 – Back-Up Light Switch
F36 – Clutch Vacuum Vent Valve Switch
F47 – Brake Vacuum Vent Valve Switch for cruise control/diesel fuel injection (DFI)
J220 – Motronic Engine Control Module (ECM)
J248 – Diesel Direct Fuel Injection (DFI) Engine Control Module (ECM)
M6 – Left Rear Turn Signal Light
M16 – Left Back-Up Light
M18 – Left, Side Turn Signal Light
M19 – Right, Side Turn Signal Light
M21 – Left Brake/Tail Light
M25 – High-mount Brake Light
M37 – Side marker light, left rear
T3a – 3-Pin Connector
T5 – 5-Pin Connector, black, on C-pillar, left
T10 – 10-Pin Connector, white, behind instrument panel, left
T80 – Connector, 80-point, on Engine Control Module (ECM)
(50) – Ground connection, in luggage compartment, left
(199) – Ground connection -3-, in instrument panel wiring harness
(218) – Ground connection -1-, in rear lid wiring harness
(A6) – plus connection (left turn signal), in instrument panel wiring harness
(A18) – wire connection (54), in instrument panel wiring harness
(A87) – Connector (reverse lamp), in instrument panel wiring harness
(A20) – wire connection (15a), in instrument panel wiring harness
** – Diesel only
*** – Gasoline only

Edition 09/98
USA.5132.05.21

Brake light switch, back-up light switch, left back-up light, left brake/tail light, hight-mount brake light, side turn signal lights

ws = white
sw = black
ro = red
br = brown
gn = green
bl = blue
gr = grey
li = violet
ge = yellow

F5 – Luggage Compartment Light Switch
J201 – Protection Diode
J393 – Central control module for comfort system
M8 – Right Rear Turn Signal Light
M17 – Right Back-Up Light
M22 – Right Brake/Tail Light
M38 – Side marker light, right rear
S14 – Fuse 14 in fuse holder
S15 – Fuse 15 in fuse holder
T3b – 3-Pin Connector
T5 – 5-Pin Connector, black, on C-pillar, left
T5a – 5-Pin Connector, black, in rear lid
T23 – 23-Pin Connector, on Central control module for comfort system
W3 – Luggage compartment Light
(98) – Ground connection, in rear lid wiring harness
(199) – Ground connection -3-, in instrument panel wiring harness
(218) – Ground connection -1-, in rear lid wiring harness
(A5) – plus connection (right turn signal), in instrument panel wiring harness
(A18) – wire connection (54), in instrument panel wiring harness
(A40) – plus connection -1- (30), in instrument panel wiring harness
(A87) – Connector (reverse lamp), in instrument panel wiring harness
(B128) – Connector (Luggage compartment lamp) in wiring harness interior

Luggage compartment light, right rear turnsignal light, right back-up light, right brake/tail light, side marker light, right, rear

Edition 09/98
USA.5132.05.21

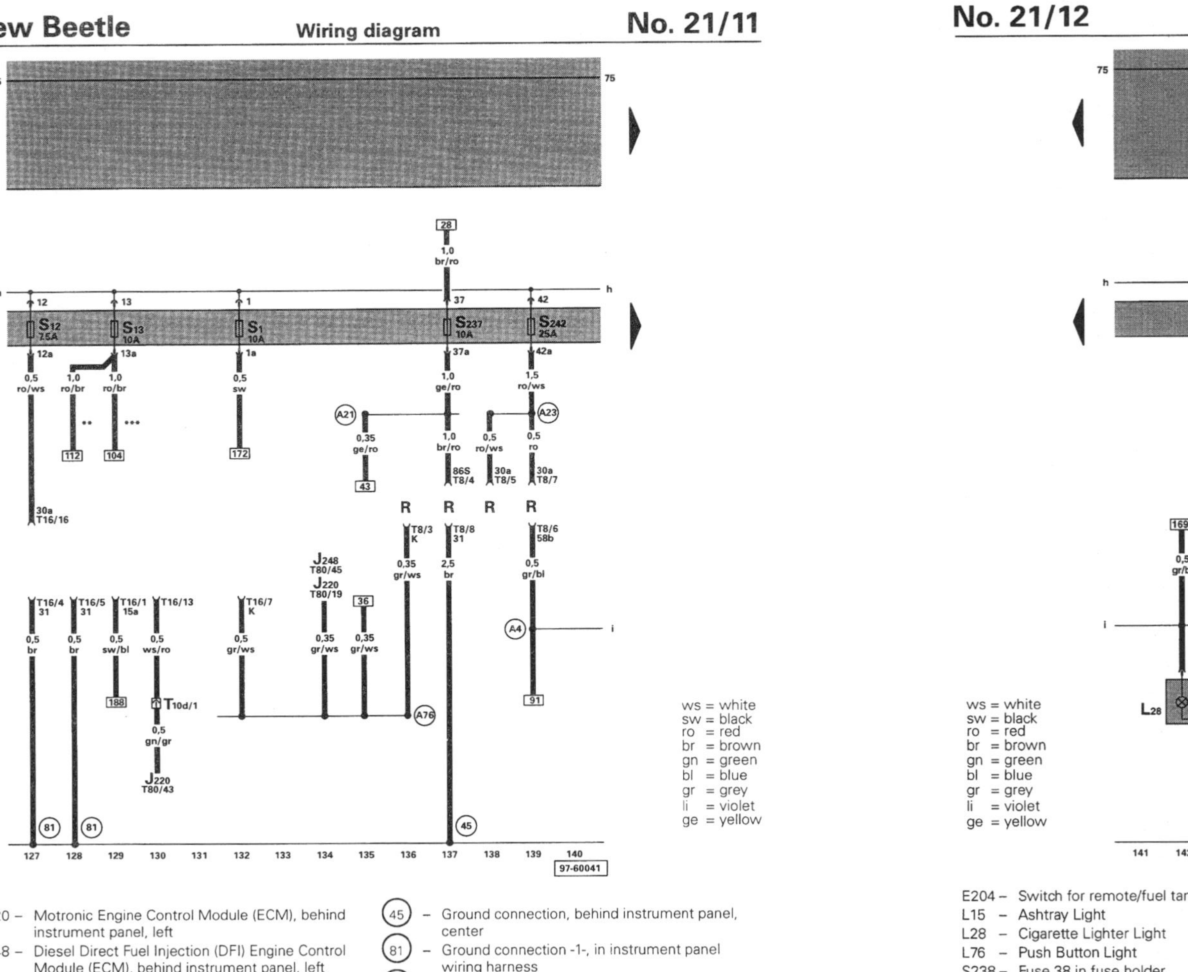

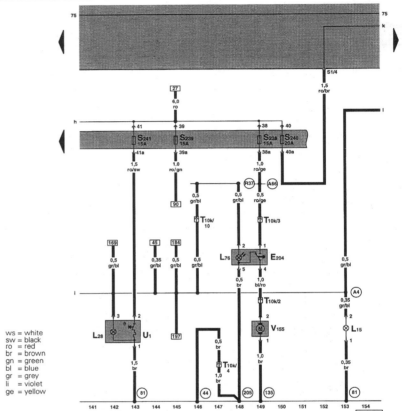

ws = white
sw = black
ro = red
br = brown
gn = green
bl = blue
gr = grey
li = violet
ge = yellow

J220 – Motronic Engine Control Module (ECM), behind instrument panel, left
J248 – Diesel Direct Fuel Injection (DFI) Engine Control Module (ECM), behind instrument panel, left
R – Radio
S12 – Fuse 12 in fuse holder
S13 – Fuse 13 in fuse holder
S237 – Fuse 37 in fuse holder
S242 – Fuse 42 in fuse holder
T8 – 8-Pin Connector, on radio
T10d – 10-Pin Connector, green, behind instrument panel, left
T16 – 16-Pin Connector, Data Link Connector (DLC), below steering column
T80 – Connector, 80 point, on Engine Control Module (ECM)

(45) – Ground connection, behind instrument panel, center
(81) – Ground connection -1-, in instrument panel wiring harness
(A4) – plus connection (58b) in instrument panel wiring harness
(A21) – wire connection (86s), in instrument panel wiring harness
(A23) – wire connection (30al), in instrument panel wiring harness
(A76) – Connector (K-diagnosis wire), in instrument panel wiring harness
** – Diesel only
*** – Gasoline only

Data Link Connector (DLC), radio connection

ws = white
sw = black
ro = red
br = brown
gn = green
bl = blue
gr = grey
li = violet
ge = yellow

E204 – Switch for remote/fuel tank door
L15 – Ashtray Light
L28 – Cigarette Lighter Light
L76 – Push Button Light
S238 – Fuse 38 in fuse holder
S239 – Fuse 39 in fuse holder
S240 – Fuse 40 in fuse holder
S241 – Fuse 41 in fuse holder
T10k – 10-pin connector, black, on conector station A-pillar, left
U1 – Cigarette Lighter
V155 – Motor for fuel tank lid unlock

(44) – Ground connection, on left A-pillar, lower part
(81) – Ground connection -1-, in instrument panel wiring harness

(135) – Ground connection -2-, in instrument panel wiring harness
(205) – Ground connection, in driver's door wiring harness
(A4) – plus connection (58b) in instrument panel wiring harness
(A66) – Connector (30a, central locking/anti-theft warning system/IR), in instrument panel wiring harness
(R37) – Connector (58b), in driver's door wiring harness

Ashtray light, cigarette lighter, cigarette lighter light, motor for fuel tank lid unlock, switch for remote/fuel tank door

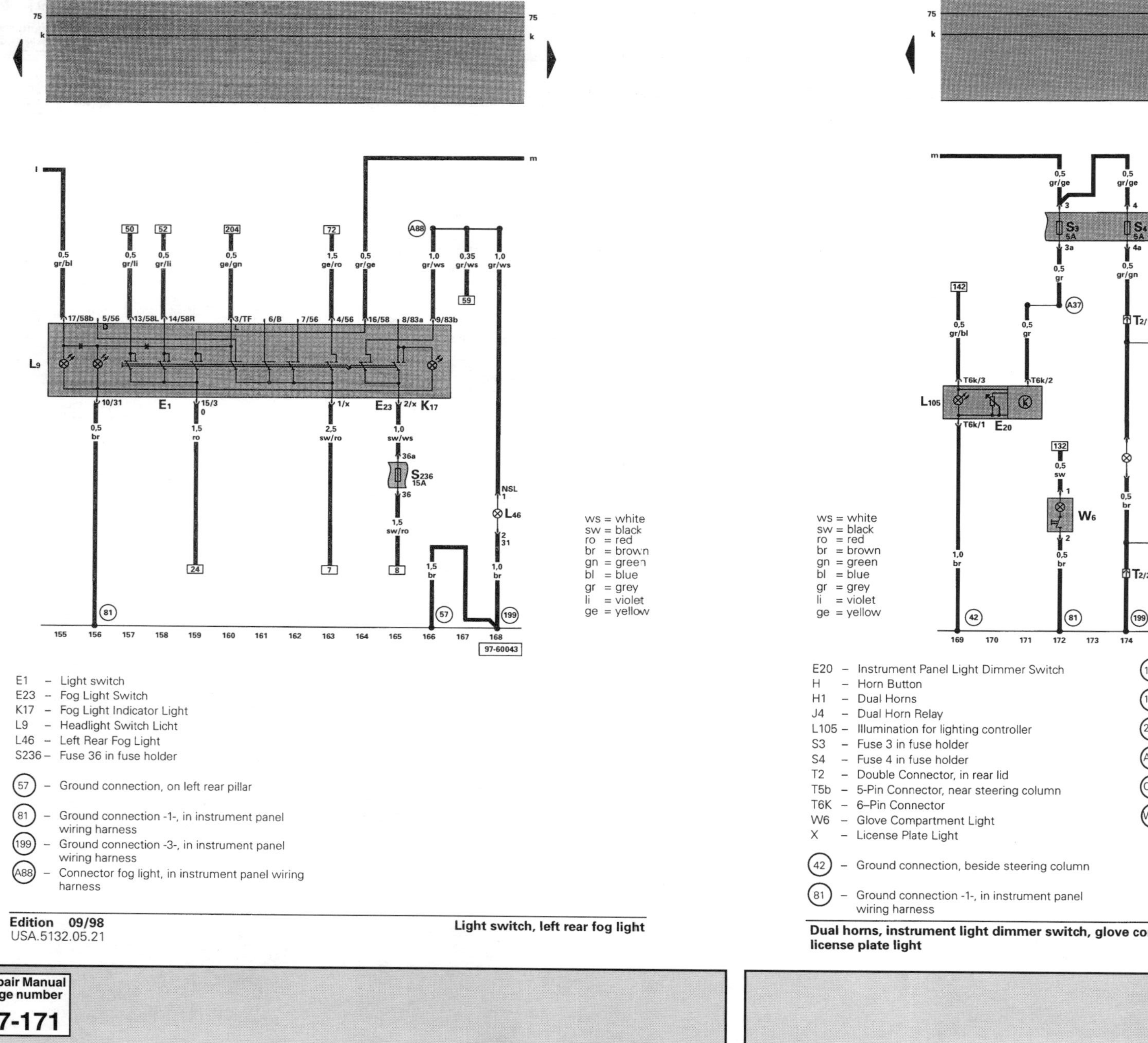

ws = white
sw = black
ro = red
br = brown
gn = green
bl = blue
gr = grey
li = violet
ge = yellow

E1 – Light switch
E23 – Fog Light Switch
K17 – Fog Light Indicator Light
L9 – Headlight Switch Licht
L46 – Left Rear Fog Light
S236 – Fuse 36 in fuse holder

(57) – Ground connection, on left rear pillar

(81) – Ground connection -1-, in instrument panel wiring harness

(199) – Ground connection -3-, in instrument panel wiring harness

(A88) – Connector fog light, in instrument panel wiring harness

Light switch, left rear fog light

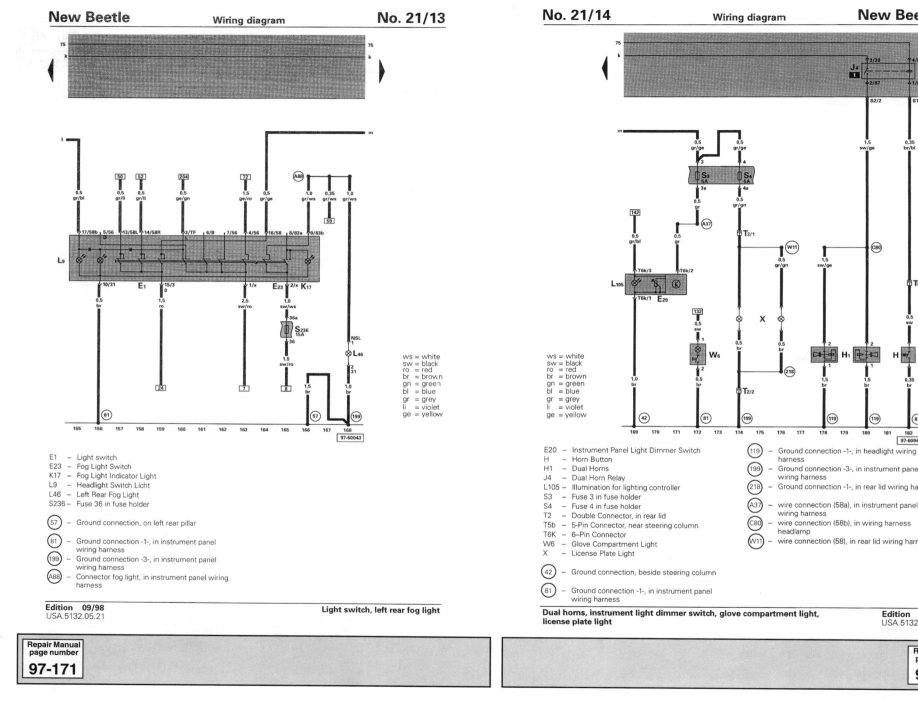

ws = white
sw = black
ro = red
br = brown
gn = green
bl = blue
gr = grey
li = violet
ge = yellow

E20 – Instrument Panel Light Dimmer Switch
H – Horn Button
H1 – Dual Horns
J4 – Dual Horn Relay
L105 – Illumination for lighting controller
S3 – Fuse 3 in fuse holder
S4 – Fuse 4 in fuse holder
T2 – Double Connector, in rear lid
T5b – 5-Pin Connector, near steering column
T6K – 6-Pin Connector
W6 – Glove Compartment Light
X – License Plate Light

(42) – Ground connection, beside steering column

(81) – Ground connection -1-, in instrument panel wiring harness

(119) – Ground connection -1-, in headlight wiring harness

(199) – Ground connection -3-, in instrument panel wiring harness

(218) – Ground connection -1-, in rear lid wiring harness

(A37) – wire connection (58a), in instrument panel wiring harness

(C80) – wire connection (58b), in wiring harness headlamp

(W11) – wire connection (58), in rear lid wiring harness

Dual horns, instrument light dimmer switch, glove compartment light, license plate light

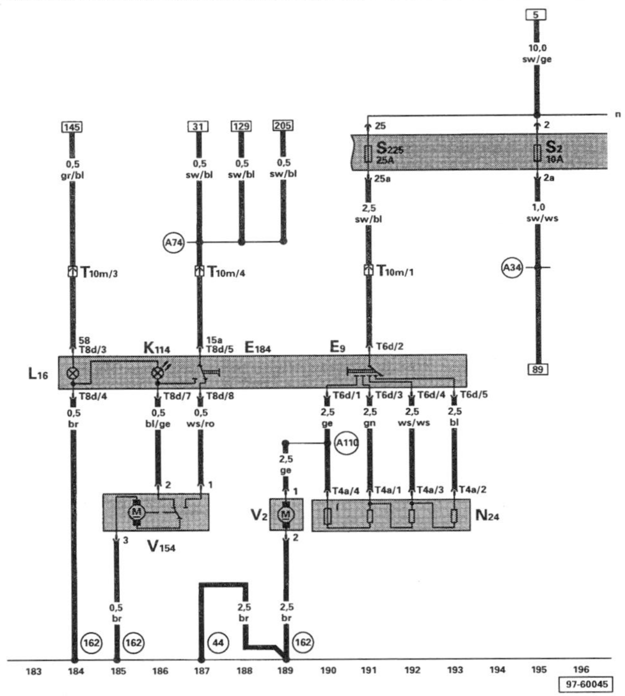

ws = white
sw = black
ro = red
br = brown
gn = green
bl = blue
gr = grey
li = violet
ge = yellow

- E9 – Fresh Air Blower Switch
- E184 – Switch for fresh air blower and recirculated air
- K114 – Fresh Air and Recirculating Air Mode Indicator Light
- L16 – Fresh Air Control Lever Light
- N24 – Fresh Air Blower Series Resistance With Fuse
- S2 – Fuse 2 in fuse holder
- S225 – Fuse 25 in fuse holder
- T4a – 4-Pin Connector
- T6d – 6-Pin Connector
- T8d – 8-Pin Connector
- T10m – 10-Pin Connector
- V2 – Fresh Air Blower
- V154 – Servo motor for fresh-/recirculating air door

- (44) – Ground connection, on left A-pillar, lower part
- (162) – Ground connection, in blower motor wiring harness
- (A34) – wire connection (75x), in instrument panel wiring harness
- (A74) – Connector (15a - fuse 5), in instrument panel wiring harness
- (A110) – Connector (fresh air blower), in instrument panel wiring harness

Edition 09/98
USA.5132.05.21

Fresch air blower, fresh air blower switch

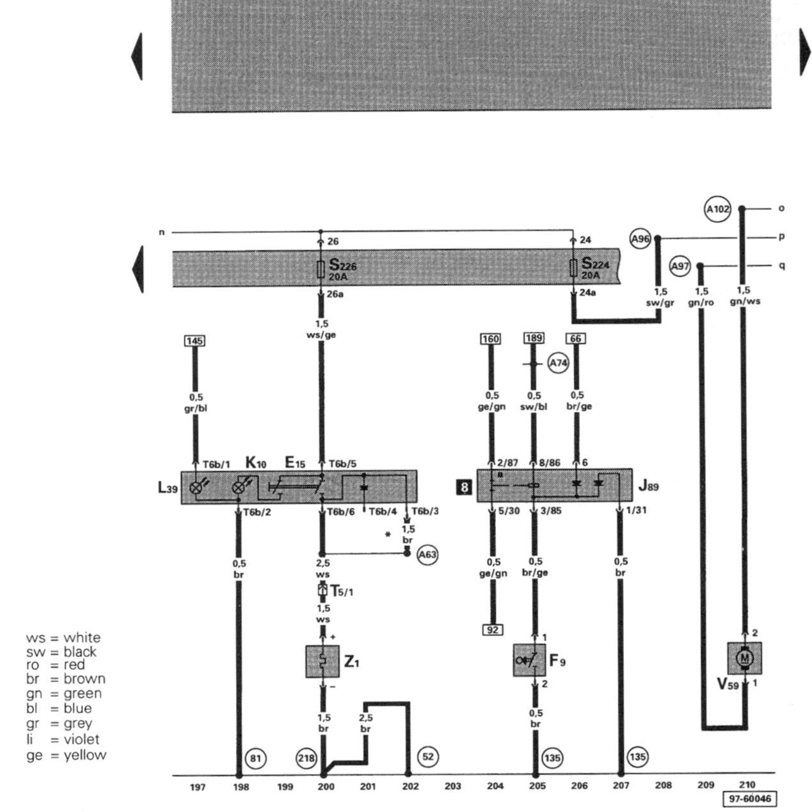

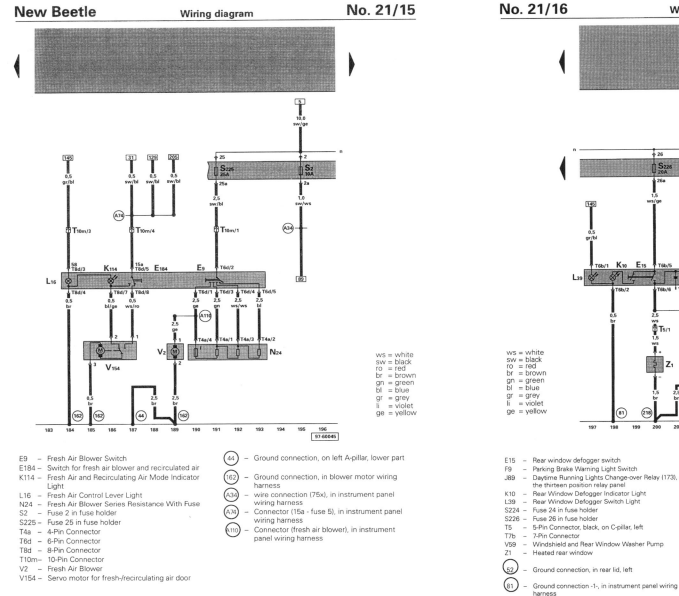

ws = white
sw = black
ro = red
br = brown
gn = green
bl = blue
gr = grey
li = violet
ge = yellow

- E15 – Rear window defogger switch
- F9 – Parking Brake Warning Light Switch
- J89 – Daytime Running Lights Change-over Relay (173), on the thirteen position relay panel
- K10 – Rear Window Defogger Indicator Light
- L39 – Rear Window Defogger Switch Light
- S224 – Fuse 24 in fuse holder
- S226 – Fuse 26 in fuse holder
- T5 – 5-Pin Connector, black, on C-pillar, left
- T7b – 7-Pin Connector
- V59 – Windshield and Rear Window Washer Pump
- Z1 – Heated rear window
- (52) – Ground connection, in rear lid, left
- (81) – Ground connection -1-, in instrument panel wiring harness

- (135) – Ground connection -2-, in instrument panel wiring harness
- (218) – Ground connection -1-, in rear wiring harness
- (A63) – Connector (mirror adjustment/ –heated) in instrument panel wiring harness
- (A74) – Connector (15a –fuse 5), in instrument panel
- (A96) – Connector (53a), in instrument panel wiring harness
- (A97) – Connector (53), in instrument panel wiring harness
- (A102) – Connector (windshield wiper), in instrument panel wiring harness
- * Manual windows, only

Heated rear window, rear window defogger switch, parking brake warning light switch, daytime running lights change-over relay

Edition 09/98
USA.5132.05.21

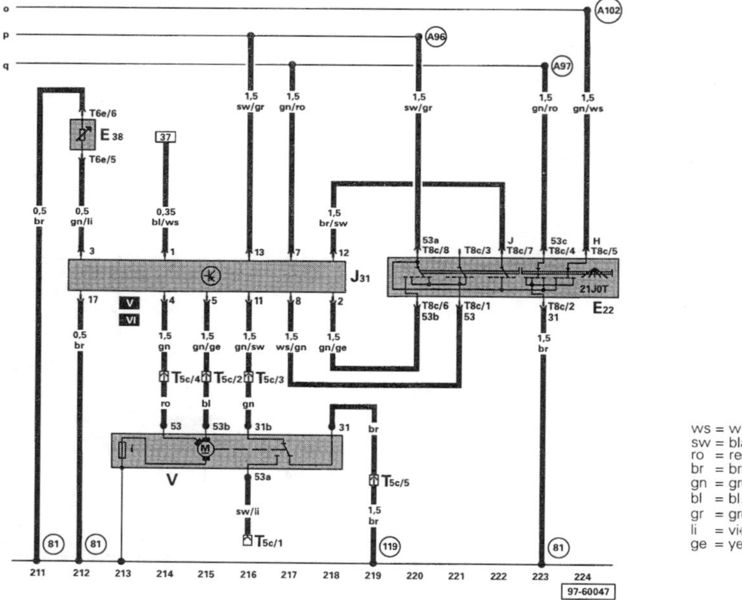

ws = white
sw = black
ro = red
br = brown
gn = green
bl = blue
gr = grey
li = violet
ge = yellow

E22 – Winshield Wiper/Washer Switch
E38 – Windshield Wiper Intermittent Regulator
J31 – Wiper/Washer Intermittent Relay, on the thirteen position relay panel, production control number (377)
T5c – 5-Pin Connector, on Windshield Wiper Motor
T6e – 6-Pin Connector, near steering column
T8c – 8-Pin Connector
V – Windshield Wiper Motor

(81) – Ground connection -1-, in instrument panel wiring harness
(119) – Ground connection -1-, in headlight wiring harness
(A96) – Connector (53a), in instrument panel wiring harness
(A97) – Connector (53), in instrument panel wiring harness
(A102) – Connector (windshield wiper), in instrument panel wiring harness

Edition 09/98
USA.5132.05.21

Windshield wiper/washer switch, windshield wiper motor, windshield wiper/washer intermittent relay

THIS PAGE INTENTIONALLY LEFT BLANK

Cruise control system (gasoline engine only)

from August 1998

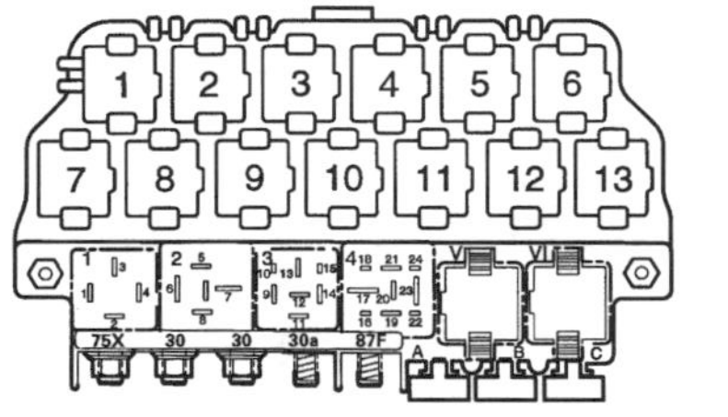

Relay panel:

2 Load Reduction Relay (100)

4 Fuel Pump (FP) Relay (409)

Note: Number in parentheses indicates production control number stamped on relay housing.

Fuse colors
30 A – green
25 A – white
20 A – yellow
15 A – blue
10 A – red
7,5 A – brown
5 A – beige

ws = white
sw = black
ro = red
br = brown
gn = green
bl = blue
gr = grey
li = violet
ge = yellow

D – Ignition/Starter Switch
F – Brake Light Switch
F47 – Brake Pedal Switch
J59 – Load Reduction Relay
J220 – Motronic Engine Control Module (ECM)
S5 – Fuse 5 in fuse holder
S13 – Fuse 13 in fuse holder
S176 – Fuse –4– (30), in fuse bracket/battery
T10h – 10–Pin Connector, black, behind instrument panel, left
T80 – Connector, 80 point
500 – Threaded connection –1– (30) on the relay plate
501 – Threaded connection –2– (30) on the relay plate
504 – Threaded connection –1– (87) on the relay plate
A2 – plus connection (15), in instrument panel wiring harness
A18 – plus connection (54), in rear wiring harness
A20 – wire connection (15a), in instrument panel wiring harness
A99 – Connector –1– (87), in instrument panel
A100 – Connector –2– (87), in instrument panel wiring harness
– – – Automatic transmission only

97-60051

Brake Light Switch, brake pedal switch, fuel pump relay, Motronic engine control module

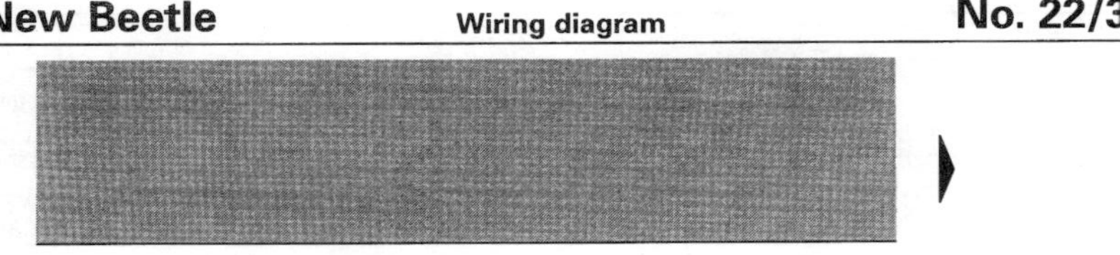

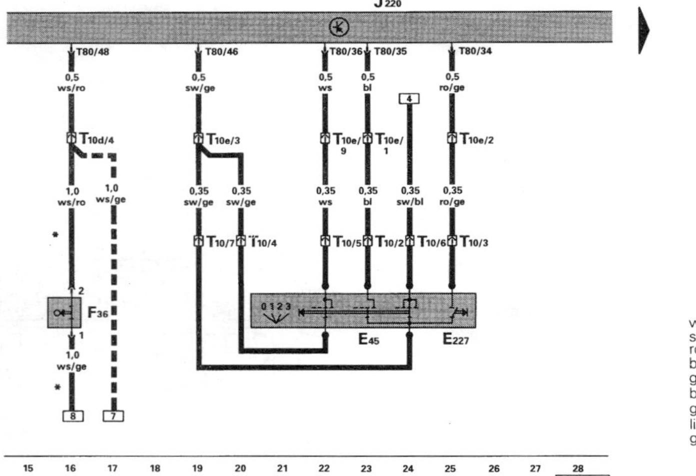

ws = white
sw = black
ro = red
br = brown
gn = green
bl = blue
gr = grey
li = violet
ge = yellow

E45 – Cruise Control Switch
E227 – Button for cruise control (set)
F36 – Clutch Vacuum Vent Valve Switch
J220 – Motronic Engine Control Module (ECM)
T10 – 10-pin connector, to right of steering column
T10d – 10-pin Connector, green, behind instrument panel, left
T10e – 10-pin Connector, black, behind instrument panel, left
T80 – 80–pin Connector, in Motronic Engine Control Module

(A100) – Connection 2 (87) (in instrument panel wiring harness)

* – Standard transmission only

– – – Automatic transmission only

Cruise control switch, button for cruise control, clutch vacuum vent valve switch, Motronic engine control module.

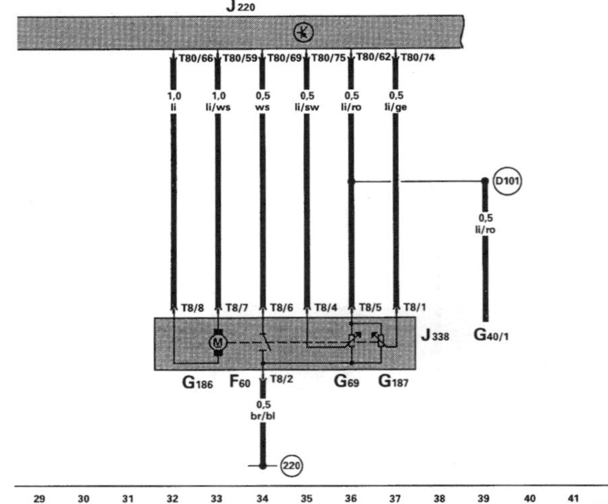

ws = white
sw = black
ro = red
br = brown
gn = green
bl = blue
gr = grey
li = violet
ge = yellow

F60 – Closed Throttle Position (CTP) Switch
G40 – Camshaft Position (CMP) Sensor
G69 – Throttle Position (TP) Sensor
G186 – Throttle Drive (electronic throttle)
G187 – Throttle Drive Angle Sensor 1 (electronic throttle)
J220 – Motronic Engine Control Module
J338 – Throttle Valve Control Module
T8 – 8–pin Connector
T80 – 80–pin Connector, in Motronic Engine Control Module

(220) – Ground Connection, Sensor Ground (in engine compartment wiring harness)

(D101) – Connection 1 (in engine compartment wiring harness)

Closed throttle position, Camshaft position sensor, Throttle position sensor, Throttle drive (electronic), Throttle drive angle sensor 1.

Power sunroof

from August 1998

Fuse colors
30 A – green
25 A – white
20 A – yellow
15 A – blue
10 A – red
7,5 A – brown
5 A – beige

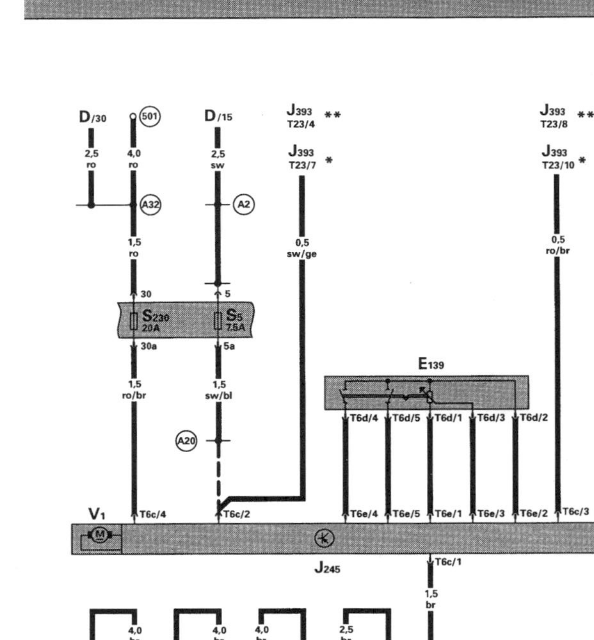

ws = white
sw = black
ro = red
br = brown
gn = green
bl = blue
gr = grey
li = violet
ge = yellow

D – Ignition/Starter Switch
E139 – Sunroof Regulator
J393 – Central control module for comfort system
J245 – Power Sunroof Control Module
S5 – Fuse 5 in fuse holder
S230 – Fuse 30 in fuse holder
T6c – 6-Pin Connector
T6d – 6-Pin Connector
T6e – 6-Pin Connector
V1 – Sunroof Motor

(42) – Ground connection, beside steering column

(81) – Ground connection –1–, in instrument panel wiring harness

(135) – Ground connection –2–, in instrument panel wiring harness

(199) – Ground connection –3–, in instrument panel wiring harness

(238) – Ground connection –1–, in wiring harness interior

(501) – Threaded connection –2– (30) on the relay plate

(A2) – plus connection (15), in instrument panel wiring harness

(A20) – wire connection (15a), in instrument panel wiring harness

(A32) – plus connection (30), in instrument panel wiring harness

– – – – without central locking (where applicable)
* with power windows
** with manual windows

Sunroof regulator, power sunroof control module, sunroof motor

WARNING

Your common sense, good judgement, and general alertness are crucial to safe and successful service work. Before attempting any work on your VW, read the warnings and cautions on page vii and the copyright page at the front of the manual. Review these warnings and cautions each time you prepare to work on your VW. Please also read any warnings and cautions that accompany the procedures in the manual.

A

B

WARNING

Your common sense, good judgement, and general alertness are crucial to safe and successful service work. Before attempting any work on your VW, read the warnings and cautions on page vii and the copyright page at the front of the manual. Review these warnings and cautions each time you prepare to work on your VW. Please also read any warnings and cautions that accompany the procedures in the manual.

> **WARNING**
>
> Your common sense, good judgement, and general alertness are crucial to safe and successful service work. Before attempting any work on your VW, read the warnings and cautions on page vii and the copyright page at the front of the manual. Review these warnings and cautions each time you prepare to work on your VW. Please also read any warnings and cautions that accompany the procedures in the manual.

I

J

K

L

M

WARNING

Your common sense, good judgement, and general alertness are crucial to safe and successful service work. Before attempting any work on your VW, read the warnings and cautions on page vii and the copyright page at the front of the manual. Review these warnings and cautions each time you prepare to work on your VW. Please also read any warnings and cautions that accompany the procedures in the manual.